RES SEVERA VERUM GAUDIUM

(True joy is a serious matter)—MOTTO OF THE LEIPZIG GEWANDHAUS ORCHESTRA (FROM SENECA, *EPISTOLAE*, I, 23)

THE NPR® LISTENER'S ENCYCLOPEDIA of CLASSICAL MUSIC

TED LIBBEY

WORKMAN PUBLISHING • NEW YORK

To Janet

For her love, support, encouragement, and forbearance

Published simultaneously in Canada by Thomas Allen & Son Limited.

Library of Congress Cataloging-in Publication Data
is available upon request.

ISBN 978-0-7611-2072-8 (paper)
ISBN 978-0-7611-3642-2 (hc)

WORKMAN PUBLISHING COMPANY, INC.
225 Varick Street
New York, NY 10014-4381
workman.com

Printed in the United States

First printing April 2006
10 9 8 7 6 5 4 3

ACKNOWLEDGMENTS

I want to thank Peter Workman for continuing to believe in this book during the many years beyond its deadline; for that belief I am grateful beyond words . . . though I hope the 600,000 of them—more or less—that appear on the following pages will justify his faith. Apart from the words I wrote, a tremendous amount of work by many hands has gone into the making of this book, and I want everybody to know it. At the head of the parade, of course, stands Ruth Sullivan, who has been the book's editor from the start, eleven years ago. This is as much her baby as mine: She has shaped it, fought for it, made every page of it better than I could possibly have managed on my own. Over the years, as we have worked together on three books, I have come to trust not only in Ruth's editorial judgment but in her counsel as a friend, her warmth, empathy, and unswerving devotion to quality. We are a team. During that time Ruth has had wonderful assistants who contributed immensely to that teamwork. I would single out Rosie Schaap, who was involved in the early phases of the creation of this book, and Beth Hatem, who has done so much to help us get it across the finish line—whose radiant smile and cheery voice at the other end of the line I have come to cherish, and whose ability to think ahead, react to emergencies, and tackle any problem has been nothing short of amazing for one so young. The whole production team at Workman has shown a tireless dedication to making this book the sort of unique, special, engaging thing a Workman book is. I owe them all my heartfelt thanks, especially Anne Cherry, who has been responsible for its production and has drawn on her remarkable musical knowledge to provide many essential enhancements; her excellent team of copyeditors, proofreaders, and typesetters deserve special mention: thank you, Dan Geist, Moraima Suarez, Jarrod Dyer, and Anne Lamb. Anita Dickhuth has done a magnificent job of finding photos and artwork to bring every page alive, and art director Janet Vicario has created a handsome design that pulls it all together magnificently, one page at a time. In the course of producing *The NPR Listener's Encyclopedia of Classical Music* we received editorial assistance from several brilliant people, including David Moran, Johanna Maria Rose, Kate McQuiston, and Carl Voss.

At various stages in the creation of this book there were many occasions when I turned to various friends—musicians, writers, record collectors—for advice on a specific subject about which they knew a great deal more than I, or asked them to look at and critique something I had written. Their number includes Tom Dixon, Richard Freed, Lawrence Dutton, Allan Kirk, Russ Hornbeck, Jacques Leiser, and Elena Park. I'd like also to thank a number of colleagues in the music business who helped during the course of this book's production, many of whom are also friends. First, Ken Richardson, my old comrade at *High Fidelity,* now music editor at *Sound & Vision,* who made his magazine's marvelous photo archive available. Next, those with whom I worked during two decades at NPR, including Ben Roe, Andy Trudeau, Martin Goldsmith (now at XM Satellite Radio), Fred Child, Miles Hoffman, Tom Huizenga, Anya Grundmann, and Barbara Vierow. I am grateful to many friends in the record business: Rebecca Pyle-Davis at Universal; Sarah Folger and Lisa Costa at harmonia mundi usa; Susan Schiffer and Doreen D'Agostino at Sony BMG; Mariko Tada at EMI; Amanda Sweet at Telarc; James Scileppi at Koch International; Lisa Pelikan at Warner; and Mark Berry at Naxos. To their names I would add those of publicists Glenn Petry at 21st Century Media, Jay Hoffman, Kerstin Hänssler, and Connie Shuman. I also happily acknowledge the publicity wings of the major musical organizations in this country and in Europe that have kept me on their mailing lists, supplied information about history and recordings (sometimes the recordings themselves), provided photos of artists and CD covers, and answered questions when I called upon them . . . all of which helped to supplement Anita's exhaustive research into archival and commercial sources. I'm grateful for the assistance given me by the staff of the music division at the Library of Congress, the greatest library in the world, and for the welcome I received at the performing arts library at the University of Alberta in Edmonton, where some of the first installments of this book were written. I'm also grateful for the encouragement and guidance I received from my agent, Bob Silverstein, as the years went by.

Finally, I want to thank my wife, Janet, without whose support this book might never have been finished. The truth is, I have been working on the book since the night we met, and for the entire time we've been married. During that period there have been plenty of times when I would rather have taken Janet to the movies, or spent a pleasant evening reading someone else's book. But Janet kept me focused on this one. I remember many occasions—at night after dinner, or on weekend afternoons—when she would silently raise her arm above her head and point to the "crow's nest," my office on the third floor. It was her way of telling me that I needed to finish the book. On a trip to Italy in 2002, while we were in Venice, she bought me a little honeybee made of Murano glass. For the last four years that honeybee has sat on top of my computer . . . so lifelike that it startled me sometimes when I saw it out of the corner of my eye. Its job, too, was to remind me to keep busy. And I can't overlook the role played by our two therapy dogs, Boojum (a 14-year-old soft-coated Wheaten terrier mix) and Jaz (a three-year-old schnoodle), who spent thousands of hours curled up at my feet, which, as all dog owners know, is their way of helping out.

INTRODUCTION

Where better to start than at the beginning?

The idea for this book came from its publisher, Peter Workman, who in the months following the publication of *The NPR Guide to Building a Classical CD Collection* suggested I write a companion volume—a comprehensive handbook on classical music for the general reader. He wanted it to be written in the same style, so that it would be approachable, informative, and fun . . . so that it would become, in effect, the hub of the wheel to which *The NPR Guide* was already one of the spokes. And he wanted it to be practical, so that someone who enjoys listening to music on the radio or CDs, and may go to a concert now and then, could learn something and be guided toward new discoveries.

I happily agreed to take on the assignment, not having the faintest idea how long it would take me or how difficult the job would be. In spite of the sizable amount of information I had accumulated over a lifetime of listening to and writing about music, there was a huge amount of research I needed to do. As I learned new things I often had to unlearn old ones, and in order to put concepts across clearly I really had to understand them myself. The task of laying all that information out in encyclopedic order as a series of individual entries on composers, performers, topics, terms, and named pieces—and making the result selective (yet inclusive), balanced, fair, and fun—proved to be the most daunting thing I've ever tried to do. But that was only part of the job. To add value to the book, we decided to include listings for well over two thousand recommended recordings. And then we went further, and arranged to have a Web site built where readers of the book could listen, over the Internet, to hundreds of hours of musical examples. The years dragged on, and so did work on the book.

One might well ask why a publisher or a writer should invest so much effort in a book about classical music. There are lots of ways one can answer that. One might remark on America's growing taste for small, affordable luxuries like $4.75 boutique-brewed cappuccinos, or budget CDs. One could point out that we live in a world that is crying out for the curatorial function, a world in which guides to the best of anything are in great demand. That is surely the case with music. But there are other handbooks out there. What makes this one special? For one thing, quite a few single-volume encyclopedias put heavy emphasis on theory and terminology, while giving short shrift to the music itself and to musicians past and present. I've tried to avoid that, in the belief that the general reader will be better served by information that relates directly to musical works, especially those that have found a place in the repertoire, and to the composers who created them and the performers who have interpreted them. Some guides seem obsessed with delving into the most arcane corners of music history and the contemporary compositional scene. While that may be appropriate for specialists, my aim has always been to connect with the broadest possible public, and to focus on those areas of the literature that are well represented on recordings and accessible to the general listener.

In the process I have tried not to oversimplify things. I do not believe in writing down to anyone, but in trying to write imaginatively and accurately about what is by any measure a complex subject. My hope is that by doing so, and communicating my enthusiasm for the literature of music and its creators, I will open a door for the reader. Which brings me to the real reason for writing this book. Nietzsche hit on it when he said, "Ohne Musik wäre das Leben unträglich." ("Without music, life would be unbearable.") For me, as I am sure for many, music has been an inestimable comfort in times of sadness and loss . . . and an inspiration at all times.

The gift of music, given to the world by composers and performers going back through the centuries, has been one of the most precious things in my life. For a long time I have felt an obligation to pay tribute to the accomplishments of music's great creators, and to honor their work as artists. Still, I was surprised when I tallied the number of people written about in this book whom I have actually encountered over the years: those I have interviewed formally, those I have heard in performance and rehearsal, and those I have known more intimately—with whom I have broken bread, clinked glasses, shared a warm embrace. This book is in part a thank-you to them. It is also, in part, a response to what happened on September 11, 2001, when the world we live in was changed forever. One of the many side effects of the attacks that occurred on that day was that, for a while, the bottom dropped out of our cultural life. In the face of such destruction and loss of life it was hard to pay attention to anything else. For me, the moment of recovery came in December 2001, with the Metropolitan Opera broadcast of Wagner's *Die Meistersinger von Nürnberg.* Here, three months after the atrocity, New York was back on its feet, lustily cheering at the end of a magnificent performance of one of the largest and most complex works in the repertoire, a comedy, but at heart a serious opera about love and loss. It was a bracing demonstration of what is of value in Western civilization, and why it is important to preserve it, protect it, and understand it.

◆◆◆

Some specifics about how entries for this book were selected and presented. There are biographical entries on major composers as well as on lesser but important figures. There are similar entries on performers of historical importance, especially those who have left meaningful recorded legacies, as well as significant performers of the present day. Other entries offer a discussion of instruments, musical terms, and concepts (forms, procedures, genres, and historical periods) that have a bearing on the performance of music and the development of style. There are entries for named pieces, including operas and other vocal works, orchestral works (symphonies, tone poems, overtures), and chamber pieces. And there are entries on institutions and organizations such as orchestras, opera companies, ensembles, festivals, and schools.

For entries on composers, the "template" has been to start with a broad evaluation, sketch the biographical details, and go on to a discussion of the oeuvre, touching on specific works as appropriate and identifying the composer's most important contributions to the repertoire. For more important figures I try to identify the hallmarks of their sound and style and offer an appreciation of their place in history. For performers, the entries take a similar approach: biographical details emphasizing major milestones in the career, followed by a discussion of the performer's artistry, drawing attention to his or her interpretive strengths. For entries on pieces, I first provide the facts relating to their genesis and composition, then try to give a description of their layout, their programmatic or expressive content, and their broader significance.

Nearly all of the entries for composers, performers, and named works include a box of "Recommended Recordings." These are selective listings of what I consider the best examples in the catalog, with information on each recording's content, the performers, and the record label, but no catalog numbers, as these are likely to change. There are more than two thousand such recommendations, and while it would have been nice to include capsule reviews of the recordings, that would have added several hundred pages to the book, and duplicated much that is already in *The NPR Guide to Building a Classical CD Collection.*

Throughout the book there are abundant cross-references to direct the reader to entries where additional information can be found: These cross-references appear at the ends of entries, or within entries as words or titles set in small caps. For example, titles of works that have their own entries appear in small caps within their composer's entry, as do references to techniques or terms that distinguish a composer's style, if they do so in a particularly significant way, or if the cross-referenced article was specifically designed to shed more light on the subject at hand.

Terms or technical words with component parts will cross-reference the component parts; for example, "suite" will refer to "bourée" and "bourée" will have a cross-reference to "suite." The book's production team gave considerable thought to the way cross-references could be used to enhance the reader's understanding of a subject, but at the same time took pains not to overuse them. Thus, important works, composers, and terms mentioned in generic entries such as "opera" are not cross-referenced, since the reader will realize that they are very likely to have their own entries anyway. The aim in cases such as this is twofold: to avoid situations that would tend to produce visual clutter, and to leave the reader free to explore items as the spirit (and his curiosity) moves him, rather than constantly pointing him typographically in this or that direction. In general, titles of musical works are listed in their original language (followed by parenthetical English translation); the exceptions are generic titles such as *Variations on a Theme by Haydn* as well as Russian, Czech, and Hungarian works. As a rule, when a composer who does not have an entry is mentioned in another entry, that composer's dates are given in parentheses following the name. Composers and conductors who have their own entries (Debussy, Toscanini) are often mentioned by last name only.

No one book can include everything that's important to everybody. I got a humorous reminder of that as this book was in its final stages. A good friend, one to whom I have often turned for advice, called one day and in the most salacious voice he could manage began, "I've put together a list of the composers that don't belong in your book."

"Oh?" I said.

"Yes. Here it is: Beethoven, Vivaldi, Bach, Schoenberg, Berg, Webern, Nielsen, Ives—I can't *stand* Ives—Elliott Carter,

Bellini, Donizetti, Verdi, Berlioz, Schubert, that horrible Pierre Boulez, Hans Werner Henze, and Hawaiian music."

I started laughing, and he kept right on going. "Now you have the master list, and if I can think of any Russian composers, I will let you know."

It was just what the doctor ordered. My friend knew how seriously I had taken the job of deciding what ought and ought not to be included in the book, and knew as well that it was time to bust things up a bit. I assured him I would take his advice very seriously. But in the end, only Henze and Hawaiian music failed to make the cut.

Behind the teasing was a point: This book should be read for what it has in it, rather than for what it doesn't. And there is a lot more to it than what is between its covers. Specifically, there is a dedicated Web site, constructed by Naxos, with links to more than 500 musical selections—entire pieces, whole movements, or passages within movements that illustrate a specific technique or procedure under discussion—each one coded in the book with a special symbol ◉. (See "Using Naxos," page xii.) In effect, *The NPR Listener's Encyclopedia of Classical Music* comes with a music library containing well over 75 hours of sound files available to all readers of this book.

The time was ripe for this. In a little more than 15 years, Naxos has grown from a budget start-up with a handful of titles into the largest classical label in the world, with a catalog of enormous breadth. Its founder, Klaus Heymann, whom I have known since the mid-1990s, learned about this book when we ran into each other at a radio conference in the winter of 2004. He immediately offered to create a Web site exclusively for readers of the book, where they could have access to a full range of music samples drawn from his catalog and others. Something on this scale could not have happened any sooner, for only in the past couple of years has sufficient bandwidth been available to permit the streaming of high-quality audio over the Internet to people using their home computers.

The result has been the most ambitious linking of any book on any subject to a dedicated Web site—certainly the most robust linkage that has ever been attempted for a book about music. You want to know what pizzicato sounds like? Now you can hear it. Never encountered the *Hebrides* Overture? It's here, as are hundreds of other excerpts and complete works. The delays I encountered in finishing the book were thus fortuitous, in that they permitted us to add an entire new dimension to it. And I'm confident that for the general reader this will be a huge value-added feature. In the course of forging these links with my editor, Ruth Sullivan, over several days of intensive work, I looked on with delight as she became a convert to early music. The more she heard, the more enthusiastic she became. I believe this feature will open many doors, and I am doubly grateful to Klaus for thinking of it and for putting his talented Hong Kong–based media team to work on it.

While on the subject of the Internet, I should point out that an increasing number of artists maintain their own Web sites. Where there was information to be gleaned from them, I went in and got it. Also, I have made judicious use of material from the official Web sites of various orchestras, opera companies, and other institutions. But I have been very leery of fan sites. Sometimes one finds interesting nuggets in such places, but often the facts are garbled. In order to check the facts against an established and respected authority, the production team at Workman settled on *The New Grove Dictionary of Music and Musicians,*

Second Edition, published in 2000, which we in the field call *Grove II* for short. In 29 volumes, filling two shelves on a standard bookcase, it is the most comprehensive reference on music in the English language. Its lists of works are remarkably thorough, and it offers an enormous amount of information about almost everything. Even so—and this is not meant to disparage Grove or its editors in any way—*Grove II* has gaps and mistakes. I have tried to make sure that errors there did not become errors in this book as well.

Doubtless there will be errors still, and for these I accept full responsibility. By the same token, there are certain cases when what may appear to be inconsistencies and errors really aren't. Some "facts" cannot be presented in a single, ironclad formulation. For example, for a large work like an opera that may have taken a composer several years to write, sometimes it is useful to cite the date of the premiere, sometimes the span of years during which the composer worked on the piece. In such cases, I have tried to make the best choice based on the context in which the information is presented in the entry.

Facts are important, but in the end it comes down to something else—one's feeling for the art of music, one's personal experience of it and one's ability to communicate that. And here I must admit that against the vastness and complexity of this subject there were many times when knowledge and memory seemed to desert me. After all, what can one say with any certainty about what made Arthur Rubinstein such a great pianist? And how could anything I might venture on the subject be enough? Trying to do justice to some of the greatest talents God has put on earth has not been easy, and I leave this book with you wishing I could have said more, and said it better.

USING NAXOS

How to Listen to This Book

As a special bonus, Naxos, the world's largest classical music label, has created a Web site expressly for the readers of *The NPR Listener's Encyclopedia of Classical Music.* Here are more than 500 pieces of music, ranging from movements to full works, that illustrate hundreds of terms, works, instruments, and composers in the book. From an example of *Alberti bass*—a compositional technique exemplified in Mozart's Sonata in C, K. 545—to six recordings that capture the range and flavor of Claude Debussy, it's a unique marriage of text and sound to educate the ear.

Every entry in the book with a corresponding sound sample is marked by the ◉ icon. The entries are searchable by composer's last name, organized alphabetically. To find Monteverdi's *L'Orfeo,* for example, just click on the "M" link on the home page, then scroll down to Monteverdi and to the *L'Orfeo* link. Links on the playlist that illustrate a particular term, such as *polytonality,* are listed as such. In this case, the example is from Ravel's *Bolero.*

Gaining access to the free Web site is easy. Just follow these steps:

1. Visit www.naxos.com/workman/

2. As a first-time user, register by following the directions where it says, "First-time users please click here to register."

3. Fill out the registration form, using this number as the log-in code: 0761120726.

4. For your convenience, write your user name (the e-mail address you used on the registration form) and password here. It is what you will need to log in on subsequent visits.

My user name: ____________________

My password: ____________________

The Web site supports Windows and Macintosh. Specific system requirements are found on the log-in page.

Happy listening!

Abbado, Claudio

(b. Milan, June 26, 1933)

ITALIAN CONDUCTOR. A veteran of the opera pit as well as the concert platform, he has brought to his work an extraordinary combination of grace and exuberance, of physical energy and intellectual refinement. At their best, his interpretations of the symphonic repertoire are masterpieces of nuance, pacing, and drama, his operatic performances models of precision and theatricality.

Son of the violinist and theorist Michelangelo Abbado, and younger brother of composer Marcello Abbado, he spent his childhood in Mussolini's Italy, not a comfortable place for a family of artists and intellectuals opposed to Fascism. He trained initially as a pianist, then studied conducting at both the Milan Conservatory and Vienna's Academy of Music under the celebrated Hans Swarowsky. In 1958 he won the Koussevitzky conducting prize at Tanglewood and in 1963, he captured first prize in the Mitropoulos Competition, which led smoothly to a five-month apprenticeship with the New York Philharmonic. From the mid-1960s to the mid-1980s, his calendar included frequent engagements with the Vienna Philharmonic and Berlin Philharmonic, as well as occasional guest-conducting appearances with major American orchestras, notably those of Boston, Philadelphia, and Chicago, where he was principal guest conductor from 1982 until 1985. Over the course of three decades, from 1972 to 2002, he filled four of the most prestigious posts in the operatic and symphonic world: music director of La Scala in Milan, the Vienna Staatsoper, the London Symphony Orchestra, and the Berlin Philharmonic.

During his tenure at La Scala (1972–86), the house enjoyed a golden age—its repertoire was broadened to include more German-language and 20th-century works, casting was strengthened, the orchestra improved, recording activity picked up, and adventurous new productions were mounted. At the Vienna Staatsoper (1986–91), he led groundbreaking productions of works by Verdi, Mussorgsky, Debussy, and Berg. During the years 1987–91 he also served as general music director of the city of Vienna.

On the symphonic front, Abbado became chief conductor of the London Symphony Orchestra in 1979 and served as its music director from 1983 to 1988. Following the death of Herbert von Karajan, the members of the Berlin Philharmonic voted to make him, as of 1990, the fifth artistic director in their history. Under Abbado's baton the orchestra quickly regained the luster it had lost during the turbulent final years of Karajan's reign, developing a new and pleasing warmth. Abbado programmed cycles of concerts dedicated to particular themes: music inspired by the poetry of Hölderlin, the legend of Faust, works centered around Greek drama. In 1998, the conductor announced that he would step down in 2002 in order to devote himself to "reading, sailing, and skiing." As it turned out, the final two years of his tenure were overshadowed by a struggle with cancer, which necessitated the removal of his entire stomach and caused him to miss many concerts. He nonetheless managed to close out his Berlin obligations triumphantly, and in 2003 the Lucerne Festival formed a handpicked orchestra especially for him to conduct, with many of Europe's top solo and orchestral players (including former Philharmoniker) in the principal chairs.

Abbado's repertoire, like his conducting, is sharply focused rather than all-embracing. At its center are three of the pillars of the Viennese symphonic tradition: Beethoven, Brahms, and Mahler. He has also championed the music of Tchaikovsky and Prokofiev, of the Second Viennese School (especially Berg and Webern), and of Luigi Nono (1924–90) and a handful of mid- and late-20th-century European serialists.

The high-voltage bravado that characterized Abbado's conducting when he was in his 30s eventually gave way to a more refined approach, one that suggested a growing concern for nuance and structural clarity. Like his best work in Berlin, his recent efforts in Lucerne (including a triumphant reunion with his old orchestra in 2004) have reflected a magnificent balance of formal integrity and expressive intensity.

RECOMMENDED RECORDINGS

BRAHMS, SYMPHONIES: BERLIN PHILHARMONIC (DG).

MAHLER, SYMPHONY NO. 2 (*RESURRECTION*); DEBUSSY, *LA MER*: LUCERNE FESTIVAL ORCHESTRA (DG).

MUSSORGSKY, *KHOVANSHCHINA*: LIPOVŠEK, BURCHULADZE, ATLANTOV, HAUGLAND; VIENNA PHILHARMONIC (DG).

VERDI, *SIMON BOCCANEGRA*: FRENI, CAPPUCCILLI, GHIAUROV, CARRERAS; LA SCALA ORCHESTRA (DG).

absolute music Music that is free of any association with a text or other extramusical idea such as a descriptive or pictorial "program." *See also* PROGRAM MUSIC.

absolute pitch Also known as "perfect pitch." The ability to identify accurately—that is, by ear without reference to an external source—the pitch of a given note or to produce a specific pitch by whistling or singing it.

Academy of Ancient Music *See box on pages 310–13.*

The church of St. Martin-in-the-Fields, London

Academy of St. Martin-in-the-Fields CHAMBER ORCHESTRA FOUNDED IN **1959** by the English violinist and conductor NEVILLE MARRINER. Originally a small, conductorless string group whose members were recruited from London's top ensembles, it spearheaded the 1960s recording boom in Baroque music. The wide dissemination of those early recordings via radio established Marriner and the ASMF as a potent brand name in classical music, enabling them to expand into 19th- and 20th-century repertoire, and add regular concerts and touring to their studio work. The Academy's artistic directors have been Iona Brown (1978–2004) and Kenneth Sillito; Marriner (Sir Neville since 1985) remains music director. With more than 1,000 recordings to its credit, the Academy is the most recorded chamber orchestra in history.

a cappella (It., "in the chapel") To be sung without instrumental accompaniment.

accelerando (It.) Becoming faster. A particularly striking example from the symphonic literature occurs in the finale of Robert Schumman's Symphony No. 1, where an *accelerando* enlivens the closing 76 measures of the score.

accent A dynamic or rhythmic emphasis given to a particular note, marking it for attention. Most accents are made by means of an increase of volume on the given note, or by a sharper attack or articulation, or by a slight lengthening of the note (known as an agogic accent). With string instruments, accents can be made by increasing the speed or pressure of the bow, or through different types of vibrato.

accidental(s) Symbol preceding a note, indicating that its pitch is to be raised or lowered by a half step—*sharp* [♯] or *flat* [♭]—or a whole step—*double sharp* [𝄪] or *double flat* [♭♭]. The *natural* sign [♮], which cancels a preceding accidental, is also considered an accidental. *See also* KEY SIGNATURE.

accompaniment The supporting part or parts in a musical composition. The term is most commonly used in reference to the vocal recital literature (in which a keybord instrument usually provides the accompaniment), to sonatas for solo instrument (in

Joseph Joachim, accompanied by Clara Schumann

which, again, the accompaniment is usually supplied by keyboard), and to concertos (in which the whole orchestra may be thought of as accompaniment). Many accompaniments are so substantive that they cannot really be considered "subordinate" elements of the texture or musical conception. In addition, composers such as Mozart and Beethoven frequently turned the tables on our modern notion of accompaniment in a sonata; both wrote sonatas "for the pianoforte with the accompaniment of a violin."

adagio (It., "in an easy manner") Generally understood as "slow." A movement in slow tempo.

Adagio for Strings WORK FOR STRING ORCHESTRA BY SAMUEL BARBER, an arrangement of the *molto adagio* opening portion of the second movement of his two-movement String Quartet in B minor, Op. 11. Arturo Toscanini and the NBC Symphony gave the first performance of the *Adagio for Strings* in 1938. The intense feeling and elegiac quality of the writing have made it a favorite of audiences ever since, and it remains the most frequently performed piece of American concert music written in the 20th century. In recent years, especially after September 11, 2001, the piece has become the American anthem of grief.

RECOMMENDED RECORDINGS

SCHIPPERS AND NEW YORK PHILHARMONIC (SONY).

SLATKIN AND SAINT LOUIS SYMPHONY ORCHESTRA (EMI).

Adam, Adolphe

(b. Paris, July 24, 1803; d. Paris, May 3, 1856)

FRENCH COMPOSER. Inclined to the theater from his youth, he became a student of Adrien Boieldieu (1775–1834) at the Paris Conservatoire and quickly emerged as one of the most prolific musical figures in 19th-century France. He composed approximately 70 operas, nearly all of them comedies, and more than a dozen ballets, of which the most famous, *Giselle,* received its premiere at the Paris Opéra in 1841. With a scenario by Théophile Gautier (based on a story by Heinrich Heine), *Giselle* was the first great Romantic ballet and the model for later works by Delibes, Tchaikovsky, and others. While Adam's operas broke little new ground, they appealed almost unerringly to Parisian tastes and enjoyed considerable popularity in their day. The best of them, *Le postillon de Longjumeau* (*The Postilion of Longjunieau*; 1836), *Giralda* (1850, set to a libretto by Eugène Scribe), and *Si j'étais roi* (*If I Were King*; 1852), are still occasionally performed. In addition to his works for the stage, Adam also wrote numerous potpourris and salon pieces, as well as a handful of sacred works and the Christmas carol "O Holy Night."

Adolphe Adam, ca. 1840

RECOMMENDED RECORDING

GISELLE: BONYNGE AND ROYAL OPERA (DECCA).

Adams, John

(b. Worcester, Mass., February 15, 1947)

AMERICAN COMPOSER. He grew up in Vermont and New Hampshire, attended Harvard, and studied composition with Leon Kirchner (b. 1919), Earl Kim (1920–98), and others. In 1971 he moved to San Francisco, teaching at the San Franciso Conservatory of Music and, from 1979 to 1985, serving as composer-in-residence of the San Francisco Symphony Orchestra. In that position he created the "New and Unusual Music" series, a springboard for the introduction of much contemporary music, including many of his own pieces. Adams achieved notoriety with two topical operas created in collaboration with Alice Goodman, Mark Morris, and Peter Sellars: *NIXON IN CHINA* (1987; dealing with Richard Nixon's epoch-making 1972 visit to mainland China), and *The Death of Klinghoffer* (1991; inspired by the at-sea hijacking of the cruise ship *Achille Lauro* in 1985). With a commission from the San Francisco Opera, he teamed with Goodman and Sellars for a third opera, *Doctor Atomic,* based on the life of physicist J. Robert Oppenheimer; the work received its premiere in October 2005.

While not quite as "high concept," Adams's orchestral and instrumental pieces have been equally adventurous. To date, the most important have been *Shaker Loops* (1978) for seven solo strings (revised in 1983 for string ensemble), *Harmonium* (1981),

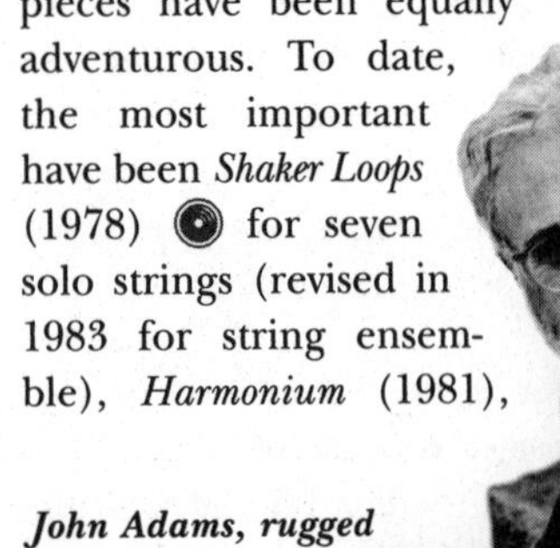

John Adams, rugged New England–California individualist

Grand Pianola Music (1982), *Harmonielehre* (1985; the title refers to a treatise by Arnold Schoenberg), *The Chairman Dances* (1986), and the fanfares *Tromba lontana* and *Short Ride in a Fast Machine* (1986). Other works of note include *The Wound-Dresser* (1988, based on Whitman) for baritone and orchestra, *On the Transmigration of Souls* (2002; Pulitzer Prize, 2003) for orchestra, chorus, and children's choir, a response to the events of September 11, 2001, and *The Dharma at Big Sur* (2003), a concerto for electric violin and orchestra that takes as its "inspirations" the writer Jack Kerouac and the composers Terry Riley and Lou Harrison. These pieces have become so popular that since the early 1990s, Adams has been America's most frequently performed living composer.

Adams's music incorporates elements of minimalism, but it also manifests an acceptance of tonality and the large-scale formal and developmental structures associated with it (particularly noticeable in his works since the 1990s). In addition, Adams's music is highly eclectic; it "raids the trash-can" of musical history, as the composer himself has said (a good example occurs in the third act of *Nixon in China,* where Mao and Jiang Ching, his wife and leader of the "Gang of Four," dance a fox-trot). In light of his engagement with tradition, Adams should be considered not merely an innovator with an astute sense of where his audience's sympathies lie, but an important renovator of the standard genres of classical music. *See also* MINIMALISM.

RECOMMENDED RECORDINGS

THE CHAIRMAN DANCES (WITH OTHER WORKS): DEWAART AND SAN FRANCISCO SYMPHONY ORCHESTRA (NONESUCH).

NIXON IN CHINA: SYLVAN, MADDALENA, FRIEDMAN; DEWAART AND ORCHESTRA OF ST. LUKE'S (NONESUCH).

SHAKER LOOPS, SHORT RIDE IN A FAST MACHINE, WOUND-DRESSER: ALSOP AND BOURNEMOUTH SYMPHONY ORCHESTRA (NAXOS).

Thomas Adès coaches a student on one of his piano pieces, 2000.

Adès, Thomas

(b. London, March 1, 1971)

ENGLISH COMPOSER, PIANIST, AND CONDUCTOR. After the 1995 premiere of his opera *Powder Her Face* he was hailed as a compositional wunderkind; the opera's lurid staging and its sensational subject, the sex-crazed Duchess of Argyll, grabbed international attention. In the decade since, the composer's vivid imagination and distinctive musical voice have kept people listening. A student of Paul Berkowitz (piano) and Robert Saxton (composition) at the Guildhall School of Music, Adès first came to notice as a performer when he won the second piano prize in the 1989 BBC Young Musician of the Year Competition. He subsequently studied music at Cambridge (with Hugh Wood, Alexander Goehr, and Robin Holloway), graduating in 1992. His compositional gift was quickly noticed: his Chamber Symphony, Op. 2, written for performance at the 1991 Cambridge Festival of Contemporary Music (which he conducted), was picked up two years later by the BBC Philharmonic and the Ensemble Modern. Numerous assignments followed. In 1993, the London Sinfonietta commissioned the cacophonous *Living Toys,* one of Adès's most-performed pieces. Between 1993 and 1995, Adès was "composer in association" with the Hallé Orchestra, which resulted in *The Origin of the Harp* (1994) and *These Premises Are Alarmed,* written for the 1996 opening of Manchester's Bridgewater Hall. *Asyla* (1997), a large-scale orchestral work commissioned for Sir Simon Rattle and the City of Birmingham Symphony Orchestra, appeared on Rattle's final program as music director of the CBSO; in September of 2002, Rattle conducted the work in his debut concert as music director of the Berlin Philharmonic. *America: A Prophecy* (1999), for mezzo-soprano, chorus, and orchestra, was one of several works commissioned by the New York Philharmonic to mark the new millennium. It offers up a vision of the destruction of Mayan civilization by Spanish invaders.

Powder Her Face, for chamber orchestra and four singers (three of whom play multiple roles), was Adès's first opera. It portrays a contemporary, wealthy, Lulu-like character whose sexual exploits finally leave her divorced, penniless, and degraded. Adès's second opera, *The Tempest,* based on Shakespeare, was commissioned by the Royal Opera House, Covent Garden, and received its premiere there in 2004 under the composer's baton. The role of Ariel is a stratospherically high part for coloratura soprano. Adès has an exclusive recording contract—as composer, conductor, and pianist—with EMI Classics, and has won numerous awards and prizes, of which the most important to date has been the 2000 Grawemeyer Prize, for *Asyla.* The Grawemeyer is the largest international award for composition, and Adès is its youngest-ever recipient.

RECOMMENDED RECORDINGS

ASYLA AND OTHER ORCHESTRAL WORKS: RATTLE AND CITY OF BIRMINGHAM SYMPHONY ORCHESTRA (EMI).

POWDER HER FACE: GOMEZ, ANDERSON; ADÈS AND ALMEIDA ENSEMBLE (EMI).

a due (It.) To be played by two instruments.

agitato (It.) Agitated, excited.

Agnus Dei (Lat., "Lamb of God") Final section of the Ordinary of the Mass. Its text is a petition for forgiveness and peace. *See also* MASS.

agréments (Fr.) Melodic ORNAMENTS. During the 17th and 18th centuries, tasteful ornamentation in the performance of solo and vocal instrumental music was de rigueur, particularly in France, where the art reached its highest refinement. The use of *agréments* served not only to draw the listener's attention to the melody but to enliven a piece's rhythm and intensify its expression. While the goal was for these ornaments—consisting of various TRILLS, TURNS, MORDENTS, and APPOGGIATURAS—to sound as though they were spontaneous "gracings" applied by the performer, their use was in fact required by convention. A number of the day's leading composers weighed in on the manner in which to sound *agréments* and the rules governing their application, among them Jean Henry d'Anglebert (1629–91) in his *Pièces de clavecin* (1689) and François Couperin in *L'art de toucher le clavecin* (1716).

Aida OPERA IN FOUR ACTS BY GIUSEPPE VERDI, to a libretto by Antonio Ghislanzoni (based on a scenario developed by Auguste Mariette and Camille du Locle), premiered December 24, 1871, in Cairo. The story, set in Egypt, concerns a love triangle with an intriguing difference: Two women (Aida, the enslaved Ethiopian princess, and Amneris, the Egyptian princess) are both in love with the same man (Radames, the Egyptian commander), who is torn between his duty to Egypt and his love for Aida.

The Triumphal Scene of Act II ("Gloria all'Egitto") ◉, with its huge choral proclamations, ballet interlude, and climactic sextet, is grand opera at its grandest. But at its core, *Aida* is an opera about love and the

Title page of Aida, *1872*

impossibility of openly revealing it. When at last Aida and Radames *can* express their love—in the opera's concluding scene, as they are being sealed alive in their tomb—Verdi shows the extraordinary depth of emotion he could generate—without plot, action, or scenery, but with music alone.

RECOMMENDED RECORDINGS

PRICE, VICKERS, MERRILL, GORR; SOLTI AND ROME OPERA (DECCA).

TEBALDI, BERGONZI, CORENA, SIMIONATO; KARAJAN AND VIENNA PHILHARMONIC (DECCA).

air [1] A solo vocal number in French opera from about 1650 to 1800. [2] From about 1600 to 1650, an English solo song to lute accompaniment, usually spelled "ayre." Later, in the 17th and 18th centuries, "air" came to mean a solo vocal or instrumental piece with a light, simple character. *See also* ARIA.

air raid/police siren *See box on pages 496–97.*

Akademie (Ger.) Term used in the 18th and early 19th centuries to refer to a subscription concert.

Akademie für Alte Musik Berlin *See box on pages 310–13.*

Albéniz, Isaac

(b. Camprodón, May 29, 1860; d. Cambô-les-Bains, May 18, 1909)

SPANISH COMPOSER. A child prodigy of the piano, he passed the entrance exam of the Paris Conservatoire when he was six and was already a seasoned touring artist at 13. He undertook further studies in Leipzig and Brussels, and had some private lessons with Liszt. The greatest influence on his development as a composer was his acquaintance with the pioneering Spanish musicologist Felipe Pedrell, who encouraged him to concentrate on creating music of specifically Spanish character.

Albéniz's first major effort along nationalistic lines was the *Suite española* (1886), eight miniatures for piano, each depicting a particular town or region. While some of the pieces exhibit the catchy rhythmic profile of Spanish folk music, others, like "Granada" ◉, spin out arabesqued melodies of an almost achingly sultry beauty. The pianistic styles of Chopin and Liszt can still be detected but the music is truly Spanish in its emotional character—volatile even when nostalgic, bittersweet even when lively. While less overtly descriptive than the sketches of the *Suite española,* the 12 vignettes that make up *IBERIA* (1906), Albéniz's masterpiece, contain music of extraordinary fantasy and complexity in which the composer's remarkable gift for pictorialism is combined with a now haunting, now exhilarating spirituality. These pieces, the majority of which deal with Andalusia, represent

Isaac Albéniz smokes at the piano.

the greatest achievement in the keyboard literature of Spain and mark the moment that a truly national musical style emerged on the Iberian peninsula.

RECOMMENDED RECORDINGS

Iberia, Suite española: Larrocha (Decca).

Suite española (arr. Frühbeck de Burgos): Frühbeck de Burgos and New Philharmonia Orchestra (Decca).

Alberti bass A "broken" figuration of the bass line in keyboard music, in which the notes of a triad (three-note chord) are played in rapid alternation as follows: lowest, highest, middle, highest, and so on. Named for Domenico Alberti (ca. 1710–46), who was the first composer to make regular use of it, Alberti basses are a common feature in keyboard pieces of the 18th and early 19th centuries. In the gentle opening measures of his Sonata in C, K. 545, Mozart graciously acknowledges the tradition, setting the sweet "drawing room" melody over a classic Alberti bass.

Albinoni, Tomaso Giovanni

(b. Venice, June 8, 1671; d. Venice, January 17, 1751)

Italian composer. Although he wrote approximately 50 operas, the music to most of them has been lost, and he is best known today as the composer of numerous concerti grossi and trio sonatas. His style has been criticized as stiff and formulaic, but he possessed an outstanding melodic gift. Unfortunately, the work most frequently associated with Albinoni's name, the Adagio in G minor, is actually a 20th-century forgery.

RECOMMENDED RECORDINGS

Concertos, Opp. 7 and 9: Standage and Collegium Musicum 90 (Chandos).

Trio sonatas, Op. 1: Parnassi Musici (CPO).

aleatoric (from Latin *alea,* "dice") Random or improvisatory; used to describe compositional approaches that involve the element of chance. Aleatoric techniques take many forms: For example, in his *Music of Changes* (1951) for piano, John Cage consulted the *I Ching* to determine the pitches, durations, and intensities of the notes in the score. Cage later utilized maps of the constellations as templates for *Atlas eclipticalis* (1961–62). Other 20th-century composers such as Stockhausen, Boulez, and Lutosławski have opted for notation that is indeterminate in some way, giving the performer latitude with regard to pitch, speed of articulation, dynamics, and other elements. In *Available Forms I* (1961) by the American composer Earle Brown (1926–2002), the performers' parts contain multiple sections of music, each consisting of five numbered segments; the number of the specific segment each musician is to play at any given time is signaled by the conductor spontaneously, using the fingers of one hand, as the performance unfolds. *See also entries for individual composers.*

Alkan, Charles-Valentin

(b. Paris, November 30, 1813; d. Paris, March 29, 1888)

French pianist and composer. A brilliant virtuoso, he wrote some of the most dazzlingly difficult piano music of the 19th century, including a set of *12 Etudes in the Minor Keys.* He was a friend and professional associate of both Franz Liszt and Frédéric Chopin, but owing to his eccentric, reclusive nature he shunned the concert stage from the age of 25 onward, preferring to concentrate on composition. His best works make tremendous technical demands and show a remarkable originality. He was also a master of the sentimental style popular in Parisian salons of his day.

Raised as an Orthodox Jew, Alkan remained a lifelong student of the Old Testament and the Talmud. This probably accounts for the oft-repeated but apocryphal story regarding the manner of his death—that in reaching for his Talmud, which he kept on top of a large bookcase, he accidentally pulled the bookcase over and was crushed by its weight.

RECOMMENDED RECORDING

12 ETUDES IN THE MINOR KEYS: HAMELIN (HYPERION).

alla breve (It., "with the breve") An instruction in early music indicating that a note of longer duration, originally the breve, got the beat in duple time, rather than the semibreve. This generally corresponds in the modern era to a time signature of $\frac{2}{2}$, with the half note getting the beat, and implies a rather fast overall tempo. The customary sign for alla breve, also known as "cut time," is ¢.

allargando (It.) Becoming broader, therefore slower.

allegretto (It., "a little fast") Slightly less fast than *allegro;* often used in place of *allegro* in pieces or movements of a lighter character or texture.

allegro (It., "cheerful") Generally understood as "fast." Often the tempo of opening and closing movements of sonatas and symphonies. As a tempo marking it is frequently modified by additional terms, e.g., *Allegro con brio, Allegro maestoso, Allegro non troppo,* or, more fancifully, *Allegro volando* (Scriabin, *Poem of Ecstasy,* m. 39).

allemande (Fr., "German [dance]") A stately dance in moderate duple meter. In the 17th and 18th centuries it was among the standard dances in orchestral and keyboard SUITES.

alphorn *See box on pages 496–97.*

Alsop, Marin

(b. New York City, October 16, 1956)

AMERICAN CONDUCTOR. The daughter of professional musicians (her father was concertmaster of the New York City Ballet Orchestra, her mother a cellist in the same orchestra), she started piano lessons at two and violin lessons at four. At nine, she decided she wanted to be a conductor after hearing a concert conducted by Leonard Bernstein. Following studies at Yale and Juilliard she made her living as a freelance violinist in New York. On the side, she studied conducting with Carl Bamberger and Harold Farberman, and formed two unusual ensembles: String Fever, a ten-piece string swing band, and the Concordia Orchestra, specializing in contemporary and crossover repertoire.

Alsop spent the summers of 1988 and 1989 at Tanglewood, studying conducting with Gustav Meier (receiving pointers along the way from Leonard Bernstein and Seiji Ozawa) and winning Tanglewood's Koussevitzky Conducting Prize. She became music director of the Colorado Symphony in 1993, and in 1999 was named principal guest conductor of the Royal Scottish National Orchestra. She was appointed principal conductor of the Bournemouth Symphony Orchestra in 2002.

On July 19, 2005, she was named to succeed Yuri Temirkanov as music director of the Baltimore Symphony Orchestra, effective at the start of the 2007–08 season. The appointment, which went through despite strong objections from the BSO's musicians, makes Alsop one of the few women ever to head a major American orchestra. Within weeks of its announcement,

she received a grant from the MacArthur Foundation, the so-called "genius award."

Alsop made her reputation conducting contemporary American repertoire, and is noted for her interpretations of the music of Bernstein, Glass, Adams, Tower, Michael Daugherty (b. 1954), and Christopher Rouse (b. 1949). She has also completed a six-CD survey of the orchestral works of Samuel Barber for Naxos.

Marin Alsop, celebrating with Champagne

RECOMMENDED RECORDINGS

BARBER, ORCHESTRAL WORKS: VARIOUS SOLOISTS; ROYAL SCOTTISH NATIONAL ORCHESTRA (NAXOS).

ROUSE, *GORGON*, TROMBONE CONCERTO: ALESSI; COLORADO SYMPHONY ORCHESTRA (RCA).

Also sprach Zarathustra (Thus Spoke Zarathustra) **TONE POEM BY RICHARD STRAUSS, OP. 30,** loosely based on Friedrich Nietzsche's philosophical tract of 1891. The score was composed in 1896 and first performed in Frankfurt, with the composer conducting, on November 27, 1896. Like his close contemporary Mahler and his predecessor Wagner, Strauss had a period of fascination with Nietzsche. By the time he decided to devote an entire composition to *Also sprach Zarathustra,* Mahler had already set a portion of the text—Zarathustra's "The Drunken Man's Song"—as an alto solo in the fourth movement of his Third Symphony. Curiously, Nietzsche himself had said some time before the publication of his tract, "To which category does my *Also sprach Zarathustra* belong? I believe to that of the symphony!" Strauss originally subtitled his tone poem: "Symphonic optimism in *fin-de-siècle form,* dedicated to the Twentieth Century," later replacing that with a note on the title page of the score that simply says, "Freely after Friedrich Nietzsche."

In composing the score, Strauss was smart enough to sidestep Nietzsche's more serious philosophical convolutions, but could not resist inserting along the way parenthetical references to the titles of eight of the 80 subsections of Nietzsche's sprawling opus, as signposts to the musical unfolding. He also prefaced the score with a long quotation, which his opening music promptly makes superfluous, if not a little silly. Although these pages of the score—beginning with a subterranean low C that is felt more than heard, and climaxing in a blazing C major sunrise of brass, pounding timpani, and organ ◉—have now acquired a life of their own thanks to Stanley Kubrick's *2001: A Space Odyssey,* they are but the prologue to one of Strauss's most profligate orchestral tapestries, full of large effects and clever attempts to depict Nietzsche's imagery in tones. Examples include the incorporation of a thunderous fugue in the section entitled "Of Science" (the fugue being music's most "learned" form), the opulently scored Viennese waltz that serves as a stand-in for "The Dance Song," and the tolling of the midnight bell to introduce "The Wanderer's Night Song" at the end of the piece.

Strauss saves one of his most striking effects for last. To suggest the enduring riddle of the cosmos—the antithetical relationship between Zarathustra's enlightenment of Man and the continuing, mysterious presence of Nature in the background—he juxtaposes the keys of C and B, leaving his musical meditation on Nietzsche's philosophy beautifully—and intentionally—unresolved.

RECOMMENDED RECORDINGS

REINER AND CHICAGO SYMPHONY ORCHESTRA (RCA).
KARAJAN AND VIENNA PHILHARMONIC (DECCA).

alto [1] In choral music, the voice range below soprano and above tenor. Alto parts are normally sung by women or boys, though adult male altos are frequently employed in performances of early music. A soloist, as opposed to a chorister, who sings in the alto range is generally called a MEZZO-SOPRANO if she is female, or a COUNTER-TENOR if he is male. [2] (Fr.) Viola.

Amati FAMILY OF VIOLIN MAKERS based in Cremona, Italy, during the 16th and 17th centuries. The dynasty was founded by Andrea Amati (ca.1510–ca.1580), and included his sons Antonio and Girolamo, grandson Nicolò, and great-grandson Girolamo. The most accomplished member of the family was Nicolò Amati (b. Cremona, December 3, 1596; d. Cremona, April 12, 1684), whose workshop flourished between about 1640 and 1670. During this period, he produced a large number of outstandingly crafted violins, notable for their elegant physical appearance (they were unusually wide, with fluid lines and a golden-orange varnish) and great beauty of tone. He also built a small number of violas (quite large-bodied) and cellos. Amati instruments continue to be highly prized for their mellow, warm sonority and easy responsiveness, though they lack the brilliance and carrying power of the best examples of STRADIVARI (an Amati pupil) and GUARNERI "DEL GESÙ."

Ameling, Elly

(b. Rotterdam, February 8, 1933)

DUTCH SOPRANO renowned as an interpreter of art songs. She studied in the Netherlands with Bodi Rapp and in Paris with Pierre Bernac, and won first prizes in the vocal competition in s'Hertogenbosch in 1956 and at the International Music Competition in Geneva in 1958. She began concertizing in Rotterdam in 1953, and devoted her lengthy career—she made a farewell recital tour in 1995—to song recitals and concert performances; on only two occasions did she take the stage in an opera, both times as Ilia in Mozart's *Idomeneo.* In 1959 she sang in the premiere of Frank Martin's *Le mystère de la Nativité;* that same year she made her Salzburg Festival debut as the soloist in the final movement of Mahler's Symphony No. 4. Ameling made her recital debut in Amsterdam in 1961, followed by her London debut in 1966 and her American debut, in New York, in 1968. As a concert artist, she appeared with many of the world's top orchestras and conductors; pianist Dalton Baldwin was her regular recital accompanist. A radiant performer, she was noted for her exquisite control of dynamics, inflection, and pitch, her agility in ornamental passages, and her superb diction, as well as for an uncanny grasp of expressive gesture that made her interpretations come to life. Her large discography encompasses most of her repertoire, especially German and French songs. In 1971 she was made a Knight of the Order of Oranje Nassau by Queen Juliana of The Netherlands.

RECOMMENDED RECORDINGS

BACH, SECULAR CANTATAS (*COFFEE, PEASANT,* AND *WEDDING*): ENGLISH; NIMSGERN AND COLLEGIUM AUREUM (RCA).
SCHUBERT, SCHUMANN, LIEDER: DEMUS (RCA).

American in Paris, An TONE POEM BY GEORGE GERSHWIN, premiered by the New York Philharmonic on December 13, 1928, with Walter Damrosch, who commissioned the score, conducting. Following the extraordinary success of his *RHAPSODY IN BLUE* and Concerto in F, Gershwin had been cast into musical high society in 1924; on a trip to Paris in the spring of 1928, he was feted by the musical establishment there and encountered composers Milhaud, Ravel, Poulenc, Stravinsky, Prokofiev, and others. His imagination fired by the lively Parisian scene, as well as by the sound of four French taxi horns he found in an auto parts store (which wound up playing a prominent part at the beginning and end of the piece), Gershwin returned to New York and threw himself into *An American in Paris,* completing the piano sketch on August 1 and the full score on November 18, 1928. His flamboyant use of percussion, idiomatic string writing, and suave scoring of a bluesy solo for trumpet "with felt crown" testify to the confidence he had gained as an orchestrator after scoring his Concerto in F, also a Damrosch commission.

In an early note, Gershwin said that he had set out to develop the opening part of the score "in typical French style" (the model could well have been Debussy's *IBÉRIA*), but stopped short of offering anything resembling a detailed program; that was added later by Deems Taylor, annotator for the Philharmonic. At no point does Gershwin try to mimic the sound of French music. Indeed, despite the color introduced at the start of the piece by the taxi horns, the tone of this exuberant fantasy—with its allusions to the blues, and even the insertion of a Charleston—is brash and American all the way. ◉ Far better than he had in the *Rhapsody in Blue,* Gershwin succeeds in maintaining the flow of ideas from one section to the next and in building a convincing overall structure out of his song and dance forms.

Karel Ančerl as music director of the Toronto Symphony

RECOMMENDED RECORDINGS

BERNSTEIN AND COLUMBIA SYMPHONY ORCHESTRA (SONY).

THOMAS AND SAN FRANCISCO SYMPHONY ORCHESTRA (RCA).

Amsterdam Baroque Orchestra and Choir *See box on pages 310–13.*

Ančerl, Karel

(b. Tučapy, April 11, 1908; d. Toronto, July 3, 1973)

CZECH CONDUCTOR. He studied at the Prague Conservatory from 1925 to 1929, then worked with Hermann Scherchen in Munich and Strasbourg, and with Václav Talich in Prague. He spent the years 1933–39 conducting in various theaters and for Prague Radio. After the German occupation of Czechoslovakia, he was removed from his positions. Deported to the Nazis' "model" concentration camp at Terezin [or Theresienstadt], he was later sent to Auschwitz, where he was the only member of his family to survive. Following the war he became conductor of the Czech Radio Symphony Orchestra (1947–50) and principal conductor of the Czech Philharmonic Orchestra (1950–68), succeeding Talich. In 1969 he left Czechoslovakia and was offered the music directorship of the Toronto Symphony Orchestra, a post he held until his death. During his years at the helm of the Czech Philharmonic, Ančerl recorded actively, achieving particular distinction in his direct and appealing interpretations of Dvořák and Janáček, as well as in the works of such 20th-century symphonists as Roussel, Martinů, and Shostakovich. His readings were characterized by a finely gauged balance of energy and lyricism, and a natural expressive warmth.

RECOMMENDED RECORDINGS

DVOŘÁK, SYMPHONY NO. 9: CZECH PHILHARMONIC (SUPRAPHON).

JANÁČEK, *SINFONIETTA*; MARTINŮ, *LES FRESQUES DE PIERO DELLA FRANCESCA, THE PARABLES*: CZECH PHILHARMONIC (SUPRAPHON).

Anda, Géza

(b. Budapest, November 19, 1921; d. Zurich, June 14, 1976)

HUNGARIAN PIANIST. He studied at the National Hungarian Royal Academy in Budapest with Ernő Dohnányi, and made his debut in 1939, playing the Brahms B-flat concerto with the Budapest Philharmonic conducted by Willem Mengelberg. In 1943 he fled Hungary for Switzerland, where he spent the rest of his life, taking citizenship in 1955. He specialized in the Mozart concertos (which he recorded in toto for Deutsche Grammophon, conducting from the keyboard) and in the music of Beethoven, Brahms, and Bartók. Anda conveyed enormous heart in everything he played, but also possessed the requisite steel for Bartók.

RECOMMENDED RECORDINGS

BARTÓK, PIANO CONCERTOS: FRICSAY AND BERLIN RADIO SYMPHONY ORCHESTRA (DG).

MOZART, PIANO CONCERTO NO. 21 IN C, K. 467 (WITH CONCERTOS NOS. 6 AND 17): ANDA AND SALZBURG MOZARTEUM ORCHESTRA (DG).

andante (It., "flowing," "walking," or "moving") Generally considered a slow tempo, although not as slow as *adagio*. It is sometimes applied to music whose character is fast (e.g., the first movement of Josef Suk's Serenade for Strings, Op. 6, marked *Andante con moto*). As a marking it is frequently modified by descriptive terms, as in Scriabin's *Poem of Ecstasy*, where the opening tempo is *Andante languido*.

andantino (It., "a little *andante*") Somewhat faster than *andante*.

Marian Anderson broke the color barrier in American opera.

Anderson, Marian

(b. Philadelphia, February 17, 1899; d. Portland, Ore., April 8, 1993)

AMERICAN CONTRALTO. She started singing in a church choir in south Philadelphia, later took voice lessons, and won a competition sponsored by the New York Philharmonic. She gave a recital at Carnegie Hall in 1929 and made her London debut in 1930. Following a series of European tours, she returned in triumph to New York and gave concerts at Town Hall and Carnegie Hall during the 1935–36 season. In 1939, when the Daughters of the American Revolution refused to allow her to perform in Washington, D.C.'s Constitution Hall because she was black, Roosevelt's secretary of the interior, Harold Ickes, invited her to give an outdoor concert at the Lincoln Memorial. Her performance there, on Easter Sunday, April 9, 1939, drew an enormous audience and was broadcast nationally. In 1955, she became the first African-American artist to sing at the Metropolitan Opera (Ulrica in Verdi's *Un ballo in maschera*). Although she lacked a refined technique, Anderson was a keenly intelligent singer gifted with a sumptuous and expressive voice. She is best known for her deeply felt interpretations of African-American spirituals.

An die ferne Geliebte (To the Distant Beloved) CYCLE OF SIX SONGS BY LUDWIG VAN BEETHOVEN to poems by Alois Jeitteles, published in 1816 as the composer's Opus 98. It is the earliest example in the German repertoire of a song cycle—a series of songs in which each constituent song tells an essential part of an ongoing story—as opposed to a collection of individual songs. *See also* LIED.

RECOMMENDED RECORDING

HAMPSON; PARSONS (EMI).

Andsnes, Leif Ove

(b. Karmøy, April 7, 1970)

NORWEGIAN PIANIST. He studied at the Bergen Conservatory and made his Oslo debut in 1987. In 1989 he made his U.S. debut performing in New York and Washington, D.C., and the following year he appeared as soloist with the Cleveland Orchestra under Neeme Järvi. His career was launched into orbit by his receipt of the Gilmore Artist Award in 1998, the most prestigious and rigorously judged honor in the pianistic universe—with a purse of $300,000 that is music's most generous prize. Since then he has solidified his place in the top international tier of performing artists via annual engagements with the world's leading orchestras, recitals at Carnegie Hall and other major venues, and with a series of acclaimed recordings for EMI that so far includes accounts of sonatas by Haydn, Chopin, and Schumann, and of concertos by Brahms, Shostakovich, Britten, and Mozart. He is particularly admired for his interpretations of the music of Janáček and of Scandinavian composers, including Grieg and Nielsen. Andsnes is co-artistic director of the Risør Chamber Music Festival in Norway, where he annually presents and collaborates with colleagues such as Maxim Vengerov, Gidon Kremer, and Ian Bostridge; with Bostridge he has also recorded selected Schubert lieder and *Winterreise*. Andsnes was made a Commander of the Royal Norwegian Order of St. Olav in 2002, and in 2004 he became the youngest artist ever to be featured in Carnegie Hall's "Perspectives" series.

RECOMMENDED RECORDINGS

BRAHMS, PIANO CONCERTO NO. 1, THREE INTERMEZZI: RATTLE AND CITY OF BIRMINGHAM SYMPHONY ORCHESTRA (EMI).

GRIEG, PIANO CONCERTO, SONATA OP. 7, *LYRIC PIECES*: KITAYENKO AND BERGEN PHILHARMONIC ORCHESTRA (VIRGIN CLASSICS).

animato (It.) Spirited, energetic.

Anonymous 4 *See* LÉONIN, PÉROTIN, *and box on pages 934–36.*

Ansermet, Ernest

(b. Vevey, November 11, 1883; d. Geneva, February 20, 1969)

SWISS CONDUCTOR. He studied clarinet, violin, and piano as a youth and graduated from the University of Lausanne with degrees in mathematics and physics. After teaching for several years, he turned seriously to musical pursuits

Victoria Hall, Geneva, where Ansermet led L'Orchestre de la Suisse Romande for five decades

and from 1912 on made his living as a conductor. An early encounter with Igor Stravinsky proved decisive: Ansermet became a champion of the Russian composer's music, eventually leading the premieres of *L'histoire du soldat* (1918) and *Pulcinella* (1922). Through Stravinsky, Ansermet also became acquainted with Sergey Diaghilev, who put him in charge of the orchestra of the Ballets Russes from 1915 to 1923. In that capacity he conducted the premieres of a number of major works, including Falla's *El sombrero de tres picos* (1919) and Ravel's *La valse* (1920). In 1918 Ansermet founded L'Orchestre de la Suisse Romande, serving as its music director until his retirement in 1967. He recorded prolifically with the OSR, specializing in French and Russian 20th-century repertoire, notably Stravinsky, as well as key orchestral works of such Swiss composers as Frank Martin and Arthur Honegger.

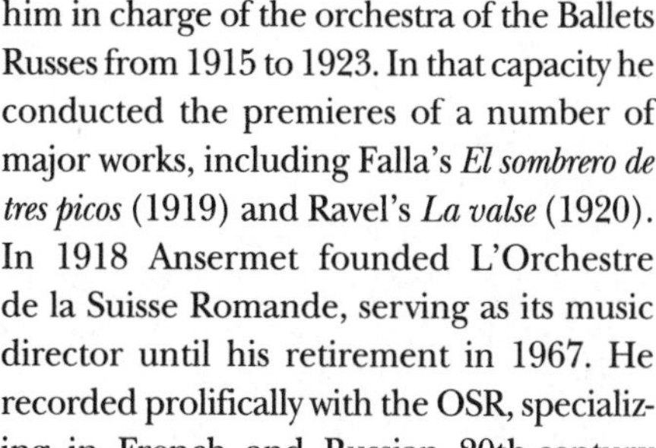

Leaf from a 15th-century illuminated antiphonary

RECOMMENDED RECORDINGS

FALLA, *EL SOMBRERO DE TRES PICOS* (WITH *EL AMOR BRUJO*): L'ORCHESTRE DE LA SUISSE ROMANDE (DECCA).

GLAZUNOV, *THE SEASONS*: L'ORCHESTRE DE LA SUISSE ROMANDE (DECCA).

MARTIN, ORCHESTRAL WORKS: L'ORCHESTRE DE LA SUISSE ROMANDE (DECCA).

Antheil, George *See box on pages 708–11.*

anthem In choral music, a setting of a religious text in English, normally intended for liturgical use.

antiphon In medieval church music, a liturgical chant with a prose text, sung before or after a Psalm.

antiphony A compositional technique utilizing separate groups of musicians who sing or play in alternation and are often placed in different parts of the performance area. Antiphonal writing was extremely popular in 16th-century Italy, particularly with the Gabrielis, who used "cori spezzati" (broken choirs) to take advantage of the superb acoustics of San Marco in Venice.

a piacere (It.) Freely.

Appalachian Spring BALLET BY AARON COPLAND, composed 1943–44 for Martha Graham on a commission from Elizabeth Sprague Coolidge, and first performed October 30, 1944, Coolidge's 80th birthday, in the Coolidge Auditorium at the Library of Congress in Washington, D.C. Owing to the intimacy of that venue, Copland found himself limited to just 13 instruments—a small group of strings plus flute, clarinet, bassoon, and piano—the maximum number that would fit on the floor between the seats and the stage. The enforced economy helped him produce a chamber score of remarkable tenderness and austere beauty—precisely the qualities of the human spirit that Graham's choreography sought to evoke. The meditative opening—especially in the original scoring—immediately sets the scene in the mind's ear. In 1945, Copland produced a suite from the ballet scored for full orchestra, which is the version best known today.

To quote from Copland's own preface to the score, the action of the ballet concerns "a pioneer celebration in spring, a newly built farmhouse in the Pennsylvania hills in the early part of the last [19th] century. The bride-to be and the young farmer-husband enact the emotions, joyful and apprehensive, their new domestic partnership invites. An older neighbor suggests now and then the rocky confidence of experience. A revivalist and his followers remind the new householders of the strange and terrible aspects of human fate. At the end the couple are left quiet and strong in their new house." At the premiere, the key roles were danced by Graham, Erik Hawkins, and Merce Cunningham.

In the final section, Copland uses the well-known Shaker hymn "Simple Gifts" as the basis for a set of variations. By this point, his own melodic style had acquired the gift of simplicity—a thrift of notes, spare and stark—so that the rest of the ballet's thematic material, which is wholly original, sounds like American folk music. This quality, in tandem with the score's vibrant energy and emotional tenderness, has made *Appalachian Spring* one of the most popular of American works. Curiously, the ballet's title, which Graham took from a line in a poem by Hart Crane simply because she liked its sound, refers to a waterfall ("O Appalachian Spring!"), not to a season of the year.

RECOMMENDED RECORDINGS

WITH *BILLY THE KID* AND *LINCOLN PORTRAIT*: COPLAND AND COLUMBIA CHAMBER ORCHESTRA, LONDON SYMPHONY ORCHESTRA (SONY).

WITH *RODEO, BILLY THE KID, FANFARE FOR THE COMMON MAN*: BERNSTEIN AND NEW YORK PHILHARMONIC (SONY).

***Appassionata* Sonata** POPULAR NAME GIVEN TO LUDWIG VAN BEETHOVEN'S PIANO SONATA IN F MINOR, OP. 57, published in 1807. The aptly chosen title (meaning "excited" or "impassioned") was bestowed on the work by the Viennese publisher A. Cranz 11 years after the composer's death. Among the most frequently performed of Beethoven's sonatas, the *Appassionata* is also one of the most immediately recognizable, thanks to the sinister opening subject, spread across two octaves, that issues sotto voce from the depths of the keyboard. The opening Allegro has precipitous changes of mood—from somber to elegiac to darkly furious—which are typical of Beethoven's minor-key expressiveness. By contrast, the ensuing Andante, consisting of four variations appended to a theme of surpassing gentleness, is tranquillity itself. The sonata's finale shatters this reverie with terrifying suddenness, and the work ends in near hysteria.

RECOMMENDED RECORDINGS

GILELS (DG).

R. SERKIN (SONY).

appoggiatura (pl., appoggiature; from It. *appoggiare*, "to lean") A note that sounds dissonant against the harmony with which it is heard, but resolves, usually downward, to a consonance. Appoggiature are frequently written as GRACE NOTES (in small type) in front of the note to which they resolve, but are usually played or sung on the beat, not ahead of it. *See also* AGRÉMENTS, ORNAMENTS.

apprenti sorcier, L' *See* THE SORCERER'S APPRENTICE.

Archduke Trio POPULAR NAME GIVEN TO BEETHOVEN'S PIANO TRIO IN B-FLAT, OP. 97, completed in 1811 and dedicated to the Archduke Rudolph. Symphonic in scale, with a broadly proportioned four-movement layout, it stands as the pinnacle of the literature for piano trio, a work of unparalleled richness and imagination that exemplifies Beethoven's middle-period manner at its best.

RECOMMENDED RECORDINGS

ASHKENAZY, PERLMAN, HARRELL (EMI).

BEAUX ARTS TRIO (PHILIPS, 1981).

arco (It., "bow") Played with the bow; usually used as an instruction to players of string instruments, indicating the end of a PIZZICATO passage.

Argerich, Martha

(b. Buenos Aires, June 5, 1941)

ARGENTINE-BORN PIANIST known for her brilliant technique and volatile temperament. She showed prodigious gifts as a child, giving her first recitals and concerto performances when she was eight. In 1955 she and her family moved to Europe, where she studied with Friedrich Gulda, among others. She won first prizes at competitions in Bolzano and Geneva in 1957, studied briefly with Arturo Benedetti Michelangeli in 1960, and hit the big time with her 1965 victory at the Warsaw Competition. Her recordings of concertos by Ravel, Prokofiev, and Liszt, made in the late 1960s in collaboration with conductor Claudio Abbado, remain among the treasures of the CD catalog, as do her recital discs devoted to the music of Chopin, Liszt, and Ravel.

Small of stature but with a remarkably sturdy build, Argerich is a spellbinding soloist whose playing—notable for its power and blazing emotional intensity—can on the same evening be both deeply engaging and undisciplined. Spontaneous in the best sense, never wayward or self-indulgent, she seems equally happy raising the roof with Rachmaninov's D minor concerto and probing the elusive mysteries of Chopin's preludes. She reduced her concertizing in the late 1980s, but still made a relatively small number of recordings, which continue to be very highly regarded. In recent years, though, she has returned with increasing frequency to the concert stage and to the studio; she remains one of the most exciting pianists alive.

aria [1] A solo vocal piece in an opera, oratorio, or cantata. Often preceded by an introductory recitative in semi-conversational style, the aria is the major set-piece of many large-scale vocal works, providing the greatest opportunity for the display of the composer's melodic gifts

Martha Argerich, mercurial genius of the keyboard

and the singer's vocal and interpretive powers. Famous arias include "Nessun dorma" from Puccini's *Turandot* ◉ and "Rejoice, greatly" from Handel's *Messiah.* [2] A movement in an instrumental composition in which the writing is songlike (e.g., the final movement of Beethoven's Piano sonata in C minor, Op. 111, which the composer designated an *arietta,* or "little aria").

Ariadne auf Naxos OPERA BY RICHARD STRAUSS, to a libretto by Hugo von Hofmannsthal, first performed in Vienna in 1916. The work occupied Strauss and Hofmannsthal for the better part of five troubled years (1912–16). Hofmannsthal's original conception was to make *Ariadne* a pendant to a staged performance—in German, with musical numbers—of Molière's *Le bourgeois gentilhomme.* A failure in that version, the score reemerged after considerable reworking; in the premieres of both versions of the work, Maria Jeritza sang the title role. The opera consists of a prologue, centering around the figure of the Composer, and the one-act opera itself, in which the unfolding of the tale about Ariadne abandoned on the island of Naxos is interrupted and commented upon by the participants in the entertainment, a raucous burlesque entourage borrowed from commedia dell'arte.

In *Ariadne,* Strauss turned away from the lavish scoring and profligate musical effects that had characterized his earlier operas; writing for an ensemble of only 37 players, a decision shaped equally by aesthetic considerations and wartime reductions in theater staffs, he managed to achieve intimate expression without sacrificing sonority or richness of texture. In the part of Ariadne he exploited the huge range he considered a hallmark of the ideal soprano, while in Zerbinetta, the coquettish leader of the burlesque troupe, he created one of the great coloratura roles in opera, climaxed by the showstopping scena "Grossmächtiger Prinzessin." He saved some of his most ardent music for the role of the Composer, who appears only in the prologue—a figure representing the artist as idealist whose passionate longing for perfection is bound to be disappointed.

Britannia rules the waves.

RECOMMENDED RECORDINGS

VOIGHT, OTTER, DESSAY, HEPPNER: SINOPOLI AND STAATSKAPELLE DRESDEN (DG).

NORMAN, VARADY, GRUBEROVÁ, FREY: MASUR AND GEWANDHAUS ORCHESTRA (PHILIPS).

arioso [1] In vocal music, a RECITATIVE passage characterized by a flowing or melismatic manner of declamation, thus resembling an ARIA. [2] A passage in an instrumental piece patterned after this kind of singing. *See also* MELISMA.

Arne, Thomas Augustine

(b. London, March 12, 1710; d. London, March 5, 1778)

ENGLISH COMPOSER. The scope and quality of his output (roughly 90 stage works, including operas and incidental music for plays and masques) made him the leading theatrical composer of mid-18th-century London. Of his many scores the finest were probably those for the masque of *Comus* (1738; based on Milton) and the serious opera *Artaxerxes* (1762). Arne is best known for the song "Rule, Britannia," which appeared as the final chorus in the masque of *Alfred* (1740), and for the anthem "God Save the King," which he was the first to arrange for public performance (1745). His symphonies are lively and elegant, though harmonically unadventurous and rather formulaic in their melodic content.

Arnold, Malcolm

(b. Northampton, October 21, 1921)

ENGLISH COMPOSER. He attended the Royal College of Music from 1938 to 1941, and later served as principal trumpet of the London Philharmonic Orchestra. From 1948 he devoted himself full-time to composition. He has written close to 100 film scores, of which the best known are those for *The Bridge on the River Kwai* (1957), *Whistle Down the Wind* (1961), and *Hobson's Choice* (1953). In addition, he has composed nine symphonies, about an equal number of concertos for various instruments (including two each for clarinet and flute), and a considerable body of chamber pieces. Arnold's music reflects the influences of jazz, the English music hall tradition, and various Latin dance styles with a liveliness and charm that almost belie the skillfulness of his craftsmanship. Their easy embrace of tonality and unfailing lyricism make even his most serious pieces readily approachable.

RECOMMENDED RECORDINGS

FILM MUSIC (INCLUDING *THE BRIDGE ON THE RIVER KWAI*): HICKOX AND LONDON SYMPHONY ORCHESTRA (CHANDOS).

SYMPHONIES NOS. 1–9: PENNY AND NATIONAL SYMPHONY ORCHESTRA OF IRELAND (NAXOS).

WORKS FOR CLARINET (INCLUDING CLARINET CONCERTOS): JOHNSON; BOLTON AND ENGLISH CHAMBER ORCHESTRA (ASV).

Malcolm Arnold conducts the English Chamber Orchestra, 1986.

arpeggio (from It. *arpeggiare,* "to play the harp") A chord of any size or configuration that is strummed—or played as if strummed, in the case of a keyboard instrument—so that the notes are sounded individually, from bottom to top or top to bottom. The conventional sign indicating that a chord is to be arpeggiated is a wavy vertical line placed before the chord. Arpeggios can also be written out as a series of small notes beamed together, with the top and bottom notes of the arpeggiation usually appearing in normal-size notes.

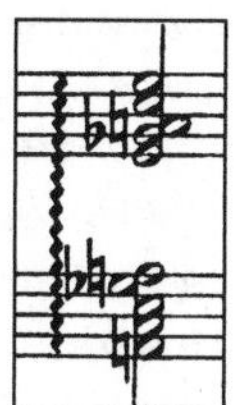

Rapidly executed arpeggios are a familiar element in much of the virtuoso piano repertoire. Chopin's turbulent Etude in C minor, Op. 25, No. 12, for example, achieves its flamboyant effect through a dazzling sequence of arpeggiated figures extended over three octaves in both hands. Chopin's Etude in E-flat, Op. 10, No. 11, consists almost entirely of arpeggiated chords in each hand.

Arrau, Claudio

(b. Chillán, February 6, 1903; d. Mürzzuschlag, Austria, June 9, 1991)

AMERICAN PIANIST OF CHILEAN BIRTH. He gave his first recital at the age of five in Santiago, and from 1912 to 1918 studied with Martin Krause in Berlin. He embarked on a European tour in 1918, made his London debut in 1922, and toured the United States for the first time in 1923. In 1924 he joined the faculty of the Stern Conservatory in Berlin, remaining there until 1940. He settled in the U.S. in 1941; for the next 50 years, with New York as his home base, he maintained a flourishing career with engagements throughout the world and a busy recording schedule. His virtuoso technique never deserted him, though he did adopt slower tempos after he entered his 80s.

Arrau was a consummate master of tone and an eloquent interpreter who communicated musical emotion—from the heroism of Beethoven to the reverie in Chopin—on a personal level. Drawn to the music of Bach, Beethoven, Brahms, and Liszt, as well as that of Chopin and Debussy (in which he achieved a sonority that can only be described as miraculous), he conveyed a firm conception of everything he played, combining elegance of articulation with a fierce inner tension. He always went his own way as an interpreter—he was perhaps the greatest ever when it came to Schumann's *Kreisleriana* and the heroic struggles of the Brahms B-flat Piano Concerto. His interests went well beyond the purely musical: He was well read, a committed Jungian, a collector of African figurines and pre-Columbian art, and a connoisseur of painting. An interview-biography by Joseph Horowitz, *Conversations with Arrau,* published in 1982, limns a fine portrait of the pianist.

RECOMMENDED RECORDINGS

BRAHMS, PIANO CONCERTO NO. 2: HAITINK AND CONCERTGEBOUW ORCHESTRA (PHILIPS).

CHOPIN, *NOCTURNES, IMPROMPTUS* (PHILIPS).

SCHUMANN, *KINDERSZENEN* (WITH *CARNAVAL* AND *WALDSZENEN*) (PHILIPS).

WORKS OF BEETHOVEN, LISZT, CHOPIN, SCHUMANN: "GREAT PIANISTS OF THE 20TH CENTURY—CLAUDIO ARRAU II" (PHILIPS).

Ars Antiqua (Lat., "the old art") [1] A term first used by Parisian theorists of the 14th century to distinguish the polyphonic music of the late 12th through early 14th centuries—specifically that emanating from the school of Notre Dame and such masters as Léonin and Pérotin between 1160 and 1260, and the music of later figures such as Jacques de Liège (ca. 1260–ca. 1330)—from the more complex and capricious music of the "modern" early-14th-century composers Johannes de Muris (ca. 1295–ca. 1355) and Philippe de Vitry, referred to as the Ars Nova. [2] In the most general sense, a synonym for 13th-century POLYPHONY.

Ars Nova (Lat., "the new art") Title of a treatise written around 1322 long attributed to Philippe de Vitry (his authorship is no longer accepted), which argued for a freer style of polyphonic composition allowing a wider range of note values and mensurations (the rhythmic relationships between them). Today the term is used generically to refer to all 14th-century POLYPHONY. Guillaume de Machaut is considered the leading composer of *Ars Nova.*

***Art of Fugue, The (Die Kunst der Fuge,* BWV 1080)** A LARGE-SCALE CONTRAPUNTAL STUDY FOR UNSPECIFIED INSTRUMENT(S) BY J. S. BACH. Compiled in the 1740s, and presumably intended for the keyboard, it consists of a series of canons and fugues (which Bach identifies by the Latin term *contrapunctus*), all derived from the same thematic material. Bach begins simply, with a slow four-voice FUGUE laying out the subject almost vocally, and adds progressive contrapuntal complications and stylistic touches, as in *Contrapunctus VI,* also a four-voice fugue, but done with dotted rhythms in the style of a French overture. ◉ The most comprehensive exercise in COUNTERPOINT ever attempted, it marks the apogee of Bach's achievement as an instrumental composer.

RECOMMENDED RECORDINGS

EMERSON STRING QUARTET (DG).

FRETWORK (HARMONIA MUNDI).

Arts Florissants, Les *See box on pages 310–13.*

Ashkenazy, Vladimir

(b. Gor'kiy [now Nizhniy Novgorod], July 6, 1937)

RUSSIAN-BORN PIANIST AND CONDUCTOR. He grew up in a musical family, and entered the class of Lev Oborin at the Moscow Conservatory in 1955. He won first prize at the Queen Elisabeth Competition in Brussels in 1956, and shared first prize (with John Ogdon) at the 1962 Tchaikovsky International Competition in Moscow. He left the Soviet Union in 1963, and began a busy international performing career as soloist, accompanist, chamber musician, and conductor. His major appointments have included engagements with two London orchestras—principal guest conductor of the Philharmonia (1981) and music director of the Royal Philharmonic (1987)—as well as posts of principal guest conductor of the Cleveland Orchestra (1987), music director of the Berlin Radio Symphony Orchestra (1989), and chief conductor of the Czech Philharmonic (1998–2003).

As a pianist, Ashkenazy plateaued early; the quality of his playing has remained constant for 40 years. He has shown an affinity for the concertos of Mozart and the solo works of Chopin, where his crystalline sound and sparkling clarity in rapid passagework are particularly welcome. Less well suited to music that requires brawn as well as brains, he has nonetheless met with success in the concertos of Brahms and Rachmaninov, and recorded the latter both as pianist (twice) and as conductor (with Jean-Yves Thibaudet as soloist). If anything, Ashkenazy's range and abilities as a conductor have been underrated: He has recorded excellent accounts of the Rachmaninov symphonies (with the Concertgebouw Orchestra), Tchaikovsky's *The Nutcracker* and Glazunov's *The Seasons* (with the Royal Philharmonic), and of Franck's Symphony in D minor (with the Deutsches Symphonie-Orchester Berlin), and his recording of Debussy's *La mer* with the Cleveland Orchestra is peerless.

Ashkenazy in his element

RECOMMENDED RECORDINGS

As pianist:

Prokofiev, complete piano concertos: Previn and London Symphony Orchestra (Decca).

Rachmaninov, piano concertos: Previn and London Symphony Orchestra (Decca).

As conductor:

Debussy, *La mer*: Cleveland Orchestra (Decca).

Glazunov, *The Seasons*: Royal Philharmonic; Prokofiev, *Cinderella*: Cleveland Orchestra (Decca).

Rachmaninov, orchestral works: Concertgebouw Orchestra (Decca).

Aspen Music Festival *See box on pages 46–47.*

assai (It.) Quite, very. Usually used to modify a basic tempo, e.g., *Allegro assai* or *Vivace assai.*

a tempo (It., "in tempo") A return to the principal tempo of a section or a piece after a passage in which the tempo has been altered.

atonal(ity) An extreme form of chromaticism that prevents the ear from recognizing or inferring a tonal center. The boundaries between tonal and atonal music were blurred in the music of Scriabin and Debussy, and further breached by Stravinsky, Bartók, and Varèse. The most enthusiastic and effective use of atonality came in the music of Schoenberg—e.g., *PIERROT LUNAIRE* (1912)—and his pupils Berg and Webern, during the decade 1911–21. *See also* CHROMATIC, *individual composers.*

aubade (Fr., "dawn song") A piece intended to "greet the dawn," or more generally to be played in the morning, often as a salute to an individual. The term implies no particular form or procedure. In the 19th century it was often used as the title of a brief characteristic piece, as in Bizet's *Aubade* for piano. Poulenc chose the title *Aubade* for a "choreographic concerto" for piano and winds. As the fourth movement of his piano suite *Miroirs* (1904–15), Ravel wrote a brilliantly colorful aubade with a sultry middle section, giving it the exotic-sounding Spanish title "Alborada del gracioso" (which roughly translates as "Jester's Morning Song"). In Ravel's orchestration, it not only greets the dawn, it is almost dazzling enough to outdo it. The greatest of all aubades, written as a Christmas-morning birthday present for his wife, is Wagner's SIEGFRIED IDYLL.

Auber, Daniel-François-Esprit

(b. Caen, January 29, 1782; d. Paris, May 12, 1871)

FRENCH COMPOSER. A late bloomer, he pursued music as a dilettante for many years, composing sporadically and at one point studying privately with Luigi Cherubini. It was only in 1819, following the death of his father and the bankruptcy of the family's art-supply business, that Auber turned seriously to the composition of opera as a means of supporting himself. Within a decade he created more than a dozen works, including *La muette de Portici* (*The Mute Girl of Portici*; 1828), which became the prototype for the style known as GRAND OPERA. With its incendiary plotline and sensational effects (the final scene depicts nothing less than the eruption of Vesuvius), *La muette de Portici* emerged as a focal point of revolutionary fervor throughout Europe; the riot at a Brussels performance on August 25, 1830 actually sparked the Belgian revolution of 1830. Auber continued to crank out operas for another 40 years, composing his last one in 1869, at the age of 87. Of the remainder of his works, the best known are *Fra Diavolo* (1830) and *Le cheval de bronze* (*The Bronze Horse*; 1835). The former is still occasionally staged, and the latter contains what is probably Auber's finest overture.

La muette de Portici, *1829*

RECOMMENDED RECORDINGS

LA MUETTE DE PORTICI: KRAUS, ANDERSON, ALER; FULTON AND MONTE-CARLO PHILHARMONIC ORCHESTRA (EMI).

OVERTURES: PARAY AND DETROIT SYMPHONY ORCHESTRA (MERCURY).

Auden, W(ystan) H(ugh)

(b. York, February 21, 1907; d. Vienna, September 29, 1973)

AMERICAN POET AND ESSAYIST OF ENGLISH BIRTH, noted for his virtuosic use of language. A dextrous versifier with a flair for the extreme, he provided the libretto for Stravinsky's THE RAKE'S PROGRESS (1951) as well as the poems set by Britten for his *Hymn to St. Cecilia* (1942). In addition, even though it is a purely instrumental work, Bernstein's Symphony No. 2 (*The Age of Anxiety*) for piano and orchestra drew its inspiration from Auden's 1947 eclogue of the same name.

Auer, Leopold

(b. Veszprem, June 7, 1845; d. Loschwitz, July 15, 1930)

RUSSIAN VIOLINIST AND PEDAGOGUE of Hungarian birth. He studied at the conservatories in Budapest and Vienna, completing his training with Joseph Joachim in Hanover (1863–64). After a successful debut at the Gewandhaus in Leipzig, he

Leopold Auer, trainer of thoroughbred violinists

was engaged as concertmaster of orchestras in Düsseldorf and Hamburg. During a visit to London in 1868, he performed Beethoven's *Archduke* Trio with Anton Rubinstein and Alfredo Piatti; on the strength of that encounter, Rubinstein arranged for him to be appointed professor at the St. Petersburg Conservatory, where he remained until 1917. He settled in the United States after the Russian Revolution, teaching in New York and at the Curtis Institute in Philadelphia.

Though best known for having spurned the dedication of Tchaikovsky's Violin Concerto (he later became its champion), Auer's real claim to fame stems from the half century he taught in St. Petersburg, where his students included Jascha Heifetz, Mischa Elman, Efrem Zimbalist, and Nathan Milstein. His influence, felt more along musical lines than technical ones, involved the cultivation of a rich, expressive tone, tastefully restrained virtuosity, and a noble singing line.

Aufstieg und Fall der Stadt Mahagonny (Rise and Fall of the City of Mahagonny) DYSTOPIAN OPERA BY KURT WEILL, to a libretto by Bertolt Brecht, premiered in Leipzig in 1930. An allegory of modern life, the story concerns the founding of an "ideal" city by a bunch of colorfully named outcasts—Leokadja Begbick, Trinity Moses, Fatty the Bookkeeper, Jim Mahoney, and Alaska Wolf Joe—and the city's inevitable decline under the weight of avarice, lust, and all manner of hypocrisy and human failing. Freighted with social commentary (the libretto is a thinly disguised critique of capitalism, fascism, and bourgeois morality), *Mahagonny* is an awkward piece of theater, but it contains some of Weill's most vivid, characterful music, including the memorable "Alabama Song." The work enjoyed a successful revival at the Metropolitan Opera in the 1970s.

RECOMMENDED RECORDING

SILJA, SCHLEMM, NEUMANN; LATHAM-KÖNIG AND COLOGNE RADIO SYMPHONY ORCHESTRA (CAPRICCIO).

augmentation [1] A procedure generally encountered in fugal writing in which a given motif or subject is set in lengthened note values. [2] The expansion of a perfect INTERVAL (fourth, fifth, or octave) or a major one (second, third, sixth, or seventh) by a half step. A major sixth expanded in this way is called an augmented sixth, and a chord based on that interval is called an augmented sixth chord.

autograph The manuscript score of a piece of music, written in the composer's own hand.

Mozart's Jupiter *Symphony (his hand can be recognized by the broken accolades)*

avant-garde (Fr., "vanguard") An aesthetic style or artistic method that departs from the conventional practices of the time. The term was first used in musicological circles to refer to the work of Karlheinz Stockhausen, Pierre Boulez, and other post–World War II European composers determined to renounce the past. It quickly came to serve as a tag for any composer whose music partook of unconventional syntax or techniques (everything from ALEATORY to electronic synthesis, from microtonality to mouth music). Since the 1970s, the European avant-garde has become the arrière-garde, as composers in Europe and America have increasingly sought a reengagement with traditional forms and means of expression. *See also individual composers.*

Ax, Emanuel

(b. Lvov, June 8, 1949)

AMERICAN PIANIST OF POLISH BIRTH. He began his musical studies at the age of six; after his family moved to New York in 1961, he enrolled at the Juilliard School as a student of Mieczysław Munz. He won the first Arthur Rubinstein International Piano Competition in Tel Aviv in 1974, and received an Avery Fisher Prize in 1979. Since then he has enjoyed a secure career as a performing and recording artist.

Pianist Emanuel Ax, reliable in the classics and a champion of his contemporaries

With an affinity for the works of Mozart, Beethoven, Chopin, and Brahms—in whose music he has had his finest pianistic moments—Ax has also taken an interest in the work of contemporary composers, including Joseph Schwantner (b. 1943), Peter Lieberson (b. 1946), Christopher Rouse (b. 1949), and Bright Sheng (b. 1955); he is the dedicatee of John Adams's piano concerto *Century Rolls* (1996). In concert he has championed the Schoenberg concerto as well as music by Bartók and Hindemith. Despite his success, Ax has a tendency to deliver what the Russians, in the old days, would have called "cosmopolitan" interpretations—meticulously polished and craftsmanlike, but lacking in individuality.

RECOMMENDED RECORDINGS

BRAHMS, *KLAVIERSTÜCKE,* OP. 118, *VARIATIONS AND FUGUE ON A THEME BY HANDEL* (SONY).

CHOPIN, PIANO CONCERTOS: ORMANDY AND PHILADELPHIA ORCHESTRA (RCA).

B

Babbitt, Milton

(b. Philadelphia, May 10, 1916)

AMERICAN COMPOSER. A child prodigy, he grew up in Jackson, Mississippi, learning to play the violin at the age of four and studying clarinet and saxophone as well. In high school, as a sideline, he played jazz and worked as a popular songwriter. Intent on becoming a mathematician, he was admitted to the University of Pennsylvania as a 15-year-old; finding himself increasingly drawn to music, he transferred to New York University, where he studied with Philip James and Marion Bauer. Later, at Princeton, he studied with Roger Sessions. Babbitt served on Princeton's faculty from 1938 to 1984, teaching mathematics during the war years (1943–45), and, from 1948 until 1984, composition. He joined the faculty of the Juilliard School in 1973.

Milton Babbitt, chairman of the avant-garde

Babbitt expanded the 12-tone technique of Arnold Schoenberg into areas not addressed by him such as dynamics, rhythm, and timbre. In 1959, with Otto Luening (1900–96) and Vladimir Ussachevsky (1911–90), he founded the Columbia-Princeton Electronic Music Center in New York City. An indefatigable innovator, he reigned as one of the most influential American composers, teachers, and theorists from the 1950s through the 1970s; but the complexity of his music, and its arcane syntax, left the broader audience cold. At its best, his music combines formidable structural rigor with an almost ethereal aural grace, as in *Philomel,* for soprano and tape. Babbitt's *All Set,* for jazz ensemble, captures his eclectic flexibility. The title of an article Babbitt wrote for *High Fidelity* in 1958—"Who Cares if You Listen?"—famously summed up the arrogance and insularity of the avant-garde then, and reads more and more like an epitaph as time goes by.

RECOMMENDED RECORDINGS

PHILOMEL, PHONOMENA, POST-PARTITIONS, REFLECTIONS: BEARDSKE, KUDERNA, ET AL. (NEW WORLD RECORDS).

PIANO MUSIC: FEINBERG (CRI).

Bach, Carl Philipp Emanuel

(b. Weimar, March 8, 1714; d. Hamburg, December 14, 1788)

GERMAN KEYBOARD PLAYER AND COMPOSER, son of Johann Sebastian Bach and Maria Barbara Bach; he became the most celebrated and influential composer among the Bach sons. When the family moved to Leipzig in 1723, he enrolled in the Thomasschule, where his father was in charge of the musical curriculum. Like his elder brother Wilhelm Friedemann (1710–84), he entered the University of Leipzig as a law student after graduating from the Thomasschule, although he continued to live at home and work as his father's chief musical assistant. The pull of music was strong, as was an early friendship with the crown prince of Prussia, who was to become King Frederick II—Frederick the Great. Emanuel spent nearly 30 years in Berlin at the monarch's court, and became the principal exponent of the *EMPFINDSAMER STIL*, or "Sensibility Style," a highly original and expressive idiom that served as an important link between the Baroque and Classical styles. He also wrote the most important musical treatise of the 18th century, *Versuch über die wahre Art das Clavier zu spielen* (*Essay on the True Art of Playing Keyboard Instruments*). Today he is mostly known through his chamber and keyboard music and for the flute concertos he wrote to please the king, who was particularly enamored of the flute.

RECOMMENDED RECORDINGS

FLUTE CONCERTOS: GALLOIS; MALLON AND TORONTO CAMERATA (NAXOS).

FLUTE SONATAS: B. KUIJKEN; VAN ASPEREN (SONY).

KEYBOARD SONATAS: SPÁNYI (BIS).

Frederick the Great plays the flute, accompanied by C. P. E. Bach (painting by Adolf von Menzel).

Bach, Johann Christian

(b. Leipzig, September 5, 1735; d. London, January 1, 1782)

ENGLISH COMPOSER OF GERMAN BIRTH, the youngest son of Johann Sebastian Bach and Anna Magdalena Bach. He came to be known as the "London Bach" because he spent most of his career in the English capital. Only 15 when his father died, Christian went to Berlin to complete his musical studies with brother Carl Philipp Emanuel. The last of the Bach boys was free-spirited and up to date, and had a soft spot for Italian music and Italian women. As a leading practitioner of the *GALANT* style he became one of the pioneers of musical Classicism, and during the 1770s, he enjoyed an enviable reputation throughout Europe as a symphonist and composer of operas. He took the eight-year-old Mozart under his wing when the child came to London, encouraging him to develop as a composer and exerting an influence that Mozart always acknowledged. Some of Christian's symphonies and overtures are still occasionally performed today.

RECOMMENDED RECORDING

SINFONIAS (COMPLETE): HALSTEAD AND HANOVER BAND (CPO).

Bach, Johann Sebastian

(b. Eisenach, March 21, 1685; d. Leipzig, July 28, 1750)

GERMAN COMPOSER AND ORGANIST whose music, in every genre but opera, spectacularly crowned the Baroque era. The most intellectual of his remarkable family—the male descendants of Hans Bach, who had served as professional musicians in Thuringia for three generations prior to his birth—he was not only the greatest composer of the Baroque era but the leading organist of his generation and an accomplished violinist and violist as well. From youth onward he undertook a self-directed

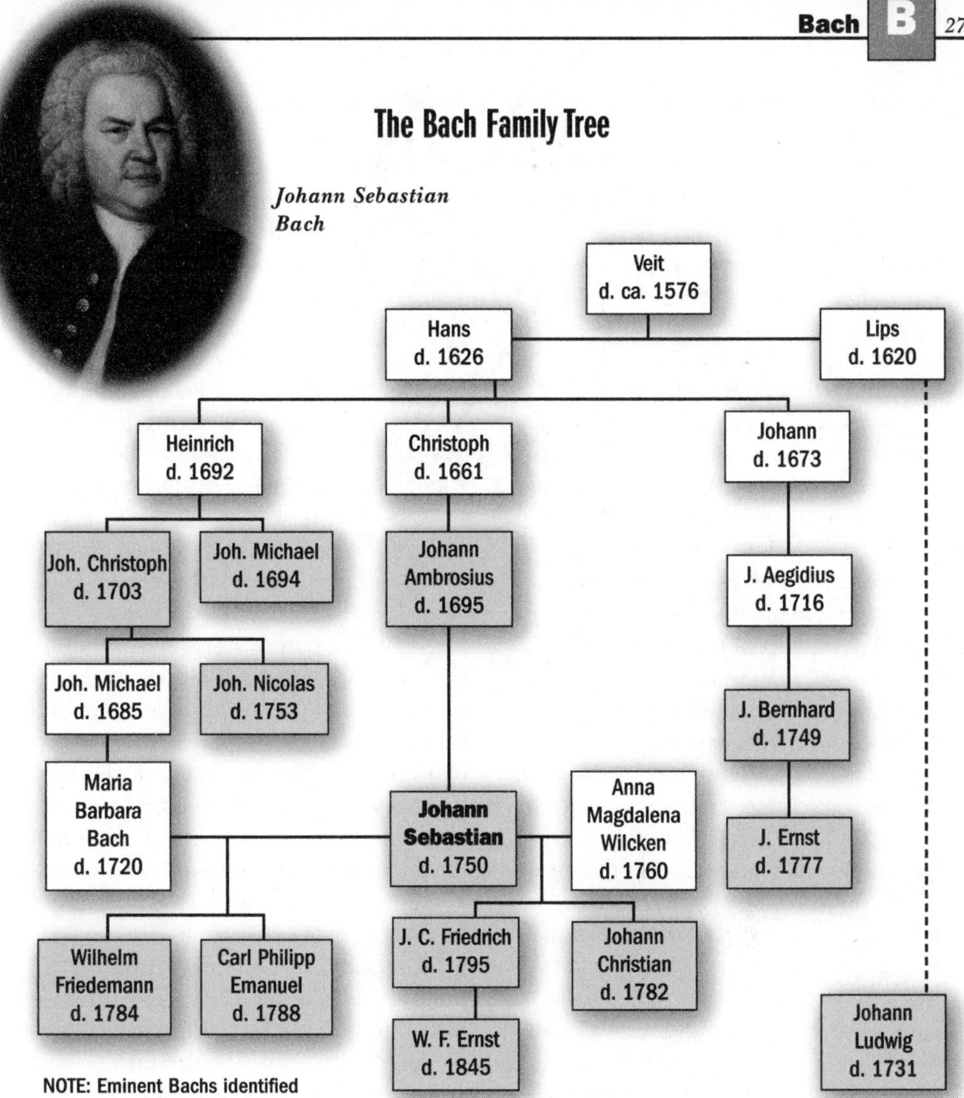

and systematic exploration of the major musical genres and styles of his day, focusing first on the keyboard, then on the broader realms of concerted vocal and instrumental music. Along the way he set himself a remarkable series of formal and aesthetic challenges and synthesized a unique personal style.

Bach received what was for the time a thorough humanistic education. After completing his studies in Lüneburg he was employed as a "lackey" at the ducal court in Weimar (1703) and as an organist in Arnstadt (1703–07). In 1705 he made a pilgrimage to Lübeck to hear Buxtehude, the greatest organist of the day and a composer whose music was to have a profound effect on his own. Inspired by what he heard there, he composed some of his greatest pieces for organ (among them the monumental Passacaglia in C minor, BWV 582) ◉ during his remaining years in Arnstadt. His next post as organist was in Mühlhausen (1707–08); after that, he served as court organist and chamber musician (and from 1714 court concertmaster as well) in Weimar (1708–17). Bach subsequently spent six productive years as Kapellmeister at the court of Cöthen (1717–23), where his young patron, Prince Leopold of Anhalt-Cöthen, a fine musician himself, enthusiastically supported his efforts. One of the ongoing concerns of Bach scholarship has been the question of what Bach composed prior to, and during, his time at Cöthen. In recent years compelling evidence has been marshaled in support of the claim that the original versions of all six of the works which in 1721 became the *BRANDENBURG* CONCERTOS, Bach's matchless contribution to the genre of the CONCERTO GROSSO, predate his Cöthen appointment. That is certainly the case in the middle movement of Concerto No. 6, where the two solo violas answer each other in an imitative pattern and eventually intertwine. ◉ If it now appears that Bach was a better and more prolific composer earlier than had previously been thought, it also appears that more than 200 of his compositions from the Cöthen years, mainly chamber and orchestral works, may be lost.

Church music in Bach's time

One of the many organs Bach played

In 1722, the death of Johann Kuhnau left vacant the position of Kantor at Leipzig's Thomaskirche, an important church and musical center. Of the six applicants for the job, Bach was neither the most famous nor the town council's first choice. But Georg Philipp Telemann could not obtain a release from his post in Hamburg, and Christoph Graupner was lured away by the city of Darmstadt. Bach was eventually offered the job, and in 1723 he moved to Leipzig.

In an average week during his first five years in Leipzig, he was expected to compose a 30-minute cantata, supervise the copying of its parts, rehearse it, and perform it on Sunday at either the Thomaskirche or the Nicolaikirche; to furnish music as required for feast days and special events such as weddings and funerals; to attend the musical training of 50-plus boarding students at the Thomasschule (he balked, however, at the demand that he teach them Latin as well); and to oversee musical activities at the two smaller churches for which he was also responsible. Somewhere in the midst of this he found time to eat and sleep, to take a hand in his sons' musical education (four of them went on to become professional musicians), and to smoke his pipe, whose pleasures he once extolled in a poem of six stanzas.

He remained Kantor at the Thomaskirche until his death in 1750, composing three complete annual cycles of church cantatas, other sacred works—including a MAGNIFICAT, the *ST. MATTHEW* PASSION, and the *MASS IN B MINOR*—numerous secular cantatas, and a large amount of keyboard and instrumental music. The cantata cycles

From **A Musical Offering**

and the other great sacred works of his Leipzig years may well have been, as scholar Christoph Wolff has suggested, the means by which Bach sought to forge "an argument for the existence of God." During his final decade he completed the score of the *Mass in B Minor,* wrote the GOLDBERG VARIATIONS, and undertook two remarkable series of contrapuntal studies that summarized his knowledge of the art and theory of music: *A MUSICAL OFFERING* and *THE ART OF FUGUE.* With these speculative, large-scale, elaborately contrapuntal works he fittingly capped his own career and sounded the last, exquisite cry of the Baroque.

Bach was the consummate student and practitioner of musical science in the 18th century, much as Sir Isaac Newton, a generation and a half older than he, had been the consummate investigator of physical science. Both, by virtue of their innate genius and systematic approach to the phenomena that interested them, brought about revolutions in their fields of study. Newton's work became the foundation of modern science and Bach's the prototype for the organically conceived, highly structured "pure music" of the 19th and 20th centuries.

The full panoply of musical style known to the late Baroque, from the rigorous imitative polyphony of the Renaissance to the breezy directness of Italian opera buffa, is recapped in Bach's works. His cantatas and large-scale sacred works make use of text-setting techniques absorbed from the Franco-Flemish composers of the 16th century, from 17th-century Italian sacred music, and from opera. His organ works respond to Italian and north-German influences, while his music for harpsichord is a brilliant amalgam of French and German elements. Bach's concertos have the grace and fluency of the finest Italian essays, with more contrapuntal density and melodic interest. His orchestral suites pay homage to the grandeur of the French style while surpassing the efforts of others (save Handel perhaps) in vitality; in the Suite No. 2 in B minor, BWV 1067, he even tips his hat in the concluding "Badinerie" to the emerging *GALANT.*

Bach cultivated virtuosity on a consistent basis, which has given his instrumental works an exceptional influence on works written subsequently, along with an enduring place in the repertoire. The sonatas and partitas for unaccompanied violin, the suites for unaccompanied cello, the sonatas for flute and harpsichord, the solo organ works, and the solo keyboard works including *DAS WOHLTEMPERIRTE CLAVIER (The Well-Tempered Clavier)* and *Goldberg* Variations are the foundation of the solo repertoire for these instruments. While the revival of interest in early music has brought the compositions of many of his predecessors back into circulation, the standard repertoire—instrumental, orchestral, and sacred—truly begins with Bach.

Nevertheless, for many years after his death the immensity of Bach's achievement as a composer remained hidden from posterity, even from the most knowledgeable and astute of his successors. Surprisingly little of his music was published during his lifetime, and the great works for which he is revered today existed only in manuscript or fair copies at the time of his death. Insiders like Mozart and Beethoven, who encountered Bach's music via these sources (or through contact with his students and sons), may have had an inkling of his greatness, but the public at large would begin to "discover" Bach only after a revival of interest in his music got under way early in the 19th century.

That revival, made possible by the efforts of enlightened performers such as Felix Mendelssohn and by the nascent academic discipline of musicology, produced a tidal wave of publication and research. Piece by piece, Bach's music was tracked down, and what could be found was published. Piece by piece, it was taken up by grateful, often awestruck, musicians and played to grateful and similarly awestruck audiences. Bach went from being a connoisseur's composer to one of the Three B's. Another of the Three B's, Beethoven, summed up Bach's importance with a pun on his name, which means "brook" in German. "Not Brook, but Ocean, should be his name!" he declared. *See also* COUNTERPOINT, FUGUE.

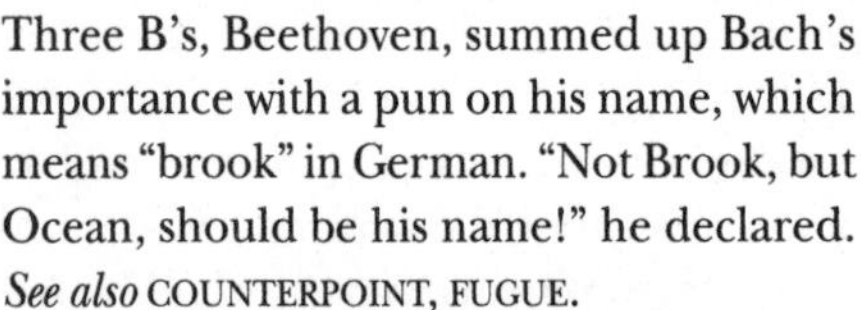

RECOMMENDED RECORDINGS

MASS IN B MINOR: SCHLICK, BRETT, CROOK, KOOY; HERREWEGHE AND COLLEGIUM VOCALE (HARMONIA MUNDI).

BRANDENBURG CONCERTOS: LAMON AND TAFELMUSIK (SONY).

BRANDENBURG CONCERTOS: PEARLMAN AND BOSTON BAROQUE (TELARC).

COMPLETE CANTATAS (SERIES): WESSEL, DE GROOT, OTHERS; KOOPMAN AND AMSTERDAM BAROQUE ORCHESTRA (CHALLENGE CLASSICS).

GOLDBERG VARIATIONS: HANTAI (MIRARE).

GOLDBERG VARIATIONS: PERAHIA (SONY).

ORCHESTRAL SUITES: GARDINER AND ENGLISH BAROQUE SOLOISTS (ERATO).

ST. MATTHEW PASSION: MONOYIOS, BONNEY, OTTER, CHANCE, ROLFE JOHNSON, CROOK; GARDINER AND ENGLISH BAROQUE SOLOISTS (ARCHIV).

Bachauer, Gina

(b. Athens, May 21, 1910; d. Athens, August 22, 1976)

GREEK-BORN PIANIST. She began her study of the piano at the age of five; later, she enrolled at the École Normale de Musique in Paris and took lessons with Alfred Cortot. She made her professional debut in Athens in 1935, playing Tchaikovsky's Piano Concerto No. 1 in B-flat minor with the Athens Symphony under Dimitri Mitropoulos. From 1937 until 1950 she lived in Alexandria, Egypt; while the Germans occupied her homeland during World War II, she gave about 40 concerts for Allied soldiers in the Middle East. She made her London debut in 1946, playing the Grieg A minor concerto, and from 1951, the year of her marriage to English conductor Alec Sherman, until her death, she spent approximately half of each year touring the United States. In 1971 she was chosen to give the first solo recital at the newly opened Kennedy Center in Washington, D.C.

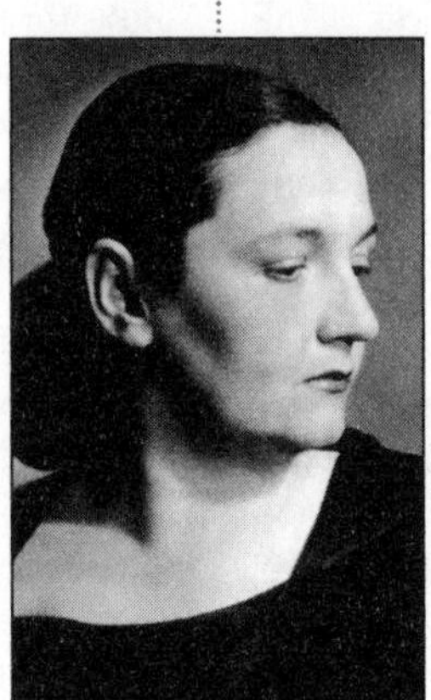

Gina Bachauer

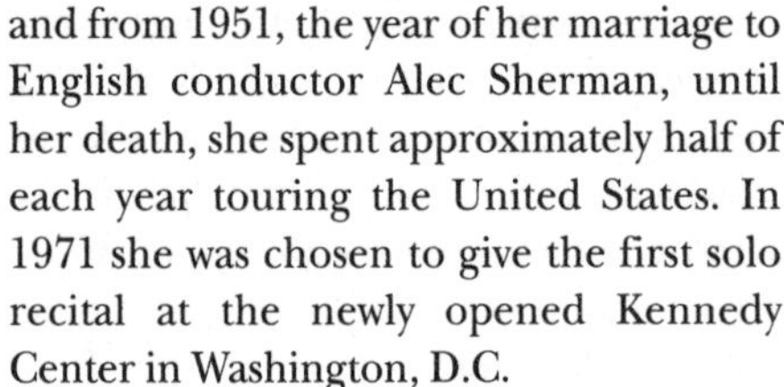

A powerful pianist most at home in thunderous works like Rachmaninov's Piano Concerto No. 2, Bachauer could also be convincing in pieces that required a delicate touch, such as the Fauré *Ballade.* She had a large repertoire, running from Bach and Mozart to Stravinsky. Sometimes the music sounded more overpowering than profound, but when she performed, there was never any doubt that an instrument was being *played*—not teased, or caressed, or put on display, but played, and with authority.

RECOMMENDED RECORDING

BRAHMS PIANO CONCERTO NO. 2: DORATI AND LONDON SYMPHONY ORCHESTRA (CHESKY).

Backhaus, Wilhelm

(b. Leipzig, March 26, 1884; d. Villach, July 5, 1969)

SWISS PIANIST OF GERMAN BIRTH. He studied at the Leipzig Conservatory, leaving in 1899 to become a pupil of Eugen d'Albert in Frankfurt. He began touring as a concert pianist in 1900, and continued to perform and record up to the time of his death, while in Austria for a concert engagement, at the age of 85. One of the last pianists to emerge from the Leipzig Conservatory tradition, Backhaus was an artist of remarkable circumspection and poise whose readings had the authority and firmness of granite. He was best known for his insightful, if "old school," interpretations of the music of Mozart, Beethoven, and Brahms.

RECOMMENDED RECORDINGS

BEETHOVEN, PIANO SONATAS: "GREAT PIANISTS OF THE 20TH CENTURY" (PHILIPS).

BRAHMS, PIANO CONCERTO NO. 2: BÖHM AND VIENNA PHILHARMONIC (DECCA).

Bacquier, Gabriel

(b. Béziers, May 17, 1924)

FRENCH BARITONE. He studied at the Paris Conservatoire, joining the company of the Paris Opéra in 1958. There, in 1960, he sang the role of Scarpia in Puccini's *Tosca,* opposite Renata Tebaldi; later that year he appeared at the festival of Aix-en-Provence in what was to become a signature role, the title part in Mozart's *Don Giovanni.* Bacquier's other roles in Paris, where he remained on the roster through 1981, included Germont in *La traviata,* Rigoletto, Simon Boccanegra, Escamillo in *Carmen,* Leporello in *Don Giovanni,* and Boris Godunov. From 1963 he was a regular guest at the Vienna Staatsoper, and he sang with the Metropolitan Opera for 18 seasons in a row. Throughout his career, especially from the 1970s onward, he was admired equally for the richness of his timbre, his nuanced delivery, and the sophistication of his acting.

Wilhelm Backhaus, young lion of the keyboard

RECOMMENDED RECORDINGS

RAVEL, *L'HEURE ESPAGNOLE*: BERBIÉ, SÉNÉCHAL; MAAZEL AND FRENCH NATIONAL RADIO ORCHESTRA (DG).

ROSSINI, *GUILLAUME TELL*: MESPLÉ, CABALLÉ, GEDDA; GARDELLI AND ROYAL PHILHARMONIC ORCHESTRA (EMI).

bagatelle (Fr. "trifle") A short work, usually for keyboard. The first use of the term dates from 1717 and a harpsichord piece by François Couperin. Beethoven's three sets of *Bagatelles,* Opp. 33, 119, and 126, are the best-known examples of the genre; the pieces of the Op. 126 set are rather formidable and ambitious in their musical content; the final one is a miniature operatic scene played out on the piano keys. Not all bagatelles are for the keyboard: Dvořák's *Five Bagatelles,* Op. 47, are scored for the delightful combination of two violins, cello, and harmonium; Webern's *Six Bagatelles* (1913) for string quartet; and Gerald Finzi's *Five Bagatelles,* Op. 23, for clarinet and piano.

RECOMMENDED RECORDINGS

BEETHOVEN, *BAGATELLES*: KOVACEVICH (PHILIPS).

DVOŘÁK, *BAGATELLES*: DOMUS (VIRGIN CLASSICS).

FINZI, *FIVE BAGATELLES*: DE PEYER; PRYOR (CHANDOS).

Baird, Julianne

(b. Statesville, N.C., December 10, 1952)

AMERICAN SOPRANO. Raised in the Appalachian Mountains, where she sang in church and listened to Mozart opera recordings, she became interested in period performance practice as a student at Eastman. She continued her studies at Stanford University and with Nikolaus Harnoncourt at the Salzburg Mozarteum; she began her career in New York as a member of the Waverly Consort and Concert Royal, with which she made her professional stage debut in 1980 in *Il pastor fido.* She quickly became known for her exquisitely musical, historically informed performances of music written before 1800. She was one of five singers on Joshua Rifkin's controversial 1982 Nonesuch recording of Bach's *Mass in B Minor,* which demonstrated Rifkin's thesis that in Bach's time soloists also sang the choruses one-on-a-part. Baird made several other Bach recordings with Rifkin; her extensive discography also includes recordings of Renaissance lute songs, Handel arias, and a considerable amount of opera, including Handel's *Imeneo* and *Berenice* and Pergolesi's *La serva padrona.* She has also recorded specially researched recital programs such as "Jane's Hand," consisting of English songs culled from Jane Austen's hand-copied music notebooks.

Baird earned her Ph.D. in musicology from Stanford in 1991. Since 1989, she has taught at Rutgers University, Camden. An expert in Baroque technique and ornamentation, she not only applies her scholarship to her singing but also teaches heavily subscribed master classes at Rutgers and other universities. In 1995, Cambridge University Press published her translation of *Introduction to the Art of Singing* by Johann Friedrich Agricola.

RECOMMENDED RECORDINGS

"ENGLISH MAD SONGS AND AYRES" (PURCELL, ARNE, BLOW): TILNEY (DORIAN).

"SONGS OF LOVE AND WAR" (CACCINI, FRESCOBALDI, MONTEVERDI): TILNEY; LUTZKE (DORIAN).

baiser de la fée, Le (Fairy's Kiss, The)

BALLET IN FOUR SCENES BY IGOR STRAVINSKY based on piano pieces and songs by Tchaikovsky, composed in 1928 to a scenario by Alexandre Benois (after Hans Christian Andersen), at the request of ballerina Ida Rubinstein. Stravinsky's longest ballet, it received its premiere on November 27, 1928, at the Paris Opéra. In creating the score, Stravinsky not only refracted the music of Tchaikovsky through his own lens, but composed much original music directly in the style of the older master, often seeking to imitate the orchestral coloring of *THE SLEEPING BEAUTY,* Tchaikovsky's greatest ballet. Compared with the revolutionary modernism of the scores to *PETRUSHKA* and *THE RITE OF SPRING* or the parodic classicizing of *PULCINELLA,* however, *LE BAISER DE LA FÉE* shows Stravinsky in a surprisingly reactionary mode, seeking to recapture, through pastiche, the tradition out of which he had so disruptively emerged.

RECOMMENDED RECORDING

JÄRVI AND ROYAL SCOTTISH NATIONAL ORCHESTRA (CHANDOS).

Baker, Dame Janet

(b. Hatfield, March 23, 1933)

ENGLISH MEZZO-SOPRANO. She studied in London, specializing early in her career in 17th- and 18th-century operatic roles, especially Handel (Rodelinda, Ariodante, and Orlando) and Purcell's Dido, which she sang at Aldeburgh in 1962 and at Glyndebourne in 1966. She also became a noted interpreter of Berlioz's Dido (in

Dame Janet Baker in 1983

Les Troyens), singing the part with the Scottish National Opera and at Covent Garden. Remarkably versatile, she excelled in contemporary opera as well, creating the role of Kate in Britten's *Owen Wingrave* and presenting Cressida in Walton's *Troilus and Cressida* at Covent Garden. She retired from the operatic stage in 1982, with the vocal world at her feet. Throughout her career she was equally celebrated for her work as a recitalist (particularly acclaimed for her renditions of Schubert and Schumann lieder) and in oratorio.

Baker possessed a voice of amazing range and richness, always superbly controlled, that made a direct emotional connection with the listener. Her precise diction and immaculate intonation were the delight of connoisseurs and the despair of all her rivals. In addition, she had an uncanny command of language—whether French, German, or English—so that her singing literally "spoke" in musical tones. Her emotional identification with, and penetrating psychological insights into, the roles she regularly sang gave her accounts an expressiveness that remains a benchmark. During the 1960s and 1970s, Baker compiled a vast discography (to which she added a few, lovely discs in the 1980s and 1990s), of which the highlights include her accounts of song cycles by Schubert and Schumann, Purcell's *Dido and Aeneas,* Elgar's *Sea Pictures,* and Mahler's *Rückert-Lieder.*

RECOMMENDED RECORDINGS

ELGAR, *SEA PICTURES*: BARBIROLLI AND LONDON SYMPHONY ORCHESTRA (EMI).

MAHLER, *KINDERTOTENLIEDER, RÜCKERT-LIEDER*: BARBIROLLI AND HALLÉ ORCHESTRA, NEW PHILHARMONIA ORCHESTRA (EMI).

SCHUBERT SONGS: JOHNSON (HYPERION).

Balakirev, Mily

(b. Nizhni Novgorod, January 2, 1837; d. St. Petersburg, May 29, 1910)

RUSSIAN COMPOSER. He had piano lessons as a child and began composing as a teenager. Entirely self-taught as a composer (though strongly influenced by the music of Beethoven, Berlioz, Schumann, Liszt, and Glinka), he became the leading figure in the St. Petersburg group of composers known as THE FIVE or the "Mighty Handful," encouraging, cajoling, and on some occasions browbeating the other members—Borodin, Rimsky-Korsakov, Mussorgsky, and César Cui (1835–1918). As the group's only full-time composer, he enjoyed prestige somewhat out of proportion to the actual quality of his music. Nonetheless, his "hands-on" combination of advice and advocacy was important to the development of a national musical style in late-19th-century Russia, and not just among the St. Petersburg composers: Tchaikovsky received detailed suggestions (some actually quite helpful) from Balakirev on the composition of his *Romeo and Juliet* Fantasy-Overture. Balakirev's best pieces, including his Symphony No. 1 (begun in 1864–66, set aside, and completed in 1893–97) and the piano fantasy *Islamey* (1869), blend advanced Western

Mily Balakirev, ca. 1870

harmony and native colorism in interesting and effective ways; their unorthodox melodic, rhythmic, and formal schemes, often derived from folk song, testify to the freshness of Balakirev's thought.

RECOMMENDED RECORDINGS

ISLAMEY (PIANO): BRONFMAN (SONY).

ISLAMEY (ARR. FOR ORCHESTRA BY LYAPUNOV): GERGIEV AND KIROV ORCHESTRA (PHILIPS).

SYMPHONY NO. 1: SVETLANOV AND PHILHARMONIA ORCHESTRA (HYPERION).

ballade [1] One of three verse forms (*formes fixes*)—the others were the rondeau and virelai—that served as templates for secular song in France during the 14th and 15th centuries. The ballade stanza adheres to an AAB pattern ending with a refrain. *See also* MACHAUT. [2] An instrumental piece of moderate length, usually for piano, in free or rhapsodic form. Chopin was the first composer to attach the name *ballade* to works of this type; his use of the term was probably inspired by the poetic ballads of his countryman Adam Miskiewicz. Chopin's four ballades are among his finest works for the piano, capturing a variety of moods from lyrical to dramatic in a narrative of almost improvisatory freedom—a quality particularly noticeable in the pointed digressions of No. 4, in F minor. ◉ Subsequent contributions to the genre have been made by Liszt, Brahms, Franck, and Fauré.

***Ballets Russes stars Tamara Karsavina and Mikhail Fokine in* The Firebird**

Ballets Russes BALLET COMPANY FOUNDED BY THE RUSSIAN IMPRESARIO SERGEY DIAGHILEV, responsible for the creation of some of the most important works of 20th-century music. The company made its debut at the Théâtre du Châtelet in Paris during the summer of 1909. Among the principal dancers were Anna Pavlova, Tamara Karsavina, Ida Rubinstein, and Vaslav Nijinsky. At their head was the choreographer Mikhail Fokine, the artistic conscience behind modern ballet. Following Diaghilev's death in 1929, a successor company was formed in Monte Carlo. Diaghilev proved an important catalyst in the development of the great ballets with which the company was associated, drawing artists such as Picasso, Rouault, Bakst, and Cocteau, and composers such as Stravinsky, Ravel, Satie, and Falla, into fascinating and mutually stimulating collaborations. The list of works first performed (mostly in Paris) by the Ballets Russes includes Stravinsky's *THE FIREBIRD* (1910), *PETRUSHKA* (1911), *THE RITE OF SPRING* (1913), *PULCINELLA* (1920), and *LES NOCES* (1923); Ravel's *DAPHNIS ET CHLOÉ* (1912); Debussy's *JEUX* (1913); Richard Strauss's *Josephslegende* (1914); Falla's *EL SOMBRERO DE TRES PICOS* (1919); and Prokofiev's *Le pas d'acier* (1927).

ballo in maschera, Un (A Masked Ball) OPERA BY GIUSEPPE VERDI, to a libretto by Antonio Somma, premiered in 1859 in Rome. Based on Eugène Scribe's *Gustave III,* about the assassination of Sweden's King Gustav III in 1792, the opera, originally meant to open in Naples, gave Verdi tremendous problems with the censors, since it depicted regicide. Eventually he agreed to turn

***Assassination scene from* Un ballo in maschera**

the king into a lesser noble and change the locale to late-17th-century America, leading to many peculiarities: Gustav III becomes Riccardo, Count of Warwick and governer of Boston (*not* Massachusetts); his enemies Count Ribbing and Count Horn are renamed Samuel and Tom; his secretary (and assassin) Captain Anckarstroem becomes Renato, a Creole; and the blond fortune-teller Mam'zelle Arvidson turns into Ulrica, the Negro fortune-teller with the remarkably Swedish-sounding name. In spite of this, Verdi's music is wonderful and the character of Riccardo emerges as one of his finest creations, which is probably why it became a favorite role of warmhearted tenors like Enrico Caruso and Luciano Pavarotti.

RECOMMENDED RECORDING

PRICE, PAVAROTTI, BRUSON; SOLTI AND NATIONAL PHILHARMONIC ORCHESTRA (DECCA).

Baltsa, Agnes

(b. Lefkas, November 19, 1944)

GREEK MEZZO-SOPRANO. She made her debut in 1968 in Frankfurt (as Cherubino in Mozart's *Le nozze di Figaro*). In 1969 she sang Octavian in Richard Strauss's *Der Rosenkavalier* at the Vienna Staatsoper, and in 1970 she made her debuts at the Salzburg Festival and the Deutsche Oper Berlin. Her Metropolitan Opera debut came in 1979, as Octavian. During the 1970s and 1980s, she was a favorite of von Karajan, recording numerous roles under his baton, including Octavian, Amneris in Verdi's *Aida,* Herodias in Strauss's *Salome,* Donna Elvira in Mozart's *Don Giovanni,* and the title part in Bizet's *Carmen.* With her husky, commanding chest voice, rock-solid top voice, and fiery delivery, Baltsa was a dramatic singer of the first order, tailor-made for roles such as Amneris and Carmen, where her ripe but not sweet tone was an asset. She was also well suited to the Rossini heroines, especially Rosina in *Il barbiere di Siviglia* and Cenerentola, both of which she recorded.

RECOMMENDED RECORDING

BIZET, *CARMEN*: CARRERAS, VAN DAM, RICCIARELLI; KARAJAN AND BERLIN PHILHARMONIC (DG).

Bang on a Can *See box on page 272.*

bar The vertical line through a musical staff, dividing the music into measures; also synonymous with "measure." *See also* METER.

Barber, Samuel

(b. West Chester, Penn, March 9, 1910; d. New York, January 23, 1981)

AMERICAN COMPOSER. He was a nephew of contralto Louise Homer and a protégé of the composer Sidney Homer, who caught on to young Samuel's gifts when, at the age of nine, he began work on his first opera. In 1924 Barber enrolled in the newly opened Curtis Institute in Philadelphia, where he studied piano with Isabelle Vengerova, composition with Rosario Scalero and conducting with Fritz Reiner. It was at Curtis that he met another young composer, Gian-Carlo Menotti, who was to become his lifelong companion and professional collaborator. Early works from Barber's student days still hold a place in the repertoire, including *Dover Beach*—a setting of a Matthew Arnold poem for voice and string quartet; Barber, who had become quite a capable baritone, sang the world premiere—and his graduation exercise, the Overture to *The School for Scandal.* These works established him as "the one to watch" in his generation of American composers, a status confirmed by his receipt of the Prix de Rome and a Pulitzer traveling grant in 1935, when he was 25 years old.

His music caught the ear of Arturo Toscanini, who led the premieres of two works: the *Essay for Orchestra* (later retitled *First Essay for Orchestra*) and the *ADAGIO FOR STRINGS*, one of the best-known works of the 20th century. The essay form—Barber's own creation, something of a musical "argument" in which one "thought" or melody is the seed from which an entire single movement springs—would be something the composer would return to at subsequent points in his life, composing a *Second Essay* in 1942 and a *Third Essay* in 1978. His beautifully lyric Violin Concerto (1940) is one of the finest string concertos of the 20th century, with a razzle-dazzle finale and a richly expressive opening movement. He also wrote a piano concerto (which won him a Pulitzer Prize) and a cello concerto. For Vladimir Horowitz he composed the Piano Sonata in E-flat minor (1949), making it as challenging as possible. Barber's other works for the piano include the *Nocturne* (*Homage to John Field*) of 1959 and the beautiful *Excursions*, Op. 20 (1942–44).

Barber's most exquisite achievements were in the realm of vocal music, particularly the songs of Opp. 10 and 13 and his 1947 setting of James Agee's *Knoxville: Summer of 1915*, for soprano and orchestra, commissioned by soprano Eleanor Steber. He also wrote a song cycle called *Hermit Songs* (1953) in which he set old anonymous Irish texts taken from the walls of monasteries.

In recognition of his preeminent place in American music, the Metropolitan Opera commissioned Barber to compose an opera, *Antony and Cleopatra* (based on Shakespeare), for the opening of its new home at Lincoln Center in 1966; while not a success in its original production, the opera, which featured Leontyne Price in the role of Cleopatra, manifested yet again Barber's unique mastery of line and color, and his extraordinarily imaginative way of setting a text.

Samuel Barber

RECOMMENDED RECORDINGS

ADAGIO FOR STRINGS (WITH OTHER WORKS): SCHIPPERS AND NEW YORK PHILHARMONIC (SONY).

HERMIT SONGS: PRICE, BARBER (RCA).

KNOXVILLE, SUMMER OF 1915: UPSHAW; ZINMAN AND ORCHESTRA OF ST. LUKE'S (NONESUCH).

ORCHESTRAL WORKS (INCLUDING *ESSAYS*): SLATKIN AND SAINT LOUIS SYMPHONY ORCHESTRA (EMI).

VIOLIN CONCERTO: OLIVEIRA; SLATKIN AND SAINT LOUIS SYMPHONY ORCHESTRA (EMI).

barbiere di Siviglia, Il (The Barber of Seville) OPERA BY GIOACCHINO ROSSINI, to a libretto by Cesare Sterbini (based on *Le barbier de Séville* by Beaumarchais), premiered in Rome in 1816. Rossini's best-known work and one of the greatest comic operas ever written, it has held the stage continuously since its premiere, making it the oldest work never to have fallen out of the repertoire. The story revolves around Figaro, the happy-go-lucky barber of the opera's title, who offers to help the young Count Almaviva in his efforts to woo Doctor Bartolo's nubile ward, Rosina. She quickly gets into the act, plotting how she will outwit her guardian and win Lindoro, which is the alias the amorous Count has adopted. Upon these machinations Rossini builds an effervescent comedy, sumptuously scored and unerringly paced. The libretto, among the finest he ever set, is full of the sort of incident and contrived confrontation on which comedy thrives. It fired the 23-year-old composer's imagination, inspiring a score full of musical riches that remains as fresh today as on the day it was first heard. The title character's spirited self-introduction in Act I, "Largo al factotum," exemplifies the brio Rossini brought to the party. ◉

RECOMMENDED RECORDINGS

Bartoli, Nucci, Matteuzzi, Burchuladze; Patanè and Teatro Communale di Bologna (Decca).

Berganza, Alva, Prey, Dara; Abbado and London Symphony Orchestra (DG).

Barbirolli, John

(b. London, December 2, 1899; d. London, July 29, 1970)

English conductor. He studied cello at the Royal Academy of Music, and in 1916 became the youngest member of the Queen's Hall Orchestra. After serving in the army during World War I he resumed playing in London orchestras; beginning in the 1920s, he conducted opera and orchestra performances in London and the provinces. In 1936–37 he spent ten weeks as guest conductor of the New York Philharmonic, and the following season, was named to succeed Arturo Toscanini as the orchestra's chief conductor. He was not quite ready for the position, and unfavorable comparisons with his predecessor ensued. In 1943 he returned to England as permanent conductor of the Hallé Orchestra in Manchester, with which he remained associated to the end of his life. Dubbed "Glorious John" by Ralph Vaughan Williams, Barbirolli had a pronounced Romantic temperament. As a conductor he wore his heart on his sleeve, urging orchestras to ardent interpretations of Mahler, Richard Strauss, and Sibelius, and excelling in the music of Elgar, Delius, Bax, and Vaughan Williams.

RECOMMENDED RECORDINGS

Bax, *Tintagel*; Vaughan Williams, Symphony No. 5: London Symphony Orchestra (EMI).

Elgar, Cello Concerto, *Sea Pictures*: du Pré; Baker; London Symphony Orchestra (EMI).

Sibelius, Symphony No. 2: Royal Philharmonic Orchestra (Chesky).

barcarolle (from It. *barcarola*) A piece in lilting $\frac{6}{8}$ meter in the style of the songs of Venetian gondoliers. A typical feature of the melody is a gentle, rocking rhythm suggestive of the side-to-side swaying of a boat. The most famous example of the genre is the barcarolle in Act IV of Offenbach's *Les contes d'Hoffmann.* ◉ Mendelssohn included several barcarolles in his *Songs Without Words* for piano, and Fauré wrote a series of

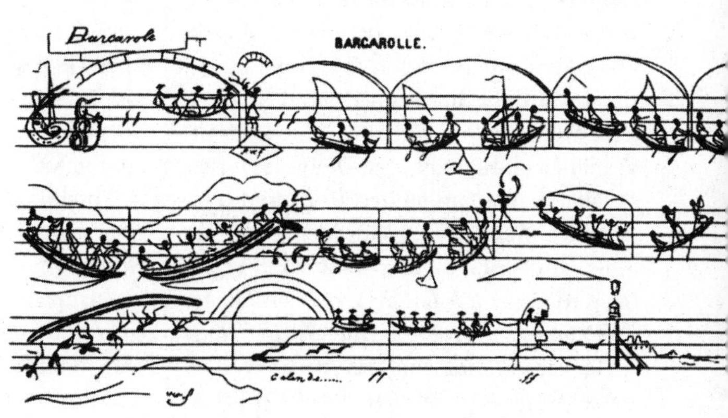

A whimsically notated barcarolle, with Venetian gondoliers for notes

13, also for piano, between 1885 and 1916. The most frequently encountered pianistic essay of this type is Chopin's *Barcarolle* in F-sharp, Op. 60.

Barenboim, Daniel

(b. Buenos Aires, November 15, 1942)

ISRAELI PIANIST AND CONDUCTOR OF ARGENTINE BIRTH. He studied piano with his mother and father and gave his first concert at the age of seven. With his parents he settled in Israel in 1952; that year he gave his first recitals in Vienna and Rome. His debuts in Paris, London, and New York followed during the years 1955–57. His conducting career began in 1962 with concerts in Israel, and in 1964 he formed a close association with the English Chamber Orchestra, subsequently performing and recording the complete Mozart piano concertos with that ensemble in the dual role of soloist and conductor. He married the English cellist Jacqueline du Pré in 1967.

The focus of Barenboim's activities shifted from the piano to conducting in the 1970s. Frequent appearances early in the decade as guest conductor of the Chicago Symphony, Berlin Philharmonic, New York Philharmonic, London Philharmonic, and L'Orchestre de Paris led to his being named music director of the latter ensemble in 1975, a post he held until 1989. He made his debut as an opera conductor at the Edinburgh Festival in 1973 with Mozart's *Don Giovanni,* and for four years he conducted at the Deutsche Oper Berlin. He was summoned to Bayreuth to conduct Wagner's *Tristan und Isolde* in 1981, and since then has returned regularly to conduct *Tristan* and *Parsifal*; in 1988 he was entrusted with his first *Ring* cycle. Clearly on a climb to the top of the music world, Barenboim stumbled badly in 1989, losing the post of music director of the Opéra de la Bastille in Paris after a

Daniel Barenboim conducting the Chicago Symphony at a Proms concert in 1998

government minister decided he was trying too hard to turn the house into a second Paris Opéra, and drawing too high a salary to do it. The setback was only momentary. In 1991, following the reunification of Germany, he was engaged to head the far more prestigious (and more generously endowed) Berlin Staatsoper. Also in 1991 he became the ninth music director of the Chicago Symphony Orchestra, succeeding Sir Georg Solti; in 2004 he announced that he would step down from the Chicago post at the expiration of his contract in 2006.

Barenboim's stock-in-trade as a pianist remains what it was at the dawn of his career: Mozart, Beethoven, Brahms, and Liszt. He has a commanding technique, but his phrasing can occasionally be sloppy and his manner bombastic. His affinities as a conductor are somewhat broader, though still mainly Germanic, with pride of place given to Beethoven, Wagner, Brahms, and Bruckner. In spite of his eminent positions in Europe and America, he remains a controversial podium figure, admired in some quarters for his visionary interpretations and flexible command of line and pacing, criticized in others for his mannered approach to the Classical and Romantic repertoire and chronic lack of attention to balances and textural detail. Talented as he is, the comparisons with Furtwängler that have been made since he first picked up a baton have yet to be justified.

RECOMMENDED RECORDINGS

AS PIANIST:

BRAHMS, CELLO SONATAS: DU PRÉ (EMI).

AS CONDUCTOR:

WAGNER, OVERTURES AND PRELUDES: CHICAGO SYMPHONY ORCHESTRA (TELDEC).

WAGNER, PARSIFAL: JERUSALEM, VAN DAM, HÖLLE, MEIER, TOMLINSON; BERLIN PHILHARMONIC (TELDEC).

bariolage (from Fr. *bariolé,* "speckled") Playing the same note in alternation on two different strings, one stopped, the other open; the rapid shift in tone color between the two creates a shimmering effect. Examples of bariolage are frequent in the solo literature (for example, in the prelude from Bach's Partita in E ◉) and can also be found in orchestral works (e.g., the finale to Brahms's Symphony No. 4 in E minor, Op. 98, in the first violin part, mm. 79–80).

baritone (from Gr. *barytonos,* "deep sounding") Male voice range between TENOR and BASS.

Baroque Stylistic period in Western music extending from the beginning of the 17th century to about 1750. The term comes from the Portuguese *barroco,* meaning an irregular, oddly shaped pearl. It was first used in a pejorative fashion to describe Italian painting and architecture of the 1600s; in the late 19th century, after art historian Heinrich Wölfflin had drawn attention to the positive aspects of Baroque style—its mixture of fantasy, grandeur, exuberance, and ornate design—the term was embraced by musicologists as well.

There is nothing convoluted or weird about Baroque music. In fact, it started out as a simplification of the rather highly stratified and artificial musical language of late Renaissance. The principal stylistic characteristic that distinguishes Baroque music from that of the Renaissance is the polarization of voices, the shift from complex polyphonic textures of five or more voices, in which all parts are of more or less equal importance, to simpler textures that emphasize only two parts: the bass line and the melody, usually in the uppermost voice. This shift occurred at the same time as another important development, the transition from a syntax based on the medieval modes to one based on functional tonality, which made possible large-scale forms such as OPERA and the SYMPHONY, as well as the CONCERTO, CANTATA, ORATORIO, and SONATA, all of which originated in the Baroque period.

As it developed, Baroque music became increasingly complex in form and utterance, placing an emphasis on ornamentation and a premium on the expression of clearly recognizable and very specific emotions, known as "affects." Among the most significant Baroque composers were Cavalli, Corelli, Vivaldi, Alessandro and Domenico Scarlatti, Schütz, Pachelbel, J. S. Bach, Handel, Lully, Couperin, and Rameau. *See also* CONTINUO, *individual composers.*

Barrios Mangoré, Agustín

(b. San Juan Bautista de las Misiones, May 5, 1885; d. San Salvador, August 7, 1944)

PARAGUAYAN GUITARIST AND COMPOSER. An outstanding virtuoso, Barrios left Paraguay in 1910 for what was expected to be a weeklong concert tour of Argentina; it proved so successful that he stayed 14 years. In 1934 he went to Europe, becoming the first Latin American guitarist to concertize there. Returning to the New World, he taught at the National Conservatory in San Salvador from 1939 until his death. His compositions, brilliantly idiomatic and often imbued with a sultry expressiveness, have become staples of the guitar repertoire. Among the most popular are the *Danza paraguaya* (1924), *Julia Florida* (1938), and the *Vals,* Op. 8, No. 4 (1923).

RECOMMENDED RECORDING

JULIA FLORIDA, VALS, OP. 8, NO. 4: VIEAUX (NAXOS).

Bartered Bride, The (Prodaná nevěsta)

COMIC OPERA BY BEDŘICH SMETANA, to a libretto by Karel Sabina, premiered in Prague in 1866. A better translation of the Czech title would be "Bride for Sale." The score is prefaced by an exuberant overture and contains a number of characteristic dances that are frequently excerpted. The plot involves a marriage contract, a case of mistaken identity, a girl (Marenka) who eventually gets to marry her sweetheart (Jeník), and a stuttering love-struck teenager who at one point masquerades as a bear (Vasek).

RECOMMENDED RECORDINGS

ORCHESTRAL EXCERPTS: KERTÉSZ AND ISRAEL PHILHARMONIC (DECCA).

OVERTURE: REINER AND CHICAGO SYMPHONY ORCHESTRA (RCA).

Bartók, Béla

(b. Nagyszentmiklós [now Sînnicolau Mare, Romania], March 25, 1881; d. New York, September 26, 1945)

HUNGARIAN COMPOSER AND PIANIST. One of the 20th century's most celebrated composers, he wrote a handful of masterpieces and a surprising amount of second-rate music, much of it for his own instrument, the piano. Both of his parents were musically inclined, but his father died when he was young and the family led a nomadic existence until 1894, leaving gaps in Bartók's education that had to be filled in during his teens. He attended the National Hungarian Royal Academy in Budapest from 1899 to 1903, honing his skills as a composer and acquiring a formidable reputation as a pianist. In 1905 he participated as both composer and pianist in the Rubinstein competition in Paris; no prize was awarded in composition, and in the piano division he lost out to Wilhelm Backhaus. He was appointed professor of piano at the Budapest Academy in 1907, a post he held until 1934.

Meanwhile, in 1904, Bartók had begun what would become a lifelong study of authentic Hungarian, Slovak, and Romanian folk music, jotting down a song as it was sung by a young peasant girl in the Gömör district. Over the next few years, he and Zoltán Kodály scoured the Eastern European countryside carrying portable recording phonographs with which they diligently captured the actual melodies of indigenous folk singers. By 1918 they had gathered more than 9,000 folk songs.

Absorbing influences from various quarters—Richard Strauss, Debussy, folk music—into his compositional lexicon, Bartók gradually developed his own distinctive voice. Among the earliest of his works to reflect this progressive synthesis of folk and modern elements was his String Quartet No. 1, Op. 7, composed in 1908. By the time of his String Quartet No. 2,

Bartók transcribing folk melodies from his phonograph

Op. 17 (1917), *DANCE SUITE* (1923), and macabre ballet-pantomime *THE MIRACULOUS MANDARIN* (composed in 1919, scored in 1924), Bartók had arrived at the idiom of his maturity, characterized by driving, anxious rhythms, angular melodies, bracingly sharp dissonances, and folklike modal harmonies. The period 1926–38 saw a broadening of Bartók's powers and a further refinement of his highly charged and intensely personal idiom. The best of his pieces from these years—the String Quartet No. 4 (1928), String Quartet No. 5 (1934), *MUSIC FOR STRINGS, PERCUSSION, AND CELESTA* (1936), the Sonata for Two Pianos and Percussion (1937), and Violin Concerto No. 2 (1938)—have a formal rigor (often based on palindromic schemes) and a rhythmic vitality that together give them impressive coherence and thrust. The expression in these works tends toward a greater austerity, even though the music retains its ties to folk song, as in the gorgeous opening melody of Violin Concerto No. 2.

Béla Bartók in America

In 1940 Bartók left Hungary and settled in America. During his final years—in the *Concerto for Orchestra* (1943) and Piano Concerto No. 3 (1945)—he turned away from the thorny complexities of the music he had written during the 1920s and 1930s, toward a more accessible language still based on the rhythmic and melodic contours of folk music. Here, in works he scarcely intended to be valedictory, he also let fall the mask of ironic detachment and cold-bloodedness that had marked much of his prior production, allowing a little real emotion to come to the surface. These late works, no less than the formidable achievements of the 1930s, show Bartók's complete mastery of his craft; the writing, notable for its melodic inspiration and sustained lines of action, is breathtakingly assured. Still, while this kinder, gentler Bartók is the one admired by audiences today, his most important achievement as a composer was to find innovative approaches to musical form that could be applied in an organic rather than systematic fashion, and to synthesize an idiom in which rhythmic, harmonic, and melodic elements of folk music were incorporated into a modern tonal framework—and this he did most impressively in the works of the 1930s. See also *MIKROKOSMOS*, STRING QUARTET.

RECOMMENDED RECORDINGS

CONCERTO FOR ORCHESTRA, MUSIC FOR STRINGS, PERCUSSION, AND CELESTA: REINER AND CHICAGO SYMPHONY ORCHESTRA (RCA).

DANCE SUITE, CONCERTO FOR ORCHESTRA, MIRACULOUS MANDARIN SUITE: SOLTI AND LONDON SYMPHONY ORCHESTRA (DECCA).

MIRACULOUS MANDARIN SUITE: MARTINON AND CHICAGO SYMPHONY ORCHESTRA (RCA).

STRING QUARTETS: EMERSON QUARTET (DG).

VIOLIN CONCERTO NO. 2: SHAHAM; BOULEZ AND CHICAGO SYMPHONY ORCHESTRA (DG).

Bartoli, Cecilia

(b. Rome, June 4, 1966)

ITALIAN COLORATURA MEZZO-SOPRANO noted for her accomplished acting and polished vocal technique. She is most identified with a handful of roles in the operas of Mozart and Rossini, among them Despina (*Così fan tutte*), Cenerentola, and Rosina (*Il barbiere di Siviglia*). She studied in Rome at the Accademia di Santa Cecilia and with her parents, Silvana Bazzoni and Angelo Bartoli, both professional singers, and made her debut in Rome, as Rosina, in 1985. Engagements at several of Italy's leading opera houses quickly followed, and in 1989 she made her recording debut, as Rosina, in a marvelous rendition of *Il barbiere di Siviglia.* Her La Scala debut, as Zerlina in Mozart's *Don Giovanni,* came in 1993, and in 1996 she made her Metropolitan Opera debut as Despina. After this meteoric start, Bartoli's career has assumed a more modest trajectory, with critics noting that her voice lacks the amplitude to fill most large opera houses. Small though the voice may be, Bartoli has cultivated a beautiful tone—honeyed in the lower register, warm and glowing at the top—and a coloratura of remarkable precision and flexibility. Capable of igniting an audience's emotions with her singing, she can also be a flamboyant comedienne.

RECOMMENDED RECORDINGS

ROSSINI, *IL BARBIERE DI SIVIGLIA*: NUCCI, MATTEUZZI, BURCHULADZE; PATANÈ AND TEATRO COMMUNALE DI BOLOGNA (DECCA).

VIVALDI, SCENES AND ARIAS: IL GIARDINO ARMONICO (DECCA).

Cecilia Bartoli as Rossini's Cenerentola

bass [1] The lowest part in a multi-voice texture. [2] The lowest male vocal range. [3] The lower half of the entire tonal range. [4] The common name for the DOUBLE BASS viol, also known as "string bass" and "bass fiddle," the lowest member of the string family in common use.

bass clarinet A member of the clarinet family pitched an octave below the standard B-flat clarinet, with a lower compass generally extending to low C-sharp, a half step above the open C on the cello. In regular use in symphonic music since the 1890s, and in opera orchestras since the 1860s, it has a remarkably rich and resonant tone in its low octave, and is capable of great agility throughout its four-octave range.

bass drum Large, two-headed drum used in orchestras, with a circumferential shell 16 inches wide and a head diameter of 30 inches (in certain cases the head diameter may be as great as 36 inches). It is played using a wooden stick with a fairly large head covered in soft felt, and may be mounted in a suspension mechanism that can be adjusted so as to put the drum heads in the horizontal plane, facilitating rolls. The bass drum produces the most sound energy of any orchestral instrument, and has been in common use since the early part of the 19th century.

basset clarinet A clarinet devised by Anton Stadler in Vienna in the 1780s with an extended lower joint that enabled it to reach A, a major third below the low C-sharp of the standard clarinet in A. Its rich, plangent sonority was what Mozart had in mind when he composed his two most important works for the clarinet: the Quintet in A, K. 581, written in September 1789, and the Concerto in A, K. 622, completed in 1791. Mozart also wrote an obbligato part for basset clarinet into the aria "Parto, parto" from his opera *La clemenza di Tito,* K. 621.

basset-horn An alto member of the clarinet family, usually pitched in F (sometimes in G) with a compass extending about a fifth below that of the standard clarinet. Developed in Germany and Austria during the second half of the 18th century, it has a plaintive sound in its upper register and a warmly sonorous low octave. Mozart used two basset-horns in his Serenade in B-flat, K. 361 (1784), where they serve primarily as a foil to the brighter sounding clarinets and oboes, and contribute a wonderful richness to the overall sonority. He included parts for three basset-horns in his *Masonic Funeral Music,* K. 477 (1785), and for two in his Requiem, K. 626 (1791), and again assigned the instrument an obbligato part in the aria "Non pìu di fiori" from his opera *La clemenza di Tito,* K. 621. Richard Strauss employed basset-horns in his operas *Elektra* and *Die Frau ohne Schatten.*

Basset-horn

basso continuo *See* CONTINUO.

basso ostinato (It., "obstinate bass") A persistently repeated pattern or melodic figure in the bass, usually consisting of just a few notes, against which other elements of a musical texture may unfold or change in a rhythmically unrestricted manner. Also called "ground" or "ground bass," the term can refer either to the bass line itself or to a recurring harmonic pattern. The opening of Orff's *Carmina Burana* and the Pachelbel Canon in D provide good examples of *basso ostinato.* The 12-bar chord progression of traditional blues can be seen as a modern application. *See also* CHACONNE.

bassoon Bass woodwind instrument fitted with a double reed. The Italian name for the bassoon, *fagotto,* means "stick," which is a good description of the instrument's loglike appearance. Most bassoons are made of maple and are assembled out of four sections: the bell joint, the bass or long joint, the butt, and the wing joint. Modern bassoons are equipped with 17 to 22 keys, and have a range from low B-flat (a whole step below the open C on the cello) up to the E a tenth above middle C. The bassoon is powerful and sonorous in the lower part of its range, svelte and creamy in its middle register, soft and slightly plaintive in the upper middle register, and increasingly tense and penetrating in the uppermost range, thinning out to a shallow squawk at the very top. The instrument can be made to sound gruff and grumbly, and is often utilized for that effect, but it has a wonderful singing tone with ample resonance and can be employed to great effect as a melodic instrument.

The modern bassoon is the descendant of the medieval dulcian and began to acquire its characteristic shape and attributes around 1700. It achieved its present form in the last decade of the 19th century. Two types of bassoon are in use today: The dominant variety is the German, or Heckel, model; less common is the French, or Buffet, model. German bassoons are usually fitted with a white ring around the bell. Within the orchestra, the bassoon has traditionally served as a foundation instrument, often doubling the bass line and adding weight and sonority to the string tutti; this was its early role, but by the 1720s, composers such as Bach were assigning solo passages to it as well. With each generation the bassoon has become more "liberated" from the strings, as its capabilities have been better understood. In the 20th century, it has frequently taken center stage—as at the very beginning of Stravinsky's *The Rite of Spring,* where it sounds the opening high C, solo, to arresting effect, and continues with a serpentine wailing in its upper register.

Bassoon

The bassoon's solo repertoire is fairly modest, but among its highlights are concertos by Mozart, Gordon Jacob (1895–1984), Nino Rota (1911–79), and Gunther Schuller (b. 1925). While the bassoon is not considered a virtuoso instrument, it has had many formidable exponents, especially in the 20th century. Among the leading players of recent years have been Bernard Garfield, Klaus Thunemann, Milan Turkovic, and Leonard Sharrow.

basso profundo (It.) An especially deep and sonorous bass voice.

baton (From Fr. *bâton,* "stick") A thin, tapered pointer, usually made of wood, used by conductors to mark the beat in a piece of music and coordinate performances by large groups of musicians. It was adopted early in the 19th century and popularized by such figures as Mendelssohn, Hummel, Moscheles, Spohr, and Berlioz. Early batons varied markedly in length and appearance, as well as materials. Mendelssohn wielded a wand of polished whalebone, wrapped at the handle in white kid leather to match the kid gloves he wore while conducting. An English critic of the 1830s reported that every motion of Mendelssohn's baton was "decisive, every glance of the eye expressive."

Berlioz, with baton, summoning an explosive climax from the orchestra

Berlioz, on the other hand, swung a stick that one observer described as "a cudgel of lime tree with the bark still on." By the end of the 19th century, the standard conductor's baton had emerged: averaging about 18 inches in length, either unfinished or painted white, frequently with a wood or cork knob as a handle.

Baton technique differs greatly from conductor to conductor. Toscanini beat time rather stiffly, like a military bandmaster, in large vertical gestures. Richard Strauss used a small stick, moving it in tiny arcs while scarcely ever taking his left hand out of his pocket. Bruno Walter's gestures were fluid, graceful, and concise, while Furtwängler's looked almost spasmodic. Bernstein made flamboyant use of his baton, often using a two-handed grip or switching the stick to his left hand for effect. In contrast, Karajan was carefully controlled, massaging the music as he conducted, the slightest motion compelling in effect. Carlos Kleiber was renowned for the broad, swashbuckling elegance of his strokes; among present-day conductors, Lorin Maazel is noteworthy for the precision of his stickwork. Conductors who do *not* use a baton include Boulez, Masur, Conlon, and Yury Temirkanov. Stokowski also eschewed the use of a stick.

Battle, Kathleen

(b. Portsmouth, Ohio, August 13, 1948)

AMERICAN SOPRANO. She attended the University of Cincinnati's College Conservatory of Music, receiving her bachelor's and master's degrees, and made her professional debut at the Spoleto Festival in a performance of Brahms's *Ein deutsches Requiem* under the baton of Thomas Schippers. Her debut with the New York City Opera came in 1976, as Susanna in Mozart's *Le nozze di Figaro*; the following year she made her Metropolitan Opera debut as the Shepherd in Wagner's *Tannhäuser.* Her career took off in the 1980s with appearances at the Salzburg Festival, Covent Garden, and a long string of reengagements at the Met, where she sang, among other roles, Zdenka in Richard Strauss's *Arabella* and Cleopatra in Handel's *Giulio Cesare.* A falling-out with the Met's management, centering on her difficult backstage personality, hastened her transition from diva to concert artist in the 1990s. Battle possessed a very light soprano that rang with bell-like clarity but in later years became increasingly breathy. André Previn composed the cycle *Honey and Rue* for Battle in 1991, to poems by Toni Morrison.

Kathleen Battle as Susanna in Mozart's **Le nozze di Figaro**

RECOMMENDED RECORDING

PREVIN, *HONEY AND RUE*: PREVIN AND ORCHESTRA OF ST. LUKE'S (DG).

Bax, Arnold

(b. London, November 8, 1883; d. Cork, October 3, 1953)

ENGLISH COMPOSER. He studied piano and composition at the Royal Academy of Music from 1900, graduating with a gold medal in piano in 1905. Fired by the poetry of Yeats, he spent the next five years in Ireland, a country whose folklore and literature fascinated him all his life. He returned to England in 1910, and entered into a highly productive phase that saw the completion of his finest tone poems—*November Woods* (1917), *The Garden of Fand* (1916) and *Tintagel* (1919), a masterpiece of scenic music named for the site of the legendary knight Tristan's castle on the coast of Cornwall. This period also saw the composition of two piano sonatas and a substantial amount of chamber music. He was appointed Master of the King's Music in 1942, the only official post he ever held.

Between 1922 and 1939 Bax composed seven symphonies, long underrated and only now beginning to receive their due. An eclectic in the best sense, Bax could meld elements of folk song with florid counterpoint, impressionistic scoring, and a sensuously rich chromatic palette. There is an almost improvisatory feel to his best music, which reveals him as one of the great musical landscape painters of the 20th century.

RECOMMENDED RECORDINGS

MATER ORA FILIUM: KING'S COLLEGE CHOIR (EMI).

SYMPHONIES: HANDLEY AND BBC PHILHARMONIC ORCHESTRA (CHANDOS).

SYMPHONIES: LLOYD-JONES AND ROYAL SCOTTISH NATIONAL ORCHESTRA (NAXOS).

TINTAGEL: BARBIROLLI AND LONDON SYMPHONY ORCHESTRA (EMI).

TONE POEMS: THOMSON AND ULSTER ORCHESTRA (CHANDOS).

Bayreuth Festival ANNUAL SUMMER FESTIVAL IN BAYREUTH, GERMANY, devoted to the works of Richard WAGNER. The first festival was held in 1876, with the complete presentation of Wagner's four-evening cycle *DER RING DES NIBELUNGEN,* including the world-premiere performances of *SIEGFRIED* and *GÖTTERDÄMMERUNG.* Hans Richter conducted. In 1882 the premiere performance of *PARSIFAL* was given at Bayreuth; for many years thereafter the opera was presented nowhere else. Cosima Wagner took over direction of the festival following her husband's death in 1883, and today it remains in the control of the Wagner family, even though it is subsidized by the German government.

Renate Hoffleit works on her microphone installation in Donaueschingen, 2000.

"The most important thing about a festival," wrote novelist E. M. Forster, "is that it be festive." Every spring and summer, there's much music to be had all over the world as orchestras, chamber ensembles, and opera companies retreat to their off-season homes, offering performances in everything from castles and "festival houses" to outdoor sheds, making spectacular occasions for concentrated listening, in black tie or alfresco, under the stars.

Aspen Music Festival

Annual summer music festival in Aspen, Colorado, inaugurated in 1949 as part of a colloquium marking the 200th anniversary of the birth of the German writer Johann Wolfgang von Goethe. The festival operates in conjunction with a school of music that is one of the most prestigious summer academies in the world.

Donaueschingen Festival

Music festival inaugurated in 1921 in Donaueschingen, Germany, the first to be devoted exclusively to contemporary music. The emphasis in the early years was on chamber music: Hindemith's *Kammermusik* No. 1 and Webern's *Six Songs,* Op. 14, were among the works premiered at Donaueschingen during the 1920s. In the 1930s the programming was coopted by Nazi party hacks, but in 1950 the festival was revived with the cooperation of Southwest German Radio, and its focus expanded to include orchestral music. Hans Rosbaud, conductor of the Southwest German Radio Symphony Orchestra from 1948 until his death in 1962, played an important part in establishing Donaueschingen as a showcase for 12-tone music, the early work of Boulez and Stockhausen in particular. During the 1970s, the festival's priorities shifted once again, to multimedia works.

The Edinburgh Festival

Inaugurated in 1947 in the aftermath of World War II, this summer festival of music and drama in Scotland sought from the beginning to be international in scope, in part to promote the healing of European culture and to bring German and Austrian ensembles back into the artistic mainstream. Under the direction of Rudolf Bing, it quickly acquired the status of a major festival. In its first year it reunited conductor Bruno Walter with the Vienna Philharmonic; other early guests were Sir Alec Guinness and mezzo-soprano Kathleen Ferrier. The festival has become a showcase for British, American, and European orchestras, and a popular venue for cutting-edge theatri-

1963 Edinburgh program featuring Martha Graham

cal productions; for many festivalgoers, the drama begins with the city's setting, on a craggy outcropping in one of Europe's most imposing landscapes.

The Glyndebourne Festival

Founded in 1934 by the obsessive music lover and estate owner John Christie, this festival—situated in East Sussex and one of the largest in England—serves as a showcase for opera. The conductor Fritz Busch, hounded out of Germany by the Nazis, was the festival's first music director. During the festival's early years the emphasis was on Mozart; the casts of many productions included leading British singers as well as talents who, like Busch, were no longer welcome in the Reich. Over the years, this festival has attracted some of the finest theatrical minds of the century, including Trevor Nunn, Peter Sellars, Jonathan Miller, and Sir Peter Hall, as well as an annual parade of world-class conductors and singers.

Bass-baritone Thomas Quasthoff sings with the Lucerne Festival Orchestra in 2005.

The Lucerne Festival

Impetus for the creation of this festival came from Ernest Ansermet, who was eager to find a summer home for his orchestra, the Geneva-based Orchestre de la Suisse Romande. The festival opened in 1938, the same year the German annexation of Austria made the Salzburg Festival off-limits to many distinguished performers, among them Fritz Busch, Bruno Walter, and Arturo Toscanini, all of whom conducted during Lucerne's first season. Following its birth as the "Counter-Salzburg," the Lucerne Festival has established an enviable reputation as a magnet for orchestras and recitalists, and with the recent addition of an Easter season and an autumn piano series, has solidified its position as one of the most elegant, wide-ranging festivals in Europe.

The Netherlands-based group Emio Greco/PC performs at the opening ceremony of Spoleto, USA, 2005.

The Marlboro Festival

Founded in 1951 by Rudolf Serkin, Adolf Busch, Marcel Blanche, and Louis Moyse, and conceived of as a place where young performers and established artists could come together on an equal footing, the festival brings the best and brightest students to the Vermont countryside every summer to play chamber music with the world's preeminent masters. Pablo Casals was among the many artists who made annual pilgrimages to Marlboro in the early years; recent mainstays have included the violinist Jaime Laredo, and the current artistic directors are the pianists Richard Goode and Mitsuko Uchida. The Guarneri Quartet was formed at Marlboro in 1964.

Mostly Mozart

The Mostly Mozart Festival at Lincoln Center—America's first indoor summer music festival—was launched as an experiment in 1966 as "Midsummer Serenades: A Mozart Festival." The first two seasons were devoted entirely to the music of Mozart. The festival acquired its present name in 1970 and since then has become a New York institution celebrated not only for its Mozart, but for attracting a procession of acclaimed soloists to Lincoln Center each summer. Its programming has expanded to include works by Mozart's predecessors, contemporaries, and successors, often in interesting juxtapositions. The festival has its own orchestra, made up of outstanding New York freelance musicians, and plays host to visiting period instrument ensembles and various chamber complements as well. Cecilia Bartoli, James Galway, and Elly Ameling all made their U.S. debuts at the Mostly Mozart Festival. From 1982 to 2001, Gerard Schwarz served as the festival's music director, becoming its conductor laureate in 2002. The French musician Louis Langrée was named music director in 2003.

The Festival of Two Worlds

Founded in Spoleto, Italy, in 1958 by composer Gian-Carlo Menotti and conductor Thomas Schippers, this annual summer affair is dedicated not only to music, but to drama, sculpture, performance art—anything in need of an art-thirsty audience. In May 1977, a satellite festival was inaugurated in Charleston, South Carolina, by Menotti and New York City Opera director Christopher Keene, bringing the same ethos of culture mixed with summer enjoyment to the second of the "two worlds." In 1993 Menotti broke with the American wing, and in 1999 the composer's adopted son took over the Italian branch.

Typically, the Bayreuth Festival presents four complete *Ring* cycles and four performances of *Parsifal,* along with a similar number of performances of two or three other Wagner operas and one or two "special" events, during a five-week period from the last week of July to the end of August. A new staging of the *Ring* is rolled out every four years or so. The orchestra is made up of players from the major German opera houses and symphony orchestras; conductors and casts are generally of the highest international rank.

The Bayreuth Festival has always had a special, and sometimes controversial, place in German musical life. During the 1930s and 1940s, it was run by Winifred Wagner, the composer's English-born daughter-in-law and a close personal friend of Adolf Hitler, who was a frequent visitor. The festival rebounded in 1951 with its first postwar season, under the direction of Wieland Wagner, the composer's grandson. The years of Wieland Wagner's artistic direction (1951–66) saw a radical reinterpretation of the canon's staging, from the naturalistic realism of Wagner's own scenic conception to a remarkably bare abstraction. Following Wieland's death in 1966, his younger brother Wolfgang took charge of the festival. In his four decades as superintendant, he has invited numerous guest directors to Bayreuth; their ideas have been all over the place, sometimes quite provocative (such as Patrice Chéreau's 1976 *Ring,* staged as a drama of bourgeois industrialists), sometimes just annoying. Numerous recordings have been made at Bayreuth, capturing the work of such great conductors as Karl Muck, Hans Knappertsbusch, Karl Böhm, Rudolf Kempe, and Herbert von Karajan.

Beach, Amy Marcy [née Cheney]

(b. Henniker, N.H., September 5, 1867; d. New York, December 27, 1944)

AMERICAN PIANIST AND COMPOSER. Precociously gifted, she could sing accurately before she was two and began playing the piano and composing when she was four. She made her debut as a pianist in 1883, shortly after her 16th birthday. In 1885 she married Henry Harris Aubrey Beach, a prominent Boston surgeon on the faculty of Harvard's School of Medicine; she was 18, he was about to turn 43. Thereafter she happily observed the propriety of identifying herself, professionally and personally, as "Mrs. H. H. A. Beach." Her *Gaelic* Symphony, given its premiere by the Boston Symphony Orchestra in 1896, was the first work of its kind by an American woman to be performed by an American orchestra; her Piano Concerto in C-sharp minor, Op. 45 (1899), even finer, shows remarkable assurance and technical accomplishment. In all, Beach composed about 300 works, in a variety of genres, principally keyboard, chamber, and choral music. Still, while her compositions show the highest competence, they rarely exhibit great originality; conventional in form, their idiom is a "safe" one derived from the music of such figures as Dvořák, Brahms, Wagner, and George Whitefield Chadwick, who played the organ at the Beaches' wedding.

A young Amy Marcy Beach

RECOMMENDED RECORDINGS

Gaelic Symphony: Järvi and Detroit Symphony Orchestra (Chandos).

Piano Concerto in C-sharp minor, Op. 45: Feinberg; Schermerhorn and Nashville Symphony Orchestra (Naxos).

beat The basic unit of time in a musical composition, felt as a regular rhythmic pulse.

Beaux Arts Trio AMERICAN PIANO TRIO FOUNDED IN **1955** by pianist Menachem Pressler, cellist Bernard Greenhouse, and violinist Daniel Guilet. Isidore Cohen replaced Guilet in 1968, and was in turn replaced by Ida Kavafian in 1992. Peter Wiley succeeded Greenhouse in 1987. As the group marked its 50th anniversary in 2005, the membership consisted of Pressler, the violinist Daniel Hope, and the cellist Antonio Meneses. Over the years the Beaux Arts Trio has performed and recorded virtually the entire literature for piano trio; while its interpretations have changed with time and the shifting of personnel, it has always played to the highest of standards. Its recordings of the trios of Beethoven, Schubert, Brahms, Chausson, and Ravel, and of works by Dvořák, Schumann, Anton Arensky (1861–1906), Joaquín Turina (1882–1949), and many others, are among the cornerstones of the catalog.

RECOMMENDED RECORDINGS

BEETHOVEN, PIANO TRIOS (PHILIPS).

RAVEL, PIANO TRIO (PHILIPS).

Beecham, Thomas

(b. St. Helens, April 29, 1879; d. London, March 8, 1961)

ENGLISH CONDUCTOR. He was the son of Sir Joseph Beecham, a manufacturer of pharmaceuticals and one of England's wealthiest men (the family business, founded in 1842 as Beecham's Pills, is known today as GlaxoSmithKline). He was educated at Rossall School and Wadham College, Oxford; the Beecham fortune allowed him to recruit orchestras, and in 1910 underwrote a London opera season devoted to such adventurous and eclectic repertoire as Richard Strauss's *Elektra* and Delius's *A Village Romeo and Juliet.* In 1915 Beecham formed the Beecham Opera Company, which lasted until 1922; in 1932 he founded the London Philharmonic

Sir Thomas Beecham on a Mediterranean holiday

Orchestra, hand-picking some of the city's finest players as principals and quickly molding the ensemble into one of Europe's elite. He served as artistic director at Covent Garden (1932–39), and during World War II was active at the Metropolitan Opera and with the New York Philharmonic (with which he had made his debut in 1928, in the same concert that witnessed the debut of Vladimir Horowitz). He turned the orchestra-founding trick a second time in 1946, creating the Royal Philharmonic Orchestra and once again managing to seed it with the cream of London instrumentalists. Many of his finest recordings were made with the RPO, including a handful of early stereo efforts.

Beecham enjoyed a career-long association with the music of Frederick Delius. As Edvard Grieg had once provided the impetus for Delius to keep composing, Delius in turn encouraged Beecham to choose conducting as his path. In return, Beecham championed the composer's music with unswerving devotion, recording a cycle of his orchestral works for Columbia between

1927 and 1936 and giving a festival of Delius's music in London in 1929. Known for his debonair manner and exuberant wit, Beecham had an enormous repertoire, extending from Handel to Stravinsky. He was an outstanding interpreter of the music of Strauss, Puccini, Sibelius, and the Russian nationalists—indeed, of anything that was large and colorful. Yet he was also the finest Haydn conductor of his generation, and he got inside French music like no Frenchman of his day, aside from Monteux and Paray: He treated French ballet as if it were Beethoven and achieved particularly convincing results in the works of Berlioz and Bizet.

RECOMMENDED RECORDINGS

DELIUS, ORCHESTRAL WORKS: LONDON PHILHARMONIC ORCHESTRA ET AL. (NAXOS).

DELIUS, ORCHESTRAL WORKS: ROYAL PHILHARMONIC ORCHESTRA (EMI).

GRIEG, *PEER GYNT* SUITE (WITH OTHER WORKS): ROYAL PHILHARMONIC ORCHESTRA (EMI).

PUCCINI, *LA BOHÈME*: LOS ANGELES, BJÖRLING, MERRILL; RCA VICTOR SYMPHONY ORCHESTRA (EMI).

SIBELIUS, SYMPHONIES NOS. 2 AND 6: ROYAL PHILHARMONIC ORCHESTRA (DUTTON).

Beethoven, Ludwig van

(b. Bonn, December 17, 1770; d. Vienna, March 26, 1827)

GERMAN-BORN COMPOSER AND PIANIST, the most important and influential musician in history. As he always took pains to admit, he was no Mozart; yet his father tried to turn him into one anyway, leaving emotional scars that would mark him for life. More than almost any other figure in the canon, Beethoven willed himself to achieve high artistic standing. Though he would reject Napoleon's imperial ambitions, he subscribed to the Napoleonic idea of "self-made greatness" and consciously shaped his growth as an artist through unrelenting work, high aspirations, and powerful, inwardly directed thought. In a career marked by unparalleled artistic achievement, he became music's great individualist and the prototype of the Romantic composer, in whose works personal liberation and spiritual triumph were evoked through transcendence of formal and stylistic limits. Beethoven's formative years were spent in Bonn, where he acquired remarkable proficiency at the piano and, thanks to instruction from Christian Gottlob Neefe, a solid foundation as a composer. In 1784 he was appointed to assist Neefe as deputy court organist, and from 1788 he played viola in court-sponsored opera and concert performances.

In November 1792, with Bonn and much of western Germany under French occupation, Beethoven made his way to Vienna. Encouraged by his Bonn patron, Count Waldstein, to "receive the spirit of Mozart from Haydn's hands," he studied on and off with Haydn, took lessons from Salieri in vocal composition, and, for about a year (1794–95) received instruction in counterpoint from Johann Georg Albrechtsberger, all as part of a well-planned campaign to advance his art by attacking the most important musical forms—the string quartet and symphony—not frontally but obliquely. His first published works were sets of piano trios and piano sonatas, which served both to announce his arrival on the musical scene and as studies for those larger forms. Thus began a lifelong pattern of using the piano sonata as a laboratory, to break new ground, consolidate ideas, and lay the foundation for his most significant works in other forms. Of his first 28 opuses, 20 involved the piano in one way or another.

In Vienna, Beethoven found patrons and princes who were willing to support him, especially Prince Karl Lichnowsky (the dedicatee of the Op. 1 Piano Trios, who gave Beethoven lodgings and from

1800 a pension), Prince Franz Joseph Lobkowitz (whose orchestra gave the first performance of the *Eroica* Symphony, and who served as one of the guarantors of Beethoven's annuity from 1809), and, most important of all, Archduke Rudolph, the son of Emperor Leopold II, who studied with Beethoven from 1803 and received the dedications of several of his works. Beethoven capitalized on his brilliance as a pianist to achieve some of his early triumphs, playing his Concertos in C major, Op. 15, and B-flat, Op. 19, on several occasions and becoming renowned for his ex tempore improvisations.

Ludwig van Beethoven in 1801

Beethoven's life and work are traditionally divided into three periods. The early period, which culminated in 1803–04 with the Symphony No. 3, in E-flat, Op. 55 (*EROICA*), marked Beethoven's conquest of the Classical style as exemplified by the works of Mozart and Haydn. Beethoven's relationship with that style was, from the beginning, subversive. While he strove to match the expressive and topical richness of Classical discourse, he also sought to make of it something surprising, to transform its poise and elegance into music that was unstable and dynamic, to deepen the argument, enlarge the scope. In works like his Op. 18 string quartets and Symphony No. 2—which display his mastery in two of the major forms of Classicism—he nonetheless managed to whip the tablecloth out from under the place settings of the style by willfully manipulating its protocols through excessive repetition of figures, disruption of flow, and the use of violent accents. The watershed year 1800 saw the completion both of the Symphony No. 1, in C, Op. 21, and the six string quartets of Op. 18. In addition to these works and the *Eroica* Symphony, the most important compositions of the early period were the Piano Sonatas in C minor, Op. 13 (*PATHÉTIQUE*), and C-sharp minor, Op. 27, No. 2 (*MOONLIGHT*), the Violin Sonata in A, Op. 47 (*KREUTZER*), and the Piano Concerto No. 3, in C minor, Op. 37.

By 1802, Beethoven had confided to a few close friends and to his brothers (in the "Heiligenstadt Testament," named for the Viennese suburb where he wrote it) that he was losing his hearing. Beethoven may have needed crises to advance his art, but deafness tested him to the very core of his being. He responded to the disaster by plunging into his work, forging scores of an increasingly bold cast. Having to rely on what he could remember and imagine, rather than on what he could hear, he became more subjective in his thinking and put himself and his emotions at the center of his music. A lesser figure might have made a wholesale retreat into the safe territory of a familiar style, but Beethoven sought freedom on the musical frontier, where he could, to an increasing degree, make his own rules. The works of Beethoven's middle period (1804–05 to 1812) are characterized by emotional directness, heightened expressiveness wedded to a feeling of rhetorical urgency, and, in most cases, the expansion of form to meet the needs of content.

The most important works of the middle period—the Fifth Symphony (1808), the Sixth Symphony (*PASTORALE*; 1808), the first *RAZUMOVSKY* Quartet (Op. 59, No. 1), the opera *FIDELIO* (1805–06, rev. 1814), and the *EMPEROR* Concerto (1809)—represent a new direction, revolutionary in its aims and methods. In their formal schemes and long-range harmonic thinking, for example, both the Fifth Symphony and the *Pastorale* are truly something new under the sun. The Fifth—which begins with urgency and foreboding and ends in triumphant celebration—is a metaphor for transcendence and probably the most influential piece of music ever written. The *Pastorale,* also a journey, but of a very different kind, is contemplative, impressionistic, and expansive; it breathes to life a whole universe of tonal possibilities and is the forerunner of all the pieces written down the years that treat sound as a constructive element. Struggle is often encountered in the works of Beethoven's middle period, expressed through conflicts in key relationships and disruptive rhetorical gestures. With *Fidelio* and the *Emperor* Concerto, written against the backdrop of the Napoleonic conquest of Europe, Beethoven's music seems to give voice to a particularly intense mode of human and political conflict, conveying, in the words of Leon Plantinga, something of the "nobility of character required to prevail." Other important works of the period include the Violin Concerto (1806), the Fourth Piano Concerto (1806), the Seventh Symphony (1812), the Eighth Symphony (1812), the *Archduke* Trio (1811), and the Piano Sonatas in C, Op. 53 (*Waldstein*), F minor, Op. 57 (*Appassionata*), and E-flat, Op. 81a (*Les adieux*).

While his isolation gave Beethoven creative freedom, he paid a terrible price in loneliness, frequent plunges into depression, and bouts of poor health. During 1809–12 his misery deepened. The Napoleonic wars reached Vienna, bringing with them currency fluctuations that undermined Beethoven's finances; his one great love interest turned to dust, and a family dispute alienated him from his brother Johann. The next few years, fallow ones for the composer, were stressful as well due to his preoccupation with the upbringing of his nephew Karl, who was left in his care. The darkly handsome, well-dressed, socially active young man of the portraits painted around 1800 became the wild, unkempt, irascible figure seen in images from 1815 on. But by 1817, even though he was almost totally deaf and his physical health was clearly in decline, Beethoven began to recover his spiritual equilibrium and with it the urge to compose. He set himself a new goal: the creation of a body of monumentally ambitious works equal to those of Bach and Handel in their scale and contrapuntal intricacy. Between 1818 and 1826—from a man who was virtually unable to communicate, who needed to carry around conversation books so that other people could "talk" to him—there poured forth a series of astonishing, visionary compositions, works whose audacity and complexity determined the course of musical thought for the remainder of the century.

Beethoven's Broadwood piano, the mighty instrument for which he wrote his **Hammerklavier** *Sonata*

In these works, unfettered by preconceptions regarding structure or content, Beethoven began to treat form in a schematic way; the number of movements in his late sonatas and string quartets varies markedly, as does their length. Fugal procedure acquires a new importance, and the inner workings of the music at times become more important than the outward effect. In the outstanding works of this period, particularly the Ninth Symphony (1824), the *Missa Solemnis* (1823), the *HAMMERKLAVIER* Sonata (1818), the three piano sonatas of 1820–22 (Opp. 109–111), the *GROSSE FUGE,* Op. 133, and the five string quartets of 1825–26 (Opp. 127, 130, 131, 132, and 135), the frame of reference is elevated from the individual to the universal, from the subjective to the metaphysical. Paradoxically, these would be the most "personal" scores Beethoven ever composed. The message of the Ninth Symphony is clear: having believed all his life in the ideals of the French Revolution, and having seen them undone by the Congress of Vienna, he rose a final time to their defense. Here is Beethoven at his most revolutionary, transforming the symphony, for the first time in its history, into an act of moral philosophy and personal confession. By choosing Schiller's ode "To Joy" as the text, sung by chorus and soloists in its final movement, he came as close as words would allow to summarizing his own spiritual credo.

Beethoven's life work, particularly his late style, represents the single greatest paradigm shift in musical history. It ushered in the modern world of subjective expression, in which content dictates form (a fact recognized by many, including Proust in his *À la recherche du temps perdu*). As he grappled initially with the achievements of Mozart and Haydn, and later with those of Bach and Handel—seeking first to emulate, then to surpass them—he created music that seems ever more surprising, personal, and forward-looking. Reinventing himself as an artist, not once but several times, and struggling to reach more deeply into the truth of things as he saw and felt it, he expressed feelings of hope, transcendence, celebration, release, and affirmation in ways that had never before been encountered in music. The power of sound was unleashed for the first time (think of the opening chords of the *Eroica* Symphony, or the cataclysmic beginning of the Ninth), but more important was the power of the ideas he unleashed. Throughout his life Beethoven remained a figure of the Enlightenment and an ardent believer in the principles of liberty, equality, and the brotherhood of man. These beliefs resound in his music, and in an unusually compassionate way. The profound personal isolation he endured over most of his life made him one of the most urgent and emotionally communicative artists in history, with a generosity of spirit such as only a few mortals have ever expressed. Where Bach's music looks up, and Mozart's outward, Beethoven's almost always looks inward first, then reaches out—coming from the heart, as he once said, so that it might go to the heart. *See also* CONCERTO, STRING QUARTET, SYMPHONY.

Beethoven, the confident master of the middle period

RECOMMENDED RECORDINGS

Fidelio: Janowitz, Kollo, Jungwirth, Popp; Bernstein and Vienna Philharmonic (DG).

Fidelio: Ludwig, Vickers, Frick, Berry; Klemperer and Philharmonia Orchestra (EMI).

Missa Solemnis: Janowitz, Ludwig, Wunderlich, Berry; Karajan and Berlin Philharmonic (DG).

Missa Solemnis: Margiono, Robbin, Kendall, Miles; Gardiner and English Baroque Soloists (Archiv).

Piano concertos: Fleisher; Szell and Cleveland Orchestra (Sony).

Piano sonatas: Gilels (DG).

Piano sonatas: Goode (Nonesuch).

String quartets: Emerson Quartet (DG).

String quartets: Guarneri Quartet (RCA).

Symphonies (complete): Böhm and Vienna Philharmonic (DG).

Symphonies: Szell and Cleveland Orchestra (Sony).

Symphony No. 3 (*Eroica*): Klemperer and Philharmonia Orchestra (EMI).

Symphonies Nos. 4 and 6 (*Pastorale*): Walter and Columbia Symphony Orchestra (Sony).

Symphonies Nos. 5 and 7: Furtwängler and Vienna Philharmonic (EMI).

Symphonies Nos. 5 and 7: C. Kleiber and Vienna Philharmonic (DG).

Symphony No. 9: Kollo, Jones, Moll, Schwarz; Bernstein and Vienna Philharmonic (DG).

Violin Concerto: Menuhin; Furtwängler and Philharmonia Orchestra (EMI).

Violin Concerto: Perlman; Giulini and Philharmonia Orchestra (EMI).

Beggar's Opera, The BALLAD OPERA WITH SONGS ARRANGED BY JOHANN CHRISTOPH PEPUSCH (1667–1752), to a libretto by John Gay (1685–1732), premiered in London in 1728. The work, a freewheeling view of lower-class London life hung on a collection of popular and borrowed songs, was a roaring success upon its premiere at Lincoln's Inn Fields, and continued to be performed in London every year for the rest of the 18th century. Its plot served as the template for Bertolt Brecht's 1928 adaptation, *DIE DREIGROSCHENOPER (The Threepenny Opera)*, with music by Kurt Weill.

***Poster for a 1920 revival of* The Beggar's Opera**

Behrens, Hildegard

(b. Vare, February 9, 1937)

GERMAN DRAMATIC SOPRANO. She made her debut in Freiburg in 1971, as the Countess in Mozart's *Le nozze di Figaro.* Engagements at Düsseldorf and Frankfurt followed, and in 1976 she took her first bows at Covent Garden (as Leonore in Beethoven's *Fidelio*) and the Metropolitan Opera (Giorgetta in Puccini's *Il tabarro*). As her voice grew in power and stamina, she took on heavier roles. She sang the title role in Richard Straussss's *Salome* at Salzburg in 1977, and was cast as Wagner's Brünnhilde in the Bayreuth *Ring* cycle (1983–86) directed by Sir Peter Hall. She was subsequently engaged by the Met for its 1988 *Ring* cycle and as Strauss's Elektra in 1992. Admired for her impassioned yet intelligently sung portrayals of the Wagner and Strauss heroines, she collaborated on record with Bernstein, Solti, Karajan, and Levine, among others.

RECOMMENDED RECORDINGS

STRAUSS, *SALOME*: BÖHME, BALTSA, VAN DAM; KARAJAN AND VIENNA PHILHARMONIC (EMI).

WAGNER, *DER RING DES NIBELUNGEN*: LUDWIG, NORMAN, MORRIS, MOLL, ET AL.; LEVINE AND METROPOLITAN OPERA ORCHESTRA (DG).

Hildegard Behrens as Elektra

bel canto (It., "beautiful singing") Operatic style of the early 19th century that called for a light, mellifluous tone and effortless delivery of florid passages. The art of writing for the voice in this manner reached its apogee in the works of the Italian composers Bellini and Donizetti, but can also be found in various operas of Rossini, Meyerbeer, Verdi, and Wagner. A setting in bel canto style could be ornamental, but did not have to be dazzling. What mattered was that it be brought off with lightness, ease, and style. *See also* FIORITURA, *entries for individual composers.*

Bell, Joshua

(b. Bloomington, Ind., December 9, 1967)

AMERICAN VIOLINIST. He studied in his hometown with Josef Gingold, and made his debut as an orchestral soloist at the age of 14, with Riccardo Muti and the Philadelphia Orchestra. His Carnegie Hall debut, in 1985, set the seal on his promise and launched a major career. In some ways his sweet-toned and soulful playing harks back to an earlier era, when subjectivity was expected of an artist. Drawn equally to the concerto, the recital, and the chamber literature, he has become a celebrated interpreter of Romantic and 20th-century showpieces, and has taken a keen interest in expanding the repertoire. He gave the world premiere of Nicholas Maw's (b. 1935) Violin Concerto in 1993, and has subsequently introduced works by John Corigliano (a chaconne and a concerto, both subtitled *The Red Violin*), Edgar Meyer (b. 1960), and Aaron Jay Kernis (b. 1960).

RECOMMENDED RECORDINGS

BARBER, VIOLIN CONCERTO; WALTON, VIOLIN CONCERTO: ZINMAN AND BALTIMORE SYMPHONY ORCHESTRA (DECCA).

BRAHMS, VIOLIN CONCERTO: DOHNÁNYI AND CLEVELAND ORCHESTRA (DECCA).

KREISLER, SELECTIONS: COKER (DECCA).

Bellini, Vincenzo

(b. Catania, November 3, 1801; d. Puteaux, September 23, 1835)

SICILIAN-BORN COMPOSER. He studied with his father and grandfather, both professional musicians, and entered the Naples Conservatory at the age of 18, under the tutelage of Rossini's archrival Niccolò Zingarelli. The triumphant 1827 premiere of his third opera, *Il pirata* (*The Pirate*), at La Scala made him a celebrity overnight and laid the foundation for his brilliant and unfortunately short-lived career. With *Il pirata,* Bellini began what was to be an extraordinarily fruitful collaboration with the librettist Felice Romani. The premiere of their *I Capuleti e i Montecchi,* based on Shakespeare's *Romeo and Juliet,* followed in 1830, and in 1831 came *LA SONNAMBULA* (*The Sleepwalker*) and *NORMA,* both featuring the celebrated soprano Giuditta Pasta in the title role. Composer and librettist had a falling-out over *Beatrice di Tenda,* which failed at its premiere in Venice in 1833. But the 1835 Paris premiere of Bellini's final opera, *I Puritani* (*The Puritans*)—with a stellar cast that included Giulia Grisi, Giovanni Battista Rubini, Antonio Tamburini, and Luigi Lablache—was a huge success. At the peak of his powers, and with the operatic world at his feet, Bellini succumbed later that year to an intestinal infection, at the age of only 33.

Bellini's operas remain the purest examples of the art of BEL CANTO. Products of a refined and sensitive musician with an unparalleled gift for melody and romantic expressiveness, their influence can be felt not only where one would expect—in the works of Verdi and Wagner—but in the beautifully spun-out melodies of Chopin's piano music, even in the Italianate lyricism of Stravinsky's *Apollon musagète* (1928). During the past half century, they have served as marvelous vehicles for interpreters such as Maria Callas, Joan Sutherland, and Montserrat Caballé, who have had the resourcefulness, imagination, and vocal flexibility needed to sing them.

Vincenzo Bellini, master of bel canto

RECOMMENDED RECORDINGS

NORMA: SUTHERLAND, HORNE, ALEXANDER; BONYNGE AND LONDON SYMPHONY ORCHESTRA (DECCA).

I PURITANI: SUTHERLAND, PAVAROTTI, CAPPUCCILLI, GHIAUROV; BONYNGE AND ROYAL OPERA (DECCA).

LA SONNAMBULA: CALLAS, MONTI, COSSOTTO, MORESI; VOTTO AND LA SCALA ORCHESTRA (EMI).

LA SONNAMBULA: SUTHERLAND, PAVAROTTI, GHIAUROV; BONYNGE AND NATIONAL PHILHARMONIC ORCHESTRA (DECCA).

berceuse (from Fr. *berceau,* "cradle") A piece in the style of a lullaby.

Berg, Alban

(b. Vienna, February 9, 1885; d. Vienna, December 24, 1935)

AUSTRIAN COMPOSER. He had little formal musical training in his youth. In 1904, at the age of 19, he became a pupil of Arnold Schoenberg, who was then 30, beginning an apprenticeship that would last until 1910. Among the works he composed under Schoenberg's guidance were the *Sieben frühe Lieder* (*Seven Early Songs*) (1905–08), the Piano Sonata, Op. 1 (1907–08) ◉, and the String Quartet, Op. 3 (1910). He struck out on his own with the *Fünf Orchesterlieder nach Ansichtkartentexten von Peter Altenberg* (*Five Songs to Picture Postcard Texts by Peter Altenberg*; 1912), brilliant and potent miniatures that look forward in many ways to the opera *Wozzeck* in their striking imagery and innovative treatment of form. The *Drei Orchesterstücke* (*Three Pieces for Orchestra*), Op. 6 (1915), the last score Berg was to complete before three years of service in the Austrian army, show him grappling with larger formal issues in response to the impact of Mahler's Ninth Symphony,

Alban Berg* (center) *and Erich Kleiber* (right) *at a rehearsal of* Wozzeck *at the Berlin Staatsoper, 1925

which he heard at its premiere in 1912.

In 1914 Berg attended the Vienna premiere of another work that would leave a lasting mark on him, Georg Büchner's *Woyzeck.* By 1918 he had begun work on an operatic setting, which he completed in the spring of 1922. The portrait of a deranged, murderous soldier and the hardly less deranged figures surrounding him, WOZZECK is one of the most gripping works in all of opera. In writing the music, Berg made use of traditional forms such as the passacaglia, rondo, sonata, and fugue as structural templates, using each for a particular dramatic purpose. He invested the individual scenes of the opera with music that is by turns edgy and urgent, haunting in its suggestiveness and in its harrowing power, drawing on the full resources of the orchestra and modern harmony in the process. Berg followed *Wozzeck* with the *LYRISCHE SUITE* (*Lyric Suite*) (1925–26) for string quartet, a masterpiece of 12-TONE writing. In 1928, he set to work on his second opera, *LULU,* based on a pair of dramas by Frank Wedekind. Composed in a full-blown 12-tone idiom, the score to *Lulu* would remain unfinished at Berg's death; but he left enough in short-score and sketches for the final act to be completed—in 1979, by the composer-musicologist Friedrich Čerha (b. 1926)—and since then the work's grand design, powerful dramatic thrust, and inspired musical treatment have been spectacularly apparent. One more great work remained, the Violin Concerto commissioned by the American violinist Louis Krasner and composed in 1935 as a requiem for the 18-year-old Manon Gropius; its final movement includes a touching reference to the chorale "Es ist genug!" from Bach's Cantata No. 60, *O Ewigkeit, du Donnerwort.* Berg died shortly after finishing it, of an infection resulting from an insect bite.

Portrait of Berg by Arnold Schoenberg

In his operas *Wozzeck* and *Lulu,* and in works such as the Violin Concerto, Berg put a human face on the 12-tone system of composition pioneered by Schoenberg. The appeal of Berg's music lies in its balance of formal rigor and emotional richness, in that it is both tightly constructed and expressive, both "cerebral" and emotional. Even the most violent, shocking pages Berg wrote have a familiar, Romantic ring to them—for in addition to observing the forms and procedures of tonal music in what he created, Berg also preserved much of its sound and spirit.

RECOMMENDED RECORDINGS

LULU: STRATAS, MINTON, SCHWARZ, MAZURA; BOULEZ AND PARIS OPERA (DG).

THREE PIECES FOR ORCHESTRA: KARAJAN AND BERLIN PHILHARMONIC (DG).

VIOLIN CONCERTO: MUTTER; LEVINE AND CHICAGO SYMPHONY ORCHESTRA (DG).

WOZZECK: FISCHER-DIESKAU, WUNDERLICH, STOLZE, LEAR; BÖHM AND DEUTSCHE OPER BERLIN (DG).

WOZZECK: WAECHTER, SILJA, WINKLER; DOHNÁNYI AND VIENNA PHILHARMONIC(DECCA).

Berganza, Teresa

(b. Madrid, March 16, 1935)

SPANISH MEZZO-SOPRANO. She made her debut in 1957 at the Festival of Aix-en-Provence as Dorabella in Mozart's *Così fan tutte.* Her debuts in England and America came the following year: at Glyndebourne as Cherubino in Mozart's *Le nozze di Figaro,* and in Dallas as Isabella in Rossini's *L'Italiana in Algeri.* During the 1960s and 1970s, she was a regular at most of the world's major houses, specializing in the Mozart and Rossini mezzo roles, and eventually making a distinguished Carmen.

RECOMMENDED RECORDINGS

BIZET, *CARMEN*: COTRUBAS, DOMINGO, MILNES; ABBADO AND LONDON SYMPHONY ORCHESTRA (DG).

MOZART, *DON GIOVANNI*: TE KANAWA, RAIMONDI, VAN DAM; MAAZEL AND PARIS OPERA (SONY).

Berglund, Paavo

(b. Helsinki, April 14, 1929)

FINNISH CONDUCTOR. After studying at the Sibelius Academy in Helsinki, he began his professional career as a violinist, cofounded the Helsinki Chamber Orchestra in 1952, and served as associate, then principal, conductor of the Finnish Radio Symphony Orchestra (1962–71). In 1972 he was engaged as music director of the Bournemouth Symphony Orchestra, a position he held until 1979. Simultaneously, he led the Helsinki Philharmonic (1975–79), later serving as principal guest conductor of the Scottish National Orchestra (1981–85) and chief conductor of the Royal Stockholm Philharmonic (1987–91). In 1993 he assumed the post of principal conductor of the Royal Danish Orchestra in Copenhagen. Berglund is a leading interpreter of the works of Sibelius, Nielsen, and Shostakovich; he has recorded complete cycles of the Sibelius symphonies with both the Helsinki Philharmonic and the Chamber Orchestra of Europe, and in 1970 he presided over the world-premiere recording of Sibelius's early choral symphony *Kullervo.*

RECOMMENDED RECORDINGS

NIELSEN, SYMPHONIES; ROYAL DANISH ORCHESTRA (RCA).

SIBELIUS, *KULLERVO*: HYNNINEN, SAARINEN; HELSINKI PHILHARMONIC ORCHESTRA (EMI).

SIBELIUS, SYMPHONIES; CHAMBER ORCHESTRA OF EUROPE (FINLANDIA).

SIBELIUS, SYMPHONIES AND TONE POEMS; HELSINKI PHILHARMONIC ORCHESTRA ET AL. (EMI).

Bergonzi, Carlo

(b. Polisene, July 13, 1924)

ITALIAN TENOR. He studied at the Arrigo Boito Conservatory in Parma, making his debut as a baritone in 1948. After further study he debuted as a tenor in 1951. He first sang at La Scala in 1953 and made his American debut in Chicago in 1955, as Turiddu in Mascagni's *Cavalleria rusticana* and Luigi in Puccini's *Il tabarro.* He appeared regularly at the Metropolitan Opera from 1956 to 1988. His stock-in-trade were the lighter Verdi and Puccini roles, and such parts as Boito's Faust and Canio in Leoncavallo's *Pagliacci.* Bergonzi was a true stylist. At its best, his singing possessed a lyric beauty of the highest order: He commanded the finest diction and most elegant legato phrasing of any Italian tenor in the second half of the 20th century, and had a delivery that was utterly distinctive. After retirement he took charge of an academy in the town of Busseto, near Verdi's birthplace.

Berio, Luciano

(b. Oneglia [now Imperia], October 24, 1925; d. Rome, May 27, 2003)

ITALIAN COMPOSER of the postwar avant-garde. Brought up in a family of professional musicians, he entered the Milan Conservatory in 1945, studying with Giorgio Federico Ghedini and receiving his doctorate in composition in 1950. That year he married the American mezzo-soprano Cathy Berberian and visited the United States for the first time. He returned the following summer to study with Luigi Dallapiccola at Tanglewood. During the early 1950s, he had stimulating contacts with the conductor Hermann Scherchen and with composers Karlheinz Stockhausen and Bruno Maderna. He founded an electronic music studio with Maderna in Milan in 1955, and became friends with John Cage, Henri Pousseur, and Umberto Eco.

Concerned that the use of serial techniques might lead to overschematization and compositional aridity, he looked for catalysts to fire his imagination—and found them in the study of structural linguistics and the work of James Joyce. In 1958 he composed *Thema* (*Omaggio a Joyce*), a work for tape whose only protagonist was the voice of Berberian. He followed this with *Sequenza III* (1966) for female voice, also written for Berberian, a piece of extraordinary interest and gestural freedom that also happens to be a lot of fun. *Sinfonia* (1968), a lively deconstructionist meditation on symphonic patterns that utilizes snippets of Debussy, Ravel, and Richard Strauss in its central movement (a collage based on the scherzo of Mahler's Symphony No. 2), proved to be one of the milestones of midcentury musical thought and a harbinger of Berio's widening horizons; from there he went to subsequent "genre" benders *Opera* (1970) and *Coro* (1976), and the restoration-via-deconstruction of Schubert's sketches for what would have been his Tenth Symphony, in *Rendering* (1990).

Freedom of thought and action characterized Berio's vast output, one of the most fascinating and provocative of modern times. These qualities can perhaps be best appreciated in the series of works for solo instruments called *Sequenze* that he began in 1958 with *Sequenza I* for flute. Intended to create a kind of polyphony through melody alone, they form a catalog of reflections on the act of playing the instruments for which they were written, as well as on the tics of virtuosity and the psychic reactions of the individual performer. What the *Brandenburg* Concertos were to the music of the first half of the 18th century, Berio's *Sequenze* are to that of the second half of the 20th.

RECOMMENDED RECORDINGS

SEQUENZE (COMPLETE): ENSEMBLE INTERCONTEMPORAIN (DG).

SINFONIA: BOULEZ AND L'ORCHESTRE NATIONAL DE FRANCE (ERATO).

Berlin Philharmonic Orchestra SYMPHONIC ENSEMBLE FORMED IN **1882** by 54 disgruntled members of the Bilsesche Kapelle. Its first regular conductors were Joseph Joachim, from 1884, and Hans von Bülow, who served as chief conductor from 1887 to 1893. Bülow's exacting standards and

Sir Simon Rattle conducts the Berlin Philharmonic at Carnegie Hall in 2003.

meticulous approach to rehearsal laid the foundation for the orchestra's disciplined style of playing and quickly turned it into one of Germany's best. Among the early guest conductors were Hermann Levi, Felix Mottl, Felix Weingartner, and Ernst von Schuch, as well as composers Edvard Grieg, Gustav Mahler, Richard Strauss, Hans Pfitzner, and Johannes Brahms (who also performed with the orchestra as a piano soloist).

Arthur Nikisch succeeded Bülow as principal conductor in 1895, remaining at the orchestra's helm until his death in 1922. Famed for his mesmerizing intensity, Nikisch championed the music of Beethoven, Schumann, Wagner, Brahms, Bruckner, and Tchaikovsky as well as works by Berlioz, Liszt, and such modern figures as Mahler and Strauss. Under Nikisch the orchestra made several international tours and gained steadily in stature. Wilhelm Furtwängler became the Philharmonic's chief conductor in 1923. Neither a disciplinarian as Bülow had been, nor a podium wizard like Nikisch, he was nonetheless one of the most profound interpretive musicians of his generation. His strengths were the music of Beethoven, Brahms, Bruckner, and Wagner, and while not particularly attuned to the music of contemporary composers, he nevertheless included works by Schoenberg, Stravinsky, and Hindemith on his programs. During his tenure, the orchestra performed with a starry roster of guest conductors, including Bruno Walter, Otto Klemperer, and Erich Kleiber. Furtwängler presided over the orchestra during the years of National Socialism, and was barred from performing with it following the end of World War II, until he had undergone denazification proceedings. In the interim, the orchestra turned first to Leo Borchard (who was shot and killed by an American sentry in the summer of 1945, on his way home from a dinner party after curfew), then to a largely unproven talent, Sergiu Celibidache, a 33-year-old Romanian. Celibidache's fiery, extreme, spontaneous brand of music making won many admirers, but his contentious personality did not go over well with the members of the orchestra. Furtwängler returned to the Philharmonic's podium in 1947 and was named conductor for life in 1952.

Following Furtwängler's death in 1954, the orchestra chose Herbert von Karajan as its permanent conductor. Throughout his tenure (1955–89, the longest in the Philharmonic's history), Karajan demanded elegance, precision, tonal refinement, and beauty of sound from the players; responding to his drive and discipline, they attained a level of perfection in their playing unmatched by any other European ensemble at the time. With Karajan the Berliners toured widely and made hundreds of recordings ranging from Vivaldi to Shostakovich, achieving particular distinction in Beethoven, Bruckner, Mahler, Strauss, and Sibelius. In spite of the extraordinary level at which they performed together, Karajan's impersonal and autocratic manner chafed; during the 1980s, tensions between conductor and players built to a level intolerable for all, and in 1989, shortly before his death, Karajan terminated his relationship with the orchestra.

In October 1989 the Berliners chose Claudio Abbado as their fifth chief conductor. Taking up his duties in 1990, Abbado quickly brought the orchestra back into trim, adding dozens of younger players to its ranks, cultivating a more intense and impassioned style of playing, and favoring a somewhat weightier and more muscular sonority than his predecessor. In the area of repertoire, he shifted the emphasis from the 19th century toward the 20th, but paid only lip service to contemporary music. With a few notable exceptions, his recordings with the orchestra had little of the impact of Furtwängler's or Karajan's. Having previously announced his intention to step down in 2002, Abbado spent his final two seasons battling stomach cancer. Sir Simon Rattle succeeded him as chief conductor beginning with the 2003–04 season.

With the reunification of Germany, Berlin has again become Europe's most important musical center. The Philharmonic continues to play a central role in the city's musical and cultural life, and remains a paragon of discipline, versatility, and virtuosity.

RECOMMENDED RECORDINGS

Brahms, Symphonies Nos. 2–4: Furtwängler (EMI).

Bruckner, Symphony No. 7: Jochum (DG).

Debussy, *La mer*; Ravel, *Boléro*; Mussorgsky, *Pictures at an Exhibition*: Karajan (DG).

Liszt, *Les préludes*; Smetana, *The Moldau*: Karajan (DG).

Mahler, Symphony No. 6: Abbado (DG).

Schoenberg, *Gurre-Lieder*: Mattila, Otter, Moser, Langridge, Quasthoff; Rattle (EMI).

Strauss, *Also sprach Zarathustra*, *Don Juan*, *Till Eulenspiegel*: Karajan (DG).

Berlioz, Hector

(b. La Côte-Saint-André, December 11, 1803; d. Paris, March 8, 1869)

FRENCH COMPOSER AND CRITIC who possessed the most daring and original voice of his age. His febrile imagination and extraordinary sensitivity to extramusical ideas drove him to fashion works that changed the scope, content, even the very sound of orchestral music in the 19th century. He was the eldest child of a country doctor, who supervised his early education and encouraged him to read the classics. He took lessons on flute and guitar, learned harmony from some textbooks, and composed his first pieces as he entered his teens. In 1821, in deference to his father, he went to Paris to study medicine. While in medical school he immersed himself in the Parisian musical scene, attending numerous performances at the Opéra and studying informally with Jean-François Le Sueur at the Conservatoire; by 1824 he had abandoned medicine, and in 1826 he entered the Conservatoire officially as a student of Le Sueur (composition) and Antoine Reicha (counterpoint and fugue).

On September 11, 1827, he attended a performance of *Hamlet* at the Odéon in which the Irish-born actress Harriet Smithson performed the role of Ophelia. Overwhelmed by her beauty and charisma he fell madly in love with her, and permanently under the spell of Shakespeare. Six months later, he heard for the first time Beethoven's dramatic, large-scale Third and Fifth Symphonies. The result of this remarkable conjunction was the *SYMPHONIE FANTASTIQUE* (*Fantastic Symphony*; 1830), an incomparably vivid self-portrait that took as its subject the experiences of a young musician in love and proved to be one of the defining works of musical Romanticism.

A string of groundbreaking efforts followed, many of them inspired by great literature: the symphony for solo viola and orchestra *HAROLD EN ITALIE* (1834), written for Paganini and loosely based on Byron's epic *Childe Harold*; the colossal Requiem, which Berlioz titled *Grande messe des morts* (1837); the "dramatic symphony" *ROMÉO ET JULIETTE* (1839) for orchestra, chorus, and soloists, a brilliant homage to Shakespeare; *La damnation de Faust* (1845–46), after Goethe's *Faust*; and, most important of all to the composer, the grand opera *LES TROYENS* (1856–58), whose story, based on Virgil's *Aeneid*, deals with the denouement of the Trojan War, the flight of Aeneas and his followers to Carthage, and the establishment of ancient Rome. In each of these grandiose scores Berlioz painted an orchestral canvas worthy of Delacroix; but his touch was

An early portrait of Berlioz; Harriet Smithson as Ophelia

Berlioz monument, Paris

equally sure in the more intimate vein of pieces such as the song cycle *Les nuits d'été* (*Summer Nights*; 1841), the quasi-oratorio *L'enfance du Christ* (*The Childhood of Christ*; 1850–54), and the opera *Béatrice et Bénédict* (1860–62), based on Shakespeare's *Much Ado About Nothing.* Unfortunately, Berlioz was his own worst enemy, unable to keep hurtful opinions of others to himself, and the prescient nature of his work too often meant that its true value eluded both the public and the establishment. He died a weary, broken man.

Unable to play a single instrument well, Berlioz nonetheless developed into the supreme orchestrator of his time. His startling innovations included the use of vastly augmented brass, multiple timpani to produce chords, esoteric percussion (like the tambourine in the *Roman Carnival* Overture ◉ and the deep bells in the *Symphonie fantastique*), riotous figurations for the strings, and unusual effects such as percussive COL LEGNO bowing. He got the orchestra to produce sonorities no one had ever imagined before: In the *Grande messe des morts* (*Grand Mass of the Dead*), to symbolize the gulf between heaven and earth, he set the groaning of eight trombones in their pedal register against dulcet chords in three flutes.

Berlioz was the quintessential Romantic, fired by a love for great literature and an unquenchable passion for the eternal feminine. He was also a classicist and an idealist, a worshipper of grace, proportion, and poise—and in the best of his works these qualities conspired to produce music of exquisite beauty and exceptional emotional power.

RECOMMENDED RECORDINGS

COMPLETE ORCHESTRAL WORKS: DAVIS AND VARIOUS ENSEMBLES (PHILIPS).

OVERTURES: DAVIS AND STAATSKAPELLE DRESDEN (RCA).

REQUIEM: SIMONEAU ET AL.; MUNCH AND BOSTON SYMPHONY ORCHESTRA (RCA).

ROMÉO ET JULIETTE: BORODINA, MOSER, MILES; DAVIS AND VIENNA PHILHARMONIC (PHILIPS).

SYMPHONIE FANTASTIQUE: DAVIS AND CONCERTGEBOUW ORCHESTRA (PHILIPS).

LES TROYENS: HEPPNER, DE YOUNG, LANG, MINGARDO; DAVIS AND LONDON SYMPHONY ORCHESTRA (LSO LIVE).

Bernac, Pierre

(b. Paris, January 12, 1899; d. Villeneuve-les-Avignon, October 17, 1979)

FRENCH BARITONE. He came to singing relatively late in life, but developed into one of the finest recitalists of the 20th century. He made his debut in 1925, and in 1926 gave the premiere of Francis Poulenc's *Chansons gaillardes.* After further study in Salzburg, he commenced a long and productive career during which he collaborated with many contemporary composers, most importantly Poulenc (his elder by five days), who frequently accompanied him in concert and on record. Among the cycles Poulenc wrote for him are the *Cinq poèmes* (1935) and *Tel jour, telle nuit* (1936), both to texts by Paul Éluard.

RECOMMENDED RECORDING

Songs of Poulenc, Ravel, Satie, Fauré, Gounod, and Duparc—"The Essential Pierre Bernac" (Testament).

Bernstein, Leonard

(b. Lawrence, Mass. August 25, 1918; d. New York, October 14, 1990)

American conductor, composer, pianist, writer, teacher, activist, and intellectual icon. If at times his talent was stretched thin by the demands of several careers, he was still the most important American musician of his generation and one of the great maestros of the 20th century. He started piano lessons when he was ten, and attended Boston Latin School and Harvard University. After graduating from Harvard in 1939, he continued his musical training at the Curtis Institute of Music in Philadelphia, studying orchestration with Randall Thompson and conducting with Fritz Reiner. He joined the conducting class of Serge Koussevitzky at the Berkshire Music Center in the summer of 1940; in 1942 he was named Koussevitzky's assistant at Tanglewood. He spent the next couple of years working as an arranger for the New York music publishing firm of Harms, Inc. (where Gershwin had once worked), using the pseudonym "Lenny Amber" (in German, *Bernstein* means "amber"). On his 25th birthday, he was named assistant conductor of the New York Philharmonic by its newly appointed music director, Artur Rodzinski; less than three months later, on November 14, 1943, he leapt into the limelight when he substituted for Bruno Walter on a few hours' notice at a Philharmonic concert. Bernstein's performance convinced *New York Times* music critic Olin Downes that he was "one of the very few conductors of the rising generation who are indubitably to be reckoned with."

In 1946 Bernstein already cast a large shadow in the musical world.

The following year Bernstein made an equally extraordinary debut as a composer with the premieres of both his First Symphony, subtitled *Jeremiah,* and his ballet *Fancy Free,* with choreography by Jerome Robbins. So successful was *Fancy Free* that by

***Shore leave: Gene Kelly goes* On the Town**

the end of 1944, with the help of lyricists Betty Comden and Adolph Green, Bernstein had adapted its scenario for *On the Town,* his first musical—as energetic and exuberant as the ballet that inspired it, but with bittersweet moments as well. As one of the songs in *On the Town* proclaims, New York in the 1940s *was* a helluva town; everything that was important in the arts was happening there, and at the center of it all was the liveliest musical scene in the world. Inevitably, the brilliant young firebrand from Cambridge became a dedicated New Yorker. The decade 1948–57 saw the completion of some of Bernstein's most important scores, including his Symphony No. 2 (1949; inspired by W. H. Auden's *The Age of Anxiety*), the *Serenade* for violin and string orchestra (1954), the film score (1954) for Elia Kazan's *On the Waterfront,* the operetta *Candide* (1956), and the musical *West Side Story* (1957; in collaboration with Robbins and the young Stephen Sondheim). In these scores, Bernstein's energetic idiom reached its maturity—serious but hip, full of jazzy animation, and with a distinctly American melodic accent derived from popular music. Several of these pieces touch on the joys and sorrows of the national experience, notably *West Side Story* and the opera *Trouble in Tahiti* (1951), which, notwithstanding its title, has nothing to do with the South Pacific and everything to do with the uniquely American malaise of life in the suburbs. For the joy, there's hardly anything that compares with *West Side Story*'s rollicking "America," a boys-versus-girls free-for-all in which the constantly shifting rhythmic accent is a metaphor for the cultural differences that drive the entire score.

Bernstein studying a score in the 1960s

In 1958, Bernstein was named music director of the New York Philharmonic, becoming one of the first U.S.-born and -trained musicians to head a major American symphony orchestra. During his years at the helm of the Philharmonic, Bernstein broadened the orchestra's repertoire and established it as a major media presence through televised Young People's Concerts and Omnibus programs for adult viewers. He not only brought a new element of glamour to the orchestra's concerts, but generated considerable excitement via his passion for Mahler, Haydn, and Beethoven, as well as for the music of the major composers of the 20th century. Bernstein recorded more than 400 pieces with the Philharmonic, garnering ten Emmy Awards and half a dozen Grammys. After stepping down as the Philharmonic's music director in 1969, he was named its laureate conductor, a post he held for the rest of his life.

During the 1970s, Bernstein was one of the most venerated and sought-after guest conductors on classical music's A-list. Forging close associations with the Vienna Philharmonic and the Israel Philharmonic, he immersed himself in the core symphonic repertoire, particularly the works of Haydn, Beethoven, Schubert, Brahms, and Mahler. Out of this reexamination of tradition emerged a new interpretive persona: Bernstein's readings became more subjective than before, acquiring in many cases a grandeur and breadth that proved deeply engaging to audiences at home and abroad. Many critics praised his interpretations, especially of the symphonies of Beethoven and Mahler, for their profundity and power—though a few, not without justification, occasionally accused him of wallowing in the emotion of the scores he championed.

In the last two decades of his life Bernstein paid a heavy price for his podium celebrity. Some observers suspected that his compositional muse was not speaking to him with the intimacy of old, citing as evidence that after *CHICHESTER PSALMS* (1965) there was little of the first order in his output. *Mass,* which opened the Kennedy Center in Washington, D.C., in 1971, had brilliant moments but more than a few flawed ones. Bernstein's last musical, *1600 Pennsylvania Avenue,* written to celebrate the Bicentennial, flopped as miserably as any show in history, while his final opera, *A Quiet Place* (1983), proved not only an audience-quieter but a theatrical bust. From this later period only the orchestral song cycle *Songfest,* premiered in 1977, can be considered a success.

Those who knew him often got the feeling that Bernstein was a man tormented by his own brilliance. He could be temperamental, even petulant, when he did not get his way. Yet he could also be surpassingly generous—sympathetic, kind, encouraging, always able to focus on the individual person no matter how large the crowd. He was amazingly clever, with a quickness of mind (especially in word games) that could hardly be believed. He was a born writer and an articulate communicator, as his scripts for the Young People's Concerts and his book *The Joy of Music* (1959) make abundantly clear. Yet despite leading a gregarious existence, and always having something to say, he seemed perpetually lonely. All this came out in his music, in which he felt compelled to take on the anguish of human existence and give voice to the frustrations and hopes that mark modern society.

What characterized Bernstein's composing and his interaction with other people also characterized his conducting: The important thing was emotion. Bernstein as conductor was never a neutral intermediary,

Bernstein on the podium in the 1980s, still passionate about music and life

but an artist who internalized the emotional world of a score and did his best to allow it to be reborn in his performance. Sometimes this approach irritated listeners, and sometimes it bothered fellow performers. The complaint was put memorably by a principal violist of the Vienna Philharmonic, who remarked, "When we play Beethoven with Bernstein, we play it Bernstein's way. But when we play Beethoven with Böhm, we play it *Beethoven's* way." Perhaps, but Bernstein's way was so compelling. . . .

Bernstein always wanted to be the center of attention, and wherever he went and whatever he did, he was. His liveliness, exuberance, and sentiment were quintessentially American, and part of what made him one of music's superstars. He wrote his best music when he was young—he was barely 39 when his masterpiece, *West Side Story,* premiered—and while his later efforts as a composer never fulfilled the extraordinary promise of his youth, they arose from an honest effort to say something meaningful. Which is hardly surprising, because that was also so clearly what motivated Bernstein when he conducted. And it is as a conductor that he seems assured of a place among the greats.

RECOMMENDED RECORDINGS

As composer:

Chichester Psalms: Bernstein and Israel Philharmonic (DG).

Serenade: Hahn; Zinman and Baltimore Symphony Orchestra (Sony).

Songfest: Dale, Elias, Gramm, Reardon; Bernstein and National Symphony Orchestra (DG).

Symphonic Dances from *West Side Story, On the Waterfront* suite, *Fancy Free, Candide* overture: Bernstein and New York Philharmonic (Sony).

As conductor:

Beethoven, Symphonies Nos. 3 and 9: Vienna Philharmonic (DG).

Copland, Symphony No. 3, *Rodeo*: New York Philharmonic (Sony).

Gershwin, *Rhapsody in Blue, An American in Paris*: Columbia Symphony Orchestra and New York Philharmonic (Sony).

Mahler, symphonies (complete): New York Philharmonic (Sony).

Mahler, Symphony No. 5: Vienna Philharmonic (DG).

Schumann, symphonies (complete): Vienna Philharmonic (DG).

Sibelius, Symphonies Nos. 4 and 5: New York Philharmonic (Sony).

Berry, Walter

(b. Vienna, April 8, 1929; d. Vienna, October 27, 2000)

Austrian bass-baritone. He studied at the Akademie für Musik in his home town, and first sang with the Vienna Staatsoper in 1950. He made his American debut at the Metropolitan Opera in 1966, as Barak in Richard Strauss's *Die Frau ohne Schatten,* a role to which, with his earthy, warm temperament, he was ideally suited. His operatic repertoire was vast, but centered on the principal Mozart roles (Masetto, Leporello, Don Alfonso, Count Almaviva, Figaro, and, to particularly charming effect, Papageno). His Strauss roles, in addition to Barak, included Ochs in *Der Rosenkavalier* and Waldner in *Arabella,* and he frequently sang the part of Telramund in Wagner's *Lohengrin,* as well as the title role in Berg's *Wozzeck,* most notably under the baton of Karl Böhm in 1955, and on the recording conducted by Pierre Boulez. Also noteworthy were his renditions of Don Pizarro in Beethoven's *Fidelio* and Bluebeard in Bartók's *Bluebeard's Castle.* Berry's voice had the mellow luster of polished mahogany. His warm, expressive delivery and *echt* Viennese accent made him a natural in comic roles, yet he could also bring a steely edge to his singing when it suited the dramatic situation. From 1957 to 1971 he was married to mezzo-soprano Christa Ludwig, frequently partnering her on stage and in recital. Of the two of them, singing Mahler, Leonard Bernstein once quipped: "They're the berries."

RECOMMENDED RECORDINGS

Bartók, *Bluebeard's Castle*: Ludwig; Kertész and London Symphony Orchestra (Decca).

Mozart, *Die Zauberflöte*: Popp, Janowitz, Gedda, Frick; Klemperer and Philharmonia Orchestra (EMI).

Berwald, Franz

(b. Stockholm, July 23, 1796; d. Stockholm, April 3, 1868)

Swedish composer. He came from a musical family and began playing the violin professionally when he was 16, as a member of the court orchestra in Stockholm. His first efforts at composition date from around 1817, but he composed nearly all his important works during the decade 1840–50. He traveled widely (St. Petersburg, Berlin, Vienna, Paris) but always returned to Sweden. In 1850 he became manager of a glass factory in the north of the country, remaining involved in its operation until 1859. During his life, he was largely overlooked in his homeland; a measure of recognition finally came in 1867 when he was appointed professor of composition at the Royal Academy of Music in Stockholm.

Berwald's early works show the influence of Beethoven and Spohr, but already reveal the presence of an independent musical personality. In his maturity he composed about a dozen operas (several now lost), a considerable amount of chamber music, and some songs, but his reputation rests almost entirely on the four symphonies he wrote during the 1840s: *Sinfonie sérieuse* in G minor (1842); *Sinfonie capricieuse* in D (1842); *Sinfonie singulière* in C (1845); and Symphony No. 4 in E-flat (1845). These works abound in fresh ideas and attest to the striking originality of Berwald's formal thought, as well as to the inventiveness with which he manipulated his material, teasing the possibilities of little two- and three-note figures into whole movements with a singular sense of fun and freedom from the rules, as he does in the first movement of the *Sinfonie singulière*.

RECOMMENDED RECORDINGS

SYMPHONIES (COMPLETE): JÄRVI AND GOTHENBURG SYMPHONY ORCHESTRA (DG).

SEPTET: GAUDIER ENSEMBLE (HYPERION).

Biber, Heinrich Ignaz Franz von

(b. Wartenberg, Bohemia, August 12, 1644; d. Salzburg, May 3, 1704)

AUSTRIAN VIOLIN VIRTUOSO AND COMPOSER, considered the most capable violinist of his age. His remarkable integration of 17th-century improvisatory practices into fantastical works for solo violin placed him among the elite of his era's performer-composers. His first major post was in Graz, followed in 1668 with an appointment as musician to the Bishop of Olmütz at Kroměříž in Moravia. In 1670 he left without giving notice and entered the service of the Prince-Archbishop of Salzburg, Maximilian Gandolph von Khuenburg, where his exceptional talents as a performer and composer won him fame and status. He was named deputy Kapellmeister in 1679, and by 1684 he had become Kapellmeister and dean of the choir school at the Salzburg Cathedral. During his years in Salzburg he composed a handful of operas and cantatas, as well as a significant body of sacred works including vespers settings, several masses, and two Requiems. He twice petitioned Emperor Leopold I to be elevated to the nobility (1681, 1690), meeting with success on his second attempt and acquiring the right to style himself Heinrich Biber "von Bibern."

Biber was a careerist and social climber of the first order. Fortunately, he showed the same dedication in his art that he brought to his personal and professional advancement. His most important achievement by far was his set of *Mystery* or *Rosary* Sonatas (named for the 15 Mysteries of the Rosary, or *Rosenkranzen*), written for violin and bass and completed ca. 1676. These works embody the most extensive use of SCORDATURA (an alternate tuning of a string instrument) in the repertoire: 14 of the 15 call for unconventional tunings, all different, creating a seemingly endless kaleidoscope of moods and colors. To cap this monumental cycle of meditations on the events of the life of the Virgin Mary, Biber composed a masterful unaccompanied passacaglia that foreshadows Bach's unaccompanied string works, written some 50 years later.

RECOMMENDED RECORDINGS

DIE ROSENKRANZEN-SONATEN: HOLLOWAY, MORONEY; WITH TRAGICOMEDIA (VIRGIN CLASSICS).

DIE ROSENKRANZEN-SONATEN): MANZE, EGARR (HARMONIA MUNDI).

VIOLIN SONATAS (INCLUDING *SONATA RAPPRESENTATIVA*): MANZE, ROMANESCA (HARMONIA MUNDI).

Billy Budd **OPERA BY BENJAMIN BRITTEN,** to a libretto by E. M. Forster and Eric Crozier (based on the novella by Herman Melville), premiered in 1951 at Covent Garden and revised in 1964. Set aboard a British man-of-war at the end of the 18th century, the story deals with the conflict between innocence (Billy Budd) and evil (Claggart), as seen through the eyes of the warship's commander (Captain Vere) many years later. It is one of Britten's finest scores—dramatic, tightly written, and tellingly orchestrated—and one of the 20th century's most compelling works of musical theater.

RECOMMENDED RECORDING

PEARS, GLOSSOP, LANGDON, SHIRLEY-QUIRK; BRITTEN AND LONDON SYMPHONY ORCHESTRA (DECCA).

Billy the Kid BALLET BY AARON COPLAND, commissioned in 1938 by Lincoln Kirstein for Ballet Caravan and the dancer Eugene Loring (who also wrote the scenario), and premiered May 24, 1939, in New York. The ballet's subject is the outlaw William Bonney, a.k.a. Billy the Kid (ca. 1859–81). Rather than focus on the details of Billy's life and death, Copland and Loring chose to explore broader issues of his story, specifically the notion of the young innocent gone wrong, and of the outlaw as both social misfit and tragic hero. The project also gave Copland an opportunity to portray the colorfulness of life in the Old West and to evoke some positive qualities of the frontier experience, a nostalgic trope quite in vogue in America during the threatening years leading up to World War II.

Billy the Kid, quintessential outlaw

In his score, Copland makes use of material from several cowboy songs. Among the tunes he quotes or adapts are "Great Granddad," "Streets of Laredo," "The Old Chisholm Trail," "Good-bye, Old Paint," and "Git Along Little Dogies." For the opening scene in the ballet, he uses a dashing *jarabe* (a traditional Mexican dance) in $\frac{5}{8}$ time based on "Come Wrangle Yer Bronco," a strange and wonderful combination of elements. Copland's melodies, favoring pentatonic scales, evoke a kind of innocence, while the lean scoring and stable harmonies built on widely spaced intervals suggest the expansiveness of the open prairie. There's a spare, clean, almost naive charm to the music, which belies its sophistication and complexity. The action of the ballet, with its love scene, saloon scene, and requisite gun battle, calls for music of lyrical tenderness, cheeky irony, and fast and furious action, along with depictions of loping cowpokes, all of which Copland's music provides with cinematic clarity.

Bing, Rudolf

(b. Vienna, January 9, 1902; d. New York, September 2, 1997)

AUSTRIAN-BORN IMPRESARIO. He worked in Berlin and Darmstadt during the 1920s and 1930s before taking charge of the Glyndebourne Opera in 1936. He became a British subject in 1946 and helped found the Edinburgh Festival, serving as its artistic director (1947–49). In 1950 he became general manager of the Metropolitan Opera in New York, remaining at the company's helm until 1972. Famous for his autocratic personality and acid tongue (to an associate's comment that conductor George Szell was his own worst enemy, Bing shot back, "Not while I'm alive"), he expanded the Met's season, raised its artistic standards, and placed a new emphasis on production values. By the end of his tenure, however, the Met had become a musically stagnant backwater desperately in need of a shakeup—which it got with the installation of James Levine as principal conductor in 1973. Bing wrote two books about his experiences:

5,000 Nights at the Opera (1972) and *A Knight at the Opera* (1981).

bitonality The employment of two tonalities (i.e., keys) simultaneously, a technique pioneered by Charles Ives and Igor Stravinsky in the early years of the 20th century and utilized by, among others, Puccini, Ravel, Milhaud, Prokofiev, and Shostakovich. Classic examples include the superimposition of chords of C major and F-sharp major in Stravinsky's *Petrushka,* and the unaccompanied duet between Peter Grimes and Ellen Orford at the end of the prologue in Benjamin Britten's *Peter Grimes*—in which Peter sings in F minor, and Ellen in E major, the two eventually coming together and reaching "agreement" on the note E-flat (enharmonically D-sharp), which is common to both keys.

Bizet, Georges

(b. Paris, October 25, 1838; d. Bougival, June 3, 1875)

FRENCH COMPOSER. After lessons from his father, a singing teacher, he entered the Paris Conservatoire in 1847, where he studied piano with Antoine-François Marmontel, harmony with Pierre-Joseph-Guillaume Zimmermann, and composition with Fromental Halévy. He composed his Symphony in C as a harmony exercise in 1855, and in 1857 won the Prix de Rome. His first important opera, *Les pêcheurs de perles* (*The Pearl Fishers*), was a failure with public and critics alike at its premiere in 1863; only Berlioz saw the score's great merit. Still trying to find his way, Bizet suffered an emotional breakdown in 1868, recovered, and married Geneviève Halévy, the daughter of his former teacher. A suite he extracted from his incidental music for Alphonse Daudet's *L'Arlésienne* (1872) met with success—little wonder, considering the tunefulness and vivid imagery of the concluding "Carillon," in which the horns toll like bells. Encouraged, Bizet turned to work on what would be his final masterpiece, the opera *CARMEN.* The failure of *Carmen* at its premiere in the spring of 1875 plunged Bizet into depression; within a few weeks of its opening he fell ill and died of a heart attack, at the age of 36.

***Georges Bizet around the time he composed* Carmen**

Carmen is the supreme accomplishment in the genre known as opéra comique, in which the musical numbers are interspersed with spoken dialogue. Beautifully scored, melodically memorable, its central characters insightfully drawn and emotionally engaging, *Carmen* can be considered one of the first "modern" operas from a psychological standpoint. Together with the music for *L'Arlésienne,* it testifies to Bizet's transcendent genius as a theatrical composer.

RECOMMENDED RECORDINGS

L'ARLÉSIENNE SUITES: BEECHAM AND ROYAL PHILHARMONIC ORCHESTRA (EMI).

L'ARLÉSIENNE SUITES: DUTOIT AND MONTREAL SYMPHONY ORCHESTRA (DECCA).

CARMEN: BALTSA, CARRERAS, VAN DAM; KARAJAN AND BERLIN PHILHARMONIC (DG).

Björling, Jussi

(b. Stora Tuna, February 5, 1911; d. Stockholm, September 9, 1960)

SWEDISH TENOR. His first teacher was his father, a professional singer. He entered the Stockholm Conservatory in 1928 and became a member of the Royal Swedish Opera in 1930, making his debut as Don Ottavio in Mozart's *Don Giovanni.* He sang at Carnegie Hall in 1937 and first appeared at the Metropolitan Opera in 1938, as Rodolfo in Puccini's *La bohème.* After spending the war years in Sweden he returned to the Met in 1945, and performed there regularly over the next decade. A versatile singer, he possessed a voice of silvery beauty that he employed with elegance and impeccable style. His command of languages was extraordinary. While he had a large repertoire, he concentrated mainly on the lyric roles of Verdi (the Duke in *Rigoletto,* Manrico in *Il trovatore,* and Riccardo in *Un ballo in maschera*) and Puccini (particularly Rodolfo, as well as Des Grieux in *Manon Lescaut* and Cavaradossi in *Tosca*).

RECOMMENDED RECORDINGS

"THE PEARL FISHERS DUET" (WITH OTHER WORKS): MILANOV, ALBANESE, MERRILL WITH VARIOUS ENSEMBLES AND CONDUCTORS (RCA).

PUCCINI, *LA BOHÈME*: LOS ANGELES, MERRILL, REARDON; BEECHAM AND RCA VICTOR SYMPHONY ORCHESTRA (EMI).

VERDI, *RIGOLETTO*: PETERS, MERRILL, TOZZI; PERLEA AND ROME OPERA ORCHESTRA (RCA).

Blitzstein, Mark *See box on pages 708–11.*

Bloch, Ernest

(b. Geneva, July 24, 1880; d. Portland, Ore., July 15, 1959)

AMERICAN COMPOSER OF SWISS BIRTH. He studied in Geneva with Jaques-Dalcroze, and in Brussels with Eugène Ysaÿe, completing his formal training in Frankfurt. For several years he worked as a lecturer and conductor, composing on the side. He came to America in 1916, teaching at the Mannes School in New York and serving as director of the Cleveland Institute of Music (1920–25) and the San Francisco Conservatory (1925–30); he took American citizenship in 1924. Important works dating from this period include the String Quartet No. 1 in B-flat minor (1916), the Piano Quintet (1921–23), and the *Concerto Grosso* No. 1 (1925). He spent most of the 1930s back in Switzerland, returning to the U.S. in 1940 and teaching at the University of California at Berkeley until 1952.

Ernest Bloch, pipe in hand, perusing one of his works

Bloch followed the currents of modernism without drifting into either dry formalism or the maelstrom of aimless experimentation. His music remained rooted in a Romantic sensibility, the best of it—including his "Hebraic rhapsody" *SCHELOMO* (1916) for cello and orchestra, and the *Avodath hakodesh* (*Sacred Service*; 1933) for baritone, chorus, and orchestra—informed by poetic or philosophical ideas and by his own deep spirituality.

RECOMMENDED RECORDINGS

CONCERTO GROSSO NO. 1: MICHAELIAN; SCHWARZ AND SEATTLE SYMPHONY ORCHESTRA (DELOS).

SCHELOMO: ISSERLIS; HICKOX AND LONDON SYMPHONY ORCHESTRA (VIRGIN CLASSICS).

Blomstedt, Herbert

(b. Springfield, Mass., July 11, 1927)

SWEDISH CONDUCTOR. He studied with Igor Markevitch in Paris and Jean Morel at the Juilliard School in New York, winning the Koussevitzky Prize in 1953. He made his professional debut in 1954 with the Stockholm Philharmonic. His most important appointments have been as chief conductor of the Danish National Radio Symphony Orchestra (1967–77) and the Dresden Staatskapelle (1975–85), and as music director of the San Francisco Symphony Orchestra (1985–95) and the Leipzig Gewandhaus Orchestra (1998–2003). A specialist in the music of Nielsen and Sibelius, but with a repertoire that includes Beethoven, Brahms, Bruckner, and Richard Strauss, as well as Hindemith and a number of other 20th-century figures, Blomstedt is admired for his gentle nature and solid musicianship. He is a fine orchestra builder whose cogent interpretations tend to be judicious and revealing, rather than exciting or uplifting.

RECOMMENDED RECORDINGS

HINDEMITH, SYMPHONY *MATHIS DER MALER* AND *SYMPHONISCHE METAMORPHOSEN NACH THEMEN VON CARL MARIA VON WEBER*: SAN FRANCISCO SYMPHONY ORCHESTRA (DECCA).

NIELSEN, SYMPHONIES (COMPLETE): SAN FRANCISCO SYMPHONY ORCHESTRA (DECCA).

Boccherini, Luigi

(b. Lucca, February 19, 1743; d. Madrid, May 28, 1805)

ITALIAN COMPOSER AND CELLIST. He grew up in musical surroundings and became a cellist in the orchestra of the Vienna Court Opera at the age of 14. In 1767, after multiple sojourns in Lucca and Vienna, he set out for Paris, where he quickly established himself and published his first works. The following year he moved again, to Madrid, and in 1770 entered the service of Don Luis, the Spanish infante and younger brother of Charles III. Over the years he enjoyed the patronage of Friedrich Wilhelm of Prussia (an amateur cellist) and Lucien Bonaparte, Napoleon's brother, who served as ambassador to Spain from 1800 to 1801; despite the offer of a position at the Paris Conservatoire, Boccherini remained in Spain the rest of his life.

A prolific composer of symphonies, cello concertos, and chamber music, Boccherini was one of the most important transitional figures between the Baroque and Classical periods, and he continued to compose right up to the dawn of Romanticism. His string quartets (nearly 100) and string quintets (more than 100, nearly all for the combination of two violins, one viola, and two cellos) are his most important legacy, and reveal a composer of marked gentleness and charm who could write with an almost improvisatory freedom of gesture. His cello concertos, of considerable significance to that instrument's repertoire, are

Painting of Luigi Boccherini, ca. 1768

notable for their courtly elegance and understated flair, qualities particularly well displayed in the Concerto No. 10 in D.
See also STRING QUARTET.

RECOMMENDED RECORDINGS

CELLO CONCERTOS: WALLFISCH; WARD AND NORTHERN CHAMBER ORCHESTRA (NAXOS).

STRING QUINTETS, OP. 11, NOS. 4–6: SMITHSONIAN CHAMBER PLAYERS (DEUTSCHE HARMONIA MUNDI).

SYMPHONIES, OP. 12: LEPPARD AND NEW PHILHARMONIA ORCHESTRA (PHILIPS).

bohème, La (Bohemian Life) **OPERA BY GIACOMO PUCCINI,** to a libretto by Luigi Illica and Giuseppe Giacosa (based on Henry Murger's autobiographical novelette *Scènes de la vie de bohème*), premiered in Turin on February 1, 1896 at the Teatro Regio, Arturo Toscanini conducting. Murger's orginal story, a kind of *Alice in Wonderland* of the Left Bank, was sharp and cynical; Giacosa and Illica made it a good deal more melodramatic and sentimental. Set in mid-19th-century Paris, the plot revolves around two pairs of lovers: The poet Rodolfo (one of a group of impoverished artists living in a chilly garret) and the seamstress Mimì (a delicate creature who embroiders flowers for a living) are the central, more serious pair, while the painter Marcello (another of the garret gang) and his flamboyant sweetheart Musetta provide a comic foil. The four come together in a marvelous way at the close of Act III, in what amounts to a double duet. One of the most popular operas in the repertoire, *La bohème* straddles the divide between comedy and tragedy, moving at lightning speed between spirited high jinks and heart-rending pathos. The score, which has a distinctive bittersweet quality, shows Puccini in the full flower of genius as the master of a radiant, supremely expressive musical portraiture.

RECOMMENDED RECORDINGS

FRENI, PAVAROTTI, PANERAI, GHIAUROV; KARAJAN AND BERLIN PHILHARMONIC (DECCA).

LOS ANGELES, BJÖRLING, MERRILL, REARDON; BEECHAM AND RCA VICTOR SYMPHONY ORCHESTRA (EMI).

Böhm, Karl

(b. Graz, August 28, 1894; d. Salzburg, August 14, 1981)

AUSTRIAN CONDUCTOR. He prepared for a career in law while attending conservatories in Graz and Vienna. In 1919, following service in World War I, he received his law degree. But the attraction of conducting proved stronger than jurisprudence, and he quickly started climbing the opera-house ladder. At the invitation of Bruno Walter he worked at the Bavarian State Opera (1921–26); he was named general music director in Darmstadt in 1927, and moved on to the Hamburg Opera in 1931. While in Darmstadt he conducted Berg's *Wozzeck* (he later made the first recording of the score). Though he never became a member of the Nazi party, he went along with the regime, accepting an appointment as general music director in Dresden in 1934, replacing Fritz Busch (who had been dismissed on political grounds). While there, he conducted the first performances of Richard Strauss's *Die schweigsame Frau* (1935) and *Daphne* (1938), forming a close association with the aging composer. In 1943, under Goebbels's patronage, and at Hitler's direction, he was given the plum job of general music director at the Vienna Staatsoper. His reign in Vienna was short-lived: Goebbels ordered the closure of Reich theaters in the autumn of 1944, and the opera house itself was destroyed by

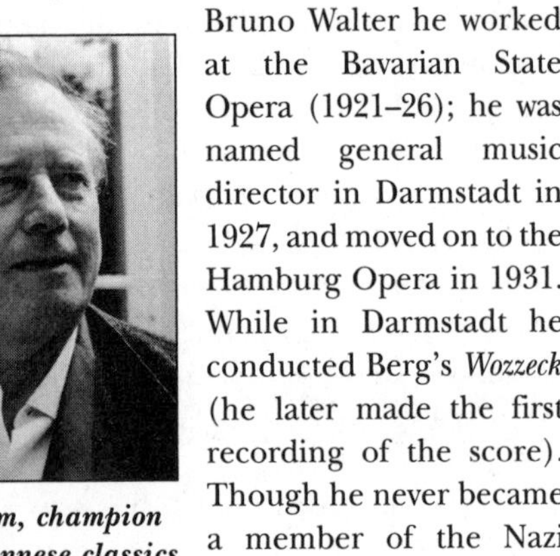

Karl Böhm, champion of the Viennese classics

bombs in 1945. Following denazification proceedings, Böhm resumed his career in 1947. He was accorded the signal honor of reopening the rebuilt Vienna Staatsoper with a performance of Beethoven's *Fidelio* in 1955. The following year he appeared for the first time in the U.S., guest-conducting the Chicago Symphony Orchestra; his Metropolitan Opera debut came in 1957. During his final two decades, he recorded extensively with the Berlin Philharmonic and Vienna Philharmonic.

Throughout his career Böhm was most closely associated with the operas and orchestral works of Mozart and Strauss. He was admired for his ability to find the perfect tempo in Mozart, for his command of complex architecture in Strauss, and for his skill at working with singers in the music of both. His repertoire also included the symphonies of Beethoven, Schubert, and Bruckner, as well as Wagner's *Ring* operas and *Tristan und Isolde* (which he conducted with notable success at Bayreuth during the 1960s). Without exception, his readings of the Austro-Germanic repertoire were authoritative, insightful, and masterfully shaped. His podium manner, much influenced by Walter and Strauss, was the antithesis of showy, and he was greatly admired by musicians for his meticulous yet patient rehearsing.

RECOMMENDED RECORDINGS

BEETHOVEN, SYMPHONIES (COMPLETE): VIENNA PHILHARMONIC (DG).

BERG, *WOZZECK*: FISCHER-DIESKAU, WUNDERLICH, STOLZE, LEAR; BÖHM AND DEUTSCHE OPER BERLIN (DG).

BRUCKNER, SYMPHONY NO. 4: VIENNA PHILHARMONIC (DECCA).

MOZART, SYMPHONIES NOS. 35–41: BERLIN PHILHARMONIC (DG).

STRAUSS, *DAPHNE*: GUEDEN, WUNDERLICH, KING; VIENNA SYMPHONY ORCHESTRA (DG).

WAGNER, *TRISTAN UND ISOLDE*: NILSSON, WINDGASSEN, LUDWIG; BAYREUTH FESTIVAL ORCHESTRA (DG).

Boito, Arrigo

(b. Padua, February 24, 1842; d. Milan, June 10, 1918)

ITALIAN POET, CRITIC, LIBRETTIST, AND COMPOSER. His collaboration with Verdi was one of the most fruitful partnerships the lyric stage has ever known. He provided Verdi with the librettos for *OTELLO* (1887) and *FALSTAFF* (1893), skillfully compressing Shakespeare's complicated plot in the former instance, and achieving a miracle of linguistic transmutation in the latter. Prior to that, in his first joint venture with Verdi, he reworked Francesco Piave's libretto for *Simon Boccanegra,* adding the scene in the council chamber (Act I, sc. ii) that proved so powerful in the work's 1881 revival. His greatest achievement as a composer was the opera *MEFISTOFELE* (to his own libretto, based on Goethe's *Faust*), which was a fiasco at its 1868 premiere, but emerged from revisions in 1875 as a work of genuine, if fitful, lyric splendor. Boito left his second opera, *Nerone,* unfinished at his death; nonetheless, its libretto is regarded by many as his finest literary achievement.

***Boito at the time of* Mefistofele**

RECOMMENDED RECORDINGS

MEFISTOFELE: GHIAUROV, PAVAROTTI, FRENI, CABALLÉ; FABRITIIS AND NATIONAL PHILHARMONIC ORCHESTRA (DECCA).

MEFISTOFELE: TREIGLE, DOMINGO, CABALLE, LIGI; RUDEL AND LONDON SYMPHONY ORCHESTRA (EMI).

Bolcom, William

(b. Seattle, May 26, 1938)

AMERICAN PIANIST AND COMPOSER. A child prodigy, he studied with Darius Milhaud at Mills College and received his D.M.A. in composition from Stanford in

1964. He joined the faculty of the University of Michigan in 1973, and won the Pulitzer Prize in 1988 for his *12 New Etudes* (1986) for piano. A versatile, brilliant eclectic, he has composed with equal success in large forms and small—everything from piano rags with colorful titles such as "Graceful Ghost" and "Brass Knuckles" (written mainly in major and minor seconds, with quite humorous effect), to songs, operas, and symphonies. His operas *McTeague* (1992) and *A View from the Bridge* (1999), both premiered by the Chicago Lyric Opera, have engendered widespread acclaim. The latter was taken up by the Metropolitan Opera during its 2002–03 season. A new opera, based on Robert Altman's film *A Wedding*, debuted in Chicago in December 2004. Bolcom is married to the singer Joan Morris, and frequently accompanies her in performances of popular American songs, including many he has written for her.

RECOMMENDED RECORDINGS

PIANO MUSIC (INCLUDING SELECTED RAGS): MURPHY (ALBANY).

SONGS OF INNOCENCE AND OF EXPERIENCE: VARIOUS SOLOISTS; SLATKIN AND UNIVERSITY OF MICHIGAN SCHOOL OF MUSIC SYMPHONY ORCHESTRA AND UNIVERSITY MUSICAL SOCIETY (NAXOS).

Boléro BALLET SCORE BY MAURICE RAVEL, commissioned by Ida Rubinstein and premiered in 1928 at the Paris Opéra. With its hypnotic repetition of the same melodic phrases over a persistent rhythmic figure (announced in the snare drum at the very start), growing ever louder over the span of a quarter of an hour, *Boléro* represents one of the greatest feats of orchestration ever attempted. The score contains the fewest dynamic and expression markings in the entire orchestral literature; there is not a single *written* crescendo anywhere in the work, and just one tempo marking. The piece's entire effect—that of a crescendo building imperceptibly from a whisper to a roar—is thus done structurally, through orchestration. All one needs to do is play the notes.

Set design for the original staging of Boléro

RECOMMENDED RECORDING

KARAJAN AND BERLIN PHILHARMONIC (DG).

View from the stage of the Bolshoi Theatre

Bolshoi Theatre OPERA HOUSE BUILT IN MOSCOW IN **1825,** where the city's principal opera and ballet companies perform. In Russian, the word *bolshoi* means "big."

Bonynge, Richard

(b. Sydney, September 29, 1930)

AUSTRALIAN-BORN CONDUCTOR. He studied piano in Sydney and London, and worked as a coach and accompanist prior to marrying soprano Joan Sutherland in 1954. He helped her to develop her high register and prepare the bel canto roles that made her famous; from the 1960s until her retirement in 1990, he often conducted performances in which she was the prima donna. The two made numerous opera recordings together as well, concentrating on forgotten 19th-century works. He had a marvelous fluency and feel for 19th-century repertoire, especially ballet, much of which he recorded.

RECOMMENDED RECORDINGS

BELLINI, *NORMA*: SUTHERLAND, HORNE; LONDON SYMPHONY ORCHESTRA (DECCA).

DONIZETTI, *LUCIA DI LAMMERMOOR*: SUTHERLAND, PAVAROTTI; ROYAL OPERA (DECCA).

DONIZETTI, *LA FILLE DU RÉGIMENT*: SUTHERLAND, PAVAROTTI; ROYAL OPERA (DECCA).

Boris Godunov **OPERA BY MODEST MUSSORGSKY,** to his own libretto (based on the play by Aleksandr Pushkin), realized by the composer in two different versions. The first version, in seven scenes, was completed in 1869 and offered to the Mariinsky Theater in St. Petersburg, which rejected it; the second version, in a prologue and four "acts" (nine scenes), was composed in 1871–72 and premiered at the Mariinsky on February 8, 1874. Part psychological study and part historical panorama, *Boris Godunov* is the first truly modern opera. It portrays 16th-century Russia in the time of turmoil following the death of Ivan the Terrible. At its center is the character of Boris Godunov, who has arranged for the murder of Ivan's son and usurped the throne. Mussorgsky's portrait of the infanticidal boyar collapsing under the weight of fear and guilt is a tour de force of characterization, the music vividly capturing the raw emotional edges of Boris's insanity, terror, and greed. In its tableau structure—both versions of the opera treat the story in a series of independent scenes rather than in continuous acts—*Boris Godunov* had a profound influence on Debussy and Berg, while its rough musical language found echoes in the operas of Janáček, Shostakovich, and Prokofiev. It is still occasionally encountered in the heavily edited, opulently rescored 1908 revision undertaken as a labor of love by Rimsky-Korsakov, but Mussorgsky's own leaner and meaner version of 1872 is now the norm.

Aleksandr Borodin in a professional pose

RECOMMENDED RECORDINGS

1869 AND 1872 VERSIONS: VARIOUS ARTISTS; GERGIEV AND KIROV OPERA (PHILIPS).

ED. RIMSKY-KORSAKOV: GHIAUROV, VISHNEVSKAYA, SPIESS, TALVELA; KARAJAN AND VIENNA PHILHARMONIC (DECCA).

Borodin, Aleksandr

(b. St. Petersburg, November 12, 1833; d. St. Petersburg, February 27, 1887)

GIFTED PART-TIME COMPOSER AND RESEARCH CHEMIST. The illegitimate son of a Georgian nobleman, Prince Luka Gedianishvili, he studied music from childhood but considered chemistry his calling and achieved early distinction for his research into acids and aldehydes. At the age of 31 he was appointed to a full professorship at the Medico-Surgical Academy in St. Petersburg, where he spent the rest of his life teaching and living adjacent to his laboratory. On the strength of his musical talent he became a leading figure in 19th-century Russian musical life, joining the St. Petersburg group of composers known as THE FIVE or the "Mighty Handful." Like his colleagues he was drawn to musical portraiture and Oriental exoticism, depicting life among Turkic nomads in his opera *PRINCE IGOR* (1869–87), and following the progress of a caravan in the tone poem *In the Steppes of Central Asia* (1880). Borodin exceeded all his peers except Tchaikovsky in melodic gift, and possessed a strong, innovative sense of musical structure that enabled him to compose successfully in abstract forms. He completed two symphonies (both of which make pioneering use of monothematic construction) and two string quartets—No. 2 in D (1881) includes a scherzo that provided the musical *Kismet* with "Baubles, Bangles, and Beads." *Prince Igor,* his most ambitious work, is best known for the dance sequence *POLOVTSIAN DANCES.* It was left unfinished at his death.

RECOMMENDED RECORDINGS

IN THE STEPPES OF CENTRAL ASIA: GERGIEV AND KIROV ORCHESTRA (PHILIPS).

POLOVTSIAN DANCES (FROM *PRINCE IGOR*): BEECHAM AND ROYAL PHILHARMONIC ORCHESTRA (EMI).

PRINCE IGOR (COMPLETE): KIT, GORCHAKOVA, OGNOVIENKO; GERGIEV AND KIROV OPERA (PHILIPS).

STRING QUARTETS: BORODIN QUARTET (EMI).

SYMPHONIES: JÄRVI AND GOTHENBURG SYMPHONY ORCHESTRA (DG).

Borodin Quartet RUSSIAN STRING QUARTET FORMED IN **1945** by the violinist Rostislav Dubinsky; the other members were cellist Valentin Berlinsky, violist Rudolf Barshai (succeeded by Dmitry Shebalin), and violinist Vladimir Rabei (replaced in 1952 by Yaroslav Aleksandrov). The quartet achieved a preeminent position in Soviet musical life during the 1960s, and was known for its interpretations of Shostakovich's string quartets. Their playing was characterized by extraordinary discipline and unanimity of phrasing, uncanny accuracy of intonation, and a huge dynamic range. The foursome's meaty tone allowed them to sound almost symphonic in the music of Beethoven, Schumann, and Brahms; in the Russian repertoire (including the two string quartets of their namesake, Aleksandr Borodin) and in modern works, the players could command every shade of color from sepulchral darkness to celestial luminosity. Dubinsky left the ensemble in 1974, prior to emigrating; with his departure the quartet's heyday came to an end, though the group, periodically reconstituted with new members, has continued to perform.

RECOMMENDED RECORDINGS

BORODIN, STRING QUARTETS (EMI).

SHOSTAKOVICH, STRING QUARTETS NOS. 1-3 (CHANDOS).

Bösendorfer Austrian manufacturer of pianos, founded by Ignaz Bösendorfer (1796–1859) in 1828, and famed for impeccable craftsmanship. Early devotees of its pianos included Franz Liszt, Anton Rubinstein, and Hans von Bülow. Modern Bösendorfers are known for the bell-like sonority of their upper notes, a somewhat reticent quality in their middle octaves, and a sustained, string bass–like bloom in their low register. The firm's "Imperial" grand (Model 290) has 97 keys, the nine extra ones extending its bass to the C below the bottom A on a conventional piano keyboard. Price: $175,000. Some artists prefer Bösendorfer instruments for their warmth and dark coloration, especially in chamber music, but Bösendorfers lack the brilliance and power of the best concert grands by Steinway & Sons. In 1966 the company was taken over by Kimball International, the American furniture giant that started out as a piano manufacturer.

Boskovsky, Willi

(b. Vienna, June 16, 1909; d. Visp, Switzerland, April 21, 1991)

AUSTRIAN VIOLINIST AND CONDUCTOR. For many years he was the first concertmaster of the Vienna Philharmonic. He succeeded Clemens Krauss as conductor of the orchestra's gala New Year's Day concerts in 1955. With the Philharmonic and other orchestras he recorded much of the music of the Strauss family and other Viennese masters in beguiling interpretations that remain unsurpassed in their *Gemütlichkeit.*

Boston Pops ANNUAL SPRING AND SUMMER OUTDOOR CONCERT SERIES OF THE BOSTON SYMPHONY ORCHESTRA. Devoted to lighter fare, the series was inaugurated in 1885 as the "Promenade Concerts" and acquired the designation the "Pops" in 1900. Since 1900 the performances have taken place in Symphony Hall; the orchestra is the regular Boston Symphony minus many of its first-desk players. The Pops became famous nationwide following the appointment of Arthur Fiedler as conductor in 1930. Fiedler led the Pops for nearly half a century, recording prolifically and truly popularizing classical music from his bully pulpit in Symphony Hall. Film-music megamaestro John Williams succeeded Fiedler and served from 1980 to 1993. Since 1995 Poughkeepsie-born Keith Lockhart has been conductor of the Pops. The typical Pops program begins with an overture or a group of light classics, followed by a short segment featuring a noted vocal or instrumental soloist or a newer talent, and usually concludes with popular pieces arranged for orchestra—film music or Broadway tunes—and a generous slate of encores.

Fireworks following a July 4 concert by the Boston Pops

Boston Symphony Orchestra ENSEMBLE FOUNDED IN 1881 BY HENRY LEE HIGGINSON and noted for its tonal refinement and stylistic versatility. It can produce the weighty sonority best suited to German music as readily as it can the luminous textures and soft woodwind colors of French Impressionism. Ever since the days of Serge Koussevitzky, music director from 1924 to 1949, it has possessed the warm string tone and well-defined light and dark timbres that are essential to Russian music, as well as the brassy punch and knife-edge rhythmic precision favored in American music. Indeed, a whole generation of American composers wrote with the sound of the Boston Symphony in their mind's ear, among them Aaron Copland, Leonard Bernstein, and Walter Piston.

The BSO's musical compass pointed toward Germany during the early decades of its existence; its first conductor was Georg Henschel, followed by Wilhelm Gericke in 1884, who in turn was succeeded by Arthur Nikisch in 1889.

The level of the orchestra's playing was raised substantially by the German-born Karl Muck, who served as the BSO's music director from 1906 to 1918. But Muck's tenure ended in fiasco when he was interned as an enemy alien following America's entry into World War I. In 1919 Pierre Monteux was engaged as music director fresh from his triumphs in Paris leading the premieres of Stravinsky's *Petrushka* and *The Rite of Spring.* Monteux served until 1924, conducting numerous premieres and bringing many younger American-born musicians into the orchestra.

In 1924 the BSO was entrusted to Koussevitzky, who transformed it into one of the world's most brilliant and responsive orchestras. Koussevitzky's programming was exceptionally adventurous. He commissioned dozens of new works from leading European composers and paid particular attention to up-and-coming young Americans such as Copland, Harris, Piston, Hanson, Barber, Schuman, and Bernstein. For the orchestra's 50th-anniversary season in 1931–32, Koussevitzky pulled out all the stops: Stravinsky's *Symphony of Psalms* and Ravel's Piano Concerto in G were among the commissions, as were works by Honegger, Hindemith, and others. In 1937, Koussevitzky took the BSO to Tanglewood in the Berkshire hills of western Massachusetts, and in 1940 the orchestra expanded its summer home there with the opening of the Berkshire Music Center, a school and musical laboratory rolled into one.

The Alsatian-born conductor Charles Munch succeeded Koussevitzky upon his retirement in 1949, serving as music director until 1962. His impassioned performances of French music and stylish work in the German repertoire are impressively documented on some of the orchestra's finest recordings. Erich Leinsdorf, a veteran of the opera pit as well as the concert stage, tightened the orchestra's ensemble during his tenure, from 1962 to 1969. The BSO referred to itself during the Leinsdorf years as "the aristocrat of orchestras," though it could be, and often was, incandescent when the occasion demanded. German-born William Steinberg served as an interim figure before the appointment of Seiji Ozawa as music director in 1973.

Ozawa served as music director until the end of 2002. His tenure, one of the longest of any music director in American history, saw the orchestra slide from the pinnacle of excellence it had achieved in the mid-1970s and proved costly to the ensemble's morale and reputation. As an interpreter Ozawa was at his best in the colorful 20th-century showpieces that he was by nature attuned to, but in Beethoven, Brahms, Mahler, and much else, his reach often exceeded his grasp.

At the start of the 2004–05 season James Levine, a proven orchestra builder, took over as the BSO's music director. The ensemble he has inherited remains stylistically one of the most flexible in the world, still a virtuoso group in the right hands. Its sonority is lighter and more transparent than one finds with the powerhouse orchestras of the American midwest—a trait that undoubtedly owes much to the exquisite acoustics of the orchestra's home, Symphony Hall, which opened in 1900, $383,000 over budget, with a performance of Beethoven's *Missa Solemnis.* Designed by architect Charles F. McKim, it was the first concert hall in America to be built in consultation with an acoustical engineer. Its classic shoe box shape and excellent natural reverberation contribute to an ambience that is regarded as one of the finest in the world.

RECOMMENDED RECORDINGS

BARTÓK, *CONCERTO FOR ORCHESTRA*: LEINSDORF (RCA).

BERLIOZ, *HAROLD EN ITALIE*: PRIMROSE; KOUSSEVITZKY (DUTTON).

COPLAND, *APPALACHIAN SPRING* SUITE, EXCERPTS FROM *THE TENDER LAND*: COPLAND (RCA).

DEBUSSY, *LA MER* (WITH WORKS OF SAINT-SAËNS AND IBERT): MUNCH (RCA).

FAURÉ, *PELLÉAS ET MÉLISANDE* (INCIDENTAL MUSIC), *DOLLY* SUITE: OZAWA (DG).

SIBELIUS, SYMPHONIES AND TONE POEMS: DAVIS (PHILIPS).

Bostridge, Ian

(b. London, December 25, 1964)

ENGLISH TENOR. He read history and philosophy at Oxford and Cambridge, receiving a doctorate from Oxford in 1990. He studied singing at the Britten-Pears School and with Dietrich Fischer-Dieskau. Possessed of a light and unusually distinctive tenor voice, he has emphasized recital work from the beginning of his career. He sang an acclaimed *Winterreise* at the Purcell Room in 1994; in 1995 he won the Royal Philharmonic Society award for his first solo recital. His extensive discography on EMI began with a 1998 recording of Schumann lieder with pianist Julius Drake, and now includes recordings of music by Schubert, Britten, Janáček, and Noël Coward, as well as collections of French and English songs, with such collaborators as Leif Ove Andsnes, Thomas Adès, Mitsuko Uchida, and the Belcea Quartet. He has also recorded for Hyperion, harmonia mundi, and other labels.

Bostridge's work in opera has included his 1996 English National Opera debut as Tamino in *Die Zauberflöte,* Quint in Britten's *The Turn of the Screw* under Sir Colin Davis at Covent Garden in 1997, and as Nerone in *L'incoronazione di Poppea* at the Munich Festival in 1998; he also took part in Deborah Warner's production of Janáček's *The Diary of One Who Vanished,* which was launched in London and toured in 1999. In 2004 he sang the role of Caliban in the world premiere of Thomas Adès's *The Tempest* at Covent Garden. Bostridge performs regularly with orchestras around the world and has recorded numerous operas, including *Die Entführung aus dem Serail, The Rake's Progress, Idomeneo,* and *L'Orfeo.* In 1997 he participated in a film of *Winterreise* directed by David Alden; his book *Witchcraft and its Transformations 1650–1750* was published the same year by Oxford University Press. He was made a Commander of the British Empire in 2004.

RECOMMENDED RECORDINGS

BRITTEN: *SERENADE* AND *OUR HUNTING FATHERS*: NEUNECKER; METZMACHER, HARDING AND BRITTEN SINFONIA (EMI).

SCHUMANN, *DICHTERLIEBE, LIEDERKREIS*: DRAKE (EMI CLASSICS).

Boulanger, Lili

(b. Paris, August 21, 1893; d. Mézy, March 15, 1918)

FRENCH COMPOSER endowed with fragile health but an exceptional talent, the first female to win the Prix de Rome. Born into a musical family (her mother was a singer, her father a professor at the Paris Conservatoire, and her elder sister Nadia an accomplished keyboard player), Boulanger showed extraordinary abilities from early childhood. She entered the Paris Conservatoire in 1909, having already composed several works, and in 1913 won the Prix de Rome for her cantata *Faust et Hélène.* The outbreak of World War I cut short her stay in Rome; she returned to France to care for the families of musicians in the army. Her sickliness and long physical suffering imbued her with both a serene, sometimes melancholic spiritual detachment and a sense of creative urgency; these qualities emerge in her music, which in its chromatic inflections and lucid contrapuntal textures stands at the juncture of Romanticism and

Impressionism, revealing the influence of both Fauré and Debussy. Her most important works were the symphonic poems *D'un soir triste* (*Of a Sad Night*) and *D'un matin de printemps* (*Of a Spring Morning*) (both dating from 1917), a cycle of 13 songs to poems of Francis Jammes (1914), and her setting of Psalm 24 (1916).

RECOMMENDED RECORDING

FAUST ET HÉLÈNE, D'UN SOIR TRISTE, D'UN MATIN DE PRINTEMPS, PSALM 24: VARIOUS ARTISTS; TORTELIER AND BBC PHILHARMONIC ORCHESTRA (CHANDOS).

Boulanger, Nadia

(b. Paris, September 16, 1887; d. Paris, October 22, 1979)

FRENCH ORGANIST, CONDUCTOR, AND PEDAGOGUE. She attended the Paris Conservatoire, studying organ with Louis Vierne and composition with Gabriel Fauré. She later taught there and at the École Normale de Musique in Paris (1920–39), as well as at the American Conservatory in Fontainebleau (from 1921), where she became the equivalent of a guru to several generations of composers and performers. She visited the United States numerous times and spent the World War II years teaching at Radcliffe, Wellesley, and Juilliard.

Boulanger was enormously influential as a shaper of tastes. Among her students were the Americans Aaron Copland, Roy Harris, Walter Piston, Virgil Thomson, Elliott Carter, David Diamond (1915–2005), and Irving Fine; others included Dinu Lipatti, Jean Françaix, Igor Markevich (1912–83), and Lennox Berkeley (1903–89). She was the first woman to conduct a regular subscription concert of the Boston Symphony Orchestra (1938) and the New York Philharmonic (1939), and the first woman to conduct a concert by *any* London orchestra (1937); in 1938 she led the premiere of Stravinsky's *Dumbarton Oaks* Concerto in Washington, D.C.

Pierre Boulez, on top of the musical world

Boulez, Pierre

(b. Montbrison, March 26, 1925)

FRENCH COMPOSER, CONDUCTOR, AND ADMINISTRATOR whose career has seen him evolve from bomb-throwing radical in the culture wars to establishment icon. He put aside an early interest in mathematics and entered the Paris Conservatoire in 1942, studying composition with Olivier Messiaen and graduating in 1945. After further instruction in 12-TONE technique from René Leibowitz, he quickly acquired a reputation as one of the brightest, fiercest, and most controversial figures in the postwar European avant-garde. He developed an extremely organized yet aurally sensuous form of 12-tone writing, which he utilized with imagination and a remarkable refinement of technique in works of extraordinary scope. Scores such as his Piano Sonata No. 2 (1948), *LE MARTEAU SANS MAÎTRE* (*The Hammer Without Master*; 1955) for alto and chamber ensemble, and *PLI SELON PLI* (*Fold upon Fold*; 1962; rev. 1989) for soprano and large orchestra, proved to be of seminal importance to the development of serialism;

in them Boulez achieved a gestural concentration and complexity of nuance that made him, by the time he was 40, already one of the most talked about, written about, and widely emulated composers of the 20th century. Since then, works such as *Éclat/Multiples* (1966), *Domaines* (1968), . . . *explosante-fixe* . . . (1973), *Répons* (1984), and *Notations* (ongoing since 1945), have shown an astonishing flexibility of approach and increasing formal plasticity; the result, in several instances, has been open-ended, modular designs that have evolved over many years.

Boulez began his conducting career with a series of Parisian concerts he organized in 1954, called "Domaine Musical" and devoted mainly to avant-garde music. He was invited to conduct at Baden-Baden in 1958, and made his American debut with the Cleveland Orchestra in 1965, at the invitation of George Szell. As that orchestra's principal guest conductor (1969–72), he served as a caretaker between the music directorships of Szell and Lorin Maazel. In 1971 he became music director of the New York Philharmonic, succeeding Leonard Bernstein. Known for his amazingly precise ear, the withering accuracy of his memory, and his ability to clarify textures and balances in the most complicated scores, he proved so demanding in rehearsal that the Philharmonic musicians dubbed him "The French Correction." Following his departure from New York in 1977, he took over the direction of the Institut de Recherche et de Coordination Acoustique/Musique (IRCAM) in Paris—a performance facility, compositional laboratory, and aesthetic thinktank rolled into one. He has kept an active conducting and recording schedule, working primarily with orchestras in Amsterdam, Berlin, Cleveland, Vienna, and London as well as with the Ensemble InterContemporain, which he founded, in Paris. Since 1995 he has served as the principal guest conductor of the Chicago Symphony Orchestra.

As composer, performer, and academician, Boulez has done more to influence the development of music since 1950 than anyone alive. He remains a huge force in French musical life, thanks as much to his political clout and control over tens of millions of francs in annual funding as to his phenomenal talent and energy. His glittering, violent, and emotional music continues to impress and disturb even though it has decidedly less importance now than it did 40 years ago. *See also box on page 272.*

RECOMMENDED RECORDINGS

ÉCLAT/MULTIPLES: BOULEZ AND ENSEMBLE INTERCONTEMPORAIN (SONY).

. . . *EXPLOSANTE-FIXE* . . .: BOULEZ AND ENSEMBLE INTERCONTEMPORAIN (DG).

LE MARTEAU SANS MAÎTRE, NOTATIONS: BOULEZ AND ENSEMBLE INTERCONTEMPORAIN (SONY).

PLI SELON PLI: SCHÄFER; BOULEZ AND ENSEMBLE INTERCONTEMPORAIN (DG).

Boult, Adrian

(b. Chester, April 8, 1889; d. London, February 22, 1983)

ENGLISH CONDUCTOR. He was educated at Westminster School and Christ Church, Oxford; during a year abroad (1912–13), he attended the Leipzig Conservatory and sat in on Arthur Nikisch's rehearsals with the Gewandhaus Orchestra. He became a staff conductor at Covent Garden in 1914, and entered the limelight in 1918 when Gustav Holst asked him to conduct the first performance of *The Planets.* He subsequently served as music director of the

Adrian Boult with the score of Wagner's* Wesendonck *Lieder

City of Birmingham Symphony Orchestra (1924–30, and again 1959–60), the BBC Symphony Orchestra (1930–50), and the London Philharmonic (1950–57). During his years with the BBC he gave the first performances of Ralph Vaughan Williams's Symphonies Nos. 3 (*Pastoral*), 4, and 6. In 1962, at the head of the London Philharmonic, he conducted Maurice Jarre's memorable soundtrack for the David Lean film *Lawrence of Arabia.* Boult recorded actively into his ninth decade, amassing a sizable discography that included much English music (Elgar, Holst, and Vaughan Williams in particular) as well as Beethoven, Brahms, and Wagner. An urbane figure famous for wielding an exceptionally long baton, he was noted for his cogent, workmanlike accounts of the traditional repertoire. When it came to English music he was a magical conductor, one who did everything right, showed exquisite tastes, and had a remarkable ear for sonorities.

RECOMMENDED RECORDINGS

HOLST, *THE PERFECT FOOL* (BALLET), *EGDON HEATH*: LONDON PHILHARMONIC ORCHESTRA (DECCA).

HOLST, *THE PLANETS*; ELGAR, *ENIGMA VARIATIONS*: LONDON PHILHARMONIC ORCHESTRA AND LONDON SYMPHONY ORCHESTRA (EMI).

VAUGHAN WILLIAMS, SYMPHONIES (COMPLETE): LONDON PHILHARMONIC ORCHESTRA (EMI).

bourrée Lively dance in $\frac{2}{2}$ or $\frac{4}{4}$ time in which the melodic phrases begin on the upbeat. A favorite dance of Baroque composers, it is frequently encountered as a movement in instrumental and orchestral suites of the 18th century. *See also* SUITE.

bow A wooden stick (usually of pernambuco) with an attached ribbon of horsehair, used to play many types of string instruments; the hair of the bow (for an average violin bow, about 150–200 strands, which must come from the tail of a white horse) is drawn across the strings, causing them to vibrate. Early bows had a convex curvature, which made them look literally like the bows from which arrows are shot. The modern violin bow, developed by François Tourte around 1785, has a reverse curvature, allowing more pressure to be applied, from which a more powerful tone can be produced. In the 19th century, Dominique Peccatte achieved distinction as a bowmaker almost as great as Tourte.

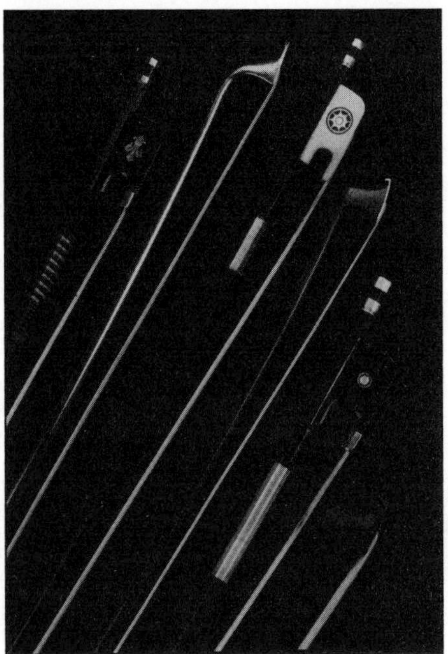

Study in wood and horsehair: a collection of bows

Bowman, James *See box on pages 155–57.*

Brahms, Johannes

(b. Hamburg, May 7, 1833; d. Vienna, April 3, 1897)

GERMAN COMPOSER. Throughout his life he clung tenaciously to the idea that he should carry on the great tradition of musical Classicism, and for 50 years after his death he was thought of as "the Classical composer born too late." With time, he has come to be seen not only as the outstanding craftsman of his era and one of the greatest masters of musical form and argument ever, but as one of the most potent and original voices of Romanticism. His father was a "beer fiddler"—a professional musician of modest attainments who worked at odd jobs—and he hoped that his son would become an orchestral musician; to that end, Brahms was given music lessons, and he quickly developed into a capable pianist. He was eventually sent to Eduard Marxsen, a prominent pedagogue who taught him without fee and helped forge his powerful musical intellect. As a teenager, he earned money playing in Hamburg waterfront dives, a degrading experience that would permanently shadow his relations with women, and from which he sought refuge in Romantic fantasizing, imagining himself as Young Kreisler, E. T. A. Hoffmann's fictitious musician-hero.

Brahms encountered his share of real musician-heroes in 1853. First came the violinist Joseph Joachim, two years his senior. Then, through Joachim, he met Franz Liszt and the Schumanns. Robert Schumann recognized his genius at once and took him under his wing; later that year he published an article in the *Neue Zeitschrift für Musik* titled "Neue Bahnen" ("New Paths"), in which he called Brahms "one of the elect." Four months later, Schumann was committed to an insane asylum, but his anointment of Brahms would remain upon the young man's head for better and for worse. During the years of Schumann's institutionalization, Brahms became emotionally attached to Clara, and although he retreated from any kind of romantic involvement with her after her husband's death in 1856, he remained devoted to her for the rest of her life. Brahms's career took him to Detmold in 1857, where he spent two years as a court musician and teacher, composed a pair of serenades for the court orchestra, and also worked on transforming what he had originally intended to be a symphony into his turbulent, emotionally charged Piano Concerto No. 1 in D minor (1859).

***Brahms in the 1860s* (above) *and the 1880s* (below)**

Brahms settled in Vienna—where music still meant more than anywhere else—in 1862. For Vienna, as for Brahms, one foot was planted in the past; the other was pointed toward a future fraught with uncertainty, desolation, and despair. He became conductor of the city's *Singakademie* in 1863, and by the end of the decade he had firmly established himself as one of Vienna's leading musical lights. In 1865, prompted by his mother's death, Brahms began the fashioning of *Ein deutsches Requiem* (*A German Requiem*), the largest and in many ways the pivotal work of his career, which with its earnest argument, rigorous craftsmanship, and mix of high purpose and intimate feeling opened the door to his mature style. While serving as artistic director of Vienna's most prestigious musical institution, the Gesellschaft der Musikfreunde (1872–75), he completed his first two string quartets and composed the *Variations on a Theme by Haydn* (1873). In 1876 he finished his Symphony No. 1, in C minor, Op. 68, a work whose genesis went back at least as far as 1862. Symphony

Pencil sketches of Brahms conducting, by his friend Willy von Beckerath

No. 2, in D, Op. 73, followed in 1877. On its heels came the Violin Concerto in D, Op. 77, written for Joachim, in 1878, its dancelike Gypsy-flavored finale a tribute to the soloist's Hungarian roots.

Over the next decade, working mostly during long summer vacations in the mountains or at lakeside retreats, Brahms composed a string of magisterial works. The rich harvest included his Piano Concerto No. 2, in B-flat, Op. 83 (1881), Symphony No. 3, in F, Op. 90 (1883), Symphony No. 4, in E minor, Op. 98 (1884–85), a substantial number of songs, and some of his finest chamber pieces—the three violin sonatas, the two cello sonatas, and the Trios in C major and C minor. In 1890, shortly after completing the Quintet in G, Op. 111, for strings, he decided to give up composition. But his muse refused to be silent, and a new round of creative fervor was sparked in the spring of 1891 by the playing of Richard Mühlfeld, the first clarinetist of the Meiningen Court Orchestra. During the next four years, with Mühlfeld in mind, Brahms would compose the Trio in A minor, Op. 114, for clarinet, cello, and piano; the Quintet in B minor, Op. 115, for clarinet and strings; and the two Sonatas for Clarinet and Piano, Op. 120. He honored Mühlfield's talents in many ways in these works, filling pages with ardent feeling and surpassing gentleness, and, in the finale to the F minor Sonata, Op. 120, No. 1, creating a virtuosic romp. Brahms also returned to writing for his own instrument after many years of neglect, penning the *Fantasien,* Op. 116, the *Three Intermezzos,* Op. 117, and the ten *Klavierstücke* (*Piano Pieces*) of Opp. 118 and 119, all between 1891 and 1893. These urgent, melancholy last works for the clarinet and the piano would prove to be among his most personal statements—intriguing in their intensity and range of expression, adventurous in their treatment of form, rhythm, and harmony.

Brahms was not a pathbreaking figure like Beethoven, but a consolidator chiefly concerned with achieving structural integrity in his music—through a thorough working out of its material and formal schemes —as well as a judicious balance of content and expression. Whereas transcendence, exuberance, and exaltation had been key elements of Beethoven's expressive brief, there is little of that in Brahms. Instead, there is formidable passion accompanied by a prevailing sense of melancholy and a notable willingness to express ambivalent feelings with unflinching honesty. Nowhere is this quality more beautifully displayed than in the bittersweet *Poco allegretto* movement of Symphony No. 3. Occasionally, Brahms's music seems overly earnest in its expression and labored in its working out of material, but at its best it combines rigorous argument with expression that is rich, nuanced, and emotionally probing.

Brahms had a fondness for VARIATION form—it played out again and again in his piano and chamber works—and for forms and procedures associated with "old" music, that is, the Baroque. Chief among these were fugue (in *Ein deutsches Requiem* and the monumental *Variations and Fugue on a Theme by Handel,* Op. 24, for piano), passacaglia (in the finales of the *Variations on a Theme by Haydn* and the Fourth Symphony), and canon (employed frequently in his works, e.g., the opening subject of the first movement of the Fourth Symphony, where it is cleverly concealed by the orchestration). Both formally and in terms of the richness of their content and discourse, Brahms's symphonies and concertos are the finest contributions to their genres penned in the second half of the 19th century; for the same reasons, his chamber pieces (especially the instrumental sonatas) and songs (a total of about 200) are essential to the repertoire. Musicians have always loved this music because, as was surely Brahms's intention, everything in it is substantive.

Brahms at the piano, by Willy von Beckerath

In his understanding of harmony Brahms was remarkably sophisticated, as he was in his predilection for rich, freely organized polyphonic textures in which the constituent lines are treated not as counterpoint in the traditional sense, but as parts of a living tissue of independent melodic elements. Mahler would continue this line of thinking, as would Schoenberg, Berg, and Webern. Perhaps most advanced of all was Brahms's acceptance of rhythm as an element of musical language on the same plane as melody and harmony, a view whose implications were felt throughout the music of the 20th century. His use of devices such as HEMIOLA, accented offbeats, and cross rhythms to build and sustain powerful climaxes remains virtually unrivaled.

Aside from Bruckner, who was nine years older, and Dvořák, who was eight years younger, it is hard to think of any contemporaries in the German-speaking world—European music's inner sanctum—who stood anywhere close to Brahms. In the final two decades of his life he fully vindicated Schumann's prediction of greatness and took his place as the greatest instrumental composer of his day, richly deserving of the salutation he received in 1879 when the University of Breslau conferred on him an honorary doctorate in philosophy: *"Artis musicae severioris in Germania nunc princeps"* ("To the leading master of serious music in Germany"). The 20th century would see even more in him than his contemporaries did. Schoenberg would hail him as the agent of "great innovations in musical language," and he would also be credited with having brought about, in a time of heady Romantic expressionism, the renovation of music as an abstract art and the resuscitation of its traditional forms. Today the repertoire is filled with his works, and his approach—that of the progressive conservative—has become a model for composers eager to connect with audiences.

RECOMMENDED RECORDINGS

CLARINET QUINTET: SHIFRIN; EMERSON QUARTET (DG).

EIN DEUTSCHES REQUIEM: SCHWARZKOPF, FISCHER-DIESKAU; KLEMPERER AND PHILHARMONIA ORCHESTRA (EMI).

HORN TRIO: TUCKWELL, PERLMAN, ASHKENAZY (DECCA).

PIANO CONCERTOS NOS. 1 AND 2: GILELS; JOCHUM AND BERLIN PHILHARMONIC (DG).

PIANO CONCERTOS NOS. 1 AND 2 (WITH OTHER PIANO WORKS): FLEISHER; SZELL AND CLEVELAND ORCHESTRA (SONY).

PIANO MUSIC, LATE PIECES: GOULD (SONY).

PIANO MUSIC, VARIOUS: KATCHEN (DECCA).

PIANO TRIOS: TRIO FONTENAY (TELDEC).

SYMPHONIES (COMPLETE): KERTÉSZ AND VIENNA PHILHARMONIC (DECCA).

SYMPHONIES (COMPLETE): WALTER AND COLUMBIA SYMPHONY ORCHESTRA (SONY).

VIOLIN CONCERTO: BELL; DOHNÁNYI AND CLEVELAND ORCHESTRA (DECCA).

VIOLIN CONCERTO: MUTTER; MASUR AND NEW YORK PHILHARMONIC (DG).

VIOLIN SONATAS: SUK, KATCHEN (DECCA).

Brain, Dennis

(b. London, May 17, 1921; d. Hatfield, September 1, 1957)

THE SUPREME HORN VIRTUOSO OF THE 20TH CENTURY. He came from a family of distinguished horn players and studied horn with his father, Aubrey Brain, at the Royal Academy of Music. He made his professional debut in 1938 and served as principal horn in the RAF Central Band during World War II. In 1945 he was engaged as principal horn of the newly formed Philharmonia Orchestra; the following year, at the behest of Sir Thomas Beecham, he took the principal's chair in the Royal Philharmonic Orchestra as well. With the Philharmonia, Brain made what many consider the finest recordings ever of the concertos of Mozart (conducted by Herbert

Dennis Brain, the horn's consummate virtuoso

von Karajan) and Richard Strauss (conducted by Wolfgang Sawallisch). His playing inspired a number of composers to write major works for him, the most celebrated of which, Benjamin Britten's *Serenade* (1943) for tenor, horn, and strings, has become a staple of the repertoire. Cultivating a bright and focused tone, Brain was unmatched in his ability to phrase a line smoothly and elegantly while articulating crisply. In his hands the modern horn retained something of the character of the valveless hunting instrument from which it is descended, speaking in a voice that was natural, lively, penetrating, and evocative.

In addition to being a musical prodigy, Brain was a passionate automobile buff. During rehearsals for his recording of the Mozart concertos with Karajan and the Philharmonia, he created a stir when his colleagues noticed he was playing the solos from memory and had the latest issue of *The Autocar* open on his music stand.

Unfortunately, Brain's love of sports cars cost him his life: Speeding back to London after a performance at the Edinburgh Festival, he lost control of his Triumph and died in a crash just 17 miles from his home.

RECOMMENDED RECORDINGS

BRITTEN, *SERENADE*: PEARS; BRITTEN AND BOYD NEEL STRING ORCHESTRA (PEARL).

MOZART, HORN CONCERTOS; KARAJAN AND PHILHARMONIA ORCHESTRA (EMI).

STRAUSS, HORN CONCERTOS; SAWALLISCH AND PHILHARMONIA ORCHESTRA (EMI).

***Brandenburg* Concertos** A COLLECTION OF SIX CONCERTI GROSSI BY J. S. BACH **(BWV 1046–1051)**, assembled by him in 1721 and dedicated to Christian Ludwig (the Margrave of Brandenburg and brother of King Friedrich Wilhelm I of Prussia). It is now thought that the original versions of the six concertos were written during the period he was court organist and chamber musician at the ducal court of Saxe-Weimar (1708–17). Nowhere is Bach's greatness as a composer of "pure music" more apparent than in these works, which stand as the supreme achievement in the CONCERTO GROSSO literature of the Baroque. The variety of the instrumental combinations they exploit sets them apart from any other collection of 18th-century concertos, as does the flexibility of Bach's writing—which allows each of the participants to play both leading and supporting roles in a constantly changing pattern of give-and-take. This is perfectly exemplified in the first movement of Concerto No. 2 in F, BWV 1047, where the four solo instruments—violin, oboe, trumpet, and recorder—take turns with the material. ◉ The *Brandenburg* Concertos, no two of which sound alike, encompass an impressive range of style and topic, and combine in wondrous ways the courtly elegance of the French suite, the exuberance of the Italian solo concerto, and the gravity of German counterpoint. A microcosm of Baroque music, they contain an astonishingly vast sample of the era's emotional universe.

RECOMMENDED RECORDINGS

LAMON AND TAFELMUSIK (SONY).

PEARLMAN AND BOSTON BAROQUE (TELARC).

brass Generic name for several families of instruments made out of brass, primarily trumpets, trombones, tubas, and horns. While the construction of standard brass instruments varies considerably, they all have several things in common: tubing (of conical bore in the case of the horn and tuba, and mostly cylindrical for trumpets and trombones), a metal mouthpiece (shallow and cup-shaped in the case of trumpet, trombone, and tuba; deep and cone-shaped for the horn), flared bells, and on modern instruments (except for the trombone, which doesn't need them), valves allowing the player to sound all the notes in the chromatic scale.

bravura (It., "bravery") Playing or singing of exceptional boldness, verve, and spirit. When an artist gives an exciting account of a piece, particularly one in which he displays complete technical mastery in passages of obvious difficulty, it is said to be a bravura performance.

Bream, Julian

(b. London, July 15, 1933)

ENGLISH GUITARIST AND LUTENIST. He studied with his father and at the Royal College of Music, and became a protégé of Andrés Segovia. In addition to mastering a vast repertoire of pieces for lute and guitar, from Dowland to Villa-Lobos, he commissioned a number of works from modern composers, most important, Benjamin Britten's *Nocturnal* (1963), an ingeniously deconstructed fantasy on John Dowland's lute song "Come, Heavy Sleep."

RECOMMENDED RECORDINGS

VILLA-LOBOS, *PRELUDES*, CONCERTO; RODRIGO, *CONCIERTO DE ARANJUEZ*: PREVIN AND LONDON SYMPHONY ORCHESTRA (RCA).

BRITTEN, *NOCTURNAL* AND OTHER WORKS (EMI).

"THE GOLDEN AGE OF ENGLISH LUTE MUSIC" (RCA).

Brecht, Bertolt

(b. Augsburg, February 10, 1898; d. Berlin, August 14, 1956)

GERMAN PLAYWRIGHT AND LYRICIST. He wrote the books for Kurt Weill's *DIE DREIGROSCHENOPER* (*The Threepenny Opera*; 1928) and *AUFSTIEG UND FALL DER STADT MAHAGONNY* (*Rise and Fall of the City Mahagonny*; 1930), as well as the text for Weill's *DIE SIEBEN TODSÜNDEN* (*THE SEVEN DEADLY SINS*; 1933). He also collaborated with Paul Hindemith, Hanns Eisler (1898–1962), and Paul Dessau (1894–1979).

Brendel, Alfred

(b. Wiesenberg, January 5, 1931)

AUSTRIAN PIANIST admired for his intellectual breadth and self-effacing interpretations of Beethoven and Schubert. He grew up in Zagreb and studied there and in Graz; in the late 1940s he participated in masterclasses with Edwin Fischer and Eduard Steuermann (a Schoenberg acolyte), further broadening his perspective by attending concerts in Vienna and devouring the recordings of Alfred Cortot and Wilhelm Kempff, among others. After receiving a prize in the 1949 Busoni Competition in Bolzano, he embarked on a solo career. In his salad days, during the 1950s, Brendel played and recorded everything, turning out Vox Boxes by the carload. He attracted international attention in 1962 when he became the first pianist ever to record Beethoven's complete works for piano. Since then he has recorded two additional complete cycles of Beethoven's piano sonatas, both times for the Philips label, and two more cycles of the Beethoven concertos, as well as the complete piano concertos of Mozart, also for Philips.

Brendel's repertoire stretches from Bach to Schoenberg and Bartók, but his sympathies are narrower than that: His recital programs typically focus on the music of Haydn, Beethoven, Schubert, and Liszt. With an adequate but not flashy technique, and very little interest in piano tone per se, Brendel neither seduces nor overpowers his audience but instead draws listeners into the performance with his thoughtful phrasing, sensitive shaping of dynamics, and emotional restraint. His playing can be imaginative and boldly characterized nonetheless. Those who admire it tend to view Brendel as a philosopher; those who don't usually dismiss him as a fusspot or a pedant. Behind the phlegmatic stage manner lurk a keen intelligence and wry wit, also evident in several books and essays Brendel has penned, as well as a collection of light verse called *Fingerzeig* (*One Finger Too Many*).

Alfred Brendel, with not a finger too many

RECOMMENDED RECORDINGS

BEETHOVEN, PIANO CONCERTOS (COMPLETE): RATTLE AND VIENNA PHILHARMONIC (PHILIPS).

SCHUBERT, PIANO SONATAS AND IMPROMPTUS (PHILIPS).

breve (from Lat. *brevis,* "short") One of the two earliest medieval note values, the other being the *longa,* or long. Gradually, as notes were divided into shorter values, the breve, in spite of its name, became the longest note in common use. Originally represented by a square black NEUME, by the late 15th century the breve had become a square white note, as can be seen in some of the earliest music imprints in "white notation," made by Ottaviano Petrucci (1466–1539). In today's fast-paced world, it is the equivalent of a double whole note, rarely used. *See also* SEMIBREVE.

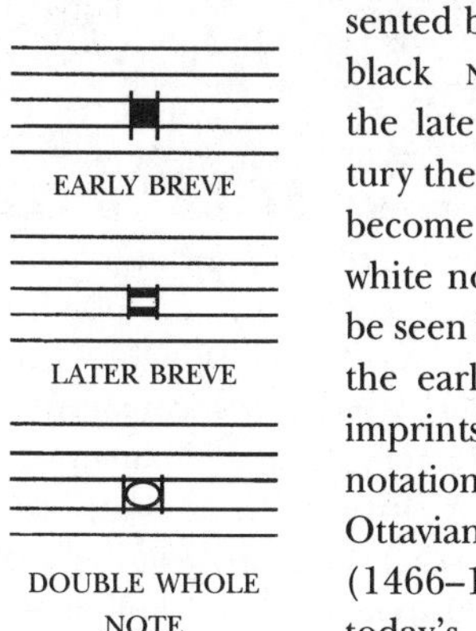

bridge [1] On string instruments, a thin piece of wood attached to the belly, or front side, of an instrument; its purpose is to raise the strings above the fingerboard so they are free to vibrate, and transmit the vibrations to the body of the instrument so the whole instrument can resonate, thereby amplifying the sound. The bridge on a lute or guitar is low and fairly flat; bridges on violins and other bowed string instruments are high and arched. Bowing close to the bridge produces a thin, edgy sound; the instruction for this is the Italian term *SUL PONTICELLO* (literally "on the little bridge"). [2] In composition or improvisation, a passage linking one section of a piece to another.

Bridge, Frank

(b. Brighton, February 26, 1879; d. Eastbourne, January 10, 1941)

ENGLISH COMPOSER, VIOLIST, AND CONDUCTOR. He learned to play the violin from his father and studied composition at the Royal College of Music with Charles Villiers Stanford (1852–1924). In 1906 he joined the Joachim Quartet as violist; he later became a member of the English String Quartet. He was active as a conductor early in his career and proved to be an able teacher, though he took on only one composition student: Benjamin Britten. As a composer Bridge enjoyed early success in the post-Romantic vein with his symphonic suite *The Sea* (1910–11), a piece whose evocative harmony and sweepingly sensuous scoring are reminiscent of the soundworld of Bax and Delius. Disillusionment over the carnage of World War I, first expressed in his poignant *Lament* (1915) for strings, led to a long period of silence and profound changes in both his personal outlook and musical idiom. Beginning with his Piano Sonata (1921–24), Bridge's music took on an increasingly advanced harmonic cast; there is an element of bitonality in many of his later works, and more than a hint of Berg's 12-tone approach in the language of String Quartets Nos. 3 and 4 (composed in 1926 and 1937). While Bridge's tone-painting skills remained evident in later orchestral works such as *Enter Spring* (1927), his modernist leanings showed through in the probing syntax and ambivalent feeling of his chamber music.

RECOMMENDED RECORDINGS

"BRITISH MUSIC COLLECTION": *ENTER SPRING, SUMMER,* "CHRISTMAS DANCE" (FROM *SIR ROGER DE COVERLEY*); MARRINER AND ACADEMY OF ST. MARTIN-IN-THE-FIELDS (DECCA).

THE SEA: HANDLEY AND ULSTER ORCHESTRA (CHANDOS).

STRING QUARTETS: BRIDGE QUARTET (MERIDIAN).

Bridgetower, George Polgreen

(b. Biala, Poland, October 11, 1778; d. London, February 29, 1860)

ENGLISH VIOLINIST OF POLISH BIRTH. The son of an African father and a Polish mother, he was brought to England as a child and entered the service of the Prince of Wales (later King George IV) at the age of 11. A year later, he played in the violin section for Joseph Haydn's London concerts of 1791. He became a noted interpreter of the music of Giovanni Battista Viotti (1755–1824) and in 1802 was given leave to visit his mother (then living in Dresden) and concertize on the continent. While encamped in Vienna he was introduced to Beethoven, and on May 24, 1803, he gave the premiere of Beethoven's Violin Sonata in A, Op. 47, with the composer at the keyboard. There was a subsequent falling-out between Beethoven and "Brischdauer" (as the composer phonetically spelled his name), apparently over a woman, and Beethoven decided to dedicate the new sonata to the eminent French violinist Rodolphe Kreutzer, who never played it. Bridgetower returned to England and took his bachelor's degree in music at Cambridge in 1811.

brio (It.) Spirit, vivacity. Usually used as a tempo modifier (e.g., *Allegro con brio*).

Britten, Benjamin

(b. Lowestoft, November 22, 1913; d. Aldeburgh, December 4, 1976)

ENGLISH COMPOSER, CONDUCTOR, AND PIANIST. In 1927, at the age of 13, he became the composition pupil of Frank Bridge, whose music and teaching were to have a decisive influence on him. From 1930 to 1933 he attended the Royal College of Music, studying composition with John Ireland and piano with Arthur Benjamin and Harold Samuel. The 1934 premiere of his *Phantasy* for oboe and strings at an

Benjamin Britten* (right) *and Peter Pears in 1943

International Society of Contempory Music concert in Florence marked his arrival as a composer of rare gifts. There followed in quick succession the song cycle *Les illuminations* (1939, to texts of Rimbaud) and the SINFONIA DA REQUIEM (1940), works of exceptional brilliance and imagination that confirmed Britten as the leading English composer of his generation. He reached a new plateau in his development with the *Serenade* (1943) for tenor, horn, and strings, a work of haunting beauty written to exploit the unique talents of Peter Pears (who was to be Britten's lifelong companion) and Dennis Brain.

With the 1945 premiere of PETER GRIMES, his second opera, Britten's genius stood fully revealed. Subsequent works such as *Albert Herring* (1947), BILLY BUDD (1951), THE TURN OF THE SCREW (1954), *A Midsummer Night's Dream* (1960), and *Death in Venice* (1973), with their probing insights into character and their dramatic—or comedic—intensity, would guarantee him a place in the operatic pantheon. In 1962 Britten's skills as a composer for large forces and his gift for the most intimate vocal expression went on display side by side in what may come to be seen as his great masterpiece, the *War Requiem*, a sublime work informed by his passionately held pacifist views. The 1960s also brought a sudden flowering of creativity in the sphere of instrumental music, thanks largely to Britten's newfound friendship with Soviet cellist Mstislav Rostropovich. For this energetic and ebullient spirit he wrote three solo suites, a sonata, and the magnificent *Cello Symphony* (1963; rev. 1964), perhaps his finest orchestral work.

Britten was a "compleat" musician: a composer, pianist, accompanist, conductor, arranger, and editor. Eclectic in the best sense, he absorbed influences from every corner—English composers of the Elizabethan era, Purcell, Verdi, Mahler, Debussy, Stravinsky—yet left his own unmistakably lyric stamp on everything he wrote. Few 20th-century composers have placed as many works in the active repertoire, and none has shown a greater gift for setting music to words.

RECOMMENDED RECORDINGS

Billy Budd: Pears, Glossop, Langdon; Britten and London Symphony Orchestra (Decca).

Cello Symphony: Hugh; Yuasa and BBC Scottish Orchestra (Naxos).

Peter Grimes: Pears, Watson, Evans; Britten and Royal Opera Orchestra (Decca).

Serenade: Pears, Tuckwell; Britten and English Chamber Orchestra (Decca).

Sinfonia da Requiem (with "Four Sea Interludes" and "Passacaglia" from *Peter Grimes*): Previn and London Symphony Orchestra (EMI).

War Requiem: Pears, Fischer-Dieskau, Vishnevskaya; Britten and London Symphony Orchestra (Decca).

Young Person's Guide to the Orchestra: Previn and Royal Philharmonic Orchestra (Telarc).

Broadwood English piano manufacturing firm, established by John Broadwood in 1782. Broadwood had produced his first instrument around 1781, and by late in that decade was turning out grand pianos whose dynamic range and powerful sonority were considered by Clementi, Haydn, and others to be state of the art. Their "new and improved" features included equalized string tension to stabilize the instruments' cases and allow a more uniform tone quality, and an extended range of five and a half, later six, octaves. Beethoven jumped on the Broadwood bandwagon in 1818, when he received as a gift a six-octave grand from London, with his name inscribed on it. It was the finest instrument he would own—though he was dissatisfied with certain characteristics and too deaf to notice when it had gone out of tune. Its heavier action and weighty tone played a recognizable part in the genesis of the *Hammerklavier* Sonata, completed that year. The firm reached the peak of its prestige around 1850, but failed to keep pace with new technological developments and by the end of the 19th century had lost all of its once formidable cachet.

Bruch, Max

(b. Cologne, January 6, 1838; d. Friedenau, October 2, 1920)

German composer. Taught the rudiments of music by his mother, a professional singer, he studied in Cologne with Ferdinand Hiller and Carl Reinecke, becoming a teacher himself at the age of 20. During the 1860s, he held conducting positions in Mannheim, Koblenz, and Sondershausen. While in Koblenz he composed his most frequently performed work, the Violin Concerto No. 1 in G minor (1866), revised in 1868 with input from Joseph Joachim; its soulful Adagio is among the most plangent expressions in the literature. Between 1868 and 1882 Bruch composed three symphonies, the rhapsody *Kol Nidrei* for cello and orchestra, and several works for violin and orchestra, including the *Scottish Fantasy,* written for Pablo de Sarasate. He taught at the Hochschule für Musik in Berlin from 1890 until his retirement in 1911.

The aesthetic axis that runs between Mendelssohn and Richard Strauss crosses right through Bruch, as can be heard in the sonorous scoring and romantic sentiment of his orchestral music. A melodist of the first rank, he was by nature suited to the rhapsodic style of writing that characterizes his symphonies and concerted works. While in later years he devoted himself increasingly to the composition of sacred and secular cantatas, his fame has been assured by the lasting popularity of his works for violin and orchestra.

RECOMMENDED RECORDINGS

Violin Concerto No. 1 and *Scottish Fantasy*: Lin; Slatkin and Chicago Symphony Orchestra (Sony).

Violin Concerto No. 1: Chung; Kempe and Royal Philharmonic Orchestra (Decca).

Bruckner, Anton

(b. Ansfelden, September 4, 1824; d. Vienna, October 11, 1896)

Austrian composer. As the first Romantic composer to take up what Deryck Cooke called the "metaphysical challenge" of Beethoven's Ninth, Bruckner renewed the symphony as an expression of transcendent emotion and a confession of personal faith. He received early instruction on the violin and organ from his father, a village schoolmaster and church organist; after his father's death in 1837 he entered the school at the Augustinian monastery of St. Florian as a chorister, studying organ, piano, violin, and theory. In 1845 he returned to St. Florian as an assistant teacher; he remained there for the next ten years, playing the organ and piano, studying the music of Bach, and composing a Requiem and a *Missa solemnis,* his first significant works.

Feeling that he needed further instruction in theory, he went to Vienna in 1855 to study with Simon Sechter (1788–1867); later that year he auditioned for, and easily won, the job of cathedral organist in Linz, where he remained for 13 years. He continued his study with Sechter by correspondence until 1861, at which point he took an examination at the Vienna Conservatory so that he would be qualified to teach harmony and counterpoint. After hearing him improvise at the organ, Johann Herbeck (1831–77), one of the examiners, exclaimed: "He should have examined us!" In 1862, he sought instruction in orchestration and symphonic form from Otto Kitzler (1834–1915), conductor at the municipal theater in Linz. As part of his work with Kitzler he studied the music of Richard Wagner for the first time; inspired by its revolutionary and sublime effects, he set off in pursuit of symphonic grandeur. He quickly found his own voice, already apparent in his Symphony No. 1 in C minor (1865–66) and the Masses in E minor (1866) and F minor (1867–68).

In 1868, at the age of 44, Bruckner went to Vienna to succeed Sechter as professor of theory at the conservatory; he would reside in the Austrian capital for the rest of his life. Despite notable triumphs, including the premieres of his

Bruckner, followed by music critics

Anton Bruckner

Symphonies Nos. 4 and 7 (in 1881 and 1884 respectively), Bruckner's doubts about his abilities fed his habit of revising his work: Hermann Levi's unfavorable opinion of his monumental Symphony No. 8, which he completed in 1887, caused him to spend three years revising. He then set about revising several of his earlier works, including Symphonies Nos. 1, 2, and 3. He began work on his Symphony No. 9 in 1891, completing the first three movements by 1894 but leaving the finale unfinished at the time of his death.

Bruckner was a devout Catholic whose innermost thoughts and feelings centered on his religious beliefs—faith in God and in the mysteries of the Church permeated his life and his work as a musician. He was also one of music's greatest late bloomers: All of his mature works date from after his 40th year. On the outside, he appeared to be a humble musician from the provinces whose awkwardness and self-doubt led many to dismiss him as a country bumpkin. On the inside, he was a powerful, visionary musical thinker whose symphonies were among the supreme accomplishments of the late 19th century. The expansive formal structures he erected, especially in Symphonies Nos. 5, 7, 8, and 9, together with the innovative rhythmic, motivic, and harmonic procedures he devised to achieve narrative continuity across vast spans of time, contributed powerfully to the advancement of symphonic language and opened the door to some of the greatest works of the 20th century, not least the symphonies of Mahler and Sibelius. With his Symphony No. 7, Bruckner succeeded in combining visionary expression with a broad yet cogent development of his material. The radiant opening subject of its first movement is one of the most beautiful ideas he would ever conceive. ◉ The mystical tranquillity and paroxysmal ecstasy he expressed in the slow movement of this symphony, and with even greater fervor in the slow movement of No. 8 ◉, remain unique in the symphonic canon, as does the desolate, mysterious beauty of the Ninth.

RECOMMENDED RECORDINGS

SYMPHONIES (COMPLETE): JOCHUM AND BAVARIAN RADIO SYMPHONY ORCHESTRA, BERLIN PHILHARMONIC (DG).

SYMPHONIES (COMPLETE): KARAJAN AND BERLIN PHILHARMONIC (DG).

SYMPHONIES (COMPLETE): TINTNER AND ROYAL SCOTTISH NATIONAL ORCHESTRA (NAXOS).

SYMPHONY NO. 4: BÖHM AND VIENNA PHILHARMONIC (DECCA).

SYMPHONY NO. 8: KARAJAN AND VIENNA PHILHARMONIC (DG).

SYMPHONY NO. 9: WALTER AND COLUMBIA SYMPHONY ORCHESTRA (SONY).

TE DEUM, MASSES, AND MOTETS: BEST AND CORYDON SINGERS (HYPERION).

Brüggen, Frans

(b. Amsterdam, October 30, 1934).

DUTCH CONDUCTOR, RECORDER PLAYER, AND FLUTIST. He distinguished himself early in his career as a recorder and Baroque flute virtuoso, becoming a professor at the

Royal Conservatory in The Hague at the age of 21. His legacy includes a treasure trove of brilliant recordings, as well as his commission of Berio's *Gesti* (1965), for recorder. His founding of the period-instrument Orchestra of the Eighteenth Century, in 1981, marked the beginning of a conducting career that has earned him engagements with the Chicago Symphony Orchestra, the Royal Concertgebouw Orchestra, and the Orchestra of the Age of Enlightenment, among others. For his operatic debut, Brüggen led the Netherlands Opera in Mozart's *Idomeneo* in 1991. Since 1992, he has shared the position of principal guest conductor of the Orchestra of the Age of Enlightenment with Simon Rattle. Brüggen is also the artistic director of the Stavanger Symphony Orchestra and the Radio Hilversum Chamber Orchestra. His recordings of Haydn's *London* symphonies, Mozart's late symphonies, and Beethoven's symphonies are especially admired for their drama, rhythmic vitality, and clarity.

Budapest String Quartet ENSEMBLE FORMED IN 1918 BY MEMBERS OF THE BUDAPEST OPERA ORCHESTRA. The original personnel were three Hungarians (violinists Emil Hauser and Alfred Indig and violist István Ipolyi) and a Dutchman (cellist Harry Son). By 1936 the roster had changed completely, but the four German-educated Russian Jews who made up the quartet—violinists Joseph Roisman and Alexander Schneider, violist Boris Kroyt, and cellist Mischa Schneider—kept the name "Budapest" just the same. The players settled in the U.S. in 1938, becoming quartet-in-residence at the Library of Congress in Washington, D.C., in 1940 (remaining there until 1962), and touring and recording widely until their disbanding in 1966. Remembered for their dynamic and brilliant performances of the Beethoven quar-

The Budapest String Quartet with Rudolf Serkin

tets (which they played in toto practically every year), for the warmth and richness of their tone, and their tightly synchronized bowing and vibrato, the Budapest Quartet pioneered the application of modern-style string playing to the quartet literature. In the Mozart quintets and in other works calling for two violas they were frequently joined by Milton Katims and Walter Trampler; in the literature for piano quartet and piano quintet their partners included Rudolf Serkin and George Szell.

RECOMMENDED RECORDING

BEETHOVEN STRING QUARTETS (SONY).

buffa, buffo (It.) Comic. An *OPERA BUFFA* is a comic opera; a *basso buffo* is a comic bass. Though sublimely elevated in their emotional content, Mozart's three collaborations with Lorenzo da Ponte are examples of *opera buffa*; the role of Leporello in *Don Giovanni* is a classic *basso buffo* part.

Bülow, Hans von

(b. Dresden, January 8, 1830; d. Cairo, February 12, 1894)

GERMAN CONDUCTOR, PIANIST, AND COMPOSER. As a child he studied piano with Friedrich Wieck (the father of Clara

Schumann and principal teacher of Robert Schumann). At the age of 21, having dropped out of law school, he went to Weimar to study intensively with Franz Liszt, becoming one of the most accomplished of Liszt's many pupils. He taught for a decade in Berlin, concertized throughout Europe, and became conductor of the Munich Court Opera in 1864, just in time to be of tremendous help to his idol, Richard Wagner. In Munich he conducted the first performances of Wagner's *Tristan und Isolde* (1865) and *Die Meistersinger von Nürnberg* (1868). There were other notable firsts in Bülow's résumé: As a pianist he gave the first performance of Tchaikovsky's Piano Concerto No. 1 in B-flat minor (1875, in Boston of all places); he was the first principal conductor of the Berlin Philharmonic (1887–94); he prepared the first performance of Brahms's Symphony No. 4 (1885; the honor of conducting it went to the composer); and he was the first husband of Cosima Liszt (from 1857 until she left him for Wagner in 1864; he granted her a divorce in 1869). Bülow reached the apex of his career during the five years he served as court music director to the Duke of Meiningen (1880–85). Under his leadership, the Meiningen Court Orchestra, though only 48 strong, was regarded as the best symphonic ensemble in all of Germany. Making a specialty of the music of Brahms, Bülow trained his musicians to play from memory and insisted that they perform standing up (which they did not particularly like).

Hans von Bülow

Busch, Fritz

(b. Siegen, March 13, 1890; d. London, September 14, 1951)

GERMAN CONDUCTOR, older brother of violinist Adolf Busch (1891–1952). He attended the Cologne Conservatory, and started his career as an opera conductor in Riga. In 1912 he was appointed music director in Aachen; following service in World War I, he returned to Aachen, and in 1918 was named music director of the Stuttgart Opera. While in Stuttgart he expanded the company's repertoire and conducted the premieres of Hindemith's daring one-act operas *Mörder, Hoffnung der Frauen* (*Murderer, Hope of Women*) and *Das Nusch-Nuschi.* In 1922 he was named music director of the Dresden State Opera, where he gave the first performances of Richard Strauss's *Intermezzo* (1924) and *Die ägyptische Helena* (1928), Busoni's *Doktor Faust* (1925), and Hindemith's *Cardillac* (1926). Busch's open contempt for the Nazis resulted in his dismissal from the Dresden post in 1933 (he was not Jewish, but suffered the same fate as his Jewish colleague Bruno Walter in Leipzig, at the hands of Saxony's particularly virulent Nazi machine). Renouncing his German citizenship, Busch continued his career in England, taking over as music director at the newly opened opera house at Glyndebourne in 1934. The six years he spent there were the apex of his career. Busch devoted his final decade to conducting in South America and the United States, though he returned to work with

Fritz Busch in 1940

the Glyndebourne company the year before his death.

Busoni, Ferruccio

(b. Empoli, April 1, 1866; d. Berlin, July 27, 1924)

PIANIST, COMPOSER, AND TEACHER OF GERMAN-ITALIAN DESCENT, one of the fathers of 20th-century modernism. Born into a family of musicians, he gave his first concert at the age of seven, and made his Viennese debut, which was acclaimed by no less a critic than Eduard Hanslick, at ten. That year the family settled in Graz, where the youth busied himself with composition and the further development of his piano technique. In 1885, on the advice of Brahms, he went to Leipzig to study composition with Carl Reinecke. The first of his virtuoso arrangements of the music of Bach appeared in 1888, and in 1890 he won the Rubinstein Prize for his *Konzertstück,* Op. 31a. Following a period of teaching in New York and Boston (1891–94), he took up permanent residence in Berlin, remaining there for the rest of his life except for a brief sojourn in Switzerland during World War I. He became a central figure in the musical life of the German capital and in the development of modernism, both in his teaching (his composition students included Kurt Weill and Edgard Varèse) and his promotion of the music of such contemporaries as Bartók, Delius, Debussy, and Sibelius. His 1907 essay *Entwurf einer neuen Ästhetik der Tonkunst* "Sketch of a New Musical Esthetic" sparked a controversy with the conservative Hans Pfitzner, who saw him as an example of the "futurist peril."

In fact, Busoni was a bridge, connecting the Latin and Germanic temperaments, the 19th and 20th centuries, and the cultural values of Romanticism and modernism, both in his music and in his personality. A remarkably innovative composer—his hourlong Piano Concerto of 1904, for example, calls for a male chorus in its final movement—he made interesting contributions to a variety of genres including chamber music, orchestral music, and opera (his unfinished *Doktor Faust,* completed in 1925 by Philipp Jarnach, is one of the most imaginative and engrossing stage works of the 20th century). The core of his output was music for the piano, comprising several dozen characteristic pieces, six sonatinas, and seven volumes of transcriptions of the music of Bach (most cel-

Two views of Ferruccio Busoni: flamboyant pianist, and thinker and dreamer

ebrated, his knuckle-busting arrangement of the D minor Chaconne). The orchestral sonority he achieved in writing for the instrument is among his most important legacies.

RECOMMENDED RECORDINGS

DOKTOR FAUST: FISCHER-DIESKAU, KOHN, COCHRAN; LEITNER AND BAVARIAN RADIO SYMPHONY ORCHESTRA (DG).

PIANO CONCERTO: HAMELIN; ELDER AND CITY OF BIRMINGHAM SYMPHONY ORCHESTRA (HYPERION).

PIANO MUSIC: KOCSIS (PHILIPS).

Butterworth, George

(b. London, July 12, 1885; d. Pozières, August 5, 1916)

ENGLISH COMPOSER. He was educated at Eaton and Trinity College, Oxford, and originally intended to take up the law. His friendship with Ralph Vaughan Williams drew him toward music, particularly the study of English folk song. He made use of folk materials in his orchestral scores *Two English Idylls* (1911) and *The Banks of Green Willow* (1913), and mimicked the style of folk music in his most celebrated work, the song set *A Shropshire Lad* (1912, to poems of A. E. Housman). At the outbreak of World War I, he enlisted in the Duke of Cornwall's Light Infantry. He was killed at the battle of the Somme.

RECOMMENDED RECORDING

ORCHESTRAL PIECES AND SONGS (INCLUDING *A SHROPSHIRE LAD*): LUXON, WILLINSON; MARRINER AND ACADEMY OF ST. MARTIN-IN-THE-FIELDS (DECCA).

Buxtehude, Dietrich

(b. Oldesloe, ca. 1637; d. Lübeck, May 9, 1707)

GERMAN COMPOSER BORN IN DENMARK. He was appointed organist at St. Mary's in Lübeck in 1668, and remained there the rest of his life. Although he spent his first 30 years on Danish soil, he was considered the leading German composer of his era. On separate occasions both Handel (1703) and J. S. Bach (1705) made pilgrimages to Lübeck to hear him play, but neither was willing to marry his by then hopelessly spinsterish daughter (it being the custom at St. Mary's, as in many German churches of the day, to keep the job of organist in the family), so neither succeeded him there. Buxtehude's powerful, imaginative, and rigorously argued organ works, as well as his cantatas, had a significant influence on Bach. The sublimely sonorous pages of his Prelude in G for organ are typical of his approach to the instrument.

A relief from St. Mary's in Lübeck showing Buxtehude at the organ with Bach standing and listening

RECOMMENDED RECORDINGS

ORGAN WORKS: KOOPMAN (NOVALIS).

CANTATAS: SCHLICK, CHANCE, JACOBS, KOOY; KOOPMAN AND AMSTERDAM BAROQUE ORCHESTRA (ERATO).

BWV Acronym standing for *Bach Werke Verzeichnis* (literally "Bach Works Catalog"), the short title of a catalog prepared by Wolfgang Schmieder and first published in 1950, in which all of Bach's compositions are listed according to type. Individual pieces are referred to by their number in the catalog, preceded by the letters BWV or, occasionally, the letter *S*. Thus, the cantata *Wachet auf, ruft uns die Stimme* is BWV 140; the Prelude and Fugue in E-flat for organ (known as the *St. Anne*) is BWV 552; and the Concerto in D minor for two violins is BWV 1043. *See also* BACH, JOHANN SEBASTIAN.

Byrd, William

(b. Lincoln, 1543; d. Stondon Massey, July 4, 1623)

ENGLISH COMPOSER. Of the generation of Edmund Spenser rather than Shakespeare, Byrd grew up Catholic at a time of dramatic upheaval in the religious sector (Henry VIII, in a feud with the Pope over the validity of his marriage to Catherine of Aragon, had ordered the dissolution of the monasteries in 1535) and became England's leading musician during the Elizabethan era, a time of equally profound change in the artistic sphere. As a boy he may have been a pupil of Thomas Tallis at the Chapel Royal in London. He was appointed organist of Lincoln Cathedral in 1563, and in 1572 was sworn in as a Gentleman of the Chapel Royal. About 1573 he joined Tallis (his elder by 38 years) as organist of the Chapel Royal, and in 1575 he and Tallis received an exclusive royal patent to print and publish music. Their first publication was a collection of Latin motets for five to eight voices, *Cantiones, quae ab argumento sacrae vocantur* (*Songs Which on Account of Their Texts Are Called Sacred*; 1575), that proved unprofitable; Byrd published nothing further until 1588, three years after Tallis's death.

William Byrd, an engraving after a contemporary portrait

A staunch Catholic, Byrd was repeatedly harassed, fined, and on several occasions prosecuted for the crime of recusancy—refusing to attend services of the Church of England. In spite of this he continued to write Latin motets (about 175 in all), and between 1592 and 1595 he composed and had published three mass settings, among his most important achievements. Their style is less florid, more declamatory than that of the High Renaissance, but still wonderfully rich; in them, Byrd often resorts to a "scoring" of the voices, giving different portions of text a distinctly different color. Their part-writing displays a virtuosity on the same level as that of the great Netherlandish composers of the 16th century. Byrd also wrote a substantial amount of music for the Anglican service, and was extremely prolific in other areas as well: He penned numerous English songs as well as pavanes and other pieces for viol consort. He also composed about 100 pieces for VIRGINAL, including fantasias, preludes, grounds, variations, pavanes, galliards, and other dances.

RECOMMENDED RECORDINGS

CONSORT MUSIC: FRETWORK (VIRGIN CLASSICS).

KEYBOARD MUSIC: MORONEY (HYPERION).

MASSES FOR THREE, FOUR, AND FIVE VOICES: PHILLIPS AND TALLIS SCHOLARS (GIMELL).

C

cabaletta In Italian opera, the concluding section of an extended two-part aria, usually in a fast tempo with a persistent, galloping rhythm. A cabaletta generally comes at an emotional turning point, often announcing a momentous decision on the part of the character singing it; in a typical cabaletta, the music is strong and assertive, generating a sense of mounting excitement. Manrico's "Di quella pira," from Part III of Verdi's *Il trovatore,* is a classic example. ◉ The opening section of an aria of this type is called a CAVATINA.

Montserrat Caballé, commanding presence on the stage

Caballé, Montserrat

(b. Barcelona, April 12, 1933)

SPANISH SOPRANO. She studied in Barcelona and worked for three years, beginning in 1956, at the Basel Opera. She made her debut at La Scala in 1960 as one of the Flower Maidens in Wagner's *Parsifal*; her breakthrough came in New York in 1965 when, on short notice, she replaced Marilyn Horne in a concert performance of Donizetti's *Lucrezia Borgia,* creating a sensation with her brilliant delivery of its taxing title role. That same year she made her debuts at the Metropolitan Opera, as Marguerite in Gounod's *Faust,* and at Glyndebourne, as the Countess in Mozart's *Le nozze di Figaro* and the Marschallin in Richard Strauss's *Der Rosenkavalier.* From 1972 she was a regular at Covent Garden, and throughout the 1970s and 1980s she was in great demand as a recording artist. Caballé possessed one of the most powerful and commanding voices of her day, notable for its superbly focused tone in the highest register and powerful, penetrating chest tones. Her technique was very well developed, allowing her to sing with remarkable agility and control for someone with such a large voice, and to achieve intense expression in the softest dynamics. Her repertoire was enormous, but she was most attuned to the bel canto style of singing, and excelled in the music of Donizetti, Bellini, and Verdi.

RECOMMENDED RECORDINGS

BELLINI, *NORMA*: SUTHERLAND, PAVAROTTI, RAMEY; BONYNGE AND WELSH NATIONAL OPERA (DECCA).

BOITO, *MEFISTOFELE*: DOMINGO, TREIGLE; RUDEL AND LONDON SYMPHONY ORCHESTRA (EMI).

PUCCINI, *TOSCA*: CARRERAS, WIXELL; DAVIS AND ROYAL OPERA (PHILIPS).

PUCCINI, *TURANDOT*: SUTHERLAND, PAVAROTTI, GHIAUROV; MEHTA AND LONDON PHILHARMONIC ORCHESTRA (DECCA).

cadence (from It. *cadere*, "to fall") A chord sequence or melodic formula that brings to a close a musical passage or section, or a whole piece. Cadences can follow a variety of harmonic pathways and be of differing degrees of finality. The typical closing cadence (called an "authentic" or "full" cadence) is DOMINANT to TONIC (e.g., in F major, a chord of C major followed by a chord of F major). A "plagal" cadence (the most common example is the "Amen" of a typical hymn) proceeds from the SUBDOMINANT to the tonic (e.g. in G major, from a chord of C major to a chord of G major). A "half" cadence ends on the dominant, and a "deceptive" cadence moves from the dominant to a chord other than the tonic, usually one based on the sixth degree of the scale, known as the submediant (e.g., in C major, a chord of G major is followed not by the expected C major, but by a chord of A minor).

cadenza In a concerto, a display passage for the soloist interpolated within a movement, usually the first one, and usually near its end. Until the 19th century, cadenzas generally did not extend beyond half a minute or a minute in length, and were not written out by the composer but left to the performer to improvise. Their purpose was to allow the soloist to display additional aspects of virtuosity and show the kind of improvisatory skill that was deemed the sine qua non of good taste, as well as to provide an opportunity, if the soloist so desired, to reflect or elaborate upon the melodic or figurative material that had gone before. With Beethoven's piano concertos, the cadenza became lengthier and more exploratory—a premeditated display of solo virtuosity rather than an improvised flash of keyboard bravura. At the same time it became a much more substantive element in the overall conception of the first movement, as control over its content shifted decisively to the composer: From Beethoven on, the written-out cadenza was the rule rather than the exception. In his *Emperor* Concerto, Beethoven underscored the integral relationship of the cadenza to the main body of the first movement by allowing the orchestra to quietly sneak in and accompany the final part of the cadenza, eliminating the seam that usually occurs at the point of transition. This process was carried forward by Mendelssohn (in his Violin Concerto) and Tchaikovsky (in his Piano Concerto No. 1 in B-flat minor). Another feature of the *Emperor* that proved influential was its opening gambit, with boldly proclaimed cadenza-like flourishes from the piano. In a bid for symphonic unity, both Liszt (in his Piano Concerto No. 1) and Brahms (in his Piano Concerto No. 2) adopted this approach and carried it a step further, front-loading cadenza-style solos for the piano into the opening pages of their scores and eschewing the conventional cadenza later on. The other part of Beethoven's legacy, the cadenza-as-showpiece, continues to be a vital part of composers' thinking. The 20th century saw some titanic achievements, culminating in the wrist-breaking alternate cadenza to Rachmaninov's Piano Concerto No. 3 and the finger-stretching cadenzas of Bartók's Violin Concerto No. 2 and Shostakovich's Cello Concerto No. 1, the latter an entire movement unto itself.

Cage, John

(b. Los Angeles, September 5, 1912; d. New York, August 12, 1992)

AMERICAN COMPOSER, ESSAYIST, AND ARTISTIC RENEGADE. He was one of the most provocative and important figures of the 20th-century avant-garde. He dropped out of Pomona College after two years to travel in Europe, later attending Henry Cowell's classes in non-Western music at the New School for Social Research in New York and studying counterpoint with Arnold Schoenberg at UCLA. In 1938 he joined Bonnie Bird's dance company in Seattle as accompanist and composer; there he met the dancer and choreographer Merce Cunningham (b. 1919), who became his partner both in life and in work. In 1942 he took up residence in New York, his base for the remaining 50 years of his life.

Cage's early notoriety was assured by several pieces written for "prepared piano"—referring to the ad hoc modification of a standard concert grand by the placement of bolts, screws, erasers, rubber bands, and other material on or between its strings, causing it to sound like a multihued percussion instrument. The landmark *Sonatas and Interludes* (1946–48) for prepared piano, a suite consisting of 16 "sonatas" (none more than a few minutes long) and four interludes, established him as a major innovator in the sonic realm. During the 1950s, Cage's music began to reflect his interest in Zen philosophy. His *Music of Changes* (1951), a major work for piano, does away with the conventional ordering of musical elements; pitches, durations, and timbres are determined not by any conscious decision on the part of the composer, but by tossing three coins and referring to charts derived from the *I Ching*. *Imaginary Landscape No. 4* (1951) calls for 12 radios, a conductor, and 24 performers—one person manipulating the tuning knob and another playing with the volume control on each of the radios. Cage's most famous composition, *4′33″* (1952), is the ultimate noncomposition: The performer (or performers; the piece is valid for any instrument or group of instruments) sits silently onstage for the duration of the piece—four minutes and 33 seconds—while the audience experiences whatever sounds occur in the performance space.

The inner workings of a prepared piano—nuts, bolts, screws, spoons

John Cage: musician, mycologist

Cage's desire to break down the distinction between life and art, and to embrace chaos rather than try to order it, continued to find new expressions in the 1960s and 1970s. In his orchestral work *Atlas Eclipticalis* (1961–62), which consists of a set of 86 instrumental parts created by tracing astronomical charts onto music paper, an instruction indicates that the score is "to be played in whole or in part, any duration, in any ensemble, chamber or orchestral." The conductor, not the composer, "determines the length of a performance and which part of the composition is to be performed." At the time of a New York Philharmonic performance of the piece in 1964 under the baton of Leonard Bernstein, many took it to be a self-indulgent exercise in zaniness. But the underlying point to this, as to many of Cage's pieces, was a profound one, namely, that the systematic ordering of musical sound is by definition an artificial process.

In thus bringing the element of chance into the musical mainstream, Cage in effect became the anti-Schoenberg. Although much of what he did struck contemporary audiences as pure rubbish and may seem hopelessly quaint and narcissistic to today's listener, the philosophical openness of Cage's music has exerted an influence on everyone from Karlheinz Stockhausen to Steve Reich.

Cage's interests outside music were wide ranging, and he pursued them with characteristic zeal. He was an expert mycologist and an accomplished writer, poet, and graphic artist. *See also* ALEATORY.

RECOMMENDED RECORDINGS

MUSIC OF CHANGES: HENCK (WERGO).

SONATAS AND INTERLUDES FOR PREPARED PIANO: KARIS (BRIDGE).

Callas, Maria

(b. New York, December 2, 1923; d. Paris, September 16, 1977)

GREEK SOPRANO OF AMERICAN BIRTH. One of the most admired if controversial figures in the history of music, she is regarded by many as the greatest of all divas, a larger-than-life personality who defined the art of operatic singing in her time; for others, including more than a few purists, she was an overpraised prima donna whose limited technique and soap-opera histrionics on and off the stage led to early burnout and vocal ruin. Few singers have embodied their chosen roles as fully as she did, or projected character and emotion with such shattering force. Fewer still have been as fanatically idolized as she was, in life and in death.

She became a student of Elvira de Hidalgo at the Athens Conservatory in 1940 and made her debut as Tosca in Athens in 1942. Subsequent roles included Santuzza in Mascagni's *Cavalleria rusticana* and Leonore in Beethoven's *Fidelio.* In 1945 she returned with her family to New York; her international career was launched in 1947 when she sang the title role of Ponchielli's *La gioconda* in Verona with Tullio Serafin conducting. Over the next few years Serafin encouraged her to drop from her repertoire the heavier roles (such as Brünnhilde, Aida, and Turandot) and concentrate on Italian bel canto heroines such as Norma, Lucia, and Amina (in Bellini's *La sonnambula*), and the lighter Verdi, including Leonora (in *Il trovatore*), Violetta, and Gilda. Matchless as Norma and Violetta, she also became identified with such esoteric parts as Cherubini's Medea and Rossini's Armida. In her detailed enactment of the role and intense vocal and musical emotion, she was arguably the most compelling Tosca ever. Callas made her debut at La Scala in 1950, as Aida, and at the Metropolitan Opera in 1956, as Norma.

Maria Callas as Cherubini's Medée

The taste for Callas is an acquired one—it does not come naturally to anyone with an ear for beauty. Her vocal prime lasted only about five years, from 1953 to 1958; after that, her voice took on a woolly quality and her high notes became increasingly strained and unreliable. She retired from the stage in 1965, emerging on rare occasions to give masterclasses, and making an ill-advised comeback tour with Giuseppe di Stefano in 1973.

Callas was married to the Italian businessman Giovanni Battista Meneghini from 1949 to 1959; at the height of her fame she left him for the Greek shipping magnate Aristotle Onassis. Callas's recordings are among the treasures of the catalog, though aficionados prefer "pirates" of her live performances to the studio versions in most cases. At her best, she was a paroxysmally great singing actress whose impassioned interpretations were characterized by a burning, direct, profoundly expressive emotionalism and seemingly superhuman coloratura and dynamic range. That her best days were over so quickly is one of the tragedies of operatic history.

RECOMMENDED RECORDINGS

BELLINI, *NORMA*: STIGNANI, FILIPPESCHI, ROSSI-LEMENI; SERAFIN AND LA SCALA ORCHESTRA (EMI).

CHERUBINI, *MEDEA*: SCOTTO, PIRAZZINI; SERAFIN AND LA SCALA ORCHESTRA (EMI).

PUCCINI, *TOSCA*: DI STEFANO, GOBBI; DE SABATA AND LA SCALA ORCHESTRA (EMI).

Cammarano, Salvatore

(b. Naples, March 19, 1801; d. Naples, July 17, 1852)

ITALIAN LIBRETTIST AND PLAYWRIGHT. His first important achievement was the libretto for Donizetti's *LUCIA DI LAMMERMOOR* (1835); his association with Donizetti continued through five more works over the next three years, including *Roberto Devereux* (1837). He furnished Verdi with four librettos: *Alzira* (1845), *La battaglia di Legnano* (1849), *LUISA MILLER* (1849), and *IL TROVATORE* (1853)—his final effort and the classic blood-and-thunder libretto of the Romantic era. His other credits include the librettos for Mercadante's *La vestale* and Pacini's *Saffo;* the latter is considered the most accomplished of all his texts.

Campion, Thomas

(b. London, February 12, 1567; d. London, March 1, 1620)

ENGLISH POET AND COMPOSER. His entire output consisted of songs for voice with the accompaniment of lute; in this genre he stood second only to John Dowland, his close contemporary. Campion's best settings exhibit a high degree of elegance and polish, and because he wrote the words for all of his songs, there is a particularly felicitous connection between the contours of his melodies and the underlying rhythm of his verse.

RECOMMENDED RECORDINGS

"THE ENGLISH AYRE": CHANCE, ELLIOTT, PADMORE; CONCORDIA ENSEMBLE (LINN).

LUTE SONGS: MINTER, O'DETTE (HARMONIA MUNDI).

canon (from Gr. *kanōn,* "rule") In polyphonic music, a procedure in which different parts take up the same melody in succession; the most familiar example is the *round* (e.g., "Row, row, row your boat"). Canon is by definition a "strict" form of imitation. In the simplest canons, the imitative entries are at the same pitch (known as canon at the unison); in more complex examples, the melody is designed so that imitation can occur at a different pitch (known as canon at the second, third, etc.). Virtually every composer has used canon. In Bach's *Goldberg* Variations, for example, every third variation is a canon; these begin at the unison and proceed through canon at the second, third, fourth, and so on, all the way up to canon at the ninth. Dvořák's *Slavonic Dance* in C minor ◉, Op. 46, No. 7, is structured as a canon at the octave. The climactic pages of both the first movement and the finale of César Franck's Symphony in D minor make use of a canon at the unison, and the aria "Glitter and Be Gay" from Leonard Bernstein's *Candide* culminates in a canon.

cantabile (It.) Songlike, in a singing manner. Often used as a tempo modifier (e.g., *Andante cantabile*).

cantata A piece for vocal soloists (with or without chorus) and orchestra, based on a sacred or secular text, usually consisting of several movements; sometimes a piece for a single solo voice with the accompaniment of an instrumental ensemble. Initially a secular form, like opera, the cantata was first developed in Italy in the early 17th century. From the 1630s until the 1720s it was the most prominent form of Italian vocal chamber music, championed by composers such as Luigi Rossi (ca. 1597–1653), Giacomo Carissimi (1605–74), Alessandro Stradella (1639–82), Agostino Steffani (1654–1728), and, most important, Alessandro Scarlatti. The German church cantata originated in the 17th century with Schütz—who, fresh from his studies in Italy, brought the new *STILE CONCITATO* back to Protestant Germany—and got a boost from Buxtehude, revered by both Bach and Handel. Around 1700, the genre gained new impetus along with a structural model, thanks to the work of Erdmann Neumeister, whose collection of sacred poems *Geistliche Cantaten statt einer Kirchen-Musik* (*Sacred Cantatas Instead of a Church Music*; 1700) consisted of texts modeled on the librettos of secular Italian cantatas, laid out as recitatives and da capo arias replete with madrigalistic imagery. Telemann and Bach were among the first composers to fashion cantatas of this type; Bach's production of several hundred is considered the core of his work, and includes such joyous pages as the opening ones of Cantata No. 80, *Eine feste Burg ist unser Gott*, based on Martin Luther's famous hymn. Since the beginning of the 20th century the term has had a very broad meaning, referring to any kind of choral-orchestral composition not belonging to a specific genre.

Cantelli, Guido

(b. Novara, April 27, 1920; d. Paris, November 24, 1956)

ITALIAN CONDUCTOR. He studied composition and conducting at the Milan Conservatory. In 1943, within months of taking his first professional position as a conductor, he was drafted into the Italian army; upon refusing to serve he was interned by the Germans. After the war he became a protégé of Arturo Toscanini, at whose invitation he made his American debut conducting the NBC Symphony Orchestra in 1949. In 1951 he began a fruitful collaboration with the Philharmonia Orchestra of London, recording symphonies of Mozart, Beethoven, Schubert, and Mendelssohn as well as works by Tchaikovsky, Debussy, Ravel, and Dukas. His appointment as music director of La Scala, to take effect in 1957, was announced just days before his death in an airplane crash at Orly airport, outside Paris. Cantelli was considered one of the most promising European conductors of his generation, with warmth and passion wedded to a keen sense of discipline and respect for the architecture of a score. Although he was closely associated with Toscanini (it was Cantelli who pulled the plug during the famous NBC Symphony broadcast in which Toscanini's memory failed him), he did not conduct like his mentor, displaying more restraint and nobility in his interpretations.

Guido Cantelli on the cusp of greatness

RECOMMENDED RECORDING

DEBUSSY, *LE MARTYRE DE SAINT SÉBASTIEN*, *LA MER*, *NOCTURNES*: PHILHARMONIA ORCHESTRA (TESTAMENT).

Canteloube, Joseph

(b. Annonay, October 21, 1879; d. Paris, November 4, 1957)

FRENCH COMPOSER. After study with Vincent d'Indy at the Schola Cantorum, he began collecting French folk songs, especially those from the Auvergne, his native region. He composed two operas, *Le mas* (1910–13) and *Vercingétorix* (1930–32), two symphonic poems, a *Poème* for violin and orchestra, and a couple of chamber pieces, but he is best known for his folk-song arrangements, particularly the four volumes of *Chants d'Auvergne* (*Songs of the Auvergne*) published 1923–30, which are among the most fetching of 20th-century cycles for voice and orchestra.

RECOMMENDED RECORDINGS

CHANTS D'AUVERGNE: LOS ANGELES; JACQUILLAT AND ORCHESTRE DES CONCERTS LAMOUREUX (EMI).

CHANTS D'AUVERGNE, VOL. 2: DAVRATH; DE LA ROCHE, KINGSLEY, AND UNNAMED ORCHESTRA (VANGUARD).

canticle A hymnlike passage in scripture that is not one of the Psalms. In the Roman and Anglican liturgies, particular importance is attached to the three canticles that appear in the New Testament—the Benedictus, the Nunc dimittis (known as the Song of Simeon) and the Magnificat—as well as to the Te Deum, known as the Hymn of St. Ambrose. Gerald Finzi's *Magnificat,* for chorus and organ, celebrates the beauty of the English text familiar to readers of the King James Bible.

cantilena (It., "singsong") A "singing" line for an instrument or a voice.

cantus firmus (Lat., "fixed melody") A preexisting melody around which a passage or a whole piece of polyphonic music is written. As a contrapuntal technique, cantus firmus can be utilized in any kind of music, but it is most often associated with sacred music, in which a portion of a PLAINCHANT melody or chorale tune usually serves as the cantus firmus. This method of composing polyphonic music was common during the Middle Ages and the Renaissance. Generally the cantus firmus appeared in the tenor voice (the meaning of "tenor" being originally "that [voice] which holds" the cantus firmus). Du Fay was among the first to utilize popular songs rather than chant melodies as the cantus firmus, (e.g., in his masses *L'homme armé* and *Se la face ay pale*). The technique ceased to be standard practice in the 17th century, but continued to be used in the sacred domain for effect, and in other types of music whenever a consciously "learned" or archaic gesture was desired. An example from the music of Bach is the opening chorus of the cantata *Wachet auf, ruft uns die Stimme,* BWV 140, composed in 1731, which uses the chorale tune of the same name, written in 1597 by Philipp Nicolai (1556–1608), as a cantus firmus.

canzona (It. "song") [1] A contrapuntal instrumental piece, originally based on the polyphonic chanson; the genre reached its high point during the 16th and 17th centuries. [2] A simple lyric poem or song.

capriccio (It., "caprice" or "whim") A piece of fanciful, spontaneous, colorful, or otherwise exceptional character, usually in a fast or dancelike tempo, for anything from a single instrument to a full orchestra. The term does not connote a specific form or procedure.

***Capriccio espagnol* (*Spanish Capriccio*)** ORCHESTRAL SHOWPIECE BY NIKOLAY RIMSKY-KORSAKOV, composed in 1887 and based on Spanish folk themes from a collection entitled *Cantos y bailes populares de España,* by José Inzenga. Originally projected as a fantasy for violin and orchestra, it retains a prominent part for solo violin and exhibits much the same festivity and flamboyance as Rimsky's two other major orchestral works of the same period, *SHEHERAZADE* and the *Russian Easter* Overture. The composer himself noted that the instrumental coloring in his *Capriccio* was "the very essence of the composition," rather than an adornment, but the score is a textbook of effects nonetheless, and one of the most satisfying display pieces in the orchestral literature.

The *Capriccio espagnol* is in five continuous movements beginning with a festive *Alborada* that puts the full resources of the percussion on display and includes energetic solos for the clarinet and violin. The ensuing theme and variation movement opens with a sultry tune in the horns over a rocking, waltzlike accompaniment in the strings; the five compact variations that follow include a dialogue between English horn and French horn against tremolo strings, and a statement of the tune in the violins, passionately punctuated by full bow strokes. A shortened reprise of the *Alborada,* in a new key and different scoring, serves as a bridge to the piece's penultimate movement, entitled *Scena e canto gitano* (*Scene and Gypsy Song*). Announced by a snare drum roll and brass fanfare, the movement begins languorously and gathers momentum until it reaches a fiery, swirling climax. Without a break the final *Fandango asturiano* erupts in a riot of color. Castanets and triangle mark the rhythm of the dance, and the *Capriccio* gallops to a dazzling conclusion, with the music of the opening *Alborada* making a final appearance in the coda.

RECOMMENDED RECORDINGS

KONDRASHIN AND RCA VICTOR SYMPHONY ORCHESTRA (RCA).

MAAZEL AND BERLIN PHILHARMONIC (DG).

MACKERRAS AND LONDON SYMPHONY ORCHESTRA (TELARC).

Capriccio italien **ORCHESTRAL SCORE BY TCHAIKOVSKY,** composed in 1880 and based on material the composer collected during an extended Roman holiday in the winter of 1879–80. A colorfully scored fantasia on four tunes, with an opening fanfare echoing the trumpet call Tchaikovsky heard daily from the army barracks next door to his hotel, it is modeled on the second of Glinka's *Spanish Overtures.* The piece received its premiere at a concert of the Russian Musical Society in Moscow on December 18, 1880.

RECOMMENDED RECORDING

DORATI AND MINNEAPOLIS SYMPHONY ORCHESTRA (MERCURY).

Carmen **OPERA BY GEORGES BIZET,** to a libretto by Henri Meilhac and Ludovic Halévy (based on a story by Prosper Mérimée), premiered in Paris in 1875. With this work Bizet transformed opéra comique into a serious, passionate, and realistic genre. *Carmen* is the tragic story of a beautiful Gypsy who works in a tobacco factory. From the moment of her opening aria, sung to the sultry rhythm of a habanera, her seductive charms mesmerize Don José, a soldier fleeing his past. He falls for her, and eventually goes AWOL for her. As Don José's love deepens into obsession, Carmen grows tired of his irrational jealousies and decides to leave him. Unable to tolerate the thought of Carmen in the arms of another man, Don José murders her. The treatment of the opera's central characters—Carmen, the freewheeling, fatalistic Gypsy, and Don José, the obsessed, morally disintegrating soldier—remains one of the great achievements of 19th-century opera; the score itself is among the most brilliantly orchestrated and melodically memorable compositions in all of music.

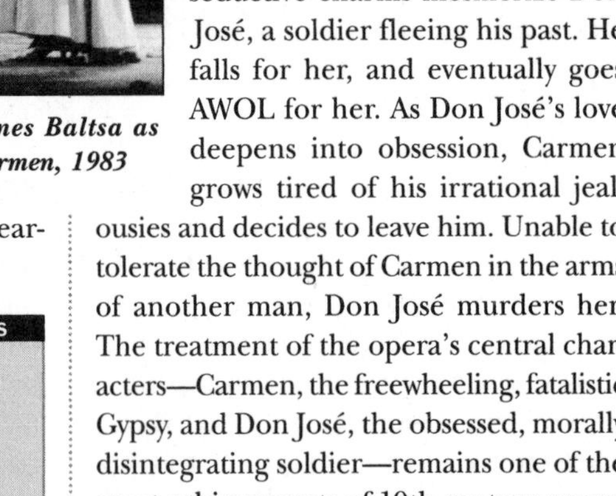

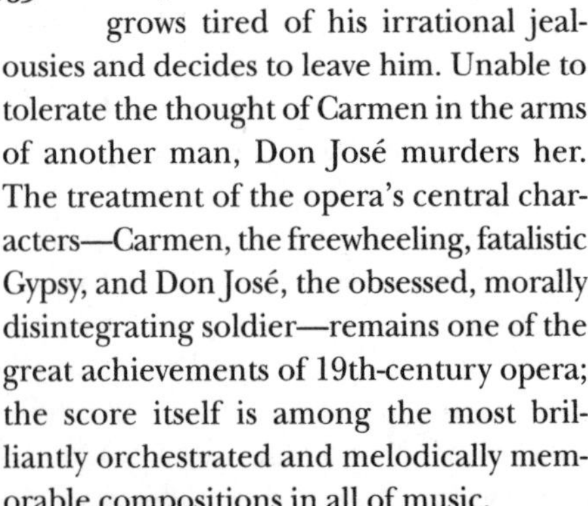

Agnes Baltsa as Carmen, 1983

RECOMMENDED RECORDING

BALTSA, CARRERAS, RICCIARELLI, VAN DAM; KARAJAN AND BERLIN PHILHARMONIC (DG).

Carmina Burana **Scenic cantata by Carl Orff,** completed in 1936 and premiered in Frankfurt on June 8, 1937. Its text is derived from some secular poems by itinerant scholars and monks known as Goliards, collected in an early-13th-century manuscript that eventually came into the possession of the Benedictine abbey of Benediktbeuren, near Munich. The score carries the elaborate Latin subtitle "Cantiones profanae cantoribus et choris cantandae comitantibus instrumentis atque imaginibus magicis" ("Profane songs to be sung by soloists and chorus with an accompaniment of instruments and magic tableaux"). The meaning of "magic tableaux" is not clear, but the term has inspired numerous concert performances using mime and dance, as well as several television productions. The piece consists of a brief prologue in the form of an address to the goddess Fortune, "Fortuna imperatrix mundi" ("Fortune, Empress of the World") followed by three main sections—the first in two parts headed "Primo vere" ("Spring") and "Uf dem anger" ("On the Green"); the second designated "In taberna" ("In the Tavern"); and the third titled "Cours d'amour" ("The Court of Love"), with a single song, "Blanziflor et Helena," as a pendant. A repeat of the opening hymn to Fortune closes the piece. Like nearly all of Orff's work, *Carmina Burana* manifests a preoccupation with music as spectacle. The writing invites the listener to participate in the hedonistic enjoyment of simple, rhythmically catchy and frequently repeated tunes, equally simple forms, consonant harmony, viscerally powerful singing, and extraordinarily colorful scoring marked by unstinting use of percussion.

RECOMMENDED RECORDINGS

Janowitz, Stolze, Fischer-Dieskau; Jochum and Deutsche Oper Berlin (DG).

Oelze, Keenlyside, Kuebler; Thielemann and Deutsche Oper Berlin (DG).

Carnaval **Piano suite by Robert Schumann, Op. 9.** Its full name is *Carnaval: Scènes mignonnes sur quatre notes* (*Carnival: Pretty Scenes on Four Notes*). Composed in 1835, it consists of 21 short numbers, all of which have titles. There are portraits of Florestan and Eusebius, as well as of characters from the commedia dell'arte ("Pierrot," "Arlequin," "Pantalon et Columbine"), and a pair of very appealing cameos devoted to two fellow composers, "Chopin" and "Paganini," the former quite striking in the way it captures Chopin's nocturnal sound and style. Schumann includes a characterization of the 15-year-old Clara Wieck ("Chiarina"), whom he would marry in 1840, as well as one of his fiancée, then just 17, Ernestine von Fricken ("Estrella"). Ernestine is the key to the piece, for she had been born in the town of Asch in Bohemia, and the four notes on which *Carnaval* is based are the four whose German names spell that out: A, Es, C, and H (A, E-flat, C, and B). Quite by chance, as the composer himself was aware, they are also the only letters in Schumann's name that signify musical pitches.

1910 costume sketch by Leon Bakst for a ballet on Schumann's Carnaval

The writing in *Carnaval* is brilliantly inventive, and the character of individual numbers so artfully varied that the waltzlike feeling of the piece as a whole never grows monotonous. It is an altogether characteristic touch that the four-note theme of *Carnaval* is revealed only in the ninth (but unnumbered) piece of the collection,

"Sphinxes," which Schumann instructs the performer *not* to play.

RECOMMENDED RECORDINGS

ARRAU (PHILIPS).

EGOROV (EMI).

RUBINSTEIN (RCA).

carnaval des animaux, Le (Carnival of the Animals) **DIVERTISSEMENT BY CAMILLE SAINT-SAËNS,** composed in 1886 in Vienna and premiered at a private soirée in Paris that same year. Saint-Saëns forbade publication of the piece during his lifetime; it first appeared in print in 1922, a year after his death. Dubbed a "Grande fantaisie zoölogique," it is scored for two pianos and a chamber ensemble consisting of two violins, viola, cello, double bass, flute, clarinet, glockenspiel, and xylophone. In *Le carnaval des animaux* Saint-Saëns pokes fun at Offenbach, Berlioz, Mendelssohn, Rossini, and not least, himself. The tortoises dance Offenbach's famous cancan in the slowest of tempos, and the elephant cavorts to the strains of both the "Dance of the Sylphs" from Berlioz's *La damnation de Faust* and the scherzo from Mendelssohn's music for *A Midsummer Night's Dream.* The swan glides along on one of the composer's most affecting melodies, played as a solo by the cello. The composer targets himself in the portrait of the "Fossils," where the xylophone plinks out his *DANSE MACABRE.*

RECOMMENDED RECORDINGS

NASH ENSEMBLE (VIRGIN).

PAHUD, CAPUÇON, OTHERS (VIRGIN).

ROBISON, CARR, OTHERS; BERNSTEIN AND NEW YORK PHILHARMONIC (SONY).

Carnegie Hall **"MUSIC HALL" IN NEW YORK CITY** founded by the Scottish-born steel magnate Andrew Carnegie (1835–1919). The structure, designed by William Burnet Tuthill and located at the intersection of Seventh Avenue and 57th Street, houses three concert halls (including a main auditorium with a capacity of 2,804 and a recital hall with a capacity of 268). For more than a century it has been regarded as the most important concert venue in the world.

Designed so that it would not require steel support beams—an irony if ever there was one, considering its founder's line of work—Carnegie Hall was built with concrete and masonry walls several feet thick and an Italian Renaissance–style facade of terra-cotta and iron-spotted brick. Construction was completed in the spring of 1891 at a total cost of slightly over $2 million, 90 percent of which was borne by Carnegie.

On opening night, May 5, 1891, horse-drawn carriages lined up for a quarter mile outside the hall as the cream of New York society—Whitneys, Sloans, Rockefellers, and Fricks—paid $1 or $2 a seat to hear the Symphony Society of New York in a program that featured a special guest-conducting appearance by the famed Russian composer Pyotr Ily'ich Tchaikovsky.

In 1892, after a fire gutted the Metropolitan Opera House, the New York Philharmonic Society joined the Symphony Society in making its home at Carnegie Hall. The Philharmonic added a glorious page to the hall's history when, on December 16, 1893, it gave the world premiere of Antonín Dvořák's Symphony No. 9 (*From the New World*) under the direction of Anton Seidl, with the composer in attendance.

In 1925, six years after its founder's death, Carnegie Hall was sold to New York realtor Robert E. Simon. For the next 30 years it was managed by Simon and his son. In 1955, when plans were announced for the construction of Lincoln Center, the New York Philharmonic decided to make its home there, and Carnegie Hall was put up for sale. When a buyer could not be found, the date of March 31, 1960, was set for its demolition. With Isaac Stern as spokesman, a number of musicians and concerned citizens banded together in a last-ditch effort to save the hall. On May 16, 1960, as a result of special state legislation, New York City was permitted to purchase Carnegie Hall for $5 million, and a new nonprofit organization called the Carnegie Hall Corporation was chartered. Stern was elected president of the corporation, a position he retained until his death in 2001.

Carnegie Hall underwent a much-needed renovation in 1986. In spite of promises that the hall's pleasantly warm and involving sound would not be altered, the reconstruction of the stage area resulted in a sound that was brighter and "harder," with a sharper focus but less warmth. After several seasons, following the discovery and removal of a concrete construction support that had inadvertently been left in place underneath the stage floor, most of the warmth and resonance of old returned. Construction of a new multipurpose venue below the main auditorium began in 1999, and the new hall, with a capacity of 640 seats, opened in September 2003.

In the 11 decades since Tchaikovsky's opening-night engagement, appearances

The main entrance to the "Music Hall founded by Andrew Carnegie"

at Carnegie Hall have stood as the litmus test of greatness for musicians. Sergey Rachmaninov made his Carnegie Hall debut in 1909, playing his Piano Concerto No. 2 in C minor as guest soloist with the Boston Symphony Orchestra. Vladimir Horowitz first rattled the rafters in 1928. Jascha Heifetz made his debut in 1917, at the age of 16, to be followed by the likes of Yehudi Menuhin, Isaac Stern, Itzhak Perlman, Anne-Sophie Mutter, Joshua Bell, and Gil Shaham. Certainly one of the greatest of the hall's great moments came in 1958 when the 23-year-old Van Cliburn staged a triumphant homecoming after winning the gold medal in the first International Tchaikovsky Competition in Moscow. And when a hall in the nation's capital was closed to her because of racial bigotry, the great Marian Anderson found herself welcome on the Carnegie Hall stage.

Carnegie Hall has played host to virtually all the world's leading orchestras and conductors. Both the Boston Symphony and Chicago Symphony made their first visits to the hall in the 19th century. Since then the orchestras of Philadelphia, Cleveland, Pittsburgh, St. Louis, Cincinnati, and Washington, D.C., and of London, Amsterdam, Vienna, and Berlin, have joined them in making regular pilgrimages to the hall. Arturo Toscanini electrified Carnegie Hall audiences for 28 years at the helm of the New York Philharmonic and the NBC Symphony, and Leonard Bernstein—whose 1943 debut with the New York Philharmonic produced one of Carnegie Hall's storied moments—later made the place a mecca for a new audience with his Young People's Concerts.

Carnegie Hall also has a distinguished jazz tradition. The indigenous art form was first heard there in 1912, in a concert of ragtime by James Reese Europe's Clef Club Orchestra. This performance was a harbinger of many stellar evenings featuring a cavalcade of jazz greats that included Fats Waller, W. C. Handy, Louis Armstrong, Count Basie, Billie Holiday, Dizzy Gillespie, Ella Fitzgerald, Charlie Parker, Oscar Peterson, Miles Davis, and John Coltrane. A 1938 concert by Benny Goodman and his orchestra, one of the most celebrated events in Carnegie Hall history, marked a turning point in the public acceptance of swing and of integrated musical ensembles. Hardly less significant was the 1943 Carnegie Hall debut of Duke Ellington, leading the New York premiere of his tone poem *Black, Brown and Beige.*

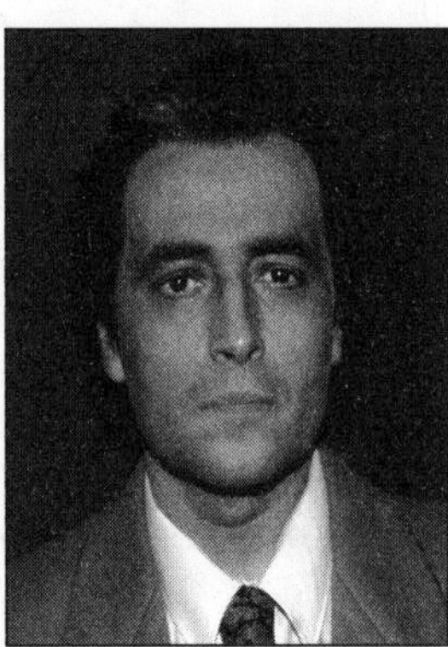

José Carreras

carol [1] A strophic song whose text is associated with Christmas. [2] A 15th-century song-form made up of uniform stanzas beginning with a burden (refrain), with a text in Latin or English usually about the Nativity or the Virgin Mary.

Carreras, José

(b. Barcelona, December 5, 1946)

SPANISH TENOR. He studied at the Barcelona Conservatory and made his debut in Barcelona in 1970, as Gennaro in Donizetti's *Lucrezia Borgia,* opposite Montserrat Caballé. His American debut, as Pinkerton in Puccini's *Madama Butterfly,* came at the New York City Opera in 1972. In 1973 he appeared with the San Francisco Opera as Rodolfo in Puccini's *La bohème,* and in 1974 he made his debuts at Covent Garden and the Metropolitan Opera. His career continued its ascent through the 1970s and 1980s as Herbert von Karajan tapped him for major roles at Salzburg and the labels jockeyed to sign him for prestigious recording projects. In 1987 he contracted leukemia and had to undergo an arduous course of treatment, including bone marrow transplants, before the disease was eradicated. Even before his illness, however, his voice had started to show signs of serious deterioration, presumably the result of his tackling roles such as Radames in Verdi's *Aida* that were far too heavy for his essentially lyrical endowment.

Carreras returned to the limelight at the World Cup soccer championships in 1990 as one of the "Three Tenors," and the success that venture has enjoyed through numerous sequels has moved him into a whole new dimension of superstardom. At his best, in the mid-1970s, Carreras was a genuinely impressive lyric tenor, one whose sweet-toned voice and ardent, caressing delivery recalled the singing of the young Giuseppe di Stefano. His singing was natural, unaffected, and disarmingly lyrical; his voice had a lustrous sheen in the upper register, with flashes of fire that set it apart.

RECOMMENDED RECORDINGS

BIZET, *CARMEN*: BALTSA, RICCIARELLI, VAN DAM; KARAJAN AND BERLIN PHILHARMONIC (DG).

VERDI, *SIMON BOCCANEGRA*: FRENI, CAPPUCCILLI, GHIAUROV, VAN DAM; ABBADO AND LA SCALA ORCHESTRA (DG).

Carter, Elliott

(b. New York, December 11, 1908)

AMERICAN COMPOSER whose formidably complex idiom has intrigued (or bewildered) and delighted (or dismayed) several generations of performers and listeners. He grew up in New York, the son of a well-to-do lace importer, and enrolled in the Horace Mann School, where he developed an interest in modern music, especially that of Scriabin and Stravinsky. In 1924 he met Charles Ives at a concert in Greenwich Village. The music of Ives exerted an important influence on Carter, as did that of Edgard Varèse. The jazz of the 1930s and 1940s—in particular the rhythmically advanced playing of Fats Waller—also came to play a role in his thinking.

In 1926 Carter went to Harvard, where he studied literature and philosophy in addition to music, then stayed to take a master's degree in music, studying composition with Walter Piston and Edward Burlingame Hill. Convinced that he needed further training, he went to study with Nadia Boulanger in Paris (1932–35), concentrating mainly on counterpoint and musical structure. Boulanger's analytical approach and concern for compositional technique tempered Carter's youthful enthusiasm for modernistic experimentation, at least temporarily. His early post-Boulanger compositions, including a ballet, *Pocahontas* (1936; rev. 1939), were in a neoclassical vein. But with the bracing *Holiday Overture* (1944; rev. 1961), a new strength and cragginess appeared in Carter's idiom, even more apparent in his next major works, the Piano Sonata (1945–46) and the Sonata for Cello and Piano (1948).

The evolution of Carter's language away from the clarities of neoclassicism toward a much thornier syntax reveling in texture and rhythm became manifest in his String Quartet No. 1 (1950–51), which, despite its complexity and 40-minute length, was performed to immediate and enormous acclaim throughout the U.S. and Europe. String Quartet No. 2 (1959) proved another watershed. Carter envisioned the instruments as four distinct "personalities" and wrote accordingly for each one. The work won Carter his first Pulitzer Prize.

With the exception of *Variations for Orchestra* (1953–55), Carter steered clear of orchestral music during the 1950s. But in the 1960s he produced three ambitious, intricately structured large-scale symphonic works: the Double Concerto (1961) for harpsichord and piano with two chamber orchestras, the Piano Concerto (1964-65), and the Concerto for Orchestra (1968–69).

Much of Carter's subsequent music has exhibited a characteristic if sometimes impenetrable complexity in its organization and superimposition of materials. Significant efforts of the 1970s and 1980s include the String Quartets No. 3 (1971, awarded the Pulitzer Prize in 1973), No. 4 (1985), and No. 5 (1995); *Night Fantasies* (1980), a substantial solo work for piano commissioned by a consortium of four pianists (Paul Jacobs, Gilbert Kalish, Ursula Oppens and Charles Rosen); and three suites for vocal soloist(s) and mixed ensembles—*A Mirror on Which to Dwell* (1975), *Syringa* (1978), and *In Sleep, in Thunder* (1981). During the 1990s, Carter composed the three-movement *Symphonia: sum fluxae pretium spei* (*Symphony: I am the prize of flowing hope*) (1993–97) and the one-act opera *What Next?* (1997–98).

Carter is one of the most important and influential figures of modern music. In many circles his works are regarded as having set the standard—in their intricacy and conceptual rigor—for "serious" composition over the past five decades. Beyond that, they testify to Carter's aesthetic position as a link between America and Europe, between the elemental, vibrant new American music of the 1920s and 1930s and the cerebral experimentalism of the

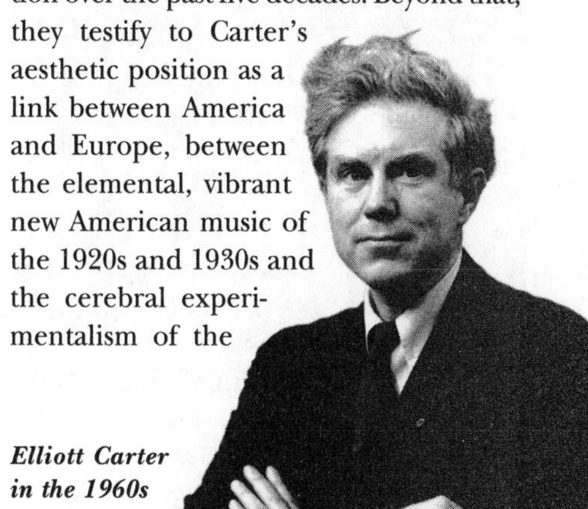

Elliott Carter in the 1960s

postwar European avant-garde. But Carter's music has yet to connect with the broader musical public, and its complexity often seems gratuitous; as impressive as its craftsmanship is, it remains an acquired taste. Though some pieces, the string quartets in particular, will likely find a permanent place in the repertoire, the bulk of Carter's music may remain the enthusiasm of no more than a small devoted coterie, as it is today.

RECOMMENDED RECORDINGS

DOUBLE CONCERTO: JACOBS, KALISH; WEISBERG AND CONTEMPORARY CHAMBER ENSEMBLE (NONESUCH).

A MIRROR ON WHICH TO DWELL (WITH OTHER WORKS): BRYN-JULSON; BOULEZ AND ENSEMBLE INTERCONTEMPORAIN (WARNER).

NIGHT FANTASIES, SONATA NO. 1: ROSEN (BRIDGE).

STRING QUARTETS: ARDITTI QUARTET (ETCETERA).

Caruso, Enrico

(b. Naples, February 27, 1873; d. Naples, August 2, 1921)

ITALIAN TENOR, one of the supreme interpretive musicians of the 20th century.

Enrico Caruso as Radames in a 1914 ad from his record label, the Victor Talking Machine Co.

His initial training was less than thorough, but his determination to overcome technical obstacles, combined with the exceptional power and appealing baritonal timbre of his voice, enabled him to develop into a vocal artist of the highest order. He made his debut in Naples in 1894 and spent the next several years singing in theaters in southern Italy. His first real triumph came at La Scala in 1901, in the role of Nemorino in Donizetti's *L'elisir d'amore,* and in 1903 he made his debut at the Metropolitan Opera in New York, as the Duke in Verdi's *Rigoletto.* The Met would become his playground over the next two decades, his name synonymous with the roles of Canio (*Pagliacci*), Rodolfo (*La bohème*), Cavaradossi (*Tosca*), Alfredo (*La traviata*), Riccardo (*Un ballo in maschera*), and Radames (*Aida*); in 1910 he would create the part of Dick Johnson in the Met's world premiere performances of Puccini's *La fanciulla del West.* His final public appearance—as Eléazar in Fromental Halévy's *La Juive*—took place at the Met on Christmas Eve, 1920, just eight months before his death.

Caruso was one of the first great singers to make commercial recordings from the beginning of his career on a regular basis; they not only served to establish him as the world's first true media celebrity, but guaranteed the public's acceptance of the phonograph as an entertainment medium. In those recordings, the sensuality and intensity of his timbre, the skill with which he varied his delivery and declamation to suit the emotion of the moment, the extraordinary breath control, unerring intonation, incomparably suave phrasing, and above all the dramatic vigor that made Caruso such a distinctive artist are engraved in vivid detail.

RECOMMENDED RECORDING

ENRICO CARUSO, VOLS. 1–11 (NAXOS).

Casadesus, Robert

(b. Paris, April 7, 1899; d. Paris, September 19, 1972)

FRENCH PIANIST AND COMPOSER. The product of a musical family, he attended the Paris Conservatoire, winning first prize in piano at the age of 14. He began concertizing internationally in 1922, the same year he met Ravel, with whom he toured and gave concerts annually through 1930. In 1936 he performed with Toscanini in New York, and following the outbreak of World War II he settled temporarily in the United States. From the 1940s through the 1960s he recorded regularly for Columbia Masterworks, both as a soloist and in collaboration with Eugene Ormandy and the Philadelphia Orchestra and with George Szell and the Cleveland Orchestra. Casadesus was a French classicist, the very opposite of Alfred Cortot, the volatile Romantic. His playing was lucid, thoughtful, exquisitely cool, and graceful—at times almost too controlled. But when provoked, by a piece like Ravel's "Scarbo" from *Gaspard de la nuit,* he could be fiery and dramatic—even a bit diabolic. He possessed an exceptionally secure technique and was admired for his insight into the music of Mozart, Beethoven, and Saint-Saëns, as well as Ravel. He composed seven symphonies, several sets of piano pieces, and a small corpus of chamber music; his works for two pianos, written for himself and his wife, Gaby Casadesus, are still occasionally encountered.

RECOMMENDED RECORDINGS

MOZART, PIANO CONCERTOS; SZELL AND CLEVELAND ORCHESTRA (SONY).
MUSIC OF RAVEL (SONY).

Casals, Pablo [Pau]

(b. Vendrell, December 29, 1876; d. Rio Piedras, Puerto Rico, October 22, 1973)

CATALAN CELLIST, CONDUCTOR, AND COMPOSER renowned for his uncompromising artistry and soulful interpretations of the classics, especially the works of Bach, Beethoven, and Brahms. He was the first modern cellist and one of the last standard-bearers of the pre–World War I European musical order.

His musician parents encouraged his precocious talent, and he had already achieved proficiency on the piano and violin by the time he first heard a cello at the age of 11. He immediately began taking lessons at the Escuela Municipal de Música in Barcelona, and had mastered the instrument by the time he was 14. He soon came to the attention of María Cristina, the Queen Regent of Spain, whose patronage enabled him to pursue subsequent studies in Madrid and Brussels. He returned to Barcelona in 1896 and was appointed principal cello in the orchestra of the Gran Teatro de Liceo; he also performed in a string quartet led by Mathieu Crickboom (Eugène Ysaÿe's favorite pupil), and in a piano trio with Crickboom and the Catalan pianist-composer Enrique Granados.

Performances in England and France in 1899 marked the beginning of Casals's international career. On January 15, 1904, at the invitation of President Theodore Roosevelt, he gave a recital at the White House (where he would be even more warmly received in 1961, at a return engagement hosted by President John F. Kennedy). In 1905 he joined forces with the pianist Alfred Cortot and the violinist Jacques Thibaud (1880–1953) to form one of the most celebrated trios in history, an ensemble whose performances and eventual recordings set the standard in the trio repertoire for many years. By 1914, the year of his marriage to the American singer and socialite Susan Metcalfe, Casals was the most acclaimed cellist in the world, a standing he maintained in the years after World War I when he resumed his international touring.

Casals enjoyed a golden decade in the studio from 1929 (following the advent of

Pablo Casals in 1972

electrical recording) until the outbreak of World War II in 1939. Recording for the HMV label, he engraved a succession of compelling accounts of major works in the repertoire: the Bach suites, the Beethoven sonatas and trios, Brahms's Cello Sonata No. 2 and Double Concerto (with Thibaud as violinist and Cortot conducting), the Dvořák concerto (with George Szell and the Czech Philharmonic). His poetic shaping of the solo part in the slow movement of the Dvořák shows him at his best.

In 1939, following the establishment of Francisco Franco's dictatorship in Spain, Casals moved to Prades, a Catalan village on the French side of the Pyrenées, refusing to perform in Spain as long as Franco remained in power. He never played another note in his homeland and for a while he withdrew from performing altogether. But in 1950, to mark the bicentennial of J. S. Bach's death, he welcomed a small group of musical friends and colleagues to Prades; the music making was of such a high order that a festival was born.

Casals settled in Puerto Rico in 1956, and in 1957, at the age of 80, married the 18-year-old Puerto Rican cellist Marta Montañez. He devoted his sunset years to teaching and conducting at the Marlboro Festival in Vermont, directing festivals in Prades, Perpignan, and Puerto Rico, and fulfilling occasional engagements as a guest conductor with major orchestras.

Like many performers of his generation, Casals found it necessary to compose. His student compositions included a mass, a symphonic poem, a concerto for piano and cello, and a string quartet. His most famous piece, *Sardana* (1927), was written for an ensemble of cellos.

Musicians admired Casals for the expressivity of his playing and above all for his commanding sense of what the music was saying and how it should go. His phrasing was enlivened by a distinctive sense of rubato, usually very subtle, sometimes not subtle at all, but always resulting in a nuance that seemed inevitable. He possessed an extraordinary awareness of the cello's range of color. His interpretations of the core repertoire, especially the Bach suites, remain benchmarks in the history of music, while his engagement as a man and musician with the important humanitarian issues of his day set a standard for artistic probity that will likely serve as a beacon for generations to come.

RECOMMENDED RECORDINGS

BACH, CELLO SUITES (NAXOS).

DVOŘÁK, CELLO CONCERTO (WITH BRAHMS DOUBLE CONCERTO): SZELL AND CZECH PHILHARMONIC (NAXOS).

Casella, Alfredo

(b. Turin, July 25, 1883; d. Rome, March 5, 1947)

ITALIAN COMPOSER, CONDUCTOR, AND ADMINISTRATOR. A gifted pianist, he studied at the Paris Conservatoire; in 1900 he entered Fauré's class in composition. Returning to Italy in 1915, he emerged as the leading composer-conductor in Italian music of the interwar years. He organized a society for the furtherance of contemporary music, and briefly embraced an avant-garde idiom in his own music. Around 1920 he turned toward neoclassicism and developed an interest in the textures and formal schemes of 18th-century music. His international career included tours of the Soviet Union and numerous performances in the United States; he made his American debut in 1921 with the Philadelphia Orchestra in the triple role of conductor, composer, and pianist on the same program, and later served as conductor of the Boston Pops (1927–29). Politically naive, he succumbed to the spell of fascism, even writing an opera glorifying Mussolini's Ethiopian adventure of 1936. After 1940 he became a victim of wartime anti-Semitism (his wife was Jewish) and suffered the onset of a debilitating and ultimately terminal illness. As a composer, Casella was cosmopolitan and eclectic—a follower rather than a leader—but his importance as a focal point for interest in instrumental music and modern currents of musical thought in post-Puccinian Italy should not be underestimated.

RECOMMENDED RECORDINGS

Paganiniana: Muti and La Scala Orchestra (Sony).

Piano pieces: Ballerini (Naxos).

cassation A term used by some Classical composers to denote a piece of chamber music similar to a serenade or divertimento. *See also* OCTET.

castanets Handheld percussion instruments of Spanish origin, usually made of wood from the chestnut tree (Sp., *castaña*). Normally they come in pairs, one slightly higher-sounding than the other; each member of a pair consists of two shallow wooden cups loosely joined by a cord that passes through holes drilled in their rims and is looped around the thumb. Castanets are a commonly used orchestral percussion instrument, particularly in pieces intended to evoke a Spanish atmosphere—examples include Bizet's *Carmen,* Chabrier's *España,* Ravel's *Rapsodie espagnole,* and Debussy's *Iberia.* Many composers have used castanets outside this context, e.g., Prokofiev in his Piano Concerto No. 3 and Violin Concerto No. 2. Orchestral percussionists frequently mount the castanets on blocks to make them easier to play.

castrato (pl., castrati) A castrated male singer. The practice of castrating boys with promising voices before they reached puberty—to ensure that their TESSITURA would remain high after they matured—was common in Italy in the 17th and 18th centuries. The procedure endowed a select few with powerful, trumpetlike voices pitched in the alto range; thus equipped, they flourished as the superstars of Baroque opera. From about 1680 until well into the 18th century, the "heroic" parts in most serious Italian operas were written for castrati, the best of whom made fortunes singing them. Even though the practice went into decline around 1740, it was still enough of a convention that Mozart, in 1781, could create the role of Idamante in *Idomeneo* for the castrato Vincenzo dal Prato.

According to contemporaneous accounts, the finest castrati possessed voices of astounding amplitude, range, and agility, almost instrumental in their size and strength. Because they underwent rigorous and uninterrupted training

A caricature of the castrato Farinelli

from childhood into their adult years, they also tended to be excellent musicians, with exceptional technique and a thorough knowledge of theory. Like bullfighters, they adopted performance names: Francesco Bernardi (ca. 1680–ca. 1759) was known as Senesino, while Carlo Broschi (1705–82) performed as Farinelli. Senesino dominated the London stage for the better part of two decades, during which Handel, who despised him on personal grounds, nevertheless penned 17 roles for him. So great was the prestige and honor accorded the leading castrati that even in retirement they remained celebrities—Farinelli, for instance, became a counselor of state to Philip V and Ferdinand VI of Spain.

Cavalleria rusticana (*Rustic Chivalry*)

OPERA BY PIETRO MASCAGNI, to a libretto by Giovanni Targioni-Tozzetti and Guido Menasci (based on a play by Giovanni Verga), premiered in Rome in 1890. It is one of the finest embodiments of the operatic style known as VERISMO, in which the stage is supposed to portray real life and real people. The central characters are Turiddu, who is carrying on an affair with Alfio's wife, Lola; Santuzza, who is carrying a torch for Turiddu; and Alfio, who is carrying a knife and eventually uses it to murder Turiddu. After completing the score, Mascagni linked the opera's two acts with an orchestral intermezzo so it would qualify in a competition for one-act operas, which it won; the music of that intermezzo is the finest thing he ever wrote. *Cavalleria rusticana* is frequently paired with Leoncavallo's *Pagliacci* as a double bill.

RECOMMENDED RECORDINGS

COSSOTTO, BERGONZI, ET AL.; KARAJAN AND LA SCALA ORCHESTRA (DG).

SCOTTO, DOMINGO, ET AL.; LEVINE AND NATIONAL PHILHARMONIC ORCHESTRA (RCA).

Cavalli, Francesco

(b. Crema, February 14, 1602; d. Venice, January 14, 1676)

ITALIAN COMPOSER OF THE EARLY BAROQUE, the leading figure in Italian opera in the years after Claudio Monteverdi. His father, Giovanni Battista Caletti, *maestro di cappella* at the cathedral of Crema, presided over his early instruction in music. At the age of 14 he was taken to Venice by Federico Cavalli, a Venetian diplomat, and enrolled in the *cappella* at the cathedral of San Marco as a soprano. There he worked in close conjunction with Monteverdi, director of music at San Marco since 1613. Other church jobs followed, including that of second organist at San Marco from 1639. In the same year, Cavalli made his debut as an opera composer at the first of Venice's public opera houses, the Teatro San Cassiano, with *Le nozze di Teti e di Peleo* (*The Marriage of Thetis and Peleus*). During the 1640s and 1650s, he was remarkably busy, composing on average one major work a year for the Venetian theaters, and producing works for Naples, Florence, and Milan as well. Among his most striking accomplishments from these years were *Egisto* (1643), *Calisto* (1651), and *Xerse* (1654), all premiered in Venice. In 1660 he was invited by Cardinal Mazarin to compose an opera for the wedding of Louis XIV to Maria Theresa of Spain; the result was *Ercole amante* (*Hercules in Love*), an ordeal two years in the making and six hours long (with ballet sequences by the young Italian expatriate Jean-Baptiste Lully). It premiered a week shy of the composer's 60th birthday. Cavalli returned to Venice and in 1668 was appointed *maestro di cappella* at San Marco, a post he held until his death.

RECOMMENDED RECORDING

CALISTO: BAYO, LIPPI, KEENLYSIDE; JACOBS AND CONCERTO VOCALE (HARMONIA MUNDI).

cavatina Originally a short aria; in 19th-century Italian opera, the term referred to a principal singer's opening aria. More recently the term has been applied to the introductory section of an extended two-part aria, the closing part of which is a CABALETTA.

celesta Keyboard instrument invented by Auguste Mustel in 1886 that produces bell-like sounds by means of a mechanism in which metal bars or plates are struck by hammers; the action is similar to that of the piano. Tchaikovsky came across the celesta during a visit to Paris; enchanted by its "divinely wonderful" sound, he became one of the first composers to use it orchestrally, featuring it in the "Dance of the Sugar-Plum Fairy," in Act II of his ballet *The Nutcracker* (1892). Ferde Grofé made colorful use of the instrument in his *Grand Canyon* Suite (1931), and Bela Bartók gave it a central role in his *Music for Strings, Percussion, and Celesta* (1936).

cello Bass member of the violin family. The instrument's proper name is *violoncello,* which means "little bass violin." The modern cello emerged at the beginning of the 18th century, having evolved from a larger form of bass violin used throughout the 17th century; its dimensions were standardized by ANTONIO STRADIVARI around 1707. In construction, materials, and overall appearance the cello bears the expected family resemblance to the violin: Spruce is used for the belly (or front) of the instrument, maple for the back and sides. The fingerboard, like those of the violin and viola, is unfretted and usually made of ebony. To produce greater bass resonance, the cello is proportionally "deeper" than the violin and viola. The instrument is held between the legs of the player, its weight supported by an extendable metal peg, called an end pin, that protrudes from a mounting on the tail piece. In addition to facilitating left-hand work high on the fingerboard, the end pin makes a firm, single-point contact with the stage floor, thus reducing the amount of sound energy lost to vibration. The standard cello bow is 28¼ inches long, a little shorter than violin and viola bows. There are four strings, tuned in fifths: C–G–D–A. The low C is pitched two octaves below middle C on the piano. The sound quality of the cello ranges from intense, warm, and penetrating, particularly in passages played on the A string, to rich and darkly resonant on the lower two strings. Its pizzicato is particularly sonorous, plump in the lower register, vibrant in the upper reaches.

Since its inception the cello has been the workhorse of string instruments, providing the sonic foundation wherever strings are used. During the 18th century it was a standard continuo instrument in chamber and orchestral music. Its capacity to "sing"—to carry the melody in an orchestral setting, rather than simply support it—came to be highly valued in the 19th century (note Beethoven's use of the cellos, with violas, for the main theme of the Andante in his Fifth Symphony). Composers with a keen interest in color, such as Schubert and Glinka, made pioneering use of the cello section in their orchestral scores (Schubert also favored the instrument in his chamber music), and later Romantics entrusted the cello section with some of the most glorious moments in the literature: e.g., the soaring opening theme of Bruckner's Symphony No. 7 (its first phrase doubled by solo horn, its second by the violas, with a single clarinet coloring the extension), or the grand proclamation that begins Richard Strauss's *Ein Heldenleben,* again with horn and violas assisting.

Cellist Yo-Yo Ma performing with Emanuel Ax at Carnegie Hall

The cello's solo repertoire is extraordinarily rich. Highlights include the six Bach suites for unaccompanied cello; Haydn's Concertos in C and D; Beethoven's five sonatas for cello and piano (Op. 5, Nos. 1 and 2, Op. 69, and Op. 102, Nos. 1 and 2) and his Triple Concerto in C for violin, cello, and piano, Op. 56; Schumann's Concerto in A minor, Op. 129; Brahms's Sonatas in E minor and F and his Concerto in A minor for violin and cello, Op. 102; Saint-Saëns's Concerto in A minor, Op. 33; Dvořák's monumental Concerto in B minor, Op. 104; Richard Strauss's *Don Quixote*; Debussy's Sonata; Prokofiev's Sonata, Op. 119, and *Symphony Concerto,* Op. 125; Shostakovich's Sonata in D minor, Op. 40, and his concertos, Opp. 107 and 126; Kodály's solo sonata, Op. 8; Walton's Concerto; and Britten's three suites for solo cello (Opp. 72, 80, and 87), Sonata for Cello and Piano, Op. 65, and *Cello Symphony,* Op. 68. Schubert's Sonata for Arpeggione (a fretted cross between cello and guitar) and Piano, D. 821, has been appropriated by cellists and is a staple of the recital repertoire, while sonatas by Chopin and Rachmaninov are occasionally performed.

Among the cello's great masters have been Anton Kraft, the brothers Jean-Pierre Duport and Jean-Louis Duport, David Popper, Pablo Casals, Emanuel Feuermann, Gregor Piatigorsky, Pierre Fournier, Janos Starker, Mstislav Rostropovich, Jacqueline du Pré, and Yo-Yo Ma.

Cenerentola, La (Cinderella) COMIC OPERA BY GIOACCHINO ROSSINI, to a libretto by Jacopo Ferretti (based on Charles Perrault's fairy tale "Cendrillon"), premiered in Rome in 1817. The title role is an outstanding vehicle for mezzo-soprano, and the score contains some of Rossini's most brilliant and imaginative music.

RECOMMENDED RECORDING

BARTOLI, MATTEUZZI, DARA; CHAILLY AND TEATRO COMMUNALE DI BOLOGNA (DECCA).

Ceremony of Carols, A WORK FOR "TREBLE" VOICES (IN THREE PARTS) AND HARP BY BENJAMIN BRITTEN, composed in March 1942 aboard the Swedish freighter *Axel Johnson* during a wartime crossing of the Atlantic from the United States to England. The texts of the various carols are medieval and 16th-century poems; as a processional to open and close the piece, Britten uses the plainsong antiphon "Hodie Christus natus est" from the Christmas Eve vespers, and at the center of the piece places an interlude for solo harp based on the same chant. The individual settings are masterly in their variety of texture and evocation of mood. *A Ceremony of Carols* was Britten's first work for boys' voices.

RECOMMENDED RECORDING

WILLIAMS; HILL AND WESTMINSTER CATHEDRAL CHOIR (HYPERION).

Chabrier, Emmanuel

(b. Ambert, January 18, 1841; d. Paris, September 13, 1894)

FRENCH PIANIST AND COMPOSER, one of the freest and most congenial musical spirits of his era. He studied law and music and for a time pursued both disciplines simultaneously, working in the French Ministry of the Interior from 1861 until 1880. He was also attracted to poetry and painting, and enjoyed close friendships with Paul Verlaine and Édouard Manet. In 1880 he went to Munich with Henri Duparc and Vincent d'Indy to hear *Tristan und Isolde,* and came away a fervent Wagnerian; the following year he decided to devote himself wholly to composition. The extent of Wagner's influence can be gauged from the harmonic complexities and seething emotionalism of Chabrier's mythic opera *Gwendoline* (1885), which in places sounds like a Gallic translation of *Tristan.* Despite his high ambitions as a dramatic composer, Chabrier's true talent lay elsewhere: as an innovative and extraordinarily skilled miniaturist with a virtually unrivaled sense of color. His piano pieces, particularly the ten *Pièces pittoresques* (1881) and the *Bourrée fantasque* (1891), significantly influenced Ravel and are among the finest French cameos after Chopin. The symphonic rhapsody *ESPAÑA* (1883)—which Ravel hailed as the first piece of "modern" music—and the "Fête Polonaise" interlude from the opera *Le roi malgré lui* (1887) rank among the most brilliant orchestral scores written in the 19th century.

RECOMMENDED RECORDINGS

ORCHESTRAL WORKS: GARDINER AND VIENNA PHILHARMONIC (DG).

ORCHESTRAL WORKS: PARAY AND DETROIT SYMPHONY ORCHESTRA (MERCURY)

PIANO PIECES: RABOL (NAXOS).

chaconne Any piece in which an extended melody or a series of variations occurs over a repeating bass line (*BASSO OSTINATO*). These were the characteristics of the French *chaconne,* a Baroque dance in slow triple time derived from a more lively dance called a *chacona* that originated in the New World during the 16th century and achieved popularity in Spain early in the 17th century. Dido's lament "When I am laid in earth" from Purcell's *Dido and Aeneas* (1689) is a chaconne, as is the second movement of Bach's Orchestral Suite No. 3 in D, BWV 1068, known as the "Air on the G string."

Chadwick, George Whitefield

(b. Lowell, Mass., November 13, 1854; d. Boston, April 4, 1931)

AMERICAN COMPOSER. His preliminary studies took place in Boston. After a year teaching music at a small midwestern college he went to Germany to study composition first with Carl Reinecke at the Leipzig Conservatory (1877–78) and subsequently with Joseph Rheinberger in Munich (1879), almost becoming a pupil of César Franck in between. He returned to Boston in 1880 as organist of the South Congregational Church and in 1882 joined the faculty of the New England Conservatory, becoming its director in 1897.

In his heyday, around the turn of the last century, Chadwick was acknowledged both in the United States and abroad as one of America's most capable composers. His output covered a broad range of genres including opera and operetta; he also composed five string quartets and a piano quintet, several choral works, and numerous songs. But his most important achievements by far were in the orchestral realm: three symphonies, a symphony-like set of four *Symphonic Sketches* ("Jubilee," "Noël," "Hobgoblin," and "A Vagrom Ballad"; 1895–1904),

George Chadwick, ca. 1895

the concert overture *Melpomene* (1887), and the symphonic ballad *Tam O'Shanter* (1915). With their German-accented idiom and full-blown late-Romantic stylistic trappings—informed by a feeling for colonial psalmody and spiked by a sense of humor—these works exemplified in a distinguished way the efforts of American composers of Chadwick's generation to join the European mainstream.

RECOMMENDED RECORDINGS

ORCHESTRAL WORKS (INCLUDING *MELPOMENE* AND *TAM O'SHANTER*): JÄRVI AND DETROIT SYMPHONY ORCHESTRA (CHANDOS).

SYMPHONIC SKETCHES: HANSON AND EASTMAN-ROCHESTER ORCHESTRA (MERCURY).

Chailly, Riccardo

(b. Milan, February 20, 1953)

ITALIAN CONDUCTOR, son of composer Luciano Chailly (1920–2002). He studied composition with his father and conducting with Piero Guarino and Franco Ferrara, and made his American debut in 1974 conducting Puccini's *Madama Butterfly* at the Lyric Opera of Chicago. From 1982 to 1988 he was conductor of the Berlin Radio Symphony Orchestra, serving concurrently as principal guest conductor of the London Philharmonic (1982–85) and music director of Teatro Comunale di Bologna (1986–93). In 1988, at the age of 35, he was named chief conductor of the Royal Concertgebouw Orchestra of Amsterdam, and in September 2005 he succeeded Herbert Blomstedt as music director of the Leipzig Gewandhaus Orchestra. Admired for his zestful performing style and adventurous programming, Chailly is a passionate interpreter of certain 20th-century repertoire, particularly post–*Rite of Spring* orchestral blockbusters. In canonic works from earlier in the century (such as Debussy's *La mer* or the Mahler symphonies), he at times suffers from an inability to see the forest for the trees, while in Romantic music he communicates only superficial enthusiasm. His recordings of Messiaen's *Turangalîla-symphonie* and the complete orchestral works of Varèse, both with the Royal Concertgebouw Orchestra, are exemplary; so is the offbeat Shostakovich "Jazz Album" he and the RCO cut in 1993, which has sold more than 200,000 copies to date.

RECOMMENDED RECORDINGS

MESSIAEN, *TURANGALÎLA-SYMPHONIE*; ROYAL CONCERTGEBOUW ORCHESTRA (DECCA).

ROSSINI, *LA CENERENTOLA*: BARTOLI, MATTEUZZI, DARA; TEATRO COMMUNALE DI BOLOGNA (DECCA).

ROSSINI, OVERTURES: NATIONAL PHILHARMONIC ORCHESTRA (DECCA).

SHOSTAKOVICH, *JAZZ ALBUM*; ROYAL CONCERTGEBOUW ORCHESTRA (DECCA).

VARÈSE, ORCHESTRAL WORKS (COMPLETE): ROYAL CONCERTGEBOUW ORCHESTRA (DECCA).

Chaliapin, Fyodor

(b. Kazan, February 13, 1873; d. Paris, April 12, 1938)

RUSSIAN BASS. As a youth he led a vagabond existence, singing in the chorus of a traveling Russian opera company from the age of 14. Upon reaching Tiflis (now Tbilisi, Georgia) in 1892, he met the singing teacher Dmitry Usatov, who recognized his extraordinary potential and gave him lessons for free. In 1894 he sang with a summer opera company in St. Petersburg and was quickly engaged for the regular season by the Imperial Opera at the Mariinsky Theater there. In 1896 he performed in Moscow, and from 1899 to 1914 was a member of that city's Bolshoi Opera. He made his international debut at La Scala as Boito's Mefistofele in 1901, and in 1907 sang the same role in his debut at the Metropolitan Opera, followed later in the season by Leporello in Mozart's *Don Giovanni* and Méphistophélès in Gounod's *Faust*. He returned to the Met in 1921 in the title role of Mussorgsky's *Boris Godunov,* and remained on the company's roster through the 1929 season. Although honored as a Peoples' Artist by the Soviet authorities, he was no friend of the Reds; he left the Soviet Union in 1921 and settled in Paris, where he resided for the rest of his life.

A perfectionist who despised mediocrity in all its forms, Chaliapin was regarded as the greatest singing actor of his day. He possessed a voice of great dramatic intensity—deep and lustrous with a baritonal glint—which together with his powerful physique and larger-than-life personality made him a vivid interpreter of such roles as Mefistofele and Philip II in Verdi's *Don Carlo,* as well as the definitive Boris of his era.

Chaliapin the matinee idol, and as Massenet's Don Quixote, a role written for him in 1910

RECOMMENDED RECORDING

CHALIAPIN: A VOCAL PORTRAIT (1907–1936) (NAXOS)

chamber music Music meant to be played in intimate surroundings, such as rooms or small auditoriums, rather than in a church, theater, or large public space. As a genre chamber music embraces everything from simple pieces for solo instruments to multimovement compositions for ensembles of a dozen or more, easily forming the largest and most diverse segment of the repertoire. The chamber inventory includes such standard complements as the instrumental sonata (with or without keyboard accompaniment), the piano trio, and the string quartet and quintet, as well as all the ad hoc combinations of instruments and voices that have struck composers' fancies over the years.

Nearly every major composer from the 17th century to the beginning of the 19th produced some chamber music. Many of the most important contributions to the repertoire—the works of Bach and Haydn are the first that come to mind—were the result of princely patronage. Bach composed the greater part of his instrumental chamber music while at the courts of Weimar and Cöthen, and Haydn turned out a vast quantity of string quartets, divertimentos, and other pieces during his years of service to the Esterházys.

Throughout the 17th and 18th centuries hundreds of other composers held court appointments and composed similarly serviceable music for a variety of courtly occasions. But as the 18th century gave way to the 19th, composers wrote less for the privileged few, more for the music-loving multitude. Then as now, music was the most stimulating form of live entertainment, and the enthusiasm of the bourgeois public for opera and symphonic music carried over to chamber music as well. Mozart and Beethoven, who preferred patronage when they could get it, adjusted to the changing reality and aimed the bulk of their chamber music at the paying public. For Mozart in particular, this meant composing a good deal of chamber music for amateurs.

Mozart refined and improved on Haydn's string quartet style in his six famous essays dedicated to the elder master, but he preferred the rich texture and more complex part writing possible in the quintet medium, and it was here that he

achieved his greatest successes in the field of chamber music. Beethoven, on the other hand, chose to stretch the string quartet toward symphonic dimensions, while enriching its expressive context through the use of parody and a breathtaking range of textures and topical devices.

As with the symphony, so in chamber music; composers of the Romantic era and in the 20th century had to acknowledge Haydn's invention, Mozart's perfection, and Beethoven's vastness in one way or another, and most did so by trying not to follow too closely in any one set of footsteps. Schubert, Mendelssohn, and Schumann were most successful when they applied themselves to unusual instrumental combinations. Brahms, too, while dutifully composing the string quartets and piano trios that were expected of Beethoven's successor, found other forms, particularly the instrumental sonata, more congenial. With Debussy, Ravel, and Bartók, the quest for new sounds and formal approaches reinvigorated the string quartet and carried over to works for other chamber complements as well.

Chance, Michael *See box on pages 155–57.*

chanson (Fr., "song") A French polyphonic song of the mid-14th through late 16th century. The genre's early development was advanced by the polished and imaginative settings of Machaut. Important contributions were subsequently made by Du Fay, Ockeghem, Binchois (ca. 1400–60), Antoine Busnois (ca. 1430–92), and Josquin. Chanson settings up to about 1450 tended to be concise, syllabic, and strongly rhythmic; the settings composed in the second half of the 15th century exhibit greater melodic and rhythmic freedom. In the latter part of the 15th century and early years of the 16th, chansons provided the raw material for many mass settings. During the 16th century, the chanson evolved away from fixed poetic forms—rondeaux, ballades, and virelais—toward more varied and free-wheeling verse forms. Settings by the likes of Clément Janequin (ca. 1485–1558) ◉, Claudin de Sermisy (ca. 1490–1562), Claude le Jeune (ca. 1530–1600), and Lassus reflect a profusion of styles; some make use of techniques borrowed from the madrigal and are highly descriptive, while others preserve the directness of expression and rhythmic simplicity that had long been a characteristic of the genre.

RECOMMENDED RECORDING

"FRICASÉE PARISIENNE": VISSE AND ENSEMBLE CLÉMENT JANEQUIN (HARMONIA MUNDI).

chanterelle The highest string on a lute, or on any instrument in the violin or lute family.

Chanticleer *See box on pages 934–36.*

Chausson, Ernest

(b. Paris, January 20, 1855; d. Limay, June 10, 1899)

FRENCH COMPOSER. He grew up in privileged surroundings and was exposed to music and art from an early age. Bowing to his father's wishes, he studied law, receiving a doctorate and gaining admission to the bar in 1877, but never practicing. His family's wealth left him free to pursue his interest in music. In 1879 he enrolled in Jules Massenet's course in orchestration at the Paris Conservatoire; while there he also audited César Franck's organ class. Like many of his generation he came to be strongly influenced by the music of Wagner: He traveled to Munich in 1879 and again in 1880 to hear *Der fliegende Holländer*, the *Ring*, and *Tristan und Isolde*, and made pilgrimages to Bayreuth in 1882 and 1883 to hear the first performances of *Parsifal*. In the 1890s he became a close friend of Claude Debussy, with whom he shared a love of literature and painting as well as a highly refined musical aesthetic. He might well have joined Debussy in the forefront of early 20th-century modernism, but his life was cut short by a freakish accident: While on holiday, he died of injuries suffered when he rode his bicycle into a wall. His finest works include the Piano Trio in G minor (1881), the *Poème de l'amour et de la mer* (*Poem of Love and the Sea*; 1882–90) for mezzo-soprano and orchestra, the Symphony in B-flat (1889–90), the *Poème* (1896) for violin and orchestra, and the symphonic poem *Soir de fête* (1897–98). He also composed a number of lovely songs and an ambitious opera, *Le roi Arthus* (1886–95), which was posthumously premiered in 1903.

RECOMMENDED RECORDINGS

PIANO TRIO IN G MINOR: BEAUX ARTS TRIO (PHILIPS).

POÈME: CHUNG; DUTOIT AND ROYAL PHILHARMONIC ORCHESTRA (DECCA).

SYMPHONY IN B-FLAT AND *SOIR DE FÊTE*: TORTELIER AND BBC PHILHARMONIC ORCHESTRA (CHANDOS).

Ernest Chausson with his wife at the piano

Chávez, Carlos

(b. Mexico City, June 13, 1899; d. Mexico City, August 2, 1978)

MEXICAN COMPOSER, CONDUCTOR, AND ADMINISTRATOR. He received lessons in piano and theory as a youth but was largely self-taught in composition; during his youth he also developed what would become a lifelong interest in Mexican Indian culture. In 1921 he made his debut as a composer and received his first official commission from the newly established democratic Mexican government. He traveled to Europe in 1922 and made the first of many extended visits to the United States in 1923. In 1928 he was chosen as conductor of the newly formed Mexico Symphony Orchestra; later that year he was appointed director of the National Conservatory in Mexico City. From 1947 to 1952 he served as director general of the National Institute of Fine Arts.

Carlos Chávez, dean of Mexican composers

If the composer Silvestre Revueltas was the "bad boy" of Mexican music, Chávez was the "good boy"—cosmopolitan, politically connected, a leading figure in the formation and guidance of many of his country's most important cultural organizations. Despite the institutional demands on his time, he was a prolific composer; his oeuvre includes seven numbered symphonies, concertos for violin and piano, a large output of chamber pieces, and several ballets. Much of Chávez's music is folkloric in character, similar to that of Copland in its directness, simplicity of line, and spare textures. His Symphony No. 2, *Sinfonía india* (1935–36), is one of his few works that makes use of actual Indian themes. Its blend of modernism and primitivism is typical of the composer's approach, as is the coloristic scoring for percussion and the use of shifting meter and other rhythmic devices to enliven the proceedings. The material is pretty thin, however, and there's a lot of repetition and window dressing; that, too, is typical of Chávez's style.

RECOMMENDED RECORDING

SYMPHONY NO. 2: BERNSTEIN AND NEW YORK PHILHARMONIC (SONY).

Cherubini, Luigi

(b. Florence, September 8, 1760; d. Paris, March 15, 1842)

FRENCH COMPOSER OF ITALIAN BIRTH. He was a central figure in French musical life from the 1790s until his death; during the last twenty years of his life, he wielded considerable influence as the administrator of the Paris Conservatoire, France's most prestigious musical institution. He studied music with his father, a harpsichordist, and later with Giuseppe Sarti in Bologna and Milan. His earliest compositions were mainly sacred pieces; in 1779 he first tried his hand at opera, and quickly became hooked. In a little less than ten years he penned a dozen Italian operas, most of them in the genre of opera seria. In the summer of 1785 he visited Paris for the first time, securing an introduction to Marie Antoinette from his countryman, the court musician Giovanni Battista Viotti (1755–1824). He soon took up residence in Paris and quickly established himself as one of the French capital's major musical figures. In 1789, with Viotti's help, he became music director of an Italian opera company, the Théâtre de Monsieur, whose repertoire included the works of Giovanni Paisiello (1740–1816) and Domenico Cimarosa (1749–1801) among others; amid the tumult of the Revolution, the company was reconstituted in 1791, and Cherubini signed a long-term contract engaging his services as composer. The result was a string of French-language operas beginning with *Lodoïska,* premiered in 1791, and culminating in the works that are regarded as his masterpieces, *Medée* (1797) and *Les deux journées* (1800). During the Napoleonic years, Cherubini remained an honored figure in spite of his royalist leanings; from the restoration of the Bourbon monarchy in 1814 until the Revolution of 1830, he served as superintendent of the Chapelle Royale, and in that capacity composed a number of sacred works, including the formidable Requiem in C minor (1816). The most important composition of his final years was a second Requiem, in D minor, completed in 1836 and intended for his own funeral. In 1841, a year before his death, he became the first musician ever designated a commander of the Légion d'Honneur.

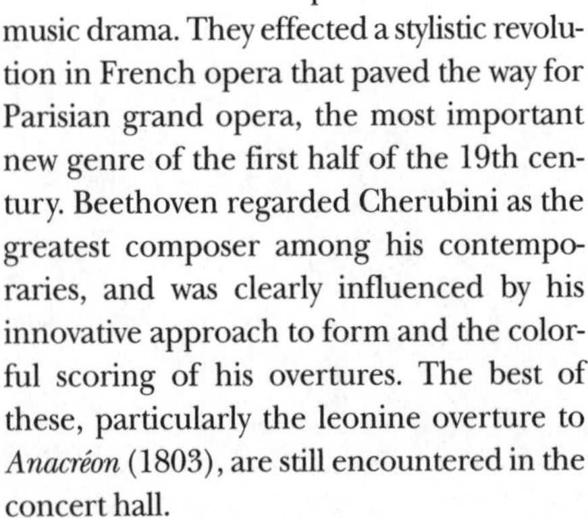

Luigi Cherubini in 1832

Although they have mostly vanished from the stage, Cherubini's French-language operas were seminal works in the development of Romantic music drama. They effected a stylistic revolution in French opera that paved the way for Parisian grand opera, the most important new genre of the first half of the 19th century. Beethoven regarded Cherubini as the greatest composer among his contemporaries, and was clearly influenced by his innovative approach to form and the colorful scoring of his overtures. The best of these, particularly the leonine overture to *Anacréon* (1803), are still encountered in the concert hall.

RECOMMENDED RECORDINGS

Anacréon Overture: Karajan and Berlin Philharmonic (EMI).

Medée (sung in Italian): Callas, Scotto, Pirazzini; Serafin and La Scala Orchestra (EMI).

Requiem in C minor: Muti and Philharmonia Orchestra (EMI).

Chicago Symphony Orchestra American orchestra founded in 1891. Over the years its music directors, beginning with the German-born Theodore Thomas and including Frederick Stock, Fritz Reiner, Georg Solti, and Daniel Barenboim, have cultivated a Central European style of playing and sound. At the time the orchestra was established (an effort spearheaded by Chicago businessman Norman Fay), Thomas was the leading conductor in America and a recognized musical pioneer. He presided over the orchestra's inaugural concerts on October 16 and 17, 1891, and served as music director for 13 years, until his death in 1905, just three weeks after the dedication of Orchestra Hall, the CSO's permanent home. Thomas's successor was Frederick Stock, who began his career in the orchestra's viola section in 1895 and became its assistant conductor four years later. A skillful musician and respected leader, Stock built the ensemble into one of America's finest during his 37-year tenure (1905–42)—though in comparison with the exploits of Stokowski in Philadelphia, Koussevitzky in Boston, and Toscanini in New York, his achievements went largely unheralded.

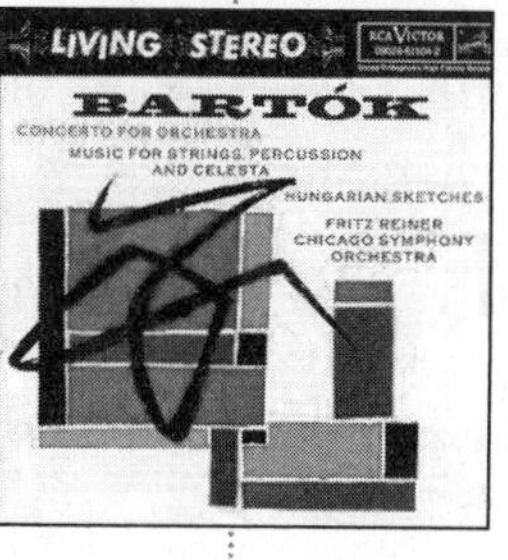

During the decade following Stock's death, the orchestra drifted through the regimes of Désiré Defauw (1943–47), Artur Rodzinski (1947–48), and Rafael Kubelík (1950–53) with no clear direction. The appointment of Fritz Reiner as music director in 1953 brought quite a sense of direction, lighting a veritable fire under the orchestra. A legendary taskmaster, Reiner exacted playing of consistently virtuoso caliber from his forces and introduced a hard core of principal players to the ranks who helped keep the orchestra's standards at the highest level for the next 50 years. Under Reiner's baton the CSO made what have become legendary recordings of the music of Beethoven, Rossini, Brahms, Tchaikovsky, Rachmaninov, Bartók, Prokofiev, and, most of all, Richard Strauss. Like many driven and demanding artists, Reiner was also difficult, and a series of heart attacks he suffered in 1960–61 hastened the decision by the orchestra's board to ease him out of his post after 1962. His replacement, the distinguished French conductor Jean Martinon, served as music director for five seasons (1963–68), making glorious recordings of the music of Ravel, Roussel, Nielsen, Bartók, Hindemith, Varèse, and Frank Martin, but never really emerging from Reiner's shadow.

Georg Solti, the orchestra's eighth music director, served from 1969 to 1991; following his retirement, he held the title of music director laureate and returned to conduct the orchestra for several weeks each season until his death in 1997. "Solti and the Chicago" proved to be one of the most acclaimed musical partnerships of the second half of the 20th century, regularly wowing New York's musical press with their performances at Carnegie Hall and laying down the law with a remarkable string of award-winning recordings. Solti took the orchestra on its first international tour in 1971, and powered it to a position of preeminence among America's orchestras. His dynamic, high-voltage approach did not suit all music equally well, nor did it please all of the critics, but he kept the CSO on its toes.

The arrival of Daniel Barenboim in 1991 was followed by a rocky period lasting several years during which the Chicagoans adjusted to their new maestro's broader, more pliant manner of music making. With its edges somewhat softened, the ensemble has taken on a darker and more burnished sound overall. Today's Chicago Symphony exhibits an esprit de corps and internal discipline that is shared by only a handful of orchestras in the world, and enjoys facilities, resources, and a depth of tradition that are the envy of all its rust-belt rivals. Every section is strong, and the brass—led for years by the solo trumpet of Adolph Herseth, a legend among American instrumentalists—remains unsurpassed. It still produces what is probably the weightiest sonority of any orchestra in the world, and it continues to attract an impressive lineup of soloists and guest conductors each season. During the past 50 years, the CSO has enjoyed fruitful associations with Carlo Maria Giulini, culminating in his being named principal guest conductor in 1969 (a post he held through 1972); with Claudio Abbado, principal guest conductor from 1982 to 1985; and most recently with Pierre Boulez, principal guest conductor since 1995.

In 1916 the CSO became the first American orchestra to record under its regular conductor, and its more than 900 recordings have earned numerous international awards and a total of 54 Grammys.

RECOMMENDED RECORDINGS

Bartók, *Concerto for Orchestra, Music for Strings, Percussion, and Celesta*: Reiner (RCA).

Mahler, Symphony No. 1: Boulez (DG).

Mahler, Symphony No. 8: Solti (Decca).

Ravel, *Daphnis et Chloé* Suite No. 2 (with other works): Martinon (RCA).

Strauss, *Ein Heldenleben, Also Sprach Zarathustra*: Reiner (RCA).

Varèse, *Arcana* (with other works): Martinon (RCA).

Wagner, overtures and preludes: Barenboim (Teldec).

Chichester Psalms **Sacred work by Leonard Bernstein for mixed choir, boy soloist, and orchestra.** It was commissioned by the Very Reverend Walter Hussey, dean of Chichester's 11th-century cathedral, for the annual summer festival sponsored by the cathedrals of Chichester, Winchester, and Salisbury. Bernstein conducted the premiere on July 15, 1965, with the New York Philharmonic, Camerata Singers, and alto John Bogart.

Asked to compose a devotional work based on the Psalms, Bernstein chose six of his favorites and set them in Hebrew. The psalms are grouped in pairs, so that the work is divided into three parts. The scoring calls for strings and brass, along with an enlarged percussion section and two harps. In the second psalm, Bernstein uses the unusual and very energetic meter of $\frac{7}{4}$ throughout ◉; the fifth is in an even more unusual meter, $\frac{10}{4}$, here treated in a wonderfully flowing manner. There is an important part for boy alto in the setting of the famous Twenty-third Psalm, in which the soloist represents the shepherd boy David.

RECOMMENDED RECORDING

Bogart; Bernstein and New York Philharmonic (Sony).

Choir of King's College, Cambridge *See box on pages 934–36.*

Chopin, Frédéric François [Fryderyk Franciszek]

(b. Żelazowa Wola, March 1, 1810; d. Paris, October 17, 1849)

POLISH-BORN PIANIST AND COMPOSER of matchless genius in the realm of keyboard music. As a pianist his talents were beyond emulation and had an impact on other musicians entirely out of proportion to the number of concerts he gave—only 30 public performances in 30 years of concertizing. No one before or since has contributed as many significant works to the piano's repertoire, or come closer to capturing its soul.

Chopin's mother was Polish, his father a Frenchman who had come to Poland as a young man and held jobs as a bookkeeper and tutor before marrying and settling in Warsaw. Young Frédéric studied piano with Wojciech Żywny and harmony and counterpoint with Józef Elsner, gave his first concert when he was eight, and rather quickly outdistanced his teachers. His name became known outside of Poland when his Variations, Op. 2, for piano and orchestra on Mozart's "Là ci darem la mano"—written when he was 17—were published in 1830, prompting Robert Schumann's famous accolade in the *Allgemeine musikalische Zeitung,* "Hats off, gentlemen! A genius!" In the spring and autumn of 1830 Chopin treated the Warsaw audience to a pair of newly composed, marvelously poetic piano concertos. Seeking to expand his horizons, he left Poland for Vienna in November 1830, and after eight months there, headed for Paris. He would never again return to his native country, but Poland's loss would be Paris's gain.

By the 1830s, Paris had become the undisputed center of European culture—a hotbed of new thinking in the arts and letters and the focal point of Romanticism in music. After a sensational debut at the Salle Pleyel on February 26, 1832, with Franz Liszt, Felix Mendelssohn, and Luigi Cherubini among those in the audience, Chopin, three days shy of his 22nd birthday, took his place as one of the celebrities of the French capital. He found himself in such demand as a teacher that he was able to make a comfortable living, and he hobnobbed with the great artists of the day, forming particularly close friendships with Eugène Delacroix, who would paint a splendid portrait of him in 1838, and Liszt. Chopin's works from his first years in Paris include the Nocturnes of Opp. 9 and 15 (1830–32), the 12 *Études,* Op. 10 (1830–32), dedicated to Liszt ◉, the 12 *Études,* Op. 25 (1835–37), dedicated to Liszt's mistress ◉, the Comtesse Marie d'Agoult, the Scherzo in B-flat minor, Op. 31 (1837), the Sonata in B-flat minor, Op. 35 (1837), and the G minor Ballade, Op. 23. In 1836 Chopin became engaged to Maria Wodzińska, but the engagement was broken off by her family the following year.

Chopin's last piano; above, a 19th-century lithograph of the composer

Frédéric Chopin plays at the salon of his patron Prince Radziwill, in 1829.

Chopin's art reached a new plateau in the late 1830s as a result of his involvement with the writer Aurore Dudevant, six years his senior, who in 1832 had taken to calling herself George Sand. Some of his greatest works emerged as a result of the emotional contentment he felt in the early days of their nine-year liaison. They spent the winter of 1838–39 together on Majorca, living in adjacent rooms in an abandoned Carthusian monastery. Chopin endured his first major bout of tuberculosis, but though seriously ill managed to complete the 24 *Préludes,* Op. 28 (1838–39). During the 1840s, in spite of emotional ups and downs and recurrent illness, he produced a remarkable body of compositions that included the Ballades in A-flat, Op. 47, and F minor, Op. 52, the Mazurkas of Opp. 50, 56, 59, 63, and 67, the A-flat major Polonaise, Op. 53, the Nocturnes of Opp. 48, 55, and 62, and the Sonata in B minor, Op. 58 (1844). The best of these works—the B minor Sonata, the Op. 55 Nocturnes, and the Op. 56 Mazurkas—are characterized by remarkable refinement and complexity, along with a newly rich sense of ambivalence. The opening movement of the sonata finds Chopin at the summit of inspiration, weaving turbulence and Romantic yearning into a beautifully seamless expression.

The situation with George Sand began to deteriorate in 1843, and in 1847 the break came. By then Chopin was gravely ill; seeking escape, he left Paris in April 1848 for an extended sojourn in England and Scotland, from which he returned, exhausted, in November. He composed virtually nothing in the final year of his life.

Chopin was the first composer of genius to devote himself uniquely to the piano—every one of his works was written for it either as solo instrument, or in combination with other instruments. The majority of his solo pieces are in shorter forms, and improvisatory by nature. These include 20 nocturnes, 25 preludes, 17 waltzes, 15 polonaises, 58 mazurkas, and 27 etudes. In these works, especially the nocturnes, preludes, and mazurkas, the emotions are fleeting, and precious because of that. Chopin also achieved success in larger forms, including the scherzo, a form he reinvented; the ballade, a genre he invented; and the sonata. The four Ballades and the Sonatas in B-flat minor and B minor are among his greatest creations, combining passionate drama and lyrical tenderness in a memorable way.

In his remarkably advanced treatment of harmony and rhythm Chopin banished the ordinary from his music and opened the door to an emotional ambiguity that continues to intrigue listeners, one whose communication requires subtleties of execution that generations of pianists have labored devotedly to achieve. The luminous textures and haunting melodies he used to express his thoughts added to the piano's sound and range of color shadings that no one before him had imagined were there, but that all who have followed recognize as his. The same is true of the harmonic question marks one finds throughout his music—the equivalent of a look of gentle longing. He created a slimmer oeuvre than any of his important contemporaries, but every piece he produced was a pearl.

RECOMMENDED RECORDINGS

BALLADES, SCHERZOS, NOCTURNES, POLONAISES, MAZURKAS, SONATAS NOS. 2 AND 3: RUBINSTEIN (RCA).

ÉTUDES: POLLINI (DG).

PIANO CONCERTOS NOS. 1 AND 2: ZIMERMAN; GIULINI AND LOS ANGELES PHILHARMONIC ORCHESTRA (DG).

WALTZES: LIPATTI (EMI).

chord Three or more tones (i.e., notes with different pitches) played simultaneously.

chorus [1] A group of singers that performs as a body. The term commonly implies a large number of singers, but is valid for any group in which two or more individuals sing the same part. [2] A work or section of a work written for such a group (e.g., the "Hallelujah!" chorus from Handel's *Messiah*).

Christie, William

(b. Buffalo, December 19, 1944)

AMERICAN CONDUCTOR. He took a B.A. in art history at Harvard before attending Yale School of Music, where he studied harpsichord and musicology. In 1971, after a brief stint teaching at Dartmouth, he moved to Paris, working as a harpsichordist with various early music ensembles. He founded Les Arts Florissants, a group specializing in Baroque vocal music, in 1979; at its helm he has presided over brilliant, standard-setting productions of works by Lully, Rameau, Purcell, and Marc-Antoine Charpentier (ca. 1645–1704), among others.

RECOMMENDED RECORDINGS

LULLY, *ATYS*: DE MEY, MELLON, LAURENS; LES ARTS FLORISSANTS (ERATO).

MOZART, *DIE ZAUBERFLÖTE*: MANNION, DESSAY, BLOCHWITZ, SCHARINGER; LES ARTS FLORISSANTS (ERATO).

PURCELL, *KING ARTHUR*: GENS, MCFADDEN, PADMORE, BEST; LES ARTS FLORISSANTS (ERATO).

***Christmas* Oratorio** SACRED WORK BY J. S. BACH (BWV 248)—actually six separate cantatas composed in 1734 for specific days during the season of Christmas and Epiphany (the first three days of Christmas, the Feast of the Circumcision, the first Sunday in the New Year, and the Feast of Epiphany). At various points in the *Christmas* Oratorio, Bach utilized material from a previously composed church cantata, his *St. Mark* Passion, and three of his secular cantatas, seamlessly integrating it into the new setting. Part I of the *Christmas* Oratorio opens with the chorus "Jauchzet, frohlocket, auf, preiset die Tage," containing some of the most festive and brilliant music Bach ever wrote, while Part II begins with a beautiful pastoral sinfonia in G major depicting the shepherds with their flocks outside Bethlehem.

RECOMMENDED RECORDING

ROLFE JOHNSON, ARGENTA, OTTER; GARDINER AND ENGLISH BAROQUE SOLOISTS (DG).

Christoff, Boris

(b. Plovdiv, May 18, 1914; d. Rome, June 28, 1993)

BULGARIAN BASS. He studied in Rome and Salzburg and made his debut in Italy, as Colline in Puccini's *La bohème,* in 1946. The following season he sang Pimen in Mussorgsky's *Boris Godunov* in Rome and Milan, stepping up to the opera's title role in 1949 at Covent Garden. He made his American debut, as Boris, in 1956 with the San Francisco Opera. In addition to Russian roles, he sang Verdi with great authority, particularly the role of Philip II in *Don Carlo,* and the Wagnerian parts of Hagen, in *Götterdämmerung,* and King Marke, in *Tristan und Isolde.* Like Chaliapin, he was a compelling actor who dominated the stage.

Boris Christoff in a Napoleonic moment

RECOMMENDED RECORDING

SELECTED SCENES AND ARIAS (EMI RÉFERENCES).

chromatic (from Gr. *khroma,* "color") In tonal music, a passage or piece characterized by the use of notes not belonging to the DIATONIC major or minor scale. By introducing notes that are "alien" to a given key, thereby destabilizing it, chromaticism has a tendency to produce a feeling of urgency, poignancy, and unrest. It has been used to this end as an expressive device since the 16th century, when it featured prominently in the madrigals of Carlo Gesualdo, Cipriano de Rore, Luca Marenzio, and others. In the 19th century, Richard Wagner pushed chromaticism to an extreme in works such as *Tristan und Isolde* (1865) and *Parsifal* (1882); the searching chromaticism and pained intensity of the Prelude to Act I of *Tristan* create a feeling of yearning that sets the tone for the rest of the opera. Here and in *Parsifal,* Wagner laid the foundation for ATONALITY and 12-TONE serialism—in which chromatic gestures, deprived of the context of functional harmony, cease to have any convincing expressive effect.

Chung, Kyung-Wha

(b. Seoul, March 26, 1948)

BRITISH VIOLINIST OF KOREAN BIRTH. The most celebrated member of a musical family (her sister Myung-Wha Chung is a cellist, her brother Myung-Whun Chung is a pianist and conductor), she was the first person of Korean birth to achieve international renown as a classical musician. She left Korea at the age of 12 to study with Ivan Galamian at the Juilliard School in New York. After winning the Leventritt competition in 1967 (sharing top honors with Pinchas Zukerman), she entered the professional ranks, appearing as a soloist with many of America's leading orchestras while continuing her studies with Galamian. In 1970 she made her European debut in London, playing the Tchaikovsky concerto at Royal Festival Hall with André Previn and the London Symphony Orchestra. She toured extensively and made numerous recordings during the 1970s and 1980s, but withdrew from the concert platform and the studio for a period of time to have children. Playing about 60 performances a year since the late 1990s, she has enjoyed a successful comeback.

Chung is a musician of unusual sensitivity who is capable of electrifying an audience with her virtuosity but is at her best in music that calls for tenderness, spontaneity, and a certain fragility of feeling. She has an affinity both for the Romantic warhorses and for the big works of the 20th-century repertoire, yet she is also marvelous in Vivaldi. Regardless of the repertoire, her playing is poetic and expressive, characterized by a wonderful, rhapsodic legato, precise intonation, an intense yet slightly attenuated tone, and an exquisite sense of detail. She plays the 1734 "ex-Rode" Guarneri del Gesù.

RECOMMENDED RECORDINGS

Franck, Violin Sonata; Debussy, Sonata; Lupu (Decca).

Mendelssohn, Violin Concerto in E minor; Tchaikovsky, Violin Concerto: Dutoit and Montreal Symphony Orchestra (Decca).

cimbalom Nineteenth-century Hungarian string instrument related to the dulcimer; its strings are struck with spoon-shaped mallets and give off a meaty, rustic-sounding twang. The cimbalom has been used as an orchestral instrument in Kodály's *Háry János* ◉, Bartók's Rhapsody No. 1 for violin and orchestra, and Stravinsky's *Renard*.

Cincinnati Symphony Orchestra Ensemble established in **1895.** It is the fifth oldest orchestra in America. Cincinnati, on the Ohio River in southern Ohio, became a locus of German immigration during the 1840s, and by the middle of the 19th century had emerged as one of the midwest's most important cultural centers. Singing societies sprang up and a choral tradition was born that gave rise to Cincinnati's oldest musical institution, the May Festival Chorus, inaugurated in 1873 under the aegis of Theodore Thomas, who continued as its music director until 1904. Cincinnati's majestic Music Hall was dedicated in 1878, at the third May Festival, and in 1894 the Cincinnati Orchestra Association Company, with a board of 15 women chaired by Mrs. William Howard Taft, was created for the purpose of supporting a professional orchestra. The 48-man orchestra gave nine concerts in its first season under the direction of Frank van der Stucken. Van der Stucken remained the orchestra's director until 1907, when the Orchestra Association disbanded the ensemble in the face of demands by the musicians' union. In 1909 the orchestra was reorganized and Leopold Stokowski was engaged as music director. Stokowski's tenure, while brief (1909–12), put the Cincinnati Symphony on the map, and in subsequent years the orchestra was entrusted to some of the most remarkable musical talents of the modern era, notably the conductors Fritz Reiner (music director from 1922 to 1931) and Thomas Schippers (1970–77). The violinist Eugène Ysaÿe served as music director from 1918 to 1922; other notable music directors have been Eugene Goosens (1931–47) and Max Rudolf (1958–70). Michael Gielen (1980–86), a provocative if not popular figure, was succeeded by Jesús López-Cobos (1986–2001), under whom the orchestra stagnated. In 2001, Paavo Järvi became the orchestra's music director. Through all of its long and distinguished history, the Cincinnati Symphony Orchestra has retained two elements of its tradition: a German heft and a pioneer spirit. It has given the American premieres of works by Debussy, Ravel, and Bartók, among others, and was responsible for the commission and world premiere of one of the most celebrated of all American works, Aaron Copland's *Fanfare for the Common Man* (1942). It has made numerous recordings since its first in 1917; now under contract with Telarc, it is one of the few American orchestras currently recording on a regular basis for a major label.

RECOMMENDED RECORDING

Berlioz, *Symphonie fantastique*: Järvi (Telarc).

"Clair de lune" The third movement of Claude Debussy's *Suite bergamasque*, composed in 1890. The opening measures of this delicate nocturne call for the use of the soft pedal; in them, Debussy employs an attenuated texture of parallel thirds and an almost static oscillation of harmony to suggest the moon's pale, ethereal light. ◉ The reverie intensifies gently, and then the stillness of the opening returns.

RECOMMENDED RECORDINGS

Cliburn (RCA).

Thibaudet (Decca) and Cliburn (RCA).

clarinet Single-reed woodwind instrument with a cylindrical bore and flared bell, made in a variety of sizes. The name is derived from *clarino,* the old term referring to the Baroque high trumpet (early clarinets tended to sound like little versions of that instrument, and to be given trumpet-like parts). Invention of the clarinet is generally credited to the Nuremberg instrument maker Johann Christoph Denner (1655–1707), who appears to have produced a two-keyed instrument around 1700. The body of a standard modern clarinet is in five sections, and is usually made of grenadilla, ebony, or African blackwood. A cane reed is attached to the mouthpiece by means of a metal screw ligature. The keywork is of nickel silver, and is patterned on the Boehm system originally developed in the mid-19th century for the flute.

The clarinet comprises the largest family of all the woodwinds, and its members all share the same fingerings. The principal members of the family are the soprano clarinets in B-flat and in A. These instruments have a usable range of more than three octaves, from E below middle C (sounding D on the B-flat clarinet, C-sharp on the A clarinet) to the G two octaves and a fifth above middle C (sounding F on the B-flat clarinet, E on the A clarinet). The actual range extends another fourth beyond that, but the uppermost notes tend to sound pinched and brittle. The standard clarinet has four main registers with distinctive colorations: The lowest octave is called the "chalumeau," after a 17th-century cousin of the clarinet, and is rich, warm, and vibrant, with a characteristic hint of buzziness; the notes from G above middle C to B-flat are called the "throat" tones, and are somewhat pale in sound; above them, from B-natural to the C two octaves above middle C, is the "clarino" register, the most characteristic part of the instrument's range, where it sounds bright, incisive, suave, and expressive; beyond that lies the "extreme" register. As with coffee, so with the clarinet—a rich, "dark" sound is desirable. The clarinet's cylindrical bore favors the odd-numbered harmonics, which impart warmth and luster to its fundamental tones. The fact that the instrument uses a single reed also gives a player excellent control of soft dynamics—indeed, the softer it gets, the more beautiful a clarinet sounds.

Other members of the clarinet family that are regularly encountered include the sopranino clarinet in E-flat, pitched a fourth higher than the standard B-flat clarinet, and the bass clarinet in B-flat, pitched an octave lower. A few pieces have been written that call for the contrabass clarinet, which is pitched two octaves lower than the standard clarinet and is capable of astonishingly sepulchral tones; they include Schoenberg's *Five Pieces for Orchestra,* Op. 16, and Corigliano's Symphony No. 1 (*Of Rage and Remembrance*). With a tube length of 106 inches, the contrabass clarinet looks like a three-and-a-half-foot-tall chrome-plated paper clip, with a mouthpiece attached.

During the 18th century, the clarinet developed from a curiosity into an essential part of the orchestra and a valued solo instrument. Clarinets began to appear in major ensembles around 1750, but were not considered part of the standard orchestral complement until the 1780s. Mozart first heard clarinets in Mannheim and used them for the first time in his *Paris* Symphony of 1778. Their luminous, poignant sound greatly appealed to him—and since they were frequently employed in serenade groups, he took to using them to accompany arias of love in his operas and to suggest the more tender emotions in his instrumental music. Many composers since Mozart have used the instrument to notable effect in a gentle, ardent solo, as Rachmaninov did in the third movement of his Symphony No. 2 (an extraordinarily long-breathed solo marked *espressivo e cantabile*). ◉ The clarinet can just as easily sound sarcastic or impudent, as it does at the beginning of the second movement of Prokofiev's Symphony No. 5, or elicit a feeling of carefree exuberance (in the same symphony's finale, mm. 28–36). Prokofiev also used the clarinet to personify the slinky elegance of the Cat in *Peter and the Wolf.*

The clarinet's solo repertoire has many highlights, foremost among them Mozart's magnificent Concerto in A, K. 622 (1791), written for Anton Stadler. Other important concerted works include a concertino and two concertos by Weber (all written in 1811), and concertos by Nielsen (1928), Stravinsky (his *Ebony Concerto,* written for Woody Herman, 1945), Copland (written for Benny Goodman, 1947–48), and Finzi (1948–49). The chamber literature for clarinet is also rich. Among its most important works are Mozart's Trio in E-flat, K. 498 (*Kegelstatt*; 1786), for clarinet, piano, and viola, and his Quintet in A, K. 581 (1789), for clarinet and strings; Schubert's song "Der Hirt auf dem Felsen" (1828) for soprano and piano with clarinet obbligato; two sonatas, a trio, and a quintet all composed late in life by Brahms ◉; and Bartók's *Contrasts* (1938), for violin, clarinet, and piano. Important works for clarinet and piano include, in addition to the Brahms sonatas, Debussy's *Rapsodie* (1909–10), Bernstein's Sonata (1941–42), Finzi's *Five Bagatelles,* Op. 23 (1941–43), and Poulenc's Sonata (1962).

Woody Herman

classical Term used to denote "longhair" or serious art music of any period, as distinct from popular music.

Classical (from Lat. *classicus,* "of the highest [social] rank") Period in Western music beginning around 1750 and extending into the early 19th century. What began as a wildly diverse style found an Italianate "middle" ground by the 1760s, displayed in the mature idioms of Haydn and Mozart. Antecedents of that style can be found in the music of Vivaldi, Sammartini, Pergolesi, and other Italian composers of the early 18th century, as well as in the *EMPFINDSAMER STIL* of C. P. E. Bach and other German composers of his time. Various dates have been proposed for the end of the Classical period—1820, 1825, 1830—but rather than a clear jump from Classicism to Romanticism, what occurred between 1800 and 1830 was a gradual transformation of rhetoric and technique along a stylistic continuum.

The notion endures that the music of the Classical period is indeed "of the highest." But the old definition of musical Classicism that relies on a complex of attributes borrowed from academic characterizations of Greek art—refinement and perfection, a balance between form and content, proportion, and a lack of irregularity—is clichéd and misleading. In fact, the music of the Classical era is remarkably vibrant and innovative, highly dramatic, often speculative, even daring—and it was designed to allow for a measure of volatility as well as a balance of diverse elements. Dynamics ranged more widely than in the Baroque, and thematic interplay (where melodies of contrasting character were pitted against one another, particularly in the dramatic interplay of SONATA FORM, which was codified in this age) superseded the generally sectional approach of the Baroque. A single prevailing affect was abandoned for a wider scope, and composers used a free play of styles and topics, along with increasingly complicated long-range harmonic schemes—as opposed to the stricter forms and contrapuntal logic of the Baroque—to guide their ever-lengthening musical works.

Some of the most important instrumental genres were developed during the Classical period, including the SYMPHONY and the STRING QUARTET. Meanwhile, the solo CONCERTO and numerous vocal genres—particularly OPERA, born in the Baroque—underwent structural and stylistic refinements. Characteristic of the instrumental genres were a new type of goal-directed harmony and a new process of argument, both made possible by the widespread use of key-area forms and the genres' expanding emotional scopes. A symphony by Haydn or Mozart could encompass the agitation of the STURM UND DRANG style on the one hand and pastoral sweetness on the other; indeed, references to several styles might be found in the same movement, often within a few bars of one another. Wind and string timbres blended to make new sounds. This expansion of sonic horizons, combined with the growing intensity of expression that Mozart and Beethoven used in their music, set the stage for Romanticism.

In addition to Haydn, Mozart, and Beethoven—the three composers whose music epitomized the Classical style—the era's other important figures included the Italians Giovanni Paisiello (1740–1816), Domenico Cimarosa (1749–1801), Antonio Salieri, and Luigi Boccherini; the Bohemians Christoph Willibald Gluck (a transitional figure between the Baroque and the Classical), Josef Mysliveček (1737–81), and Antoine Reicha; the Austrians Johann Nepomuk Hummel and Carl Ditters von Dittersdorf; the Spaniard Juan Crisóstomo de Arriaga (1806–26); Denmark's Friedrich Kuhlau (1786–1832); and Sweden's Joseph Martin Kraus (1756–92). *See also* GALANT.

***Classical* Symphony** SYMPHONY BY SERGEY PROKOFIEV, completed in 1917 and premiered in Leningrad, with the composer conducting, on April 21, 1918. The work was so named because it is intentionally "Classical" in spirit and layout, despite being modern in terms of its phraseology, instrumentation, and harmonic language.

RECOMMENDED RECORDING

KARAJAN AND BERLIN PHILHARMONIC (DG).

clavichord Keyboard instrument in use from the early 15th century through the mid-18th century, prized for its remarkably gentle and expressive sound. The mechanism of a clavichord is elegantly simple compared with that of a harpsichord or piano: When a key is depressed a brass blade at the back of the key, called a tangent, contacts a pair of strings, causing them to vibrate; the tangent remains in contact with the strings until the key is released, allowing the player to influence the sound by touch, even create a delicate vibrato. The instant the key is released, the

Clavichord

strings are damped by strips of cloth that lace between them. The clavichord was par excellence a "private" instrument, meant to be played for one's own pleasure. Its intimate sound, almost inaudible in any space larger than a drawing room, has a fragile beauty that is difficult to describe but resembles a cross between a harmonica and a long-toothed comb.

clavier (Ger.) Generic word for a keyboard instrument, usually referring to a HARPSICHORD or PIANO.

clef (Fr., "key") A symbol placed on a musical staff indicating where a specific note lies on that staff, used as a reference point to facilitate the location of pitches on all the staff's lines and spaces. The first clefs, which appeared in the 11th century, were simply the written letter F or C , placed on the appropriate line of the staff (then only 4 lines) to keep the musician oriented. Common practice through the Renaissance and even into the Baroque period was to change the placement of the clef as needed, in order to keep all the notes on the staff and avoid drawing ledger lines (additional lines above or below the staff which wasted precious ink). Over time, the different letters evolved into the more stylized signs known today.

Of these, the most commonly encountered clefs are the G clef, also called the treble clef, and the F clef, also called the bass clef. The "belly" of the treble clef circles the second line of the staff, indicating that this is the G above middle C. The "eye" of the bass clef is set on the fourth line of the staff, marking this as the F below middle C. Also in common use is the C clef, which indicates middle C and is movable; when the "brace" of the C clef is centered on the middle line of the staff, it is known as an alto clef, and when set on the fourth line as a tenor clef. In rare cases, one encounters the C clef on the bottom line of the staff (where it is called a soprano clef) or the second (a mezzo-soprano clef). The tenor clef is regularly used by the trombone, and can be presed into service for high notes for the cello and bassoon. The viola uses the alto clef normally, and for high notes, the treble clef.

Clementi, Muzio

(b. Rome, January 23, 1752; d. Evesham, March 10, 1832)

ENGLISH KEYBOARDIST, COMPOSER, PUBLISHER, AND BUSINESSMAN OF ITALIAN BIRTH. He studied music as a child and became organist at the Roman church of San Lorenzo in Damaso when he was 13. The following year, he was taken to England as an indentured servant by Peter Beckford, at whose country estate he practiced and studied for the next seven years. In the winter of 1774–75, freed from his obligations, Clementi moved to London, where he performed on the harpsichord and worked as a conductor—leading ensembles from the keyboard—at the King's Theatre in Haymarket. His six keyboard sonatas, Op. 2, were published in 1779, followed in 1779–80 by two more sets of accompanied sonatas and keyboard duets. In 1780 Clementi set out on a tour of the continent, performing in Paris and, at the invitation of Joseph II, engaging in a keyboard "duel" with Mozart in Vienna on December 24, 1781. During five years of wandering in Europe he composed upward of 25 sonatas, including some of his best. He returned to London in 1785 and stayed put—occupied mainly with the business of music publishing and piano manufacturing.

In the course of several visits to Vienna, he arranged to become Beethoven's publisher. Returning to London in 1810, he settled into a life of prosperity and domestic contentment, marrying at the age of 59 and becoming a director of the Philharmonic Society upon its founding in 1813. He continued to appear as a conductor, often leading his own symphonies from the keyboard, until 1824. His *Gradus ad Parnassum, or The Art of Playing on the Piano Forte,* a compendium of keyboard compositions from all periods of his life, was published in three volumes between 1817 and 1826.

Muzio Clementi, English country gentleman

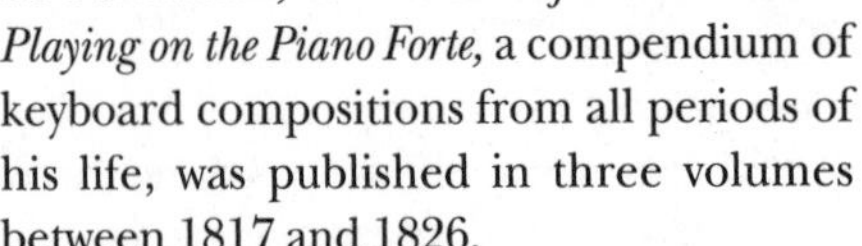

Although his symphonies were eclipsed in his lifetime—first by those of Haydn, then by those of his own client, Beethoven—Clementi was an important figure in the development of a pianistic style of keyboard writing from about 1780, when he started playing the piano in public, until well into the 19th century. His music had a discernible influence on Beethoven, as well as on the generation of Field, Meyerbeer, Hummel, and Jan Dussek. In showing what the piano could do, as well as in his enlightened activities as a publisher, he helped usher in the Romantic era.

RECOMMENDED RECORDINGS

PIANO SONATAS: ALEXANDER-MAX (NAXOS).

SYMPHONIES: BAMERT AND LONDON MOZART PLAYERS (CHANDOS).

Cleveland Orchestra ENSEMBLE FOUNDED IN **1918** thanks to the support and encouragement of music patron Adella Prentiss Hughes, and counted among the world's finest since the days of music director George Szell, who turned it into a paragon of flexibility, brilliance, and discipline during the 1950s and 1960s. The orchestra's first music director, the Russian-born violinist Nikolay Sokolov, served from 1918 until 1933. A highlight of his tenure was the construction and opening of the orchestra's permanent home, Severance Hall (seating 2,000) in Cleveland's University Circle area. Artur Rodzinski was music director from 1933 to 1943; during his decade on the podium, the orchestra presented 15 fully staged opera productions in Severance Hall, including the American premiere of Shostakovich's *Lady Macbeth of Mtsensk District.* Rodzinski was succeeded by Viennese-born Erich Leinsdorf, only 31 at the time of his appointment. Leinsdorf presided over the orchestra in absentia for the first half of his brief tenure (1943–46) while he served in the U.S. military.

In 1946 George Szell was chosen as the Cleveland Orchestra's fourth music director. An accomplished pianist and chamber musician, he honed the Cleveland ensemble to razor sharpness and presided over an illustrious run of recordings for Epic, Columbia Masterworks, and EMI that catapulted the orchestra to international prominence. Szell led the orchestra on its first tours of Europe and the Far East, and presided over annual visits to Carnegie Hall from 1948. Szell's formidable musicianship and paternal authority commanded equal measures of respect and devotion from the Cleveland players, who under his baton achieved what was probably the highest executant standard of any orchestra in the world.

In 1968, as Szell entered the final stages of a battle with cancer, Pierre Boulez was appointed principal guest conductor. Following Szell's death in 1970, Boulez served for two seasons as the orchestra's musical adviser and principal conductor. He and the Cleveland Orchestra seemed to have been made for each other; after 24 years with Szell, the ensemble was as polished and faultless and precise as Boulez himself, and could follow him anywhere he wanted to go. Their early-1970s recordings of Debussy's *Images,* Stravinsky's *The Rite of Spring,* and a sampling of Ravel's showpieces are extremely charismatic.

Lorin Maazel became the orchestra's fifth music director in the fall of 1972. During his decade-long tenure, he maintained the ensemble discipline and virtuoso standards of the Szell era while broadening the orchestra's repertoire and giving it a darker and more voluptuous sound. Under his guidance the orchestra's string of successful recordings continued, mainly with Decca and the Cleveland-based Telarc label.

Following Maazel's departure for Vienna in 1982, the title of music director was conferred on Christoph von Dohnányi, who had previously been in charge of the Hamburg Opera. Despite his tendency toward cool, emotionally uninvolved interpretations of big Romantic scores, the orchestra prospered under his direction. Austrian-born Franz Welser-Möst became music director at the start of the 2002–03 season.

In terms of sonority and stylistic flexibility, the Cleveland Orchestra is very nearly in a league of its own, a crack ensemble with an esprit de corps matched by only a handful of orchestras in the world. Its recordings are the discographic gold standard.

RECOMMENDED RECORDINGS

BEETHOVEN, SYMPHONIES: SZELL (SONY).

DEBUSSY, *IMAGES*: BOULEZ (SONY).

DEBUSSY, *LA MER, PRÉLUDE À L'APRÈS-MIDI D'UN FAUNE*: ASHKENAZY (DECCA).

DVOŘÁK, SYMPHONIES NOS. 7–9 AND *SCHERZO CAPRICCIOSO*: DOHNÁNYI (DECCA).

MAHLER, SYMPHONY NO. 4: RASKIN; SZELL (SONY).

MOZART, PIANO CONCERTOS: CASADESUS; SZELL (SONY).

PROKOFIEV, *ROMEO AND JULIET*: MAAZEL (DECCA).

Cliburn, Van [Harvey Lavan Cliburn Jr.]

(b. Shreveport, La., July 12, 1934)

AMERICAN PIANIST. One of the most accomplished classical musicians America has ever produced, he was catapaulted to fame in 1958 by his victory at the first International Tchaikovsky Competition in Moscow. He began his piano studies at the age of three with his mother, Rildia Bee O'Bryan Cliburn. The family moved to Kilgore, Texas, the following year; there, Cliburn gave his first public performance and quickly attracted attention as a prodigy. He continued to study with his mother into his teens, winning a Texas State Prize in 1947 and appearing with the Houston Symphony Orchestra. He entered the Juilliard School in 1951. In 1954, the year he graduated, he won the Roeder Award and the Leventritt competition, which earned him his first concert date as a soloist with the New York Philharmonic. His big break came in the spring of 1958 when he was invited to compete in the Tchaikovsky Competition. It was the height of the Cold War, a mere six months after the October 1957 launch of *Sputnik* had brought American self-esteem to a post–World War II low; no one dreamed that a non-Russian would prevail. But Cliburn performed on such a superlative level that the jury, which included Sviatoslav Richter, awarded him the gold medal—but only after Emil Gilels, its chairman, placed a late-night call to Soviet premier Nikita Khrushchev to get his approval.

Cliburn's victory in Moscow generated international headlines. Twenty-three years old, tall and lanky, and still pretty much of an ingenue, he seemed an unlikely figure for the role of cultural hero. Yet upon his return to the United States he was honored by the City of New York with a ticker-tape parade, the only one ever held for a classical musician. On May 19, 1958, the same day his picture graced the cover of *Time* magazine, the sandy-haired Texan repeated his Moscow triumph at a sold-out concert in Carnegie Hall, playing Tchaikovsky's First and Rachmaninov's Third Piano Concertos. During the next 20 years, he performed thousands of concerts around the globe, in recital and as a soloist with major orchestras. In 1971 he was the featured soloist at the opening of Wolf Trap Park for the Performing Arts in Virginia, and in 1976 he appeared with André Previn and the New York Philharmonic on the first-ever *Live From Lincoln Center* PBS broadcast. He had a way of reaching out to his audiences through playing that was not only virtuosic, but full of nobility and expressiveness.

Van Cliburn, fresh from triumphs in Moscow and New York

Unwilling or unable to deal with the strain of celebrity and the demands of his career, Cliburn withdrew from the concert stage in 1978. Subsequent "comebacks" in the 1980s and 1990s proved ineffectual, and in the few public appearances he has made since retiring he has shown little of his former command of the piano. That a figure who was one of the giants of keyboard history could have withered so completely remains cruelly disappointing. Today, Cliburn's name is most often associated with the Van Cliburn International Piano Competition, organized in 1962 by friends of the pianist, which takes place every four years in Fort Worth.

Throughout his career Cliburn championed the Romantic repertoire. His calling cards were the concertos of Brahms, Tchaikovsky, Rachmaninov, and MacDowell, which he played in the grand manner and with magnificent weight and beauty of tone. He was also a marvelous interpreter of the music of Chopin. At its best, his playing incomparably combined technical brilliance, emotional warmth, power, sonority, sensitivity, and insight. The sound he achieved conveyed at once why a concert instrument is called a "grand" piano, and could carry thrillingly above an orchestra in full cry. His recorded legacy, most of which is available on CD, remains a source of inspiration and delight, and a reminder of interpretive benchmarks brilliantly engraved by a master stylist.

RECOMMENDED RECORDINGS

BRAHMS, PIANO PIECES (RCA).

CHOPIN, PIANO PIECES (RCA).

MACDOWELL, PIANO CONCERTO NO. 2; BRAHMS, PIANO CONCERTO NO. 2: HENDL, REINER AND CHICAGO SYMPHONY ORCHESTRA (RCA).

TCHAIKOVSKY, PIANO CONCERTO NO. 1; RACHMANINOV, PIANO CONCERTO NO. 2: KONDRASHIN AND RCA SYMPHONY ORCHESTRA; REINER AND CHICAGO SYMPHONY ORCHESTRA (RCA).

***Clock* Symphony** NICKNAME FOR JOSEPH HAYDN'S SYMPHONY NO. 101 IN D, premiered in London on March 3, 1794. The name was inspired by the regular "tick-tock" of the chords—in bassoons and plucked strings—that accompany the principal tune of the second movement.

RECOMMENDED RECORDING

DAVIS AND CONCERTGEBOUW ORCHESTRA (PHILIPS).

coda (It., "tail") A section that brings a movement to a conclusion. Many 19th-century symphonies incorporate substantial codas in their first or last movement, e.g. Beethoven's *Eroica* (first movement) and his Fifth (finale, a 126-measure-long celebration of C major that starts softly and ends in thunderous affirmation).

***Coffee* Cantata** POPULAR NAME FOR J. S. BACH'S SECULAR CANTATA *SCHWEIGT STILLE, PLAUDERT NICHT*, BWV 211. Written sometime between 1732 and 1735 to a text by Picander (the pen name of the poet C. F. Henrici), the cantata takes as its model the standard opera buffa situation in which a headstrong young woman is pitted against an easily exasperated older male. The Italians usually made the antagonists a husband and his wife; here, Picander makes them a father and his coffee-crazed daughter. Just as the consumption of gin was becoming a problem in England (Hogarth's famous engravings graphically portray its social cost), so that of coffee was creating a stir on the Continent. The habit, adopted from the Turks, had spread from those parts of Europe most affected by the Ottoman incursion all the way to France, Germany, and Scandinavia, where it remains as strongly entrenched today as 250 years ago.

The *Coffee* Cantata stands out among Bach's works as the closest he ever came to writing operatically. While many of his liturgical cantatas reveal the formal influences of Italian opera seria, this one shows him actually thinking like an opera composer. Indeed, it would scarcely be brewing controversy to describe the *Coffee* Cantata as Bach's answer to *La serva padrona* (1733), the miniature opera buffa by Giovanni Pergolesi.

RECOMMENDED RECORDINGS

GRIMM, MERTEN; KOOPMAN AND AMSTERDAM BAROQUE ORCHESTRA (COMPLETE BACH CANTATAS, VOL. 4) (ELEKTRA)

KERTESI, GATI; ANTAL AND FAILONI ORCHESTRA (NAXOS).

Collegium Vocal Ghent *See box on pages 934–36.*

col legno (It., "with the wood") An instruction to the player of a string instrument to play a note or a passage by bouncing the wooden part of the bow against the strings, or by drawing it across the strings rather than using the hair of the bow in the conventional manner. The technique had been used by solo players for coloristic effect from the early 17th century; its earliest orchestral application occurs in the finale of Berlioz's *Symphonie fantastique* (mm. 444–60), where the bizarre, scratchy sounds produced by the violins and violas serve to evoke the grotesquery of a witches' sabbath. To create an ominous effect at the beginning of "Mars," in *The Planets,* Holst has the entire string section tap out a martial ostinato, *col legno.*

coloratura (It., "coloring") In vocal music, florid, elaborately decorative, and generally high-lying figuration or ornamentation. Coloratura parts are most often the province of sopranos, though Rossini had a particular fondness for writing this type of music for mezzo-soprano (e.g., the part of Rosina in *Il barbiere di Siviglia* and the title role in *La Cenerentola*), and even created coloratura parts for tenor and bass. Celebrated roles for coloratura soprano include the Queen of the Night in Mozart's *Die Zauberflöte* ◉, and the title roles in Donizetti's *Lucia di Lammermoor* and Delibes's *Lakmé*. Some noted coloratura sopranos of the past and present are Natalie Dessay (b. 1965), Galli-Curci, Gruberová, Pons, Popp, and Sutherland.

comprimario (It., "subprincipal") [1] A secondary or supporting role in an opera. Originally the term referred to those roles in which the singer might be expected to sing in a duet or an ensemble but did not receive a solo aria. Later, the term came to mean any lesser part. [2] A singer who specializes in smaller roles, the operatic equivalent of a character actor in the movies. Singing *comprimario* roles requires good acting ability, a well-developed knowledge of style, and thorough command of several languages. Examples of *comprimario* roles include the Sacristan in Puccini's *Tosca,* Monostatos in Mozart's *Die Zauberflöte,* Flora Bervoix in Verdi's *La traviata,* and the four commedia dell'arte suitors in Richard Strauss's *Ariadne auf Naxos.* The term is sometimes used in a derogatory fashion by one singer jealous of another.

Concentus Musicus Wien *See box on pages 310–13.*

concert (from It. *concertarsi,* "to agree") A presentation of music to an audience by a group of performers.

concertante [1] A musical passage, or a piece, that is concerto-like, in which a solo instrument or group is set off against a larger group. [2] A synonym for the genre known as the *symphonie concertante,* popular in Paris in the late 18th and early 19th centuries. Haydn and Mozart both wrote works in this form; Beethoven's Triple Concerto can also be considered an example of the French-style concertante.

Concert des Nations, Le *See box on pages 310–13.*

Concertgebouw (Dutch, "Concert Building") Concert hall in Amsterdam built between 1883 and 1886 and opened on April 11, 1888. With an interior design patterned after that of the Neue Gewandhaus in Leipzig, the Concertgebouw's Grote Zaal (Main Hall) has some of the finest acoustics of any large concert venue in the world. Following the hall's construction, Dutch conductor Willem Kes was given the task of forming and leading the orchestra that would thenceforth reside there. Kes quickly recruited an ensemble of 65 mostly Dutch musicians, and on November 3, 1888, the Concertgebouw Orchestra gave its first "Philharmonic Concert." Kes, a stern but admired taskmaster, departed in 1895 and was replaced by a charismatic 24-year-old from Utrecht, Willem Mengelberg, who during five decades in the job of music director transformed the Concertgebouw Orchestra into one of Europe's most admired and accomplished virtuoso ensembles.

Mengelberg was a champion of Mahler and Richard Strauss, and their music

Riccardo Chailly, music director of Royal Concertgebouw Orchestra (1988–2004)

quickly found a place in the core repertoire of the orchestra alongside that of Beethoven, Brahms, and Wagner; in gratitude, Strauss would dedicate *Ein Heldenleben* to Mengelberg and the ensemble. Mahler and Strauss were also among the many guest conductors to share the Concertgebouw's podium during Mengelberg's tenure. Others of note included composers Grieg, Debussy, Schoenberg, and Stravinsky, as well as conductors Busch, Beecham, Boult, Monteux, and Bruno Walter. Because of his pro-German conduct during World War II, Mengelberg was prohibited from conducting the orchestra for a period of six years beginning July 1, 1945 (he died in 1951, three months before the end of his banishment). His place was taken by Eduard van Beinum, who had been appointed second conductor of the orchestra in 1931 and promoted to the position of first conductor in 1938. Van Beinum's integrity, humility, and warmth contrasted sharply with his predecessor's dynamism, egocentricity, and volatility. After the liberation of Holland, Van Beinum began the process of rebuilding the orchestra—which had lost almost all its Jewish members—and of refining both its palette and its manner of playing. In effect, he transformed the orchestra into a big chamber ensemble, which it still is today. His advocacy of Bruckner and of the 20th-century English and French repertoire further broadened the orchestra's stylistic base.

The venerable Concertgebouw Orchestra fills an equally venerable stage.

Van Beinum's sudden death on April 13, 1959, while conducting a rehearsal, left the orchestra in a bind, which it addressed in typically pragmatic fashion by appointing two conductors to fill the vacancy. The respected German-born veteran Eugen Jochum, and an up-and-coming young Dutchman, Bernard Haitink, shared the responsibilities of music director from 1961 until 1964, when Haitink, having proven himself, took over sole authority. The orchestra recorded prolifically during Haitink's 24 years at the helm, and solidified its reputation as one of the world's finest and most versatile ensembles. Haitink's understated but eloquent interpretations of the symphonic works of Brahms, Bruckner, Mahler, and Strauss, his poised and atmospheric accounts of the music of Debussy and Ravel, and his vibrant readings of scores by Stravinsky, Shostakovich, and other 20th-century figures remain among the glories of the CD catalog.

In 1988, in celebration of its centenary, the Concertgebouw Orchestra was officially renamed the Royal Concertgebouw Orchestra. For the first time in its history it embraced a "non-Dutch" musician as its chief conductor, tapping the 35-year-old Italian maestro Riccardo Chailly to succeed Haitink. Chailly's passionate commitment to 20th-century music and his special flair for pieces with a Mediterranean accent resulted in some very adventurous programming during his years in Amsterdam; to his credit, he plunged into the orchestra's traditional repertoire, Bruckner and Mahler in particular, with enthusiasm if not always resounding success.

Mariss Jansons succeeded him as music director in 2004.

RECOMMENDED RECORDINGS

DEBUSSY, ORCHESTRAL WORKS: HAITINK (PHILIPS).

HAYDN, *LONDON* SYMPHONIES: DAVIS (PHILIPS).

MAHLER, *DAS LIED VON DER ERDE*: BAKER, KING; HAITINK (PHILIPS).

MAHLER, SYMPHONY NO. 1: HAITINK (PHILIPS).

SIBELIUS, SYMPHONY NO. 2: SZELL (PHILIPS).

STRAVINSKY, *FIREBIRD*, *PETRUSHKA*, *THE RITE OF SPRING*: DAVIS (PHILIPS).

VARÈSE, ORCHESTRAL WORKS: CHAILLY (DECCA).

WAGENAAR, OVERTURES: CHAILLY (DECCA).

concertmaster Title given to the "leader" or principal first violinist of an orchestra. In addition to being regularly called upon to play solos when they appear in standard reportory works (e.g., the extended violin solo in the second movement of Brahms's Symphony No. 1), the concertmaster has an important managerial role in the day-to-day work of an orchestra—deciding in conjunction with the conductor what bowings the first violin section (and by extension the entire string body) will use for specific passages in the music it is to play. In performance, the concertmaster's most important function is to lead by example, in particular to convey to the rest of the string group the phrasing and the manner and intensity of attack appropriate at any given moment.

concerto (It., "agreement") A work for one or more solo instruments and orchestra. Though a child of the Baroque era, the solo concerto did not come of age until the last decades of the 18th century, largely as a result of Mozart's efforts. As both an outstanding violinist and the preeminent pianist of his day, he was able to shape the concerto to his own exacting standards of musicianship. In his hands, and in the works of Joseph and Michael Haydn, among other, lesser-known contemporaries, it became the form we know today, usually consisting of three movements (in a fast-slow-fast sequence) and combining serious content with virtuosic display.

Mozart's Viennese piano concertos represent the pinnacle of his achievement in instrumental composition. Those from 1785 on, beginning with K. 466 in D minor, are particularly rich in their invention and formal sophistication, expansive in their scale, and brilliant in their exploitation of the inherently dramatic relationship between soloist and orchestra. Mozart's other instrumental concertos of this period, for the horn and the clarinet, were composed for supremely talented colleagues and exhibit the same depth of expression and wealth of content.

In a Classical concerto, the first movement is typically in sonata form, like the first movement of a Classical symphony, though in a concerto the structural demarcations are often less clear than they are in a symphony. There is usually an opportunity for a CADENZA toward the end of the movement. The second movement is in a slow tempo, often laid out in the manner of an aria (usually in three-part song form). This showcases the solo instrument's capacity for intimate expression and gives the player an opportunity to inflect lines and improvise ornaments as a singer would. The finale, usually in rondo form or a hybrid of sonata and rondo, is almost always fast, light, tuneful, and display-oriented. Mozart's finales, like his slow movements, often have an operatic quality—where the slow movements resemble arias of love and emphasize tender sentiments, the finales have the rapid repartee and exciting shifts of mood of act-ending ensembles.

Beethoven built his concertos on this model, greatly expanding the scale and altering the relationship between the solo instrument and the orchestra. His first two piano concertos clearly follow Mozart—carefully approached and painstakingly reworked, energetic and imaginative if occasionally unbalanced, they already strain at the confines of the Classical style. In short order these were superseded by the Concertos in C minor, G major, and E-flat major, works of breathtaking originality and imagination in which the balance between piano and orchestra, inherently unequal, becomes a dynamic element of the conception. The nature of that balance is less the back-and-forth shifting of a seesaw (as in Mozart), and more a dynamic process in which soloist and orchestra jointly shape the musical material into a vast, overarching structure. Remarkably, this transformation in the aesthetics of the concerto, one of the great achievements of Beethoven's middle period, took little more than ten years. In his Violin Concerto, Beethoven attained a similar enlargement of form along with a majestic integration of soloist and orchestra.

As his symphonies had done, Beethoven's concertos left the early Romantics with a dilemma—it was all but impossible to carry the same ideas further. In the works of Chopin, Mendelssohn, Schumann, and Liszt there is a new focus on the element of virtuosity, with the soloist often being treated as a heroic protagonist. These composers were all preoccupied with conveying the impression that the concerto had emerged from a single inspiration—not from the topical stage-play of Mozart or the constructive struggles of Beethoven, but from an elevated, rhapsodic state of feeling within which the listener was free to wander. Still, Beethoven's example forced his successors to think about unity. The connected movements of his Violin Concerto and the Piano Concerto in E-flat (*Emperor*) were emulated by Mendelssohn in his E minor Violin Concerto and by Schumann in his Piano Concerto. Liszt, in his Piano Concerto in E-flat, took the more daring step of conjuring a multimovement structure from a sonata-form design. Only Brahms managed to equal Beethoven in the scale of his concerto structures and the way he forged their musical material into powerful symphonic arguments.

The 20th century was a particularly rich period for the concerto. While the three-movement form survived as the norm, multiple alternatives were successfully tried; in addition, composers posited new relationships between solo instrument and orchestra, demanded a heightened virtuosity, and showed a new eclecticism in their choice of material. Among the ideas and procedures explored were jazz (in Ravel's two piano concertos), film music (Korngold's Violin Concerto), the 12-tone row (Berg's Violin Concerto), and folk-inspired rhythms and melodies (Bartók, Falla, Rodrigo). Concertos in the grand manner, such as those written early in the century by Rachmaninov, Elgar, and Sibelius, were still being produced in the 1990s by the likes of Stephen Albert (1941–92) and Lowell Liebermann (b. 1961).

concerto grosso In Baroque music, an instrumental work in which a small group of soloists, called a concertino, is set off against a larger ensemble, called the RIPIENO or concerto grosso, hence the genre's name. The most common solo group, two violins and a cello, was utilized in the 12 concerti grossi of Corelli's Op. 6 (1714), the seminal essays in the form, as well as in Handel's Op. 6 collection of 1740. Bach, in his *Brandenburg* Concertos (1721), opted for more variety in the concertino groupings, scoring Concerto No. 2 for a solo quartet of violin, recorder, oboe, and trumpet, and Concerto No. 4 for violin and two recorders. Typically, a concerto grosso consists of three or four movements, sometimes more. The division of forces into a larger and smaller group enables composers to exploit the contrast between loud and soft, or "near" and "far," a characteristic exercise in Baroque music.

Concert Spirituel (Fr., "sacred concert") **A Parisian concert series founded in 1725** by Anne Danican Philidor, devoted to the performance of instrumental music and sacred works with Latin texts (hence the name), eventually expanded to include secular works with French texts as well. For most of the 18th century, until its demise in the post-Revolution year of 1790, the series stood at the center of nonoperatic Parisian musical life. Mozart composed his *Paris* Symphony (No. 31 in D, K. 297) for the Concert Spirituel, where it received its premiere on June 18, 1778. The orchestra of the Concert Spirituel was large even by today's standards, and famed for its virtuosity and discipline.

***Concord* Sonata** **Subtitle of Charles Ives's second piano sonata,** composed between 1911 and 1915. The full subtitle reads "Concord Mass., 1840–60." Ives arranged for a private printing of the score, prefaced by his *Essays Before a Sonata,* in 1920. The work was premiered by John Kirkpatrick in 1939, and was officially published in 1947. The four movements—"Emerson," "Hawthorne," "The Alcotts," and "Thoreau"—are intended as both character sketches and ruminations on the ideals that were espoused by the New England Transcendentalists. In a way, the work is also Ives's spiritual autobiography: It speaks of his Transcendentalist spirit, his Emersonian self-reliance, his feeling of a lost Eden.

Like much of Ives's work, the *Concord* Sonata came into being not by design but through a process of accretion and discovery. Three of the four movements ("Thoreau" being the exception) were originally conceived for orchestra and recast for the piano. At various points in the score, Ives creates dense polyphonic textures of thickly layered counterpoint; at others, an impressionistic haze. He employs conflicting tonalities and meters, throws in fistfuls of tone clusters, and makes constant use of the pedals, reveling in dissonance and extremes of register. It is a combustible idiom (partly to show that "manliness" which was such an issue for Ives), even more remote and tonally ambivalent than that of Debussy's *Préludes,* of exactly the same vintage. Throughout, Ives employs a collage structure involving quotation (including Beethoven's Fifth, "Columbia, the Gem of the Ocean," and some of his own songs and instrumental works, for example, his *Country Band March*).

The first movement, "Emerson," is the longest and densest, almost disorderly in its swirling free association of ideas and gestures—near the movement's end there is even a part for offstage solo viola. The second movement, "Hawthorne," is a rollicking, all-but-impossible scherzo, a fantastic journey back to Ives's Danbury childhood; in its sheer virtuosic demands, it literally "transcends" the limits of the piano. In the third movement, a portrait of the philosopher Amos Bronson Alcott and his family, the music is quiet, introspective, and sentimental in tone, and features moments of hymn-like beauty and simplicity—a projection of the domestic integrity and "spiritual sturdiness" Ives associated with the Alcotts. The final movement, "Thoreau," is a day on Walden Pond, from morning mists to dusk. Here, Ives's music merges with the hum of nature, reflecting man absorbed in the infinite and the mysteries of transcendence. It ends with a brief solo for flute (Thoreau's own instrument) sounding over the quietude of the pond.

RECOMMENDED RECORDING

Hamelin (New World).

conductor An individual who leads a performance by a group of musicians, coordinating their actions by means of gestures and often using a baton to mark the beat. Conducting of one sort or another has been a necessary and accepted means of shaping performances by vocal and instrumental ensembles since the Middle Ages. The practice of conducting an orchestra from the podium, rather than leading from within the group, emerged in the early 19th century; among the first to do it were Carl Maria von Weber, Louis Spohr, Hector Berlioz, and Felix Mendelssohn. In modern orchestral performances, the conductor is responsible not only for the cohesion of the ensemble but for the "interpretation" of the music as well, and conductors have developed a remarkable repertoire of glances, cues, facial expressions, dance steps, and body English to mime the piece for their audiences and get the message across to the players—though what orchestras really want from a conductor is focused rehearsing, a clear beat, and cues and dynamic correction when necessary.

Conlon, James

(b. New York, March 18, 1950)

AMERICAN CONDUCTOR. He completed his training at the Juilliard School in 1972 and rose quickly to the top of the musical ladder. He made his New York Philharmonic debut in 1974 as the youngest maestro ever to conduct a subscription concert of the orchestra, and first conducted at the Metropolitan Opera in 1976. He was named music director of the Cincinnati May Festival in 1979, a position he still holds, but during the 1980s and 1990s his career was based mainly in Europe. From 1983 to 1991 he was music director of the Rotterdam Philharmonic, and from 1989 to 2002 he served as general music director of the city of Cologne. In 1996 he assumed the post of principal conductor of the Paris Opéra, where the works he conducted during his first four seasons included *Tristan und Isolde, Lohengrin, Parsifal, Pelléas et Mélisande, Le nozze di Figaro, Don Giovanni, Carmen, Rigoletto, La traviata, Don Carlo, Falstaff,* and *Turandot.* Stepping down in 2004, he began a new tenure as music director of the Ravinia Festival in 2005, and becomes music director of the Los Angeles Opera at the start of the 2006–07 season. One of the most gifted, versatile, and intelligent conductors of his generation, Conlon has a penchant for exploring new repertoire and has become in recent years a champion of the works of Zemlinsky. In all that he does he tries to look beneath the surface of the music; for example, prior to making a recording of Liszt's *Legend of St. Francis of Assisi,* he went to the hermitage where the saint lived and crawled through the cave-like passage to the secluded grove where, legend has it, Francis once preached to the birds—a true pilgrimage, undertaken with the goal of conveying the spirit of the piece. In 2002 he was awarded the Légion d'Honneur by Jacques Chirac.

RECOMMENDED RECORDING

Zemlinsky, Operas and Orchestral Works: Various Artists and Gürzenich Orchestra (EMI).

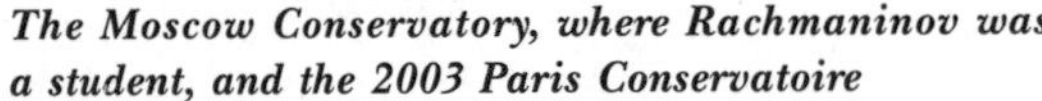

The Moscow Conservatory, where Rachmaninov was a student, and the 2003 Paris Conservatoire

conservatory (from It. *conservatorio,* "orphanage") A music school. The term refers to Italian orphanages of the 17th and 18th centuries at which music was taught. Nearly all were run by the Catholic Church and had been founded as hospitals—their purpose in teaching music was to give poor and orphaned children a trade by which they might support themselves. Vivaldi taught at one such conservatory in Venice, the Pio Ospedale della Pietà, one of four in the city established solely for girls. Among the world's most celebrated conservatories are the Accademia di Santa Cecilia in Rome, the Paris Conservatoire, the Moscow Conservatory (whose Great Hall is one of the finest concert halls in the world), the Royal Academy of Music, the Juilliard School in New York, the Peabody Institute in Baltimore, and the Curtis Institute in Philadelphia.

consort A group of instruments. The term, originally synonymous with the Italian *concerto* and the French *concert,* came into use in England in the late 16th century. Consorts of the 16th and 17th centuries typically consisted of plucked and bowed string instruments of different types—such as lutes, violins, and viols—with the occasional wind instrument, although consorts could also be composed of instruments belonging to a single family, e.g., a consort of viols. Purcell wrote some lovely works for this formation.

contes d'Hoffmann, Les (The Tales of Hoffmann) "FANTASY OPERA" IN FOUR ACTS AND AN EPILOGUE BY JACQUES OFFENBACH, to a libretto by Jules Barbier (derived from his 1851 play based on stories of E. T. A. Hoffmann), premiered February 10, 1881, at the Opéra-Comique in Paris. The historical Ernst Theodor Amadeus Hoffmann (1776–1822), one of the great literary and musical figures of German Romanticism (he was a composer of modest talent but a very perceptive critic), here becomes a character in the musical retelling of his own stories. The libretto follows a series of unhappy love affairs with three paramours: Olympia, a breathtakingly lifelike mechanical doll (the creation of the physician Spalanzani, with porcelain eyes supplied by the mad scientist Coppélius); Antonia, the beautiful, mysteriously ailing daughter of the instrument maker Crespel; and Giulietta, a Venetian courtesan. The opera's most famous music is the barcarolle "Belle nuit, ô nuit d'amour" that opens Act IV, set in a palace overlooking the Grand Canal.

RECOMMENDED RECORDINGS

Domingo, Gruberova, Schmidt, Bacquier; Ozawa and L'Orchestre National de France (DG).

Sutherland, Domingo, Bacquier; Bonynge and Orchestre de la Suisse Romande (Decca).

continuo In Baroque music, the custom of assigning the bass line to one or more low-pitched instruments (e.g., cello, viola da gamba, or bassoon) while a keyboard instrument (e.g., harpsichord or organ) plays a version of the bass line that is "figured"—i.e., with numbers placed below the notes, so that the player can determine which harmonies are to be played above it, and how they are to be voiced. The practice of writing figured bass began in Italy around 1600, as a form of shorthand. It became obsolete during the second half of the 18th century as the emergence of larger ensembles and more powerful-sounding string instruments made it unnecessary to use keyboard instruments to fill out musical textures.

contrabassoon Double-reed woodwind instrument with an air column 18 feet, 4 inches long and a compass an octave below that of the standard bassoon. It has been part of the standard complement of a symphony orchestra since the time of Beethoven, who called for its use in the finale of his Fifth Symphony and again in the Ninth. Its key system and construction are similar to those of the bassoon; as with the bassoon, the air column of the contrabassoon is folded upon itself—not once, however, but twice. The lowest notes are buzzy when sounded by any but the most exceptional players, and the upper register has a tendency to sound shaky and strained. Nonetheless, the instrument is quite effective in its lower octave when doubled by the bassoons an octave above, or in combination with the string basses.

Brahms preferred the contrabassoon to the tuba, using it to anchor the wind section in three of his four symphonies (the exception: Symphony No. 2, in the bright, brassy key of D major). Richard Strauss wrote some extraordinary parts for the instrument as well: It joins the organ and the bass section in sounding the pianissimo low C at the start of *Also sprach Zarathustra,* and in *Salome* is assigned an eerie solo with several A-sharps in it—which, during performances many years ago at the Chicago Lyric Opera, caused the eyeballs of the young principal who was playing them to vibrate uncontrollably, thereby rendering him unable to see the music on the page and unsure of when to release the notes. The problem was remedied when the player memorized the passage. Mahler used the contrabassoon to remarkable effect in the Ländlerlike second movement of his Symphony No. 9, and Ravel charmingly made it the "voice" of the beast during the "Conversation of Beauty and the Beast" in his ballet *Ma mère l'oye.*

contralto The lowest female voice range. The term originally referred to a high male voice part found in music of the 15th and 16th centuries, the *contratenor altus,* which became the domain of castrati during the 17th century. The use of the term to designate a female singer with an especially deep voice dates from the 18th century. Contralto parts in opera are relatively rare. Among the most important are Ulrica in Verdi's *Un ballo in maschera,* Ortrud in Wagner's *Lohengrin,* Erda in *Das Rheingold* and *Siegfried,* and Madame de Croissy in Poulenc's *Dialogues des Carmélites.* Azucena, in Verdi's *Il trovatore,* and Dalila, in Saint-Saëns's *Samson et Dalila,* can also be considered contralto roles despite the fact that they are usually sung by MEZZO-SOPRANOS. Concert works that call for a contralto soloist include Mahler's Symphony No. 3 and *Das Lied von der Erde,* Brahms's *Alto Rhapsody,* and Elgar's *Sea Pictures.* Ernestine Schumann-Heink, Clara Butt (1872–1936), Kathleen Ferrier, and Maureen Forrester (b. 1930) are among the great contraltos of the past 100 years.

contredanse (Fr., "country dance") A dance in moderate to lively duple or triple time.

Copland, Aaron

(b. New York, November 14, 1900; d. North Tarrytown, December 2, 1990)

AMERICAN COMPOSER. Regarded by many as the finest composer the United States has yet produced, he created important works from the 1920s to the 1970s, defining American music in the process and helping to liberate it from an often hidebound imitation of European models. His role in the development of America's musical identity was uniquely broad.

He was the youngest of five children born to Harris and Sarah Copland, Lithuanian Jewish immigrants who owned a department store in Brooklyn. He started taking piano lessons in 1913, and in 1917 embarked on the study of harmony and counterpoint with Rubin Goldmark. Following his graduation from Boys' High School in Brooklyn in 1918, he decided to continue his studies with Goldmark (with whom he remained until 1921) rather than go to college. In 1921 Copland took the decisive step of leaving New York to enroll at the newly established American Conservatory at Fontainebleau, outside Paris. He studied piano with Ricardo Viñes, conducting with Albert Wolff, and composition and orchestration with Nadia Boulanger. Paris also brought contact with the conductor Serge Koussevitzky, who would become a major champion of Copland's work. At the conclusion of Copland's Paris sojourn, Koussevitzky suggested he compose a work for Boulanger to play on an upcoming tour of America. The result was the *Symphony for Organ and Orchestra* (1924), premiered January 11, 1925, at Carnegie Hall by Walter Damrosch and the New York Symphony Society, with Boulanger as soloist. Copland himself was the soloist when Koussevitzky and the Boston Symphony Orchestra premiered his Piano Concerto in 1927. In 1929 Copland entered a competition sponsored by RCA Victor and won a $5,000 prize for his *Dance Symphony,* completed in 1925. In 1930 he composed the *Piano Variations,* a work of uncompromising rigor and austere beauty, and one of the most imposing pieces for solo piano written in the 20th century.

Copland's greatest achievement as a composer was his creation of a musical language at once original and familiar, contemporary yet comprehensible, and capable of conveying a wide range of emotion. The works he composed in this style during the 1930s and 1940s, while no less modern than the edgy, Stravinsky-inspired scores of his youth, were formally more accomplished and at the same time easier for audiences to follow. The first score to fully embody this approach was EL SALÓN MÉXICO (1932–36), which subjects simple Mexican dance tunes to a harmonically advanced and rhythmically dazzling rethinking. Copland continued in this vein with his next major works, the ballets BILLY THE KID (1938) and RODEO (1942), in which he drew on traditional cowboy songs, and the LINCOLN PORTRAIT (1942), for speaker and orchestra, which quotes carefully selected and edited passages from Lincoln's letters and speeches and makes use of two popular American songs—"Camptown Races" and "Springfield Mountain." In these works Copland evoked the expansiveness of the American landscape and the optimism of the American character by using melodies based on fairly large intervals and allowing them to sound in wide-open harmonic spaces.

The ballet *Appalachian Spring* (1943–44), written for Martha Graham, and the Third Symphony (1944–46) marked the apex of this phase in Copland's career. With the exception of a single Shaker tune in *Appalachian Spring,* the melodies are no longer quotations but original conceptions. The feeling is the same: a mix of tenderness and triumph, shaded here and there by moments of desolation and mystery and by a bittersweet sense of nostalgia, enlivened elsewhere by jaunty syncopations, not always "happy," but ultimately positive.

Because of the success of his symphonic works, Copland tended to be overlooked as a composer of chamber and vocal music. But several of his shorter instrumental works, including the *Piano Variations* and the Duo for Flute and Piano (1971), have become classics of their type, and his song settings are among the finest by any American, particularly the cycle *Twelve Poems of Emily Dickinson* (1950), and the deft arrangements of *Old American Songs* (1950, 1952). Copland's "populist" style carries over to his opera *The Tender Land,* premiered by the New York City Opera in 1954. It also shows up in his film scores, of which the most important are *The Red Pony* (1948) and *The Heiress* (1949), for which Copland won an Oscar.

Aaron Copland in rehearsal; he called conducting "hot work, if you can get it."

Copland's career took a new turn with the large orchestral piece *Connotations* (1962), commissioned by the New York Philharmonic for the opening of Philharmonic Hall at Lincoln Center, and the shorter *Inscape* (1967), commissioned by the same orchestra for its 125th anniversary. Both works explore the 12-tone method. Copland began to be affected by dementia in the early 1970s. He made few appearances during his last decade, although he recorded many reminiscences in conversations with historian Vivian Perlis, which provided the material for two autobiographical volumes, *Copland: 1900 Through 1942* (1984) and *Copland: Since 1943* (1989).

Through his music, Aaron Copland pronounced a benediction upon America. Other composers have created music that is identifiably "American" in spirit and have developed idioms that are distinctive and unique, but Copland did something more—in works such as *El Salón México, Billy the Kid, Rodeo, Appalachian Spring,* and the Third Symphony he gave voice to America's character. Prior to the creation of these justifiably popular works, he composed valid, accomplished essays in the jazzy, cosmopolitan, Stravinsky-accented language of the 1920s; and in later years he showed that he could achieve success using the rigorous methodology of 12-tone composition. Even when he was writing pieces in a popular vein, he also wrote music that was demanding and made no effort to be popular, but which has retained a place in the repertoire simply because it is good.

In addition to creating a formidable body of work, Copland wrote perceptively about music, conducted his own and other composers' scores with passion and understanding, encouraged young talent wherever he saw it, and acted with generosity and respect toward his admirers, of which there were many. He wrote three books for the general reader: *What to Listen for in Music* (1939), *Music and Imagination* (1952), and *Copland on Music* (1960).

RECOMMENDED RECORDINGS

BILLY THE KID, RODEO: SLATKIN AND SAINT LOUIS SYMPHONY ORCHESTRA (EMI).

"COPLAND THE MODERNIST" (*SHORT SYMPHONY,* PIANO CONCERTO, *ORCHESTRAL VARIATIONS*): THOMAS AND SAN FRANCISCO SYMPHONY ORCHESTRA (RCA).

"COPLAND THE POPULIST" (*BILLY THE KID, RODEO, APPALACHIAN SPRING*): THOMAS AND SAN FRANCISCO SYMPHONY ORCHESTRA (RCA).

LINCOLN PORTRAIT, FANFARE FOR THE COMMON MAN: JONES; SCHWARZ AND SEATTLE SYMPHONY ORCHESTRA (DELOS).

EL SALÓN MÉXICO, BILLY THE KID, RODEO, APPALACHIAN SPRING, SYMPHONY NO. 3: BERNSTEIN AND NEW YORK PHILHARMONIC (SONY).

THE TENDER LAND (CHAMBER ARRANGEMENT): HANSON, VARGAS, MACNEIL, WEBSTER; SIDLIN AND THIRD ANGLE NEW MUSIC ENSEMBLE (KOCH).

THE TENDER LAND (SUITE): COPLAND AND BOSTON SYMPHONY ORCHESTRA (RCA).

Corelli, Arcangelo

(b. Fusignano, February 17, 1653; d. Rome, January 8, 1713)

ITALIAN VIOLINIST AND COMPOSER. He was the most influential violin teacher of the 17th century, and in his sonatas and concerti grossi he established the norms for both those genres, exerting an influence that lasted well into the 18th century. He was born into a well-to-do family and studied violin in Bologna from about 1666, becoming a member of its Accademia Filarmonica in 1670. From 1675 he was active in Rome, where he quickly established himself as one of the city's foremost violinists and attracted the attention of notable patrons such as Queen Christina of Sweden and Cardinal Benedetto Pamphili. His first publication, a set of 12 trio sonatas, appeared in 1681, and was followed by additional sets of sonatas in 1685 and 1689. In 1690 the 22-year-old Cardinal Pietro Ottoboni, nephew of Pope Alexander VIII, became Corelli's patron; his generosity made Corelli a rich man and enabled him to concentrate increasingly on composition (to the detriment of his playing, according to several eyewitness accounts, including one from Handel, who met Corelli in Rome in 1707). He retired from concertizing in 1708 and spent the final five years of his life perfecting his last works, a set of 12 concerti grossi that were published posthumously in Amsterdam, as his Op. 6, in 1714.

Corelli was the first important composer to focus his efforts primarily on instrumental music, beginning a trend that would culminate in the 19th century's enthronement of symphonic and chamber music as the loftiest pursuits of "serious" music. The elegance of his instrumental writing and the sure handling of form in his sonatas and concerti grossi impressed all his peers; so imaginative was his instrumentation, so poetic the expression of his concertos, that one contemporary dubbed

Title page of an early edition of Corelli's Trio Sonatas, Opus 1

him "the new Orpheus of our days." His works were among the first by any composer to be considered "canonic," and held up as examples of the art of composition long after he was dead.

RECOMMENDED RECORDINGS

CONCERTI GROSSI, OP. 6: BIONDI AND EUROPA GALANTE (HARMONIA MUNDI).

CONCERTI GROSSI, OP. 6: KRECHEK AND CAPPELLA ISTROPOLITANA (NAXOS).

VIOLIN SONATAS, OP. 5: HUGGETT AND TRIO SONNERIE (VIRGIN CLASSICS).

Corigliano, John

(b. New York City, February 16, 1938)

AMERICAN COMPOSER, one of the most versatile and successful figures in American music during the past quarter century. Prominent among the group of Americans who, in the 1980s, began to turn the tide of mainstream classical composition away from dogmatic serialism to a more inclusive and eclectic view of musical style, he has developed an accessible, kaleidoscopic idiom that incorporates tonality and glimpses of historical styles as well as more contemporary serial, microtonal, and aleatoric writing. His orchestral works and concertos are performed regularly, and his opera *The Ghosts of Versailles* (1987), commissioned by the Metropolitan Opera, played to sold-out houses at the Met in 1991 and 1994, and at Lyric Opera of Chicago in 1995.

The son of a piano teacher and the violinist John Corigliano Sr., who was concertmaster of the New York Philharmonic for 23 years, Corigliano studied with Otto Luening at Columbia but never adopted the Columbia conviction that tonality was dead. After graduating in 1959 he worked in radio, at WQXR and WBAI, and in television, as an assistant to Leonard Bernstein on his *Young People's Concerts* (1961–72). He gained early recognition as a composer when his Sonata for Violin and Piano won the chamber music prize at the 1964 Spoleto Festival. He taught at the Manhattan School of Music from 1971 to 1986 and joined the faculty of Lehman College, City University of New York, in 1973, attaining the rank of distinguished professor in 1984; since 1992 he has also served on the faculty of the Juilliard School. From 1987 to 1990, he was engaged by the Chicago Symphony Orchestra as its first-ever composer-in-residence.

Corigliano's *Pied Piper Fantasy* (1981) for flute and orchestra (his third woodwind concerto, following on the heels of concertos for oboe and clarinet), was among the first of his works to gain widespread popularity. Written for James Galway, the piece's vivid musical imagery (and the fact that it concludes with a parade of children playing drums and tin whistles) gave it instant audience appeal. The next work to attract widespread notice, the composer's Symphony No. 1 (1989), was an anguished response to the loss of many of his friends and colleagues to AIDS. Commissioned by the Chicago Symphony Orchestra and premiered under the baton of Daniel Barenboim on March 15, 1990, it quickly entered the repertoire; it has been twice recorded, and has been played by nearly 125 orchestras worldwide.

The Ghosts of Versailles, with a libretto by William M. Hoffman, presents a phantasmagorical reimagining of the world of the

French Revolution in which the ghost of the playwright Beaumarchais and characters from the third play of the Figaro series (*La mère coupable*) coexist with Marie Antoinette and the rest of the doomed French aristocracy. A lively work that weaves together historical and modern musical ideas, it is Corigliano's musical manifesto, a rejection of revolutions that feel they must destroy everything old and start over. In keeping with this theme, Corigliano's progress as a composer has been evolutionary rather than revolutionary. His roots can be found in the world of "Americana," particularly the elegant beauty of the music of Aaron Copland and Samuel Barber. Over time, as he became more aware of influences from outside this tradition, he made skillful use of aleatoric techniques, nontonal modes and scales, and the sounds of Eastern music, specifically the gamelan. "When we add things," he has said of his idiom, "we don't have to give up things." Throughout his career Corigliano has also recycled material when new possibilities or appealing commissions presented themselves; for example, his early orchestral piece *Three Hallucinations* (1981) was based on the score he composed for the film *Altered States* (1979). In recent years he has turned this process into a cottage industry, with notable success. He has worked themes from *The Ghosts of Versailles* into a piece called *Phantasmagoria* (1993), which exists in versions for cello and piano, and for orchestra. His score for *The Red Violin* (1997), which won the Academy Award for best film score, has provided material for two concert works so far—*The Red Violin: Chaconne for Violin and Orchestra* (1997), which has been championed and recorded by Joshua Bell, and the Concerto for Violin and Orchestra (*The Red Violin*), which Bell premiered in 2003. Most successful of all perhaps has been Corigliano's transformation of his String Quartet (1995), commissioned by Lincoln Center for the valedictory appearance of the Cleveland Quartet, into his Symphony No. 2, which was premiered in November of 2000 by Seiji Ozawa and the Boston Symphony Orchestra and won the composer the 2001 Pulitzer Prize for music. Other works of note include *A Dylan Thomas Trilogy*, originally three pieces composed between 1960 and 1976, put together as a "choral symphony" in 1976, and revised and expanded as a "memory play in the form of an oratorio" in 1999; and *The Mannheim Rocket* (2001), an orchestral fantasy of Munchausenesque extravagance.

RECOMMENDED RECORDINGS

Phantasmagoria (*Three Hallucinations*, other works): Klas and Tampere Philharmonic (Ondine).

The Red Violin (film score): Bell; Salonen and Philharmonia Orchestra (Sony).

Symphony No. 1, "Of Rage and Remembrance": Slatkin and National Symphony Orchestra (RCA).

cornet Valved brass instrument invented in France around 1825, more closely related to the posthorn than to the trumpet, which it resembles. The cornet has the same range as the B-flat trumpet; its bore is two-thirds conical and one-third cylindrical, which imparts a mellowness of tone to the instrument that sets it apart from the more powerful-sounding trumpet. Because of its ease of speaking, it is the most agile of all the brass instruments, ideally suited to florid, decorative figuration. Berlioz, always quick to take advantage of a new sonority, used two cornets in his *Symphonie fantastique* (1830); they are particularly promi-

Cornet

nent in the fourth movement ("Marche au Supplice"). Sometime after the symphony's premiere, he added an obbligato solo for cornet to the second movement ("Un bal"). In the final movement of *La mer* (1903), Debussy augmented the brass complement with two cornets, and in *Petrushka* (1911), Stravinsky used a pair throughout the score, giving a prominent solo to the instrument in the "Dance of the Ballerina." Tchaikovsky included a marvelous solo for cornet in the "Neapolitan Dance" from Act III of his *Swan Lake.*

cornett; cornetto (It., "little horn") A wind instrument made of leather-covered wood, often curved like a cow's horn, with a conical bore, cup-shaped mouthpiece, and finger holes. From about 1550 to 1650, it was the preferred instrument for virtuosic passage work wherever large instrumental or vocal-instrumental forces were called for, and was often heard in wind ensembles along with SACKBUTS. As its tone is remarkably vocal—velvety yet piercing—it was used to double or accompany voices in large concerted works, such as Gabrieli's *Symphoniae sacrae* (1597 and 1615), Monteverdi's *Vespro della Beata Vergine* (1610), *Polyhymnia caduceatrix* (1619 and 1620) by Michael Praetorius (1571–1631), and Schütz's *Symphoniae sacrae* (1629–50). In the canzonas he wrote for the resident instrumental ensemble at the basilica of San Marco in Venice, Gabrieli included highly ornamented lines for his two virtuoso cornettists. Solo sonatas and canzonas by Italian composers, mostly Northerners, were often marked "canto" or "soprano" and could be played on cornetto or violin; sometimes the instrument was specified. Important collections include Frescobaldi's 38 canzonas from *Il primo libro delle canzoni* (1628); *Affetti musicali* (1617) by Biagio Marini (1594–1663); seven books of sonatas and canzonas by Mario Uccellini (1610–80); *Sonate à 1.2.3. per violino o cornetto* (1641) by Giovanni Fontana (d. ca. 1630); *Sonate concertante in stil moderno* (1621 and 1629) by Dario Castello (fl. early 17th century); and four books of canzonas (1615–51) by Tarquinio Merula (1544–ca. 1625). Merula's *Canzona La Gallina à 2* is a comical duo in which the cornetti virtuosically mimic clucking chickens.

RECOMMENDED RECORDINGS

"EFFETTI E STRAVANGANZE": DICKEY AND CONCERTO PALATINO (ACCENT).

"QUAL LASCIVISSIMO CORNETTO": DICKEY; TRAGICOMEDIA (ACCENT).

Cortot, Alfred

(b. Nyon, Switzerland, September 26, 1877; d. Lausanne, June 15, 1962)

FRENCH PIANIST famed for the elegance of his phrasing and the ravishing beauty of his tone. His father was French, his mother Swiss. He studied in Paris at the Conservatoire, winning first prize in piano in 1896. He worked as a *répétiteur* at Bayreuth during the summers of 1898–1901, and conducted the French premiere of Wagner's *Götterdämmerung* in Paris in 1902. From 1905 he performed as a trio partner of violinist Jacques Thibaud and cellist Pablo Casals, and between 1907 and 1917 he taught piano at the Conservatoire. In 1919 he founded the École Normale de Musique in Paris, becoming its director and leading an annual summer class there for many years. His love of Teutonic culture—the music of Beethoven, Wagner, and Schumann in particular—allowed him to get cozy with the Germans during their uninvited stay in France from 1940 to 1944, and turned French hearts against him after the war.

A lapidary artist and supreme teacher, Cortot was a celebrated interpreter of the music of Chopin, Debussy, and, above all, Schumann. His recordings reveal a technique that was accident-prone but not shoddy, as well as a perfumed sonority that remains one of most remarkable musical signatures of the 20th century.

RECOMMENDED RECORDING

CHOPIN, PIANO CONCERTO NO. 1; SCHUMANN, PIANO CONCERTO: BARBIROLLI; RONALD AND LONDON PHILHARMONIC ORCHESTRA (NAXOS).

Così fan tutte OPERA BY MOZART, to a libretto by Lorenzo da Ponte, premiered at the Burgtheater in Vienna on January 26, 1790. The title, which defies elegant translation, can be loosely rendered in English as "All Women Are Like That." The libretto for *Così fan tutte* was the most formally perfect of the three that Da Ponte produced for Mozart. It takes off on the old opera buffa convention of paired lovers, which leads to a plethora of symmetries in plot and construction. At the center are two sisters, Fiordiligi and Dorabella, and their officer/lovers, Guglielmo and Ferrando—who, to test their fiancées' faithfulness, dress up as Albanians and woo each other's betrothed. Rounding out the cast are the wry old philosopher Don Alfonso, the prime mover in the whole charade, and the sisters' quick-witted maid Despina, who aids in the deception by impersonating, as necessary, a doctor and a notary.

Mozart's music has the polish and seamless elegance typical of the works of his last two years. The scoring is especially beautiful, at times luminously atmospheric in a way that points toward Weber and beyond. A lovely example is the trio "Soave sia il vento" from Act I. Yet there is a strong element of parody in Mozart's treatment of the material—emotions and their expression are projected with considerable beauty and animation, but not always with a naive acceptance of their value. This is one reason *Così fan tutte* seems as much an opera about opera as it is an opera about love.

RECOMMENDED RECORDINGS

FLEMING, OTTER, LOPARDO, BÄR; SOLTI AND CHAMBER ORCHESTRA OF EUROPE (DECCA).

LOTT, MCLAUGHLIN, HADLEY, CORBELLI; MACKERRAS AND SCOTTISH CHAMBER ORCHESTRA (TELARC).

counterpoint A type of POLYPHONY in which two or more independent and essentially melodic lines (often called "voices") proceed simultaneously, creating harmonious, rhythmically complex textures through their interaction. Modern tonal counterpoint emerged from the elaborate vocal polyphony of the 16th century, epitomized in the works of Josquin, Palestrina, and Lassus. As an element of instrumental composition, it was brought to a high state of development in the later Baroque, achieving a notable richness, rigor, and complexity in the music of J. S. Bach. Significantly, Bach thought of music as both a science and an art, and on the scientific side he devoted much energy in the last decade of his life to two purely speculative, large-scale contrapuntal studies: *A MUSICAL OFFERING* (1747) and *THE ART OF FUGUE* (finalized in 1748–49).

Because it is an especially difficult task to produce counterpoint that is lively, effective, and natural sounding, the writing of counterpoint continued to be considered a test of a composer's skill (and an essential part of proper training), even as the evolution of musical style from the Classical era into the 20th century tended to marginalize the use of contrapuntal textures. Still, there are great manifestations of contrapuntal art to be found, for example, in the music of Mozart (the finale of the *Jupiter* Symphony), Beethoven, Wagner (the Act I prelude to *Die Meistersinger von Nürnberg*), Franck (the canonic finale of the Sonata in A for violin and piano), Bruckner, Brahms, Mahler, Richard Strauss, and Reger. *See also* FUGUE; *individual composers.*

Men have sung in the alto range for hundreds of years, in traditional and church music, opera, and popular music. In the Middle Ages and Renaissance, countertenors (the part "against [i.e., above] the tenor"), sang alto in church choirs and in secular art music; in the 17th century, Purcell wrote parts for countertenors in his operas and semioperas, and in the 18th century, Handel wrote operatic roles for both castrati and countertenors. But with the demise of Baroque *opera seria* and the rise of *opera buffa* in the 19th century, the solo countertenor voice disappeared from the operatic scene.

In the late 1960s and early 1970s, the movement to revive Baroque opera began to create a need for voices that could sing the roles originally written for countertenors and castrati. At first these roles were either sung at pitch by mezzos or transposed for basses or baritones, but these solutions were often less than optimal. A new generation of countertenors began to fill the void, particularly Britons James Bowman and Paul Esswood, and the Belgian René Jacobs.

As Baroque opera has become a repertoire staple, there has been an explosion in the number of virtuoso countertenors with the range (both alto and soprano) and volume to undertake demanding roles and project in larger venues. While there may never be a perfect solution for castrato roles, it is now possible to cast them with men, already a step forward. Today's countertenors are also breaking out of the usual repertoire to sing music ranging from Mozart and Schubert to Cole Porter to contemporary works, establishing the countertenor—no longer just a curiosity—as an accepted and legitimate modern voice type.

Alfred Deller

(b. Margate, May 31, 1912; d. Bologna, July 16, 1979) The modern countertenor revival began in Britain, which had kept an unbroken tradition of using male altos in church and chapel choirs. The pioneering singer/scholar Deller brought to light much of the repertoire now sung by countertenors, particularly the works of Dowland, Blow, Purcell, and Handel. In 1948 he founded the Deller Consort, one of the first groups dedicated to historical performance practice. The ensemble's international tours and numerous recordings introduced the countertenor voice to audiences around the world. Deller's voice inspired Britten to write the first 20th-century operatic role for countertenor, that of Oberon in *A Midsummer Night's Dream.* Deller's unmistakable timbre, still allied with the flutelike English choral sound, was penetrating yet full, agile, and appealingly plangent.

RECOMMENDED RECORDING
"PORTRAIT OF A LEGEND": DELLER CONSORT, DUPRÉ (HARMONIA MUNDI).

Russell Oberlin

(b. Akron, Ohio, October 11, 1928) Another pioneering countertenor, Oberlin did not use falsetto (head voice), but instead had the quality of a very high, light tenor. After graduating from the Juilliard School in 1951, he became a founding member of Noah Greenberg's New York Pro Musica Antiqua, the first American ensemble to focus on medieval and Renaissance repertoire. In 1960 Oberlin stepped in for Deller, who was ill, to premiere the role of Oberon at Covent Garden. He had an active career as a recitalist, but retired from singing at age 36 to become an educator.

RECOMMENDED RECORDING
DOWLAND, LUTE SONGS: IADONE (LYRICHORD).

James Bowman

(b. Oxford, November 6, 1941) He began his career with Britten's English Opera Group as Oberon in Britten's *A Midsummer Night's Dream,* and was the first countertenor to sing at Glyndebourne, where he appeared in Cavalli's *La Calisto* in 1970. In 1971 he appeared in Handel's *Semele* with the English National Opera, and in Peter Maxwell Davies's *Taverner* at Covent Garden in 1972. During a 30-year career, he has premiered works by Britten, Tippett, Davies, and others and performed with conductors such as Harnoncourt, Gardiner, Norrington, and Leonhardt. His pure vocal color and elegant, heartfelt interpretations have been a revelation to listeners and an inspiration to following generations of countertenors.

RECOMMENDED RECORDING
VIVALDI, *STABAT MATER, NISI DOMINUS*: HOGWOOD AND ACADEMY OF ANCIENT MUSIC (POLYGRAM).

Paul Esswood

(b. West Bridgford, June 2, 1942) Educated at the Royal College of Music (1961–64), he made his operatic debut in Cavalli's *Erismena* in Berkeley in 1968, and went on to become the first countertenor to sing at La Scala. He appeared at the Zurich Festival in Jean-Pierre Ponelle's production of Monteverdi's three surviving operas, filmed for television. The title role in Philip Glass's *Akhnaten* and the role of Death in Penderecki's *Paradise Lost* were written for Esswood, whose rich, expressive voice has a fairly prominent

James Bowman in 1992

vibrato. Among his recordings are many in Teldec's complete Bach cantata series with Harnoncourt and Leonhardt.

RECOMMENDED RECORDING
BACH, "FAMOUS CANTATAS": KWEKSILBER, EQUILUZ, VAN EGMOND, HAMPSON; LEONHARDT AND LEONHARDT CONSORT (ELEKTRA/WEA).

René Jacobs

René Jacobs

(b. Ghent, October 30, 1946) He was a boy chorister at the Cathedral of Ghent. While studying classics at the University of Ghent, he continued voice studies as a tenor in Brussels. There he met Alfred Deller, with whose encouragement he retrained his voice, becoming the most successful European countertenor of his generation, performing and recording extensively with Hans Martin Linde, Leonhardt, Herreweghe, Sigiswald Kuijken, and others. After enthusiastically immersing himself in the Baroque repertoire, he began to conduct as well. In 1977 he founded Concerto Vocale, and he continues to direct often controversial and cutting-edge productions of Baroque and Classical operas. *See box on pages 310–13.*

RECOMMENDED RECORDING
RECITAL (WORKS BY CACCINI, PURCELL, MONTEVERDI, MOZART, OTHERS): JUNGHANEL (HARMONIA MUNDI).

Drew Minter

(b. Washington, D.C., January 11, 1955) He was a boy soprano at Washington National Cathedral and studied at Indiana University and the Vienna Musikhochschule. His light, extremely flexible voice is equally suited to medieval troubadour songs, 16th-century lute songs, and Baroque repertoire. A Handel specialist and expert in 18th-century vocal and stage practice, he has sung in and directed numerous performances of Handel operas in the United States and abroad. He is especially admired for his elegant portrayal of Tolomeo in Peter Sellars's film of *Giulio Cesare.*

RECOMMENDED RECORDING
HANDEL, "ARIAS FOR SENESINO": MCGEGAN AND PHILHARMONIA BAROQUE ORCHESTRA (HARMONIA MUNDI).

Michael Chance

(b. Penn Bucks, England, March 7, 1955) He has performed roles in Baroque and contemporary opera at Glyndebourne, Covent Garden, the Paris Opéra, and the Netherlands Opera. Also active in recital and oratorio, he appears regularly at major venues and festivals worldwide, with conductors such as Gardiner, Marriner, Leonhardt, Koopman, and Trevor Pinnock. A keen interest in transcending the standard repertoire

Michael Chance

has led to collaborations with Tan Dun, John Tavener, Elvis Costello, and others. He is noted for the velvety, seamless quality of his voice; his interpretive and expressive gifts are especially affecting in his recordings of Bach's Passions and cantatas with Sir John Eliot Gardiner.

RECOMMENDED RECORDING
"THE ART OF COUNTERTENOR": CANTATAS AND ARIAS BY BACH, HANDEL, PURCELL, SCHÜTZ, VIVALDI (UNIVERSAL/ARCHIV).

Gérard Lesne

(b. Montmorency, France, July 15, 1956) While studying musicology at the Sorbonne, Lesne began his career as a jazz and rock singer, but turned to early music at the urging of conductor René Clemencic. After touring Europe with the Clemencic Consort, Lesne joined Marcel Pérès's Ensemble Organum, specializing in medieval chant and polyphony. He has performed and recorded Baroque repertoire with William Christie's Les Arts Florissants and the Collegium Vocale under Philippe Herreweghe. In 1985, Lesne founded Il Seminario Musicale, producing many award-winning recordings of Italian and French Baroque repertoire. He possesses a warm, dark voice with a rich low register that lends an unmistakable virility to his interpretations.

RECOMMENDED RECORDING
VIVALDI, *SALVE REGINA* AND OTHER SACRED CANTATAS: BIONDI AND IL SEMINARIO MUSICALE (EMI).

Derek Lee Ragin

(b. West Point, N.Y., June 17, 1958) He made a spectacular switch to a singing career after graduating from Oberlin Conservatory with degrees in piano and education. The sheer beauty of his voice, as well as a natural, unaffected interpretive style, led to his acclaimed 1998 Metropolitan Opera debut in Handel's *Giulio Cesare.* In 1990 he sang the title role in Gluck's *Orfeo ed Eurydice* at the Salzburg Festival under Sir John Eliot Gardiner.

Ragin sang several roles in the world premiere of Peter Eötvös's *Angels in America,* and has premiered works by Giya Kancheli, Jonathan Dawes, and others. His voice was blended with that of coloratura soprano Ewa Mallas Godlewksa for the1993 film *Farinelli: Il Castrato.*

RECOMMENDED RECORDING
Gluck, *Orfeo ed Euridice*: McNair, Sieden: Gardiner and English Baroque Soloists (Philips).

David Daniels

(b. Spartanburg, S.C., 1966) The son of two voice teachers, he began as a boy soprano; while studying as a tenor with George Shirley at the University of Michigan, he discovered his countertenor voice. Since then he has become one of most sought-after artists of his generation—his powerful, masculine, yet soft-edged vocal quality, incomparable coloratura, and ability to fully inhabit his roles have been widely praised. In 1999, he made his Metropolitan Opera debut as Sesto in Handel's *Giulio Cesare,* and in 2004 triumphed as Bertarido in *Rodelinda* opposite Renée Fleming. Appearing at major opera houses and festivals around the world, he has performed the title roles in *Rinaldo, Tamerlano,* and *Giulio Cesare,* Orfeo in Gluck's *Orfeo ed Eurydice,* Oberon in *A Midsummer Night's Dream,* and Farnace in Mozart's *Mitridate.* He is an accomplished recitalist, and has recorded American contemporary and folk music as well as songs by Beethoven, Gounod, Schubert, and Poulenc.

David Daniels

RECOMMENDED RECORDING
Handel, *Rinaldo*: Bartoli, Fink, Orgonasova, Mehta: Hogwood and Academy of Ancient Music (Decca).

Andreas Scholl

Andreas Scholl

(b. Eltville-am-Rhein, November 10, 1967) He sang as a boy in the Kiedricher Chorbuben, and was still singing soprano and alto long after his voice had changed. Recruited by René Jacobs at age 19, he entered the Schola Cantorum Basiliensis, where he studied with Richard Levitt and Jacobs. His professional break came in 1993 when he stepped in for Jacobs, singing Bach's *St. John* Passion in Paris. Conductor William Christie heard a broadcast of the performance and was impressed; Scholl's 1994 recording of *Messiah* with Christie's Les Arts Florissants made him a star virtually overnight. With a voice of uncanny beauty and clarity, he is renowned for his sensitive and nuanced Bach interpretations. Preferring to focus on Renaissance and Baroque repertoire, he has performed and recorded with every major Baroque orchestra, under conductors such as Gardiner, Herreweghe, Norrington, McGegan, and Hogwood. Aside from oratorio and recitals, he has sung the role of Bertarido in Handel's *Rinaldo* at Glyndebourne, and the title role in *Giulio Cesare* with the Royal Danish Opera. Beyond his usual repertoire, he has recorded "Wayfaring Stranger," a program of folk songs, with Orpheus Chamber Orchestra, and writes and performs pop songs with fellow countertenor Roland Kunz.

RECOMMENDED RECORDING
Bach, Cantatas for Alto: Herreweghe and Collegium Vocale Gent (harmonia mundi).

Bejun Mehta

(b. North Carolina, June 29, 1968) Born into a musical family (his pianist father is a cousin of Zubin Mehta), he had a brilliant career as a boy soprano soloist; later he tried unsuccessfully to make the transition to baritone. After attending Yale University (where he studied cello with Aldo Parisot) and becoming an award-winning record producer, he was inspired by David Daniels's story and reemerged in 1997 with a remarkable countertenor voice. He made sensational debuts in 1998 at New York City Opera as Armindo in Handel's *Partenope,* and in 2002 at the Metropolitan Opera as Oberon in *A Midsummer Night's Dream.* With his ringing, clarion sound and charismatic stage presence, he is well suited to the heroic Handel roles, singing Unulfo in the Met's 2004 production of *Rodelinda,* the title role in *Tamerlano* with Netherlands Opera, and Bertarido in *Rodelinda* with the Bavarian State Opera. Other roles include Ottone in *L'incoronazione di Poppea,* the title roles in *Giulio Cesare* and *Orlando,* and Farnace in *Mitridate.* He has sung at major opera houses as well as appearing with orchestras such as the Israel Philharmonic, San Francisco Symphony, Scottish Chamber Orchestra, and Les Musiciens du Louvre.

RECOMMENDED RECORDING
Handel, *Giulio Cesare*: Mijanovic, Kozena, Otter: Minkowski and Les Musiciens du Louvre (Archiv).

Couperin, François

(b. Paris, November 10, 1668; d. Paris, September 11, 1733)

FRENCH KEYBOARD PLAYER AND COMPOSER, with Rameau the most important figure in French music during the first half of the 18th century. He was known as "le grand" ("the Great") because he was the most illustrious member of a family of musicians that dominated the French keyboard scene for more than a century. In 1685 he succeeded his father as organist at the church of St. Gervais, taking his rightful place in the family dynasty (Couperins would eventually rule the organ loft at St. Gervais for 173 years). In 1693 he was named *organiste du roi* (court organist), a position that carried considerable prestige and financial benefit, and brought Couperin into contact with the movers and shakers at the court of Louis XIV. A second royal appointment came in 1717, when he was finally named *ordinaire de la musique de la chambre du roi pour le clavecin* (court harpsichordist), after having deputized for the incumbent d'Anglebert for many years. Couperin's prosperity continued after Louis XV ascended the throne in 1715; he kept a busy teaching schedule into the 1720s, but gradually had to give up performing as his health failed. He continued composing and publishing music right up to the time of his death.

Manuscript page of a prelude by Couperin

Naturally enough, Couperin's output consisted mainly of keyboard works and the sacred vocal pieces expected of a church organist. Of prime importance to his legacy were the four books of harpsichord pieces, called *Ordres* ◉, that he published in 1713, 1716, 1722, and 1733. He also composed several collections of chamber pieces, including *Les goûts réunis* (1724) and *Les nations* (1726), both much influenced by Corelli, and wrote a treatise on harpsichord playing, *L'art de toucher le clavecin* (1716).

RECOMMENDED RECORDINGS

HARPSICHORD PIECES: ROUSSET (HARMONIA MUNDI).

LEÇONS DE TÉNÈBRES: DANEMON, PETIBON; CHRISTIE AND LES ARTS FLORISSANTS (ERATO).

courante (Fr., "running [dance]") A flowing, fast-paced dance in triple meter. In the 17th and 18th centuries it was among the standard dances incorporated in orchestral and keyboard suites. *See also* SUITE.

Covent Garden London neighborhood where the city's principal opera house has stood since 1732. The first building to occupy the site, the Theatre Royal, was built in 1732; it was replaced by a new structure in 1809, which burned in 1856. The building that currently occupies the site, the Royal Opera House, was built in 1858 and extensively renovated in the 1990s. Covent Garden was the first housing development in history, laid out in the 1630s by Inigo Jones.

cowbells *See box on pages 496–97.*

Cowell, Henry

(b. Menlo Park, Calif., March 11, 1897; d. Shady, N.Y., December 10, 1965)

AMERICAN COMPOSER. Like Thomas Edison (who hailed from the *other* Menlo Park, in New Jersey) he was an inventor. He created (independent of Charles

Ives, who came up with it as well) the pianistic device known as the "tone cluster"—a dissonant clump of notes played using the fist or entire forearm—and introduced elements from various non-Western musics, including Asian and American Indian, to the vocabulary of mainstream classical composition. He was the first serious composer to synthesize an idiom based on what today is referred to as "world music," and the first to advance the concept of indeterminacy, which he called "elastic form." His large output included 20 symphonies and more than a dozen concerted works, numerous short pieces for orchestra and concert band, a large body of chamber music, and dozens of pieces for piano. He was also a prolific essayist. While few of his works are played today, the influence he exerted on the development of 20th-century musical thought—through his prose as well as his music—was profound, particularly in the way it opened the door to an acceptance of sparse textures and unconventional sounds.

RECOMMENDED RECORDINGS

"INSTRUMENTAL, CHAMBER, AND VOCAL MUSIC," VOLS. 1 AND 2: SACHS AND CONTINUUM (NAXOS).

MUSIC FOR STRINGS: FRANCIS AND NORTHWEST CHAMBER ORCHESTRA SEATTLE (CPO).

Craft, Robert

(b. Kingston, N.Y., October 20, 1923)

AMERICAN CONDUCTOR AND WRITER. He graduated from the Juilliard School in 1946, studied at the Berkshire Music Center at Tanglewood, and worked as an assistant to Pierre Monteux. In his early years as a conductor, he became enthralled with serialism and the music of Arnold Schoenberg and his circle. He met Igor Stravinsky in 1948, beginning an artistic relationship that lasted until the composer's death in 1971. Craft became personal assistant, musical collaborator, and a kind of adopted son to Stravinsky; he shared conducting duties on many concerts, apparently had a significant role in Stravinsky's late-in-life adoption of 12-tone techniques, and conducted the world premieres of several late works, including *In Memoriam Dylan Thomas* and *Requiem Canticles.* After Stravinsky's death, Craft continued to conduct, record, write about, and advocate Stravinsky's music. He is the author of a dozen books about the composer, including a three-volume edition of his letters and *Stravinsky: Chronicle of a Friendship, 1948–71.* After the death of Stravinsky's wife, Craft inherited many of the composer's papers, as well as a portion of the copyright. His closeness to Stravinsky, and longtime control over material pertaining to him, has led to some speculation from music scholars as to the degree to which Stravinsky's words, as reported by Craft, are accurate, particularly after Stravinsky's papers at the Paul Sacher Foundation in Basel, Switzerland, were opened to researchers in 1986. In 2003, Vanderbilt University Press published Craft's autobiography, *An Improbable Life: Memoirs.*

Craft also championed the music of early composers such as Monteverdi, Schütz, and Gesualdo, as well as the works of Schoenberg, Berg, Webern, Stockhausen, Varèse, and Boulez. He conducted the first performance of Varèse's *Nocturnal* and, at the Santa Fe Opera, the American premieres of Berg's *Lulu* and Hindemith's *Cardillac.*

RECOMMENDED RECORDINGS

SCHOENBERG, *FIVE PIECES FOR ORCHESTRA, A SURVIVOR FROM WARSAW*: VARCOE; LONDON CHAMBER CHORUS, LONDON SYMPHONY ORCHESTRA (KOCH).

STRAVINSKY, *THE FIREBIRD, PETRUSHKA*: PHILHARMONIA ORCHESTRA (NAXOS).

Creation, The (Die Schöpfung) **ORATORIO BY FRANZ JOSEPH HAYDN,** to a libretto by Gottfried van Swieten (based on Milton's

Paradise Lost), premiered April 29, 1798, in a private performance at the Schwarzenberg Palace in Vienna. The first public performance took place in Vienna on March 19, 1799, Haydn's name day. The oratorio is in three parts: the first represents the first four days of Creation, the second the fifth and sixth days, and the third the blissful existence of Adam and Eve before the Fall. The score contains some of Haydn's most powerful and imaginative music, in particular the prologue's magnificent depiction of chaos, the opening chorus's blazing C major declamation of the word "LIGHT!" as it recounts the first act of Creation, and the second part's colorful portrait of animal life in Eden, including a roaring lion (in the brass), a leaping tiger (rising scale passages in the strings), a bounding stag, the oxen in the meadows (a pastorale for flute), buzzing insects (soft string tremolos), and even a lowly earthworm.

RECOMMENDED RECORDINGS

Janowitz, Ludwig, Wunderlich, Fischer-Dieskau; Karajan and Berlin Philharmonic (DG).

McNair, Brown, Schade, Finley, Gilfry; Gardiner and English Baroque Soloists (DG).

Credo Third section of the Ordinary of the Mass. Its text is the Nicene Creed, which begins with the words "Credo in unum Deum . . ." ("I believe in one God . . .") and states the fundamental tenets of Christian belief. In the archlike structure of the Mass, the Credo forms the keystone. Its text is the longest of any section of the Ordinary, and at the center of it are the words that express the mystery that is central to the faith: "Qui propter nos homines et propter nostram salutem, descendit de coelis, et incarnatus est de Spiritu Sancto ex Maria Virgine, et homo factus est." ("For us men and for our salvation he came down from heaven: by the power of the Holy Spirit he was born of the Virgin Mary, and became man.") Because of the importance of its text the Credo tends to receive an especially rich treatment in most polyphonic settings of the Mass. *See also* MASS.

crescendo Growing louder. A crescendo is often notated by the abbreviation *cresc.* or by a wedge-shaped marking under the phrase or passage where it is to occur [<]. Among the most common expressive devices in music, crescendos typically produce a heightened sense of tension, drama, and excitement. One of the most effective uses of crescendo in the literature is the 8-measure buildup (from *pp* to *ff*) at the end of the transition passage between the third movement and the finale of Beethoven's Fifth Symphony. *See also* DECRESCENDO.

Crumb, George

(b. Charleston, W.V., October 24, 1929)

AMERICAN COMPOSER. Both of his parents were musical. His study of music began at home and continued at Mason College in Charleston and the University of Illinois, where he received a master's degree in 1952. In 1955, on a Fulbright Fellowship, he studied with Boris Blacher in Berlin, and in 1959 he obtained his doctorate in composition at the University of Michigan; his principal teacher there was Ross Lee Finney. From 1959 to 1964 he taught piano and composition at the University of Colorado, and in 1965 he joined the faculty of the University of Pennsylvania. Like many mid-20th-century composers, Crumb began as a serialist and metamorphosed into an eclectic; his pointillistic idiom is one of the most delicately nuanced and evocative of the past 40 years, remarkable not only for its sonic daring but also for its concision. His most important works are *Makrokosmos,* Volume I (1972) and *Makrokosmos,* Volume II (1973), both subtitled "12 Fantasy-Pieces After the Zodiac for Amplified Piano"; *Ancient Voices of Children*

(1970) for soprano, boy soprano, oboe, mandolin, harp, electric piano/toy piano, and three percussionists; and several books of vocal-instrumental "madrigals" to texts by Federico García Lorca.

RECOMMENDED RECORDINGS

Ancient Voices of Children: DeGaetani; Dash, Kalish; Weisberg and Contemporary Chamber Ensemble (Nonesuch).

Makrokosmos I and II: Crumb, Hudicek (Furious Artisans).

Music for a Summer Evening, Makrokosmos III: Freeman, Kalish, Fitz, DesRoches (Nonesuch).

crumhorn A family of double-reed wind instruments in common use during the Renaissance. The body of a crumhorn was shaped like the letter "J," and the instrument made a buzzing sound similar to that of a kazoo, only far more raucous.

Curtin, Phyllis

(b. Clarksburg, W.V., December 3, 1922)

AMERICAN SOPRANO. She spent the early years of her career on the roster of the New York City Opera, where she sang a variety of roles including the major Mozart heroines, Violetta in Verdi's *La traviata,* Salome, Cressida in Walton's *Troilus and Cressida,* and the title role in Carlisle Floyd's *Susannah,* which she created in 1955. During the 1960s, she performed in Vienna, Milan, Frankfurt, and Buenos Aires, as well as at the Metropolitan Opera. A gifted teacher with an impeccable technique, she possessed a voice of great lyrical beauty but could sing with fire and dramatic urgency when the occasion demanded.

RECOMMENDED RECORDING

"Phyllis Curtin: Opera Arias 1960–1968" (selections from Floyd, Charpentier, Giordano, Mozart, Puccini, Verdi, Strauss): Various (VAI).

Curtis Institute of Music CONSERVATORY IN PHILADELPHIA FOUNDED IN 1924 by newspaper heiress Mary Louise Curtis Bok, who remained president of the school until her death in 1970. The institute's directors have been John Grolle (1924–26), Josef Hoffmann (1926–38), Randall Thompson (1939–41), Efrem Zimbalist (1941–68), Rudolf Serkin (1968–76), John de Lancie (1976–86), and Gary Graffman (1986–2006), and its faculty has included Leopold Auer, Carl Flesch, Wanda Landowska, Carlos Salzedo, William Primrose, Gregor Piatigorsky, and Leonard Rose. Among its most notable students have been composers Samuel Barber, Leonard Bernstein, Lukas Foss, and Ned Rorem, pianists Jorge Bolet, Walter Hendl, and Richard Goode, and violinists Young-Uck Kim and Hilary Hahn. Roberto Diaz will assume the post of director at the end of the 2005–06 academic year.

The Curtis Institute of Music on Rittenhouse Square

Curzon, Clifford

(b. London, May 18, 1907; d. London, September 1, 1982)

ENGLISH PIANIST. He entered the Royal Academy of Music in 1919, was appointed to its faculty in 1926, and left two years later in order to continue his studies with Artur Schnabel in Berlin. He subsequently studied in Paris with Wanda Landowska and Nadia Boulanger. His American debut took place in 1939; following the end of World War II he returned to the United States and toured throughout Europe. He was knighted in 1977. Dignified and introverted, Curzon was an artist of patrician taste and gentleness. Schubert, Schumann, and Brahms formed the core of his repertoire, but there was no better pianist in Mozart and no finer chamber musician in any setting. Because he had a tendency to be an anxious performer and could come unglued when the red light went on in the recording studio, he concertized infrequently and made relatively few recordings (approving still fewer). But in those he did approve, the depth of his musical and spiritual insights can be readily sensed.

RECOMMENDED RECORDINGS

BRAHMS, PIANO QUINTET; SCHUBERT, *TROUT* QUINTET: AMADEUS QUARTET (BBC).

MOZART, PIANO CONCERTOS: BRITTEN AND ENGLISH CHAMBER ORCHESTRA; KERTÉSZ AND LONDON SYMPHONY ORCHESTRA (DECCA).

cyclical form In multimovement works, a thematic procedure in which a motive or melodic idea from the opening movement serves as the basis for the thematic material of subsequent movements, or is reintroduced verbatim in a later movement, either for dramatic effect or to lend coherence to the overall formal plan. Beethoven pioneered the process of thematic recall in the finale of his Ninth Symphony, and Schubert the principle of monothematic construction in his *WANDERERFANTASIE*. Berlioz attempted a mix of both techniques with the use of an idée fixe in his *SYMPHONIE FANTASTIQUE*, and Liszt greatly refined the concept in works such as his *Faust Symphony* and Piano Sonata in B minor. Liszt's approach strongly influenced many composers, particularly the Russians Borodin (both of whose completed symphonies are cyclic in their thematic construction) and Tchaikovsky (who incorporated a cyclical return of first-movement material in the finales of his Symphony No. 4 and *Manfred* Symphony). In fin-de-siècle French music, cyclical form reached its peak in the works of Franck (his Violin Sonata and String Quartet) and Debussy (his String Quartet in G minor, Op. 10).

cymbals Dish-shaped plates made of brass alloy that can produce a loud, ringing vibration when forcefully clashed together, or a tingling, whisper-soft swoosh when brushed gently. Cymbals generally come in matched pairs, and can be of differing thicknesses, from paper-thin to bulletproof. When two cymbals are struck or brushed together they are referred to as "crash" cymbals; they are held by looped leather straps passed through small holes drilled in the center of each dome. When a single cymbal is mounted on a stand, it is called a "suspended" cymbal; it can be struck with a soft stick, a snare-drum stick, or a metal object such as a penknife blade or triangle beater, rolled using a pair of soft sticks, or brushed with metal or fiber implements.

Cymbals were appropriated from the Janissary bands of the Ottoman Turks and made their way into European classical music toward the end of the 18th century. Mozart used them to provide "local" color in the overture to *Die Entführung aus dem Serail*, set in Turkey; Haydn employed them in his Symphony No. 100 in G (*Military*); and Beethoven made notable use of them in the finale of his Symphony No. 9, where they accompany a Turkish march. Never willing to get by with just one or two of an instrument if he could muster three or four, Berlioz, in the Sanctus of his *Grand messe des morts*, calls for three pairs of cymbals to be softly brushed, in an imaginatively scored passage that David Cairns has described as an "audible equivalent of the swinging censers around God's throne."

Czech Philharmonic The leading orchestra of the Czech Republic, and through much of its history one of Europe's most distinguished symphonic ensembles. Originally the orchestra of the Prague National Opera, it was first designated as the Česká Filharmonie (Czech Philharmonic) for a pension-fund concert conducted by Antonín Dvořák in Prague's Rudolfinum Hall, on January 4, 1896. Following a strike by members of the opera orchestra, the Czech Philharmonic became an independent body in 1901. In 1908 Gustav Mahler led it in the premiere of his Symphony No. 7. The orchestra entered a golden age when Václav Talich was appointed principal conductor in 1919. Talich remained in that post until 1941, by which time he had transformed the Philharmonic into a world-class ensemble; he was succeeded by the young Rafael Kubelík, whose tenure (1942–48) lasted through the war years and up to the Communist takeover. Karel Ančerl sustained the orchestra during some of the darkest years in Czech history (1950–68). Forced to abandon his position when the reform government of Alexander Dubček was crushed, he left a valuable legacy of recordings. Václav Neumann brought stability and a measure of prestige to the orchestra during his long tenure (1968–89), which saw numerous international tours and a plethora of recordings. Following the "Velvet Revolution" and the slashing of state subsidies, the orchestra went through a period of adjustment in the 1990s, including an uneasy marriage with conductor Gerd Albrecht (1992–95). Vladimir Ashkenazy was appointed chief conductor in 1997; following his installation in January 1998 he began a series of recordings for the Finnish label Ondine, and in recent years he has led the Czechs on tours of Europe, the Far East, and North America. The Czech-American conductor Zdeněk Mácal (b. 1936), a native of Brno, became chief conductor at the start of the 2003–04 season.

The Czech Philharmonic is one of the few major orchestras in the world with an unmistakable sound, which it has maintained throughout its turbulent history. At its core is a unique string sonority—full-bodied without being heavy, and magically luminous, especially in the violins. While the brass can be reticent and rather light in weight, the winds, particularly the clarinets, are colorful and play with a "vocal" character that is marvelously expressive.

RECOMMENDED RECORDINGS

DVOŘÁK, CELLO CONCERTO: ROSTROPOVICH, TALICH (SUPRAPHON).

DVOŘÁK, *SLAVONIC DANCES*: SEJNA (SUPRAPHON).

JANÁČEK, *GLAGOLITIC MASS*: MACKERRAS (SUPRAPHON).

JANÁČEK, *SINFONIETTA* (WITH WORKS OF MARTINŮ): ANČERL (SUPRAPHON).

MARTINŮ, SYMPHONIES NOS. 3 AND 4: BĚLOHLÁVEK (SUPRAPHON).

SMETANA, *MÁ VLAST*: KUBELÍK (SUPRAPHON).

da capo (It., "from the top") Instruction to return to the beginning of a movement or a section of a piece, and sing or play it again. This procedure was frequently used in arias of 17th- and 18th-century operas and oratorios. A typical da capo aria consisted of two clearly differentiated sections, the first of which had to be repeated—with elaborations improvised by the singer—following the conclusion of the second, resulting in a lengthy ABA form. An example familiar to many in the English-speaking world is "I know that my Redeemer Liveth," from Handel's *Messiah.*

"Dance of the Seven Veils" ORCHESTRAL INTERLUDE IN RICHARD STRAUSS'S *SALOME* **(1905),** during which the opera's title character performs a seductive striptease for her lecherous stepfather, King Herod. Having sworn an oath to give Salome anything she wants if she will only dance for him, Herod learns to his horror (after she's finished dancing) that what she wants is the head of John the Baptist brought to her "on a silver platter." The dance is usually done by a member of the corps de ballet, who substitutes herself for the soprano singing the part of Salome in the moments before the dance begins. The luxurious pages of the "Dance of the Seven Veils" set a new standard for eroticism in orchestral music, and remain among the most ravishing examples of Strauss's penchant for putting waltzes into his operas and symphonic poems.

RECOMMENDED RECORDING

KARAJAN AND BERLIN PHILHARMONIC (DG).

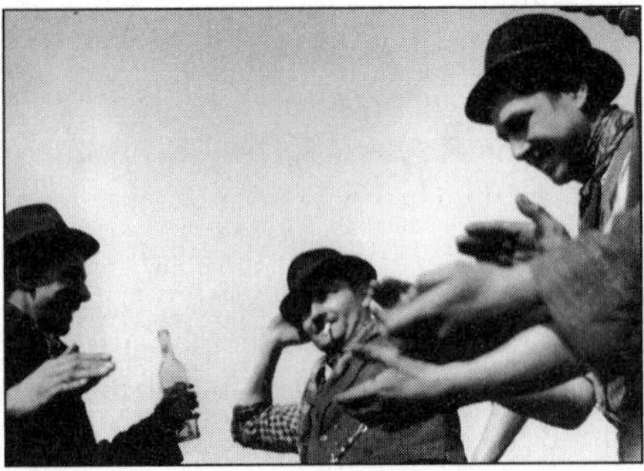

A Gypsy spirit pervades the **Dances of Galánta.**

Dances of Galánta ORCHESTRAL WORK BY ZOLTÁN KODÁLY, composed in 1933 in honor of the 80th anniversary of the Budapest Philharmonic Society and premiered October 23, 1933. Raised in the little town of Galánta, where his father worked as a railroad stationmaster, Kodály absorbed a variety of musical influences, among them the spirited music making of Gypsy bands. Years later, he drew upon that experience to fashion the *Dances of Galánta.* Borrowing some of his thematic material from anthologies of popular and Gypsy melodies, he created a colorfully scored sequence of five connected dances, part suite, part symphonic rondo. There is a languorous, improvisatory quality to the opening dance; gradually gaining momentum with each ensuing dance, the piece builds to a wild, *molto vivace* conclusion.

RECOMMENDED RECORDING

DORATI AND MINNEAPOLIS SYMPHONY ORCHESTRA (MERCURY).

Dance Suite ORCHESTRAL WORK BY BÉLA BARTÓK, first performed on November 19, 1923, with Ernő Dohnányi conducting, at a concert celebrating the 50th anniversary of the merger of Buda and Pest into a single city. The work is in six sections—five dances and a finale—played without a break and linked by a *ritornello,* or recurring interlude, in the style of a Hungarian dance. The dances are shaped by elements drawn from Hungarian, Romanian, and Arabic folk music. The work brought Bartók his first popular success.

RECOMMENDED RECORDINGS

DORATI AND PHILHARMONIA HUNGARICA (MERCURY).

SOLTI AND LONDON SYMPHONY ORCHESTRA (DECCA).

Daniels, David *See box on pages 155–57.*

Danse macabre WALTZ FANTASY FOR SOLO VIOLIN AND ORCHESTRA BY CAMILLE SAINT-SAËNS, composed in 1874. The composer's inspiration was a poem by Henri Cazalis in which Death is depicted as a fiddler playing in a churchyard on a wintry night, making skeletons dance to his tune. The piece begins with the soft chiming of midnight; without much ado, the spectral violin makes its entrance and—introducing itself with a gruesome tritone, a.k.a. "the Devil's interval," produced by playing the open A string against the open E string, tuned down a half step—launches into a waltz grotesque enough to send a shiver up the spine. This is answered by an animated solo on the xylophone (a parody of the *DIES IRAE*), depicting the dance of the skeletons. The dance becomes increasingly frenzied and exultant, though always retaining a certain balletic grace, until, at the climactic moment, the cock's crow, played by the oboe, announces daybreak. With that, the spirits depart the scene as mysteriously as they arrived.

Danses concertantes SUITE BY IGOR STRAVINSKY in neoclassical style for small orchestra, composed in Hollywood in 1941–42 on a commission from the Werner Janssen Orchestra, and premiered by that group in Los Angeles on February 8, 1942, with the composer conducting. Though created as a concert piece, the score is unabashedly balletic; in 1944 the dances were choreographed by George Balanchine for the Ballets Russes de Monte Carlo.

RECOMMENDED RECORDING

ORPHEUS CHAMBER ORCHESTRA (DG).

Daphnis et Chloé BALLET IN THREE TABLEAUX BY MAURICE RAVEL, to a scenario by Mikhail Fokine (based on a pastoral drama by the Greek poet Longus), commissioned by Sergey Diaghilev and his Ballets Russes and premiered in Paris on June 8, 1912, at the Théâtre du Châtelet. Considered the composer's masterpiece, it is one of the most gratifying showpieces in the symphonic repertoire. The setting is ancient Greece, though Ravel later pointed out that in writing the music, his intention had been "to compose a vast musical fresco in which I was less concerned with archaism than with faithfully reproducing the Greece of my dreams, which is quite similar to what was imagined and painted by French artists at the end of the 18th century." The ballet depicts the tender love of the shepherd Daphnis for the maiden Chloé; her abduction by pirates and miraculous escape (thanks to Pan); and the young lovers' joyous reunion. The work's voluptuous score—308 pages of astonishingly precise and demanding notation—is a fascinating, subtly organized tissue of changing colors, textures, and effects. It calls for an enormous orchestra with expanded percussion (13 separate instruments plus timpani, requiring six players) and a chorus behind the scene, all used to superbly atmospheric effect, as in the depiction of dawn that opens the ballet's final tableau. Pierre Monteux, who was 37 at the time and had already presided over the first performance of Stravinsky's *Petrushka,* conducted the premiere, with Vaslav Nijinsky and Tamara Karsavina as Daphnis and Chloé.

RECOMMENDED RECORDING

DUTOIT AND MONTREAL SYMPHONY ORCHESTRA (DECCA).

da Ponte, Lorenzo

(b. Ceneda, March 10, 1749; d. New York, August 17, 1838)

ITALIAN POET AND LIBRETTIST, best known for his collaboration with Mozart on *LE NOZZE DI FIGARO, DON GIOVANNI,* and *COSÌ FAN TUTTE.* Though he had a tendency, displayed in his *Memoirs,* to embellish the truth, he did lead a remarkably eventful life. He was born Emmanuele Conegliano, the son of a Jewish tanner, and took the name of the Bishop of Ceneda, Lorenzo da Ponte, when he and his family were received into the Catholic Church in 1763. He was ordained in 1773, and taught at several seminaries in the region around Venice before his noncelibate lifestyle resulted in his being banned from teaching and, in 1779, excommunicated. He went to Dresden, where he worked briefly with the poet Caterino Mazzolà, but after failing to land a position at the Saxon court he moved on to Vienna bearing a letter of recommendation from Mazzolà to court-composer Antonio Salieri, arriving in late 1781. There he succeeded in ingratiating himself with Emperor Joseph II, who in 1783 appointed him poet to the court theater.

Lorenzo da Ponte in later years

Da Ponte met Mozart in the spring of that year. "If he is in league with Salieri," Mozart wrote his father on May 7, "I will never get anything out of him. But I would dearly love to show what I can do in an Italian opera." Finally, in the summer of 1785, Mozart asked Da Ponte if he would be willing to provide him with a libretto based on Beaumarchais's *Le mariage de Figaro. Le nozze di Figaro* premiered May 1, 1786, and was so satisfying to both Mozart and Da Ponte that they teamed up on two further efforts: *Il dissoluto punito, o sia Il Don Giovanni* (premiered October 29, 1787, in Prague) and *Così fan tutte, o sia La scuola degli amanti* (premiered January 26, 1790). During these years, Da Ponte also collaborated with Vicente Martín y Soler—*Una cosa rara* (1786) and *L'arbore di Diana* (1787)—and Salieri, of whose *Tarare* he made an Italian adaptation, *Axur, re d'Ormus,* in 1788. Between 1794 and 1804 he crafted a dozen original librettos and revised an equal number of existing ones, including that to Cimarosa's *Il matrimonio segreto.* In 1805, after various exploits and bankruptcies in Europe, he came to America, set up shop as a greengrocer in New York City, spent time as a book dealer in Philadelphia, returned to New York in 1819, and was appointed professor of Italian literature at Columbia College in 1825. He helped establish New York's first Italian opera company, and died an American citizen during the presidency of Martin Van Buren, at the age of 89.

Darmstadt City in western Germany where, since 1946, summer courses in advanced composition have been offered. Inaugurated by Wolfgang Steinecke, the courses were held annually until 1970 and since then have taken place every two years.

During the 1960s and 1970s, when figures such as Maderna, Stockhausen, Ligeti, and Xenakis were involved in its programs, Darmstadt was considered the center of the post–World War II avant-garde.

Daugherty, Michael *See box on pages 708–11.*

Davidsbündlertänze (Dances of the Tribe of David) PIANO PIECE BY ROBERT SCHUMANN, OP. 6, composed in the summer of 1837. It consists of 18 miniatures (arranged in two groups of nine) in a kaleidoscopic array of moods. One of Schumann's favorite conceits was the *Davidsbund* ("Tribe of David"), peopled by imaginary characters who, like the biblical David, had decided to stand up to the artistic Philistines of the day. The members of this society included the impetuous extrovert, Florestan, and the pale, studious, introverted Eusebius, reflecting two sides of Schumann's own character, as well as a figure he called Meister Raro, who may have represented Schumann's teacher, Friedrich Wieck, the father of his bride-to-be, Clara. At the time he composed the *Davidsbündlertänze,* Schumann's courtship had just passed through a particularly tense phase, with the happy result that Clara had secretly pledged herself to him. Feelings of joy, giddiness, and anxiety succeed one another in the cameos of the *Davidsbündlertänze* with remarkable ease, as though Schumann were keeping a diary of his emotions in music. The intensity of these feelings translates into music of remarkable affective power.

RECOMMENDED RECORDING

PERAHIA (SONY).

Sir Peter Maxwell Davies

Davies, Sir Peter Maxwell

(b. Salford, September 8, 1934)

ENGLISH COMPOSER. A prolific and decidedly individualistic figure, he was part of a vibrant British new-music scene during the 1960s; his music underwent a profound stylistic shift in the years following 1971, when he settled in the Orkney Islands at the northern extreme of Scotland. A maverick from an early age, he began studying piano at four and reached an important milestone—the first public performance of one of his compositions—when he was eight. He received much of his early compositional education through reading and the radio, which fostered a profound interest in such nonstandard repertoire as medieval and Renaissance music and Indian ragas (on which he wrote his master's thesis). The most influential aspect of his studies at the Royal Manchester College of Music and Manchester University was his association with fellow students Harrison Birtwistle, Alexander Goehr, Elgar Howarth, and John Ogdon, all of whom were interested in avant-garde musical styles. Known as the Manchester Five, they formed an ensemble to perform their own work and other new music.

Studies in Rome with Goffredo Petrassi and at Princeton with Roger Sessions and Earl Kim prompted Davies to develop a more rigorous underpinning to his composition, including his own mathematically developed version of serial technique; he also incorporated techniques and ideas from his much-admired early composers as well as various avant-garde models. Returning to London in 1967, he and Birtwistle founded the Pierrot Players, consisting of the Schoenberg *Pierrot lunaire* ensemble (flute/piccolo, clarinet/bass clarinet, violin/viola, cello, and piano), plus percussion, and this became for a while the focus of his compositional life. One of Davies's best-known works, the wildly expressionistic *Eight Songs for a Mad King* (1969), a dramatic setting of fictional rantings by George III, is emblematic of his music from this period.

In 1970, Davies took a summer trip to the Orkney Islands. By the following year, he was living there, as he has ever since, first on Hoy and then, after 1998, on Sanday. As a result of this relocation, his composition took a profoundly different turn. Inspired by the writings of the Orcadian poet George Mackay Brown (1921–96), Davies became fascinated by the landscape, seascape, culture, and people of these remote islands, and his work began to reflect that inspiration. Examples include his chamber opera, *The Martyrdom of St Magnus* (1976), about a local saint, and the orchestral work *An Orkney Wedding, with Sunrise* (1985), one of Davies's most frequently heard pieces, in which the "sunrise" brings an obbligato solo for Scottish bagpipes. Although he continued to work until 1987 with the Pierrot Players (reconstituted as the Fires of London in 1971, without Birtwistle), Davies allowed his music to move toward a more expansive style. He began a cycle of symphonies in 1976, and from 1985 to 1994, as associate composer-conductor of the Scottish Chamber Orchestra, he wrote a series of chamber concertos (called the *Strathclyde Concertos*) and orchestral pieces. Later associations included conductor-composer posts with the Royal Philharmonic Orchestra and the BBC Philharmonic in Manchester.

Davies is regularly commissioned, and his catalog now includes nearly 300 works, ranging from the well-known chamber opera *The Lighthouse* (1979) and his second full-scale opera, *The Doctor of Myddfai* (1995), commissioned by the Welsh National Opera, to a recently launched series of string quartets for the Maggini String Quartet and the orchestral cycle *The Orkney Saga.* Davies's commitment to his adopted home has included founding the St. Magnus Festival in 1977 (which he directed until 1986), writing many pieces for the local community, particularly for schoolchildren, and establishing a summer school for student composers on Hoy in the late 1980s. Queen Elizabeth made him a Commander of the British Empire in 1981; in 1987, he received a knighthood.

RECOMMENDED RECORDINGS

EIGHT SONGS FOR A MAD KING: EASTMAN; DAVIES AND FIRES OF LONDON (UNICORN).

THE LIGHTHOUSE: COMBOY, KEYTE, MACKIE; DAVIES AND BBC PHILHARMONIC ORCHESTRA (COLLINS CLASSICS).

"MAXIMUM MAX" (*AN ORKNEY WEDDING, WITH SUNRISE*; *OJAI FESTIVAL* OVERTURE; CHORAL WORKS): DAVIES AND BBC PHILHARMONIC ORCHESTRA (COLLINS CLASSICS).

Davis, Sir Colin

(b. Weybridge, September 25, 1927)

ENGLISH CONDUCTOR, equally at home in the opera house and the concert hall. He did not come from a musical family and began his musical training late, taking his first lessons on the clarinet when he was 11. He later won a scholarship to study at the Royal College of Music in London, but because he was not a pianist was barred from the conducting course. He learned the skills he needed on his own, and in 1957 was named to his first professional post—assistant conductor of the BBC Scottish Orchestra. He subsequently served as music director at Sadler's Wells (1961–65) and principal conductor of the BBC Symphony Orchestra (1967–71). In 1965 he made his debut at the Royal Opera, Covent Garden with Mozart's *Le nozze di Figaro.* He enjoyed one of the great triumphs of his career con-

Sir Colin Davis, a shining knight on the podium

ducting a Covent Garden production of *Les Troyens* during the Berlioz centennial year of 1969, and served as the company's music director from 1971 to 1986. He made his debut at the Metropolitan Opera in 1967, conducting Benjamin Britten's *Peter Grimes,* and was engaged for 12 seasons as principal guest conductor of the Boston Symphony Orchestra (1972–84). From 1983 to 1992 he served as music director and principal conductor of the Bavarian Radio Symphony Orchestra, and during the 1980s and 1990s he also worked with the Staatskapelle Dresden, with which he recorded symphonies of Mozart, Beethoven, and Schubert. In 1995 he was named principal conductor of the London Symphony Orchestra (a post he will relinquish in 2007), and in 1998 he became principal guest conductor of the New York Philharmonic.

Admired by orchestral musicians for his professionalism and erudition, and by critics for his penetrating and immaculately polished interpretations, Davis established himself as one of the most important conductors of his generation largely through recordings. His vast discography includes distinguished readings of symphonic works by Haydn, Mozart, Beethoven, Sibelius, and Stravinsky, as well as of operas by Mozart, Puccini, and Britten. His collaboration with Michael Tippett was particularly close: He conducted the first performances of *The Knot Garden* (1970), *The Ice Break* (1977; the score is dedicated to him), and *The Mask of Time* (1984). On disc, his greatest achievement to date is the survey of Berlioz's operas and orchestral works he recorded for Philips during the 1960s and 1970s, crowned by a magnificent account of *Les Troyens* recorded at the time of the Covent Garden performances. For his services to music, Davis was made a Commander of the British Empire in 1965, and knighted in 1980.

RECOMMENDED RECORDINGS

BERLIOZ, *SYMPHONIE FANTASTIQUE*; CONCERTGEBOUW ORCHESTRA (PHILIPS).

BERLIOZ, *LES TROYENS*: VICKERS, VEASEY, LINDHOLM, GLOSSOP; ROYAL OPERA (PHILIPS).

SIBELIUS, SYMPHONIES NOS. 5 AND 7: BOSTON SYMPHONY ORCHESTRA (PHILIPS).

STRAVINSKY, *PETRUSHKA, THE RITE OF SPRING*: CONCERTGEBOUW ORCHESTRA (PHILIPS).

Death and the Maiden. *See* TOD UND DAS MÄDCHEN.

Death and Transfiguration. *See* TOD UND VERKLÄRUNG.

Death in Venice OPERA IN TWO ACTS BY **BENJAMIN BRITTEN,** to a libretto by Myfanwy Piper (based on Thomas Mann's novella *Der Tod in Venedig*), premiered by the Aldeburgh Festival on June 16, 1973, at the Maltings, Snape. Britten's last completed opera, it was intended, like many of his stage works, as a vehicle for tenor Peter Pears. The refined musical idiom and economical scoring are well suited to the opera's underlying theme, which is the inability of even the most articulate to express, or suppress, their innermost feelings in the face of beauty.

Of particular interest is the way in which Britten focuses on the opera's central figure,

Gustav von Aschenbach, a novelist. Present in each of the opera's 17 scenes, Aschenbach undergoes an emotional journey from fascination to infatuation to all-consuming homoerotic passion. The role of Tadzio, the boy who becomes the object of his love, is a mute one, however, performed by a dancer rather than a singer.

RECOMMENDED RECORDING

PEARS, SHIRLEY-QUIRK; BEDFORD AND ENGLISH CHAMBER ORCHESTRA (DECCA).

Debussy, Claude

(b. St. Germain-en-Laye, August 22, 1862; d. Paris, March 25, 1918)

FRENCH COMPOSER. He created a body of works whose innovative treatment of sonority and imaginative approach to form, harmony, and texture opened the door to a new century of musical possibility. Born outside Paris, the son of a salesman/shopkeeper and a seamstress, he moved to the capital with his family in 1867. Debussy was nine when his father served a year in prison for participating in the 1871 Paris Commune (the nine-week socialist takeover of the city following the Franco-Prussian War); during the crisis, the family took refuge in Cannes, where the youngster had his first piano lessons, and where glimpses of the Mediterranean left a lasting impression.

Portrait of Claude Debussy, 1907

By the age of ten, Debussy was well enough prepared to be admitted to the Paris Conservatoire, where he studied piano with Antoine Marmontel, solfège with Albert Lavignac, and harmony with Emile Durand. During the summers of 1880–82 he was engaged as pianist in a trio employed by Tchaikovsky's patroness, Nadezhda von Meck. As a result of this experience, "Bussik"—as his young Russian colleagues in the trio called him—was exposed to a considerable amount of Russian music. In December 1880 he entered the composition class of Ernest Guiraud, who was tolerant of his student's antiorthodox attitude and would exert an important influence. The young composer honed his skills writing songs, and in 1884 won the Prix de Rome with the lyrical scene *L'enfant prodigue.* In January 1885 he took up residence at Villa Medici; later that year he met Liszt, who encouraged him to investigate the works of Palestrina and Lassus. Upon his return to Paris in 1887, he composed *Printemps,* an orchestral fantasy with piano, and *La damoiselle élue,* a "poème lyrique" for female voices and chorus, to words by Dante Gabriel Rossetti.

Lured to the Bayreuth Festival in 1888 and 1889, Debussy heard *Parsifal, Die Meistersinger von Nürnberg,* and *Tristan und Isolde.* He was impressed by the orchestration of *Parsifal,* but it was the Javanese GAMELAN at the 1889 Exposition Universelle in Paris that opened his imagination to a new universe of sonority. In 1892 he began to fashion the first great work of his maturity, the orchestral *PRÉLUDE À L'APRÈS-MIDI*

D'UN FAUNE ◉, inspired by Mallarmé's sultry eclogue. In 1893 he saw Maurice Maeterlinck's play PELLÉAS ET MÉLISANDE and immediately went to work setting it as an opera. ◉ The opera's premiere in 1902 created a minor scandal—offering as it did a suggestive glimpse of a dark interior world, without the slightest bow to operatic convention or even much "singing"—and drew critical disapproval. It would remain Debussy's only work in the genre: In the years that followed he would contemplate several other operatic projects (including one based on Poe's *The Fall of the House of Usher*), but none would come to fruition.

In 1903 Debussy began work on his orchestral masterpiece *LA MER* (*The Sea*) ◉, a magnificent hybrid of symphony and tone portrait in which a kaleidoscopic array of motifs, textures, and timbres is transformed into an aural canvas of dazzling beauty and power. The reaction of the critics to the work's initial performance, in 1905, was hostile; even the composer's friends and staunchest admirers had difficulty comprehending the score's brilliantly complex imagery.

The cover of the first edition of **La Mer**, *showing Hokusai's* **Great Wave**; *below, a gaunt Debussy with daughter Chouchou in 1916*

Meanwhile, Debussy, something of a cad even by the standards of his day, had left his wife for Emma Bardac (in anguish, his wife shot herself, though the wound wasn't fatal). In 1905, Bardac and Debussy had a daughter, Claude-Emma ("Chouchou," to whom the composer would dedicate the piano suite *Children's Corner*); they married in 1908. The liaison with Bardac brought a creative surge. Among the works Debussy produced were the two books of *IMAGES* for piano (published in 1905 and 1907); the *IMAGES* for orchestra (1905–12), centering on the magnificent *IBÉRIA* ◉; two sets of preludes for piano ◉; incidental music for *Le martyre de Saint Sébastien*, a "mystery" in five scenes by Gabriele d'Annunzio staged as a hybrid of oratorio and ballet; and the ballet *JEUX* (1912–13), written for Sergey Diaghilev's Ballets Russes.

Despite symptoms of colorectal cancer that appeared in 1909, Debussy kept up the creative pace, also performing extensively. He took narcotics for his pain, and in 1915 had surgery, but gradually wasted away. He managed to complete *En blanc et noir* (1915), for two pianos, and the *Études* for piano (1915), along with three magnificent chamber sonatas (of six projected), composed during World War I in a climate of nationalist reaction: On the title page Debussy identified himself as *"musicien français."* Depressed by the toll the war was taking and despondent over the fact that his disease could not be arrested, Debussy died in 1918, in the final spring of the war, as Germany's "Big Bertha" was pounding the Paris suburbs.

Aside from music, Debussy was largely self-educated. His intellectual horizon was vast, and many of his most important works were influenced and inspired by literature, especially poetry. He was strongly attracted to the work of Baudelaire, Verlaine (many of whose verses he set as songs), and Mallarmé, and to the stories of Poe. The associative techniques of literary symbolism—connecting sensory, emotional, and imaginative experiences to

Debussy at the piano, chez Ernest Chausson, in August 1892

one another—were fundamental to his own way of thinking, and played a role in many of his songs, as well as his *Prélude à l'après-midi d'un faune,* the three *Nocturnes* for orchestra (1897–99), the opera *Pelléas et Mélisande,* and other works. Debussy was similarly influenced by the visual arts, not just the Impressionism of Monet but the fantastic, swirling colorism of Turner, the analytical coolness of Whistler (certainly an influence on his *Nocturnes*), and Asian art, from Japanese lacquer panels (the inspiration for "Poissons d'or," the final piece of his 1907 *Images*) to the work of Hokusai and Hiroshige. As attuned to sound as he was to the poetic and the visual, he drew inspiration from a wide range of sources: the sylvan beauty of Weber's overtures, the primary colors of Russian music, the magically veiled sonority of Wagner's orchestration, and, always, the suggestive, tonally vague tintinnabulation and shimmer of the gamelan he heard in Paris.

Debussy was the first Western musician to use WHOLE-TONE SCALES with any consistency, and his harmonic language was revolutionary in its emphasis of the subdominant and its predilection for chord progressions with missing steps. All of these traits show up in his orchestral music, lending nostalgia to the pastel shadings of *Prélude à l'après-midi d'un faune,* imparting mystery to the harmonic ambiguity of "Nuages" and zest to the colorful whirl of "Fêtes" in the *Nocturnes,* and contributing impressively to the dazzling beauty and organic complexity of *La mer.*

Debussy's keyboard music was no less harmonically advanced, and perhaps even more revolutionary in its timbral explorations, which culminate in the extraordinary refinement of the second book of *Préludes* (1913) and the *Études.* While Debussy wrote a remarkably small amount of chamber music, his works in the genre are well established in the repertory. The early Quartet in G minor, Op. 10 (1893) is a turbulent mix of barely restrained passion and exquisite poetry, wrapped in modal harmony, and cast in a cyclical structure; its beauty and emotional warmth conceal tremendous intellectual accomplishment. The late sonatas are from a different world, composed in a telegraphic style that is remarkably rich in feeling, nuance, and poetic suggestiveness.

Sensitive, introverted, and arrogant in a characteristically French way, Debussy confided in a few close friends and remained guarded with almost everyone else. He was prickly, but his genius was one of the greatest music has known. His influence extended not just to composers such as Ravel, Stravinsky, and Falla—figures in his immediate aesthetic vicinity—but to Puccini, Bartók, Gershwin, Messiaen, Britten, Dutilleux, and countless others down to the present day. His new concepts of sound, musical time, and structure, and his emancipation of music from received notions of form, argument, and the function of tonality, are initiatives that composers today are nowhere near finished exploring.

RECOMMENDED RECORDINGS

La Mer: Munch and Boston Symphony Orchestra (RCA).

Orchestral works: Dutoit and Montreal Symphony Orchestra (Decca).

Pelléas et Mélisande: Stillwell, Von Stade, Van Dam; Karajan and Berlin Philharmonic Orchestra (EMI).

Piano works: Jacobs (Nonesuch).

Sonatas: Nash Ensemble (Virgin Classics).

decrescendo (It.) Becoming less loud. A decrescendo is often notated by a wedge-shaped marking under the phrase or passage where it is to occur [>]. *See also* CRESCENDO.

DeGaetani, Jan

(b. Massillon, Ohio, July 10, 1933; d. New York, September 15, 1989)

AMERICAN MEZZO-SOPRANO. She was one of the foremost interpreters of contemporary vocal music in the latter part of the 20th century. She studied at the Juilliard School and made her New York debut in 1958. In 1970, she took part in the first performance of George Crumb's *Ancient Voices of Children* at the Library of Congress in Washington, D.C. The work's premiere recording on Nonesuch with DeGaetani and the Contemporary Chamber Ensemble under Arthur Weisberg was a hit, raising the profiles of both singer and composer. DeGaetani performed regularly with the Contemporary Chamber Ensemble (making a much-praised recording of *Pierrot lunaire*) and her artistic partnership with pianist Gilbert Kalish, one of the founders of the group, lasted 30 years.

In addition to championing Crumb's music, DeGaetani performed and made important recordings of works by Elliott Carter, Charles Ives, Peter Maxwell Davies, Stephen Foster, and others. She first appeared with the New York Philharmonic in 1973, and subsequently sang with many other orchestras, including the BBC Symphony Orchestra, the Chicago Symphony Orchestra, the Concertgebouw Orchestra, and the Scottish National Orchestra, with which she gave the premiere, in 1973, of Davies's *A Stone Litany*. DeGaetani also performed and recorded medieval and Renaissance music, as well as works by Mahler, Brahms, and other 19th-century composers. In 1973, she became a professor at the Eastman School of Music in Rochester, where she taught until her death. She was appointed artist-in-residence at the Aspen Festival in 1973, and frequently gave masterclasses and concerts at American universities. As a teacher and role model, she had an enormous influence on many younger singers, particularly Dawn Upshaw and Renée Fleming.

RECOMMENDED RECORDINGS

Crumb, *Ancient Voices of Children*: Dash, Kalish; Weisberg and Contemporary Chamber Ensemble (Nonesuch).

Ives, songs: Kalish (Nonesuch).

degree A note of a diatonic scale, identified by a number between one and seven representing its place in the stepwise order of the scale. For example, the second degree in the scale of E-flat major is F, and the third degree in the scale of G minor is B-flat.

Delibes, Léo

(b. St. Germain-du-Val, February 21, 1836; d. Paris, January 16, 1891)

FRENCH COMPOSER. He enrolled at the Paris Conservatoire in 1847 and studied composition with Adolphe Adam. With the exception of several choral works, a few songs, and some piano pieces, his entire output consisted of works for the stage. The earliest were operettas in the style of Adam and Ferdinand Hérold, most of them written for the Bouffes-Parisiens, a popular theater run by the king of Parisian operetta, Jacques Offenbach. In 1864

Delibes became chorusmaster at the Paris Opéra, giving him the opportunity to write for the Opéra's ballet. The success of his first full-length ballet, *Coppélia* (1870), based on E. T. A. Hoffmann's tale "Der Sandmann," allowed him to give up his conducting job and devote himself wholly to composition. While it created less of a sensation, his second ballet, *Sylvia* (1876), based on a pastoral drama by Torquato Tasso, was musically even finer; when Tchaikovsky first heard the score, he was so dismayed by its excellence he told composer Sergey Taneyev that, had he come across it sooner, he would never have had the nerve to write *Swan Lake.* With the 1883 premiere of his opera *LAKMÉ*, a tragic love story set in colonial India, Delibes achieved the crowning success of his career. In it, as in the two ballets, his gifts as an orchestrator and tunesmith are readily apparent, as are the qualities of elegance and lightness that made his music so popular in its day and continue to charm listeners today.

Léo Delibes, luminary of the Opéra's ballet

RECOMMENDED RECORDINGS

COPPÉLIA AND SYLVIA (BALLETS): BONYNGE AND NEW PHILHARMONIA ORCHESTRA (DECCA)

LAKMÉ: DESSAY, KUNDE, VAN DAM; PLASSON AND L'ORCHESTRE DU CAPITOLE DE TOULOUSE (EMI).

Deller, Alfred *See box on pages 155–57.*

Delius, Frederick

(b. Bradford, January 29, 1862; d. Grez-sur-Loing, France, June 10, 1934)

ENGLISH COMPOSER OF GERMAN PARENTAGE. As the son of a well-to-do wool merchant, he was able to travel widely in his youth, and his exposure to different locales profoundly influenced both his personal outlook and his development as a musician. In his early 20s he persuaded his father to lend him the money to go to Florida and put himself in business as an orange grower; there he met Thomas Ward, a teacher from Jacksonville, who gave him a six-month course in technique that was the foundation of his musical education. He also came into contact with the music of American blacks, which would figure in several of his early scores, including the *Florida Suite* (1887), a rhapsodic tribute to his year on the plantation, and the opera *Koanga* (1895–97). In 1886 he made his way to Germany for study at the Leipzig Conservatory. It was in Leipzig that he met Edvard Grieg—who encouraged him to continue composing, and, more important, persuaded Delius's father to keep supporting him.

After completing his studies in 1888, Delius moved to Paris, where he joined the circle of Paul Gauguin, Edvard Munch, and August Strindberg, living a bohemian life through the artistically vibrant 1890s. Late in the decade he met the painter Jelka Rosen, whom he married in 1903. With his opera *A VILLAGE ROMEO AND JULIET* (1899–1901), in which the tale of two star-cross'd young lovers is given a Swiss setting, Delius reached maturity as a composer.

Delius listening to his own music, 1929

In the decade that followed, Delius continued his celebration of the idyllic with a pair of pieces for small orchestra, *Summer Night on the River* (1911) and *ON HEARING THE FIRST CUCKOO IN SPRING* (1912), that were first performed in Leipzig under the baton of Arthur Nikisch.

The latter mimics the cuckoo's distinctive two-note call and also quotes the tune "In Ola Valley, in Ola Lake" from Grieg's *Norwegian Folk Songs.*

The outbreak of World War I forced Delius to return temporarily to England. After the war, the syphilis he had contracted in Florida began to attack his nervous system, eventually leaving him blind and paralyzed. With the help of an English amanuensis, Eric Fenby, he was able to complete a handful of scores during his final years, among them the beautiful *Irmelin* Prelude (1931). By that time, his music had found a steadfast champion in Sir Thomas Beecham, who had first come under its spell in 1907. Beecham organized a Delius festival in London in 1929, and between 1934 and 1938 undertook to record most of the orchestral works for Columbia (two decades later he re-recorded some of them in stereo, with the Royal Philharmonic, for EMI). Delius's death, following those of Holst and Elgar earlier in 1934, marked the end of an era in English music.

RECOMMENDED RECORDING

ORCHESTRAL WORKS: BEECHAM AND ROYAL PHILHARMONIC ORCHESTRA (EMI).

del Monaco, Mario

(b. Florence, July 27, 1915; d. Mestre, October 16, 1982)

ITALIAN TENOR. He studied at Pesaro and in Rome, and made his debut in 1941 at the Teatro Puccini in Milan as Pinkerton in *Madama Butterfly.* In 1946 he sang Radames in Verdi's *Aida* at the Arena di Verona, and in 1950 he made his American debut with the San Francisco Opera, appearing both as Radames and in the title role of Umberto Giordano's *Andrea Chénier,* followed by his Metropolitan Opera debut as Des Grieux in Puccini's *Manon Lescaut.* He continued to sing at the Met until 1959. He possessed a true spinto voice of prodigious power and ringing top notes. His most famous role was Otello, a part particularly well suited to his stentorian delivery.

de Larrocha, Alica *See* LARROCHA, ALICIA DE.

de Los Angeles, Victoria *See* LOS ANGELES, VICTORIA DE.

de Luca, Giuseppe

(b. Rome, December 25, 1876; d. New York, August 26, 1950)

ITALIAN BARITONE. He made his debut at Piacenza in 1897 as Valentin in Gounod's *Faust.* In 1902 he appeared opposite Enrico Caruso and Angelica Pandolfini as Michonnet in the world premiere of *Adriana Lecouvreur* by Francesco Cilea (1866–1950), and in 1904 at La Scala he created the role of Sharpless in the world premiere of Puccini's *Madama Butterfly.* He made his American debut at the Metropolitan Opera in 1915, as Figaro in *Il barbiere di Siviglia,* and remained on the company's roster for 20 consecutive seasons, eventually commanding all the leading baritone roles in the Italian repertoire. Superbly well trained, he continued to sing with undiminished brilliance into his 60s and made his farewell appearance at a concert in New York when he was 70. Among his favorite roles were Rossini's Figaro, with which—at the age of 58 and after an absence of 25 years—he made a

Giuseppe de Luca as Rigoletto

triumphant comeback at Covent Garden in 1935, and Rigoletto, with which he closed out his career at the Met in 1940.

de Reszke, Jean [Jan Micezislaw]

(b. Warsaw, January 14, 1850; d. Nice, April 3, 1925)

POLISH TENOR. He started out as a baritone; by 1876 he had sung the role of Alphonse XI in productions of Donizetti's *La favorite* in Venice and London, and that of Figaro in Rossini's *Il barbiere di Siviglia* in Paris. His debut as a tenor, in the title role of Meyerbeer's *Robert le diable* in 1879, was not a success. He returned to the stage in 1884, this time triumphantly, as John the Baptist in Massenet's *Hérodiade,* and in 1885 he created the role of Rodrigue in the premiere of Massenet's *Le Cid* at the Paris Opéra. He remained at the Opéra for the next five seasons, singing the title roles in Meyerbeer's *Le prophète* and Gounod's *Faust* as well as Radames in Verdi's *Aida.* He made his American debut as Lohengrin with the Metropolitan Opera on tour in Chicago in 1891, followed that same year by his debut at the Metropolitan Opera House in New York, as Roméo in Gounod's *Roméo et Juliette*; he remained on the Met's roster through the next ten seasons. During the 1890s, he took on the heavier Wagnerian roles, beginning with Tristan in New York in 1895 and progressing to the title role of *Siegfried* in 1896 and the *Götterdämmerung* Siegfried in 1898. He retired in 1902. His good looks, excellent musicianship, and superior control of dynamics made him a standout in the French repertoire, and endowed his Wagner with an uncommon degree of warmth and expressiveness.

Deutsche Oper Berlin GERMAN OPERA COMPANY originally established in Charlottenburg in 1912 as the Deutsches Opernhaus. It was designated the Städtische Oper when the city of Berlin took over its operation in 1925, but reverted to the name Deutsches Opernhaus during the Nazi years (1933–44). It reopened in September 1945, once again as the Städtische Oper, and was renamed the Deutsche Oper Berlin upon moving into a newly built opera house on Bismarckstrasse in 1961. That year also saw the construction of the Berlin Wall. With the city divided, the Deutsche Oper Berlin became the chief opera company of West Berlin; since reunification, it has ceded pride of place to the Berlin Staatsoper—historically the city's principal opera house—on Unter den Linden in what was formerly East Berlin.

The quartet from Beethoven's* Fidelio *at the Deutsche Oper Berlin, 1962

From 1981 to his death in 2000, the company's *Intendant,* or director, was Götz Friedrich, a Walter Felsentein pupil known for unconventional and often thought-provoking productions. Over the past four decades its music directors have included Lorin Maazel (1965–71), Jesús López-Cobos (1980–90) and Christian Thielemann (since 1997). Giuseppe Sinopoli, named music director in 1990, never accepted the post owing to issues over his contract, but he died in the Deutsche Oper's pit, conducting a performance of *Aida* in 2001.

development [1] The extension, elaboration, or transformation of a musical idea by means of repetition, subtle variation, or a refractory process of breaking it into constituent parts. [2] The second section in what is commonly called SONATA FORM (exposition–development–recapitulation).

devil's interval *See* INTERVAL.

Diabelli Variations **WORK FOR PIANO BY LUDWIG VAN BEETHOVEN,** begun in 1819 and completed in 1822–23. It is his most extensive composition for the piano and the most important work in VARIATION form written during the Classical period. The full title translates as *33 Variations on a Waltz by Diabelli.* It was published in 1823 by Anton Diabelli as Beethoven's Op. 120. The work's genesis is unusual: In 1819 Diabelli (1781–1858), himself a composer of modest talent, sent copies of a waltz tune he had written to a number of Austrian composers, asking each to write a variation on it and offering to publish them all in a collection. Beethoven described the original waltz as a "Schusterfleck" (cobbler's patch) and initially refused to participate in the project. Then, realizing the potential of the cobbler's patch, he conceived not one but 23 variations on it, which he called "transformations" (*Veränderungen*). In 1822–23 he added ten more, setting the crown on a magnificent cycle. In Beethoven's finished essay—which Diabelli generously saw into print before his long-anticipated collection (containing contributions from, among others, Schubert, Czerny, and the 11-year-old Liszt)—the waltz's simple structure becomes the point of departure for an extraordinary journey of musical imagination. As is the case with many of his late works, the *Diabelli Variations* reflect Beethoven's preoccupation with achieving small-scale variety and large-scale cohesion in the same piece.

RECOMMENDED RECORDING

ANDERSZEWSKI (VIRGIN CLASSICS).

diatonic Belonging to a major or minor SCALE, or one of the ancient or medieval modes, as opposed to a whole-tone scale or a CHROMATIC scale. The term, derived from the Greek *dia tonos* ("proceeding by tones"), refers to a scalar arrangement of whole steps and half steps in which the half steps are separated by at least two whole steps.

Dichterliebe (A Poet's Love) **SONG CYCLE BY ROBERT SCHUMANN,** composed in a single week at the end of May 1840, the year of Schumann's marriage to Clara Wieck. A setting of 16 poems from Heinrich Heine's 1823 collection *Lyrischen Intermezzo,* it is one of the supreme achievements in the field of German lied. The songs exhibit a tremendous amount of emotion, compressed into the tightest musical space; in contrast with Schubert, who tended to let sentiment blossom flowerlike in his songs, Schumann extracts the essence from Heine's verses as if

Robert and Clara Schumann, at home with music

each one were a single petal. The piano is an active participant in the process, conveying much of the message and contributing considerable nuance as well in the astonishing variety of its figuration.

Most of the songs are brief cameos, a few more thoroughly worked tableaux. "Im wunderschönen Monat Mai" ("In the lovely month of May"), which opens the cycle, is one of the most remarkable songs in the entire literature. Its rarefied texture, ambiguous harmonies tinged with suspensions, and prescient sentiment create an extraordinary impression—this is the moment in a man's soul when he becomes aware that something is happening to him, and Schumann, in a mere 26 measures, captures it perfectly. The scherzolike third song, "Die Rose, die Lilie, die Taube, die Sonne" ("The rose, the lily, the dove, the sun"), has all the giddiness of puppy love, while the martial, angry "Ich grolle nicht" ("I don't complain") seems to exult in the sadness of rejection. The desolation and quiet despair of later numbers in the set, particularly the 12th, "Am leuchtenden Sommermorgen" ("On a gleaming morning in summer"), and 13th, "Ich hab' im Traum geweinet" ("I wept in my dreams"), are potent without descending into self-pity, while the downward course of the closing song, "Die alten, bösen Lieder" ("The old and evil songs"), from sarcastic rage to heartbreak effectively recaps the concluding half of the cycle. The piano has the last word, a tender envoy that seems to say, "'Tis better to have loved and lost than never to have loved at all."

RECOMMENDED RECORDINGS

FISCHER-DIESKAU, MOORE (DG).

WUNDERLICH, GIESEN (DG).

Dido and Aeneas OPERA BY HENRY PURCELL, to a text by Nahum Tate (based loosely on Virgil's *Aeneid*), composed around 1685 and premiered prior to December 1689 by the students of Josias Priest's School for Young Ladies in Chelsea. It was created for the court of Charles II, whose sudden death in 1685 may have been the reason it did not get performed sooner. *Dido and Aeneas* deals in rather fanciful form with the story told in Book IV of the *Aeneid,* concerning the passionate entanglement of the Carthaginian queen and the wandering Trojan warrior, which ends in Dido's death from a broken heart. Its arias show that Purcell was acquainted with the Venetian style, and the choruses and dances suggest that he was conversant with French opera as well. Dido is among the most beautifully realized tragic heroines in opera, and her final "When I am laid in earth," set over a CHACONNE bass, remains one of the most moving laments ever written.

RECOMMENDED RECORDINGS

BAKER, HERINCX; LEWIS AND ENGLISH CHAMBER ORCHESTRA (DECCA).

HUNT LIEBERSON, SAFFER, ELLIOTT, BRANDES; MCGEGAN AND PHILHARMONIA BAROQUE ORCHESTRA (HARMONIA MUNDI).

Dies irae (Lat., "Day of Wrath") Sequence used in the Latin Requiem, or Mass for the Dead. The text, attributed to Thomas of Celano (d. ca. 1250), vividly describes the horrors of the Last Judgment. The medieval plainchant melody associated with the text has been quoted numerous times in concert works to evoke death or the supernatural. Among the most familiar appropriations are those of Berlioz (in the final movement of his *SYMPHONIE FANTASTIQUE*), Liszt (*Totentanz*), and Rachmaninov (*ISLE OF THE DEAD, RHAPSODY ON A THEME OF PAGANINI,* and *Symphonic Dances*).

diminish To reduce a perfect INTERVAL (fourth, fifth, or octave) or a minor one (especially the seventh) by a half step. A seventh so reduced is called a diminished seventh (e.g., C-sharp–B-flat), and a chord built on that interval (e.g., C-sharp–E–G–B-flat) is called a diminished seventh chord.

diminuendo (It.) A gradual decrease in loudness. *See also* DECRESCENDO.

diminution A procedure generally encountered in fugal writing in which a given motif or subject is set in shortened note values.

dissonance A simultaneous sounding of two or more notes that the ear judges to be unstable or discordant, according to the harmonic context of the surrounding sounds. Over centuries the line between consonance and dissonance has blurred, until, in the 20th century, Shoenberg declared the concept of dissonance null and void. But human ears still recognize certain intervals—tritones, minor seconds, major sevenths—as dissonant, just as human eyes instinctively regard some faces as beautiful, others as plain or ugly. One of the most sublime uses of dissonance in the entire repertoire occurs at the very beginning of the final movement of Beethoven's Ninth Symphony, symbolizing the ugliness and confusion out of which the composer will wrest joy and brotherhood.

di Stefano, Giuseppe

(b. Motta Santa Anastasia, July 24, 1921)

ITALIAN TENOR. He studied in Milan, and, having survived wartime service in the Italian army, made his La Scala debut in 1947, followed a year later by his Metropolitan Opera debut as the Duke in Verdi's *Rigoletto,* and in 1950 by his San Francisco Opera debut as Rodolfo in Puccini's *La bohème.* He possessed one of the most alluring lyric voices ever to issue from the mouth of a tenor, and for a few glorious years in the early 1950s he held audiences in thrall with the elegance of his singing and the sheer beauty of his sound. By decade's end, however, his ill-advised efforts to take on heavier roles—such as Radames in Verdi's *Aida,* Cavaradossi in Puccini's *Tosca,* and Canio in Leoncavallo's *Pagliacci*—had ruinously degraded his timbre, effectively ending his career when it should have been reaching its peak.

Dittersdorf, Carl Ditters von

(b. Vienna, November 2, 1739; d. Schloss Rothlhotta, Bohemia, October 24, 1799)

AUSTRIAN COMPOSER. He was born Carl Ditters, into a well-to-do Viennese family, and ennobled by Empress Maria Theresa in 1773. As a child he learned to play the violin and as a teen he received instruction in composition from Giuseppe Bonno. He held several positions as a Kapellmeister in minor courts, but inexplicably turned down an offer from Joseph II to succeed Leopold Gassmann as imperial court Kapellmeister in Vienna in 1774 (the job went to Bonno, who was succeeded by Salieri). Instead, he spent the greater part of his career at the castle of Johannisberg, as Kapellmeister to the Prince-Bishop of Breslau. He composed approximately 120 symphonies, including a set of 12 based on Ovid's *Metamorphoses,* and more than 40 solo concertos, as well as several oratorios and masses and about 40 works for the stage.

Portrait of Carl Ditters von Dittersdorf, ca. 1780

divertimento (from It. *divertire,* "to entertain") A multimovement composition consisting of music in a light and pleasing vein, often including dance movements. The genre was common in the later 18th century, when a piece of this kind might also be referred to as a "cassation," "serenade," "partita," or "notturno"—the terms were used more or less interchangeably. Mozart composed approximately 35 works that he identified as divertimentos; among the best known are the three for string quartet written in 1772 (K. 136–38), and the Divertimento in D, K. 334, written in Salzburg in 1779 or 1780, which contains one of the most tuneful of Mozart's minuets. Other 18th-century contributions to the genre were made by Dittersdorf, Boccherini, Gassmann, Johann and Carl Stamitz, and Michael and Joseph Haydn. The divertimento has enjoyed something of a comeback in the 20th century. Examples of note include Bartók's *Divertimento* (1939) for strings, commissioned by Paul Sacher, and Stravinsky's *Divertimento* (1934; rev. 1949), actually a suite drawn from his ballet *Le baiser de la fée,* based on music by Tchaikovsky.

divisi (It., "divided") Usually abbreviated *div.,* the term is used as an instruction to string section players in orchestras and ensembles that intervals, chords, or passages in multiple voices written in a single part are to be divided among the players in such a way that each instrument plays only one note at a time. Divisions into more than two parts are usually spelled out *div. in 3* or *div. in 4,* as appropriate. The instruction is canceled by the direction *non divisi* or *unisoni*—abbreviated *non div.* and *unis.,* respectively.

dodecaphonic *See* 12-TONE.

Dohnányi, Christoph von

(b. Berlin, September 8, 1929)

GERMAN CONDUCTOR. Born into a prominent, musically cultivated family, he studied piano and flute as a child. He was 15 when, on April 9, 1945, his

Christoph von Dohnányi in 1997

father, Hans von Dohnányi, an eminent jurist, and his uncle Dietrich Bonhoeffer, a respected Protestant theologian, were hanged by the Nazi authorities for their complicity in several unsuccessful plots to assassinate Hitler. Following World War II, he enrolled as a law student at the University of Munich, and while there he decided to devote himself full-time to music. After winning the Richard Strauss Conducting Prize in 1951 he spent a brief period studying with his grandfather, Ernő Dohnányi, at Florida State University. In 1957 he was appointed music director of the opera in Lübeck; he served there for six years before moving on to posts in Cologne and Kassel. In 1968 he succeeded Georg Solti as artistic and musical director of the Frankfurt Opera, and from 1978 to 1984 he was the director and chief conductor of the Hamburg State Opera, where critics of his administration—in a play on his name aimed at his frequent conducting assignments elsewhere—referred to him as Herr

"Doch-nie-da" (Mr. "He's Never Here"). In 1982, after just a single guest-conducting engagement, he was chosen to succeed Lorin Maazel as music director of the Cleveland Orchestra, a post he held from 1984 through the end of the 2001–02 season. He was named principal guest conductor of London's Philharmonia Orchestra in 1994, and has served as that orchestra's principal conductor since 1997.

A thoughtful musician with a solid grounding in the works of Mozart, Beethoven, Schubert, and the German Romantics, Dohnányi is a conductor who eschews all forms of showmanship. In repertoire that is often prone to heated emotionalism he tends toward restraint, keeping a gentle distance that appears at times to be philosophical detachment. With the Cleveland Orchestra he has made distinguished recordings of symphonies by Beethoven, Schumann, Brahms, Tchaikovsky, and Dvořák, and of works by Ives, Varèse, and Webern. Though he has recorded relatively few operas for someone with his experience in the pit, his mastery in that arena can be gauged from his magnificent account with the Vienna Philharmonic of Wagner's *Der fliegende Holländer.*

RECOMMENDED RECORDINGS

DVOŘÁK, SYMPHONIES NOS. 7–9: CLEVELAND ORCHESTRA (DECCA).

WAGNER, *DER FLIEGENDE HOLLÄNDER*: HAK, BEHRENS, RYDL, PROTSCHKA; VIENNA PHILHARMONIC (DECCA).

Dohnányi, Ernő [Ernst von]

(b. Pozsony [now Bratislava], July 27, 1877; d. New York, February 9, 1960)

HUNGARIAN PIANIST, TEACHER, AND COMPOSER. He graduated from the National Hungarian Royal Academy in Budapest in 1897 and moved to Berlin for further piano study with Eugen d'Albert. From 1908 to 1915 he served as professor of piano at the Hochschule für Musik in Berlin; returning to Budapest, he taught piano and composition at the Academy, became its director in 1934, and served as chief conductor of the Budapest Philharmonic (1919–44) and music director of Hungarian Radio (1931–44). He left Hungary in 1944, after his son Hans von Dohnányi was implicated in the failed Stauffenberg plot to kill Hitler. In 1949, following a brief hiatus in South America, he became composer-in-residence at Florida State University in Tallahassee.

Dohnányi suffered grievously from the jealousies aroused by his enormous talent, especially in Hungary after World War II. Only recently has his reputation begun to recover. He was one of the 20th century's most brilliant and accomplished pianists, a discerning conductor, and a composer of the first rank, especially in the field of chamber music. In addition, he was a formidable teacher whose students included Géza Anda, Annie Fischer, and Georg Solti. His output as a composer was remarkably balanced, encompassing works for the stage, chamber pieces, vocal music, orchestral works, and piano pieces. His most famous score, *Variations on a Nursery Tune* (1914) for piano and orchestra, is an engaging theme-and-variations treatment of "Twinkle, Twinkle, Little Star."

RECOMMENDED RECORDING

VARIATIONS ON A NURSERY TUNE: SHELLEY; BAMERT AND BBC PHILHARMONIC ORCHESTRA (CHANDOS).

dolce (It.) Soft, sweet.

dominant In harmonic analysis, a chord based on the fifth degree of a given scale or key. For example, in the key of F major, the dominant is the triad C–E–G. Such a chord with an added seventh (e.g., C–E–G–B-flat), a configuration frequently encountered in cadential formulas, is called a dominant seventh chord.

Domingo, Plácido

(b. Madrid, January 21, 1941)

SPANISH TENOR, CONDUCTOR, AND ADMINISTRATOR. His parents were zarzuela performers who brought him to Mexico when he was eight. As a child he took part in some of the productions in which they were involved, and developed a taste for life on the stage. He studied piano and conducting at the Mexico City Conservatory, turning his attention to vocal studies when his potential became apparent. He made his operatic debut in 1961, singing Alfredo in Verdi's *La traviata* at Monterrey, Mexico; later that year, in Dallas, he made his American debut as Arturo in Donizetti's *Lucia di Lammermoor.* From 1962 to 1965 he was a member of the Israel National Opera, appearing in 12 different roles and singing much of the time in Hebrew. He made his New York City Opera debut in 1965 as Pinkerton in Puccini's *Madama Butterfly,* and took his first bows at the Metropolitan Opera in 1968, as Maurizio in Cilea's *Adriana Lecouvreur.* Since then he has given more than 400 performances in 40 different roles at the Met, and sung on more opening nights than any singer in the company's history. He made his debut at La Scala in 1969 in the title role of Verdi's *Ernani,* and first sang at Covent Garden in 1971, as Cavaradossi in Puccini's *Tosca* (a role he has sung more than 225 times over the years). His long-awaited Bayreuth Festival debut occurred in 1992.

Domingo's repertoire is the largest of any tenor in the history of music. He has sung virtually every important tenor part in Italian and French opera, and in recent years he has taken on much Wagner (Parsifal, Lohengrin, Siegmund in *Die Walküre,* and, on record, Walther in *Die Meistersinger von Nürnberg* and Tristan). In 1999, he added Tchaikovsky to his inventory, singing Herman in *The Queen of Spades* at both the Met and the Vienna Staatsoper. He has created roles in operas by Ginastera (the title role in *Don Rodrigo,* 1966) and Menotti (the title role in *Goya,* 1986). He made his debut as the title character in Franco Alfano's *Cyrano de Bergerac* (his 121st role) at the Met, in May 2005.

Domingo made his U.S. conducting debut at the New York City Opera in 1973, in *La traviata,* and has conducted on numerous occasions at the Met, where his credits include *La bohème, Roméo et Juliette, Carmen,* and *Tosca.* He has also guest-conducted the Chicago Symphony Orchestra, the London Symphony Orchestra, the Vienna Symphony, and the National Symphony Orchestra in purely symphonic repertoire. In 1996 he became artistic director of the Washington National Opera, and in 2000, having served as the Los Angeles Opera's artistic advisor for many years, he was named artistic director of that company as well.

Domingo's burnished, argent tenor is one of the supreme voices of the past century, equally remarkable for its power, flexibility, richness of color, and expressive intensity. In using it with taste, intelligence, and the most thorough musicianship, Domingo has set a standard for vocal artistry that future operatic tenors will be

Domingo as Otello

hard pressed to surpass. His enormous discography includes more than 90 full-length opera recordings and dozens of recital and crossover discs, as well as the phenomenally popular showcase albums in which he has participated, along with Luciano Pavarotti and José Carreras, as one of the "Three Tenors." Of these he will certainly be remembered as the greatest, a commanding presence in Verdi (perhaps the greatest Otello of all time), an outstanding exponent of Puccini and verismo, a fervent Don José in *Carmen,* and a truly noble, suavely appealing Wagnerian hero.

RECOMMENDED RECORDINGS

VERDI, *OTELLO*: SCOTTO, MILNES; LEVINE AND NATIONAL PHILHARMONIC ORCHESTRA (RCA).

VERDI, *IL TROVATORE*: PRICE, MILNES, COSSOTTO; MEHTA AND NEW PHILHARMONIA ORCHESTRA (RCA).

WAGNER, *LOHENGRIN*: NORMAN, NIMSGERN, RANDOVÁ; SOLTI AND VIENNA PHILHARMONIC (DECCA).

Donaueschingen Festival *See box on pages 46–47.*

Don Carlo OPERA IN FIVE ACTS BY GIUSEPPE VERDI, to a libretto in French by Joseph Méry and Camille du Locle (based on Friedrich von Schiller's *Don Carlos, Infant von Spanien*), written for the Paris Opéra and premiered there on March 11, 1867. It was Verdi's second work for the Parisian stage, coming 12 years after his first, *Les vêpres siciliennes.* Only after being translated into Italian and recast first into four acts, then back into five—a process Verdi and his publisher completed in 1883—did *Don Carlo* find a place in the repertoire. Grand-opera elements survive in the larger-than-life trappings of the story, which is set in the 1560s against the backdrop of the Spanish Inquisition and the Protestant insurrection in the Low Countries, and has at its center the historical personage of Philip II, King of Spain, who ruled from 1556 to 1598. Philip, the father of the opera's title character Don Carlo, is a figure torn between his devotion to the state, the responsibilities of his position, and the inflexible demands of the Catholic church, represented by the sightless yet terrifying Grand Inquisitor. Don Carlo (who was also a real person, though nothing like Schiller's and Verdi's hero), is in love with Elisabeth of Valois, a French princess whose fate is to be married not to him, as she hopes, but to his father the king. Carlo and his friend Rodrigo, Marquis of Posa, support the insurgents in Flanders, further complicating the relationship with Philip. There is also the one-eyed Princess Eboli, whose love for Don Carlo is unrequited, and whose "fatal gift," her ravishing beauty, leaves Philip enamored of her but unable to act on his feelings. Verdi's music rises to inspired heights in Philip's "Ella giammai m'amò!" and Eboli's "O don fatale," and imparts sharp point to a series of dramatic duets: between Carlo and Elisabeth, Carlo and Rodrigo, Rodrigo and Philip, and most extraordinary of all, between Philip and the Grand Inquisitor, a memorable scene whose dark orchestral tones offer a chill reminder of the power of the church to compel even a king.

RECOMMENDED RECORDING

DOMINGO, CABALLÉ, VERRETT, MILNES, RAIMONDI; GIULINI AND ROYAL OPERA (EMI).

Don Giovanni OPERA IN TWO ACTS BY WOLFGANG AMADEUS MOZART, to a libretto by Lorenzo da Ponte (based on a story by Tirso de Molina), commissioned by Pasquale Bondini and premiered in Prague on October 29, 1787. The work's full title is *Il dissoluto punito, o sia Il Don Giovanni* (*The Rake Punished, or Don Giovanni*). Da Ponte's libretto—a clever patchwork lifted in large part from Giovanni Bertati's libretto for

Giuseppe Gazzaniga's *Don Giovanni, o sia Il convitato di pietra*—fired Mozart's imagination like nothing the composer had worked on before. Most of the opera was composed in Vienna during the summer of 1787; the overture, several numbers, and many of the recitatives were fashioned in Prague a matter of days before the first performance.

Although successful in Prague, *Don Giovanni* was less enthusiastically received when it was staged in Vienna, with two new arias, in the spring of 1788. Mozart's treatment of the opera's principal figures—Don Giovanni, his servant Leporello, the two high-born ladies Donna Anna and Donna Elvira, and the peasant girl Zerlina—is virtuosic. Don Giovanni, the chameleon, moves easily in both the highest and lowest circles, as the varied stylistic shading of his arias makes clear. Leporello, who would like to be a cavalier, proves adept at mimicking the stations of others (in his catalog aria), and is ultimately more honest than his master. The discarded Elvira, easily wronged and a little absurd, has the most florid music in the opera, while Anna, the cold goddess of fury, conveys a masculine authority in her arias that her suitor, the wimpy Don Ottavio, lacks. There is even a subtle polish to the rusticity of Zerlina—in the duet "Là ci darem la mano," she plays on Don Giovanni's reflexes, allowing him to chase her until *she* catches him. The extraordinary detail Mozart brings to the opera's characters and situations, and the way his music balances the comic and the serious, transcending the limits of genre, combine to make *Don Giovanni* one of the greatest works of musical theater ever created.

Thomas Hampson as Don Giovanni

RECOMMENDED RECORDINGS

GHIAUROV, FRENI, GEDDA, BERRY; KLEMPERER AND NEW PHILHARMONIA ORCHESTRA (EMI).

TERFEL, FLEMING, MURRAY, GROOP; SOLTI AND LONDON PHILHARMONIC ORCHESTRA (LONDON).

WAECHTER, SCHWARZKOPF, SUTHERLAND; GIULINI AND PHILHARMONIA ORCHESTRA (EMI).

Donizetti, Gaetano

(b. Bergamo, November 29, 1797; d. Bergamo, April 8, 1848)

ITALIAN COMPOSER, one of the leading operatic lights of early-19th-century Italy. His music stands at the crossroads between the decorative style of bel canto, then on its way out, and the more direct, sensational, and melodramatic manner of the mid-19th century, which soon after Donizetti's death was to find its greatest exponent in Verdi. Born into a poor family, Donizetti was sent to study at the Lezioni Caritatevoli ("Charitable Lessons"), a music school run by Simon Mayr. Mayr played an active part in his education, and in 1815 sent him on to Bologna for two years of study with Stanislao Mattei, who had been Rossini's teacher. By the end of 1818, Donizetti had seen two of his operas produced in Venice, and in 1822 the triumphant success of his "heroic melodrama" *Zoraide di Grenata* brought him to the attention of the leading impresario of the day, Domenico Barbaia, who quickly arranged for him to come to Naples. There, over the next 16 years, Donizetti became one of the most renowned figures of Italian opera. His most popular work, *LUCIA DI LAMMERMOOR*, received its premiere in Naples at the Teatro San Carlo in 1835. Composed to an especially skillful libretto by Salvatore Cammarano (based on Walter Scott's novel *The Bride of Lammermoor*), it rapidly entered the international repertoire, firmly establishing Donizetti's reputation and taking on iconic status as

Caricature of Gaetano Donizetti writing with two pens

one of the cornerstones of Italian Romanticism thanks to its felicitous melding of a virtuosic role for the heroine (capped by an incomparable "mad scene") with a moody and emotional score. Other significant works from this period include *Lucrezia Borgia* (1833) and *Gemma di Vergy* (1834), both premiered at La Scala, *Roberto Devereux* (1837), one of several operas Donizetti wrote on Elizabethan subjects, and *L'ELISIR D'AMORE* (1832), his first great comedy.

In 1838, Donizetti left Naples for Paris, where in 1840 he produced one of his most brilliant comedies, *La fille du régiment,* and one of his finest dramas, *La favorite.* He reached the pinnacle of his achievement with the comic masterpiece *DON PASQUALE,* premiered in Paris in 1843 at the Théâtre Italien. In the autumn of that year the composer began to suffer the ravages of syphilis; within two years he was unable to work, and by the spring of 1847 paralysis had set in. In the final months of his life friends arranged for him to be taken back to Bergamo, where he was cared for until his death by the Baroness Rota-Basoni Scotti.

Donizetti's success in both comic and dramatic genres, and his amazing fecundity (65 completed operas in a career spanning 25 years), argue for his being considered one of the greatest opera composers of the 19th century. He possessed a sure theatrical instinct that, together with his miraculous gift for melody, enabled him to create memorable and affecting situations on the stage. Even if he had written nothing but *Lucia di Lammermoor,* he would be assured of a place in the pantheon of operatic history, but his legacy includes at least ten other works that remain in the active repertoire all over the world.

RECOMMENDED RECORDINGS

DON PASQUALE: BRUSON, MEI, ALLEN; ROBERTO ABBADO AND MUNICH RADIO ORCHESTRA (RCA).

L'ELISIR D'AMORE: BATTLE, PAVAROTTI, NUCCI, DARA, UPSHAW; LEVINE AND METROPOLITAN OPERA ORCHESTRA (DG).

LA FILLE DU RÉGIMENT: SUTHERLAND, PAVAROTTI; BONYNGE AND ROYAL OPERA (DECCA).

LUCIA DI LAMMERMOOR: SUTHERLAND, PAVAROTTI, MILNES; BONYNGE AND ROYAL OPERA (DECCA).

Don Juan SYMPHONIC POEM FOR LARGE ORCHESTRA BY RICHARD STRAUSS, OP. 20, composed in 1888–89 and premiered in Weimar on November 11, 1889, with the composer conducting. Strauss was only 24 when he completed the piece, yet the orchestral writing is astonishingly brilliant and complex—strings, winds, and especially the brass are required to play passages virtuosic enough to belong in concertos—and the control of form is remarkably sure. There is no specific program, but at the head of the score Strauss quotes portions of a poem by Nikolaus Lenau, an early-19th-century Austrian poet. Lenau's Don Juan is not the lusty, high-living rake of Mozart's *Don Giovanni* but an idealist eternally in search of feminine perfection. One of the unusual elements of the poet's conception is that it is Don Juan himself, the seducer rather than the seduced, who suffers most from his ultimately fruitless quest. But Strauss, to judge by his music, sees swashbuckling, heroic ardor and longing as the main point. The opening pages of the score contain some of the most ebullient music he ever composed. A lyrical reprieve is provided by a languorous oboe solo, one of the lengthiest in the symphonic literature, before a reprise of the heroic opening material gives way to an ambivalent ending.

RECOMMENDED RECORDINGS

Karajan and Berlin Philharmonic (DG).

Szell and Cleveland Orchestra (Sony).

Don Pasquale **Comic opera by Gaetano Donizetti,** to a libretto by Giovanni Ruffini, premiered in Paris at the Théâtre Italien on January 3, 1843. The composer's 64th opera, it is arguably the finest and deepest of all his comedies. The wealthy bachelor Don Pasquale is angry with his nephew Ernesto because he refuses to accept the bride Pasquale has selected for him. Instead, Ernesto declares his intent to marry a pretty young woman named Norina. Pasquale enlists the aid of his physician, Dr. Malatesta, to help him deal with his stubborn nephew. But Malatesta, who has much affection for Ernesto, has other ideas. Convincing Pasquale that by marrying he could produce his own heirs, Malatesta offers him his sister—who, when the ceremony comes to pass, is actually Norina in disguise. Norina declares that now that she is married to a wealthy man, she intends to live a life of unbridled pleasure. Don Pasquale, miserable at this turn of events, spends his days worrying that his wife will squander his fortune. By the time her identity is revealed, he is glad to be rid of his shrewish bride and happily hands her over to his nephew. The overture to *Don Pasquale* is the finest instrumental piece Donizetti ever penned; a classic pastiche as brilliant and rambunctious as anything by Rossini, it is frequently encountered in the concert hall.

RECOMMENDED RECORDING

Bruson, Mei, Allen; Roberto Abbado and Munich Radio Orchestra (RCA).

Don Quixote **Symphonic poem for large orchestra in theme-and-variation form by Richard Strauss, Op. 35,** composed in 1897 and premiered in Cologne on March 8, 1898. Based on the famous romance by Miguel de Cervantes, and subtitled "Fantastic variations on a theme of knightly character," the piece features prominent solo parts for cello and viola, the former representing Don Quixote, and the latter his squire, Sancho Panza. It is Strauss's supreme achievement in the field of symphonic portraiture, and one of the surest of his scores.

Each of the quixotic escapades portrayed in *Don Quixote*—from the hero's tilting at windmills and attacking a flock of sheep he has mistaken for an enemy army, to his ride through the air, nightlong vigil, and final combat with the Knight of the White Moon—is cast as a variation on Don Quixote's own theme, suggesting at once

Mstislav Rostropovich with the Boston Symphony and Seiji Ozawa in Strauss's **Don Quixote**

the imaginary aspect of his chivalry. There are ten variations in all, prefaced by an introduction and the theme itself, and followed by an epilogue-like finale in which the solo cello soars to a high A in an ecstatic embrace of the ideal, then gives up the ghost with an octave slide to the low D. Nowhere is Strauss's skill as an orchestrator more evident than in variation 2, when he depicts the bleating of a herd of sheep by having the muted brass flutter-tongue a series of dissonant intervals. He is even able to conjure up a vision with all the glory of a full orchestra, and deny it by a single note—his portrayal of Don Quixote's flight through the air (variation 7) involves a host of atmospheric effects in the strings, whooshing figures in the winds, even a wind machine. But does the Knight of the Rueful Countenance ever leave the ground? The persistent low D in the basses tells the listener that it was a flight of fancy only.

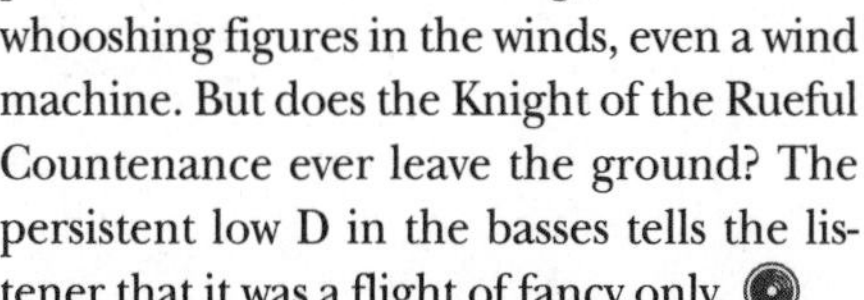
RECOMMENDED RECORDING

ROSTROPOVICH; KARAJAN AND BERLIN PHILHARMONIC (EMI).

Dorati, Antal

(b. Budapest, April 9, 1906; d. Gerzensee, November 13, 1988)

AMERICAN CONDUCTOR AND COMPOSER OF HUNGARIAN BIRTH. Born during the final years of the Austro-Hungarian Empire, he belonged to the last generation of performers steeped in the musical traditions of prewar Europe. He studied at the Royal Academy of Music in Budapest (where his teachers included Bartók and Kodály, as well as Leo Weiner), and upon graduating landed a job as a *répétiteur* at the Budapest Opera (1924–28). He served as assistant to Fritz Busch in Dresden in 1928, and was general music director in Münster from 1929 to 1932. He next moved to France, where he worked as conductor of the Ballets Russes de Monte Carlo (1933–39). Having made his American conducting debut in 1937, he took up permanent residence in the United States in 1940 and spent the war years in New York as music director of the American Ballet Theater; he became an American citizen in 1947. Over the next three decades he acquired a reputation as a builder and maintainer of first-class orchestras, serving as music director of the Dallas Symphony (1945–49) and the Minneapolis Symphony (1949–60), chief conductor of the BBC Symphony Orchestra (1963–66) and Stockholm Philharmonic (1966–70), music director of the National Symphony Orchestra in Washington, D.C. (1970–77) and the Detroit Symphony (1977–81), and principal conductor of London's Royal Philharmonic Orchestra (1975–79).

Antal Dorati, old-world maestro and builder of orchestras

A musician's musician, Dorati could, with equal sureness, write a brilliant solo work for oboe, lead a Haydn symphony from the harpsichord, or conduct from memory a massive choral-orchestral score. He was one of the first conductors to take full advantage of modern musicology and the phonographic medium (his landmark integral recording of the symphonies of Haydn stands as an early example of both), and his recorded legacy remains one of the largest in history, amounting to more than 500 discs, including a number of important recording premieres. His repertoire encompassed everything from J. S. Bach to Luigi Dallapiccola (1904–75), and was especially deep in ballet and music of the 20th century. Volatile, high-strung, energetic, and quick-witted, he brought together the best of the old school and the new. From 1969 until his death, he was married to the Austrian-born pianist Ilse von Alpenheim.

RECOMMENDED RECORDINGS

KODÁLY, ORCHESTRAL WORKS: MINNEAPOLIS SYMPHONY ORCHESTRA (MERCURY).

STRAVINSKY, ORCHESTRAL WORKS: LONDON SYMPHONY ORCHESTRA (MERCURY).

dotted rhythm A relationship of unequal duration between two consecutive notes, which most commonly is represented in notation by a first note, with a dot next to it, that is three times the length of the second. (A dot following a note or a rest increases the duration of the note or rest by one half its normal rhythmic value.) In some practices, the inequality is not calculated precisely; the short note is to be played as short, and as late within the beat, as possible. Dotted rhythms are easiest to recognize when in a series, so that a repeating long-short pattern ("tum-tee-tum-tee-tum-tee . . .") is established.

The effect of dotted rhythms depends in part on the tempo of the music. In the slow *Marcia funèbre* movement of Chopin's Piano Sonata No. 2 in B-flat minor, the dotted figures sound heavy and downcast. In French overtures, which are characterized by dotted rhythms, the tempo is so slow that the long note fades before the short one is played; the short notes seem to be attached not to the notes immediately preceding them, but to the notes immediately following. The result approximates a verbal "Ta-da!" The overture to Handel's *Water Music* is a clear example. ◉ In quick tempi, dotted rhythms create propulsive excitement and an effect that can be reminiscent of skipping or galloping. The main theme of the Allegro in the first movement of Schubert's Symphony No. 9 cavorts in this manner. Less common are double-dotted rhythms (the second dot adds half the value added by the first dot). In double-dotted figures the first note is seven times the length of the second. The opening of Beethoven's Piano Sonata in C minor, Op. 111, is notated in this fashion. In some dotted rhythms, two or three notes can take the place of the short note; this is the case with the lugubrious subject that opens Mahler's Symphony No. 7.

double bass Bass member of the viol family. The largest and lowest-pitched string instrument in standard use, it is known by many names, including "string bass," "contrabass," "bass fiddle," and plain old "bass." There are many variations in the size and shape of double basses, but most of the instruments in use today are examples of what is called a "three-quarter" bass, which has an overall length of 73 to 74 inches, a body length of about 44 inches, and strings with a sounding length of 42¾ inches. Whereas the other orchestral string instruments—cello, viola, and violin, all members of the violin family—have softly rounded backs and round shoulders that join the neck at a perpendicular angle, the double bass has a flat back whose upper section slopes inward toward the neck, and a pear-shaped body with steeply sloped shoulders—anatomical features typical of a VIOL.

The four strings of the double bass are tuned in a manner that is also typical of viols, in fourths: E–A–D–G. In order to produce notes lower than the low E, many basses are fitted with what is called a C-extension on the E string, which sticks up above the pegbox; five-string basses with a low B or C string are also frequently encountered, and are preferred in European orchestras. The pegbox on a modern double bass is itself a distinctive mechanism, adjusting string tension with cogwheels and worm gears rather than the friction pegs found on violins, violas, and cellos.

Two quite different types of bow are employed by double bass players. The "French" bow, common not only in France and other Mediterranean countries, but England and Scandinavia, is similar in appearance to a cello bow, but slightly shorter (averaging 26 inches in length) and sturdier; like a cello bow, it is played using an overhand grip. The "German" bow, long used in Germany and Austria, and now supplanting the French bow in America, is deeper at the frog (the heel end) and shaped more like a traditional viol bow; it is played with an underhand grip, but different from that used by viol players.

The useful range of the double bass, from low B or C to the D an octave and a fifth above the open G, is about an octave lower than that of the cello. In order to facilitate sight-reading and avoid a jungle of ledger lines, music written for the double bass is generally notated an octave higher than it sounds. Because of the instrument's remarkable resonance, notes played pizzicato sustain themselves marvelously. And because the strings are quite long, natural harmonics are easy to produce and of excellent quality.

Double bass

The double bass appeared on the scene around the beginning of the 16th century, finding use both as a continuo instrument and as the bass "voice" in consorts of viols. From there it made its way into the orchestra, earning a place in the standard string complement by the beginning of the 18th century. The double bass section of a modern symphony orchestra usually consists of eight, sometimes nine or ten, instruments. Alone or, more frequently, in combination with the cellos and various low wind and brass instruments, the bass section's role is to provide the harmonic foundation of the orchestral sonority.

Though it may be thought of as an elephantine instrument, the double bass has surprising agility, a fact many knowledgable composers have taken advantage of. A remarkable example comes in the opening pages of Richard Strauss's *Ein Heldenleben* (beginning at bar 76), where the basses, doubling the cellos and playing *ff* and *fff*, get to sing the hero's theme as it vaults from low G's and A's to high C's. For 27 swashbuckling measures the section plays without a rest. Other sectional passages worthy of note include: Beethoven, Symphony No. 5, third movement (where the basses and cellos carry the mysterious main theme of the scherzo and also lead the manic fugato of the trio section); Tchaikovsky, Symphony No. 6, third movement (an obstacle course of scurrying eighth-note triplets); Stravinsky, *The Firebird,* introduction; Holst, *Egdon Heath,* the somber opening measures; and Mahler, *Das Lied von der Erde,* first movement (in which closely spaced chords, played pizzicato, are used to reinforce the brass in lieu of strokes on the timpani). Passages for solo double bass are rare in the orchestral literature. One of the best-known examples is the solo for muted double bass (playing a minor-key version of the tune "Frère Jacques") that begins the third movement of Mahler's Symphony No. 1.

The chamber literature contains a smattering of works that feature the double bass, of which the most frequently encountered are Mozart's Serenade in B-flat,

K. 361, Beethoven's Septet, Op. 20, and two works by Schubert, the Octet, D. 803, and the celebrated *Trout* Quintet. In contrast, a large number of concertos, more than 200, have been written for the double bass. Among the most successful are the operatically styled works of Giovanni Bottesini (1821–89), who ranks among the instrument's greatest virtuoso players and was also a conductor of considerable distinction (he led the premiere of Verdi's *Aida* in 1871). The leading virtuoso of the Classical and early Romantic period was the Venetian-born Domenico Dragonetti, (1763–1846), who composed extensively for the instrument. He spent most of his career in London and was on friendly terms with Haydn, Beethoven, Cherubini, and Rossini. In the early 20th century, Serge Koussevitzky made a name for himself as a bass player before gaining even greater fame as a conductor. More recently, notable soloists have included Gary Karr, Bertram Turetzky, James VanDemark, and Edgar Meyer. It should not be forgotten that for many years the bass, usually without its bow, has moonlighted as a jazz instrument. The honor roll of top jazz bassists includes Charles Mingus, Ray Brown, Charlie Haden, and Ron Carter.

double stop On a string instrument, two notes played simultaneously on two strings. A three-note chord, or triple stop, is achieved by playing three notes on three strings. The Ragtime from Stravinsky's *L'histoire du soldat* features a solo violin playing in double stops.

Dowland, John

(b. prob. London, 1563; d. London, February 20, 1626)

ENGLISH COMPOSER-LUTENIST. A close contemporary of Shakespeare, he received his bachelor's degree in music from Oxford in 1588, the year of the Spanish Armada. He spent much of his life abroad—first in France (1580–84), later in Germany and Italy (1594–96; while in Italy he sought out the famed madrigal composer Luca Marenzio), and finally in Denmark (1598–1606), where he served as lutenist to King Christian IV. His life's ambition was to find preferment at the English court, which finally materialized in 1612, when he was named to a minor position as one of the King's Lutes; thereafter he composed little of any importance. Dowland's works are about evenly divided between songs and solo compositions for lute. His *Firste Booke of Songes or Ayres,* a collection of 21 songs—including some for solo voice with lute accompaniment, and some for four voices, mostly without accompaniment—appeared in 1597. His *Second Booke* was published in 1600, and his *Third and Last Booke* in 1603. As a song writer and performer on a "gentleman's" instrument, Dowland was, in effect, a pop musician. But the expressive content of his music is serious, and in most of his songs darker sentiments predominate. His early songs were strophic, patterned on dance types, and influenced by the madrigal styles of Marenzio and others. In his later works, of which fewer are strophic, he gradually moved away from madrigalistic word-painting toward a freer and more subtle style closely attuned to the rhythms of speech, and marked by a keen, often biting, expressiveness.

RECOMMENDED RECORDINGS

FIRST BOOK OF SONGS OR AYRES: COVEY-CRUMP; LINDBERG (BIS).

LUTE MUSIC: O'DETTE (HARMONIA MUNDI).

LUTE SONGS (*FLOW MY TEARS AND OTHER SONGS*): RICKARDS, LINELL (NAXOS).

Dreigroschenoper, Die (Threepenny Opera)

PLAY WITH MUSIC IN A PROLOGUE AND THREE ACTS BY KURT WEILL AND BERTOLT BRECHT (after John Gay's *THE BEGGAR'S OPERA*), composed in 1928 and premiered August 31, 1928, at the Theater am Schiffbauerdamm in Berlin. The score contains an abundance of memorable numbers, the most celebrated of which is "Die Moritāt von Mackie Messer," known to English-speaking audiences as "Mack the Knife."

Dresden Staatskapelle *See* STAATSKAPELLE DRESDEN.

drum A large and morphologically varied family of percussion instruments featuring a membrane made of animal skin or some other pliable material (the "head"), which is stretched across a casing and vibrates when struck. *See also* BASS DRUM, SNARE DRUM, TAMBOURINE, TIMPANI.

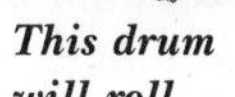

This drum will roll.

duet A piece (or a passage within a piece) for two performers. Vocal duets are a common feature of operas and cantatas, and may occur in symphonic works with multiple vocal soloists. Delibes's opera *Lakmé* contains a particularly lovely duet, "Dôme épais le jasmin," also known as the "Flower Duet." Instrumental duets usually involve two instruments of like type—such as violin and viola, or clarinet and bassoon—both of which are treated melodically; works of this type are thought of as being distinct from sonatas, which generally involve a keyboard instrument and a single "melody" instrument. Examples of instrumental duets include Mozart's Duos, K. 423 in G, and K. 424 in B-flat, for violin and viola; Kodály's Duo, Op. 7, for violin and cello; Koechlin's *15 Duos* for two clarinets; and Ravel's Sonata for Violin and Cello.

Du Fay, Guillaume

(b. Cambrai, ca. 1400; d. Cambrai, November 27, 1474)

FRENCH COMPOSER, acknowledged by his colleagues as the preeminent musician of the mid-15th century, and described by Piero de' Medici in 1467 as "the greatest ornament of our age." Du Fay (his name was pronounced in three syllables—*Doo-fah-ee*) was accepted as a choirboy at Cambrai Cathedral in August 1409 and served in that capacity until 1414, when, presumably, his voice broke. Between 1414 and 1418 he is thought to have attended the Council of Constance in the retinue of Cardinal Pierre d'Ailly. While there, he came into contact with members of the Malatesta family, who commissioned some of his earliest works, including the motet *Vasilissa ergo gaude* (1420). By the late 1420s he had become a priest as well as one of the most famous, and well traveled, musicians in Europe. From 1428 (the year he was ordained) until 1433, he was a member of the papal choir in Rome. He appears to have been held in great esteem by Pope Eugene IV, who commissioned six motets, one of which, *Ecclesie militantis,* was sung at his coronation in 1431.

Following a stint as *maître de la chapelle* to the Duke of Savoy in 1434, Du Fay rejoined the papal choir (1435–37), which by then had moved, along with the pope, to Florence. He wrote the motet *Nuper rosarum flores* for the dedication of the Florence Cathedral in 1436, and probably came into contact with the cathedral's architect, Filippo Brunelleschi, as well as the sculptor Donatello. Du Fay spent two further periods in Savoy (1437–39 and 1451–58), in between which he was resident at Cambrai, becoming choirmaster in 1442. He returned to Cambrai in 1458 and spent the rest of his life there, completing

Guillaume Du Fay* (left) *with Gilles Binchois, from a contemporary manuscript

a Requiem in 1470 (unfortunately lost) and the mass *Ave regina celorum* in 1472.

Du Fay composed at least seven settings of the complete Ordinary of the Mass and about a dozen independent settings of the Kyrie and Gloria, as well as hymns, antiphons, motets, and nearly 100 secular songs in French and Italian. Most important were the mass settings—which exhibit great refinement and exceptional polyphonic skill, as well as groundbreaking innovations in their conception and organization—and the motets, particularly the 13 isorhythmic motets that are among the masterpieces of medieval art. Du Fay was the first composer to base a setting of the mass on a popular song, using one of his own, the chanson "Se la face ay pale," as the CANTUS FIRMUS for his mass *Se la face ay pale* (composed around 1455). The four great mass cycles of Du Fay's later years—*Se la face ay pale, L'homme armé* (also based on a popular song, and composed most likely in the 1460s), *Ecce ancilla Domini* (ca. 1463), and *Ave regina celorum*—are works of extraordinary richness and beauty whose lucid counterpoint, exquisite sonority, and cogent organization are supreme musical achievements. *See also* ISORHYTHM.

RECOMMENDED RECORDINGS

MISSA "ECCE ANCILLA DOMINI": VELLARD AND ENSEMBLE GILLES BINCHOIS (VIRGIN).

MISSA "L'HOMME ARMÉ": SUMMERLY AND OXFORD CAMERATA (NAXOS).

MOTETS: VAN NEVEL AND HUELGAS ENSEMBLE (HARMONIA MUNDI).

Dukas, Paul

(b. Paris, October 1, 1865; d. Paris, May 17, 1935)

FRENCH COMPOSER. Despite the fact that his reputation rests on fewer than half a dozen works, albeit of the highest quality, he is considered one of the greatest masters France has produced. Between 1882 and 1889 he attended the Paris Conservatoire, joining the composition class of Ernest Guiraud in 1883 and winning first prizes in counterpoint and fugue in 1886; during his student years, he became friends with both Debussy and d'Indy. In 1892, following a year in the military, he began to write criticism for the *Revue hebdomadaire,* the first of a string of Parisian journals to which he contributed over the years. He was named a chevalier of the Légion d'Honneur in 1906, and twice served on the faculty of the Conservatoire, where he taught orchestration (1910–13) and composition (1928–35) and numbered among his students Duruflé and Messiaen.

By nature conservative and self-critical, he allowed only 15 of his compositions to survive. Among these are the exuberant Symphony in C (1895–96), with its echoes of Franck, d'Indy, and Chausson (but with a palette closer to that of Roussel and the late-19th-century Russians), and the popular *THE SORCERER'S APPRENTICE* (1897), a masterpiece of orchestration as well as rhythmic and metrical sophistication. Many regard as his supreme achievement the opera *Ariane et Barbe-Bleu* (*Ariane and Bluebeard*) based on a "tale in three acts" by Maurice Maeterlinck, which received its premiere at the Opéra-Comique in 1907. His final gift to the public was the 20-minute-long ballet *La péri* (1911–12) ◉, a work of exotic, *Tristan*-esque harmonies and coruscatingly brilliant scoring that he "composed on a bet," and whose exquisite fanfare was added just prior to the premiere as an afterthought.

RECOMMENDED RECORDING

ORCHESTRAL WORKS (INCUDING *LA PÉRI* AND *THE SORCERER'S APPRENTICE*): SLATKIN AND L'ORCHESTRE NATIONAL DE FRANCE (RCA).

Dun, Tan *See box on pages 708–11.*

Dunstable [Dunstaple], John

(b. ca. 1390; d. December 24, 1453)

ENGLISH COMPOSER. Only a few remnants are known of his life: also a mathematician and astrologer, he worked under the patronage of John, Duke of Bedford, the Dowager Queen Joan, and Humfrey, Duke of Gloucester. Humfrey's friendship with Leonello d'Este in Ferrara may explain why most of Dunstable's compositions ended up in Italian rather than English manuscripts, though it is doubtful whether Dunstable himself spent time in Italy. His numerous works preserved in manuscripts in Bologna, Modena, and Trent, as well as Munich, attest to his near-mythic status in Europe as the inventor of what Continental musicians termed "contenance angloise" ("English style"): a warm, full sonority, extensive use of thirds and sixths, resulting in triadic motion with a characteristic melodic suppleness, and suspended, slowly shifting harmony, similar to that of modern minimalism. Despite the presence of these qualities in earlier English music, and their rich manifestation in the late-14th- or early-15th-century collection known as the Old Hall Manuscript—which also contains works by Dunstable's brilliant contemporary, Leonel Power (1370–1445)—Dunstable alone was credited with this "great flowering" and its overwhelming influence on Franco-Flemish composers, particularly Du Fay and Gilles Binchois (ca. 1400–60).

Although Machaut owns the distinction of producing, in the late 14th century, the first truly unified mass cycle, in which all the movements of the Ordinary are structurally and/or melodically connected, it took more than half a century for this approach to become the norm. Dunstable and Power were pioneers in bringing the change about; they each wrote connected pairs of mass movements, and the five movements of the *Missa Rex seculorum* (attributed to both men) appear to be based on the same tenor, though the upper parts contain no unifying melodic material.

The true glories of Dunstable's output are his isorhythmic motets and polyphonic settings of sacred Latin texts. In these works, for example the incomparably luscious "Quam pulcra es," the rich, expressive "pan-consonance" of the new style reaches its apogee. The spellbinding, seductive effect it must have had on Continental composers can easily be imagined.

RECOMMENDED RECORDINGS

MOTETS: HILLIARD ENSEMBLE (EMI).

"MUSICIAN TO THE PLANTAGENETS" (MOTETS, ANTIPHONS, MASS MOVEMENTS): ORLANDO CONSORT (METRONOME).

duo [1] A pair of musicians who perform together. [2] A DUET.

du Pré, Jacqueline

(b. Oxford, January 26, 1945; d. London, October 19, 1987)

ENGLISH CELLIST. She studied from the age of ten with William Pleeth, and attended the Guildhall School of Music in London. After some additional coaching from Paul Tortelier and Mstislav

Jacqueline du Pré in performance

Rostropovich, she made her professional debut at London's Wigmore Hall in 1961. She toured America for the first time in 1965 (as a soloist with the BBC Symphony Orchestra), and in 1967 she married the pianist Daniel Barenboim, with whom she made a number of recordings. Her career, which lasted only about ten years, was cut tragically short by the onset of multiple sclerosis. She nonetheless managed to record the main works of the concerto literature—both of Haydn's concertos and those of Schumann, Saint-Saëns, Dvořák, and Elgar, plus Richard Strauss's *Don Quixote*—as well as the sonatas by Beethoven, Brahms, Chopin, and Franck. An engaging performer whose striking looks and animal magnetism charmed audiences and lent extra excitement in concerts, she exuded personality. Her playing was impassioned and intense, sometimes raw and reckless, but never reticent.

RECOMMENDED RECORDINGS

BRAHMS, CELLO SONATAS: BARENBOIM (EMI).

ELGAR, CELLO CONCERTO: BARBIROLLI AND LONDON SYMPHONY ORCHESTRA (EMI).

Duruflé, Maurice

(b. Louviers, January 11, 1902; d. Paris, June 16, 1986)

FRENCH ORGANIST AND COMPOSER. He studied in Paris with Charles Tournemire and Louis Vierne, and entered the Paris Conservatoire in 1920. There, over the next four years, he received first prizes in organ, accompaniment, harmony, and fugue; he also studied composition with Paul Dukas. In 1930 he was named organist of St. Étienne-du-Mont, and from 1943 to 1969 served as professor of harmony at the Conservatoire. Like Dukas he was an extremely fastidious composer—in 60 years he allowed the publication of only ten works. His best-known score is his Requiem, Op. 9 (1947), based on plainchant melodies.

RECOMMENDED RECORDING

REQUIEM: LARMORE, HAMPSON; LEGRAND AND PHILHARMONIA ORCHESTRA (TELDEC).

Dutilleux, Henri

(b. Angers, January 22, 1916)

FRENCH COMPOSER. His family moved to Douai when he was two, and it was at the conservatory there that he began his formal study of music. He entered the Paris Conservatoire in 1933, studying with Henri Büsser and winning the Prix de Rome upon his graduation in 1938; his stay in Rome was cut short by the outbreak of European hostilities. During the occupation of France, he served as chorusmaster at the Paris Opéra, and in 1943 he joined the staff of Radio France, where he subsequently served as head of the music department (1945–63). From 1961 to 1970 he was professor of composition at

Henri Dutilleux, master of colors, space, movement

the École Normale de Musique in Paris, and during 1970–71 he taught at the Paris Conservatoire. Although he has contributed several works to the chamber literature—including an early, charming Sonatine for Flute and Piano (1943) and a masterly Piano Sonata (1946–48)—the greater part of his output consists of works for orchestra, among which the most important to date are two symphonies (premiered in 1951 and 1959); the variation work *Métaboles* (1959–64); a cello concerto composed for Mstislav Rostropovich titled, after Baudelaire, *Tout un monde lointain . . .* (*A Faraway World*; 1967–70); *Timbres, espace, mouvement (ou "La nuit étoilée")* (1978; rev. 1990), inspired by Van Gogh's famous painting *Starry Night*; and a violin concerto, *L'arbre des songes* (*Tree of Dreams*; 1985), written for Isaac Stern.

A meticulous composer whose integrity, imagination, and independence of thought have kept his work on the highest artistic plane, Dutilleux has proven to be one of the 20th century's most resourceful and intrepid explorers of musical time and space, without ever departing from the time-honored French tradition of giving pleasure to the senses through one's art. His music, all of it exquisitely crafted, is characterized by rhythmically alert textures and luminous, pulsating sonorities, by the unusual combination of spontaneity and organic continuity, and by expression that can be explosive, seductive, poetic, and, to an exceptional degree, exhilarating, without ever resorting to cliché, e.g., the opening minutes of the Cello Concerto, which progress from mysterious to fulminant.

RECOMMENDED RECORDINGS

CELLO CONCERTO: ROSTROPOVICH; BAUDO AND ORCHESTRE DE PARIS (EMI).

SYMPHONIES (COMPLETE): TORTELIER AND BBC PHILHARMONIC (CHANDOS).

Elegance personified: Charles Dutoit

Dutoit, Charles

(b. Lausanne, October 7, 1936)

SWISS CONDUCTOR. As a youth he learned to play violin, viola, piano, and percussion. He studied at the conservatories of Lausanne and Geneva, attended Ernest Ansermet's rehearsals with the Orchestre de la Suisse Romande, and took summer conducting courses in Siena and at Tanglewood (studying with Charles Munch in 1959). In 1963, after a short stint playing viola in the Lausanne Chamber Orchestra, he made his debut as a conductor with the Berne Symphony Orchestra; he became the orchestra's assistant conductor the following year, and subsequently served as its principal conductor (1967–77). He was named music director of the Montreal Symphony Orchestra in 1977 and rapidly transformed that ensemble into what was arguably the finest French orchestra in the world, and certainly one of North America's best. He resigned abruptly in 2002, after the orchestra's union boss badmouthed him in the press. Dutoit's recordings with the Canadians, which focused on coloristic early-20th-century repertoire—Ravel, Debussy, Stravinsky, and Falla—as well as the music of Berlioz, Tchaikovsky, and Prokofiev, are among the most consistent and successful efforts of the past

25 years, and have been highly praised. Affable and energetic, Dutoit has a fine ear and an exceptionally elegant podium manner. He has had notable success as a guest conductor with the Philadelphia Orchestra and the Boston Symphony, among others, and remains a dark-horse candidate for the music directorship of one of America's top orchestras.

RECOMMENDED RECORDINGS

BERLIOZ, OVERTURES: MONTREAL SYMPHONY ORCHESTRA (DECCA).

DEBUSSY, ORCHESTRAL WORKS: MONTREAL SYMPHONY ORCHESTRA (DECCA).

FAURÉ, REQUIEM, *PELLÉAS ET MÉLISANDE* (INCIDENTAL MUSIC): MONTREAL SYMPHONY ORCHESTRA (DECCA).

Dvořák, Antonín

(b. Nelahozeves, September 8, 1841; d. Prague, May 1, 1904)

CZECH COMPOSER. Despite the widespread popularity of much of his music, in particular the Symphony *From the New World*, he remains, more than a century after his death, one of the most underrated major composers in the history of music. He achieved distinction in all the important fields of his day: His remarkably balanced production included 13 operas, nine symphonies, dozens of orchestral works (including concert overtures and symphonic poems), three concertos (a mediocre one for piano, a very good one for violin, and a monumentally great one for cello), more than 50 chamber pieces, several large sacred and choral works, and numerous songs. His symphonies—he composed one every four or five years for some three decades—are among the most important 19th-century contributions to the genre.

Antonín Dvořák

Dvořák was brought up in a village near Prague where his father was butcher and innkeeper. Impressed by his aptitude for music, his father, who played the zither, arranged for him to take violin lessons from a local teacher. His musical education continued in the nearby town of Zlonice from 1853, and in 1857 he entered the Prague Organ School, completing his studies there in 1859. For a short while following graduation Dvořák played viola in a dance band, and in 1862 he was appointed principal viola of the orchestra of the newly established Provisional Theater, the first Czech theater in Prague. He remained in the orchestra until 1871, playing French, German, and Italian operas and performing frequently under Smetana's direction following the latter's appointment as chief conductor in 1866. During his years as an orchestral musician, he also played in occasional concerts, including three all-Wagner programs in 1863 under the baton of Wagner himself. Like many composers of his era, Dvořák succumbed early to the influence of Wagner, showing his indebtedness in works such as the first version of his opera *King and Charcoal Burner* (1871) and the opulently lyrical Symphony No. 3 (1873). Smetana's premiere of the symphony in 1874 gave Dvořák's reputation a major boost.

The 1870s brought significant personal and professional fulfillment. In 1873, having failed in his courtship of her elder sister, Dvořák married Anna Čermáková. It would be a happy union. In 1875 he won an Austrian state stipend, the first of five consecutive yearly grants he would receive. Brahms, one of the judges, was so impressed by the sample works Dvořák sent in that he took the remarkable step of recommending Dvořák to his own publisher, Fritz Simrock, in Berlin. Simrock straightaway commissioned a set of eight *Slavonic Dances.*

Composed in 1878 and published in a version for piano four-hands and in marvelous orchestrations by the composer, the *Slavonic Dances,* Op. 46, catapulted Dvořák to fame outside Bohemia and made a fortune for Simrock. In 1886–87 Dvořák composed and orchestrated a second set of eight *Slavonic Dances,* Op. 72.

Dvořák became a figure of international importance during the 1880s. His brilliant Symphony No. 6 (1880), a masterpiece of symphonic design in the line of Beethoven and Brahms—but with a heart that is all Czech—was written for Hans Richter. He composed his Symphony No. 7 (1884–85) on a commission from the London Philharmonic Society. A work of dark eloquence and titanic grandeur, it shows Dvořák at the pinnacle of his powers and ranks as one of the 19th century's greatest symphonic scores. Other important works of the decade include *The Jacobin* (1888)—Dvořák's finest comic opera—and the Quintet in A for piano and strings, Op. 81 (1887), as well as the bucolic Symphony No. 8, completed in 1889. A remarkable set of three thematically linked concert overtures—*In Nature's Realm,* Op. 91, *Carnival,* Op. 92, and *Othello,* Op. 93—followed in 1891–92.

In September 1892, on an invitation from Jeannette Thurber, the wife of a wealthy New York businessman, Dvořák came to America to head the newly established and ambitiously named National Conservatory of Music (his initial salary of $15,000 was 25 times what he was making at the Prague Conservatory). He spent most of the next three years in the United States teaching and composing, until Thurber ran out of money and the conservatory failed. During the summer of 1893, separated from Bohemia by an ocean and half the width of Europe, Dvořák found a home away from home in the tiny farm community of Spillville, situated near the Turkey River in northeastern Iowa, 110 miles due west of Madison, Wisconsin. Spillville's population of 300 consisted mostly of Czech immigrants who preserved the language and culture of their homeland; the town even had a butcher named Dvořák.

Dvořák composed his most celebrated work, the Symphony No. 9 in E minor, Op. 95 (*From the New World*; 1893), entirely in the United States, following it with his most popular chamber piece, the String Quartet in F (*American*), Op. 96 (1893), and the equally fine though less well known String Quintet in E-flat, Op. 97 (1893). After hearing a performance of the Second Cello Concerto by Victor Herbert (1859–1924) in Brooklyn (and being impressed by the younger composer's skill in scoring the work so that the cello could be heard), he decided to compose a cello concerto of his own for his friend and colleague, the Czech cellist Hanuš Wihan. The score, revised after his return to Bohemia in the spring of 1895, is grand in scale and at the same time one of his most personal and emotionally poignant utterances.

Antonín Dvořák reading a score

Antonín Dvořák conducting his music at the World's Columbian Exposition in Chicago, 1893

The major works of Dvořák's final years were the operas *The Devil and Kate* (1899), *Rusalka* (1901)—a radiant "lyric fairy tale" that is now gaining a foothold in the standard repertoire—and *Armida* (1904). In 1896 he also created a group of four symphonic poems based on tales by K. J. Erben—*The Water Goblin, The Noonday Witch, The Golden Spinning-Wheel,* and *The Wood Dove,* Opp. 107–110—in the music of which Mahler can be seen peeking out from behind the rocks and trees.

Dvořák knew only one way to compose: from the heart. He was an extraordinarily hard worker and possessed an exceptional facility, so that pieces that might occupy another composer for months or years took only weeks to pour from his pen. He was an outstanding orchestrator. He wrote idiomatically for the strings and had a special fondness for pure woodwind colors—oboes in thirds, clarinets in sixths—as opposed to the mixtures that were typical of Germanic music in his day. Perhaps because he spent so many years as a professional violist, he also felt it his duty to create interesting inner parts and countermelodies, which lend his music not only a unique felicity, but a marvelous richness of texture. He communicated emotions directly, powerfully, and in an utterly sincere and engaging manner, and his best scores stand out for their vibrant energy, dramatic shifts of mood, and wealth of melodic ideas.

RECOMMENDED RECORDINGS

Cello Concerto: Rostropovich; Karajan and Berlin Philharmonic (DG).

Overtures and symphonic poems: Kertész and London Symphony Orchestra (Decca).

Rusalka: Fleming, Heppner; Mackerras and Czech Philharmonic (Decca).

Slavonic Dances: Kubelík and Bavarian Radio Symphony Orchestra (DG).

Symphonies (complete): Kertész and London Symphony Orchestra (Decca).

dynamic [1] The loudness or softness of a given note, passage, or part within a musical texture. [2] A marking used to indicate the appropriate dynamic (e.g., *ppp, mf,* or *ff*), or the treatment of a musical gesture (e.g., *cresc., poco a poco dim., sfz,* or *subito f*).

E

early music European music created before 1600—i.e., before the emergence of Baroque style and systematic use of tonal harmony. In practice, this consists of the music of the Middle Ages and the Renaissance, from the earliest written forms of ninth-century plainchant and organum through the complex modal polyphony of the 16th century. An allied concept is that of historically informed performance (also referred to as "authentic" or "period-instrument" performance), which has become a major force on the concert and recording scene today. It involves not just the use of period instruments (or modern copies of them) in performances of any music written prior to about 1900, but also the adoption of the style of playing and singing current at the time the music was written, which takes into account such things as tuning, articulation, ornamentation, tempo, and phrasing. *See also box on pages 310–313.*

Edinburgh Festival, The *See box on pages 46–47.*

Egmont VERSE DRAMA BY JOHANN WOLFGANG VON GOETHE about the struggles of Count Egmont (1522–68), the Flemish statesman and soldier who opposed Spain's occupation of the Low Countries during the 16th century. For an 1810 revival of the play in Vienna, the Burgtheater commissioned Beethoven to compose about an hour of incidental music, consisting of the *Egmont* Overture ◉—one of his most powerful and dramatic concert pieces—as well as four orchestral interludes, two songs for soprano (setting the words of Egmont's beloved Clärchen), a scene depicting Clärchen's death, a Melodrama, and a final "Triumphant Symphony" that recapitulates the heroic ending of the overture.

Got lute? An early-music group rehearses.

RECOMMENDED RECORDINGS

COMPLETE INCIDENTAL MUSIC: LORENGAR; SZELL AND VIENNA PHILHARMONIC (DECCA).

OVERTURE: BÖHM AND VIENNA PHILHARMONIC (DG).

eighth blackbird *See box on page 272.*

Eine kleine Nachtmusik (A Little Night Music) TITLE GIVEN BY MOZART TO HIS SERENADE IN G, K. 525, for string quartet with added double bass. In the catalog of his works that he kept from 1784 until his death, Mozart's entry dated August 10, 1787, describes the piece as having *five* movements: an Allegro, a minuet, a Romance, a second minuet, and a finale. The page containing the first minuet was removed from the manuscript at an early date, by whom and for what reason no one knows; thus, the piece as we know it is actually a little less night music than Mozart originally composed. Notwithstanding that, and the fact that its musical content is rather modest (nowhere near as sophisticated as the String Quintets in C major and G minor penned earlier the same summer), *Eine kleine Nachtmusik* has become the most frequently played and familiar of Mozart's works. Yet, far from being a piece Mozart expected to be remembered by, it seems rather to have been a particularly exalted case of musical joinery, whose greatness—like that of an exquisite piece of furniture—lies not in the materials from which it was made, but in the craftsmanship of the maker.

RECOMMENDED RECORDING

Mackerras and Prague Chamber Orchestra (Telarc).

Einstein on the Beach **MINIMALIST OPERA IN FOUR CONTINUOUS ACTS** (framed by five intermezzos) by Philip Glass, with mise-en-scène by Robert Wilson to a "libretto" by Christopher Knowles, Lucinda Childs, and Samuel M. Johnson, premiered July 25, 1976, in Avignon. The work is scored for chamber choir, including soprano and tenor soloists, a chamber ensemble consisting of two electronic keyboards, three wind players and soprano, and a solo violin. Glass's first opera, and the first installment in a trilogy of operas about great men (*Satyagraha,* about Gandhi, followed in 1980, and *Akhnaten* in 1984), *Einstein on the Beach* was the work that put Glass on the map both in Europe and the United States.

RECOMMENDED RECORDING

Various soloists; Philip Glass Ensemble (Nonesuch).

Elgar, Edward

(b. Lower Broadheath, June 2, 1857; d. Worcester, February 23, 1934)

ENGLISH COMPOSER. His father, a piano tuner by trade and a capable musician, opened a music shop in Worcester in 1863; during Elgar's youth the family lived in rooms over the shop. Though he received only rudimentary formal training, he was exposed to music on a daily basis and learned to play the violin (well enough to perform in the orchestra of the Three Choirs Festival), bassoon, and organ. He began to compose when he was ten, teaching himself theory and technique as he went along and mastering formal principles from the study and playing of the classics. By the age of 16 he had embarked on the career he

Einstein on the Beach *at the Brooklyn Academy of Music*

Elgar with his bicycle, "Mr. Phoebus," in 1903

would have for the rest of his life, that of a freelance musician. He taught violin for a while, and conducted amateur orchestras and choruses in the area around Worcester. In 1885 he succeeded his father as organist of St. George's Church in Worcester.

In 1889, over the objections of her family, Elgar married Caroline Alice Roberts. He was 31, she was 40; he was Catholic, she was not; he came from a lower-class tradesman's family, she was the daughter of the late Major General Sir Henry Gee Roberts. Alice was strong willed, devoted to her young husband, and supportive of his efforts to succeed as a creative artist. Following their marriage, he was able to turn his attention wholly to composition.

Sir Edward with a portable gramophone, ca. 1926

Elgar was temperamentally inclined toward larger undertakings, and the bulk of his output consists of weighty choral-orchestral works and dramatic, big-boned symphonic scores. The first of his large-scale symphonic canvases, and the one that made him famous, was the *ENIGMA* VARIATIONS (1899). Buoyed by its success, he composed a song cycle for contralto and orchestra, *Sea Pictures* (1899), whose finest number, "Sabbath Morning at Sea" (to a poem by Elizabeth Barrett Browning), is a grand expression of religious rapture. Elgar gave voice to his strongly held spiritual beliefs in several sacred works, of which the most important was *The Dream of Gerontius* (1900), an ambitious, oratorio-like setting of a text by John Henry Cardinal Newman that portrays the soul's experience of bodily death, judgment, and purgatory according to Catholic doctrine. The work's premiere was a fiasco, but with the passage of time this dramatic, visionary, and intensely expressive score has come to be seen as one of Elgar's finest achievements.

Elgar soldiered on after the heartbreaking setback of *Gerontius,* penning his celebrated *POMP AND CIRCUMSTANCE* March No. 1 (1901) and a pair of wonderfully upbeat concert overtures—*Cockaigne* (1901) and *In the South* (1904), the former a portrait of London, the latter an ebullient paean to Italy. Knighted in 1904, he completed a string of masterpieces during the next 15 years: his Symphony No. 1 (1907–08), a majestic, nobly poignant work that received nearly 100 performances in the year following its premiere; the darkly passionate Violin Concerto (1909–10); Symphony No. 2 (1909–11); the tone poem *Falstaff* (1913); and the brooding, relentlessly pessimistic Cello Concerto (1919). Along with the melancholy feelings that permeate these scores one finds strength, energy, nobility, and grandeur. Sir Edward also completed his first major chamber works during this intense twilight phase of his career—a violin sonata, string quartet, and piano quintet, all dating from the years 1918–19. Following the death of Lady Elgar in 1920, he composed almost nothing.

Elgar was among the first composers to recognize the potential of the phonograph and systematically record his own music. He began in 1914, the heyday of acoustical recording, and continued until shortly before his death in 1934, well into the electrical era. No other composer of his generation is as well represented by his own recordings. Among Elgar's most celebrated studio achievements was the premiere recording of his Violin Concerto, captured in July 1932 with the 15-year-old Yehudi Menuhin as soloist. Elgar himself had just turned 75.

The dignified variety of nostalgia to which Elgar frequently gave voice was balanced in the best of his works by a sense of panache—and by a vigorous, often swashbuckling use of instruments and of the orchestra as a whole—that keeps what he wrote from sounding staid or old-fashioned. It may well sound like the work of someone who was as much a European as an Englishman, but that is no weakness. In his music Elgar was always himself, and he was unquestionably one of Romanticism's last great masters.

RECOMMENDED RECORDINGS

CELLO CONCERTO: DU PRÉ; BARBIROLLI AND LONDON SYMPHONY ORCHESTRA (EMI).

THE DREAM OF GERONTIUS: GEDDA, WATTS; BOULT AND NEW PHILHARMONIA ORCHESTRA (EMI).

ENIGMA VARIATIONS: BOULT AND LONDON SYMPHONY ORCHESTRA (EMI).

SYMPHONIES NOS. 1 AND 2: SOLTI AND LONDON PHILHARMONIC ORCHESTRA (DECCA).

VIOLIN CONCERTO: HAHN; DAVIS AND LONDON SYMPHONY ORCHESTRA (DG).

Elijah **ORATORIO BY FELIX MENDELSSOHN,** composed to a text by Julius Schubring (translated into English by William Bartholomew) and premiered on August 26, 1846, at the Birmingham Festival, the composer conducting. The story, drawn from various Old Testament sources, depicts the major events in the life of the prophet. With *Elijah,* Mendelssohn reached the pinnacle of his fame and made a crucial contribution to what had become a moribund genre. *Elijah* would serve as a majestic bridge between the works of Handel and Haydn and those of Elgar and Walton that would mark the resurgence of the oratorio in the 20th century; today, for all intents and purposes, it is the only mid-19th-century English oratorio in the active repertoire.

RECOMMENDED RECORDING

WHITE, PLOWRIGHT; HICKOX AND LONDON SYMPHONY ORCHESTRA (CHANDOS).

elisir d'amore, L' (The Elixir of Love) **COMIC OPERA IN TWO ACTS BY GAETANO DONIZETTI,** to a libretto by Felice Romani (based on Eugène Scribe's libretto for Daniel-François-Esprit Auber's *Le philtre*), premiered at the Teatro Cannobiana in Milan on May 12, 1832. The story revolves around the lovesick peasant Nemorino, who pines for the beautiful and well-off Adina, but is too timid to declare his feelings openly. Dr. Dulcamara, a smooth-talking purveyor of patent remedies, comes to the rescue with an "elixir" of love (nothing more than a bottle of cheap Bordeaux) that proves to be just the thing for Nemorino's shyness. The suddenly outgoing young man ultimately wins Adina's heart and hand, and comes into a tidy inheritance as well. *L'elisir d'amore* is a deft, lighthearted comedy, upbeat and melodically engaging, whose showpiece roles for bass (Dulcamara) and tenor

(Nemorino) have provided star turns over the years for the likes of Luigi Lablache, Enrico Caruso, Giuseppe di Stefano, and Luciano Pavarotti. With its plaintive bassoon obbligato and bittersweet line, Nemorino's Act II *romanza* "Una furtiva lagrima" ("A Furtive Tear") is not only the opera's most striking number but one of the most celebrated tenor arias in the bel canto repertoire.

RECOMMENDED RECORDING

BATTLE, PAVAROTTI, NUCCI, DARA, UPSHAW; LEVINE AND METROPOLITAN OPERA ORCHESTRA (DG).

Elman, Mischa

(b. Talnoye, January 20, 1891; d. New York, April 5, 1967)

AMERICAN VIOLINIST OF RUSSIAN BIRTH. As a child of 11 he came under the wing of Leopold Auer, who taught him at the St. Petersburg Conservatory during the years 1903–04. He made his debut in Berlin on October 14, 1904, conquering London (with the Glazunov concerto) the following year and making a triumphant New York debut in 1908. He settled permanently in the United States in 1911, becoming a citizen in 1923. He performed with all of America's major orchestras and made numerous recordings. During the 1936–37 season, he gave a series of five concerts at Carnegie Hall in which he surveyed the concerto literature for his instrument, playing more than a dozen works. He was one of the last of the great Romantic violinists, noted for his warm, expressive tone.

Mischa Elman, known for his warm tone

embouchure (Fr., "mouthpiece") [1] The mouthpiece of a wind or brass instrument. [2] The proper shaping and tensioning of the player's lips so as to direct a stream of air into or across an instrument's mouthpiece, to produce vibration within a mouthpiece, or to control the vibration of a reed, while at the same time regulating the tone that is produced.

Emerson Quartet STRING QUARTET FOUNDED IN **1976** and named in honor of the 19th-century American poet and essayist Ralph Waldo Emerson. Since 1979 its members have been violinists Philip Setzer and Eugene Drucker (who share first violin duties equally), violist Lawrence Dutton, and cellist David Finckel. The group has established itself as one of the preeminent string foursomes in the world today. Celebrated for their high-octane performances of the 20th-century repertoire, in particular the quartets of Bartók and Shostakovich, they are equally at home in the music of Haydn, Beethoven, Schubert, Brahms, and Dvořák. Since 2002, the group has performed without the aid of chairs—Messrs Setzer, Drucker, and Dutton standing, cellist Finckel seated on a piano bench atop a low podium.

RECOMMENDED RECORDINGS

BARTÓK, STRING QUARTETS (COMPLETE): (DG).

SCHUBERT, QUARTET IN D MINOR, D. 810 (*TOD UND DAS MÄDCHEN*; *DEATH AND THE MAIDEN*) (DG).

***Emperor* Concerto** NICKNAME GIVEN TO BEETHOVEN'S PIANO CONCERTO NO. 5 IN E-FLAT, OP. 73, composed in 1809 and dedicated to Archduke Rudolph. The opening of the concerto, with piano flourishes boldly punctuating a majestic chord progression in the orchestra, is at once magnificent and arresting; the ensuing Allegro strikes a remarkable (and notably dynamic) balance between festivity and fantasy. Time virtually stands still during the meditative

Adagio that follows, set in the lofty key of B major, and so gently scored that the piano converses for nearly the whole of its duration in the softest tones. The impetuous rondo finale—which, with its $\frac{6}{8}$ meter and emphasis on dotted rhythms, foreshadows the treatment Beethoven would soon apply to the first movement of his Seventh Symphony—ends the work in a bacchanalian release of energy. Through all three movements Beethoven contrives to give the piano's solo passages, by virtue of their brilliance and distinctiveness, an impact and dramatic presence equal to that of the orchestra, in effect treating the piano as a "field marshal" (or, indeed, an "emperor") and the orchestra as an "army."

RECOMMENDED RECORDINGS

FLEISHER; SZELL AND CLEVELAND ORCHESTRA (SONY).

R. SERKIN; BERNSTEIN AND NEW YORK PHILHARMONIC (SONY).

***empfindsamer Stil* ("Sensibility Style")** Compositional style championed in the mid-18th century by C. P. E. Bach and J. J. Quantz among others, in which the arousal of emotions—in particular, feelings of poignancy, sorrow, and tender melancholy—was deemed to be the highest aspiration of the composer. While the precise meaning of "sensibility," a watchword of 18th-century arts and letters, is difficult to convey, it might best be rendered in today's language as "heightened sensitivity." To achieve the most direct expression of emotion, composers working in the *empfindsamer Stil* sought to strip music of the merely ornamental embellishment that characterized much of the writing of the high Baroque.

Enescu, George

(b. Liveni-Vîrnav [now George Enescu], August 19, 1881; d. Paris, May 4, 1955)

ROMANIAN VIOLINIST, PIANIST, CONDUCTOR, AND COMPOSER. A musical prodigy of the first magnitude, he was the preeminent Romanian composer of the 20th century. Pablo Casals called him "the most amazing musician since Mozart," and Yehudi Menuhin, who was his student and friend, held him in similarly high esteem. He began taking violin lessons when he was four, and continued his musical studies at the Gesellschaft der Musikfreunde in Vienna (1888–94), under the tutelage of Joseph Hellmesberger and Robert Fuchs, among others, and subsequently at the Paris Conservatoire (1895–99), where his teachers included Gabriel Fauré and Jules Massenet. He launched his performing career with an unprecedented double demonstration of instrumental mastery, playing the violin at the first performance of his Violin Sonata No. 1 in 1898 (accompanied by Alfred Cortot), and the piano in the first performance of his Violin Sonata

Cover artist George Enescu, one of the greatest musical talents of his era

No. 2, in 1900 (accompanying Jacques Thibaud). Paris would remain his artistic base for the rest of his life, though he would spend long periods in Romania, holing up there for the duration of World War I and again during World War II, and seeking throughout his career to contribute to his native country's musical life as conductor, musicologist, and educator. He conducted frequently in Bucharest; among his many engagements was one in 1903 in which he led the premiere of what would become his most popular work, the uncharacteristically gaudy *Romanian Rhapsody* in A, Op. 11, No. 1, composed two years earlier. He was also active in Iasi, where he served as an honorary chairman of the conservatory, and in 1917 inaugurated a series of symphony concerts bearing his name. Prior to 1915, and during the interwar years, he traveled and concertized widely in Europe and America as well, appearing as conductor and violinist with the Philadelphia Orchestra in 1923, and guest conducting the New York Philharmonic several times during the 1937–39 seasons. Following the Communist takeover of his homeland in 1946, he returned to Paris in self-imposed exile; his last years there were clouded by illness and financial duress.

Enescu was a formidable teacher whose students included the American prodigy Menuhin (from 1927), and later Arthur Grumiaux, Ida Haendel, Christian Ferras, and Ivry Gitlis. His list of works as a composer, necessarily short because of his career as a virtuoso and his obligations as a teacher and administrator, nonetheless includes contributions to a variety of vocal, instrumental, and orchestral genres. Just as he had a divided loyalty to two countries—his native Romania and his adopted France—he also had a dual personality as a composer—the one part nationalistic and folk-oriented (reflected in the two *Romanian Rhapsodies,* and, much later, in 1948, the *Ouverture de concert sur des thèmes dans le caractère populaire roumain*), the other cosmopolitan and progressive. His greatest work was the four-act opera *Oedipe,* based in part on the dramas of Sophocles. Sketched in 1910 and composed mainly between 1921 and 1931, it received its premiere at the Paris Opéra on March 13, 1936. Other compositions that have found a place in the repertoire include the Violin Sonata No. 3 (1926), two string quartets, and three symphonies.

RECOMMENDED RECORDINGS

Oedipe: Van Dam, Hendricks, Fassbaender; Foster and Monte-Carlo Philharmonic Orchestra (EMI).

Romanian Rhapsody No. 1: Dorati and London Symphony Orchestra (Mercury).

String quartets: Ad Libitum Quartet (Naxos).

Violin Sonata No. 3: A. Oprean and J. Oprean (Hyperion).

enfant et les sortilèges, L' (The Child and the Magic Spells) Opera in one act by Maurice Ravel, to a libretto by Colette, premiered in Monte Carlo on March 21, 1925, Victor de Sabata conducting. The story revolves around a bratty little boy who defies his mother, bangs up the furniture, and torments animals. After some of the household items he has mistreated rise up and give him a taste of his own medicine (taking on magically human qualities in the process), the outdoor creatures he has victimized decide to attack him. He astonishes them all by showing compassion for a pet squirrel that gets hurt in the fray. Seeing that he is exhausted, alone, and afraid, they take pity on him and help him call for his mother, who appears as the curtain descends.

Ravel's imaginative score evokes the mood of enchantment and wonder at the heart of the story through an exquisite and subtle use of the orchestra, while conveying the child's aimless nature—and the emotional ambivalence of his relationship to the world around him—by means of harmonic ambiguities and occasional recourse to bitonality. The characterization of various objects and animals gains added piquancy from the witty use of allusion: for example, a jazzy fox-trot accompanies the dialogue of the Black Wedgwood Teapot and the Chinese Teacup, and when the Armchair and the Louis XV Chair dance, it's to an 18th-century sarabande. Cat lover that he was (as was Colette), the composer also makes something special of the "Meowed Duet."

RECOMMENDED RECORDING

STEPHEN, OWENS, JOHNSON, TUCKER; PREVIN AND LONDON SYMPHONY ORCHESTRA (DG).

English Baroque Soloists *See box on pages 310–13.*

English Chamber Orchestra ENSEMBLE FOUNDED IN **1948** by Arnold Goldsborough for the purpose of performing the music of the Baroque era (in particular, that of Purcell, J. S. Bach, and Handel), and originally known as the Goldsborough Orchestra. The group adopted its present name in 1960, and since then has specialized in a broader repertoire that includes much 20th-century music. The members of the ECO enjoyed a particularly close association with Britten, playing in the 1960 premiere of his opera *A Midsummer Night's Dream* at the Aldeburgh Festival and in the first performance of his *Cello Symphony* (1964), and making several distinguished recordings with him as conductor—of Bach's *Brandenburg* Concertos, of select Mozart symphonies and concertos, and of Britten's operas *Albert Herring* and *The Rape of Lucretia.* Other maestros with whom the band has worked closely over the years are Barenboim, Raymond Leppard, and Jeffrey Tate. The ECO has taken part in several noteworthy recorded surveys of Mozart's piano concertos: with Barenboim playing and conducting, with Murray Perahia playing and conducting, with Mitsuko Uchida as soloist and Tate conducting, and with Alicia de Larrocha as soloist and Sir Colin Davis conducting. The group's discography also includes a marvelous cycle of the Mozart violin concertos with Cho-Liang Lin as soloist, conducted by Leppard.

The English Chamber Orchestra

English Concert, The *See box on pages 310–13.*

English horn Alto member of the OBOE family. Still known in England by its French name, *cor anglais,* it has nothing to do with the English. How it got its name remains, in fact, a mystery. One theory holds that "anglais" may be a corruption of an old French word meaning "angled"—which, for ease of playing, the instrument *has* to be on account of its length. The modern English horn has a bent metal crook that holds the reed, and a distinctively bulbous bell with a smallish opening, rather than a flared one; the keywork and fingering are similar to those for the oboe. Its range is a fifth lower than the oboe's, extending to the E below middle C, and it possesses a darker, more nasal tone, plaintive in the upper reaches, rich and resonant in the lower.

Originally a denizen of the opera pit, the English horn entered the symphony orchestra in the early 19th century. Berlioz was among the first composers to appreciate its expressive potential, and he used it to magnificent effect in the third movement of his *Symphonie fantastique* (1830)—where call-and-response solos on oboe and English horn evoke a duet of shepherds—as well as in his *Roman Carnival* Overture (1844). With its exotic sound, the English horn remained a particular favorite of French composers through the 19th century. Debussy entrusted it with an important role in *La mer* (1905), where it lends a distinctive yet subtle coloration to important lines, doubling a pair of solo cellos at one point, and a muted trumpet at another. The symphonic repertoire is rife with extended solos for the English horn. One of the most familiar graces the Largo of Dvořák's Symphony *From the New World* (1893) ◉, evoking a mood of pastoral calm; around the same time, Sibelius used the English horn in *The Swan of Tuonela* to conjure up a scene of Nordic gloom. Perhaps the most taxing solo in the literature is the one Shostakovich includes in the first movement of his Symphony No. 8, which lasts three minutes without a break. There are few concertos for the English horn, but the repertoire includes several interesting works in which it is treated as a solo instrument. The best of these are Honegger's *Concerto da camera* (1948) for flute, English horn, and strings, and Copland's *Quiet City* (1940), in which the English horn carries on a pensive dialogue with the solo trumpet.

***English* Suites** SET OF SIX SUITES FOR HARPSICHORD (BWV 806–811) BY J. S. BACH, composed around 1715 in Weimar. There is nothing specifically "English" about the *English* Suites; according to Johann Forkel, Bach's first biographer, they acquired the name because they were written "for an Englishman of rank." Bach himself called them "Suites avec prelude," because each one begins with a prelude, which distinguishes the *English* Suites from Bach's *French* Suites and the Partitas. The order of the remaining movements in each of the *English* Suites is typical of the French style: allemande, courante, sarabande, and gigue, with an optional dance (variously a bourrée, gavotte, minuet, or passepied) between the sarabande and gigue.

RECOMMENDED RECORDINGS

LEONHARDT (VIRGIN CLASSICS).

PERAHIA (SONY).

***Enigma* Variations** SUBTITLE OF ELGAR'S VARIATIONS ON AN ORIGINAL THEME, OP. 36, composed in 1898–99 and premiered in London on June 19, 1899, Hans Richter conducting. The melancholy theme in G minor on which the variations are based is the "enigma" of the work's title—the composer never revealed its source, if it had one, though he hinted early on that "another and larger theme 'goes,' but is not played" through the work. Years later, Elgar confided that the theme "expressed when written (in 1898) my sense of the loneliness of the artist . . . and to me, it still embodies that sense." Each of the 14 variations is a portrait of someone known to the composer, though the only clues to the identity of these subjects come in the form of initials, code words, or, in one case, a mysterious cipher. For a long time the names of the "friends pictured within" to whom Elgar dedicated the score remained an enigma as well, but the composer eventually revealed them in the notes he wrote to accompany a set of player piano rolls of the piece. The *Enigma* Variations is among the finest free-standing variation works in the repertoire, revealing a technique on the same level as Brahms's in his *Variations on a Theme by Haydn* and Richard Strauss's in *Don Quixote.* But it offers an even richer emotional experience, for in portraying the salient qualities of each of his friends—whether melancholy or tenderness, bluster or coy reserve, delicacy, mirth, or soaring passion—Elgar was actually characterizing himself and the feelings that friendship aroused in him. The work is thus more than a series of clever vignettes—it is a touchingly confessional self-portrait and a glowing tribute to the values of Edwardian England. In the final variation, "E. D. U.," Elgar steps forward and takes a bow, as himself.

RECOMMENDED RECORDINGS

Boult and London Symphony Orchestra (EMI).

Solti and Vienna Philharmonic (Decca).

ensemble [1] Generic term for any group of musicians that performs together. [2] The accuracy and unanimity of execution attained in the performance of a piece, or of a particular passage within a piece, by any group of two or more musicians.

Ensemble InterContemporain *See box on page 272.*

Érard French manufacturer of pianos and harps founded in 1777 by Sébastian Érard. The company built its first grand piano in 1796, modeled on the type of piano then being produced in England. Beethoven's acquisition, in 1803, of one of these Érard grands with a six-octave range expanded his sonic horizons impressively—the immediate result can be heard in the *Waldstein* Sonata, completed the following year. In 1821 Érard patented the double-escapement action, allowing the rapid repetition of single notes. Under the direction of Pierre Érard, the founder's nephew, the firm reached its peak during the 1850s, winning the gold medal at the Paris Exhibition of 1855 and garnering the plaudits of performers all over Europe. But as time went by the company proved unable to keep up with technological innovations coming mainly from America, and in 1960 its name was bought and it ceased producing its own pianos.

Sébastian Érard also developed the double-action harp in the first decade of the 19th century, with the pitch-adjustment mechanism still in use on the modern concert harp. Unfortunately, Érard's harps suffered the same fate as their pianos, and by the 1970s the company was producing only one or two instruments a year.

"Erlkönig" ("Erlking") **Song by Franz Schubert, D. 328,** to a text by Johann Wolfgang von Goethe, composed in 1815 and published in 1821 as Schubert's Op. 1. The composer made 84 settings of 55 different Goethe texts (31 in 1815 alone), and created four separate versions of "Erlkönig," all in G minor. The text describes a wild night ride in which a father, carrying his young son in his arms, reassures the delirious child even as the malevolent Erlking,

A mid-19th-century rendering of the scene depicted in Goethe's "Erlkönig"

whom the father cannot see, ravishes him and ultimately takes his life. With its dramatic use of the minor mode and the insistent triplet rhythm of the accompaniment, "Erlkönig" achieves an urgency entirely new to the art of song.

RECOMMENDED RECORDING

Fischer-Dieskau, Moore (DG).

***Eroica* Symphony** Title given by Ludwig van Beethoven to his Symphony No. 3 in E-flat, Op. 55, composed in 1803. Intending to honor Napoleon, Beethoven originally inscribed the name "Buonaparte" on the score. But after Napoleon proclaimed himself emperor in 1804, the angry composer scratched it out so vehemently that he tore the title page. The symphony received its first public performance on April 7, 1805, at the Theater an der Wien; when it was published the following year it carried the inscription "Sinfonia Eroica, composta per festeggiare il sovvenire di un grand Uomo" ("Heroic Symphony, composed to celebrate the memory of a great man"), along with a dedication to Prince Franz Joseph von Lobkowitz, one of Beethoven's most prominent patrons.

The accepted view of the *Eroica*—that it was a revolutionary departure heralding the age of symphonic Romanticism—tends to misrepresent the work. What the score embodies is not so much a break with the past as a culmination, in which the 18th-century ideal of the symphony is carried to its theoretical limit. Throughout the piece Beethoven observes the formal protocols of Classicism—in the layout, disposition, and relative weights of the four movements, as well as in the way long-range harmonic goals are established and reached. What sets the *Eroica* apart and truly does break new ground, is the scope and forcefulness of the argument and the intensity with which expressive gestures are hammered home. In the first movement of the *Eroica,* for the first time in any of his symphonies, Beethoven symbolically raises a clenched fist—violently pounding out offbeat accents and wrenching the scansion in a manner that is clearly meant to shock, while forcing the harmony into regions unsettlingly distant from the home key. Equally remarkable, in all four movements, is the power and brilliance of Beethoven's orchestration, which creates a sonic gravitas no 18th-century symphony had even approached. Thus, while the *Eroica* belongs formally to the Classical period, it leans toward the Romantic in its expression and tone, and in that sense, it truly is a new species.

Title page of the Eroica *Symphony, with the name "Buonaparte" scratched out*

RECOMMENDED RECORDINGS

BÖHM AND VIENNA PHILHARMONIC (DG).

KLEMPERER AND PHILHARMONIA ORCHESTRA (EMI).

España SYMPHONIC RHAPSODY BY EMMANUEL CHABRIER, completed in 1883 following an extended holiday in Spain, during which the composer jotted down some of the melodies utilized in the piece. On the surface a tuneful and brilliantly orchestrated pastiche, *España* proved an important forerunner of 20th-century modernism not only in its metrical complexity and assertive, at times even violent, rhythmic accentuation, but also in its boldly unorthodox scoring, which includes scintillating effects on the harp, bravura solos by the bassoon, and saucy proclamations from the trombones. Mahler and Ravel, among others, hailed it as a groundbreaking work; the general public found it so enjoyable that in 1886 Emil Waldteufel could capitalize on its popularity by recasting it as a waltz for ballroom dancing.

RECOMMENDED RECORDINGS

GARDINER AND VIENNA PHILHARMONIC (DG).

PARAY AND DETROIT SYMPHONY ORCHESTRA (MERCURY).

Esswood, Paul *See box on pages 155–57.*

etude (Fr., "study") Term used to denote a focused technical exercise for the performer or, in some cases, the composer, and most commonly written for the piano. In the hands of Chopin (among others), the etude became a genre in which concentration on a particular aspect of keyboard technique (i.e., scales for the left hand, fast octaves, use of a particularly weak finger to play the melody) or on a particular texture was coupled with the expression of mood or imagery. The result could often be quite dramatic and intense, for example, the surging chromatic octaves in the outer sections of Chopin's Étude in B minor, Op. 25, No. 10, or the stormy arpeggiations and hammered right-hand chords of his *Revolutionary* Étude in C minor, Op. 10, No. 12.

Liszt, in his *Études d'exécution transcendante* (1851), a set of 12 tone-pictures for the piano, adopted a more freewheeling approach to the genre, piling technical challenges one upon another as a pretense for the most flamboyant sort of virtuosity. Ten of the studies come with poetic titles—"Mazeppa," "Vision," "Wilde Jagd"—Liszt's way of suggesting the kind of imagery a pianist should have in mind when performing them. In 1859 the Bohemian composer Bedřich Smetana, much influenced by Liszt (and, like him, a brilliant pianist), did his idol one better by composing a chromatic *Concert Étude* of stupendous difficulty.

In the 20th century, Leopold Godowsky created 53 transcriptions of Chopin's etudes, making them fiendishly difficult (for example, recasting Op. 10, No. 5, for the left hand only). Rachmaninov enriched the genre with two groupings of *Études-tableaux* (Opp. 33 and 39), melancholy set pieces that capture a range of moods from dark introspection and funereal gloom to impassioned reverie. Late in his career Debussy penned a dozen etudes for the piano that, in a nod to pedagogic tradition, address specific technical challenges: thirds, fourths, sixths, octaves, grace notes, repeated notes, arpeggios, chords, etc. Beyond that, hardly anything in these pregnant works is traditional; their luxuriant harmony and dense, intricate textures reflect Debussy's idiom at its most advanced. And as studies of compositional technique—of the ways in which a particular sonority or texture can be developed into a whole piece—they point the way to much of what has since been explored in the piano works of Messiaen, Boulez, Stockhausen, Ligeti, and Carter. In this regard the etudes of Ligeti are particularly important, for they link the traditions of Chopin, Liszt, and Debussy to the present, posing many of the same challenges, punching up the dynamic extremes, redefining virtuosity in the most modern terms. Among the most striking are the "Cordes vides" etude, with its eerily translucent sonorities, and "L'escalier du diable," which spirals up the keyboard, reaches a dynamic of *ffffffff*, and ends in what has been described as "sonic pandemonium."

RECOMMENDED RECORDINGS

CHOPIN, ÉTUDES: PERAHIA (SONY).

DEBUSSY, ÉTUDES: JACOBS (NONESUCH).

LIGETI, ÉTUDES: AIMARD (SONY).

Eugene Onegin OPERA IN THREE ACTS BY PYOTR IL'YICH TCHAIKOVSKY with a libretto by Tchaikovsky and Konstantin Shilovsky based on the verse tale by Aleksandr Pushkin, composed in 1878 and premiered the following year. The scenic elements of Pushkin's tale clearly appealed to the composer, but it was the character of Onegin—a jaded egotist at the beginning, a crumbling figure by the end—that really fired his imagination. Some of Tchaikovsky's finest music is contained in the score, in the first-act soliloquy for Tatyana (the so-called "Letter Scene"), in Lensky's poignant meditation "*Kuda, kuda, kuda vï udalilis*" ("*Where have you gone?*"), and in the extended final scene for Onegin and Tatyana. Two large dance numbers—the second-act waltz and the third-act polonaise—are popular orchestral excerpts.

A. V. Nezhdanova in the Bolshoi's **Eugene Onegin**

Europa Galante *See box on pages 310–13.*

Euryanthe OPERA IN THREE ACTS BY CARL MARIA VON WEBER, to a libretto by Helmina von Chézy based on a medieval French romance, premiered at the Kärntnertortheater in Vienna on October 25, 1823, with the composer conducting. The plot is a Gothic farrago, involving ghostly visitations, ghastly snakes, poison rings, treachery, abandonment, and betrayal, in which the innocent Euryanthe, bride of Count Adolar, is pitted against the jealous Eglantine and the deceitful Count Lysiart. Good ultimately prevails. For this, his penultimate opera, Weber composed a brilliant overture—today a staple of the concert repertoire—and much beautiful music, but owing to the execrable libretto the work is rarely staged.

RECOMMENDED RECORDING

OVERTURE: KARAJAN AND BERLIN PHILHARMONIC (DG).

exposition The section of a fugue or of a movement in sonata form in which the subject or the main thematic ideas are initially stated and elaborated. *See also* FUGUE, SONATA FORM.

F

f hole On string instruments, particularly those belonging to the violin and viol family, the symmetrical openings (one shaped like an italic *f*, the other like its mirror image) on the front or "belly" of the instrument that allow sound to radiate from its interior.

The f hole and bridge, secrets of string sound

Fairy-Queen, The "SEMIOPERA" IN FIVE ACTS BY PURCELL, very loosely based on Shakespeare's *A Midsummer Night's Dream*, premiered in London on May 2, 1692, at the Queen's Theatre, Dorset Garden. Purcell's music consists of two instrumental suites and five masques lasting between 10 and 40 minutes, one for each act of the play.

RECOMMENDED RECORDINGS

HARRHY, STAFFORD, HILL, VARCOE; GARDINER AND ENGLISH BAROQUE SOLOISTS (ARCHIV).

VARIOUS SOLOISTS; CHRISTIE AND LES ARTS FLORISSANTS (HARMONIA MUNDI).

Falla, Manuel de

(b. Cádiz, November 23, 1876; d. Alta Gracia, Argentina, November 14, 1946)

SPANISH COMPOSER, the most important figure in his country's 20th-century musical reawakening. He learned to play the piano from his mother and had a childhood interest in writing short stories; his endeavors then, and for the rest of his life, were informed by a devout Catholicism. He studied harmony and counterpoint at the conservatory of Cádiz and continued his study of piano in Madrid, where he came into contact with composer Felipe Pedrell (1841–1922), who encouraged him to work with Spanish folk material and subjects. In 1905 Falla's Gypsy-themed opera *La vida breve* (*The Short Life*) won a major contest, solidifying his reputation as a nationalist. Falla spent the years 1907–15 in Paris, where he met the leading figures of French musical life. Particularly impressed with the work of Debussy, he made a thorough study of *Pelléas et Mélisande.* Debussy helped create connections for Falla in Paris (providing introductions to Dukas and Ravel) and advised him on compositional matters. Falla intended to settle in Paris, but returned to Spain after World War I broke out.

Back home, Falla entered his most productive period. Finding inspiration in the rich cultural matrix of Andalusia, in 1915 he completed *NOCHES EN LOS JARDINES DE ESPAÑA* (*Nights in the Gardens of Spain*), whose impressionistic scoring shows how thoroughly he had absorbed the French approach to orchestral colorism. Other compositions inspired by Andalusia followed, including the one-act "Gypsy revel" *El amor brujo* (*Love, the Magician*; 1915), which became in subsequent revisions an orchestral work (1916) and a ballet (1916–17), and the ballet *EL SOMBRERO DE TRES*

PICOS (*The Three-Cornered Hat*; 1916–19), commissioned by Sergey Diaghilev for the Ballets Russes, with sets designed by Picasso. The success of *El sombrero de tres picos* prompted Diaghilev to offer Falla the commission for *Pulcinella,* which he turned down (the work thus went to Stravinsky).

Seeking tranquillity and spiritual renewal, Falla moved to Granada in 1920. He formed a close friendship with the poet Federico García Lorca (whom he had met in 1915) and began writing in a neoclassical vein: Key works from this period include the puppet opera *El retablo de maese Pedro* (*Master Peter's Puppet Show*; 1919–23), based on a section of Cervantes's *Don Quixote,* and the Harpsichord Concerto (1923–26), written for Wanda Landowska. Falla's idyll was shattered by the outbreak of the Spanish Civil War (1936–39) and Lorca's execution in its very first year (to no avail, and at some risk to his own life, the composer had tried to intercede for his friend). Falla sat out the rest of the conflict, and in the spring of 1939 left Spain for Argentina. By then his best work was long behind him, and the Spain it told of was gone forever. He spent his last years struggling in vain to complete the "scenic cantata" *Atlantida,* an epic in which he fantastically tried to tie together Spain, the myth of the lost continent of Atlantis, and the forward march of Catholic Christianity.

Falla moved freely in several currents of 20th-century musical thought, composing colorful, folk-flavored orchestral showpieces, warmly romantic stage works, and spiky essays in the neoclassical style. He subtly endowed his scores with sensuality and an exotic flavor that invariably rings true, yet he also achieved a formal rigor that frequently eluded his contemporaries. Much like Bartók, he was able to assimilate the distinctive rhythmic and melodic patterns of folk music into a highly developed and eclectic compositional language. To create the Andalusian atmosphere that characterizes much of his music he used arabesque-like melodic figures and simple chord progressions hovering ambiguously between major and minor. Behind this approach was a concept typical of Moorish-influenced art: the ornamental made substantive. Nearly all of his works are distinguished by first-rate musical ideas.

Manuel de Falla, ascetic, colorist, the hero of Spain

RECOMMENDED RECORDINGS

EL AMOR BRUJO: FRÜHBECK DE BURGOS AND NEW PHILHARMONIA ORCHESTRA (DECCA).

NOCHES EN LOS JARDINES DE ESPAÑA: LARROCHA WITH FRÜHBECK DE BURGOS AND LONDON PHILHARMONIC ORCHESTRA (DECCA).

EL SOMBRERO DE TRES PICOS: DUTOIT AND MONTREAL SYMPHONY ORCHESTRA (DECCA).

LA VIDA BREVE: COSSUTTA, LOS ANGELES, MORENO; FRÜHBECK DE BURGOS AND NATIONAL ORCHESTRA OF SPAIN (EMI).

falsetto A singing technique, more properly called second-mode phonation, which produces in men a pure head-voice resonance, higher than the usual chest voice; since ancient times, men have sung in alto range in this manner. *See also* COUNTERTENORS.

Falstaff OPERA IN THREE ACTS BY GIUSEPPE VERDI, to a libretto by Arrigo Boito (based on Shakespeare's *The Merry Wives of Windsor* and *Henry IV*), composed 1890–92 and premiered at La Scala in Milan on February 9, 1893. Verdi's last work for the stage (he was 79 at its premiere), *Falstaff* was also his first comedy in more than 50 years. The opera begins in musical midsentence, with a cadence, and ends with what may be the most exhilarating fugue in all of music, as one by one the characters follow Falstaff in admitting that "Tutto nel mondo è burla" ("The whole world is crazy"). Between this beginning and this end, there is not a dull moment in the entire opera. The familiar story is treated energetically, and with deep insight into the emotions of the characters. Boito's felicitous language and the quick-hitting spontaneity of his dialogue are matched point for point by Verdi's robust score, a miracle of rhythmic, melodic, and harmonic animation that propels the action to uproarious climaxes.

Bryn Terfel, outsized singing personality, as Falstaff

Verdi's most ensemble-dominated opera, *Falstaff* is also in many ways his most human and profound statement, a compassionate view of youth and age, and a knowing look at life through the battle of the sexes. As the parting gift of a great master and the crowning glory of a life's work, it has no real rival in the operatic repertoire.

RECOMMENDED RECORDING

GOBBI, SCHWARZKOPF, PANERAI, MOFFO; KARAJAN AND PHILHARMONIA ORCHESTRA (EMI).

fanciulla del West, La (The Golden Girl of the West) **OPERA IN THREE ACTS BY GIACOMO PUCCINI,** to a libretto by Carlo Zangarini and Guelfo Civinini based on David Belasco's play *The Girl of the Golden West.* The premiere, on December 10, 1910, at the Metropolitan Opera in New York, was a star-studded affair: Arturo Toscanini, the composer's friend and an ardent champion of his music, conducted, Emmy Destinn created the title role of Minnie, and Enrico Caruso was cast as the "good guy" bandit Ramerrez (a.k.a. Dick Johnson). The action, set in Gold Rush–era California, involves the comings and goings of various miners, an Indian and his squaw, a Wells Fargo agent, a Pony Express rider, and a saloon keeper, but centers on the love triangle of Minnie, Ramerrez, and the local sheriff, Jack Rance. Minnie cheats Rance at cards in order to save Ramerrez's life, and later holds off a posse at gunpoint. The opera ends with Minnie and Ramerrez riding off into the sunset together. The music of *La fanciulla del West* is fierce and masculine, as befits the rough-and-tumble world it depicts. Puccini's harmony takes on a decidedly modern edge in this opera, and his scoring at times conveys an almost barbaric splendor, marking a departure from the pastel language of *Madama Butterfly* and pointing clearly toward *Turandot.*

RECOMMENDED RECORDING

TEBALDI, DEL MONACO, MACNEIL; CAPUANA AND ORCHESTRA DELL'ACCADEMIA DI SANTA CECILIA (DECCA).

fandango A lively Spanish dance in triple meter. Rimsky-Korsakov inserted one in his *Capriccio espagnol* (1887) and Falla used one in the ballet *El sombrero de tres picos* (1916–19). The dreamy opening piece ("Evocación") of Albéniz's *Iberia,* Book I (1906), is also based on a fandango rhythm.

fanfare A festive call to attention, usually played by one or more brass instruments (though wind and string instruments may participate as well), often accompanied by percussion. Most fanfares feature triadic figures, DOTTED RHYTHMS, and repeated flourishes of one kind or another. The term is commonly used to identify a freestanding piece that is essentially ceremonial or incantatory in nature; examples of this type of fanfare include Copland's *Fanfare for the Common Man* and a whole series of works by Joan Tower that bear the title *Fanfare for the Uncommon Woman,* as well as the prefatory fanfare Dukas appended to his ballet *La péri.* But the term can also apply to passages within a larger work that make prominent use of the brass.

RECOMMENDED RECORDINGS

COPLAND, *FANFARE FOR THE COMMON MAN*: DORATI AND DETROIT SYMPHONY ORCHESTRA (DECCA).

TOWER, FANFARES: ALSOP AND COLORADO SYMPHONY ORCHESTRA (KOCH).

Fantasia on a Theme by Thomas Tallis WORK FOR DOUBLE STRING ORCHESTRA BY RALPH VAUGHAN WILLIAMS, composed in 1910 and revised in 1919. The theme on which the fantasia is based comes from *Tunes for Archbishop Parker's Psalter,* a set of nine psalm tunes by Tallis, specifically from the third, which sets the words "Why fum'th in fight the Gentiles spite, in fury raging stout?" (Psalm 2, known in the language of the King James version of the Bible as "Why do the heathen rage and the people imagine a vain thing?"). Vaughan Williams had looked into the music of Tallis during his revision of the English hymnal in 1904–06, and had been impressed by both its serenity and its soaring lyricism. In this brief work, his first masterpiece, he was able to achieve a combination of grandeur and intimacy similar to that in Tallis's music, while at the same time finding his own voice and setting the tone for much of his future output.

RECOMMENDED RECORDING

MARRINER AND ACADEMY OF ST. MARTIN-IN-THE-FIELDS (PHILIPS).

fantasy (from Greek *phantasia,* "idea," "image") An instrumental piece in free form. The term was first used in the 16th century, to refer to music that was freely "invented" rather than based on a preexisting (usually vocal) melody or a particular dance form. By the beginning of the 18th century it had come to designate a type of keyboard piece in which the emphasis was on virtuosity, daring modulation, and the improvisatory development of ideas. The pianist-composers of the Romantic era fully embraced this notion—along with its implication that the imagination was free to roam unfettered by any fixed formal design—even though most of their fantasies adhered to fairly standard forms, and many derived their thematic content from existing music.

In many ways a Romantic ahead of his time, Mozart set a precedent with his Fantasia in C minor, K. 475 (1785), a work of extraordinary emotional intensity, by turns dark, dramatic, and despondent. Schubert, in his *Wandererfantasie* (1822), and Schumann, in his *Fantasie,* Op. 17 (1836–38)—both for solo piano—boldly expanded the scale of the genre by utilizing spacious multimovement designs similar to what they might have employed in a sonata or a symphony. The same traits are apparent in Schubert's Fantasy in F minor, D. 940 (1828), for piano four-hands. Liszt penned dozens of large, rhapsodic fantasies on everything from popular Spanish tunes to Paganini's "La campanella"—showing particular affinity for bel canto and grand-opera themes. Among his most impressive achievements were the *Réminiscences de Don Juan* (1841), based on Mozart's *Don Giovanni,* and *Réminiscences de Boccanegra* (1882), on themes from Verdi's *Simon Boccanegra.* Numerous 19th-century virtuosos followed Liszt's lead, among them Balakirev, whose *Islamey* (1869), subtitled an "Oriental Fantasy," epitomized the genre at its most flamboyant. Sarasate brought a Lisztian panache to several concert fantasies for violin and piano, of which the most celebrated was his Fantasy on *Carmen,* Op. 25 (1883).

By the end of the 19th century, "fantasy" and "fantasia" had become catchall terms suitable for describing any work in which a borrowed theme or themes were used, or a work in which ideas were developed or sequenced in an essentially free manner, whether the treatment of the material was virtuosic or not. Notable 20th-century examples include Vaughan Williams's *Fantasia on a Theme by Thomas Tallis* (1910) for double string orchestra; Thomas Canning's *Fantasy on a Hymn Tune by Justin Morgan* (1944) for double string quartet and orchestra; Martinů's Symphony No. 6 (1953), subtitled *Fantaisies symphoniques;* Rodrigo's *Fantasía para un gentilhombre* (1954) for guitar and orchestra; and Elliott Carter's *Night Fantasies* (1980) for piano.

***Farewell* Symphony** NICKNAME OF JOSEPH HAYDN'S SYMPHONY NO. 45 IN F-SHARP MINOR, composed in 1772. A paragon of the STURM UND DRANG style, it is the only known 18th-century symphony in the inhospitable key of F-sharp minor, and would have been unplayable by Haydn's orchestra at Esterháza without the special crooks he ordered for the two horns. The score's finale is a clever musical plea from Haydn to his patron, Prince Nikolaus Esterházy, to allow the musicians of the orchestra to go home to their families as winter approached (hence the name). It calls for the players to perform little solos one by one and then leave the stage, blowing out the candles at their music stands as they go, until only two violins are left to play the final notes in near darkness.

RECOMMENDED RECORDING

WORDSWORTH AND CAPPELLA ISTROPOLITANA (NAXOS).

Stefano Dionisi as Farinelli, in the film by Gerard Corbian

Farinelli [Broschi, Carlo]

(b. Andria, January 24, 1705; d. Bologna, September 16, 1782)

ITALIAN CASTRATO. He grew up in Naples and was a student of the composer Nicola Porpora, of whose work he became a devoted interpreter. He made his debut in 1720, as Tirsi in Porpora's *Angelica e Medoro,* composed to the first printed libretto by Pietro Metastasio, and rapidly rose to prominence. After successful residencies in Bologna (1727–34) and London (1734–37), he was whisked off to Madrid by the queen of Spain, Italian-born Elisabetta Farnese, in hopes that his singing would ease the suffering of her chronically depressed husband, Philip V. Farinelli sang for Philip every night until the king's death in 1746; his role at court eventually came to include service as a counselor of state both to Philip and to his heir, Ferdinand VI. Expelled from Spain following Ferdinand's death in 1759, Farinelli retired to his country estate outside Bologna, where he spent the remaining years of his life enjoying visits from the musical and political elite of Europe, and showing off his collection of paintings and musical instruments.

Farinelli's extraordinary range, power, and agility, together with his highly cultivated musicianship and tasteful improvisation, exerted a major influence on the vocal style of Baroque opera seria. His singing—and, no less important, his artistry and intelligence—made a tremendous impression on all who came into contact with him and won great praise from his fellow musicians.

Farrar, Geraldine

(b. Melrose, Mass., February 28, 1882; d. Ridgefield, Conn., March 11, 1967)

AMERICAN SOPRANO. A liberated woman long before the term came into use, she studied in Boston, New York, and Paris prior to making her operatic debut on October 15, 1901, in Berlin, as Marguerite in Gounod's *Faust* under the baton of Karl Muck. She subsequently studied with Lilli Lehmann and spent three seasons with the Monte Carlo Opera. She made her Metropolitan Opera debut in 1906, as Juliette in Gounod's *Roméo et Juliette,* and remained on the company's roster until 1922. During her Met career, Farrar became a celebrated exponent of Gounod's Marguerite and Bizet's Carmen, sang the title roles in Massenet's *Manon* and *Thaïs,* and above all triumphed in the role of Cio-Cio-San in Puccini's *Madama Butterfly,* which she sang at its American premiere on February 11, 1907, opposite Caruso, and on 138 further occasions. While at the Met she also created the title role in Puccini's *Suor Angelica* (1918), and the role of the Goose Girl in Humperdinck's *Königskinder* (1910). Farrar retired from the operatic stage in 1922, after turning 40, but continued to sing in recital until 1931. She also enjoyed a brief but lucrative career as a silent-film star following the outbreak of World War I, when touring in Europe was out of the question. During the summer of 1915, she made three films with the legendary director Cecil B. DeMille, including a wildly popular adaptation of Bizet's *Carmen.* Her captivating aura came across on the big screen just as it did on the stage.

Farrar's exceptional beauty was complemented by great intelligence, solid musicianship (she was an accomplished pianist), and a racy sense of humor. One example of her high jinks was preserved for posterity when she and Caruso made a recording of the love duet from *Madama Butterfly.* The tenor, having imbibed heavily during a lunch break, flubbed take after take; when he finally got one right, Farrar took exuberant revenge at the duet's climactic moment, singing "He had a highball!" to Puccini's soaring melody.

A recumbent Geraldine Farrar, enjoying stardom in an age of glamour

Farrell, Eileen

(b. Willimantic, Conn., February 13, 1920; d. Park Ridge, N.J., March 23, 2002)

AMERICAN SOPRANO. She possessed one of the largest and most radiant operatic voices of the 20th century. But she first attracted the attention of the music world as a pop vocalist, singing on radio and television and, in 1959, stepping in for Louis Armstrong at the Spoleto Festival (where she had been

Eileen Farrell belts one out.

engaged to sing Verdi's Requiem), after which Columbia Records signed her to a contract. She made her operatic debut in 1956, as Santuzza in a Tampa production of Mascagni's *Cavalleria rusticana.* Engagements in San Francisco and Chicago followed; finally, on December 6, 1960, at the age of 40, she made her Metropolitan Opera debut, singing the title role in Gluck's *Alceste.* No slave to career (she was married to a New York City policeman and was a dedicated housewife and mother), she sang at the Met a total of only 46 performances in six roles over five seasons. Her relationship with the company's management was an uneasy one, and most of her triumphs took place on the concert stage. She was a favorite of the conductor Leonard Bernstein, who engaged her to sing the Wagnerian roles of Brünnhilde and Isolde in concert performances with the New York Philharmonic.

Known for the expressive warmth and sheer size of her voice, she was also a cunning artist whose phrasing and pacing revealed a keen intelligence. Her physique was on the large side as well, and its amplitude occasioned a famous backstage tiff with the conductor Eugene Ormandy, who pointedly asked her in front of others how much she weighed. Farrell slammed her fists onto her saddlebag hips, glared down at the 5-foot 4-inch conductor, and hooted: "None of your goddamn business. I don't ask you how tall *you* are, do I?"

Fassbaender, Brigitte

(b. Berlin, July 3, 1939)

Brigitte Fassbaender; angst with artistry

GERMAN MEZZO-SOPRANO, called by some the "Queen of Angst," a tribute to her emotionally charged singing and the engaging dramatic intensity of her acting. She studied in Nuremberg with her father, the baritone Willi Domgraf-Fassbaender, and made her debut in 1961 at the Bavarian State Opera in Munich, as Nicklausse in Offenbach's *Les contes d'Hoffmann.* Her repertoire included several Mozart roles (Cherubino in *Le nozze di Figaro,* Dorabella in *Così fan tutte,* Sextus in *La clemenza di Tito*) as well as Octavian in Richard Strauss's *Der Rosenkavalier,* with which she made her debuts at both Covent Garden (1971) and the Metropolitan Opera (1974). She was also much admired for her Orlofsky in Johann Strauss Jr.'s *Die Fledermaus,* and for her gripping performances as Countess Geschwitz in Berg's *Lulu* and the Nurse in Richard Strauss's *Die Frau ohne Schatten.* She was an outstanding lieder singer whose gift for characterization made her an appealing interpreter of the songs of Schubert, yet she happened also to possess a sardonic edge particularly suited to the music of Kurt Weill.

RECOMMENDED RECORDING

WEILL, *DIE SIEBEN TODSÜNDEN (THE SEVEN DEADLY SINS)*; GARBEN AND NORTH GERMAN RADIO PHILHARMONIC ORCHESTRA (HARMONIA MUNDI).

Fauré, Gabriel

(b. Pamiers, May 12, 1845; d. Paris, November 4, 1924)

FRENCH COMPOSER, PIANIST, AND TEACHER. Though not a virtuoso, he was a genius at the keyboard, and his works in all forms show an innovative and advanced use of harmony. He was one of the great masters of French song, and with his gift for expressive understatement he excelled in the art of the vignette. But over a career that spanned seven decades, he longed to be known for larger and more widely popular works, an ambition in which he was for the most part to be disappointed.

Born into a family of the petty nobility, Fauré showed a childhood love of music. At nine he was enrolled in the École Louis Niedermeyer for training as a church choirmaster; he boarded there for 11 years, studying plainchant, organ, harmony, counterpoint, and piano. Camille Saint-Saëns took over the piano department in 1861, and thanks to him Fauré received exposure to contemporary music that was not part of the curriculum. He finished in 1865, with first prizes in composition, counterpoint, and fugue. The following year he became organist at the church of St. Sauveur in Rennes; he spent four years there, finding ample time to compose, and returned to Paris in 1870, just in time to help lift the siege of the city during the Franco-Prussian War. He left Paris during the Commune, and spent the summer of 1871 teaching at his alma mater, the École Niedermeyer, which had taken refuge in Switzerland. Upon his return to the capital in the fall, he was appointed assistant organist at St. Sulpice, and was introduced to all of musical Paris by Saint-Saëns.

Gabriel Fauré, age 18

Together with Vincent d'Indy, Édouard Lalo, Emmanuel Chabrier, and Henri Duparc (1848–1933), Fauré founded the Société Nationale de Musique in 1872. With its concerts as an outlet he turned his attention to chamber music, producing the exquisite, lyrical Violin Sonata No. 1 in A and the bold, emotionally direct Piano Quartet No. 1 in C minor. Fauré left St. Sulpice in 1874 to assist Saint-Saëns at the Madeleine, one of Paris's leading churches, and within three years was named choirmaster. A failed romance with Marianne Viardot (daughter of the soprano Pauline Viardot) led him to seek solace in travel. In Weimar in 1877 he met Liszt, who was then premiering Saint-Saëns's *Samson et Dalila*), and between 1879 and 1882 he attended numerous performances of Wagner operas in Germany and London. He was fascinated by this revolutionary music but unlike most of his peers did not fall under its spell.

Fauré married in 1883 and was forced to teach, in addition to working his church jobs, in order to support his family. His creative work, which earned him little money in any case, was relegated to the summer months. Fauré's career peaked in 1896, when he became chief organist at the Madeleine and was named professor of composition at the Paris Conservatoire.

Considered radical in his day, he now became a father figure to a whole generation of French composers, attracting a circle of students that would eventually include Maurice Ravel, Charles Koechlin, George Enescu, Nadia Boulanger, Florent Schmitt, and others. He was appointed director of the Conservatoire in 1905. A few years later, after the Société Nationale became ossified in its resistance to modern music, he backed the renegades (including Ravel, Koechlin, and Schmitt) who left it to create the Société Musicale Indépendente, and served as the new organization's first president. By this point he had taken up journalism as well, serving as music critic for *Le Figaro* (1903–21). He spent World War I teaching at the Conservatoire, retired in 1920, and died four years later.

Fauré's output was relatively small, one of the occupational hazards of being not only a regular performer in churches but also a working critic, teacher, and administrator. He was most at home in songs, music for the piano, and chamber music, almost all of which includes the piano (the exception: his final work, the String Quartet in E minor, Op. 121). His works in these genres are notable for their refinement and fastidious craftsmanship; among the characteristics that betray Fauré's authorship are the dense textures, often with flowing arpeggiated piano figuration—Copland called Fauré "the French Brahms"—and the rhapsodic linkage of ideas. The music is emotional yet restrained, suffused with a feeling halfway between melancholy and gentle rapture. Fauré's harmonic language is remarkably sensuous (full of perfumed ninth chords) and ardent: "intensity on a background of calm," as Alfred Cortot put it. Taken together, these traits produce, in a worklike the Piano Quartet No. 2 in G minor, Op. 45, the finest embodiment in music of the aesthetic so memorably proposed by Baudelaire in the lines, "Là, tout n'est qu'ordre et beauté, / Luxe, calme et volupté."

Fauré wrote surprisingly little orchestral music; he appears not to have been particularly interested in the orchestra as a medium, coloristic or otherwise. He had others do most of his scoring, though he frequently revised the final product, as was the case with his incidental music for *PELLÉAS ET MÉLISANDE.*

Fauré's decades-long work as a church musician (he referred to it as his "mercenary job") entailed the composition and performance of a sizable amount of sacred music. He might have been forgiven for not wanting to spend any more time on liturgical pieces than the job required, but "purely for the pleasure of it" he composed a setting of the Requiem, the work for which he is best known today. The score is uniquely consoling—in conscious reaction to the immensity and over-the-top emotionalism of the Berlioz Requiem—which in large part accounts for its ongoing popularity. Perhaps only Fauré could have made such a riposte. "The piece," he said, "is as gentle as I am myself."

RECOMMENDED RECORDINGS

PELLÉAS ET MÉLISANDE (INCIDENTAL MUSIC) AND REQUIEM: DUTOIT AND MONTREAL SYMPHONY ORCHESTRA (DECCA).

PIANO QUARTETS AND PIANO QUINTETS: DOMUS (HYPERION).

STRING QUARTET: AD LIBITUM QUARTET (NAXOS).

VIOLIN SONATAS: KANG, DEVOYON (NAXOS).

Faust OPERA IN FIVE ACTS BY CHARLES GOUNOD, to a libretto by Jules Barbier and Michel Carré (based on Goethe's *Faust*), premiered as an opéra comique (i.e., with spoken dialogue in place of recitative) on March 19, 1859, at the Théâtre Lyrique in Paris. The first performance of *Faust* at the Paris Opéra followed in 1869, and it was the work with which New York's Metropolitan Opera opened its doors in 1883. Outwardly, with its five-act structure and closed forms, its obligatory ballet and dramatic soldiers' chorus, *Faust* carries forward many of the conventions of grand opera. But it does so in a fashion that, for the most part, avoids the grandiose. Gounod's focus is on the pull of intimate emotions, and thanks to his superior craftsmanship the grand tableaux are absorbed into a lyric piece about love, morality, and redemption with a finesse that belongs to the sphere of

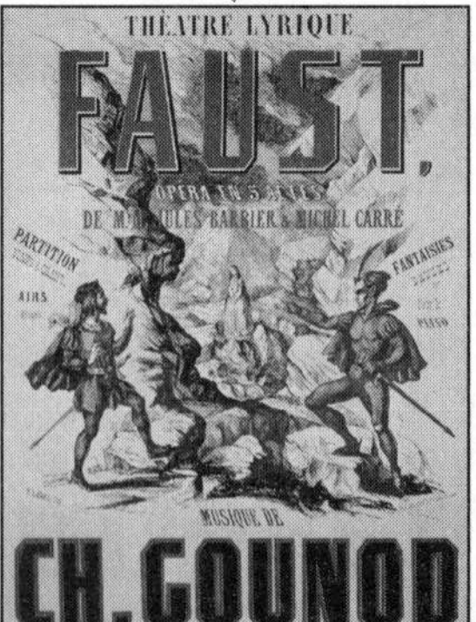

comic opera. The comic element is particularly apparent in the characterization of Méphistophélès, as much the soul of the piece as Faust or Marguerite. The score is notably tuneful, but the drama occasionally veers toward sentimentality, which has made *Faust* an easy target of critics, especially those with jaded ears.

A tale of idealism gone wrong in which a man's soul becomes the prize in a battle between God and the devil, Goethe's *Faust* has inspired numerous works of music. The character of Faust particularly appealed to the Romantics, who often saw themselves in similar peril. A partial list of composers and their treatments of *Faust* includes:

Wagner–*Eine Faust-Ouverture* (1839–40)
Berlioz–*La Damnation de Faust* (1846)
Schumann–*Szenen aus Goethe's Faust* (1844–53)
Liszt–*Faust-Symphonie* (1854–57)
Gounod–*Faust* (1859)
Boito–*Mefistofele* (1868; rev. 1875)
Mahler–Symphony No. 8, second movement (1906–07)
Busoni–*Doktor Faust* (1925)

In addition, Goethe's story has inspired treatments by Ludwig Spohr, Wolfgang Rihm, and Giacomo Manzoni.

RECOMMENDED RECORDING

Hadley, Gasdia, Ramey; Rizzi and Welsh National Opera (Teldec).

***Faust-Symphonie* (*Faust Symphony*)** Symphony in three movements by Franz Liszt, based on the verse drama by Goethe, composed in 1854, revised in 1857 (with the addition of a "Chorus mysticus" for tenor soloist and men's voices in the closing pages of the finale), and premiered September 5, 1857, at Weimar in a performance conducted by the composer. Liszt's original title for the work was "A *Faust* Symphony in Three Character Sketches After Goethe: (1) Faust, (2) Gretchen, (3) Mephistopheles."

Liszt was introduced to *Faust* by Berlioz, who in 1830 slipped his friend a copy of Gérard de Nerval's French translation of Part 1. He was immediately captivated, but it was not until 1848, when he settled in Weimar (where Goethe had spent the greater part of his life), that he began to fashion a musical response to the text. The resulting work, like the B minor Piano Sonata of 1853, is Liszt at his most incandescent. Notable for its advanced harmonic thinking (its first theme is a 12-tone row, and the "Tristan" chord shows up a few pages later, seven years before *Tristan und Isolde*), as well as its telling use of motive and thematic transformation, the dazzling score shows Liszt in the act of coining the language of Romanticism. While Berlioz and Beethoven are evident models, the overall conception is so original and remarkable as to be sui generis. Of particular note is the way Liszt portrays Mephistopheles as the spirit of negation—by making his movement a parody of the "Faust" movement and building its music upon sinister transformations of Faust's motives.

RECOMMENDED RECORDING

I. Fischer and Budapest Festival Orchestra (Philips).

fauxbourdon Technique mainly found in works by Franco-Flemish composers to enrich the sonority of certain pieces of sacred music, employed mainly during the 15th century. In essence it involved adding a middle voice between the tenor and the superius, or descant, part ranging above the tenor in sixths and octaves; the middle voice, called a *contratenor altus,* moved parallel to the descant a fourth below, creating a succession of what today would be called $^6_3$ chords or first-inversion triads, whose distinctively warm, harmonious sound is characteristic of the *fauxbourdon* style. A fourth voice, called a *contratenor bassus,* could be added below the tenor, moving parallel to it in thirds and fifths; this produced an even richer sonority, with the bass often sounding a tenth below the descant. "Faburden," a similar technique, though improvised rather than written down, was widely employed in English music during the 15th and early 16th centuries and became a hallmark of later English choral music. In the 20th century, composers such as Holst, Finzi, and Vaughan Williams would employ this effect in their orchestral music whenever they wanted to sound "English."

Kathleen Ferrier

fermata (from It. *fermarsi,* "to stop"; "to dwell on") Symbol [𝄐] indicating that a note or rest should be held longer than its written value. The extent of the lengthening is at the discretion of the performer.

Ferrier, Kathleen

(b. Higher Walton, April 22, 1912; d. London, October 8, 1953)

ENGLISH CONTRALTO. She originally intended to become a pianist, but decided on a career as a singer when she was in her mid-20s. During World War II, she sang with the Bach Choir in London and gave concerts throughout England. She made her stage debut at Glyndebourne in 1946, as Lucretia in the premiere of Benjamin Britten's *The Rape of Lucretia.* The following year, also at Glyndebourne, she appeared as Orfeo in Gluck's *Orfeo ed Euridice.* These would be her only operatic roles. She was more comfortable on the concert stage, where her repertoire included Bach, Handel, Mozart, and Elgar (the Angel in *The Dream of Gerontius,* which she performed to great acclaim with Sir John Barbirolli conducting). Her earnest delivery and consoling tone made her an ideal interpreter of Elgar's music, as well as of Brahms's *Alto Rhapsody* and, most important, Mahler's *Das Lied von der Erde,* which she performed under Bruno Walter's baton at the Edinburgh Festival in 1947 and again at the Salzburg Festival in 1949. In 1952, already suffering from the cancer that would end her life, she recorded the Mahler with Walter and the Vienna Philharmonic (the tenor was Julius Patzak), delivering one of the most poignant statements of the closing "Abschied" ever committed to disc. She appeared for the last time in public in February 1953, singing two performances of Gluck's *Orfeo* at Covent Garden.

Although she never developed a truly commanding technique, Ferrier had a voice of remarkable size and regal beauty, which she used with unfailing expressiveness. During the final months of her life, knowing that the end was near, she allowed her singing to take on an emotional intensity that, more than 50 years later, still arouses the deepest sentiments in listeners.

RECOMMENDED RECORDING

MAHLER, *DAS LIED VON DER ERDE*; PATZAK; WALTER AND VIENNA PHILHARMONIC (DECCA).

Festival of Two Worlds, The *See box on pages 46–47.*

Feuermann, Emanuel

(b. Kolomed [now Kolomyja, Ukraine], November 22, 1902; d. New York, May 25, 1942)

AUSTRIAN CELLIST, one of the most accomplished string players of the 20th century. He began cello lessons as a youth after his family moved to Vienna, studying with his father and Anton Walter. He made his debut in Vienna in 1912, with Felix Weingartner conducting, and continued his studies in Leipzig, where he was appointed to the faculty of the conservatory at age 16. He became principal of the Gürzenich Orchestra of Cologne in 1919, and served on the faculty of the Berlin Hochschule für Musik from 1929 until

1933, when he was dismissed, one of many victims of a Nazi law barring Jews from civil service positions. During the next five years, he toured widely, making his New York debut in 1935 under the baton of Bruno Walter, and performing in Asia and South America. He took up permanent residence in the United States in 1938, and was appointed to a teaching position at the Curtis Institute in 1941. His brilliant career was cut tragically short when, at the age of 39, he died of complications from surgery for hemorrhoids.

Feuermann's playing set a new technical standard for the cello and proved enormously influential. His tone was intense, his intonation flawless, his sonority powerful and brilliantly focused. His virtuosity was comparable to that of the greatest violinists of his day, one of whom, Jascha Heifetz, became a regular partner both on the concert stage and in the studio; together they recorded the Brahms Double Concerto with Eugene Ormandy and the Philadelphia Orchestra, and trios by Beethoven, Schubert, and Brahms with pianist Arthur Rubinstein. Some of the finest cellists of the mid-20th century were Feuermann's students, among them Bernard Greenhouse, Zara Nelsova, and Claus Adam, for many years the cellist of the Juilliard String Quartet.

Fidelio OPERA BY LUDWIG VAN BEETHOVEN, to a libretto in German by Joseph von Sonnleithner (based on Jean-Nicolas Bouilly's *Léonore, ou L'amour conjugal*), composed in 1804–05 and premiered on November 20, 1805, at the Theater an der Wien. In the months following the premiere, Beethoven created a second version of the opera, with revisions to the libretto by his longtime friend Stephan von Breuning, which was first presented on March 29, 1806, also at the Theater an der Wien. The opera's third and final version, incorporating further alterations to the libretto (this time by Georg Friedrich Treitschke), as well as substantial revisions in the music, was premiered on May 23, 1814, at the Kärntnertortheater in Vienna.

Fidelio is the central work of Beethoven's middle period. Its story, a celebration of idealism and courage in the face of mortal danger, resonated keenly in the composer's imagination and gave rise to some of his greatest music. The action takes place in a prison near Seville, where Florestan, a nobleman, has been unjustly incarcerated by the vicious warden, Pizarro. Hoping to save him, Florestan's wife, Leonore, disguises herself as a young man and, using the alias Fidelio, becomes a jailor in the prison. She finds Florestan, delirious and nearly dead, in the prison's deepest dungeon. When Pizarro appears, intent on murdering Florestan, she draws a pistol on the warden; at this moment, an offstage trumpet call heralds the arrival of the King's minister. Pizarro's treachery is exposed, and amid general rejoicing Leonore releases the shackles that have held her husband captive.

It has often been suggested that in the prison of his deafness, still hoping for his own Leonore to appear, Beethoven identified with Florestan. There can be little doubt that he also identified personally and ideologically with the high-minded Leonore. In the music he wrote for her, particularly the recitative "Abscheulicher!" and aria "Komm, Hoffnung," Beethoven created an embodiment of

***Wilhelmine Schröder-Devrient as Leonore in* Fidelio**

the "eternal Feminine" as powerful as the image Goethe would conjure at the end of *Faust.* It is the extraordinary quality of that music which makes *Fidelio,* despite the stiffness of its libretto, one of the most gripping and uplifting operas ever written.

RECOMMENDED RECORDINGS

JANOWITZ, KOLLO, POPP, SOTIN, JUNGWIRTH; BERNSTEIN AND VIENNA PHILHARMONIC (DG).

LUDWIG, VICKERS, HALSTEIN, BERRY, FRICK; KLEMPERER AND PHILHARMONIA ORCHESTRA (EMI).

Fiedler, Arthur

(b. Boston, December 17, 1894; d. Brookline, Mass., July 10, 1979)

AMERICAN CONDUCTOR. His Austrian-born father, Emanuel Fiedler, was a violinist and a member of the Boston Symphony Orchestra for 25 years; his mother was a pianist. As a child he took lessons from both parents, receiving his regular education at Prince Grammar School and Boston Latin. Following Emanuel's retirement from the BSO, the family moved back to Austria. The younger Fiedler worked in publishing houses in Vienna and Berlin and entered the Royal Academy in Berlin to study violin, piano, and conducting. He returned to Boston at the start of World War I, and in 1915 joined the Boston Symphony as a violist, serving in that capacity under Karl Muck, Pierre Monteux, and Serge Koussevitzky. He organized the free outdoor Esplanade Concerts in 1929, which proved so popular with audiences that in 1930 he was named conductor of the Boston Pops, succeeding Alfredo Casella. He remained the ensemble's conductor until his death, a tenure of nearly 50 years.

Despite his limited conducting technique and stolid approach to the orchestral showpieces that figured so prominently in his repertoire, Fiedler became an American icon, "Mr. Pops." Under his direction the Pops became one of the top recording entities in the world—their recording of *Jalousie,* the celebrated tango by Danish composer Jacob Gade, sold more than a million copies. Fiedler's insights as a programmer, and his ability to mix popular favorites, light classics, and more serious fare, established a new paradigm and brought pleasure to millions of listeners who might otherwise have been reluctant to enter Symphony Hall.

Arthur Fiedler with personalized towel, listening to playbacks at a recording session

RECOMMENDED RECORDING

OFFENBACH, *GAITÉ PARISIENNE*; RESPIGHI, *LA BOUTIQUE FANTASQUE*: BOSTON POPS (RCA).

Field, John

(b. Dublin, July 26, 1782; d. Moscow, January 23, 1837)

IRISH PIANIST AND COMPOSER. After preliminary instruction in music from his grandfather, an organist, he took piano lessons in Dublin, giving his first concerts at the age of nine. He became a student of Muzio Clementi in London in 1793, and his playing drew Haydn's approval during his second visit to London in 1794–95. Field traveled with Clementi to Paris, Vienna, and St. Petersburg in 1802–03; finding the musical climate in St. Petersburg to his liking, he remained there on and off, teaching and performing, until 1807, when he settled in Moscow. The years 1811–21 proved particularly productive ones for him as a composer, and he enjoyed a prosperous career as a teacher until the 1830s, when changing tastes and his failing health began to work against him. During his final years, battling rectal cancer, he undertook several concert tours and spent nine months in a hospital in Naples. Friends brought him back to Moscow, where he spent the last months of his life revising some of his earlier compositions.

Apart from a handful of chamber pieces and songs, Field's compositional output consists entirely of works for the piano, either solo or with orchestra. He wrote seven brilliant concertos for his instrument, which treat the orchestra in a manner redolent of late Haydn and early Beethoven, with many lovely, imaginative touches. He is best known for his 16 nocturnes, composed between 1812 and 1836. These luminous works gave birth to a genre that has attracted numerous later composers, beginning with Chopin and Liszt and their colleagues Johann Baptist Cramer (1771–1858), Frédéric Kalkbrenner (1785–1849), and Sigismond Thalberg (1812–71), and including Glinka, Balakirev, Tchaikovsky, Fauré, Scriabin, and Barber. The "nocturne" texture explored in them, consisting of an ornamentally elaborated melody over a steady left-hand accompaniment, usually chordal or in broken figures, became not only a characteristic of the genre itself but an essential part of the language of pianism, especially during the Romantic era. *See also* NOCTURNE.

John Field, father of the nocturne

RECOMMENDED RECORDINGS

NOCTURNES (COMPLETE): FRITH (NAXOS).

NOCTURNES (SELECTED): O'CONNOR (TELARC).

PIANO CONCERTOS: FRITH; HASLAM AND NORTHERN SINFONIA (NAXOS).

PIANO CONCERTOS: O'ROURKE; BAMERT AND LONDON MOZART PLAYERS (CHANDOS).

figured bass *See* CONTINUO.

finale [1] The last movement of a multimovement piece such as a symphony, concerto, sonata, or string quartet. [2] The concluding scene of an opera, or of an act within an opera.

Fine, Irving

(b. Boston, December 3, 1914; d. Boston, August 23, 1962)

AMERICAN COMPOSER. An accomplished pianist, he attended Harvard, where he studied theory and composition with Walter Piston and choral conducting with Archibald T. Davison. He continued his studies with Nadia Boulanger in France and in Cambridge, and studied conducting with Serge Koussevitzky at Tanglewood, joining the Harvard faculty in 1939. By the age of 30, he had developed a sure mastery of technique and form, together with a lyrical fluency few members of his generation could rival. His early music had a pronounced neoclassical bent and revealed the influence of Stravinsky, by way of Boulanger. In some of his later works he experimented with 12-tone techniques. Yet while his music grew increasingly more involved and probing, it always retained an expressive lyricism. His last work, *Symphony (1962)*, reveals these qualities in excelsis. Premiered by the Boston Symphony under Charles Munch just five months before Fine's death, it is a work of refinement and brilliance, and remains one of the outstanding American contributions to the genre. Fine also composed several delightfully inventive chamber works, of which his Sonata for Violin and Piano (1946) and the beautifully crafted Partita for Wind Quintet (1948) are the most frequently encountered. He was one of the most promising voices on the American musical scene at the time of his death.

RECOMMENDED RECORDINGS

SPIEGELMAN AND MOSCOW RADIO SYMPHONY (DELOS).

SYMPHONY (1962): LEINSDORF AND BOSTON SYMPHONY ORCHESTRA (PHOENIX).

fingerboard On string instruments, a tapered strip of wood (usually ebony) affixed to the neck of the instrument and aligned so as to run beneath the strings from the pegbox toward the bridge, against which the player's fingers stop the strings.

Finlandia **ORCHESTRAL PIECE BY JEAN SIBELIUS,** composed in 1899. The original version of the score, entitled *Suomi herää* (*Finland Awakes*), was written to accompany the last in a set of six "historical tableaux" staged at the Swedish Theater in Helsinki on November 4, 1899, as part of a three-day pageant called the "Press Pension Celebrations." The declared aim of the event was to benefit a newspaper writers' pension fund, but its real purpose was to protest the efforts of tsarist censors to muzzle the Finnish press. The scenario to *Finland Awakes* included images of the national poet J. L. Runeberg, the folklorist Elias Lönnrot, an elementary school classroom, and Finland's first steam locomotive. Its narrative began: "The powers of darkness menacing Finland have not succeeded in their terrible threats. Finland awakes."

Sibelius's music—a brooding Andante introduction followed by a stirring, martial Allegro—powerfully distills the emotion of Finland's situation at the close of the 19th century. The snarling wind and brass chords at the beginning of the piece certainly suggest an oppressive presence, while the Allegro's hymnlike second subject seems to offer up a reassuring vision of the future, full of solace and hope. A triumphant conclusion spurred by the repeated clashing of cymbals points confidently to the victory that lies ahead. The piece proved so compelling that Sibelius decided to publish it separately, as *Finlandia*, Op. 26, in 1900.

Finzi, Gerald

(b. London, July 14, 1901; d. Oxford, September 27, 1956)

ENGLISH COMPOSER whose gentleness of spirit, combined with a sometimes painful sense of the ephemeral, brought forth music notable for its austere beauty and rhapsodic lyricism. In 1915, after his family settled in Harrogate, he became a student of Ernest Farrar. He subsequently studied with Sir Edward Bairstow at York Minster, and, in 1925, on the advice of Adrian Boult, took a course in counterpoint from R. O. Morris. The following year he moved to London, where he came into contact with Gustav Holst and Arthur Bliss and became friends with Ralph Vaughan Williams. From 1930 to 1933 he taught at the Royal Academy of Music, and in 1940 he founded the Newbury String Players, a group of mostly amateur musicians, with which he performed a wide variety of 18th-century and contemporary music. That same year his breakthrough work, the song cycle *Dies natalis* for high voice and strings, received its premiere in London.

After serving in the Ministry of War Transport from 1941 to 1945, Finzi returned to composition with a renewed sense of purpose and turned out a series of masterpieces that included his Clarinet Concerto (1949) and the ode *Intimations of Immortality* (1950). In 1951 he learned that he was suffering from Hodgkin's disease and had at most ten years to live; during what turned out to be the five years remaining to him, he composed an exquisite English setting of the *Magnificat* (1952) for chorus with organ accompaniment, his Cello Concerto (1955), and the cantata *In terra pax* (1956).

As a composer Finzi took after Elgar—in his essentially conservative idiom, carefully wrought counterpoint, and the rich textures he favored—as well as Vaughan Williams—in the modal flavor of his melodies and the patoral feeling conveyed in many of his pieces. But his voice was decidedly his own: frequently contemplative, often melancholy, it was also occasionally "tough" and astringent—witness the string recitative that opens the Clarinet Concerto. He could look beyond mundane life, as he did in his *Romance* (1928) for string orchestra, a piece typical of his pastoral vein, but could also be gloriously caught up in it, as in the Cello Concerto, with its turbulent, impassioned opening movement, rapturous Andante, and exuberant, dancelike finale. Though an agnostic, Finzi wrote some of the most beautiful sacred music of the 20th century, specifically the *Magnificat* and the anthems "Lo, the full, final sacrifice" (1946) and "God is gone up" (1951). He was above all a composer of songs. Drawn particularly to the poetry of Hardy (whose bleak view of life he shared) and Shakespeare, he created beautiful, natural settings of their words in cycles such as *Earth and Air and Rain,* (1928–32), *Till Earth Outwears* (1927–56), and *Let us garlands bring* (1929–42).

Introspective and retiring, Finzi cherished the life of the mind and sought to preserve good things, whether they were books, apple trees, or fleeting perceptions of truth. Though he was a man "acquainted with grief," as the line from Isaiah goes, he expressed ecstasy better than anyone. He did it with a passion that was all the more engaging for not being excessive or obvious.

RECOMMENDED RECORDINGS

CELLO CONCERTO: WALLFISCH; HANDLEY AND ROYAL LIVERPOOL PHILHARMONIC ORCHESTRA (CHANDOS).

CLARINET CONCERTO: A. MARRINER; N. MARRINER AND ACADEMY OF ST. MARTIN-IN-THE-FIELDS (DECCA).

MAGNIFICAT AND ANTHEMS: CLEOBURY AND CHOIR OF KING'S COLLEGE, CAMBRIDGE (EMI).

fioritura (pl. fioriture; It., "flowering") In vocal music, embellishments such as rapid scale passages, trills, and turns, whether improvised or written out, that serve to ornament a line or show off a singer's technique and agility. Lisa's cavatina "Tutto e gioia," from Bellini's *La sonnambula,* is a fine example of an aria that incorporates fioritura. *See also* BEL CANTO.

Firebird, The BALLET BY IGOR STRAVINSKY, to a scenario by Mikhail Fokine, composed on a commission from Sergey Diaghilev and the Ballets Russes, and premiered June 25, 1910, at the Paris Opéra. The scenario offered abundant opportunities for pictorialism, of which the 27-year-old composer took full advantage. The resulting score, though padded and discursive in some sections, contained effects of such spectacular brilliance that it set the musical establishment of 1910 on its ear.

The action centers on Ivan, the Tsarevich, who captures the Firebird but spares its life in return for one of its magic plumes, which will summon the Firebird to the Tsarevich's assistance should he ever be in jeopardy. Ivan comes across the enchanted palace of the evil Kastchey, where 13 princesses are held captive, guarded by Kastchey's monstrous retainers. He enters, is captured, and summons the Firebird. The Firebird casts a spell over the retainers, who try to counter its effect with an infernal dance of their own; they collapse and are lulled to sleep, and the Firebird guides Ivan to a treasure chest where the egg containing Kastchey's soul is hidden. The egg is smashed, Kastchey's sorcery evaporates, and Ivan and the 13th princess are united amid general rejoicing.

The sound-world of Rimsky-Korsakov's fairy-tale opera *The Golden Cockerel,* composed in 1906–07 and first performed in 1909, is very much in evidence in *The Firebird.* Stravinsky shows complete mastery of the exotic orchestral colorism his teacher had employed in that work, and carries even further the practice of characterizing the supernatural world by means of chromaticism, and the human protagonists by diatonic harmonies, a technique going all the way back to Glinka's *Ruslan and Lyudmila* (1842). He also makes use of Russian folk music in his score, the most prominent example being the main subject of the final tableau, an almost literal quotation of a tune published by Balakirev in an anthology of 1873.

Tamara Karsavina as the Firebird, 1910

Stravinsky extracted a suite from the complete ballet in 1911, which he subsequently revised twice; all three versions of the suite are encountered in concert and on record.

RECOMMENDED RECORDINGS

COMPLETE: DAVIS AND CONCERTGEBOUW ORCHESTRA (PHILIPS).

SUITE: DORATI AND LONDON SYMPHONY ORCHESTRA (MERCURY).

SUITE: STRAVINSKY AND COLUMBIA SYMPHONY ORCHESTRA (SONY).

Fireworks **ORCHESTRAL SHOWPIECE BY IGOR STRAVINSKY, OP. 4,** composed in 1908 as a wedding present for Nadia Rimsky-Korsakov (daughter of the composer Rimsky-Korsakov, Stravinsky's teacher) and Maximilian Steinberg. Subtitled "A Fantasy for Large Orchestra" and cast in the form of a scherzo, it is a dazzling evocation, not so much of fireworks' explosivity, as of their ephemeral brilliance and delightful, shimmering colors. The piece begins with an eerily suspenseful introduction as the winds and strings flicker to life. Excitement builds, the orchestra starts to give off sparks, and brass and percussion erupt in brief dramatic outbursts. In the climactic final measures, a furiously fast scale passage makes a blazing, rocketlike ascent to cap the spectacle.

Like the first Roman candle at the beginning of a fireworks display—bursting unexpectedly overhead—this potent, masterfully orchestrated vignette heralded the arrival of its 25-year-old composer as a brilliant new star on the musical scene.

RECOMMENDED RECORDINGS

ASHKENAZY AND ST. PETERSBURG PHILHARMONIC (DECCA).

DORATI AND LONDON SYMPHONY ORCHESTRA (MERCURY).

Fischer-Dieskau, Dietrich

(b. Berlin, May 28, 1925)

GERMAN BARITONE, one of the supreme vocal artists of the 20th century. His father, a music-loving classical scholar, served as headmaster of a secondary school in Berlin; his mother was a teacher. The future singer came under the spell of music in early childhood, and the excellence of his voice was already noted when he was in elementary school. He took his first piano lessons as a lad of nine and began serious study of singing at 16. He was briefly enrolled at the Academy of Music in Berlin, but the war made a normal career path impossible: His first public recital, a performance of Schubert's *Winterreise* on January 31, 1942, was interrupted by an air raid, and in 1943, immediately after his graduation from high school, he was drafted into the Wehrmacht. He received training as a veterinarian and was packed off to the Russian front. He was subsequently sent to Italy, where he was taken prisoner on May 5, 1945, three days before the end of the war in Europe. He spent the following two years in American POW camps, studying the repertoire by any available means and frequently performing for fellow prisoners.

Dietrich Fischer-Dieskau as Don Giovanni

Released in the spring of 1947, he made his stage debut on November 18, 1948, at Berlin's Städtische Oper (the predecessor of the Deutsche Oper Berlin, which would become his home company), as Rodrigo in Verdi's *Don Carlo*; the conductor was Ferenc Fricsay, who would exert an important influence on the young singer. In 1949 Fischer-Dieskau was signed as a guest artist by both the Vienna Staatsoper and the Bavarian State Opera in Munich, and he began to make commercial recordings. In 1951 he made his Salzburg Festival debut, singing Mahler's *Lieder eines fahrenden Gesellen* with Wilhelm Furtwängler conducting, and the following year he was invited to sing the role of Kurwenal on Furtwängler's monumental recording of Wagner's *Tristan und Isolde.* During the summers of 1954–56 he was engaged by the Bayreuth Festival; his roles there included the Herald in *Lohengrin* (conducted by Eugen Jochum), Kothner in *Die Meistersinger von Nürnberg,* Amfortas in *Parsifal,* and, most important, Wolfram in *Tannhäuser* (conducted by Joseph Keilberth), a particularly compelling characterization.

In 1960, at the Städtische Oper, Fischer-Dieskau stepped into the role of Berg's Wozzeck for the first time; he would later participate in a magisterial recording of the opera under the baton of Karl Böhm. In 1961, he created the role of Gregor Mittenhofer, the villainous central figure in *Elegie für junge Liebende* (*Elegy for Young Lovers*) by Hans Werner Henze (b. 1926), and in 1962 he was one of three soloists in the world premiere of Britten's *War Requiem.* The following year, at the long-awaited reopening of the National Theater in Munich, he sang the role of Barak in Richard Strauss's *Die Frau ohne Schatten.* He made his Covent Garden debut in 1965 as Mandryka in Strauss's *Arabella,* one of his best roles. Later highlights in his operatic career included his 1976 debut in the role of Hans Sachs in *Die Meistersinger von Nürnberg* and his performance of the title role in the world premiere of *Lear* (1978) by Aribert Reimann (b. 1936), in Munich.

Notwithstanding his impressive credentials in opera, Fischer-Dieskau's main sphere was lieder. He had a gigantic career on the recital stage, where over the course of 45 years he performed and made distinguished recordings of vast stretches of the repertoire. With Gerald Moore, in 1970–71, he recorded all of Schubert's songs for male voice, an epic traversal. He premiered Britten's *Songs and Proverbs of William Blake* (1965) and Ernst Krenek's (1900–91) *Spätlese* (*Late Harvest*; 1974), each with the composer at the piano, and several works by Reimann, including his *Fünf Lieder nach Paul Celan* (1962), *Zyklus* (1971), and *Shine and Dark* (1991). Fischer-Dieskau's stature can be gauged from even a partial list of the musicians who have accompanied him; they include Vladimir Ashkenazy, Daniel Barenboim, Leonard Bernstein, Alfred Brendel, Benjamin Britten, Jörg Demus, Christoph Eschenbach, Vladimir Horowitz, Wilhelm Kempff, Murray Perahia, and András Schiff. In the songs of Schubert, Schumann, Brahms, Wolf, and Mahler—indeed, in the whole German repertoire and much else besides—he set the standard for interpretation, in renderings notable for their fine diction and their wealth of linguistic and musical nuance. He performed infrequently in the United States, reflecting, perhaps, a lack of sympathy for the inattentiveness of American audiences. He made a few recordings as a conductor (Schubert, Brahms), none too successful.

The artist in retirement, still an eminence

Fischer-Dieskau relied most on his intelligence to achieve his goals as a singer, but he possessed one of the most remarkable voices in history, with a sound—honeyed and suavely expressive, when not barking—that, once heard, cannot be forgotten. His singing has been a major influence on several generations of vocalists, including students of his—among them Matthias Goerne, Christine Schäfer, and Andreas Schmidt—as well as others who have looked to him as an example and inspiration, such as Olaf Bär, Thomas Quasthoff, the Danish baritone Bo Skovhus, and England's Ian Bostridge.

Fischer-Dieskau retired from the stage on December 31, 1992, and has devoted considerable time in the years since to teaching and writing. His artistic temperament runs deep: He is a painter and has written more than a dozen books, including studies of Schumann and Debussy, two explorations of the songs of Schubert, and an analysis of the relationship between Nietzsche and Wagner. But he is above all a singer. It is impossible to imagine the postwar musical scene without him, nor will it be possible for lieder singers far into the future to escape being compared with him.

RECOMMENDED RECORDINGS

SCHUBERT, *DIE SCHÖNE MÜLLERIN*: MOORE (DG).

SCHUMANN, SELECTED LIEDER, INCLUDING *DICHTERLIEBE*: DEMUS, ESCHENBACH (DG).

STRAUSS, *CAPRICCIO*: SCHWARZKOPF, WAECHTER, GEDDA; SAWALLISCH AND PHILHARMONIA ORCHESTRA (EMI).

Five, the GROUP OF COMPOSERS active in St. Petersburg from the mid-1860s to the early 1880s, consisting of Mily Balakirev, Nikolay Rimsky-Korsakov, Aleksandr Borodin, Modest Mussorgsky, and César Cui (1835–1918). Of them, only Balakirev was a full-time composer. Borodin was a professor of chemistry, Cui was a military engineer (with a special expertise in fortifications) and part-time music critic, Rimsky-Korsakov served as a naval officer and later joined the civil service as an inspector of military bands, and Mussorgsky worked in the tsarist ministries of communications and forestry. Celebrated in their homeland as the "Moguchaya Kuchka" (the "Mighty Handful," a term coined by the critic Vladimir Stasov), the five composers played a central role in the development of a Russian "national" style—a process begun by Glinka and Aleksandr Dargomïzhsky (1813–69) during the middle third of the 19th century. Their style emphasized emotional directness, vivid extramusical imagery, and bold, sometimes raw, orchestral colorism, while seeking to avoid Western European (particularly German) formal and developmental procedures.

Flagstad, Kirsten

(b. Hamar, July 12, 1895; d. Oslo, December 7, 1962)

NORWEGIAN SOPRANO. She was the reigning Wagnerian of her generation, particularly admired for her sublime portrayals of Isolde and Brünnhilde. Her voice was all but incomparable in its amplitude and beauty of tone, and she possessed as well an extraordinary stamina that allowed her to sing the most taxing roles without any evident strain. She came from a musical family: Her father was a conductor, her mother a pianist and voice coach. She studied in Oslo and Stockholm, and at the age of 18 made her debut at the National Theater in Oslo. Her early career was confined entirely to Scandinavia, but after singing Isolde in Oslo in 1932, she was engaged by the Bayreuth Festival in 1933. The following summer at Bayreuth she took on the roles of Sieglinde (*Die Walküre*) and Gutrune (*Götterdämmerung*), which brought an immediate engagement by the Metropolitan Opera. On February 2, 1935, she made her Met debut as Sieglinde in a matinee performance of *Die Walküre*; four nights later she created a sensation with the first of many Isoldes she would sing at the house. Later that season she added Brünnhilde (in *Die Walküre*) to her Met repertoire, completing, in a matter of weeks, the transition from debutante to world celebrity and establishing herself as the Met's top box-office attraction.

Kirsten Flagstad, the Nordic wonder

The Met became Flagstad's base of operations for the next six seasons. She opened the seasons of 1936–37 and 1937–38, teaming with Lauritz Melchior on both occasions, and astonished the Met faithful with regular demonstrations of her superhuman endurance, the most impressive occurring when she sang *Götterdämmerung, Lohengrin,* and *Tristan und Isolde* on three successive days (March 2–4, 1937). She was in the United States when World War II began, and might easily have sat out the war as the Met's number-one star. But in 1941 she returned to occupied Norway in order to be with her husband—who during her absence had become a collaborator. Flagstad herself refused to sing in Norway (or for that matter in Germany or any of the occupied countries) for the duration of the war, and after the war was acquitted of any wrongdoing by a Norwegian tribunal. But she was nonetheless considered a quisling in the United States, and was never again invited to sing at the Met.

In 1948, Flagstad resumed her career at Covent Garden as Isolde, and over the next three seasons she reprised additional Wagnerian roles there. At the Salzburg Festival during the summers of 1948–50, she sang Leonore in Beethoven's *Fidelio* under Furtwängler's baton, and in 1950, honoring a request that Richard Strauss had made before he died, she gave the world premiere of his *Vier letzte Lieder* (*Four Last Songs*), with Furtwängler and the Philharmonia Orchestra. In 1952, retired but still in spectacular voice, she recorded *Tristan und Isolde* with Furtwängler, and in 1958 she came out of retirement once again to record the role of Fricka for Decca's epoch-making stereo *Das Rheingold,* under the baton of Georg Solti.

Flagstad was blessed with the rare combination of outstanding musicianship *and* a magnificent instrument, a voice with remarkable power, steadiness, and beauty of tone. As a singer her manner was regal rather than impassioned, but that quality was indisputably well suited to the roles she espoused.

RECOMMENDED RECORDING

WAGNER, *TRISTAN UND ISOLDE*: SUTHAUS, FISCHER-DIESKAU, THEBOM; FURTWÄNGLER AND PHILHARMONIA ORCHESTRA (EMI).

flat [1] Sign placed before a note [♭] indicating that its pitch is to be lowered by one semitone. [2] Sounding lower than the correct pitch.

Fledermaus, Die (The Bat) COMIC OPERA IN THREE ACTS BY JOHANN STRAUSS JR., to a libretto by Richard Genée and Carl Haffner (based on Henri Meilhac and Ludovic Halévy's *Le réveillon*), premiered in Vienna on April 5, 1874, at the Theater an der Wien. The plot, which makes virtuosic use of the device of assumed identities, revolves around the character of Gabriel von Eisentein, a "man of means," and the complicated but good-natured bit of revenge he endures for a practical joke he once inflicted on his friend, Dr. Falke (the "Bat" of the work's title). Strauss's treatment unashamedly takes after Offenbach's works—quite naturally, as the original story was created by the same writers who provided Offenbach with some of his most brilliant librettos, including those to *La belle Hélène* and *La Grand-Duchesse de Gérolstein.* Yet the way in which Strauss brings the complications of the story to a head, and his sharp characterization, make *Die Fledermaus* uniquely pleasing, one of the handful of perfect works in musical theater. The work's overture, a classic example of the pastiche form, is a popular concert selection.

RECOMMENDED RECORDING

GRUBEROVÁ, TE KANAWA, FASSBAENDER, BRENDEL; PREVIN AND VIENNA PHILHARMONIC (PHILIPS).

Fleisher, Leon

(b. San Francisco, July 23, 1928)

AMERICAN PIANIST. He combined fireball virtuosity and extraordinary musical intelligence in his playing, establishing himself as one of America's most impressive concert artists before falling victim at the height of his powers to a career-changing ailment. He gave his first public performance when he was six and received instruction from Artur Schnabel between 1938 and 1948. During his years as Schnabel's student, he appeared as a soloist with both the San Francisco Symphony Orchestra and the New York Philharmonic under the baton of Pierre

Monteux. His rise to prominence began with his victory in the Queen Elisabeth of Belgium International Competition in 1952, when he was 24. In the years that followed he dazzled audiences with his sensational technique, which was all the more impressive for being subordinated to interpretive decisions of exceptional insight and sensitivity. During the 1950s and 1960s, he made recordings of several major works—including accounts of the Beethoven and Brahms concertos with George Szell and the Cleveland Orchestra—that have yet to be bettered.

This phase of his career came to a precipitous end in 1964, when he lost the use of his right hand to what would eventually be diagnosed as dystonia, a common neurological disorder, and had to give up playing the standard repertoire. He turned to the concerto repertoire for the left hand and began a second career as a conductor and coach, serving as the artistic director of the Theater Chamber Players of the Kennedy Center, music director of the Annapolis Symphony, and associate conductor of the Baltimore Symphony.

For nearly four decades Fleisher's condition resisted treatment. In September 1982 he valiantly essayed Franck's *Variations symphoniques* at the gala opening of Baltimore's Meyerhof Symphony Hall—his first public performance as a two-handed pianist in 17 years. Dissatisfied after that outing, he resumed playing the left-hand repertoire. In 1992 he enrolled in a clinical trial at the National Institutes of Health, and by 2004, thanks to treatments with Botox, he was able to begin playing again with two hands.

At his peak, Fleisher was without peer for the weight of tone he produced, for the solidity of his left hand, and, in particular, for the ringing brilliance of his right. His playing left an indelible impression, which the best of his recordings vividly convey.

RECOMMENDED RECORDINGS

BEETHOVEN, PIANO CONCERTOS (COMPLETE); SZELL AND CLEVELAND ORCHESTRA (SONY).

BRAHMS, PIANO CONCERTOS NOS. 1 AND 2 AND SOLO WORKS; SZELL AND CLEVELAND ORCHESTRA (SONY).

"LEON FLEISHER RECITAL" (WORKS AND TRANSCRIPTIONS FOR PIANO, LEFT HAND, BY BRAHMS, SCRIABIN, SAINT-SAËNS, GODOWSKY) (SONY).

Fleming, Renée

(b. Rochester, N.Y., February 14, 1959)

AMERICAN SOPRANO. Her distinctive warm vocal timbre, onstage vulnerability, and versatile repertoire have made her one of the most beloved singers of her generation. Raised in upstate New York, the daughter of two voice teachers, she studied at SUNY and Eastman, and then with Beverley Johnson at Juilliard. Her receipt of a Fulbright grant to study in Europe with Arleen Augér and Elisabeth Schwarzkopf (1984–85) led to her professional debut as Constanze in Mozart's *Die Entführung aus dem Serail* at the Salzburg Landestheater. She worked for several years in American regional opera companies; her breakthrough came in 1988, when she won the Metropolitan Opera Auditions and made her debut with the Houston Grand

Renée Fleming

Opera as the Countess in Mozart's *Le nozze di Figaro.* In 1991 she made her Met debut as the Countess. Her 1995 opening night engagement at the Met as Desdemona in Verdi's *Otello,* opposite Plácido Domingo, cemented her reputation as one of the world's leading sopranos. She has been heard in all of the world's major opera houses, and has recorded exclusively for Decca since 1995.

Fleming's repertoire has ranged widely, from Mozart and Richard Strauss (including a much-heralded Marschallin) to the title roles in Massenet's *Manon,* Dvořák's *Rusalka,* and Carlisle Floyd's *Susannah.* She has investigated bel canto (*Il pirata* at the Met in 2002) as well as Handel—beginning with *Alcina,* partnered by William Christie and a period instrument orchestra in Paris in 1999, and including *Rodelinda* at the Met in 2004. André Previn wrote the role of Blanche DuBois in *A Streetcar Named Desire* (1998) for her, and she has incorporated the songs of contemporary American composers into her recital work. Her substantial discography reflects these preoccupations, and her 2005 release, "Haunted Heart," in which she collaborates with jazz artists on jazz and popular songs, represents still another intriguing direction. Fleming has won two Grammy Awards, and in 2005 she was named a Chevalier de la Légion d'Honneur. Her book *The Inner Voice: The Making of a Singer,* which combines memoir with explorations of vocal training and career development, was published in 2004.

RECOMMENDED RECORDINGS

"BY REQUEST" (OPERA ARIAS): VARIOUS CONDUCTORS AND ORCHESTRAS (DECCA).

PREVIN, *A STREETCAR NAMED DESIRE*: GILFRY, FUTRAL, GRIFFEY; PREVIN AND SAN FRANCISCO OPERA ORCHESTRA (DG).

"STRAUSS HEROINES" (SCENES FROM *DER ROSENKAVALIER, ARABELLA, CAPRICCIO*: BOUNEY, GRAHAM; ESCHENBACH AND VIENNA PHILHARMONIC (DECCA).

fliegende Holländer, Der (The Flying Dutchman) "ROMANTIC" OPERA IN THREE ACTS BY RICHARD WAGNER, to his own libretto (after Heinrich Heine's *Aus den Memoiren des Herren von Schnabelewopski*), composed 1840–41 and premiered January 2, 1843, at the Royal Saxon Court Theater in Dresden. The first truly distinctive work to come from Wagner's pen, it marks a revolutionary step forward both in the continuity of its musical ideas and the Teutonic power of its orchestration; nonetheless, it clings to the Franco-Italian trappings and structure of grand opera. The dark side of Romanticism, glimpsed briefly in Weber's *Der Freischütz,* emerges here with overwhelming force in the person of the Dutchman, the legendary sailor condemned to roam the seas perpetually in search of a woman who will be faithful unto death. The Dutchman's Act I monologue ("Die Frist ist um") is a masterpiece of psychological portraiture ◉, and the musical effects that bring his ghost ship to life are among the eeriest in opera. The crowd scenes and splendid effects of grand opera are carried to new heights in the work's climax, which ends with the Dutchman's theatrically artificial redemption.

The ominous subject matter of *Der fliegende Holländer* excited Wagner's imagination to incandescence, lending the scenes of the Dutchman's inner agonies a sweep and intensity that would characterize later and greater works. In the best pages of the opera, the tight compression of the drama creates a remarkable sense of urgency.

RECOMMENDED RECORDING

HALE, BEHRENS, RYDL, PROTSCHKA; DOHNÁNYI AND VIENNA PHILHARMONIC (DECCA).

Flight of the Bumblebee, The ORCHESTRAL ENTR'ACTE FROM THE OPERA THE TALE OF TSAR SALTAN (1900) BY NIKOLAY RIMSKY-KORSAKOV. It depicts the aerial journey of the opera's hero, Prince Guidon (the son of

Tsar Saltan), who has transformed himself into a bumblebee so that he can fly across the ocean to visit his father's court. Because its rapid notes (suggesting the buzzing of a bee's wings and its darting flight) make it an ideal virtuoso showpiece, *The Flight of the Bumblebee* is frequently performed in arrangements for solo instrument.

flugelhorn (Ger., Flügelhorn, "wing horn") Valved brass instrument related to the keyed bugle. It gets its name from a valveless 18th-century horn used by riders on one or another wing of a hunting party to signal each other, which made its way into European military bands of the 19th century. The flugelhorn has the same compass as a cornet, but its wider bore and larger bell give it a mellow sound that has been particularly prized in the jazz world, where players such as Miles Davis, Thad Jones, and Clark Terry have championed it as a solo instrument. While there are few pieces in the classical literature that call for the flugelhorn, it can be pressed into service to play parts written for exotic or ceremonial brass. Respighi specified flugelhorns for the six offstage *buccine* that signal the triumphant approach of a consular army in the finale of his *Pini di Roma.*

flute Wind instrument, which in its simplest form consists of a hollow tube, closed at one end, with the embouchure near the closed end, and a series of holes drilled along its length that can be covered by the player's fingers. The instrument is sometimes called the "transverse" flute to distinguish it from instruments such as the recorder that are held end-on. A flutist uses the lips to direct a tightly focused stream of air at the edge of the embouchure; when it strikes the edge, the stream is split into eddies, producing vibrations that cause the column of air inside the flute to resonate. Flutes can be made of anything—wood, bone, bamboo, clay, ivory, glass, or metal. The best instruments are made of precious metal: solid sterling silver, gold, or platinum.

The standard modern flute is assembled from three sections, called "joints" (head, body, and foot). The lowest note is middle C (though some flutes come with an extended foot joint allowing a B), and the usable range extends up to C three octaves above. There is a soft, velvety quality to the lower notes; while with weaker players these notes tend to be breathy, a good player can produce a weighty, even fat, tone when sounding them. There is a brightening of tone as one goes up the scale, and a notable clarity and silvery brilliance in the second octave, the ideal part of the flute's range. Higher than that the flute acquires a penetrating brilliance, tending eventually toward shrillness in the third octave, though when played by a master like James Galway these high notes are of glistening purity, and sweet. The uppermost notes require a considerable amount of breath, however, and cannot be played softly.

No wind instrument surpasses the flute in agility or the fleetness with which it can execute rapid passagework, scales, and runs. Staccato articulation and skips between registers are practicable and idiomatic, but it is difficult to play long, smoothly sustained phrases without pauses for breath. Among the qualities players try to cultivate are powerful projection, rich tone, and timbral balance across the instrument's range.

A coterie of virtuoso players, mainly French, developed the instrument's repertoire and technique, and by the second decade of the 18th century it had become a hugely popular solo instrument. Its popularity spread to Germany and England, and keys, which had first appeared in the 17th century, continued to be added to facilitate playing of the chromatic scale. Theobald Boehm (1794–1881), a flutist and goldsmith in Munich, devised a revolutionary key system for the flute (1847) that proved such a breakthrough it was quickly applied to other wind instruments as well; his system was adopted by other makers and repeatedly modified by French makers later in the 19th century, in whose hands the flute attained its modern form about 1900.

The flute has been part of the orchestra since the middle of the 18th century, and has been used to good effect by composers from Gluck to Glass. Distinctive solos can be found in many works, notably: Brahms, Symphony No. 4, finale (mm. 92–105 ◉); Dvořák Symphony No. 9, first movement (mm. 149–56, lying in the lower part of the flute's range); Mahler, Symphony No. 4, first movement (mm. 126–41, played by four flutes in unison); Debussy, *Prélude à l'après-midi d'un faune* (several prominent solos in the opening pages of the score); Fauré, *Pelléas et Mélisande* Suite, "Sicilienne"; Ravel, *Daphnis et Chloé,* (Chloé's dance in the final tableau, which features an extended "solo" for the four players of the flute section—two flutes, piccolo, and alto flute—written to sound like a single superflute).

Among the flute's greatest masters have been Jacques Hotteterre (1673–1763; author of the 1707 treatise *Principes de la flûte traversière*); Johann Joachim Quantz; Paul Taffanel (1844–1908), and his student Philippe Gaubert (1879–1941), who completed the work begun by Taffanel of creating a *Méthode complète* for the flute, published in 1923 and used ever since; Georges Barrère (1876–1944) and Marcel Moyse (1889–1984), also students of Taffanel; Barrère's student William Kincaid (1895–1967); Jean-Pierre Rampal; and Galway. Other notables include Julius Baker, Samuel Baron, Aurèle Nicolet, Alain Marion, Jeffrey Khaner, Ransom Wilson, Carol Wincenc, and Paula Robison.

As a solo instrument the flute flourished in the 18th century, was largely overlooked in the 19th century, and enjoyed a revival of interest in the 20th. It has a distinguished repertoire that includes several sonatas by J. S. Bach as well as his Orchestral Suite in B minor, BWV 1067 (ca. 1738–39); numerous solo and concerted works by Georg Philipp Telemann, Quantz, C. P. E. Bach, and Frederick the Great; two concertos by Mozart (1778); Griffes's *Poem* (1918); Nielsen's Concerto (1926); Ibert's Concerto (1932–33); and Corigliano's *Pied Piper Fantasy* (1981). Works for flute and piano include the Prokofiev Sonata (1943), Dutilleux's *Sonatine* (1943), the Poulenc Sonata (1956–57), and Copland's Duo (1971). There are also some wonderful pieces for unaccompanied flute, including Debussy's *Syrinx* (1913), Varèse's *Density 21.5* (1936, rev. 1946), Messiaen's *Le merle noir* (1951), and Berio's *Sequenza I* (1958).

The most important auxiliary members of the flute family are the PICCOLO (pitched an octave above the standard flute) and the alto flute (pitched in G, a fourth lower); the family also includes a bass flute (in C, an octave lower than the standard flute) and a sub-bass in G. Among makers, supremacy was wrested from the French in the first half of the 20th century by the Boston-based firms of William S. Haynes and Verne Q. Powell. Other esteemed makers include Brannen Brothers (who produce flutes based on Albert K. Cooper's revision of the Boehm system), and Japan's Muramatsu and Yamaha.

Foote, Arthur

(b. Salem, Mass., March 5, 1853; d. Boston, April 8, 1937)

AMERICAN COMPOSER, PIANIST, ORGANIST, AND TEACHER. He was the first important American composer of concert music trained wholly in the United States. He began his study of music at the age of 14. In 1870 he entered Harvard, where he became a pupil of John Knowles Paine and a conductor of the Harvard Glee Club. He remained at Harvard for graduate study with Paine (whose models were Beethoven, Mendelssohn, and Schumann), and in 1875 he received the first M.A. in music awarded by an American university. During the summer of 1876, he attended the first Bayreuth Festival, coming under the spell of Wagner, and in 1878 he was appointed organist and choirmaster of the First Unitarian Church of Boston, a post he would hold until 1910. He founded a chamber music society in 1880 and was active as a solo recitalist, quickly becoming one of the most prominent musicians on the Boston scene. His first compositions to be published—Three Pieces, Op. 1, for cello and piano, and a set of piano pieces—appeared in 1882.

Foote continued to devote himself to chamber music for the remainder of his career, producing two piano trios, three string quartets, a piano quartet, a piano quintet, and several pieces for solo string instruments and piano. He also composed a handful of orchestral works, of which the best known is the Suite in E, Op. 63 (1907), for strings. His warmly lyrical style took its formal and expressive cues from the tradition of mid-19th-century German Romanticism. And while quite a few of his mature works reveal the influence of Brahms and Dvořák in their instrumental textures and harmony, he tempered those elements with a stateliness and serenity of his own.

RECOMMENDED RECORDING

SUITE IN E: KENNETH KLEIN AND LONDON SYMPHONY ORCHESTRA (EMI/ALBANY).

forte (It., "strong") Loud. A passage to be played forte is marked by an *f* in the score. Greater degrees of loudness are indicated by the dynamic *fortissimo*—sometimes called "double forte" and marked *ff*—and *fortississimo*—called "triple forte" and marked *fff*. In some music of the late Romantic and modern eras, even greater loudness is specified by the use of additional *f*'s, up to six or more in rare cases.

fortepiano Generic term used to refer to pianos of the 18th and early 19th centuries, as distinct from the iron-framed "grand" pianos that emerged in the middle of the 19th century, from which the modern concert grand evolved around 1900.

forza del destino, La (The Power of Fate) OPERA IN FOUR ACTS BY GIUSEPPE VERDI, to a libretto by Francesco Maria Piave (based on Angel de Saavedra's play *Don Alvaro, o La fuerza del sino*), premiered at the Imperial Theater in St. Petersburg, Russia, on November 10, 1862. A revised version of the opera, with new text by Antonio Ghislanzoni and some major dramaturgical changes, received its premiere in 1869 at La Scala. The opera's sprawling story deals with the usual subject matter of Spanish and Italian melodrama—love, offended honor, and revenge—and centers on the triangle of Donna Leonora, her brother Don Carlo di Vargas, and her lover Don Alvaro. The scene is set in several different locales in Spain and Italy.

The role of Alvaro is one of the most demanding tenor roles in all of Verdi, while that of Leonora (the "other" Leonora in the Verdi canon, after the Leonora of *La traviata*) has served as a vehicle for some of the greatest Verdi sopranos, among them Teresa Stolz (who premiered the 1869 version), Rosa Ponselle (who made her Metropolitan Opera debut in the role, opposite Caruso), Leontyne Price, and Mirella Freni. The original version of *La forza del destino* exerted significant influence on Mussorgsky's *Boris Godunov,* apparent in several scenes and in the treatment of the character of Varlaam, who is clearly derived from Verdi's Fra Melitone. For the 1869 version of *La forza del destino,* Verdi composed a full-blown overture in the conventional potpourri mold. Far and away his finest curtain-raiser, this potent, gripping essay has had broad exposure as a concert work.

RECOMMENDED RECORDING

PRICE, DOMINGO, MILNES, COSSOTTO; LEVINE AND LONDON SYMPHONY ORCHESTRA (RCA).

Foss, Lukas

(b. Berlin, August 15, 1922)

AMERICAN PIANIST, CONDUCTOR, AND COMPOSER. He studied piano as a child in Berlin and began to compose when he was seven. Forced to leave Germany with his family in 1933, he continued his musical education in Paris. Upon arriving in America in 1937, he enrolled in Philadelphia's Curtis Institute of Music, where his teachers included Isabelle Vengerova (piano), Rosario Scalero (composition), and Fritz Reiner (conducting). He was the "baby" in the first group of young Americans to study conducting with Serge Koussevitzky at Tanglewood (1939–43), but managed to hold his own with fellow students Richard Bales, Thor Johnson, and Leonard Bernstein. Like Bernstein, with whom he formed a lifelong friendship, Foss seemed to excel at everything.

Lukas Foss, presenting a nosegay to the camera

Foss received a Guggenheim Fellowship as a composer in 1945. As a pianist he played in the 1949 premiere of Bernstein's Symphony No. 2 (*The Age of Anxiety*) under the composer's baton, and was the soloist in the 1951 premiere of his own Piano Concerto No. 2, in Venice. He joined the faculty of UCLA in 1953, and from 1963 to 1970 was music director of the Buffalo Philharmonic. He subsequently served as music director of the Brooklyn Philharmonia (1971–90; the orchestra changed its name to the Brooklyn Philharmonic in 1982), and of the Milwaukee Symphony Orchestra (1981–86). Among his most important accomplishments during the two decades he spent in Brooklyn was the inauguration of the "Meet the Moderns" series in 1973. This series, and Foss's innovations in concert format—which included thematic programs, one-composer marathons, and pre- and postconcert discussions—proved very popular.

Concurrent with his career as a performer, Foss remained active as a composer. He has produced a voluminous body of work with a chameleonic diversity of style. His first important piece, *Song of Songs* (1946) for mezzo-soprano and orchestra, which sounds equally indebted to Stravinskian neoclassicism and Copland's "American" idiom, still astonishes with its virtuoso orchestration and sensuous lyricism. During the 1950s and 1960s, Foss's compositions turned wildly experimental, embracing group improvisation and ALEATORIC techniques. In his best-known work from this period, *Time Cycle* (1960), a set of four songs for voice and chamber ensemble, Foss managed to unite the seemingly irreconcilable poles of the avant-garde: SERIALISM and indeterminacy.

From serialism Foss moved on to surrealism. His *Baroque Variations* (1967) are a dreamlike reformulation of motives, figurations, and other stylistic gestures drawn from some of the most familiar pieces of Handel, Scarlatti, and Bach. The writing is virtuosic, especially in variation 3, called "Phorion" (Greek for "stolen goods"), a delightfully manic deconstruction of the prelude from Bach's Partita in E for solo violin. Foss continued this line of exploration in his *Renaissance Concerto* (1985) for flute and orchestra, which weaves 16th-century dances into a gently exuberant postmodernist tapestry.

Foss the composer has been praised—and criticized—as an eclectic's eclectic, a man who never met a style he didn't like, and never found a technique he couldn't use. Over the years this trait kept him busy, but it also kept him from developing a truly distinctive voice: In the end, what he has produced is a few impressive pieces and a large body of amusing but mostly unimportant work. Yet even if Foss fooled around too much for his own good, he remains one of the most versatile musicians of his generation.

RECOMMENDED RECORDING

Time Cycle, Phorion: Addison; Bernstein and New York Philharmonic (Sony).

Four Last Songs *See* VIER LETZTE LIEDER.

Fournier, Pierre

(b. Paris, June 24, 1906; d. Geneva, January 8, 1986)

FRENCH CELLIST, considered one of the most accomplished players in the history of his instrument. He began his study of music with his mother, at the piano, but

Pierre Fournier on the A string

after contracting polio at the age of nine, he switched to the cello. He studied at the Paris Conservatoire and subsequently taught at the École Normale de Musique (1937–39) and the Conservatoire (1941–49). His willingness during World War II to take Pablo Casals's place in trio performances with Jacques Thibaud and Alfred Cortot, and to appear as a soloist with Furtwängler and the Berlin Philharmonic, caused consternation in anti-Fascist circles; however, his patriotism was never questioned by the French government, and he was made a Chevalier of the Légion d'Honneur in 1953, and an Officier in 1963. In 1970 he settled in Switzerland. From the late 1940s until the late 1970s, when he was disabled by a stroke, he had a thriving international career.

Fournier played with patrician grace and possessed an utterly fluent technique; his interpretations of the major works in the literature were considered paragons of style and subtlety. Among the works written for him were Frank Martin's Cello Concerto (1965–66) and Francis Poulenc's Cello Sonata (1940–48). In 1937 he gave the premiere of Albert Roussel's last orchestral work, the Concertino for Cello and Orchestra.

RECOMMENDED RECORDINGS

BRAHMS, DOUBLE CONCERTO: FRANCESCATTI; WALTER AND COLUMBIA SYMPHONY ORCHESTRA (SONY).

SAINT-SAËNS, CELLO CONCERTO NO. 1; LALO, CELLO CONCERTO; MARTINON AND LAMOUREUX ORCHESTRA (DG).

Four Saints in Three Acts **OPERA IN A PROLOGUE AND *FOUR* ACTS** (with roles for about 40 saints) by Virgil Thomson, to a libretto by Gertrude Stein, composed in Paris in 1927–28 and premiered at the Wadsworth Atheneum in Hartford, Connecticut, on February 8, 1934. The original production, which featured an all-black cast, was one of the outstanding collaborative efforts in the history of American opera. In addition to Stein's words and Thomson's music, it boasted choreography by Frederick Ashton and up-to-the-minute set designs by Florine Stettheimer in cellophane and glass beads, and was directed by John Houseman. The casting of black singers and dancers in a serious work *not* about black life, something that was done more or less on a whim by the work's creators, raised eyebrows on both sides of the Atlantic. Stein's freewheeling, not to say nonsensical, libretto broke with all convention, and Thomson's score—in which the stage directions were set to music along with the dialogue—went against the grain of traditional operatic writing in both its studiously naive tunefulness and its reliance on hymnlike musical elements reconstituted from the composer's Southern Baptist upbringing. For all these reasons, while it continues to be regarded as an icon of 20th-century American intellectualism, *Four Saints in Three Acts* is rarely performed.

Four Seasons, The (Le Quattro Stagione) **GROUP OF CONCERTOS FOR SOLO VIOLIN, STRINGS, AND CONTINUO BY ANTONIO VIVALDI,** Nos. 1–4 of his Op. 8 collection of 12 concertos, *Il Cimento dell'Armonia e dell'Invenzione* (*The Contest Between Harmony and Invention*), published in Amsterdam in 1725. The four works depict the different seasons of the year, beginning with spring and ending with winter. The wealth of effect Vivaldi was able to achieve in these pieces, using nothing more than string instruments, compels the greatest admiration, and the imagery—of birds in spring, storms in summer, hunters in autumn, and icy landscapes in winter—remains as vivid today as when the notes were penned.

RECOMMENDED RECORDINGS

CARMIGNOLA; MARCON AND VENICE BAROQUE ORCHESTRA (SONY).

LOVEDAY; MARRINER AND ACADEMY OF ST. MARTIN-IN-THE-FIELDS (DECCA).

Four Temperaments, The [1] **TITLE OF A BALLET FOR PIANO AND STRING ORCHESTRA BY PAUL HINDEMITH,** composed in 1940 on a commission from George Balanchine, and first performed September 3, 1944, in Boston with Lukas Foss as soloist. [2] **SUBTITLE OF CARL NIELSEN'S SYMPHONY NO. 2, OP. 16,** composed during 1901–02 and premiered December 1, 1902, in Copenhagen.

Françaix, Jean

(b. Le Mans, May 23, 1912; d. Paris, September 25, 1997)

FRENCH COMPOSER AND PIANIST. His father was the director of the Le Mans Conservatoire, his mother a professional singer. He began writing music around the age of six, and was soon accepted at the Paris Conservatoire, where he studied piano with Isidor Philipp (taking first prize at the age of 18); on the side, he studied composition with Nadia Boulanger. His early works include a Concertino for Piano and Orchestra (1932), a Wind Quartet and a String Trio (both 1933), and the intriguingly titled *Cinq portraits de jeunes filles* (*Five Portraits of Girls*; 1936) for piano.

His first ballets, *Beach* and *Scuola di ballo* (*School of Dance*), were created in 1933 for the Ballets Russes de Monte Carlo, and in 1938 Boulanger conducted the premiere of his first opera, *Le diable boiteux* (*The Limping Devil*), at a private performance for the Princesse de Polignac. He remained productive as a composer into his 80s.

A spiritual descendant of Haydn and Mozart, as well as a self-avowed follower of Chabrier, Françaix composed more than 150 works, including five operas, 13 ballets, three symphonies (one for strings), ten film scores, and more than 30 concertos. He wrote several large-scale works of fairly serious import, including the oratorio *L'apocalypse selon Saint Jean* (*The Apocalypse According to Saint John*; 1939) for four soloists, mixed chorus, and two orchestras; the opera *La princesse de Clèves* (1965); and the ballets *Les demoiselles de la nuit* (*The Women of the Night*; 1948) and *Les camélias* (1950). But most of his music was intended to be entertaining and easygoing. This included a large amount of chamber and solo instrumental music as well as a substantial number of vocal pieces. Among his most felicitous creations is *L'horloge de Flore* (*The Flower Clock*) for oboe and strings, written in 1959 for John DeLancie, then the principal oboist of the Philadelphia Orchestra. Similarly charming are his Wind Quintet (1948), Quintet for Clarinet and Strings (1977), and octet *À huit* (1972). Françaix was also a skillful orchestrator, and scored Poulenc's *L'histoire de Babar* as well as all 24 of Chopin's *Préludes*.

Françaix's music is gentle and bucolic, yet bracing in its urbanity—full of wit, animation, and high spirits. Like Poulenc, Françaix filled his works with allusions to jazz and the music hall; like Ibert, he had a parodistic bent and a love of pranks, all the while displaying impeccable craftsmanship, elegance, lucidity, and polish.

RECOMMENDED RECORDINGS

APOCALYPSE: SIMONIS AND GÖTTINGEN SYMPHONY ORCHESTRA (WERGO).

CHAMBER WORKS (INCLUDING *À HUIT* AND CLARINET QUINTET): GAUDIER ENSEMBLE (HYPERION).

Franck, César

(b. Liège, December 10, 1822; d. Paris, November 8, 1890)

FRENCH COMPOSER OF BELGIAN BIRTH. He was one of the 19th century's most formidable musicians—a brilliant organist capable of extraordinary feats of improvisation, an inspiring teacher with a reverence for Bach and Beethoven yet open to new ideas, and a hardworking perfectionist who, in his compositions, sought to blend rigorous formal organization with soaring lyricism. Idolized by his students and reviled by his more conservative colleagues, he was neither prolific nor an early bloomer: his greatest works are late ones, and to such important forms as the symphony and string quartet he contributed but a single effort.

Franck's father, recognizing his son's precocious talent, sought to capitalize on it by grooming him for a career as a piano prodigy. The boy was enrolled at

César Franck, master and mentor

the Liège Conservatoire at seven and sent on his first concert tour at 12. The family moved to Paris in May 1835 to facilitate young César's anticipated conquest of the French capital; preparation for the Paris Conservatoire's entrance exams included private piano lessons with Pierre-Joseph-Guillaume Zimmerman and study of harmony and counterpoint with Antoine Reicha. At first Franck was refused admission to the Conservatoire because he was a foreigner; in 1837, he was admitted and he subsequently received first prizes in piano and counterpoint. He began studying organ in 1841, but was pulled out of his classes by his father so he could be sent on a concert tour of Belgium in 1843.

Franck's performing career fizzled. In 1846 he moved out of his parents' home and started to support himself by teaching. He married in 1848 and got a job as a church organist in 1851. His big break came in 1858, when he became organist at the newly finished basilica of St. Clothilde, where he would serve until the end of his life. The basilica housed an outstanding instrument by the king of French organ builders, Aristide Cavaillé-Coll, and Franck's post-service improvisations became legendary. In 1871, Franck was named professor of organ at the Conservatoire; his class quickly turned into an advanced seminar in composition, and a whole generation of French composers took it in order to study with him, among them Henri Duparc, Vincent d'Indy, Ernest Chausson, Paul Dukas, Gabriel Pierné, and Albéric Magnard.

Franck's oratorio *Rédemption* was a failure at its first performance, in 1873, but the following year Franck's artistic redemption began when he heard the Prelude to Act I of *Tristan und Isolde*; Wagner's CHROMATICISM was to have a major impact on his own harmonic language, notably in the symphonic poem *Les Éolides* (1875–76) and the Symphony in D minor (1886–88). The final 15 years of Franck's life saw the production of a string of masterpieces. Among these were three great chamber works: the Piano Quintet in F minor (1879), the Sonata in A for violin and piano (1886, composed as a wedding present for Franck's countryman, the violinist Eugène Ysaÿe), and the String Quartet in D (1889). There were also three great orchestral works: the *Variations symphoniques* for piano and orchestra (1885), the symphonic poem *Psyché* (1887–88), and the Symphony in D minor—arguably the greatest symphony composed in France between Berlioz and the 20th century, though far less likely to be heard nowadays than Saint-Saëns's contemporaneous *Organ Symphony*. In the breadth of their conception and the density of their harmonic syntax, these late works reveal a willingness to go to the edge of tonality to convey restlessness, yearning, and a feeling of transcendence. Yet as powerful as their emotional undercurrents are, these scores embody the art of a composer who remained more architect than sensualist, and whose main concerns were with contrapuntal and formal matters. For all his heated chromaticism, Franck never strayed far from the asethetic and metaphysical footsteps of Beethoven.

RECOMMENDED RECORDINGS

SYMPHONY IN D MINOR: BEECHAM AND FRENCH NATIONAL RADIO ORCHESTRA (EMI).

VARIATIONS SYMPHONIQUES: CURZON; BOULT AND LONDON PHILHARMONIC (DECCA).

VIOLIN SONATA: CHUNG, LUPU (DECCA).

Frauenliebe und -leben (Woman's Love and Life) **CYCLE OF EIGHT SONGS BY ROBERT SCHUMANN, OP. 42,** composed in 1840 to texts by Adelbert von Chamisso and published in 1843. The cycle, into which Schumann poured much of his own feeling for his young bride, Clara, tells the story of a woman in love, from the first glimpse of her beloved, through marriage, motherhood, and the heartbreak of being widowed.

Frau ohne Schatten, Die (The Woman Without a Shadow) **OPERA IN THREE ACTS BY RICHARD STRAUSS,** to a libretto by Hugo von Hofmannsthal, premiered at the Vienna Staatsoper on October 10, 1919. Its fairy-tale plot concerns a spirit Empress who wants to have children but, because her husband has no interest in her, is unable to (hence, she casts no shadow). She and her guardian, the Nurse, become servants in the hut of a poor, hardworking dyer named Barak, and using various forms of deception try to get the dyer's young wife to part with her shadow. In the end, Barak and his wife remain true to each other and their love blossoms anew; by refusing to intervene in their happiness, the Empress redeems both herself and her husband and acquires a shadow. Despite the extraordinary power and grandeur of much of Strauss's music, the opera's allegorical complexities—to say nothing of the philosophical freight of Hofmannsthal's libretto—make *Die Frau ohne Schatten* heavy going in the theater.

Freischütz, Der (The Free Shooter) **OPERA IN THREE ACTS BY CARL MARIA VON WEBER,** to a libretto by Johann Friedrich Kind, premiered at the Berlin Schauspielhaus on June 18, 1821. The plot, rich in the trappings of German folklore, also touches on some of the grand themes of Romanticism, among them the individual's transcendence of the social hierarchy, supernatural interference in the natural order, and redemption through love. At the center is Max, a young assistant forester desperately in love with Agathe, the daughter of the head forester, Cuno. With the help of Caspar, another assistant forester (but one

Der Freischütz: ***Casting "free" bullets in the Wolf's Glen. (Don't try this at home.)***

who is in league with the diabolical "black huntsman" Samiel), Max goes to the Wolf's Glen at midnight to cast a batch of "free" bullets, which six times out of seven magically strike the target; with these he hopes to win a shooting contest, the prize being Agathe's hand in marriage. Max's deal with the devil is found out after a bullet he fires misses the mark and kills Caspar instead. He is on the point of being banished when a hermit (opera's first "monk ex machina") intervenes on his behalf. Prince Ottokar sentences Max to a year of probation, after which he may marry Agathe. The opera ends with a joyous celebration proclaiming the virtues of constancy and faith in providence.

Der Freischütz is one of the cornerstones of musical Romanticism. Its appealing story and rich emotional content—running the gamut from the nightmarish terrors of Max's encounter with Samiel in the Wolf's

Glen to Agathe's "Leise, leise, fromme Weise," one of the most soulful arias of the 19th century—proved enormously popular and set the tone for much of what Wagner would later attempt. Even more important, perhaps, was Weber's imaginative use of the orchestra, which plays a role equal to that of any character in the opera. Here for the first time (one year before Schubert's *Unfinished* Symphony and nine years before Berlioz's *Symphonie fantastique*) one encounters a recognizably Romantic palette, heightened by the liberal use of trombones, ominous tremolos in the strings, and colorful shadings in the woodwinds (the opera's overture really marks the dawn of Romanticism). This, and the striking harmonic language of *Der Freischütz* (radiant C major for the happy conclusion, hair-raising F-sharp minor for the demonic seance in the Wolf's Glen), would have far-reaching consequences, influencing the operas not only of Berlioz and Wagner, but of Rimsky-Korsakov, Strauss, Berg, and others.

RECOMMENDED RECORDING

JANOWITZ, MATHIS, SCHREIER, ADAM; KLEIBER AND STAATSKAPELLE DRESDEN (DG).

French horn *See* HORN.

French overture A prefatory movement with a slow introductory section featuring DOTTED RHYTHMS and fanfare figures, followed by an Allegro with a fugal texture. Developed by Lully in the 1650s, it quickly established itself as the standard for opera and ballet overtures in France, hence its name. Adopted in Germany and England as well, it saw widespread use until the mid-18th century, when it was supplanted by the Italian *sinfonia*. French overtures prefaced numerous odes and oratorios, including Purcell's "Hail, bright Cecilia" (1692) and Handel's *Messiah* (1742), and they were commonly used as the opening movements of Baroque orchestral suites. The overtures to Bach's Orchestral Suite No. 3 in D (1731) and Handel's *Music for the Royal Fireworks* (1749) are especially grand examples of the genre. Mozart echoed the convention in the slow introduction to his Symphony No. 39 in E-flat, K. 543 (1788), as did Beethoven in the first movement of his *Pathétique* Sonata, Op. 13 (1798).

French Suites SET OF SIX SUITES "SANS PRELUDE" FOR HARPSICHORD (BWV 812–17) BY J. S. BACH. They were published in 1731 but composed earlier, probably in the final years of Bach's service in Cöthen; the original versions of the first five appear in the *Clavier-Büchlein* ("keyboard notebook") that he started in 1722 for his second wife, Anna Magdalena. All incorporate the four standard dances found in Baroque suites in the French style (in order, an ALLEMANDE, COURANTE, SARABANDE, and GIGUE), as well as one or more additional movements between the sarabande and gigue. Among these are airs (in Nos. 2 and 4) and a variety of optional dances (including GAVOTTES, MINUETS, BOURRÉES, an "Anglaise" in Suite No. 3, a *loure* in No. 5, and a "menuet polonaise" in No. 6).

RECOMMENDED RECORDINGS

HEWITT, PIANO (HYPERION).
SCHIFF, PIANO (DECCA).

Freni, Mirella

(b. Modena, February 27, 1935)

ITALIAN SOPRANO. She studied in Bologna and made her debut in Modena in 1955, as Micaëla in Bizet's *Carmen*. Her breakthrough came at La Scala in 1962, when she was invited to sing the role of Mimì in a production of Puccini's *La bohème* staged by Franco Zeffirelli and conducted by Herbert von Karajan. She was among the last great singers to make her Metropolitan Opera debut in the old Metropolitan Opera

House at Broadway and 39th Street—on September 29, 1965, again as Mimì—and one of the first to grace the company's new home at Lincoln Center, appearing there during the 1966–67 season as Liù in Puccini's *Turandot* and as Marguerite in Gounod's *Faust.* She was a welcome if irregular visitor to the Met during the 1970s and 1980s, known best for her memorable performances as Elisabeth in Verdi's *Don Carlo.* During the course of her career, Freni developed from a lyric soprano into a dramatic soprano, but at all times was noted for her exquisite artistry and the beautiful, even coloration of her voice, a quality apparent in her lovely realization of Cio-Cio-San in Puccini's *Madama Butterfly,* a role she recorded twice but never performed in its entirety on stage. Her powerful dramatic instincts and outstanding command of language and diction added an extra dimension to her interpretations of more than 40 roles, including, in the adventurous final years of her career, three Tchaikovsky heroines, Tatyana in *Eugene Onegin,* Liza in *The Queen of Spades,* and Joan of Arc in *The Maid of Orleans.*

RECOMMENDED RECORDINGS

PUCCINI, *LA BOHÈME*: PAVAROTTI, PANERAI, HARWOOD; KARAJAN AND BERLIN PHILHARMONIC (DECCA).

PUCCINI, *MADAMA BUTTERFLY*: PAVAROTTI, LUDWIG, KERNS; KARAJAN AND VIENNA PHILHARMONIC (DECCA).

Frescobaldi, Girolamo

(b. Ferrara, September 1583; d. Rome, March 1, 1643)

ITALIAN COMPOSER AND KEYBOARD VIRTUOSO. A brilliant organist and harpsichordist, he was one of the most important, and widely published, composers of keyboard music in the first half of the 17th century. He was also noted for his vocal music, particularly madrigals, as well as sonatas and canzonas for various instruments. He was active mainly in Rome,

Girolamo Frescobaldi and a page from one of his toccatas

where he served as organist at St. Peter's, as well as in Mantua and Florence, and his influence extended to Germany, France, and Flanders. The brilliance he showed in the most rigorously contrapuntal of his works had a profound impact on Bach, who is known to have possessed a copy of Frescobaldi's *Fiori musicali* of 1635.

fret On string instruments such as guitars, lutes, and viols, a thin strip of wood or ivory placed on the fingerboard that allows a player to stop a string cleanly and play notes in tune.

From My Life (Z mého života) SUBTITLE GIVEN BY BEDŘICH SMETANA TO HIS STRING QUARTET NO. 1 IN E MINOR, composed in 1876, the first entirely programmatic work in the string quartet literature. The four movements constitute a sort of autobiographical self-portrait, touching on different phases of the composer's life: youthful abandon shadowed by premonitions of tragedy in the first movement; the unbearable lightness of a young man's being in the ensuing scherzo (Smetana, using a polka, fondly recalls his love of dancing the night away); a recollection of marital bliss in the lovely Andante; and the busy happiness of maturity in the finale. The sudden interruption of the finale by a sustained high E in the first violin mimics the attack of tinnitus that Smetana suffered on the night of October 19, 1874, which left him totally deaf. At the first public performance of the quartet, in 1878, the 37-year-old Antonín Dvořák was the violist. An orchestral version of the piece was prepared in 1940 by George Szell, who recorded it in 1949.

RECOMMENDED RECORDINGS

QUARTET: CLEVELAND QUARTET (TELARC).

SZELL ORCHESTRATION: SIMON AND LONDON SYMPHONY ORCHESTRA (CHANDOS).

From the House of the Dead (Z mrtvého domu) OPERA IN THREE ACTS BY LEOŠ JANÁČEK based on Fyodor Dostoyevsky's *Notes from the House of the Dead,* composed between February 1927 and July 1928, and posthumously premiered at the National Theater in Brno on April 12, 1930.

From the New World (Z nového světa) TITLE GIVEN BY ANTONÍN DVOŘÁK TO HIS SYMPHONY NO. 9 IN E MINOR, OP. 95,composed between January 10 and May 24, 1893, and first performed December 16, 1893, at Carnegie Hall by the New York Philharmonic, Anton Seidl conducting. The symphony's Prague premiere, given by the orchestra of the National Theater on October 13, 1894, was conducted by the composer.

The E minor Symphony was the first work Dvořák composed entirely—from sketches to finished orchestration—in the United States. Taking his cue from American popular song and from the few examples of American Indian music and African-American spirituals he had heard, Dvořák sought to give the symphony's melodic material an "American" accent, without actually quoting from existing tunes. Several of his themes are based on PENTATONIC scales (good examples being the subject for oboe and flute at measure 91 in the first movement, and the famous English horn melody of the second movement), sounded over simple drones or PEDAL POINTS. This artful naïveté, enhanced by folklike instrumental colorings and rhythmic inflections, was what the composer had in mind when he said that "everyone who has a nose must smell America in this symphony." American literature, specifically Longfellow's poem "The Song of Hiawatha," also played a part in the symphony's genesis. The second movement took its inspiration from the tale of Minnehaha's forest funeral, and the third was meant to depict "a feast in the woods where the Indians dance."

Dvořák's intention in writing the symphony was to show American composers how to transform the raw material of authentic American music into a grand symphonic gesture in the best European manner. In keeping with that goal, he made a point of building cyclical returns of the first movement's main theme into the structure of the second and third movements, and he went even further in the finale, tying citations from all three prior movements into a climax that is a rhetorical tour de force.

In contriving to make the material of this symphony seem "American," Dvořák may have surrendered some of his native eloquence, and in trying to prove a point, he may have sacrificed a measure of subtlety. But the very directness and tunefulness of the ideas themselves, and the energy with which they are treated, are precisely what have made this the most popular of Dvořák's symphonies. The music has a ruggedness, openness, brassy confidence, and lyric generosity that are American in the best sense.

RECOMMENDED RECORDING

KERTÉSZ AND LONDON SYMPHONY ORCHESTRA (DECCA).

fugato A section of a piece that is written in the manner of a fugue, but less fully developed, such as the passage led by cellos and basses that begins the trio section to the scherzo of Beethoven's Fifth Symphony (mm. 141 et seq.). Other examples include the breezy opening music of Smetana's Overture to *The Bartered Bride* (mm. 14–100) and the passage that launches the presto coda in the final movement of Dvořák's Symphony No. 6 in D, Op. 60 (mm. 441–75). Shostakovich makes use of the procedure in the interlude between scenes 2 and 3 of Act I in his opera *Lady Macbeth of Mtsensk District.*

fugue (from It. *fuga,* "flight") A contrapuntal procedure in which a subject in one voice is answered, successively and in fairly strict imitation, in at least two additional voices, usually at the interval of a fourth or fifth; also, the title of a piece, or of a section of a piece, in which such a procedure is employed. The successive entries in a fugue transpose the subject (rather than echoing it at the same pitch, as in a round), creating a harmonically "open" framework that lends itself to extension and development. Within this framework, there is room for a considerable amount of free COUNTERPOINT, and opportunity for the harmonizing to lead in any number of directions. The "flight" of a fugue is thus one of fancy, largely unfettered despite the orderliness of the procedure. Fugue developed out of the "point of imitation" style characteristic of the vocal music of Josquin and his successors, in which a phrase of text, set melodically, is stated in one voice and loosely imitated in others. This process made its way into instrumental music during the 16th century and was developed into an art of the greatest rigor and refinement by the end of the 17th century. Fugal technique reached a high-water mark in the keyboard works of J. S. Bach, particularly the 48 fugues in the two books of *DAS WOHLTEMPERIRTE CLAVIER* and the great stand-alone fugues for organ such as the *St. Anne* Fugue in E-flat, BWV 552. The unsurpassed brilliance of Bach's fugal writing has echoed down through the centuries. Beethoven put a personal stamp on the technique in the fugues that figure in many of his late works, including the *HAMMERKLAVIER* SONATA, the *MISSA SOLEMNIS,* the String Quartet in C-sharp minor, Op. 131, and the *GROSSE FUGE,* Op. 133. Mendelssohn followed Bach a bit more slavishly, but also quite stylishly, in the final chorus of his oratorio *ELIJAH,* while Brahms looked as much to Handel as to Bach in the fugal sections of *Ein deutsches Requiem,* not to mention the fugue that concludes his *Variations and Fugue on a Theme by Handel,* Op. 24, for piano. While such full-blown efforts were relatively rare (and smacked of antiquarianism), less rigorous allusions to the mechanism of fugue found their way into many works of the 19th century. The 20th century brought a renewed interest in fugue, both as a serious formal device (as in Bartók's *Music for Strings, Percussion, and Celesta* and Berg's *Wozzeck*) and as a showcase for razzle-dazzle contrapuntal virtuosity (as in Reger's *Variations and Fugue on a Theme of Mozart* and Hindemith's *SYMPHONISCHE METAMORPHOSEN NACH THEMEN VON CARL MARIA VON WEBER*).

funeral march *See* MARCH.

Für Elise **BAGATELLE IN A MINOR BY LUDWIG VAN BEETHOVEN,** composed in 1808. The long-lost manuscript may actually have been inscribed "Für Therese" and meant for Therese Malfatti, the niece of

Beethoven's physician Giovanni Malfatti. In 1810, the year of the bagatelle's first performance, Beethoven made an unsuccessful proposal of marriage to Therese. *See also* BAGATELLE.

furiant Czech dance in quick triple time in which every second beat is accented, so that the rhythmic emphasis cuts across the meter. Smetana included one in Act II of his opera *The Bartered Bride,* and Dvořák patterned two of his eight *Slavonic Dances,* Op. 46, on the furiant: No. 1, in C, and No. 8, in G minor. Dvořák also incorporated a furiant rhythm in several symphonic movements, most notably the third movement of his Symphony No. 6 in D, Op. 60, and the finale of his Violin Concerto in A minor, Op. 53.

Furtwängler, Wilhelm

(b. Berlin, January 25, 1886; d. Baden-Baden, November 30, 1954)

GERMAN CONDUCTOR AND COMPOSER. He was the most important German musician of this generation and remains among history's most penetrating and persuasive interpreters of the 19th-century Austro-Germanic symphonic repertoire. Son of an archaeologist father and a mother who was a gifted painter, he was a precocious child in every way, showing special aptitude for literature, philosophy, and the arts. At the age of four he began his studies at the piano; as a teenager he pursued composition under the tutelage of both Joseph Rheinberger (1839–1901) and Max von Schillings (1869–1933). At the age of 19, around the same time he received the equivalent of a university degree from his private tutors, he took his first job in the musical profession, serving as *répétiteur* at the Breslau Stadttheater for two years; following this, he became third conductor at the Zurich Opera. In Munich in 1906, Furtwängler led his first orchestral concert, featuring music by Beethoven, Bruckner, and his own Largo in B minor.

Wilhelm Furtwängler, portrait by Trude Fleischmann, 1927

After two years serving as assistant conductor at the Munich Court Opera, in 1910 Furtwängler moved on to Strasbourg, working as third conductor under Hans Pfitzner. At the age of 25 he was given his first important post, the directorship of the Lübeck Opera, where he stayed until 1915. Following this, he became director of the Mannheim Opera, and it was there he conducted his first performances of the major operas of Verdi, Mozart, Richard Strauss, and Wagner. In 1920, Furtwängler succeeded Richard Strauss as director of the Berlin Staatsoper's concert series and Willem Mengelberg as conductor of the Frankfurt Museum Concerts, and in 1922, on the death of Arthur Nikisch (one of his artistic heroes) he inherited what were widely viewed as the two most important conducting posts in Germany: director of the Leipzig Gewandhaus Orchestra (where he remained until 1928) and director of the Berlin Philharmonic, to which he would be wedded for the rest of his life.

By the time Hitler became Chancellor in 1933, Furtwängler was far and away the most respected (and financially successful) musician in Germany, and his stature only increased during the years of the Third Reich—despite being intellectually and philosophically at cross-purposes with them, he had the ear of propaganda minister Joseph Goebbels and of the Führer himself. During the entire Nazi period, as his artistry reached its zenith, Furtwängler clung to the naive belief that a true German artist could remain above politics, even in the face of vicious tyranny. Feeling the need to keep music alive, and protective of his powerful musical positions, he engaged in a delicate tap dance with the Nazis, mixing compliance with defiance, becoming essentially the Führer's conductor on the one hand, but using his influence to protect many Jewish musicians on the other. This flirtation with the Reich, regardless of how politically innocent the conductor truly was, compromised him in the eyes of many.

Furtwängler was also twice shot down after being approached to head American orchestras. On Arturo Toscanini's suggestion he was offered the position of chief conductor of the New York Philharmonic in 1936; Göring told him that if he left the Reich he could never return, and a boycott was mounted in New York, effectively killing the plan. After the war he was invited to serve as principal conductor of the Chicago Symphony Orchestra for the 1949–50 season. A campaign was mounted against him to which such musicians as Toscanini, Vladimir Horowitz, and Arthur Rubinstein lent their names. Only a few prominent musicians voiced support for the conductor, chiefly Yehudi Menuhin. Bruno Walter, like Menuhin a Jew, refused to join the attack on Furtwängler, though he was personally at odds with his colleague's decision to remain in Germany during the Nazi years. In the end, the orchestra's board withdrew its offer.

In early 1945 Furtwängler ducked out of Germany to take refuge in Switzerland; after the war he underwent a humiliating denazification proceeding and was for bidden to conduct until 1947. His return to the podium—leading the Berlin Philharmonic in an all-Beethoven program—was greeted with a 15-minute ovation. From that point on, Furtwängler was essentially back in the saddle as director of the orchestra, and in 1952, two years before his death, he was named its "conductor for life." During the fruitful postwar years, he was a frequent guest conductor of the Vienna Philharmonic, and in 1951 he conducted a remarkable performance of Beethoven's Ninth Symphony at the reopening of the Bayreuth Festival. He also led London's Philharmonia Orchestra in the world premiere of Richard Strauss's *Vier letzte Lieder* with soprano Kirsten Flagstad, and remained active in the studio. Among the greatest of his recordings from those years was an epochal account with the Philharmonia of *Tristan und Isolde* featuring Flagstad, Ludwig Suthaus, and Dietrich Fischer-Dieskau.

Though he composed throughout his life, writing three sprawling Romantic symphonies, Furtwängler was not the creative genius in his own music that he was on the podium. Rather, he was an epigone of the music he deeply loved to perform. At the heart of Furtwängler's repertoire were Beethoven and Brahms, followed by Wagner, Schubert, Bruckner, and Strauss. His affinity for his contemporaries was limited—though he did give the premieres of Schoenberg's Variations, Op. 31 (1928), and of Hindemith's Symphony *Mathis der Maler* (1934), suffering the wrath of Goebbels after the latter. It was the 19th-century masterworks in which he primarily excelled, and within that repertoire he conducted with an unmatched urgency and intensity of vision, lunging for the music's emotional heart while groping at the limits of sustainable sound. He sought spontaneity in performance—a transformation of the music as it had been rehearsed into an experience that went beyond what could be communicated in rehearsal—with the result that he hardly ever presented a piece the same way twice. Every account was its own revelation. More than any other conductor of the 20th century, Furtwängler brought to his work a musical perception and temperament that commanded the respect of his peers, won the admiration of younger colleagues, and inspired devotion among players.

RECOMMENDED RECORDINGS

Beethoven, Symphonies Nos. 5 and 7: Vienna Philharmonic (EMI).

Beethoven, Symphony No. 9: Bayreuth Festival Orchestra (EMI).

Brahms, symphonies (complete): Vienna Philharmonic (No. 1), Berlin Philharmonic (Nos. 2–4) (EMI).

Bruckner, Symphony No. 8: Berlin Philharmonic (Testament).

Furtwängler 1942–44 (including works of Mozart, Beethoven, Schubert, Schumann, Brahms, Bruckner, Strauss, Sibelius, Ravel): Berlin Philharmonic (DG).

Schumann, Symphony No. 4: Berlin Philharmonic (DG).

Strauss, *Don Juan, Till Eulenspiegel, Tod und Verklärung* (with Smetana, Vltava): Vienna Philharmonic (EMI).

Wagner, *Tristan und Isolde*: Suthaus, Flagstad, Thebom, Fischer-Dieskau; Philharmonia Orchestra (EMI).

Gabrieli, Giovanni

(b. prob. Venice, ca. 1557; d. Venice, August 1612)

ITALIAN ORGANIST AND COMPOSER, one of the most important figures in Venetian music at the end of the 16th century and the beginning of the 17th. He was the nephew of composer Andrea Gabrieli (1532–85) and, like his uncle, apprenticed with Orlande de Lassus in Munich. He returned to Venice around 1584, and in 1585 succeeded Claudio Merulo as organist at the basilica of San Marco, a post he held until his death. In later years he became an important teacher of northern European composers, of whom the most famous was Heinrich Schütz.

Nearly all of Gabrieli's music was written for ecclesiastical use. His works for instrumental ensemble—sonatas and canzonas—were intended for use as interludes in large liturgical settings, and were tailored to the acoustics of San Marco and to the talent available there (in particular, two virtuoso cornettists). He also wrote several dozen pieces for organ and composed a large number of liturgical settings. He produced little secular music—a handful of madrigals and some occasional pieces.

Gabrieli specialized in antiphonal treatments of voices and instruments, a typical feature of Venetian music of the 16th century. He went beyond mere statement-and-answer, the approach generally employed by his uncle Andrea, toward a dynamic development of material between or among the various antiphonal groups, integrating the antiphonal effects within a broader line of argument. He had only a limited influence on the music of the Baroque period (Monteverdi was far more important), but was "rediscovered" in the 20th century. His collection of sacred vocal works titled *Symphoniae sacrae* (1597) was quickly reprinted north of the Alps, which was part of the reason several German and Scandinavian princes sent their best young musicians to him for training. His principal instrumental collection, *Canzoni e sonate* (1615), appeared posthumously.

RECOMMENDED RECORDINGS

CANZONAS AND SONATAS FROM *SACRAE SYMPHONIAE* 1597: ROBERTS AND HIS MAJESTY'S SAGBUTTS AND CORNETTS (HYPERION).

CREES AND LONDON SYMPHONY ORCHESTRA BRASS (NAXOS).

"MUSIC FOR SAN ROCCO": MCCREESH AND GABRIELI CONSORT AND PLAYERS (DG ARCHIV).

SAVALL AND HESPÉRION XX (VIRGIN CLASSICS).

Gabrieli Consort and Players *See box on pages 310–13.*

Gade, Niels

(b. Copenhagen, February 22, 1817; d. Copenhagen, December 21, 1890)

DANISH COMPOSER, CONDUCTOR, AND VIOLINIST. The son of an instrument maker, he studied in Copenhagen and joined the Royal Orchestra as a violinist in 1834. His concert overture *Efterklange af Ossian* (*Echoes of Ossian*) won first prize in a competition sponsored by the Copenhagen Music Society in 1840. After his First Symphony (1841–42) was rejected for performance by the Royal Orchestra, he sent the manuscript (with a dedication) to Felix Mendelssohn, who premiered the work with the Gewandhaus Orchestra in Leipzig on March 2, 1843. A Danish government stipend soon enabled Gade to follow his score to Leipzig, where Mendelssohn engaged him as assistant conductor at the Gewandhaus and found him a spot on the faculty of the newly opened Leipzig Conservatory. On March 13, 1845, Gade conducted the premiere of Mendelssohn's Violin Concerto in E minor at the Gewandhaus, with Ferdinand David as the soloist, and in 1847, following Mendelssohn's untimely death, Gade became chief conductor of the orchestra. He kept the post only a year, returning to Copenhagen in 1848 when war broke out between Prussia and Denmark.

Niels Gade in 1845

During the remainder of his life Gade presided over musical life in Denmark, heading up the Copenhagen Music Society and conducting its orchestra. His output as a composer centered on orchestral music—eight symphonies, eight concert overtures, a violin concerto, and some smaller pieces—but included music in a variety of other genres. In addition to some chamber music (including three violin sonatas, three string quartets, and two piano trios), several sets of piano pieces, and a few songs and choral pieces, he contributed music to three ballets and penned several large cantatas, the most famous of which, *Elverskud* (*The Elf-King's Daughter*; 1854), brought Danish folk music into the concert hall and remains a cherished piece of Denmark's musical patrimony. Gade, who saw himself as part of the European mainstream, has long been viewed as a figure of peripheral importance outside Scandinavia. But scholars are beginning to take a fresh look at his music and to discern lines of influence running from it to that of Mendelssohn and Brahms, among others—suggesting that as a musical stylist he played a more important role than has previously been acknowledged.

RECOMMENDED RECORDINGS

ELVERSKUD: VARIOUS SOLOISTS; SCHØNWANDT (DA CAPO).

STRING QUARTETS: KONTRA QUARTET (BIS).

SYMPHONIES NOS. 3 AND 6, *EFTERKLAUGE OF OSSIAN*: HOGWOOD AND DANISH NATIONAL RADIO SYMPHONY ORCHESTRA (CHANDOS).

galant Dominant musical style of the second half of the 18th century, also known as the "free" style to distinguish it from the "strict" or "learned" style. Whereas the "learned" style derived from Renaissance vocal polyphony and exhibited counterpoint and fugal procedure, the *galant* was associated with theatrical, symphonic, and chamber music and contained allusions to various topics—among them the singing style, the brilliant style, Sturm und Drang, and Turkish music, as well as to the rhythms of popular and courtly dances. J. C. Bach, one of the leading practitioners of the *galant* style during the 1760s and 1770s, was an early model for Mozart, in whose music the *galant* reached its peak in the 1780s.

Galli-Curci, Amelita

(b. Milan, November 18, 1882; d. La Jolla, Calif., November 26, 1963)

ITALIAN SOPRANO. She graduated from the Milan Conservatory in 1903 with a first prize in piano but was essentially self-taught as a singer. She made her debut in 1906 as Gilda in Verdi's *Rigoletto,* and during the next decade appeared in a variety of coloratura roles in opera houses throughout Europe and in Central and South America. Her career entered a new phase with her debut in Chicago on November 18, 1916, as Gilda. She was engaged to sing in Chicago each of the next eight seasons, appearing in lyric and coloratura roles in operas by Rossini, Donizetti, Verdi, Gounod, Massenet, and Delibes. Her long-awaited Metropolitan Opera debut, as Violetta in an opening-night performance of Verdi's *La traviata,* took place on November 14, 1921. She remained at the Met for nine seasons, making her farewell appearance in Rossini's *Il barbiere di Siviglia* on January 24, 1930. By then vocal problems had become evident; she underwent throat surgery in 1935 but was disappointed in her subsequent efforts to return to the stage.

In her prime, Galli-Curci possessed a coloratura of great naturalness and ease, well documented on numerous recordings made before about 1925. Along with Caruso, McCormack, and Chaliapin, she was one of the brightest early stars of the phonograph.

James Galway, impeccable player, impeccably tailored

Galway, Sir James

(b. Belfast, December 8, 1939)

IRISH FLUTIST. That he is one of the world's most popular performers has led some to underestimate his musicianship and artistry, but he is the most technically proficient flutist to have appeared in the past 50 years, and among colleagues—wind players in particular—he is acknowledged as a paragon.

As a child, he took up the pennywhistle before switching to the flute. In less than two years he won top prizes in three categories at a local flute contest. He studied at London's Royal College of Music (1956–59) and Guildhall School (1959–60), subsequently taking classes at the Paris Conservatoire with Jean-Pierre Rampal and studying privately with Marcel Moyse. His professional career began with the Wind Band of the Royal Shakespeare Theater at Stratford-upon-Avon. Subsequent posts at Sadler's Wells and Covent Garden led to positions with the BBC Symphony Orchestra, the London Symphony Orchestra, and the Royal Philharmonic. In 1969 he became principal flute of the Berlin Philharmonic, playing with great distinction during the orchestra's glory years under Herbert von Karajan and contributing to some of the finest recordings the BPO has made. He relinquished his chair in 1975 to embark on a solo career, and within a year had played 120 concerts and made appearances with all five of the major London orchestras.

In his 30 years as a solo performer, Galway has set a new standard for virtuosity on the flute. In matters of breath control and tone production he is unsurpassed, and his sound—clear, bright, focused, almost bell-like in the purity of its upper range—is instantly recognizable. His engaging personality and roguish sense of humor have charmed listeners all over the world, and helped to make the flute more popular than at any time since the 18th century. Works written for him include the *Pied Piper Fantasy* (1981) by John Corigliano, *Orfeo II* (1975) by Thea Musgrave, *Varianten* (1968) for flute and orchestra by Hanning Schröder (1896–1987), and concertos by Jindřich Feld (b. 1925), Lowell Liebermann (b. 1961), and Lorin Maazel. He was knighted in 2001.

Mary Garden

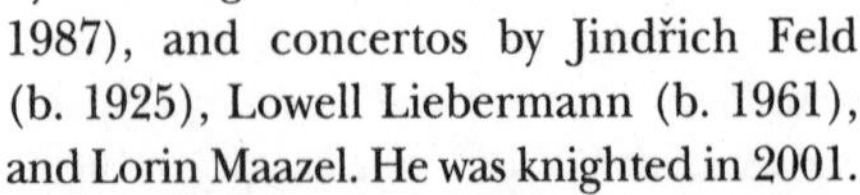
RECOMMENDED RECORDING

MOZART, FLUTE CONCERTOS: ROBLES, HARP; MARRINER AND ACADEMY OF ST. MARTIN-IN-THE-FIELDS (RCA).

gamelan *See box on pages 496–97.*

Garden, Mary

(b. Aberdeen, February 20, 1874; d. Inverurie, Scotland, January 3, 1967)

AMERICAN SOPRANO OF SCOTTISH BIRTH. She came to the United States when she was seven. Soon after settling in Chicago with her family, she began to study violin, piano, and voice. In 1896 she moved to Paris to continue her vocal training. In 1900, as an understudy at the Opéra-Comique, she made her debut in the title role of *Louise* by Gustave Charpentier (1860–1956). The lead roles in Massenet's *Thaïs* and *Manon* were quickly offered her, but she was still virtually unknown when, in 1902, Debussy chose her to create the role of Mélisande in his opera *Pelléas et Mélisande,* over the objections of the play's author, Maurice Maeterlinck (who wanted his mistress, Georgette Leblanc, to sing the part). Debussy's judgment was vindicated: Garden's light, unoperatic voice and ethereal pre-Raphaelite beauty made her perfect for the part, and it became her signature role. Her first recordings, made a short time later, were of Debussy songs, accompanied by the composer.

Garden's success as Manon convinced Massenet to compose *Chérubin* for her (1905). In 1907 she sang in the American premiere of his *Thaïs,* at Oscar Hammerstein's Manhattan Opera House, and in 1910 she began a long association with the Chicago Grand Opera, as Mélisande. Garden spent 20 seasons in Chicago, including a brief stint as director (1921–22), during which she presided over the world premiere of Prokofiev's *The Love for Three Oranges.* Though she was known mainly for lyric and coloratura roles, she also took on heavier roles, including Carmen, Tosca, and Salome. While others may have possessed more impressive voices and technique, in her day Garden was considered the supreme singing actress. Her recordings give evidence of a smallish voice, technical limitations, and a tendency to sing on the flat side of the pitch.

Gardiner, Sir John Eliot

(b. Fontmell Magna, April 20, 1943)

ENGLISH CONDUCTOR. He majored in history and Arabic at Cambridge. In 1964, while still an undergraduate, he founded the Monteverdi Choir in order to put on a performance of Monteverdi's *Vespers* of 1610. Following graduation, he studied with harpsichordist Thurston Dart in London and with Nadia Boulanger in Paris, and in 1968 he formed the Monteverdi Orchestra. He made his London debut, conducting Mozart's *Die Zauberflöte* at the English

National Opera, in 1969, and in 1973 he bowed at Covent Garden, conducting Gluck's *Iphigénie en Tauride.*

In 1977, with the establishment of the English Baroque Soloists (formed from members of the Monteverdi Orchestra), Gardiner put himself at the cutting edge of the early music movement. The group, which made its debut at the Innsbruck Festival of Early Music, performing Handel's *Acis and Galatea,* continues to be one of the most important period-instrument ensembles in the world. In 1990, Gardiner formed a new period-instrument orchestra for the performance of Classical and Romantic music, the Orchestre Révolutionnaire et Romantique.

In addition to his work in the early music field, Gardiner has had a wide-ranging career as a guest conductor, crowned by engagements with the leading orchestras of Amsterdam, Berlin, Boston, Cleveland, Dresden, London, Prague, and Vienna. He served as principal conductor of the CBC Vancouver Orchestra (1980–83), music director of the Opéra de Lyon (1983–88), and artistic director of the Göttingen Handel Festival (1981–90). His tenure as principal conductor of the NDR (North German Radio) Symphony Orchestra in Hamburg, from 1991 to 1994, was short-lived and shadowed by reports of friction between conductor and players.

Sir John Eliot Gardiner rehearsing the Orchestre Révolutionnaire et Romantique

Gardiner has been very successful as a recording artist. His large portfolio includes outstanding recordings of the cantatas and major sacred works of Bach, of Beethoven's symphonies and piano concertos, the operas of Mozart, Haydn's oratorios, and orchestral music by Chabrier and Elgar. In 1989, to mark the 25th anniversary of the Monteverdi Choir, he brought that group to San Marco in Venice and made what is still the definitive recording of the *Vespers.* With the Philharmonia he presided over one of the best recordings ever of Holst's *The Planets,* and he won a Grammy for his colorful rendition of Stravinsky's *The Rake's Progress.*

RECOMMENDED RECORDINGS

BACH, *ST. MATTHEW* PASSION: ROLFE JOHNSON, BONNEY, OTTER, CHANCE, CROOK; MONTEVERDI CHOIR WITH ENGLISH BAROQUE SOLOISTS (ARCHIV).

HANDEL, *MESSIAH*: MARSHALL, QUIRKE, ROBBIN, BRETT, ROLFE JOHNSON, HALE; MONTEVERDI CHOIR WITH ENGLISH BAROQUE SOLOISTS (PHILIPS).

HOLST, *THE PLANETS*: PHILHARMONIA ORCHESTRA (DG).

MONTEVERDI, *VESPERS*: MONTEVERDI CHOIR WITH ENGLISH BAROQUE SOLOISTS (ARCHIV).

Gaspard de la nuit **PIANO PIECE IN THREE MOVEMENTS BY MAURICE RAVEL,** inspired by Aloysius Bertrand's *Gaspard de la nuit,* a collection of lugubrious prose poems posthumously published in 1842. Composed in 1908, it is Ravel's most ambitious work for the piano and one of the supreme accomplishments of musical Impressionism. The three movements are entitled "Ondine" (after the fatally alluring water nymph of numerous fairy tales), "Le gibet" ("The Gallows"), and "Scarbo" (the name of a malevolent medieval dwarf). With its fiendish hand crossings and wicked, repeated-note figures broken out into octaves, "Scarbo" aptly characterizes its subject and is one of the most difficult pieces in the piano literature. Ricardo Viñes, the literarily-minded Catalan pianist who introduced Ravel to Bertrand's book, gave the premiere of *Gaspard de la nuit* on January 9, 1909.

RECOMMENDED RECORDING

POGORELICH (DG).

Gavotte: a German illustration showing how it was done "in the era of Louis XV"

gavotte An elegant dance in moderately paced duple time, in which melodic phrases begin on the third beat of a measure and carry a strong accent on the downbeat of the following measure; in the dance, the characteristic step—called a *contretemps de gavotte*—involves a plié on the upbeat followed by a kick on the downbeat. The gavotte is frequently encountered as one of the optional dances in Baroque suites. Melodies in gavotte rhythm are also found in later 18th-century music: The festive principal subject of the final movement of Mozart's Piano Concerto No. 26 in D, K. 537 is one, and so is the innocent little cadential tune that appears three times (mm. 49–52, 164–67, 352–55) in the first movement of Mozart's Clarinet Concerto, K. 622. Because they must begin and end in mid-measure, melodies in gavotte rhythm are not easily sustained. Their tendency toward brevity and fragility gives them a special beauty. *See also* SUITE.

gazza ladra, La (The Thieving Magpie)
OPERA IN TWO ACTS BY GIOACHINO ROSSINI, to a libretto by Giovanni Gherardini, premiered at La Scala on May 31, 1817. The serving girl Ninetta is arrested for the theft of a spoon (actually purloined by the avian kleptomaniac of the opera's title). She is put on trial, found guilty, and marched to the scaffold. Only then, thanks to the fortuitous discovery of the magpie's thievery (it has been storing stolen coins and cutlery in its nest in a church tower), is the young woman freed. Not an opera buffa per se, but a *melodramma* with serious overtones in the way it depicts the social order, *La gazza ladra* foreshadows the more explicit political stance of much of Verdi's work. The overture is one of Rossini's strongest and most expertly crafted.

RECOMMENDED RECORDING

OVERTURE: NORRINGTON AND LONDON CLASSICAL PLAYERS (VIRGIN CLASSICS).

Gedda [Ustinov], Nicolai

(b. Stockholm, July 11, 1925)

SWEDISH TENOR. His mother was Swedish, his father a White Russian immigrant who had sung in the Don Cossack Choir. After a brief stint as teller in a Stockholm bank, he studied with Carl Martin Oehman at the Royal Academy of Music in Stockholm; he made his debut at the Swedish Royal Opera in 1951, in the premiere of Heinrich Sutermeister's *Der rote Stiefel,* and was engaged the following season to sing Chapelou in Adolphe Adam's *Le postillon de Longjumeau.* From the beginning, his stylistic discernment and a phenomenal gift for languages stood out, and very quickly demand for his burnished tone led to a succession of debuts at the world's leading houses: La Scala in 1953 (as Don Ottavio in Mozart's *Don Giovanni*), the Paris Opéra in 1954 (as Sir Huon in Weber's *Oberon*), Covent Garden in 1955 (as the Duke of Mantua in Verdi's *Rigoletto*), and the Metropolitan Opera in 1957 (singing the title role in Gounod's *Faust*). With his native fluency in Russian, he was a commanding singer of Tchaikovsky—a distinguished Hermann in *The Queen of Spades* and the outstanding Lensky of modern times in *Eugene Onegin.* His beautiful, essentially lyric voice remained well preserved through a career that lasted more than 30 years, and has been documented on more than 200 recordings.

RECOMMENDED RECORDINGS

MOZART, *DIE ZAUBERFLÖTE*: POPP, JANOWITZ, BERRY; KLEMPERER AND PHILHARMONIA ORCHESTRA (EMI).

STRAUSS, *CAPRICCIO*: SCHWARZKOPF, FISCHER-DIESKAU; SAWALLISCH AND PHILHARMONIA ORCHESTRA (EMI).

"THE VERY BEST OF NICOLAI GEDDA" (OPERA ARIAS) (EMI CLASSICS).

Nikolai Gedda, reflecting on the score

Geminiani, Francesco

(b. Lucca, December 3, 1687; d. Dublin, September 17, 1762)

ITALIAN COMPOSER, VIOLINIST, AND THEORIST. The son of a violinist, he inherited his father's position with the Cappella Palatina in Lucca in 1707, presumably after a period of study with Arcangelo Corelli and Alessandro Scarlatti in Rome. He left Italy in 1714 to seek his fortune in England. His first London patron was King George I's adviser Baron Kielmansegge, who in 1717 would commission Handel to compose his *Water Music*; Kielmansegge arranged for Geminiani to perform for the king with Handel as accompanist, and received the dedication of Geminiani's Op. 1, a set of 12 sonatas for violin and continuo, in 1716. In his heyday—from 1716 to 1732—Geminiani was one of the most admired musicians on the London scene. During the final three decades of his life, he divided his time between London, Paris, and Dublin, teaching, performing, publishing various editions of his music, and establishing a business as an art dealer.

The bulk of Geminiani's output consists of sonatas and concertos. The former are in the style popularized by Corelli and reflect his influence; the latter are also indebted to Corelli—indeed, quite a few of them are outright arrangements of sonatas from Corelli's Op. 3 and Op. 5 collections. Geminiani was also the author of six treatises that contained additional pieces and arrangements, the most important and influential of which was *The Art of Playing the Violin,* Op. 9, published in London in 1751.

RECOMMENDED RECORDINGS

CONCERTI GROSSI: KREČEK AND CAPPELLA ISTROPOLITANA (NAXOS).

CONCERTI GROSSI (WITH OTHER COMPOSERS): LAMON AND TAFELMUSIK (SONY).

Gergiev, Valery

(b. Moscow, May 2, 1953)

RUSSIAN CONDUCTOR of enormous drive and talent, if sometimes questionable musicianship. Raised in the Caucasus, he started his musical studies in 1961, continuing them at the Leningrad Conservatory (1972–76) under Ilya Musin. Two important prizes followed his graduation: the All-Soviet Conducting Prize and first prize in the Herbert von Karajan Conducting Competition. This led to his engagement by the Kirov Theater (renamed the Mariinsky Theater in 1992) as assistant conductor to Yury Temirkanov in 1977. Gergiev subsequently served as chief conductor of the Armenian State Orchestra (1981–85). In 1988 he made his London debut with the London Symphony Orchestra; that same year, by vote of the musicians of the orchestra, he was chosen to succeed Temirkanov as conductor and artistic director of the Kirov. When, after the end of Communist rule in Russia, the company fell on hard times, Gergiev kept it going by the sheer force of his energy and personality, and by taking it on lucrative tours to the West.

During the 1990s, Gergiev became a figure of international prominence. He made his debuts with the opera companies of Munich and San Francisco in 1991, launched the Stars of the White Nights Festival in St. Petersburg in 1992, and in 1993 conducted for the first time at both Covent Garden and the Metropolitan Opera. In 1995 he became principal conductor of the Rotterdam Philharmonic, and the next year he was appointed artistic and general director of the Mariinsky Theater. In 1997 he became principal guest conductor of the Metropolitan Opera, and he is slated to become principal conductor of the London Symphony Orchestra in 2007.

With his menacing gaze and fierce five-day beard, Gergiev looks more like a wild man of the Caucasus than one of the world's busiest maestros. His sometimes brilliant, always high-voltage accounts of operas and symphonic scores by Mussorgsky, Rimsky-Korsakov, Prokofiev, and Shostakovich have established him as an interpreter to be reckoned with; in 15 years he has recorded vast stretches of the Russian repertoire, greatly enriching the discography and making a particularly strong case for the less familiar operas of Tchaikovsky, Rimsky-Korsakov, and Prokofiev. Praised for his passionately intense performing style, he has also been criticized for his idiosyncratic technique and his tendency to burn the candle at both ends, which sometimes leaves insufficient time for preparation and rehearsal. In repertoire sympathetic to his fierce nature, he is capable of delivering riveting performances of a white-hot intensity that few can match.

RECOMMENDED RECORDINGS

MUSSORGSKY, *BORIS GODUNOV* (1869 AND 1874 VERSIONS): VARIOUS SOLOISTS; KIROV OPERA (PHILIPS).

PROKOFIEV, *THE FIERY ANGEL*: KIROV OPERA (PHILIPS).

RIMSKY-KORSAKOV, *SHEHERAZADE*: KIROV OPERA (PHILIPS).

RIMSKY-KORSAKOV, *THE TSAR'S BRIDE*: KIROV OPERA (PHILIPS).

Gershwin, George

(b. New York, September 26, 1898; d. Hollywood, July 11, 1937)

AMERICAN COMPOSER, PIANIST, AND SONGWRITER. With an unsurpassed melodic gift and a sure instinct for the rhythms of his nation's musical vernacular, he created a body of works that has kept a hold on the public for more than three generations. Forever young, fresh, and American, his scores convey the assertive spirit and the charged emotions of the Jazz Age, and remain among America's most popular musical exports.

Gershwin's parents came to the United States from Russia sometime around 1891; they met in New York, got married in 1895, and settled in a poor Jewish neighborhood on Manhattan's Lower East Side. Originally Gershovitz and then Gershvin, the family moved to Brooklyn, where George was born in 1898 (birth name Jacob; he was the family member who eventually decided upon "Gershwin," with everyone else following his lead). Gershwin had little exposure to music until his 12th year, when the family bought an upright piano that he quickly taught himself to play; before then, he said, he had been a rowdy child both in and out of school, a "nuisance." He subsequently studied with a number of teachers, but had acquired no more than a rudimentary knowledge of theory, harmony, counterpoint, and orchestration by the time he went to work, at 15, for Remick & Co., plugging songs for $15 a week on Tin Pan Alley. He later worked as a rehearsal pianist on Broadway and an accompanist to pop singers; in 1918 he was hired as a staff composer by the music firm of T. B. Harms at $35 a week. He quickly made a mark as a songwriter, hitting the big time in 1919 with "Swanee," which Al Jolson recorded the following year.

From 1920 to 1924 Gershwin wrote the music for the annual revue *George White's Scandals.* Subsequent Broadway shows included *Lady Be Good!, Oh, Kay!* (book by P. G. Wodehouse), *Strike Up the Band, Girl Crazy,* and *Of Thee I Sing* (awarded the Pulitzer Prize for drama in 1932). His principal collaborator in these was his elder brother, Ira Gershwin (1896–1983). Their extraordinary partnership produced some of the greatest songs in the English language, including "'S Wonderful," "Somebody Loves Me," "Fascinating Rhythm," "The Man I Love," "Someone to Watch Over Me," "Strike Up the Band," "Embraceable You," "Let's Call the Whole Thing Off," "They All Laughed," "They Can't Take That Away From Me," and "A Foggy Day."

In light of their Broadway success, it was natural that George and Ira would be called to Hollywood to conjure up hit songs for the movie musicals that were fast becoming the Depression era's number-one escape from reality. They spent the winter of 1930–31 there working on songs for the film *Delicious,* and in the summer of 1936 they returned under contract to RKO; in the space of a year, they provided numbers for *Shall We Dance?, A Damsel in Distress,* and *The Goldwyn Follies.* It would be a tragic year, however. While Gershwin settled easily into the California lifestyle—hobnobbing with the rich and famous, even playing tennis with Arnold Schoenberg (also painting his portrait)—in the winter of 1937 he began to experience symptoms of the brain tumor that would shortly kill him. With the Hollywood craze for psychoanalysis then in its initial full swing,

George Gershwin at the keyboard, ready to rhapsodize

***Gene Kelly and Leslie Caron in Vincente Minelli's film* An American in Paris**

his complaints of dizziness, headaches, despondency, and of the recurrent smell of burning rubber were dismissed as "hysteria brought on by the pressures and artificiality of Hollywood life." In July, Gershwin abruptly fell into a coma, and, too late, his tumor was diagnosed. A five-hour operation ensued but he died the following morning, Ira at his bedside.

Gershwin's reputation as a "serious" composer had been secured in 1924 with the creation of *RHAPSODY IN BLUE*. Drawing on the dynamic language of jazz, the piece communicated an entirely new range of moods and emotions in a classical context. Among the impressed listeners at its premiere was Walter Damrosch, the conductor of the New York Symphony (soon to be amalgamated with the New York Philharmonic). He approached Gershwin with a commission for a full-blown piano concerto, which received its premiere December 3, 1925, at Carnegie Hall, with the composer as soloist. The work—which Gershwin thought of calling *New York* Concerto before settling on the more conventional-sounding Concerto in F—reflects the same jazzy influences that shaped the *Rhapsody*; if not as spontaneous or melodically memorable, it is formally more coherent.

Gershwin returned to the tuneful manner of *Rhapsody in Blue* with his next big piece, the exuberant, colorfully rendered tone poem *AN AMERICAN IN PARIS* (1928). Brilliantly inventive, *An American in Paris* ranks second only to the *Rhapsody* in popularity among Gershwin's works, and in scope and craftsmanship it can rightly be considered his symphonic masterpiece. Looking for a sequel to *Rhapsody in Blue,* Gershwin fashioned another fantasy for piano and orchestra in 1931, which he premiered in 1932 with Serge Koussevitzky and the Boston Symphony. Glamorously scored and every bit as energetic as its predecessor, the Second Rhapsody might be more widely known today had the composer stuck with either of the titles he originally considered, *Manhattan Rhapsody* or *Rhapsody in Rivets.* Gershwin turned to a Latin sound in his next concert work, the *Cuban* Overture (1932), which makes colorful use of a rhythm section consisting of claves, guiro, maracas, and bongos. Still looking for another piano-and-orchestra hit, Gershwin strutted his stuff one more time with his *"I Got Rhythm" Variations* (1934), based on the wildly popular song he and Ira had written for *Girl Crazy.*

In *PORGY AND BESS* (1935), which he called an American folk opera, Gershwin's two talents as a composer for the musical stage and for the concert hall were united in a work of extraordinary accomplishment, which represented not only something new in American music but a new height in Gershwin's artistic development. Though the action is discursive as Gershwin originally conceived the piece (he tightened it by making cuts to the score), the music of *Porgy and Bess* is rich and emotionally compelling. What Gershwin might have done after *Porgy and Bess* one can only speculate, but it is obvious that a rich vein in American music came into view with this work, only to be lost with Gershwin's death.

RECOMMENDED RECORDINGS

An American in Paris, Second Rhapsody, Concerto in F: Thomas and San Francisco Symphony Orchestra (RCA).

Porgy and Bess: White, Mitchell, Boatwright; Maazel and Cleveland Orchestra (Decca).

Rhapsody in Blue and *An American in Paris*: Bernstein and New York Philharmonic Orchestra (Sony).

Gesualdo, Carlo

(b. prob. Naples, ca. 1561; d. Gesualdo, September 8, 1613)

ITALIAN COMPOSER whose extraordinary chromatic inventiveness anticipated centuries of musical development. He came from an aristocratic family and upon his father's death in 1591 succeeded to the title of Prince of Venosa. Astonishing as his music was, Gesualdo is also notorious for the double murder he committed on October 16, 1590, when he surprised his wife, Maria d'Avalos, in bed with her lover, Don Fabrizio Carafa, Duke of Andria. The execution-style slaying, using swords and pistols, was carried out with the help of three men hired by Gesualdo, who, by virtue of his station and because he had indeed caught his wife in flagrante delicto, went unpunished for the deed.

A contemporary image of Carlo Gesualdo

Gesualdo wrote dozens of motets, most of them for five or six voices, and six books of madrigals, the last three of which are filled with lavish chromaticism, irregular and unresolved dissonances, and surprising juxtapositions of unrelated harmonies, all intended mainly for his own delectation. The boldness and extravagance of these pieces, though not characteristic of all of his work, have led to his being admired in modern times as the composer of a polyphony of "inspired disorder."

RECOMMENDED RECORDINGS

Motets: Phillips and Tallis Scholars (Gimell).

"O Dolorosa Gioia" (madrigals): Galassi; Alessandrini and Concerto Italiano (Opus 111).

Tenebrae Responsories: Hilliard Ensemble (EMI).

Gewandhaus Orchestra ENSEMBLE FOUNDED IN **1743** by a group of 16 Leipzig merchants. The original orchestra was the same size as its board of directors—16 players—and presented a series of "Grand Concerts" at the Three Swans Inn in Leipzig's commercial district. In 1781 the orchestra moved to the 500-seat hall of the cloth traders, known as the Gewandhaus ("Garment House"). The first concert in the Gewandhaus took place on November 25, 1781, and was directed by J. A. Hiller. Since then, nearly all of Europe's most important composers and conductors have stood upon its podium, beginning with Wolfgang Mozart in 1789.

The appointment of Felix Mendelssohn as music director was a milestone in the orchestra's history. Mendelssohn led the Gewandhaus ensemble from 1835 until his death in 1847, and transformed it into one of the finest in Europe. He conducted the world premiere of Schubert's Symphony No. 9 at the Gewandhaus in 1839, the premiere of Schumann's *Spring* Symphony in 1841, and the premiere of his own Symphony No. 3

Watercolor of the Gewandhaus by Felix Mendelssohn, 1836

(*Scottish*) in 1842. In the half century following Mendelssohn's death, Leipzig became a bastion of musical conservatism, a trend reflected throughout the tenure of Carl Reinecke as the orchestra's music director (1860–95). In 1884, after more than a century in the cloth merchants' hall, the orchestra moved into a newly constructed 1,500-seat hall. Dubbed the Neues ("New") Gewandhaus, it proved to be one of the finest concert halls ever built in Europe, and served as the model for Boston's outstanding Symphony Hall.

By the turn of the century, the orchestra's strength was almost 100 players. And with the arrival of Arthur Nikisch as music director in 1895, the Gewandhaus programs again became adventurous and forward-looking. Nikisch restored Berlioz, Liszt, and Wagner to the repertoire, introduced works by Bruckner and Richard Strauss, and even programmed the music of Arnold Schoenberg during his tenure, which lasted until 1922. Nikisch was succeeded by a pair of luminaries: Wilhelm Furtwängler, who held the reins from 1922 to 1928, and Bruno Walter, who served from 1929 until he was removed from the position by the Nazis in 1933. Hermann Abendroth led the Gewandhaus Orchestra during the remainder of the Third Reich; the Neues Gewandhaus itself was destroyed by Allied bombing in February 1944.

The orchestra's fortunes declined under the Communists, who installed Franz Konwitschny as music director after World War II. In 1964 the Czech conductor Václav Neumann succeeded Konwitschny, and in 1970 Kurt Masur became music director. Masur brought stability and a renewed sense of pride and purpose to the orchestra, and pushed for the construction of a new 1,900-seat hall on the Augustusplatz. The third concert hall to be called the Gewandhaus opened on October 8, 1981. By the time he stepped down in 1996, Masur had brought the Gewandhaus Orchestra back into the ranks of world-class ensembles and contributed extensively to its discography. In 1998, following an unsucessful transition involving Gerd Albrecht, the Swedish conductor Herbert Blomstedt took over as caretaker until a new music director could be found. Riccardo Chailly inherited the mantle in 2005.

The Gewandhaus Orchestra has been an important venue for new music for much of its 260-year history. Among the works it has premiered are Beethoven's Triple Concerto (1808) and *Emperor* Concerto (1811), Wagner's *Meistersinger* Prelude (1862), Brahms's Violin Concerto (1879, with the composer conducting), and Bruckner's Symphony No. 7 (1884). More recently, it has given the world premieres of Schnittke's Symphony No. 3 (1981) and Hans Werner Henze's (b. 1926) *Seconda Sonata per Archi* (1996), dedicated to the string players of the orchestra.

RECOMMENDED RECORDINGS

BEETHOVEN, SYMPHONIES (COMPLETE): MASUR (PHILIPS).

HINDEMITH, SYMPHONY *DIE HARMONIE DER WELT* AND *SYMPHONIA SERENA*: BLOMSTEDT (DECCA).

Ghiaurov, Nicolai

(b. Velingrad, September 13, 1929; d. Modena, June 2, 2004)

BULGARIAN BASS. He studied at the Bulgarian State Conservatory as well as in Moscow and Leningrad, and in 1955 made his debut in Sofia as Don Basilio in Rossini's *Il barbiere di Siviglia.* His debut at the Vienna Staatsoper, as Ramfis in Verdi's *Aida,* followed in 1957, and within a decade he had taken his first curtain calls at La Scala, Covent Garden, and the Metropolitan Opera. A regular in Vienna from 1962, he also appeared frequently at the Salzburg Festival, where he was one of Herbert von Karajan's favorite collaborators and scored triumphs in Mussorgsky's *Boris Godunov* (1965) and as Philip II in Verdi's *Don Carlo* (1975). Ghiaurov's dependable musicianship, stylistic versatility, and dramatic flair made him one of the most frequently engaged basses of his generation; his distinctively rich timbre and warm expressiveness made him one of the most admired as well.

Ghislanzoni, Antonio

(b. Lecco, November 25, 1824; d. Caprino, July 16, 1893)

ITALIAN JOURNALIST AND LIBRETTIST. Originally destined for the priesthood, he left the seminary to study medicine in Pavia and eventually gave that up to pursue a career as a singer. Burning out early, he focused his attention on writing; he produced his first opera libretto in 1857 and quickly became Italy's most sought-after librettist. Giuseppe Verdi asked for his help with the revision of *LA FORZA DEL DESTINO* in 1869, then assigned him to fashion the libretto for *AIDA* from the composer's own prose text. In 1872 Ghislanzoni supplied Verdi with new verses for an early Italian production of *DON CARLO.* His style, though not as incandescent as Arrigo Boito's, was sturdy and free of hackneyed phraseology.

***Ghost* Trio** NICKNAME OF LUDWIG VAN BEETHOVEN'S TRIO IN D, OP. 70, NO. 1, for piano, violin, and cello, composed in 1808. The trio's middle movement, a Largo, incorporates an eerie passage lifted from sketches for music intended to accompany the witches' scene in Shakespeare's *Macbeth,* a project Beethoven never completed. The mysterious effect of tremolos and measured trills in the piano is unlike anything he had tried before; heard against this backdrop, a series of ominous crescendos and poignant phrases in the strings creates a mood of tense expectation. ◉ The *Ghost* Trio and its sister work, the Trio in E-flat, Op. 70, No. 2, were published in 1809 with a dedication to the Countess Anna Maria Erdödy.

Giacosa, Giuseppe

(b. Colleretto Parella, October 21, 1847; d. Colleretto Parella, September 2, 1906)

ITALIAN PLAYWRIGHT AND LIBRETTIST. Following the success of his one-act comedy *Una partita a scacchi* (*A Game of Chess,* 1873), he gave up the practice of law to devote himself full-time to writing. He penned a number of successful prose plays and served as chairman of the

Giuseppe Giacosa, polisher of prose

department of literature and dramatic art at the Milan Conservatory (1888–94). In 1894 he was recruited by the Milanese music publisher Giulio Ricordi to work on the libretto for Giacomo Puccini's *La bohème,* in tandem with the writer Luigi Illica. Illica's job was to draft the scenario and sketch out the dialogue, which Giacosa, a master versifier, turned into polished final text. The collaboration proved so successful that Giacosa and Illica were again teamed for the librettos to *Tosca* (1900) and *Madama Butterfly* (1904).

Gianni Schicchi **Comic opera in one act by Giacomo Puccini,** to a libretto by Giovacchino Forzano (based on a passage in canto 30 of Dante's *Inferno*), composed 1917–18 and premiered December 14, 1918, at the Metropolitan Opera in New York as the third part of *Il trittico.* The action, set in 13th-century Florence, centers on a scheme by the avaricious relatives of a well-to-do merchant, Buoso Donati, to claim his assets following his recent death. They call in a quick-witted and warmhearted scoundrel, Gianni Schicchi, who agrees to impersonate his deceased neighbor and dictate a new will from his "deathbed." But he turns the tables on the conspirators by leaving them token gifts while making himself the dead man's heir. The title role is a showcase for a baritone gifted with acting ability (he gets to sing most of the part as a creaky-voiced caricature, lying in bed). The comedy is rounded out by the love interest of Schicchi's daughter, Lauretta, and Rinuccio, her beau. Lauretta's "O mio babbino caro" ("O Dearest Little Daddy") is the quintessential Puccini aria for soprano.

RECOMMENDED RECORDINGS

Gobbi, Te Kanawa, Cotrubas, Malaga, Domingo; Maazel and London Symphony Orchestra (Sony).

Van Dam, Gheorghiu, Palmer, Alagna; Pappano and London Symphony Orchestra (EMI).

Gieseking, Walter

(b. Lyons, November 5, 1895; d. London, October 26, 1956)

German pianist of French birth. He grew up in the south of France and at the age of 16 began serious study of the piano at the Hanover Conservatory. Gifted with a phenomenal memory, he mastered the Beethoven sonatas by the time he was 20. He made recital debuts in Berlin (1920) and London (1923), and showed an early devotion to contemporary music, giving the premiere of Pfitzner's Piano Concerto in 1923 and playing Hindemith's Piano Concerto at his American debut in 1926. He made his Paris debut in 1928. Gieseking remained in Germany during World War II, and toed the Nazi line without being an enthusiast. In American eyes, he was tainted nonetheless. A planned performance at Carnegie Hall in 1949 sparked vehement protests and had to be canceled, but the pianist later revisited America successfully.

Gieseking had stupendous technique and perhaps the keenest understanding of sonority of any pianist ever: he was unrivaled in the use of the pedals and in his ability to convey a full tone in the softest dynamics. This made him an ideal interpreter of the music of Debussy, for whose music (and that of Ravel) he retained a deep and abiding affinity.

RECOMMENDED RECORDINGS

Beethoven, Mozart, Debussy, Ravel, works for piano (Philips).

Debussy, works for piano (EMI).

Gigli, Beniamino

(b. Recanati, March 20, 1890; d. Rome, November 30, 1957)

Italian tenor. He entered the international arena just as Caruso's career was coming to an end, and emerged during the 1920s as the dominant lyric tenor of his generation. The son of a shoemaker, Gigli joined the choir of his local cathedral as a boy of six. From the age of 17 he studied privately in Rome, and at 21 he received a scholarship to attend the Accademia di Santa Cecilia. In 1914 he won first prize at an international singing competition in Parma and made his professional debut at Rovigo, as Enzo in Ponchielli's *La gioconda.* Italy's leading opera houses quickly snapped him up, and in 1918 he made a triumphant La Scala debut as Faust in Boito's *Mefistofele* under the baton of Arturo Toscanini. Following those performances, HMV signed him to a recording contract, and he cut his first discs that year in Milan. In 1919 Gigli made his debut at the Teatro Colón in Buenos Aires, and on November 26, 1920, he bowed for the first time at the Metropolitan Opera, once again as Faust in *Mefistofele.*

Beniamino Gigli

Gigli remained on the Met roster for 12 seasons, during which he became the company's (and the world's) highest-paid tenor. Among his bread-and-butter parts were the title role in Giordano's *Andrea Chénier* (which he also sang at his Covent Garden debut in 1930), Des Grieux in Puccini's *Manon Lescaut,* Roméo in Gounod's *Roméo et Juliette,* Lionel in Flotow's *Martha,* Fenton in Verdi's *Falstaff,* and Don Ottavio in Mozart's *Don Giovanni.* In 1928 he sang in the American premiere of Puccini's *La rondine.* The Depression brought a premature end to Gigli's career at the Met, as management sought salary concessions from its most expensive artists even as the IRS upped the tax rate on their earnings. Gigli returned to Italy in 1932; he was welcomed with open arms and became a favorite of the music-loving Mussolini. Listeners at the Met heard him only once more, in five performances during the 1938–39 season.

Following the end of World War II, Gigli was cleared of charges that he had collaborated with the Fascist regime and the German occupation, and he resumed his career with engagements in Rome, London, Lisbon, and Buenos Aires. He did not sing again in America until 1955, where he made the final stops on a farewell concert tour of 41 cities worldwide. During a career that lasted 41 years, Gigli gave 2,249 performances on the opera stage, appearing in 62 roles. He made more than 400 recordings and appeared in nearly 20 films. His voice, one of the most ravishing of the 20th century, was admired more for its beautiful timbre than for its power or brilliance; many listeners remarked on the sensuous quality of Gigli's mezza voce—his singing in the middle part of the range. While some found his expression mannered and overly sentimental, others were struck by the emotional charge he brought to his performances.

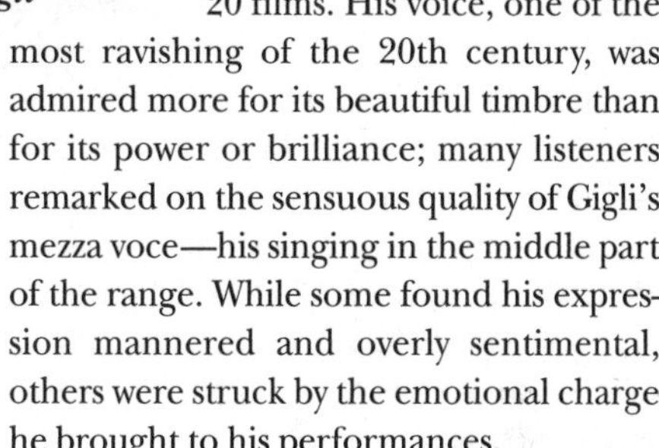

gigue A lively dance, usually in rapid $\frac{6}{8}$ time with a regular, skipping rhythm. It was typically used as the concluding dance in dance suites and partitas of the 17th and 18th centuries. *See also* SUITE.

Gilbert, William *See* SULLIVAN, ARTHUR.

Gilels, Emil

(b. Odessa, October 19, 1916; d. Moscow, October 14, 1985)

SOVIET PIANIST. He was a dazzling performer, and a magisterial interpreter of Beethoven, Brahms, and Tchaikovsky. His American debut in 1955 broke the ice of the Cold War, astonishing the musical world in much the same way that *Sputnik* would astonish the scientific community two years later. He began studying the piano at the age of five, gave his first public recital when he was nine, and made his formal concert debut at 13. He studied at the Odessa Conservatory, graduating in 1935, then attended the Moscow Conservatory, where he worked with Heinrich Neuhaus, also the teacher of Sviatoslav Richter. In 1936, Gilels played outside Russia for the first time, winning second prize at a competition in Vienna. Two years later he became a professor at the Moscow Conservatory and won first prize at the Concours Ysaÿe in Brussels. He was scheduled to make his American debut in 1939 but was prevented by the outbreak of World War II.

Emil Gilels, at the office

Gilels joined the Communist Party in 1942. On December 30, 1944, he gave the first public performance of Prokofiev's monumental Piano Sonata No. 8. He was awarded his country's second-highest honor, the Stalin Prize, in 1946. In the years that followed he was allowed to accept engagements outside the Soviet Union, first in the Eastern European countries and then in the West, beginning with Italy in 1951. His American debut, on October 3, 1955, marked the first time a Soviet artist had performed in the U.S. since the 1930s. He played Tchaikovsky's Piano Concerto No. 1 in B-flat minor with Eugene Ormandy and the Philadelphia Orchestra in Philadelphia and New York, and gave recitals in six cities. His British debut followed in 1959.

Over the next three decades Gilels concertized internationally and recorded prolifically, both in the Soviet Union and in Europe. Among his most important discographic achievements were a nearly completed cycle of the Beethoven sonatas for Deutsche Grammophon and several accounts of the Beethoven concertos.

The only Soviet pianist who could rival Richter, Gilels commanded extraordinary tone and no less extraordinary virtuosity. He was never a note-perfect pianist—not on recordings, and certainly not in performance—and he was not afraid to push himself beyond his limits when that was what the music called for. His playing was masculine in the best sense, remarkably powerful yet capable of great gentleness, and his willingness to commit everything he had to a performance gave his readings a reserved yet heroic intensity that set them apart from the efforts of the self-consciously flashy.

RECOMMENDED RECORDINGS

BEETHOVEN, *WALDSTEIN*, *APPASSIONATA*, *LES ADIEUX* SONATAS (DG).

GRIEG, SELECTED *LYRIC PIECES* (DG).

TCHAIKOVSKY, PIANO CONCERTO NO. 1: REINER AND CHICAGO SYMPHONY ORCHESTRA (RCA).

Ginastera, Alberto

(b. Buenos Aires, April 11, 1916; d. Geneva, June 25, 1983)

ARGENTINE COMPOSER. Born to parents of Italian and Catalan descent, he developed an early interest in music, entering the Williams Conservatory at age 12, and completing his studies at the National Conservatory of Music in Buenos Aires (1936–38). He received a Guggenheim Foundation grant in 1942, but waited to use it until 1945, when he traveled to the United States. Upon his return to Buenos Aires, he helped found the Argentine chapter of the International Society for

Contemporary Music, the La Plata Music and Performing Arts Conservatory, and the Latin American Center for Advanced Music Studies at the Instituto Torcuato di Tella in Buenos Aires. He was constantly at odds with the government of Argentine strongman Juan Perón as well as with the military regime that toppled him; in 1969 he emigrated to Switzerland, where he lived the rest of his life.

As a composer, Ginastera was a slow and meticulous worker, a perfectionist like Ravel. Extraordinarily self-critical, he amassed a catalog of only 54 numbered opuses, yet the majority of them remain in the active repertoire. Stravinsky, Bartók, Falla, and Ravel were among the influences on his early works, yet his style was always original, absorbing these influences rather than echoing them.

Ginastera identified three phases in his compositional career: objective nationalism, subjective nationalism, and neo-Expressionism, by which he meant music in an explicitly modernist style that was less reliant on imagery and folk elements than the music of his early years. There were no clear-cut breaks between these phases, rather a gradual shift in the composer's approach and techniques. He came out of the box impressively with the ballet *Panambí,* his Op. 1, written between 1934 and 1937. In a coloristic, folk-flavored idiom, the work relies on energetic rhythms and brilliant orchestral writing for much of its effect; but it is also notable for intensely poetic, quiet passages that evoke the mystery and solitude of Argentina's open spaces.

The *Danzas Argentinas* for piano, Op. 2 (1937), also typical of Ginastera's folk-flavored early idiom, celebrate the world of the gauchos, southern cowboys who could dance as well as they could ride. The ballet *Estancia,* Op. 8 (1941), is another representative work of the composer's overtly nationalist period. Around 1948, after his American sojourn, Ginastera's approach became more cosmopolitan. Working in standard musical forms, he imbued them with the rhythmic energy and rhapsodic flourishes of Argentine folk music, now thoroughly assimilated into his own increasingly bold and incisive idiom. The popular Piano Sonata No. 1 and the *Variaciones concertantes* for chamber orchestra date from this time. After 1958, Ginastera began regularly employing compositional techniques from the modernist arsenal (including 12-tone rows), composing music that was harmonically and texturally more complex but no less vibrant and approachable. Among the notable works he produced in this phase of his career were the operas *Bomarzo* (1966–67) and *Beatrix Cenci* (1971); concertos for piano, violin, and cello; and the orchestral suite *Popol Vuh,* Op. 44, a sprawling work based on the sacred book of the Mayas that was commissioned by the Philadelphia Orchestra in 1975.

In 1971 Ginastera married the cellist Aurora Nátola, his muse and companion for the remainder of his life. The years of his marriage to Aurora were among the most productive of the composer's life; indeed, the flow of inspiration was such that in 1981 he warmly confided to an interviewer that he had enough ideas to

Alberto Ginastera: craftsman at work

keep him busy until he was 100. His death from cancer less than two years later deprived the world of several potentially important works, including the planned opera *Barabbas,* on a drama by Michel de Ghelderode.

Personally as well as professionally, Ginastera was one of the most admirable composers of the 20th century, a master craftsman who showed remarkable imagination in his work and arrived at a style of great expressiveness and depth. The balance of his oeuvre—he made valuable contributions to the orchestral repertoire as well as to the chamber and instrumental literature, and he wrote magnificently for voices and the stage—marks him as a major figure, while the marvelous amalgam of refinement and flair he produced in so many pieces shows that he was a true son of Argentina.

RECOMMENDED RECORDINGS

PANAMBÍ, ESTANCIA: BEN-DOR AND LONDON SYMPHONY ORCHESTRA (CONIFER).

PIANO MUSIC: RODRIGUEZ (ELAN).

VARIACIONES CONCERTANTES: BEN-DOR AND LONDON SYMPHONY ORCHESTRA (KOCH).

gioconda, La **OPERA IN FOUR ACTS BY AMILCARE PONCHIELLI,** to a libretto by "Tobia Gorrio" (an anagrammatic alias of Arrigo Boito), premiered at La Scala on April 8, 1876. Conceived along the lines of a grand opera (much like Verdi's *Aida*) and requiring vast performing forces, it offers, in Enzo's "Cielo e mar," one of the greatest of all tenor arias, and in the title character's "Suicidio!" a melodramatic tour de force for the prima donna. But the opera is best known for its Act III ballet, the "Dance of the Hours." Time really flies in this ballet, a brilliant piece of scenic music whose final galop was memorably sent up by Disney in *Fantasia* as a combat of hippos in tutus and crocodiles, and whose opening tune was used by Allan Sherman in the song "Hello Muddah, Hello Fadduh, Here I am at Camp Granada."

RECOMMENDED RECORDINGS

CABALLÉ, PAVAROTTI, MILNES, BALTSA; BARTOLETTI AND NATIONAL PHILHARMONIC ORCHESTRA (DECCA).

URMANA, DOMINGO, ATANELI, D'INTINO; VIOTTI AND MUNICH RADIO ORCHESTRA (EMI).

Giordano, Umberto

(b. Foggia, August 28, 1867; d. Milan, November 12, 1948)

ITALIAN COMPOSER. He was educated at the Naples Conservatory and composed his first opera while still a student there. He is remembered chiefly for the opera *Andrea Chénier* (1896), a splashy melodrama in the VERISMO style set against the backdrop of the French Revolution; its title role, a prestige vehicle for tenor, has been championed by Beniamino Gigli, Franco Corelli, Luciano Pavarotti, and Plácido Domingo. Giordano wrote a dozen operas in all, but aside from *Chénier,* the only one to have retained a place in the repertoire is *Fedora* (1898), once again thanks mainly to its glamorous title role, which has served as a showcase for adventurous sopranos from Maria Caniglia and Magda Olivero to Eva Marton.

RECOMMENDED RECORDINGS

ANDREA CHÉNIER: DOMINGO, SCOTTO, MILNES; LEVINE AND NATIONAL PHILHARMONIC ORCHESTRA (RCA).

ANDREA CHÉNIER: OLIVERO, DEL MONACO, GOBBI; GARDELLI AND MONTE CARLO OPERA (DECCA).

Giulini, Carlo Maria

(b. Barletta, May 9, 1914; d. Brescia, June 14, 2005)

ITALIAN CONDUCTOR, renowned equally for his work on the concert stage and in the opera house. He studied viola and composition at the Accademia di Santa Cecilia in Rome and played in its orchestra under Otto Klemperer and Bruno Walter. He later recalled that with Walter on the

Urgings from an old string player: Carlo Maria Giulini in rehearsal

podium, he felt as though he was playing "Brahms's Symphony No. 1 for viola obbligato and orchestra." Such experiences contributed to his own wish to be a conductor, but, like Walter, one who truly served the music. He studied conducting with Bernardino Molinari and made his debut with the Orchestra of the Accademia di Santa Cecilia in 1944. Following World War II, he was named music director of Italian Radio; in 1950 he made his stage debut conducting Verdi's *La traviata* at Bergamo, and in 1952 he bowed at La Scala with Falla's *La vida breve.* After Victor de Sabata stepped down in 1953, Giulini became principal conductor at La Scala, serving in that capacity until 1956. While there he introduced a number of new pieces to the company's repertoire and worked with the directors Luchino Visconti and Franco Zeffirelli. He made his American debut in 1955 with the Chicago Symphony Orchestra, developing a close rapport with the ensemble that eventually led to his serving as its principal guest conductor (1969–78). In 1958 he made an acclaimed debut at Covent Garden conducting the Visconti production of Verdi's *Don Carlo,* and began making recordings with the Philharmonia Orchestra.

Giulini absented himself from the opera house for 15 years, from 1967 to 1982, while he concentrated on symphonic conducting. From 1973 to 1976 he was principal conductor of the Vienna Symphony Orchestra and in 1978 he succeeded Zubin Mehta as music director of the Los Angeles Philharmonic, remaining there until 1984. Refusing to live or work like a jet-set maestro, Giulini focused nearly all his performing energies on Los Angeles and devoted the rest of the year to family and study. When his wife, Marcella, suffered a debilitating stroke, he packed up and headed home to Milan to take care of her, thereafter limiting his conducting activities to a few guest appearances. He quietly retired from the podium in the 1990s.

As a conductor, Giulini was the spiritual heir to the maestros under whom he played as a young man, Klemperer in particular, and Walter, with whom he shared an elegance and aristocratic restraint. Giulini always thought of himself as a vehicle for the music (his favored metaphor was that of a mason carefully laying stones in a great edifice), yet in spite of this self-effacing attitude he was a knowledgeable, penetrating, and ardent interpreter, always learning, always seeking new insights. In opera, he had a particular affinity for Mozart, Rossini, and Verdi; in the symphonic repertoire, his advocacy extended from Mozart, Beethoven, and Schubert to Schumann, Brahms, Dvořák, and Tchaikovsky, and he embraced with equal fervor particular works by Bruckner, Mahler, Webern, Debussy, and Ravel. His profound knowledge and gentle yet passionate nature made him an ideal collaborator for solo artists and an inspiring leader.

RECOMMENDED RECORDINGS

BRAHMS, SYMPHONY NO. 4: CHICAGO SYMPHONY ORCHESTRA (EMI).

BRAHMS, VIOLIN CONCERTO: PERLMAN; CHICAGO SYMPHONY ORCHESTRA (EMI).

BRUCKNER, SYMPHONY NO. 9: VIENNA PHILHARMONIC (DG).

VERDI, *DON CARLO*: DOMINGO, CABALLÉ, VERRETT, MILNES, RAIMONDI; ROYAL OPERA (EMI).

Glagolitic Mass (Mša glagolskaja) MASS BY LEOŠ JANÁČEK, composed in the summer of 1926 to a text in Church Slavonic (Glagolitic), and scored for a large orchestra with organ, mixed chorus, and four soloists. The original version of the piece, which contained passages of remarkable rhythmic complexity, was revised and simplified by the composer at the time of the premiere, and further modified following his death in 1928. As published in 1929, the score consists of five movements corresponding to the five main sections of the Latin Mass—"Gospodi pomiluj" (Kyrie), "Slava" (Gloria), "Věruju" (Credo), "Svet" (Sanctus), and "Agneče Božij" (Agnus Dei)—framed by an orchestral introduction and an organ postlude. An orchestral "Intrada" closes the work, though Janáček's original conception called for it to be played twice—as a preface to the mass, and again at the end. The original version of the score was recorded in 1994 by Sir Charles Mackerras and the Danish National Radio Symphony Orchestra and Choir, and has been performed on a few occasions since then; it uniquely conveys the modernity, and unorthodox intentions, both of Janáček's musical language and his conception of the mass itself.

Notwithstanding Janáček's insistence that he was "no believer," the *Glagolitic Mass* represents a strikingly sincere expression of its composer's pantheistic spirituality. Mixing haunting beauty with pagan exuberance, it is vibrant, earthy, electric, and deeply moving.

RECOMMENDED RECORDINGS

KIBERG, SVENSSON; MACKERRAS AND DANISH NATIONAL RADIO SYMPHONY ORCHESTRA (CHANDOS).

KUBIAK, TEAR; KEMPE AND ROYAL PHILHARMONIC (DECCA).

Glass, Philip

(b. Baltimore, January 31, 1937)

AMERICAN COMPOSER AND PERFORMER. Though Steve Reich, Terry Riley (b. 1935), La Monte Young (b. 1935), and others had been working at it longer, it was the runaway success of Glass's music in the late 1970s and early 1980s that established MINIMALISM as the hot (and commercially viable) trend in composition. As the idiom caught on, Glass acquired a cult following, particularly among younger listeners already comfortable with the sound of amplified instruments. His style of minimalism has aptly been described as "motoric Romanticism."

Glass began studying the violin at the age of six and started flute lessons when he was eight. During his second year of high school,

Philip Glass checking a score, 1987

he was admitted to the University of Chicago, where he majored in mathematics and philosophy; he took piano lessons and continued his music studies on the side, briefly becoming interested in 12-tone techniques. During his four years at the Juilliard School (1957–61), he studied composition with William Bergsma and Vincent Persichetti. He developed an interest in the music of the American mavericks—Ives, Cowell, Harry Partch (1901–74)—and spent two years in Paris (1964–65) as a Fulbright scholar, studying with Nadia Boulanger. During his Parisian sojourn, he was hired by the French filmmaker Conrad Rooks to transcribe music Ravi Shankar had created for his film *Chappaqua* into notation readable by conventionally trained musicians. With this assignment, Glass was introduced to the elaborate rhythmic structure of Indian music. He undertook further research in North Africa and India, returned to New York in 1967, hooked up with Alla Rakha, Shankar's tabla accompanist, and began methodically applying non-Western techniques in his own music.

To present this music, Glass formed the Philip Glass Ensemble—an ad hoc group of six to a dozen musicians playing amplified keyboard, wind, and string instruments. Between 1971 and 1974 he composed *Music in 12 Parts,* which along with Reich's *Music for 18 Musicians* (1974–76) marked a culmination in the development of minimalism and the arrival of a new phase in which its characteristic techniques began to be absorbed into more "maximal" works organized along scenic or structural lines and adhering, at least to some degree, to the principles of functional tonality.

For Glass this phase began in 1976, via his collaboration with the American director Robert Wilson on the opera *EINSTEIN ON THE BEACH.* An epic five-hour, nonnarrative celebration of the irrational, *Einstein* was revolutionary, and since its creation Glass has had an ongoing partnership with Wilson. Glass's production of theatrical works includes the operas *SATYAGRAHA* (1980), *Akhnaten* (1983), *The White Raven,* about Vasco da Gama (composed in 1991, but not staged until 1998), and *The Voyage* (premiered at the Metropolitan Opera in 1992); the chamber operas *The Juniper Tree* (1984) and *The Fall of the House of Usher* (1988); and the "music theater" works *1000 Airplanes on the Roof* (1988), *Hydrogen Jukebox* (1990), and *Monsters of Grace* (1998; a collaboration with Wilson).

Glass is renowned for his film scores, particularly those for the Godfrey Reggio films *KOYAANISQATSI* (1982), *Powaqqatsi* (1987), *Anima Mundi* (1992), and *Naqoyqatsi* (2002). He has also provided the music for Errol Morris's *The Thin Blue Line* (1988) and *A Brief History of Time* (1991), Martin Scorsese's *Kundun* (1997), Peter Weir's *The Truman Show* (1998), and Stephen Daldry's *The Hours* (2002). Glass has written a handful of string quartets and several symphonies, including a pair of titled works, *Low Symphony* (1992) and *Heroes Symphony* (1996), based on themes from pop records by David Bowie and Brian Eno. His orchestral works include a Violin Concerto (1987) and the numbingly amateurish tone poem *The Light* (1987).

Once a radical and unpredictable innovator, Glass has become a victim of his own overproduction. Since the late 1980s he has been little more than a musical cartoonist, trotting out the same thing—with slight variations—every Sunday. *See also* MINIMALISM *and box on page 272.*

RECOMMENDED RECORDINGS

EINSTEIN ON THE BEACH: VARIOUS SOLOISTS; PHILIP GLASS ENSEMBLE (SONY).

KOYAANISQATSI: VARIOUS SOLOISTS; PHILIP GLASS ENSEMBLE (NONESUCH).

MUSIC IN 12 PARTS: PHILIP GLASS ENSEMBLE (NONESUCH).

STRING QUARTETS: KRONOS QUARTET (NONESUCH).

In the last century, in the opinion of Leonard Bernstein among others, the symphony orchestra became a museum, favoring the works of long-dead composers over those of the living. But certain groups—many of them founded by composers—have made it their mission to win audiences for the music written, if not by living composers, then at least by composers not so long ago departed.

Bang on a Can

A large-scale, New York-based new-music concern, it was founded in the early 1980s by three composers—Julia Wolfe, Michael Gordon, and David Lang—who felt that their kind of music (often called "postminimalist") was not being played enough. What began as marathon concert "happenings" (people were encouraged to move freely in and out of the hall) grew into an empire. Bang on a Can now gives concerts all over the world, has a record label and a dedicated performing group (the Bang on a Can All-Stars), and has helped hundreds of composers find an audience for their music.

Ensemble InterContemporain

A group sponsored by the city of Paris, it was founded in 1976 by Pierre Boulez and then-Minister of Culture Michel Guy, with a mission to play the masterworks of the 20th century, and those to come in the 21st. Over the years it has acquired a reputation as being one of the fiercest, most unwavering champions of the most difficult music—especially when helmed by the maître himself, the inexhaustible M. Boulez.

Nouvel Ensemble Moderne

Canada's first chamber orchestra dedicated to new music, it was founded in 1989 by pianist and conductor Lorraine Vaillancourt. It has since become fearless in its programming choices and stylistically wide-ranging in its repertoire, playing everything from David Lang to Elliott Carter, as well as championing less well known composers.

Philip Glass Ensemble

In 1968, composer Philip Glass decided to do things his way: rather than trying to write for standard ensembles and orchestras, he took to the streets, forming his own touring ensemble—three keyboards, some wind instruments, and a singer—dedicated to playing his music alone. It exists to this day, with many of its original members, touring the world, making recordings, as appealing (and loud) as any rock group, and as well honed as any of the world's leading chamber ensembles.

Steve Reich and Musicians

This group, much like the Philip Glass Ensemble, was dedicated solely to performing the works of its founder-composer—though its instrumentation is a little more flexible and the group hasn't stayed as close or performed as often. Steve Reich and Musicians gave the premiere (and subsequent performances of) Reich's seminal *Music for 18 Musicians.*

Speculum Musicae

Founded in 1971, this group consisting of an ever-shifting roster of the most talented freelance musicians in New York has been commissioned and has premiered works by dozens of America's most important composers.

eighth blackbird

Formed at Oberlin Conservatory in 1996, this contemporary-music sextet takes its name from the eighth stanza of Wallace Stevens's poem *Thirteen Ways of Looking at a Blackbird* and consists of Molly Alicia Barth, flute, Michael J. Maccaferri, clarinet, Matt Albert, violin, Nicholas Photinos, cello, Matthew Duvall, percussion, and Lisa Kaplan, piano. In its ten years on the scene it has commissioned works from George Perle (b. 1915), Frederic Rzewski (b. 1938), Joseph Schwantner, Paul Moravec (b. 1957), and Jennifer Higdon (b. 1962), among others. Its recordings and concert programs have featured the music of George Crumb, Joan Tower, Osvaldo Golijov (b. 1960), Perle, Rezewski, and Higdon, and it has presented Schoenberg's *Pierrot lunaire* as a cabaret opera, playing its complex score from memory. The group maintains residencies at the University of Richmond and the University of Chicago, "uses 12 hands, plays over 50 instruments," and records for the Chicago-based Cedille label as well as for Naxos.

glass harmonica *See box on pages 496–97.*

Glazunov, Aleksandr

(b. St. Petersburg, August 10, 1865; d. Paris, March 21, 1936)

RUSSIAN COMPOSER. He began musical studies at nine, progressing so rapidly that by the time he was 14 he was accepted as a private composition pupil by Nikolay Rimsky-Korsakov. His talent was precocious and enormous: He completed his first symphony and first string quartet when he was 16, and at 22 was able to assist Rimsky-Korsakov in completing and orchestrating Borodin's unfinished opera *Prince Igor.* His capacity for work and his compositional output were likewise huge, in spite of an increasingly bibulous nature. By 1906 he had completed eight symphonies, composed numerous overtures and symphonic poems, penned the two ballets for which he is best known—*The Seasons* (1899) with a wonderful autumn bacchanale as its final tableau, and *Raymonda* (1896–97)—and written a violin concerto (1904) that remains a staple of the repertoire.

His appointment in 1905 as director of the St. Petersburg Conservatory opened a new phase of his career, one to which he devoted himself with typical energy and purposefulness. He remained the institution's titular director until 1930, though by 1928 he had left the Soviet Union, disillusioned and largely written out. Though denigrated as a composer of facile charm, Glazunov was a musician of formidable abilities, perfectly attuned to the aesthetic of his youth but unable to adjust to the currents of modernity.

Portrait of Glazunov by Ilya Repin, 1887

RECOMMENDED RECORDINGS

THE SEASONS: ASHKENAZY AND ROYAL PHILHARMONIA ORCHESTRA (DECCA).

SYMPHONIES NOS. 5 AND 8: ANISSIMOV AND MOSCOW SYMPHONY ORCHESTRA (NAXOS).

VIOLIN CONCERTO: HEIFETZ; HENDL AND RCA VICTOR SYMPHONY ORCHESTRA (RCA).

Glier, Reyngol'd

(b. Kiev, January 11, 1875; d. Moscow, June 23, 1956)

RUSSIAN COMPOSER known for the brilliant pictorialism of his ballets. An heir to the tradition of Borodin, Rimsky-Korsakov, and Glazunov, he strove for cinematic colorism in his orchestration, and is considered the father of Soviet—as opposed to Russian—ballet. He studied violin, theory, and composition at the Moscow Conservatory, where his teachers included Mikhail Ippolitov-Ivanov, Anton Arensky, and Sergey Taneyev. He joined the faculty himself in 1920, serving until 1941 as professor of composition. In 1938 he received the title People's Artist of the U.S.S.R., the highest honor for an artist in the Soviet Union.

Glier retained a lifelong interest in the music of the ethnic populations of the Soviet Union, particularly those of the Transcaucasus and his native Ukraine. Many of his stage works derive their subject matter from the folk cultures of these far-flung regions. His reputation outside the Soviet Union rests primarily on his Symphony No. 3 (1909–11), titled *Il'ya Muromets* after a Russian folk hero, and on two of his ballets, *The Red Poppy* (1927) and *The Bronze*

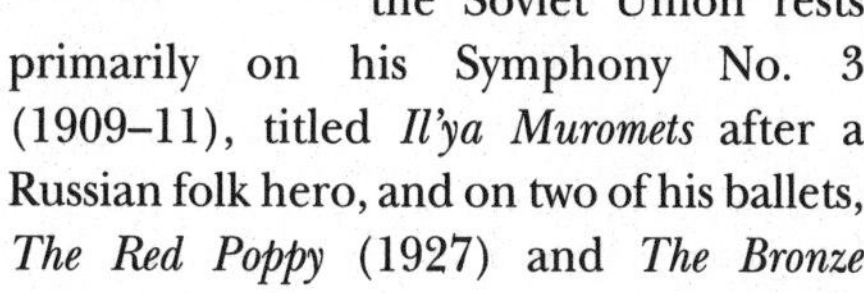

Horseman (1949). The colorful score to *The Red Poppy* includes Glier's most frequently encountered piece, the stirring "Yablochko," or "Russian Sailors' Dance."

RECOMMENDED RECORDINGS

The Red Poppy (complete): Anichanov and St. Petersburg State Symphony Orchestra (Naxos).

The Red Poppy (suite): Downes and BBC Philharmonic Orchestra (Chandos).

Symphony No. 3: Downes and BBC Philharmonic Orchestra (Chandos).

Glinka, Mikhail

(b. Novospasskoye, June 1, 1804; d. Berlin, February 15, 1857)

Russian composer, acknowledged as the father of Russian nationalism. He was born into the landed gentry—his father was a retired army captain—and his musical education was essentially that of a dilettante, albeit a very gifted one. His early interest in music was whetted by hearing and working with the serf musicians on his uncle's estate. He attended boarding school in St. Petersburg (1818–22), where he took a few piano lessons from John Field; later, he received some singing lessons and, during the winter of 1833–34, studied composition with Siegfried Dehn in Berlin. During his adult years he frequently went abroad for extended periods. He spent three years in Italy (1830–33), taking in the latest works of Vincenzo Bellini and Gaetano Donizetti and acquiring a working knowledge of the art of bel canto; ten months in France (1844–45), where he developed a close rapport with Berlioz (whom he had met during his sojourn in Italy); two years in Spain (1845–47); and two more years in France (1852–54).

Mikhail Glinka, father of Russian nationalism, 1852

The influences on Glinka's compositional style included Russian folk music, the BEL CANTO idiom of Bellini in particular, and the "magical" vein of German Romanticism that runs through the works of Carl Maria von Weber. Rather than writing in the Italian style he admired, he was determined to create a distinctively Russian style in opera. He made his breakthrough with *A Life for the Tsar,* composed in 1834–36 to a libretto by Yegor Fyodorovich Rozen, with contributions from several other well-connected literary figures, and premiered December 9, 1836, in St. Petersburg. The opera's story, set in 1613, celebrates the virtues of patriotism and self-sacrifice. The tsar of the title (who does not appear as a character in the opera) is Mikhail Romanov, founder of the Romanov dynasty, the "life" that of the peasant Ivan Susanin, who sacrifices himself to prevent a contingent of Polish soldiers from capturing the tsar. Italian operatic elements abound, but for the first time one finds genuine Russian melodic inflections in the music, particularly in the scenes with chorus.

Immediately after the premiere of *A Life for the Tsar,* Glinka began work on an operatic setting of Pushkin's *Ruslan and Lyudmila.* Pushkin's demise early in 1837 deprived Glinka of the opportunity to work directly with him on the libretto; it took him five years of fitful work to finish the score. *Ruslan and Lyudmila,* while dramatically weaker than *A Life for the Tsar,* is musically stronger. It too is an amalgam of different elements: There is an "Eastern" flavor to some of the material, enhanced by a few borrowings from folk material, and there are allusions to European, specifically Viennese, dance music. What stands out above all is the decidedly advanced treatment of harmony. This is immediately apparent in the overture, by far the most widely known of Glinka's creations—which, thanks to its razzle-dazzle writing, especially for the strings, has won an unassailable place in the orchestral repertoire.

Glinka wrote only a handful of works for the concert stage, but even there he proved an innovator. He was the first Russian composer to draw upon the rhythms and sounds of Spanish music in an orchestral work: his *Capriccio brillante* on the traditional "jota aragonesa," composed in 1845. His other works include the orchestral fantasy *Kamarinskaya* (1848) and *Recuerdos de Castilla* (1848; sometimes referred to as his Second *Spanish Overture*), which he expanded into *Souvenir d'une nuit d'été à Madrid* (*Memory of a Summer Night in Madrid*) in 1851. He composed a significant amount of salon music—variations, dances, characteristic pieces for piano and various chamber groupings—and songs to both Italian and Russian texts, including the cycle *A Farewell to St. Petersburg* (1840).

At once eclectic and inventive, Glinka opened the door for the triumphs of Russian music that would soon follow. His stage works provided models for the historically themed and fantastical operas of Mussorgsky and Rimsky, while his colorful evocations of central-Asian and Iberian settings influenced the orchestral imaginings of Balakirev, Rimsky, and Tchaikovsky. Most significant of all, the harmonic novelty of *Ruslan and Lyudmila* left its mark on the development of musical syntax in Russia right up to Stravinsky.

glissando (pl., glissandi; from Fr. *glisser,* "to slide") A smooth, rapidly executed scale passage. On keyboard instruments glissandos can be produced by drawing the thumb or the knuckles across the keys; on pitched percussion instruments (such as marimba, xylophone, vibraphone, and glockenspiel) by sliding a mallet across the sound bars; and on the harp by sweeping the fingers across the strings. The difference between a glissando and a PORTAMENTO is that a portamento connects two notes of different pitches seamlessly, as though one were bleeding into the other, whereas in a glissando the individual tones or semitones of the scale between the two notes are distinctly sounded, as when one runs a thumbnail across the teeth of a comb. A pair of dreamy glissandos from the harp help set the languorous mood in the opening moments of Debussy's *Prélude à l'après-midi d'un faune.*

glockenspiel Percussion instrument consisting of up to 30 tuned steel bars mounted in a wooden case, arrayed in two ranks like the white and black keys of a piano. It is played using mallets that have small, spherical heads made of rubber, yarn, wood, or metal. When struck, the bars emit a bright, bell-like tone capable of penetrating even the thickest orchestral texture. The glockenspiel can be used to provide reinforcement for flutes, piccolos, and other high-pitched instruments, or by itself for its distinctive color—especially magical when it is played softly. Among notable uses are passages in the works of Mahler (Symphony No. 4, first movement; *Das Lied von der Erde,* second movement), Debussy (*La mer,* second and third movements), and Shostakovich (Symphony No. 5, third movement).

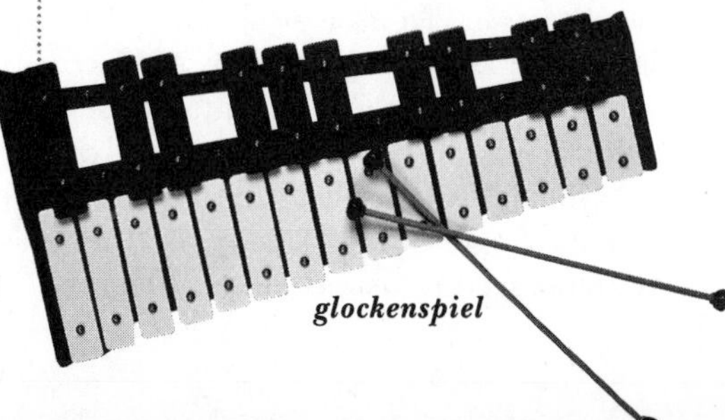
glockenspiel

Gloria Hymn of praise used as the second part of the Ordinary of the Latin Mass, following the Kyrie. The text begins with the words of acclamation delivered by the heavenly host in the account of the Nativity that appears in the Gospel of Luke (2:14): "Gloria in excelsis Deo, et in terra pax hominibus bonae voluntatis . . ." ("Glory to God in the highest, and on earth peace to men of good will . . .") *See also* MASS.

Gluck, Christoph Willibald

(b. Erasbach, July 2, 1714; d. Vienna, November 15, 1787)

BOHEMIAN COMPOSER. He achieved an important reform of serious opera in the mid-18th century, paring back the excesses of Baroque vocal style in favor of a purer, more direct melding of words and music. He was the son and grandson of gamekeepers in the employ of the Lobkowitz family, large landowners in what is today northeastern Bavaria, bordering the Czech Republic. As a child he studied music in school and learned to sing and to play the violin and cello; one early account of his life claims that rather than acquiesce to his father's wishes that he too become a gamekeeper, he ran away from home and supported himself by singing and playing the Jew's harp. He enrolled at the University of Prague in 1731, left without taking a degree, and probably spent a couple of years in Vienna as a chamber musician to the Lobkowitz family. By 1737 he was in Milan, where he came into contact with Sammartini, picking up much of his style and getting first-hand exposure to Italian opera seria. Four years later he composed his first opera, to a libretto by Pietro Metastasio, Vienna's imperial court poet.

Christoph Willibald Gluck

Between 1741 and 1756, Gluck set more than a dozen Metastasian librettos. Residing in London during 1745 and 1746, he encountered the operas of Handel (and may even have met the great man) and showed his skill playing the glass harmonica. For the next six years he was a traveling musician, crisscrossing between Europe's musical capitals—Dresden, Vienna, Hamburg, Copenhagen, Prague, Munich, Naples—with an itinerant opera troupe. He settled in Vienna in 1752 and was active there for more than two decades, becoming musical director at a local theater, responsible both for Lenten concerts and for productions of French *opéra comique.*

The course of Gluck's career changed in 1761, when the Tuscan poet Ranieri Calzabigi arrived in Vienna. Full of the new ideas of the day concerning dramatic aesthetics, Calzabigi was the most notable and effective opponent of Metastasian opera seria, and in him Gluck found the ideal collaborator. The classicizing spirit and sharp point of Calzabigi's librettos for *ORFEO ED EURIDICE* (1762) and *Alceste* (1767) proved tailor-made for Gluck's austere, yet genuinely passionate, music. Both are majestic operas that avoid the vocal display characteristic of opera seria; plots unfold in a straight line, and music and action are powerfully integrated. Just as Calzabigi's terse dramas were a welcome change from the effusions and platitudes that marked opera seria, Gluck's melodic simplicity and chaste scoring, along with his reliance on arioso and his fluid sense of form, were necessary correctives to the florid musical

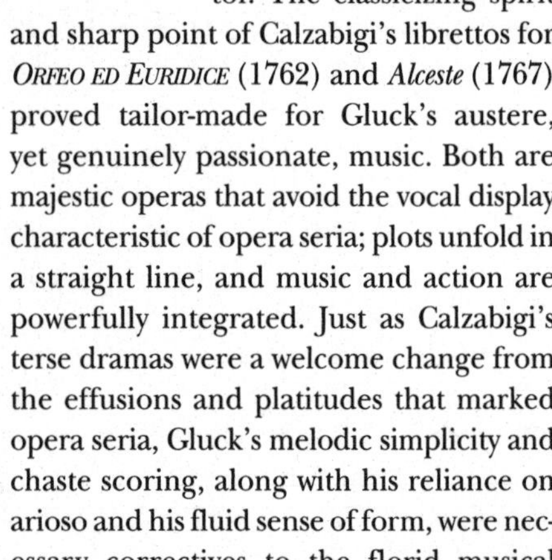

styles of many opera composers. *Orfeo ed Euridice,* which premiered in Vienna right under Metastasio's nose, was hugely successful.

Gluck took over the financial administration of Vienna's main theaters in 1769 and had little success, nearly losing his shirt (he quit the next year). Soon he found a new mission, the renewal of *tragédie lyrique,* the French equivalent of opera seria. In Paris between 1774 and 1779 he produced two new masterpieces, *IPHIGÉNIE EN AULIDE* and *IPHIGÉNIE EN TAURIDE,* and new French versions of earlier hits—*Orphée et Eurydice* and *Alceste.* He spent his final years in Vienna, in semiretirement and declining health, but greatly honored by the Hapsburg dynasty.

An avant-garde figure in his day, Gluck was outdated by the time of his death, overtaken by Mozart and the younger Italians, who were all writing comedies. Gluck's music was a dead end: It lacked the variety of scoring and texture, the play of style, and the long-range harmonic schemes that would allow opera to advance as a dramatic art. Gluck's works quickly disappeared from the repertoire, though the transformation of operatic conventions that he helped bring about—a greater naturalness of action and an increased emphasis on visual and other nonverbal elements to energize the plot—had a profound influence on the genre. Also important was Gluck's use of musical pictorialism: for example, his gloomy portrayal of the underworld in *Orfeo,* or his deft rendering of Orestes' psychological situation in *Iphigénie en Tauride*—when Orestes sings "Le calme rentre dans mon coeur," the ostinato in the violas shows he's anything but calm. These are among the numerous cases in Gluck where the music *is* the drama and where the composer set an example much admired by Berlioz and Wagner. With the recent revival of interest in him, there is a new opportunity for Gluck's works to be better appreciated.

RECOMMENDED RECORDINGS

IPHIGÉNIE EN TAURIDE: MONTAGUE, ALER, ALLEN; GARDINER AND LYON OPERA (PHILIPS).

ORFEO ED EURYDICE: RAGIN, MCNAIR, SIEDEN; GARDINER AND ENGLISH BAROQUE SOLOISTS (PHILIPS).

Glyndebourne Festival, The *See box on pages 46–47.*

Gobbi, Tito

(b. Bassano del Grappa, October 24, 1913; d. Rome, March 5, 1984)

ITALIAN BARITONE. He studied voice in Rome and made his debut at Rome's Teatro Adriano in 1937, as Germont in Verdi's *La traviata.* The conductor Tullio Serafin, in attendance, was impressed enough to offer Gobbi an engagement at the Rome Opera, where, protected from the draft, he sang through the fall of Mussolini's regime and the German occupation, and then on an occasional basis for many seasons. In 1942 he made his La Scala debut, as Belcore in Donizetti's *L'elisir d'amore,* and sang the title role in the Italian premiere of Berg's *Wozzeck* in Rome. Gobbi's international career gained pace after World War II with appearances in Stockholm and at the San Francisco Opera, where he made his American debut, as Figaro in Rossini's *Il barbiere di Siviglia,* in 1948. From 1954 to 1973 he sang regularly in Chicago, and in 1956 he made his Metropolitan Opera debut, as Scarpia in Puccini's *Tosca* opposite Zinka Milanov.

Gobbi was best known for his partnership with Maria Callas, in which

Tito Gobbi

he played a formidable Scarpia to her incendiary Tosca; their legendary chemistry can be heard in the recording of *Tosca* they made in 1953, and seen in a video of the opera's second act, filmed in conjunction with the soprano's farewell performances of the role at Covent Garden in 1964. A magisterial actor, Gobbi possessed a voice of remarkably rich coloration that he used with outstanding intelligence and expressiveness. He proved as gifted in comedy as in more melodramatic parts, and produced a memorable Falstaff and Gianni Schicchi.

RECOMMENDED RECORDINGS

PUCCINI, *TOSCA*: CALLAS, DI STEFANO; DE SABATA AND LA SCALA ORCHESTRA (EMI).

VERDI, *FALSTAFF*: SCHWARZKOPF, ZACCARIA, MOFFO; KARAJAN AND PHILHARMONIA ORCHESTRA (EMI).

***Goldberg* Variations** HARPSICHORD PIECE BY **J. S. BACH,** published in 1741–42 as the fourth part of Bach's *Clavier-Übung* ("keyboard exercise"). The title given there is "Aria with 30 Variations." The variations get their name from Johann Gottlieb Goldberg, who is thought to have been one of Bach's pupils and who from an early age was in the service of Count Kaiserling, the Russian ambassador to the Kingdom of Saxony. Legend has it that Bach composed the variations for Goldberg to play during the small hours of the night when his employer, a noted insomniac, had difficulty getting to sleep. Kaiserling supposedly rewarded Bach with the gift of a golden goblet filled with 100 louis d'or. The reason there is some doubt about the connection between the music and Count Kaiserling is that Goldberg was barely 14 when the variations were published.

The only large-scale set of variations Bach is known to have composed, the *Goldberg* set is based on a lyrical two-part theme in G major from the notebook (*Clavier-Büchlein*) Bach prepared for his second wife, Anna Magdalena, about 1725. The 30 variations function not only as a brilliant investigation of the theme, but as a masterly compendium of Baroque style and a study in how to write idiomatically for the keyboard. The fifth variation, for instance, calls for crossed hands; the seventh is a siciliana; the tenth a fughetta. Variations Nos. 13 and 25 are both embellished arias, while No. 16 is a French overture. The final variation is a quodlibet in which Bach weaves two popular German songs into the texture. After this variation, he repeats the aria, going full circle; it is a wonderful touch, and the final demonstration of Bach's art, for, try as one might, it is impossible to hear the aria the same way *after* the variations as before them. ◉ *See also* CANON, VARIATION.

RECOMMENDED RECORDINGS

HANTAÏ, HARPSICHORD (MIRARE).

PERAHIA, PIANO (SONY).

Golden Cockerel, The OPERA IN A PROLOGUE, THREE ACTS, AND AN EPILOGUE BY **NIKOLAY RIMSKY-KORSAKOV,** to a libretto by Vladimir Bel'sky (based on the tale by Aleksandr Pushkin), composed 1906–07 and premiered in Moscow on October 7, 1909. The fairy-tale plot is an allegory of monarchical foolishness, which Rimsky underscores with outlandishly exaggerated musical gestures and a parodistic treatment of character. ◉ In its sharply colorful scoring and complex harmony—especially in its evocation of the "magical" world of the Astrologer—*The Golden Cockerel* had an immediate influence on the Stravinsky of *The Firebird* and *Petrushka*.

RECOMMENDED RECORDING

(SUITE): MAAZEL AND CLEVELAND ORCHESTRA (DECCA).

Golijov, Osvaldo *See box on pages 708–11.*

gong *See* TAM-TAM.

Górecki, Henryk

(b. Czernica, December 6, 1933)

POLISH COMPOSER. He studied composition at the Music Academy in Katowice, subsequently joining its faculty and serving for four years (1975–79) as its rector. Born less than two weeks after his countryman Krzysztof Penderecki, of the generation following that of Witold Lutosławski and Andrzej Panufnik, his course as a composer has been guided by the centrality of Catholicism to his views of life and art. In much of his music he has drawn on elements of chant to create an austere spirituality similar to that expressed in the music of Arvo Pärt and Sir John Tavener, tapping into the sense of religious hunger that emerged in late-20th-century Europe in countries that, like Poland, spent decades behind the Iron Curtain.

Górecki's three-movement Symphony No. 3 (1976) ◉, known as the SYMPHONY OF SORROWFUL SONGS (*Symfonia piesni żalosnych*), proved to be a work of singular importance to his career and to the unfolding of a postmodernist aesthetic in Europe. Along with Pärt's *Tabula Rasa* (1977), it marked the coming-of-age of European minimalism. What can be said of it can also be said of much of Górecki's other work—where some find it deeply inspiring, others find it unbearably tedious and predictable.

RECOMMENDED RECORDING

SYMPHONY NO. 3: UPSHAW; ZINMAN AND LONDON SINFONIETTA (NONESUCH).

Götterdämmerung (Twilight of the Gods)

OPERA IN THREE ACTS AND A PROLOGUE BY RICHARD WAGNER, to his own libretto, composed 1869–74 as the final part of the *RING* cycle, and premiered August 17, 1876, at the Festspielhaus in Bayreuth, Hans Richter conducting. The opera's complicated plot is advanced by some of the greatest music Wagner wrote. In the first scene of the prologue, the three Norns, spinning the thread of fate, recall some of the events that have already occurred in the saga of the *Ring*; becoming agitated by a vision of the stolen Rhine gold, they break the thread, presaging the end of the world. The scene shifts to Brünnhilde's rock. From the mouth of the cave where they have cohabited since the end of *SIEGFRIED*, Siegfried and Brünnhilde greet the dawn and celebrate their happy union. Siegfried sets off on a journey down the Rhine, magnificently reported by Wagner's orchestra.

In the opera's first act, Siegfried visits the Gibichungs, Gunther and Gutrune, and meets their gloomy half-brother Hagen, son of the Nibelung, Alberich. Administered a magic potion, Siegfried loses all memory of Brünnhilde and their love; swearing an oath of brotherhood with Gunther, he returns to Brünnhilde's rock disguised as Gunther, and forcibly claims the horrified Brünnhilde as a prize. In Act II, Siegfried, still in the dark, prepares to marry Gutrune, while against her will Brünnhilde is compelled to be Gunther's bride. In fury at her betrayal by Siegfried, the Valkyrie avenges herself by revealing his one weakness to Hagen. Act III opens with an encounter between Siegfried and the Rhine Maidens. In the forest, Hagen murders Siegfried, who in his dying moments returns to his senses, remembering Brünnhilde. In the opera's mind-boggling denouement, Brünnhilde immolates herself on Siegfried's funeral pyre, sparks from which set Valhalla on fire. The Rhine overflows its banks and the Rhine Maidens get back the ring. Thus the reign of the gods ends, and the world is redeemed by love.

The culmination of the scene with the three Norns in the opera's prologue is among the most powerful moments in all of Wagner, while the second act is a tour de force of musical tension, with gripping ensemble passages and a glorious choral finale. Yet Wagner manages to trump all this in the paroxysmal music of Brünnhilde's immolation scene, a finale of superhuman scale, and the fitting end to a cycle that remains the crowning glory of Romantic opera.

RECOMMENDED RECORDING

NILSSON, WINDGASSEN, FISCHER-DIESKAU, FRICK; SOLTI AND VIENNA PHILHARMONIC (DECCA).

Gottschalk, Louis Moreau

(b. New Orleans, May 8, 1829; d. Tijuca, Brazil, December 18, 1869)

AMERICAN PIANIST AND COMPOSER, the first American musician to achieve international celebrity. Born to a German Jewish father and a French Creole mother, he showed prodigious talents as a child and was sent to Paris at the age of 12; though barred from auditioning at the Conservatoire because he was a foreigner, he studied privately, first with Charles Hallé, then with Camille Stamaty, who was also teaching another prodigy, Camille Saint-Saëns. Gottschalk made his official debut in 1849, creating a sensation with the public and earning praise from the critics for both his compositions and his keyboard virtuosity, which was compared with Chopin's. After returning to the United States in 1853, heaped with European accolades, he devoted the next three years to touring and to composing pieces tailored to American sentiments and musical tastes.

In 1857 he headed to Havana with the not quite 14-year-old soprano Adelina Patti in tow; he decided to stay on in the West Indies for the next five years, based first in Guadeloupe, then Havana. He played a bit, composed in the Caribbean style, and wrote articles for the American and French press. Impelled by strong pro-Union sympathies, he returned to the United States after the outbreak of the Civil War, and between 1862 and 1865 gave more than 1,000 concerts, anywhere there was a piano, living what he called "la vie de carpetbag." By the end of the Civil War, he had racked up 95,000 miles on the rails, and had done more to further the Union cause than any other American musician.

His last four years were spent in South America, feverishly devoted to concertizing as he toured through Peru, Chile, Argentina, Uruguay, and Brazil. His death at the age of 40—most likely from an overdose of quinine administered to treat malaria—broke the hearts of fans all over the world. Gottschalk created more than 300 works, mostly piano pieces. His compositional skills were limited if not rudimentary, but many of his notions were brilliantly original—throughout his music there are adumbrations of Ives (particularly his use of quotation as a musical device) as well as of ragtime (in his syncopated rhythms). His First Symphony, subtitled *La nuit des tropiques* (*A Night in the Tropics*), composed 1858–59 and first performed in Havana in 1860, is a particularly effective concert piece, as is his *Grand Tarantelle* for piano and orchestra (1858–64). Among his early hits were the "Creole" solo piano pieces *Bamboula* (ca. 1846–48) and *Le bananier, chanson nègre* (ca. 1848). Later triumphs included *Union* (1852–62), a concert paraphrase on the "Star Spangled Banner," "Yankee Doodle," and "Hail Columbia"; *The Dying Poet* (1863); and *Morte!!* (*She Is*

Louis Moreau Gottschalk in the 1860s

Dead!!), his tear-jerking lamentation of 1868. Though Gottschalk's output is dismissed by many highbrows as flashy or sentimental, there is a seductive charm in much of it. At its best, it displays brilliant vitality, originality, and irrepressible rhythmic drive.

RECOMMENDED RECORDINGS

A Night in the Tropics, *Grand Tarantelle*: Abravanel and Utah Symphony Orchestra (Vanguard).

Piano music (including *Bamboula*, *Union*, *The Dying Poet*): Licad (Naxos).

Gould, Glenn

(b. Toronto, September 25, 1932; d. Toronto, October 4, 1982)

CANADIAN PIANIST, WRITER, AND COMMENTATOR. A mix of wild intellectual flamboyance and Zen-like introspection, he was one of the most probing and unorthodox musicians of the 20th century. He took an illuminating if idiosyncratic approach to nearly everything he played, electrifying audiences during the course of a performing career that lasted less than a decade—from 1955, the date of his American debut, until he retired from concertizing in 1964 at the age of 31—and tantalizing music lovers thereafter with an extraordinary body of radio and television essays and recordings, his true legacy.

Gould's father was a furrier and his mother a skilled musician who gave him lessons at the piano practically from his infancy. An only child, he developed into a precociously gifted adolescent misfit. He enrolled at the Toronto Conservatory at the age of ten, studying with Alberto Guerrero and dropping out of school when he was 19 to concentrate full-time on music. He did not attend college. After performing to local acclaim in Canada, he made his American debut in Washington, D.C., on January 2, 1955, at the Phillips Collection. A performance in New York's Town Hall the following week, in front of an audience of 35 (there would have been fewer had word of his Washington performance not preceded him), created a sensation. By the time he left New York a few days later, he had a contract with Columbia Records.

Glenn Gould, tamer of the wild Steinway, 1955

He performed in the Soviet Union in 1957 and undertook an extended concert tour of Europe and Israel in the summer of 1958. The following year he played a career-high 51 concerts, not a particularly large number. In April 1962, his performances of the Brahms D minor concerto with Leonard Bernstein and the New York Philharmonic—in which he opted for a glacial tempo in the first movement—were prefaced by an all but unprecedented podium disclaimer from Bernstein, and elicited a scathing review from Harold Schonberg in *The New York Times*. Gould gave only two concerts in 1964, then retired from the stage for good. For the rest of his life he led a reclusive existence, doing radio and television work for the

Canadian Broadcasting Company, recording occasionally, sleeping during the day, and keeping in touch with a handful of friends via late-night phone calls. He died of a stroke a few days after his 50th birthday.

What made Gould a great pianist—a strong mother-son bond formed at the piano and expressed through music—also made him a psychic cripple his entire life. As an adult he was incapable of dealing with emotion outside the musical realm and unable to form close personal relationships. He was anxious, obsessive, and afraid—of crowds, travel, anger, germs—and gripped by a hypochondria so severe that it led to dangerous forays into self-medication.

As a musician, Gould's primary interest was in polyphony, which caused him to develop a highly articulate style of playing and to emphasize, sometimes in strikingly unconventional ways, the individual strands of a musical texture. His fascination with the inner workings of scores resulted in performances that were often more like provocations than anything else, though he could be remarkably contemplative, even sensuous in an intensely ascetic way. Gould was a natural for the medium of radio—he loved the microphone and hated the audience, the opposite of most performers.

Throughout his career Gould was closely identified with the music of J. S. Bach, which he played in a manner that could be as infuriating to some as it was illuminating to others. His antiheroic stance toward the Beethoven sonatas was also controversial, as was his playing of Brahms's late piano pieces, which Gould himself characterized as "sexy," though his performances of them seemed informed by the most profound melancholy. Gould championed the music of Schoenberg, and dismissed most of Mozart and Chopin.

Ever the narcissist, Gould found his perfect companion in the piano—it said only what he wanted it to say, and never talked back. More than two decades after his death, he remains one of the most significant performing artists of recent times, about whom more has been written than any other musician of his generation, save Elvis Presley.

RECOMMENDED RECORDINGS

BACH, *GOLDBERG* VARIATIONS (SONY; REC. 1955).

BACH, *THE WELL-TEMPERED CLAVIER*, BOOKS I AND II (SONY).

BEETHOVEN, SYMPHONIES NOS. 5 AND 6, ARR. LISZT (SONY).

BRAHMS, LATE PIANO PIECES (SONY).

Gounod, Charles

(b. Paris, June 17, 1818; d. Saint-Cloud, October 18, 1893)

FRENCH COMPOSER, best known for his opera *Faust* (1859), which became one of the most popular works in the repertoire. His father was a highly regarded painter and engraver, and his mother was an accomplished pianist; the talents of both rubbed off on Charles, who early on showed gifts for music and drawing. He studied privately with Antoine Reicha, and then at the Paris Conservatoire with Ferdinando Paer, Jean-François Le Sueur, and Fromental Halévy, and won the Prix de Rome in 1839. Gounod adored Italy and immersed himself in the study of Renaissance polyphony, especially the music of Palestrina, which he echoed in a pair of early masses written in 1841 and 1843. While in Rome he met Fanny Mendelssohn Hensel; on his way back to Paris he stopped in Leipzig to visit Felix Mendelssohn, whose music and character left an indelible impression. In 1843, Gounod became music director at the Séminaire des Missions Etrangères in Paris. In 1847 he began to study for the

Charles Gounod in 1841

priesthood, a course he abandoned after a few months. He married in 1851 and played an active role in Parisian musical life during the following decade. Opera was still at the center of the compositional scene, and Gounod quickly established himself as a force to be reckoned with. His first effort, *Sapho* (1851), received only four performances in spite of having the great Pauline Viardot in its title role. This was followed by *La nonne sanglante* (1854) and *Le médecin malgré lui* (1858), whose libretto, after Molière, was provided by the team of Jules Barbier and Michel Carré. The same partnership had already supplied Gounod with the libretto for FAUST, which after a slow start met with extraordinary success, catapulting its composer to international prominence. *Faust* richly earned its popularity. A work of enormous accomplishment—colorful, engaging, and tuneful, if not very deep dramatically—it demonstrated a mastery of all the clichés of French grand opera and achieved a remarkable scenic splendor. Gounod never again managed anything quite as magnificent, though his ROMÉO ET JULIETTE (1867) came close.

Fatigued by the labor he expended on the 12 operas he wrote (notwithstanding the fame and wealth they brought), Gounod felt the need to turn periodically to sacred music as a restorative. His production in that area was substantial, and included 21 masses, three oratorios, and numerous cantatas, motets, and informal settings of sentimental religious texts. In 1870, during the Franco-Prussian War, Gounod fled to London. The English, with their strong choral tradition, loved his religious music, and he stayed in Britain for nearly four years, becoming the first conductor of the Royal Albert Hall Choral Society.

In addition to works for the stage and sacred music, Gounod wrote some piano pieces, many songs, and a small amount of chamber music. One of his piano pieces, the "Funeral March of a Marionette" (1872), became well known as the theme music for television's *Alfred Hitchcock Presents.* And while *Faust* is more famous, Gounod's most widely performed creation is the little *mélodie religieuse* "Ave Maria" that he arranged in 1859, based on Bach's C major prelude from Book I of *Das wohltemperirte Clavier.* Because of music like this, many of Gounod's younger contemporaries looked down on him as bourgeois. But, as even the hypercritical Debussy had to admit, Gounod represented an era in French art, and the accomplishment of works such as *Faust* and *Roméo et Juliette* provided an important bulwark against the encroachments of Wagnerism.

RECOMMENDED RECORDINGS

FAUST: HADLEY, GASDIA, RAMEY: RIZZI AND WELSH NATIONAL OPERA (TELDEC).

ROMÉO ET JULIETTE: ALAGNA, GHEORGHIU, VAN DAM; PLASSON AND ORCHESTRE DU CAPITOLE DE TOULOUSE (EMI).

Goyescas, o Los majos enamorados (Young Men in Love) PIANO SUITE BY ENRIQUE GRANADOS consisting of six pieces, each a musical reflection on a portrait by Francisco José de Goya, the composer's favorite artist. The first four pieces, including the hauntingly beautiful nocturne "Quejas, o La maja y el ruiseñor" ("Laments, or The Maiden and the Nightingale") ◉, were published in 1912; the remaining two pieces appeared in 1913. The suite as a whole is remarkable for its melodic expressiveness and for Granados's exquisite, highly improvisatory treatment of color, harmony, and rhythm. He later used the music from the piano suite in an opera of the same title.

A scene from the premiere of Goyescas *at the Metropolitan Opera, 1916*

RECOMMENDED RECORDING

LARROCHA (DECCA).

grace note An ornamental note, usually of short duration, appended to another note. In written notation, grace notes appear smaller than the notes they ornament, and are often written with a slash through the stem. *See also* APPOGGIATURA.

Graham, Susan

(b. Roswell, N.M., July 23, 1960)

AMERICAN MEZZO-SOPRANO. She studied at Texas Tech University and the Manhattan School of Music, and won the Metropolitan Opera National Council Auditions in 1988. After engagements with Opera Theatre of Saint Louis (Erika in Samuel Barber's *Vanessa*) and in Seattle, Chicago, and Washington, she made her first Met appearances during the 1991–92 season, as Octavian in Richard Strauss's *Der Rosenkavalier* and Cherubino in Mozart's *Le nozze di Figaro.* Pants roles continued to be her calling card in opera houses in Europe and the U.S.: In 1993 she sang Cecilio in Mozart's *Lucio Silla* at the Salzburg Festival and in 1994 made her Covent Garden debut in the title role of Massenet's *Chérubin.*

Graham has premiered several important new works, creating the title role in Alexander Goehr's *Ariana* (1995, Covent Garden), Jordan in John Harbison's *The Great Gatsby* (1999, Metropolitan Opera) and Sister Helen in Jake Heggie's *Dead Man Walking* (2000, San Francisco Opera). In December 2005 she created the role of Sondra Finchley in Tobias Picker's *An American Tragedy* at the Metropolitan Opera. In 2003, she turned to comedy, taking on the title roles in Offenbach's *La belle Hélène* and Lehár's *Die lustige Witwe.* She has also worked with period-instrument specialists William Christie, for a Paris production of Handel's *Alcina* with Renée Fleming, and Emanuelle Haim, for Purcell's *Dido and Aeneas,* both of which were recorded. In 2003, she sang her first Didon in Berlioz's *Les Troyens,* in Paris. She has often sung Marguerite in Berlioz's *La damna-*

The eyes of the world are on Texas's Susan Graham.

tion de Faust and has been praised for her performances of Berlioz's *Les nuits d'été* and Ravel's *Shéhérazade,* as well as for her interprations of the songs of Debussy, Ravel, and Reynaldo Hahn.

Graham's extensive discography reflects her wide interests, ranging from the songs of Ned Rorem to overlooked operas such as Gluck's *Iphigénie en Tauride,* Berlioz's *Béatrice et Bénédict,* and Barber's *Vanessa.* Her recording of Charles Ives's songs with pianist Pierre-Laurent Aimard won the 2005 Grammy for Best Classical Vocal Performance.

RECOMMENDED RECORDINGS

"ARTIST'S PORTRAIT" (ARIAS BY HANDEL, GLUCK, OTHERS): BICKET AND CITY OF BIRMINGHAM SYMPHONY; NELSON AND LYON OPERA; OTHERS (WARNER CLASSICS).

HANDEL, *ALCINA*: FLEMING, DESSAY, KUHLMANN; CHRISTIE AND LES ARTS FLORISSANTS (ELEKTRA).

RAVEL, *SHÉHÉREZADE*: TORTELIER AND BBC SYMPHONY ORCHESTRA (WARNER).

Grainger, Percy

(b. Brighton, Australia, July 8, 1882; d. White Plains, N.Y., February 20, 1961)

AUSTRALIAN/AMERICAN PIANIST AND COMPOSER. Home-schooled by his mother, he made his debut as a pianist in Melbourne in 1894. From 1895 to 1901 he attended the Hoch Conservatory in Frankfurt, where he studied with James Kwast. Between 1901 and 1914 he resided mainly in London, moving to the United States after the outbreak of World War I. He served as a musician in the U.S. Army during 1917–19. Following his mother's suicide in 1922, he spent several years wandering the world trying to get his bearings. He married in 1928 and settled down in the New York area, where he devoted himself to teaching, lecturing, composing, and giving the occasional performance of his own music. He was among the great piano virtuosos of his time and a composer of

Percy Grainger

some merit, though his reputation today rests on such lighter fare as "Handel in the Strand" and folk-song arrangements like "Country Gardens" and "Molly on the Shore." His most significant extended work was *The Warriors* (1916), a splashily scored piece for three pianos and orchestra, which he subtitled "music for an imaginary ballet."

Athletic, energetic, eccentric, Grainger was a tireless proponent of music as a visceral and imaginative exercise rather than an intellectual "art." In his studio he would jump over the piano rather than walk around it when he needed to show a fingering to a student; as a performer he was fond of walking to the town where he was performing, and famed for his muscular accounts of works like the Grieg concerto. Behind his physical bravado lay deep neuroses that for most of his life made him an emotional wreck. Yet there was a wonderfully gentle and sentimental side to his musicianship, which can be felt in works like his *Ramble on Love,* a meltingly beautiful arrangement of the love duet from the end of Richard Strauss's *Der Rosenkavalier*, written as a tender tribute to his mother, Rose.

RECOMMENDED RECORDINGS

PIANO MUSIC: HAMELIN (HYPERION).

THE WARRIORS: GARDINER AND PHILHARMONIA ORCHESTRA (DG).

Granados, Enrique [Enríc]

(b. Lérida, July 27, 1867; d. at sea aboard the Sussex, *March 24, 1916)*

CATALAN COMPOSER AND PIANIST. Like his elder colleague Isaac Albéniz, he composed in a variety of genres but achieved his most effective expression at the piano. Also like Albéniz, he was influenced by the musicologist Felipe Pedrell to seek a Spanish direction in his art. He studied piano as a child in Barcelona, and at the age of 13 became a student of Joan Pujol, who had been Albéniz's teacher. He later audited classes at the Paris Conservatoire (1887–89), and in 1890 made his recital debut at Barcelona's Teatro Lírico. He won short-term success with an early opera, *María del Carmen*, premiered in Madrid in 1898, and in 1901 he founded his own music school, the Academia Granados.

Enrique Granados

Granados's music is sophisticated, intimate, suffused with a gentle ardor—as the man himself was. His most important work was the piano suite in two books *GOYESCAS, O LOS MAJOS ENAMORADOS* (*Young Men in Love*; 1909–12), inspired by the tapestry cartoons of Francisco José de Goya on display at the Prado in Madrid. ◉ He subsequently created an opera, also titled *Goyescas* (based on the music of the piano suite), which received its premiere at the Metropolitan Opera on January 28, 1916. Following the work's premiere, Granados accepted an invitation to the White House from President Woodrow Wilson, a gesture that turned out to have fatal consequences. In order to make the journey to Washington, he had to cancel his planned return to Europe and book passage at a later date. Following an uneventful Atlantic crossing, Granados and his wife were aboard the SS *Sussex* when it was torpedoed in the English Channel by a German U-boat. Granados survived the attack, but jumped out of his lifeboat in a desperate attempt to save his wife, and drowned with her. On May 7, 1916, the Met presented a benefit concert for the six orphaned children the couple left behind.

RECOMMENDED RECORDINGS

DANZAS ESPAÑOLAS: LARROCHA (RCA).

GOYESCAS (PIANO SUITE): LARROCHA (DECCA).

grand opera Style of opera characterized by spectacular scenery, elaborate effects, and grandiose staging, developed in Paris during the early decades of the 19th century. Its *spiritus rector* was the librettist Eugène Scribe, an inexhaustible writer who worked an endless number of variations on the same basic formula: the parade of history in five acts of pageantry and extravagance, with central characters caught in the flux of religious or patriotic movements, huge tableaux involving the chorus, solemn processionals, and awesome denouements. In its heyday, during the 1830s and 1840s, grand opera was big business. Fortunes were made and lost on a regular basis, often depending upon the whim of the claque, whose caesar, Auguste Levasseur, was another of the era's aptly named figures.

Among the first works in the style was Daniel-François-Esprit Auber's *La muette de Portici* (1828), which took as its subject the 1647 Neapolitan revolt against Spain and ended with no less than the eruption of Vesuvius (poetic license, as the eruption portrayed occurred in 1631). Rossini's *Guillaume Tell* (1829), on another historico-patriotic theme, brought the Swiss Alps to the stage of the Paris Opéra, concentrated on the protagonist's feelings of duty to his family and society, and relied for much of its effect on superbly gauged crowd scenes. Fromental Halévy (1799–1862), whose *La Juive* received its premiere in 1835, was another leading composer in the style. But for more than 30 years, it was the German-born Giacomo Meyerbeer who ruled the roost in Paris. Meyerbeer's debut effort, *Robert le diable* (1831), became one of the most popular of all grand operas. He achieved even greater glory with *Les Huguenots* (1836) and *Le prophète* (1849), both touching on themes of religious fanaticism and political tumult, the latter creating a sensation with its Act III depiction of the rising sun—the first use of electric lighting on the stage. Finally, with *L'Africaine* (posthumously premiered in 1865), Meyerbeer gave impetus to the orientalist vogue that would influence *Aida.* Gounod stole plenty of grand-opera thunder in his setting of *Faust* (1859), and elements of the genre survived all the way up to Debussy's *Pelléas et Mélisande* (1902). In between came what many would argue was the greatest of all grand operas by a Frenchman, Berlioz's *Les Troyens,* which was spurned by the Paris Opéra and not performed in its entirety until 1890 (and then in Germany), 21 years after the composer's death.

Ever since the mid-19th century, critics have condemned grand opera as a dramatically shallow premise, a magnificent ship with an inadequate engine that went straight to the bottom as soon as it was launched. But Parisian grand opera provided a blueprint for many of the finest works of the mid- and late 19th century: Tchaikovsky's *The Maid of Orleans* and *Mazeppa,* Mussorgsky's *Boris Godunov* and *Khovanshchina,* and numerous creations of Verdi and Wagner—among them *Don Carlo, Il trovatore, Otello, Aida, Der fliegende Holländer, Tannhäuser, Lohengrin, Parsifal,* and *Götterdämmerung*—would have been unthinkable without it. The influence of grand opera continued to be felt in the 20th century in works such as Britten's *Peter Grimes* (1945) and Poulenc's *Dialogues des Carmélites* (1957), and will doubtless be felt in the 21st as long as composers and operagoers retain a taste for the sublime.

The interior of the Paris Opéra

RECOMMENDED RECORDINGS

AUBER, *LA MUETTE DE PORTICI*: KRAUS, ANDERSON, ALER; FULTON AND MONTE-CARLO PHILHARMONIC ORCHESTRA (EMI).

HALÉVY, *LA JUIVE*: VARADY, ANDERSON, CARRERAS; ALMEIDA AND PHILHARMONIA ORCHESTRA (PHILIPS).

MEYERBEER, *LES HUGUENOTS*: SUTHERLAND, VRENIOS, BACQUIER; BONYNGE AND NEW PHILHARMONIA ORCHESTRA (DECCA).

Graun, Carl Heinrich

(b. Wahrenbrück, 1704; d. Berlin, August 8, 1759)

GERMAN COMPOSER, considered with Johann Adolf Hasse (1699–1783) the leading exponent of Italian opera seria in Germany during the 18th century. He was educated at the Kreuzschule in Dresden and spent a year at the University of Leipzig. Starting out as a boy chorister, he developed into a capable cellist and keyboard player. His first professional appointment, from 1724, was as tenor at the ducal court in Brunswick, where his duties also included composing. His first operas, composed for the Brunswick court, betray an Italian influence—not surprising for one brought up in Dresden, the center of Italian opera in 18th-century Germany.

In 1735 Graun was hired away from Brunswick by the Prussian crown prince Frederick, later to rule as Frederick the Great, whose dream was to establish a court opera in Berlin. Following his ascent to the throne in 1740, Frederick sent Graun to Italy to recruit singers for the venture. Graun was appointed Kapellmeister in 1741 and quickly built a first-rate company, which took its place in a magnificent new opera house on Unter den Linden (now the home of the Deutsche Staatsoper). During his career, Graun set librettos by Apostolo Zeno, Pietro Metastasio, and Francesco Algarotti, as well as several by his royal employer, including those to *Silla* (1753) and *Montezuma* (1755). His work was closely scrutinized by that most musical of monarchs, which led an earlier generation of scholars to presume that some of his stylistic innovations—particularly the use of cavatinas in place of da capo arias in works such as *Semiramide* (1754) and *Montezuma* —were imposed on him by Frederick; that no longer seems to have been the case. In addition to operas, Graun also composed a number of cantatas in the Italian style for solo voice, strings, and continuo; several dozen sinfonias and concertos; and a small amount of chamber music.

RECOMMENDED RECORDING

CLEOPATRA E CESARE: WILLIAMS, VERMILLION; JACOBS AND CONCERTO KÖLN (HARMONIA MUNDI).

grave (It.) Serious. As a tempo marking it implies an extremely slow pace, slower than *adagio* or *largo*.

grazioso (It.) Dainty, gracious, pretty. It is most often encountered as the pendant to a standard tempo marking (e.g., *Allegretto grazioso,* in Dvořák's Symphony No. 8 in G, third movement, and in Brahms's Symphony No. 2 in D, third movement). Occasionally it serves as a tempo indication in its own right, as in the rondo finale of Beethoven's Piano Sonata in A, Op. 2, No. 2.

Greeting Prelude ORCHESTRAL PIECE BY IGOR STRAVINSKY, composed for the 80th birthday of conductor Pierre Monteux and played for the first time as a surprise gift to him on April 4, 1955, by the Boston Symphony Orchestra under the baton of Charles Munch. Lasting less than a minute, it is an arrangement of the song "Happy Birthday to You," deconstructed, reharmonized, and scored in Stravinsky's typically spiky, mosaic-like manner.

RECOMMENDED RECORDING

THOMAS AND LONDON SYMPHONY ORCHESTRA (RCA).

Grieg, Edvard

(b. Bergen, June 15, 1843; d. Bergen, September 4, 1907)

NORWEGIAN COMPOSER AND PIANIST OF SCOTTISH ANCESTRY. Grieg's mother was a pianist, his father a merchant who also served as British consul at Bergen (as had his father before him). The connection to Scotland came from Edvard's great-grandfather, Alexander Greig, who emigrated from Aberdeen to Bergen in 1779 and changed the name. Grieg began piano lessons with his mother at six, and at the urging of the Norwegian violin virtuoso Ole Bull was sent to study piano, theory, and composition at the Leipzig Conservatory (1858–62). The separation

Edvard Grieg

from his family made him homesick, and he was unhappy with the hidebound German curriculum, but he stuck it out, and while in Leipzig acquired a taste for Schumann's piano music. After a year back in Norway he decided to continue his studies in Copenhagen (1863–65), where he came to the attention of the Danish composer Niels Gade, who encouraged him to write a symphony. Grieg did so, although even then he knew that he possessed greater gifts as a miniaturist. (He later withdrew the piece from performance.)

In a search for roots, Grieg developed a keen interest in Norwegian folk music. He moved back to Norway and in 1867 married his cousin, Nina Hagerup, a talented singer. Grieg's repatriation and the marriage produced a musical awakening; his first set of *Lyric Pieces* for the piano was closely followed by the immensely popular Piano Concerto in A minor, composed in 1868 and premiered in Copenhagen on April 3, 1869, with dedicatee Edmund Neupert as soloist. ◉ For the concert's finale Grieg drew on a characteristic Norwegian dance, the *halling,* and saved one of his most soulful melodies for use as the second subject. First heard in the flute, it returns in brassy splendor for the end of the work, a glorious unison between piano and full orchestra in A major.

While on a sojourn in Rome in 1869–70, Grieg had several encounters with Liszt; at one of them Liszt played Grieg's concerto at sight and gave it a ringing endorsement. In 1874, the playwright Henrik Ibsen asked Grieg to compose incidental music for the first staging of *Peer Gynt*; that same year Grieg was awarded an annual stipend by the Norwegian national assembly. From 1880 to 1882, he was conductor of the Bergen Philharmonic Society, and in 1884, to mark the bicentennial of the birth of the great Norwegian playwright Ludvig Holberg, he composed the suite for strings *From Holberg's Time.* Around this time the Griegs began building a villa south of Bergen. Here Grieg would spend spring and summer composing and wandering the countryside; the winter and fall were for travel and concert tours throughout Europe. Grieg's health went into decline around 1900 (he had a history of lung trouble). He composed little in his final years, but kept up an active performing schedule right to the end.

Grieg was first and foremost a composer of songs and keyboard miniatures. His exceptional craftsmanship, combined with his intuitive feel for the rhythmic patterns, harmonic oddities, and melodic characteristics of folk music, is what gives these pieces their unique appeal. The songs show Grieg at his best, not surprising in view of his extraordinary melodic gift. There are 25 sets in all, to German and Scandinavian texts, and they reflect Grieg's characteristic blend of Romantic sentiment and nationalistic inflection. Notable is the heart-melting *"Jeg elsker dig"* ("I Love You"), set to the words of Hans Christian Andersen.

Grieg was an excellent pianist, and his deep understanding of the instrument shows throughout the solo piano music.

The beautiful, idiomatic *Lyric Pieces* (Grieg wrote ten sets of them) are not virtuoso concert efforts but are rewarding to the capable amateur, with enough in them to be treasured by the accomplished professional. Of chamber works there are just a few; the String Quartet in G minor, from 1878, is a serious, well-crafted score worthy of comparison with similar efforts by Smetana and Dvořák.

The most popular of Grieg's works are the Piano Concerto and the music for *PEER GYNT.* The former was a special triumph, establishing the composer on the international scene and, for the remainder of his life, winning acclaim as the most successful of his large-scale concert works. The influence of Schumann is evident, but the work's ardor and melodic freshness sweep all reservations aside. *Peer Gynt* is particularly notable for its evocation of mood and atmosphere, an area in which Grieg can be seen as a forerunner of 20th-century musical Impressionism, and an influence on the thinking not only of Debussy, Ravel, and Delius, but of Sibelius and Bartók as well.

RECOMMENDED RECORDINGS

LYRIC PIECES: GILELS (DG).

PEER GYNT (COMPLETE): JÄRVI AND GOTHENBURG SYMPHONY ORCHESTRA (DG).

PEER GYNT SUITES, *HOLBERG* SUITE: BERLIN PHILHARMONIC (DG).

PIANO CONCERTO: PERAHIA; DAVIS AND BAVARIAN RADIO SYMPHONY ORCHESTRA (SONY).

Griffes, Charles Tomlinson

(b. Elmira, N.Y., September 17, 1884; d. New York, April 8, 1920)

AMERICAN COMPOSER. During his brief life, cut short by influenza when he was just 35, he created a valuable body of work that was distinctive in tone and exquisitely well crafted. Intent on a career as a concert pianist, he went to Berlin in 1903 to study at the Stern Conservatory, taking private lessons from Engelbert Humperdinck. He returned to the United States in 1907 and became a schoolmaster at the Hackley School for Boys in Tarrytown, New York, where he taught until his death. His early works were substantially indebted to German late Romanticism, but beginning around 1911 his music took on an Impressionist cast, its scoring and harmony clearly influenced by Debussy. A fondness for exotic scales and other "orientalisms" became apparent about 1917, and in the works of Griffes's final years—particularly the Piano Sonata (1917–18) and the *Three Poems of Fiona McLeod* (1918)—a darker, more dissonant and emotionally urgent idiom began to emerge.

Charles Tomlinson Griffes

Griffes was a first-rate colorist, and the best known of his compositions, the sultry, languorous piano vignette *The White Peacock* (1915; orchestrated 1919), is as fine a piece of tone-painting as anything by Debussy or Ravel. Yet as outstanding as he was in the Impressionist vein, Griffes inclined emotionally toward the Romantic, and in works such as *The Pleasure-Dome of Kubla Khan* (1912; orchestrated 1917) and the *McLeod* songs, one quickly becomes aware of a volcanic passion lying just beneath the music's sensuous surface.

RECOMMENDED RECORDINGS

PIANO WORKS (WITH WORKS OF MACDOWELL): TOCCO (GASPARO).

THE PLEASURE-DOME OF KUBLA KHAN, THE WHITE PEACOCK, THREE POEMS OF FIONA MCLEOD: FALLETTA AND BUFFALO PHILHARMONIC ORCHESTRA (NAXOS).

Grofé, Ferde

(b. New York, March 27, 1892; d. Santa Monica, Calif., April 3, 1972)

AMERICAN COMPOSER AND ARRANGER who found his niche as a musical landscape painter. In the early years of his career he was a viola player in the Los Angeles Philharmonic and the San Francisco Symphony Orchestra. He joined Paul Whiteman's band in 1920, and had the great luck of being in the right place at the right time—as Whiteman's arranger when George Gershwin came along with his *Rhapsody in Blue.* Grofé's orchestration of the piece was magnificently adept, and in subsequent works such as his *Mississippi: A Journey in Tones* (1925) and *Grand Canyon Suite* (1931)—both produced for Whiteman—he showed that he could write brilliantly atmospheric and descriptive music of his own, notable above all for its spectacular orchestration. He remained something of a one-trick pony, never again achieving the cinematic breadth and glorious coloration of his *Grand Canyon Suite,* but in that one work—with its iconic representation of a mule ride down the side of the canyon, the clarinet braying and the temple blocks providing the "clip-clop" of the hooves—he earned a place in the pantheon of symphonic poetry.

Ferde Grofé, master of tone pictures, at the piano

RECOMMENDED RECORDING

GRAND CANYON SUITE: BERNSTEIN AND NEW YORK PHILHARMONIC (SONY).

Grosse Fuge (Grand Fugue) WORK FOR STRING QUARTET BY LUDWIG VAN BEETHOVEN, composed in 1825 and published posthumously as his Op. 133 in 1827. Beethoven originally conceived of it as the concluding movement of his String Quartet in B-flat, Op. 130. Following the quartet's first performance, on March 21, 1826, the composer was persuaded by several friends, including Karl Holz (second violinist of the Schuppanzigh Quartet, which had given the premiere), to drop the *Grosse Fuge* and substitute a less difficult movement as the finale. A staggering 741 measures long, with a layout resembling that of a four-movement symphony, the *Grosse Fuge* is the most radical and imposing of all Beethoven's fugal compositions. The writing is thorny, at many points ungrateful, calling for extreme skips in register and jarring dissonances—one of the rare instances in Beethoven's music for string quartet where idiomatic fluency is thrown out the window. But the power of the conception is overwhelming. The fugue's two main ideas are worked out under relentless tension, with a gestural ferocity beyond anything previously attempted in music, producing climaxes of mounting force until the work reaches a cataclysmic conclusion. *See also* FUGUE.

RECOMMENDED RECORDING

ALBAN BERG QUARTETT (EMI).

Gruberová, Edita

(b. Raca, December 23, 1946)

SLOVAK SOPRANO. She studied at the Bratislava Conservatory and made her debut in Bratislava in 1968, as Rosina in Rossini's *Il barbiere di Siviglia.* In 1970 she gave her first performances with the Vienna Staatsoper, as the Queen of the Night in Mozart's *Die Zauberflöte,* a role she continued to sing there through 1984; she became a regular member of the Vienna company in 1972, adding to her repertoire the roles of Zerbinetta in Richard Strauss's *Ariadne auf Naxos* (1973), Konstanze in Mozart's *Die Entführung aus dem Serail* (1974), and Lucia in Donizetti's *Lucia di Lammermoor* (1978). Her sensational performances as Zerbinetta in a new production of *Ariadne,* which opened in 1976 under the baton of Karl Böhm, established her as one of the opera world's brightest stars. She made her Metropolitan Opera debut in 1977, as the Queen of the Night, and appeared for the first time at Covent Garden in 1984, as Giulietta in Bellini's *I Capuleti e i Montecchi.* As her career developed she increasingly devoted herself to bel canto heroines such as Lucia, Elisabetta in Donizetti's *Roberto Devereux,* and Elvira in Bellini's *I puritani.* She possessed a stupendous technique marked by easy production of high notes and an uncanny accuracy of intonation, along with a considerable flair for acting.

RECOMMENDED RECORDINGS

BELLINI, *I CAPULETI E I MONTECCHI*: BALTSA, RAFFANTI, HOWELL; MUTI AND ROYAL OPERA (EMI).

STRAUSS, *ARIADNE AUF NAXOS*: PRICE, TROYANOS, KOLLO; SOLTI AND LONDON PHILHARMONIC ORCHESTRA (DECCA).

Grumiaux, Arthur

(b. Villers-Perwin, March 21, 1921; d. Brussels, October 16, 1986)

BELGIAN VIOLINIST. He began his musical studies at the age of four and attended the conservatories of Charleroi and Brussels, where he was a pupil of Alfred Dubois. He received the Prix Henri Vieuxtemps in 1939 and in 1940 became the first recipient of a "prix de virtuosité" awarded by the Belgian government, after which he studied briefly with George Enescu in Paris. Within weeks of his debut with the Brussels Philharmonic, at which he played Mendelssohn's E minor concerto under the baton of Charles Munch, Germany invaded Belgium and his career as a concert artist was nipped in the bud. Rather than perform for the occupiers, Grumiaux withdrew from public life and turned to chamber music, which would remain a lifelong interest. Following the war, he quickly established himself on the international scene, touring regularly in Europe, Great Britain, and the United States, and becoming a prolific recording artist. He formed an especially rewarding partnership with the pianist Clara Haskil, with whom he recorded the sonatas of Mozart and Beethoven; in addition, with violist Georges Janzer and cellist Eva Czako, he established the Grumiaux Trio, a collaboration that yielded recordings of Beethoven's string trios and the complete Mozart string quintets.

Grumiaux's playing was elegant, refined, and wonderfully lucid. He was particularly admired for his Mozart, which was exquisite; his repertoire included the concertos of Bach, Beethoven, and Mendelssohn as well as a significant number of 20th-century masterpieces, among them Walton's concerto, which he introduced to the European continent, and the concertos of Stravinsky and Berg. In 1949 Grumiaux succeeded his teacher Dubois as professor of violin at the Brussels Conservatory. He received the title of baron in 1973.

RECOMMENDED RECORDINGS

BEETHOVEN, STRING TRIOS: GRUMIAUX TRIO (PHILIPS).

MOZART, VIOLIN CONCERTOS: DAVIS AND LONDON SYMPHONY ORCHESTRA (PHILIPS).

MOZART, VIOLIN SONATAS: HASKIL (PHILIPS).

Guarneri "del Gesù," Giuseppe

(b. Cremona, August 21, 1698; d. Cremona, October 17, 1744)

ITALIAN VIOLIN MAKER, grandson of Andrea Guarneri (1626–98) and son of Giuseppe Giovanni Battista Guarneri (1666–1739), both prominent Cremonese luthiers. His instruments, together with those of Antonio STRADIVARI, are the supreme achievements of the art of violin making. Even as a young man he was alert to the tonal qualities of Stradivari's violins, which he sought to capture in his own early efforts, produced jointly with his father, for whom he worked. His total production was probably not more than 250 violins, of which about 150 are still extant; there is no evidence that he made any other type of instrument. He did his best work in the 1740s; experts have noted the irregularity of his craftsmanship after 1738 and evidence of an increasingly impetuous style of working, as though the wood were being attacked in the heat of inspiration.

The best instruments of Guarneri del Gesù adhere to a pattern based on that of Stradivari, but with some notable modifications suggesting the influence of Giovanni Paolo Maggini and other Brescian makers of the early 17th century. In most cases, the length of the body is 13⅞ inches, sometimes 1/16 inch less. The f-holes are longer than with Stradivari and almost Mannerist in appearance—less refined in their cut, somewhat pointed at the top. Where Stradivari worked to perfect every detail, Guarneri del Gesù's method was more spontaneous, resulting in violins that were intensely original in style yet stunning and rich-toned; the best are able to take more bow pressure and consequently produce a more powerful sound than the best Strads.

The label on a Guarneri del Gesù violin typically reads *Joseph Guarnerius fecit Cremonae anno 17__ IHS.* (From 1730 on, he added IHS to his label—an abbreviation of the name Jesus, in Greek—hence his nickname "del Gesù.") Niccolò Paganini owned a 1742 instrument known as "Il cannone" ("The Cannon"), and Fritz Kreisler played a particularly fine 1733 instrument. Another 1742 Guarneri del Gesù, the celebrated "David," was played in the 19th century by Ferdinand David (Mendelssohn's concertmaster at the Leipzig Gewandhaus Orchestra), in the 20th century by Jascha Heifetz, and now in the 21st by Alexander Barantschik, concertmaster of the San Francisco Symphony Orchestra. Other soloists who have favored a Guarneri del Gesù are Arthur Grumiaux, Isaac Stern, Henryk Szeryng, and Pinchas Zukerman.

Guarneri Quartet AMERICAN STRING QUARTET FORMED IN **1964** at the Marlboro Festival in Vermont. The four founding members—violinists Arnold Steinhardt and John Dalley, violist Michael Tree, and cellist David Soyer—played together for 35 years, an extraordinary accomplishment in an arena where burnout often comes after ten. In 2000 Soyer retired and was replaced by Peter Wiley, formerly the cellist of the Beaux Arts Trio. Celebrated for the vitality of their playing and the ravishing beauty of their sound, the Guarneri players have a repertoire that extends from Haydn to Bartók and includes a smattering of works by contemporary composers (in recent years they have given the first performances of a string quartet by Lukas Foss and of a concerto for string quartet and orchestra by Richard Danielpour). They

No strings attached: the founding members of the Guarneri Quartet

are best known for their Beethoven, which is distinguished not only by its sweep and cogency—the later works seem almost symphonic in scale—but by a unique fusion of energy, elegance, and wit. Their Dvořák is fresh and exuberant, their Debussy sensuous, expressive, and exquisitely refined. Though less adventurous—both interpretively and in their programming—than the Juilliard Quartet or the Emerson, the Guarneri are second to none in polish and panache, and remain among the most insightful current interpreters of the quartet literature.

Since 1965, the Guarneri Quartet has performed an annual series of six concerts at the Metropolitan Museum of Art. Over the decades its members have toured widely and made dozens of recordings—including one that is now journeying through interstellar space aboard the *Viking II* spacecraft. They are the subject of several books, including a memoir by first violinist Steinhardt, *Indivisible by Four* (1998).

RECOMMENDED RECORDINGS

BEETHOVEN, STRING QUARTETS (COMPLETE): (RCA).

DEBUSSY, QUARTET IN G MINOR, OP. 10 (RCA).

DVOŘÁK, STRING QUARTET IN F, OP. 96 (*AMERICAN*); PIANO QUINTET IN A, OP. 81: RUBINSTEIN (RCA).

Gubaydulina, Sofiya

(b. Chistopol, Tartar Republic, October 24, 1931)

RUSSIAN COMPOSER. She received instruction in piano and composition at the Kazan Conservatory and continued her study of composition at the Moscow Conservatory under Nikolay Peyko and Vissarion Shebalin. The work that brought her to the attention of listeners in the West was her violin concerto *Offertorium* (1980), written for Gidon Kremer. Based on the subject from Bach's *A Musical Offering,* it is not a concerto in the conventional sense, but closer to an extended rhapsody in which the solo instrument has the concertante function and the orchestra the obbligato. The imaginative scoring lends certain pages of the work a gripping intensity, and others an equally intense but fragile and haunting beauty, and the writing for the violin has considerable bite and brilliance. Since first being allowed to travel to the West in 1985, Gubaydulina's international reputation has soared, and she has received a steady stream of honors and commissions. In 1992 she left Russia for Germany.

Sofiya Gubaydulina

Gubaydulina's champions among performers include, in addition to Kremer, Mstislav Rostropovich (for whom she wrote *Seven Words,* for cello, bayan [a type of accordion], and strings, in 1982), the Kronos Quartet, violist Yuri Bashmet, and conductors Kent Nagano and Kurt Masur. Among her recent works are *Two Paths ("A Dedication to Mary and Martha"),* premiered by the New York Philharmonic in 1999, and the two-part cycle *Passion and Resurrection of Jesus Christ According to St. John,* premiered in 2002. Gubaydulina's intensely expressive music has led some observers to hail her as the truest successor to Dmitry Shostakovich. As with Henryk Górecki and John Tavener, there is a strong spiritual dimension to her art.

RECOMMENDED RECORDINGS

OFFERTORIUM: KREMER; DUTOIT AND BOSTON SYMPHONY ORCHESTRA (DG).

SEVEN WORDS: GERMAN CHAMBER PHILHARMONIC ORCHESTRA (BERLIN CLASSICS).

Guillaume Tell (William Tell) Opera in four acts by Gioachino Rossini, to a libretto by Étienne de Jouy and Hippolyte-Louis-Florent Bis (based on Friedrich von Schiller's *Wilhelm Tell*), premiered at the Paris Opéra on August 3, 1829. Rossini's final opera, it is a work of monumental proportions with which the composer, still in his 30s, helped to lay the foundations of French grand opera. The familiar story involves the struggle of the first Swiss cantons to free themselves from Austrian domination. Tell, a renowned crossbowman and leader in the struggle, is captured along with his son Jemmy after defying the Austrian governor, and is ordered to shoot a bolt through an apple that has been placed on Jemmy's head; a secondary plot involves the young Swiss patriot Arnold Melcthal, thrust into the eye of the storm by Tell's capture, torn between his love for the Hapsburg princess Mathilde and his determination to avenge his father's murder by the Austrians.

Tell's Act III aria "Sois immobile," sung as he prepares to shoot the apple, and Arnold's Act IV aria "Asil héréditaire," in which he laments the loss of his father, are two of Rossini's most inspired and affecting creations, and the crowd scenes are marvels of color and characterization. But the best-known music in *Guillaume Tell* is the opera's overture, a four-part tone poem that foreshadows the dramatic progression of the opera from pastoral innocence through storm and strife to the triumphant dawn of liberty. A masterpiece of orchestration, its notable effects include the opening passage for five solo cellos, a ferocious storm scene led by the trombones, a bucolic English horn solo, and the famous concluding galop.

Rossini lived to see the 500th performance of *Tell* at the Paris Opéra in 1868, but the work almost disappeared from the French (and Italian) repertoire in the 20th century, a victim of changing tastes and the inability of modern audiences to sit through operas lasting as long as a transcontinental flight.

RECOMMENDED RECORDING

Caballé, Bacquier, Gedda; Gardelli and Royal Philharmonic Orchestra (EMI).

guitar String instrument of the lute family with a fretted fingerboard, a wooden body with a flat back and incurved sides, and several courses of strings that are strummed or plucked. The modern six-stringed classical guitar became standardized in the mid-19th century, primarily through the work of Spanish luthier Antonio de Torres Jurado (1817–92). Typically, it has a round soundhole, a table made of spruce or cedar, and sides and back of rosewood or maple. Instruments thought to be forerunners of the modern guitar include the gittern, a three- or four-course lutelike instrument of Moorish origin that came to Spain in the 13th century, and the gittern's Spanish offspring, the six- or seven-course *vihuela,* which had a flat back and curved sides and was primarily an instrument of the court. By the 16th century, the smaller four-string guitar, used more in popular music, began to replace the *vihuela*; the five-string Renaissance guitar came into its own with its first tutorial, by Juon Carles Amat, *Guitarra española,* published in 1596.

Guitar tablature was established late in the 18th century, and composer-performers championed their instrument throughout Europe during the 19th—among them the

Spanish-born Fernando Sor (1778–1839), Dionysio Aguado (1784–1849), and Francisco Tárrega (1852–1909) and the Italian-born Ferdinando Carulli (1770–1841) and Mauro Giuliani (1781–1829). Niccolò Paganini loved the guitar and became an extremely fine performer on it. The most famous 20th-century proponent of the classical guitar was Andrés Segovia, a virtuoso performer, transcriber, and highly sought-after teacher. His students included Julian Bream (who also did a great deal to revive the lute), Christopher Parkening, and John Williams (not the Hollywood composer of the same name), a versatile performer equally brilliant in the classical repertoire and in jazz and pop. Many 20th-century composers have written works for the guitar, the most significant being Falla, Villa-Lobos, Ponce, Joaquín Turina (1882–1949), Britten, Ginastera, and Rodrigo, whose *Concierto de Aranjuez* (1940) has become the most frequently performed concerto for the instrument. ◉ Joseph Schwantner and Christopher Rouse (b. 1949) are among the contemporary composers who have written concertos for the guitar; in both cases their works were conceived for the talented player Sharon Isbin. A who's who of current masters would include, in addition to Isbin, David Russell, David Starobin, Eliot Fisk, and Jason Vieaux.

Andrés Segovia gave the guitar new cachet.

Guntram **OPERA IN THREE ACTS BY RICHARD STRAUSS,** to his own libretto, premiered in Weimar on May 10, 1894. Set in medieval Germany, it is a sprawling, dramatically turgid affair whose music and plot—a study of love with religious overtones, along the lines of *Tannhäuser* and *Parsifal*—betray the influence of Wagner.

A success in Weimar, *Guntram* failed miserably at its premiere in Munich the following year, and has never held a place in the repertoire. Nonetheless, Strauss was deeply fond of this, his first opera, and he made a point of quoting its music in his tone poem *Ein Heldenleben*.

RECOMMENDED RECORDING

ORCHESTRAL EXCERPTS: THIELEMANN; ORCHESTER DER DEUTSCHEN OPER BERLIN (DG).

Gurre-Lieder (Songs of Gurre) **WORK BY ARNOLD SCHOENBERG** for speaker, five soloists, three men's choirs, large eight-part mixed chorus, and gargantuan orchestra, to a German translation of texts by the Danish poet Jens Peter Jacobsen, composed 1900–01 and orchestrated 1901–03 and 1910–11. The premiere, on February 13, 1913, in Vienna, with Franz Schrecker conducting, brought the composer the greatest triumph of his career.

Gurre is a small, ruined medieval fortress in what is now a cow pasture in the northern part of the Danish island of Seeland, not far from Elsinore. Jacobsen's poem tells of a mythical past when the castle of Gurre was inhabited by King Waldemar, and of his ill-fated love affair with the commoner Tove, which brings about Tove's death and Waldemar's damnation. Schoenberg originally conceived of *Gurre-Lieder* as a song cycle with piano accompaniment, but in the course of compiling it he decided to flesh things out by orchestrating the songs and connecting them with symphonic interludes, in effect turning the piece into a gigantic cantata. The result is a succession of quasi-operatic tableaux, yet the song-cycle structure remains—thus, the main figures, Waldemar and Tove, Waldtaube (the voice of a wood dove), the fool Klaus-Narr, and the peasant Bauer, sing at each other, never with each other as they would in a true opera.

Gurre-Lieder nonetheless marks Schoenberg's closest encounter with Wagner on the themes of love, death, and redemption, conveyed in a musical language reminiscent of Wagner's operas, especially *Götterdämmerung.* Musically, it is a celebration of the interval of the sixth, and a work whose sonic grandeur and heated emotion represent, in the words of Dennis Libby, "the last, glorious ascent of the Wagnerian gasbag." Philosophically, the score pays fulsome homage to the Romantic notion of Nature as an animate force, capable of redeeming Man from the sins of pride and blasphemy.

RECOMMENDED RECORDING

Mattila, Otter, Moser, Quasthoff; Rattle and Berlin Philharmonic (EMI).

Gymnopédies Name given by Erik Satie to a set of three languorous, waltzlike piano pieces composed in 1888 and inspired by Flaubert's *Salammbô.* The first and third of the set were orchestrated by Debussy in 1895. The name, from *gymnopaedic,* refers to ritual dances and exercises of ancient Greece.

RECOMMENDED RECORDING

Ciccolini (EMI).

habanera Sultry dance in duple time named for the city of Havana. Its characteristic feature is a dotted figure on the downbeat of each measure. Of Afro-Cuban origin, the habanera emerged around 1800 and became enormously popular with French and Spanish composers of the later 19th and early 20th centuries. Bizet immortalized the dance in his opera *Carmen,* where it serves to introduce the title character. Among the many other composers who have made use of the habanera rhythm are Chabrier (*Habanera*), Saint-Saëns (*Havanaise* for violin and orchestra), Debussy (*Ibéria*; *La puerta del vino,* from the second book of *Préludes* for piano), and Ravel (*Rapsodie espagnole*).

Habanera, with castanets

Haffner Serenade NICKNAME OF WOLFGANG AMADEUS MOZART'S SERENADE IN D, K. 250, composed for the marriage of Marie Elisabeth Haffner to Franz Xaver Späth on July 21, 1776. The bride was the daughter of the merchant Sigmund Haffner the Elder (1699–1772), a leading citizen of Salzburg and friend of the Mozart family. The weightiest and most symphonic of the occasional pieces Mozart had produced up to that point in his life, the serenade consists of eight movements and is scored for two oboes (alternating with flutes in some movements), two bassoons, two horns, two trumpets, and strings. The second, third, and fourth movements—an Andante, minuet, and rondo—also call for a solo violin, in effect making them an embedded violin concerto. Mozart himself was undoubtedly the soloist on the evening of the first performance, and his writing for the violin, especially in the ebullient rondo, reflects that he was one of the most accomplished violinists of his day.

RECOMMENDED RECORDINGS

BROWN AND ACADEMY OF ST. MARTIN-IN-THE-FIELDS (HANSSLER).

MARRINER AND ACADEMY OF ST. MARTIN-IN-THE-FIELDS (PHILIPS).

WEIL AND TAFELMUSIK (SONY).

Haffner Symphony NICKNAME OF WOLFGANG AMADEUS MOZART'S SYMPHONY NO. 35 IN D, K. 385. Its four movements originally belonged to a six-movement serenade commissioned by Sigmund Haffner the Younger (1756–87) to celebrate his ennoblement by Emperor Joseph II on July 29, 1782. Mozart penned the serenade in Vienna between July 20 and August 7, 1782, sending the movements to Salzburg in installments, the final one apparently arriving just in time for the festivities in mid-August. Later that year, in need of a symphony for a concert he was planning to give on March 23, 1783, he asked his father to return the manuscript to him in Vienna; it arrived in February, and Mozart quickly reworked it into the form in which it is known today. The opening march was dropped, as was one of the minuets (now lost), and the scoring of the outer movements was augmented by the addition of flutes and clarinets.

With its bravura and headlong energy, the *Haffner* has established itself as one of Mozart's most popular symphonies. The muscularly scored first movement is a rousing, lively affair with a dynamic opening subject that leaps up an octave, and a plethora of racy scale passages designed for grand effect. ◉ As befits movements originally from a serenade, the two middle ones are lighter and more modestly contrived, while the finale, one of the few that Mozart designated a true *Presto,* is a tour de force of the brilliant style that contains a fascinating hint of darker sentiments.

RECOMMENDED RECORDING

SZELL AND CLEVELAND ORCHESTRA (SONY).

Hagegård, Håkan

(b. Sunne, November 25, 1945)

SWEDISH BARITONE catapulted to stardom by his appearance as Papageno in Ingmar Bergman's film version of *Die Zauberflöte* (1975). He studied at the municipal school of music in Sunne, the Royal Academy of Music in Stockholm, and the Mozarteum in Salzburg, and worked privately with Tito Gobbi in Florence and Gerald Moore in London. He made his operatic debut in Stockholm in 1968, as Papageno, and first appeared at the Metropolitan Opera in 1978, as Malatesta in Donizetti's *Don Pasquale.* Among the many roles he has sung with distinction are Figaro in Rossini's *Il barbiere di Siviglia,* Wolfram in Wagner's *Tannhäuser,* and the title role in Mozart's *Don Giovanni.* He created the role of Beaumarchais in *The Ghosts of Versailles* by John Corigliano at the Met in 1991, and sang in the premiere of Corigliano's *A Dylan Thomas Trilogy* with the National Symphony Orchestra in 1999. In 2000, as part of the Met's televised 25th anniversary tribute to James Levine, he gave a memorable cameo performance as Eisenstein (opposite the Rosalinde of Karita Mattila) in the repeating watch duet from Johann Strauss Jr.'s *Die Fledermaus,* delighting an audience of millions with his burnished tone and comic suggestiveness. Hagegård has enjoyed considerable success as a concert soloist in works such as Britten's *War Requiem,* and is also an admired recitalist. His voice and presence are large enough to fill any hall, but it is his refined musicianship and remarkable command of language and diction that have made him a standout. Among fellow musicians he is greatly liked, not least for having founded in 1992 the HageGården Music Center in Brunskog, Sweden, where artists of all kinds can recharge their batteries amid the beauty of the Scandinavian countryside.

RECOMMENDED RECORDINGS

FAURÉ, *REQUIEM,* SONGS: BONNEY; OZAWA AND BOSTON SYMPHONY ORCHESTRA (RCA).

ORFF, *CARMINA BURANA*: BLEGEN, BROWN; SHAW AND ATLANTA SYMPHONY ORCHESTRA (TELARC).

WOLF, *ITALIENISCHES LIEDERBUCH*: BONNEY, PARSONS (TELARC).

Hahn, Hilary

(b. Lexington, Va., November 27, 1979)

AMERICAN VIOLINIST. Her family moved to Baltimore when she was three, and she enrolled in the Suzuki program at the Peabody Conservatory a month before her fourth birthday. At the age of five she became a student of Klara Berkovich, and at ten she entered the Curtis Institute in Philadelphia, where from 1990 to 1997 she studied with Jascha Brodsky, the last surviving student of Eugène Ysaÿe. She made her orchestral debut with the Baltimore

Symphony Orchestra in December 1991, after which she was more or less "adopted" by the orchestra and its music director David Zinman. Her Philadelphia Orchestra debut occurred in 1993, and was followed by appearances with the Cleveland Orchestra, the Pittsburgh Symphony, and the New York Philharmonic, as well as by recital debuts in Chicago and Washington, D.C., in 1994. She signed a recording contract with Sony in 1996, and over the next six years recorded works of Bach, Barber, Beethoven, Bernstein, Brahms, Mendelssohn, Edgar Meyer (b. 1960; his violin concerto was written for her), Shostakovich, and Stravinsky. In 1999, at the age of 19, she received her bachelor's degree from Curtis, and in 2002 she joined the artist roster of Deutsche Grammophon.

Thanks to parents and teachers who wanted her to develop as a person and not just as a performer, Hahn has emerged from her student and early professional years with a remarkably mature musical personality. Her playing is suave, technically accomplished, and powerfully expressive.

RECOMMENDED RECORDINGS

BERNSTEIN, *SERENADE*: ZINMAN AND BALTIMORE SYMPHONY ORCHESTRA (SONY).

ELGAR, VIOLIN CONCERTO: DAVIS AND LONDON SYMPHONY ORCHESTRA (DG).

Haitink, Bernard

(b. Amsterdam, March 4, 1929)

DUTCH CONDUCTOR admired for his cogent readings of the symphonies of Mahler, Bruckner, Beethoven, and Brahms and his wide-ranging commitment to the music of the 20th century, particularly the works of Debussy, Ravel, Stravinsky, Shostakovich, Vaughan Williams, and Britten. He studied violin at the Amsterdam Conservatory and was a member of the Netherlands Radio Symphony Orchestra. In 1955, following conducting studies with Ferdinand Leitner, he was engaged as

Bernard Haitink rehearsing at the Edinburgh Festival

second conductor of the Netherlands Radio Union. He made his debut with the Concertgebouw Orchestra in 1956 and the following year was named principal conductor of the Netherlands Radio Philharmonic. In 1961, following the death of Eduard van Beinum, he was appointed joint principal conductor of the Concertgebouw Orchestra with Eugen Jochum. He became the orchestra's music director in 1964 and remained in that post until 1988.

Haitink served as the London Philharmonic Orchestra's principal conductor from 1967 to 1979. He made his operatic debut at Glyndebourne (where the LPO played in the pit) in 1972, conducting Mozart's *Die Entführung aus dem Serail*, and was invited back to do Mozart's *Die Zauberflöte* in 1973 and Stravinsky's *The Rake's Progress* in 1975 (in a production designed by David Hockney). He succeeded Sir John Pritchard as music director at the Glyndebourne Festival in 1977, stepping down in 1988. In 1987 he was appointed music director at the Royal Opera, Covent Garden, in which capacity he served until 2002.

Haitink came to the podium after working as an orchestral violinist (like Charles Munch and Neville Marriner, among others), and has always avoided histrionics and display in his conducting. Impatient with "tricks," as he calls them, he is a painstaking musical craftsman whose main interest is in getting an orchestra to play cohesively and produce a sonority suited to the music in front of it. His interpretations, notably free of exaggeration, exhibit an emotional restraint that occasionally makes them seem understated, but rarely miss the mark stylistically. Over the past 40 years he has made a distinguished contribution to the discography through his recordings with the Concertgebouw Orchestra and the London Philharmonic. His later efforts with the Berlin Philharmonic and Boston Symphony have enjoyed somewhat less success.

RECOMMENDED RECORDINGS

DEBUSSY, ORCHESTRAL WORKS (INCLUDING *LA MER, NOCTURNES, IMAGES*): CONCERTGEBOUW ORCHESTRA (PHILIPS).

MAHLER, SYMPHONIES (COMPLETE): CONCERTGEBOUW ORCHESTRA (PHILIPS).

VAUGHAN WILLIAMS, *SINFONIA ANTARTICA*: LONDON PHILHARMONIC ORCHESTRA (EMI).

Hamelin, Marc-André

(b. Montreal, September 5, 1961)

AMERICAN PIANIST OF CANADIAN BIRTH. He studied at the Vincent d'Indy School of Music and earned his B.A. and M.M. degrees at Temple University in Philadelphia. Since winning the Carnegie Hall International American Music Competition in 1985, he has enjoyed a burgeoning career highlighted by recital appearances at London's Wigmore Hall and other major venues throughout Europe and North America, by engagements with the orchestras of Amsterdam, Chicago, Detroit, Houston, Montreal, Philadelphia, and Toronto, and by an acclaimed series of recordings on the Hyperion label. In the past decade Hamelin has won an avid following among piano aficionados thanks not only to his remarkable artistry, which combines sensational technique and superior taste, but to his adventurous pursuit of esoteric repertoire. On record he has conquered the most challenging works of Alkan, Busoni, Leopold Godowsky (1870–1938; the fiendishly difficult *53 Studies on Chopin's Etudes*), Grainger, Liszt, Nikolay Medtner (1880–1951; the complete sonatas), Reger, Nikolay Roslavets (1881–1944), Frederick Rzewski (b. 1938; his mammoth variation piece *The People United Will Never Be Defeated!*), Scriabin (the complete sonatas), and Szymanowski. The more difficult the music is, the better Hamelin plays it. But he can also melt the heart of even the most jaded listener, as in his rapturous realization of Grainger's *Ramble on Love,* as beautiful a take as has ever been committed to disc.

RECOMMENDED RECORDINGS

GODOWSKY, *53 STUDIES ON CHOPIN'S ETUDES* (HYPERION).

SCRIABIN, SONATAS (HYPERION).

***Hammerklavier* Sonata** NAME ATTACHED TO LUDWIG VAN BEETHOVEN'S PIANO SONATA IN B-FLAT, OP. 106, which the composer designated "für das Hammer-Klavier," mainly to avoid using the French word for his instrument, the pianoforte, in the piece's title. Its composition, which took nearly a full year from the autumn of 1817 to the autumn of 1818, marked Beethoven's recovery from five years of emotional crisis and creative inertia.

The sonata's opening movement contains some of Beethoven's most powerfully assertive music, which is juxtaposed with material of a much more courtly and lyrical cast to produce a study in contrast between incisiveness and flow. The ensuing scherzo shows how Beethoven could create music of remarkable complexity out of material that is simple, even aphoristic. Its subject outlines the interval of a third, which is the main building block of the melodic material of the sonata's first movement as well.

The Adagio of the *Hammerklavier* Sonata is one of the most overwhelmingly affecting expressions in all of Beethoven's sonatas. It opens in a mood of quiet contemplation and builds like a great hymn toward a climax that is painful and ecstatic at the same time; just when Beethoven appears to have reached the limit of spirituality, he goes off still further into an utterly ethereal realm. An entire line of development in Romantic music—passing through Schubert, Chopin, Schumann, Brahms, and Liszt—springs from this movement. The sonata's finale, mysteriously prefaced by a series of meditative and violent asides, is a gigantic three-voice FUGUE so elaborate and eventful it seems more like a fantasy in which long arcs of invention are sustained by brilliant imitative writing.

RECOMMENDED RECORDING

ARRAU (PHILIPS) AND GILELS (DG).

Hampson, Thomas

(b. Elkhart, Ind., June 28, 1955)

AMERICAN BARITONE. He grew up in Spokane and attended Eastern Washington University and Fort Wright College, where he received voice lessons from Sister Marietta Coyle (who prior to taking the veil had studied with Lotte Lehmann). In 1980, after spending two summers at the Music Academy of the West, he enrolled in the San Francisco Opera's Merola program and received coaching from Elisabeth Schwarzkopf. The following year he won the Metropolitan Opera Auditions and began a European apprenticeship with the Düsseldorf Opera. In 1984 he was engaged as a principal by the Zurich Opera, and in 1986 he made his debuts at the Vienna Staatsoper, as Guglielmo in Mozart's *Così fan tutte,* and the Metropolitan Opera, as the Count in *Le nozze di Figaro.*

By the late 1980s Hampson's sizable talent, packed into a suitably imposing 6-foot 4-inch frame, was winning recognition everywhere. Leonard Bernstein tapped him for performances and recordings of Mahler's *Rückert-Lieder* and *Lieder eines fahrenden Gesellen.* Nikolaus Harnoncourt chose him for the title role in performances and a recording of Mozart's *Don Giovanni.* And the Salzburg Festival welcomed him as the Count in performances of *Figaro* conducted by James Levine. During the 1990s, Hampson returned to the Met to sing the title roles in Britten's *Billy Budd* (1992) and Massenet's *Werther* (1999); in Vienna he took on the title roles in Tchaikovsky's *Eugene Onegin* (1997) and Rossini's *Guillaume Tell* (1998). He also sang the title role in Szymanowski's *King Roger* at Salzburg Festival (1998).

From the beginning of his career Hampson has been a prolific and thoughtful recitalist. His programs often showcase songs by American composers, particularly Samuel Barber and Charles Ives, and he has earned praise for exploring the work of the legendary American tunesmith Stephen Foster as well as for his penetrating evening-length examination of songs to texts by Walt Whitman.

At his best, Hampson is a commanding performer, fiery yet capable of a seductive gentleness. His intelligence, together with the carefully controlled forcefulness of his delivery, occasionally reminds one of the young Dietrich Fischer-Dieskau. But in recent years a tendency to overload his singing with narcissistic posturing has detracted from his artistry.

RECOMMENDED RECORDINGS

BERNSTEIN, *ON THE TOWN*: THOMAS AND LONDON SYMPHONY ORCHESTRA (DG).

SCHUMANN, SONGS: PARSONS (EMI).

"TO THE SOUL: SONGS TO TEXTS OF WALT WHITMAN" (EMI).

(Left) ***Portrait of Handel by Hudson, ca. 1736.*** **(Right)** ***Caught red-handed: The young George Frideric Handel practicing in the attic.***

Handel, George Frideric

(b. Halle, February 23, 1685; d. London, April 14, 1759)

ENGLISH COMPOSER OF GERMAN BIRTH. One of the most cosmopolitan and eclectic musicians of the 18th century, and a true celebrity in his day, he created works of lasting value in every important musical form known to his age. He was a pioneer in the field of opera, and all but invented the genre of English oratorio, of which *MESSIAH* is the most famous example.

The son of a barber-surgeon in the service of the Duke of Saxe-Weissenfels, the young Handel was discouraged in his efforts to learn music. He nonetheless practiced the clavichord in the attic and became so skilled that, at the Duke's urging, he was allowed to study with Friedrich Zachow, an organist in Halle. From this teacher, he received a thorough grounding in keyboard technique and composition. In 1703 he left Halle for Hamburg, where he played violin and harpsichord in the city's opera house. It was here, in 1704, that he composed his first opera, *Almira,* which, though it bears the stamp of a 19-year-old's freshman attempt at vocal composition, shows evidence of the many influences that would eventually make Handel an opera composer par excellence: elements of French tragic opera and German singspiel and an uncanny understanding of Italian opera, extremely popular at the time.

In 1706, Handel set off for Italy, quickly establishing himself in Rome, where he realized that the native composers were circumventing the papal ban on opera by composing oratorios and cantatas in a theatrical style—in essence, operas without staging, costumes, or sets. Following their example, he fashioned a pair of oratorios—*Il trionfo del Tempo e del Disinganno* (1707) and *La resurrezione* (1708)—and many cantatas before heading north back to his homeland.

In 1710, at the age of 25, Handel was appointed Kapellmeister to the Elector of Hanover—the future King George I of England—and was granted an immediate leave of absence to spend the better part of a year in London. He returned to Hanover in the summer of 1711, but in the fall of 1712 again asked to be relieved of his duties in order to visit London, agreeing to return "within a reasonable time."

During his first London sojourn, in 1711, Handel had written the well-received Italian opera *Rinaldo,* which premiered on the night he turned 26; his librettist, Giacomo Rossi, was knocked out by the sheer speed at which the composer had worked. "Mr. Handel," he wrote, "the Orpheus of our century, while composing the music, scarcely gave me time to write, and to my great wonder I saw an entire opera put to music by that surprising genius, with the greatest degree of perfection, in only two weeks." Following his return to London, early in 1713, Handel penned a birthday ode for Queen Anne, *Eternal Source of Light Divine,* which went unperformed due to her flagging health. He was beginning to make a name for himself as a composer for both the stage and the concert hall—and making a fair amount of money as well. But his love affair with London came at a cost: In June 1713 he was summarily dismissed from his Hanover post, despite the fact that he had been feeding useful information on the queen's condition to his employer's representatives in London. When George became King, following Anne's death in August 1714, he reinstated Handel's back wages from Hanover; the following month, as a sign of favor to his Kapellmeister, George attended a performance of Handel's "Caroline" *Te Deum* in the Chapel Royal at St. James's, and subsequently doubled Handel's salary.

Handel commemoration at Westminster Abbey, 1784

After a number of successes on the stage—*Teseo, Il Pastor Fido,* and *Amadigi di Gaula*—Handel was the toast of London, just the person to create the music for a spectacular royal journey by barge up the Thames. The notion that a contrite Handel wrote the *Water Music* (1717) as a means of restoring himself to his king's good graces (passed down by John Mainwaring, the composer's first biographer) is a myth. George in fact remained a staunch supporter and patron to the end of his life, just as the Prince of Wales, the future George II, would be. Part of the reason was that Handel, like Purcell and John Blow (1649–1708) before him, and Elgar and Walton later on, proved to be a consummate master of ceremonial music. The four *Coronation Anthems,* composed for the coronation of King George II and Queen Caroline in 1727, and the *Music for the Royal Fireworks,* commissioned by George II to mark the signing of the Peace of Aix-la-Chapelle in 1749, are of the highest quality and exemplify the effort Handel put into his works of musical pageantry.

Handel also published two magnificent collections of concerti grossi—Op. 3, consisting of six works, in 1734, and Op. 6, containing 12 concertos, in 1740—as well as two collections of trio sonatas (Opp. 2 and 5) and dozens of suites for harpsichord, of which the eight collected in 1720 as the first *Suites de pièces pour le clavecin* are the most important.

But by temperament and training, Handel was, above all else, inclined to the theater. Between 1711 and 1741 he produced no fewer than 36 Italian operas, establishing himself as one of the supreme masters of the genre. Among the finest of his contributions were *Tamerlano* (1724), *Giulio Cesare in Egitto* (1724, a huge success with the castrato Senesino in the title role), *Orlando* (1733), *Ariodante* (1735), and *Alcina* (1735). By the time these later works appeared, the style of opera seria Handel had done so much to advance was on its way out. Moreover, the cost of staging these extravagant epics, and of engaging the finest singers to perform them, was starting to wreak havoc on Handel's bottom line. Remembering what he had learned in Rome, Handel hit upon the idea of the oratorio as a way to keep writing Italian opera in all but the words themselves (the texts would henceforth be in English), and simultaneously save the cost of mounting lavish productions in the theater.

***Royal Mail commemorative honoring the* Water Music**

The success of the oratorio *SAUL* (1739) confirmed Handel in his commitment to the new genre. Still, he had much to learn about popular taste. Despite being one of his most imaginative and majestic works, his very next venture, *Israel in Egypt* (1739), failed to please because it offered relatively few solo numbers. But Handel's successes were many and dazzling. Among the greatest was *Messiah* ◉, which premiered in Dublin in 1742, and was revived numerous times in London during Handel's lifetime. On the same lofty plane are a pair of oratorios that received their premieres in 1749. *SOLOMON* boasts fine writing for the solo singers, many magnificently composed pages for a large orchestra, and some of the biggest and greatest of Handelian choruses. *Susanna,* a more intimate and subtle work, presents a vivid characterization of its biblical heroine. Handel's production effectively ceased a few years later as blindness brought the curtain down on his career. He continued working to the end, however, and attended a performance of *Messiah* just a week before his death. As a sign of the esteem in which his adopted country held him, he was interred in Westminster Abbey.

Handel's talent was prodigious, and the range of his musical interests enormous. His style was synthetic in the best sense: He absorbed the best of what French, German, Italian, and English music of the late 17th and early 18th centuries had to offer, and made of it something wonderfully alive and boldly communicative.

RECOMMENDED RECORDINGS

GIULIO CESARE: LARMORE, SCHLICK, RAGIN, VISSE; JACOBS AND CONCERTO KÖLN (HARMONIA MUNDI).

MESSIAH: HALE, MARSHALL, ROLFE JOHNSON, ROBBIN; GARDINER AND ENGLISH BAROQUE SOLOISTS (PHILIPS).

SOLOMON: WATKINSON, ARGENTA, ROLFE JOHNSON, HENDRICKS; GARDINER AND ENGLISH BAROQUE SOLOISTS (PHILIPS).

WATER MUSIC AND *MUSIC FOR THE ROYAL FIREWORKS*: GARDINER AND ENGLISH BAROQUE SOLOISTS (PHILIPS).

WATER MUSIC AND *MUSIC FOR THE ROYAL FIREWORKS*: LAMON (SONY).

Handel and Haydn Society CHORAL SOCIETY FOUNDED IN BOSTON IN 1815, the second oldest musical organization (after the U.S. Marine Band) in continuous existence in the United States. Established for the purpose of "cultivating and improving a correct taste in the performance of sacred music, and also to introduce into more general practice the works of Handel, Haydn, and other eminent composers," it gave the first performances in America of Handel's complete *Messiah* (1818) and Haydn's *The Creation* (1819). The great American hymnodist Lowell Mason was its president from 1827 to 1832. Under the guidance of Christopher Hogwood (music director from 1986 to 2001), it transformed itself into a professional chorus with an associated period-instrument ensemble.

Handful, The *See* FIVE, THE.

Hänsel und Gretel OPERA IN THREE ACTS BY ENGELBERT HUMPERDINCK, to a libretto by his sister, Adelheid Wette (based on the fairy tale by the Brothers Grimm), premiered at the Hoftheater in Weimar on December 23, 1893. The story is the familiar one about a brother and sister on the point of becoming dinner and dessert, who outwit a witch and are happily reunited with their parents. With its delightful mix of humor, sentiment, and classic "good triumphs over evil" plot, the opera—which the composer designated a "Märchenspiel" ("fairy-tale play")—has held a cherished place in the repertoire ever since its debut. Humperdinck's use of folk songs along with simple chorales and folklike melodies establishes an appropriate musical framework for the drama, while his skill in subjecting these materials to rich polyphonic development and clothing them in the opulent colors and textures of Wagnerian orchestration allows the deeper emotional nuances of the story to be revealed in an especially appealing way.

RECOMMENDED RECORDING

LARMORE, ZIESAK, SCHWARZ, BEHRENS, WEIKL, SCHÄFER; RUNNICLES AND BAVARIAN RADIO SYMPHONY ORCHESTRA (TELDEC).

Hanslick, Eduard

(b. Prague, September 11, 1825; d. Baden, August 6, 1904)

AUSTRIAN MUSIC CRITIC. He was one of the first to treat music criticism as a career rather than a sideline, and he became the most influential and powerful figure in his field during the second half of the 19th century. Both of his parents were artistically inclined, and he was well educated in music, philosophy, and literature. As preparation for a career in the Austrian civil service he studied law at the University of Vienna; after receiving his degree in 1849, he worked for several years in the Austrian ministries of finance and education. He began writing criticism in 1844, and started contributing to the *Wiener Zeitung* in 1848. He subsequently served as critic for *Die Presse* and, from 1864 until 1895, as the critic of the *Neue freie Presse.* Hanslick's writing was marked by taste and perception, but he had limited enthusiasm for music before Mozart's ("I would rather see all of Schütz go up in flames than lose the *German Requiem,*" he is reported to have said) and antipathy toward some of the most important music of his own time (that of Liszt, Tchaikovsky, Bruckner, and Wagner, in particular). The avant-garde of the day saw him as inflexible and dogmatic, while his adherents saw him as the steadfast guardian of tradition, logic, and beauty. Wagner avenged himself on Hanslick in *Die Meistersinger von Nürnberg,* trundling out the hapless, pedantic, supercilious character of Sixtus Beckmesser as a parody (in early drafts of the work going so far as to name him "Veit Hanslich"). But Hanslick rightly judged the importance of much contemporary music. He was an ardent supporter and close friend of Brahms, encouraged Dvořák from the beginning, and found much to value in the French and Italian opera of his day.

Eduard Hanslick

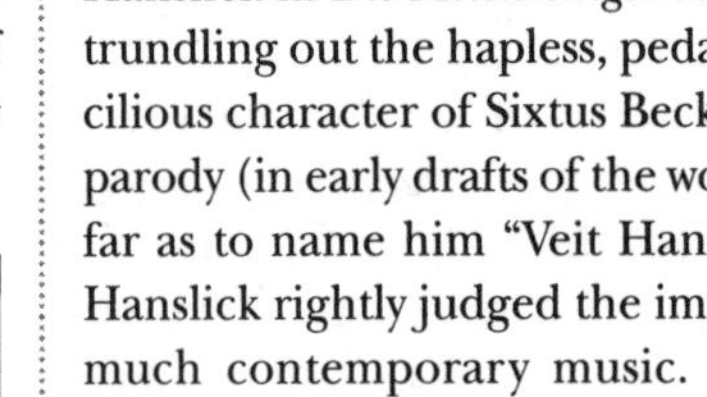

Hanson, Howard

(b. Wahoo, Nebr., October 28, 1896; d. Rochester, N.Y., February 26, 1981)

AMERICAN COMPOSER, CONDUCTOR, AND EDUCATOR OF SWEDISH DESCENT. A prominent figure in American musical life for much of the 20th century, he was often described as a "prairie Romantic" because he grew up in the heartland and wrote music that was lush, emotionally expansive, and unapologetically tonal. Intellectually as well as musically precocious, he received his B.A. from Northwestern University in 1916 and subsequently taught at the College of the Pacific in San Jose, California, becoming dean in 1919. He won the Prix de Rome in 1921 and spent the next three years in Italy, immersing himself in the arts and studying orchestration with Ottorino Respighi. In 1924, upon his return to the United States, he made his conducting debut with the New York Symphony Orchestra and assumed the directorship of the newly created Eastman School of Music in Rochester, New York, where he stayed until 1964. Following his retirement, he remained active into his 80s as a composer and conductor.

Hanson was a jack of all musical trades who proved himself a master in each. As a conductor he was admired for his strongly stated, straightforward, and propulsive style. With the Eastman Rochester Symphony Orchestra he made the first recordings of many major works, not just his own. Through his teaching he trained generations of students and was a tireless champion of American music and musicians. As a composer, he worked in an idiom that was at once modern, vital, and approachable, taking full advantage, in his seven symphonies, of the virtuosity and sonic splendor of America's orchestras. His harmonic language remained virtually unchanged from his Symphony No. 1 (*Nordic*), written in 1923, to his Symphony No. 7 (*A SEA SYMPHONY*), composed in 1977. His best-known work, the Symphony No. 2 (*ROMANTIC*), has become so emblematic of rugged American individualism that it was used in the final scene of the movie *Alien* (1979) as Ripley (Sigourney Weaver) prepares for the long voyage home from outer space. The score demonstrates Hanson's gift for memorable melody and grand gestures, but it also reveals his music's most common flaw: a tendency to boil the pot for half an hour by gussying up five minutes of real material in various orchestral costumings.

Howard Hanson in rehearsal

RECOMMENDED RECORDINGS

SYMPHONIES (COMPLETE, WITH OTHER WORKS): SCHWARZ AND SEATTLE SYMPHONY ORCHESTRA (DELOS).

SYMPHONIES NOS. 1 AND 2: HANSON AND EASTMAN ROCHESTER ORCHESTRA (MERCURY).

Harbison, John

(b. Orange, N.J., December 20, 1938)

AMERICAN COMPOSER. He began improvising at the piano when he was five and started a jazz band at the age of 12. He studied with Walter Piston at Harvard, where he received his B.A. in 1960, and with Roger Sessions and Earl Kim at Princeton, where he earned an M.F.A. in 1963. He joined the faculty of the Massachusetts Institute of Technology in 1969 and was named Institute Professor there in 1996. During his career, he has served as composer-in-residence of the Pittsburgh Symphony (1981–83) and the Los Angeles Philharmonic (1985–88); in 1987 he won the Pulitzer Prize for his cantata *The Flight into Egypt*, and in 1989 he received a MacArthur Fellowship. He has composed three operas, four symphonies, concertos for piano, violin, flute, and cello, a substantial amount of chamber music (including four string quartets), two piano sonatas, a ballet, and a Requiem (premiered by the Boston Symphony in 2003). His opera *The Great Gatsby*, based on F. Scott Fitzgerald's novel, was commissioned by the Metropolitan Opera and was a succès d'estime when it premiered there in 1999.

John Harbison

RECOMMENDED RECORDING

THE FLIGHT INTO EGYPT (WITH OTHER WORKS): SYLVAN, GOLD; PREVIN, HOOSE AND LOS ANGELES PHILHARMONIC (NEW WORLD).

harmonics [1] Overtones or "partials," i.e., tones above the fundamental frequency of a given musical note that are component parts of the sound of that note. Harmonics occur at integral multiples of the fundamental frequency of a note, meaning that if the note is pitched at 64 Hz, harmonics sound at 128 Hz, 192 Hz, 256 Hz, 320 Hz, and so on. In music, the harmonic series for a given fundamental includes the fundamental itself. Thus, for the note C, the harmonic series consists of the note itself followed by the C an octave above and, continuing upward, G, C, E, G, B-flat, C, D, E, F-sharp, G, A, B-flat, B, and the 16th harmonic, the C four octaves above the fundamental.

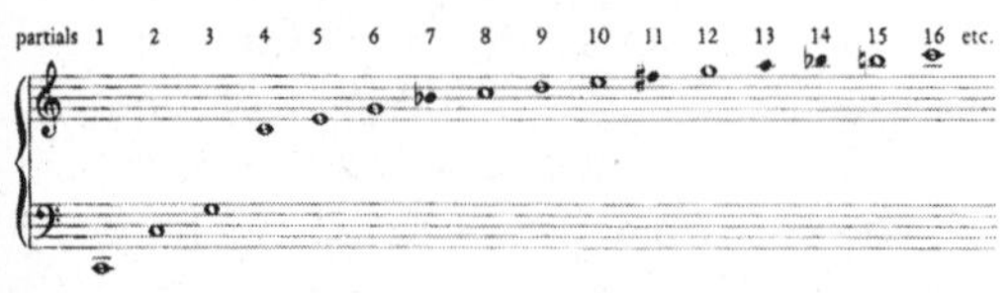

Harmonics are usually much weaker than the fundamentals from which they arise, and typically get weaker as the series proceeds, but it is the relative strength of particular harmonics that determines the quality and color of notes produced by an instrument, giving instruments of different families their distinctive timbres. For example, tones produced by the clarinet in the lower part of its range have particularly strong odd-numbered partials, which helps account for their warmth and richness (because the third and fifth partials produce the tones belonging to a major triad, whereas the second and fourth merely replicate the fundamental note one and two octaves higher).

[2] Notes of high pitch produced artificially on string and wind instruments by fingering or overblowing in such a way as to select and strengthen an overtone while suppressing the fundamental that normally produces it. Notes to be played as harmonics are indicated by small circles over the note heads, or, in parts written for string instruments, by the insertion of a diamond-headed note above the fingered note, showing where the string is to be lightly touched in order to produce the desired harmonic.

harmonium SMALL REED ORGAN PATENTED IN **1842** by the Parisian instrument builder Alexandre-François Debain (1809–77). The standard version of the instrument has a pedal-operated bellows mechanism and a five-octave keyboard. During the 19th century, the harmonium became a popular instrument for domestic music-making. It also saw use in churches lacking a full-size pipe organ, and eventually in movie theaters, providing accompaniment for silent films. It began to be superseded by the electronic organ and other devices around 1930.

The repertoire for harmonium includes a number of fine solo pieces composed by Sigfrid Karg-Elert (1877–1933) in the early years of the 20th century. There is also a substantial part for harmonium in Mahler's Symphony No. 8. But the most celebrated examples of its use are Rossini's *Petite messe solennelle* (1863), for solo voices, harmonium, and two pianos, and Dvořák's *Bagatelles,* Op. 47 (1878), for two violins, cello, and harmonium. Less well known but equally charming are Schoenberg's chamber arrangements of Johann Strauss Jr.'s *Rosen aus dem Süden* and *Lagunen* waltzes, for a salon orchestra of piano, harmonium, and string quartet. At the premiere of these arrangements in Vienna in 1921, the harmonium parts were played by Alban Berg.

RECOMMENDED RECORDINGS

DVOŘÁK, *BAGATELLES*: DOMUS (VIRGIN CLASSICS).

DVOŘÁK, *BAGATELLES*: PANOCHA QUARTET, ET AL. (SUPRAPHON).

SCHOENBERG, *ROSEN AUS DEM SÜDEN*: BIEDERMEIER ENSEMBLE (CAMERATA).

harmony (from Gr. *harmonia,* "a joining [of sounds]") [1] The simultaneous sounding of different tones to produce chords. [2] The process whereby a contextual relationship of chords to one another can be deduced through their linear progression and evaluated in terms of the structural significance or function each chord has within an established theoretical framework.

Harnoncourt, Nikolaus

(b. Berlin, December 6, 1929)

AUSTRIAN CONDUCTOR, CELLIST, AND VIOL PLAYER. He grew up in Graz, the capital of Styria: His father was a scion of the de la Fontaine-d'Harnoncourt-Unverzagt family, his mother the great-granddaughter of Archduke Johann of Styria. His interest in music ultimately won out over a childhood fondness for puppet theater. He studied cello at the Vienna Academy of Music before joining the ranks of the Vienna Symphony Orchestra, where he was a member of the cello section from 1952 to 1969. In 1953, together with his wife, Alice, a violinist, he founded the Concentus Musicus Wien for the purpose of performing 17th- and 18th-century repertoire on period instruments. He began making recordings with the group in 1962, winning praise for his historically informed accounts of Monteverdi's operas and Bach's *St. John* and *St. Matthew* Passions. In 1971, in cooperation with Gustav Leonhardt, he began a monumental effort to record all 200 of Bach's surviving church cantatas; the project, a landmark in recording history, was completed in 1990. He began teaching performance practice and historical instruments at the Salzburg Mozarteum in 1972, and during the 1970s and 1980s he collaborated with Jean-Pierre Ponnelle on productions of the operas of Monteverdi and Mozart at the Zurich Opernhaus.

Harnoncourt's forays into the Romantic repertoire have become increasingly numerous since the late 1980s. His integral recording of the Beethoven symphonies with the Chamber Orchestra of Europe, released in 1991, is among the more compelling of recent realizations. He has

Nikolaus Harnoncourt at work, 1997

The 1950s saw the beginnings of an effort to rediscover how music of earlier periods might have sounded on original instruments, and period instrument ensembles have proliferated since the early 1970s. At first focused on Baroque repertoire, many period instrument orchestras bring similar scholarship to the Classical and Romantic periods. Research into stylistic matters such as phrasing, tone, and vibrato has also influenced the ways in which mainstream players and orchestras approach these repertoires.

Academy of Ancient Music

Founded by Christopher Hogwood in 1973. The name was inspired by the original Academy of Ancient Music, established in 18th-century London by Samuel Pepusch, with a mission to perform "old" music, which Dr. Pepusch defined as anything that had been written more than 20 years earlier. In the 1980s, the present-day AAM completed a landmark traversal of the Mozart symphonies with Jaap Schröder as concertmaster and Hogwood playing continuo, followed by the complete symphonies of Beethoven in 1989 and ongoing cycles of the Haydn symphonies and the Mozart piano concertos, all under Hogwood's direction. The group has also recorded numerous works of Bach, Vivaldi, and Handel, including the first period instrument recording of the *Messiah* in 1980. In 1996 violinist Andrew Manze was appointed AAM's associate director

and concertmaster; in 2005 harpsichordist Richard Egarr took his place as the new associate director.

RECOMMENDED RECORDINGS
BACH, SOLO AND DOUBLE VIOLIN CONCERTOS: MANZE, PODGER; MANZE (HARMONIA MUNDI).
HANDEL, *MESSIAH:* KIRKBY, NELSON, WATKINSON, ELLIOTT, THOMAS; HOGWOOD (OISEAU-LYRE).

Akademie für Alte Musik Berlin

Founded in 1982 by musicians culled from East Berlin's leading orchestras, it became the first world-class period instrument ensemble in the former German Democratic Republic. Working with top-rank artists such as Ton Koopman, Reinhard Goebel, Monica Huggett, and Marion Verbruggen, the ensemble began touring throughout East Germany and Western Europe, and is now regarded as one of most exciting of the new breed of period instrument orchestras. Since 1994, under the direction of René Jacobs, it has produced a series of award-winning recordings for harmonia mundi france. Aside from performances at major concert venues worldwide, the orchestra regularly collaborates with the Berlin Staastoper and the RIAS-Kammerchor, under the direction of Marcus Creed.

RECOMMENDED RECORDING
BACH, *CHRISTMAS* ORATORIO: RÖSCHMANN, SCHOLL, GÜRA, HÄGER; JACOBS (HARMONIA MUNDI).

Amsterdam Baroque Orchestra and Choir

Founded in 1979 by the Dutch organist and harpsichordist Ton Koopman. Focusing on repertoire from 1600 to 1791, the ensemble is made up of international Baroque specialists who convene throughout the year to perform and record. In 1992 the Amsterdam Baroque Choir made its debut in Utrecht with the modern pre-

mieres of Biber's *Requiem* and *Vespers*, receiving the Cannes Classical Award for its recording of the works. In 1994 the group made a commitment to perform and record the complete cantatas of Bach; after recording 12 critically acclaimed vol-

The Academy of Ancient Music

William Christie in Lucerne, 1996

umes for Erato, the project has continued on the Antoine Marchand label, which also has reissued volumes 1-9.

RECOMMENDED RECORDING
BUXTEHUDE, COMPLETE CANTATAS: SCHLICK, FRIMMER, CHANCE, JACOBS, PRÉGARDIEN, KOOY (ERATO).

Les Arts Florissants

Founded in Paris in 1979 by the American-born harpsichordist William Christie, it takes its name from an opera by the French Baroque composer Marc-Antoine Charpentier. Through Christie's pioneering research and brilliant productions, the ensemble has been almost solely responsible for the rediscovery of 17th- and 18th-century French opera. Beginning with its legendary 1987 production of Lully's *Atys* at the Opéra-Comique in Paris, "Les Arts Flo" has mounted operas of Rameau, Charpentier, Monteverdi, Handel, Purcell, and Mozart, as well as giving concert performances of operas by Campra, Montéclair, Landi, and Rossi. The group has made more than 60 recordings of opera, oratorio, and concert repertoire, and received four Gramophone Awards.

RECOMMENDED RECORDING
LULLY, *ATYS*: DE MEY, LAURENS, MELLON, GARDEIL (HARMONIA MUNDI).

Concentus Musicus Wien

Formed in 1957 by the cellist and conductor Nikolaus Harnoncourt. For two decades, until the emergence of the major English early-music groups, the Vienna-based ensemble stood at the vanguard of the period instrument movement. Under Harnoncourt's direction it has recorded most of the sacred and orchestral works of Bach (including numerous cantatas), several Handel oratorios, the major sacred works of Mozart, selected Mozart and Haydn symphonies, and all three of Monteverdi's surviving operas.

RECOMMENDED RECORDING
MOZART, *REQUIEM*: SCHÄFER, FINK, STREIT, FINLEY; HARNONCOURT (DEUTSCHE HARMONIA MUNDI).

Le Concert des Nations

Named after a work by François Couperin, the group was created in 1989 by the Spanish viola da gamba virtuoso Jordi Savall to work in collaboration with his vocal ensemble, La Capella Reial de Catalunya. Made up of early-music specialists from mainly Latin countries, Le Concert des Nations has brought spirit and fire to repertoire from Bach and Handel to Haydn, Mozart, and Beethoven. In 1991, Savall turned to opera, starting with Vicente Martín y Soler's *Una cosa rara* and *Il Burbero di buon cuore;* at the 1999 Salzburg Festival, the ensemble gave the world premiere of *Celos aun de ayre matan* by Calderón de la Barca and Juan Hidalgo.

RECOMMENDED RECORDING
BACH, *BRANDENBURG* CONCERTOS (ASTRÉE).

English Baroque Soloists

Founded by John Eliot Gardiner in 1977, the group was initially made up of members of the Monteverdi Orchestra (which Gardiner also founded, in 1968), and now collaborates with the Monteverdi Choir *(see pages 934–36)*. Since its formation, the London-based ensemble has performed and recorded repertoire ranging from Monteverdi's *L'Orfeo* (1607) and *Vespro della Beata Vergine* (1610) to Beethoven's *Missa Solemnis* (1823), and has established itself at the forefront of the early-music movement. Among the highlights of its extensive discography are superlative accounts of the major sacred works of J. S. Bach and the best-known oratorios of Handel, as well as the first integral cycle of Mozart's piano concertos played on period instruments.

RECOMMENDED RECORDING
HANDEL, *SOLOMON*: WATKINSON, ARGENTA, HENDRICKS, ROLFE JOHNSON, VARCOE (PHILIPS).

The English Concert

Established in 1973 by harpsichordist Trevor Pinnock, has long been considered one of the world's most dependable period instrument orchestras, with a performing and recording repertoire ranging from Baroque instrumental works to the sacred masterpieces of Bach and, in 2001, a celebrated production of Handel's *Tamerlano,* co-produced with the Halle Handel Festival and Théâtre des Champs Elysées, and recorded live at Sadler's Wells. In 2003, the violinist Andrew Manze took over as artistic director, bringing to the ensemble his inimitable brand of high-voltage music making.

Recorder and lute

RECOMMENDED RECORDINGS
Handel, Concerti Grossi, Op. 6, Nos. 1-12: Pinnock (Archiv).
Mozart, *Eine Kleine Nachtmusik*, Serenade No. 6 in D Major, other works: Manze (harmonia mundi).

Europa Galante

Founded in 1990 by the idiosyncratic virtuoso violinist Fabio Biondi, Europa Galante is a prime representative of the blossoming Italian presence in the period instrument movement. Since its first award-winning recording of Vivaldi's *L'estro armonico,* the ensemble has brought its sparkling, spicy interpretive touch to works of Vivaldi, Scarlatti, Locatelli, and other Italian Baroque composers. The orchestra has established an ongoing collaboration with Rome's Ente Santa Cecilia to produce little-known operas by composers such as Caldara, Leonardo Leo, and Alessandro Scarlatti.

RECOMMENDED RECORDING
Vivaldi, *Il cimento dell'armonia e dell'inventione* (12 concertos, including *The Four Seasons*) (Virgin Veritas).

Gabrieli Consort and Players

Founded in 1982 by the British conductor Paul McCreesh, the group first became known for fastidiously researched and magnificently performed historical reconstructions, such as its *Venetian Coronation Mass* (1595), Biber's 40-voice *Missa Salisburgensis,* and J. S. Bach's *Epiphany* Mass. In the late 1990s the ensemble began to tackle the great oratorios of Handel with a critically acclaimed recording of *Messiah,* followed by *Solomon, Saul,* and *Theodora*. The group is also admired for its interpretations of Bach's large-scale works, such as the *Passion* settings, *Mass in B Minor,* the *Easter* Oratorio, and the *Magnificat*.

RECOMMENDED RECORDING
Venetian Vespers: Works of Gabrieli, Monteverdi, Cavalli, Grandi, Marini, and others (Archiv).

Musica Antiqua Köln

Formed as a chamber group in 1973 by Reinhold Goebel and fellow students from the Cologne Conservatory. After a breakthrough performance in London in 1979, Goebel expanded the forces to explore 17th- and 18th-century orchestral repertoire. The ensemble has made important contributions to the rediscovery of German Baroque repertoire, producing a multi-award-winning disc of the

Marc Minkowski in 2002

Dresden Concertos by Johann David Heinichen (1683-1729). Recent recording projects include previously unrecorded works by Telemann and the lesser-known members of the Bach family.

RECOMMENDED RECORDING
Heinichen, *Dresden* Concertos (Archiv).

Les Musiciens du Louvre

Formed in Paris in 1982 and directed by Marc Minkowski, the ensemble spent its first years exploring French Baroque repertoire and reviving lesser-known Handel operas such as *Amadigi, Ariodante,* and *Teseo*. Based in Grenoble since 1996, the ensemble is recognized for its superb opera productions, at the Paris Opéra, Versailles Opera, Houston Opera, and the Salzburg Festival. The orchestra's discography includes instrumental works such as Rebel's *Les éléments* and the symphonies and sonatas of Mondonville; among its numerous opera recordings are Lully's *Acis et Galatée,* Rameau's *Hippolyte et Aricie, Anacréon,* and *Platée,* and Handel's *Teseo*.

RECOMMENDED RECORDING
Rameau, *Platée:* Ragon, Smith, de Mey, Gens, Laurens (WEA International).

Orchestra of the Age of Enlightenment

Formed in 1986 by a group of British period instrument specialists. As a self-governing ensemble, the OAE works with various conductors, among them Roger Norrington, Sir Charles Mackerras, Gustav Leonhardt, and Sir Simon Rattle. Since its 1989 Glyndebourne debut, with performances of *Le nozze di Figaro* under Rattle, the OAE has been the festival's associate orchestra. The ensemble has had great success with its forays into the Romantic repertoire, with programs featuring the works of Mahler, Verdi, Glinka, and Borodin. Based in London, the ensemble is also the associate orchestra of the Royal Festival Hall, where it presents an annual series.

RECOMMENDED RECORDING
C. P. E. Bach, symphonies and cello concertos: Bylsma; Leonhardt (Virgin Veritas).

Philharmonia Baroque Orchestra

Founded in 1981, it is considered America's finest period instrument orchestra. Under the direction of Nicholas McGegan since 1985, the San Francisco-based ensemble has performed at major venues worldwide and released over 30 recordings of Baroque and Classical repertoire. In 1990 the orchestra embarked on a long-term collaboration with the Mark Morris Dance Group, creating innovative productions of Handel's *L'Allegro, il Penseroso ed il Moderato* for Lincoln Center's Mostly Mozart Festival, Purcell's *Dido* and *Aeneas* at the Brooklyn Academy of Music, and the American premiere of Rameau's *Platée* in Berkeley and Los Angeles.

RECOMMENDED RECORDING
Corelli, *Concerti Grossi,* Op. 6 (harmonia mundi).

Tafelmusik

Founded in 1979 and based in Toronto, the group has been under the musical direction of the American-born violinist Jean Lamon since 1981. With a core of 18 members, the ensemble has toured internationally and made more than 70 recordings of repertoire from the Baroque to the Romantic. *Le Mozart Noir,* the orchestra's award-winning recording of music by the Chevalier de Saint-Georges, is also the soundtrack for a film about this remarkable 18th-century French black composer. An adjunct to the orchestra, the Tafelmusik Chamber Choir, was formed in 1981.

RECOMMENDED RECORDING
Bach, *Brandenburg* Concertos (Sony Classical).

Taverner Consort, Choir, and Players

Established in 1973 in response to an invitation by Sir Michael Tippett to perform at the Bath Festival. Under the direction of conductor Andrew Parrott, also a widely respected scholar, the ensemble has made more than 50 recordings, including, in 1999, the first period instrument recording of Purcell's *Dido and Aeneas*. In 2000, Parrott and the Taverner Choir released the recording *Out of the Night,* featuring works by the contemporary minimalists Arvo Pärt and John Tavener.

RECOMMENDED RECORDING
Purcell, *Ode for St. Cecilia's Day:* Kirkby, King, Covey-Crump, Elliott, George, Thomas (EMI).

***Mark Morris Dance group performing* L'Allegro, il Penseroso ed il Moderato**

formed particularly close associations with the Royal Concertgebouw Orchestra of Amsterdam (with which he has recorded the complete symphonies of Schubert, as well as works by Johann Strauss Jr., Dvořák, and Bruckner) and the Vienna Philharmonic (with which he has begun a series of recordings for RCA Red Seal that includes Bruckner's Symphonies Nos. 5 and 9 and Smetana's *Má vlast*). The Philharmonic accorded him a signal honor when it invited him to conduct its millennial New Year's Day 2001 concert; Harnoncourt was again on the Musikverein podium for New Year's Day 2003. Orchestral musicians have said that they like to play for Harnoncourt because of the way he shapes phrases, clarifies structure, and approaches the familiar with a fresh perspective. Despite the flashes of genius that sometimes light up his performances, he remains a notably eccentric, at times fussy, interpreter, whether conducting Bach or Dvořák.

RECOMMENDED RECORDINGS

BEETHOVEN, SYMPHONIES: CHAMBER ORCHESTRA OF EUROPE (TELDEC).

MOZART, *REQUIEM*: YAKAR, WENKEL, EQUILUZ, HOLL; CONCENTUS MUSICUS WIEN (DEUTSCHE HARMONIA MUNDI).

Harold en Italie SYMPHONY FOR VIOLA AND ORCHESTRA BY HECTOR BERLIOZ after Lord Byron's epic poem *Childe Harold,* composed in 1833 for Nicolò Paganini. The owner of a fine Stradivari viola, Paganini had his sights set on a flamboyantly virtuosic concerto; when Berlioz responded with a four-movement symphony lasting three quarters of an hour with a solo part "too full of rests"—especially in the brooding first movement and the freewheeling finale—the Genoese virtuoso was more than a little chagrined. He never played the piece, but after attending a performance of it in 1838 he sent Berlioz a check for 20,000 francs, the equivalent of about $35,000 today, a sum that enabled Berlioz to devote himself full-time to the composition of *Roméo et Juliette,* which was dedicated to Paganini upon its completion.

The four movements of *Harold en Italie* are titled "Harold in the Mountains," "Pilgrims' March," "Serenade," and "Orgy of the Brigands." The opening movement begins with a remarkable orchestral fantasia in the form of a fugato, and the finale includes a series of reminiscences of themes from the preceding movements, in the manner of Beethoven's Ninth Symphony. As in the *Symphonie fantastique,* Berlioz makes use of an IDÉE FIXE (played by the viola and representing the figure of Harold, the Romantic loner and distant observer) to unify the composition.

RECOMMENDED RECORDING

ZUKERMAN; DUTOIT AND MONTREAL SYMPHONY ORCHESTRA (DECCA).

harp Framed string instrument of ancient lineage. Though the physical characteristics and mechanisms of harps have changed through the years, the essential elements in nearly all European harps have been a neck, forepillar, and resonator—generally joined in a triangular arrangement—and strings of graduated length strung between the neck and the resonator.

The modern double-action pedal harp, today's standard concert instrument, was patented by Sébastien Érard in 1810 with a mechanism consisting of two sets of rotating, pedal-activated discs placed along the neck on the left-hand side of the instrument, which by shortening the sounding length of the strings can sharpen their pitch by either a half step or a whole step, allowing the harp to sound all the notes of the chromatic scale. There are 47 strings—seven per octave—tuned to the diatonic C-flat major scale: C-flat, D-flat, E-flat, F-flat, G-flat, A-flat, B-flat. Each of the harp's seven pedals controls the discs for all of the strings tuned to its note, and can be set in one of three positions. With a pedal in its uppermost position, the strings for that particular note are "open" and vibrate freely; depressing the pedal to its middle position raises the pitch by a semitone, and depressing it to its lowest position raises it by another semitone. Thus, with the D pedal in its uppermost position, each of the harp's D strings will sound a D-flat. With the pedal set to the middle position, each will sound a D-natural, and in the lowest position, a D-sharp. Pedal changes can be made quickly and noiselessly while the instrument is being played, enabling the harpist to change tunings on the fly and keep up with all but the most rapid modulation of the harmony. To keep individual strings in tune—a constant challenge, owing to the complexity of the mechanism and the harp's sensitivity to ambient temperature and humidity—harpists use a keylike wrench that fits tuning pins on the right side of the neck. For more than a century, the firm of Lyon & Healy in Chicago has set the standard in the manufacture of harps.

The development of a virtuoso technique followed quickly on Érard's invention of the double-action harp, spearheaded by the playing of English-born Elias Parish Alvars (1808–49) and the teaching of Alphonse Hasselmans (1845–1912), professor at the Paris Conservatoire from 1884 until his death. Among Hasselmans's students were three of the greatest performers and teachers of the 20th century—Carlos Salzedo (1885–1961), whose *Modern Study of the Harp* (1921) remains the bible of technique, Marcel Grandjany (1891–1975), and Lily Laskine (1893–1988).

Like the English horn and the bass clarinet, the harp came into the symphony orchestra by way of the opera pit. Berlioz was the first composer to appropriate it—in his *Symphonie fantastique* (1830), which calls for "at least four" harps, and in *Harold en Italie* (1834), where a note in the score indicates that the single harp is to be placed close to the solo violist, making clear its role as the protagonist's helpmate.

Thereafter, French and Russian composers led the way in employing the harp as an orchestral instrument, both on the concert stage and in the pit, though nearly everybody with an interest in color got into the act. Berlioz himself later wrote discrete parts for six harps in his opera *Les Troyens,* and Liszt gave the harp a prominent role in his *Faust* Symphony. Wagner was extraordinarily fond of the harp, though his writing for it was not particularly idiomatic. He went over the top in the final pages of *Das Rheingold* ◉, calling for six harps in the pit, all with separate parts—their voluminous, sparkling sound limning the Rainbow Bridge over which the gods make their entrance into Valhalla—plus a seventh offstage, cavorting with the Rhine Maidens in the river below. Bruckner followed suit in the second and third movements of his Symphony No. 8, writing a single part to be played by three harps.

There are beautifully idiomatic parts for one or more harps in the ballets of Tchaikovsky and Glazunov, in Rimsky-Korsakov's *Sheherazade* and *Capriccio espagnol* ◉, in Franck's Symphony in D minor, in several of Richard Strauss's tone poems (especially *Don Juan, Tod und Verklärung,* and *Ein Heldenleben*) and in his opera

Fashion has changed in a century, but the harp is pretty much the same.

Salome. The pinnacle comes with Debussy, whose *Prélude à l'après-midi d'un faune* and *La mer* are scored with parts for two harps that are essential to the atmosphere of the pieces and unsurpassed in their musical interest and variety of figuration. Not far behind is Ravel, who makes masterly use of paired harps in his *Rapsodie espagnole* and the ballet *Daphnis et Chloé,* where the instruments are kept particularly busy in the final tableau (familiar to concertgoers as Suite No. 2). The harp is used effectively by Roussel in *Le festin de l'araignée* (without it the spider of the piece's title would have no web), Shostakovich (Symphony No. 5), Britten (an exquisitely challenging part in *Peter Grimes*), and Bartók (Violin Concerto No. 2, *Concerto for Orchestra*).

Many composers have cast the harp as the "bardic" instrument, a descendant of Apollo's lyre. Following the lead of Gluck in *Orfeo ed Euridice,* Wagner armed the minstrel hero of his opera *Tannhäuser* with a harp, on which he accompanies his Act I hymn to Venus. And to begin *Vyšehrad,* the first movement of *Má vlast,* Smetana wrote an extended preamble for two harps, signaling that a "story of old" is about to be told. In much the same vein, Charles Villiers Stanford (1852–1924) gave the harp a prominent role in his Symphony No. 3 (*Irish*).

The concert and recital repertoire for harp includes solo pieces written for the single-action harp by Jan Ladislav Dussek (1760–1812), Jean-Baptiste Krumpholtz (1742–90), and Louis Spohr (1784–1859), all of whom happened to be married to harpists. The gems of the chamber literature are Ravel's Introduction and Allegro (1905) for flute, clarinet, harp, and string quartet and Debussy's Sonata for Flute, Viola, and Harp (1915). The concerto repertoire is not large, and several of the best works have the harp share center stage with the flute—for example, Mozart's Concerto for Flute and Harp, K. 299 (1778), and Hanson's *Serenade* (1945). Major works include Debussy's *Danses* (1903) for harp and string orchestra; concertos by Glier (1938), André Jolivet (1905–74; 1952), and Ginastera (1965); and Hans Werner Henze's (b. 1926) Double Concerto (1966) for oboe, harp, and strings, written for Heinz and Ursula Holliger. The obbligato part for harp in Britten's *Ceremony of Carols* (1942) is as taxing as a concerto.

Among the outstanding virtuosos of the past half century have been the Welsh harpist Osian Ellis, for whom Britten wrote a number of pieces; Alice Chalifoux, the longtime principal of the Cleveland Orchestra, and Marilyn Costello, the longtime principal of the Philadelphia Orchestra, both students of Salzedo; and Nancy Allen, who had a distinguished solo career before becoming principal of the New York Philharmonic and one of Grandjany's successors as professor of harp at the Juilliard School.

harpsichord Keyboard instrument with strings of graduated length, usually strung perpendicular to the keyboard on a wooden frame enclosed within a wooden case. The earliest harpsichords appeared around 1400. The development and refinement of the instrument's design continued for several centuries, and it remained in widespread use until around 1800. The mechanism makes use of individual jacks (one for each string) to which small plectra of quill, leather, or plastic are attached; when a key is depressed, it raises one or more of the jacks, allowing the plectrum, mounted near the top of the jack, to pluck its designated string. When the key is released, the jack drops (a hinged fitting allows the plectrum to slide back over the string more or less silently) and the string is silenced by a damper at the top of the jack. Harpsichords normally have two sets of strings tuned to the same pitch (and two corresponding rows of jacks) for each key, with a shift mechanism that allows the player to engage one set or both. For greater body and variety of tone, many harpsichords built from the mid-17th century on had two manuals, which could be played separately (for contrast) or coupled (for added sonority). The primary reason the harpischord was eventually superseded by the piano was that a player could not achieve substantive dynamic gradations by means of touch.

The emergence around 1600 of a new musical style—the Baroque—one of whose characteristics was the polarization of melody (in the upper voices) and harmony (in the lower ones), established an important niche for the harpsichord in the instrumental ensembles of the period. Alone or in combination with other accompanying instruments, it could sound the bass line and fill in the inner voices of the harmony, a function known as basso continuo. Because of its range the harpsichord was also well suited to the simultaneous playing of melody and accompaniment, which made it particularly attractive as a solo instrument. This ability to function both as a foundation and a solo instrument gave the harpsichord a utility that ensured its long-term survival.

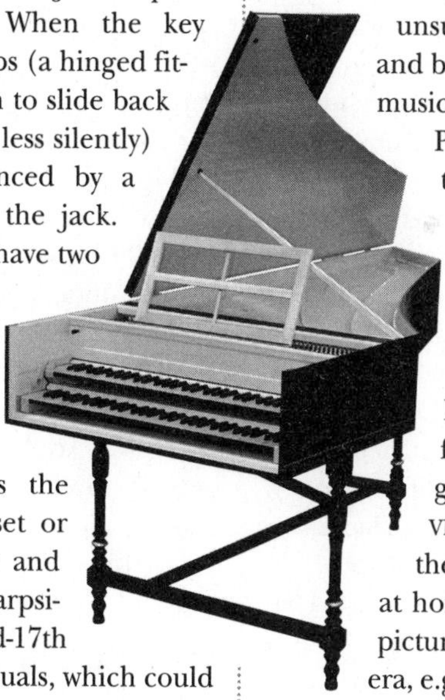

The full-size instruments made by Flemish and French builders from the late 16th century to the mid-18th, often magnificently decorated, were unsurpassed in their sonority and beauty of tone and prized by music lovers throughout Europe. Particularly influential were the instruments produced during the 17th century by the Ruckers family of Antwerp, which possessed a sound that has been emulated ever since. The Flemish makers also were famous for smaller, rectangular instruments known as VIRGINALS, so called because they were almost always played at home by females (and are so pictured in many paintings of the era, e.g., Vermeer's).

The heyday of the solo harpsichord came during the 17th and early 18th centuries. The literature grew impressively in the 17th century, with major contributions from Jacques Champion de Chambonnières (ca. 1601–72) and Louis Couperin (ca. 1626–61) in France, William Byrd, John Bull (ca. 1562–1628), and Thomas Tomkins (1572–1656) in England,

Girolamo Frescobaldi and Bernardo Pasquini (1637–1710) in Italy, and Johann Jacob Froberger (1616–67) in Austria. The supreme works for the harpsichord date from the first half of the 18th century, when Bach, Handel, Rameau, François Couperin, and Domenico Scarlatti produced a matchless body of suites and sonatas ideally tailored to the instrument's capabilities, including the masterpiece of masterpieces for the two-manual harpsichord, Bach's *Goldberg* Variations (1741).

By about 1810 the harpsichord had been fully supplanted by the piano. But with the 20th-century revival of interest in early music came a revival of interest in the harpsichord as well. The instrument was popularized anew by Wanda Landowska (1879–1959)—who had a preference for overbuilt instruments and played them as though they were a peculiarly clangorous species of piano—and a cadre of virtuoso players whose approach was more scholarly and appropriate, including Ralph Kirkpatrick, Gustav Leonhardt, and Rafael Puyana. Robert Levin, Davitt Moroney, Christophe Rousset, and Pierre Hantaï are among the leading harpsichordists of the current generation. Numerous modern builders have produced excellent instruments, including William Dowd, John Lyon, Thomas and Barbara Wolf, and the firms Henk Klop and Bizzi.

Harrell, Lynn

(b. New York, January 30, 1944)

AMERICAN CELLIST. The son of baritone Mack Harrell, he studied with Leonard Rose at Juilliard and with Orlando Cole at Curtis. At 18 he joined the Cleveland Orchestra under George Szell, and in 1964, at 20, he became the orchestra's principal cellist, a chair he kept until 1971, when he embarked on a solo career. He made his New York recital debut in 1971 and his European debut in 1974, and was corecipient of the first Avery Fisher Prize in 1975. Since then Harrell has appeared as a soloist with many of the world's leading orchestras and has performed frequently in chamber music settings with a variety of collaborators. His trio partnership with Itzhak Perlman and Vladimir Ashkenazy was among the most successful of modern times; the group made many outstanding recordings, winning Grammys in 1981 for their account of the Tchaikovsky Piano Trio and in 1987 for their traversal of the complete Beethoven piano trios. More recently, Harrell has performed in a trio with Anne-Sophie Mutter and André Previn.

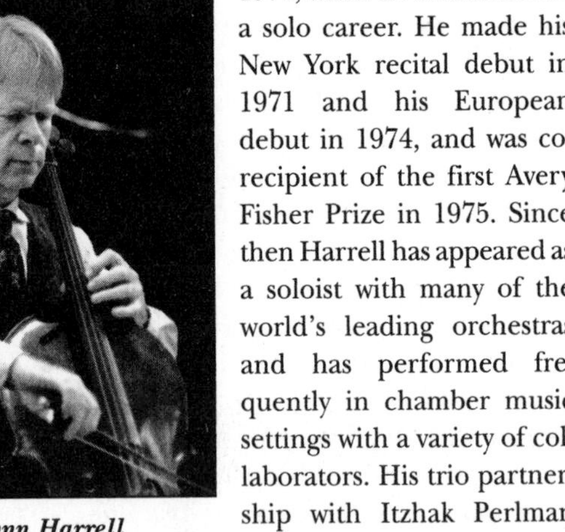

Lynn Harrell

Harrell has taught at the Cincinnati College-Conservatory, the Juilliard School, the University of Southern California, and the Royal Academy of Music in London, serving briefly (1993–95) as the latter's director. Since 2002, he has taught cello at Rice University in Houston, Texas. He plays a 1720 Montagnana.

RECOMMENDED RECORDINGS

BACH, CELLO SUITES (DECCA).

PROKOFIEV, CELLO CONCERTOS: PREVIN AND LONDON SYMPHONY ORCHESTRA; DUTOIT AND MONTREAL SYMPHONY ORCHESTRA (DECCA).

Harris, Roy

(b. near Chandler, Okla., February 12, 1898; d. Santa Monica, Calif., October 1, 1979)

AMERICAN COMPOSER. His parents were farmers. Like many rural midwesterners in search of a better life, they moved to California, where as a child Harris helped out on the farm and studied piano and clarinet. After high school he farmed his own land, drove a delivery truck for a dairy, studied on and off at UCLA and Berkeley, and tried his hand at composition. His teachers included Arthur Farwell, Modeste Altschuler, and Arthur Bliss. He studied with Nadia Boulanger in Paris from 1926 to 1929 and later taught at Mills College. He composed his first symphony, *Symphony 1933,* on a commission from Serge Koussevitzky. The work's successful premiere encouraged Harris in his symphonic ambitions, and he produced another 14 symphonies at regular intervals over the next 40 years. Four of these (Nos. 3, 7, 8, and 11) were single-movement works, a form Harris found particularly congenial.

Roy Harris

With his Symphony No. 3 (1939), composed on a commission from Hans Kindler and the National Symphony Orchestra but premiered by Koussevitzky and the Boston Symphony, Harris established himself as a figure of major importance on the American scene at a crucial moment in history. The work, a true American epic, electrified concert and radio audiences with its stark yet uncomplicated melodic content and accessible gestures, and is considered a landmark of mid-20th-century American symphonic thought.

Harris's best music—which includes his orchestral variations on *When Johnny Comes Marching Home* (1934) and Symphony No. 6 (*Gettysburg*), composed in 1944—is forceful in its expression and original in construction. The salient features of his style are modal inflections in the melody, harmony based on fourths, lean textures, asymmetrical rhythms and phrases, frequent ostinatos and long pedal points, orchestration by choir, and a predilection for continuous unfolding and variation rather than standard development. Harris's idiom was flavored by his association during the 1930s with students and practitioners of folk music, among them Burl Ives, Woody Guthrie, and the Lomaxes.

Harris is seen by some as the father of a distinctively American school of symphonic composition, and by others as a cantankerous if well-intentioned primitive —short on training and craft, long on bombast— who embraced so many peculiar notions that by the end of his career he could not be taken seriously. The truth lies in between: Harris started out as a visionary and trailblazer, and lived long enough to devolve into a crackpot.

RECOMMENDED RECORDINGS

SYMPHONY NO. 3: BERNSTEIN AND NEW YORK PHILHARMONIC (SONY).

SYMPHONY NO. 6 (*GETTYSBURG*): CLARK AND PACIFIC SYMPHONY ORCHESTRA (ALBANY).

***WHEN JOHNNY COMES MARCHING HOME*: SCHWARZ AND SEATTLE SYMPHONY ORCHESTRA (DELOS).**

Harrison, Lou

(b. Portland, Ore., May 14, 1917; d. Lafayette, Ind., February 2, 2003)

AMERICAN COMPOSER. A West Coast original, he wrote works for the stage (including opera), orchestra (including symphonies and concertos), chorus, mixed ensembles, solo voices, and keyboard. He experimented with unusual sonorities and esoteric tuning systems—he was especially fond of "just intonation," in which the thirds are pure—and sought to integrate in new and surprisingly beautiful ways the sounds and textures of Asian music with the notational procedures and formal schemes of Western classical music.

Harrison grew up in northern California, where his family moved in 1926. In 1935, after graduating from high school, he became a composition student of Henry Cowell in San Francisco, and in 1937 he was hired by the dance department at Mills College as an accompanist. During the late 1930s, he formed a close association with John Cage. The two spent hours rummaging through San Francisco junkyards seeking out brake drums, oxygen bottles, automobile springs—anything that made an interesting sound when struck—and founded the first Western percussion ensemble. Additional musical stimulus came from frequenting performances of Cantonese opera in Chinatown.

By the time he left San Francisco in 1942, Harrison had composed more than 175 works. He moved to Los Angeles, where he studied with Arnold Schoenberg (1942–43), and went to New York in 1943 along with Lester Horton and his dance troupe. There he revived his associations with Cage and Cowell and developed a close friendship with Virgil Thomson, who added him to his stable of reviewers at the *New York Herald Tribune* and became a powerful advocate of his music. Harrison worked as a critic from 1943 to 1947, and, like Thomson, remained active on both sides of the footlights. On April 6, 1946—35 years after it was written—he conducted the premiere of Charles Ives's Symphony No. 3 (*Camp Meeting*), which he had edited from the manuscript score. The piece won Ives a Pulitzer Prize the following year.

After suffering a nervous breakdown in 1947, Harrison sought solace from the noise and stress of New York City by spending two summers at Reed College in Oregon, and in 1951 he joined the faculty at Black Mountain College in North Carolina. He returned to California in 1953, settling in Aptos, south of Santa Cruz, living on grants and doing odd jobs, including a three-year stint working by day (as an orderly) at an animal hospital and composing at night. During these years, Harrison again found himself looking to Asia for inspiration, and he made trips to Japan, Korea, and Taiwan in 1961–62. In 1971 he and his companion William Colvig, a craftsman and amateur musician, built a gamelan out of various found metal objects. A few years later he met gamelan master K. R. T. Wasitodiningrat and began a study of traditional gamelan techniques.

Harrison's music is wonderfully eclectic, original, and personal. Early on, after becoming fatigued with equal temperament and rigorous argument (each a sine qua non of most Western music of the past three centuries), he experimented with alternative tuning systems (especially just intonation), the use of irregular rhythmic patterns repeated ostinato-fashion, and the creation of an unbroken melodic flow over drones or the sparest of background textures (like much Asian art). Ten years before he made his first trip to the Far East, Asian influences were already apparent in his Suite for Violin, Piano, and Small Orchestra (1951), whose ensemble consists of three winds, two cellos, bass, harp, celesta, tam-tam, and "tack piano." Over the years Harrison turned out dozens of works for gamelan, of which two of the most interesting are the 1972 *La Koro Sutro* ("The Heart Sutra") for 100-voice chorus, gamelan, harp, and organ, based on Buddhist scriptures from the first century B.C. onward, and the Double Concerto for Violin and Cello, with Javanese Gamelan (1981–82). Toward the end of his career he returned to his roots in dance with *Rhymes with Silver,* a 12-movement suite for solo cello and chamber ensemble commissioned by

The Sneeze—an Edison film strip, ca. 1896

choreographer Mark Morris and premiered in 1997 with Yo-Yo Ma as soloist.

Like Mozart's, Harrison's music often contains beautiful "parting gifts," for example, "Round Dance" (the final movement of *Rhymes with Silver*) and the concluding chorale of the Suite for Violin, Piano, and Small Orchestra. Everything he created testified to his love of beautiful sound—derived from many of the same influences as Debussy's, including the gamelan—and his fascination with the unexpected. These qualities made his one of the most distinctive voices in American music.

RECOMMENDED RECORDINGS

DOUBLE CONCERTO (WITH TRIO FOR VIOLIN, CELLO, AND PIANO): MILLS COLLEGE GAMELAN ENSEMBLE (MUSIC ARTS).

LA KORO SUTRO (WITH *SUITE FOR VIOLIN AND AMERICAN GAMELAN*): VARIOUS ARTISTS (NEW ALBION).

RHYMES WITH SILVER: JEAN RENAUD ENSEMBLE (NEW ALBION).

Háry János A MUSICAL ENTERTAINMENT IN THE STYLE OF A *SINGSPIEL*—with spoken dialogue—composed by Zoltán Kodály to a libretto by Béla Paulini and Zsolt Harsányi (based on the humorous verse epic *Az obsitos* [*The Veteran*] by János Garay), and premiered in Budapest on October 16, 1926. The plot follows the made-up exploits of a hussar in the Napoleonic Wars named János Háry (the Hungarians put family names first, so he is Háry János to them)—a Hungarian Everyman who triumphs over adversity, defeats the tyrant, and gets the girl. The colorfully orchestrated score, which includes a prominent part for the cimbalom, consists of a prelude and a number of characteristic dances, marches, and vocal pieces strung together with dialogue to make a fairy-tale romance lasting an hour and three quarters. The prelude begins with the musical depiction of a sneeze—Hungarian folklore maintaining that anything a person says after a sneeze is bound to be untrue.

A year after its premiere, Kodály excerpted the prelude and five numbers from the score to form a concert suite, which received its premiere in Barcelona on October 24, 1927. This suite has since become one of the most popular pieces of 20th-century orchestral music. It includes a sprightly depiction of a Viennese musical clock and an intermezzzo in the style of a *VERBUNKOS*, with the cimbalom going full tilt.

RECOMMENDED RECORDINGS

COMPLETE: USTINOV; KERTÉSZ AND LONDON SYMPHONY ORCHESTRA (DECCA).

SUITE: SZELL AND CLEVELAND ORCHESTRA (SONY).

Haydn, [Franz] Joseph

(b. Rohrau, March 31, 1732; d. Vienna, May 31, 1809)

AUSTRIAN COMPOSER. Although he did not actually invent either genre, he is rightly regarded as the father of both the symphony and the string quartet. During most of his career, he was considered the world's greatest living composer, and he deserves much of the credit for developing the Classical style out of the Baroque and Rococo and for advancing it to the very threshold of Romanticism.

The son of a wheelwright and a cook, he had a gift for singing and a phenomenal musical memory, and by the age of seven had been recruited to sing in the choir of St. Stephen's Cathedral in Vienna. In 1749, when his voice changed, he left the choir and began to make his living as a teacher and freelance musician, playing serenades in the streets for pocket change, composing at night, and living in an unheated garret. Around 1753 he landed a job as an assistant to Nicola Porpora, accompanying the elder master's singing students and absorbing many of the finer points of the Italian style in the process. His big break came in 1757, when he was engaged as music director by Count Morzin, the Bohemian nobleman whose grandfather had been a patron of Vivaldi. While in Morzin's service he composed his first symphonies and possibly his first string quartets, as well as keyboard sonatas, trios, and several divertimentos and wind serenades.

In 1761 the newly married Haydn accepted an offer of employment from Prince Paul Anton Esterházy. The prince died the following year and was succeeded by his brother Nicolaus, who encouraged Haydn to stay on by raising his salary 50 percent. Haydn served Nicolaus for nearly 30 years, first as vice-Kapellmeister, then as Kapellmeister, working in Eisenstadt and, from 1767, spending long periods with the prince's orchestra at Esterháza, his newly built summer residence on the shores of Lake Neusiedl, in what is now western Hungary.

Joseph Haydn, portrait in gouache by Johann Zitterer, ca. 1790

Haydn's output while in the service of the Esterházys was immense—roughly 80 symphonies, 50 quartets, and 45 keyboard sonatas, about a dozen Italian operas, half a dozen singspiels for the marionette theater at Esterháza, and even 126 baryton trios (the baryton, resembling a viola d'amore with frets, being the instrument Prince Nicolaus himself played). Haydn produced about 25 symphonies during his years as vice-Kapellmeister (1761–65) that exhibit great variety of style and treatment, and uniform brilliance of execution. During the early 1770s he emphasized strength and passion more than elegance, and the works of this period are often referred to as his Sturm und Drang symphonies—something of a misnomer, since the literary movement to which the term refers came into existence later.

On January 1, 1779, Haydn signed a new contract with Nicolaus that freed him to accept outside commissions, in effect declaring his independence as a composer. His work at Esterháza centered on opera for the next few years, and he produced a string of first-rate works—*L'isola disabitata* (1779), *La fedeltà premiata* (1781), *Orlando paladino* (1782), and *Armida* (1784). But in 1785 he took advantage of his newly won freedom to compose a set of six symphonies on commission from the Count d'Ogny for the Concert de la Loge Olympique in Paris. Written for a large orchestra, led by the swashbuckling Chevalier de Saint-Georges, the PARIS SYMPHONIES are notable for their vigorous opening movements, their elegant slow movements, and their imaginative use of the orchestra throughout—one example of many being the oboe's vivid "clucking" that inspired the Parisians to dub Symphony No. 83 in G minor *La poule* (*The Hen*).

Between 1787 and 1789 Haydn followed these symphonies with five more (Nos. 88–92) in which his sovereign command of musical imagery leaps out from every page. Nothing could be more wonderfully rustic than the animated country-dance finale of Symphony No. 88 in G, yet behind the bucolic facade, the workmanship is extraordinary. Following the death of Prince Nicolaus in 1790, Haydn was approached by Johann Peter Salomon to write a set of six symphonies for London. Haydn, who had not traveled widely, spent much of 1791–92 in England supervising the performance of six new symphonies. They were so successful that another six were commissioned, which he returned to London to present in 1794–95. In their stylistic sophistication and the richness of their ideas, Haydn's 12 LONDON SYMPHONIES stand among the very highest peaks of symphonic art. They mark, as the American musicologist Leonard Ratner has noted, "the culmination of a long period of growth in skill, fluency, and fantasy." In their rhetorical strength, assured handling of form, robust scoring, and bold gestures they surpass everything he had done previously and epitomize the formal and expressive aims of the Classical style, inviting comparison with the best of Mozart's work. They are particularly rich in topical gestures—like the incursion of "hostile" Turkish elements (triangle, cymbals, and bass drum) into the Allegretto, and later the finale, of Symphony No. 100 in G, known for this reason as the *Military*. No group of works better exemplifies Haydn's unique ability to combine elevated discourse and playfulness, or shows to better effect his delight in the unexpected. This quality is apparent not just in the surprise that gives Symphony No. 94 in G its famous nickname, but in many other touches, for example, the sparkling violin solos strewn throughout the *presto* finale of Symphony No. 98 in B-flat, which Salomon would have played at the premiere from the concertmaster's desk. These are answered at the end of the movement by a slowed-down, ornamented reprise of the movement's rondo theme, played as a solo on the harpsichord—a jolly little tip of the cap from Haydn himself that must have sent the symphony's first audience into transports.

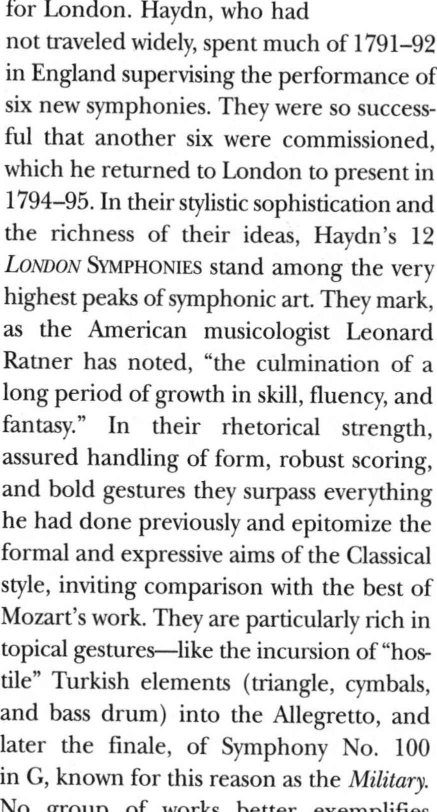

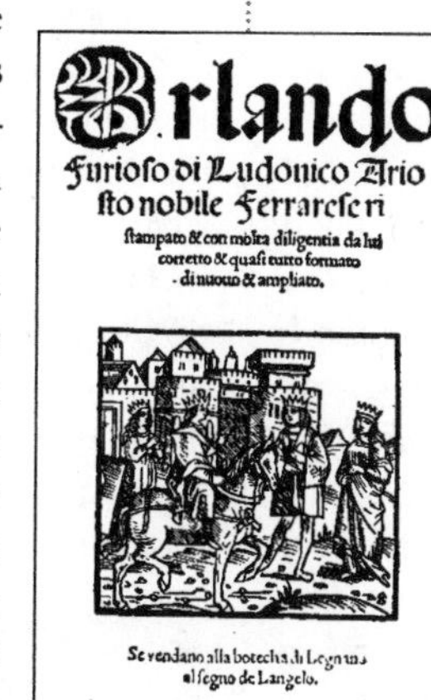

***Ariosto's* Orlando furioso**

There is more to Haydn than his symphonies, splendid as they are. The nearly 70 string quartets he composed between 1762 and 1799, along with the piano sonatas and piano trios he produced after 1790, are the bedrock of the active chamber music literature. With his six *Russian* Quartets, Op. 33 (1781), he effectively brought the quartet genre into its maturity, and in the quartets he composed from 1787 onward (Opp. 50, 54, 55, 64, 71, 74, 76, and 77), so brilliant in their formal and melodic invention, he defined the state of the art of quartet writing in the 18th century.

The great works of Haydn's final years were the oratorios *THE CREATION* (1796–98) and *THE SEASONS* (1799–1801) and the six masses composed between 1796 and 1802 for the name day (September 8) of Princess Maria Hermenegild, wife of young Prince Nicolaus Esterházy, the grandson of Haydn's longtime patron. The glorious architecture, rich musical characterization, and unfettered invention of the *London*

Symphonies and the late string quartets and piano trios are carried forward in these radiant works, which additionally testify to their composer's robust and deeply rooted Catholic faith.

Haydn's work as an instrumental composer proved particularly important to the evolution of musical thought. At the time he began working in the genres, around 1760, the symphony and string quartet had few formal or procedural norms. By the mid-1780s he had established lasting models for both. Even more important, he devised a novel manner of developing thematic material in such works, by breaking it down into units of several notes that through repetition and extension could be turned into "engines" capable of driving a movement's line of action forward in a very dramatic way. Most of the music of the past two centuries has to some extent used this procedure. *See also* STRING QUARTET.

RECOMMENDED RECORDINGS

THE CREATION: JANOWITZ, LUDWIG, WUNDERLICH; KARAJAN AND BERLIN PHILHARMONIC (DG).

LATE MASSES: VARIOUS SOLOISTS; HICKOX AND COLLEGIUM MUSICUM 90 (CHANDOS).

LONDON SYMPHONIES: DAVIS AND CONCERTGEBOUW ORCHESTRA (PHILIPS).

LONDON SYMPHONIES: JOCHUM AND LONDON PHILHARMONIC ORCHESTRA (DG).

PARIS SYMPHONIES: KUIJKEN AND ORCHESTRA OF THE AGE OF ENLIGHTENMENT (VIRGIN CLASSICS).

STRING QUARTETS, OP. 33: MOSAÏQUES QUARTET (ASTRÉE).

STRING QUARTETS, OP. 76: MOSAÏQUES QUARTET (ASTRÉE).

Haydn, [Johann] Michael

(b. Rohrau, September 14, 1737; d. Salzburg, August 10, 1806)

AUSTRIAN COMPOSER, younger brother of Joseph Haydn. He received his education at the choir school of St. Stephen's in Vienna, and by the age of 12 was serving as a substitute organist there. He left Vienna when he was about 20 and served for several years as Kapellmeister to the bishop of Grosswardein (now Oradea, Romania). In 1763 he became court concertmaster to the Archbishop of Salzburg; his colleagues in the Salzburg musical establishment included Leopold Mozart and, soon enough, the young prodigy Wolfgang Amadeus Mozart, who found much to admire in his music and remained a friend over the years.

Haydn served in Salzburg for the rest of his life, achieving distinction as a composer of sacred music and producing a body of instrumental work that included about 40 symphonies as well as serenades, marches, minuets, and some chamber pieces.

RECOMMENDED RECORDING

SELECTED SYMPHONIES: BAMERT AND LONDON MOZART PLAYERS (CHANDOS).

***Haydn* Quartets** SET OF SIX STRING QUARTETS BY WOLFGANG AMADEUS MOZART (in G, K. 387; in D minor, K. 421; in E-flat, K. 428; in B-flat, K. 458; in A, K. 464; and in C, K. 465) composed between December 1782 and January 1785 and published in September 1785 with a dedication to Joseph Haydn. In deference to Haydn, Mozart withheld publication and performance of the individual quartets until all six were ready; they were performed for their dedicatee at a private reading on January 15, 1785. Haydn had a second opportunity to hear three of the quartets—K. 465, K. 428, and K. 464—played for him by Wolfgang and Leopold Mozart and the Barons Anton and Bartholomäus Tinti in February 1785. It was on this occasion that he paid his celebrated compliment to the composer's father: "I tell you before God and as an honest man, that your son is the greatest composer I know personally or by reputation. He has taste and, what is more, the greatest knowledge of the technique of composition."

In their structural integrity, richness of character, and warm expressiveness, the *Haydn* Quartets represent Mozart's finest achievement in the genre. They exhibit an extraordinarily high level of melodic and harmonic invention along with a remarkable degree of contrapuntal sophistication; and while they are clearly indebted to Haydn's own example (especially that of his Op. 33 quartets), they repay their obligation with interest. *See also* HUNT QUARTET.

RECOMMENDED RECORDINGS

COMPLETE: MOSAÏQUES QUARTET (ASTRÉE).

K. 458 AND 465: ALBAN BERG QUARTETT (WARNER).

***Hebrides* Overture** CONCERT OVERTURE BY FELIX MENDELSSOHN, subtitled "Fingal's Cave," inspired by a trip to Scotland in the summer of 1829, and composed and revised between 1830 and 1832. The work's opening was conceived on the spot, in a flash of inspiration. The key is a brooding B minor, and undulating figures in the lower strings suggest the regular motion of the sea; over this, the violins sustain octave F-sharps, the fifth of the chord, creating an effect that is eerie and unsettled. The piece's stormy climax is gripping and expertly gauged. The *Hebrides* Overture is one of the seminal works in a whole vein of Romantic music, a masterpiece of pictorialism (as opposed to programmatic narrative) in which texture and sonority are used to remarkably expressive ends. In its vivid evocation of a restless, mysterious sea viewed in bleak northern light, it is as stark and powerful as the paintings of C. D. Friedrich, and as evocative as the nature poetry of Wordsworth.

heckelphone Double-reed woodwind instrument with a wide conical bore, large tone holes, and a perforated spherical bell, sounding an octave below the oboe—in effect a baritone oboe. The reed is set into a curved crook, like that of the English horn, and is similarly shaped, though somewhat larger; the key system is based on that of the German oboe. The standard version of the instrument is pitched in C and has a range from the A a tenth below middle C to the G a twelfth above. It is most effective in its lower two octaves, where it produces a reedy and robust sound. The original *Heckelphon* was developed around 1904 by Wilhelm Heckel, of the German family famous for their bassoons, in response to an idea originally suggested to him by Richard Wagner. The first composer to write for the instrument was Richard Strauss, who included a prominent part for it in his opera *Salome* (1905). Later works of Strauss calling for a heckelphone include *Elektra* (1909) and *Eine Alpensinfonie* (1915). Among others who have written for the instrument are Orff, Hindemith, and Varèse (*Arcana*).

Heckelphone

Heifetz, Jascha

(b. Vilna, February 2, 1900 or 1901; d. Los Angeles, December 10, 1987

AMERICAN VIOLINIST OF RUSSIAN BIRTH. He possessed the most accomplished technique of any violinist in history, and set the standard of virtuosity on the instrument in the 20th century. He began his study of the violin with his father in 1903 and started formal training with Ilya Malkin at the Imperial School of Music in Vilna in 1905. In 1907 he gave his first public performance, playing the Mendelssohn E minor concerto. He became a student of Leopold Auer at the St. Petersburg Conservatory in 1910 and made his concert debut on April 30, 1911, in St. Petersburg. He created a sensation in Berlin in 1912 playing the Tchaikovsky concerto with the Berlin Philharmonic under Arthur Nikisch (despite hostile reviews), and he subsequently toured Austria and Scandinavia.

Heifetz made his American debut in Carnegie Hall on October 27, 1917. In the audience that afternoon, violinist Mischa Elman turned to pianist Leopold Godowsky, and, dabbing at his forehead with a handkerchief, whispered, "It's warm in here, isn't it?" "Not for pianists," Godowsky shot back. Overnight, Heifetz became the musical idol of America; in the span of a year he made 30 appearances in New York alone. He made his first recording in November 1917 and his debuts in London and Paris in 1920. In 1930, five years after becoming an American citizen, he published a transcription of Grigoraş Dinicu's *Hora staccato* (it would become one of his favorite encore pieces), and in 1934 he undertook a 17-day tour of Russia, the only time he would return to his homeland. He made several USO tours in 1942–44, on one occasion playing 45 concerts in eight weeks in North Africa and Italy. During the 1940s, he settled in Beverly Hills, where he lived until his death. In 1946, using the alias Jim Hoyl, he penned his first popular song, "When You Make Love to Me—Don't Make Believe." The tune was recorded by Bing Crosby and Margaret Whiting.

Heifetz spent the 1950s and 1960s concertizing and recording for RCA Victor as the label's marquee artist. He was named professor of violin at the University of Southern California in 1961; that same year he inaugurated a series of concerts in Los Angeles with cellist Gregor Piatigorsky. He gradually curtailed his appearances and gave his last public performance in 1972 at the Los Angeles Music Center. Ending his association with USC in 1983, Heifetz devoted the final years of his life to private teaching. His students included Eugene Fodor and Glenn Dicterow, concertmaster of the New York Philharmonic since 1980.

Heifetz's repertoire encompassed all the major concertos of the 19th century, as well as the concertos of Glazunov, Sibelius, and Elgar. A number of important pieces were written for or premiered by him, including the violin concertos of William Walton (1936–39) and Erich Wolfgang Korngold (1947). Heifetz also championed works by Hollywood composers Franz Waxman (1906–67; his *Carmen Fantasy* of 1947) and Miklós Rózsa (1907–95; his Violin Concerto, written in 1953).

Heifetz's virtuosity was astonishing. He had the instinct for speed of a thoroughbred racehorse, together with extraordinary fingers capable of articulating passagework at exorbitantly fast tempos. His intonation was uncannily exact, his tone powerful and—thanks to his intense, fast vibrato—distinctively "hot." Though he seemed distant on the stage, barely moving as he played, he was hardly unemotional; if anything, his playing suffered from hyperexpressiveness and a tendency toward flamboyance. (These qualities led to his being criticized by Virgil Thomson as a purveyor of "silk underwear music," a comment that said more about Thomson than about Heifetz.) He rarely rethought an interpretation, but for many listeners he epitomized the art of violin playing. For most of his career, Heifetz played

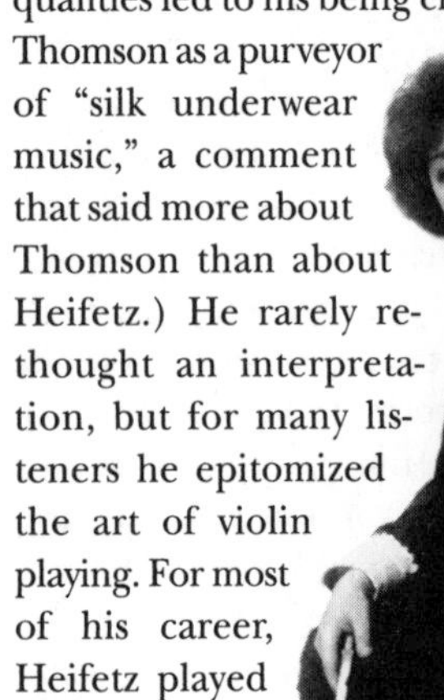

Jascha Heifetz, child prodigy

the 1742 "David" Guarneri del Gesù (named for the violinist Ferdinand David), on which the Mendelssohn E minor concerto received its premiere. At the beginning of the 21st century that instrument (valued at $10 million) went on loan to Alexander Barantschik, concertmaster of the San Francisco Symphony Orchestra.

RECOMMENDED RECORDINGS

Brahms, Violin Concerto: Reiner and Chicago Symphony Orchestra (RCA).

Tchaikovsky, Violin Concerto; Mendelssohn, Violin Concerto: Reiner and Chicago Symphony Orchestra (RCA).

Heldenleben, Ein (A Hero's Life) **Tone poem by Richard Strauss, Op. 40.** The "hero," thinly disguised, is Strauss himself. Composed in 1898 and dedicated to Willem Mengelberg and the Concertgebouw Orchestra of Amsterdam, the score was premiered on March 3, 1899, in Frankfurt, under the composer's direction. It is in a single continuous movement lasting about 40 minutes, but falls into six distinct parts.

The opening section is a glorified march clothed in the most sumptuous of orchestral colors. The Hero's theme, proclaimed by strings and first horn, strides broadly through it, triumphant from the start. In the second section, called "The Hero's Adversaries," the critics are depicted by strident, querulous solos in the wind and brass. The scene shifts to a portrayal of "The Hero's Companion," whose capricious, complicated nature is represented by a series of flighty solos on the violin. In part 4, "The Hero's Battlefield," the Hero and his adversaries clash mightily, and by the battle's end the field is littered with the corpses of the critics. The music of the opening returns, and the Hero parades in victory. Triumph is savored, but soon gives way to contemplation in the fifth section. Motives from a number of Strauss's previous compositions are woven into "The Hero's Works of Peace," in which the Hero revels not only in his past triumphs but in his ongoing and absolute mastery of the orchestra. There are prominent references to *Don Juan, Don Quixote,* and *Till Eulenspiegel,* and a fond look back at less familiar works, including Strauss's first opera, *Guntram,* and one of the loveliest of his songs, "Traum durch die Dämmerung" ("Dream in the Twilight"). In the work's closing section, the Hero, joined by his companion, withdraws from the world in search of an inner peace that is lit, in the final measures, by a briefly flickering memory of his earlier heroism.

RECOMMENDED RECORDING

Reiner and Chicago Symphony Orchestra (RCA).

hemiola (from Gr. *hemiolios,* "a half and a whole") Any rhythmic pattern in which units consisting of two beats are set against a prevailing triple meter, or three-beat units against duple meter, resulting in metric ambiguity. The procedure originated in medieval music with the substitution of three "imperfect" notes (each taking two beats) for two "perfect" (three-beat) ones. It became a common feature of Baroque dance music, and was frequently employed by Brahms (who had a great fondness for past practices) in his instrumental works.

Heppner, Ben

(b. Murrayville, B.C., January 14, 1956)

Canadian tenor. One of nine children in a British Columbia farm family, he studied music at the University of British Columbia and sang with the Canadian Opera Company's Ensemble Studio in Toronto during the mid-1980s. In 1987, he began studies with tenor William Neill, switching from lighter lyric repertoire into spinto territory, and in 1988 was a

Ben Heppner as Peter Grimes at the Royal Opera, Covent Garden, 2004

winner of the Metropolitan Opera National Council Auditions, taking the Birgit Nilsson Prize. (Soprano Renée Fleming and mezzo Susan Graham were also winners that year.) He was quickly engaged by major houses to sing roles such as Bacchus in Strauss's *Ariadne auf Naxos,* the Prince in Dvořák's *Rusalka,* Laca in Janáček's *Jenůfa,* and Florestan in Beethoven's *Fidelio.* He made his Metropolitan Opera debut in 1991 in the title role of Mozart's *Idomeneo.*

Heppner's Wagner career began in 1989, with the title role in *Lohengrin* at the Royal Swedish Opera; in 1990, he made his debut at La Scala as Walther in *Die Meistersinger von Nürnberg.* In 1998, he sang his first Tristan at the Seattle Opera, repeating the role at the Met in 1999; he has since made it a central part of his repertoire. Heppner has also been praised for his performances as Peter Grimes, and as Énéo in Berlioz's *Les Troyens,* which he first sang in concert in 2000 with the London Symphony Orchestra and Sir Colin Davis and first performed on stage at the Metropolitan Opera in 2003. Heppner created the title role in William Bolcom's *McTeague* at the Lyric Opera of Chicago in 1992, and took on Verdi's Otello in Chicago in 2001 and at the Met in 2004.

Heppner's concert repertoire includes Mahler's *Das Lied von der Erde,* Schoenberg's *Gurre-Lieder,* Kodály's *Psalmus Hungaricus,* Beethoven's Ninth Symphony, Mahler's Eighth Symphony, Britten's *War Requiem,* and the Verdi Requiem. He has taken part in recordings of Strauss's *Die Frau ohne Schatten,* Puccini's *Turandot,* and Dvořák's *Rusalka*; he has also recorded several recital discs, including one devoted to the songs of Paolo Tosti (1846–1916). His voice, that of a true Heldentenor, is sizable yet firmly focused, with clarion top notes. At its best his singing is characterized by an affecting combination of intelligence and emotive thrust.

RECOMMENDED RECORDINGS

BERLIOZ, *LES TROYENS*: DE YOUNG, MATTEI, LANG, MINGARDO; DAVIS AND LONDON SYMPHONY ORCHESTRA (LSO LIVE).

MAHLER, *DAS LIED VON DER ERDE*: MEIER; MAAZEL AND BAVARIAN RADIO SYMPHONY ORCHESTRA (RCA).

WAGNER: *DIE MEISTERSINGER*: STUDER, KALLISCH, MOLL; SAWALLISCH AND BAVARIAN STATE ORCHESTRA (EMI/ANGEL).

Herreweghe, Philippe

(b. Ghent, May 2, 1947)

BELGIAN CONDUCTOR. He studied medicine and psychiatry while attending the conservatory in Ghent, and received piano and organ lessons from Marcel Gazelle. He founded the choral group Collegium Vocale Gent in 1969. His performances with the Collegium attracted the attention of Nikolaus Harnoncourt and Gustav Leonhardt, who invited the group to participate in their project to record Bach's complete cantatas. In 1977 Herreweghe founded La Chapelle Royale, a period instrument ensemble based in Paris, with which he has recorded a substantial amount of 17th- and 18th-century music, including major sacred works of

J. S. Bach and hitherto neglected masterpieces by such luminaries of the French Baroque as Lully, Marc-Antoine Charpentier (ca. 1645–1704), and André Campra (1660–1744). He branched out yet again in 1991, establishing the Orchestre des Champs-Elysées to perform Romantic works on original instruments.

A perfectionist with heart, Herreweghe is one of the most perceptive and penetrating musicians active today. His recordings of the great choral works of the Baroque are formidable achievements notable for their polish and beauty, and for a spiritual elevation that approaches the sublime.

RECOMMENDED RECORDINGS

BACH, *MASS IN B MINOR*: GENS, SCHOLL, PRÉGARDIEN, KOOY; COLLEGIUM VOCALE (HARMONIA MUNDI).

LASSUS, *LAMENTATIONS OF JEREMIAH*: CHAPELLE ROYALE (HARMONIA MUNDI).

MENDELSSOHN, OVERTURE AND INCIDENTAL MUSIC TO *A MIDSUMMER NIGHT'S DREAM*: ORCHESTRE DES CHAMPS ELYSÉES (HARMONIA MUNDI).

Hess, Dame Myra

(b. London, February 25, 1890; d. London, November 25, 1965)

ENGLISH PIANIST, famous for her lunch-hour recitals in London's National Gallery during World War II. She studied at the Guildhall School of Music and with Tobias Matthay at the Royal Academy of Music. She made her debut in 1907, playing Beethoven's Piano Concerto No. 4 with the Queen's Hall Orchestra under Thomas Beecham, and in 1908 appeared for the first time at the Proms, beginning a long series of collaborations with Henry Wood. She made her American debut in 1922, and was a regular visitor in the years before and after World War II. Hess identified herself most closely with the music of Mozart, Beethoven, and Schumann, and was at her best in the Mozart concertos. Although she possessed a thoroughly respectable technique, her finest qualities were musical rather than pianistic, and included her supple way of treating rhythm and figure and her refreshingly straightforward manner of expression.

RECOMMENDED RECORDINGS

BEETHOVEN, PIANO CONCERTOS NOS. 2 AND 5: SARGENT AND BBC SYMPHONY ORCHESTRA (BBC LEGENDS).

MOZART, PIANO CONCERTO NO. 23, K. 488 (WITH BEETHOVEN, PIANO CONCERTO NO. 4): BOULT WITH LONDON PHILHARMONIC ORCHESTRA (BBC LEGENDS).

hexachord (from Gr. *hex* and *chorde*, "string of six") [1] A stepwise arrangement of six notes (rather than the seven of the DIATONIC scale) used as a mnemonic device in the teaching of music during the Middle Ages. The concept was introduced by Guido of Arezzo (ca. 991–ca. 1035); the tones of the hexachord were named after the opening syllables—*ut, re, mi, fa, sol, la*—of the first six lines of the plainchant *Ut queant laxis*, each of which began a step higher than its predecessor. This became the basis of the technique of solmization—sight-singing by means of syllables—still in use today. [2] In 12-TONE music, either of the two groups of six pitches that make up a 12-tone row.

Higdon, Jennifer *See box on pages 708–11.*

Hildegard von Bingen

(b. Bermersheim, 1098; d. Rupertsberg, September 17, 1179)

GERMAN ABBESS, COMPOSER, AND WRITER. Her parents, Hildebert and Mechtild von Bermersheim, were of the nobility and gave her as a tithe to the Benedictine Convent of Disibodenberg, southwest of Mainz, when she was eight. She took the veil at 15 and succeeded her mentor, Jutta von Spanheim, as mother superior in 1136. She later founded a convent on the

Rupertsberg, near Bingen (1147–50), and another (ca. 1165) at Eibingen, on the opposite bank of the Rhine.

In between her convent duties and travels throughout Germany to push for ecclesiastical reform, Hildegard turned her attention to health and medicine, natural history, and music. Until the fairly recent surge of interest in her music and her ideas on natural healing, she was remembered principally for her religious writings, which consist mainly of accounts of her mystical experiences and prophetic visions. Although attempts in the early 13th century to have her canonized did not succeed, she has long been venerated by German Catholics and has come to be recognized as a major historical figure.

Hildegard von Bingen, postcard image ca. 1910

From the time of her childhood, Hildegard had seen visions and experienced strange ecstatic states. She began recording the visions when she was in her 40s; included in these "inspirations" was a great deal of music, which has come down to us in two manuscripts that have largely the same content: the Dendermonde codex, completed by 1158, and the Rupertsberger "Riesencodex," which dates from the decade after her death. Hildegard's main work was the *Symphonia armonie celestium revelationum,* consisting of 77 poems with music. The majority of these, 43, are antiphons. There are 18 responds, melismatic and complex, as well as seven sequences and four hymns, which are less elaborate. The pieces of the *Symphonia armonie celestium revelationum* are devoted to praise of the Holy Trinity, the Virgin Mary, and various angels, apostles, martyrs, and confessors. They represent a complete "body," organized so as to form a liturgical cycle.

This staggering production is all the more remarkable because it stands completely outside the line of 12th-century musical development. The characteristic melodic formulas on which Hildegard based most of her music are not derived from chant, and they are combined in an extremely flexible manner, suggesting a sort of "plug and play" approach to composition. The formulas crop up in different pieces of the same mode, with different elaborations, and even appear in pieces of different modes, creating what some have described as the "fearful symmetries" in her music—an apt metaphor, considering that William Blake was a visionary, too.

What is distinctive about Hildegard's music is its almost ecstatic opulence, an opulence with perhaps a hint of elitism. For all its richness, so appealing to listeners of the present day, the music of Hildegard had little impact outside her immediate orbit. While she was dictating her quasi-improvisatory pieces to a scribe, the real work was going on in Paris, with the development of polyphony and the systematic approach to composition it required. But it no longer counts against Hildegard's musical production that it epitomized the flow of "inspiration" rather than a dependence on "proper" construction. She is a reminder that the real history of music has many fascinating eddies in addition to the mainstream.

RECOMMENDED RECORDINGS

"11,000 VIRGINS": ANONYMOUS 4 (HARMONIA MUNDI).

"CANTICLES OF ECSTASY": SEQUENTIA (DEUTSCHE HARMONIA MUNDI).

"A FEATHER ON THE BREATH OF GOD": KIRKBY, GOTHIC VOICES (HYPERION).

"THE ORIGIN OF FIRE": ANONYMOUS 4 (HARMONIA MUNDI).

Hilliard Ensemble, The *See box on pages 934–36.*

Hindemith, Paul

(b. Hanau, November 16, 1895; d. Frankfurt, December 28, 1963)

GERMAN COMPOSER, PERFORMER, TEACHER, AND THEORIST, influential though largely unloved, one of the most important musicians of the 20th century. In addition to being a powerful musical thinker and a formidable pedagogue, he was a world-class violist, an excellent violinist, and a capable conductor. He began taking violin lessons in 1902, and entered the Hoch Conservatory in Frankfurt at age 13. He commenced serious study of composition in 1912, and the next year became concertmaster of a local orchestra. Just two years after that he was appointed concertmaster of the Frankfurt Opera orchestra, and his String Quartet No. 1, Op. 2, was performed at the conservatory. In September of 1915 Hindemith's father was killed at the front in Flanders. Drafted in August 1917, Hindemith was stationed first in Frankfurt, which enabled him to keep his orchestra job, and then sent as a military musician to Alsace, where he served for the remainder of World War I.

Following the war, Hindemith returned to the Frankfurt Opera and played viola in the Amar Quartet (his younger brother Rudolf was the quartet's cellist). In 1921 the joint premiere in Stuttgart of his cheeky modernist operas *Mörder, Hoffnung der Frauen* (*Murderer, Hope of Women*), to a text by Oskar Kokoschka, and *Das Nusch-Nuschi* caused a scandal; they were followed the next year by another one-act opera, *Sancta Susanna,* whose erotic subject matter raised eyebrows even higher. Hindemith gave up his post as concertmaster at the Frankfurt Opera in 1923 to devote more time to composition, and began cranking out a stream of chamber and small-ensemble works, including several written as solo vehicles for himself and his quartet partners.

In 1926 Hindemith's first full-length opera, *Cardillac* (based on a story by E. T. A. Hoffmann) received its premiere. The following year he was appointed professor of composition at Berlin's Academy of Music. The 1930s saw the growth of Hindemith's reputation outside Germany, particularly in England and America. He was one of the distinguished group of composers—including Stravinsky, Honegger, and Prokofiev—who received commissions from Serge Koussevitzky for new works to celebrate the 50th anniversary of the Boston Symphony Orchestra; the result was his *Konzertmusik* for Strings and Brass, which Koussevitzky premiered with the BSO in 1931.

When the Nazis came to power in 1933 they branded Hindemith's music "culturally Bolshevist." The following year they intensified their campaign against Hindemith after Wilhelm Furtwängler led the premiere of his three-movement Symphony *MATHIS DER MALER* (*Mathias the Painter*) at a concert of the Berlin Philharmonic. The conductor's staunch defense of the music and its composer, published in the *Deutsche allgemeine Zeitung,* was answered three days later by a stinging rebuke in the Nazi party paper and a flamboyant denunciation by propaganda minister Joseph Goebbels, who called Hindemith an "atonal noisemaker." Thenceforth, Hindemith's works received their premieres outside of Germany: the viola concerto *Der Schwanendreher* (*The Swan-Turner*; 1935) in Amsterdam, with Willem Mengelberg conducting the Concertgebouw Orchestra and the composer as soloist; *Trauermusik* (*Mourning Music*; 1936), in London, with Adrian Boult conducting and the composer again as soloist; the opera *Mathis der Maler* in Zurich; and the ballet *Nobilissima Visione* (1938; based on the life of St. Francis of Assisi) in London, conducted by the composer.

The Nazis officially banned Hindemith's music in 1936, and in May 1938 they accorded him a prominent place in their "Degenerate Music" exhibition in Düsseldorf. The following September the composer fled Germany for temporary exile in Switzerland. He settled in the United States in 1939, and from 1940 to 1953 taught composition and theory at Yale, becoming an American citizen in 1946. His important works of the 1940s were the *SYMPHONISCHE METAMORPHOSEN NACH THEMEN VON CARL MARIA VON WEBER* (*Symphonic Metamorphoses After Themes of Carl Maria von Weber*; 1943) and the requiem *When Lilacs Last in the Dooryard Bloom'd* (1946), commemorating the death of FDR. In 1953 Hindemith moved back to Switzerland, where he finished work on the opera *Die Harmonie der Welt* (*The Harmony of the World*), about the life and times of the astronomer Johannes Kepler. During the final decade of his life, he was showered with honors and awards.

In his journey as a composer, Hindemith started out as a radical and ended up a conservative. That he took himself more and more seriously as time went by is scarcely surprising; current events and the European avant-garde's increasingly dismissive attitude toward tradition gave him ample reason. What makes Hindemith's case interesting is that in a certain sense it was his own music that he was reacting to, as he moved from such farcical, irreverent gestures as *Das Nusch-Nuschi* to reverent, high-concept, "serious" works like *Mathias der Maler* and *Die Harmonie der Welt*.

The criticism most frequently leveled at Hindemith's later music is that it sounds academic. It is true that he had a predilection for chorales, canons, fugal passages, and other "learned" procedures, for the rigorous working out of traditional formal schemes, and for contrapuntal textures. And it can be argued that even his best music tends to sound melodically "brittle," his less-than-best downright arid. On the other hand, he composed idiomatically for every kind of instrument (writing sonatas for all of the major ones), showed an exceptional command of the orchestra, and made lasting contributions to the chamber, choral, organ, operatic, and symphonic repertoires. He also accomplished the by no means easy feat of writing music that was modern in style yet thoroughly approachable, with a distinctive sound that was immediately recognizable as his.

RECOMMENDED RECORDINGS

NOBILISSIMA VISIONE: MARTINON AND CHICAGO SYMPHONY ORCHESTRA (RCA).

SYMPHONISCHE METAMORPHOSEN: SZELL AND CLEVELAND ORCHESTRA (SONY).

SYMPHONY *MATHIS DER MALER* AND *SYMPHONISCHE METAMORPHOSEN*: BLOMSTEDT AND SAN FRANCISCO SYMPHONY ORCHESTRA (DECCA).

WHEN LILACS LAST IN THE DOORYARD BLOOM'D: DEGAETANI, STONE; SHAW AND ATLANTA SYMPHONY ORCHESTRA (TELARC).

Paul Hindemith with viola, ca. 1930

Hines, Jerome

(b. Los Angeles, November 8, 1921)

AMERICAN BASS. He made his debut in San Francisco at the age of 20, and joined the roster of the Metropolitan Opera in 1946, appearing in the small role of the Officer in Mussorgsky's *Boris Godunov.* He went on to spend more than four decades with the Met in leading roles, including Sparafucile in *Rigoletto,* Philip II in *Don Carlo,* Sarastro in Mozart's *Die Zauberflöte,* Hunding in Wagner's *Die Walküre,* and, perhaps most memorable of all, the Grand Inquisitor in the company's 1979 production of *Don Carlo.* He appeared with the Bolshoi Theatre as Boris in 1962, and at Bayreuth from 1958 to 1963 as Gurnemanz, King Marke, and Wotan. Remarkably tall, he cut an impressive figure on the stage and possessed a booming, sepulchrally dark voice well suited to the characters he portrayed.

Jerome Hines as Boris Gudonov

Hirt auf dem Felsen, Der (The Shepherd on the Rocks) SONG FOR HIGH VOICE AND PIANO, with clarinet obbligato, to a text by Wilhelm Müller and possibly Helmine von Chézy, composed by Franz Schubert in October 1828 and published posthumously, in 1830, as his Op. 129. (In the Deutsch catalog it carries the designation D. 965.) A miniature scena rich in color and fantasy, the song tells the romantic story of a lonely, isolated shepherd who is consoled by the approach of spring. Schubert lived less than a month after completing the piece; one senses that he knew he would not see another spring when he wrote it.

RECOMMENDED RECORDING

AUGÉR, JOHNSON (HYPERION).

histoire du soldat, L' (The Soldier's Tale) MUSICAL FABLE BY IGOR STRAVINSKY, to a text by C. F. Ramuz, composed in 1918 and premiered September 28, 1918, in Lausanne, Ernest Ansermet conducting. The story is that of a soldier who trades his violin to the devil for a book that contains the secrets to acquiring great riches. The soldier gets his violin back by purposely losing all his money to the devil in a game of cards, but in the end it is the devil who possesses the violin, and the soldier. The work has speaking parts for a narrator and two actors, and is scored for an ensemble of violin, string bass, clarinet, bassoon, trumpet, trombone, and percussion.

Taking its cue from the text, Stravinsky's music is at once irreverent, mock serious, and sarcastic. Ribaldry and a much blacker kind of humor coexist in many of the numbers, two sides of the same musical coin. Here Stravinsky turns away from the preoccupation with Russian folk materials that had shaped much of his music in the years following *The Rite of Spring,* embracing an eclectic mix of elements that includes American ragtime (which he had absorbed from sheet music Ansermet gave him) and popular dance forms such as the tango. The rhythmic complexities of the score give the music considerable bite and are still quite challenging to performers, while the use of high and low instruments from string, wind, and brass families, with no attempt to blend their sonorities, introduces an additional piquancy. In assigning several percussion instruments to a single player, Stravinsky pioneered what has come to be called "multiple percussion," a usage subsequently taken up in hundreds of 20th-century chamber pieces.

RECOMMENDED RECORDING

WILSON AND SOLISTI NEW YORK (CHESKY).

hocket (from Fr. *hoquet,* "hiccup") In medieval polyphony, the staggered interruption of one or more lines by rests, creating the effect of a single line that moves among the different voices. The technique, which turned the resulting silences into contrapuntal elements, often to humorous ends, arose around 1200 and disappeared from use around 1400. In a more serious vein, Machaut used the technique in the Kyrie to his *Messe de Nostre Dame.*

Hofmann, Josef

(b. Kraków, January 20, 1876; d. Los Angeles, February 16, 1957)

AMERICAN PIANIST OF POLISH BIRTH. A child prodigy, he became one of the most brilliant and charismatic virtuosos in the history of the piano. He made his New York debut at the Metropolitan Opera House on November 29, 1887, amazing the public and critics but bringing the wrath of the Society for the Prevention of Cruelty to Children upon the heads of his promoters. A wealthy New Yorker put up $50,000 to see that the young Hofmann was educated rather than exploited; he studied briefly with Moritz Moszkowski before becoming a pupil of Anton Rubinstein in Dresden in 1892. Hofmann eventually made his adult debut in the United States at the acceptable age of 22. By then he was a finished pianist, his virtuosity all the more hair-raising for its elegance and seeming effortlessness, and all the more surprising considering that his hands were so small Steinway had to build a concert grand with slightly narrower keys just for him. He concertized widely until the 1940s, and served as director of the Curtis Institute from 1926, two years after its founding, until 1938.

Joseph Hofmann next to his favorite instrument

Hofmann was the first pianist ever to record: In 1887 he sat on Thomas Edison's lap and played into a prototype of the cylinder machine. Some of Edison's genius may have rubbed off on him, for in later years, Hofmann secured more than 70 patents for various inventions and mechanical devices of his own. A masterful interpreter of the music of Chopin, Schumann, and Liszt, he was also the dedicatee of Rachmaninov's Piano Concerto No. 3 and was regarded as a pianistic paragon by his colleagues, the critics, and the public alike. He had an unerring sense of line and pace that kept his pronounced rubato from ever sounding mannered. His recordings show as well that he was capable of extraordinary effects of color and delicacy (e.g., his achingly tender playing in the second movement of Chopin's Piano Concerto No. 2).

In his interpretive liberties, but also in his profound emotional engagement with the music he played, Hofmann epitomized the Romantic tradition. His playing, while inimitable like that of all true greats, remains an inspiration to pianists in search of fluidity and grace.

RECOMMENDED RECORDING

WORKS OF SCHUBERT, CHOPIN, MENDELSSOHN, LISZT, OTHERS: "GREAT PIANISTS OF THE 20TH CENTURY—JOSEF HOFMANN" (PHILIPS).

Hofmannsthal, Hugo von

(b. Vienna, February 1, 1874; d. Vienna, July 15, 1929)

AUSTRIAN POET AND LIBRETTIST. He was born into a cultivated Viennese family and showed precocious gifts as a poet. His collaboration with Richard Strauss—which resulted in seven operas, a ballet scenario, and a suite over a period of 23 years—is one of the most celebrated in musical history. The partnership began in 1906 when Strauss, who had seen a staged performance of Hofmannsthal's one-act play *Elektra* (1903), asked the poet for permission to set it as an opera. Hofmannsthal agreed, and the two got down to business. Work on the operatic *Elektra* occupied Hofmannsthal from 1906 to 1908. Within weeks of its premiere, early in 1909, he and Strauss had embarked on a new project, *DER ROSENKAVALIER,* which kept them busy through 1910. Both works are among the mainstays of the repertoire.

While all of the Strauss-Hofmannsthal operas from *Der Rosenkavalier* on are studies of love, each proceeds from its own distinct premise. The list includes *ARIADNE AUF NAXOS* (first version 1911–12; second version 1916), *DIE FRAU OHNE SCHATTEN* (1914–17), *Die ägyptische Helena* (1923–27), and *Arabella* (1929–32). Strauss's penultimate opera, *Die Liebe der Danae* (1938–40), though it dates from well after the poet's death, was based on a sketch Hofmannsthal had supplied in 1920.

Hofmannsthal's refinement and intellectual depth, his extraordinary sense for the pacing of dialogue, and his insight into character contributed greatly to the beauty and complexity of the operas he and Strauss created. Rarely have a composer and librettist worked so closely, on such a wide range of topics, and in such a complementary fashion to produce so many works of the first rank.

Hogwood, Christopher

(b. Nottingham, September 10, 1941)

ENGLISH KEYBOARD PLAYER AND CONDUCTOR. He studied harpsichord with Raphael Puyana in 1961 and received his B.A. from Cambridge in 1964. He subsequently attended Charles University in Prague (1964–65), earned an M.A. at Cambridge (1967), and studied with Gustav Leonhardt (1968–69). In 1965 he became one of the founding members of the Early Music Consort of London, a group led by the charismatic David Munrow. That same year he joined the Academy of St. Martin-in-the-Fields as a continuo player, becoming the group's keyboard soloist in 1970. But because of what he calls his "criminal thumbs" (unusually short thumbs that made it difficult to position the hand properly for certain intervals), he soon gave up on a solo career and threw his energies into conducting.

In 1973, he formed the Academy of Ancient Music, where he put into practice his ideas about the performance of Baroque, Classical, and pre-Romantic music on original instruments. During his years as the AAM's director, he has made more than 200 recordings with the group—including the first complete cycle of Mozart's symphonies on period instruments. From 1986 to 2001, he served as artistic director of the Handel and Haydn Society of Boston, where he guided the group's transition to period instruments; from 1987 to 1992 he was a director of the St. Paul Chamber Orchestra; and during nine summers, from 1993 to 2001, he presided over the National Symphony's Mozart Festival at the Kennedy Center in Washington, D.C. In 1999 he began an association with the Basel Chamber Orchestra; he is currently its principal conductor.

Since the mid-1970s, Hogwood has

Christopher Hogwood

done as much as anyone to advance the "historically informed" performance movement. He has also proven himself as a conductor with conventional forces and as an interpreter of much 19th- and 20th-century repertoire, including works of Dvořák, Gade, Stravinsky, Martinů, Tippett, and Britten. He has an exceptionally acute mind, and has written a penetrating study of Handel (1984), as well as a book on Haydn (1980) and a number of important scholarly articles.

RECOMMENDED RECORDINGS

DVOŘÁK, SERENADES: LONDON PHILHARMONIC ORCHESTRA (DECCA).

HONEGGER, SYMPHONY NO. 4 (WITH WORKS BY STRAVINSKY AND MARTINŮ): BASEL CHAMBER ORCHESTRA (ARTE NOVA).

MOZART, CLARINET CONCERTO: PAY; ACADEMY OF ANCIENT MUSIC (OISEAU-LYRE).

MOZART, SYMPHONIES: ACADEMY OF ANCIENT MUSIC (OISEAU-LYRE).

Holst, Gustav

(b. Cheltenham, September 21, 1874; d. London, May 25, 1934)

ENGLISH COMPOSER OF GERMAN DESCENT. Best known as the composer of *The Planets,* he gave voice in other, less frequently encountered works to a mystical, visionary, and deeply personal spirituality. As he matured, he developed an idiom that combined the melodic contours of English folk music and the bracing clashes of modern harmony in a way that was utterly individual and distinctive.

Gustav Holst at 22

The son of a musician, Holst learned to play piano, violin, and trombone as a boy, and in 1893 he was admitted to the Royal College of Music, where he studied with Charles Villiers Stanford and Hubert Parry and became friends with fellow student Ralph Vaughan Williams. His proficiency on the piano and organ was hampered by chronic neuritis in his right hand, so he made the trombone his major instrument; while still a student he played in the Queen's Hall Orchestra, on one occasion under the guest baton of Richard Strauss. He left school in 1898 to play in a touring opera company; he joined the Scottish Orchestra (now the Royal Scottish National Orchestra) as a trombonist in 1900, performing with it until the end of 1903. In 1905 he became head of the music department at St. Paul's Girls' School in Hammersmith, where he remained for the rest of his life (he honored the school in the title of his *St. Paul's Suite* for strings, composed 1912–13). He concurrently served as director of music at Morley College (1907–24). During the 1920s he also held teaching posts at the Royal College of Music and at University College, Reading. In 1932 he taught briefly at Harvard, where one of his students was Elliott Carter. He spent the last 18 months of his life as an invalid, composing to the end.

Bookish, introverted, and gentle, Holst maintained an ascetic lifestyle and refused to court fame or popularity, though *THE PLANETS,* composed in 1914–16 and premiered in 1918 under the baton of Adrian Boult, made him a very popular figure. His lifelong interest in languages and philosophy led him in a number of interesting directions, most of them off the beaten path: He studied Sanskrit at University College, London, out of which emerged his *Hymns from the Rig Veda* (1907–08) for voice and piano, four groups of *Choral Hymns from the Rig Veda*

(1908–12), and the chamber opera *Sāvitri* (1908), based on an episode from the *Mahabharata.* As a professional brass player, he came honestly by his extraordinary skills as an orchestrator, particularly his knowledge of, and flair in using, the brass. These skills are abundantly displayed in several symphonic suites and put to profligate use in *The Planets.* Surprisingly for a composer so often thought of as an orchestral master, the bulk of Holst's output consists of songs, choral pieces, and works for the stage.

The real Holst was a far more profound composer than one might assume from first acquaintance with the all-stops-out orchestral showmanship of *The Planets.* Yet even here, along with the remarkable rhythmic vitality, one encounters characteristics of the deeper musician—the gift for melody, displayed on nearly every page of the score, and the pervasive mysticism. Holst touched on the mystical numerous times in his music, sometimes in earnest and sometimes parodistically. An example of the latter is his one-act opera *The Perfect Fool* (1918–19), a send-up of grand opera, which begins with a ballet overture portraying the spirits of Earth, Water, and Fire. The orchestration of this 11-minute curtain-raiser is as brilliant as anything in *The Planets.* The serious vein of Holstian mysticism comes to the fore in the symphonic sketch *Egdon Heath* (1927), inspired by Thomas Hardy's *The Return of the Native,* which Holst rightly considered his best work.

Holst's friendship with Vaughan Williams was among the closest ever between two composers of genuine stature. They critiqued each other's work and had a beneficial influence on one another. Holst's music continued to exert an influence after his death, not only on Vaughan Williams, but tangentially on composers such as Tippett and Britten. Yet he was too individualistic—in his interests, aims, and methods—to have left any stylistic heirs. While the "sound" of *The Planets* has been imitated countless times, especially in Hollywood, Holst's voice—strange, esoteric, conveying both earthiness and spirituality—remains unique.

RECOMMENDED RECORDINGS

Choral Hymns for the Rig Veda: Wetton and Holst Singers (Hyperion).

"The Essential Holst" (including *The Planets, The Perfect Fool, Egdon Heath*): Various soloists (Decca).

The Perfect Fool and *Egdon Heath*: Previn and London Symphony Orchestra (EMI).

The Planets: Boult and London Philharmonic Orchestra (EMI).

The Planets: Gardiner and Philharmonia Orchestra (DG).

homophony Polyphonic music in which the various voices or lines move in more or less the same rhythm, in effect producing a series of chords. The chorales in Bach's cantatas and passions are homophonic settings, as are most standard hymns. *See also* MONOPHONY, POLYPHONY.

Honegger, Arthur

(b. Le Havre, March 10, 1892; d. Paris, November 27, 1955)

FRENCH COMPOSER OF SWISS PARENTAGE. He learned to play the violin as a child, attended the Zurich Conservatory from 1909 to 1911, and enrolled at the Paris Conservatoire at a time when the city's musical life was being energized by Diaghilev's Ballets Russes and the annual appearance of new works by Debussy, Ravel, and Stravinsky. At the Conservatoire, he studied violin with Lucien Capet and counterpoint with André Gédalge, and became friends with fellow students Darius Milhaud and Jacques Ibert; after a brief stint in the Swiss Army he returned to the Conservatoire and studied composition with Charles-Marie Widor (1844–1937). He graduated in 1918, scarcely a standout, with a modest second prize in counterpoint.

Honegger was soon pulled into the orbit of artistic jack-of-all-trades Jean Cocteau and composer Erik Satie and the association of younger musicians known as Les Six. In keeping with his Swiss nature, he maintained an aesthetic independence. He quickly established his reputation with a pair of strikingly original yet approachable scores: *Le roi David,* composed for a theatrical depiction of the life of King David (recast as an oratorio with narrator in 1924), and the "symphonic movement" *Pacific 231,* a tour de force of sonic imagery and orchestral mayhem—yet as tightly organized as a Bach chorale—which was given its premiere by Serge Koussevitzky. *Pacific 231* was followed by *Rugby,* even more audacious in its treatment of rhythm and dissonance, and by his Symphony No. 1, commissioned by Koussevitzky for the 50th anniversary of the Boston Symphony Orchestra, which gave its premiere in 1931.

Arthur Honegger depicted on the Swiss franc

Hard hit by the failure of the symphony (and several other works of the same vintage) to connect with audiences, Honegger temporarily stopped composing. Looking for a new direction, he turned to the cinema. He had already composed music for two films by Abel Gance, including the epic silent *Napoléon* (1927). Between 1934 and 1939 he penned 24 film scores. At the same time, he entered into a collaboration with Paul Claudel on the dramatic oratorio *Jeanne d'Arc au bûcher* (*Joan of Arc at the Stake*), which was finished in 1935 and premiered in 1938 in Basel, thanks to the efforts of Honegger's countryman Paul Sacher, who would henceforth become one of his greatest champions.

The onset of World War II had a profound impact on Honegger, who refused to abandon his adopted city and country, remaining in Paris during the German occupation. In 1941 he composed his three-movement *Symphonie pour cordes* (*Symphony for Strings*), a tense, tightly wound creation, quite possibly his masterpiece and certainly one of the finest works for strings of the 20th century. The symphony's finale concludes with a chorale tune played by the strings, which is brightened by the sudden introduction of a solo trumpet doubling the melody *ad libitum*—a gesture of hope, perhaps even liberation. The symphony, dedicated to Sacher, was premiered by him in Zurich in 1942.

Although he had certainly been no collaborator, Honegger's music was briefly banned in France after the liberation, an affront that left him embittered. In 1945–46 he composed two new symphonies: his Third Symphony (*Symphonie liturgique*), dedicated to Charles Munch and premiered in 1946 by the Zurich Tonhalle Orchestra under Munch's baton—a desolate commentary on the war just ended and the bleak prospects for civilization that lay ahead—and the Fourth Symphony, subtitled *Deliciae basiliensis* (*The Delights of Basel*), dedicated to Sacher and the Basel Chamber Orchestra, and premiered by them in 1947.

In the summer of 1947, at Koussevitzky's invitation, Honegger came to the U.S. to teach at Tanglewood. Two weeks after arriving he experienced shortness of breath; a heart condition was diagnosed and a month later Honegger suffered a massive coronary, necessitating a long convalescence. He returned to France in November and for a while remained stubbornly active, attending concerts and traveling. But composition became more and more difficult. Among the works of the 1950s, which reflect the composer's deepening gloom, was at least one masterpiece, the Fifth Symphony, subtitled *Di tre ré* (*Of the Three D's,* a reference to the notes—three low D's, played pizzicato by the double basses—that end each of its movements). It is a work of grim solemnity, of chill and shadow, which after a catastrophic climax closes with an agonizingly quiet contemplation of death. The composer spent his final year virtually a prisoner in his Paris apartment, saying farewell to his friends and writing nothing. He was the first of Les Six to pass from the scene.

Honegger appreciated fine craftsmanship, athletic flair, and horsepower. Passionate about trains, on a visit to America in 1929 he donned engineer's overalls and rode from Boston to Providence in the cab of a locomotive. Later that year, back in Europe and flush with royalties from performances of *Pacific 231,* he bought a Bugatti, which he immediately took on a solo drive through Switzerland. His music was every bit as well built as that Bugatti. In it he made use of the revolutionary advances in musical language brought into currency by Stravinsky but, admittedly in a very innovative way, he remained committed to the formal traditions of the 19th century. "It is pointless," he said, "to break down doors that one can open." He kept his distinctive voice, contributing a host of impressive works to the repertoire, particularly in the symphonic realm, and, in *Le roi David* and *Jeanne d'Arc au bûcher,* giving the oratorio genre a new lease on life.

RECOMMENDED RECORDINGS

Complete symphonies: Dutoit and Bavarian Radio Symphony Orchestra (Erato).

Jeanne d'Arc au bûcher: Keller, Wilson; Ozawa and L'Orchestre National de France (DG).

Pacific 231 and *Rugby*: Bernstein and New York Philharmonic (Sony).

Symphony No. 2 (with *Pacific 231* and other works): Zinman and Zurich Tonhalle Orchestra (Decca).

horn Brass instrument with a relatively deep, funnel-shaped mouthpiece, tubing of conical bore, and a widely flared bell. Because of the length of tubing necessary to make a horn sound like a horn (upward of eight feet), early instruments were curved or corkscrewed for ease of handling. During the 17th century, French instrument makers worked the tubing into a "hoop" (i.e., a circular coil); this became the standard arrangement and probably accounts for the instrument's common name among English-speaking people, the French horn. Because of its origin as an instrument of the hunt, composers have frequently used the horn to evoke nobility or to suggest elemental nature and the spirit world. Its burnished warmth and weight of tone lend solos a golden radiance and give passages played by an entire horn section a drama, color, and heft unmatched by the sound of any other instruments.

Until the early part of the 19th century the horn was a natural instrument, meaning that it lacked valves and thus produced only the natural harmonic series (the overtones) of a given fundamental note. As with all early brass instruments, the player sounded different notes by varying his lip tension to produce the proper overtone from the series. Some notes were inevitably out of tune, so along with making other minute adjustments in lip tension, players learned to control the pitch by inserting the right hand into the horn's bell, partially closing the instrument's throat (thus shortening the length of the column of air inside it) and raising the pitch of the note being sounded. If notes outside the harmonic series were called for, all a player could do was switch to a horn in a different key. By the mid-18th century this process was simplified with the introduction of crooks (insertable sections of tubing) in different keys.

The development of valved horns, spearheaded by German makers in the early 19th century, made it possible for hornists to play a continuous chromatic scale. Further refinement followed at the end of the 19th century with the introduction of the modern double horn, basically a valved horn in F with a trigger that switches the entire valve action to a set of tubing sized for B-flat. The B-flat division has a somewhat harder and brighter sound than the F, which is notable for its richness and warmth; good horn players are skilled at minimizing the tonal differences between the two.

As the natural horn began to take on its more or less recognizable form in the Baroque period, composers and players made a virtue of its limitations and exploited the upper octave of the range, where the overtones lie close enough together to permit scale runs and trills; by the end of the Baroque a florid style of playing, similar to the clarino trumpet style, had raised the horn to a high station among orchestral instruments. While players with the requisite technique specialized in the higher-lying parts, others specialized in the lower, a distinction that is still recognized among orchestral musicians today. The decline of guilds (which had fostered mastery of the florid technique) and the emergence of a new, less ornate musical style in the middle of the 18th century brought an end to the "high" horn era. During the Classical era, most composers used the horn as a foundation instrument, rarely entrusting a solo to it and usually keeping it in the lower part of its range.

Beethoven was one of the first to restore the horn to prominence in the symphonic sphere. Notable examples include the boisterous writing for three horns in the scherzo of the *Eroica* Symphony, redolent of the hunt, and the sublime solo (for fourth horn!) in the slow movement of the Ninth; Beethoven also included a striking obbligato for three horns in the aria "Abscheulicher!/Komm, Hoffnung" in his opera *Fidelio.* Weber wrote magically for the horn—the overture to *Oberon* begins with a three-note solo that is wonderfully evocative of an enchanted forest, and the overture to *Der Freischütz* has an interlude featuring a quartet of hunting horns. Wagner brought the horn to the forefront of his orchestral forces: In the ten-minute-long Prelude to Act I of *Die Meistersinger von Nürnberg,* there are barely 20 bars in which one or more of the four horns is not playing, and *Siegfried* and *Götterdämmerung* feature solos that are among the touchstones of the horn player's repertoire. Brahms composed in the era of the valved horn, but persisted in writing for the horn as though it were a natural instrument, feeling that to be more in its character. Examples include the majestic solo for two horns early in the final movement of his Symphony No. 1 (mm. 30–61) and the melancholy rumination in the third movement of Symphony No. 3 (mm. 98–110). Richard Strauss used horns the way a dyspeptic uses antacids—all the time, the more the better, calling for eight in the opera *Elektra,* 20 in

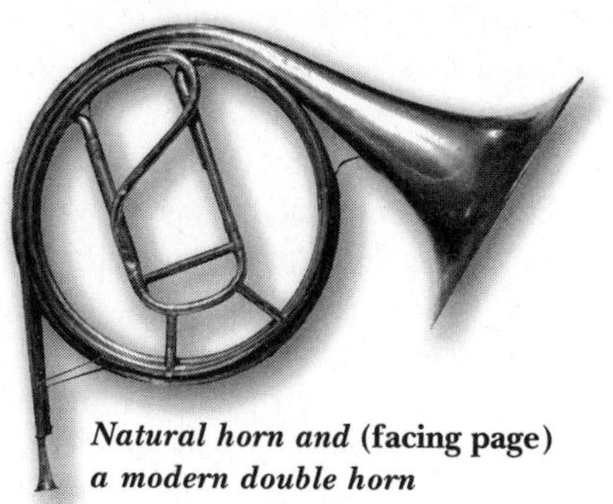

Natural horn and* (facing page) *a modern double horn

Eine Alpensinfonie. As he did for so many other instruments, Strauss placed virtuoso demands not just on the principal, but on the entire section. Two particularly fine examples are the heroic section solo for four horns in *Don Juan* (17 mm. before letter Q), and the exuberant solo horn tune that serves as the main theme of *Till Eulenspiegel.* The 20th century produced many outstanding pages for the horn, from the pounding chords and whooping glissandos of Stravinsky's *The Rite of Spring,* to Holst's use of six horns in unison in the "Jupiter" movement of his *Planets,* to the uneasy reverie near the end of the first movement of Shostakovich's Symphony No. 5, where the first horn, playing in canon with the flute, rises to a high E that must be played *piano.*

The solo repertoire for horn, while not large, includes concertos by Telemann, Mozart, Carl Stamitz (1745–1801), Richard Strauss, and Hindemith; Britten's *Serenade* for tenor, horn, and strings (1943); and Schumann's mighty *Conzertstück* for four horns and orchestra (1849), one of his most brilliant creations. Important works in the chamber literature include Brahms's Trio, Op. 40, for violin, horn, and piano ◉, and the sonatas for horn and piano by Beethoven and Hindemith; the horn is also part of the complement in Schubert's Octet, D. 803, Beethoven's Septet, Op. 20, Janáček's sextet *Mládí,* and the quintets for piano and winds by Mozart and Beethoven.

The honor roll of hornists who have helped enrich the repertoire begins with Joseph Leutgeb, for whom Mozart wrote four concertos and several other pieces. Celebrated as Leutgeb is today, the Bohemian master who styled himself Giovanni Punto (1746–1803) was regarded as the supreme horn soloist of the late 18th century; it was for him that Beethoven composed his Sonata in F, Op. 17. In the 19th century one player stands out, as much for his influence upon a composer as for his technical supremacy. The composer was Richard Strauss and the virtuoso was his father, Franz Strauss (1822–1905), for many years principal horn with the Court Opera at Munich. From childhood Richard had a love affair with the horn, and during his extraordinary six-decades-long career, he left two concertos for it, one from his student days in the 1880s and the other from 1942 when he was 78 years old; they are the only horn concertos truly fit to stand alongside those of Mozart. In the 20th century the English virtuoso Dennis Brain set a new standard of technical excellence and artistry; Britten's *Serenade* and the Hindemith concerto are among the works that owe their existence to him. Notable among Brain's younger colleagues were Alan Civil and the Australian-born Barry Tuckwell, whose recordings have been among the best of the stereo era. Gerd Seifert, Peter Damm, Mason Jones, Myron Bloom, John Cerminaro, and Dale Clevenger are some of the other significant soloists to emerge in the second half of the 20th century.

Horne, Marilyn

(b. Bradford, Penn., January 16, 1929)

AMERICAN MEZZO-SOPRANO. She studied at the University of Southern California and made her debut in Los Angeles

Mezzo-soprano Marilyn Horne

in 1954, as Háta in Smetana's *The Bartered Bride.* She sang the role of Marie in Berg's *Wozzeck* at her San Francisco Opera debut (1960) and again at her Covent Garden debut (1964). On March 3, 1970, she made her Metropolitan Opera debut as Adalgisa in Bellini's *Norma,* opposite Joan Sutherland, and in 1972 she sang the title role in Bizet's *Carmen* in a new Met production conducted by Leonard Bernstein. With a chest voice of astonishing power and a rich and creamy top, she had a particular affinity for the operas of Handel and Rossini, and played an important part in restoring several of the latter's less well-known works to the repertoire. She excelled as a recitalist, and was as comfortable with the songs of Stephen Foster as she was with Schubert and Schumann lieder. She retired from performing in 1998 but continues to devote herself to the nurturing of young talent.

RECOMMENDED RECORDINGS

BIZET, *CARMEN*: MCCRACKEN, KRAUSE, MALIPONTE; BERNSTEIN AND METROPOLITAN OPERA ORCHESTRA (DG).

HANDEL, *SEMELE*: MCNAIR, BATTLE, RAMEY; NELSON AND ENGLISH CHAMBER ORCHESTRA (DG).

ROSSINI, *IL BARBIERE DI SIVIGLIA*: NUCCI, DARA, RAMEY; CHAILLY AND LA SCALA ORCHESTRA (SONY).

Horowitz, Vladimir

(b. Berdichev, Ukraine, October 1, 1903; d. New York, November 5, 1989)

UKRAINIAN/AMERICAN PIANIST. With his daunting technique he was the defining pianist of the mid-20th century, for better and for worse. Since his death, no one has loomed over the keyboard as he did.

Born into a cultured Jewish family, he began taking piano lessons from his mother, a professional musician (his father was an engineer), when he was six. At the age of 15 he entered the conservatory in Kiev, where he studied with Felix Blumenfeld and Sergey Tarnowski and graduated with honors in two years. He made his official debut in the neighboring town of Kharkov; triumphant debuts in Moscow and Leningrad soon followed.

In 1925, Horowitz embarked on a European tour on a six-month visa; he did not return to the Soviet Union for 61 years. He gave his first concert in Berlin on January 2, 1926, and subsequently performed in Hamburg and Paris. News of his phenomenal playing spread quickly, and in Paris the American concert manager Arthur Judson heard him and signed him to a tour of the United States the following season.

Horowitz made his American debut at Carnegie Hall on January 12, 1928, performing Tchaikovsky's Piano Concerto No. 1 in B-flat minor with the New York Philharmonic under Sir Thomas Beecham, who was making *his* American debut on the same program. The performance, which ended with Horowitz racing a full measure ahead of Beecham and the orchestra, left an indelible impression on the audience and is still regarded as one of the most significant debuts in New York's musical history.

Horowitz shared a stage with Arturo Toscanini for the first time in 1933, playing the *Emperor* Concerto as part of a

Beethoven cycle the conductor was leading with the New York Philharmonic. During preparations for the concert, he met Toscanini's daughter Wanda, whom he married later that year in Milan. As successes in Europe and North America continued to pile up, Horowitz was recognized as one of the titans of the keyboard well before he turned 40. He settled in New York in 1940, and became an American citizen in 1942. During World War II, he helped raise millions of dollars for the War Bond effort through benefit performances. A single concert at Carnegie Hall on April 25, 1943, at which he performed the Tchaikovsky concerto with Toscanini and the NBC Symphony, brought in an astounding $11,000,000 for the cause.

Drawing of Horowitz by Hilda Wiener

Gripped by severe depression over the suicide of his only daughter, Horowitz withdrew from the public arena in 1953. He began to emerge from his cocoon in 1962 with the signing of a long-term recording contract with Columbia, and on May 9, 1965, he returned in triumph to the concert platform, delivering a sensational recital at Carnegie Hall. He took another sabbatical between 1969 and 1974, and again stormed back, this time for good, in the late 1970s. It was front-page news when, in the spring of 1986, he returned to his native Russia to give concerts in Moscow and Leningrad. He continued to perform and record almost to the end of his life, making his last visit to the studio just four days before his death.

The most recognizable features of Horowitz's playing were his fiery virtuosity and unique brilliance of tone. He had the ability to achieve an almost orchestral sonority, sometimes coming off the piano bench to do so. His performances of showpieces by Chopin, Liszt, Scriabin, and Prokofiev were admired for their technical precision, color, and dynamic range, while his trademark renditions of Scarlatti sonatas and keyboard miniatures such as Schumann's *Kinderszenen* were noted for their delicacy. He was recognized as a preeminent interpreter of the music of Rachmaninov; the composer in turn acknowledged Horowitz as the greatest pianist of the 20th century, paying him the ultimate compliment of giving up performing his Third Piano Concerto after he heard Horowitz play it.

Not everyone esteemed Horowitz's musicianship or warmed to his neurotic, sometimes nasty, personality, but it was hard not to respect his command of the piano, and impossible to ignore the spell he cast on audiences wherever he played. Only a few pianists of his generation could match him as a technician, and none possessed his uniquely dazzling brand of showmanship, which gave him the power to bring down the house with thundering octave cascades, or leave audiences on the edge of their seats as his concert grand whispered *pianissimo* from the stage.

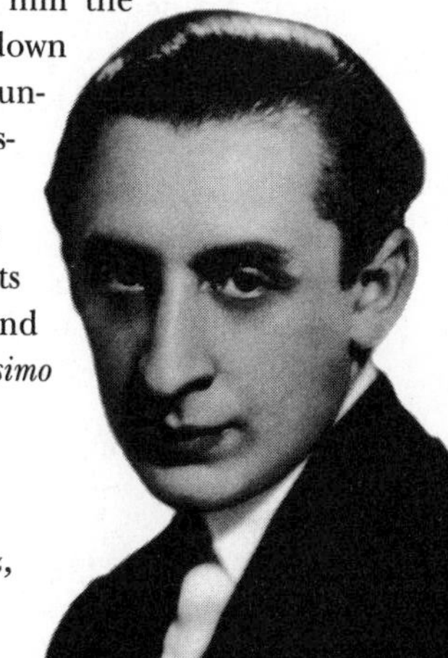

Vladimir Horowitz, the young titan

RECOMMENDED RECORDINGS

Carnegie Hall recital, May 9, 1965 (Sony).

Rachmaninov, Piano Concerto No. 3: Coates and London Symphony Orchestra (Biddulph).

Scarlatti, sonatas (Sony).

Scriabin, piano pieces (Sony).

Tchaikovsky, Piano Concerto No. 1: Toscanini and NBC Symphony Orchestra (Naxos).

Hotter, Hans

(b. Offenbach-am-Main, January 19, 1909; d. Grünwald, December 6, 2003)

German bass-baritone, widely regarded as the greatest Wagnerian of the post-war era. He studied philosophy at the University of Munich and worked briefly as an organist and choirmaster, with the aim of becoming a conductor. Voice lessons with Matthäus Roemer convinced him to pursue a career as a singer instead. In 1930 he made his operatic debut in Troppau; this was followed by engagements in Breslau, Prague, and Hamburg, where in 1936 he earned the designation Kammersänger, a high honor for a singer only 27 years old. In 1937 Hotter was summoned to Munich by Clemens Krauss, and began an affiliation with the Bavarian State Opera that continued until 1972; he settled in Munich in 1940. After the war, he appeared as a guest artist with the Vienna Staatsoper, and in 1948 he made his Covent Garden debut as Hans Sachs in Wagner's *Die Meistersinger von Nürnberg.* Hotter sang at the Metropolitan Opera for four seasons starting in 1950, and from 1952 he sang for 12 glorious seasons at Bayreuth, where he came to own the roles of Sachs, Gurnemanz, and Wotan. As he gradually retired from the demanding Wagner repertoire, he became more active as a stage director, putting on the *Ring* cycle at Covent Garden (1961–64), *Der fliegende Holländer* in Munich (1964), and Pfitzner's *Palestrina* in Vienna (1966). His later operatic appearances included memorable performances in the speaking part of Moses in Schoenberg's *Moses und Aron,* and in the character role of Schigolch in Berg's *Lulu.*

Hotter made his recital debut in 1941, and remained throughout his career a distinguished interpreter of the lieder of Schubert, Schumann, Brahms, and Wolf. His book *Vox humana—Eine Studie über das Singen* (*The Human Voice—A Study on Singing*) appeared in 1951, and in 1996 he published his memoirs, *Der Mai war mir gewogen* (*May Was Kind to Me*), a line taken from *Winterreise.* During his long career, Hotter brought an unmatched clarity of diction and expressive warmth to the big Wagnerian roles for which he was best known, particularly the role of Wotan. His authoritative delivery and the remarkably focused tone, clear edge, and heroic ring of his voice represent the gold standard against which the accomplishments of future interpreters are certain to be judged.

RECOMMENDED RECORDINGS

Lieder recital (songs by Schubert, Schumann, Loewe, Brahms, R. Strauss, and Pfitzner): Moore (Testament).

Schubert, *Winterreise*: Moore (EMI).

Wagner, arias: Nilsson; Ludwig and Philharmonia Orchestra (Testament).

Hovhaness, Alan *See box on pages 708–11.*

Huguenots, Les Grand opera in five acts by Giacomo Meyerbeer, to a libretto by Eugène Scribe, premiered at the Paris Opéra on February 29, 1836. The opera is set in 1572 and deals with the tensions between the Huguenots (French Protestants) and Catholics at the time of the marriage of Henri of Navarre (who in 1594 would become Henri IV, King of France) to Marguerite of Valois. Its plot centers on the ill-fated love of Raoul de Nangris, a Huguenot nobleman, for Valentine, the daughter of the Comte de Saint-Bris, a Catholic nobleman. The final act portrays the St. Bartholomew's Day massacre, in which more than 3,000 Huguenots perished.

Les Huguenots was the first work to receive 1,000 performances at the Opéra (so far only Gounod's *Faust* has surpassed it), and it remains one of the few Parisian grand operas never to have lost its place in the active repertoire. The cast of the premiere included several of the great singers of the day: soprano Cornélie Falcon as Valentine, tenor Adolphe Nourrit as Raoul, and bass Nicholas Levasseur as Marcel. Among the work's early admirers was Richard Wagner, who, though he despised Meyerbeer, found much to emulate—particularly its Act IV "consecration of the swords" and lovers' duet, which influenced his handling of large scenes right up through *Götterdämmerung*.

RECOMMENDED RECORDING

SUTHERLAND, ARROYO, VRENIOS, TOURANGEAU, BACQUIER; BONYNGE AND NEW PHILHARMONIA ORCHESTRA (DECCA).

Hummel, Johann Nepomuk

(b. Pressburg [now Bratislava, Slovakia], November, 14, 1778; d. Weimar, October 17, 1837)

AUSTRIAN COMPOSER AND PIANIST. The most gifted student of Wolfgang Amadeus Mozart, he lived in the Mozart home as a member of the composer's family for several years, developing remarkable skills as a pianist along with a fluency in the topics of 18th-century music that frequently puts one in mind of his master. A good deal of Mozart's facility as an orchestrator also rubbed off on him. Hummel's lessons with Mozart ended when he was ten; for the next four years he toured with his father, a capable conductor, through Germany, the Netherlands, Scandinavia, and the British Isles. Returning to Vienna in 1793, he spent the next decade teaching the piano and studying counterpoint and composition with Johann Albrechtsberger and Antonio Salieri. In April 1804 he was installed as Kapellmeister to the Esterházy family at Eisenstadt, succeeding Haydn (who nonetheless kept the title). He returned to Vienna in 1811, married the singer Elisabeth Röckel in 1813, and resumed his career as a concert pianist in 1814. But Beethoven's sun burned too brightly for Hummel to shine in Vienna. In need of a secure position, he spent two years as Kapellmeister in Stuttgart (1816–18) before settling in as Kapellmeister at the ducal court of Weimar in 1819.

Mozart protégé Johann Nepomuk Hummel

Hummel composed a sizable body of piano pieces, mostly in smaller forms, as well as six piano concertos. He also wrote more than ten operas and singspiels, numerous sacred works, a great deal of chamber music, and several orchestral pieces—everything except symphonies. Nowadays his most frequently encountered work is the Concerto in E for trumpet, composed in 1803 for Anton Weidinger, the trumpet soloist of the Vienna Court Opera (for whom Haydn wrote his celebrated concerto in E-flat). Essentially conservative at a time when changing tastes and revolutionary advances in musical language were transforming the scene, Hummel upheld the values of the Classical style—clarity, elegance, and lyricism—in an age enthralled by subjectivity, drama, and heightened emotionalism. Through his piano music he exerted an important influence on Schubert (who dedicated his last three piano sonatas to Hummel), Mendelssohn, Chopin, and, to a lesser extent, Liszt.

RECOMMENDED RECORDINGS

SELECTED PIANO CONCERTOS: HOUGH; THOMSON AND ENGLISH CHAMBER ORCHESTRA (CHANDOS).

TRUMPET CONCERTO: HARDENBERGER; MARRINER AND ACADEMY OF ST. MARTIN-IN-THE-FIELDS (PHILIPS).

Humperdinck, Engelbert

(b. Siegburg, September 1, 1854; d. Neustrelitz, September 27, 1921)

GERMAN COMPOSER. He studied at the Cologne Conservatory with Ferdinand Hiller, and in Munich with Franz Lachner and Joseph Rheinberger. A meeting with Richard Wagner in Naples in 1880 shifted his musical direction completely. Wagner invited Humperdinck to Bayreuth to assist him in preparing the premiere of *Parsifal*; from January 1881 to August 1882, Humperdinck lived in Bayreuth, copying out the score, training a boys' chorus, assisting the master in myriad details, and in the process becoming a devoted Wagnerite. After periods of residence in Paris, Cologne, Barcelona, and Mainz, Humperdinck eventually settled in Frankfurt, where he taught at the Hoch Conservatory and wrote criticism for the *Frankfurter Zeitung*. In 1893 he produced his enduring masterpiece, *HÄNSEL UND GRETEL*, based on the brothers Grimm tale, with a libretto provided by his sister, Adelheid Wette. The work received its premiere on December 23 and was an immediate hit. Within a few years, it had been staged all over Europe and by 1909 had made it to China; it is the only opera in the Wagnerian idiom not written by Wagner to have earned a place in the repertoire. The work's charmed life extended to the radio—it was the first opera to receive a European broadcast from the Royal Opera House in London (in 1923) and was heard on the first ever national broadcast from the Metropolitan Opera in New York, on Christmas Day, 1925. Humperdinck's later operas, *Dornröschen* (*Sleeping Beauty*; 1902) and *Königskinder* (*King's Children*; 1910), though not significantly inferior, never caught on; by the time they appeared, the musical tide in Europe had left Humperdinck and his Wagnerian style behind. *Hänsel und Gretel* remains something of a miracle—for all its sumptuous orchestration and sophisticated compositional technique, it ushers the listener into a world of childlike simplicity and emotional innocence that make its familiar story newly wonderful. The enchanting woodland scene with the cuckoos and the Dew Fairy presiding over the lost siblings is as magical as anything in *Der Ring des Nibelungen,* without taking nearly as long to unfold.

Would the real Engelbert Humperdinck please twirl his mustache?

Humperdinck's name entered the lexicon of pop culture in the 1960s when it was assumed by the smooth-voiced English ballad singer Arnold George Dorsey (b. 1936). As Engelbert Humperdinck, Dorsey achieved stardom in 1967 with his version of "Release Me," and for several years after that was a regular on the charts in the United States and the United Kingdom.

RECOMMENDED RECORDINGS

HÄNSEL UND GRETEL: LARMORE, ZIESAK, SCHWARTZ, WEIKL; RUNNICLES AND BAVARIAN RADIO SYMPHONY ORCHESTRA (TELDEC).

KÖNIGSKINDER: MOSER, SCHELLENBERGER; LUISI AND BAVARIAN RADIO SYMPHONY ORCHESTRA (CALIG).

Hunt Lieberson, Lorraine

(b. San Francisco, March 1, 1954)

AMERICAN MEZZO-SOPRANO. A voice of unusually plangent richness and expressivity, combined with extraordinary musical and dramatic intensity, has made her a unique performer. The daughter of two music teachers, she studied viola at San Jose State University and made a living as a freelance violist until, at 26, she moved to Boston and changed her focus to singing. While a student in the Boston Conservatory opera program, she began working as a violist with Craig Smith and Emmanuel Music (an ensemble based in that Boston church) and met Peter Sellars, who was putting on Baroque operas in radically updated stagings. In 1985, playing Sesto as a gun-toting terrorist in Handel's *Giulio Cesare,* Hunt (as she was then known) gave a breakthrough performance at the PepsiCo Summerfare Festival in Purchase, New York. She continued to work with Sellars on operas and, later, on stagings of Bach cantatas. For the label harmonia mundi usa she made many recordings of Handel operas and oratorios with Nicholas McGegan and the Philharmonia Baroque. Other major achievements included, in 1993, her seething accounts of the title role in Marc-Antoine Charpentier's *Médée* with William Christie's Les Arts Florissants in Paris and New York and, in 1996, her transcendent performance as Irene in the Sellars production of Handel's *Theodora* at Glyndebourne.

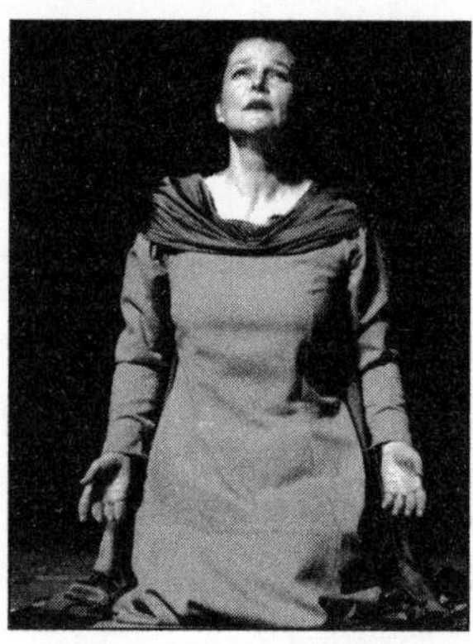
Lorraine Hunt Lieberson

In 1997, Hunt sang in the world premiere of Peter Lieberson's *Ashoka's Dream* at the Santa Fe Opera. She and Lieberson subsequently married, and she now often performs his songs. She made her Metropolitan Opera debut as Myrtle Wilson in John Harbison's *The Great Gatsby* in 1999, and returned to the house in 2003 as Didon in Berlioz's *Les Troyens.* In 2000 she sang in the premiere of John Adams's oratorio *El Niño* at the Théâtre du Châtelet in Paris. Hunt Lieberson's concert work has included performances of Britten's *Phaedra* and Berlioz's *Les nuits d'été* as well as an appearance with the Boston Symphony Orchestra as Mélisande in a concert production of Debussy's *Pelléas et Mélisande.* In addition to her opera recordings with McGegan and Christie, she has recorded several recital discs.

RECOMMENDED RECORDINGS

HANDEL, ARIAS: BICKET AND ORCHESTRA OF THE AGE OF ENLIGHTENMENT (AVIE).

PURCELL, *DIDO AND AENEAS*: SAFFER, ELLIOTT, BRANDES; MCGEGAN AND PHILHARMONIA BAROQUE ORCHESTRA (HARMONIA MUNDI).

***Hunt* Quartet** NICKNAME OF WOLFGANG AMADEUS MOZART'S STRING QUARTET IN B-FLAT, K. 458, composed in 1784 and included in the set of six quartets dedicated to Joseph Haydn that was published in 1785 as Mozart's Op. 10. The opening theme of the first movement is in the $\frac{6}{8}$ rhythm of a hunting gigue, and the writing for the violins mimics the paired-horn fanfares associated with the hunting topic in 18th-century music.

RECOMMENDED RECORDING

MOSAÏQUES QUARTET (ASTRÉE).

Hvorostovsky, Dmitri

(b. Krasnoyarsk, Siberia, October, 16, 1962)

RUSSIAN BARITONE. He studied singing and choral conducting in his native city. In 1989, his victory in the Cardiff Singer of the World competition (over fellow baritone Bryn Terfel, the local favorite), launched an international career that has included appearances with the world's major opera companies and a recording contract with Philips Classics. His operatic work has centered on such Verdi roles as Count di Luna (*Il trovatore*), Posa (*Don Carlo*), Germont (*La traviata*), Renato (*Un ballo in maschera*), and the title roles in *Rigoletto* and *Simon Boccanegra,* as well as in Tchaikovsky's Onegin and the role of Prince Yeletsky in *The Queen of Spades.* He is also a distinguished interpreter of the title role in Mozart's *Don Giovanni,* of Almaviva in *Le nozze di Figaro,* and of Valentin in Gounod's *Faust.* On record and in concert, he has championed the music of his native Russia, ranging widely from works such as Mussorgsky's *Songs and Dances of Death* to folk songs, romances, Russian sacred music, and even a program of Russian war songs, which he toured through Russia in 2005 with the Moscow Chamber Orchestra and conductor Constantine Orbelian in commemoration of the 60th anniversary of the end of World War II. He has performed and recorded the music of Georgi Sviridov, who wrote a song cycle, *St. Petersburg,* for him; with the San Francisco Symphony Orchestra, he premiered Giya Kancheli's *Do Not Grieve* (2002), also written for him. He starred in *Don Giovanni Unmasked,* a film by Rhombus Media based on Mozart's opera.

RECOMMENDED RECORDINGS

"Russian Romances" (songs of Tchaikovsky and Rachmaninov): Boshnyakovich (Philips).

Tchaikovsky, *Eugene Onegin*: Focile, Borodina, Shicoff; Bychkov and L'Orchestre de Paris (Philips).

hymn In Greek and Roman times, any song in honor of a god or hero; in the Middle Ages, a strophic song of religious praise. The Christian hymn originated in the 4th century, possibly with St. Ambrose, bishop of Milan, and Latin hymn texts without melodies began to be collected in manuscripts in the 7th century. The first monophonic hymn melodies are found in manuscripts of the 10th century, the oldest known being the Corpus Christi hymn (ca. 900). Thereafter, numerous monophonic hymns for the Divine Office appear in manuscript sources such as hymnaries and antiphoners, usually copied and kept in monasteries. In the 15th century, hymn cycles (alternating monophonic verses with three- or four-voice polyphonic verses) became popular; the first important cycle was Du Fay's, which includes settings for nearly every feast of the liturgical year (1433–35). The alternation of chant and polyphony continued throughout the Renaissance, and composers such as Lassus, Victoria, Palestrina, Byrd, and Tallis contributed to the repertoire.

With the Reformation, hymns in the vernacular were introduced and were quickly accepted as a standard aspect of Lutheran worship, eventually becoming integrated into the sacred works of Bach and other German composers. In England, however, owing to Calvinist influences at court, the hymn was shunned by the Anglican church in favor of the metrical psalm. During the 18th century John Wesley, the founder of Methodism, reinstated hymns in his services, and by the 19th century the Anglicans had fully embraced the form. The Anglican Hymnal formed the basis for the present-day American Episcopal Hymnal, which includes both original and modern polyphonic settings of an enormous range of sources, from Ambrose to Martin Luther to American spirituals.

I J

Iberia **Suite for solo piano by Isaac Albéniz,** composed 1905–08. A collection of 12 "impressions" in four books, it is universally regarded as Albéniz's masterpiece and as one of the greatest achievements in the keyboard literature of Spain. As the titles of the individual pieces make clear, the focus of the suite is Andalusia, the southern region of Spain rich in Moorish influences. The composer conjures up a Corpus Christi processional ("Fête-Dieu à Séville"), the tranquil gaiety of a fishing village ("El Puerto") ◉, a melancholy Gypsy song ("El Albaicín"), and numerous dances, writing in a manner that is at once deliciously evocative and flamboyantly virtuosic.

RECOMMENDED RECORDING

Larrocha (Decca).

Ibéria **Symphonic score in three movements by Claude Debussy,** composed 1905–08 and published in 1910. The second of his three *Images* for orchestra, it is a brilliantly executed portrait of Spain. The mood of the outer movements ("Par les rues et par les chemins" and "Le matin d'un jour de fête") is festive and energetic, while the middle movement ("Les parfums de la nuit") is one of the most enchanting of Debussy's many nocturnes. In its motivic concentration and rhythmic complexity, *Ibéria* represents a fascinating step forward in the composer's thinking, toward the stream-of-consciousness style of his late piano and chamber works. The orchestration is a delight, relying on a palette mixed with bold, bright colors to produce a "harder" sonority than that of *La mer,* yet one which is superbly evocative. ◉

RECOMMENDED RECORDINGS

Boulez and Cleveland Orchestra (Sony).

Dutoit and Montreal Symphony Orchestra (Decca).

Ibert, Jacques

(b. Paris, August 15, 1890; d. Paris, February 5, 1962)

French composer. His mother, an excellent pianist, encouraged his interest in music and began teaching him when he was four. He entered the Paris Conservatoire in 1910, studying harmony with Émile Pessard (who had also taught Ravel) and counterpoint with André Gédalge

Jacques Ibert at the piano

(whose other students included Milhaud and Honegger). After service as a naval officer in World War I he was awarded the Prix de Rome for his cantata *Le poète et la fée* (*The Poet and the Fairy*; 1919). The most important product of his stay in Rome was the symphonic suite *Escales . . .* (*Ports of Call . . .*), composed in 1922 and premiered by Paul Paray and the Lamoureux Orchestra on January 6, 1924. An evocative, sensuously scored souvenir of three Mediterranean destinations (Rome, Tunis, and Valencia), the work immediately entered the repertoire and secured Ibert's reputation both within France and beyond.

In 1936 Ibert was named director of the French Academy in Rome, a prestigious position that he held—apart from an interruption of six years during World War II—until 1960. Happily ensconced at the Villa Medici, he proved both a capable administrator and a sympathetic guide to the younger artists who came there as winners of the Prix de Rome, among them Henri Dutilleux (in 1939). In 1955, he was named director of the Paris Opéra, but was forced to resign after less than a year because of ill health.

In spite of the amount of time his administrative duties took up, Ibert remained a prolific composer. His well-balanced oeuvre includes seven operas, half a dozen ballets, incidental music for numerous plays, and around 60 film scores, as well as a handful of concertos, songs, and chamber pieces (among them a string quartet and several works for unusual combinations of instruments), and a small amount of piano music. His most frequently encountered works, aside from *Escales . . .* , are the *Divertissement* (1929)—a delightful pastiche for chamber orchestra drawn from his incidental music for *Un chapeau de paille d'Italie* (*An Italian Straw Hat*)—his Flute Concerto (1932–33), and the *Concertino da camera* (1935) for alto saxophone and chamber ensemble. Lively, lucid, and engaging, each of these flawlessly crafted works exudes the warmth at the heart of Ibert's style.

RECOMMENDED RECORDINGS

DIVERTISSEMENT: TORTELIER AND ULSTER ORCHESTRA (CHANDOS).

ESCALES . . . (*PORTS OF CALL*): MUNCH AND BOSTON SYMPHONY ORCHESTRA (RCA).

FLUTE CONCERTO: GRAF; LEPPARD AND ENGLISH CHAMBER ORCHESTRA (CLAVES).

idée fixe (Fr., "obsession") A theme used on a recurring basis in a piece of program music to represent a specific person, idea, or action. The term was coined by Hector Berlioz, whose use of the procedure in his *Symphonie fantastique* (1830) and *Harold en Italie* (1834) influenced a number of his contemporaries. Franz Liszt incorporated an idée fixe in his *Faust* Symphony (1857), and the device later found its way into the music of numerous Russian composers, including Rimsky-Korsakov (an idée fixe represents the title character in *Sheherazade*), Tchaikovsky (*Manfred* Symphony), and Glier (*Il'ya Muromets*).

Idomeneo, re di Creta **OPERA IN THREE ACTS BY WOLFGANG AMADEUS MOZART,** to a libretto by Giovanni Battista Varesco (after Antoine Danchet's *Idomenée*), premiered January 29, 1781, at the Residenztheater in Munich. Mozart's first mature opera, it combines elements of Italian opera seria and French *opéra-ballet.* The integration of the chorus into the proceedings follows the French tradition, as does the incorporation of several dance numbers to form a divertissement. Mozart was particularly impressed by the Munich court orchestra of Elector Carl Theodor (which he had gotten to know during the 1770s when it, and the elector, resided in Mannheim), and in the score to *Idomeneo* he gives the band ample opportunity to show off its virtuosity, particularly the wind players. His characterization of the opera's central figures—world-weary Idomeneo, shrewish, self-pitying Elettra, idealistic Idamante—is no less virtuosic, and in the carefully considered harmonic plan of the whole he already shows the technical mastery that would set his later operas on a plane above all the others of the 18th century.

RECOMMENDED RECORDING

McNair, Otter, Rolfe Johnson; Gardiner and English Baroque Soloists (Archiv).

Illica, Luigi

(b. Castell'Arquato, May 9, 1857; d. Colombarone, December 16, 1919)

ITALIAN PLAYWRIGHT AND LIBRETTIST. As a youth he ran away from home and went to sea; he ended up fighting the Turks, in 1876. In 1879 he settled in Milan and began his literary career. He wrote his first play in 1883, and fashioned his first libretto in 1889. In 1892, at the suggestion of Ruggero Leoncavallo, he was brought in to retool the libretto to Giacomo Puccini's *MANON LESCAUT*. That led to his being teamed with Giuseppe Giacosa on the librettos for *LA BOHÈME* (1896), *TOSCA* (1900), and *MADAMA BUTTERFLY* (1904). In addition to his work for Puccini, Illica also wrote the librettos for *La Wally* (1892), by Alfredo Catalani (1854–93), and Umberto Giordano's *Andrea Chénier* (1896), the latter based on a story of his own devising. Illica's use of language was direct rather than elegant. He had a proclivity for lines of irregular length that often came closer to conversation than poetry, along with an extraordinary feel for local detail. These qualities were ideally suited to the requirements of VERISMO.

Images [1] TITLE GIVEN TO THREE SETS OF PIANO PIECES BY CLAUDE DEBUSSY. The earliest set, which dates from 1894, was suppressed by the composer and remained unpublished until 1977. The two later sets, composed between 1901 and 1907, are Debussy's most substantial works for piano. The first of them, published in 1905, opens with "Reflets dans l'eau" ("Reflections in the Water"), one of the greatest pieces in the piano literature and among the finest examples of the way Debussy could use techniques resembling those of Impressionist painters to achieve similarly suggestive effects in music. The second piece in the series, "Hommage à Rameau," is a probing meditation written "in the style of a Sarabande but without rigor," while the toccata-like finale, entitled "Mouvement," calls for notes to be sustained bell-like in the middle of a fluid sixteenth-note texture, and for a chorale to emerge from a pointillistic haze. The second of the later sets of *Images*, published in 1907, begins with one of the most aphoristic of Debussy's piano pieces, "Cloches à travers les feuilles" ("Bells Through the Leaves"). Using a WHOLE-TONE SCALE to create a sense of mystery, the composer suggests that the left-hand accompaniment sound "as in a rainbow-colored mist." The title of the second piece, "Et la lune descend sur le temple qui fût" ("And the Moon Descends on the Temple That Was"), was chosen because it forms a perfect alexandrine, the classic 12-syllable line of French poetry. With its dreamy stasis and delicate use of parallel fourths and fifths, the music expresses Debussy's enchanted notions of the Orient. "Poissons d'or" ("Gold Fish"), the exuberant concluding piece, was inspired not by the fish themselves, but by a Japanese lacquer panel Debussy kept in his study showing two carp swimming beneath the branch of a tree. The writing incorporates tonal smears suggesting rapid, darting movement, and trills and arpeggios to depict the flowing water and the glint of light off the shiny forms beneath its surface.

[2] CYCLE OF THREE PIECES FOR ORCHESTRA BY CLAUDE DEBUSSY, composed between 1905 and 1912, and first performed as a set on January 26, 1913, with the composer conducting. The three pieces—*Gigues* (1909–12), *IBÉRIA* (1905–08), and *Rondes de printemps* (*Spring Rounds*; 1905–09)—are linked by common thematic elements. In addition, *Rondes de printemps* carries on a game Debussy had begun in his early, unpublished set of *Images* for piano (1894) and continued in the piano piece *Jardins sous la pluie* (*Gardens in the Rain*; 1903), quoting the French folk song "Nous n'irons plus aux bois" ("We're Not Going into the Woods Anymore") as an evocation of lost innocence.

RECOMMENDED RECORDINGS

PIANO:
JACOBS (NONESUCH).
KOCSIS (PHILIPS).
ORCHESTRA:
BOULEZ AND CLEVELAND ORCHESTRA (SONY).
DUTOIT AND MONTREAL SYMPHONY ORCHESTRA (DECCA).
HAITINK AND CONCERTGEBOUW ORCHESTRA (PHILIPS).

imitation A contrapuntal procedure involving the repetition of a melodic figure in a different voice from the one in which it is first heard; in most cases the repetition overlaps the initial statement. Imitation is "strict" if it involves a more or less exact repetition of the figure (CANON and FUGUE are examples); it is "free" if the repetition departs from the figure in any substantial way. The art of imitation was raised to exalted heights in the Renaissance, particularly by Josquin, whose motet *Ave Maria* offers a clear example. The technique was carried forward in various genres of Baroque instrumental music including ricercares, canzonas, and fugues, and remains an essential element of many modern styles as well.

impromptu A piece, usually for a solo instrument such as the piano, written in a spontaneous or improvisatory manner. The term was first used by the Bohemian composer Jan Václav Voříšek (1791–1825) in 1817 as the title of a piano piece, and was quickly appropriated by various publishers and by composers such as Schubert, Chopin, and Schumann. In their hands it acquired a more generic meaning, as a suitable designation for any relatively brief instrumental work that was not based on a common dance rhythm. Schubert's two sets of Impromptus for piano (D. 899 and 935), composed in 1827, are studies in motif and texture, rather less rigorously argued than his piano sonatas but still highly organized and scarcely "improvisatory" in manner. Chopin applied the title to four of his piano pieces, all quite similar to one another in figuration and thematic construction, suggesting that the later three were conceived as improvisatory "take-offs" on the material of the first one, the Fantaisie-Impromptu in C-sharp minor, Op. 66—a notion not far removed from the sphere of jazz.

RECOMMENDED RECORDINGS

CHOPIN: RUBINSTEIN (RCA).
SCHUBERT: PERAHIA (SONY).

incidental music Music written for ancillary use in the presentation of a play or other dramatic work. Examples include Beethoven's music for *Egmont,* Mendelssohn's for *A Midsummer Night's Dream,* Grieg's for *Peer Gynt,* Bizet's for *L'Arlésienne,* Fauré's and Sibelius's for *Pelléas et Mélisande,* Debussy's for *Le martyre de Saint Sébastien,* and Vaughan Williams's for *The Wasps.*

incoronazione di Poppea, L' OPERA IN A PROLOGUE AND THREE ACTS BY CLAUDIO MONTEVERDI, to a libretto by Giovanni Francesco Busenello based on Tacitus and other sources, premiered in 1643 at the Teatro Santi Giovanni e Paolo in Venice. Monteverdi's final opera, and the only one from his Venetian years (1613–47) to have survived in toto, it was also the first opera to have a historical as opposed to mythological subject. The drama centers on the sharply differentiated personalities of the Roman emperor Nerone (the same Nero who allegedly fiddled while Rome burned), his wife Ottavia, his scheming mistress Poppea, and his erstwhile preceptor Seneca, the Stoic philosopher. Propelled by the conflicts between these characters, the drama rises to remarkable heights of emotion, which Monteverdi's music conveys with extraordinary precision and force. Evil triumphs over good in the conclusion, which finds Seneca dead by his own hand, Ottavia banished, and Nero and the newly crowned Poppea rhapsodically duetting on the pleasures of carnal love.

RECOMMENDED RECORDING

Borst, Laurens, Köhler, Larmore; Jacobs and Concerto Vocale (harmonia mundi).

Indy, Vincent d'

(b. Paris, March 27, 1851; d. Paris, December 2, 1931)

FRENCH COMPOSER AND TEACHER. Born into an aristocratic family from the south of France, he studied piano and theory as a youth, but was equally interested in the military, in which his forebears had served. After a stint in the National Guard during the Prussian seige of Paris in 1870–71, he enrolled at the Conservatoire, studying organ and composition with César Franck and graduating in 1875. Seeking to broaden his horizons, d'Indy traveled to Germany, sitting in on Liszt's masterclasses in Weimar and, in 1876, attending the premiere of Wagner's *Ring* at Bayreuth. Back in France, he gained additional experience as a timpanist and chorus master. His best-known work, the *Symphonie sur un chant montagnard français* (*Symphony on a French Mountain Air*; 1886), for piano and orchestra, draws on a folk tune from his ancestral home in the Ardèche, and like many of his other works, including the symphonic triptych *Jour d'été à la montagne* (1905), demonstrates masterly handling of orchestral textures in its scene-painting and soulful evocation of nature's majesty. His operas include *Fervaal,* premiered in Brussels in 1897, which the composer (who wrote the libretto) situated in the Ardèche, and *L'étranger,* based on Ibsen's play *Brand,* which received its premiere in Brussels in 1903. A devout Catholic as well as a political right-winger, d'Indy was drawn to religious subject matter in a number of his works. His 1920 music drama, *La légende de St. Christophe* (1908–15), upholds traditional Catholic values while rather crudely parodying musical modernism, and fancifully places St. Christopher in—where else?—the Ardèche.

On safari: Vincent d'Indy (with parasol) hunting for folk music

Vincent d'Indy dressed as a gentleman of the Ardèche

Dissatisfied with the increasingly archaic style of teaching at the Conservatoire, d'Indy joined Charles Bordes and

Alexandre Guilmant in founding the Schola Cantorum in 1894, taking over as director in 1904. The Schola's initial goal was the reform of the music of the Catholic liturgy, but it soon developed into a complete musical academy. There, d'Indy established his own method of teaching composition, attracting such students as Roussel and Satie, and creating a community of scholars distinguished by the full admission of women to all courses, and the abolition of prizes. His composition course, edited and published by his assistants, was studied as far afield as Brazil, by the young Villa-Lobos. D'Indy and the Schola also served as pioneers in the revival of forgotten works from the medieval, Renaissance, and Baroque eras. His efforts included giving concert performances of Monteverdi's *L'Orfeo* and *L'incoronazione di Poppea,* in his own editions, derived from manuscript sources discovered in Italian libraries. In 1906, d'Indy published an adoring study of his mentor César Franck, and in 1911 he produced a monograph on his other hero, Beethoven.

RECOMMENDED RECORDINGS

STRING QUARTETS NOS. 1 AND 2: KODALY QUARTET (MARCO POLO).

SYMPHONY ON A FRENCH MOUNTAIN AIR; (FRANCK, SYMPHONY IN D MINOR): THIBAUDET; DUTOIT AND MONTREAL SYMPHONY ORCHESTRA (DECCA).

SYMPHONY ON A FRENCH MOUNTAIN AIR, SYMPHONY NO. 2: SCHAPIRO; MONTEUX AND SAN FRANCISCO SYMPHONY ORCHESTRA (RCA).

Inextinguishable, The (Det Uudslukkelige) TITLE OF CARL NIELSEN'S SYMPHONY NO. 4, OP. 29, composed in 1916 while World War I raged across Europe. Nielsen's aim was to show that amid the terror, the life-seeking force, the counterpart of the destructive forces all around, could be as strong. The symphony is in four continuous movements and draws much of its effect from the buildup of towering contrasts of sound. The outbursts are violent, rhythmically insistent; the moments of tranquillity, with their echoes of folk song and a pastoral calm, seem to come from another world. In the final movement, Nielsen portrays almost literally the struggle between chaos and the affirmative force of life, in a battle involving two groups of timpani—placed on opposite sides of the orchestra—and the orchestra itself. In the end, harmony triumphs.

RECOMMENDED RECORDINGS

BLOMSTEDT AND SAN FRANCISCO SYMPHONY ORCHESTRA (DECCA).

MARTINON AND CHICAGO SYMPHONY ORCHESTRA (RCA).

interlude/intermezzo [1] A relatively short instrumental number (sometimes referred to as an entr'acte) played between scenes or acts of a theatrical work such as a ballet or an opera. Examples of this type of interlude can be found in numerous works, including Wagner's *Parsifal,* Debussy's *Pelléas et Mélisande,* and Britten's *Peter Grimes.* [2] In instrumental works, a connecting episode placed between movements or sections of a larger piece. Examples of this type of interlude appear in Stravinsky's *Symphony in Three Movements* (a seven-bar passage between the second and third movements) and Elgar's *Falstaff.*

interval The distance between two notes of different pitches, expressed in terms of the number of diatonic steps they compass. For example, the interval C–G is referred to as a *fifth* because the two notes span five steps (C, D, E, F, G), while the interval A-flat–C is a called a *third,* because those two notes span three steps (A-flat, B-flat, C). Fifths and fourths, as well as octaves, are referred to as *perfect* (a parlance going back to the Middle Ages), *augmented,* or *diminished.* According to the ancient Greeks, upon whom the medieval theorists relied for their authority, the intervals of the fourth, fifth, and octave were derived from the numerical ratios of 4:3, 3:2, and 2:1, respectively; consequently they could be described as "perfect." Stopping a string at different points along its length, they were able to show that a tone sounding a fifth higher than another vibrated in the ratio of 3:2 relative to the lower tone. Varieties of these intervals that are not perfect have come to be known as augmented if they include a half step more than the perfect interval and diminished if they span a half step less. Thus, the interval F–C-sharp is called an augmented fifth, since it reaches a half step beyond the perfect fifth F–C, while E–A-flat is a diminished fourth, since it falls a half step short of the perfect fourth E–A. A special name—the *tritone*—was coined for the interval of the augmented fourth (e.g., C–F-sharp), owing to the fact that it spans the equivalent of three "whole" tones: C–D, D–E, and E–F-sharp. Because of its strikingly dissonant sound and obdurate imperfection (falling in the crack between the perfect fourth and the perfect fifth), the tritone was often referred to as the "devil's interval."

The remaining intervals found within the octave—seconds, thirds, sixths, and sevenths—are identified as either *major* (i.e., greater) or *minor* (lesser), depending on whether they span a full complement of diatonic steps (in which case they are major intervals) or are reduced by a semitone (minor intervals). A major sixth, such as B-flat–G, encompasses six diatonic steps (B-flat, C, D, E-flat, F, G, with D–E-flat being a half step, all the rest being whole steps), while a minor sixth, such as E–C, spans a semitone less (E, F-sharp, G, A, B, C, where both F-sharp–G and B–C are semitones). Similarly, a minor seventh (e.g., C–B-flat) spans one semitone less than a major seventh (C–B).

inversion [1] A voicing of the notes of a chord in which a note other than the root of the chord is heard as the bass. For example, a chord of D major (D–F-sharp–A) is said to be in first inversion if the F-sharp is in the bass. If A is the lowest note, the chord is said to be in second inversion. [2] The complementary interval that results when the notes forming a given interval "trade places" by means of octave transposition. The inversion of a third (such as from C to E) is a sixth (E–C), while the inversion of a seventh (such as G–F) is a second (F–G). [3] The process of turning a succession of notes or an entire theme "upside down." For example, if a particular melody ascends by a fourth, then makes a stepwise descent of a third, its inversion descends a fourth, then makes a stepwise ascent of a third. Inversion of this kind is frequently encountered in contrapuntal music, especially in fugues, and is a ubiquitous feature of 12-TONE composition.

Iphigénie en Aulide (Iphigenia in Aulis) OPERA IN THREE ACTS BY CHRISTOPH WILLIBALD GLUCK, to a libretto by Marie François Louis Gand Leblanc Roullet after Racine's eponymous tragedy (based on Euripides), premiered April 19, 1774, at the Paris Opéra. The first of seven operas Gluck composed for Paris, it melded Italianate lyricism with the stately declamation characteristic of French *tragédie lyrique,*

***Iphigénie en Aulide,* engraving ca. 1780**

enlivening the drama and breaking down the barriers between the Italian and French styles.

RECOMMENDED RECORDING

Dawson, Van Dam, Otter, Aler: Gardiner and Lyon Opera (Erato).

Iphigénie en Tauride (Iphigenia in Tauris)

Opera in four acts by Christoph Willibald Gluck, to a libretto by Nicolas-François Guillard after Guymond de la Touche's eponymous tragedy (based on Euripides), premiered May 18, 1779, at the Paris Opéra. With its tight dramatic fabric (the result of a superior libretto), fluid musical structure, and inspired characterization, it marks the pinnacle of Gluck's achievement as an operatic composer.

RECOMMENDED RECORDING

Montague, Aler, Allen with Gardiner and Lyon Opera (Philips).

Isaac, Heinrich

(b. Flanders, ca. 1450; d. Florence, March 26, 1517)

Flemish composer. Though he received his earliest musical training in the Netherlands, Isaac, like many of his contemporaries, traveled widely, absorbing the influences of different European countries and writing sacred and secular music in all forms, including masses, motets, and songs. One of many Flemish musicians recruited by the Medici, he served from 1485 to 1493 as a singer at the baptistry of San Giovanni in Florence, and became a valued member of the circle of artists and musicians assembled by Lorenzo the Magnificent. In 1496, shortly after the Medici were banished from Florence, Isaac found a new patron in Emperor Maximilian I, and in 1497 he was installed as court composer at Maximilian's newly established chapel in Vienna. In 1515, he returned to Florence, where he spent the remaining years of his life, continuing to draw his imperial salary and to enjoy the favor of the Medici.

Isaac's oeuvre is remarkably large and varied and includes many stunningly inventive mass settings, for four, five, and six voices. He wrote 36 mass cycles that have survived. In 1508, he was contracted by the cathedral of Konstanz to compose a cycle of polyphonic Mass Propers for the year. This project, which occupied him for much of the rest of his life, eventually resulted in a collection of 99 settings, most of them for four voices, published between 1550 and 1555 in Nuremberg as the *Choralis Constantinus.* Isaac is also remembered for his many songs, in a variety of languages, including "Innsbruck, ich muss dich lassen," which was later given a sacred text and became "O welt, ich muss dich lassen."

RECOMMENDED RECORDINGS

Missa *de Apostolis* and motets: Phillips and Tallis Scholars (Gimell).

Motets for Emperor Maximilian I: Procter and Ensemble Hofkapelle (Christophorus).

Isbin, Sharon

(b. Minneapolis, August 7, 1956)

American guitarist. She began her study of the guitar at the age of nine in Italy, and later studied with Andrés Segovia and Oscar Ghiglia. While a student at Yale (where she earned both a B.A. and a master's) she coached privately with the pianist and Bach specialist Rosalyn Tureck and won several major international guitar competitions. She made her New York debut in 1979 and taught at the Manhattan School of Music from 1979 to 1989. In 1989 she became the first director of the guitar department at the Juilliard School. The list of composers who have written works for her includes Leo Brouwer (b. 1938), John Corigliano, David Diamond (1915–2005), Tan Dun (b. 1957), Aaron

Jay Kernis (b. 1960), Ned Rorem, Christopher Rouse (b. 1949), Joseph Schwantner, and Joan Tower.

Isbin's recording "Dreams of a World: Folk-inspired Music for Guitar" won a Grammy Award in 2001, and her recording of Rouse's *Concert de Gaudí* brought the composer a Grammy in 2002. In addition to being a champion of contemporary composers and a distinguished interpreter of the standard repertoire for her instrument, Isbin has been an eloquent and imaginative advocate of the music and culture of South and Central America.

RECOMMENDED RECORDINGS

"DREAMS OF A WORLD" (TELDEC).
"JOURNEY TO THE AMAZON" (TELDEC).
RODRIGO: *CONCIERTO DE ARANJUEZ, FANTASIA PARA UN GENTILHOMBRE*; SCHWANTNER: *FROM AFAR . . .* (VIRGIN CLASSICS).

Isle of the Dead, The [1] TONE POEM BY SERGEY RACHMANINOV, OP. 29, inspired by Arnold Böcklin's gloomy painting *Die Toteninsel.* Between 1880 and 1886, Böcklin produced five versions of the painting, all of which depict a desolate island mausoleum with crypts hewn from solid rock and a forbiddingly dark stand of cypresses at its center, surrounded by ebony-black water. In the foreground a rowboat approaches, its oarsman ferrying a solitary standing figure and a coffin, both shrouded in white. Rachmaninov saw a black-and-white reproduction of the painting in 1907; after making a trip to Leipzig to see one of the original paintings, he finished his musical representation in 1909. The rowboat's slow passage across the water is suggested by the opening music's unsettling $\frac{5}{8}$ meter; later in the piece, Rachmaninov makes use of the *Dies irae* chant from the Latin Mass for the Dead, one of his favorite musical mottoes. [2] THE THIRD OF MAX REGER'S *Vier Tondichtung nach Arnold Böcklin* (*Four Tone Poems After Arnold Böcklin*), Op. 128, composed in 1913.

RECOMMENDED RECORDINGS

RACHMANINOV:
ASHKENAZY AND CONCERTGEBOUW ORCHESTRA (DECCA).
PLETNEV AND RUSSIAN NATIONAL ORCHESTRA (DG).

isorhythm (Gr., "equal rhythm") A procedure evident in some polyphonic compositions of the 14th and early 15th centuries, especially motets, in which a slow-moving melody in the tenor (usually derived from Gregorian chant) is repeated according to a fixed rhythmic pattern while the upper voices unfold above it. The tenor melody might consist of 20 notes (medieval theorists called such a melodic pattern the *color*), and be set to a rhythmic sequence 15 units long (called the *talea*). Thus, three statements of the color would occur during the course of four statements of the talea. This complex overlapping of basic chant material with a recurrent rhythmic scheme created a structural and textural richness hitherto unprecedented in the history of music. Isorhythmic settings by Vitry, Machaut, Dunstable, and others have survived. Du Fay's isorhythmic motets, of which *Supremum est mortalibus bonum* is one, illustrate the technique at its most accomplished.

Istomin, Eugene

(b. New York, November 26, 1925; d. Washington, D.C., October 10, 2003)

AMERICAN PIANIST. His parents, Russian émigrés, were both professional singers. At the age of six he became a pupil of Alexander Siloti and at 12 entered the Curtis Institute to study with Rudolf Serkin and Mieczyslaw Horszowski. He won the Leventritt competition in 1943, when he was 17; later that year he made his debuts with the Philadelphia Orchestra and the New York Philharmonic in the space of a single week, playing Brahms's Piano Concerto No. 2 with the latter. He was the youngest performer invited to the first Prades Festival in 1950, where he worked with Pablo Casals. He became known as one of the "OYAPs" (for "Outstanding Young American Pianists"), a designation worn tongue in cheek by the whiz-kid pianists who, with William Kapell in the vanguard, came to prominence in the 1950s. While many of his colleagues later succumbed to the pressures of life in music's fast lane, Istomin continued to win laurels as a soloist, recitalist, and chamber musician, combining intelligence and pure virtuosity in a manner as satisfying as it was unusual.

Admired for his aristocratic interpretations of the concertos of Mozart, Beethoven, Schumann, and Rachmaninov, Istomin performed with many of the great conductors on the mid-20th-century American scene, including Bruno Walter, Fritz Reiner, George Szell, Charles Munch, Dimitri Mitropolous, Eugene Ormandy, and Leonard Bernstein. He joined with violinist Isaac Stern and cellist Leonard Rose in forming the Istomin-Stern-Rose Trio in 1960, and partnered with Stern in an integral recording of the Beethoven violin sonatas. His old-fashioned barnstorming tour of the American hinterland in 1988—a four-month affair using a specially fitted truck carrying two Steinway concert grands—made national news. An artist with intellect, though hardly the ivory-tower type, Istomin was equally at home talking about the music of Schumann and Rachmaninov, the latest novel of Milan Kundera, or the Yankees' hot new .300 hitter. A die-hard Detroit Tigers fan, he is probably the only concert pianist in history who kept a complete regulation baseball uniform—from cap to tube socks—in the closet next to his tails.

RECOMMENDED RECORDINGS

BEETHOVEN, PIANO TRIOS: STERN, ROSE (SONY).

SCHUMANN, PIANO CONCERTO: WALTER AND COLUMBIA SYMPHONY ORCHESTRA (SONY).

Italiana in Algeri, L' (The Italian Girl in Algiers) COMIC OPERA IN TWO ACTS BY GIOACHINO ROSSINI, to a libretto by the composer based on an existing libretto by Angelo Anelli, premiered May 22, 1813, at the Teatro San Benedetto in Venice. The score was cranked out in a mere 27 days, under time pressure so extreme that some of the material (the recitatives and one or two arias) had to be provided by another composer, whose identity remains unknown. Rising to the occasion, Rossini produced a youthful masterpiece notable for its sophistication and innovative approach to form. The work caught on immediately, and became the first of Rossini's operas to be performed in Germany and in France.

RECOMMENDED RECORDINGS

OPERA: BALTSA, RAIMONDI, LOPARDO, DANA; ABBADO AND VIENNA PHILHARMONIC (DG).

OVERTURE: NORRINGTON AND LONDON CLASSICAL PLAYERS (VIRGIN CLASSICS).

Portrait of a European woman, showing the 19th-century vogue for Turkish dress

Italian Concerto HARPSICHORD PIECE IN THREE MOVEMENTS BY J. S. BACH (BWV 971), actually a sonata in the style of a "modern" Italian solo concerto (i.e., one by Vivaldi). The work's full title is *Concerto nach italienischem Gusto* (*Concerto after the Italian*

Taste); it was published in the second part of the *Clavier-Übung* in 1735. Pianists have long since appropriated the piece for their recital programs. ◉

RECOMMENDED RECORDING

HARPSICHORD: ROUSSET (OISEAU-LYRE).

Italian Serenade **PIECE FOR STRING QUARTET BY HUGO WOLF,** composed May 2–4, 1887. A single movement lasting six and a half minutes, it is a parody of a sunny Italian dance, full of cheeky chromaticism, displaced accents, and sly turns of phrase.

RECOMMENDED RECORDING

FINE ARTS QUARTET (HÄNSSLER).

***Italian* Symphony** **TITLE OF FELIX MENDELSSOHN'S SYMPHONY NO. 4 IN A, OP. 90.** The music was inspired by a journey Mendelssohn made to Italy from October 1830 to July 1831. He composed the symphony following his return to Berlin in 1832 and conducted it in London on May 13, 1833. The first movement, with its racing eighth-note pulse and exuberant main theme, conveys a feeling of unbridled joy. The brief second movement, in D minor, suggests a procession of penitents with its walking bass line and chorale-like inner voices, while the third movement, ostensibly a scherzo, has the easy flow and ornamental grace of a moonlight serenade. Passions seethe and erupt with Vesuvian force in the finale, a tarantella in the fierce key of A minor (though Mendelssohn calls it a saltarello). ◉

While it remains the most popular of his five symphonies, the *Italian* was a problem child for Mendelssohn. He was dissatisfied with many details of the composition and did not allow publication during his lifetime. When the score finally did appear, in 1851, it was in a form that eschewed Mendelssohn's revisions (considered much weaker by nearly everyone who has heard them) in favor of his original conception of the piece.

RECOMMENDED RECORDING

KARAJAN AND BERLIN PHILHARMONIC (DG).

Italienisches Liederbuch (Italian Songbook) **COLLECTION OF 46 LIEDER BY HUGO WOLF,** to texts translated from Italian poetry by Paul Heyse. Part I (consisting of songs Nos. 1–22) was composed between September 1890 and December 1891 and published in 1892. Following a hiatus of five years, Part II (songs Nos. 23–46) was written at great speed between March 25 and April 30, 1896, and published later the same year. The songs of the *Italienisches Liederbuch,* all of which deal with love, are radiant and beautifully limned, exhibiting a remarkable clarity of texture. They mark the apex of Wolf's achievement as a composer.

RECOMMENDED RECORDINGS

BONNEY, HAGEGÅRD, PARSONS (TELDEC).

LOTT, SCHREIER, JOHNSON (HYPERION).

Ives, Charles

(b. Danbury, Conn., October 20, 1874; d. New York, May 19, 1954)

AMERICAN COMPOSER. The son of a maverick Connecticut bandmaster, he grew up in the rich intellectual soil of late-19th-century New England, and was exposed to a wide gamut of musical stimuli from an early age by his irreverent experimentalist father. By the time Ives was a teenager, he was composing, playing the organ—becoming the youngest-ever salaried organist in the state of Connecticut—and drumming in his father's band. He left Danbury for New Haven in 1893, spending a preparatory year at the Hopkins Grammar School before entering Yale.

Ives had a complex relationship with his German-trained composition teacher, Horatio Parker (1863–1919). Parker stoically suffered Ives's insubordinate attitude, and in the end prevailed a little: Ives became more disciplined in his counterpoint and orchestration, and above all acquired a deeper grasp of formal processes. It was under Parker's tutelage that Ives composed his Symphony No. 1, written as a graduation exercise, and more redolent of Dvořák and Brahms than anticipatory of the cantankerously dissonant works he would soon be creating. While at Yale, Ives also composed his String Quartet No. 1 (1900), titled *From the Salvation Army*; despite occasional piquancies it is a beautiful piece of chamber music.

After graduating from Yale in 1898, Ives moved to New York and went into the insurance business. He pioneered the idea of estate planning, and wrote a classic promotional guide called *The Amount to Carry*. During his years in business, he composed music on the side, piling up score after score atop his piano, his experimental notions expanding as his hope of having any career as a composer dwindled. He married Harmony Twitchell, the daughter of a prominent Hartford minister, in 1908. His health was always frail, and in 1918, after years of composing at night and on the train, added to long days at the office, he suffered a heart attack from which he never fully recovered. He essentially stopped composing in 1927, retired from his business in 1930, and spent the rest of his life as a semi-invalid, using his money to publish his own work as well as that of other composers. During his retirement, performers (as well as other composers, including Aaron Copland) began to discover his work—a fact which Ives viewed with typical self-deprecating humor. In 1947, his Symphony No. 3 (*The Camp Meeting*), sketched 1908–11, was awarded the Pulitzer Prize.

Much of Ives's music is characterized by a nostalgic fascination with the vernacular: the music of the church services, marching bands, camp meetings, and holiday parades of his youth. With typical Yankee ingenuity, he transformed these elements—hymns, patriotic songs, and sentimental ditties—into increasingly more complicated and speculative collages. If Ives had a weakness, it was in the way he elevated local over cumulative effect: he believed in casting his ideas in the large forms carried over from the European tradition—symphony, sonata, string quartet—but tended to turn out works that were more collections of movements than organic wholes.

His Symphony No. 2 (1909), which did not receive its premiere until 1951 (when Leonard Bernstein performed it with the New York Philharmonic), is rooted in material drawn from both hymnody and such popular songs as "Turkey in the Straw," "Columbia, Gem of the Ocean," "Bringing in the Sheaves," "Camptown Races," and "Reveille." Between the years 1917 and 1919 Ives compiled *A Symphony: New England Holidays,* whose four movements—"Washington's Birthday," "Decoration Day," "The Fourth of July," and "Thanksgiving"—are sonic depictions of these fondly remembered times, in effect, an American *Four Seasons.* His Symphony No. 4 (1912–25) was premiered in 1965 by Leopold Stokowski and the American Symphony Orchestra. The first of its four movements, a setting of the hymn "Watchman, Tell Us of the Night," includes a part for small chorus along with an instruction from Ives that it would be preferable to omit it—a characteristic touch of levity. Parts of the score to the Fourth are metrically so complex that performances used to call (as at the premiere) for two assistant conductors in addition to the principal one.

Three Places in New England and the frequently paired single-movement essays *The Unanswered Question* (ca. 1908) and *Central Park in the Dark* (ca. 1909) play with background/foreground relationships between tonal and atonal music.

Ives's mature efforts also included four violin sonatas, a Piano Trio (1909–10), the Second String Quartet (1913–15), and two numbered piano sonatas. The second of these, completed in 1919 and popularly known as the *Concord Sonata,* is one of the supreme masterpieces of American music. Its four movements—"Emerson," "Hawthorne," "The Alcotts," and "Thoreau" —are character studies of the New England Transcendentalists. Ives also wrote nearly 50 choral works, both sacred and secular, and more than 180 art songs.

As anarchic as Ives seemed to be in his composing, he never strayed from the classic idea of composition as an exercise involving form, technique, and a grasp of tradition. He also never strayed from his roots in the American experience: His music was always about it, in one way or another. In nearly every work he wrote, the sound imagery is extraordinarily vivid and evocative, as though each score were really a sonic home movie. Ives's music had to wait many years to be received by a comprehending audience, and in many ways it is still waiting. But in its materials and manner—and its stance, somewhere between freethinking orneriness and rugged individualism—no music is more thoroughly American.

Charles Ives: Stand up and use your ears like a man!

RECOMMENDED RECORDINGS

Concord Sonata: Kalish (Nonesuch).

Songs: DeGaetani, Kalish (Nonesuch).

String quartets: Emerson Quartet (DG).

Symphony No. 2: Bernstein and New York Philharmonic (Sony).

Three Places in New England: Thomas and San Francisco Symphony Orchestra (RCA).

Jacobs, René *See box on pages 156–57.*

Janáček, Leoš

(b. Hukvaldy, July 3, 1854; d. Moravská Ostrava, August 12, 1928)

Czech composer. The greatest late bloomer in the history of music, he composed half a dozen of the most beautiful and compelling operas of the 20th century and was one of its most original musical thinkers. His father and grandfather were village musicians and teachers. At the age of 11, he was sent to the Augustinian monastery in the Moravian capital Brünn, where he served as a chorister. He later studied in Brünn at the German high school and at the Czech Teachers' Training Institute. After graduating, he worked as a choral conductor and teacher. In 1881 he married a 15-year-old pupil, Zdenka Schulzova; their domestic life would be troubled, and both their children would die young. Also in 1851 he founded an organ school in Brünn, beginning a directorship that would last until

1919. After the Provisional Czech Theater opened in Brünn in 1884, Janáček launched a music journal to report on its productions. A few years later he composed his first opera, *Sarka* (which went unperformed until 1925), and in 1894 he began work on *Jenůfa*, the opera that would bring about his artistic breakthrough. *Jenůfa* received its premiere in 1904, but it would be another dozen years before it was accepted for performance by the National Theater in Prague. Its successful premiere there, in 1916, established Janáček—about to turn 62—as the leading figure in Czech (not just Moravian) musical life.

In 1917 Janáček met Kamila Stösslová—35 years younger than he, and married—with whom he fell deeply in love. His passionate attachment to her, which built inexorably over a decade to a first kiss in the summer of 1928, just a month before he died, powered Janáček to the completion of an extraordinary body of work. The 1920s saw the composition of four first-rate operas: *Káťa Kabanová* (1921), *The Cunning Little Vixen* (*Příhody Lišky Bystroušky*; 1924), *The Makropulos Case* (*Věc Makropulos*; 1926), and *From the House of the Dead* (*Z mrtvého domu*; premiered posthumously, in 1930). All are now regularly performed in houses outside the Czech Republic; another opera, the two-part *Excursions of Mr. Broucek* (1917), may someday join their ranks. There were two phenomenally original string quartets—the first, subtitled *The Kreutzer Sonata* (after Tolstoy), composed in 1923; the second, subtitled *Intimate Letters* (a reference to the 700-plus letters Janáček wrote to Stösslová), composed in 1928 (written

Leoš Janáček: music written in fire

"in fire," as Janáček put it in one of the letters, as distinct from earlier works "written only in hot ash"). Also from this exceptionally fertile period came the effervescent wind sextet *Mládí* (*Youth*)—for flute (doubling piccolo), oboe, clarinet, bassoon, horn, and bass clarinet—composed in 1924; the ebullient, idiosyncratically colorful *Sinfonietta* (1926); and the magnificent *Glagolitic Mass* (*Mša glagolskaja*; 1926).

Many composers start out ahead of their time and fall behind. Janáček did just the opposite. His early music emerged from the mainstream of Czech nationalism and was indebted to Smetana and Dvořák (who had befriended the young composer in the 1870s). The later operas, as well as works like the *Sinfonietta*, the orchestral rhapsody *Taras Bulba* (1915–18), and the *Glagolitic Mass* are striking in their modernity. They embody a highly advanced harmonic language marked by daring modulations, and an orchestral palette that was leaner and more

***Scene from* The Cunning Little Vixen**

schematic than that of most late-Romantic composers. Janáček's distinctive manner of scoring emphasized athletic string ostinatos and jubilant brass fanfares, plaintive wind solos, and growling, sepulchral chords in the trombones—all of which make the occasional long-breathed melody in the violins that much more beautiful.

RECOMMENDED RECORDINGS

The Cunning Little Vixen: Popp, Randová; Mackerras and Vienna Philharmonic Orchestra (Decca).

Glagolitic Mass: Kiberg, Stene, Svensson, Cold; Mackerras and Danish National Radio Symphony Orchestra (Chandos).

Jenůfa: Söderström, Ochman, Dvorsky, Randová, Popp; Mackerras and Vienna Philharmonic Orchestra (Decca).

Kát'a Kabanová: Söderström, Dvorsky, Kniplová; Mackerras and Vienna Philharmonic Orchestra (Decca).

Mládí (with other works): Chamber Orchestra of Europe (ASV).

Sinfonietta, Taras Bulba: Mackerras and Vienna Philharmonic Orchestra (Decca).

String quartets: Talich Quartet (Calliope).

Janowitz, Gundula

(b. Berlin, August 2, 1937)

German soprano. She trained in Graz and made her debut at the Vienna Staatsoper in 1960, as Barbarina in Mozart's *Le nozze di Figaro,* remaining on the roster of the Vienna company for the next three decades. She made her Metropolitan Opera debut in 1967 as Sieglinde in Wagner's *Die Walküre,* also performing that role at the Salzburg Easter Festival (1967–68) and recording it under the baton of Herbert von Karajan. She was one of Karajan's favorite collaborators, and one of the few who could endure his often autocratic manner without bridling. The core of her repertoire was Mozart, Wagner, and Richard Strauss, where she excelled in roles such as the Countess (in *Figaro*), Fiordiligi (in *Così fan tutte*), Elisabeth (in *Tannhäuser*), and Ariadne (in *Ariadne auf Naxos*) that favored her opulent yet essentially lyric instrument. She was an outstanding concert artist and participated in notable recordings of Beethoven's *Missa Solemnis* and Symphony No. 9 (with Karajan), Haydn's oratorios *The Creation* (Karajan) and *The Seasons* (Karl Böhm), and Orff's *Carmina Burana* (Eugen Jochum).

Gundula Janowitz in 1983

Jansons, Mariss

(b. Riga, January 14, 1943)

Latvian conductor. His father was the conductor Arvid Jansons. He studied violin, piano, and conducting at the Leningrad Conservatory. Following his graduation, he refined his conducting skills with Hans Swarowsky in Vienna (1969–72) and worked with Herbert von Karajan in Salzburg. In 1971 he won the Karajan Foundation conducting competition in Berlin. He was appointed associate conductor of the Leningrad Philharmonic in 1973 and became music director of the Oslo Philharmonic Orchestra in 1979. In 1985, following the death of Evgeny Mravinsky and the selection of Yury Temirkanov as music director of the Leningrad Philharmonic, Jansons was elevated to the post of principal conductor of that orchestra. He was named music director of the Pittsburgh Symphony Orchestra in 1997. A heart attack forced him to slow down his career, but only briefly. He assumed the title of music director of the Bavarian Radio Symphony Orchestra in 2003, and of principal conductor of the Royal Concertgebouw Orchestra of Amsterdam in 2004 (leaving Pittsburgh in a lurch from which it began to extricate itself with the appointment of Sir Andrew Davis as artistic adviser in 2005).

Though versatile, Jansons is most comfortable in music of the late 19th and early 20th centuries, and he has a particular affinity for the scores of Tchaikovsky and Rachmaninov. Polish and precision, rather than passion, are the hallmarks of his conducting—an approach that is refreshing to many orchestras and some listeners, though others find it too emotionally distant. Nonetheless, every now and then, Jansons can turn on the grand manner and get an orchestra such as the Leningrad (now St. Petersburg) Philharmonic to play with a splendor that verges on perfection. Many of his recordings, particularly those with the Oslo orchestra, have been overrated.

RECOMMENDED RECORDINGS

Rachmaninov, Symphony No. 2: St. Petersburg Philharmonic (EMI).

Shostakovich, Symphony No. 13: Aleksashkin; Bavarian Radio Symphony Orchestra (EMI).

Järvi, Neeme

(b. Tallinn, June 7, 1937)

AMERICAN CONDUCTOR OF ESTONIAN BIRTH. He attended the Tallinn Music School and studied at the Leningrad Conservatory (1955–60) under Nikolay Rabinovich and Evgeny Mravinsky, and served briefly as a percussionist in the Estonian State Symphony Orchestra. In 1963, at the age of 26, he was appointed chief conductor of the Estonian Radio and Television Orchestra; shortly after that he took on the additional responsibilities of principal conductor and artistic director of the State Academic Opera and Ballet Theater of the Estonian Soviet Socialist Republic (renamed the Estonian National Opera Theater after the restoration of independence). He made his North American debut in 1979, conducting *Eugene Onegin* at the Metropolitan Opera, and emigrated to the United States in 1980. He was named principal conductor of the Göteborg Symphony Orchestra in 1982 (a position he still holds), and was appointed music director of the Scottish National Orchestra in 1984. He became an American citizen in 1987, and in 1990 he was engaged as music director by the Detroit Symphony; that same year he accepted the title Conductor Laureate for Life from the (by then) Royal Scottish National Orchestra. In the fall of 2003 he was named principal conductor of the New Jersey Symphony Orchestra; in 2005 he became the New Jersey orchestra's music director and assumed the title of music director emeritus in Detroit.

Since coming to the West, Järvi has built his reputation primarily on recordings of less frequently heard repertoire, broadening his focus from the Russian and Scandinavian literature to include works by many American composers, especially since he began his stewardship in Detroit. Over the last 20 years he has amassed one of the largest discographies—totaling more than 350 CDs—of any active conductor, earning high praise for cycles devoted to orchestral works of Berwald, Sibelius, Nielsen, Grieg, Eduard Tubin (1905–82), Franz Schmidt (1874–1939), Dvořák, Martinů, Rimsky-Korsakov, and Prokofiev. A true journeyman—he is a quick study, but also a fine craftsman—he has in recent years developed into a truly individualistic conductor capable of bringing profound insights to his work, ready and willing to delve into any corner of the repertoire that hasn't been overexplored. Both of his sons are conductors as well: Paavo Järvi became music director of the Cincinnati Symphony Orchestra in 2001, and is enjoying phenomenal success there, while Kristjan Järvi is principal conductor of the Norrlands Opera in Sweden.

RECOMMENDED RECORDINGS

BERWALD, SYMPHONIES: GOTHENBURG SYMPHONY ORCHESTRA (DG).

GRIEG, ORCHESTRAL WORKS: GOTHENBURG SYMPHONY ORCHESTRA (DG).

RIMSKY-KORSAKOV, SUITES FROM OPERAS: SCOTTISH NATIONAL ORCHESTRA (CHANDOS).

SCHMIDT, SYMPHONIES: CHICAGO SYMPHONY ORCHESTRA, DETROIT SYMPHONY ORCHESTRA (CHANDOS).

Jenůfa **OPERA IN THREE ACTS BY LEOŠ JANÁČEK,** to a libretto by the composer based on Gabriela Preissová's play *Její pastorkyňa* (*Her Stepdaughter*), premiered at the National Theater in Brünn on January 21, 1904. The story, set in a Moravian mill town, is a study of spiritual transformation with two women at its center: a widow, the Kostelnička, and her stepdaughter Jenůfa. After Jenůfa, disfigured by a jealous suitor, falls for the wrong guy and secretly has his baby, the Kostelnička murders the infant so that Jenůfa can marry the man who had slashed her face, but who truly loves her and feels remorse for his deed. The Kostelnička tries to keep her appalling act a secret, but when the baby's corpse is discovered, she must step forward and acknowledge what she has done out of love for her stepdaughter. With this grisly tale of hardship, rage, despair, and forgiveness, Janáček created his first masterpiece, at the age of 50. The music is superb—edgy, vital, and disturbing, in many places intentionally raw and coarse, but at crucial moments, particularly in the final scene, poignantly lyrical and deeply moving.

RECOMMENDED RECORDING

SÖDERSTRÖM, OCHMAN, DVORSKY, RANDOVÁ, POPP; MACKERRAS AND VIENNA PHILHARMONIC ORCHESTRA (DECCA).

Jeritza, Maria

(b. Brünn, October 6, 1887; d. Orange, N. J., July 10, 1982)

MORAVIAN SOPRANO. She studied in Brünn and Prague, and made her debut in 1910 at Olmütz, as Elsa in Wagner's *Lohengrin*. She was quickly snapped up by the Vienna Volksoper, appearing in the roles of Agathe in Weber's *Der Freischütz*, Senta in Wagner's *Der fliegende Holländer*, and Marguerite in Gounod's *Faust*. In 1912, supposedly at the urging of Emperor Franz Josef, she was engaged by the Vienna Court Opera; later that year, in Stuttgart, she sang the title role in the world premiere of Richard Strauss's *Ariadne auf Naxos* in a production staged by Max Reinhardt and conducted by the composer.

Maria Jeritza

When the Vienna Court Opera premiered the second version of *Ariadne* in Vienna in 1916, Jeritza was again cast as the heroine. She sang the title role in the first Viennese performance of Janáček's *Jenůfa* in 1918 (reprising it at the Metropolitan Opera in 1924, the work's American premiere), and in 1919—at what by then had become the Vienna Staatsoper—she was entrusted with the role of the Empress in the world premiere of Strauss's *Die Frau ohne Schatten*, under the baton of Franz Schalk. In 1921 she performed the role of Marietta/Marie in both the Viennese and the American premieres of *Die tote Stadt* by the wunderkind composer Erich Wolfgang Korngold; the latter performance, on November 19, 1921, was her debut at the Metropolitan Opera.

During the next 11 years, Jeritza simultaneously reigned over the Staatsoper and the Met. She found time between engagements to write her autobiography—*Sunlight and Song: A Singer's Life* (1924)—and to sing in other houses, among them the Semper Opera in Dresden, where, in 1928, she performed the title role in the world premiere of yet another Strauss opera, *Die ägyptische Helena.* At the Met, her gripping portrayals of three Puccini heroines—Tosca, Turandot, and Minnie (in *La fanciulla del West*)—made her an audience favorite. In all, she gave 344 performances in 19 roles at the Met before bidding the house adieu at the end of the 1931–32 season, her departure hastened by the management's Depression-era austerity measures. In 1935 she announced her retirement from the Vienna Staatsoper, and in 1943, having married a American film mogul, she became a U.S. citizen. She later forsook California for New York, where on the night of February 22, 1951, she returned to the stage of the Met for a final bow, as Rosalinde in a gala performance of Johann Strauss Jr.'s *Die Fledermaus.*

No soprano of the 20th century participated in as many premieres of major operas as Jeritza, and only a few enjoyed the kind of acclaim she earned as *prima donna assoluta* in not one but two of the world's leading opera houses. Her triumphs were dramatic as much as musical, and hinged on her ability as a singing actress to inhabit the roles she performed, making the characters come to life. Throughout her career, operetta remained a part of her portfolio, particularly the works of Suppé and Lehár (who was one of her many admirers among composers of the day). She lived as colorfully off the stage as on, and during her long life collected four wealthy husbands, discarding the first two and outliving both the third and the fourth.

Jeu de cartes (Game of Cards) BALLET "IN THREE DEALS" BY IGOR STRAVINSKY, written in 1936 on a commission from Lincoln Kirstein for his newly established American Ballet, with original choreography by George Balanchine, premiered at the Metropolitan Opera in New York on April 27, 1937, with the composer conducting. The game is poker, and the dancers are decked out as cards; the progress of various hands is continually disrupted by the Joker, who is eventually sent packing when a group of spades he has assembled is routed by a Royal Flush in hearts. The effervescent score is a delightful example of Stravinsky's neoclassical style, and contains witty references to Rossini's Overture to *Il barbiere di Siviglia,* Johann Strauss Jr.'s *Die Fledermaus,* Ravel's *La valse,* Beethoven's Symphonies Nos. 5 and 8, and Stravinsky's own youthful Symphony in E-flat. All three deals begin with a marchlike introduction,

Jeu de cartes, *danced by the Stuttgart Ballet*

representing the shuffling of the cards. The second deal incorporates a set of variations on a suave march given out by the brass.

RECOMMENDED RECORDING

JÄRVI AND CONCERTGEBOUW ORCHESTRA (CHANDOS).

Jeux (Games) **"POÈME DANSÉ" BY CLAUDE DEBUSSY,** to a scenario by Vaslav Nijinsky, commissioned by Sergey Diaghilev for the Ballets Russes and premiered on May 15, 1913, at the Théâtre des Champs-Elysées in Paris, Pierre Monteux conducting. The action takes place on a summer's evening in the vicinity of a tennis court and involves a chance encounter between two young girls and a young man (danced by Nijinsky at the premiere) searching for a lost ball. Debussy's music—at once mysterious and mercurial, erotically charged and evanescent—yearns for an ecstatic climax but never reaches it. The score is considered by many to be Debussy's most important legacy to the 20th century, a masterful study of subtly shifting timbres and muted colorism. As a ballet, *Jeux* enjoyed a modest success, quickly overshadowed by the premiere, two weeks later in the same theater, of Stravinsky's *The Rite of Spring*.

RECOMMENDED RECORDINGS

DUTOIT AND MONTREAL SYMPHONY ORCHESTRA (DECCA).

HAITINK AND CONCERTGEBOUW ORCHESTRA (PHILIPS).

Jeux d'enfants (Children's Games) **SUITE IN 12 MOVEMENTS FOR PIANO FOUR-HANDS BY GEORGES BIZET,** composed in 1871. The "Trompette et tambour" march foreshadows the Act I street urchins' chorus in *Carmen* ("Avec la garde montante"), while the concluding galop, "Le bal," is a jaunty tip of the cap to Rossini. Bizet subsequently orchestrated six of the pieces, and grouped five of them (Nos. 6, 3, 2, 11, and 12) under the title *Petite suite*; this compilation received its premiere on March 2, 1873, under the baton of Édouard Colonne. *Jeux d'enfants* was the model for Debussy's *Petite suite* (1888), Fauré's *Dolly* (1894–96), and Ravel's *Ma mère l'oye* (1908–10), all conceived for piano four-hands and later orchestrated.

RECOMMENDED RECORDINGS

ORCHESTRA: MARTINON AND FRENCH NATIONAL RADIO ORCHESTRA (DG).

PIANO: KATIA AND MARIELLE LABÈQUE (PHILIPS).

Joseph Joachim by Ludwig Michalek Gmunden, 1898

Joachim, Joseph

(b. Kittsee, June 28, 1831; d. Berlin, August 15, 1907)

AUSTRO-HUNGARIAN VIOLINIST, CONDUCTOR, COMPOSER, AND PEDAGOGUE, among the most important and influential performers of the 19th century. Born near Pressburg (now Bratislava) into a Jewish family, he began his study of the violin in the Hungarian capital of Pest, where his parents had moved in 1833. He gave his first public performance in 1839, and was sent to Vienna for further study with Georg Hellmesberger and Joseph Böhm. In the spring of 1843 he became a student at the newly founded Leipzig Conservatory and a protégé of its director, Felix Mendelssohn. Under Mendelssohn's watchful eye the not-yet-teenaged phenomenon was groomed for stardom. Mendelssohn accompanied him in his Leipzig debut at the Gewandhaus in August 1843, and arranged for him to receive lessons in composition. Mendelssohn then whisked him off to London, where, in May 1844, with Mendelssohn conducting, he gave a performance of Beethoven's Violin Concerto that created a sensation and effectively guaranteed the work a lasting place in the repertoire.

It took Joachim a while to find his bearings after Mendelssohn's death in 1847. By 1850 he had taken his first professional position, as Franz Liszt's concertmaster in Weimar, but in 1852—unable to reconcile himself to Liszt's radical aesthetic—he left to become principal violinist at the court in Hanover. The following year he met and befriended the 20-year-old Johannes Brahms, with whom he forged an intimate artistic relationship that eventually gave rise to some of Brahms's greatest works.

In 1868 Joachim was summoned to Berlin to supervise the music curriculum at the newly established Königliche Akademie der Künste. He remained in Berlin the rest of his life, teaching, and serving as one of the first regular conductors of the Berlin Philharmonic. Although his activity as a composer tapered off after 1860, he continued to act as a kind of "technical adviser" to others, aiding Max Bruch in the revision of his G minor Violin Concerto (1868), serving as muse and midwife for Brahms's great D major Violin Concerto (1878), and helping Dvořák fine-tune his Violin Concerto in A (1882). Despite a falling-out with Brahms (who had sided with Joachim's wife when the violinist sought to divorce her), Joachim continued to champion Brahms's music. In 1887 he received the dedication of the latter's Concerto for Violin and Cello in A minor, Op. 102, and participated in the work's first performance, with Brahms conducting.

Joachim's style, hints of which can be gleaned from a few gramophone recordings he made in the final years of his life, emphasized nobility of line, long-breathed phrasing, and the subtle use of rubato; his vibrato was sparing. He was among the few virtuosos of the Romantic era who avoided displays of bravura and made a point of subordinating himself to the music. In that respect he proved to be not only a throwback to an earlier era, but a forerunner of 20th-century objectivity.

Jochum, Eugen

(b. Babenhausen, November 1, 1902; d. Munich, March 26, 1987)

GERMAN CONDUCTOR. The second of three brothers, all musicians, he learned to play piano and organ in his youth and attended the Akademie der Tonkunst in Munich, where he studied conducting and composition. His first job was as a *répétiteur* at the National Theater in Munich (1924–25); he moved on to the opera house in Kiel in the same capacity in 1926, and became music director there in 1927. He subsequently held posts in Mannheim (1929–30) and Duisburg (1930–32). From 1932 to 1934 he conducted at the Berlin Radio and the Berlin Staatsoper, and from 1934 until 1949 he was the general music director in Hamburg,

Eugen Jochum, a picture of Swabian warmth, 1976

succeeding Karl Böhm. Jochum happily remained there for the duration of World War II, conducting music that was banned elsewhere in Germany. He later quipped that it was in Hamburg that he learned to speak English, knowing that the British and Americans were coming.

Jochum became the principal conductor of the newly established Bavarian Radio Symphony Orchestra in 1949, and in 1961, as a caretaker, he assumed the helm of the famed Concertgebouw Orchestra in Amsterdam, sharing the duties of principal conductor with Bernard Haitink. Over the years he also conducted at the Bayreuth Festival and enjoyed a close relationship with the Berlin Philharmonic as guest conductor. From 1969 to 1973 he served as music director of the Bamberg Symphony, and from 1975 to 1978 he was conductor laureate of the London Symphony Orchestra.

A man of keen intelligence and probing musicianship, Jochum also exhibited a typically Swabian warmth and good humor. Particularly admired for his magnificent, deeply felt interpretations of Bruckner's symphonies, he was also an outstanding exponent of the music of Bach, Beethoven, and Brahms, of the symphonies of Haydn, Mozart, and Schubert, and of works by Reger, Pfiztner, and Orff. His repertoire ranged all the way from Lassus to Karl Amadeus Hartmann (1905–63), whose Symphony No. 6 he premiered in 1953. His daughter is the pianist Veronica Jochum.

RECOMMENDED RECORDINGS

BEETHOVEN, SYMPHONIES: CONCERTGEBOUW ORCHESTRA (PHILIPS).

BRUCKNER, SYMPHONIES: BERLIN PHILHARMONIC; BAVARIAN RADIO SYMPHONY ORCHESTRA (DG).

HAYDN, *LONDON* SYMPHONIES: LONDON PHILHARMONIC ORCHESTRA (DG).

ORFF, *CARMINA BURANA*: JANOWITZ, STOLZE, FISCHER-DIESKAU; DEUTSCHE OPER BERLIN (DG).

Pages from Josquin's **Missa Pange lingua**

Josquin des Prez

(b. near St. Quentin, ca. 1450–55; d. Condé-sur-l'Escaut, August 27, 1521)

FRENCH COMPOSER acknowledged as the most important musician of the Renaissance, in whose works the rigor of the northern style and the sensuality of the southern were uniquely synthesized. Linking the soundscape of the medieval world with that of the Renaissance, he struck much of the stylistic coinage that circulated in music throughout the 16th century.

Josquin was born in the region then known as Vermandois, most likely near the town of St. Quentin, which lies halfway along a straight line between Paris and Brussels. The first certain documentation of Josquin's career places him as a singer in the chapel of René "the Good," Duke of Anjou, in 1475. Josquin remained at the court of Duke René at least until the spring of 1478.

By June 1484 Josquin was in the entourage of the wealthy Milanese prelate Ascanio Sforza, who had been elevated to the rank of cardinal that year. Josquin traveled with

Sforza to Rome in the summer of 1484, and continued in his service until the spring of 1489. He joined the Sistine Chapel in June 1489 and served there at least until 1495, working for two Popes, Innocent VII and Alexander VI. In 1499 he left Italy for a position at the court of Louis XII, the newly crowned French king. By this point Josquin's reputation as the finest composer in Europe was established, and it was on the basis of that reputation that he won the job of *maestro di cappella* to Ercole d'Este, Duke of Ferrara, in April 1503—beating out the estimable Heinrich Isaac. Josquin left Ferrara a year later, following an outbreak of plague; he was ready to return to his native country. From May 1504 until his death, he served as canon and provost of the collegiate church of Notre Dame in Condé-sur-l'Escaut, working with its choir and managing several dozen canons, chaplains, and vicars.

Of the music Josquin is known or believed to have composed, 18 masses, more than 100 motets, and around 80 polyphonic chansons survive. Josquin's motets are wonderfully refined, and show how skilled he was at setting text in a clear, sensitive manner. They achieve an extraordinary balance of expressiveness and rhetorical effect with intellectual rigor and formal brilliance (a good example is his *Ave Maria*). These qualities can also be found in the best of Josquin's secular settings, which include the poignant "Regretz sans fin" and "Nymphe des bois," his five-voice *déploration* on the death of Ockeghem (1497).

Josquin's masses are likewise works of towering genius, notable for the purity and expressiveness of their musical language. The Venetian music publisher Ottaviano Petrucci, the first anthologizer of polyphonic music, allotted three entire volumes to Josquin's masses, which he published in 1502, 1505, and 1514. Among them are the *Missa Ave maris stella* (based on a plainchant hymn), two different masses based on "L'homme armé," a popular tune of the 15th century, the *Missa Hercules dux Ferrariae,* and the *Missa de Beata Virgine.* One late mass, probably composed around 1514, is the four-voice *Missa Pange lingua* (based on the plainchant hymn for the Feast of Corpus Christi). Stylistically, the *Missa Pange lingua* is the summit of Josquin's work in the genre. Its free-flowing polyphony, less rigorously canonic than that of his earlier works, is supple, expressive, and extraordinarily beautiful, and contributes to a sonority that is unusually rich and luminous. The theological message of the chant on which the mass is based is driven home by a remarkable "flowering" of the chant melody in the final section of the Agnus Dei. Musicologist Gustav Reese described this mass as "a fantasy on a plainsong."

Josquin was the greatest composer of his age, respected and emulated by his contemporaries, and as significant a figure in his own day as Beethoven was in the early 19th century. His fame during his lifetime was such that many works not his were attributed to him, making posterity's effort to assess his stature somewhat more difficult. An innovator of the first order, he was the principal architect of the "point of imitation" style, in which a motif introduced in one voice is imitated in another, then another, enabling the polyphonic texture to grow from a pair of voices to four, five, or six before a cadence is reached and the process begins again with a new round of entries. This became the fundamental modus operandi for serious composers of the 16th century. In addition, Josquin pioneered the techniques of word-painting, sequence, and stretto that played an important role in the music of the late Renaissance and were carried into the Baroque, Classical, Romantic, and modern eras. As more is learned about his music, it becomes ever more apparent that he deserves to be considered one of a handful of monumentally great composers.

RECOMMENDED RECORDINGS

Missa de beata virgine and motets: A Sei Voci (Astrée).

Missa Pange lingua: Phillips and Tallis Scholars (Gimell).

Missa "L'homme armé" super voces musicales, *Missa "L'homme armé" sexti toni*: Phillips and Tallis Scholars (Gimell).

Motets and *Stabat Mater*: Herreweghe and La Chappelle Royale (harmonia mundi).

Selected motets and chansons: Hilliard Ensemble (Virgin Classics).

Juilliard School CONSERVATORY FOUNDED IN NEW YORK IN **1905** by Frank Damrosch and James Loeb, and known originally as the Institute of Musical Art. In 1926 the Institute merged with the Juilliard Graduate School (founded in 1924 on a bequest from the will of Augustus D. Juilliard) and became known as the Juilliard School of Music. The first president of the combined institutions, John Erskine, had previously served as a professor at Columbia University. He was succeeded in 1937 by Ernest Hutcheson. William Schuman became president of Juilliard in 1945. He established Juilliard's dance division in 1951 and presided over a restructuring of the school's curriculum. Peter Mennin, like Schuman a respected composer, was named president in 1961 following Schuman's departure to head Lincoln Center. During Mennin's administration, the school's drama division was created (with John Houseman as its first director), and the school moved to its present location at Lincoln Center, changing its name officially to the Juilliard School to reflect an artistic scope that had widened considerably beyond music.

Ensemble performance at the Juilliard School

In 1984, following Mennin's death, Joseph Polisi was put in charge. Juilliard has grown and prospered on his watch, widening its curriculum and developing new interdisciplinary programs to link its divisions more closely. The school's core mission remains the training of professional musicians, and it continues to do an outstanding job. Even a tiny list of Juilliard's most famous alums reads like a who's who of American classical music: Van Cliburn, Renée Fleming, Philip Glass, Yo-Yo Ma, Midori, Itzhak Perlman, Leontyne Price, Steve Reich, Leonard Slatkin, Pinchas Zukerman. . . .

Juilliard String Quartet ENSEMBLE ESTABLISHED IN **1946** by William Schuman, then president of the Juilliard School of Music. Founding members were violinists Robert Mann and Robert Koff, violist Raphael Hillyer, and cellist Arthur Winograd. Subsequent members of the ensemble have included violinists Isidore Cohen, Earl Carlyss, Joel Smirnoff (second violinist 1986–97, currently first violinist), and Ronald Copes (second violinist since 1997); violist Samuel Rhodes (since 1969); and cellists Claus Adam (1955–74) and Joel Krosnick (since 1974). Mann dominated the "personality" of the quartet for more than 50 years, his influence readily apparent in the ensemble's sharply chiseled, high-intensity style of playing. While this driven manner did not suit all works and composers equally, it often produced performances of memorable excitement. Today's foursome retains much of that stamp.

Since 1962 the Juilliard has been in residence at the Library of Congress in Washington, D.C., where it performs on a rare matched set of Stradivari instruments belonging to the library. The ensemble has an enormous repertoire that includes all the masterpieces of the 18th- and 19th-century quartet literature as well as 150 compositions from the 20th century. Over the years, it has given the premieres of numerous works by American composers, including the String Quartets Nos. 2 and 3 of Elliott Carter, the String Quartet No. 1 of Leon Kirchner (b. 1919), and quartets by William Schuman, Roger Sessions, Milton Babbitt, George Perle (b. 1915), and David Diamond (1915–2005), among others. Arguably the most versatile quartet ever, the Juilliard players have shared the stage with all manner of musical luminaries, from Glenn Gould and Dietrich Fischer-Dieskau to Maurizio Pollini and Yo-Yo Ma.

RECOMMENDED RECORDINGS

BEETHOVEN, STRING QUARTETS (SONY).

CARTER, STRING QUARTETS (SONY).

***Jupiter* Symphony** SOBRIQUET, DATING FROM EARLY IN THE 19TH CENTURY, ATTACHED TO WOLFGANG AMADEUS MOZART'S SYMPHONY NO. 41 IN C, K. 551. It is believed to have originated in England with Johann Peter Salomon, the violinist-impresario who commissioned Joseph Haydn's *London* Symphonies. In view of the work's expansive character and the Olympian grandeur of its formal plan, no nickname could be more fitting.

Completed on August 10, 1788, the *Jupiter* was the last of Mozart's symphonies; it represents the embodiment of his artistic philosophy, which saw perfection as the gathering of diverse expressive elements into a coordinated structure of exalted cast. The opening movement is a tour de force of symphonic argument, marked by sparkling invention and a seamless connection of ideas. The brilliant style predominates, but Mozart mixes in a singing-style second subject, a Sturm und Drang episode, and elements of the fantasy style to create an extraordinarily rich and elevated discourse. The second movement, a sarabande poignantly colored by muted violins, is an orchestral aria in which Romantic anguish is expressed with an almost Baroque elegance. The Ländlerlike minuet seems more down-to-earth, but its tone is complicated by an unusually intense chromaticism, while Sturm und Drang elements darken the rustic innocence of the movement's trio.

The finale is Mozart's greatest symphonic movement, a majestic demonstration of the art of finding the maximum number of different arrangements of a set of musical figures. The process reaches its climax in the coda, with a FUGATO in which five of the movement's six principal thematic ideas are presented in gradual superimposition on one another, until all five are going at once—then, over the span of 20 measures, the counterpoint is inverted five times so that each of the string sections (first violins, second violins, violas, cellos, and basses) carries a different motif in succession. It is a matchless display of musical technique, and with it Mozart brings his greatest symphony, and his life's work as a symphonist, to a spectacular close.

RECOMMENDED RECORDINGS

BÖHM AND BERLIN PHILHARMONIC (DG).

JOCHUM AND BOSTON SYMPHONY ORCHESTRA (DG).

HARNONCOURT AND CHAMBER ORCHESTRA OF EUROPE (TELDEC).

K. [1] Abbreviation of the name Köchel, author of the standard catalog of Mozart's compositions. Ludwig Ritter von Köchel (1800–77) was an Austrian scholar of independent means with interests in history, botany, mineralogy, and music, especially the music of Mozart. As a botanist he was familiar with the Linnaean classification of plants; as an amateur musicologist, he recognized the need for an orderly assessment of Mozart's music that would identify when each work had been composed and where the manuscript, if it survived, could be found. Köchel's *Chronologisch-thematisches Verzeichnis sämtlicher Tonwerke Wolfgang Amadé Mozarts* (*Chronological-Thematic Catalog of the Complete Works of Wolfgang Amadé Mozart*), published in Leipzig in 1862, was the first comprehensive catalog of any composer's works, and the model for subsequent tomes devoted to the music of Schubert (by Otto Erich Deutsch, hence "D" numbers), Haydn (Anthony van Hoboken, "Hob."), and Vivaldi (Peter Ryom, "RV"—for *Répertoire Vivaldi*), among others, though of these only the Deutsch classification is chronological. Köchel's devotion to the music of Mozart extended to his subsidizing the first printed edition of the composer's collected works, published by Breitkopf & Härtel between 1877 and 1883. His catalog has appeared in six editions so far, with a seventh, *Der neue Köchel,* currently in preparation.

[2] Abbreviation of the name Kirkpatrick, used in association with the music of Domenico Scarlatti. The harpsichordist RALPH KIRKPATRICK published a study of Scarlatti's works in 1953 and edited all the sonatas in facsimile. Kirkpatrick's numbering of the sonatas is the preferred one, though references to "L" numbers (from a catalog by Alessandro Longo, published 1906–08) and "P" numbers (Giorgio Pestelli, 1967) are also encountered.

Kapell, William

(b. New York, September 20, 1922; d. King's Mountain, Calif., October 29, 1953)

AMERICAN PIANIST. One of the most gifted performers the United States has ever produced, he died at the age of 31 in a plane crash outside San Francisco, returning from a tour of Australia. He left behind a handful of recordings testifying to an artistry that was already distinctive and well developed. Kapell studied first with Dorothy Anderson LaFollette and subsequently in Philadelphia and at the Juilliard School in New York with Olga Samaroff. In 1941 he walked off with the prestigious Naumburg Award; his New York debut later that year won the Town Hall Award for the season's outstanding

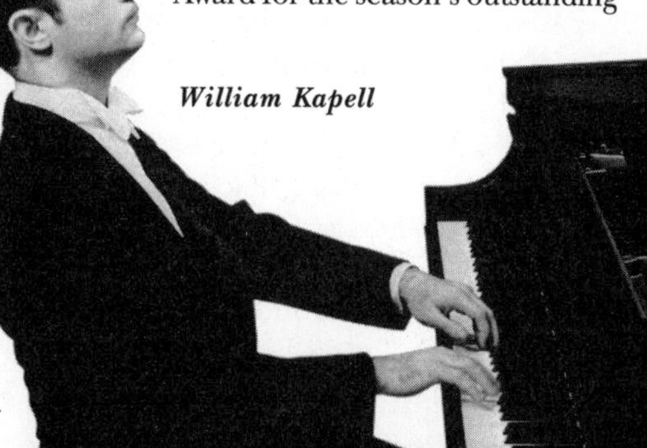

William Kapell

concert by a musician under 30 (he was not yet 20). His career developed quickly, and by the early 1950s he had emerged as the foremost among a new generation of American pianists that included Gary Graffman, Eugene Istomin, Leon Fleisher, and Julius Katchen.

Kapell possessed a sovereign technique born of prodigious practice, and his interpretations were marked by a maturity and firmness of conception that belied his age. His performances of Khachaturian's Piano Concerto, a trashy yet splendidly virtuosic work, created a sensation, as did his later magisterial accounts of the Brahms D minor concerto (No. 1) and his hair-raising renditions of Rachmaninov's Second and Third. He was equally attuned to the solo and chamber repertoires. His playing was informed by a rare blend of communicative intensity and sensitivity to structure that made his realizations of Bach, Chopin, Mozart, Schubert, Brahms, Prokofiev, and Copland not only technically impressive but emotionally satisfying. He also believed in programming works by living composers and was a staunch champion of 20th-century repertoire. At the time of his death he had plans to commission works from a number of American composers, including Ned Rorem and Vincent Persichetti (1915–87); Aaron Copland, whose sonata and *Piano Variations* he programmed frequently, subsequently dedicated his *Piano Fantasy* (1955–57) to Kapell's memory.

Among Kapell's most impressive achievements in the studio were his recordings of the Khachaturian concerto (with Koussevitzky and the Boston Symphony), Prokofiev's Piano Concerto No. 3 in C (with Dorati in Dallas), Rachmaninov's *Rhapsody on a Theme of Paganini,* and the Chopin B minor sonata. In the virile power of his playing and his sober yet intense expressiveness, Kapell—not Horowitz—was Rachmaninov's true pianistic heir.

RECOMMENDED RECORDING

"The William Kapell Edition" (RCA).

Kapellmeister (Gr., "master of the chapel") In German-speaking lands, a term originally used to describe the music director of a court chapel, which later came to be used as a designation for the leader of any large ensemble, such as an orchestra or a court opera. In the modern era of glamorous podium princes, the term has acquired a pejorative ring in some circles, denoting a journeyman rather than a star. But many "star" conductors of the present day, including Kurt Masur, have worn it as a badge of honor, a title linking them to a distinguished centuries-old tradition.

Karajan, Herbert von

(b. Salzburg, April 5, 1908; d. Anif, July 16, 1989)

AUSTRIAN CONDUCTOR AND STAGE DIRECTOR. A headstrong and controversial figure whose energy, ambition, capacity for work, and insistence on getting his way were legendary, he was the preeminent European conductor of the postwar period. Though small in stature he had a charismatic presence that gave him enormous authority on the podium. A supremely assured conducting technique, athletic grace, and aristocratic good looks—slender build, sharply chiseled features, piercing blue eyes, a dramatic shock of light-brown hair that turned silver in later years—contributed to the effect, as did the mystique of power that influenced his behavior from youth, imparting a relentless drive for control and perfection.

Christened Heribert Ritter von Karajan, the child who would become Salzburg's most famous son after Mozart was brought up in a cultivated musical environment. His great-grandfather, Theodor Georg von Karajan, had been an eminent musicologist,

Herbert von Karajan conducting Brahms

and his father, Ernst, chief of the surgical clinic in Salzburg, was an accomplished clarinetist who played in the town's chamber music society. The young Karajan studied piano at the Salzburg Mozarteum before enrolling in the University of Vienna, where he studied musicology, and at the Vienna Music Academy, where he became a conducting pupil of Franz Schalk. He made his conducting debut in 1928 and took a post in Ulm, Germany, the following year. The experience of hearing Toscanini conduct Verdi's *Falstaff* and Donizetti's *Lucia di Lammermoor* with the La Scala company in Vienna in 1929, and of attending one of Toscanini's performances with the New York Philharmonic on its European tour of 1930, proved a revelation—for the first time, Karajan became aware of a conductor's enormous capacity to transform a piece of music in performance and make it compelling by sheer force of conviction. In the summer of 1930 he bicycled 250 miles from Salzburg to Bayreuth to hear Toscanini conduct Wagner's *Tannhäuser,* and came away from the encounter strengthened in his resolve to get to the top of the musical world.

The ascent began when Karajan joined the Nazi party in Salzburg on April 8, 1933—three days after his 25th birthday, barely two months after Hitler had been named chancellor of Germany, and just one day after the promulgation of a law effectively removing Jewish civil servants (including conductors) from their positions in state opera houses in Germany. No zealot, but already a shrewd opportunist, Karajan realized that the new law would create vacancies at every rung on the career ladder and that party membership would speed his rise to the top.

With his credentials in hand he went to Aachen in 1934 and was appointed general music director there in 1935; he made his debuts at the Vienna Staatsoper and the Berlin Staatsoper in 1937, and with the Berlin Philharmonic on April 8, 1938. The turning point in Karajan's career came with a performance of Wagner's *Tristan und Isolde* at the Berlin Staatsoper in 1938; one review of the event hailed "Karajan the Miracle." Under the patronage of Hermann Göring, Karajan was brought from Aachen to Berlin permanently in 1941, and presided over the Staatsoper and the Berlin State Orchestra through 1944, competing for glory in the heart of the Reich with the one and only Wilhelm Furtwängler.

Following the end of World War II, Karajan underwent denazification proceedings, which stalled his career until 1947, when he was officially cleared. Anticipating that result, the English record producer Walter Legge had signed Karajan to a contract with EMI in 1946, which allowed Karajan to record with the Vienna Philharmonic even though he was still barred from performing with the orchestra in public. In 1948, Legge put Karajan in front of the Philharmonia Orchestra, handpicked from London's best musicians; his recording of the Schumann Piano Concerto with Dinu Lipatti marked the beginning of a fruitful association with that orchestra. Karajan reopened the Bayreuth Festival in 1951, and returned to conduct *Tristan und Isolde* in 1952, but was never invited back; he made his first postwar appearance with the Berlin Philharmonic in 1953.

On April 5, 1955, his 43rd birthday, Karajan was appointed music director for life by the Berlin Philharmonic, while he and the ensemble were on tour in the United States. Furtwängler's shoes were big ones to fill, but in the years that followed, Karajan painstakingly rebuilt the orchestra into one of the finest in the world. Appointments as music director of the Vienna Staatsoper and the Salzburg Festival came in 1956 and 1957, the latter year also marking the commencement of a short-lived relationship with La Scala. Because he had so many irons in the fire Karajan came to be known in the press as the "General Music Director of Europe." But controversy ended his reign at the Vienna Staatsoper in 1964, and his relationship with the Berlin Philharmonic soured in the mid-1980s as a result of disputes over personnel (specifically, Karajan's wish to engage Sabine Meyer as principal clarinet) and other matters. Karajan's final concerts, tours, and recordings were made with the Vienna Philharmonic; he resigned his Berlin post in the spring of 1989, and died at his home in Austria later that year.

Karajan's concert repertoire ranged from Bach and Vivaldi to Berg and Webern, but was anchored in the music of Mozart, Beethoven, Brahms, Bruckner, and Richard Strauss. In the opera house he gravitated toward the works of Mozart, Verdi, Wagner, and Puccini. He had a remarkable affinity for the music of Sibelius and Debussy as well, and a natural flair for the waltzes of Johann Strauss Jr. and his brother Josef. As a conductor, Karajan put a premium on beauty of sound, constantly admonishing his players to make things *schön.* This led to the "massaged" style of performance Karajan cultivated in Berlin during the 1970s and 1980s, and that critic Andrew Porter so famously likened to Kobe beef. Karajan preferred a weighty sound in Brahms, but opted for chamber-music textures in Wagner, and his Mozart could be, in the words of Alan Rich, "powerful and prissy at the same time." Karajan's readings tended to emphasize musical line and architecture over emotional expression (in this he was the opposite of Bernstein), but one of the most satisfying aspects of a Karajan performance was the grip it could exert on a listener.

During a media career that spanned more than 50 years, Karajan made approximately 800 recordings, including groundbreaking stereo, digital, and video efforts. From the 1960s through the 1980s he towered over European musical life as no one had before, and in the process amassed a personal fortune worth about $300 million at the time of his death. His strong-willed and autocratic personality clashed with many other egos along the way—one of the reasons he enjoyed few successful long-term collaborations with top-flight singers or soloists—but assured him an artistic scope and freedom no other conductor in history has achieved.

RECOMMENDED RECORDINGS

BEETHOVEN, SYMPHONIES (1962): BERLIN PHILHARMONIC (DG).

BRUCKNER, SYMPHONY NO. 8: VIENNA PHILHARMONIC (DG).

DEBUSSY, *LA MER, PRÉLUDE À L'APRÈS-MIDI D'UN FAUNE*: BERLIN PHILHARMONIC (DG).

HONEGGER, SYMPHONIES NOS. 2 AND 3: BERLIN PHILHARMONIC (DG).

MAHLER, SYMPHONY NO. 9: BERLIN PHILHARMONIC (DG).

PUCCINI, *MADAMA BUTTERFLY*: NIMSGERN, FRENI, LUDWIG, PAVAROTTI; VIENNA PHILHARMONIC (DECCA).

SIBELIUS, SYMPHONIES NOS. 4 AND 7: BERLIN PHILHARMONIC (DG).

WAGNER, *PARSIFAL*: HOFFMAN, MOLL, VAN DAM, VEJZOVIC; BERLIN PHILHARMONIC (DG).

Kát'a Kabanová OPERA IN THREE ACTS BY LEOŠ JANÁČEK, to his own libretto (based on Aleksandr Ostrovsky's play *The Storm*), premiered at the National Theater in Brno on November 23, 1921. The score, which occupied Janáček from January 1920 to April 1921 and marks the beginning of his amazingly fruitful final period as a composer, is dedicated to Kamila Stösslová. Janáček's tender feelings for the dedicatee informed his treatment of the opera's title character, a gentle, conscience-stricken young woman who, having given in to the advances of a passionate admirer, chooses suicide as the only means of escape from her drunken husband and vindictive, domineering mother-in-law.

RECOMMENDED RECORDING

SÖDERSTRÖM, DVORSKY, KNIPLOVÁ; MACKERRAS AND VIENNA PHILHARMONIC (DECCA).

kazoo *See box on pages 496–97.*

Kempe, Rudolf

(b. Niederpoyritz, June 14, 1910; d. Zurich, May 12, 1976)

GERMAN CONDUCTOR. He was principal oboist with the Leipzig Gewandhaus Orchestra from 1928 to 1935 and made his conducting debut at the Leipzig Opera in 1935. In the course of his military service during World War II he worked for a time at the Chemnitz Opera; following the war, he returned to Chemnitz to serve as the company's music director (1946–48). He was music director at Dresden's Semper Opera (1950–53) and head of the Bavarian State Opera in Munich (1952–54). He achieved a wider European reputation as a result of successful visits to the Vienna Staatsoper in 1951 and regular guest performances at Covent Garden beginning in 1953. He made his Metropolitan Opera debut on January 26, 1955, conducting Wagner's *Tannhäuser,* and over the next 14 months revisited its pit for performances of Richard Strauss's *Arabella* and *Der Rosenkavalier* and Wagner's *Die Meistersinger von Nürnberg* and *Tristan und Isolde.* He appeared for the first time as a conductor at the Bayreuth Festival in 1960. Also in 1960, at the request of Sir Thomas Beecham, he became associate conductor of the Royal Philharmonic Orchestra; following Beecham's death in 1961, he was elevated to the post of principal conductor. He became the RPO's artistic director in 1963 and was named "conductor for life" in 1970, but resigned in 1975. He was music director of the Zurich Tonhalle Orchestra from 1965 to 1972 and of the Munich Philharmonic from 1967 until his death.

Though little known in America (apart from recordings) he was considered a figure of major importance in England. As a former orchestra player he knew how to get musicians to give their all, and his athletic, tightly wound interpretations of the music of Beethoven, Wagner, and Strauss typically show the orchestra in full cry, but always under control. During the 1960s and 1970s he made many distinguished recordings with the RPO (among them Dvořák's Symphony *From the New World,*

Strauss's *Eine Alpensinfonie,* and Janáček's *Glagolitic Mass*) and recorded a landmark set of the complete orchestral works of Strauss with the Staatskapelle Dresden. He is well represented in the operatic catalog by recordings of Wagner's *Lohengrin* and *Die Meistersinger von Nürnberg,* and of Strauss's *Ariadne auf Naxos.*

RECOMMENDED RECORDINGS

JANÁČEK, *GLAGOLITIC MASS*: KUBIAK, COLLINS, TEAR, SCHÖNE AND ROYAL PHILHARMONIC (DECCA).

R. STRAUSS, ORCHESTRAL WORKS: STAATSKAPELLE DRESDEN (EMI).

Kempff, Wilhelm

(b. Jüterbog, November 25, 1895; d. Positano, May 23, 1991)

GERMAN PIANIST. Raised in the rich cultural and intellectual soil of Wilhelmine Prussia, he studied philosophy and music history at the University of Berlin while taking a diploma in piano at that city's Hochschule für Musik. He gave his recital debut in Berlin in 1917 (characteristically, his program included Beethoven's *Hammerklavier* Sonata and Brahms's *Variations on a Theme of Paganini,* tough nuts to crack) and the following year appeared for the first time as a soloist with the Berlin Philharmonic. He served as director of the Stuttgart Musikhochschule from 1924 to 1929 and taught a summer course in piano at Potsdam from 1931 to 1941. His international reputation waxed considerably after World War II. In 1951 he made his recital debut in London, and in 1964 he made his American debut, in New York. During the 1950s and 1960s, he recorded extensively for Deutsche Grammophon.

Kempff was the preeminent German pianist of the postwar decades. He was also among the last musical emissaries of German Romanticism, and it was in this role that he functioned as an interpreter. He could relate the emotional world of a Schubert sonata to feelings expressed in Goethe's poetry, or explain its structure using analogies drawn from classical architecture, as easily and convincingly as he could phrase a singing line at the piano. Beauty of tone, clarity of texture, and graceful phrasing were the hallmarks of his playing, which frequently conveyed a spiritual elation. He was devoted to the music of Beethoven and Schubert, and was also a formidable interpreter of Mozart, Chopin, Schumann, and Brahms. His integral recording of the Schubert sonatas is among the gilt-edged securities in the discographic marketplace, and his two recorded cycles of the Beethoven sonatas (one in mono from the 1950s, the other in stereo from the 1960s) are interpretive landmarks, though the latter set reveals an approach more deliberate than fiery.

Wilhelm Kempff in performance

RECOMMENDED RECORDINGS

BEETHOVEN, PIANO CONCERTO NO. 5: LEITNER AND BERLIN PHILHARMONIC ORCHESTRA (DG).

BEETHOVEN, PIANO SONATAS (DG).

SCHUBERT, PIANO SONATAS (DG).

SCHUMANN, *KINDERSZENEN, KREISLERIANA* (DG).

Kernis, Aaron Jay *See box on pages 708–11.*

Kertész, István

(b. Budapest, August 28, 1929; d. Kfar Saba, Israel, April 16, 1973)

HUNGARIAN CONDUCTOR, one of the most gifted and versatile musicians of his generation. He learned to play the violin and piano as a child. At the Franz Liszt Academy in Budapest he studied violin, composition (his teachers included Zoltán Kodály and Leo Weiner), and, from 1949 to 1953, conducting (with László Somogyi). His outlook was strongly influenced by the artistry of an earlier generation, particularly that of conductors Bruno Walter and Otto Klemperer, who was then chief conductor at the Budapest Opera. Kertész began his career working in Györ (1953–55) and at the Budapest Opera (1955–56). He left Hungary after the brutal Soviet crackdown that brought an end to the Hungarian revolution of 1956. In 1958 he put the finishing touches on his podium technique, studying with Fernando Previtali at the Accademia di Santa Cecilia in Rome. Taking up residence in West Germany, he began a short but spectacular career in Germany, England, and the United States. He served as chief conductor at the Augsburg Opera (1958–63) and the Cologne Opera (from 1964 until his death). In Cologne he was hailed for a wide-ranging repertoire that included Wagner's *Tristan und Isolde* and a number of 20th-century works; while there he introduced operas as diverse as Verdi's *Stiffelio* and Britten's *Billy Budd* to the German stage and developed a reputation as a fine Mozartean. He served as principal conductor of the London Symphony Orchestra (1965–68), continuing to record with that ensemble after quitting his post in a dispute over artistic control. He made his Covent Garden debut in 1966 with Verdi's *Un ballo in maschera,* worked regularly with the Vienna Philharmonic, and became a favorite guest conductor of major American orchestras, including those of Philadelphia and Cleveland. In 1972 he was passed over for the music directorship of the Cleveland Orchestra, despite an overwhelming vote in his favor by the members of the orchestra. Shortly before his death he was named chief conductor of the Bamberg Symphony. Kertész's death at the age of 43 remains a mystery; officially, he drowned while swimming in the Mediterranean. Certain colleagues, including his countryman Antal Dorati, believed he was despondent over not getting the music directorship in Cleveland and that he committed suicide by intentionally swimming into a riptide. Others who were close to Kertész have said that he was prone to sudden seizures and may simply have suffered one while in the water.

Kertész was a spontaneous musician, not a disciplinarian, one who enjoyed "winging it" with orchestras during rehearsal but had such a natural feeling that things almost invariably clicked. His polished, physically elegant technique evoked a bygone era, yet there was nothing old-fashioned about his repertoire or his sensibilities: He was known for performances that were incisively shaped and exciting, yet warmly expressive, never driven. His repertoire ranged from Mozart, Haydn, Beethoven, and Schubert to Bruckner, Brahms, and Dvořák, and was particularly broad in the music of the 20th century, where he inclined toward Bartók, Kodály, Hindemith, Shostakovich, Britten, and Hans Werner Henze (b. 1926). On records he is represented by a mere sliver of his operatic repertoire—Mozart's *La clemenza di Tito,* Donizetti's *Don Pasquale,* Bartók's *Bluebeard's Castle*—each outstanding. He recorded complete cycles of the symphonies of Schubert and Brahms (with the Vienna Philharmonic) and of the major orchestral works of Dvořák (with the

London Symphony). The latter effort remains, nearly 40 years after it was finished, the preeminent traversal of the music on disc. Kertész's accounts of Kodály's *Háry János, Psalmus Hungaricus,* and *Peacock* Variations, also with the LSO, likewise have yet to be bettered.

RECOMMENDED RECORDINGS

BARTÓK, *BLUEBEARD'S CASTLE*: BERRY, LUDWIG; LONDON SYMPHONY ORCHESTRA (DECCA).

BRAHMS, SYMPHONIES: VIENNA PHILHARMONIC (DECCA).

DVOŘÁK, SYMPHONIES, OVERTURES, TONE POEMS: LONDON SYMPHONY ORCHESTRA (DECCA).

KODÁLY, *PEACOCK* VARIATIONS: LONDON SYMPHONY ORCHESTRA (DECCA).

kettledrum *See* TIMPANI.

key [1] Tonal disposition of a passage, a movement, or a piece of music, referred to by the name of the tonic (i.e., first note) of the major or minor scale that is predominant. [2] On instruments such as the piano, harpsichord, and organ, one of a set of levers corresponding to the notes of the chromatic scale that, when depressed, causes a specific note to sound. [3] On woodwind instruments such as the flute, oboe, clarinet, and bassoon, a metal lever that opens or closes one or more tone holes, thus permitting the player to sound specific notes. *See also* TONALITY.

key signature The group of sharp or flat signs placed on a staff at the beginning of a piece of music (immediately after the clef), indicating the key in which the music is written. Each signature corresponds to one major and one minor key: Three flats, for example, signifies either E-flat major or C minor, two sharps either D major or B minor. The key signature for C major/A minor is blank since the scales of those keys contain neither sharps nor flats.

Khachaturian, Aram Il'yich

(b. Tiflis, Georgia, June 6, 1903; d. Moscow, May 1, 1978)

SOVIET COMPOSER OF ARMENIAN DESCENT. In his fiery, energetic, and impulsive music he spoke for his people in a way that won the hearts of listeners everywhere. While studying biology at the University of Moscow (1922–25), he enrolled as a cello student at the Gnessin Institute, then shifted his focus to composition, where his teachers were Mikhail Gnessin and Reyngol'd Glier. He earned his diploma from the Moscow Conservatory in 1934 and did postgraduate work there from 1934 to 1936. In the dozen years that followed he became one of the Soviet Union's most successful composers, admired for music that blended folkloristic color and Romantic sentiment. Despite his conservative stance, he was denounced by the central committee of the Communist Party in 1948 for "formalist tendencies," along with Prokofiev, Shostakovich, and others. He quickly rehabilitated himself and was named a People's Artist of the U.S.S.R. in 1954. In later years he spent time on the international circuit as a guest conductor of his own music.

Khachaturian was best known for his ballets *Gayane* (1942) and *Spartacus* (1950–54), and for his incidental music for Lermontov's *Masquerade* (1941); effective concert suites were drawn from all three scores. His efforts in more "serious" genres, such as the concerto and symphony, were not as successful—though a few pianists have made hay with his Piano Concerto (1936), particularly William Kapell. His Violin Concerto (1940), written for David Oistrakh, has won a place in the repertoire, if not of violinists, at least of flutists in need of a rousing 20th-century work. Khachaturian composed a handful of chamber pieces and ten film scores. But his most important movie credit came with Stanley Kubrick's *2001: A Space Odyssey,*

Aram Il'yich Khachaturian, 1968, on a visit to Rochester, New York

which made haunting use of the Adagio from *Gayane*, alongside snippets from Richard Strauss, Johann Strauss Jr., and György Ligeti—strange bedfellows.

Khachaturian was the Rimsky-Korsakov of the Caucasus—he took the idiom of *Sheherazade* and punched it up to 20th-century standards of gaudiness, as in the Lezghinka from *Gayane,* which takes riffs and harmonies directly from Rimsky's famous suite. His ability to transplant colorful, rhythmically distinctive folk material from Armenia, Georgia, Ukraine, or Belarus into a more formal musical setting, without losing its essence, was unmatched by any of his Soviet contemporaries.

RECOMMENDED RECORDINGS

Gayane and *Spartacus* (excerpts): Khachaturian and Vienna Philharmonic (Decca).

Piano Concerto: Kapell; Koussevitzky and Boston Symphony Orchestra (RCA).

Violin Concerto: Kogan; Monteux and Boston Symphony Orchestra (RCA).

Khovanshchina **Opera in six scenes by Modest Mussorgsky,** to his own libretto, premiered posthumously in St. Petersburg on February 21, 1886. The original performing version of the score, left unfinished and unorchestrated by Mussorgsky at his death in 1881, was the work of Rimsky-Korsakov; in 1913, Ravel and Stravinsky collaborated on a version, and Shostakovich tried his hand in 1958–59. Mussorgsky described *Khovanshchina* as a "national music drama." Set in and around Moscow in the 1680s, it deals with the political infighting from which Peter the Great emerged as unchallenged ruler of Russia; caught up in the action is a group of religious zealots known as the "Old Believers," whose opposition to Peter's rule ends in their self-immolation. While it remains difficult to bring coherence to this sprawling work on stage, it has received a new lease on life in recent years thanks to productions at the Mariinsky Theater and the Metropolitan Opera. The Prelude, a beautiful tone poem depicting dawn on the Moscow River, appears frequently on concert programs.

RECOMMENDED RECORDING

Lipovšek, Burchuladze, Haugland; Abbado and Vienna Philharmonic (DG).

Kinderszenen (Scenes from Childhood) **Cycle of 13 vignettes by Robert Schumann,** composed in 1838 and published the following year as his Op. 15. It is the most intimate of Schumann's major works for the piano, and it contains what is probably the best known of all his musical utterances, the gentle "Träumerei" ("Reverie"), epitomizing the Romantic sentiment of poetic yearning.

RECOMMENDED RECORDINGS

Curzon (Decca).

Kempff (DG).

Kindertotenlieder (Songs on the Deaths of Children) **Cycle of five songs for low voice and orchestra by Gustav Mahler,** to poems by Friedrich Rückert, composed 1901–04 and premiered in Vienna on January 29, 1905, the composer conducting.

At the time of the premiere, Mahler might well have appeared to be tempting fate in his choice of texts, for he and his wife, Alma, had two daughters. It surely must have seemed so when, on July 5, 1907, Maria Anna, the elder of the two, died of scarlet fever, four months shy of her fifth birthday. But work on the cycle had begun even before Mahler married; Rückert's grim poetry resonated in Mahler's mind in part because he had already witnessed many childhood deaths, including those of eight of his siblings. The songs mark the beginning of a new phase in Mahler's work—the treatment is no longer essentially folkloric (nor intentionally coarse, rustic, or mawkish, as often before), but austere, reserved, elevated, aphoristic, and powerfully concentrated. ◉ The orchestration, sparing compared with that of Symphonies Nos. 5 and 6 from the same period, looks ahead to the manner of the Symphony No. 7 and *Das Lied von der Erde.*

RECOMMENDED RECORDINGS

BAKER; BARBIROLLI AND HALLÉ ORCHESTRA (EMI).

FERRIER; WALTER AND VIENNA PHILHARMONIC (EMI).

King Arthur "SEMIOPERA" IN FIVE ACTS WITH MUSIC BY HENRY PURCELL, first performed at the Queen's Theater, London, in the spring of 1691. The text, written in 1684 by John Dryden, was intended for festivities the following year marking the 25th anniversary of the restoration of Charles II, but was not used at that time. After hearing Purcell's *Dioclesian* in 1690, Dryden revised the text at the composer's request. The musical numbers are among the most vivid and imaginative of the 17th century, particularly Act III's "Frost Scene," with its shivering aria for the Cold Genius.

RECOMMENDED RECORDING

GENS, MCFADDEN, PADMORE; CHRISTIE AND LES ARTS FLORISSANTS (ERATO).

King's Sisters, The *See box on pages 934–36.*

Kipnis, Alexander

(b. Zhitomir, February 13, 1891; d. Westport, Conn., May 14, 1978)

UKRAINIAN/AMERICAN BASS. He began singing in a synagogue as a boy soprano of unusual purity and musicality. He studied music at the Warsaw Conservatory (graduating as a bandmaster), and went to Berlin to study voice for three years with Ernst Grenzebach, also the teacher of Lauritz Melchior and Max Lorenz. Briefly interned as an enemy alien at the beginning of World War I, he made his operatic debut in Hamburg. His early career centered on Berlin, where from 1919 to 1930 he sang at the Deutsche Oper (renamed the Städtische Oper in 1925), and from 1930 to 1935 at the Staatsoper. Between 1923 and 1937 he appeared in Vienna, Buenos Aires, Bayreuth, Munich, Salzburg, and at the Chicago Lyric Opera. He made his Covent Garden debut in 1927, as Marcel in Meyerbeer's *Les Huguenots,* and later sang the roles of Gurnemanz and Ochs there as well.

Alexander Kipnis

In 1934 Kipnis became an American citizen, and from 1935 to 1938, no longer welcome in Germany, he sang with the Vienna Staatsoper. In 1940, at the age of 48, he made a late debut at the Metropolitan Opera, as Gurnemanz; he continued to sing at the Met until 1946, appearing in half a dozen Wagnerian roles, as Arkel in Debussy's *Pelléas et Mélisande,* as Sarastro in Mozart's *Die Zauberflöte,* and in the title role of Mussorgsky's *Boris Godunov.*

Kipnis's voice was not unusually powerful, but it was extremely refined and flexible. He was capable of achieving remarkable nuance and gradations of tone and color, and with his highly developed musical instincts he enjoyed a distinguished career as a concert singer. In addition to the Wagner and Mozart roles that figured prominently in his career, one of his specialties was Méphistophélès in Gounod's *Faust.* His son was the harpsichordist and fortepianist Igor Kipnis (1930–2002).

Kirkby, Emma

(b. Camberley, Surrey, February 26, 1949)

ENGLISH SOPRANO. Her crystalline voice, used with minimal vibrato, is the epitome of the so-called "white sound" associated with the English period-performance style of the 1970s and 1980s. She read classics at Oxford and began singing in small choirs, developing an interest in Renaissance and Baroque music. Through her studies with Jessica Cash, and her work with instrumentalists, singers, and conductors specializing in period performance, she acquired a technique suitable for singing early music, along with fluency in a considerable range of styles. In 1973, she joined lutenist Anthony Rooley's Consort of Musicke, an ensemble dedicated to rediscovering early English and Italian repertoire. She made many landmark recordings with them, as well as recordings of Baroque vocal works with Christopher Hogwood and the Academy of Ancient Music. She made her operatic debut in Bruges in 1983, as Mother Nature in *Cupid and Death* by the team of Matthew Locke (1621–77) and Christopher Gibbons (1615–76), and in 1989 she sang the role of Dorinda in an American tour of Handel's *Orlando.* Her extensive discography on a variety of labels includes, among many other things, a pioneering disc devoted to the music of Hildegard von Bingen ("A Feather on the Breath of God"), as well as recordings of Bach cantatas, Vivaldi opera arias, duos with Anthony Rooley, and the first recording (2001) of the newly rediscovered *Gloria* by Handel, with the Royal Academy Baroque Orchestra under Lawrence Cummings. In 2000, Kirkby received the Order of the British Empire.

RECOMMENDED RECORDING

"THE EMMA KIRKBY COLLECTION" (MUSIC OF PURCELL, HANDEL, MONTEVERDI, AND OTHERS); ROOLEY, PAGE, PARROTT; CONSORT OF MUSICKE, TAVERNER CONSORT, AND OTHERS (HYPERION).

Kirkpatrick, Ralph

(b. Leominster, Mass., June 10, 1911; d. Guilford, Conn., April 13, 1984)

AMERICAN HARPSICHORDIST, CLAVICHORDIST, AND PIANIST. Having studied piano from the age of six, he took up the harpsichord in 1930, while attending Harvard on scholarship. After earning his bachelor's degree in fine arts, he spent 1931–32 in Paris on a Paine Travelling Scholarship. His studies included research at the Bibliothèque Nationale, harpsichord lessons with Wanda Landowska and Paul Brunold (1875–1948), and classes in theory with Nadia Boulanger. In 1933 he made his European debut in Berlin, playing the *Goldberg* Variations to great acclaim. Over the years he performed widely in Europe and America. His repertoire was extensive and included all of Bach's music for harpsichord and clavichord, the sonatas of Domenico Scarlatti, a good deal of 18th-century French keyboard music, and Mozart, which he played on the fortepiano.

Kirkpatrick's groundbreaking critical and biographical study of Scarlatti, supported early on by a Guggenheim Fellowship, was a major contribution to the music literature. Published in 1953 by Princeton University Press, *Domenico Scarlatti* established the standard numbering of Scarlatti's keyboard sonatas. Kirkpatrick also prepared an edition of Scarlatti's complete sonatas in facsimile, and recorded 60 of them. He was an authority on the music of Bach as well; in addition to creating a critical edition of the *Goldberg* Variations he wrote a penetrating study of the interpretation of *Das wohltemperirte Clavier.* His academic career took him to posts at the Salzburg Mozarteum (1933–34), Yale (1940–76), and the University of California at Berkeley, where in 1964 he taught as the first Ernest Bloch Professor of Music.

Reacting to Romantic excesses typical of the first generation of modern harpsichordists, Kirkpatrick reined in his own expressiveness, cultivating a rhythmically vital and authoritative style that was incisive and direct, if sometimes dry. His brilliance nonethelesss came across in his interpretations, and he continues to be regarded as one of the most influential harpsichordists of the 20th century.

RECOMMENDED RECORDINGS

BACH, *GOLDBERG* VARIATIONS (POLYGRAM).
D. SCARLATTI, 53 SONATAS FOR HARPSICHORD (URANIA).

Kissin, Evgeny

(b. Moscow, October 10, 1971)

RUSSIAN PIANIST. He began to play the piano at the age of two, and was six when he entered Moscow's Gnessin School of Music, where he studied under Anna Pavlovna Kantor. He came to international attention in 1984 when, at the age of 12, he performed both Chopin concertos at the Great Hall of the Moscow Conservatory with the Moscow State Philharmonic conducted by Dmitry Kitaenko. By the time he was a teenager he was being hailed in the Western press as the next genius of the piano, with record companies in hot pursuit. In 1988, a year after making his Western European debut in Berlin, he toured Europe with the Moscow Virtuosi and Vladimir Spivakov. He made his American debut in September 1990, again playing the Chopin concertos, with Zubin Mehta and the New York Philharmonic. A week later he opened Carnegie Hall's centennial season with one of the most eagerly anticipated solo recitals in the hall's history.

While Kissin's artistry and career have yet to develop to the extraordinary degree his early triumphs foreshadowed, he remains an artist to watch, one who has already made a significant contribution to the record catalog with his fiery, virtuosic interpretations of the Romantic repertoire, particularly the works of Chopin, Schumann, Liszt, and the Russians.

RECOMMENDED RECORDING

CHOPIN, FANTAISIE IN F MINOR; NOCTURNES, OP. 27, NOS. 1 AND 2; SCHERZO IN B-FLAT MINOR (RCA).

klagende Lied, Das (The Song of Lamentation) **CANTATA IN THREE MOVEMENTS BY GUSTAV MAHLER,** to his own text (based on "The Singing Bone" by the brothers Grimm), composed 1878–80. In this, his first sym-

Evgeny Kissin, 2004

phonic score, Mahler showed an acute awareness of the expressive possibilities of orchestral song, along with a striking mastery of the orchestra itself. Many of the emotional themes and musical devices he explored here for the first time—for example, the use of offstage forces to dramatic effect—were to occupy him for the rest of his life.

RECOMMENDED RECORDING

Döse, Hodgson, Tear; Rattle and City of Birmingham Symphony Orchestra (EMI).

Kleiber, Carlos

(b. Berlin, July 3, 1930; d. Konjsic, Slovenia, July 13, 2004)

Austrian conductor, son of Erich Kleiber. He grew up in Argentina, where his family had moved in 1935 following his father's resignation as general music director of the Berlin Staatsoper. As a youth Kleiber studied piano, learned to play timpani, and attended boarding schools in Argentina and Chile. He studied chemistry at the Technische Hochschule in Zurich (1949–50), and returned to South America in 1950 to finish his musical training in Buenos Aires. In 1951 he started his conducting career at the bottom rung, as an unpaid rehearsal pianist at the Gärtnerplatztheater in Munich. He subsequently became a vocal coach at the Vienna Volksoper, then joined the staff of the Deutsche Oper am Rhein in Düsseldorf in 1956, becoming conductor there in 1958. He served as conductor at the Zurich Opera (1964–66) and as principal conductor at the Württembergisches Staatstheater in Stuttgart (1966–68). From 1968 to 1979 he was engaged as a regular conductor at the Bavarian State Opera in Munich; until 1988 he returned occasionally as a guest conductor. He made his debuts at the Vienna Staatsoper (1973) and the Bayreuth Festival (1974) conducting Wagner's *Tristan und Isolde,* and at Covent Garden and La Scala (both 1974) conducting Richard Strauss's *Der Rosenkavalier.* He made his American debut with the San Francisco Opera in 1977, leading Verdi's *Otello,* and took his first bows at New York's Metropolitan Opera in 1988, with Puccini's *La bohème.* He became an Austrian citizen in 1980; soon after, he began limiting himself to a mere handful of guest-conducting engagements, mostly in Europe.

Kleiber was one of the most capable conductors of the past 50 years; some would say he was among the greatest of all time. His talent was huge, his technique magnificent. His brilliance and innate musicianship—together with a remarkable facility for languages and a profound knowledge of the scores he conducted (often revealed in detailed written messages to players that came to be known as "Kleibergrams")—made him a darling of the orchestral musicians lucky enough to work with him. On the other hand, his mercurial personality, combined with a penchant for walking out of rehearsals and canceling performances if things were not exactly to his liking, made him the despair of orchestra and opera house managers. He appeared almost unconcerned with career matters (years ago, one European impresario said Kleiber was just as happy napping in his hammock as conducting), and he held no permanent positions after 1979. In later years his active repertoire consisted of only a handful of pieces, which he knew with something approaching divine authority. His few recordings—including exquisite, impassioned accounts of Beethoven's Symphonies Nos. 5 and 7, a magisterial Brahms Fourth, and two New Year's Day concerts (1989, 1992), all with the Vienna Philharmonic—exemplify the art of conducting at its highest. For anyone fortunate enough to have witnessed him in performance, the experience was unforgettable.

RECOMMENDED RECORDINGS

BEETHOVEN, SYMPHONIES NOS. 5 AND 7: VIENNA PHILHARMONIC (DG).

BRAHMS, SYMPHONY NO. 4: VIENNA PHILHARMONIC (DG).

NEW YEAR'S DAY CONCERTS (1989, 1992): VIENNA PHILHARMONIC (SONY).

Kleiber, Erich

(b. Vienna, August 5, 1890; d. Zurich, January 27, 1956)

AUSTRIAN CONDUCTOR, father of Carlos Kleiber. He studied violin in Vienna and attended both the University of Prague—where he studied philosophy and the liberal arts—and the Prague Conservatory. He was appointed chorusmaster at the German Theater in Prague in 1911; from 1912 to 1918 he conducted at Darmstadt. After holding posts in Barmen-Elberfeld, Düsseldorf, and Mannheim, he was named general music director of the Berlin Staatsoper in 1923 at the age of only 33. In Berlin he distinguished himself as a conductor of contemporary repertoire, presiding over an acclaimed production of Janáček's *Jenůfa* in 1924 and leading the world premieres of Berg's *Wozzeck* (1925) and Milhaud's *Christophe Colombe* (1930). Outraged by Nazi cultural policies, he resigned his position in 1934, but not before conducting a suite from Berg's *Lulu* at his last concert. He left Germany with his family in 1935 and moved to Argentina; he conducted frequently at the Teatro Colón in Buenos Aires and maintained a busy guest-conducting schedule in Latin America. After the war, he conducted frequently at Covent Garden, including productions of Mozart's *Die Zauberflöte,* Richard Strauss's *Der Rosenkavalier,* and Tchaikovsky's *The Queen of Spades.* He was once again named director of the Berlin Staatsoper in 1954, but he resigned before taking up the post, citing difficulties with the Communist authorities. He died on the 200th anniversary of Mozart's birth.

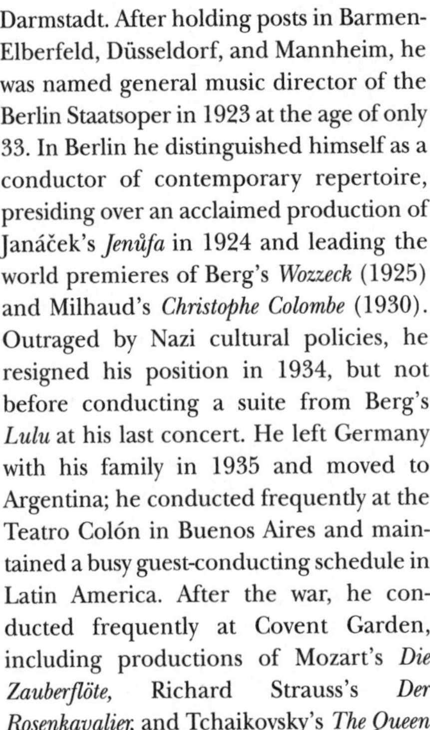

Erich Kleiber

Kleiber's reputation as a conductor was based on his unwavering fidelity to the score and the scrupulous care he took in rehearsing, traits he shared with such contemporaries as Fritz Reiner and George Szell. In addition to being a champion of 20th-century works, he was also widely acknowledged as an outstanding conductor of Mozart and Beethoven. He was himself an accomplished composer whose output included concertos for violin and piano, a *Capriccio* for orchestra, and several songs, piano pieces, and chamber works.

RECOMMENDED RECORDINGS

MOZART, *LE NOZZE DI FIGARO*: SIEPI, DELLA CASA, CORENA, DANCO; VIENNA PHILHARMONIC (DECCA).

STRAUSS, *DER ROSENKAVALIER*: REINING, JURINAC, GUEDEN, WEBER; VIENNA PHILHARMONIC (DECCA).

Klemperer, Otto

(b. Breslau [now Wrocław, Poland], May 14, 1885; d. Zurich, July 6, 1973)

GERMAN CONDUCTOR of intermittent greatness who was at his best in the core works of the Austro-Germanic repertoire, especially the symphonies of Beethoven. He began his studies in Frankfurt and continued them in Berlin, where he studied composition and conducting with Hans Pfitzner. In 1905 he led the offstage ensemble in a Berlin performance of Mahler's Symphony No. 2, and in 1907, on Mahler's recommendation, he was appointed chorusmaster at the German Theater in Prague. He subsequently became conductor there, moving to the Hamburg Opera (1910–12) and serving as first Kapellmeister in Barmen-Elberfeld (1913–14). He then worked as assistant to Pfitzner at the Stadttheater in Strasburg (1914–17), music director at the Cologne Opera (1917–24), and music director at the Wiesbaden Opera (1924–27).

Klemperer's next post was one of the most significant of his career. From 1927 to 1931 he was director of the Kroll Opera in Berlin, a newly opened subsidiary of the Berlin Staatsoper whose purpose was to present nontraditional stagings of standard repertoire pieces and to offer challenging new works in topflight productions. At the Kroll, where he worked alongside Alexander von Zemlinsky and Fritz Zweig, Klemperer staged and conducted Stravinsky's *Oedipus rex* and *Mavra,* and conducted performances of Schoenberg's *Erwartung* and *Die glückliche Hand,* Hindemith's *Cardillac* and *Neues vom Tage,* and Janáček's *From the House of the Dead.* He also presided over highly acclaimed productions of Beethoven's *Fidelio* and Mozart's *Don Giovanni*; in 1929 he directed a production of Wagner's *Der fliegende Holländer* whose spare, stylized staging anticipated the look Wieland Wagner would bring to Bayreuth in the 1950s. After the Prussian ministry of culture closed the Kroll in 1931, Klemperer moved to the Berlin Staatsoper, where on February 13, 1933, he conducted a performance of *Tannhäuser* marking the 50th anniversary of Wagner's death. By then the Nazis had taken power; in April 1933 Klemperer, who was Jewish, left Germany and headed for the United States.

Otto Klemperer in a victorious moment

Klemperer worked as principal conductor of the Los Angeles Philharmonic from 1933 to 1939. During the 1930s, he took advantage of Schoenberg's proximity in Brentwood to study composition with him, and he fulfilled guest-conducting engagements with the orchestras of Chicago, San Francisco, New York, Philadelphia, and Pittsburgh. He underwent an operation for a brain tumor in 1939, which left him partially paralyzed and gave him a permanent scowl, and effectively sidelined him for several years. He returned to Europe after World War II and from 1947 to 1950 served as music director of the Budapest Opera. After that he worked briefly alongside Walter Felsenstein at the Komische Oper in Berlin. He was again put out of action in 1951, by a broken leg, and his conducting days appeared close to over when, in October 1954, the English record producer Walter Legge took a gamble and invited him to begin making recordings with the Philharmonia Orchestra. As a result, a whole new career in the recording studio and on London's concert stage opened up for Klemperer just as he was about to turn 70. In 1955 Herbert von Karajan, the Philharmonia's chief conductor, was summoned to Berlin; in the years that followed, Klemperer became the orchestra's de facto chief conductor and recorded an enormous swath of the symphonic repertoire with it. In 1960, he had an astonishing year in the studio, taping a two-disc collection of Wagner preludes and overtures, Bach's *Brandenburg* Concertos, several tone poems of Richard Strauss, and symphonies of Haydn, Mozart, Beethoven, Bruckner, Schubert, Schumann, and Mendelssohn, as well as Mendelssohn's music for *A Midsummer Night's Dream.* Klemperer gave many memorable concert performances with the Philharmonia as well, and he continued at its helm when its players reconstituted themselves as the New Philharmonia Orchestra in 1964. He made his Covent Garden debut in 1961, conducting *Fidelio,* and retired in 1972.

During the first part of his career, spent in German opera houses, Klemperer acquired a reputation not only as an advocate for contemporary works but as a penetrating interpreter of the standard repertoire. In the second part, working mainly with the Philharmonia Orchestra in London, he became a major figure, widely admired for his authoritative grasp of the symphonic canon. In particular, he was praised for his puissant readings of the symphonies of Beethoven, which with their raw sonority sounded as if they had been hewn from granite. His Wagner was burnished to gleaming perfection, and his Bruckner and Mahler had a grandeur and tempered edge that can still take a listener's breath away. Unsentimental, powerfully intelligent, and armed with a quick, sometimes caustic wit, Klemperer was never a flamboyant figure on the podium; in later years his readings became increasingly slow, eventually losing the shape and cohesion for which they once had been known. Yet even then, something about the way Klemperer conducted could make the music glow with purposefulness and inner fire.

Over the years Klemperer dabbled in composition: His works include the opera *Das Ziel* (1915), six symphonies, nine string quartets, and about 100 lieder. His son Werner Klemperer (1920–2000) played the long-suffering and easily outmaneuvered Colonel Klink on the television series *Hogan's Heroes.*

RECOMMENDED RECORDINGS

BEETHOVEN, *FIDELIO*: LUDWIG, VICKERS, FRICK, BERRY; PHILHARMONIA ORCHESTRA (EMI).

BEETHOVEN, SYMPHONIES: PHILHARMONIA ORCHESTRA (EMI).

BRAHMS, *EIN DEUTSCHES REQUIEM*: SCHWARZKOPF, FISCHER-DIESKAU; PHILHARMONIA ORCHESTRA (EMI).

MAHLER, SYMPHONY NO. 2: SCHWARZKOPF, RÖSSL-MAJDAN; PHILHARMONIA ORCHESTRA (EMI).

WAGNER, OVERTURES AND PRELUDES: PHILHARMONIA ORCHESTRA (EMI).

Knaben Wunderhorn, Des (The Youth's Magic Horn) **ANTHOLOGY OF GERMAN FOLK POEMS** compiled by Achim von Arnim (1781–1831) and Clemens Brentano (1778–1842), published in three volumes between 1805 and 1808. In addition to influencing the style of several 19th-century poets, among them Joseph Freiherr von Eichendorff and Heinrich Heine, the anthology attracted the attention of composers from Weber and Carl Loewe (1796–1869) through Schumann, Mendelssohn, Brahms, Wolf, and Richard Strauss to Zemlinsky, Schoenberg, Webern, and Ives. But by far the most frequently encountered settings of *Wunderhorn* poetry are those of Gustav Mahler.

Between 1887 and 1890, Mahler composed nine songs for voice and piano to *Wunderhorn* poems. He created another 14 songs (in versions for voice and piano and for voice and orchestra) between 1892 and 1901, plus a setting of "Das himmlische Leben," which he expanded on to create the finale of his Symphony No. 4 (1900). Twelve of these later settings were grouped in a cycle entitled *Des Knaben Wunderhorn,* published in 1899. The songs Mahler wrote to *Wunderhorn* texts are among his most important contributions to the literature, potent examples of dramatic music in small, brilliantly condensed forms; they are notable for their emotional directness and sharp characterization. Five of them became working templates for symphonic movements—in addition to recycling "Das himmlische Leben" in his Fourth Symphony, Mahler drew upon "Des Antonius von Padua Fischpredigt" for the scherzo of the Second, "Urlicht" for its fourth movement, "Ablösung im Sommer" for the scherzo of the Third, "Es sungen drei Engel" for its fifth movement, and "Lob des hohen Verstandes" for the finale of his Symphony No. 5.

RECOMMENDED RECORDING

SCHWARZKOPF, FISCHER-DIESKAU; SZELL AND LONDON SYMPHONY ORCHESTRA (EMI).

Kocsis, Zoltán

(b. Budapest, May 30, 1952)

HUNGARIAN PIANIST AND COMPOSER. He began piano lessons when he was five and enrolled in the Béla Bartók Conservatory in 1963 as a student in piano and composition. In 1968 he gained admission to the prestigious Franz Liszt Academy, and in 1970, while still a student, he won first prize in Hungarian Radio's Beethoven Competition. In 1973, upon his graduation from the Franz Liszt Academy, he was appointed to the school's piano faculty. That same year he became the youngest musician ever to win Hungary's Liszt Prize. Kocsis's international career developed rapidly during the 1970s and 1980s, and subsided almost as rapidly during the 1990s as his interests turned elsewhere—to composition, criticism, and conducting. His work as a conductor has centered on the Budapest Festival Orchestra, of which he was a co-founder, and the Hungarian National Philharmonic Orchestra (formerly the Hungarian State Orchestra), of which he became music director in 1997. As a pianist he still commands a magnificent, world-class technique; his recordings, especially of the music of Liszt, Bartók, and Rachmaninov, testify to a major interpretive talent.

RECOMMENDED RECORDINGS

BARTÓK, PIANO CONCERTOS: I. FISCHER AND BUDAPEST FESTIVAL ORCHESTRA (PHILIPS).

DEBUSSY, *IMAGES* (WITH OTHER PIANO PIECES) (PHILIPS).

Kodály, Zoltan

(b. Kecskemét, December 16, 1882; d. Budapest, March 6, 1967)

HUNGARIAN COMPOSER AND ETHNOMUSICOLOGIST. His father was a stationmaster for the Hungarian state railways on the line between Budapest and Pressburg (now Bratislava). Kodály spent his youth in the countryside of what is now Slovakia, including seven impressionable years (1885–92) in Galánta, a rail junction. He grew up in musical surroundings—his father played the violin, and his mother sang and played the piano. Kodály

Zoltán Kocsis, ca. 1985

became proficient at violin, viola, cello, and piano, and he played chamber music at home and performed in the school orchestra. After graduating from high school in 1900, he enrolled at the University of Budapest (Péter Pázmány University), and studied composition at the National Hungarian Royal Academy of Music, receiving diplomas in composition (1904) and teaching (1905). His university work centered on ethnomusicology. His first expedition to collect folk songs took place in August of 1905, and he was awarded a Ph.D. in 1906—the title of his dissertation was *The Strophic Structure of Hungarian Folk Songs.* His interest in folk song was shared by a fellow student at the Academy, Bela Bartók; they began a lifelong friendship collaborating on the collection and cataloging of Hungarian folk songs. During 1906–07, Kodály pursued studies in Berlin and Paris; in Paris he encountered the music of Debussy, which was to have a lasting impact on him. He returned to Budapest in the autumn of 1907 to teach at the Academy, where his students over the years would include Eugene Ormandy, Antal Dorati, and István Kertész.

During the early years of his career Kodály was so busy teaching and hunting for folk songs that he produced only a few compositions, which were heard in a handful of performances. He made significant strides with the Duo for Violin and Cello, Op. 7 (1914), and Solo Sonata for Cello, Op. 8 (1915). He was active as a music critic 1917–19, and in February 1919, with the establishment of the Hungarian Republic, he became assistant director of the Academy, under Ernő von Dohnányi. But with the fall of the republic four months later, there was a crackdown, and Kodály was relieved of his post, on trumped-up charges, and suspended from teaching. It took him two years to get himself cleared, and he returned to teaching in 1921. A lifelong leftist, Kodály had had his first taste of political oppression, and it is tempting to assume that he put some of that experience into his next major work, a setting of Psalm 55 for tenor solo, chorus, and orchestra, entitled *Psalmus Hungaricus.* The piece was premiered November 19, 1923, with Dohnányi conducting, at a concert celebrating the 50th anniversary of the union of Pest, Buda, and Obuda to form the city of Budapest. It marked Kodály's breakthrough as a figure of international importance, and is one of the finest choral works of the 20th century.

Kodály's star continued to rise with the premiere of *HÁRY JÁNOS* at the Budapest Opera, on October 16, 1926. His works were starting to be noticed abroad (the first foreign performance of *Psalmus Hungaricus* took place in Zurich in 1926; he made his debut as conductor leading another performance of the piece in Amsterdam, in 1927). At home, Kodály continued his scholarly work, and in 1929 he formulated his pedagogical principles in a study entitled "Children's Choirs." The 1930s saw the premieres of three important orchestral works: the *Dances of*

Zoltan Kodály in his study

Marosszék (Dresden, 1930, conducted by Fritz Busch); *DANCES OF GALÁNTA* (Budapest, 1933, conducted by Dohnányi); and the *PEACOCK* VARIATIONS (Amsterdam, 1939, conducted by Willem Mengelberg).

Kodály spoke out against the hard right turn Hungarian politics took in the late 1930s, to no avail. During World War II, with Hungary as part of the Axis, he kept his mouth shut and entered a self-imposed retirement. He continued to compose, and was also instrumental in assisting some less fortunate than he to escape persecution. Following the war, Kodály made trips to America (1946–47) and the Soviet Union (1947), and took a few honorary and official positions, serving as head of the Hungarian academy of Arts and Sciences (1947–50), where he used his influence to advance the study and dissemination of folk music. He spent his last years traveling (making a second trip to the U.S. in July–August 1965), still engaged with folk music and pedagogy.

Kodály maintained an unshakable conviction that the roots of good concert music lay in folk music, which kept him from embracing the artificial systems and methods so many of his contemporaries felt compelled to use. His idiom was colorful and folk-flavored (though not as rhythmically complex as that of Bartók), with a floating sense of tonality. In addition to a handful of symphonic works that are firmly entrenched in the repertoire (and in which he made brilliant use of the orchestra), Kodály created a large body of choral work, both accompanied and a cappella (including a number of especially beautiful settings for girls' voices), several sets of songs with piano and chamber accompaniment, and an enormous number of exercises and teaching pieces. His system of music instruction for children has won universal acclaim and is utilized throughout the world.

RECOMMENDED RECORDINGS

HÁRY JÁNOS (COMPLETE): USTINOV, KERTÉSZ WITH LONDON SYMPHONY ORCHESTRA (DECCA).

HÁRY JÁNOS (SUITE): DORATI AND MINNEAPOLIS SYMPHONY ORCHESTRA (MERCURY).

PEACOCK VARIATIONS: KERTÉSZ AND LONDON SYMPHONY ORCHESTRA (DECCA).

PEACOCK VARIATIONS: SOLTI AND VIENNA PHILHARMONIC (DECCA).

PSALMUS HUNGARICUS: KOZMA, KERTÉSZ AND LONDON SYMPHONY ORCHESTRA (DECCA).

SONATA FOR SOLO CELLO: STARKER (DELOS).

Koechlin, Charles

(b. Paris, November 27, 1867; d. Le Canadel, December 31, 1950)

FRENCH COMPOSER. He came from a well-to-do Alsatian family with a successful textile business. His father sent him to the École Polytechnique to train for a career in the artillery, but while he was a student there he contracted tuberculosis, which left him unfit for military service. During a long convalescence in Algeria, he turned his attention to music. He entered the Paris Conservatoire in 1890, studying counterpoint with André Gédalge (teacher of Ravel, Enescu, Honegger, and Milhaud) and composition with Jules Massenet. In 1896, when Massenet resigned his professorship, Koechlin became a student of Gabriel Fauré, whose music and personality were to have a lasting influence on him.

To support himself, Koechlin took up teaching, worked as a critic, and wrote frequent articles on music theory. In 1909, together with Ravel and Florent Schmitt, he founded the Société Musicale Indépendente to advance the cause of new music. He was an exceptionally productive composer, if also an exceptionally flaky one, and proved fascinatingly esoteric in his choice of extramusical inspirations. Between 1899 and 1940 he composed seven works based on Rudyard Kipling's *Jungle Book* stories, the most celebrated of which (thanks to a recording by Antal Dorati) is the symphonic poem *Les bandar-log* (1939–40), subtitled *Scherzo des singes* (*Scherzo of the Monkeys*). In 1933 he created a seven-movement symphonic suite, the *Seven Stars Symphony,* inspired by Douglas Fairbanks, Lilian Harvey, Greta Garbo, Clara Bow, Marlene Dietrich, Emil Jannings, and Charlie Chaplin. He also composed more than 100 bagatelles—songs, piano pieces, and small chamber works—inspired by Lilian Harvey, as well as paeans to Ginger Rogers and Jean Harlow. His output includes numerous interesting works for solo wind and brass instruments, several ballets, more than 20 sets of songs, and a vast quantity of chamber pieces for unusal combinations of instruments. In addition, he orchestrated the original version of Fauré's incidental music for *Pelléas et Mélisande* (1898) and all but the prelude of Debussy's pseudo-Egyptian ballet *Khamma* (1912–13).

RECOMMENDED RECORDINGS

SEVEN STARS SYMPHONY: JUDD AND DEUTSCHES SYMPHONIE ORCHESTER BERLIN (RCA).

SYMPHONIC POEMS FROM *THE JUNGLE BOOK* (INCLUDING *LES BANDAR-LOG*): ZINMAN AND BERLIN RADIO SYMPHONY ORCHESTRA (RCA).

Koopman, Ton

(b. Zwolle, October 2, 1944)

DUTCH CONDUCTOR, HARPSICHORDIST, AND ORGANIST. A prominent figure in early music circles, he has focused on music of the 17th and 18th centuries from the outset of his career. He studied organ with Simon Jansen and harpsichord with Gustav Leonhardt at the Sweelinck Conservatory in Amsterdam from 1965 to 1970, while also studying musicology at Amsterdam University, and in 1968 won first prize in both the solo and continuo categories of the Bruges International Competition. He founded his first period instrument orchestra in 1970, as a student. In 1979, he founded the Amsterdam Baroque Orchestra, followed by the Amsterdam Baroque Choir in 1992. In 1994, with these two ensembles, he embarked on a project to record all 215 surviving Bach cantatas. Erato released the first 12 volumes of the survey, which garnered important prizes, including the Deutsche Schallplattenpreis Echo Klassik and the Grand Prix from France's Académie du Disque Lyrique. In 2003, Koopman founded his own label, Antoine Marchand Records, to release the remaining volumes. Koopman guest-conducts orchestras in Europe and the U.S., performs as a harpsichord and organ soloist, and has a discography of more than 180 recordings. From 1978 to 1988 he was professor of harpsichord at the Sweelinck Conservatory. Since 1988, he has been professor of harpsichord at the Royal Conservatory in The Hague. He is admired for his lively, rhythmically alert, and idiomatically persuasive accounts of Baroque keyboard and orchestral music.

RECOMMENDED RECORDINGS

AS ORGANIST:

BACH, COMPLETE FANTASIAS, PRELUDES, AND FUGUES (ELEKTRA).

AS CONDUCTOR:

COMPLETE BACH CANTATAS (SERIES): WESSEL, DEGROOT, OTHERS; AMSTERDAM BAROQUE ORCHESTRA (CHALLENGE CLASSICS).

Ton Koopman at the podium, 1996

Korngold, Erich Wolfgang

(b. Brünn [now Brno, Czech Republic], May 29, 1897; d. Los Angeles, November 29, 1957)

AUSTRIAN/AMERICAN COMPOSER. Best known as the author of some of the greatest film scores of the 20th century, his accomplishments, still undervalued in many quarters, extended to opera, symphonic works, chamber music, and songs. The son of the music critic Julius Korngold (Eduard Hanslick's deputy, and later successor, at the *Neue freie Presse* in Vienna), he was one of the greatest child prodigies in the history of music. His cantata *Gold,* written when he was nine (and unfortunately now lost), was shown to Mahler, who, thoroughly impressed, suggested that the boy be sent to study with Alexander von Zemlinsky. Among the scores Korngold wrote under Zemlinsky's tutelage was a ballet entitled *Der Schneemann* (*The Snowman*), which received its premiere at the Vienna Court Opera in 1910. By then he had already penned his Piano Trio in D, Op. 1, and Piano Sonata in E, Op. 2, precocious works that immediately entered the repertoire. Korngold came to prominence as the result of two exceptionally fine one-act operas, *Violanta* and *Der Ring des Polykrates,* which were written in 1914 and premiered as a double bill in Munich under the baton of Bruno Walter on March 28, 1916, two months shy of the composer's 19th birthday. His first masterpiece, the opera DIE TOTE STADT (*The Dead City*), received simultaneous premieres in Hamburg and Cologne on the night of December 4, 1920, when Korngold was 23. He was a venerable man of 30 when his next opera, *Das Wunder der Heliane*—less well known but arguably an even greater work than *Die tote Stadt*—received its premiere in 1927.

Korngold was brought to Hollywood by Max Reinhardt in 1934 to adapt Felix Mendelssohn's incidental music for *A Midsummer Night's Dream* to a production

Erich Wolfgang Korngold arriving in New York with his family, 1936

of the Shakespeare play at the Hollywood Bowl and subsequent Warner Bros. film. He proved so adept in the cinematic medium that Warner Bros. invited him back the following year to compose the score for *Captain Blood* (1935), the first of the Errol Flynn swashbucklers. With trouble brewing in Europe, Korngold stayed on, creating the scores for 17 more feature films including *Anthony Adverse* (1936) and *The Adventures of Robin Hood* (1938), both of which won Academy Awards for Best Original Score, *The Private Lives of Elizabeth and Essex* (1939), *The Sea Hawk* (1940), *King's Row* (1942; starring Ronald Reagan), *Between Two Worlds* (1944), and *Escape Me Never* (1946). Each of these scores was the musical equivalent of a large symphonic poem, containing close to an hour of motivically integrated, spectacularly descriptive music. In 1943 Korngold became an American citizen.

After a heart attack in 1947, Korngold was forced to bring down the curtain on his career as a film composer. But as a composer of "serious" symphonic music he was not quite finished. He had already enjoyed an enormous triumph with the premiere early in 1947 of his Violin Concerto, played by the master of masters, Jascha Heifetz. Conceived in 1937 and set aside, then taken up again and finished in 1945 (at the request of Bronislaw Huberman), the work has since established itself as one of the supreme masterpieces in the literature. Its wealth of melody is no accident: In the first movement Korngold drew on themes he had composed for the films *Another Dawn* (1937) and *Juarez* (1939)—creating a movement whose first and second subjects are *both* love themes ◉—while in the slow movement he recycled material from *Anthony Adverse,* and in the finale used a scurrying subject from *The Prince and the Pauper* (1937). Korngold's brief, single-movement Cello Concerto (1946) was even more closely tied to his movie music; indeed, it *was* movie music, written directly into the story line of *Deception* (1946). Korngold's last major work was his monumental Symphony in F-sharp, Op. 40. Written in 1951–52 and dedicated to the memory of Franklin Delano Roosevelt, the 50-minute work combines the orchestral opulence and melodic sweep of Korngold's finest soundtracking efforts with the structural rigor characteristic of the great Viennese symphonists.

Like his colleague Miklós Rózsa (1907–95), Korngold came to be despised because of his success as a film composer. In the minds of Europeans he went from being a genius in the years before 1934 to a minor talent once the dust of World War II had settled. Only now is that perception changing. In the summer of 2004 the Salzburg Festival belatedly recognized Korngold by making him its featured composer, mounting a new production of *Die tote Stadt* and offering performances of the Symphony in F-sharp, the *Symphonic Serenade* (1947) for strings, the Violin Concerto, the delicious *Much Ado About Nothing* Suite, Op. 11 (1918–19), and several chamber works. It has taken two generations, but Korngold's reputation is returning. He was one of the most identifiable film composers who ever lived. As an orchestrator he was on a par with Richard Strauss—a master at painting colors that were lush yet transparent, and whose characteristic touches included a particular fondness for vibraphone and celesta. Most important, he was the true heir to the grand line of Austro-Germanic symphonic thought that ran from Mozart through Beethoven, Weber, and Schubert to Wagner, Bruckner, Mahler, and Strauss. He kept that tradition alive, in America, while it was being stamped out in Europe.

RECOMMENDED RECORDINGS

BETWEEN TWO WORLDS: MAUCERI AND BERLIN RADIO SYMPHONY ORCHESTRA (DECCA).

SYMPHONY IN F-SHARP: PREVIN AND LONDON SYMPHONY ORCHESTRA (DG).

DIE TOTE STADT: MUTTER, NEBLETT; LEINSDORF AND MUNICH RADIO ORCHESTRA (RCA).

VIOLIN CONCERTO: MUTTER; PREVIN AND LONDON SYMPHONY ORCHESTRA (DG).

DAS WUNDER DER HELIANE: TOMOWA-SINTOW, WELKER, PAPE, GEDDA; MAUCERI AND BERLIN RADIO SYMPHONY ORCHESTRA (DECCA).

Koussevitzky, Serge

(b. Vyshniy Volochyek, July 26, 1874; d. Boston, June 4, 1951)

RUSSIAN/AMERICAN CONDUCTOR whose first flush of fame came as a double bass virtuoso. He learned to play the trumpet as a boy and performed alongside his brothers in an amateur wind band. At 14 he went to Moscow to study double bass at the Music-Dramatic Institute of the Moscow Philharmonic (as a Jew, he had to be baptized in order to live in Moscow). In 1894 he joined the orchestra of the Bolshoi

Koussevitzky after his last concert as the music director of the Boston Symphony, 1949

Theatre as a bass player, becoming principal in 1901. That year he made his debut as a soloist, in Moscow, and in 1903 he created a stir with a solo recital in Berlin. With help from Reyngol'd Glier he composed a double bass concerto in 1905; that same year he married Natalie Ushkov. The couple moved to Berlin, where Koussevitzky continued to concertize on the double bass while keeping his eyes on a bigger prize, the podium. He observed Nikisch, Weingartner, and Richard Strauss at work, and practiced conducting with a student orchestra. In 1908 he bought his conducting debut by hiring the Berlin Philharmonic; the program, which featured Sergey Rachmaninov playing his Piano Concerto No. 2, received positive notices in the press. Koussevitzky returned to Russia and in 1909 founded his own publishing company, Éditions Russes de Musique, through which he established a rapport with the most significant Russian composers of the day—Scriabin, Rachmaninov, Prokofiev, Stravinsky, and Nikolay Medtner (1880–1951). He formed his own orchestra to give concerts in Moscow, and toured by steamship up and down the Volga in 1910, 1912, and 1914.

Koussevitzky stayed in Russia through the Revolution, conducting the State Symphony Orchestra in Petrograd from 1917 until 1920. He subsequently settled in Paris, where he organized the Concerts Koussevitzky and continued his work as a staunch advocate of living composers. In Paris he conducted the first performances of Stravinsky's *Symphonies of Wind Instruments* (1921), Prokofiev's Violin Concerto No. 1 (1923), and Honegger's *Pacific 231* (1924); he also commissioned and premiered Ravel's brilliant orchestration of Mussorgsky's *Pictures at an Exhibition* (1922).

In 1924 Koussevitzky succeeded Pierre Monteux as music director of the Boston Symphony Orchestra, a post he would hold for 25 years. His first seasons with the BSO were shaky—the orchestra quickly learned that Koussevitzky possessed neither the baton technique nor the score-reading abilities of his predecessors. Nevertheless, a chemistry developed, aided by the conductor's undeniable zeal and charisma. At their best, the performances Koussevitzky conducted were compelling and full of character. In Boston he continued to champion contemporary music. For the orchestra's 50th anniversary season, 1930–31, he commissioned Stravinsky's *Symphony of Psalms,* Ravel's Piano Concerto in G, Roussel's Symphony No. 3, Hindemith's *Konzertmusik* for strings and brass, and works by Prokofiev, Respighi, and Honegger. He was commited to American composers as well; during his tenure he led first performances of scores by Copland, Harris, Piston,

Hanson, Schuman, and others, many of them major works.

Koussevitzky became an American citizen in 1941. Following the death of his wife in 1942, the conductor established a foundation in her memory to commission new works. The glorious results included Bartók's *Concerto for Orchestra* (1944), premiered by Koussevitzky and the BSO, and Benjamin Britten's *Peter Grimes* (1945), which received its American premiere at the Berkshire Music Center, conducted by Koussevitzky's young protégé Leonard Bernstein.

The establishment of the Berkshire Music Center and Tanglewood's summer music festival was Koussevitzky's other great achievement as music director of the Boston Symphony. Koussevitzky himself taught the summer course in conducting-during the festival's early years, where his students included Bernstein, Lukas Foss, and Thor Johnson.

"You must 'heep-notize' the orchestra," Koussevitzky was fond of telling his students. Passionate, egocentric, and colorful—both musically and linguistically—he was the most important advocate of contemporary orchestral music in the 20th century, with an enormous impact on the repertoire. His work in Boston compared in importance and brilliance with that of Toscanini in New York and Stokowski in Philadelphia, contributing to a golden age in American musical life.

RECOMMENDED RECORDINGS

BERLIOZ, *HAROLD EN ITALIE*; R. STRAUSS, *TILL EULENSPIEGEL*): PRIMROSE; BOSTON SYMPHONY ORCHESTRA (DUTTON).

COPLAND, *EL SALÓN MÉXICO*; HARRIS, SYMPHONY NO. 3: BOSTON SYMPHONY ORCHESTRA (PEARL).

TCHAIKOVSKY, SYMPHONY NO. 5 (WITH RACHMANINOV, *ISLE OF THE DEAD*): BOSTON SYMPHONY ORCHESTRA (EMI).

Koyaanisqatsi FILM SCORE IN EIGHT SECTIONS FOR BASS VOCALIST, small chorus, orchestra (consisting of low strings and brass), and contemporary instrumental ensemble, composed by Philip Glass for the 1983 film by Godfrey Reggio. The film takes as its title the Hopi word meaning "life out of balance, a state of life that calls for another way of living." Glass's minimalist music plays a prominent part throughout the 87-minute-long movie, which conveys an apocalyptic vision of late-20th-century America.

RECOMMENDED RECORDING

PHILIP GLASS ENSEMBLE (NONESUCH, 1998).

Kraft, Anton

(b. Rokycany, December 30, 1749; d. Vienna, August 28, 1820)

AUSTRIAN CELLIST. He joined the court orchestra of Prince Nicolaus Esterházy in 1778, remaining until the ensemble was disbanded in 1790. While in Nicolaus's employ he worked under the supervision of the prince's Kapellmeister, Joseph Haydn, with whom he also studied composition. Haydn composed his Cello Concerto in D (1783) for Kraft, and the work's technical challenges suggest that Kraft collaborated closely with Haydn on the shaping of the solo part. From 1793, Kraft was active in Vienna, as a member of the Kapelle of Prince Joseph Lobkowitz and as founding cellist of the Schuppanzigh Quartet, with which he participated in the premieres of many of Beethoven's chamber works. Beethoven composed the solo cello part of the Triple Concerto, Op. 56 (1808), for Kraft, and the two musicians enjoyed a cordial friendship. Kraft left the Schuppanzigh Quartet in 1809, but remained in the service of Prince Lobkowitz to the end of his life. As a player he was admired not only for his technical finesse but for his especially beautiful and expressive tone.

Kraus [Trujillo], Alfredo

(b. Las Palmas, Canary Islands, September 24, 1927; d. Madrid, September 10, 1999)

SPANISH TENOR. He studied with Mercedes Llopart and made his professional debut in Cairo in 1956, as the Duke of Mantua in Verdi's *Rigoletto.* During the 1957–58 season, he sang the role of Alfredo opposite Maria Callas in a legendary series of performances of Verdi's *La traviata* at the Teatro Saõ Carlos in Lisbon. He made his Covent Garden debut in 1959, as Edgardo opposite Joan Sutherland's Lucia in Donizetti's *Lucia di Lammermoor,* and bowed for the first time at La Scala in 1960, as Elvino in Bellini's *La sonnambula.* At the Metropolitan Opera, where he made his debut in 1966 as the Duke in *Rigoletto,* his repertoire included Ernesto in Donizetti's *Don Pasquale,* Tonio in Donizetti's *La fille du régiment,* and the title role in Massenet's *Werther,* a role he sang with incomparable elegance. Considered one of the finest lyric tenors of his generation, Kraus sang with nobility, taste, and an impeccable sense of style. He took such care of his voice that in his 70th year he was able to sing the same roles he had sung when he was 30, with little diminution of quality.

RECOMMENDED RECORDING

VERDI, *LA TRAVIATA*: CALLAS, SERENI; GHIONE AND TEATRO SÃO CARLOS (EMI).

Krauss, Clemens

(b. Vienna, March 31, 1893; d. Mexico City, May 16, 1954)

AUSTRIAN CONDUCTOR. His father was Hector Baltazzi, a gentleman at the court of Emperor Franz Josef, and his mother was Clementine Krauss, a 17-year-old dancer at the Court Opera. As their illegitimate offspring, he was brought up by his maternal grandparents and took his mother's name. At the age of eight he entered the Vienna Boys' Choir (following in the footsteps of Haydn, Schubert, and Hans Richter), and from 1905 to 1912 he studied at the Vienna Conservatory. Following graduation, he held conducting posts at opera houses in Brünn, Riga, Nuremberg, and Stettin (where he availed himself of every opportunity to visit Berlin and observe the work of Arthur Nikisch with the Philharmonic). In 1922 he became Franz Schalk's assistant at the Vienna Staatsoper. While there he formed a close relationship with Richard Strauss, who with Schalk was codirector of the Staatsoper. Strauss would later entrust Krauss with the first performances of several operas: *Arabella* in 1933, *Friedenstag* in 1938, *Capriccio* (for which Krauss wrote the libretto) in 1942, and finally, *Die Liebe der Danäe* in 1944.

Clemens Krauss in 1925

Krauss served as director of the Frankfurt Opera from 1924 to 1929 and as director of the Vienna Staatsoper from 1929 to mid-1934. Concurrent with that appointment he had responsibility for the concerts of the Vienna Philharmonic (1930–33). Like many Austrians he was openly pro-Nazi, and during the 1930s and 1940s, he benefited from the regime's interference in cultural affairs. In 1935, he was named director of the Berlin Staatsoper, taking the post after Erich Kleiber resigned. In 1937 he became Intendant and general music director of the Bavarian State Opera in Munich, stepping into the vacancy left after Hans Knappertsbusch refused to kowtow to Hitler's cronies. Krauss's years in Munich, the high point of his career, came to an abrupt end after the

National Theater, the company's home, was bombed in 1943. In the spring of 1945, having returned to Vienna, Krauss conducted the last Philharmonic concert before the Russians entered the city, and, three weeks later, led the first one following the "liberation" of Austria.

Though he was not a member of the Nazi party, Krauss underwent denazification proceedings and did not resume his career until 1947. He toured with the Vienna Philharmonic and the Bamberg Symphony, guest conducted at Covent Garden and La Scala, led Wagner's *Parsifal* and the *Ring* at Bayreuth (1953), and kept up a busy recording schedule. He died of a heart attack a few hours after conducting a concert in Mexico.

Krauss had little contact with America during his career, aside from guest conducting engagements with the New York Philharmonic and the Philadelphia Orchestra in 1929. But his postwar recordings were, and still are, widely admired. Fifty years after his death, he is perhaps best remembered for the New Year's Day concerts of the Vienna Philharmonic, which he inaugurated on January 1, 1941. He conducted the waltzes of Johann Strauss Jr. with an unmatched ease and naturalness and an irresistible panache, and there has been no more insightful and authoritative interpreter of the music of Richard Strauss.

RECOMMENDED RECORDINGS

SELECTIONS FROM NEW YEAR'S DAY CONCERTS, 1952–54: VIENNA PHILHARMONIC (ARCHIPEL).

STRAUSS, *SALOME*: GOLTZ, PATZAK, BRAUN; VIENNA PHILHARMONIC (DECCA).

Kreisler, Fritz

(b. Vienna, February 2, 1875; d. New York, January 29, 1962)

AUSTRIAN/AMERICAN VIOLINIST. His life was remarkably eventful, and his radiant charm and incomparably expressive playing delighted audiences and aroused the admiration of his fellow musicians for more than 50 years. He studied violin in Vienna and Paris, won prizes at the conservatories in both cities, and as a lad of 14 toured the United States with Moriz Rosenthal in 1889–90. He returned to Vienna and set aside his fiddle for a while, studying art and then medicine, each for two years, whereupon he entered the Austrian army. He resumed playing in 1896. In 1898 he appeared as a soloist with the Vienna Philharmonic and in December 1899 he made a sensational debut with the Berlin Philharmonic under Arthur Nikisch. He revisited the United States during the 1900–01 season and made his London debut in 1902, with Hans Richter conducting. This phase of his career climaxed in 1910 when he gave the premiere of Edward Elgar's Violin Concerto in London, with the composer conducting.

Kreisler rejoined his old regiment in 1914 at the outbreak of World War I, was

Fritz Kreisler, the embodiment of panache, produced a golden tone using only half of the violin's bow.

wounded fending off a Russian cavalry charge during the first weeks of the war, and spent the remainder of the conflict in the United States, deliberately keeping a low profile as sentiment against Austria and Germany mounted. Continuing his career in Europe after the war, he lived in Berlin from 1924 to 1934, then moved to France. In 1938, following the annexation of Austria by Germany, he became a French citizen. In 1939 he returned once again to the U.S., becoming an American citizen in 1943. He gave his last performance in Carnegie Hall on November 1, 1947.

Famous for his effortless technique and the extraordinary warmth and beauty of his tone, Kreisler was not only a virtuoso of the first rank but an outstanding interpreter of the classics. During the course of his long life, his career intersected with many others: In the 1880s, while attending conservatory in Vienna, he studied theory with Anton Bruckner; in the 1890s he clowned around with Arnold Schoenberg in the "fröhliches Quintett" (Schoenberg was the group's cellist); during the 1920s he played and recorded much of his recital repertoire with Sergey Rachmaninov at the piano. Kreisler composed admirable cadenzas for the Beethoven and Brahms concertos as well as many short concert pieces, some of them clever fakes written in the style of (and impishly attributed to) various minor 17th- and 18th-century masters, some of them sentimental Viennese bonbons to which he attached his name from the start. The best known of these—*Liebesfreud, Liebesleid* ◉, *Schön Rosmarin, Caprice viennois,* and *Tambourin chinois*—have become fixtures of the encore repertoire.

RECOMMENDED RECORDING

BEETHOVEN, GRIEG, SCHUBERT, VIOLIN SONATAS (WITH *LIEBESFREUD* AND *LIEBESLEID*): RACHMANINOV (RCA).

Kreisleriana **SET OF EIGHT "FANTASIES" FOR PIANO BY ROBERT SCHUMANN,** composed in April 1838 and published that year as his Op. 16. The title is an allusion to the nom de plume under which E. T. A. Hoffmann occasionally wrote music criticism: "Johannes Kreisler, Kapellmeister." The individual numbers of *Kreisleriana* are substantial and well contrasted, the writing coherent and expressive, with a broad range of emotion—Schumann's hallmark tenderness, Romantic bombast, and even wit. ◉ The piece is dedicated to Chopin.

Gidon Kremer in 1996

Kremer, Gidon

(b. Riga, February 27, 1947)

LATVIAN VIOLINIST OF GERMAN DESCENT. He began violin lessons at home (his father and grandfather were professional violinists) and subsequently studied at the Latvian Academy of Music. He continued his studies with David Oistrakh at the Moscow Conservatory (1965–73), winning second prize at the Queen Elisabeth Competition in Brussels (1967) and first prizes at competitions in Genoa and Montreal (both in 1969) and the International Tchaikovsky Competition in Moscow (1970). After several years of concertizing in the Soviet Union, he made his London debut in 1975 and soon had a flourishing career in the West.

In addition to playing the standard repertoire, Kremer has championed the music of contemporary composers such as Alfred Schnittke, Arvo Pärt, Giya Kancheli (b. 1935), Sofiya Gubaydulina, Valentin Silvestrov (b. 1937), Luigi Nono (1924–90), Aribert Reimann (b. 1936), and Peteris Vasks (b. 1946); a number of works have been written for him, including Pärt's *Tabula Rasa* and Gubaydulina's *Offertorium.* He has been particularly influential in his advocacy of the music of Astor Piazzolla (1921–92), demonstrating the range and virtuosity of the Argentinian's tango-based repertoire through violin-centered interpretations, including a landmark Teldec recording of the composer's "tango opera" *María de Buenos Aires* (1968). Kremer's entreprenurial endeavors include the Lockenhaus Festival in Austria, which he founded in 1981, and Kremerata Baltica, an orchestra of young string players from Latvia, Estonia, and Lithuania, founded in 1997. With this group he has disseminated, through concerts and recordings, the work of Baltic and other Eastern European composers. The antithesis of a flashy virtuoso—he does not indulge in showmanship, and no one would characterize his tone as opulent—Kremer stands out among his colleagues for his restless, rigorously intellectual approach to the repertoire, and for playing that, while often not beautiful, can be intensely expressive nonetheless.

RECOMMENDED RECORDINGS

"FROM MY HOME: MUSIC FROM THE BALTIC COUNTRIES" (INCLUDING WORKS BY PÄRT, VASKS, PLAKIDIS, AND TÜÜR): SACHAROV; DEUTSCHE KAMMERPHILHARMONIE (TELDEC).

PÄRT, *TABULA RASA*: JARRETT; DAVIES AND STAATSORCHESTER STUTTGART (ECM).

Kreutzer, Rodolphe

(b. Versailles, November 16, 1766; d. Geneva, January 6, 1831)

Rodolphe Kreutzer

FRENCH VIOLINIST AND COMPOSER. He was taught the rudiments of music by his father, a German-born wind player, and received instruction in violin and composition from Anton Stamitz beginning in 1778. He made his debut in 1780 at the Concert Spirituel in Paris, playing one of Stamitz's concertos. After hearing Giovanni Viotti perform in the early 1780s, he began to model his own style of playing on that of the Italian master. Following the deaths of his parents in 1784–85, he was taken under the wing of Marie Antoinette and the Comte d'Artois; in 1789 he moved from Versailles to Paris. Talented and astute enough to keep ahead of the political curve, he associated himself with the Paris Conservatoire upon its establishment in 1795, remaining there as professor of violin until 1826. He joined Napoleon's private orchestra in 1806, served as chief conductor at the Paris Opéra from 1817 to 1824, and closed his career with a brief stint as the Opéra's music director (1824–26).

Kreutzer's most important work for violin, the set of *42 études ou caprices,* appeared in 1796 and was published a decade later by the Conservatoire. A second set of pieces, *18 nouveaux caprices ou études,* was published in Leipzig around 1815. He also composed approximately 50 stage works (including operas, ballets, and various hybrids), 19 violin concertos, and a handful of chamber pieces.

***Kreutzer* Sonata** TITLE OF LUDWIG VAN BEETHOVEN'S SONATA FOR VIOLIN AND PIANO IN A, OP. 47, composed in 1803 for the young English violinist George Polgreen Bridgetower, but dedicated, upon its publication in 1805, to Rodolphe Kreutzer. In one of his sketchbooks Beethoven described the work as "a sonata written in a very concertante style—almost a concerto,"which is borne out by the composition's vast scale and virtuosic violin part. The proportions of all three movements resemble those of a concerto, and the writing for the piano is often dense, producing an orchestral texture. The raw energy of Beethoven's ideas and their development in a symphonic manner, both decidedly novel, presage the *Eroica* Symphony.

Bridgetower gave the first performance of the sonata, with Beethoven at the keyboard, on May 24, 1803, in Vienna's Augarten. The composer's decision to dedicate the work to the more celebrated Kreutzer, whom he had met in 1804, was typical: Beethoven always aimed high in such matters. According to Berlioz, Kreutzer found the piece "outrageously unintelligible." He never played it or acknowledged the dedication.

RECOMMENDED RECORDING

PERLMAN, ASHKENAZY (DECCA).

Kreutzer Sonata SHORTENED SUBTITLE OF LEOŠ JANÁČEK'S STRING QUARTET NO. 1, composed between October 30 and November 7, 1923. The full subtitle, "after Tolstoy, *The Kreutzer Sonata,*" is significant: Janáček had in mind not Beethoven's Violin Sonata in A, but Tolstoy's eponymous novella, in which the institution of marriage is critiqued as a destroyer of, and constraint upon, pure love. At the time he composed the quartet, Janáček was 69 years old, and six years into a platonic infatuation with Kamila Stösslová; his choice of title suggests that he must have seen his own marriage, and hers, in such Tolstoyesque terms. The four movements of the quartet follow no narrative plan, but express the urgent, all-consuming force of human passion through music of almost feral energy.

RECOMMENDED RECORDINGS

TALICH QUARTET (CALLIOPE).

VLACH QUARTET (NAXOS).

Kronos Quartet AMERICAN STRING FOURSOME BASED IN SAN FRANCISCO, specializing in contemporary music. Founded by violinist David Harrington in 1973, the highly regarded quartet's core membership consisted for many years of Harrington, violinist John Sherba, violist Hank Dutt, and cellist Joan Jeanrenaud. In 1999 Jennifer Culp became the group's cellist, and in 2005 Jeffrey Zeigler succeeded her. The Kronos Quartet has greatly expanded the quartet literature during its three decades; more than 450 pieces have been written or arranged for the group, and about a dozen new works are commissioned each season.

The Kronos String Quartet

The ensemble's repertoire includes works by Alban Berg, George Crumb, Morton Feldman (1926–87), Osvaldo Golijov (b. 1960), Thomas Oboe Lee (b. 1945), Steven Mackey (b. 1956), Harry Partch (1901–74), Steve Reich, Terry Riley (b. 1935), Alfred Schnittke, and many others. In the manner and style of their dress the Kronos players appear to have more in common with rock musicians than with their tuxedo-clad counterparts in other string quartets, but they play with the precision and unanimity one would expect of a first-rate classical ensemble.

RECOMMENDED RECORDINGS

KRONOS QUARTET, 25 YEARS (NONESUCH).

"SHORT STORIES" (INCLUDING WORKS BY ZORN, OSWALD, MACKEY, AND GUBAYDULINA) (NONESUCH).

Kubelík, Rafael

(b. Býchory, June 29, 1914; d. Lucerne, August 11, 1996)

CZECH/SWISS CONDUCTOR AND COMPOSER. Son of the noted violinist Jan Kubelík and the Countess Marianne Csaky-Szell, he was born the day after the assassination of Archduke Franz Ferdinand in Sarajevo, the event that precipitated World War I. He studied violin, piano, composition, and conducting at the Prague Conservatory, and made his conducting debut with the Czech Phiharmonic on January 24, 1934. After conducting at the National Theater in Brno from 1939 to 1941, he became chief conductor of the Czech Philharmonic in 1942. During World War II, he refused to collaborate with the Nazi authorities; in 1948, shortly after the Communists had taken control of the Czech government, he defected in the middle of a guest-conducting engagement at the Edinburgh Festival.

He became music director of the Chicago Symphony Orchestra in 1950, but was driven out after only three seasons by a combination of managerial dyspepsia over his adventurous programming and hostile press from music critic Claudia Cassidy. Thereafter he concentrated his career in Europe, serving briefly as music director at Covent Garden (1955–58) and for nearly two decades (1961–79) as music director of the Bavarian Radio Symphony Orchestra in Munich. With that orchestra, and in continuing guest conducting engagements with many of the world's top ensembles—including the Vienna and Berlin Philharmonics, the Boston Symphony Orchestra, and the New York Philharmonic—he won vindication as a podium figure of the first rank. Kubelík became a Swiss citizen in 1967, and in 1972 he was named music director of the Metropolitan Opera by its newly installed general manager, Gören Gentele, becoming the first conductor to hold that title since Felix Mottl 70 years earlier. Kubelík made his Met debut on October 22, 1973, conducting a new production of Berlioz's *Les Troyens*; by then Gentele had been dead more than a year, having perished in an automobile accident during a brief vacation in Sardinia. Kubelík left the Met in the spring of 1974.

Kubelík was outstanding in the music of Mozart, Schumann, Brahms, Smetana, Dvořák, Mahler, and Janáček. He preferred the old European left/right seating of first and second violins, and cultivated a luminous sonority (which came naturally to him as a string player). He was also a successful composer. His opera *Veronica* (1947) was especially popular in Czechoslovakia prior to the Communist takeover. In later years he composed music that reflected his concerns as a Czech expatriate, offering up, in his Requiem No. 3 *Libera nos,* a plea for the liberation of his homeland, and giving voice to fresh hopes in his *Symphony in One Movement,* written during the spring and summer of 1968. In 1990 he finally went home to conduct a triumphant performance of

Rafael Kubelík in action, ca. 1966

Smetana's *Má vlast* with the Czech Philharmonic at the Prague Spring Festival, ending his sometimes troubled career in a blaze of glory.

RECOMMENDED RECORDINGS

DVOŘÁK, *SLAVONIC DANCES*: BAVARIAN RADIO SYMPHONY ORCHESTRA (DG).

DVOŘÁK, SYMPHONIES NOS. 8 AND 9: BERLIN PHILHARMONIC (DG).

JANÁČEK, *TARAS BULBA, SINFONIETTA*: BAVARIAN RADIO SYMPHONY ORCHESTRA (DG).

MAHLER, SYMPHONIES: BAVARIAN RADIO SYMPHONY ORCHESTRA (DG).

SMETANA: *MÁ VLAST*: CZECH PHILHARMONIC (SUPRAPHON).

Kuijken FAMILY OF BELGIAN MUSICIANS FROM DILBEEK AND BRUGES.

Wieland Kuijken *(b. August 31, 1938)*, viola da gambist and Baroque cellist. Considered one of the foremost exponents of the viola da gamba, at 15 he began studying cello and piano at Bruges Conservatory; he graduated from the Brussels Conservatory in 1962 with the *prix d'excellence*. During his time at school he experimented with avant-garde music in the ensemble Musiques Nouvelles, and with Baroque music, teaching himself to play the viola da gamba. Baroque music won out, and he spent the years 1959–72 performing with the Brussels-based Ensemble Alarius. He developed an international career, working with artists such as Gustav Leonhardt, Frans Brüggen, and René Jacobs, and performing in his brother Sigiswald's orchestra, La Petite Bande. Since the early 1970s he has taught at the conservatories in The Hague, Brussels, and Antwerp. Admired for the spirit of his playing and his beauty of tone, he is in demand both as continuo player and soloist; in the latter capacity he has specialized in the works of J. S. Bach and the French viol masters.

Sigiswald Kuijken *(b. February 6, 1944)*, Baroque violinist and conductor. He studied violin at the conservatories of Bruges and Brussels, earning the *premier prix* in 1964. Like his brother, he performed with Musiques Nouvelles and Ensemble Alarius. Self-taught on the Baroque violin, his research resulted in a revolutionary change in current performance practice—resting the violin on the chest rather than under the chin—a technique adopted by many other Baroque violinists. As a soloist, he made an award-winning recording of the Bach sonatas with Gustav Leonhardt. He has held posts at the conservatories of The Hague and Brussels, and has taught at the Royal College of Music in London. In 1972 he turned his attention to conducting, forming La Petite Bande to focus on French Baroque repertoire, later branching out to record Bach's *St. John* Passion as well as stylish accounts of Handel and Mozart operas and Haydn symphonies and oratorios. In 1986 he founded the Kuijken String Quartet to perform Classical repertoire.

Barthold Kuijken *(b. March 8, 1949)*, Baroque flutist and recorder player. He studied flute at the conservatories of Bruges and Brussels, and recorder with Frans Brüggen in The Hague. Following his brothers' example, he taught himself the Baroque flute, using 18th-century treatises as his guide; he has performed with La Petite Bande, the Collegium Aureum, and the Parnassus Ensemble and toured extensively as a soloist. He is professor of Baroque flute at the conservatories of The Hague and Brussels, and has brought to light much 17th- and 18th-century flute repertoire as well as editing a new Urtext edition of Bach's flute works for Breitkopf and Härtel. He is known for his warm, full tone and rhythmic sensitivity, evident on many recordings, including accounts of the complete Telemann fantasias for solo flute, the Bach and Handel sonatas, and the Vivaldi flute concertos; his discography also includes the Mozart flute quartets and the flute sonatas of C. P. E. Bach.

RECOMMENDED RECORDINGS

BARTHOLD:

TELEMANN, *12 FANTASIAS FOR SOLO FLUTE* (ACCENT).

SIGISWALD:

(AS VIOLINIST): BACH, VIOLIN SONATAS NOS. 1–6; LEONHARDT (DEUTSCHE HARMONIA MUNDI).

(AS CONDUCTOR): RAMEAU, *HIPPOLYTE ET ARICIE* (DEUTSCHE HARMONIA MUNDI).

WIELAND:

MARAIS, *PIÈCES DE VIOLE,* BOOK 5: KOHNEN (ACCENT).

Kullervo SYMPHONY FOR SOPRANO AND BARITONE SOLOISTS, MALE CHORUS, AND ORCHESTRA BY JEAN SIBELIUS, composed 1891–92 and premiered April 28, 1892, in Helsinki, with the composer conducting. With this work—based on the story of the hard-luck hero Kullervo, from the Finnish national epic the *Kalevala*—Sibelius tapped into the wellsprings of Finnish mythology for the first time and found the craggy, strikingly original voice that would become his hallmark. *Kullervo* takes as its point of departure a tale that is gloomy even by Finnish standards. Kullervo, the blond-haired youth, comes across his sister while she's out picking berries; he deflowers her, unaware of who she is. When their identities are revealed to one another, she runs away and drowns herself in a river, while he, guilt-stricken, sets off in search of his family's worst enemy, whom he murders along with his whole clan. When Kullervo comes home from his wanderings he finds only his dog still alive, and he goes off and kills himself. Out of this, Sibelius fashioned an epic symphonic score in five movements, a sprawling yet magnificent creation full of the brooding energy that would mark subsequent works such as the tone poem *En saga* and the four-part *Lemminkäinen* Suite. In setting the work's two vocal movements he also established a new standard for the idiomatic handling of the Finnish language.

RECOMMENDED RECORDING

PAASIKIVI, LAUKKA; VÄNSKÄ AND LAHTI SYMPHONY ORCHESTRA (BIS).

"kutchka" *See* FIVE, THE.

Kyrie Opening section of the Latin Mass. The text, actually in Greek, is quite short, consisting of three two-word utterances, each of which is repeated three times: "Kyrie eleison, Christe eleison, Kyrie eleison" ("Lord, have mercy; Christ, have mercy; Lord, have mercy"). One of the most beautiful is in Bach's *Mass in B Minor.* *See also* MASS.

L

Lady Macbeth of Mtsensk District **Opera in four acts, by Dmitry Shostakovich, Op. 29,** to a libretto by the composer and Aleksandr Preis based on a story by the 19th-century Russian writer Nikolay Leskov. Written between 1930 and 1932, and premiered on January 22, 1934, at the Maly Theater in Leningrad, it was Shostakovich's second opera and one of the most brilliant achievements of his career. Notwithstanding its title, *Lady Macbeth of Mtsensk District* has nothing to do with Shakespeare's *Macbeth*; it does have quite a lot to do with Dostoyevsky. The plot has all the elements of a Russian epic—boredom, need, irresistible sexual longing, infidelity, murder, suicide—and the music is vintage Shostakovich, swinging between farce and tragedy with astonishing sureness, magnificently intense, deeply absorbing, yet approachable. The opera's climactic scenes are driven by music of fierce power, and there are pages of haunting lyric beauty as well, such as Katarina's aria ("The foal runs after the filly") in Act I, sc. 3, and the extraordinary music that begins the love scene between Katarina and Sergey a few moments later—mysterious, edgy, sensuous, and vast.

Lady Macbeth was a huge success with critics and public alike, but it proved to be the costliest of all Shostakovich's triumphs. After Stalin attended a performance in Moscow in 1936, he ordered the publication of a scathing article in *Pravda* ("Muddle Instead of Music"), attacking the work for its dissonant musical language and distorted dramatic characterizations—the opening shot in a ruthless campaign to reduce all the arts in Soviet Russia to a state of dogmatic subservience to the regime. *Lady Macbeth* disappeared from the repertoire for 40 years (though a cleaned-up version, called *Katerina Ismailova*, would be approved for production in 1963), and Shostakovich, despite his great gifts in the genre, never completed another opera.

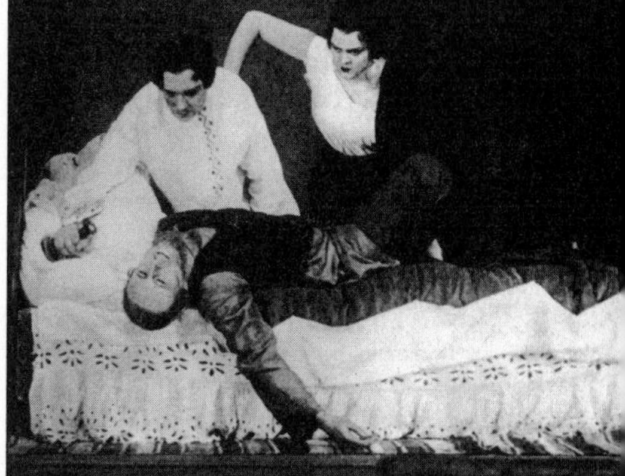

Lady Macbeth of Mtsensk District ***premiere in Moscow, produced by Vladimir Nemirovich-Danchenko, 1934***

RECOMMENDED RECORDING

Vishnevskaya, Gedda, Petkov; Rostropovich and London Philharmonic Orchestra (EMI).

Lakmé **Opera in three acts by Léo Delibes,** to a libretto by Edmond Gondinet and Philippe Gille, first staged by the Opéra-Comique in Paris on April 14, 1883. The story, set in India during the British regency, centers on the love between Lakmé, the beautiful daughter of a vengeful Brahmin priest, and Gérald, an English officer, making the opera a sort of *Norma* of the subcontinent. The duet "Dôme épais le jasmin," sung by Lakmé and her handmaid Mallika as they are canoeing down a tree-shaded stream, known as the "Flower Duet," was used for years by British Airways as its theme music and testifies to Delibes's extraordinary gift for memorable melody. Equally celebrated is Lakmé's "Où va la jeune indoue," known as the "Bell Song," which has become a coloratura standard embraced by grateful interpreters from Lily Pons to Natalie Dessay.

RECOMMENDED RECORDING

DESSAY, KUNDE, VAN DAM; PLASSON AND L'ORCHESTRE DE CAPITOLE DE TOULOUSE (EMI).

Lalo, Édouard

(b. Lille, January 27, 1823; d. Paris, April 22, 1892)

FRENCH COMPOSER. As a youngster, he studied both the violin and cello at the Lille Conservatoire; in 1839, his parents withdrew their support of his musical pursuits, and he made his way to Paris on his own. Accepted at the Conservatoire, he continued his study of violin with François Habeneck and received private instruction in composition from Joseph Crèvecoeur. For many years he supported himself by playing the violin and teaching. His early compositions were mostly chamber pieces, and in 1855 he became a founding member of the Armingaud Quartet, in which he played viola and second violin. By the early 1860s he had grown despondent about his future as a composer. He married the singer Julie de Maligny in 1865 and, with the encouragement of his new bride, started to compose again in earnest. His opera *Fiesque* (1868) went unperformed, but a ballet suite extracted from it, called *Divertissement,* was favorably received at the Concert Populaire in 1872. Nearly 50, Lalo finally hit his stride. His reputation skyrocketed after the premieres of his Violin Concerto in F, Op. 20 (1874) and *SYMPHONIE ESPAGNOLE,* Op. 21 (1875), both written for the brilliant Spanish violinist Pablo de Sarasate. Lalo's Cello Concerto followed in 1877; like the *Symphonie espagnole,* it has earned a permanent place in the repertoire. Recognition for these accomplishments came quickly: Lalo was named to the Légion d'Honneur in 1880. But his greatest wish was for a success on the stage. The premiere of his ballet *Namouna* at the Paris Opéra in 1882 was a disappointment, but his opera *Le roi d'Ys,* which premiered at the Opéra-Comique in 1888, was a triumph. The work, performed 100 times in its first year, is considered by the French to be Lalo's masterpiece. Nowadays it is rarely staged elsewhere, though its overture is still found on symphony programs from time to time. Lalo was, with Saint-Saëns and Franck, one of the most important composers of instrumental music in France during his era. While his music rarely attains the sublime, it is well crafted and notable for its melodic charm and colorful, energetic scoring.

Édouard Lalo, stagestruck colorist

RECOMMENDED RECORDINGS

CELLO CONCERTO: DU PRÉ; BARENBOIM AND CLEVELAND ORCHESTRA (EMI).

SYMPHONIE ESPAGNOLE: CHANG; DUTOIT AND CONCERTGEBOUW ORCHESTRA (EMI).

Ländler A moderately paced Austrian country dance in triple time. Frequently encountered in the music of Mozart and Haydn (often as the trio to a minuet, e.g., in Mozart's Symphony No. 39), the Ländler was a predecessor of the waltz. Over the course of the 19th century the waltz acquired an urban sophistication, whereas the Ländler never lost its rustic innocence; in the music of later composers such as Mahler (his *Wunderhorn* songs, and Symphonies Nos. 1, 4, and 9 ◉) and Berg (his Violin Concerto), one often finds nostalgic or parodistic allusions to it.

larghetto (It., "a little broadly") A tempo slightly faster than *largo,* closer to *adagio.*

largo (It., "broadly") Usually interpreted as a very slow tempo, between *adagio* and *grave.*

Lark Ascending, The "ROMANCE" FOR VIOLIN AND ORCHESTRA BY RALPH VAUGHAN WILLIAMS, written in 1914 and revised in 1920. The score is prefaced by several lines of verse that make it clear that the music represents not so much the *song* of the lark as its graceful flight. Here at his pastoral best, Vaughan Williams paints an almost motionless sonic landscape, as static, yet exultant, as a warm summer day. The music is gentle and rhapsodic, and the feeling of folk song that permeates the setting perfectly complements the natural stirrings suggested in the orchestra and, at times, in the figuration for the solo violin itself. ◉

RECOMMENDED RECORDINGS

BEAN; BOULT AND NEW PHILHARMONIA ORCHESTRA (EMI).

NOLAN; HANDLEY AND LONDON PHILHARMONIC ORCHESTRA (CFP).

***Lark* Quartet** SOBRIQUET OF JOSEPH HAYDN'S STRING QUARTET IN D, OP. 64, NO. 5 (Hob. III:63), composed in 1790 and published in 1791. Part of a set of six quartets written for the violinist Johann Tost, it gets its nickname from the chirpily songful entrance of the first violin in the eighth measure of the opening movement. Haydn's writing throughout the piece exhibits a feathery delicacy that by itself might easily have justified the name.

RECOMMENDED RECORDING

KODÁLY QUARTET (NAXOS).

Larrocha, Alicia de

(b. Barcelona, May 23, 1923)

SPANISH PIANIST. She began her study of the piano at age three and gave her first public recital when she was five. She subsequently studied with Frank Marshall, a student of Enrique Granados, and made her Madrid debut at the age of 11, playing a Mozart concerto with the Orquesta Sinfónica de Madrid under the baton of Enrique Arbós. She first toured outside of Spain in 1947, and gave her first American concerts in 1955, performing with Alfred Wallenstein and the Los Angeles Philharmonic in works by Mozart and Falla—a coupling she revisited with the same orchestra in 1980, on the occasion of the 25th anniversary of her debut.

A peerless performer of Spanish music, Larrocha acquired an enviable reputation via recordings and concert performances all over the globe. Her poetic interpretations of piano pieces by Albéniz and Granados won those composers many admirers among listeners who might otherwise never have encountered their music, while her easygoing renditions of a handful of Mozart concertos wore well even though they changed little over the years. Outside of Mozart and the Spanish repertoire, she had little to say; from her Granados to her Beethoven was a long step down. Her best playing had an appealing liveliness, beauty of tone, and sparkle, if not great depth of feeling. She maintained

Alicia de Larrocha

an active recording schedule until the early 1990s and retired from concertizing in 2003.

RECOMMENDED RECORDINGS

ALBÉNIZ, *IBERIA*, AND GRANADOS, *GOYESCAS* (DECCA).

MOZART, PIANO CONCERTOS NOS. 9 AND 21: DAVIS AND ENGLISH CHAMBER ORCHESTRA (RCA).

Lassus, Orlande [Roland] de

(b. Mons, ca. 1532; d. Munich, June 14, 1594)

FRANCO-FLEMISH COMPOSER. His name was styled, by himself and others, in various ways: Orlando di Lasso, Orlando de Lasso, Orlandus Lassus. Legend has it that as a boy he had an uncommonly beautiful voice, as a consequence of which he was kidnapped three times by parties desirous of placing him in their choirs. His first documented service was as a boy singer in the retinue of the Mantuan nobleman Ferrante Gonzaga, who passed through the Low Countries in 1544 and presumably made a deal with Lassus's parents to educate and care for the young musician. Lassus spent the next decade in Italy, first with Gonzaga, later with Constantino Castrioto in Naples. By 1553 he was choirmaster at the church of San Giovanni in Laterano, in Rome; on the news that both his parents were ill he returned home, only to find they had died. He subsequently spent time in Antwerp, where in 1556 his first book of five- and six-part motets was published. That same year, Lassus was invited to Munich by Albrecht V, Duke of Bavaria, to serve as a tenor in his court chapel; he was one of several Flemish singers contemporaneously imported to Munich in what appears to have been a bid to improve the state of singing there. Lassus married the daughter of a Munich court official in 1558. In 1560 the duke sent him back to Flanders to recruit another round of Netherlandish singers for the chapel. Lassus became *maestro di cappella* in 1563, a position he would hold for 30 years. Following Albrecht's death in 1579, he continued in the service of Wilhelm V, Albrecht's son, with whom—to judge from the bantering letters they exchanged, often with plays on words—he had a close, affectionate relationship. Wilhelm was also knowledgeable about music, and even though one of his first acts as duke was to reduce the size of the chapel ensemble, Lassus remained his loyal "servitor," turning down an offer from Dresden in 1580. Both Andrea and Giovanni Gabrieli came to study with Lassus during his long career in Munich, and he undertook periodic travel—to France, Italy, and Austria—befitting a person of recognized importance at court and in the world at large. In later years he suffered from depression ("melancholia hypocondriaca") and what today would be called burnout.

Orlandus Lassus, musician to the Duke of Bavaria

Lassus was among the most prolific and versatile composers of the 16th century. He produced more than 2,000 works encompassing all the important liturgical and secular genres of his day and touching on nearly every manner and style of expression. Of his roughly 60 mass settings—the majority for four to six voices, a few for eight—most are parody settings based either on Italian madrigals (by figures such as Adrian Willaert and Cipriano de Rore [ca. 1515–65]), French chansons (by Nicolas Gombert [ca. 1495–ca. 1560], among others), or Latin motets (often ones Lassus had written himself). As a body, the masses call on an enormous and intriguing range of styles and techniques. For example, the eight-voice *Missa osculetur me*—a double-choir parody mass based on Lassus's own motet of 1582—exhibits many of the trappings of the Italian style and shows how masterfully Lassus could play one manner of text setting (contrapuntal) against another (homophonic) in the same piece.

Lassus also composed more than 100 settings of the *Magnificat,* and between 1575 and 1582 made settings of each of the four passion narratives. Most important of all, he created approximately 530 motets. These works are varied in style and tone, and particularly notable for their expressiveness, rhetorical strength, and contrapuntal fluidity. The six-voice *Timor et tremor* (published in 1564) is especially fascinating—both for its brevity and its breathtaking use of chromaticism. Among Lassus's most effective compositions in this vein is his five-voice *Lamentations of Jeremiah* (published in 1585) ◉, in effect a motet cycle for Holy Week and one of the peaks of Renaissance polyphony. On the secular side, Lassus is credited with the creation of 175 Italian madrigals, about 150 French chansons, and nearly 100 German songs.

Flemish by birth, Italian by training, Lassus managed to bring the best of the northern and Italian traditions together, and he did it in Munich, a place that had not been considered a musical center until he arrived. Among composers of the later 16th century, he stands out not only for the quantity of his work, but for his richness of technique, expressivity, formal elegance, and architectural organization. Everything he did was characterized by the highest craftsmanship; his works were taken as models by other composers, and his influence extended through several generations, even up to Bach and Beethoven. The esteem in which he was held by his contemporaries can best be judged by the fact that he was appointed a Knight of the Golden Spur by Pope Gregory XIII, awarded the cross of the Order of Malta by Charles IX of France, and, on December 7, 1570, raised to the nobility by Emperor Maximilian II. It was uncommon for even important musicians to be so honored—and quite remarkable that the same musician could have compelled the respect of a king, a pope, and an emperor, none of whom was his employer. The music of Lassus was also fancied by the incomparable Sherlock Holmes, who, according to Arthur Conan Doyle, penned a monograph on the motets in 1895.

RECOMMENDED RECORDINGS

LAMENTATIONS OF JEREMIAH: HERREWEGHE AND CHAPELLE ROYALE (HARMONIA MUNDI).

MISSA *OSCULETUR ME* (WITH MOTETS): PHILLIPS AND TALLIS SCHOLARS (GIMELL).

Lauri-Volpi, Giacomo

(b. Rome, December 11, 1892; d. Valencia, March 17, 1979)

ITALIAN TENOR. He studied at the Accademia di Santa Cecilia in Rome and made his debut in Viterbo, as Arturo in Bellini's *I puritani,* in 1919. He quickly worked his way up to more important houses, appearing at La Scala in 1922 and making his debut at the Metropolitan Opera on January 26, 1923. Over the next 11 seasons he was a fixture at the Met, singing 308 performances and appearing in a total of 27 roles, sharing much of

***Lauri-Volpi in* Guillaume Tell**

what had been the Caruso repertoire with Beniamino Gigli. The highlight of his Met career came on November 16, 1926, when he sang the role of Calaf in the American premiere of Puccini's *Turandot.* Renowned as a singer of Verdi, he also made frequent appearances as the Duke in *Rigoletto* and Alfredo in *La traviata.* A lyric tenor at home in *lirico spinto* roles such as Radames in *Aida* and Manrico in *Il trovatore,* he was admired for his vibrant manner and gleaming tone in the upper register. He wrote several volumes of reminiscences and two books about celebrated vocalists and the art of singing.

legato (from It. *legare,* "to tie") A manner of playing in which notes are effectively "tied" to one another (i.e., smoothly connected). Legato phrasing is normally indicated by slur markings over or under the notes that are to be elided in this fashion. When two or more notes of the same pitch are "tied," especially across a bar line, the note is sounded once and held for the duration of the combined note values. The instruction *non legato* means that a performer should clearly articulate each note.

Lehár, Franz

(b. Komáron, April 30, 1870; d. Bad Ischl, October 24, 1948)

AUSTRO-HUNGARIAN COMPOSER AND CONDUCTOR. The eldest son of an army bandmaster, he entered the Prague Conservatory at the age of 12 to study violin and theory; on the side, he studied composition with Zdeněk Fibich and received some pointers from Antonín Dvořák. After his graduation he played violin in the theater orchestra at Barmen-Elberfeld before donning a uniform and joining his father's band, that of the 50th Austrian infantry regiment. Within a year he was put in charge of his own ensemble, making him the youngest bandmaster in the Austrian army. Rising through the ranks, he was posted to Vienna in 1899 as bandmaster of the 26th infantry regiment; there he won recognition following the success of his *Gold and Silver* Waltz, written for a society ball in 1902. He left the military that year and began a new career as a freelance composer and conductor. In 1905, after one hit and several misses, the premiere of his operetta *Die lustige Witwe* (*The Merry Widow*) at the Theater an der Wien made him famous; the work has since enjoyed the greatest worldwide success in the history of operetta.

Franz Lehár and the piano-vocal score to **The Ideal Wife**

Though Lehár recalled that he stumbled into the genre, his 20 subsequent works (including *The Count of Luxembourg, Gypsy Love,* and *Eva*) show how surefooted he became while bringing a warm glow to the sunset years of Viennese operetta. In the 1920s Lehár found his muse in the incomparable singing of tenor Richard Tauber, an artist of rare charm and charisma. Most of the remaining operettas were written with him in mind, and included the requisite "Tauber-lied" as a hallmark. These included *Paganini, Frasquita, Der Zarewitsch, Schön ist die Welt!* and the universally adored *Das Land des Lächelns* (*The Land of Smiles*), for which the composer wrote the most famous of all his Tauber songs, "Dein ist mein ganzes Herz." Rich and successful, Lehár composed his final and most ambitious stagework, *Giuditta,* in 1933 for the Vienna Staatsoper and a cast featuring Tauber and Jarmila Novotná in the lead roles. In 1935 he founded his own publishing house to control the production rights and availability of his works. He spent the war years in retirement.

RECOMMENDED RECORDINGS

GOLD AND SILVER (WITH OTHER WALTZES): BOSKOVSKY AND VIENNA JOHANN STRAUSS ORCHESTRA (EMI).

DIE LUSTIGE WITWE: STUDER, SKOVHUS, BONNEY, TERFEL; GARDINER AND VIENNA PHILHARMONIC (DG).

Lehmann, Lilli

(b. Würzburg, November 24, 1848; d. Berlin, May 17, 1929)

GERMAN SOPRANO. She made her debut in Prague in 1865 and joined the Berlin Court Opera in 1870, following a successful debut there as Marguerite de Valois in Meyerbeer's *Les Huguenots.* Although she started out as a coloratura, as her career developed she became closely identified with Wagnerian repertoire, without losing the vocal sparkle of her youth. She sang in the first Bayreuth *Ring* cycle (1876) in the roles of Woglinde (*Das Rheingold* and *Götterdämmerung*), Helmwige (*Die Walküre*), and the Forest Bird (*Siegfried*). She made her debut in Vienna in 1882 and appeared at Covent Garden in 1884 both as Isolde and as Elisabeth in *Tannhäuser.* Lehmann's career at the Metropolitan Opera was a brief one (six seasons between 1885 and 1892) but very big (262 performances). She made her debut as Carmen on November 25, 1885, during the Met's third season, and became the vocal cornerstone of the company during its "German interval" (1884–91) when Wagner's heroines, led by conductor Anton Seidl, ruled the roost. She was celebrated especially as Brünnhilde, Isolde, and Venus in *Tannhäuser,* but also sang Marguerite in Gounod's *Faust* and several major Verdi roles, including Aida, Amelia in *Un ballo in maschera* (sung in German!), and Leonore in *Il trovatore.* When *Götterdämmerung* received its American premiere at the Met, on January 25, 1888, she was the Brünnhilde, and she sang all three Brünnhildes in the Met's first integral staging of the *Ring,* March 5–11, 1889. It would have been hard to imagine a greater triumph, but she achieved one the following year when she sang the title role in Bellini's *Norma* at the Met. Her extraordinary flexibility and exquisite command of diction and ornamentation astonished New Yorkers who had thought of her only as a power singer.

Lehmann was in fact a total vocal artist, brilliant in opera, a distinguished lieder performer, and an outstanding teacher whose students included Geraldine Farrar and Olive Fremstadt.

Lehmann, Lotte

(b. Perleberg, February 27, 1888; d. Santa Barbara, August 26, 1976)

GERMAN SOPRANO, one of the most accomplished and expressive singers of the 20th century. She studied in Berlin and was put under contract by the Hamburg Opera in 1910, stepping into her first big role, Elsa in Wagner's *Lohengrin,* in 1912. She made her debuts in London and with the Vienna Court Opera in 1914, and was chosen by Richard Strauss to sing the role of the Composer in the Court Opera's 1916 premiere of the second version of *Ariadne auf Naxos,* with a cast that included Maria Jeritza as Ariadne. In 1919 Strauss engaged Lehmann for the role of the Dyer's Wife in the world premiere of *Die Frau ohne Schatten* in Vienna, again casting her opposite Jeritza, who sang the role of the Empress. In 1924 Lehmann created the role of Christine in the world premiere of Strauss's *Intermezzo* in Dresden.

Lehmann spent 12 seasons at the Metropolitan Opera, making her debut on January 11, 1934, as Sieglinde in Wagner's *Die Walküre* (with Lauritz Melchior as Siegmund) and returning later in the season to sing Elisabeth in *Tannhäuser.* During her Met tenure, she owned the role of the Marschallin in Strauss's *Der Rosenkavalier,* singing it 33 times. She also appeared as Tosca, and as Eva in Wagner's *Die Meistersinger von Nürnberg.* Outside the Met she was noted for her performances as Leonore in Beethoven's *Fidelio,* the Countess in Mozart's *Le nozze di Figaro,* and in several Puccini roles including Mimì in *La bohème* and the title role in *Suor Angelica.* Retiring from the opera stage in 1946, she starred in the MGM feature *Big City* the following year. A superb lieder singer, she continued to give recitals through 1951. She enjoyed an active retirement, helping to establish the Music Academy of the West in Santa Barbara and distinguishing herself as a teacher—among the many outstanding singers who came to her for coaching were Marilyn Horne, Grace Bumbry, Jeanine Altmeyer, and Carol Neblett.

In her singing Lehmann combined a spontaneous, almost impulsive expressiveness with exceptional refinement, beauty of tone, and charisma. She was one of the greatest exponents of the role of Sieglinde and perhaps the greatest Marschallin of all time. Strauss was not alone in adoring her. The conductor Bruno Walter became a favorite collaborator, both as pianist and conductor ("When he conducts, I feel as though I'm being cradled by the tip of his baton," she once said). Walter was on the podium with the Vienna Philharmonic in 1935 when Lehmann and Melchior, joined by the bass Emanuel List as Hunding, teamed up for a memorable recording of Act I of *Die Walküre*; part of a projected complete recording that was never finished owing to the political turmoil of the time, it shows what a splendid singer Lehmann was.

Lotte Lehmann as the Marschallin at the Met

RECOMMENDED RECORDING

WAGNER, *DIE WALKÜRE,* ACT I: MELCHIOR, LIST; WALTER AND VIENNA PHILHARMONIC (EMI).

Leider, Frida

(b. Berlin, April 18, 1888; d. Berlin, June 4, 1975)

GERMAN SOPRANO, one of the great Wagnerians of the 20th century. She made her debut in Halle, as Venus in Wagner's *Tannhäuser,* in 1915. She subsequently sang in Rostock, Königsberg, and Hamburg before joining the Berlin Staatsoper in 1923, where she remained a principal for 15 seasons. She gave her first performances at Covent Garden in 1924, singing the roles of Isolde and Brünnhilde; she returned every year until 1938. For four seasons beginning in 1928 she was the leading dramatic soprano with the Lyric Opera of Chicago. Also in 1928 she made her debut at the Bayreuth Festival, where for ten years she was the dominant Brünnhilde, Isolde, and Kundry.

On January 16, 1933, within days of Hitler's appointment as Chancellor of Germany, Leider made her debut at the Metropolitan Opera in *Tristan und Isolde,* singing opposite Lauritz Melchior. She remained on the company's roster just two seasons, taking on, in addition to Isolde, the roles of Kundry and the three Brünnhildes, and giving a single performance as Venus. The Nazis refused to let her sing in America after 1934 because her husband Rudolf Deman, concertmaster of the Berlin Staatsoper orchestra, was Jewish. Her appearances at Covent Garden and elsewhere outside Germany came to an end in 1938, and by 1940 her operatic career was essentially over. Leider's husband sat out the war in Switzerland, while she stayed behind in Berlin, her loyalty to the city of her birth and to the Staatsoper taking precedence. She continued to give recitals during the war with the pianist Michael Raucheisen; she and her husband were reunited in 1946. Following the war she headed up a studio for young singers at the Staatsoper and later taught at the Berlin Hochschule für Musik.

Part of what made Leider such a sensational Isolde, possibly the greatest, was the feeling of dignity she brought to the role, the intelligent conviction that shaped her singing so that it was full not only of passionate intensity (to paraphrase Yeats) but of great nuance and depth. Leider was also an outstanding Kundry and Brünnhilde and a superb interpreter of numerous Mozart and Verdi roles.

RECOMMENDED RECORDING

WAGNER, *LIEBESTOD* FROM *TRISTAN UND ISOLDE* (WITH OTHER WAGNER EXCERPTS): BARBIROLLI AND LONDON SYMPHONY ORCHESTRA (PEARL).

Leinsdorf [Landauer], Erich

(b. Vienna, February 4, 1912; d. Zurich, September 11, 1993)

AUSTRIAN/AMERICAN CONDUCTOR. During the course of a peripatetic career, he held important positions in European and American musical life, emerging as one of the 20th century's most versatile, experienced, and respected conductors. He began studying music when he was six and started piano lessons when he was eight. In the summer of 1930 he participated in a masterclass for conductors at the Salzburg

Erich Leinsdorf in performance

Mozarteum, and after a term at the University of Vienna he completed his studies at Vienna's State Music Academy, making his conducting debut with its student orchestra upon graduation in 1933. He worked for a while as rehearsal pianist for Anton Webern's Singverein der Sozialdemokratischen Kunststelle (Choral Society of the Social Democratic Arts Council) and as a vocal coach in Vienna; in the summer of 1934 he was appointed assistant to Arturo Toscanini and Bruno Walter at the Salzburg Festival, where he served through the summer of 1936. He came to the United States in the fall of 1937 to work as an assistant conductor at the Metropolitan Opera. As a Jew he had no choice but to remain in America following the annexation of Austria by Germany in March 1938; a young congressman from Texas named Lyndon Baines Johnson helped him get his visa extended, and he became a U.S. citizen in 1942.

Leinsdorf made his professional conducting debut on January 21, 1938, leading a performance of Wagner's *Die Walküre* at the Met (astonishingly, the house's management had engaged him without solid evidence that he *could* conduct). He took over the Wagner portfolio at the Met following the death of Artur Bodanzky in 1939. In 1943 he succeeded Artur Rodzinski as music director of the Cleveland Orchestra, but his stewardship was interrupted in December of that year when he was inducted into the U.S. Army. He received his discharge in 1944, but the orchestra's board decided to relieve him of command in 1946 and appoint George Szell in his stead. Leinsdorf subsequently served as music director of the Rochester Philharmonic (1947–56); in 1956, after an absence of ten seasons, he resumed working at the Met. He remained on the Met's roster through 1962 and returned periodically after that until 1983. His career climaxed with his tenure as music director of the Boston Symphony Orchestra (1962–70). During the 1970s and 1980s, he was active as a guest conductor with major American and European orchestras, and from 1977 to 1980 he served as principal conductor of the Berlin Radio Symphony Orchestra.

Leinsdorf's personality combined elegance with cutting politeness, a Germanic formality, and notable intensity. He knew every nook and cranny of the repertoire, every gesture, every trick of the trade. He had a keen and pitiless eye, a sharply analytical ear, an exacting if at times pedantic rehearsal style, and an enormous and very keen intellect. His programs usually contained a twist, or at least a lesson, though occasionally he conducted like a traffic cop rather than a teacher. Seemingly indifferent in performance, always reined in, he was the pure antithesis of Leonard Bernstein; he valued warmth and transparency of sound and had a remarkable way of bringing out the inner voices of a complex texture. As a symphonic conductor he was at his best in Mozart (in whose music he conveyed the seemingly contradictory qualities of aristocratic grace and earthy vitality), Beethoven, Wagner, Mahler, and Stravinsky; he was naturally attuned to the Second Viennese School as well, and he championed a good deal of American music. In the sphere of opera he was an outstanding interpreter of Wagner and Richard Strauss, and also of Verdi and Puccini.

When Leinsdorf guest-conducted it was usually to the benefit of the host ensemble ("Playing with Leinsdorf for two weeks is like going back to school," a string player with a major orchestra once remarked). He wrote cogently on music and conducting in two highly regarded books—*Cadenza: A Musical Career* (1976) and *The Composer's Advocate: A Radical Orthodoxy for Musicians* (1981). In addition, a posthumous collection of essays and writings, *Erich Leinsdorf on Music* (1997), was seen into print by his widow, Vera.

RECOMMENDED RECORDINGS

BARTÓK, *CONCERTO FOR ORCHESTRA*: BOSTON SYMPHONY ORCHESTRA (RCA).

MAHLER, SYMPHONIES NOS. 1 AND 3: BOSTON SYMPHONY ORCHESTRA (RCA).

leitmotif (Ger., "leading motif") A musical representation of a specific object, person, or idea in a descriptive piece such as an opera or symphonic poem, which is used not only as a thematic "tag" but as a substantive element of the musical discourse. This combination of referential and structural utility was pioneered by Wagner principally in *Der Ring des Nibelungen* (the "spear" motif in *Die Walküre,* gloriously transformed, also serves as the basis for the "love" theme in Wotan's farewell to Brünnhilde ◉), as well as *Tristan und Isolde* and *Parsifal.* Richard Strauss made use of Wagnerian-style leitmotifs in his operas *Salome* and *Elektra,* and in several of his tone poems. Debussy, while taking great pains not to sound like Wagner, took advantage of the technique in his opera *Pelléas et Mélisande*.

***Leningrad* Symphony** TITLE OF DMITRY SHOSTAKOVICH'S SYMPHONY NO. 7 IN C, OP. 60, composed in 1941. Shostakovich was already at work on the score when, in the summer of 1941, Hitler sent his armies to invade the Soviet Union. Leningrad came under attack almost immediately, and Shostakovich became a symbol of his country's spirited resistance—*Time* magazine ran a portrait of him in firefighter's gear on its cover. The siege of Leningrad lasted 900 days; Shostakovich was evacuated from the city early on, and continued work on the symphony at Kuibyshev on the Volga, where a composers' retreat had been established by the Soviet government. Writing at a feverish pace, he completed the symphony's finale on December 27, 1941. The score received its premiere in Kuibyshev on March 5, 1942, played by members of the Bolshoi Theatre Orchestra under the direction of Samuil Samosud.

Following this performance, the manuscript was smuggled out of the Soviet Union on microfilm. Taken by air to Tehran, by truck to Cairo, and finally flown over the Sahara and the Atlantic, the score eventually reached New York, where Arturo Toscanini, having outmaneuvered Leopold Stokowski, claimed the privilege of conducting the American premiere. His performance, on July 19, 1942, was broadcast nationwide, and the work became an overnight sensation. Subsequent performances conducted by Stokowski, Serge Koussevitzky, and Artur Rodzinski had the effect of saturating the American ear (and the amusing side effect of eliciting Bartók's famous parody of the first movement's march in his *Concerto for Orchestra*). From the start, the critics were divided over the work's merit, and it was not long before the consensus emerged that the symphony had been a facile, bombastic attempt at creating a patriotic potboiler.

In fact, the score's banality and repetitiveness are fully intentional, its sense of grotesquery and desolation hauntingly keen. But whether the first movement's agonizingly long crescendo is actually a portrayal of Hitler's advancing military machine, or of Stalin's crushing totalitarianism, remains an open issue. Shostakovich is supposed to have said, "I have nothing against calling the Seventh the *Leningrad* Symphony, but it's not about Leningrad under siege, it's about the Leningrad that Stalin destroyed and that Hitler merely finished off." For all its tragic weight, the symphony ends with a magnificent paean to victory—a necessary gesture under the circumstances, but also, as it has turned out, a prophetic one in view of the post-Soviet transformation of Leningrad back into the composer's beloved St. Petersburg.

RECOMMENDED RECORDINGS

BERNSTEIN AND CHICAGO SYMPHONY ORCHESTRA (DG).

TERMIRKANOV AND ST. PETERSBURG PHILHARMONIC (RCA).

lento (It., "slow") A tempo midway between *andante* and *adagio*.

Leoncavallo, Ruggero

(b. Naples, March 8, 1957; d. Montecatini, August 9, 1919)

ITALIAN COMPOSER. With Pietro Mascagni, he was the leading early exponent of opera's VERISMO style, in which subjects are taken from the darker side of life and treated in a realistic manner. Not only did he share the same fate as Mascagni—as a composer of a single-hit, single-act opera, but their famous works are often inseparable as the "Cav and Pag" double bill.

Leoncavallo graduated from the Naples Conservatory at the age of 18. His first opera was *Chatterton* (ca. 1876), based on Alfred de Vigny's life of the English poet. The impresario who had agreed to produce it disappeared at the last moment, leaving the project in a shambles and the composer in debt. After that fiasco, Leoncavallo spent some time in Egypt before moving to Paris, where he supported himself by teaching and playing the piano at café concerts. Upon his return to Italy, he received a contract from the publishing house Ricordi and started to write an opera based on the Medici family, the first installment of a trilogy he hoped would bear comparison with Wagner's *Ring* cycle. While in the midst of that project he was inspired by the recent success of Mascagni's *Cavalleria rusticana* to write an opera in a similar style, based on a true story he remembered from his childhood told by his father, a police magistrate. He wrote his own libretto (later adding the famous prologue, "Si può?" that is delivered in front of the curtain). The first performance of PAGLIACCI was given in Milan in 1893 at the Teatro dal Verme, conducted by Arturo Toscanini. It created an immediate sensation, and within two years *Pagliacci* had been produced all over Italy, as well as at the Vienna Staatsoper, Covent Garden, the Metropolitan Opera, and in Prague, Budapest, Buenos Aires, Stockholm, Dublin, and Moscow. Leoncavallo's next opera, based on Henri Mürger's *Scènes de la vie de bohème* (*Scenes from the Bohemian Life*) and finished in 1897, had the extraordinary bad luck of appearing 15 months after Puccini's *La bohème,* based on the same novel. The public, enamored of Puccini's stunning operatic rendering of the story, paid little attention to Leoncavallo's worthy but lesser effort. It was a bitter moment for Leoncavallo, who accused Puccini of stealing his idea. In 1900 Leoncavallo's *Zaza* enjoyed only a modest success; *Der Roland von Berlin* (1904), an opera commissioned by Kaiser Wilhelm II to celebrate the House of Hohenzollern, did well in Berlin thanks to its royal theme and patronage, but was a bust at its Italian premiere in 1905. Try as he might, Leoncavallo could not duplicate the passionate dramatic flow of *Pagliacci* or the emotional paroxysm of its famous aria "Vesti la giubba," which has become a showpiece for hot-blooded tenors the world over. ◉ He spent the final years of his career writing operettas.

Ruggero Leoncavallo

RECOMMENDED RECORDING

Pagliacci: Carlyle, Bergonzi, Taddei; Karajan and La Scala Opera (DG).

Leonhardt, Gustav

(b. Graveland, May 30, 1928)

DUTCH HARPSICHORDIST, ORGANIST, AND CONDUCTOR. He studied organ and harpsichord at the Schola Cantorum Basiliensis from 1947 to 1950, and made his debut in Vienna in 1950, playing Bach's *Art of Fugue* on the harpsichord. Following a year of studying musicology in Vienna, he served as professor of harpsichord at the Vienna Music Academy (1952–55). He enjoyed a lengthy tenure as professor at the Amsterdam Conservatory (1954–88), and also served as organist at the Waalse Kerk; over the years he became a key figure in the period instrument movement in the Netherlands, inspiring other early-music artists, including keyboardist Bob Van Asperen, flutist and recorder soloist Barthold Kuijken, and cellist Anner Bylsma.

The world's most recorded harpsichordist, Leonhardt prefers historically replicated instruments to modern ones, and takes care to play the instrument most appropriate to each composer's time and place. He is known for his tasteful approach to ornamentation and his fine yet flexible sense of rhythm. Leonhardt has made numerous recordings as a conductor, including a groundbreaking project of the complete Bach cantatas on period instruments in collaboration with Nikolaus Harnoncourt. He has published an acclaimed edition of Sweelinck's fantasias and toccatas and, in a more thespian mode, played the role of J. S. Bach in Jean-Marie Staub's biographical film, *Die Chronik der Anna Magdalena Bach.* He received the Erasmus Prize in 1980 and holds a number of honorary doctorates.

By integrating his thorough knowledge of Baroque performance practice with active concertizing and recording, Leonhardt has won new audiences for composers such as Johann Jacob (1616–67), Froberger, Frescobaldi, and Couperin, and has been a major force in bringing period instrument performance into the classical mainstream.

Léonin

(fl. Paris, ca. 1150–1201)

FRENCH COMPOSER. Also known as Magister Leoninus or Leonius, his exact identity is uncertain, but his role in Western music should not be underestimated. Probably a priest, and certainly a teacher of arts and functionary at the Cathedral of Notre Dame in Paris, Léonin's great undertaking was the creation of the *Magnus liber organi* (*Great Book of Polyphony*) for use in the cathedral services. The significance of this earliest collection of polyphonic music lies in its transformation of what had been essentially an improvised tradition, perhaps a couple of centuries old, into a written art of actual composition, encompassing both pitch and rhythm.

Léonin's very existence as a composer and the compiler of the *Magnus liber* is known only from the writings of the late-13th-century English theorist designated Anonymous 4, who discusses both Léonin and his slightly younger contemporary, Pérotin. From this treatise, it is clear that Léonin was considered the "best" composer of organum of his generation, although as yet no specific works have been identified as his. Since Léonin's *Magnus liber* no longer exists, its original content is unknown; however, versions of pieces it is believed to have contained were disseminated and survive in other manuscripts.

In these are found various styles of polyphonic writing in two, three, and even four voices. Probably the best-known form is *organum purum,* in which one or more voices move in a highly florid manner over a much slower-moving tenor; other techniques include descant, in which all the voices move at a more active rate, and *conductus,* in which the text is set more or less syllabically and all the parts move in the same rhythm. The melodic and rhythmic language of the School of Notre Dame, part of the same creative flowering that brought the Gothic style in architecture into being, became the basis of Western musical art in the centuries that followed.

RECOMMENDED RECORDING

"THE AGE OF CATHEDRALS": HILLIER AND THEATRE OF VOICES (HARMONIA MUNDI).

Lesne, Gérard *See box on pages 156–57.*

Leutgeb, Joseph

(b. Vienna, October 8, 1732; d. Vienna, February 27, 1811)

AUSTRIAN HORN VIRTUOSO for whom Wolfgang Amadeus Mozart composed several concertos. He worked as a freelancer in Vienna during the 1750s, and in the early 1760s performed solo works by Carl Ditters von Dittersdorf (1739–99) and the brothers Michael and Joseph Haydn in a series of concerts at the Burgtheater. In 1763 he entered the service of the Elector of Salzburg as a horn player in the court orchestra, remaining, with frequent periods of leave for touring, until 1777, when he moved back to Vienna to open a cheese shop. He continued playing until 1792.

The manuscript of Concerto No. 2 in E-flat, K. 417, the first of the pieces Mozart finished for Leutgeb, is inscribed: "Wolfgang Amadé Mozart has taken pity on Leutgeb—that ass, ox, and fool—in Vienna on 27 May, 1783." In his next work for Leutgeb, Concerto No. 4 in E-flat, K. 495 (completed on June 25, 1786), Mozart wrote the solo part in four different colors of ink—red, green, blue, and black—thinking perhaps to distract the hornist as he tried to cope with the part's many challenges. Concerto No. 3 in E-flat, K. 447, composed in 1787 or 1788, is the greatest of the set, its harmonic language richer and noticeably more chromatic than that of the others. Concerto No. 1 in D, K. 412, long thought to have been composed in 1782 (hence the misnumbering of the whole set), has been established as belonging to 1790–91, the last years of Mozart's life. The work's lower key and the somewhat narrower compass of the solo part may have been concessions to Leutgeb's eroding technique (he was by then nearly 60), but the music here and in the other concertos makes it clear that Mozart had the highest regard for Leutgeb's abilities, and fully recognized that he was neither ox, ass, nor fool, but a supremely gifted virtuoso.

Hermann Levi in 1893

Levi, Hermann

(b. Giessen, November 7, 1839; d. Munich, May 13, 1900)

GERMAN CONDUCTOR. With Felix Mottl and Hans Richter, he was the third member of the "Holy Trinity" responsible for the initial performances, at Munich and Bayreuth, of all of Wagner's operas after *Lohengrin.* He studied theory, composition, and conducting at the Leipzig Conservatory (1855–58) and became music director at Saarbrücken in 1859. After brief stints in Mannheim and Rotterdam he served as court Kapellmeister in Karlsruhe (1864–72), where he came into contact and formed close personal friendships with Clara Schumann and Johannes Brahms. He was named court Kapellmeister in Munich in 1872, becoming the city's general music director in 1894. He retired in 1896.

Levi entered Wagner's orbit in 1871, and in 1875 he took part in early rehearsals for the first Bayreuth Festival. His skills as a conductor were highly esteemed by Wagner; the fact that he was a Jew did not stop the composer, known for his anti-Semitic views, from choosing him to conduct the premiere of *Parsifal* at Bayreuth in 1882. Levi continued to conduct *Parsifal* at Bayreuth until 1894; he became a staunch champion of the symphonies of Anton Bruckner as well, presenting the Adagio from the Seventh Symphony in Munich in 1884 and hailing Bruckner as the true successor to Beethoven. Levi's interest proved to be a mixed blessing when, in 1887, he expressed in a letter to Bruckner misgivings about the score of his Eighth Symphony; for three years thereafter the pathologically insecure composer agonized over revisions to the work.

Levine, James

(b. Cincinnati, June 23, 1943)

AMERICAN CONDUCTOR AND PIANIST. He began piano lessons at the age of four and made his debut with the Cincinnati Symphony Orchestra when he was ten. He subsequently studied at the Marlboro Music Festival with Rudolf Serkin and at Aspen with Rosina Lhévinne. He entered the Juilliard School in 1961, continuing his piano studies with Lhévinne and studying conducting with Jean Morel. From 1964 to 1970 he worked with George Szell as assistant conductor of the Cleveland Orchestra. On June 5, 1971, Levine made his conducting debut at the Metropolitan Opera, leading a performance of Puccini's *Tosca.* Associated with the Met ever since, he was named principal conductor in 1973, music director in 1976, and artistic director (the first in the company's history) in 1986.

In the spring of 2004, despite growing concern that tremors in his left arm and leg were impairing his work on the rostrum, the Met's management extended his contract through 2011. During his Met tenure, Levine has conducted more than 2,000 performances of more than 75 different pieces (including the Met premieres of works by Mozart, Rossini, Verdi, Schoenberg, Stravinsky, Weill, Berg, and Gershwin, and world premieres of operas by Harbison and Corigliano), taken the company on numerous domestic and international tours, and built the Met Orchestra into one of the most brilliant and responsive ensembles in the world. Since 1991, he and the Met Orchestra have also presented works from the standard symphonic repertoire on tour and in much-admired concert performances at Carnegie Hall.

Apart from his duties at the Met, Levine spent 20 years (1973–93) as music director of the Ravinia Festival and enjoys ongoing associations with the Vienna Philharmonic and the Berlin Philharmonic. He filled annual engagements at the Salzburg Festival from 1975 to 1993, and at the Bayreuth Festival he was entrusted with both *Parsifal* (1982–93) and the *Ring* cycle (1994–98). He became music director of the Munich Philharmonic in 1998, and in the fall of 2004 he succeeded Seiji Ozawa as music director of the Boston Symphony Orchestra.

James Levine, with ubiquitous rehearsal towel

Throughout his four-decade career Levine has remained active on the recital stage as a chamber musician and as accompanist and partner to outstanding singers, from Jennie Tourel, Hans Hotter, and Eleanor Steber in the 1960s to a 2004 Schubertiade at Carnegie Hall with René Pape, Anne Sophie von Otter, Renée Fleming, and Matthew Polenzani.

Criticized early in his career for conducting that was loud, fast, and showy, and later on for performances that were impeccably played but said to be lacking in nuance, Levine has risen above it all, developing into a musician of enormous range, ability, and stature. The Met has flourished artistically under his direction, and even the critics have to admit that his leadership is the reason.

RECOMMENDED RECORDINGS

VERDI, *LA FORZA DEL DESTINO*: PRICE, DOMINGO, MILNES; LONDON SYMPHONY ORCHESTRA (RCA).

VERDI, *OTELLO*: DOMINGO, MILNES, SCOTTO; NATIONAL PHILHARMONIC ORCHESTRA (RCA).

WAGNER, *DER RING DES NIBELUNGEN*: BEHRENS, JERUSALEM, MORRIS; METROPOLITAN OPERA ORCHESTRA (DG).

libretto (It., "booklet") The sung text of an opera or other work for the musical theater.

lied (Ger., "song") A song with a text in German, usually with piano accompaniment. The modern lied arose in the mid- to late 18th century; interest in it exploded during the second and third decades of the 19th, with Schubert, who composed approximately 660 such songs, leading the way. Other principal exponents of the genre include Mozart, Beethoven, Schumann (who wrote 260, 140 of them in 1840, his "year of song"), Carl Loewe (1796–1869; 375), Brahms (200), Wolf (300), Mahler, Richard Strauss, and Korngold. Many other German and Austrian composers have contributed songs to the repertoire, even the American Charles Ives (who set Heinrich Heine's "Ich grolle nicht," in German, 58 years after Schumann). Important works include the cycles and collections *AN DIE FERNE GELIEBTE,* by Beethoven; Schubert's *DIE SCHÖNE MÜLLERIN* and *WINTERREISE*; Schumann's *DICHTERLIEBE* and *LIEDERKREIS* (literally "song cycle") on poems of Heine and Joseph von Eichendorff; Brahms's *Magelone-Lieder* on poems of Ludwig Tieck; Wolf's *Gedichte von Eduard Mörike, Spanisches Liederbuch,* and *ITALIENISCHES LIEDERBUCH*; and numerous individual settings by these composers and others.

While other forms of music may deal with the abstract or the theatrical elements of experience, art songs such as lieder typically concern themselves with matters of the heart, with perceptions of beauty, with the play of senses—in short, with those things in which we recognize our relationship to life and to our own humanity. Thanks to their fusion of musical and poetic elements, such songs have a communicative appeal that transcends both the spoken word and the imagery of instrumental sound.

Lieder eines fahrenden Gesellen (Songs of a Wayfarer) CYCLE OF FOUR SONGS FOR PIANO AND LOW VOICE composed 1883–85 by Gustav Mahler, to his own texts. During the 1890s, the songs were revised and orchestrated; in this guise they received their premiere on March 16, 1896, in Berlin, with the composer conducting the Berlin Philharmonic. The fruit of an unhappy love affair with the singer Johanna Richter, the *Wayfarer* songs are Mahler's first masterpiece; portraying as they do the musings of a jilted lover who seeks solace in nature and is ultimately plunged into despair by his loss, they also constitute his first confessional work.

There is a close connection between the *Songs of a Wayfarer* and Mahler's Symphony No. 1. The main theme of the symphony's first movement is taken from the second of the *Wayfarer* songs ("Ging heut' morgen übers Feld"), and a quote from the final song of the *Wayfarer* cycle ("Die zwei blauen Augen von meinem Schatz") appears in the symphony's third movement, piercing its gloom with a short-lived ray of consolation.

RECOMMENDED RECORDINGS

FISCHER-DIESKAU; KUBELÍK AND BAVARIAN RADIO SYMPHONY ORCHESTRA (DG).

PREY; HAITINK AND CONCERTGEBOUW ORCHESTRA (PHILIPS).

Liederkreis (Ger., "song circle") Generic name occasionally given to song cycles. The most celebrated example is Schumann's *Liederkreis,* Op. 39 (1840), to poems of Joseph von Eichendorff.

Lied von der Erde, Das (The Song of the Earth) SYMPHONY FOR TENOR AND CONTRALTO (or baritone) soloists and orchestra by Gustav Mahler, based on texts from *Die chinesische Flöte* (*The Chinese Flute*), a collection of Chinese poetry translated into German by Hans Bethge; composed in 1908–09, it was premiered posthumously on November 20, 1911, in Munich, Bruno Walter conducting. Each of the six movements is set for a single solo voice and orchestra. Mahler specified the use of tenor for movements 1, 3, and 5, and either contralto or baritone for movements 2, 4, and 6 (nearly all performances make use of a contralto).

Das Lied von der Erde is the summation of Mahler's work as a song symphonist, a profound and intimate joining of those two modes of expression. Aware that his own death was imminent, the composer here came face-to-face emotionally and personally with a subject on which he had often dwelt philosophically. The result was an outpouring of feeling new even to him, climaxed by the half-hour-long concluding movement "Der Abschied" ("The Farewell"), one of the most beautiful and heartbreaking finales in the symphonic literature and the most perfectly realized of all Mahler's creations. Like brushstrokes in a Chinese landscape, touches of color from celesta, two harps, and mandolin are applied to pages almost bare of sound to create a fragile, haunting backdrop for the solo voice. The final pages of the setting, in which the earth's eternal cycle of self-renewal is observed and embraced, brings a feeling of spiritual release unprecedented in music.

A mandarin listens to a Chinese flute.

RECOMMENDED RECORDINGS

BAKER, KING; HAITINK AND CONCERTGEBOUW ORCHESTRA (PHILIPS).

FERRIER, PATZAK; WALTER AND VIENNA PHILHARMONIC (DECCA).

Lieutenant Kijé FILM BY ALEKSANDR FAJNTSIMMER based on a story by Yury Tynyanov, with music by Sergey Prokofiev. The score, completed in 1933, was the first important Soviet commission to be offered to Prokofiev following his emigration from the Soviet Union in 1918. The farcical plot of *Lieutenant Kijé*—about a nonexistent officer in the Russian army who comes into being as the result of a clerical error—hides a serious attack on bureaucratic stupidity and the love of the lie that has marked Russian officialdom for centuries. Prokofiev's music captures the pomposity and sham at the heart of the story with marvelous bite, and breathes splendid life into Kijé's invented escapades. In some of the music, an ironic undertone brings the satire close to tragedy. From the 16 musical segments he wrote for the film, Prokofiev extracted five to form the *Lieutenant Kijé* Suite, Op. 60 (1934), one of his most popular symphonic works. The depiction of a horse-drawn sleigh ride in the suite's fourth movement, "Troika," is especially vivid.

RECOMMENDED RECORDING

SZELL AND CLEVELAND ORCHESTRA (SONY).

Life for the Tsar, A OPERA IN FIVE ACTS BY MIKHAIL GLINKA, premiered in St. Petersburg on December 9, 1836. Set in Russia and Poland in the year 1613, it deals with the period immediately following the death of Boris Godunov, when Polish elements were attempting to win control of Russia. The opera's central figure is the peasant Ivan Susanin, who, at the cost of his own life, prevents a Polish search party from finding the hiding place of Russia's newly elected tsar, the 16-year-old Mikhail Romanov (founder of what would become his country's last ruling dynasty). The opera ends with Mikhail's coronation in Red Square. *A Life for the Tsar* was the first full-fledged Russian opera, a cornerstone of the national repertoire that emerged with remarkable speed in Russia over the next 70 years. While its scenic structure shows the influence of the Italian tragedies and French rescue operas of the day, its musical style is distinctive to Glinka and recognizably Russian.

Ligeti, György

(b. Dicsöszentmárton, May 28, 1923)

HUNGARIAN COMPOSER. One of the most inventive composers of the 20th century, he has been called "the poet of sonorous matter." Born into a Jewish Hungarian family, he moved with his parents to Kolozsvár (present-day Cluj-Napoca) shortly after his birth. He wanted to be a scientist, but the Jewish quota at the university was filled—so in 1941 he began studying composition at the conservatory in Kolozsvár, taking summer instruction in Budapest (he commuted on foot). During World War II, Ligeti's father and brother lost their lives in concentration camps, and in 1944 the Nazis placed Ligeti in a labor camp. He resumed his studies in September 1945, enrolling at the Franz Liszt Academy in Budapest. For a year after his graduation in 1949 he did research on Romanian folk music; in 1950 he took a position teaching harmony and counterpoint at the Academy. After the Soviets crushed the 1956 Hungarian uprising he left Budapest for Vienna and then Cologne, where from 1957 to 1959 he worked with Karlheinz Stockhausen and others at the Electronic Music Studio of Westdeutscher Rundfunk. Ligeti joined the Darmstadt crowd in 1958, but disliking systems and artificial methods, he soon broke ranks with his fellow European avant-gardists and set off on what would become his lifelong quest—finding new, unusual, and beautiful sounds in all sorts of unorthodox aggregations of voices and conventional instruments.

György Ligeti

In works such as *Apparitions* (1958–59), *Atmosphères* (1961), and *Lontano* (1967), Ligeti pioneered the use of tone clusters in orchestral music—creating remarkable cloudlike effects of slowly changing texture and color—and developed a concept he called micropolyphony, based on an incredibly densely woven tissue of imitation in which individual lines can no longer be discerned. The graphic precision required to notate these effects gave some of Ligeti's scores (e.g., *Atmosphères*) the appearance of geometric art.

In 1968 Ligeti's *Lux aeterna* (1966) for 16-voice unaccompanied chorus was used by Stanley Kubrick in his blockbuster *2001: A Space Odyssey* for the scene depicting the rocket shuttle trip to the moon monolith site. Its ethereal dissonances aptly suggest the strangeness of the lunar landscape and the mysterious beckoning of the otherworldly object that awaits the shuttle passengers. Parts of *Atmosphères* and of Ligeti's Requiem (1963–65) were also used in that film, which introduced an enormous new audience to the composer's music. The 1960s also saw Ligeti embrace the absurd in a series of brief, wordless, vocal/instrumental pieces, *Aventures* (1962) and *Nouvelles aventures* (1965), even as he satirized some of the more outrageous conceits of fellow modernists in works such as *Poème symphonique* (1962) for 100 metronomes set at different speeds. The climax of this phase came with *Le grand macabre* (1978; rev. 1996), an opera based on the darkly comical doomsday play by the Belgian dramatist Michel de Ghelderode, which has become one of Ligeti's most widely performed works (though its American premiere had to wait until the 2004–05 season at the San Francisco Opera).

During the 1970s and 1980s, influenced by the music of the American composers Conlon Nancarrow (1912–97) and Steve Reich, by various strands of non-European music, and by the drawings of M. C. Escher (which he encountered while teaching at Stanford in 1972), Ligeti began to move away from the stasis of his earlier micropolyphonic works toward writing of greater rhythmic complexity. Around the same time he developed a new interest in unconventional scales and tunings and in the use of microtones and fractal patterns. These trends are evident in his Piano Concerto (1985–88) and an ongoing series of piano etudes begun in 1985.

For four decades, notwithstanding his rejection of serialism and other modernist methodologies, Ligeti has been idolized and imitated by the avant-garde, though both the fascinating originality and the whimsicality of his music remain unique. Ligeti himself best characterized the mix of mechanistic activity and diffuse, subtly changing textures and sonorities in his music in the title he gave to a 1973 piece for female voices and orchestra: *Clocks and Clouds.* His great accomplishment has been to bring certain elements of the "old" musical language, especially rhythm and melody, back from exile so that they could be explored once again, which has led to the discovery of a whole new world of sound between music and noise.

RECOMMENDED RECORDINGS

ATMOSPHÈRES, APPARITIONS, LONTANO: NOTT AND BERLIN PHILHARMONIC (TELDEC).

ATMOSPHÈRES: BERNSTEIN AND NEW YORK PHILHARMONIC (SONY).

ETUDES: AIMARD (SONY).

LE GRAND MACABRE: EHLERT, CLARK, WHITE; SALONEN AND PHILHARMONIA ORCHESTRA (SONY).

LUX AETERNA (WITH OTHER A CAPPELLA VOCAL WORKS): EDWARDS AND LONDON SINFONIETTA VOICES (SONY).

Lincoln Center Performing arts complex in New York City. Home to 12 resident arts organizations, it is the largest performing arts center in the world and a mecca for opera, symphonic music, chamber music, and dance. The site, on 16.3 acres adjacent to the intersection of Broadway and 65th Street on Manhattan's Upper West Side, was designated by the mayor's Slum Clearance Commission in 1955 as a target for urban renewal. At the time, it was one of the most depressed neighborhoods in the New York (two years later it would become the storied backdrop to the gang warfare in Leonard Bernstein's *West Side Story*). Its development driven by the indefatigable Robert Moses, the center was incorporated in 1956 and began the process of attracting "constituents," essentially tenants, to the property. By early 1957

***The fountain and plaza at Lincoln Center, with Avery Fisher Hall* (right) *and the Metropolitan Opera House* (left)**

the New York Philharmonic, the Juilliard School, and the Metropolitan Opera had committed to taking up residence at Lincoln Center, and ground was broken for its construction by President Dwight D. Eisenhower on May 14, 1959.

The composer William Schuman was named president of Lincoln Center in 1962, and on September 23, 1962, Philharmonic Hall, the new home of the New York Philharmonic, opened its doors to the public. The New York State Theater, designed by Philip Johnson, opened in 1964, and became the home of the New York City Opera and the New York City Ballet. The summer of 1966 saw the launch of "Midsummer Serenades—A Mozart Festival," the first indoor music festival in the United States (made possible by air conditioning in the center's new buildings); in 1972 the festival acquired the name by which it is still known, "Mostly Mozart." On September 16, 1966, the Metropolitan Opera moved into its new building on the center's main plaza with a gala season-opening performance of Samuel Barber's *Antony and Cleopatra,* commissioned for the occasion. A second concert venue, Alice Tully Hall, opened in September of 1969, and the following month the Juilliard School moved into its new building next door.

In 1973, in recognition of a generous gift from a leading maker of high-fidelity audio equipment, Philharmonic Hall was renamed Avery Fisher Hall. Two and a half years later its interior was gutted for a not altogether successful acoustical reconstruction. The New York State Theater underwent the same process in 1982, with similar results. During the 1980s and 1990s additional buildings opened on the campus and new constituents set up shop. In 1994, the soprano Beverly Sills (whose career had included many starry nights at the New York State Theater, and a few at the Met) was elected chairman of the board of Lincoln Center, a post she held until 2002. During the summer of 1996, Jazz at Lincoln Center became a constituent of the center and the first Lincoln Center Festival took place. In 2002, Reynold Levy became president of Lincoln Center, succeeding Gordon Davis, and Bruce Crawford became chairman of the board, succeeding Sills. In 2004, Jazz at Lincoln Center moved to a new off-campus home in the Time Warner Building.

The 12 resident organizations of Lincoln Center together put on thousands of performances and events each year and have an economic impact of $1.5 billion annually. Their payrolls currently support approximately 9,000 full- and part-time jobs. The work of the Metropolitan Opera, the New York Philharmonic, and the Juilliard School sets world-class standards and is of the highest national and international importance. The New York City Opera, though often thought of as the "number two" company at Lincoln Center, is an extraordinarily resourceful institution with an admirable track record; over the years it has mounted unforgettable stagings of works (such as Handel's *Giulio Cesare* and Boito's *Mefistofele*) that are somewhat off the beaten track, presented fresh interpretations of more familiar repertoire, premiered many new operas, and earned a gleaming reputation for cultivating American singers and conductors. Lincoln Center Presents draws many of the world's great orchestras and soloists to New York City, sharing that role in the city's cultural life with Carnegie Hall, and is responsible for the Emmy Award-winning series of national television broadcasts "Live From Lincoln Center," which made its PBS debut in 1976. The Chamber Music Society of Lincoln Center, currently under the artistic direction of cellist David Finckel and pianist Wu Han, concentrates on 19th- and 20th-century repertoire and each year brings the talents of an outstanding assemblage of artist members to Alice Tully Hall, while Jazz at Lincoln Center provides a showcase for a distinctive repertoire and some of the great jazz musicians of the present day.

Lincoln Portrait, A **WORK FOR SPEAKER AND ORCHESTRA BY AARON COPLAND,** to a text by the composer incorporating the words of Abraham Lincoln, composed in 1942 and premiered May 14, 1942, by the Cincinnati Symphony Orchestra under the direction of André Kostelanetz. The text excerpts several short passages from the letters and speeches of the 16th president, concluding with a quote from the Gettysburg Address. Kostelanetz, who commissioned the work in January 1942, within days of the attack on Pearl Harbor, left the choice of subject open, saying only that he wanted a musical portrait of "a great American." Virgil Thomson and Jerome Kern were also asked to write portraits. Copland originally intended to portray Walt Whitman, but when Kern opted for Mark Twain, Kostelanetz asked Copland if he would choose a "statesman" as subject rather than another literary figure. Lincoln was the obvious choice. The music of *A Lincoln Portrait* is in Copland's majestic "American" style and makes use of two songs from Lincoln's era, Stephen Foster's "Camptown Races" and the popular ballad "Springfield Mountain."

RECOMMENDED RECORDINGS

JONES; SCHWARZ AND SEATTLE SYMPHONY ORCHESTRA (DELOS).

SANDBERG; ORMANDY AND PHILADELPHIA ORCHESTRA (SONY).

Lind, Jenny

(b. Stockholm, October 6, 1820; d. Wynds Point, England, November 2, 1887)

SWEDISH SOPRANO, famed as the "Swedish Nightingale." The illegitimate child of neglectful parents, she was placed in the opera school of the Royal Theater in Stockholm at the age of nine. The theater became her true home, and she appeared in many leading roles during her teen years, including Agathe in Weber's *Der Freischütz* (with which she made her debut in 1838) and the title role in his *Euryanthe,* Julia in Spontini's *La vestale,* and the title roles in Donizetti's *Lucia di Lammermoor* and Bellini's *Norma.* By 24, she was a huge star in Stockholm, but in vocal distress and in need of serious retraining. She went to Paris to study with the great teacher Manuel García, and returned to Stockholm in 1842 with improved technique and in resplendent voice. She added several new roles to her repertoire, including Valentine in Meyerbeer's *Les Huguenots* and Amina in Bellini's *La sonnambula,* and began singing at houses in Germany and Austria. She made her London debut in 1847 with Queen Victoria and Prince Albert in attendance; later that year, still in London, she created the role of Amalia at the world premiere of Verdi's *I masnadieri.* She retired from the operatic stage in 1849, and embarked on a second, wildly successful career as a recitalist. Engaged by P. T. Barnum, she undertook a monumental tour of the United States, making her New York debut on September 11, 1850, and appearing in 95 concerts over the next ten months, for which she received a fee of $176,675.09, the equivalent of millions of dollars today (Barnum netted a whopping $535,486.25). Lind gave 35 concerts in New York alone, made 12 appearances in New Orleans, eight in Philadelphia, and seven in Boston, and sang in more than a dozen other American cities. In 1852 she married her accompanist, Otto Goldschmidt, a German pianist and composer; from 1856 until her death she lived in England. Lind continued to sing in concerts and oratorios for many years, and in 1883 she became a professor at the Royal Academy of Music. She was the first woman buried in Westminster Abbey.

Jenny Lind, the Swedish Nightingale

Much was written about Lind's supreme vocalism. Though her lower register was apt to sound weak and veiled, her upper register was rich and brilliant, and her breath control allowed her to spin out endless streams of a pure and nuanced legato sound often described as "otherworldly." Her command of fioritura was sophisticated and tasteful, and she had an incredible trill. These attributes enabled her to become one of the great exponents of the art of bel canto during its golden age. Lind also successfully brought high art into the popular culture of the day. As a singer and an artist, she impressed not only her adoring throngs but such serious and skeptical composers as Chopin, Schumann, and Mendelssohn.

***Linz* Symphony** **NICKNAME OF WOLFGANG AMADEUS MOZART'S SYMPHONY NO. 36 IN C, K. 425,** composed in Linz and first performed there on November 4, 1783. In the summer of 1783, nearly a year after he had married her, Mozart finally took his wife, Constanze, to Salzburg so that she could be introduced to his father. On their way back to Vienna following a three-month stay, the couple passed through Linz, where they were lavishly hosted by Johann Joseph Thun, a wealthy nobleman and the father of Franz Joseph Thun, one of Mozart's staunchest Viennese supporters. In a letter to his father dated October 31, 1783, Mozart reported that "old" Count Thun had arranged for him to give a concert there on November 4, "and as I haven't got a single symphony with me, I'm writing a new one at breakneck speed." The resultant work, the first of Mozart's symphonies to have a slow introduction, is a fashionably *galant* essay that almost, but not quite, hides the fact that it was written in four or five days. Here and there the seams *do* show, particularly in the uncharacteristic squareness of the phrase structure and the way the strings do nearly all the work, while wind and brass are relegated to an auxiliary role.

RECOMMENDED RECORDINGS

MARRINER AND ACADEMY OF ST. MARTIN-IN-THE-FIELDS (PHILIPS).

WALTER AND COLUMBIA SYMPHONY ORCHESTRA (SONY).

lion's roar *See box on pages 496–97.*

Lipatti, Dinu

(b. Bucharest, March 19, 1917; d. Geneva, December 2, 1950)

ROMANIAN PIANIST. He came from a musical family—his father was an outstanding violinist and his mother a capable pianist. He studied at the Bucharest Conservatory from 1928 to 1932. Following a second-place finish at the Vienna International Piano Competition in 1934, he was taken as a pupil by Alfred Cortot, who had been one of the jurors. While working with Cortot in Paris, Lipatti also studied composition with Paul Dukas and Nadia Boulanger. He waited until 1939 to play his first major Paris recital, and when France became involved in World War II he returned to Romania to work in relative isolation. He made his way to Switzerland in 1943, where he was diagnosed with a rare form of lymphatic cancer.

In 1946 Lipatti was signed by Walter Legge to a recording contract for the English Columbia label. For the next three years he was able to travel to London for studio sessions; in 1948 he was the soloist in the recording of the Schumann Piano Concerto that marked Herbert von Karajan's debut with the Philharmonia Orchestra. He was appointed professor at the Geneva Conservatory in 1949, but by 1950 he was gravely ill. Thanks to experimental cortisone treatments he rallied briefly in the summer of 1950 and was able to make a few more recordings in Geneva. That September, against his doctors' wishes, he traveled to France to play a final recital at the Besançon Festival, which produced a memorable recording.

Lipatti's playing was characterized by elegance, warmth of feeling, and a haunting restraint that could sparkle with flashes of virtuosity. An outstanding Chopin interpreter, he was also noted for his Schumann and Bach. Though some have disputed his claim to greatness, more than half a century after his death he retains a cult following, particularly in Europe.

RECOMMENDED RECORDINGS

BESANÇON RECITAL (MUSIC OF BACH, MOZART, AND CHOPIN) (EMI).

CHOPIN, WALTZES; *BARCAROLLE*, OP. 60 (WITH OTHER WORKS) (EMI).

SCHUMANN, PIANO CONCERTO: KARAJAN AND PHILHARMONIA ORCHESTRA (EMI).

Liszt, Franz

(b. Raiding, October 22, 1811; Bayreuth, July 31, 1886)

HUNGARIAN COMPOSER AND PIANIST. He was the greatest pianist of his age and one of the most important of the Romantic composers, a figure whose novel ideas of musical form were to have sweeping influence throughout the second half of the 19th century and into the modern era. His father was an official on the Esterházy estates in western Hungary, a capable cellist who had played in the court orchestra under Haydn and Beethoven. A prodigy, Franz studied in Vienna with Beethoven's most important student, Carl Czerny (the boy also played for Beethoven, took lessons from Salieri, and met Schubert). In 1823, Liszt was refused entry to the Paris Conservatoire because he was a foreigner, so he studied privately in the French capital with Antoine Reicha and Ferdinando Paër. With his father he toured England three times in three years (1824–27). His father's death in 1827 left the 16-year-old Franz as the family breadwinner, and forced him to teach.

Portrait of Liszt by Ingres, Rome, 1839

His rise to fame was rapid. Well read, sociable, endowed with a magnetic personality, burning intelligence, and compelling good looks, he was drawn to Paris, then the epicenter of Romanticism in music as well as literature and art. He formed friendships with the leading lights of the arts and letters: Lamartine, Heine, Balzac, de Musset, Chopin, Berlioz, Rossini, Delacroix, and Hugo, among many others. "What speaks most for Liszt," wrote Heine, "is the respect with which even his enemies recognize his personal merits. He is a man of unruly but noble character, not self-seeking and without falseness."

Liszt was introduced to the married Countess Marie d'Agoult in 1832; soon they were lovers, then parents. They would spend 12 years together, and Marie would bear Liszt three children. Her first pregnancy necessitated a move by the couple to Geneva to escape scandal, which marked the beginning of Liszt's "years of pilgrimage," 1835–39. In Paris in 1837 Liszt had a famous face-off against the great pianist Sigismond Thalberg, with no losers: Thalberg was hailed as the first pianist of the world and Liszt was declared unique. In Vienna in 1838 the unique pianist gave concerts for victims of Danube flooding in Hungary; he returned to his homeland the next year for the first time since his childhood. There he encountered native Gypsy music, an influence on his *Hungarian Rhapsodies,* in which he sought to re-create on the piano the sound and style of Gypsy orchestras.

Lizst on keyboard with* (from left to right) *Josef Krieheeber, Hector Berlioz, Karl Czerny, and Heinrich Ernst

During the 1840s Liszt toured Europe. He coined the term "recital" and was the first to turn the piano sideways so his profile (and flashing hands) could be admired by the audience. Liszt retired from public concertizing in 1847, at the age of 35. On his final tour he met Princess Carolyne von Sayn-Wittgenstein, and in 1848 the two settled in Weimar, where Liszt worked as Kapellmeister to Carl Alexander, the Grand Duke of Saxe-Weimar. They lived in a house called the Altenburg, surrounded by a circle of student acolytes known as the "Altenburg eagles" that included at one time or another Carl Tausig, Karl Klindworth, Peter Cornelius, Joachim Raff, and Hans von Bülow (who would marry Liszt's daughter Cosima in 1857). During his years in Weimar, Liszt concentrated on composition, and as the ducal Kapellmeister he regularly conducted his own and other composers' works, making extraordinary efforts on behalf of the music of

Beethoven, Berlioz, and Wagner. He presided over "Berlioz Weeks" in 1852 and 1855, and gave the world premiere of Wagner's *Lohengrin* in 1850.

In 1861 Liszt retired yet again, this time settling in Rome, where his planned marriage to Princess Carolyne was sidetracked on orders from the Vatican. By the end of the decade he had begun a triangular circuit between Weimar, Rome, and Budapest (where in 1875 he was made head of the newly created National Hungarian Royal Academy of Music, subsequently named for him). During his Weimar periods of residence, he taught master classes three times a week, encouraging another generation of students—including Moriz Rosenthal, Emil von Sauer, Rafael Joseffy, and Alexander Siloti—to polish their technique and deepen their interpretations. Over a period of nearly 60 years Liszt worked with perhaps as many as 400 students, and never charged any of them a penny. Liszt continued this tripartite existence to the end of his life, covering thousands of miles each year by rail and, as the spirit moved him, making additional trips to Paris, Vienna, and—to lend public support to Wagner's grandiose festival and be near Cosima, now married to Wagner—Bayreuth, where he died in 1886.

Liszt's output as a composer was voluminous and varied. He composed a vast amount of music for the piano: etudes, fantasias, and "reminiscences" of various popular operas; all sorts of character pieces; transcriptions of Schubert's songs, the nine Beethoven symphonies, and symphonic works by Berlioz; cycles like the *Harmonies poétiques et religieuses* and the *Années de pèlerinage*; and a single magnificent sonata. He penned 13 "symphonic poems" (a term and a genre he invented), of which the most frequently encountered is *LES PRÉLUDES*; two symphonies (the *FAUST* Symphony and the *Dante* Symphony), two piano concertos, and several other concerted works. In addition, he wrote close to 100 songs, a great deal of sacred music (including two oratorios), and some imposing music for organ, particularly the Fantasy and Fugue on "Ad nos, ad salutarem undam" (from Meyerbeer's) and the Prelude and Fugue on the name *B–A–C–H.*

If one looks at the Romantic period as the era of the soloist, of Prometheus unbound, then this handsome, energetic, generous, dazzling keyboard artist was its hero, and his piano music—in which he carried to breathtaking heights the process begun by Beethoven of treating the piano as an orchestra—its purest expression. Liszt pushed the frontiers of pianistic technique beyond all previous bounds, requiring unprecedented velocity *and* power from the performer. At the same time, he explored new regions of sonority and created entirely new kinds of keyboard imagery. The greatest of his piano works, the Sonata in B minor (1853), could well be said to be *the* work of the age: With

Franz Liszt, "hurling his lance into the future"

this vast, single-movement composition Liszt achieved a synthesis of symphonic and sonata form that has yet to be surpassed for cogency, scope, and imaginative range. In his late music for the piano, Liszt looked *beyond* his age, creating works that are impressionistic and austere, whose seemingly fragmentary nature anticipates the 20th century's love of aphorism, and whose chromaticism verges on atonality. The message of these pieces from the 1880s was not lost on Debussy and Schoenberg; they exemplify what Princess Carolyne meant when she described Liszt as "hurling his musical lance far into the future."

RECOMMENDED RECORDINGS

Années de pèlerinage: Jando (Naxos).

Faust Symphony: I. Fischer and Budapest Festival Orchestra (Philips).

Hungarian Rhapsodies: Cziffra (EMI).

Piano Concertos Nos. 1 and 2: Richter; Kondrashin and London Symphony Orchestra (Philips).

Les préludes: Karajan and Berlin Philharmonic (DG).

Sonata in B minor: Hough (Hyperion).

Selected piano works: Hough (Virgin Classics).

Litton, Andrew

(b. New York, May 16, 1959)

American conductor and pianist. He studied piano and conducting at the Juilliard School, where his teachers included Nadia Reisenberg and Sixten Ehrling. In 1982 he was tapped by Mstislav Rostropovich to serve as assistant (later associate) conductor of the National Symphony Orchestra in Washington, D.C. That same year he won the Rupert Foundation International Competition in Britain, which brought him a debut with the BBC Symphony Orchestra and led to a successful career in Great Britain, including his engagement as music director of the Bournemouth Symphony Orchestra (1988–94). He made his Metropolitan Opera debut in 1989 with Tchaikovsky's *Eugene Onegin,* gamely conducting the entire opera while suffering from a case of appendicitis that would require him to be hospitalized the next day. In 1994 he became music director of the Dallas Symphony Orchestra, a post he is due to relinquish at the end of the 2005–06 season. In 2005 he assumed the title of music director of the Bergen Philharmonic in Norway.

Litton's ebullient personality and keen musical instincts have catapulted him to the top rank of American conductors and filled his calendar with international guest-conducting engagements. At his best in music that calls either for sweeping Romanticism or a jaunty, rhythmically upbeat approach, he has made more than 60 recordings, among them impressive accounts of symphonies and orchestral works by Elgar, Walton, Rachmaninov, Tchaikovsky, and Shostakovich, and spirited renditions of music by Gershwin, Copland, and Bernstein, his birthright as an American. A spontaneous and unaffected performer, he remains a good enough pianist to be his own soloist in works such as Ravel's G major concerto and Gershwin's *Rhapsody in Blue.*

RECOMMENDED RECORDINGS

Gershwin, *Rhapsody in Blue*; *American in Paris* (with works by Copland, Grofé, and Sousa): Dallas Symphony Orchestra (Delos).

Rachmaninov, piano concertos: Hough; Dallas Symphony Orchestra (Hyperion).

Walton, *Belshazzar's Feast*: Terfel; Bournemouth Symphony Orchestra (Decca).

Lohengrin **"Romantic" opera in three acts by Richard Wagner,** to his own libretto, premiered August 28, 1850, at the Court Theater in Weimar, Franz Liszt conducting. The setting is Antwerp in the first half of the tenth century. The opera's central characters are Lohengrin, a mysterious knight from a "distant land" who appears,

Plácido Domingo and Anna Tomowa-Sintow in **Lohengrin** *at the Met, 1984*

as if by magic, on a boat drawn by a swan; the gentle Elsa of Brabant, who stands falsely accused of murdering Gottfried, her younger brother, and whom Lohengrin champions and marries on the condition that she never ask his name or origin; and the black-hearted Telramund and his sorceress wife, Ortrud (who, unbeknownst to the others, has cast a spell on Gottfried). Ortrud and Telramund attempt to undo Elsa by sowing doubts in her mind about Lohengrin; she eventually gives in to those doubts and asks Lohengrin the forbidden question. In the opera's climactic final scene, Lohengrin, having identified himself as a Knight of the Holy Grail and the son of its guardian Parsifal, undoes Ortrud's sorcery and restores Gottfried to life, proclaiming him Duke of Brabant, before departing forever. As he disappears from view, Elsa falls lifeless.

Lohengrin marks a turning point in Wagner's development, a decisive step away from the conventions of grand opera toward the continuous music drama of *Tristan und Isolde* and the *Ring*. Set pieces and numbers are abandoned as such, and the action unfolds more or less continuously in lengthy scenes with powerful, dramatic climaxes based on confrontations between the central characters. Wagner builds the opera to a potent climax in which good triumphs, without the protagonists' living happily ever after. His music for the final scene, prefigured in the opera's luminous orchestral prelude ◉, is richly Romantic and has an emotive power new to the operatic sphere.

RECOMMENDED RECORDINGS

Domingo, Norman, Nimsgern, Randová; Solti and Vienna Philharmonic (Decca).

Preludes to Acts I and III: Karajan and Berlin Philharmonic (EMI).

Thomas, Grümmer, Ludwig, Fischer-Dieskau; Kempe and Vienna Philharmonic (EMI).

London, George

(b. Montreal, May 30, 1920; d. Armonk, N.Y., March 24, 1985)

Canadian-born bass-baritone whose powerfully theatrical interpretations of such roles as Wotan, Amfortas, Boris Godunov, Scarpia, Figaro, Don Giovanni, Amonasro, and Escamillo established him as one of the preeminent singers of his generation. His family moved to Los Angeles when he was 15 and he made his operatic debut there in 1941. After further studies he joined Frances Yeend and Mario Lanza for two seasons as a member of the Bel Canto Trio. His breakthrough came in 1949, when he appeared at the Vienna Staatsoper as Amonasro in Verdi's *Aida*. He subsequently became a regular at the Bayreuth Festival, starting out in 1951 with the role of Amfortas in Wagner's *Parsifal* (under Hans Knappertsbusch), and eventually stepping into the title role of Wagner's *Der fliegende Holländer.* On November 13, 1951, he made his Metropolitan Opera debut, again as Amonasro; he remained on the company's roster for 15 seasons, singing 19 roles plus the four villains in Offenbach's *Les contes d'Hoffmann.* Among his most notable roles at the Met were the title roles of Mozart's *Don Giovanni* and Wagner's *Der fliegende Holländer,* as well as Almaviva in Mozart's *Le nozze di Figaro* and Scarpia in Puccini's *Tosca.*

In 1960 London became the first non-Russian to perform the role of Boris Godunov at the Bolshoi Theatre. He had barely entered his vocal prime when paralysis of the larynx abruptly ended his singing career. He became artistic director of the Kennedy Center in 1968 and was named general director of the Washington Opera in 1975. In 1977 a massive coronary ended this second phase of his career. His arrestingly powerful voice is well documented on recordings, and archival films and videos testify to his extraordinary skills as an actor.

RECOMMENDED RECORDINGS

MOZART, *DON GIOVANNI*: DELLA CASA, JURINAC, SEEFRIED; BÖHM AND VIENNA PHILHARMONIC (RCA).

WAGNER, *DER FLIEGENDE HOLLÄNDER* (SELECTIONS): RYSANEK, TOZZI; DORATI AND ROYAL OPERA (DECCA).

London Philharmonic Orchestra ENGLISH ENSEMBLE FOUNDED IN 1932 BY SIR THOMAS BEECHAM. For its debut concert, on October 7, 1932, Beecham prepared with no fewer than 12 rehearsals; the program—Berlioz's *Roman Carnival* Overture, Mozart's *Prague* Symphony, Delius's *Brigg Fair,* and Richard Strauss's *Ein Heldenleben*—was carefully chosen to show the orchestra's versatility and virtuosity. Under Beecham's leadership the LPO toured and recorded the works of Borodin, Delius, Mozart, Sibelius, and many more, and soon came to be regarded as one of the finest orchestras in Europe. With Beecham absent during the war years, the orchestra became a self-governing body; Beecham's association with it ended when he formed the Royal Philharmonic in 1946. Sir Adrian Boult was tapped as the orchestra's permanent conductor in 1950. Under his baton the orchestra made splendid recordings of the music of Elgar, Vaughan Williams, and Holst, among others, and resumed extensive international touring; in 1956 it became the first British orchestra to perform in the Soviet Union. In 1964 the London Philharmonic became the resident orchestra of the Glyndebourne Festival, and later it was the first Western orchestra to play in China. Its principal conductors have included William Steinberg, John Pritchard, Bernard Haitink, Sir Georg Solti, Klaus Tennstedt, Roger Norrington, Franz Welser-Möst, and, since 2000, Kurt Masur. In 1992 the LPO became resident orchestra of the Royal Festival Hall at London's South Bank Centre.

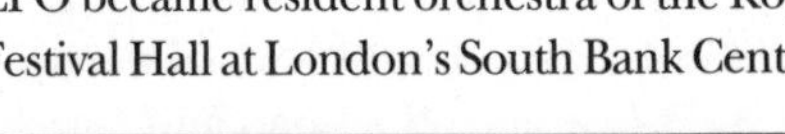

RECOMMENDED RECORDINGS

ELGAR, SYMPHONIES NOS. 1 AND 2: SOLTI (DECCA).

ELGAR, VIOLIN CONCERTO; HAENDEL; BOULT (TESTAMENT).

HOLST, *THE PLANETS*: BOULT (EMI).

MUSIC OF DELIUS: BEECHAM (NAXOS).

MUSIC OF VAUGHAN WILLIAMS: HANDLEY (CFP).

VAUGHAN WILLIAMS, SYMPHONIES: BOULT (EMI).

***London* Symphonies** GENERIC TERM FOR JOSEPH HAYDN'S LAST 12 SYMPHONIES (Nos. 93–104), commissioned by the London-based impresario Johann Peter Salomon, and composed between 1791 and 1795. They are considered the composer's supreme achievements in the form, a compendium of late-18th-century symphonic thought embracing the full range of style and topic found in the music of the Classical period.

The first six *London* Symphonies (Nos. 93–98) received their premieres in 1791 and 1792; the final six (Nos. 99–104) were premiered in 1794 and 1795.

Symphony No. 104 in D, the last of the group and a particularly splendid work, has long individually borne the title *London* as a tribute to its pride of place within the group. It begins with a weighty, austere introduction in the style of a French overture, with pathetic accents in the violins and not a hint of the major mode. That has to wait for the arrival of the Allegro, which dispels the clouds in a gentle instant. Haydn proceeds joyously to working out a tune that ingeniously combines an affectionate lyricism with the vitality of the march. The stormy development is of an unparalleled contrapuntal brilliance, but Haydn, never one to take himself too seriously, allows moments of utter innocence to leaven the music lesson. The theme of the Andante picks up the dotted rhythm from the symphony's slow introduction; here the element of fantasy is strong, and, as in the first movement, the variety of treatment to which the material is subjected seems extraordinary even for Haydn. The minuet is a brilliant country dance with a hint of the hurdy-gurdy, the trio a witty affair in which winds and strings play with a modest two-note motif while spinning out a little "specious" counterpoint. The sonata-form finale opens with a Croatian folk tune over a musette-style drone bass. Throughout the movement, the drone effect provides a sonorous anchor for Haydn's exuberant treatment of this subject, while the madrigal-like second subject allows both breathing room and a few forays into unexpected harmonic territory. The joyous conclusion blends the two main ideas into a heady affirmation of D major.

RECOMMENDED RECORDINGS

COMPLETE: DAVIS AND CONCERTGEBOUW ORCHESTRA (PHILIPS).

COMPLETE: JOCHUM AND LONDON PHILHARMONIC ORCHESTRA (DG).

London Symphony, A **TITLE GIVEN BY RALPH VAUGHAN WILLIAMS TO HIS SYMPHONY NO. 2,** composed 1911–13, and premiered March 27, 1914. Vaughan Williams's original aim was to compose a symphonic poem on the subject of London, but his friend and fellow composer George Butterworth suggested that he instead fashion a true four-movement symphony out of the material. In the summer of 1914, shortly after the symphony's premiere, Vaughan Williams sent the only copy of the full score off to Germany at the request of Fritz Busch, who was interested in conducting the symphony there. A few weeks later World War I broke out, and the manuscript was lost in the mails. It was only through the efforts of several of the composer's close friends—including Butterworth and the musicologist Edward J. Dent, who teamed up to reconstruct the score from the orchestral parts—that the work survived. Vaughan Williams revised the score substantially in 1918 (excising almost 20 minutes of music, much of it

Piccadilly Circus at the time of Ralph Vaughan Williams's **A London Symphony**

quite exotic and colorful), and made smaller revisions in 1920 and 1933. Upon its publication he dedicated the symphony to Butterworth, who had been killed during the war. Despite quotations of the Westminster chimes in the first and last movements, there is no actual program to *A London Symphony*; it is impressionistic, seeking to convey something of the energy and the now wistful, now bracingly extrovert character of London, rather than any specific images. The score confirmed Vaughan Williams's greatness as an orchestral composer and revealed for the first time his remarkable gift for investing deeply personal, even visionary expression in conventional forms.

RECOMMENDED RECORDINGS

FINAL VERSION: BOULT AND LONDON PHILHARMONIC ORCHESTRA (EMI).

ORIGINAL VERSION: HICKOX AND LONDON SYMPHONY ORCHESTRA (CHANDOS).

London Symphony Orchestra ENGLISH ENSEMBLE FORMED IN **1904** by disaffected members of the Queen's Hall Orchestra. It was initially set up as a "commonwealth," owned and operated by the musician members, who took responsibility for organizing their own season of concerts and engaging conductors, beginning with Hans Richter. In 1911 Arthur Nikisch was engaged as principal conductor and led the LSO on a European tour. The orchestra has always championed Britain's leading composers, and in its early years developed a special relationship with Sir Edward Elgar, a frequent guest conductor. Faced with complacency in its ranks and new competition after the founding of the BBC Symphony Orchestra in 1930 and Sir Thomas Beecham's organization of the London Philharmonic Orchestra in 1932, the LSO lost some of its luster. But it endured, weathering even stiffer postwar competition from the newly founded Royal Philharmonic and Philharmonia Orchestras. During the 1960s, it regained its reputation as the top London orchestra and one of the premier ensembles in Europe. Principal conductors since 1960 have included Pierre Monteux, István Kertész, André Previn, Michael Tilson Thomas, Claudio Abbado, and Sir Colin Davis, the incumbent since 1995. In 2007, Valery Gergiev will assume the mantle. Although it has always attracted excellent players and engaged in prestigious tours and residencies, the orchestra did not have a permanent home until 1982, when it took up residency at the Barbican Centre; the center's hall, refurbished in 2001, is now considered London's finest concert venue. One of the most widely recorded orchestras in the world, the LSO has contributed some spectacularly successful efforts to the discography, including cycles devoted to the symphonic works of Berlioz and Sibelius (with Davis) and Dvořák (with Kertész), as well as many distinguished recordings of the music of Elgar, Holst, Vaughan Williams, Walton, and Britten. Its myriad film credits include the *Star Wars* movies. Since 2000, it has operated its own recording label, LSO Live.

The London Symphony Orchestra in Royal Festival Hall

RECOMMENDED RECORDINGS

Britten, *Sinfonia da Requiem*; Holst, *Egdon Heath*: Previn (EMI).

Britten, *War Requiem*: Vishnevskaya, Pears, Fischer-Dieskau; Britten (Decca).

Dvořák, Symphonies: Kertész (Decca).

Elgar, Cello Concerto, *Sea Pictures*: Du Pré, Baker; Barbirolli (EMI).

Music of Berlioz: Davis (Philips).

Music of Sibelius: Davis (RCA).

Walton, Symphony No. 1: Previn (RCA).

Long, Marguerite

(b. Nîmes, November 13, 1874; d. Paris, February 13, 1966)

FRENCH PIANIST. She studied at the Paris Conservatoire, winning first prize in piano in 1891. Fauré praised her playing of Franck's *Variations symphoniques* in 1903 and later dedicated his Fourth Impromptu (1906) to her. She reciprocated by championing his music all her life, and by recording his Ballade, Op. 19. From 1906 to 1940 she served as a professor at the Paris Conservatoire, where her students included Samson François, Jacques Février, and Nicole Henriot-Schweitzer. Long was married to the musicologist 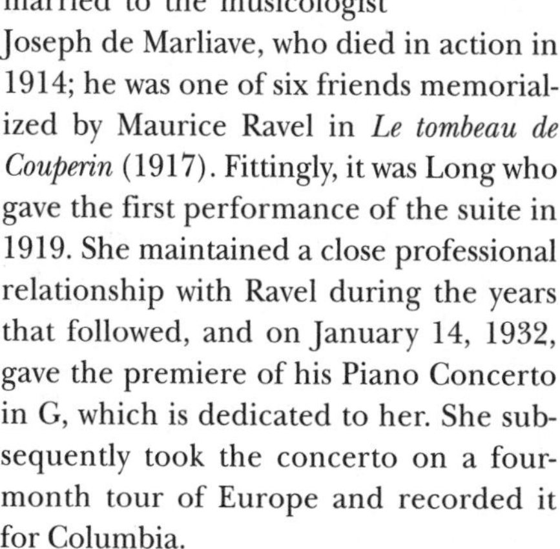Joseph de Marliave, who died in action in 1914; he was one of six friends memorialized by Maurice Ravel in *Le tombeau de Couperin* (1917). Fittingly, it was Long who gave the first performance of the suite in 1919. She maintained a close professional relationship with Ravel during the years that followed, and on January 14, 1932, gave the premiere of his Piano Concerto in G, which is dedicated to her. She subsequently took the concerto on a four-month tour of Europe and recorded it for Columbia.

RECOMMENDED RECORDINGS

Ravel, Piano Concerto in G: Ravel and Lamoureux Orchestra (Pearl).

Music of Debussy and Fauré (including Ballade, Op. 19) (Pearl).

Los Angeles, Victoria de

(b. Barcelona, November 1, 1923; d. Barcelona, January 15, 2005)

SPANISH LYRIC SOPRANO. She studied piano and guitar, as well as voice, at the Barcelona Conservatory, and made her debut in Barcelona in 1941 as Mimì in Puccini's *La bohème.* After World War II she rapidly became an international star, singing for the first time at Covent Garden in 1950 and making her Metropolitan Opera debut in 1951 as Marguerite in Gounod's *Faust.* Although best known for her exquisite work in the French and Italian repertoire, she was also a notable Wagnerian whose credits included Eva in *Die Meistersinger von Nürnberg* and Elsa in *Lohengrin,* as well as Elisabeth in the Bayreuth production of *Tannhäuser* in 1961 and 1962. She remained active as a recitalist through the 1970s. No singer of the 20th century could bring out the 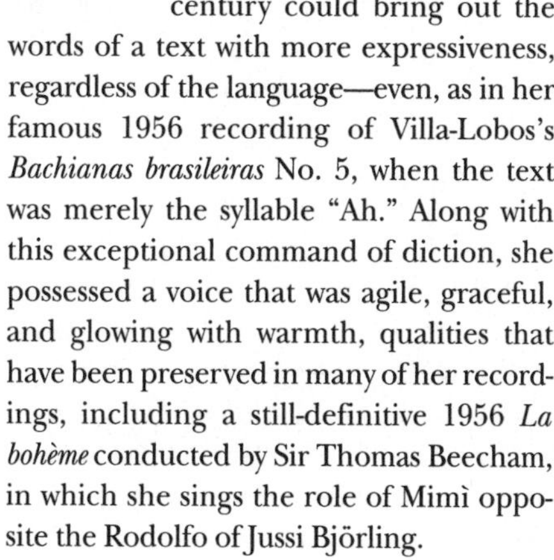words of a text with more expressiveness, regardless of the language—even, as in her famous 1956 recording of Villa-Lobos's *Bachianas brasileiras* No. 5, when the text was merely the syllable "Ah." Along with this exceptional command of diction, she possessed a voice that was agile, graceful, and glowing with warmth, qualities that have been preserved in many of her recordings, including a still-definitive 1956 *La bohème* conducted by Sir Thomas Beecham, in which she sings the role of Mimì opposite the Rodolfo of Jussi Björling.

Victoria de Los Angeles

RECOMMENDED RECORDINGS

PUCCINI, *LA BOHÈME:* BJÖRLING, MERRILL, AMARA; BEECHAM AND RCA VICTOR SYMPHONY (EMI).

VILLA-LOBOS, *BACHIANAS BRASILEIRAS* (NO. 5): VILLA-LOBOS AND ORCHESTRA NATIONAL DE LA RADIODIFFUSION FRANÇAISE (ANGEL).

Love for Three Oranges, The OPERA IN A PROLOGUE AND FOUR ACTS BY SERGEY PROKOFIEV, to his own libretto (in Russian) based on Carlo Gozzi's 1761 comedy *L'amore delle tre melarance.* Composed in New York in 1919, the work was premiered in Chicago on December 30, 1921, as *L'amour des trois oranges* (in a French translation by the composer and Vera Janacopoulos), with the composer conducting. Prokofiev's raucous, hyperactive music perfectly complements the burlesque absurdity of Gozzi's story, which concerns a Prince who is cursed with a consuming passion for three oranges and who keeps running afoul of characters from the commedia dell'arte. The score wears the influence of Rimsky-Korsakov and Stravinsky (especially *Petrushka*) at a rather rakish angle, and includes a cheeky little march that has become one of the best known of all Prokofiev's creations.

RECOMMENDED RECORDING

DIADKOVA, MOROZOV; GERGIEV AND KIROV OPERA (PHILIPS).

Lucerne Festival, The *See box on pages 46–47.*

Lucia di Lammermoor OPERA IN THREE ACTS BY GAETANO DONIZETTI, to a libretto by Salvatore Cammarano (based on Walter Scott's novel *The Bride of Lammermoor*), premiered at the Teatro San Carlo in Naples on September 26, 1835. The plot is a typically gothic affair involving a family feud, an arranged marriage, a forged letter, betrayal, murder, and madness; Cammarano's libretto skillfully pares away the novel's excess detail to create a taut line of action. The score, one of Donizetti's strongest, stands at the crossroads between the decorative style of bel canto, then on its way out, and the more direct, sensational, and melodramatic manner soon to find its greatest exponent in Verdi. With its memorable characterization of Scott's unhinged heroine, climaxed by one of the great mad scenes in opera ◉, *Lucia* firmly established Donizetti's reputation and served as one of the cornerstones of Italian Romanticism.

RECOMMENDED RECORDING

SUTHERLAND, PAVAROTTI, MILNES, GHIAUROV; BONYNGE AND ROYAL OPERA (DECCA).

Ludwig, Christa

(b. Berlin, March 16, 1928)

GERMAN MEZZO-SOPRANO. During a career that lasted nearly 50 years, she established herself as one of the finest mezzos of the 20th century. The daughter of two professional singers, she made her debut in 1946 at the Frankfurt Opera, as Orlovsky in Johann Strauss Jr.'s *Die Fledermaus.* She sang in Frankfurt until 1952, moving on to engagements in Hanover and Darmstadt. In 1955, the year its bombed-out house on the Ringstrasse reopened, the Vienna Staatsoper signed her to its roster; she remained with the company for more than 30 years. She made her American debut in Chicago in 1959, as Dorabella in Mozart's *Così fan tutte,* and her Covent Garden debut in 1968, as Amneris in Verdi's *Aida.* Audiences at the Metropolitan Opera first heard her on December 10, 1959, as Cherubino in Mozart's *Le nozze di Figaro*—the beginning of a love affair that lasted through her final Met performance in 1990.

***Christa Ludwig as Octavian in Strauss's* Der Rosenkavalier**

In 1966, at Bayreuth, she sang the role of Brangäne, opposite the Isolde of Birgit Nilsson, in a series of incandescent performances of Wagner's *Tristan und Isolde* conducted by Karl Böhm. The following summer she returned to Bayreuth as Kundry in Wagner's *Parsifal.* During the course of her career, she also sang at Hamburg, San Francisco, Munich, La Scala, and the Paris Opéra. She made her farewell appearance in Vienna in 1994, as Klytämnestra in Richard Strauss's *Elektra.*

Ludwig's repertoire centered on Mozart, Wagner, and Richard Strauss—particularly the roles of Octavian in *Der Rosenkavalier,* Brangäne in *Tristan und Isolde,* Kundry in *Parsifal,* and the Dyer's Wife in *Die Frau ohne Schatten.* In later years she was a sensational Waltraute in the Met's highly naturalistic staging of Wagner's *Götterdämmerung,* and her forays into less familiar repertoire included the roles of Judit in Bartók's *Bluebeard's Castle* and Didon in Berlioz's *Les Troyens.* Over the years she collaborated with a distinguished array of conductors, including Böhm, Otto Klemperer, Herbert von Karajan, Leonard Bernstein, and James Levine. She was a noted lieder singer and concert artist as well. Ludwig possessed a voice of exquisite richness and, when needed, breathtaking amplitude. She had the ability to impart dramatic urgency to a performance, the hallmark of a great singer. She was married to the Austrian bass-baritone Walter Berry from 1957 to 1971.

RECOMMENDED RECORDINGS

BEETHOVEN, *FIDELIO*: VICKERS, FRICK; KLEMPERER AND PHILHARMONIA ORCHESTRA (EMI).

MAHLER, *RÜCKERT-LIEDER*: KARAJAN AND BERLIN PHILHARMONIC (DG).

STRAUSS, *DER ROSENKAVALIER*: SCHWARZKOPF, STICH-RANDALL, EDELMANN; KARAJAN AND PHILHARMONIA ORCHESTRA (EMI).

WAGNER, *TRISTAN UND ISOLDE*: NILSSON, WINDGASSEN; BÖHM AND BAYREUTH FESTIVAL ORCHESTRA (DG).

Luisa Miller OPERA IN THREE ACTS BY GIUSEPPE VERDI, to a libretto by Salvatore Cammarano (based on Friedrich von Schiller's *Kabale und Liebe*), premiered at the Teatro San Carlo in Naples on December 8, 1849. With its potent climaxes, beefed-up sonority, and dramatic toughness, Verdi's score exhibits an indebtedness to Donizetti, while pointing the way toward the even more powerful and energetic manner of *Il trovatore.*

RECOMMENDED RECORDING

CABALLÉ, PAVAROTTI, MILNES; MAAG AND NATIONAL PHILHARMONIC ORCHESTRA (DECCA).

Lully, Jean-Baptiste [Lulli, Giovanni Battista]

(b. Florence, November 29, 1632; d. Paris, March 22, 1687)

ITALIAN/FRENCH COMPOSER. His works played a dominant role in establishing many of the stylistic conventions of the French Baroque and of *tragédie lyrique,* including the five-part division of orchestral strings (violins, three sizes of viola, and basses) and the use of the French overture and accompanied recitative.

His father, of peasant stock, married a miller's daughter and took over the business. The boy probably received his musical education from Franciscan friars in Florence, learning to play the guitar and violin. He left Italy for Paris in 1646 to serve as an Italian tutor to Anne-Marie-Louise d'Orléans, a cousin of Louis XIV. While working in that capacity he completed his musical education, studying harpsichord and composition, and became an accomplished dancer. He entered the service of Louis XIV in 1652, when the Sun King was 14 years old. In 1653 the king appointed him composer of instrumental music, and from that post he began a steady ascent to the top of French musical life, receiving the title of superintendent of the king's chamber music in 1661. His work as a violinist and orchestra leader won him a sterling reputation, which grew even more lustrous as a result of his collaboration with the playwright Molière on a series of *comédie-ballets* beginning in 1664. (When Molière pocketed a disproportionate share of the proceeds from their joint ventures, the relationship cooled.)

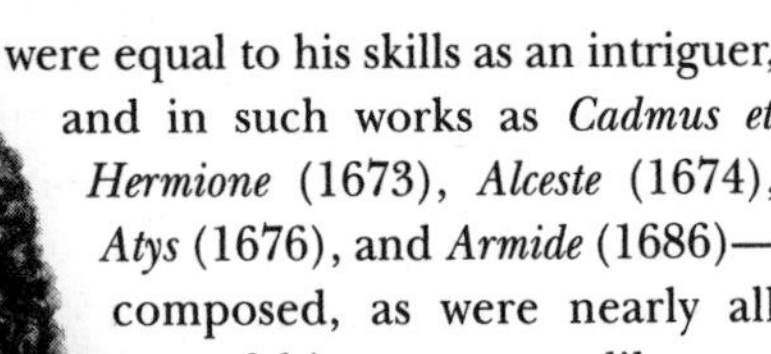

Jean-Baptiste Lully

Lully professed to be unperturbed when, in 1669, the librettist Pierre Perrin was granted letters patent by the king to form an opera company. In due course Perrin and some perfidious business associates produced *Pomone* (1671), to music by Robert Cambert; the first French opera and the first opera of any kind to be publicly performed in France, it was an overnight success. Sensing the profit that awaited him—and taking advantage of the scandal that ensued when Perrin's partners failed to pay those who had created *Pomone*—Lully in 1672 persuaded the king to withdraw the monopoly from Perrin and award it to him. With this coup, Lully put himself firmly in control of opera in France. Fortunately, his gifts as a musician were equal to his skills as an intriguer, and in such works as *Cadmus et Hermione* (1673), *Alceste* (1674), *Atys* (1676), and *Armide* (1686)—composed, as were nearly all of his operas, to librettos by Philippe Quinault—he achieved an extremely elegant yet lively fusion of ballet, choral music, and solo singing highlighted by richly varied airs and duets, expressively charged recitatives, and vibrant orchestral colorism. Lully died a wealthy man, able to command the highest ticket prices in Paris for the splendid entertainments he put on.

The broad plan of Lullian opera—a prologue and five acts, each with its own set, a divertissement with chorus and dance, and special effects (with the fantastic a necessary element of the conception)—would remain the model for serious opera in France for almost a century, all the way up to Gluck. His style would be emulated in the *opéra-ballets* of André Campra (1660–1744) and the *tragédies* of Jean-Philippe Rameau, and his colorful use of the orchestra would influence composers from Purcell to Vivaldi to Bach and Telemann. In addition to his many works for the stage

Scene from Lully's* Alceste*, staged at Versailles, 1674

(16 *tragédies* and several dozen ballets), Lully composed a small but significant body of sacred choral works for double choir with orchestral accompaniment, intended for use at the royal chapel.

When conducting his music Lully was accustomed to using a pointed ballet master's cane to beat time on the floor. In the winter of 1686–87, during a performance of his Te Deum (1677) at a Parisian church, Lully accidentally jabbed his foot with the cane. The wound became infected, gangrene set in and eventually spread to his leg, and he died three months later.

Ambitious and fiercely competitive, Lully remained a brutish figure all his life. In the high-stakes cultural politics at the court of Louis XIV he brought not only a powerful personality but an equally powerful artistic vision to bear. He transformed French music in the 17th century, assimilating its speech-derived rhythms and cadences and introducing an Italian lightness and grace along with a novel sense of animation and color. His music, with its appealing lyricism and quick-hitting emotive power, was revolutionary long before the Revolution.

RECOMMENDED RECORDINGS

Atys: De Mey, Mellon, Laurens; Christie and Les Arts Florissants (harmonia mundi).

Motets: Nicquet and Concert Spirituel (Naxos).

Lulu **Opera in three acts by Alban Berg** to his own libretto, based on the plays *Erdgeist* (*Earth Spirit*) and *Die Büchse der Pandora* (*Pandora's Box*) by Frank Wedekind, composed 1929–35. At the end of 1935, when Berg died, the first two acts of the opera were fully scored. The concluding act, the crux of the work from a dramatic standpoint, lay virtually complete on Berg's desk, awaiting orchestration of some 600–700 measures already sketched, and the fresh composition of another 80–90. Yet this final act was suppressed for almost 40 years by Berg's widow, Helene, who eventually took steps to see that the sketches were locked away. In 1963 the American composer George Perle (b. 1915) was granted access to the sketches for a period of two weeks, sufficient for him to realize that *Lulu*'s all but complete third act was not only performable, but essential to the musical and dramatic integrity of the opera. Some years later the Austrian composer Friedrich Čerha (b. 1926), who had also studied the sketches, was secretly contracted by Berg's publisher, Universal Edition, to finish the scoring of Act III. Nevertheless, the completed opera could not be staged until after Helene Berg's death in 1976.

Lulu is the first 12-TONE opera, a devastating psychological portrait of lust, destructiveness, and moral and spiritual decay. Its prologue introduces the principal characters as if they were beasts in a menagerie—each one is endowed with the characteristics of a particular animal, which will emerge during the course of the work. The character of Lulu is one of the most remarkable in all of opera. She is the snake, a sexual predator compulsively seducing men, crushing them with the force of her need, consuming and extinguishing them without even being aware of what she is doing. She finds herself married to three husbands in succession: the Professor of Medicine, the Painter, and Dr. Schön, an editor in chief. She destroys them all, sinking lower each time. In the closing scene of the third act, set in the London brothel where Lulu now works, her three dead husbands return in alter egos—the Professor of Medicine as a professor (a silent role), the Painter as a Negro, and Dr. Schön as Jack the Ripper—to debase and finally destroy her. This chilling denouement completes the opera's fearful symmetry. The squalor and despair of Lulu's situation finally humanizes her, and Berg's powerful, enveloping music compels the listener to pity her horrible end.

The cast is rounded out by three other main characters: Alwa, Dr. Schön's son, who is in love with Lulu; the lesbian Countess Geschwitz, also in love with Lulu; and Schigolch, a distasteful old lecher who in some strange way may also be in love with Lulu. By the end of the opera, only Schigolch is left alive. Alwa has been beaten to death by the Negro, and Geschwitz lies dying of a stab wound from Jack the Ripper, singing of her love for Lulu.

Acts I and II of *Lulu* were premiered June 2, 1937, at the Stadttheater in Zurich; the American premiere took place at the Santa Fe Opera in 1963. The three-act version of the opera was premiered at the Paris Opéra on February 24, 1979, with Teresa Stratas in the title role and Pierre Boulez conducting. The Santa Fe Opera gave the American premiere of the three-act version of *Lulu* in July 1979 under the baton of Michael Tilson Thomas.

RECOMMENDED RECORDING

STRATAS, MINTON, SCHWARZ, MAZURA; BOULEZ AND PARIS OPERA (DG).

Lupu, Radu

(b. Galati, November 30, 1945)

ROMANIAN PIANIST. Beginning his study of the piano when he was six, he made his debut (in a program of his own works) at the age of 12. In 1963 he was awarded a scholarship to study at the Moscow Conservatory, where his teachers included Galina Eghyazarova and Heinrich Neuhaus. While still a student he won two major competitions, the 1966 Van Cliburn and the 1967 Enescu International. He finished his studies in 1969; that same year he won the Leeds International Piano Competition and made his London recital debut. His first major American engagements came in 1972, with the Cleveland Orchestra and the Chicago Symphony Orchestra. Since the late 1970s he has repeatedly appeared as a soloist with major European and American orchestras and in recitals around the world.

A probing artist with a versatile technique, Lupu is capable of producing a ravishing tone and an almost infinite variety of coloration. He exhibits profound interpretive insights and has the ability to inhabit the music in a way that deeply involves his audience; he has often been described as a poet, yet his accounts never lack grip. As a soloist with orchestra he is noted for his readings of concertos of Mozart and Beethoven. In recital, he is especially compelling in Schubert, Schumann, and late Brahms, where he can be as impassioned as he is tender and delicate, as called for. He has a limpid touch and can produce tones of crystalline clarity. But he is also able to generate a powerful sonority in works such as the Liszt sonata, which he unfolds with a visionary intensity.

RECOMMENDED RECORDINGS

BRAHMS, PIANO PIECES (DECCA).

FRANCK AND DEBUSSY, VIOLIN SONATAS: CHUNG (DECCA).

SCHUBERT, IMPROMPTUS (DECCA).

SCHUMANN, *KREISLERIANA, KINDERSZENEN* (DECCA).

Radu Lupu, poet of the piano

lute Family of fretted string instruments in various sizes, having these general characteristics: a rounded, pear-shaped back made up of separate ribs of thin wood; a flat belly with an ornately carved soundhole (called a *rose*) in the middle and a bridge near the base; a pegbox bent at nearly a right angle toward the back; and strings arranged in pairs (referred to as *courses*). The Western lute is derived from the archaic Arabian instrument known as the *ud,* whose name means "wood." Early lutes (the instrument was well established in Europe by about 1350) had four courses; by about 1500, six-course lutes were the standard, and the number of courses continued to increase as time went by, reaching 13 in some late-17th-century German lutes. To notate music for the lute, a system of tablature was developed in the second half of the 15th century.

The lute was the preeminent "gentleman's" (and sometimes "lady's") instrument of the 16th through the early 18th century, suitable to accompany oneself in song or to be played solo. The Italians Joan Ambrosio Dalza (fl. 1508), Francesco Spinacino (fl. 1507), Vincenzo Capirola (1474–1548), and above all Francesco Canova da Milano (1497–1543) were important figures in the development of playing style and repertoire of the lute during the first half of the 16th century. Later masters included Vincenzo Galilei (ca. 1530–91; father of the astronomer Galileo) and Alfonso Ferrabosco (1543–88; active in England 1562–78). John Dowland, the leading English lutenist of the early 17th century, contributed richly to the instrument's repertoire. A significant body of work for the fuller-sounding Baroque lute was developed mainly by French composers, including Denis Gaultier (ca. 1600–72) and Robert de Visée (ca. 1655–1732), and by the German Silvius Leopold Weiss (1686–1750).

A lute at rest, and in a lady's embrace

RECOMMENDED RECORDINGS

"Baroque Lute" (Weiss, Bach, Vivaldi): North (Linn).

Dowland, lute music: O'Dette (harmonia mundi).

Early 16th-century lute music: O'Dette (harmonia mundi).

"Rosa" (Elizabethan lute music): Wilson (Virgin Classics).

Lutosławski, Witold

(b. Warsaw, January 25, 1913; d. Warsaw, February 7, 1994)

Polish composer. He experimented with aleatoric and improvisatory techniques aimed at freeing the performer from the literal execution of a fixed sequence of notes. Yet even in works where he permitted a certain freedom of performance, he always maintained firm control of the composition's harmonic structure and formal outline, developing several very personal, identifiable idioms.

Lutosławski inherited his musical talent from his father, a politically active member of the Polish landed gentry who was

Witold Lutosławski, making a point

executed by the Bolsheviks in 1918. He received piano lessons from the age of six, and took up the violin when he was 13. He spent a year at the Warsaw Conservatory as a part-time student (1927–28) and entered the University of Warsaw as a math major in 1931. The following year he enrolled at the Conservatory as a composition student, and in 1933 he dropped out of the university in order to pursue his musical training full time; he received a degree in piano in 1936 and one in composition in 1937.

In the summer of 1939, shortly after finishing a year of compulsory military service, Lutosławski was ordered back into uniform as an officer cadet in the signal corps; captured by the Germans, he escaped after eight days and made his way to Warsaw, where he supported himself for the duration as a café pianist, even forming a piano duet with his countryman and fellow composer Andrzej Panufnik (1914–91). It was for this wartime partnership with Panufnik that Lutosławski wrote the earliest of his pieces to earn a place in the repertoire, the *Variations on a Theme by Paganini* (1941) for two pianos, based on the same A minor caprice that had previously inspired Schumann, Liszt, Brahms, and Rachmaninov. Only a handful of Lutosławski's other early works survived the destruction of Warsaw in 1944–45.

Following the war, Lutosławski completed his Symphony No. 1 (1947) and served briefly as music director of Polish Radio. After the Communist takeover in 1948 his music was branded as "formalist," and for a while he had to keep his more experimental harmonic ideas to himself. He had already begun to explore the use of folk material in some of the pieces he was writing for Polish Radio and for the new state publishing house, and with his *Concerto for Orchestra* (1950–54) he successfully incorporated folk elements in a major concert work. Commissioned by conductor Witold Rowicki, the *Concerto for Orchestra* ◉ secured Lutosławski's reputation in Poland while simultaneously offering a bold riposte to the concept of "socialist realism" then being bandied about by the Communists, since it was a work that reveled in "form" (its finale, for example, begins with a passacaglia) but was in no sense academic. With his *Musique funèbre* (*Funeral Music*) for strings, completed in 1958 and dedicated to the memory of Bartók, Lutosławski established himself on the international scene. His stature was confirmed by the 1961 premiere of *Jeux vénitiens* (*Venetian Games*) for chamber orchestra, in which he made use for the first time of an aleatoric technique that would become one of his trademarks—the deployment of carefully structured ostinato episodes in various parts, cued by the conductor, to produce an exceptionally dynamic contrapuntal fabric of rhythmically independent threads.

Lutosławski pursued this technique in his Symphony No. 2 (1965–67) and *Livre pour orchestre* (1968), and used it to particularly dramatic effect in his Cello Concerto (1970), written for and premiered by Mstislav Rostropovich. Elements of indeterminacy remained a feature of Lutosławski's

Symphony No. 3 (1981–83), which, along with the Cello Concerto, has become one of his most widely performed works. During the 1980s and 1990s Lutosławski's work became more openly melodic—less concerned with texture and the accretion of sound, more concerned with the linkage of ideas. He wrote three pieces exploring the idea of linkage in which the beginnings and ends of sections overlapped like links in a chain—*Chain 1* (1983) for chamber ensemble, *Chain 2* (1984–85) for violin and orchestra, and *Chain 3* (1986) for orchestra—and applied the same approach in the finale of his Piano Concerto (1987–88). Lutosławski's last major work was his Symphony No. 4 (1988–92), commissioned by the Los Angeles Philharmonic and premiered, under his own baton, in 1993. He was at work on a violin concerto for Anne-Sophie Mutter when he died.

Lutosławski was a figure of intense energy and great intelligence—alert, articulate, engaging, and impeccably elegant, both on the podium and off. His music bears the stamp of his personality: Sure of its direction, it exudes vitality and drama, making its points astutely, imaginatively, and with compelling clarity.

RECOMMENDED RECORDINGS

CELLO CONCERTO: ROSTROPOVICH; LUTOSŁAWSKI AND ORCHESTRE DE PARIS (EMI).

ORCHESTRAL WORKS (INCLUDING *CONCERTO FOR ORCHESTRA, JEUX VÉNITIENS, LIVRE POUR ORCHESTRE,* SYMPHONIES NOS. 1 AND 2): LUTOSŁAWSKI AND POLISH NATIONAL RADIO SYMPHONY ORCHESTRA (EMI).

SYMPHONIES NOS. 3 AND 4: SALONEN AND LOS ANGELES PHILHARMONIC (SONY).

SYMPHONY NO. 4 (WITH OTHER WORKS): WIT AND POLISH NATIONAL RADIO SYMPHONY ORCHESTRA (NAXOS).

Lyric Pieces NAME GIVEN TO TEN SEPARATE SETS OF PIANO VIGNETTES BY EDVARD GRIEG, composed between 1864 and 1901 and published as his Opp. 12, 38, 43, 47, 54, 57, 62, 65, 68, and 71. Among the 66 miniatures that make up the *Lyric Pieces*—variously titled *Lyriske småstykker, Neue lyrische Stückchen, Lyrische Stückchen,* and *Lyrische Stücke* in the original Danish and German—are some of Grieg's most delightful inspirations, including "Schmetterling" ("Butterfly"), Op. 43, No. 1.

RECOMMENDED RECORDING

(SELECTION) GILELS (DG).

Lyric Suite (Lyrische Suite) COMPOSITION IN SIX MOVEMENTS FOR STRING QUARTET BY ALBAN BERG, composed 1925–26 and premiered by the Kolisch Quartet on January 8, 1927, in Vienna. The work was shaped by a detailed autobiographical program (which Berg kept secret from his wife and the rest of the world) documenting a love affair between the composer and Hanna Fuchs-Robettin, the wife of a Czech businessman and sister of the novelist Franz Werfel. The work's main motive—A, B-flat, B, F—is formed from the initials of the two protagonists (in German, the note B is known as "H").

RECOMMENDED RECORDING

ALBAN BERG QUARTETT (EMI).

M

Yo-Yo Ma soars on the D string.

Ma, Yo-Yo

(b. Paris, October 7, 1955)

AMERICAN CELLIST OF CHINESE DESCENT. He began lessons with his father, the music educator Hiao-Tsuin Ma, when he was four, and gave his first public recital when he was five. He subsequently studied with Janos Scholz, and in 1962 became a pupil of Leonard Rose at the Juilliard School. He attended Harvard University, earning his B.A. in 1976 (the school would add an honorary doctorate in music in 1991). He received the prestigious Avery Fisher Prize for career development in 1978; by the time he was 30 he had emerged as the leading cellist of his generation, well on his way to becoming one of the most popular and respected classical musicians in the world.

Over the past decade Ma has conceived several projects that expand the classical performer's traditional role. One of these, *Inspired by Bach,* was a series of six films with artists in other media (including the Japanese Kabuki actor Tamasaburo Bando and the Olympic ice-dancing champions Jayne Torvill and Christopher Dean) geared to the music of the six Bach cello suites. Another, the three-year Silk Road project begun in 1999, explored the musical traditions of peoples and cultures along the ancient silk trading route between China and Europe. An undertaking of major cultural significance, it attracted enormous media attention at its climax in 2002 during the Fourth of July holiday at the National Folklife Festival on the Mall in Washington, D.C.

As a performer, Ma has had productive associations with many contemporary composers, including Tan Dun (b. 1957), John Williams, Edgar Meyer (b. 1960), Richard Danielpour (b. 1956), Leon Kirchner (b. 1919), and Christopher Rouse (b. 1949). He has collaborated with Ton Koopman in performances and recordings of Classical and Baroque repertoire (adjusting his bowing and vibrato to conform with period style), and has worked as a chamber-music partner with Emanuel Ax, Isaac Stern, Jaime Laredo, and Pamela Frank, among others. His playing is outgoing and intense, characterized by a passionate address and an emphasis on the singing line. He plays a

1733 Montagnana and the 1712 "Davidoff" Stradivarius formerly owned by Jacqueline du Pré.

RECOMMENDED RECORDINGS

Bach, cello suites (Sony).

Boccherini, cello concertos: Koopman and Amsterdam Baroque Orchestra (Sony).

Haydn, cello concertos: Garcia and English Chamber Orchestra (Sony).

Kirchner, Danielpour, Rouse, cello concertos: Zinman and Philadelphia Orchestra (Sony).

Maazel, Lorin

(b. Neuilly-sur-Seine, France, March 6, 1930)

American conductor, violinist, and composer. He received his first violin lessons when he was five and as a child studied conducting with Vladimir Bakaleinikov in Los Angeles and Pittsburgh. He was invited by Arturo Toscanini to conduct the NBC Symphony Orchestra in 1937 at the age of seven, and he made his New York debut in 1939, conducting the Interlochen Orchestra at the New York World's Fair. That summer he also conducted the Los Angeles Philharmonic at the Hollywood Bowl, sharing a program with Leopold Stokowski. On August 5, 1942, he made his debut with the New York Philharmonic at Lewisohn Stadium, conducting a full program that included Beethoven's Symphony No. 5 and a suite from Tchaikovsky's *The Nutcracker*. Engagements with several other major orchestras followed.

Lorin Maazel

At the age of 16, Maazel entered the University of Pittsburgh, where he studied languages, mathematics, and philosophy. He joined the Pittsburgh Symphony Orchestra violin section in 1948, while still a student, and in 1951 received a Fulbright scholarship to study Baroque music in Italy. On December 23, 1953, he made his European conducting debut, stepping in for an ailing conductor at the Massimo Bellini Theater in Catania. In 1960 he became the first American to conduct at Bayreuth (leading performances of *Lohengrin*) and, in spite of disparaging ethnic comments from members of the Wagner family, he returned there in 1968–69 to conduct the *Ring* cycle, becoming the first non-German to do so.

Maazel served concurrently as artistic director of the Deutsche Oper Berlin (1965–71) and music director of the Berlin Radio Symphony Orchestra (1965–75), and spent ten years as music director of the Cleveland Orchestra (1972–82), maintaining the ensemble at the pinnacle of discipline it had achieved under George Szell, while broadening its repertoire and deepening and darkening its sound. He subsequently served as general manager and artistic director of the Vienna Staatsoper (1982–84), music director of the Orchestre National de France (1988–90), music director of the Pittsburgh Symphony Orchestra (1988–96), and music director of the Bavarian Radio Symphony Orchestra (1993–2002). He became music director of the New York Philharmonic at the start of the 2002–03 season, and in June of 2004 his contract was extended through 2009.

In the half century preceding the start of his New York tenure, Maazel led more than 150 orchestras in more than 5,000 opera and concert performances, making him easily the most experienced active conductor in the world. He has enjoyed long associations with the Vienna Philharmonic (which has honored him with invitations to conduct 11 of its New Year's Day concerts), the Salzburg

Maazel, maestro and master of the baton

Festival, the Berlin Philharmonic, and La Scala in Milan. In recent years he has devoted considerable time to composition, creating a trilogy of concerted works for cello, flute, and violin (written for Rostropovich, Galway, and himself) as well as several symphonic pieces, some with narration. His opera *1984,* based on the George Orwell novel, received its premiere at the Royal Opera House, Covent Garden, on May 3, 2005.

Brilliant, articulate, ambitious, self-assured, and formidably capable, Maazel is one of the world's premiere conductors. His performances, though often criticized for their emotional detachment, and occasionally for signs of willfullness and calculation, never fail to convey a point of view and are usually marvels of clarity and precision. Beneath his frosty exterior, which frequently produces a reciprocal chill among orchestral musicians, hide a playfulness and sophisticated sense of humor; he is ready to match wits with anyone or to spring a practical joke for the sheer fun of it.

RECOMMENDED RECORDINGS

GERSHWIN, *CUBAN OVERTURE, RHAPSODY IN BLUE, AN AMERICAN IN PARIS*: CLEVELAND ORCHESTRA (DECCA).

GERSHWIN, *PORGY AND BESS*: WHITE, MITCHELL, BOATRIGHT; CLEVELAND ORCHESTRA (DECCA).

PROKOFIEV, *ROMEO AND JULIET*: CLEVELAND ORCHESTRA (DECCA).

RESPIGHI, *FONTANE DI ROMA, PINI DI ROMA, FESTE ROMANE*: PITTSBURGH SYMPHONY ORCHESTRA (SONY).

TCHAIKOVSKY, SERENADE NO. 3: VIENNA PHILHARMONIC (DECCA).

MacDowell, Edward

(b. New York, December 18, 1860; d. New York, January 23, 1908)

AMERICAN PIANIST AND COMPOSER, the most formidably talented of the American Romantics and one of the first American composers to be recognized internationally. He began learning piano as a child; from 1878 to 1888 he studied in Europe (Paris, Frankfurt, Wiesbaden) and established his career in Germany. There he met and married an American student, Marian Nevins. Returning to the U.S. in 1888 and settling in Boston, he rapidly established himself as the country's leading serious musician, writing in an idiom influenced by mainstream European composers such as Liszt (who praised his Piano Concerto No. 1), Tchaikovsky, and Grieg.

In 1896, at the height of his powers, MacDowell was appointed the first professor of music at Columbia University. He left after eight years, following the arrival of a new president whose ideas about music and curriculum he found unsympathetic. That same year he was injured in a hansom accident, which led to a rapid mental and physical decline. The shy, beleaguered composer and his loyal wife retired to their quiet summer home in New Hampshire, which, after his death, was turned into the now-renowned MacDowell artists' colony.

MacDowell's Piano Concerto No. 2 in D minor, the work by which he is best known to concert audiences today, is his masterpiece. Written in Germany during the winter of 1884–85, when the composer was 24, it received its premiere in New York four years later. Its rich lyricism, European accent, and accomplished orchestration mark it as one of the great Romantic concertos, even if the writing is imbued with enough diminished-seventh chords to sink a transatlantic steamer. ◉ From the same time, the paired symphonic poems *Hamlet* and *Ophelia* show a debt to Tchaikovsky's *Francesca da Rimini*. MacDowell's most substantial symphonic works are his two Suites for orchestra. No. 1 consists of five movements with German titles alluding in pure Romantic fashion to nature scenes; No. 2, the *Indian* Suite, is a five-movement symphony in the best European style, but based on American motifs (MacDowell mentions "Iroquois and Chippewa themes"). Each movement is a descriptive piece ("Legend," "Love Song," "Wartime," "Dirge," "Village Festival").

MacDowell published 11 song collections and numerous piano miniatures, most gathered in collections: *Idyllen, Sea Pieces, Fireside Tales, New England Idyls,* and the best known, *Woodland Sketches,* which opens with "To a Wild Rose." Of his four piano sonatas, he considered the fourth, in E minor (named the *Keltic*), his finest effort; though he appended a poetic preface asserting that the piece should be thought of as "a 'bardic' rhapsody," the work is tightly organized. The thematic material of all three movements is based on the interval of a descending minor third that becomes a sort of IDÉE FIXE, motivically unifying in a manner reminiscent of Liszt.

Edward Macdowell

In the years following his death, the explosive infusion of ragtime, jazz, and blues into American music (and the rise of anti-German sentiment during World War I) quickly pushed MacDowell—brilliant pianist, gifted composer, pioneering educator, the American Grieg—into the shadows. He has yet to fully reemerge.

RECOMMENDED RECORDINGS

ORCHESTRAL SUITES NOS. 1 AND 2: YUOSA AND ULSTER ORCHESTRA (NAXOS).

PIANO CONCERTO NO. 2: CLIBURN; HENDL AND CHICAGO SYMPHONY ORCHESTRA (RCA).

PIANO MUSIC (INCLUDING SONATAS AND SHORTER WORKS): BARBAGALLO (NAXOS).

PIANO MUSIC: TOCCO (GASPARO).

Machaut, Guillaume de

(b. near Reims, 1300; d. Reims, April, 1377)

FRENCH COMPOSER AND POET. The leading figure of the ARS NOVA, he was regarded during his lifetime not only as his era's finest composer, but as its finest poet as well, probably the last time supremacy in both fields was united in one person. His talent and good fortune placed him at the center of power and wealth in 14th-century France, which allowed him to produce a large oeuvre and gave him the means to ensure its survival as well.

Machaut was educated in the cathedral town of Reims and, possibly, in Paris. For a period of about 17 years, from 1323 to 1340, he was employed as clerk, then notary, and eventually personal secretary to Jean de Luxembourg, King of Bohemia, a formidable figure known in English-speaking countries as John the Blind. King John was closely allied with the French court by blood and marriage. As a result, many important doors were opened for his young scribe. Machaut visited the French court in 1323–24 as part of John's retinue, and at that time probably came into contact with the composer and theorist Philippe de Vitry, a seminal figure in the emergence of the Ars Nova.

By the time he was 30, Machaut already enjoyed considerable fame for his verse accounts of King John's exploits. His initial achievements as a composer were his motets, of which 23, mostly three-part, ISORHYTHMIC pieces, have survived, 19 of them dating from before 1350. He also made important early contributions to the art of the courtly love song. Building on the tradition of the TROUBADOURS and trouvères, he began by introducing the more elaborate metrical schemes of the Ars Nova, and ultimately succeeded in creating a new genre, the polyphonic chanson, by applying compositional techniques pioneered by Vitry. His settings occupy a number of genres: lays and virelais, ballades, and rondeaux. One of his most impressive is the lay "Je ne cesse de prier" ("I do not cease praying"), known as the "Lay de la Fonteinne," a meditation on the Holy Trinity delivered as a prayer to the Virgin Mary in the guise of a love song. Equally fascinating is the rondeau "Ma fin est mon commencement" ("My end is my beginning"), a song about itself composed as a retrograde canon, in which Machaut airily demonstrates the self-awareness of the true artist.

The cathedral of Notre Dame in Reims

The greatest of Machaut's compositional achievements is his *Messe de Nostre Dame,* created sometime in the early 1360s. The earliest integral, stylistically coherent polyphonic setting of the Ordinary of the Mass (including the "Ite missa est"), it remains the only surviving complete mass by a composer of the 14th century, at once marking a watershed in the history of the musical genre and an extraordinarily innovative step in compositional technique. The writing still sounds "open" and organum-like, but the polyphony is elevated, beautiful, and arresting, testifying to Machaut's extraordinary powers of invention. The setting incorporates isorhythmic structure everywhere except in the Gloria and Credo and, while not based on a specific cantus firmus, is unified by a number of melodic, rhythmic, and harmonic elements that are consistent throughout. The first masterpiece of polyphonic music, it is one of the most vital expressions of the Ars Nova.

During his years of service to King John, Machaut had received a string of benefices, culminating in a canonicate at the cathedral of Notre Dame in Reims. In April of 1340 he settled into a comfortable residence near the church, where he remained for the rest of his life. (John would die a valiant death in 1346 at the battle of Crécy, when he and a handful of retainers, tied to each other by the reins of their horses, charged the English lines.) Thanks to the esteem in which he continued to be held by various members of the French royal family, Machaut in later years was able to have his works copied into a number of lavishly illuminated manuscript volumes, which, owing to their striking visual beauty, were preserved through the centuries. These have provided scholars with the most extensive sources for any composer of the 14th century (only 12 or 13 compositions securely attributable to Vitry have survived, while Machaut's known works number 143). Thanks to these sources, which exist in large part due to Machaut's unique foresight in preserving his artistic legacy, posterity has come to recognize him as one of the first truly "modern" artists. It is with him, too, that polyphony transcended its status as a mere technique, becoming an art for the first time.

RECOMMENDED RECORDINGS

Messe de Nostre Dame: Hilliard Ensemble (Hyperion).

Messe de Nostre Dame: Summerly and Oxford Camerata (Naxos).

Selected ballades, rondeaux, virelais: Kirkby; Page and Gothic Voices (Hyperion).

Mackerras, Sir Charles

(b. Schenectady, N.Y., November 17, 1925)

Australian conductor. He studied in Sydney and became principal oboe of the Sydney Symphony Orchestra in 1945. In 1947 he studied conducting with Václav Talich in Prague, and the following year he made his debut at Sadler's Wells (later the English National Opera), conducting Johann Strauss Jr.'s *Die Fledermaus*. He served as principal conductor of the BBC Concert Orchestra (1954–66), first conductor of the Hamburg State Opera (1966–69), and music director at Sadler's Wells (1970–77). Subsequent activities have included stints as chief conductor of the Sydney Symphony Orchestra (1982–85), music director of the Welsh National Opera (1987–92), principal conductor of the Orchestra of St. Luke's (1998–2001), and appointments as principal guest conductor of the Scottish Chamber Orchestra (1992–95), the San Francisco Opera (1993–96), and the Czech Philharmonic (from 1999). He has appeared frequently as a guest conductor at Covent Garden, as well as in Munich, Vienna, and Paris. He made his Metropolitan Opera debut in 1972, conducting Gluck's *Orfeo ed Euridice,* and in recent years has returned there to conduct Janáček's *Kát'a Kabanová* and *The Makropulos Case,* Britten's *Billy Budd,* and Mozart's *Die Zauberflöte.*

Australian Czechmate: Sir Charles Mackerras

With his wide-ranging interests and encyclopedic knowledge of the repertoire, Mackerras is regarded as a musician's musician. For more than half a century he has specialized in the Czech literature, in particular the music of Janáček, which he conducts with unique authority. (His recorded cycle of Janáček's operas with the Vienna Philharmonic remains one of the most admirable discographic achievements of the stereo era.) He is also notably well versed in the performance practice of the 18th and 19th centuries, and ranks as one of the world's foremost Mozarteans, having made outstanding recordings of the complete symphonies with the Prague Chamber Orchestra and of the major operas with the Scottish Chamber Orchestra. He was knighted in 1979.

RECOMMENDED RECORDINGS

Janáček, *Jenůfa, Kát'a Kabanová, The Cunning Little Vixen, The Makropulos Affair, From the House of the Dead*: Various artists with Vienna Philharmonic Orchestra (Decca).

Mozart, *Così fan tutte*: McLaughlin, Lott, Hadley, Corbelli; Scottish Chamber Orchestra (Telarc).

Mozart, symphonies (complete): Prague Chamber Orchestra (Telarc).

Madama Butterfly OPERA IN THREE ACTS BY GIACOMO PUCCINI to a libretto by Giuseppe Giacosa and Luigi Illica based on David Belasco's stage version of a magazine story by John Luther Long. A two-act version of the work, composed and premiered in 1904, was a complete failure, but three subsequent revisions over the next two years shaped *Butterfly* into the three-act masterpiece we know today, first performed at the Opéra-Comique in Paris on December 28, 1906. The composer's love of exotic locations was clearly one of the factors that drew him to Belasco's play about a young Japanese geisha who marries and is abandoned by an American naval officer. The scoring is especially beautiful: whole scenes of the opera are suffused with a luminous, pastel glow that perfectly suggests the gentle emotional world of the heroine. In the well-known aria "Un bel dì, vedremo," the glow intensifies as Butterfly radiantly affirms that her beloved will return. The opera's denouement is fierce and expertly gauged.

RECOMMENDED RECORDINGS

FRENI, PAVAROTTI, LUDWIG, KERNS; KARAJAN AND VIENNA PHILHARMONIC (DECCA).

PRICE, TUCKER, ELIAS, MAERO; LEINSDORF AND RCA ITALIANA OPERA ORCHESTRA (RCA).

madrigal [1] A literary-musical vocal form originating in northern Italy in the early 14th century, part of the "dolce stil nuovo" ("sweet new style") as characterized by Dante. The poetic form, at first on arcadian courtly subjects and later on autobiographical or moralizing texts, consisted generally of two- or three-line strophes, followed by a ritornello, and was set for one or two very active upper voices over a slower-moving lower voice. Major composers associated with the genre were Jacopo da Bologna (fl. 1340–60), Johannes Ciconia (ca. 1370–1412), and the Florentines Lorenzo da Firenze (d. 1372/73) and Francesco Landini (ca. 1325–97), a blind poet, organist, and figure of near-mythic status who was the author of over 150 compositions, and whose modern legacy is the so-called "Landini cadence." The 14th-century madrigal disappeared by about 1415.

[2] A polyphonic vocal setting of a piece of secular verse. Also Italian in origin, it became one of the most important musical genres of the 16th century. The madrigal's emergence coincided with the poet Pietro Bembo's (1470–1547) revival of interest in the poetry of Petrarch (1304–74). Petrarch's sonnets—elegant, refined, and fanciful, emotionally charged and astonishingly virtuosic in their imagery—were a particularly popular source of madrigal texts, as were the richly allusive verse epics of Ludovico Ariosto (1474–1533), Torquato Tasso (1544–95), and Giovanni Battista Guarini (1538–1612). The madrigal's musical antecedents are to be found mainly in the frottola, a popular strophic song of the 15th century, usually for four voices and essentially homophonic. Since many of the early madrigalists were transplanted northerners working in Italian courts, the contrapuntal techniques of the Franco-Flemish motet became integral to madrigal composition: a continuous musical unfolding (not strophic) consisting of a series of overlapping sections, frequently imitative, marked off by cadences, each treating a phrase or line of text. The best madrigal settings showed their artistry by achieving an emotionally compelling synthesis of word painting and often dramatic changes in vocal texture and affect, while still maintaining a sense of continuity and well-proportioned climax.

Typically, madrigal settings called for three to six voice parts. Three- and four-voice settings predominated up to about 1550; after that, five- and six-voice settings became the norm. The madrigal's early

Madrigal singers in **A Concert,** *16th-century Venetian painting*

development, during the second quarter of the 16th century, was spearheaded by the settings of the Italian Costanzo Festa (d. 1545) and northerners Jacques Arcadelt (ca. 1507–68), Adrian Willaert, and Philippe Verdelot (ca. 1485–ca. 1530), whose first two books of four-voice madrigals (first published in 1533–34 and reprinted many times over the next 25 years) became one of the most popular collections of the time. The style was carried forward in the third quarter of the century by Cipriano de Rore (ca. 1516–65), Orlande de Lassus, Andrea Gabrieli (ca. 1532–85), and Giaches de Wert (1535–96), and in the final quarter of the century by Wert, Luca Marenzio, Luzzasco Luzzaschi (ca. 1545–1607), and Carlo Gesualdo. During the 1570s and 1580s, a hybrid style developed, combining the influence of the dancelike Neapolitan villanella with an increasingly sensuous and expressionistic manner, each line of poetry and nuance set off by extravagant musical gestures and luxuriant use of pictorialism.

This hybrid became the most representative style of the Italian madrigal, and rapidly traveled outside of Italy to the rest of Europe. It reached England via Nicolas Yonge's "Musica Transalpina," two collections (1588 and 1597) of Italian madrigals translated into English, which inspired an entire body of Italianate madrigals by composers such as Thomas Morley (1557–1603), William Byrd, Thomas Weelkes (1576–1623), and John Wilbye (1574–1638). With his "Triumphs of Oriana" (1601), Morley collected the compositions of 23 composers into a tribute to Queen Elizabeth, and created the concept of an English madrigal school.

The later years of the 16th century saw new developments in Italy as the forms of poetry chosen for setting began to diverge. Some composers followed a trend begun by Andrea Gabrieli in the 1560s, away from the Petrarchan texts and toward lighter, more pastoral subjects. Others followed the example of Wert, continuing to set the serious literary texts of Petrarch and Ariosto, but allowing the changes of texture to become bolder, even disruptive, and making freer use of expressive dissonance. This more audacious style, which Monteverdi called the *seconda prattica,* reached its summit in Luzzaschi's Fourth, Fifth, and Sixth Books (1594–96), in the rich, masterfully conceived settings of Marenzio's Ninth Book for five voices (1599), and in Monteverdi's Fourth and Fifth Books (1603–05) ◉. Also during these years, the madrigal underwent a transformation from being social music, written for amateurs, to the status of concert piece, intended for performance by groups of skilled professional singers (both men and women) such as were maintained at the courts of Mantua and Ferrara. Toward the end the century, Marenzio, Luzzaschi, and Monteverdi, again following Wert's lead, began setting a new type of text: the dramatic scena, represented by Guarini's popular pastoral play *Il pastor fido,* and Tasso's epic poem *La Gerusalemme liberata,* which ultimately provided Monteverdi with the text for his masterpiece in the *STILE CONCITATO, Il Combattimento di Tancredi e Clorinda* (1624).

Throughout the history of the madrigal, text and music remained closely intertwined. At its height, the style was one in which word painting abounded—so much so that the practice of mimicking a poetic gesture or image in music is still referred to as "madrigalism." An allusion to "pain" or "anguish" in the text might provoke a sharp dissonance; similarly, "suffering" or "longing" might be expressed by chromaticism, "despair" and "hopelessness" by a descending melodic figure, "flight" or "joy" by a lively ascending figure.

The madrigal was the most progressive of late 16th-century forms, as the motet had been in the early part of the century, and the mass before that. Through its emphasis on the expressive relationship between text and music, and its refinement of music's affective capabilities, it served as a proving ground for the development of the Baroque style.

RECOMMENDED RECORDINGS

ENGLISH AND ITALIAN MADRIGALS: HILLIARD ENSEMBLE (VIRGIN CLASSICS).

"FLORA GAVE ME FAIREST FLOWERS" (MORLEY, WEELKES, WILBYE, GIBBONS): RUTTER AND CAMBRIDGE SINGERS (COLLEGIUM).

"THE MANNERIST REVOLUTION" (WERT, GESUALDO, MARENZIO, MONTEVERDI): BLACHLY AND POMERIUM (DORIAN).

maestoso (It., "majestic") Occasionally encountered as a tempo marking, e.g., *Maestoso alla marcia* (Vaughan Williams, Symphony No. 2, finale), more commonly used as a modifier for a standard tempo, e.g., *Allegro ma non troppo, un poco maestoso* (Beethoven, Symphony No. 9, first movement), *Andante maestoso* (Tchaikovsky, Symphony No. 5, beginning of finale).

maestro (It., "master") Term used when addressing or referring to a conductor, derived from *maestro di cappella* ("master of the chapel"), the Italian designation for the director of music at a court or church.

Magnificat A musical setting of the passage identified in the King James version of the Bible as "Mary's song of thanksgiving" (Luke 1: 46–55), which begins, "My soul doth magnify the Lord" or, in the Latin of the Vulgate, "Magnificat anima mea Dominum."

As Luke tells it, the angel Gabriel has visited Mary and announced to her that she will bring forth a son whom she will call Jesus, who will "reign over the house of Jacob for ever." He tells her further that her cousin Elisabeth, who had been barren, has also conceived a son and is in her sixth month. Mary goes immediately to visit Elisabeth; when Elisabeth hears Mary's voice, the unborn child in her womb (who will grow up to be John the Baptist) leaps for joy. Understanding the meaning of all this, Elisabeth greets Mary as "the mother of my Lord." And Mary responds with her wondrous song of praise for God.

The words of the Magnificat came to play an important role in Christian worship as a part of the Vespers service, and they have been set to music countless times—more frequently during the Renaissance and Baroque than any liturgical text save the Ordinary of the Mass. So numerous and prominent have these settings been (Lassus alone set the text about 100 times, and Palestrina more than 30) that it is fair to characterize the Magnificat as the equivalent in music of the Annunciation in painting.

Monteverdi included two settings of the Magnificat in his Vespers of 1610. Among the most impressive modern settings of the text have been those by Gerald Finzi (1952), Krzysztof Penderecki (1974), and Arvo Pärt (1989).

No setting of the text has been more widely admired and performed than that of J. S. Bach. Composed in 1723 for evensong of Bach's first Christmas in Leipzig, it calls for five soloists, a five-part chorus, and the largest orchestra available to Bach—three trumpets with drums, two flutes, two oboes (doubling oboe d'amore), strings, and continuo. The setting divides the text into 12 separate numbers, in which Bach creates a moving characterization of each phrase of Mary's proclamation.

Mahler, Gustav

(b. Kalischt, July 7, 1860; d. Vienna, May 18, 1911)

AUSTRIAN COMPOSER AND CONDUCTOR. Although he managed to compose an impressive series of ambitious, large-scale scores in his spare time, Mahler was a working musician throughout his career. Brought up in a large Jewish family, he taught himself to play the piano. In 1875 he was accepted as a student at the Vienna Conservatory, where he studied piano, harmony, and composition. In the Viennese musical scene, Mahler aligned himself with the Wagner-Bruckner faction; he twice tried and failed to win the Beethoven Prize, the second time with his dark, folk tale–inspired cantata *DAS KLAGENDE LIED* (*The Song of Lamentation*; 1881), in which many elements of his mature musical style are already present.

At age 20 Mahler started his professional career, conducting operetta at a spa in Upper Austria; over the next few years he led opera performances at increasingly larger venues. He went to hear *Parsifal* at Bayreuth in July 1883, the summer after Wagner's death, prior to taking his first major position in Kassel (1883–85). He subsequently held posts in Prague, Leipzig, and Budapest (his first as chief conductor), before taking charge of the operas in Hamburg (1891–97) and Vienna (1897–1907) and finishing his career in New York (1908–11). In the early 1890s he began making an annual summer retreat to the Austrian countryside to compose and indulge in his favorite physical activities—hiking, cycling, and swimming. In 1897, motivated as much by career considerations in an anti-Semitic milieu as by his spiritual inclinations, he converted to Catholicism.

Gustav Mahler in 1907

When Mahler was ousted from his post at the Vienna Opera in 1907 (becoming one in a long line of conductors to be ground up by Austrian cultural politics), he moved to the Metropolitan Opera, where he conducted works of Wagner, Mozart, Beethoven, Smetana, and Tchaikovsky. After three seasons of continuous bickering with management and resentment over having to share the limelight with Arturo Toscanini, he left for the New York Philharmonic. His tenure there (1909–11) proved similarly tumultuous, although he retained warm feelings for America and Americans. An extraordinarily gifted but demanding conductor, he was considered one of the greatest maestros of his day; from the beginning of his career to its end, his conducting was intense, impassioned, revelatory, and very physical—a frenzied, sublime communion with the music, in which he was all over the podium.

Mahler's symphonies are works of confession that offer insight into one of the most fascinating and complex of modern minds. In contrast to his contemporary Richard Strauss, who exercised sovereign control over his music, Mahler was powerless to keep his personal life from invading his compositions. Self-expression was as important as formal procedure to him, and what emerged is what Mahler *was*, a volatile mix of optimism and irony, sublimity and vulgarity, melancholy and stormy transcendence. His music has an emotional fervor born of insecurity, reflecting lifelong spiritual turmoil; evocations of childhood, such as the marches and dance tunes he heard garrison bands play in his hometown, fill the fanciful world of his symphonies, as do passages of consciously naive expression and dreamlike elation.

Die Auferstehungs-Sinfonie

Sinfonie der Welttraurigkeit

Kammersinfonie in Dur

Der Werther des Achtundzwanzigjährigen

Gustav Mahler conducts: caricatures depicting the agony and the ecstasy of his podium persona

Song and symphony were intertwined in Mahler's mind, and his first five symphonies are closely related in spirit and content to two of his song cycles, *LIEDER EINES FAHRENDEN GESELLEN* (*Songs of a Wayfarer*) and *DES KNABEN WUNDERHORN* (*The Youth's Magic Horn*). In programmatic terms, the First Symphony deals with man's earthly struggles and the Second with his death and potential for resurrection, though in a philosophical rather than religious sense. The Third is Mahler's *summa theologiae,* his musical evocation of the great chain of being from primordial chaos up through plants and animals to man and, finally, God. In his Fourth Symphony, Mahler steps back to take a fond look at Mozart and Haydn, giving the score an intentionally Classical shape and ending it with a song about a child's view of heaven.

Mahler's Fifth Symphony, the last of his song-based symphonies, was completed in 1902, the year of his marriage to Alma Schindler. (A painter's daughter, she was an outstanding composer in her own right, and also one of the most magnetic personalities of her time, famously marrying first Mahler, then the architect Walter Gropius, then novelist Franz Werfel, as well as carrying on affairs with several others, notably the Czech painter Oskar Kokoschka.) Mahler's marriage marked a turning point in his life, and the symphony his maturity as a composer, ushering in the most fruitful years of his career. The Fifth employs a richer, more colorful orchestral palette and a new, contrapuntally denser style of writing inspired by Bach. It also marks an important advance in style toward a more unified concept of structure and a greater reliance on thematic linkages among movements. Yet, in spite of the symphony's more objective stance, its emotional trajectory—

from the funereal weight and violence of the first two movements, through the dreamlike digressions of the Scherzo and the yearning of the well-known Adagietto, to the almost giddy optimism of the finale ◉—is intensely subjective and Romantic. The tragic mood of the Sixth, Mahler's most menacing symphony, is clear enough; in the finale there are three percussive crashes representing what the composer called "the three hammer blows of fate." The Seventh is lugubrious, mysterious, and nocturnal. Its buoyant C major finale can be a problematic movement, unless the glorious cacophony of its closing pages is seen as a last evocation of fin-de-siècle optimism amid the ruins of Romanticism. Majestic in its conception and magnificent in its technical assurance, the Eighth, a choral symphony in two huge movements (the second a setting of the final scene of Goethe's *Faust*), is unique in Mahler's canon both in size and in lack of ambivalence. Dubbed the *Symphony of a Thousand,* it fuses religious mysticism, symphonic argument, and the greatest of all German lyric poetry, and marks the end of the line for German Romanticism.

Alma Mahler

In 1907, a year after completing the Eighth, Mahler suffered the three great blows: dismissal from the directorship of the Vienna Court Opera, the death of his eldest daughter from scarlet fever, and diagnosis of his own terminal heart condition. Confronted by mortality, Mahler's gaze turned inward, yet the outpouring of emotion in his music became greater than ever. The works of this short but productive final period—*Das Lied von der Erde* (*The Song of the Earth*), the Ninth Symphony, and the unfinished Tenth—filled with otherworldly beauty and resignation, constitute a three-part valedictory. In *Das Lied von der Erde,* Mahler gives voice to his sadness and loneliness while still embracing life. ◉ With the Ninth, fear and anger are vented in a searing cry from the heart, prior to the passionate leave-taking of the final Adagio. Pain, dreamlike detachment, and an elegiac acceptance of the inevitable merge in the sketches of the Tenth. While working on it, Mahler discovered that Alma had fallen in love and was having an affair with Gropius; in emotional agony, he sought out Sigmund Freud, who led him to a more forgiving insight into his wife's psyche. In this final work, Mahler can be seen looking beyond death, though toward what he was unable to tell us fully.

To anyone who loves the orchestra, or who views music as a medium in which expression is paramount, Mahler's symphonies offer endless fascination. Each one is a world unto itself, as the composer himself took pains to point out: "The term 'symphony,'" Mahler said after completing the Second, "means creating a world with all the technical means available. The constantly new and changing content determines its own form." Challenging as his music was, Mahler was convinced his time would come. By the 1960s, the unprecedented scope and self-conscious emotionalism of his symphonies, along with the uneasy mix of nostalgia and vision that sets them apart, had become much easier for the concertgoing public to understand. Mahler did not live to witness World War I, much less the Third Reich, and the disintegration of 19th-century European society they brought about, but he foresaw the coming of a violent end to his own era and the eventual demise of Romantic art and culture. His music gives prophetic voice to the fears and aspirations that would characterize the remainder of the 20th century: the anxiety of the individual overwhelmed by forces beyond his control, the painful longing for love in the midst of alienation, the need to find meaning in life, and the fleeting dream of spiritual transcendence.

RECOMMENDED RECORDINGS

Kindertotenlieder and *Rückert-Lieder*: Baker with Barbirolli and Hallé Orchestra, New Philharmonia Orchestra (EMI).

Des Knaben Wunderhorn: Schwarzkopf, Fischer-Dieskau; Szell and London Symphony Orchestra (EMI).

Das Lied von der Erde: Patzak, Ferrier; Walter and Vienna Philharmonic (Decca).

Symphonies (complete): Bernstein and New York Philharmonic (Sony).

Symphony No. 1: Boulez and Chicago Symphony Orchestra (DG).

Symphony No. 1: Kubelík and Bavarian Radio Symphony Orchestra (DG).

Symphony No. 2: Cundari, Forrester; Walter and New York Philharmonic (Sony).

Symphony No. 4: Raskin; Szell and Cleveland Orchestra (Sony).

Symphony No. 8: Various soloists with Solti and Chicago Orchestra (Decca).

Symphony No. 9: Karajan and Berlin Philharmonic (DG).

Symphony No. 9: Walter and Vienna Philharmonic (EMI).

major Literally, "greater" or "larger." When used to identify a key or a scale, it refers to the fact that the third degree of that key or scale is a major third (i.e., four semitones) above the fundamental or tonic note. Intervals of the second, third, sixth, and seventh variety can be either major or minor; the major spans one semitone more than the minor. Of the major keys, C major seems to sound particularly rich and satisfying to our ears (doctors tell us it has to do with the crystalline structure of bone). The ebullience of this key is wonderfully conveyed in Dvořák's *Slavonic Dances,* Op. 46, No. 1. *See also* INTERVAL; MODE; MINOR.

Makropulos Case, The (Věc Makropulos) OPERA IN THREE ACTS BY LEOŠ JANÁČEK, to his own libretto after Karel Čapek's comedy *Věc Makropulos,* premiered December 18, 1926, at the National Theater in Brno. The complicated plot, involving a lawsuit in progress as the opera begins, centers around the enigmatic figure of Emilia Marty, a celebrated opera singer who seems to know a lot about the past, including many details pertinent to the lawsuit. It turns out, in the opera's concluding act, that Emilia Marty is more than 300 years old. She has been living under a variety of aliases, all sharing the initials "E. M."—for a while she was the Spanish Gypsy dancer Eugenia Montez, and before that she was Elian MacGregor (making her the plaintiff's great-great-grandmother). But her true name is Elina Makropulos, and she was born on Crete in the year 1585. The secret of her longevity: an elixir given to her by her father, who served as physician to Rudolf II, the Holy Roman Emperor. Or so she claims. She dies with the words of the Lord's Prayer on her lips, which she repeats in Greek, her mother tongue. *The Makropulos Case* is one of Janáček's finest achievements. Its score is masterfully constructed, sustaining a remarkable tension from the opera's opening scene to its surprising denouement. The orchestration is typically bold and imaginative, and the characterization powerful and compelling, particularly the portrait of the mysterious, alluring woman at the heart of the work.

RECOMMENDED RECORDING

Söderström, Dvorsky, Blachut; Mackerras and Vienna Philharmonic (Decca).

Malibran, Maria

(b. Paris, March 24, 1808; d. Manchester, September 23, 1836)

SPANISH MEZZO-SOPRANO. She was the daughter of the tenor Manuel García and the older sister of mezzo-soprano Pauline Viardot. The training she received from her father was painstaking, even harsh, but it produced impressive results: Malibran possessed an enormous range, from G to high E, quickly mastered a very large repertoire, and was hailed from the start of her career as a singer of exquisite refinement. She made her London and New York debuts in 1825, at the age of 17, singing Rosina in Rossini's *Il barbiere di Siviglia.* During her first New York season, she sang alongside her father in several other Rossini operas, including *La cenerentola, Otello,* and *Il turco in Italia,* as well as in Mozart's *Don Giovanni* (presented at the request of Lorenzo da Ponte, then living in New York). These were the first performances of opera in Italian in the United States. Malibran made her Paris debut in 1828, singing the title role in Rossini's *Semiramide* at the Théâtre Italien, and remained active in Paris and London until 1832, when she turned her attention to Italy.

Malibran made her Italian debut on June 30, 1832, singing Rossini's Desdemona at the Teatro Valle in Rome. Later that year, at the Teatro San Carlo in Naples, she achieved a string of triumphs in the Rossini operas *Il barbiere di Siviglia, La cenerentola, La gazza ladra, Semiramide,* and *Otello.* She returned to San Carlo the following season, appearing in the title role of Bellini's *Norma* on February 23, 1834, before heading off to Milan to sing *Norma* at La Scala. Now at the height of her career, she could command a fee of 3,000 Austrian lire per performance at La Scala, where, on December 30, 1835, she created the title role in Donizetti's *Maria Stuarda.* Her meteoric career came to a tragic end the following September as a result of a riding accident. With her ravishing good looks and equally ravishing vocal artistry, Malibran blazed, albeit briefly, as one of bel canto's brightest stars.

Maria Malibran

Ma mère l'oye (Mother Goose) SUITE CONSISTING OF "CINQ PIÈCES ENFANTINES" ("FIVE CHILDLIKE PIECES") FOR PIANO FOUR-HANDS BY MAURICE RAVEL, composed 1908–10 and first performed at the inaugural concert of the Société Musicale Indépendente on April 20, 1910, by Jeanne Leleu (age 11) and Geneviève Durony (age 14). The individual pieces carry descriptive titles relating them to various fairy-tale characters and scenes. Ravel transformed the work into a ballet in 1911, orchestrating the five pieces and adding a prelude, a "Danse du rouet" ("Spinning Wheel Dance"), and a series of imaginatively scored passages connecting all the pieces to one another. The ballet received its premiere on January 29, 1912, in Paris.

RECOMMENDED RECORDINGS

BALLET: BOULEZ AND NEW YORK PHILHARMONIC (SONY).

PIANO, FOUR-HANDS: LORTIE, MERCIER (CHANDOS).

SUITE FOR ORCHESTRA: MARTINON AND CHICAGO SYMPHONY ORCHESTRA (RCA).

mandolin Small plucked string instrument with a pear-shaped, round-backed body, a fretted fingerboard, and four double courses of strings (in the same tuning as those of a violin) that are sounded by a

La Mandoline ***(1921) by Juan Gris, and*** **(right)** ***the real thing***

plectrum. Developed in Naples during the 1740s, it became popular during the second half of the 18th century, and its use as a serenade instrument inspired numerous allusions and parodies in opera, the most famous of which is the aria "Deh, vieni alla finestra" from Mozart's *Don Giovanni.* Classical composers of the 19th and 20th centuries occasionally made use of the mandolin in orchestral scores to create an appropriately Italianate color or to evoke a nocturnal mood: Prokofiev used four in *Romeo and Juliet* ◉, and Mahler called for a single mandolin in his Symphonies Nos. 7 and 8 as well as in *Das Lied von der Erde,* where its sound conveys a haunting sense of fragility and nostalgia. Schoenberg included a part for mandolin in his *Variations for Orchestra,* Op. 31 (1926–28), and Boulez has used the instrument in *Pli selon pli* (1962) and *Éclat/ Multiples* (1966). The literature contains a small number of mandolin concertos, including one written by Johann Nepomuk Hummel in 1799 for the Italian virtuoso Bartholomeo Bortolazzi. Far more likely to be encountered are Vivaldi's concertos for one and two "mandolins" (RV 425 and RV 532), which were actually composed for the mandolino, a smaller, higher-pitched predecessor of the Neapolitan mandolin.

Manfred VERSE DRAMA BY GEORGE GORDON, LORD BYRON, written in 1817. Byron's works—particularly *Childe Harold's Pilgrimage, Manfred,* and *Don Juan*—exerted a profound influence on the Romantics, not only in literature (the "hero" of Aleksandr Pushkin's *Eugene Onegin,* for example, is a typically isolated, self-regarding Byronic figure) but in music, where composers from Berlioz to Busoni found inspiration in his words. Both Schumann and Tchaikovsky created important works based on *Manfred.*

Schumann's *Manfred,* composed in 1848–49 and published in 1853 as his Op. 115, is a respectfully abridged setting of the bulk of Byron's drama, as translated into German by K. A. Suckow. In typically obsessive fashion, Schumann began work on the score the day after he finished his opera *Genoveva.* His treatment of the text represents one of the most extensive uses of melodrama (dramatic speech accompanied by illustrative instrumental music). The first performance of the complete score was given on June 13, 1852, in Weimar, under the direction of Franz Liszt (who had recently penned a work of his own based in part on Byron, the symphonic poem *Tasso*). Today, the only music from *Manfred* that is performed with any regularity is the overture, a fiery, dramatic essay whose convulsive syncopations and restless chromaticism aptly convey the hero's disturbed, guilt-ridden state of mind. Schumann conducted the overture's premiere at a concert of the Leipzig Gewandhaus Orchestra on March 14, 1852.

Tchaikovsky composed his *Manfred* Symphony between April and October of 1885, to a program devised by Vladimir Stasov in 1867–68 and originally offered to Mily Balakirev. Stasov's inspiration had been Hector Berlioz's great Byronic essay *HAROLD EN ITALIE,* and he proposed to

Balakirev a program that would make similar use of an IDÉE FIXE to represent Byron's brooding, melancholy hero. In an amusingly circular bit of intellectual recycling, Balakirev, finding Stasov's ideas unsuitable for his own use, tried at first to pawn them off on Berlioz himself, appealing to the Frenchman's love of Byron; but Berlioz, seriously ill and with less than a year to live, had no interest. There things stood until 1882, when Balakirev pitched the same program to Tchaikovsky, whose initial response was utterly unenthusiastic. Balakirev kept working, suggesting exactly how the music should go (with a particularity remarkable for someone who had no intention of composing the piece himself), until Tchaikovsky eventually was persuaded.

In the end, what engaged Tchaikovsky's sympathies was not Stasov-by-way-of-Balakirev, but the character of Manfred himself. Byron's Alpine wanderer, the lonely individual burdened by feelings of guilt and hopelessness, was a figure with whom Tchaikovsky had much in common, and he responded with one of his most powerful and imaginative symphonic essays. The grim, emotionally intense first movement, marked *Lento lugubre,* is particularly strong, and the magically atmospheric effects of the scherzo show that Tchaikovsky knew his Berlioz very well indeed. The *Manfred* Symphony received its first performance on March 23, 1886, in Moscow, and was published the same year as Tchaikovsky's Op. 58.

RECOMMENDED RECORDINGS

SCHUMANN (OVERTURE): SZELL AND CLEVELAND ORCHESTRA (SONY).

TCHAIKOVSKY: PLETNEV AND RUSSIAN NATIONAL ORCHESTRA (DG).

Mannheim Court Orchestra ENSEMBLE OF THE ELECTOR PALATINE, resident at Mannheim from 1720. During the period of Carl Philipp (reigned 1716–42) and Carl Theodor (1742–78), it established itself as one of the most brilliant orchestras in Europe—"an army of generals," in the words of English musician Charles Burney—numbering among its ranks virtuosos such as the violinists Johann Stamitz (employed 1741–57, concertmaster from 1744) and Christian Cannabich (concertmaster from 1759; music director 1774–98), flutist Johann Baptist Wendling, and oboist Friedrich Ramm. Many of its members were capable composers as well. Under the tutelage of Stamitz and Cannabich, the orchestra developed a remarkable unanimity of ensemble and attack. The Mannheim compositions emphasized bold, powerful tuttis, breathtaking crescendos (an effect known as the "Mannheim steamroller"), and brilliant effects in the strings and winds. In addition to the trademark crescendo, a favorite compositional device was the use of themes built on major or minor triads, which ascended rapidly from the lowest to the highest note. Arrestingly bold themes of this type came to be called "Mannheim rockets," and were a favorite musical topic of the late 18th century (Mozart used a rocket to launch the finale of his Symphony in G minor, K. 550, and Beethoven touched one off at the start of his First Piano Sonata).

The Mannheim orchestra was one of the first in Europe to engage clarinets (beginning in 1758–59), and it was on his visits to Mannheim in 1777–78 that Mozart first heard the instruments and fell in love with their sound. "You cannot imagine the glorious effect of a symphony with flutes, oboes, and clarinets," he wrote to his father. But Leopold Mozart probably *could* imagine: He had already declared the Mannheim orchestra "undeniably the best in Germany." The roster of singers and instrumentalists associated with the Mannheim court included 52 names in 1748, and had expanded to 78 in 1778, when Carl

Theodor became the ruler of Bavaria as well as the Palatinate. Upon his assumption of the new seat, the majority of the Mannheim players went to Munich as well, forming the nucleus of the orchestra that early in 1781 gave the premiere of Mozart's *Idomeneo, re di Creta.*

Manon **Opera in five acts by Jules Massenet,** to a libretto by Henri Meilhac and Philippe Gille (based on the 1731 novel *L'histoire du Chevalier des Grieux et de Manon Lescaut* by Abbé Prévost), premiered January 19, 1884, at the Opéra-Comique in Paris. The original novel's grim story of amorous ambition and moral and financial ruin is told with a fairly gentle touch, but Massenet's portrayal of the heroine has dimension and depth, and his score is full of well-judged effects. Highlights include Manon's Act II farewell to the happy life she has shared with Des Grieux, which is sung not to him but to the kitchen table ("Adieu, notre petit table"), and the meltingly seductive number in which she asks his forgiveness at the end of Act III ("N'est-ce plus ma main?").

RECOMMENDED RECORDING

Gheorghiu, Alagna, Van Dam; Pappano and Orchestre Symphonique de la Monnaie (EMI).

Manon Lescaut **Opera in four acts by Giacomo Puccini,** to a libretto by Domenico Oliva and Luigi Illica (based on the same 1731 novel, *L'histoire du Chevalier des Grieux et de Manon Lescaut* by Abbé Prévost, as Massenet's *Manon*), premiered February 1, 1893, at the Teatro Regio in Turin. The premiere was an unqualified success, establishing Puccini as the leading figure among Italian opera composers of his generation, and as Verdi's heir apparent. Although the libretto underwent a complicated process of creation and revision, Puccini's treatment proved remarkably sure, coming much closer to the gritty realism of the Prévost novel than Massenet's had. The vitality and symphonic sweep of the first two acts are particularly noteworthy. The score includes a number of memorable scenes and one of the most grateful arias ever written for tenor, Des Grieux's Act I confession "Donna non vidi mai"—its melody taken from a student exercise Puccini completed in 1883.

RECOMMENDED RECORDING

Freni, Pavarotti, Croft, Taddei; Levine and Metropolitan Opera (Decca).

Manze, Andrew

(b. Beckenham, England, January 14, 1965)

English violinist and conductor. One of today's foremost exponents of the Baroque violin, he is highly regarded for the improvisatory freedom of his playing and for his dazzling virtuosity. Manze read classics at Cambridge, and studied violin at the Royal Academy of Music and with Marie Leonhardt in Amsterdam. With the trio Romanesca, and with keyboard player Richard Egarr, he pioneered a red-hot, fantastical style of playing 17th- and 18th-century repertoire; his recordings with these colleagues have collected numerous awards. Manze was concertmaster of the Amsterdam Baroque Orchestra from 1989 to 1993. He began to conduct as well, serving as associate director of the Academy of Ancient Music from 1996 to 2003, and guest-conducting many ensembles. In 2003, he succeeded Trevor Pinnock as director of the English Concert.

RECOMMENDED RECORDINGS

As performer:

Biber, violin sonatas: Romanesca (Harmonia Mundi).

Tartini, *Devil's Trill* Sonata, other works (Harmonia Mundi).

As conductor:

Handel, concerti grossi, Op. 6; Academy of Ancient Music (Harmonia Mundi).

marcato (It., "marked") A direction to the performer that a particular line or gesture (usually embodying an important melodic or motivic idea) should be brought out and emphasized, often occurring in passages where the texture is dense or rhythmically complicated. In music for string instruments, the term carries the additional implication that each individual note be forcefully accented.

march Music with a fixed, strong, repetitive rhythmic profile, usually in $\frac{2}{2}$ or $\frac{4}{4}$ time, used to accompany formalized military processions, or—in the words of Peter Schickele, alias P. D. Q. Bach—"to coordinate stylized walking." The earliest known military marches date from the late 17th century, though it can be reasonably assumed that the use of march music, or at least the rhythmic patterns associated with it, dates back to ancient times. By the middle of the 18th century, a time when everything of importance occurred either on the battlefield or in the boudoir, the march had thoroughly infiltrated the vocabulary of classical music.

Among the best-known true military marches are the *Marseillaise,* written by Claude-Joseph Rouget de Lisle (1760–1836) in 1792, and the masterly creations of John Philip Sousa, many of them composed during the 12 years (1880–92) he served as conductor of the United States Marine Band in Washington, D.C. Other notable contributions to the genre were made by England's Kenneth J. Alford (1881–1945), particularly his *Colonel Bogey* of 1914, and the Czech Julius Fučik (1872–1916), whose *Entrance of the Gladiators* is familiar to anyone who has been to a circus. Many classical composers have written concert marches as standalone compositions or included them in larger works such as suites: Among the most familiar examples are Berlioz's arrangement of the *Rákóczi* March (in *La damnation de Faust*), the "Wedding March" from Mendelssohn's incidental music for *A Midsummer Night's Dream* ◉, Elgar's *Pomp and Circumstance* Marches, and Walton's two coronation marches, *Crown Imperial* and *Orb and Sceptre.*

Marches first made their way into classical music via the opera house, where, by the 18th century, they had become a common device. Two notable examples from the 19th century are the "Entrance of the Guests" from Wagner's *Tannhäuser,* and the triumphal scene (Act II, sc. ii) of Verdi's *Aida.* Symphonic movements with the character of a march are everywhere in the literature. They include the first movements of Mozart's *Jupiter* Symphony and Piano Concerto No. 21 in C, of Beethoven's *Emperor* Concerto and *Archduke* Trio, of Bruckner's Symphony No. 8, of Mahler's Symphonies Nos. 3, 5, 6, and 7, and of Shostakovich's Symphonies Nos. 1 and 9; the opening of Stravinsky's *Jeu de cartes* and the Act I prelude to Wagner's *Die Meistersinger von Nürnberg*; the second movements of Beethoven's Symphony No. 7 and Schubert's Symphony No. 9; the third movement of Tchaikovsky's Symphony No. 6; and the finales of Beethoven's

Symphony No. 5, Mendelssohn's *Scottish* Symphony, Mahler's Symphony No. 7, and Shostakovich's Symphony No. 10. One of the literature's more speculative treatments of the march topic can be found in "Mars," the first movement of Holst's *The Planets*: Its $\frac{5}{4}$ time signature makes it a march with an extra step, designed to leave listeners feeling distinctly uneasy.

When a march is slow and in the minor mode, it becomes a funeral march (e.g., the first movements of Bruckner's Symphony No. 8 and Mahler's Symphonies Nos. 5 and 7; the second movement of Beethoven's *Eroica*; and the third movements of Chopin's Piano Sonata in B-flat minor, Op. 35, and Mahler's Symphony No. 1). Another variant is the Turkish march, whose "foreign" coloration is achieved through the use of piquant dissonances, surprising melodic turns, or manic little runs and repeated notes—and is confirmed in orchestral settings by the prominent use of cymbals, triangle, and bass drum. Some of the best-known examples are the finale of Mozart's Piano Sonata in A, K. 331 (the celebrated "Rondo alla Turca"), the march interludes in the second movement of Haydn's Symphony No. 100 (*Military*), and the march from Beethoven's *Die Ruinen von Athen* (it was, after all, the Turks who ruined Athens). Greatest of all is the Turkish march that accompanies the tenor soloist's "Froh, wie seine Sonnen" in the final movement of Beethoven's Ninth Symphony.

Marenzio, Luca

(b. Coccaglio, 1553; d. Rome, August 22, 1599)

ITALIAN COMPOSER, one of the most accomplished and prolific madrigalists of the 16th century. Though details of his early life and musical education are sketchy, he appears to have studied with Giovanni Contino in Mantua and probably entered the service of Cardinal Cristoforo Madruzzo in Rome in the early 1570s. Following Madruzzo's death in 1578, he joined the staff of Cardinal Luigi d'Este, which connected him to the cardinal's brother, Alfonso II, Duke of Ferrara, and sister, Lucrezia (joint dedicatees of Marenzio's second and third books of five-part madrigals); he remained with the d'Este household until Luigi's death in 1586. From 1587 to the end of his life Marenzio was associated with several noble and ecclesiastical patrons and lived and worked mostly in Rome.

Between 1580 and 1587 Marenzio published a total of 12 books of madrigals. Another seven volumes followed between 1588 and 1599. In all, he composed roughly 500 madrigals, 80 villanellas, four or five masses, and about 70 motets.

Marenzio's achievements as a madrigal composer were extraordinary. His versatility made him a natural match for so varied a musical form, and he was second to none in the imagination he brought to the art of word painting. He was able to chart, even within a highly virtuosic texture, an extraordinarily economical path to a musical point. Then as now, there was near-universal admiration for his talent at finding the perfect musical gesture to characterize a word, a mood, an event. His finest works, whether the pastoral settings of his earlier books or the dazzling and adventurous ones of his Ninth Book for five voices (1599), essentially brought the genre to perfection.

RECOMMENDED RECORDINGS

MADRIGALS: ALESSANDRINI AND CONCERTO ITALIANO (OPUS 111).

IL NONO LIBRO DI MADRIGALI: LA VENEXIANA (GLOSSA).

marimba Percussion instrument of the xylophone family, consisting of wooden bars of graduated length set on a frame with metal resonators underneath. It is played with yarn-wrapped mallets (one or two in each hand) and has a range of four to five octaves. Its sound is mellow, not as bright as that of a xylophone, and, thanks to the resonators, richly expressive. Developed around 1910, the marimba is a high-tech adaptation of an instrument that has been used for centuries in Latin America, which in turn traces its lineage back to Africa. The instrument's solo repertoire includes the Concertino for Marimba and Orchestra, Op. 21 (1940), by Paul Creston (1906–85), and Milhaud's Concerto for Marimba, Vibraphone, and Orchestra, Op. 278 (1947).

Marlboro Festival, The *See box on pages 46–47.*

Marriner, Sir Neville

(b. Lincoln, April 15, 1924)

ENGLISH CONDUCTOR AND VIOLINIST. He studied violin at the Royal College of Music in London and the Paris Conservatoire and spent a year teaching at Eton College (1947–48). He subsequently taught violin at the Royal College of Music (1949–59) while playing in the Martin String Quartet and the Philharmonia Orchestra. From 1956 to 1968 he served as principal second violin of the London Symphony Orchestra. In 1959 he took the summer course in conducting given by Pierre Monteux in Hancock, Maine; having spent the early years of his career watching the baton rather than wielding it, he made the shift with remarkable ease. Also in 1959 he organized the Academy of St. Martin-in-the-Fields, an ensemble consisting of top London freelancers that is devoted chiefly to studio work, and began recording everything in sight—so successfully that his name became almost synonymous with classical music for many radio listeners. He served as music director of the Los Angeles Chamber Orchestra (1969–78), the Minnesota Orchestra (1978–86), and the Stuttgart Radio Symphony Orchestra

Sir Neville Marriner, founder of the Academy of St. Martin-in-the-Fields

(1986–89), and has appeared as a guest conductor with many major American and European orchestras. Knighted in 1985, he continues to make recordings with the Academy of St. Martin in the Fields, interpreting and reinterpreting the great works of the 18th and 19th centuries with singular success.

RECOMMENDED RECORDINGS

MOZART, PIANO CONCERTOS (COMPLETE): BRENDEL; ACADEMY OF ST. MARTIN-IN-THE-FIELDS (PHILIPS).

MOZART, PIANO CONCERTOS NOS. 20, 23, 24, AND 25: MORAVEC; ACADEMY OF ST. MARTIN-IN-THE-FIELDS (HÄNSSLER).

VAUGHAN WILLIAMS, *FANTASIA ON A THEME OF THOMAS TALLIS* (WITH OTHER ORCHESTRAL WORKS): ACADEMY OF ST. MARTIN-IN-THE-FIELDS (PHILIPS).

VIVALDI, *THE FOUR SEASONS*: LOVEDAY; ACADEMY OF ST. MARTIN-IN-THE-FIELDS (ARGO).

marteau sans maître, Le WORK FOR ALTO VOICE AND SIX INSTRUMENTALISTS (playing alto flute, xylorimba, vibraphone, mixed percussion, guitar, and viola) by Pierre Boulez, composed 1953–55 and premiered June 18, 1955, in Baden-Baden by members of the Sudwestfunk Symphony Orchestra under the direction of Hans Rosbaud, to whom the score is dedicated. The composition consists of nine pieces, four of which (pieces III, V, VI, and IX) are settings of poems by René Char ("L'artisanat furieux," "Bourreaux de solitude," and "Bel édifice et les pressentiments") and involve the alto soloist, while the others, for various combinations of instruments, function as "commentaries," prologues to or meditations on the texts. The work's scoring pays homage to Schoenberg's *Pierrot lunaire* in certain places, and to the "exotic" sound worlds of African, Balinese, and Japanese music. The labyrinthine organization of the score into three interpenetrating cycles of pieces is one of its most fascinating aspects; the extraordinary metrical and textural complexity of the writing and sudden, dramatic shifts in tempo are a characteristic; so is a sometimes subtle, sometimes sharp contrast of dynamics from note to note within nearly every part. *Le marteau sans maître* (the title means, literally, "The hammer without master") established Boulez as the leading figure in postwar SERIALISM and is widely acknowledged as one of the supreme achievements of the 20th-century avant-garde.

RECOMMENDED RECORDING

Boulez and Ensemble InterContemporain (DG).

Frank Martin

Martin, Frank

(b. Geneva, September 15, 1890; d. Naarden, The Netherlands, November 21, 1974)

SWISS COMPOSER. The son of a Calvinist minister, Martin was the last of ten children. He began composing when he was eight, and was deeply affected at the age of 12 by a performance of Bach's *St. Matthew* Passion; its majestic harmony and the rigor of its construction would have a lasting influence on his own musical thinking. He never attended conservatory; to please his parents, he studied mathematics and physics at the University of Geneva for two years, but music's pull was too strong and he ended up studying piano, harmony, and composition privately with Joseph Lauber. His early works drew on Chopin, Schumann, and Franck; close contact with the Swiss conductor Ernest Ansermet—who conducted the 1918 premiere of Martin's *Les dithyrambs* for chorus and orchestra, as well as many subsequent first performances—deepened his appreciation for the music of Debussy and Ravel as well as that of Bach. Between 1918 and 1926 Martin lived in Zurich, Rome, and Paris. He then returned to Geneva, where he taught improvisation and history of rhythm at the Institut Jaques-Dalcroze and founded the Société de Musique de Chambre de Genève. In 1933 he became founder and director of the Technicum Moderne de Musique, a private school, and at the same time began to explore the 12-tone techniques of Schoenberg, which he applied after his own fashion in a number of subsequent works. In 1938 he was commissioned to compose a work for a madrigal choir. The result, completed in 1941, was the secular oratorio *Le vin herbé* (*The Drugged Wine*) for 12 solo voices and an ensemble of seven string instruments and piano. In this piece, based on the Tristan legend in a retelling by Joseph Bédier, Martin successfully synthesized triadic harmony with 12-tone thematic elements. It was an international success; Martin's two-movement *Petite symphonie concertante* of 1944–45, composed on a commission from Paul Sacher, solidified his reputation.

In 1946 Martin moved to Amsterdam, where he lived for ten years before settling in nearby Naarden. During the quarter century between 1949 and his death in 1974, Martin produced a stream of works in different genres that included many masterpieces, among them his Concerto for Seven Wind Instruments (1949), Harpsichord Concerto (1951–52), Cello Concerto (1965–66; written for Pierre Fournier), and *Ballade* for Viola (1972). Between 1950 and 1957, he also taught at the Staatliche Hochschule für Musik in Cologne.

Though he is thought of primarily as an instrumental composer, over the years Martin made several very important contributions to the sacred literature, including the *Messe pour double choeur a cappella* (*Mass for Double Choir*; 1926), the Passion oratorio *Golgotha* (1945–48; inspired by Rembrandt's *The Three Crosses*), *Le mystère de la Nativité* (*The Mystery of the Nativity*; 1957–59), and a Requiem (1971–72).

The music of Martin's maturity, from *Le vin herbé* onward, is marked by elegance of gesture, an extraordinary formal command, remarkable grace, energy, and lyricism. Its emotion is restrained yet intense, at times even haunting, its scoring economical yet sensuous, reflecting Martin's keen ear for sonority. Few composers of the 20th century succeeded so well at writing music that was suave, expressive, and modern, and at the same time utterly original.

RECOMMENDED RECORDINGS

BALLADES FOR SOLO INSTRUMENT AND ORCHESTRA: VARIOUS SOLOISTS WITH BAMERT AND LONDON PHILHARMONIC ORCHESTRA (CHANDOS).

***CONCERTO FOR SEVEN WIND INSTRUMENTS*: CHAILLY AND ROYAL CONCERTGEBOUW ORCHESTRA (DECCA).**

***CONCERTO FOR SEVEN WIND INSTRUMENTS*: MARTINON AND CHICAGO SYMPHONY ORCHESTRA (RCA).**

***CONCERTO FOR SEVEN WIND INSTRUMENTS, PETITE SYMPHONIE CONCERTANTE, IN TERRA PAX, ETUDES FOR STRING ORCHESTRA*, OTHER WORKS (2 DISCS): ANSERMET AND ORCHESTRE DE LA SUISSE ROMANDE; MUNCHINGER AND STUTTGART CHAMBER ORCHESTRA (DECCA).**

***MASS FOR DOUBLE CHOIR*: O'DONNELL AND WESTMINSTER CATHEDRAL CHOIR (HYPERION).**

***LE VIN HERBÉ*: THARP, WHYTE; SHAPIRO AND I CANTORI DI NEW YORK (NEWPORT CLASSICS).**

Martinelli, Giovanni

(b. Montagnana, October 22, 1885; d. New York, February 2, 1969)

ITALIAN TENOR. He studied in Milan and made his debut there in 1910, in Verdi's *Ernani.* His breakthrough came the following year in Rome, when he sang the role of Dick Johnson (a.k.a. Ramerrez) in Puccini's *La fanciulla del West* under Arturo Toscanini. Martinelli made his Metropolitan Opera debut as Cavaradossi in Puccini's *Tosca,* on November 18, 1913. With his clarion tenor and compelling gifts as an actor, he immediately became the company's workhorse, taking over the Verdi repertoire in the 1920s after the death of Caruso, in particular Manrico (in *Il trovatore*), Radames (*Aida,* of which he gave 123 performances), and Don Alvaro (*La forza del destino*). Martinelli sang with the Met for 32 seasons, taking his final bows in 1946 after 926 performances in 38 roles. He demonstrated uncommon versatility and musicianship, singing Eléazar (in Halévy's

La Juive), Jean (in Meyerbeer's *Le prophète*), and Avito (in *L'amore dei tre re* by Italo Montemezzi [1875–1952]), while proving a durable lead in mainstays such as Gounod's *Faust* and Bizet's *Carmen*. His final decade at the Met was crowned by 26 performances as Verdi's Otello, a role in which he was particularly admired.

Martinon, Jean

(b. Lyon, January 10, 1910; d. Paris, March 1, 1976)

FRENCH CONDUCTOR AND COMPOSER. He studied violin at the conservatories of Lyon and Paris, graduating from the latter with a first prize in violin in 1928. He then studied conducting with Charles Munch and Roger Desormière, and composition with Albert Roussel. Drafted following Germany's attack on France in 1940, he was captured and spent two years as a prisoner of war, during which he composed several works, including a setting of Psalm 136 and a piece for jazz orchestra titled *Stalag IX (Musique d'exil)*. In 1946 he became conductor of the Paris Conservatoire Orchestra, and the following year he made his London debut as a guest conductor of the London Philharmonic. His American debut came in 1957 with the Boston Symphony. In 1963 he was named music director of the Chicago Symphony, a post he held until 1968. His adventurous programming, which placed a pronounced emphasis on music of the 20th century, did not enjoy widespread support, and he was forced out to make way for Georg Solti. Martinon returned to France, where he worked with both the French National Radio Orchestra and the Orchestre de Paris in the years prior to his death. His recordings of the orchestral music of Debussy and Ravel, and of various works by Nielsen, Bartók, Hindemith, Prokofiev, Martin, Roussel, and Varèse, are among the finest in the catalog.

The composed conductor: Jean Martinon

Martinon remained active as a composer throughout his career. Among his compositions were four symphonies as well as concertos for flute, violin, and cello (the latter two written for Henryk Szeryng and Pierre Fournier, respectively) and a small amount of chamber music.

RECOMMENDED RECORDINGS

DEBUSSY, ORCHESTRAL WORKS: ORCHESTRE NATIONAL DE L'O.R.T.F. (EMI).

RAVEL, *DAPHNIS ET CHLOÉ* SUITE NO. 2 (WITH OTHER WORKS): CHICAGO SYMPHONY ORCHESTRA (RCA).

RAVEL, ORCHESTRAL WORKS: ORCHESTRE DE PARIS (EMI).

ROUSSEL, *BACCHUS ET ARIANE* SUITE NO. 2: CHICAGO SYMPHONY ORCHESTRA (RCA).

VARÈSE, *ARCANA* (WITH BARTÓK, *MIRACULOUS MANDARIN* SUITE; HINDEMITH, *NOBILISSIMA VISIONE*): CHICAGO SYMPHONY ORCHESTRA (RCA).

Martinů, Bohuslav

(b. Polička, Bohemia, December 8, 1890; d. Liestal, Switzerland, August 28, 1959)

CZECH COMPOSER. After Leoš Janáček, he was the most important Czech composer of the 20th century. Up to the age of 11 he lived in the family quarters atop the tower of St. James's Church in Polička, where his father was watchman and bell ringer. He later said that this unique environment—with its isolation, elevation, eerie quietness (except when bells were ringing), and "differentness"—played an important role in shaping his music. While he absorbed a variety of influences over the years, some of the most consistent features of his idiom lend credence to that assertion, not least the airy spaciousness of the orchestral textures he favored and the wistful, distant emotions many of his works convey. Martinů began violin lessons as a child, and at 15, on a scholarship provided by the town of Polička, entered the Prague Conservatory to study violin and composition. Resistant to discipline, he skipped classes and was suspended for ten weeks for performing in public without permission. He transferred in 1909 to the conservatory's organ department to focus on composition, but after a year was expelled for "incorrigible carelessness." Largely self-taught, and henceforth answering only to his muse, he began to compose more or less continuously.

For several years Martinů supported himself by teaching violin and playing as an occasional substitute in the violin section of the Czech Philharmonic under Václav Talich. In 1918 he wrote the patriotic cantata *Česká rapsódie* (*Czech Rhapsody*), celebrating the end of World War I and the arrival of Czech independence; it was premiered by the Philharmonic, and soon afterward Martinů became a regular in the second violins.

In the early 1920s Martinů returned briefly to the Prague Conservatory to study composition with Josef Suk. In the fall of 1923 he left Prague for Paris, where he studied with Albert Roussel, was exposed to the music of Stravinsky, Debussy, and Les Six, and came under the spell of jazz. His music, richly reflecting this stylistic mélange, began to be noticed, and the conductor Serge Koussevitzky became an early champion. Martinů lived in Paris for 17 years, marrying a Frenchwoman and producing new pieces at a prolific rate. The 1930s saw Martinů's aesthetic compass align with the prevalent neoclassical style, resulting in a simplification of his idiom and a preoccupation with forms and procedures of the Baroque, evident in works such as the *Concerto grosso* (1937) for chamber orchestra, and the Double Concerto (1938) for two string orchestras, piano, and timpani. This work also reflects, in its edgy, anguished expressiveness, the prewar tensions then gripping Europe.

With the fall of France in 1940, the composer fled Paris for Provence, then traveled by boat to Lisbon and on to the United States. In America, Martinů's career entered a new phase, characterized by the production of larger orchestral works such as symphonies and concertos. He wrote his first symphony at 52, on a commission from Koussevitzky, and

Bohuslav Martinů, out for a stroll

completed four more in as many years; his Symphony No. 6, commissioned by Charles Munch and subtitled *Fantaisies symphoniques,* brought the cycle to a brilliant conclusion in 1953. ◉ That year Martinů returned to Europe, where, except for a brief stint back in New York, he spent the rest of his life. Among the most important works of his final years were his Piano Concerto No. 4 (1956), *Fresky Piero della Francesca* (*The Frescoes of Piero della Francesca*; 1955) for orchestra, and an opera, *Řecké pašije* (*The Greek Passion*; 1954–57).

Martinů produced music easily, and despite periods of illness and depression was remarkably prolific for a 20th-century composer. Notwithstanding the many influences he absorbed into his style over the years, his mature idiom is immediately recognizable; pleasantly triadic, its hallmarks include spiky ostinatos, luminous string textures, and distinctive, unorthodox chord progressions that defy traditional tonal logic. He contributed valuable works to nearly every area of the repertoire, though his operas (including several works written for radio and television) have so far failed to gain a foothold in the international arena. His surviving stage works include more than a dozen ballets, among them several jazz-inspired efforts from the 1920s; the best-known of these, *Kuchyňská revue* (*The Kitchen Review*; 1927), scored for a sextet of violin, cello, clarinet, bassoon, trumpet, and piano, Martinů rightly regarded as one of his finest compositions. Martinů's instrumental works are his most important legacy, especially the six symphonies, the Double Concerto ◉, the *Sinfonia Concertante* No. 2 (1949), and the impressive portfolio of chamber pieces he created over the years, which includes, in addition to *The Kitchen Review,* string and wind quintets, seven numbered string quartets, three piano trios, and an adorable sonata for flute and piano.

RECOMMENDED RECORDINGS

DOUBLE CONCERTO: BĚLOHLÁVEK AND CZECH PHILHARMONIC (CHANDOS).

FLUTE SONATA: GISLER-HAASE, MORI (CAMERATA).

THE KITCHEN REVIEW: HOGWOOD AND CZECH PHILHARMONIC (SUPRAPHON).

SINFONIA CONCERTANTE, CONCERTO GROSSO: BĚLOHLÁVEK AND CZECH PHILHARMONIC (SUPRAPHON).

SYMPHONIES NOS. 3 AND 4: BĚLOHLÁVEK AND CZECH PHILHARMONIC (SUPRAPHON).

SYMPHONY NO. 6: BĚLOHLÁVEK AND CZECH PHILHARMONIC (CHANDOS).

Mascagni, Pietro

(b. Livorno, December 7, 1863; d. Rome, August 2, 1945)

ITALIAN COMPOSER. Against his father's wishes, he contrived to study music by enrolling secretly in the Instituto Luigi Cherubini, the discovery of which led to a family blowup that was resolved when an uncle agreed to adopt the boy. His musical education continued, and positive notice of his early compositions facilitated a reconciliation with his father and his acceptance at the Milan Conservatory, where he was sponsored by Count Florestano Larderel, a wealthy musical amateur. Mascagni studied with Ponchielli, who encouraged his talent, and

Pietro Mascagni

he became friends, then roommates, with Puccini, whose fascination with the music of Wagner he shared. Impatient with the tedium of conservatory training, and anxious to make a name for himself in the professional world, Mascagni left Milan without receiving a diploma. After a year as conductor of a touring opera troupe he settled into the life of a municipal music teacher in Cerignola in southeastern Italy. In 1889 he entered and won a competition for new one-act operas sponsored by the publishing house of Sonzongo. His winning entry, CAVALLERIA RUSTICANA (*Rustic Chivalry*), produced in 1890 at Rome's Teatro Costanzi, was a sensation, turning its 26-year-old composer into an overnight celebrity. It immediately entered the standard repertoire, a position it retains today, usually sharing the bill with its stylistic first cousin, Leoncavallo's *Pagliacci*. In fact, "Cav and Pag," as the double bill is affectionately known, proved to be the high-water mark of the VERISMO style in opera. Mascagni's popularity faded after *Cavalleria rusticana,* the one true hit of his career. He would subsequently compose a handful of songs, some choral-orchestral music and 15 additional operas, only three of which—*L'amico Fritz* (1891), *Zanetto* (1896), and *Iris* (1898)—had any success. Mascagni was also active as a conductor, holding the directorship of the Liceo Rossini in Pesaro from 1895 until 1903. From then until 1911 he directed the Scuola Musicale in Rome, where he resided for the rest of his life.

RECOMMENDED RECORDINGS

L'AMICO FRITZ: PAVAROTTI, FRENI, SARDINERO; GAVAZZENI AND ROYAL OPERA (EMI).

CAVALLERIA RUSTICANA: COSSOTTO, BERGONZI, ALLEGRI; KARAJAN AND LA SCALA ORCHESTRA (DG).

CAVALLERIA RUSTICANA: SCOTTO, DOMINGO, ELVIRA; LEVINE AND NATIONAL PHILHARMONIC ORCHESTRA (RCA).

Maskarade COMIC OPERA IN THREE ACTS BY CARL NIELSEN, to a libretto by Vilhelm Andersen (based on Ludwig Holberg's 1724 play *Mascarade*), premiered November 11, 1906, at the Royal Theater in Copenhagen. The story revolves around a masked ball and the escapades of the love-struck young Leander and his servant Henrik, whose clever machinations, Figaro-style, bring about a happy end in which love triumphs. Nielsen's music creates a world deliciously full of gaiety and complexity, bringing the central characters to life while probing deeper (and sometimes troubling) aspects of the human situation, particularly the link between love and mortality. This balance between the comic and the serious reminds one of Mozart, as well as Milan Kundera's considerations of "the unbearable lightness of being." Certainly no work of the 20th century comes closer to Mozart than *Maskarade*—not in the way it sounds, which is pure Nielsen, but in the way it functions. For too long the opera was known only by its ebullient, sparklingly bright overture and the third act's "Dance of the Cockerels," but recent productions, together with a recording based on a new edition of the score published by Edition Wilhelm Hansen, have gone a long way toward helping the work gain its rightful place in the repertoire outside Denmark.

RECOMMENDED RECORDING

HAUGLAND, RESMARK, HENNING, SKOVHUS; SCHIRMER AND DANISH NATIONAL RADIO SYMPHONY ORCHESTRA (DECCA).

Mass Christian liturgical ceremony consisting of prayers, acclamations, readings from scripture, and a eucharistic meal in which the body and blood of Christ (in the form of bread and wine) are consumed, recalling the Last Supper and Christ's sacrificial death on the Cross. As the central act of

Christian worship, the Mass held a place of unique importance in European civic and cultural life for centuries and gave rise to a vast body of music intended to amplify the emotional impact and spiritual meaning of its text. The singing or chanting of psalms at Mass probably occurred from the earliest days of the Church; as time went by, the musical trappings became ever richer, achieving an extraordinary complexity and beauty in the late Middle Ages and Renaissance. Since then a large number of musically important settings of the Mass have been created not with actual liturgical use in mind but as pendants to special occasions or as freestanding works of art.

The text of the Mass as it was fixed by the Roman Catholic Church in the first millennium is in Greek and Latin. The five main sections that are spoken or intoned at every celebration—the Kyrie, Gloria, Credo, Sanctus, and Agnus Dei—are referred to as the Ordinary. The sections of the text that are specific to a particular day in the church year are referred to as the Proper.

During the early Middle Ages PLAINCHANT settings of texts belonging to both the Proper and the Ordinary (except for the Credo) proliferated throughout Christendom. By the beginning of the 8th century a substantial number of these were available for use in celebrations of the mass. The 9th century saw the development of more elaborate chant settings of the Ordinary.

The creation of POLYPHONIC settings of portions of the Mass, based on existing plainchant, began with a group of composers centered in the Isle de France. The most striking early activity occurred at Notre Dame in Paris, with the polyphonic elaboration of two important sections of the Proper: the Gradual and the Alleluia, which is sung on feast days. Settings of these sections, in two-voice ORGANUM, possibly by Léonin, survive in the *Magnus liber organi,* compiled at Notre Dame during the second half of the 12th century and the early years of the 13th. Léonin's successor Pérotin subsequently contributed more intricate settings, in three- and four-voice organum, to the same compilation. The experiments of the school of Notre Dame had a catalytic effect, prompting emulation throughout Europe, especially in England and Spain, and catapulting polyphonic composition to the forefront of musical endeavor. By the early decades of the 14th century French composers were creating true polyphonic settings of individual sections of the Ordinary. In some manuscript sources these treatments, by different hands, are found grouped to create a polyphonic setting of the entire Ordinary, referred to as a mass "cycle." The earliest of these is the Tournai Mass, found in several medieval sources.

Guillaume de Machaut created a new paradigm with his *Messe de Nostre Dame,* the earliest-known complete polyphonic mass cycle conceived as an integral work by a single composer. Written for the Reims Cathedral in the early 1360s, it is one of the outstanding achievements of the French ARS NOVA. Still, for some years afterward, Gloria-Credo pairs, rather than complete settings of the Ordinary, were the predominant focus of liturgical composition.

For a good part of the period 1400–1600, polyphonic settings of the Ordinary represented the most important and prestigious sphere of musical activity in Europe. The masses of this period were the proving ground for innovations in compositional technique that produced a polyphonic language of extraordinary richness and complexity, which was not only one of the great artistic achievements in history but the foundation for four centuries of development in Western music—the preludes and fugues of Bach, Mozart's concertos, Beethoven's symphonies, Wagner's operas, Stravinsky's ballets, Webern's hyper-refined serialism, and even—indeed especially—the Beach Boys.

A celebration of Mass from the Psalter of Alfonso V of Aragon (1442), showing male choir, organist, and an assistant working the bellows

Behind the stylistic trends of the 15th century was a striving for structural coherence. Two general approaches found favor: the "motto" mass, in which the music for each section of the Ordinary began with a similar opening motif, and the "CANTUS FIRMUS" or "tenor" mass, in which each section was based on the same borrowed melody, usually appearing as a cantus firmus in the tenor voice. This practice of unifying a polyphonic setting of the Ordinary by employing the same cantus firmus tenor in all five sections originated in England, in the works of Leonel Power (d. 1445) and John Dunstable. It spread quickly to the Continent, and ruled as the basic mass type of the later 15th century. Up to about 1450, the cantus firmus almost always was taken from chant; afterwards, it became fashionable to import it from a polyphonic secular song. Examples of this practice include Guillaume Du Fay's *Missa "Se la face ay pale"* (ca. 1455), based on one of his own ballades, and his *Missa "L'homme armé,"* (ca. 1460), based on a popular medieval song (one that would inspire, over the course of 150 years, at least 40 further settings by the likes of Ockeghem, Josquin, and Palestrina).

The mass enjoyed its heyday as the dominant musical genre in Europe during the 100 years between 1450 and 1550, a period when supremacy in the field of composition belonged to a remarkable assemblage of Franco-Flemish masters. The dynasty began with Du Fay, whose innovative approach proved highly influential; the seven masses that survive are among the glories of late medieval music. The masses of Johannes Ockeghem (13 settings can be attributed to him, plus a Requiem) are equally fine and demonstrate amazing originality as well as a magnificent artifice. Nearly every one takes a different compositional approach: the source material for five of them comes from chansons, while others are based on chant. Two, the *Missa prolationum* and *Missa cuiusvis toni,* are musical puzzles. Ockeghem's counterpoint tends to be free rather than imitative, a noteworthy departure from the norms of the day. Other important figures of the era were Antoine Busnois (ca. 1430–92), whose *Missa "L'homme armé"* may have been the very first based on this tune (indeed, he may have written the tune), and Jacob Obrecht (1457–1505), who composed nearly three dozen masses and whose music undoubtedly exerted an influence on the greatest composer of the age, Josquin des Prez.

Josquin's masses, of which 18 have survived, exhibit an astonishing mastery of a variety of styles and unifying techniques, and are remarkable for their virtuosic counterpoint. Conceptually they are quite rich. The *Missa Hercules dux Ferrariae,* for example, is based on a cantus firmus derived from the vowels of its title; his *Missa "L'homme armé" sexti toni,* based on the same chanson as Busnois's and Du Fay's earlier settings, allows the cantus firmus to migrate to every voice. Perhaps the greatest of Josquin's contributions to the genre, the *Missa Pange lingua,* is plainchant-based but remarkably sophisticated in its approach, coming closer to an "imitative paraphrase" than a true tenor mass. The flexibility and beauty of Josquin's point-of-imitation style, displayed in many of these works, had a profound impact on the music of nearly every important figure of the 16th century.

The 16th century saw the ascendancy of a new style of mass, called the "imitation" or "parody" mass, in which the unifying element was no longer a single thread—a borrowed melody from a plainchant or popular song—but the whole polyphonic cloth of another, preexisting piece, e.g., a three-part chanson or a four-part motet. The works of Josquin and Obrecht helped establish this new procedure, which figures prominently in the masses of Jean Mouton (ca. 1459–1522) and his student Adrian Willaert, as well as Nicolas Gombert (ca. 1495–ca. 1560), Cristóbal de Morales (ca. 1500–53), and Jacobus Clemens non Papa (ca. 1510–ca. 1555). Also popular during the 16th century were polyphonic masses based on a freely invented subject rather than a preexisting one, such as Giovanni Pierluigi da Palestrina's *Missa Papae Marcelli.* While settings of the Ordinary continued to be the gold standard in serious composition, the early years of the 16th century also brought forth the *Choralis Constantinus* of Heinrich Isaac, a vast compendium of polyphonic settings of the Proper.

The high polyphonic style of the Renaissance enjoyed a final flowering in the closing decades of the 16th century, in the works of Palestrina, Orlande de Lassus, and Tomás Luis de Victoria. Palestrina's 104 masses are remarkable both for the variety of approaches they embrace and their technical resourcefulness, and notable most of all for their magisterial polyphony, still a model of purity. About 60 settings by Lassus survive, also quite splendid in their craftsmanship; many are based on secular models. Victoria's 20 masses, most of which are imitation masses, include settings for four, five and six voices, as well as two-choir settings for eight and nine voices and a three-choir setting for 12 voices. William Byrd's three mass settings, all dating from the 1590s—one for three voices, one for four, and one for five—are, by comparison with the work of Palestrina and Victoria (or Byrd's own earlier sacred music), relatively chaste, choosing straightforward text setting rather than elaborate polyphony. Like Isaac, Byrd also contributed important collections of Proper settings to the literature, his *Gradualia* of 1605 and 1607.

With the arrival of the 17th century and the birth of a new musical style built on the primacy of a single melodic line set above a basso continuo, the development of the mass as a polyphonic vocal genre stalled. Opera's dominance forced changes in the sound and structure of liturgical music, and by the 18th century an entirely new manner of setting the mass—utilizing instrumental accompaniment and solo singers as well as chorus—had superseded the old. The greatest musical influence on mass settings of the 18th century was the so-called Neapolitan style, which combined elements of cantata and opera and made a practice of breaking up the standard sections of the Ordinary into shorter numbers. Exemplars of this style included works by Alessandro Scarlatti, Nicola Porpora (1686–1768) and Niccolò Jommelli (1714–74). Bach, the great Lutheran, tapped into the Neapolitan model in his monumental *Mass in B Minor,* which includes many passages summarizing the earlier polyphonic tradition as well.

The fact that the mass was merely one of many musical genres in circulation during the second half of the 18th century did not keep composers in Catholic Europe from devoting their attention to it. Mozart created a plethora of masses and mass sections during his years in Salzburg, capped by the *Coronation* Mass in C, K. 317, of 1779. He soon topped that effort with his Mass in C minor, K. 427 (1782–83); though unfinished, it offers majestic tribute in its scale and style to the grand vocal manner of Handel's oratorios. Joseph Haydn composed only a handful of masses during the first part of his career; but the six late works he created between 1796 and 1802 to celebrate the name day of Princess Maria Hermenegild—the *Missa Sancti Bernardi von Offida, Missa in tempore belli, Nelsonmesse, Theresienmesse, Schöpfungsmesse,* and *Harmoniemesse*—qualify him as the most important mass composer of the Classical era. Written after he had completed the last of his symphonies, at roughly the same time as his oratorios *The Creation* and *The Seasons,* they are among the greatest of his achievements.

The most salient quality of Beethoven's Mass in C, Op. 86 (1807), is its comforting routineness; it is scarcely an earth-shaking statement. His *Missa solemnis,* on the other hand, is precisely that, a work of enormous scope and great modernity that also manages, like Bach's *Mass in B Minor,* to summarize the tradition from which it emerged. The Romantics saw more in the Requiem text, with its allusions to tears and fiery punishments, than they did in the Mass, though multiple settings of the Mass were made by Franz Schubert, Anton Bruckner, and Charles Gounod. One of the most remarkable of all 19th-century contributions to the genre was Gioacchino Rossini's *Petite messe solennelle* (1864) for 12 solo voices, with the whimsical accompaniment of piano and harmonium—a precious late gift, modest and full of gentle devotion, spiced by more than a touch of the operatic.

With the 20th century came sweeping reinterpretations of what the Mass meant, both in liturgical terms and musical ones, along with bracing stylistic renewal, which in some cases meant a return to the earlier manner of writing for unaccompanied voices and creating settings based on plainchant. Leoš Janáček's *Glagolitic Mass,* with a text in Church Slavonic, is a wonderfully vital statement in which not only the form of the mass but the roles of chorus, soloists, and orchestra are newly imagined; there is a prominent solo part for organ, the composer's own instrument, and the orchestration is dazzling. Stravinsky also took a novel approach to the scoring of his *Mass* (1944–48), which calls for an accompaniment of ten wind and brass instruments. Notable 20th-century a cappella settings include Poulenc's *Mass in G* (1937) and a pair of masses for double choir: Vaughan Williams's Mass in G minor (1920–21) and Frank Martin's *Mass* (1922–26). Whereas these composers chose to pare things back, Leonard Bernstein's *Mass,* written for the opening of the Kennedy Center in 1971 and described as a "theatre piece for singers, players and dancers," sought to embrace everything from electronic tape to marching bands and rebellious rock stars. In a sense, Bernstein brought the mass full circle: as Beethoven had inserted the music of war in the Agnus Dei of his *Missa Solemnis,* and as Ockeghem and Josquin had inserted popular song, he inserted rock and roll, the blues, and a "street chorus" that sings in American slang. More recent contributions to the genre have included Arvo Pärt's *Berliner Messe* (1990) for soloists, chorus, and organ; Libby Larsen's (b. 1950) *Missa Gaia: Mass for the Earth* (1992), with a text drawn from various sources including the poetry of Gerard Manley Hopkins; and Sven-David Sandström's (b. 1942) *The High Mass* (1993–94), a 90-minute-long setting of the Latin Mass for soloists, chorus, organ, orchestra.

RECOMMENDED RECORDINGS

Bach, *Mass in B Minor*: Gens, Zomer, Scholl, Prégardien, Kooy; Herreweghe and Collegium Vocale (Harmonia Mundi).

Beethoven, *Missa Solemnis*: Janowitz, Ludwig, Wunderlich, Berry; Karajan and Berlin Philharmonic (DG).

Bernstein, *Mass*: Bernstein and various soloists (Sony).

Byrd, Masses for 3, 4, and 5 voices: Carwood and The Cardinall's Musicke (ASV).

Haydn, masses: Various soloists; Hickox and Collegium Musicum 90 (Chandos).

Josquin, *Missa Hercules Dux Ferrarie*: Blachly and Pomerium (Glissando).

Machaut, *Messe de Nostre Dame*: Hilliard Ensemble (Hyperion).

Mozart, Mass in C (*Coronation*): Bonney, Gadd, McDougall; Pinnock and The English Concert (Archiv).

Ockeghem, *Missa prolationum*: Wickham and The Clerk's Group (ASV).

"1000: A Mass for the End of Time" (Aquitanian chant and polyphony): Anonymous 4 (Harmonia Mundi).

Pärt, *Berliner Messe*: Kaljuste and Estonian Philharmonic Chamber Choir (ECM).

Poulenc, *Mass in G*: Christophers and The Sixteen (Virgin Classics).

Vaughan Williams, *Mass in G Minor*: Best and Corydon Singers (Hyperion).

Massenet, Jules

(b. Montaud, May 12, 1842; d. Paris, August 13, 1912)

French composer. The youngest of 12 children, he received his first musical instruction from his mother, a capable pianist; the family settled in Paris in 1847 after his father, a businessman, retired. Entering the Paris Conservatoire at the age of ten, he eventually studied composition with Ambroise Thomas (1811–96). Before leaving the Conservatoire, he took first prize in piano, and in 1863 he won the Prix de Rome, which supported a two-year residency in the Eternal City. There, as a result of an introduction from Franz Liszt, he met Ninon de Sainte-Marie, who became his piano student. The two were married in 1866 and settled in Paris, where Massenet occupied himself with musical odd jobs and piano instruction. In 1867 his one-act opera *La grand'tante* (*The Great-Aunt*) was produced at the Opéra-Comique, and in the decade that followed, his reputation grew steadily, boosted first by the 1873 triumph of *Marie-Magdeleine,* a "sacred drama" with Pauline Viardot in the title role, and then in 1877 with *Le roi de Lahore,* his first premiere at the Paris Opéra. In 1876 Massenet was decorated with the Légion d'Honneur, and in 1878 he became the youngest member ever elected to the Académie des Beaux-Arts. That same year he succeeded his old teacher as professor of composition at the Conservatoire, following Thomas's appointment as director. By 1881, with the premiere of *Hérodiade,* Massenet had established himself as France's preeminent opera composer. In the period that followed, he created the operas for which he is famous today: *MANON* (1884), *Le Cid* (1885), *Esclarmonde* (1889), *WERTHER* (1892), *THAÏS* (1894), and *Cendrillon* (*Cinderella*; 1899). Though less well known, several other operas in the Massenet canon—including *La Navarraise* (1894), *Sapho* (1897), *Chérubin* (1905), and *Don Quichotte* (1910)—are occasionally revived. In all, Massenet contributed 40 works to the genre; four ballets and incidental music for more than a dozen plays make up the remainder of his output for the stage. In addition, he composed nearly 300 songs, a number of short orchestral pieces and suites, a piano concerto, a handful of chamber works, and a small number of pieces for piano.

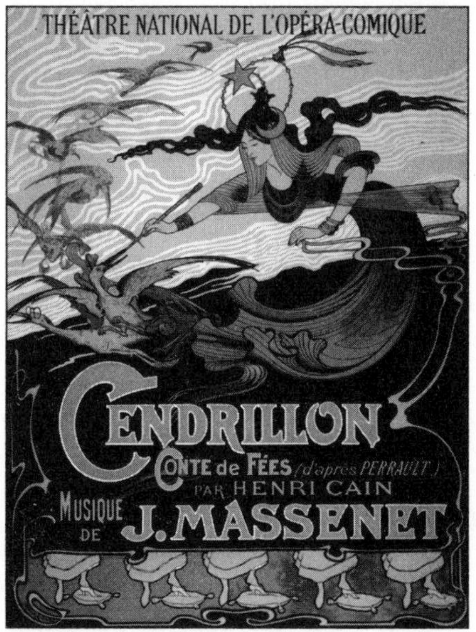

***Poster for Massenet's* Cendrillon**

At a time when Wagner was beginning to dominate French musical and artistic life, Massenet bucked the trend, employing a fluent and decidedly French idiom in his operas, whether run-of-the-mill or enduring masterpieces such as *Manon, Werther,* and *Cendrillon.* These works exhibit a rare sympathy for their characters, and their refinement and dramatic cohesion reflect a very high standard of craftsmanship. Massenet's influence can be felt in the music of Debussy and Ravel, much as those composers might have wished otherwise, and was more gratefully absorbed by several of his students at the Conservatoire, particularly Gustave Charpentier (1860–1956) and Reynaldo Hahn (1874–1947).

RECOMMENDED RECORDINGS

LE CID (BALLET SUITE): BONYNGE AND NATIONAL PHILHARMONIC ORCHESTRA (DECCA).

MANON: GHEORGHIU, ALAGNA, VAN DAM; PAPPANO AND ORCHESTRE SYMPHONIQUE DE LA MONNAIE (EMI).

WERTHER: ALAGNA, GHEORGHIU, HAMPSON; PAPPANO AND LONDON SYMPHONY ORCHESTRA (EMI).

Mass in B Minor **SACRED WORK BY J. S. BACH,** scored for soloists (two sopranos, alto, tenor, and bass), chorus, orchestra, and continuo. It is one of several instances in Bach's music of a piece created not for practical use but as an example of what could be achieved within a given form. It represents an attempt to fuse the liturgical tendencies of two confessions—the Catholic and the Lutheran— into a single work conceived on a monumental scale and unprecedented in its stylistic scope. While the vastness of the conception would have made the score inappropriate for liturgical use in Bach's day (or any other), it is necessary and altogether fitting on musical and theological grounds as a reflection of the artist's devotion to his faith. Most of the component parts of the score date from various times in Bach's long residence in Leipzig (1723 until his death in 1750), but were not assembled into a complete mass until near the end of his life. Bach never heard the work in its entirety, and though it consists of a collection of movements in a variety of styles, including some deliberately archaic elements, it transcends the inconsistency of its origins. There is a powerful unity to the conception as a whole, expressed in rhythmic and motivic connections between parts composed at different times, in the profound harmonic logic of the overall plan, and not least in the compelling beauty of the music itself and the depth of feeling that underlies Bach's setting of the text.

The score is divided, like an opera, into choral and solo numbers, 27 in all. The pillars of the work are the nine massive choruses of praise in D major, with their celebratory trumpets and drums. Between them, Bach deploys a remarkable variety of choruses, arias, and duets, some with instrumental obbligatos.

The contrast of style and treatment Bach achieves throughout the mass is as noteworthy as the work's underlying expressive unity. In the second Kyrie, for example, he harks back to the polyphony of the 16th century, while in the eight-part setting of *Osanna in excelsis* the treatment is modeled on the Venetian double-choir style of the early 17th century. A motet-like CANTUS FIRMUS technique is applied in the choral writing of the *Credo in unum Deum* and *Confiteor.* Serene diatonic harmony underscores the restful message of the *Dona nobis,* while the most intense chromaticism serves to convey the stabbing pain of the *Crucifixus*—a movement whose "walking" bass, in the style of a CHACONNE, literally makes the sign of the cross 13 times on the page of the score. The joyous *Et resurrexit* chorus that immediately follows marks the spiritual apogee of the mass, and of Bach's entire life as a musician.

RECOMMENDED RECORDINGS

ARGENTA, DAWSON, CHANCE, STAFFORD, VARCOE; GARDINER AND ENGLISH BAROQUE SOLOISTS (ARCHIV).

GENS, ZOMER, SCHOLL, PRÉGARDIEN, KOOY; HERREWEGHE AND COLLEGIUM VOCALE (HARMONIA MUNDI).

Masur, Kurt

(b. Brieg, July 18, 1927)

GERMAN CONDUCTOR. As a teenager he studied piano and cello in Breslau (now Wrocław, Poland) and after World War II he enrolled at the Leipzig Conservatory, where he studied piano, composition, and conducting. He began his apprenticeship in 1948 as orchestra coach at the Landestheater in Halle, subsequently working as Kapellmeister at the city theaters of Erfurt (1951–53) and Leipzig (1953–55). He served two appointments as conductor of the Dresden Philharmonic (1955–58 and 1967–72), and between those was engaged as general music director at the Mecklenburg State Theater in Schwerin (1958–60) and senior music director of the Komische Oper Berlin (1960–64). He was in Berlin when the Wall went up.

Kurt Masur, modern-day Kapellmeister

In 1970 he was named music director of the Leipzig Gewandhaus Orchestra. During his tenure, which lasted until 1996, he brought the orchestra back into the ranks of world-class ensembles and restored its faded reputation through recordings and international tours. In his effort to stabilize it both artistically and financially at a time of political tension and economic stagnation, he pushed for construction of a second "new" Gewandhaus concert hall, which opened in 1982. He became a pivotal figure in the peaceful anti-Communist revolution of 1989; his position at the center of Leipzig's cultural life during the collapse of the former German Democratic Republic enabled him to help convince that government's leaders not to use force against their own people.

Masur assumed the leadership of the New York Philharmonic in 1991, inheriting an orchestra in dire need of discipline and artistic shaping. This he provided during 11 seasons at the helm, earning the respect of critics and most (though not all) of the Philharmonic players for his painstaking (some viewed it as intimidating) approach to music making; he built the orchestra once again into a cohesive unit that, stand-for-stand, may be the strongest in the world. In 2002, a few days before conducting his final subscription concerts as music director, he was named the Philharmonic's music director emeritus; he subsequently became music director of the Orchestre National de France.

What stands out about Masur as a conductor—in addition to his command of a broad symphonic repertoire centering on the works of Beethoven, Mendelssohn, Schumann, Bruckner, and Brahms—is his deep engagement with the music and the musicians who are making it. Averse to any kind of podium display, he coaches an orchestra as it performs, molding and polishing its sound like a sculptor, using gestures not so much to convey a choreographic equivalent as to suggest the appropriate intensity of expression. It is the classic, old-school approach, and Masur is one of its last true representatives.

RECOMMENDED RECORDINGS

BEETHOVEN, SYMPHONIES (COMPLETE): GEWANDHAUS ORCHESTRA (PHILIPS).

BRAHMS, SYMPHONIES (COMPLETE): NEW YORK PHILHARMONIC (TELDEC).

MENDELSSOHN, SYMPHONIES (COMPLETE): GEWANDHAUS ORCHESTRA (EURODISC).

STRAUSS, *VIER LETZTE LIEDER (FOUR LAST SONGS)*: NORMAN; GEWANDHAUS ORCHESTRA (PHILIPS).

Mathis der Maler (Mathias the Painter)

OPERA IN SEVEN SCENES BY PAUL HINDEMITH, to his own libretto (based on the life of the painter Mathias Grünewald), composed between July 1933 and July 1935 and premiered May 28, 1938, at the Stadttheater in Zurich. Set in and around Mainz against the background of the Reformation and the Peasants' War of 1524, the opera depicts

Concert of Angels—*a panel from the Isenheim altarpiece*

Grünewald's struggle to act conscientiously in the face of cruelty and repression; the libretto is a commentary on the artist's role in times of social upheaval. The analogy with Hindemith's own situation—that of an artist in Nazi Germany in the mid-1930s—did not escape those in power there.

While at work on the opera, in response to a request from the conductor Wilhelm Furtwängler, Hindemith extracted a three-movement suite from the score that he titled Symphony *Mathis der Maler,* which Furtwängler premiered with the Berlin Philharmonic on March 12, 1934. The public's response was enthusiastic, but the official reaction was predictably hostile. In spite of Furtwängler's staunch defense of the music and its composer (published in the November 25, 1934, issue of the *Deutsche allgemeine Zeitung*), the opera's planned premiere in Berlin was blocked. Hindemith thereupon took a leave of absence from his teaching position at the Berlin Hochschule, and for the first time considered emigrating. The eventual premiere of *Mathis der Maler* made his situation untenable, and in September 1938 he left Germany for Switzerland.

Though the opera is rarely performed owing to its cumbersome plot, the Symphony *Mathis der Maler* has become one of Hindemith's best-known pieces. Its three movements are named after panels from Grünewald's most famous work, the altarpiece in the Church of St. Anthony at Isenheim, which he painted between 1512 and 1515. The music of the first movement ("Concert of Angels") is identical to that of the opera's prelude. The second movement ("The Entombment") appears as an orchestral interlude in the opera's final scene. The music of the concluding movement ("The Temptation of St. Anthony") comes from the opera's sixth scene, in which Mathis experiences a series of visions akin to scenes portrayed in the altarpiece, culminating in the meeting of St. Anthony and St. Paul. Even removed from its operatic context, the music of the symphony retains a remarkable eloquence and dramatic urgency. Hindemith's radiant scoring for the strings and magnificent use of the brass make it an impressive modern orchestral showpiece.

RECOMMENDED RECORDINGS

FISCHER-DIESKAU, KING, KOSZUT, WAGEMANN; KUBELÍK AND BAVARIAN RADIO SYMPHONY ORCHESTRA (EMI).

PROTSCHKA, HERMANN, VON HALEM; ALBRECHT AND WEST GERMAN RADIO SYMPHONY ORCHESTRA, COLOGNE (WERGO).

SYMPHONY (WITH *TRAUERMUSIK* AND *SYMPHONIC METAMORPHOSIS*): BLOMSTEDT AND SAN FRANCISCO SYMPHONY ORCHESTRA (DECCA).

Maurel, Victor

(b. Marseilles, June 17, 1848; d. New York, October 22, 1923)

FRENCH BARITONE. A singer of extraordinary intelligence and accomplishment, he was Verdi's choice to create the roles of Iago and Falstaff. Trained as an architect, he decided early on to pursue a career as a singer. He studied in Marseilles and at the Paris Conservatoire, and as a student sang in the chorus of the Paris Opéra at the premiere of Verdi's *Don Carlo.* He made his Opéra debut as a solo singer in 1868, appearing as Count di Luna in Verdi's *Il trovatore* and in productions of Meyerbeer's *Les Huguenots* and *L'Africaine.* Following a decade in foreign houses—during which he made his debut at La Scala in Milan (1870) and sang the role of Amonasro in the first American production of Verdi's *Aida* (1873)—he returned to the Opéra in 1879, remaining on its roster until 1894.

On March 24, 1881, at La Scala, Maurel sang the title role in the premiere of the revised version of Verdi's *Simon Boccanegra.* His success in that venture, overcoming Verdi's doubts that he was mature enough for the role, encouraged the composer to entrust him with the part of Iago at the premiere of *Otello* in 1887 and with the title role of *Falstaff* in 1893. In between, he created the role of Tonio in Leoncavallo's *Pagliacci* (1892). Maurel made his Metropolitan Opera debut, as Iago, on December 3, 1894, and on February 4, 1895, sang the title role in the Met premiere of *Falstaff.* During the three seasons he spent at the Met, between 1894 and 1899, he also appeared as Amonasro, Rigoletto, Don Giovanni, and Escamillo in Bizet's *Carmen.* Following his retirement from the stage, he returned to New York, where he taught from 1909 until his death.

Victor Maurel as Iago

Má vlast (My Country) CYCLE OF SIX SYMPHONIC POEMS BY BEDŘICH SMETANA, composed 1874–79, and first performed as a whole on November 5, 1882, in Prague. The cycle celebrates the history, folklore, and landscape of Smetana's native Bohemia. In order, the six tone poems that make up the work are: *Vyšehrad* (the "high fortress" overlooking Prague, fabled seat of the oldest Czech dynasty), *Vltava* (the river that flows past Prague, known in German as the Moldau), *Sárka* (the name of a legendary warrior princess), *Z ceskych luhu a háju* (*From Bohemia's Woods and Fields*), *Tábor* (the town where a courageous Hussite force was defeated), and *Blaník* (the name of the mountain where, according to legend, the Hussite warriors of old sleep away the passing centuries, to be summoned at the time of the Czech nation's greatest need). The two concluding sections form a continuous musical narrative; in both of them Smetana quotes the Hussite chorale "Ye Who are God's Warriors." In the final pages of *Blaník,* the Hussite hymn is transformed into a victorious march, and its strains are joined with the theme of *Vyšehrad* to bring the work to a glorious conclusion.

RECOMMENDED RECORDING

KUBELÍK AND CZECH PHILHARMONIC (SUPRAPHON).

Mazeppa TITLE OF A SYMPHONIC POEM BY FRANZ LISZT AND AN OPERA BY PYOTR IL'YICH TCHAIKOVSKY. Both works are studies of Ivan Stepanovic Mazeppa (ca. 1644–1709), a Russian nobleman who became a Cossack leader. As an opponent of the Russian assimilation of the Ukraine, Mazeppa became an early rallying figure for the 19th-century nationalists, and his life and colorful exploits were celebrated in verse by Lord Byron, Aleksandr Pushkin, and Victor Hugo. It was Hugo's treatment in two poems from his *Orientales* that especially appealed to Liszt. Following Pushkin's

Poltava, Hugo tells of how the young Mazeppa, secretly in love with the Countess Palatine, is caught in the act and, as punishment, strapped naked on the back of his horse and chased out onto the steppe. Hugo concludes his narrative with an optimistic vision of the future for Mazeppa and the Cossack people. Liszt follows the structure of Hugo's poem; Mazeppa's apprehension and wild ride onto the steppe are portrayed, and the tone poem ends with a martial flourish as the Cossacks liberate their hero and advance to victory. *Mazeppa,* the sixth of Liszt's 13 symphonic poems, was composed 1851–54 and received its premiere April 16, 1854, in Weimar, with Liszt conducting.

Tchaikovsky's opera, to a libretto by Victor Burenin based directly on Pushkin, shows a darker and considerably less heroic side of the Cossack hetman. Its plot revolves around Mazeppa's betrayal of a close friend, the Cossack judge Vasily Kochubey, out of love for Kochubey's daughter, Maria. Mazeppa has his friend tortured and beheaded; Maria subsequently loses her mind, and Mazeppa, without Kochubey's aid, loses his struggle against the Tsar. The opera contains some rousing battle music ("The Battle of Poltava") and portrays the conflicted title character with considerable sympathy. *Mazeppa* received its premiere February 15, 1884, at the Bolshoi Theatre in Moscow.

RECOMMENDED RECORDINGS

LISZT: KARAJAN AND BERLIN PHILHARMONIC (DG).

LISZT: MASUR AND GEWANDHAUS ORCHESTRA (EMI).

TCHAIKOVSKY: LEIFERKUS, GORCHAKOVA, DYADKOVA, KOTCHERGA; JÄRVI AND GOTHENBURG SYMPHONY ORCHESTRA (POLYGRAM).

TCHAIKOVSKY: PUTILIN, LOSKUTOVA, DYADKOVA, ALEKSASHKIN; GERGIEV AND KIROV OPERA (PHILIPS).

mazurka Polish dance in $\frac{3}{4}$ time originating in the Mazovia region around Warsaw, where Frédéric Chopin spent his childhood. The mazurka rhythm is similar to that of the waltz, but with a characteristic emphasis—occasionally on the second and more usually on the final beat of the measure—that produces a sense of syncopation.

Chopin was not the first to write pieces enlivened by the mazurka rhythm, but his 50-odd contributions to the genre are the most important by any composer. Nearly all display the clear sectional layout characteristic of Chopin's dance-based piano pieces. But Chopin's frequent use of modal harmony and chromaticism transforms the mazurka from something a peasant might recognize into music of an exceptionally rarefied cast. A number of the later mazurkas belong to the works Chopin wrote not for his students but for himself, to be shared with a small circle of sympathetic friends. Their emotion—a distillation, one part nationalism to two parts febrile sensitivity—is intense yet restrained, their expression subtly nuanced and refined. Among the best are two in Chopin's much-loved key of C-sharp minor: Op. 50, No. 3, is at once elegiac, troubled, and bold, while Op. 63, No. 3, begins as if it were a waltz, grows increasingly speculative, questioning, and surprising, and ends with a remarkable canon at the octave. Equally fine is the Mazurka in C minor, Op. 56, No. 3, suspended between agitation and sultry yearning.

RECOMMENDED RECORDING

CHOPIN: RUBINSTEIN (RCA).

McCormack, John

(b. Athlone, June 14, 1884; d. Dublin, September 16, 1945)

IRISH TENOR. He cultivated a burnished beauty of tone from bottom to top and could deliver even the most familiar ballad

Smiling Irish eyes: John McCormack, tenor

so that it sparkled. His career as an opera star was relatively brief, though it included a number of engagements at Covent Garden and the Metropolitan Opera between 1907 and 1919, as well as frequent stage appearances in Boston and Chicago. As a recitalist, however, he was without peer. He had the ability to turn his listeners into confidants, smiling as he told a story in music. In this role, from about 1910 until the mid-1930s, he enjoyed immense popularity, bolstered to a great extent by the success of his phonograph recordings.

The arrival of the phonograph as a home entertainment device coincided precisely with the apogee of McCormack's operatic career; a not-very-good actor but a smart man and a magnificent singer, he was quick to take advantage of the new technology and became a household name to generations of Americans. His 791 surviving recordings, made between 1904 and 1942, cover a formidable range of material. From the start, though less so in later years, he championed the songs and ballads of Ireland, and it is with these, rather than with any particular part of the operatic or art song repertoire, that his name is associated today. His vibrant timbre and clarion brilliance—even in 75-year-old transcriptions—are happy reminders of a time when popular singers really knew how to sing.

RECOMMENDED RECORDINGS

FAVORITES, VOL. 1 (NAXOS).
"MY WILD IRISH ROSE" (RCA).

McGegan, Nicholas

(b. Sawbridgeworth, January 14, 1950)

ENGLISH CONDUCTOR, FLUTIST, AND HARPSICHORDIST. After studies at Oxford and Cambridge, he led performances of Baroque opera at the English Bach Festival (1979–81). He became the founding music director of the Philharmonia Baroque Orchestra in Berkeley, California, in 1985. He is partly credited with the resurgence of interest in Handel's dramatic music, which he so adroitly champions, and has produced remarkable recordings of many of that composer's oratorios and operas. Since 1990, he has been the music director of the Göttingen Handel Festival. Over the years he has made regular conducting appearances in opera houses in the U.S. and Europe. In 1992, he founded the Arcadian Academy, an ensemble with which he has toured and made a few recordings, and in 1999 he was appointed Baroque series director of the St. Paul Chamber Orchestra.

measure A unit of musical duration consisting of the number of beats specified in the time signature, set off in conventional notation by bar lines before and after.

Mefistofele OPERA BY ARRIGO BOITO, consisting of a "prologue in heaven," four acts, and an epilogue, which premiered October 4, 1875, at the Teatro Comunale in Bologna. Boito wrote his own libretto based on Goethe's *Faust*; an earlier version of the opera, in five acts, was a fiasco at its premiere in 1868, forcing the composer to make sweeping revisions and eliminate several scenes altogether. The work has kept its place in the international repertoire mainly as a vehicle for leading bassos—its title role has attracted the likes of Chaliapin, Ramey, and Treigle. The opening and closing scenes, replete with angelic chorus and offstage brass, have a sublime effect in the theater, and there are several first-rate numbers, especially the title character's mocking "Ave signor" in the prologue, Faust's "Dai campi dai prati" in Act I, and the Act III duet of Margherita and Faust, "Lontano, lontano."

RECOMMENDED RECORDINGS

GHIAUROV, PAVAROTTI, FRENI, CABALLÉ; FABRITIIS AND NATIONAL PHILHARMONIC ORCHESTRA (DECCA).

TREIGLE, DOMINGO, CABALLÉ; RUDEL AND LONDON SYMPHONY ORCHESTRA (EMI).

Mehta, Bejun *See box on pages 155–57.*

Mehta, Zubin

(b. Bombay, April 29, 1936)

INDIAN CONDUCTOR. His father, Mehli Mehta, a violinist and conductor, was the founder of the Bombay Symphony and later joined the Hallé Orchestra in England. Zubin, whose given name means "the powerful sword," learned violin and music theory as a youth. At the age of 18 he abandoned medical studies to study conducting with Hans Swarowsky at the Academy of Music in Vienna, where he also played double bass in the school's orchestra. In 1958 he entered a conducting competition sponsored by the Royal Liverpool Philharmonic and won a year's appointment as assistant conductor. Miserable in Liverpool, he went back to Vienna. A successful guest-conducting engagement with the Philadelphia Orchestra was fol-

Zubin Mehta

lowed by debuts with the Vienna Philharmonic and the Berlin Philharmonic in 1961, and an appointment as music director of the Montreal Symphony Orchestra (1961–67).

In 1962, following a performance of Richard Strauss's *Don Quixote* with the Los Angeles Philharmonic in which he stepped in as a last-minute substitute for Fritz Reiner, Mehta was engaged as the orchestra's associate conductor—without the approval of its music director, Georg Solti. Solti promptly quit, and Mehta assumed the position; at the age of 26, he was the youngest music director of any major American orchestra. He remained 16 years, developing an excellent rapport with the Angelenos. In spite of some tactless remarks about the New York Philharmonic in 1967, when he compared it unfavorably with his group in Los Angeles, Mehta was engaged by the New York ensemble as music director following the departure of Pierre Boulez. His lengthy tenure (1978–91) was controversial: the notoriously finicky New York press became increasingly hostile, with criticism centering on lack of discipline within the orchestra and the occasional superficiality of Mehta's interpretations. But there were many triumphs amid the routine, and Mehta took the orchestra on numerous prestige tours.

Mehta became chief music adviser of the Israel Phiharmonic in 1969 and was named that orchestra's music director for life in 1981. After a distinguished career as an opera conductor in some of the world's major houses—including those of Vienna, Rome, Chicago, and London—he was appointed music director of the Bavarian State Opera in Munich from 1998 to 2006, when he will be succeeded by the American Kent Nagano. For decades he has returned regularly to guest-conduct the Berlin Philharmonic and the Vienna Philharmonic, and from time to time adds recordings to the large discography he has amassed with those orchestras. He has given outstanding accounts of the symphonies of Mahler and Franz Schmidt (1874–1939), and of the operas of Wagner, Verdi, and Puccini, and is both a sensitive Mozartean and a brilliant exponent of a large swath of 20th-century repertoire, centering on the most colorful works of Stravinsky and Bartók.

RECOMMENDED RECORDINGS

MAHLER, SYMPHONY NO. 3: LOS ANGELES PHILHARMONIC ORCHESTRA (DECCA).

PUCCINI, *TURANDOT*: SUTHERLAND, PAVAROTTI, GHIAUROV, CABALLÉ; LONDON PHILHARMONIC ORCHESTRA (DECCA).

SCHMIDT, SYMPHONY NO. 4: VIENNA PHILHARMONIC (DECCA).

SCRIABIN, *POEM OF ECSTASY*: LOS ANGELES PHILHARMONIC ORCHESTRA (DECCA).

Meiningen Court Orchestra ENSEMBLE FORMED IN THE MID-19TH CENTURY at the court of the Dukes of Sachsen-Meiningen. It flourished under the leadership of Hans von Bülow, its music director from 1880 to 1885, rivaling (even surpassing, in the minds of some) the larger and longer-established orchestras of Leipzig and Vienna. Bülow trained the group (numbering 49 in 1880) to play from memory, and made a specialty of the music of Brahms; in 1885 he rehearsed it for the premiere of Brahms's Symphony No. 4, which it played under the composer's baton. Richard Strauss served briefly as music director (1885–86), and was succeeded by Fritz Steinbach (1886–1903), like Bülow a friend and champion of Brahms. Steinbach took the ensemble on several successful tours of Germany, as well as to England in 1902. Max Reger presided over the orchestra from 1911 to 1914.

Meistersinger von Nürnberg, Die (The Mastersingers of Nuremberg) OPERA IN THREE ACTS BY RICHARD WAGNER to his own libretto, composed 1862–67 and premiered June 21, 1868, at the National

Painting of Ludwig II, next to the original score of Die Meistersinger von Nürnberg

Theater in Munich. The only comedy Wagner essayed in his maturity (the youthful *Das Liebesverbot* dates from 1836), it is nonetheless a very serious work, probing the emotions of love and longing with remarkable wisdom as well as reassuring warmth. The story revolves around a historical figure, the 16th-century Nuremberg cobbler-poet Hans Sachs, who teaches the mastersinger's art to Walther von Stolzing, a young Franconian knight, so that he may court Eva, the daughter of another mastersinger, Veit Pogner. It is Sachs's yearning for what he cannot have—the hand of the beautiful but younger Eva and the freedom to break the rules as Walther does—that gives the work its extraordinary psychological resonance and poignant air of nostalgia. Calling for enormous resources (there are 17 principal parts as well as choruses in each act, and a proper staging requires hundreds of extras), it is, along with *Tristan und Isolde,* the most autobiographical of Wagner's creations. A part of the composer resides in the character of Sachs and another part in Walther, whose triumph over the odds and in spite of the railings of the critics is an allegory of Wagner's own.

It is Sachs, though, who has the opera's most moving and profound music, who sees more and feels more than the others, yet must do his best to make another man happy and triumphant. Sachs's two monologues—"Was duftet doch der Flieder" in the second act, and "Wahn! Wahn! Überall Wahn!" in the third—and the Act III quintet "Selig, wie die Sonne" are among the finest and most human pages in all of Wagner's output. They round out a work filled with big choruses and magnificent orchestral music (the Act I prelude is a tour de force of symphonic composition), whose joyful C major conclusion remains the most unambiguously optimistic statement Wagner ever made.

RECOMMENDED RECORDINGS

FISCHER-DIESKAU, DOMINGO, LIGENDZA, HERMANN; JOCHUM AND DEUTSCHE OPER BERLIN (DG).

PRELUDE TO ACT I: BARENBOIM AND CHICAGO SYMPHONY ORCHESTRA (TELDEC).

VAN DAM, HEPPNER, MATTILA, PAPE; SOLTI AND CHICAGO SYMPHONY ORCHESTRA (DECCA).

Melba, Nellie [Mitchell, Helen Porter]

(b. Melbourne, May 19, 1861; d. Sydney, February 23, 1931)

AUSTRALIAN SOPRANO. She left Australia in 1886 but honored her hometown througout her career by adopting the stage name Melba. Following a year in Paris as a student of Mathilde Marchesi, she made her European debut in Brussels on October 13, 1887, as Gilda in Verdi's *Rigoletto.* Within a year she had also appeared at Covent Garden, singing the title role in Donizetti's *Lucia di Lammermoor,* and at the Paris Opéra, as Ophélie in *Hamlet* by Ambroise Thomas (1816–96). Her radiant coloratura and refined technique—which permitted her to sing with beautiful evenness of tone from the bottom of her range to the top—captivated audiences and critics alike, and her fame spread quickly. On December 4, 1893, she made her Metropolitan Opera debut as Lucia, beginning a relationship that lasted, off and on, until 1910. During the eight seasons she sang at the Met, Melba achieved notable success in the roles of two Gounod heroines, Marguerite in *Faust* and Juliette in *Roméo et Juliette,* both of which she had studied with the composer. Her amazing versatility can be gauged from the fact that during her Met

Nellie Melba, 1890

career she also sang Marguerite in Meyerbeer's *Les Huguenots,* Mimì in Puccini's *La bohème,* and Brünnhilde in Wagner's *Siegfried.* But Covent Garden remained Melba's favorite house, and it was there, in 1926, that she bade farewell to opera. As Luisa Tetrazzini's predecessor in most of the major coloratura roles, Melba was one of the operatic superstars of her day. She gave her name to peach melba and to melba toast.

RECOMMENDED RECORDING

COLLECTIONS: COMPLETE GRAMOPHONE RECORDINGS (NAXOS).

Melchior, Lauritz

(b. Copenhagen, March 20, 1890; d. Santa Monica, Calif., March 18, 1973)

DANISH TENOR. He studied in Copenhagen and in 1913 made his professional debut there as a baritone, singing the role of Silvio in Leoncavallo's *Pagliacci.* In 1918 he made his debut as a tenor, singing the title role in *Tannhäuser.* Following a period of intensive study, including a year in Munich with Anna Bahr-Mildenburg and some final polishing from Cosima Wagner (who relayed comments to the singer via her son, Siegfried), Melchior made a third debut in 1924, taking on the role of Siegmund in *Die Walküre* at Covent Garden. That summer he sang Siegmund and Parsifal at Bayreuth, returning each year until 1931. He made his Metropolitan Opera debut, as Tannhäuser, on February 17, 1926, adding appearances as Siegmund, Siegfried, and Parsifal before the season was out. Melchior immediately became the anchor of Wagner productions at both Covent Garden, where he was on the roster from 1926 to 1939, and the Met, where he sang every season from 1928 to 1950. During his Met career, he concentrated on the heaviest roles, singing 128 Tristans and 98 Siegfrieds (47 in *Siegfried* and 51 in *Götterdämmerung*), along with 83 Siegmunds, 68 Lohengrins, and 70 Tannhäusers. Gifted with prodigious stamina—as the numbers make clear—he was able to celebrate his 70th birthday back in Denmark by singing Siegmund in a performance of *Die Walküre* with the Danish Radio Symphony Orchestra.

Melchior's voice was a unique amalgam of baritone and tenor. He never lost the baritonal resonance and heft that were his natural endowment, but his top notes had a clarion ring that any tenor might envy, and were extraordinarily powerful and secure. These attributes, combined with his innate expressiveness and phenomenal endurance, made him the greatest Heldentenor of the 20th century.

RECOMMENDED RECORDINGS

SELECTIONS FROM OPERAS OF WAGNER, VERDI, LEONCAVALLO (PEARL).

WAGNER, *DIE WALKÜRE,* ACT I: LEHMANN, LIST; WALTER AND VIENNA PHILHARMONIC (EMI).

melisma (Gr., "song") A group of several notes, usually more than five or six, sung to a single syllable. Bach's setting of the initial choral entries in his Magnificat provides a good example.

melodrama A passage in spoken dialogue accompanied by music. Examples include the dungeon scene in Beethoven's *Fidelio* and the "Wolf's Glen" scene in Weber's *Der Freischütz,* Schumann's *Manfred,* and the final measures of Berlioz's *Lélio.*

Lauritz Melchior, golden-age Heldentenor in Wagnerian garb

Mendelssohn-Bartholdy, [Jakob Ludwig] Felix

(b. Hamburg, February 3, 1809; d. Leipzig, November 4, 1847)

GERMAN COMPOSER, CONDUCTOR, PIANIST, AND ORGANIST. He possessed one of the most cultivated sensibilities of his age, along with an imagination capable of turning impressions of travel, literature, and history into works of unparalleled charm and vitality. He belonged to an extraordinary German family, cultured and rich. His paternal grandfather was the Jewish philosopher Moses Mendelssohn, a leading figure of the Enlightenment. His parents, Lea and Abraham Mendelssohn, were devoted to Felix and his amazingly talented elder sister, Fanny (who became a fine composer in her own right and married the painter Wilhelm Hensel). To ensure that society's doors would be open to them, the parents were determined to bring the children up as Lutherans, and on March 21, 1816, the clandestine conversion and baptism of Felix and his three siblings occurred, and the surname Bartholdy was added. Felix, who always signed his name "Mendelssohn-Bartholdy," remained a staunch Lutheran throughout his life.

Portrait of Mendelssohn at 12

Mendelssohn was exposed to superior teaching (lessons with Carl Friedrich Zelter until 1827) and all manner of cultural stimulus. Recitals as a piano prodigy, and many early string symphonies, prepared the way for two adolescent breakthroughs: the Octet in E-flat for Strings, Op. 20 (1825), and the Overture to *A Midsummer Night's Dream* (*Ein Sommernachtstraum*), Op. 21 (1826). In its élan and brilliance the Octet still outshines anything ever written by a 16-year-old, Mozart included. And what Mendelssohn achieved a year later in the Overture to *A Midsummer Night's Dream,* translating Shakespeare's spirit world into sound, borders on the miraculous: In the vast number of musical works inspired by Shakespeare, there is hardly another that is so perfect a creation.

Mendelssohn matriculated at the University of Berlin in the spring of 1827 and spent four semesters studying history and geography. The school's remarkable faculty included Humboldt, Schleiermacher, Fichte, and Hegel; Feuerbach and Heine were students a few classes ahead of Mendelssohn. This phase of his life climaxed on March 11, 1829, when Mendelssohn led the first public performance in 100 years of Bach's *St. Matthew* Passion, albeit reorchestrated and with significant cuts. This undertaking by the 20-year-old (he had spent five years readying himself) led to the reawakening of wide interest in the music of Bach.

Of the composers of his generation, Mendelssohn, avid reader and indefatigable traveler, had the best eye for nature and scenery—he was a more than competent watercolorist and draftsman. In the summer of 1829 he toured Scotland, whose historical and natural sights inspired what was to become the *Scotch* (today *SCOTTISH*) Symphony and the *Hebrides* Overture. A journey to Italy followed in 1830–31. Well acquainted with Italy's musical tradition, Mendelssohn's ear must have delighted in the stimulus it received daily, from the streets as well as the churches and opera houses. The *ITALIAN* SYMPHONY, reflecting these influences, is animated, vividly pictorial, almost spontaneous, yet with the most polished construction and felicitous scoring.

From 1835 Mendelssohn was conductor of the Leipzig Gewandhaus Orchestra, and he made it one of the best ensembles in Germany. He led the world premieres of Schubert's then recently discovered *Great* Symphony in C major and his own *Scotch* Symphony. He was among the first to conduct with a baton, and he pioneered the modern approach to programming concerts and seasons with a mix of repertoire staples and new works. He was also the guiding force behind the founding of the Leipzig Conservatory, in 1843.

Looking at Mendelssohn's career, one gets the impression of a figure in motion, in great demand everywhere music mattered—the first performing artist of the "steamship" set, making multiple visits to England (where he was revered) and constantly on the go in Germany. But what began as the kind of adventure only the privileged could enjoy turned into a grueling, stressful routine. Mendelssohn experienced burnout, then exhaustion. He died in 1847 a few months after his beloved elder sister, and in the same way, following a series of strokes.

The maestro at the height of his powers

Mendelssohn's overtures are seminal for a whole vein of Romantic music: *A Midsummer Night's Dream* for its shining synthesis of formal and descriptive elements; *Calm Sea and Prosperous Voyage* as a masterpiece of tone painting, in which Mendelssohn offers up a paean to modern capitalism, using trumpet fanfares to proclaim a merchant ship's arrival in port. Most brilliant of all is the *Hebrides* Overture, its opening composed in a flash of inspiration as Mendelssohn contemplated the craggy seascape of Fingal's Cave in Scotland.

***Title page of Mendelssohn's* Three Etudes for Piano**

In symphonies as in overtures, Mendelssohn was a master of pictorialism (as opposed to programmatic narrative). The most satisfying are the *Italian*, with which the composer tinkered needlessly, and the *Scotch*. The Violin Concerto from 1844 belies the notion that Mendelssohn became uninspired as he got older; it is a great, "late" work of perfected, intimate craftsmanship, dazzling and memorable. The Piano Concertos in G minor and D minor are scintillating, vivacious works that put a premium on fleet-fingered virtuosity. Mendelssohn ranked among his era's best pianists, and was probably its finest organist as well. He wrote much good organ music and a large amount for the piano—most important the *Lieder ohne Worte* (*Songs Without Words*), the *Rondo capriccioso,* and *Variations sérieuses.* His important chamber works after the Octet include two piano trios and half a dozen string quartets. He penned two impressive oratorios, *Paulus* (1836) and *ELIJAH* (1846), effectively reviving the tradition and bringing a new symphonic cogency to the genre.

With his compositions' pristine scoring, poise, and formal balance, Mendelssohn exerted an influence on the music of the mid-19th century that was second only to Beethoven's. The effervescent brilliance of the *Midsummer Night's Dream* Overture and of his scherzos left Mendelssohn's mark on every composer of "spirited" music from Berlioz and Lalo to Richard Strauss and Korngold, while the more festive style of the symphonies and the concert overtures influenced composers from Gounod and Gade to Strauss and Elgar.

Mendelssohn is sometimes critically lamented as an artist who did not live up to the potential of his early works. The problem was not that his inspiration failed him but that the range and variety of his endeavors, the many small compositions he felt compelled to produce, the conducting, the need to maintain contact with other musicians, all deflected him from works of "greater" purpose—from the kind of grand, audacious, and troubling efforts to which Berlioz and Wagner devoted their lives. Mendelssohn's Classical formal sense and Romantic palette make it easy to categorize him as a "Classical Romantic." Yet he was more forward-looking than that characterization implies. He was a creator of sonic marvels and in some ways the father of musical Impressionism, who understood even as a teenager the significance of what Weber had achieved in his orchestration, and took it further. The persistent view that Mendelssohn was a lightweight is, rightly, coming in for reassessment.

RECOMMENDED RECORDINGS

ELIJAH: WHITE, PLOWRIGHT, FINNIE; HICKOX AND LONDON SYMPHONY ORCHESTRA (CHANDOS).

A MIDSUMMER NIGHT'S DREAM (OVERTURE AND INCIDENTAL MUSIC): HERREWEGHE AND L'ORCHESTRE CHAMPS-ELYSÉE (HARMONIA MUNDI).

A MIDSUMMER NIGHT'S DREAM (OVERTURE AND INCIDENTAL MUSIC): PREVIN AND LONDON SYMPHONY ORCHESTRA (EMI).

A MIDSUMMER NIGHT'S DREAM (SELECTIONS), SYMPHONY NO. 3: MAAG AND LONDON SYMPHONY ORCHESTRA (DECCA).

OCTET: ACADEMY OF ST. MARTIN-IN-THE-FIELDS CHAMBER ENSEMBLE (PHILIPS).

OVERTURES: FLOR AND BAMBERG SYMPHONY ORCHESTRA (RCA).

PIANO MUSIC: FRITH (NAXOS).

PIANO TRIOS: GOULD PIANO TRIO (NAXOS).

SYMPHONIES NOS. 3 AND 4; *HEBRIDES* OVERTURE: KARAJAN AND BERLIN PHILHARMONIC (DG).

VIOLIN CONCERTO: CHUNG; DUTOIT AND MONTREAL SYMPHONY ORCHESTRA (DECCA).

Mengelberg, Willem

(b. Utrecht, March 28, 1871; d. Zuort, Switzerland, March 21, 1951)

DUTCH CONDUCTOR. He studied music in Utrecht, and at 17 was sent to the Cologne Conservatory to complete his formal education; while there he studied composition and conducting with Franz Wüllner, who in 1898 would be entrusted with the first performance of Richard Strauss's *Don Quixote.* In 1892 Mengelberg assumed his first professional post, music director of the municipal theater in Lucerne. Just three years later, on Wüllner's recommendation, he was appointed conductor of the Concertgebouw Orchestra in Amsterdam, a position he retained for 50 years. During his tenure, Mengelberg transformed the Concertgebouw from a second-tier orchestra into one of the world's leading ensembles. In 1905 he made his debut with the New York Philharmonic as a guest conductor, and in 1922 he assumed the role of the Philharmonic's principal conductor, sharing it unhappily with Arturo Toscanini from 1928 to 1930. Throughout his career Mengelberg championed the music of Mahler and Richard Strauss. In 1898 he and the Concertgebouw Orchestra shared the dedication of Strauss's *Ein Heldenleben,* and in 1920 they put on the first ever festival devoted to the works of Mahler. Mengelberg possessed an unerring ear, a solid baton technique, boundless energy for performing, and a remarkably complex and quirky character that often led him to impose his own ideas on the music he conducted. He was at his best in works of the 19th century that projected great excitement, drama, and emotional turbulence. Not insensitive to modern fare, he gave the premieres of Kodály's *Peacock Variations,* Bartók's Violin Concerto No. 2, and Hindemith's *Der Schwanendreher,* with the composer as soloist. Regardless of the music on the stand, Mengelberg had no compunction about rearranging or reorchestrating the score to boost the excitement of his interpretation, and characteristically took huge liberties with tempo.

Willem Mengelberg, ca. 1940

In spite of his extraordinary musical talent, Mengelberg tarnished his reputation late in his career by readily accommodating to the German occupation of the Netherlands and by accepting a position on the German Cultural Cabinet in 1941, conducting in Germany and other occupied countries during World War II. In 1945 he was barred from participation in Dutch musical life; he died in self-imposed exile in Switzerland, a few months before the ban on his activities was to have been lifted.

RECOMMENDED RECORDINGS

BRAHMS, SYMPHONIES NOS. 1 AND 3, *ACADEMIC FESTIVAL* OVERTURE, *TRAGIC* OVERTURE: CONCERTGEBOUW ORCHESTRA (NAXOS).

BRAHMS, SYMPHONIES NOS. 2 AND 4: CONCERTGEBOUW ORCHESTRA (NAXOS).

STRAUSS, *EIN HELDENLEBEN, TOD UND VERKLÄRUNG*: HELMAN; CONCERTGEBOUW ORCHESTRA (NAXOS).

Menotti, Gian Carlo

(b. Cadegliano, July 7, 1911)

ITALIAN/AMERICAN COMPOSER. He exhibited an early predilection for opera, and had already composed two by the time he entered the Milan Conservatory at 13. In 1928 he became a composition student of Rosario Scalero at the Curtis Institute of Music in Philadelphia, and also formed an immediate friendship with fellow student Samuel Barber. Menotti and Barber traveled together to Europe in the summer months, and subsequently shared a home, named Capricorn, in Mount Kisco, New York, for 30 years. Menotti completed his first mature opera, *Amelia al ballo* (*Amelia Goes to the Ball*), in 1937. Subsequent works in the genre included *The Old Maid and the Thief* (1939; the first opera written specifically for radio), *The Medium* (1945), *The Consul* (1949), *Amahl and the Night Visitors* (1951; the first opera written specifically for television), *The Saint of Bleecker Street* (1954), and a number of children's operas. Menotti also composed cantatas and other choral works, several concertos, and a small amount of chamber and instrumental music; in addition, he provided the librettos for two of Barber's operas, *Vanessa* (1957) and *A Hand of Bridge* (1959). In 1958 Menotti founded

Gian Carlo Menotti in 1937

the Festival of Two Worlds in Spoleto, Italy, and in 1977 he expanded the festival's scope by giving it a second home in Charleston, South Carolina. He was still actively involved in the direction of both at the start of his tenth decade. Menotti's importance as a custodian of operatic tradition cannot be underestimated. He created some of the most popular stage works of the 20th century, but his production was at best uneven. In addition to works of merit—*Amahl and the Night Visitors, The Saint of Bleecker Street*—there were stupidities such as *Help, Help, the Globolinks!* (1968) and catastrophes such as *Goya* (1986), a vehicle for Plácido Domingo that was such a clunker it had to be towed to the junkyard.

RECOMMENDED RECORDINGS

Amahl and the Night Visitors: Kuhlman, Allen; Schippers and NBC Symphony Orchestra (RCA).

The Saint of Bleecker Street: Melinek, Richards, Howard; Hickox and Spoleto Festival Orchestra (Chandos).

Menuhin, Yehudi

(b. New York, April 22, 1916; d. Berlin, March 12, 1999)

American violinist and conductor. The son of Russian Jewish parents who had emigrated from Palestine, he was brought up in San Francisco, where he began violin lessons at the age of five, studying with Sigmund Anker and Louis Persinger. One of the most remarkable prodigies of the 20th century, he began his professional career when he was seven. He played his New York recital debut and made his first appearance as a soloist with orchestra at the age of nine. His Paris debut, in February 1927, created a sensation; he remained in Paris afterward to study with George Enescu, whose deep musicianship left a lasting impression. His stature was confirmed later that year by a

Menuhin in his study

performance of the Beethoven concerto at Carnegie Hall, with the New York Symphony Orchestra under the baton of Fritz Busch. Following a 1929 concert with the Berlin Philharmonic in which Menuhin, a few days shy of his 13th birthday, played concertos by Bach, Beethoven, and Brahms, Albert Einstein rushed backstage, embraced the young soloist, and declared, "Now I *know* there is a God." Three years later Menuhin recorded the Elgar concerto in London, with the 75-year-old composer conducting. Menuhin continued working with Enescu during the 1930s and embarked on a world tour in 1935. He settled in California and was married in 1938. During World War II, he gave roughly 500 concerts for U.S. and Allied troops; he played in Paris in 1944 following the liberation, and immediately after the war, with Benjamin Britten at the piano, he played in Germany for survivors of the Nazi concentration camps. He returned to

Germany to perform with Wilhelm Furtwängler and the Berlin Philharmonic two years after the end of the war, defying those in the music world who were attempting to ostracize the conductor; he contributed his fee to the purchase of CARE packages for the Philharmonic's hungering players, a gesture that brought him an automatic annual reengagement with the orchestra. He married the ballet dancer Diana Gould in 1947.

Over the years, Menuhin the pudgy prodigy became a slender, spiritual aesthete, admired not only for the nobility and expressiveness of his playing but for his personal gentleness and intellectual sophistication. He also developed troubles with his technique, particularly matters of bowing. In later years he had so much difficulty with the change from upbow to downbow that he resorted to rebowing the repertoire in order to play as much on the upbow as possible. These difficulties, along with his innate musical curiosity, eventually led Menuhin to conducting. He founded the Bath Festival Orchestra in 1959, making nearly 100 recordings with it, and subsequently formed close associations with the Royal Philharmonic Orchestra (serving as its president from 1982 to his death) and the Sinfonia Varsovia, a Polish chamber orchestra. He was in Berlin to conduct the Sinfonia Varsovia when he died of a heart attack.

For much of his life Menuhin was deeply involved in teaching. In 1963 he founded an international school for children in Stoke d'Abernon in Surrey, and in 1977 he created the Menuhin Academy in Gstaad, Switzerland, dedicated to training young professional musicians. He served as director of the Bath Festival (1959–68) and of an annual festival in Gstaad (1957–96). During his career, Menuhin commissioned works from more than 40 composers, the most important being Bartók's Sonata for Solo Violin (1944) and Walton's Sonata for Violin and Piano (1947–49). He received an honorary knighthood in 1966 and a real one after he became a British subject in 1985. In 1993 he was elevated to the peerage, trading up from "Sir Yehudi" to the considerably more august "Lord Menuhin of Stoke d'Abernon."

Menuhin was an artist of unusual breadth and curiosity—a man whose inquiring mind and philosophical promptings enabled him to look both outward and inward at the same time and to draw upon all of life's experiences in pursuit of musical insights. His manner was polished and worldly, yet otherworldly as well, lending a mystical quality to his frequent verbal musings. He held deep moral convictions and could defend them in an exceptionally articulate manner, as on the many occasions when he spoke out for human rights and world peace. In all that he did, Menuhin offered a shining reminder that the greatest artists are always to some extent self-educated—not self-taught, but motivated to continue to learn about their art and the world at large long after they have ceased to be students.

RECOMMENDED RECORDINGS

As violinist:

Beethoven, Violin Concerto: Furtwängler and Philharmonia Orchestra (EMI).

Beethoven, Violin Sonatas Opp. 24 (*Spring*) and 47 (*Kreutzer*): Kempff (DG).

Elgar, Violin Concerto: Elgar and London Symphony Orchestra (EMI).

As conductor:

Elgar, Symphonies Nos. 1 and 2, *Pomp and Circumstance Marches*: Royal Philharmonic Orchestra (Virgin Classics).

For nearly half a century Menuhin was a devoted practitioner of yoga—so devoted that in 1982, during the centenary celebrations of the Berlin Philharmonic, he disarmingly mounted the podium, stood on his head, and conducted the great orchestra with his feet.

Cover of the first edition of* La Mer, *with Hokusai's depiction of the great wave

mer, La (The Sea) **SET OF THREE SYMPHONIC SKETCHES BY CLAUDE DEBUSSY,** composed 1903–05 and premiered October 15, 1905, by the Lamoureux Orchestra under the baton of Camille Chevillard (whose interpretation satisfied neither the composer nor the critics). One of the great masterpieces of 20th-century music—admired for its motivic and structural coherence, the brilliance of its orchestration, its extraordinarily vivid imagery and, above all, for its breathtaking grandeur and originality—it is Debussy's finest symphonic work and the supreme example of Impressionism in orchestral music.

Debussy's occasional encounters with the sea—from childhood visits to Cannes to travels in Italy as a recipient of the Prix de Rome to a holiday spent on the coast of Brittany—gave him a rich store of memories with which to work as he sketched the sea in his imagination. These sources were supported by secondary ones almost as potent. The paintings of J. M. W. Turner had a profound effect on him; their mysterious, atmospheric depiction of the sea took hold of his imagination and influenced his choice of palette. Another graphic image, Hokusai's *The Hollow of the Wave Off Kanagawa,* exerted a compelling influence on the composer, particularly in his translation into music of the sea's sheer, awesome power in the finale.

La mer is divided into three movements: "De l'aube à midi sur la mer" ("From dawn to midday on the sea") explores the sometimes subtle, sometimes dramatic changes of lighting and intensity that accompany the progress of morning on the water. The music suggests a gradual coming to life, from calm gray to almost blinding noonday brilliance, ending in a blaze of brass and percussion breaking over the full sonority of the orchestra.

In "Jeux de vagues" ("Play of waves"), one senses the rocking of the waves, unexpected shifts of current, the iridescent glint of sunlight on the surface of the water, and mysterious depths half-lit and teeming with life. Here one is *in* the water, not merely upon it. Of the three movements this is the least heavily scored, yet the most intricate in texture.

The final movement, "Dialogue du vent et de la mer" ("Dialogue of the wind and the sea"), is at once ominous and urgent: the orchestra heaves and subsides in great washes of sound, thrillingly suggestive of the danger of the sea. Near the end, a moment of suspenseful calm is reached, then a last great buildup shows the sea in triumph, dazzling and full of elemental force.

RECOMMENDED RECORDINGS

ASHKENAZY AND CLEVELAND ORCHESTRA (DECCA).

KARAJAN AND BERLIN PHILHARMONIC (DG).

MUNCH AND BOSTON ORCHESTRA (RCA).

Merrill, Robert

(b. New York, June 4, 1917; d. New York, October 23, 2004)

AMERICAN BARITONE. He got his start singing popular music on the radio, and made his operatic debut in 1944 in Trenton, as Amonasro in Verdi's *Aida.* He subsequently sang for 31 straight seasons at the Metropolitan Opera (1945–76), making his debut there on December 15, 1945, as Germont in Verdi's *La traviata,* a role he would eventually sing 132 times on the Met stage. As the Met's leading Verdi baritone, he was also entrusted with the roles of Rigoletto, Amonasro, Renato in *Un ballo in maschera,* Count di Luna in *Il trovatore,* and Rodrigo in *Don Carlo.* In addition to these he also sang Escamillo in Bizet's *Carmen,* Valentin in Gounod's *Faust,* and Rossini's Figaro in *Il barbiere de Siviglia,* reportedly his favorite opera.

Robert Merrill, all-American baritone

Merrill made many recordings, collaborating with Toscanini, Leinsdorf, and Karajan among others, and contributed a memorable Marcello to Sir Thomas Beecham's 1956 taping of Puccini's *La bohème.* His voice was noted for its amplitude, warmth, and resonance. A rabid baseball fan, he sang "The Star-Spangled Banner" on opening day at Yankee Stadium every season for three decades, from 1969; he died at home watching Game 1 of the 2004 World Series on television.

RECOMMENDED RECORDINGS

PUCCINI, *LA BOHÈME*: BJÖRLING, LOS ANGELES, PEARDON; BEECHAM AND RCA VICTOR SYMPHONY ORCHESTRA (RCA).

VERDI, *LA TRAVIATA*: MOFFO, TUCKER, REYNOLDS; PREVITALI AND ROME OPERA ORCHESTRA (RCA).

Messiaen, Olivier

(b. Avignon, December 10, 1908; d. Paris, April 27, 1992)

FRENCH COMPOSER, ORGANIST, AND TEACHER. As a pedagogue and through his works, he played a pivotal role in the development of modern music from well before World War II until the 1970s. His best works are models of how rhythmic complexity, timbral refinement, and an innovative approach to sonic architecture can be brought into expressive balance. In nearly all of his music he sought to express the joy and rapture that were roused in his soul by what lay beyond music.

Messiaen was raised in a cultivated environment; his mother was a poet and his father an English teacher and Shakespeare translator. Without promptings from them, he found himself drawn to music and also to an ardent, freewheeling mystical Catholicism. In 1919 the family moved to Paris, where the precocious 11-year-old entered the Conservatoire and became one of the most brilliant students in its history, taking five first prizes between 1926 and 1929. His teachers included Marcel Dupré for improvisation and organ and Paul Dukas for composition; the latter became an important champion of the young artist. The music of Debussy significantly influenced Messiaen's early direction, but the composer quickly developed his own modal system, and his music from 1930 onward had a unique sound and flavor. After finishing his studies, he was appointed organist at La Trinité in Paris, where he would serve more than 60 years. He passed the 1930s composing music for organ and orchestral works, including his first significant piece, *L'Ascension,* a set of

Olivier Messiaen in the organ loft

four "symphonic meditations." His scores from those years, emphasizing passion and sensuality, are full of exuberance, very much counter to the decade's prevailing neoclassical style. In 1932 he married violinist and composer Claire Delbos, and in 1936 he began teaching at the École Normale de Musique; the next year the couple had a son.

At the outbreak of World War II, Messiaen was called up; taken prisoner by the Germans in 1940, he was interned in Silesia. There, at Stalag VIII A in Görlitz, he composed the eight-movement *QUATUOR POUR LE FIN DU TEMPS* (*Quartet for the End of Time*), inspired by the Book of Revelation. Released in the spring of 1941, he took a position teaching harmony and, later, analysis, at the Conservatoire. His wife became ill around 1940 and was confined thereafter to a sanatorium, where she remained until her death in 1959. During the 1940s, Messiaen developed a close relationship, both personal and professional, with the pianist Yvonne Loriod; in 1962 she would become his second wife. He wrote a considerable amount of music taking advantage of Loriod's virtuoso capabilities during the decade: *Visions de l'Amen,* for piano duo, and *Vingt regards sur l'Enfant-Jésus* (*Twenty Contemplations of the Baby Jesus*), a two-hour cycle for solo piano, are among his most important, as is the huge *TURANGALÎLA-SYMPHONIE*, which has a prominent part for piano (as well as one for ONDES MARTENOT). His teaching inspired the young avant-garde: Boulez was a student during the 1940s, Stockhausen and Xenakis in the 1950s.

Throughout his life Messiaen was fascinated by birdsong and spent much time noting down the rhythms and inflections of his avian muses. This element came obsessively to the fore in his compositions of the 1950s, including *Le merle noir* (*The Blackbird*), for flute and piano, *Réveil des oiseaux* (*Awakening of the Birds*), for piano and orchestra, *Oiseaux exotiques* (*Exotic Birds*), for piano, 11 winds, and percussion, and the huge *Catalogue d'oiseaux* (*Catalog of Birds*), for solo piano. Messiaen also experienced throughout his life a pronounced form of synesthesia, the association of color with sound. His coloristic concerns were acknowledged in the titles of works like *Chronochromie* (1959–60) and *Couleurs de la Cité Céleste* (*Colors of the Celestial City*; 1963) for piano, three clarinets, ten brass, and six percussion.

By the late 1960s, all these elements, together with Messiaen's increasingly peculiar metaphysics, lading a symbolist aesthetic with religious freight, had led to music of meandering aimlessness such as the two-hour-long *Méditations sur le mystère de la Sainte Trinité* for organ. Other sprawling works of his final decade include *La Transfiguration de notre Seigneur Jésus-Christ* (1965–69) for seven instrumental soloists (flute, clarinet, cello, piano, xylorimba, vibraphone, marimba), large orchestra, and 100-voice chorus, and *Des canyons aux étoiles* (*From the Canyons to the Stars*; 1971–74) for piano, 23 winds, seven percussion, and 13 string instruments, inspired by the birds and canyons of Utah, and the stars above the desert sky.

Still more grandiose, the five-hour opera *Saint François d'Assise* (1975–83) was intended, the composer explained, to show "the progress of grace in St. Francis's soul." Adherents regard it as one of the great operas of the 20th century; detractors have described it as a heavenly bore. All agree that Assisi's gentle saint—celebrated for his holiness, humility, and connection to nature—was the ideal subject for Messiaen. Messiaen's last major work was *Éclairs sur l'Au-delà* (*Illuminations of the Beyond*; 1988–92), commissioned by the New York Philharmonic.

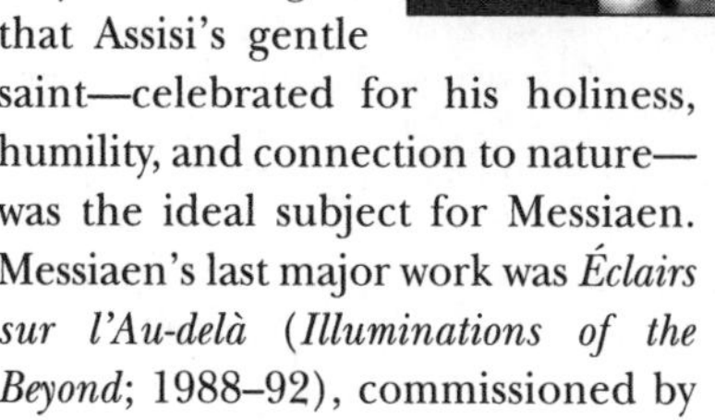

Messiaen was a composer of blazing imagination, inspired by constant thoughts of the afterlife and of the glory of God, to which he responded in a way that was musically unique. His main vehicles were the keyboard and the orchestra, and his great accomplishment was to show that there were compositional possibilities beyond traditional tonality other than 12-tone and serial procedures. He found new sonic resources, particularly in novel complements of wind and percussion (taking a cue from Varèse) and in the Balinese GAMELAN. He developed new harmonic resources, which he called "modes of limited transposition"—scales with eight tones to the octave whose symmetrical intervallic arrangement effectively eliminates tonal centers. And he cultivated new rhythmic resources, drawn from his study of Indian and Asian music.

Messiaen's language was the product of a system he created and that only he could follow. At its best, his music is brilliantly original, striking in its sounds and colors, ecstatic. At its worst it is manic, directionless, repetitious, inane—Satie with a pedigree. His most important contributions to the repertoire date from the 1930s and 1940s: *L'Ascension, Turangalîla, Vingt regards,* and the *Quatuor pour le fin du temps*. By the 1960s his music was coming to be seen as a backwater. When a leading American classical-music periodical asked prominent critics who was the most inexplicably overrated contemporary composer, more than half named Messiaen. That dismissiveness has now abated, and there can be little doubt that future generations will find more personality in Messiaen's better works than in the drab production of most of the serialists, spectralists, and other academically fashionable types who were the European mainstream of the late 20th century.

RECOMMENDED RECORDINGS

L'Ascension: Wit and Polish National Radio Symphony Orchestra (Naxos).

Quatuor pour le fin du temps: Shaham, Meyer, Wang, Chung (DG).

Quatuor pour le fin du temps: Tashi (RCA).

Turangalîla-Symphonie: Beroff, Loriod; Previn and London Symphony Orchestra (EMI).

Turangalîla-Symphonie: Thibaudet, Harada; Chailly and Royal Concertgebouw Orchestra (Decca).

Vingt regards sur l'enfant-Jésus: Hill (Unicorn).

Vingt regards sur l'enfant-Jésus: Osborne (Hyperion).

What's that sound? Exotic instruments occasionally supplement the conventional orchestra; their evocative sounds are especially vivid in program music. **Cowbells** (*Herdenglocken* in German) help set an idyllic tone for Strauss's *Eine Alpensinfonie* and Mahler's Symphonies Nos. 6 and 7. **Sleighbells** paint a wintry picture in the opening bars of Mahler's Symphony No. 4 and in Prokofiev's *Lieutenant Kijé.* In his *Arcana,* Varèse uses the **string drum,** also known as the **lion's roar**, in which the friction produced by rubbing a taut cord affixed to a drum approximates the animal's cry. Bernstein calls for **kazoo** in his *Mass.* Britten displays the **whip**, or **slap stick**, in *A Young Person's Guide to the Orchestra,* while Ravel uses it to transport his jazzy Piano Concerto in G to the world of vaudeville. Other noise-making devices can find their way into the orchestra as well. You'll hear **air raid** or **police sirens**, in Varèse's *Ionisation,* Korngold's *Between Two Worlds,* and Prokofiev's *Cantata for the Twentieth Anniversary of the October Revolution.*

Listen for these other unusual instruments:

alphorn

The alphorn is *the* national instrument of Switzerland. Originally carved by shepherds and used by them to call their flocks over long distances, they are natural horns, meaning that changes in pitch are not achieved by fingerholes, valves, or keys. Alphorn melodies were always improvised or played by memory until musicians started to write down the tunes in the 18th century, and the distinctive resonance of the instrument inspired such composers as Liszt, Wagner, and Rossini. Wagner specifies that the joyous little horn call in the third act of *Tristan und Isolde,* heralding the safe passage of Isolde's ship through the rocks offshore, is to sound as though it is being played on a natural instrument like an alphorn. The part is written for English horn, but at Bayreuth they use something like an English horn with a trumpet mouthpiece. There are several passages in Richard Strauss's opera *Daphne* that call for alphorn, though the parts are usually played by the trombones, but for a 1983 recording of the work played by the Bavarian Radio Symphony Orchestra conducted by Bernard Haitink, EMI commissioned the construction of an alphorn by the Swiss firm Pilatus. The instrument—22 feet, 3 inches long—was made in 11 sections to facilitate intonation.

alphorn

lion's roar

gamelan

Instrumental ensemble of Indonesia. Gamelans vary widely in size and instrumentation by geographic region, but consist primarily of xylophones, metallophones, gongs, gong-chimes, double-headed drums, and sometimes a lone woodwind instrument. Instruments in the gamelan are never played individually, but work together as a whole, one player per instrument, to create interlocking layers of long, underlying rhythmic patterns, melody, and elaboration. Patterns in each of the three layers periodically coincide at strong gong hits that mark the beginnings of rhythmic cycles. Providing accompaniment for a variety of dramatic performances and social functions that last all night, the gamelan is a living tradition dating from at least the first century B.C., and has long fascinated Western musicians. The gamelan inspired exoticism in the music of Debussy, who was enchanted by the Javanese ensemble he heard at the World Exhibition in Paris in 1889, as well as Poulenc, Ravel, Messiaen, Britten, and Cage, all of whom wrote music inspired by gamelan rhythm and timbre.

glass harmonica

A collection of glasses, graded by size, which are rubbed or struck to produce a bell-like sound. Water can be added to the glasses to change their pitch. The instrument enjoyed its height of popularity in Western music in the 18th century, owing largely to Benjamin Franklin, who heard it while visiting England. Franklin was so taken with the instrument that he improved upon its design. His version, devised around 1761, consisted of a concentric arrangement of the bowls of the glasses upon a rotating, horizontal rod. The close arrangement of the glasses, the practice of moistening them before playing, and the simplification of the performer's movements made it much easier to play. Franklin's glass harmonica caught the interest of Wolfgang Mozart, who wrote a quintet for glass harmonica, flute, oboe, viola, and cello in 1791.

ondes martenot

Electronic instrument invented by **Maurice Martenot** *(b. Paris, October 14, 1898; d. Clichy, October 8, 1980)* after he was inspired by meeting Leon Theremin, inventor of the theremin (see below), in 1923. The ondes martenot, first heard in public in 1928, would gain favor and eventually replace the theremin in orchestral works that used it, for example in Edgard Varèse's *Ecuatorial,* written in 1934. Like the theremin, the ondes martenot produces only one pitch at a time, but unlike the theremin, the pitches are determined by striking a keyboard with the right hand. Wiggling the keys produces vibrato. The left hand determines the signal of the variable oscillator, which produces the pitch, which is then amplified through a loudspeaker that stands separate from the keyboard. The left hand is used to change timbre and volume. The instrument has often been used for its eerie approximation of the human voice, most notably in Messiaen's *Turangalîla-symphonie.* Recently, the ondes martenot has enjoyed an unexpected—perhaps unprecedented—surge in popularity in the music of Radiohead.

ratchet

In addition to coloring the most rambunctious pages of Richard Strauss's *Till Eulenspiegel,* the ratchet is called upon to play a run-up to the opening of "The Great Gate of Kiev" in Ravel's orchestration of Mussorgsky's *Pictures at an Exhibition.* It is also used to suggest the play of children in the first part of Respighi's *Pini di Roma.* Although it makes a racket, the ratchet is not to be confused with the medieval woodwind instrument called the racket.

theremin

One of the first electronic instruments, invented around 1920 by Russian inventor **Lev Termen** *(later, Leon Theremin, b. St. Petersburg, August 15, 1896; d. Moscow, November 3, 1993).* The sound, produced in vacuum tubes, is a combination of signals from a fixed frequency radio oscillator and a variable one controlled by the player. This variable oscillator depends upon the capacitance (a measure of ability to transmit electricity) of the player's hands. The principles behind the instrument are the same as those observed by walking toward or away from a radio or television and hearing a change in sound. A wooden cabinet conceals the oscillators and vacuum tubes, and antennae emerge from the cabinet's top and left side. Much of the theremin's novelty and appeal owes to the fact that it is played without being physically touched, and that a theremin, unlike many other instruments, can be easily built at home. The instrument can produce only one pitch at a time. The distance between the left hand and the vertical antenna controls volume. Because of the lack of a system of set pitches, a portamento between one pitch and the next is unavoidable. This technical idiosyncrasy lends the theremin its vocal quality. Edgard Varèse used two theremins in *Ecuatorial* (1934). The instrument's unique sound has been used liberally in movie soundtracks—especially for science fiction, or eerie moments—such as Miklós Rózsa's 1945 scores for *Spellbound* and *The Lost Weekend,* and Bernard Herrmann's for *The Day the Earth Stood Still* (1951). The theremin is also significant for having sparked the imaginations of a generation of experimental composers and musical inventors, most notably Robert Moog (1934–2005), manufacturer of theremins and inventor of the Moog synthesizer.

ondes martenot

wind machine

A thick wheel mounted on a stand, covered with canvas that is turned by a hand crank so that the canvas rubs against wooden slats to produce a wind like sound. The intensity, technically the volume and pitch, of the "wind" is adjusted by increasing or decreasing the speed of turning, or tightening or loosening the canvas. Another version of the instrument consists in an electric fan with blades made of cane. A novelty item in the percussion section, its evocative howl enlivens Richard Strauss's *Don Quixote,* Ravel's *Daphnis et Chloé,* and Vaughan Williams's *Sinfonia antartica.*

Messiah **ORATORIO IN THREE PARTS BY GEORGE FRIDERIC HANDEL,** to a text by Charles Jennens based on passages from the Old and New Testament. It was composed between August 22 and September 14, 1741, and premiered in Dublin on April 13, 1742, the proceeds going to benefit local charities. The oratorio's first part establishes God's plan to redeem the world through a Savior and presents the story of the Nativity. The second part touches upon Christ's ministry on earth as well as His death, resurrection, and ascension; it ends with the famed "Hallelujah!" chorus, a joyous processional proclaiming Christ's triumphant reign over creation. One of Handel's most moving airs, "I know that my Redeemer liveth," opens the final part of the oratorio, which builds magnificently to a conclusion climaxed by a lengthy "Amen" fugue.

Since the day of its premiere, *Messiah* has enjoyed a popularity with English-speaking audiences that is unparalleled. Surely part of the reason is that so much of the oratorio's best music is in its choruses, which are wonderfully pointed in their depictions of innocence, joy, grief, and exaltation. Equally significant is that by keeping recitative to a minimum and relying on the direct, openly theatrical expression of the arias—in which the full persuasiveness of Baroque vocal art is brought to bear—Handel taps into the feeling of his great story in a way that cannot fail to move any sensitive listener.

RECOMMENDED RECORDINGS

ROBBIN, MARSHALL, ROLFE JOHNSON, HALE; GARDINER AND MONTEVERDI CHOIR, ENGLISH BAROQUE SOLOISTS (PHILIPS).

SCHLICK, PIAU, SCHOLL, PADMORE, BERG; CHRISTIE AND LES ARTS FLORISSANTS (HARMONIA MUNDI).

Metamorphosen **"STUDY" FOR 23 SOLO STRING INSTRUMENTS BY RICHARD STRAUSS,** inspired by Goethe's poem "Nieman wird sich selber kennen" ("No one can know himself"), and completed April 12, 1945. Goethe's meditation on the bestial nature of man resonated with Strauss, who saw how humanity's potential for good had metamorphosed into the evil of Nazi Germany and the terrible destruction wrought by it and upon it in the final months of World War II. At the end of the piece, a quote of the funeral march from Beethoven's *Eroica* Symphony emerges from the texture as a final, perhaps ironic, reminder of what has been lost. The work was premiered in January 1946 by the Collegium Musicum of Zurich, under the direction of Paul Sacher.

RECOMMENDED RECORDING

KARAJAN AND BERLIN PHILHARMONIC (DG).

Metastasio [Trapassi], Pietro

(b. Rome, January 3, 1698; d. Vienna, April 12, 1782)

ITALIAN POET AND LIBRETTIST. Born into modest circumstances, he benefited during childhood and adolescence from the patronage of the most privileged cadre of Roman society. His godfather was Cardinal Pietro Ottoboni, a grand-nephew of Pope Alexander VIII, and he was adopted at the age of ten by Gianvincenzo Gravina, a distinguished Roman jurist who saw to his education and arranged for his name to be changed from Trapassi (meaning "change" or "passage") to its Greek equivalent, Metastasio.

Following Gravina's death in 1718, Metastasio made his way as a poet, producing works on commission for a number of noble families. Thanks to the connections that had been forged for him during his youth, he was a shoo-in for the job of imperial court poet in Vienna when it came open on the retirement of Apostolo Zeno (court poet 1718–29). He retained the position for the rest of his life.

The early 18th century had seen Hapsburg Vienna emerge as one of Europe's operatic centers. During Metastasio's 53-year tenure as court poet, the literary conventions of opera seria became firmly fixed. His 27 opera seria librettos, written between 1723 and 1771, attracted the attention of more than 300 composers, including Johann Adolf Hasse (the poet's favorite), Antonio Caldara, Nicola Porpora, Gluck, Georg Christoph Wagenseil, Niccolò Jommelli, Graun, Cherubini, and Mozart. Most of Metastasio's librettos were set dozens of times; some received more than 50 settings during a century or more of use. Metastasio's most famous libretti are *Artaserse* (1730), set by Hasse, Gluck, Graun, Jommelli, Arne, Paisiello, and Cimarosa, among others; *Il re pastore* (1751), by Mozart, et al.; *La clemenza di Tito* (1734), by Hasse, Gluck, Jommelli, Mozart, et al.; *L'olimpiade* (1733), by Vivaldi, Pergolesi, Hasse, Arne, Cimarosa, and Paisiello, among others.

Pietro Metastasio

The standard Metastasian plot involves three pairs of lovers, usually of noble birth, and a set of complications that is resolved in a happy, elevated ending. Invariably, virtue is exalted, vice reviled. The scene structure generally follows a three-act plan, with 12 scenes (determined by the entrance or exit of a character) to each act. The focal point of each scene is a da capo aria. Such a moralistic, hierarchical, and slow-moving formula was bound to give way as tastes changed, but it provided Italian opera seria with a durable foundation during a period of remarkable metastasis in society and musical art.

meter (from Gr. *metron,* "measure") In musical notation, the recurring pattern in which a succession of rhythmic units or pulses is organized. The meter of a given passage—whether it consists of a single measure, several measures, or an entire piece—is indicated by a "time" signature, which resembles a fraction. The top number states how many units of a specified value are present in each succeeding measure, but not necessarily the number of beats. The bottom number specifies the rhythmic value that is considered the unit. Common meters include $\frac{2}{2}$ (i.e., the unit is the half note, and there are two to a measure), $\frac{4}{4}$ (the unit is the quarter note, and there are four to a measure), $\frac{3}{4}$, $\frac{2}{4}$, and $\frac{6}{8}$; meters of $\frac{3}{8}$, $\frac{9}{8}$, and $\frac{12}{8}$ are also fairly common. Less common are $\frac{5}{4}$ (Tchaikovsky, Symphony No. 6, second movement), $\frac{7}{4}$, and $\frac{10}{4}$ (both used in Bernstein's *Chichester Psalms*). Even further out is $\frac{13}{8}$, which appears several times in the second movement of Janáček's *Sinfonietta.*

In a meter such as $\frac{3}{4}$, there may well be a feeling of three quarter-note beats to each measure, but in many cases—the typical waltz, for example—there is a feeling of one beat to a measure. Similarly, there may be six eighth-note beats in a measure of $\frac{6}{8}$, if the tempo is very slow. But in most cases, the meter of $\frac{6}{8}$ produces a feeling of *two* beats per measure, which usually fall on the first eighth note and the fourth eighth note of each measure.

Meter is usually stable through a given movement in most music written before the middle of the 19th century. But with the arrival of the 20th century, frequent shifts of meter within a movement became a part of musical syntax. On the fifth page of

Stravinsky's *Petrushka* (1911), for example, where the hustle and bustle of the Shrovetide fair are marvelously evoked, two bars of superimposed $\frac{3}{4}$ and $\frac{7}{8}$ are followed by two bars of $\frac{2}{4}$ and $\frac{5}{8}$ and one of $\frac{3}{4}$ and $\frac{8}{8}$. Yet while all seems to be clash and clatter on the surface, the complexity of this passage produces an extraordinary sense of animation and drive.

metronome (from Gr. *metron,* "measure," and *nomos,* "law") Device patented by Johann Nepomuck Maelzel in 1815, using a double-ended pendulum with an adjustable weight to sound a steady beat at any speed from approximately 50 beats per minute to 160. It is one of the few precision instruments still manufactured according to the original specifications (though models in use today operate at speeds from 40 beats per minute to 208 or 212). Beethoven was among the first composers to make use of metronome markings to indicate appropriate tempos for performance of his music, including them in the score to his Ninth Symphony and retroactively applying them to earlier symphonies as well.

Maelzel's metronome—it keeps on ticking.

Metropolitan Opera COMPANY FOUNDED IN **1880** and based at the Metropolitan Opera House in New York. With an annual budget in excess of $200 million, it is America's largest musical institution, and by far its busiest, maintaining an orchestra of 150 and a chorus of 80 (plus 75 extras), engaging more than 200 solo artists a year as well as dozens of directors, designers, choreographers, and conductors, and employing a staff of hundreds. During an average 32-week season, it puts on upward of 220 performances of as many as 25 operas, far more than any other American company. For more than a century it has been one of the most important operatic venues in the world.

The company's creation was backed by a group of 20 well-to-do New Yorkers, essentially the cream of the city's nouveaux riches, who had no entrée to the old-money boxes at the Academy of Music on 14th Street. They paid for the construction of a new opera house on West 39th Street between Broadway and Seventh Avenue, then the largest in the world, which opened October 22, 1883, with Gounod's *Faust* (sung in Italian, as were all the operas presented at the Met during its first season). The company, managed by Henry E. Abbey, lost $250,000 that first season, a financial debacle that prompted the board to seek a new general manager. For its second season, the Met hired Leopold Damrosch as general manager and music director. As part of the arrangement Damrosch brought his own orchestra, the New York Symphony Society, into the pit. When Damrosch died in the middle of the season, his 23-year-old son, Walter, who would later be instrumental in the creation of Carnegie Hall, stepped in to help with the conducting. Walter Damrosch remained on the company's roster until 1891 and returned to conduct during the 1930s. Anton Seidl, a protégé of Wagner, became the Met's music director and principal conductor at the start of the 1885–86 season, remaining six years. He presided over a great era of Wagner performances, with casts led by Lilli Lehmann. Seidl was still on the scene for much of the Met's first golden age, 1891–1903, during which it attracted many of the greatest singers in the world—Lehmann, Jean and Edouard De Reszke, Emma Eames, Lillian Nordica, and Adelina Patti among them.

The company's engagement of Gustav Mahler in 1907 confirmed its international stature. Mahler made his debut conducting a new production of Wagner's *Tristan und Isolde* on January 1, 1908. The following season marked the beginning of a new era with the arrival of Giulio Gatti-Casazza as general manager. His tenure would last 27 seasons, to 1935, and its early years saw a huge expansion of the Met's roster and repertoire. One of Gatti-Casazza's major coups was to engage conductor Arturo Toscanini, who became the company's de facto music director, hastening Mahler's departure (Mahler's last assignment, in March 1910, was to conduct the U.S. premiere of Tchaikovsky's *The Queen of Spades*). Toscanini made his debut conducting a new production of *Aida* on November 16, 1908, opening the 1908–09 season. He remained on the roster through the 1914–15 season, conducting a large repertoire (34 works) and leading the world premiere of Puccini's *La fanciulla del West* and the American premieres of Mussorgsky's *Boris Godunov,* Puccini's *Le villi,* Catalani's *La Wally,* Dukas's *Ariane et Barbe-Bleue,* Montemezzi's *L'amore dei tre re,* and Gluck's *Armide.*

The Depression forced austerity on the company. Its lowered fees drove many stars back to Europe, but the company carried on. The 1930s, in fact, brought a second golden age with casts dominated by the likes of Lotte Lehmann, Kirsten Flagstad, Lily Pons, Rosa Ponselle, Lauritz Melchior, Giovanni Martinelli, Friedrich Schorr, and Lawrence Tibbett—and the beginning of the Met's radio broadcasts (whose sponsorship was picked up by Texaco in 1940). During the war years, still more European artists found refuge on the Met roster, including singers Alexander Kipnis and Jarmila Novotna and conductors Bruno Walter and George Szell, though increasingly the company was able to rely on American-born talent such as Richard Tucker, Robert Merrill, and Risë Stevens to carry its productions.

The Austrian-born Rudolf Bing, a British subject who had managed the Glyndebourne Festival, served as the Met's general manager from 1950 to 1972. A powerful, domineering figure, Bing insisted on high standards of production and strong international casts. He sought out and engaged many new singers, including Leontyne Price, George London, Marian Anderson, Otto Edelmann, Tito Gobbi, Carlo Bergonzi, Maria Callas, Renata Tebaldi, Birgit Nilsson, Sherrill Milnes, Plácido Domingo, Frederica Von Stade, and James Morris. Among the conductors he brought to the house were Thomas Schippers, Karl Böhm, Herbert von Karajan, and a young, Ohio-born maestro named James Levine. The high point of Bing's tenure was the company's move to its current home at Lincoln Center, which opened September 16, 1966, with the world premiere of Barber's *Antony and Cleopatra,* conducted by Schippers, directed by Franco Zeffirelli, and with Price as Cleopatra. The Swedish impresario Göran Gentele was

Metropolitan Opera House at Lincoln Center, opening night 1989

named to succeed Bing as general manager, beginning with the 1972–73 season, but he died the summer before he would have taken office; Schuyler Chapin stepped into the breach and served through the end of the 1974–75 season.

Since 1975, Levine's has been the principal artistic voice at the Met, in various managerial arrangements, from a triumvirate (with John Dexter and Anthony Bliss) that lasted six seasons (1975–81) to partnerships with Bruce Crawford, Hugh Southern, and Joseph Volpe (since 1990). In the fall of 2004 the company announced that recording executive Peter Gelb would succeed Volpe as general manager at the start of the 2006–07 season. The 30 years in which Levine has been a power have seen a vast improvement in the playing of the Met Orchestra (which had languished too long under the batons of *routiniers*) and a steady expansion of the repertoire (works of Stravinsky, Schoenberg, Berg, Janáček, Dvořák, and Prokofiev, among others, have been added), along with a substantial number of new productions—some brilliant, some not—of core works. On his watch there has been a renewal of the house's stagecraft, and a decline and subsequent recovery in its standard of singing.

Despite the company's leadership position in the world of opera it has had a poor record of commissioning and performing new work. In the early years of the 20th century it gave the world premieres of operas by Puccini, Giordano, Granados, and Humperdinck, among others. But in the half century from 1940 to 1990 the Met gave only four world premieres: Menotti's inconsequential *Ilo e Zeus,* Barber's *Vanessa* and *Antony and Cleopatra,* and Marvin David Levy's (b. 1932) *Mourning Becomes Electra.* John Corigliano's *Ghosts of Versailles* (1991) was the first new work put on since 1967 and has been followed by Glass's disastrous *The Voyage* (1992), Harbison's *The Great Gatsby* (1999), and Tobias Picker's *An American Tragedy* (based on Theodore Dreiser's novel), which received its premiere December 2, 2005.

RECOMMENDED RECORDINGS

BARBER, *VANESSA*: STEBER, ELIAS, GEDDA; MITROPOULOS (RCA).

PUCCINI, *MANON LESCAUT*: FRENI, PAVAROTTI, TADDEI, BARTOLI; LEVINE (DECCA).

ROSSINI, *IL BARBIERE DE SIVIGLIA*: PETERS, VALLETTI, MERRILL, TOZZI, CORENA; LEINSDORF (RCA).

WAGNER, *DER RING DES NIBELUNGEN*: BEHRENS, NORMAN, MORRIS, MOLL, OTHERS; LEVINE (DG).

Meyerbeer, Giacomo [Beer, Jakob Liebmann Meyer]

(b. Vogelsdorf, September 5, 1791; d. Paris, May 2, 1864)

GERMAN COMPOSER. The most successful composer of GRAND OPERA, he responded to the Zeitgeist of post-1830 France—socially conservative but hungry for vicarious thrills, earth-shaking spectacle, and awe-inspiring demonstrations of wealth, power, and prestige—by creating lavish escapist entertainments for the bourgeois multitude. His concepts in orchestration, visual effect, scene structure, and pacing were innovative and revolutionary, and his works powerfully influenced the development of opera in the 19th century, shaping the vision and style of Richard Wagner in particular, and echoing through the scores of Berlioz, Verdi, Gounod, and many others.

Giacomo Meyerbeer

Meyerbeer was born into a wealthy, accomplished, cultivated Berlin Jewish family. His parents and grandparents were successful in banking and business, and he had prominent rabbinical ancestral roots as well.

The eldest of three boys, Jakob was a child prodigy on the piano and had lessons in composition with Carl Friedrich Zelter (later Mendelssohn's teacher) and Georg Joseph Vogler. He befriended his contemporary Carl Maria von Weber (who regarded him as one of the finest pianists of the day), and in 1816, after showing promise with a couple of German operas and several cantatas and occasional pieces, he turned his attention to Italian opera. He began using the Italian form of his first name, Giacomo, and during the course of nearly a decade spent in Italy, developed his skills and built an impressive portfolio of half a dozen theatrical successes. By the mid-1820s, he was being seen as an heir to Mozart and a figure worthy to stand alongside Rossini, who recognized his rival's talent and furthered his career by producing *Il crociato in Egitto* (*The Crusader in Egypt*), the last of Meyerbeer's Italian operas, at the Théâtre Italien in Paris in 1825. With its success Meyerbeer was securely established in Paris; with Rossini's retirement in 1829 he got down to business . . . the business of grand opera.

Despite his relatively small output—four grand operas and two comic operas in 33 years—Meyerbeer loomed large in Parisian operatic life. His debut effort for the Paris Opéra, *Robert le diable* (1831), set to a libretto by Eugène Scribe, became one of grand opera's touchstone works and cast a potent spell on many other artists; among its most ardent admirers were Balzac, Berlioz, and Chopin. Five years later, *Les Huguenots* brought the style to new heights of dramatic and musical sophistication (in many ways it remains the quintessential grand opera). *Le prophète* (1849) was important in several respects; its staging was a technological tour de force involving the first use of an electric spotlight, its crowd scenes gave new meaning to the word "sublime," and the role of Fidès, sung by Pauline Viardot at the premiere, proved to be one of

***Depiction of a scene from Meyerbeer's* Il crociato in Egitto**

the most magnificent and challenging parts of the 19th century. With *L'Africaine* (premiered posthumously, in 1865) Meyerbeer created a work at once intimate and spectacular, and introduced a taste for the exotic that was to be an influence on *Aida.*

Independently wealthy, Meyerbeer was able to maintain artistic control over composition and presentation to an unusual degree. All four of his grand operas were written to librettos by Scribe, and, without being formulaic in any way, all dealt with the drama that arises when individuals are caught in the flux of forces larger than themselves, whether metaphysical, religious, political, or historical (or any combination thereof). For Parisians, who liked their tumult on the stage, not in the street, they proved matchlessly entertaining. In *Les Huguenots, Le prophète,* and *L'Africaine,* the plots involve the struggle of one group against another and the efforts of individuals to deal with the tragic complications love brings to their situation. In many ways it is not so much the particular historical events that are the crux of these dramas—the massacre of St. Bartholomew's Day, the Anabaptist revolt, the voyages of Vasco da

Gama—as the historical process itself, which Meyerbeer views as his subject. This aspect gives them a richness that is lacking in many other works of the era, and looks forward to the theatrical concerns of the 20th century.

While Meyerbeer's main focus was on pacing and scenic impact, he was not indifferent to color and characterization. His treatment of the orchestra was masterful; he was one of the first composers to exploit solo divisi strings, a technique both Wagner (*Lohengrin*) and Verdi (*Aida, Otello*) later employed to great advantage. He also made innovative use of obbligato instruments to comment on a character's state of mind, e.g., the solo viola d'amore in Raoul's Act I romance "Plus blanche que la blanche hermine" in *Les Huguenots.* These touches were not lost on Wagner, nor were Meyerbeer's distinctive, darkly expressive shadings of the orchestral tutti—using low horns, bassoons, bass clarinet—which found their way into *Rienzi, Der fliegende Holländer,* and *Tannhäuser,* and became part of the lexicon of 19th-century orchestration.

RECOMMENDED RECORDINGS

LES HUGUENOTS: SUTHERLAND, TOURANGEAU, VRENIOS, BACQUIER; BONYNGE AND NEW PHILHARMONIA ORCHESTRA (DECCA).

ROBERT LE DIABLE: ANDERSON, RAMEY, VANZO; FULTON AND PARIS OPÉRA (ADONIS).

mezza/mezzo (It., "half," "middle") Descriptive modifier indicating a medium degree of intensity or character. Thus, *mezzo-forte* suggests a moderate loudness, somewhere between *piano* and *forte.* The term *mezza voce* ("half voice") indicates that a particular passage should be sung or played with a restrained tone.

mezzo-soprano Female voice type midway between soprano and contralto. Operatic roles typically sung by a mezzo-soprano ("mezzo" for short) include Cherubino in Mozart's *Le nozze di Figaro,* Rosina in Rossini's *Il barbiere di Siviglia,* Eboli in Verdi's *Don Carlo,* the title role in Bizet's *Carmen,* and Octavian in Richard Strauss's *Der Rosenkavalier.*

Michelangeli, Arturo Benedetti

(b. Brescia, January 5, 1920; d. Lugano, June 12, 1995)

ITALIAN PIANIST. He entered the Milan Conservatory at the age of ten, graduating with honors at 14. In 1939 he won first prize in the first ever Geneva International Piano Competition, and in 1940 he made a sensational debut in Rome. After serving in the Italian air force during World War II, he resumed his career, performing at London's Royal Albert Hall in 1946, making his Carnegie Hall debut in 1948, and in 1949 taking part in Warsaw's celebration of the 100th anniversary of Chopin's death. Following a fallow period in the 1950s, during which he devoted himself mainly to study and teaching, he returned to the fray, performing widely in Europe and making extended tours of South America, the USSR and the United States. He reached the height of his powers in the late 1950s and remained at the summit through the 1970s, delivering mythic performances on concert stages throughout Europe and in front of the microphone. Though he suffered a serious heart attack during a recital in Bordeaux in 1988, he was able to continue performing and teaching the following year.

An eccentric, reclusive, and charismatic figure, Michelangeli was as unpredictable as he was chimerically brilliant—if he felt like playing, he would play, often magnificently, and if he didn't, he would sulk. He became as legendary for canceling concerts as for playing them. He possessed a formidable technique and could produce an absolutely breathtaking sonority, with a huge dynamic range and endless gradations of color. At his best, his interpretations exhibited both a pianistic brilliance and a conceptual brilliance. But like all the greats, except for Rubinstein, he had as many faults as virtues: though he knew every corner of the literature, he offered the public a very narrow repertoire, and he was prone to turning interpretations into ego trips that did not always serve the music he was playing. Still, he is remembered for his titanic accounts of Rachmaninov's Piano Concerto No. 4 and Ravel's Concerto in G, recorded for EMI (an issue that has never been out of print), and for what is arguably the greatest recording ever made of the Grieg concerto, captured in a 1965 performance with Rafael Frühbeck de Burgos and the New Philharmonia Orchestra. His readings of Ravel's *Gaspard de la nuit* and Debussy's *Préludes* and *Images* (the latter recorded by Deutsche Grammophon) are considered interpretive touchstones.

At one time or another, Michelangeli held posts at the Conservatories of Bologna, Venice, and Bolzano, and he gave masterclasses throughout his career. As a teacher, he was notoriously whimsical. Students would be summoned from their sleep to play for him in the small hours of the night, sent packing in minutes, or kept at the keyboard for hours. Yet some of the greatest sought him out, including Maurizio Pollini and Martha Argerich—brilliant musicians in their own right, on whom some of Michelangeli's magic and perfectionism undoubtedly rubbed off.

RECOMMENDED RECORDINGS

DEBUSSY, *IMAGES* AND *PRELUDES*, BOOK I (DG, WARNER CLASSICS).

GRIEG, PIANO CONCERTO: FRÜHBECK DE BURGOS AND NEW PHILHARMONIA ORCHESTRA (BBC LEGENDS).

RACHMANINOV, PIANO CONCERTO NO. 4; RAVEL, PIANO CONCERTO IN G: GRACIS AND PHILHARMONIA ORCHESTRA (EMI).

Midori [Goto, Midori]

(b. Osaka, October 25, 1971)

JAPANESE/AMERICAN VIOLINIST. Her study of the violin began at the age of four with lessons from her mother. In 1980 she received a scholarship to study with Dorothy DeLay at the Aspen Music School, and two years later she became one of DeLay's full-time students at Juilliard. In 1982, with Zubin Mehta on the podium, she made her debut with the New York Philharmonic as a surprise guest soloist at its traditional New Year's Eve concert; she subsequently joined the orchestra on a tour of Asia. In the summer of 1988 her career received a huge boost when she appeared in a gala concert at Tanglewood honoring Leonard Bernstein on his 70th birthday, breaking two strings during her performance and playing on to a tumultuous ovation. She made her Carnegie Hall recital debut in 1990. In 1992 she established a foundation, Midori & Friends, to bring the performing arts, especially music, into the everyday lives of children through free lecture-demonstrations.

Midori's youthful charm, combined with the fiery intensity of her playing, helped create the mania for girl-prodigy violinists that began in the 1980s. Her playing, while technically proficient, has been criticized by some as lacking interpretive depth, though in recent years she has emerged from a period of quiescence as a more interesting and probing artist, and an engaging blogger to boot. A 2001 recipient of the Avery Fisher Prize, she plays the 1734 "Ex-Hubermann" Guarneri del Gesù, on lifetime loan to her from the Hayashibara Foundation.

Mikrokosmos **COLLECTION OF PEDAGOGICAL PIANO PIECES BY BÉLA BARTÓK,** begun in 1926 and completed in 1939. Beginning with extremely simply rhythms and melodies, the six books of etude-like pieces build in complexity and sophistication, especially rhythmically, introducing the pianist first to meters based on units of 5 and 7, then 11 and 13, then to different meters in different hands, and so on. The melodies and harmonies are most often based on modes found in the folk music that Bartók had studied so thoroughly, and have a haunting and sometimes fierce beauty. The pieces also explore techniques found in both contrapuntal and 12-tone writing, such as retrograde (presenting a melody "backward"), thus linking several seemingly disparate musical traditions.

RECOMMENDED RECORDINGS

COMPLETE: KOCSIS (PHILIPS).
SELECTIONS: SZOKOLAY (NAXOS).

Milanov, Zinka

(b. Zagreb, May 17, 1906; d. New York, May 30, 1989)

CROATIAN SOPRANO. She studied at the Zagreb Academy of Music and made her debut in Ljubljana in 1927, as Leonora in Verdi's *Il trovatore.* From 1928 to 1935 she assumed leading roles in operas of Wagner, Richard Strauss, and Puccini with the Zagreb Opera, and in 1937 she sang at the Salzburg Festival, giving a memorable performance of the Verdi Requiem under Arturo Toscanini. She made her Metropolitan Opera debut on December 17, 1937, in *Il trovatore,* and became the Met's reigning Aida during the 1940s. During the 25 seasons she sang at the Met, Milanov also appeared frequently as Santuzza in Mascagni's *Cavalleria rusticana,* as Amelia in Verdi's *Un ballo in maschera,* and in the title role in Ponchielli's *La gioconda.* Later in her career she took on the roles of Tosca (which she would also sing at La Scala and Covent Garden) and Desdemona, and became a celebrated Maddalena in Giordano's *Andrea Chénier.* On April 16, 1966, at the gala farewell performance in the old Metropolitan Opera House at Broadway and 39th Street, she sang the duet "Vicino a te" from *Chénier* with Richard Tucker, and went gloriously into retirement.

Milanov's lyric spinto soprano was a paragon of beauty and power, firmly controlled in pianissimo and majestic in full cry.

Milhaud, Darius

(b. Marseilles, September 4, 1892; d. Geneva, June 22, 1974)

FRENCH COMPOSER. The personification of musical eclecticism, he absorbed *everything*—from Stravinskian polytonality to popular ethnic dance music to jazz—and made it his own. He was a folklorist who was interested not in folk music but in popular music, especially urban expressions such as the samba. He was a serious composer, but was branded a comedian because he embraced the animated musical styles of Brazil and Harlem and because he knew how to swing.

Milhaud was born into a well-to-do Jewish family. He grew up in Aix-en-Provence and absorbed music at home: His father was an accomplished amateur pianist, his mother, Italian by birth, a capable singer. He started piano when he was three and picked up violin at seven, becoming skilled on both it and viola. (In 1916 he would be the violist in the first performance of Debussy's Sonata for Flute, Viola, and Harp.) He wanted to be a composer and in 1909 enrolled in the Paris Conservatoire, where he studied with Charles-Marie Widor and Paul Dukas and was exposed to all sorts of new music, including the work of Fauré, Roussel, Ravel, and Stravinsky.

In 1912 Milhaud met Paul Claudel (1868–1955), a poet/dramatist (and diplomat) of the preceding generation and a devout Roman Catholic; they developed a close friendship and Milhaud would

Darius Milhaud, the composer who could swing

later compose several works to texts by Claudel. Medically unfit for World War I, Milhaud worked on behalf of refugees and then joined the propaganda section of the foreign ministry. Claudel was appointed minister to Brazil and offered Milhaud the job of attaché; in 1917 Milhaud set out for Rio. Impressions of the rain forest and of urban street scenes began to make their way into his music. He returned to Paris two years later and renewed ties with friends from Conservatoire days, including Arthur Honegger and Francis Poulenc. He encountered Erik Satie as well and became associated with the group known as Les Six. During the 1920s and 1930s, Milhaud was energetic on several fronts: composing, writing music criticism, and conducting (he led the French premiere of Schoenberg's *Pierrot lunaire,* in 1922). Much of his musical output in the 1930s took the form of film scores and incidental music. Around this time he suffered his first crippling attacks of rheumatoid arthritis.

With the fall of France in 1940, the composer left for the United States. He was welcomed with open arms by Mills College, in Oakland, California. After the war he was named professor of composition at the Paris Conservatoire, but kept his post at Mills, leaving only in 1971. In addition, he spent 16 summers teaching at Aspen. By all accounts he was inspiring; his students included William Bolcom, Richard Felciano, and Dave Brubeck.

Milhaud was an amazingly fecund composer, producing some 440 works, a prodigious output for the 20th century. He contributed again and again to the standard genres: 12 numbered symphonies, six chamber symphonies, more than 35 concerted works (including 21 concertos), 18 string quartets (nos. 14 and 15 are also playable simultaneously, as an octet), and dozens of film scores. But his most important compositions were the one-offs. *Les choëphores* (1915–16), incidental music for a drama by Claudel after Aeschylus, exemplifies the advanced, rhythmically adventurous idiom of the composer's youth. The ballet *Le boeuf sur le toit* (*The Ox on the Roof*; 1919), the product of his Rio years, is a kind of rondo—Milhaud called it a "cheerful, unpretentious divertissement"—raucous fun, like Gottschalk on a bender. In it Brazilian dances (sambas, maxixes, even a Portuguese fado and an Argentine tango) are transformed by polytonality. It was used by Cocteau for a ballet, set in America during Prohibition, which premiered in 1920. *Saudades do Brasil* (*Homesick for Brazil*; 1920–21), for piano solo, starts out like Albéniz but quickly curdles the harmony; we are, after all, well into the 20th century. Perhaps Milhaud's best-known piece today, the ballet *La création du monde* (*The Creation of the World*; 1923), was inspired by a pilgrimage to Harlem. It is a free-form fantasia for small ensemble imbued with an authentic jazzy feeling

(Milhaud was there ahead of Gershwin)—gentle, loving, in no sense a parody. Indeed, Milhaud's musical expression as a whole was genuine and free, never awkward or embarrassed, and among the most generous and appealing gifts of modernism.

RECOMMENDED RECORDINGS

LE BOEUF SUR LE TOIT: DORATI AND LONDON SYMPHONY ORCHESTRA (MERCURY).

LES CHOËPHORES: VARIOUS SOLOISTS WITH BERNSTEIN AND NEW YORK PHILHARMONIC (SONY).

LA CRÉATION DU MONDE: HOBSON AND SINFONIA DA CAMERA (ARABESQUE).

LA CRÉATION DU MONDE: TORTELIER AND ULSTER ORCHESTRA (CHANDOS).

SAUDADES DO BRASIL: LESAGE (RCA).

SAUDADES DO BRASIL: THARAUD (NAXOS).

Milnes, Sherrill

(b. Hinsdale, Ill., January 10, 1935)

AMERICAN BARITONE. He studied at Northwestern University and privately with Rosa Ponselle, gradually working his way up to the Metropolitan Opera by way of Santa Fe, Boston, Baltimore, and the New York City Opera (which engaged him for its 1964–66 seasons). He made his Met debut on December 22, 1965, as Valentin in Gounod's *Faust,* and served as a mainstay of the company for nearly 30 seasons. For most of that time he owned the major Verdi roles, earning repeated accolades as Iago, Macbeth, Carlo in *Ernani,* Simon in *Simon Boccanegra,* Renato in *Un ballo in maschera,* Germont in *La traviata,* the Count di Luna in *Il trovatore,* Miller in *Luisa Miller,* and Rodrigo in *Don Carlo.* He was also a splendid Don Giovanni, and an intriguingly complex figure in roles such as Tonio in Leoncavallo's *Pagliacci* and Scarpia in Puccini's *Tosca.*

A virile, stylish actor who never resorted to mugging, Milnes was a commanding presence on stage. His voice, with its lustrous metal core, had remarkable firmness at the low end and a beautifully burnished quality at the top. In combination with his unequaled reliability, these attributes made Milnes one of opera's most admired blue chips.

RECOMMENDED RECORDINGS

VERDI, *DON CARLO*: DOMINGO, CABALLÉ, VERRETT, RAIMONDI; GIULINI AND ROYAL OPERA (EMI).

VERDI, *OTELLO*: DOMINGO, SCOTTO; LEVINE AND NATIONAL PHILHARMONIC ORCHESTRA (RCA).

VERDI, *LA TRAVIATA*: COTRUBAS, DOMINGO, MALAGÙ; KLEIBER AND BAVARIAN STATE OPERA (DG).

Milstein, Nathan

(b. Odessa, December 31, 1904; d. London, December 21, 1992)

RUSSIAN-AMERICAN VIOLINIST. His childhood studies with Pyotr Stolyarsky (also the teacher of David Oistrakh) in Odessa were followed by a year and a half with Leopold Auer in St. Petersburg. The young Milstein returned to Odessa to start playing concerts. After a performance in Kiev, he met Vladimir Horowitz; he subsequently developed a close relationship with the pianist and his family. The two young virtuosos played concerts together, and in 1920 made their debuts in St. Petersburg, Milstein playing the Glazunov Concerto with the composer conducting, Horowitz playing the Liszt First Concerto

Nathan Milstein, showing his impeccable form

and the Rachmaninov Third. Both scored successes, but the pianist's was the more spectacular. In 1925, both Milstein and Horowitz left Russia. Whereas Horowitz's career took off immediately, Milstein's developed more slowly. In 1926 he went to Brussels to coach with Eugène Ysaÿe, under whose tutelage he grew into a deeper interpretive artist.

Milstein made his American debut with the Philadelphia Orchestra on October 17, 1929; his debut with the New York Philharmonic followed on January 23, 1930. He settled in New York and became a naturalized citizen in 1942. He toured extensively and made many recordings, which display an impeccable technique, magnificent virtuosity, and unfussy, intelligent artistry. Universally admired by his colleagues, Milstein earned a reputation as a "thoughtful" and intellectually probing violinist. His playing was characterized by a pure, silvery tone and direct and convincing musicianship. Although he eschewed cheap effects, he was in Heifetz's league as a technician and was capable of producing hair-raising fireworks, as was evident whenever he played his own bravura showpiece *Paganiniana* or launched into the cadenza of any one of the dozen concertos he kept in his repertoire. Milstein's recordings of the concertos of Dvořák and Karl Goldmark are unsurpassed, and his traversal of the unaccompanied sonatas and partitas of Bach remains an account of enormous stature.

Milstein played with almost unimpaired command into his 80s, a rare accomplishment for violinists. His sterling qualities remain remarkably in evidence in a live recording of his last public recital, given in Switzerland on June 17, 1986, when he was 82; the program included Bach's *Chaconne* with all its sweep and drama intact. His instrument was a Stradivari violin of 1716, which he renamed the "Marie-Thérèse," after his wife and daughter.

RECOMMENDED RECORDINGS

BACH, SONATAS AND PARTITAS (DG).

GLAZUNOV, DVOŘÁK, VIOLIN CONCERTOS: STEINBERG AND PITTSBURGH SYMPHONY ORCHESTRA (EMI).

MENDELSSOHN, TCHAIKOVSKY, VIOLIN CONCERTOS: ABBADO AND VIENNA PHILHARMONIC (DG).

minim (from Lat. *minima,* "smallest") In medieval notation, the shortest of the five note values in common use, represented by a solid black (or hollow) diamond-shaped note head with a vertical stem [♩]. It is equivalent to a half note in modern notation.

minimalism Musical style that emerged in America in the 1960s. The term is borrowed from the field of visual art, where minimalist painting and sculpture shaped conceptual art of the late 1950s and 1960s. The roots of musical minimalism can be traced to the simplified, repetitive textures and intentionally static harmonics of Carl Orff, Henry Cowell, Alan Hovhaness (1911–2000), and Bernard Herrmann (1911–75), among others; composers working in the style have also acknowledged the influence of various strains of African, Indian, and Asian/Pacific music, and more recently, the pop genres of hip-hop, house music, and trance. The founding fathers of musical minimalism were the American composers La Monte Young (b. 1935), Terry Riley (b. 1935), Steve Reich, and Philip Glass. A characteristically minimalist fixation on stasis appeared in Young's music as early as his Trio for Strings (1958), but it was Riley's *In C* (1965), with its motoric rhythmic pulsations, that proved to be the seminal work in the style. Initially, minimalism marked an extension of the textural and procedural reductivism that was a characteristic of rigorously serial music, particularly that of Anton Webern. Very quickly, however, it developed into a reaction against that style. Much as minimalism in the visual arts was a riposte to the complexities of Abstract Expressionism, musical minimalism rejected the complex, rigidly organized, dissonant, and emotionally crabbed language of serialism—the prime post–World War II modernist orthodoxy—as well as the anarchy of indeterminacy put forward by John Cage and others as a corrective. Using simple procedures and relying on various kinds of formulaic repetition of short, melodic cells in which any single rhythmic or melodic element might change at any time, minimalism marked an attempt to embrace the living and intuitive side of music, after years of abstraction in wildly divergent directions.

By the 1970s, Riley and Young had moved on to other things. Reich and Glass, along with their younger colleague John Adams, were left to carry the minimalist torch, which they did in a series of vibrant and imaginative works: Reich in his *Drumming* (1970–71) and *Music for 18 Musicians* (1974–76); Glass in his *Music in 12 Parts* (1971–74), the operas *Einstein on the Beach* (1976) and *Satyagraha* (1980), and the film score *Koyannisqatsi* (1982); Adams in *Shaker Loops* (1978, rev. 1983), *The Chairman Dances* (1986), and the opera *Nixon in China* (1987). These scores show the broad characteristics of the style—a reiterative, at times manic, fixation on a particular rhythm, melodic figure, or chord; a progression of subtle, incremental changes within a texture of incessant repetition, resulting in the very gradual establishment and subversion of large-scale patterns by small-scale patterns; and a feeling of restlessness and pulsing energy within harmonic stasis, which can be at once hypnotic and intense. Reich, Glass, and Adams utilized the methods of minimalism in their own particular ways, and developed their own distinctive sounds, but each produced music that is incisive and energetic, vibratingly "alive" and colorful. Classic examples include the motoric pulsing of amplified keyboard and wind instruments in Glass's *Music in 12 Parts,* the extraordinary phased color shifts of Reich's *Music for 18 Musicians,* and the shimmering effects of Adams's *Shaker Loops.*

Over the past two decades Reich and Adams in particular, along with younger composers like Michael Daugherty (b. 1954), Steven Mackey (b. 1956), and Michael Torke (b. 1961), have developed a kind of "maximal" minimalism that utilizes more and more of the expressive resources of conventional tonal music—including discrete melodies, rich ensemble scoring, and long-range harmonic action—in a sense rejoining the mainstream of musical thought, but in a light, fast-moving craft. Adams's *Short Ride in a Fast Machine* (1986) and *The Wound Dresser* (1988), Daugherty's *Metropolis Symphony* (1993), and Reich's *City Life* (1995) show how the style has matured.

In Europe, minimalism has developed along different, no less interesting lines. In the mid-1970s, as the American minimalists were coming to prominence, a number of European composers also turned away from the abstract, highly systematized procedures of the avant-garde in search of a language that would allow them to communicate in a direct yet profound way with listeners. In the vanguard of this movement have been four composers—Arvo Pärt, Henryk Górecki, Sofiya Gubaydulina, and John Tavener—who, though they come from quite different backgrounds, have at least two things in common: a distaste for the intellectual aridity of most contemporary music and a strong religious orientation. Their melding of minimalism with religious mysticism is realized in such works as Górecki's Third Symphony (1976), Pärt's *Tabula Rasa* (1977) and *Fratres* (1977), Gubaydulina's *Seven Last Words* (1982), and Tavener's *The Protecting Veil* (1987). Their masterful achievements have proven extraordinarily popular as well. While a final determination may be years away, it appears that the growth of minimalism as a musical style—in the work of both the European and the American minimalists—is likely to rank as the most significant musical development in the final third of the 20th century. Without question, minimalism has broadened the audience for classical music through its appeal to new and younger listeners. *See also entries for individual works and composers.*

minor Literally, "lesser" or "smaller." When used to identify a key or a scale, it means that the third degree of that key or scale is a minor third (i.e., three semitones) above the fundamental or tonic note. In most cases the sixth and seventh degrees of a minor scale are also "flatted," i.e., a semitone lower than in a major scale. In certain situations, they are raised when the scale ascends, and lowered only when it descends, to produce what is called a "melodic minor" scale. Minor keys are often associated with the expression of sadness, pain, or agitation, as in Mozart's Symphony in G minor, K. 550. *See also* INTERVAL, MODE, MAJOR.

Minter, Drew *See box on pages 155–57.*

minuet French dance in moderately slow $\frac{3}{4}$ time, often found in suites of the Baroque era. During the Classical period, the character of the minuet changed from stately to rather brisk, and it became the standard dance movement in four-movement forms such as the symphony and the string quartet. *See also* SUITE.

"Minute Waltz" NAME FOR FRÉDÉRIC CHOPIN'S WALTZ IN D-FLAT, OP. 64, NO. 1. The nickname comes from the French word for "small," not a measure of duration; in fact, though brief, it still takes nearly two minutes to play.

Miraculous Mandarin, The "PANTOMIME" (I.E., BALLET) FOR ORCHESTRA AND WORDLESS CHORUS BY BÉLA BARTÓK, OP. 19, to a scenario by Menyhért Lengyel (who also wrote the screenplay for *Ninochka* [1939]). Bartók completed a draft of the score in 1919 but did not orchestrate it until 1924; the first performance took place November 27, 1926, in Cologne. The ballet's plot is a macabre variation of the Flying Dutchman story. Thugs force a prostitute to lure men to her dingy room, where they set upon and rob the unlucky victims. The first two—a doddering old cavalier and a student—are thrown out because they have no money. The third—a wealthy Mandarin—is of such forbidding appearance that he frightens the girl. When she attempts to seduce him by means of a provocative dance, the aroused Mandarin embraces her. Alarmed by the intensity of his desire, she tries to escape. There is a chase, the Mandarin catches her, and just as he is about to have his way with her, the thugs break in to rob him. They suffocate him with pillows, run him through with a sword, and hang him from a light fixture—but he proves impossible to kill. The girl, seeing that the yearning Mandarin's gaze is ever upon her, takes him into her arms, whereupon his wounds begin to bleed, and he dies.

Bartók's music is appropriately garish, violent, and bizarre; the flamboyantly orchestrated score is a catalog of the cataclysmic effects that entered European musical language in the wake of Stravinsky's *The Rite of Spring,* with many exotic twists of Bartók's own devising, such as his characterization of the Mandarin via a pentatonic melody on muted trombones accompanied by eerily wailing woodwinds. In 1924 Bartók extracted several scenes from the pantomime for concert performance; this abridged version of the score was premiered on April 1, 1927, by the Cincinnati Symphony Orchestra under the baton of Bartók's former student Fritz Reiner. Further revisions resulted in *The Miraculous Mandarin* Suite, completed in 1927 and published in 1929. More frequently programmed today than the complete ballet, the suite, which omits the ballet's final scene and concludes with the chase, received its premiere in Budapest on October 15, 1928, conducted by Ernő Dohnányi.

RECOMMENDED RECORDINGS

COMPLETE BALLET: CHAILLY AND ROYAL CONCERTGEBOUW ORCHESTRA (DECCA).

SUITE: MARTINON AND CHICAGO SYMPHONY ORCHESTRA (RCA).

SUITE: SOLTI AND CHICAGO SYMPHONY ORCHESTRA (DECCA).

missa brevis (Lat., "short mass") Typically, a mass setting consisting of only the Kyrie and Gloria. The term is also used to refer to complete settings of the Ordinary that are relatively brief in duration or are conceived for fairly modest performing forces. Examples of the latter include Kodály's *Missa brevis* (1942–44) for soloists, chorus, and organ, and Britten's *Missa brevis* in D (1959) for boys' choir and organ.

missa solemnis (Lat., "solemn mass") Any mass in which the entire Ordinary is sung. By the 18th century the term had come to signify a lavish setting with full orchestra, chorus, and soloists in which each section of the Ordinary was typically subdivided into a sequence of musical numbers, with the text treated at length in many of them. Examples include Bach's *Mass in B Minor* (completed in the 1740s) and Beethoven's *Missa solemnis* in D, Op. 125 (1823). *See also* MASS.

Mitropoulos, Dimitri

(b. Athens, March 1, 1896; d. Milan, November 2, 1960)

GREEK/AMERICAN CONDUCTOR, COMPOSER, AND PIANIST. He graduated from the Athens Conservatory in 1919 after winning the gold medal in piano, and continued his education in Brussels and at the Berlin Hochschule, studying piano and composition with Ferruccio Busoni. While working as a coach at the Berlin Staatsoper, he studied conducting with Erich Kleiber. Mitropoulos returned in 1924 to Athens, where he taught at the city's conservatory and served as conductor of its symphony orchestra. During the early years of his career, he was also active as a composer, writing an opera, *Soeur Béatrice* (based on a play by Maurice Maeterlinck), a couple of large-scale orchestral works, some chamber music, and several piano pieces. In 1930 he accepted the position of professor of composition at the Athens Conservatory, and in 1933 he was elected to the Academy of Athens.

Mitropoulos's international breakthrough came on February 27, 1930, when he made his debut with the Berlin Philharmonic Orchestra as soloist in Prokofiev's Third Piano Concerto, which he conducted from the keyboard. He subsequently appeared as soloist and guest conductor with many European orchestras, and in 1936 he made his American debut with the Boston Symphony Orchestra. In 1937 he was appointed principal conductor of the Minneapolis Symphony (now the Minnesota Orchestra), where he remained for 12 seasons. In 1949 he accepted the position of co-conductor of the New York Philharmonic with Leopold Stokowski. Following Stokowski's departure in 1950,

Dimitri Mitropoulos

Mitropoulos served as the orchestra's music director until 1958; in that capacity he introduced many contemporary scores to New York audiences, including Berg's *Wozzeck,* Schoenberg's *Erwartung,* Milhaud's *Les choëphores,* Busoni's *Arlecchino,* and Shostakovich's Tenth Symphony. He conducted at the Metropolitan Opera for six seasons (1954–60), leading performances of works by Verdi, Puccini, Mussorgsky, Tchaikovsky, Bizet, Wagner, and Richard Strauss, as well as the world premiere of Barber's *Vanessa* (1958).

One of the most gifted conductors of the 20th century, Mitropoulous had an extraordinary photographic memory and excelled in scores of great complexity. He was completely comfortable in contemporary music and was one of the few conductors of his day to program serial music. He was also a wholehearted advocate of Mahler's music, at a time when that was neither fashionable nor easy, considering the difficulty most orchestras had performing it. His conducting was marked by a combination of missionary zeal and physical exertion, and he was able to wrest spectacular performances from the orchestras he faced—his recorded legacy abounds in readings in which the playing is beautiful, limpid, and hauntingly expressive, the conception brilliant and incisive. He died of a heart attack during a rehearsal of Mahler's Third Symphony with the La Scala Orchestra in Milan.

RECOMMENDED RECORDINGS

Mahler, Symphony No. 1: Minneapolis Symphony Orchestra (Sony).

Shostakovich, Violin Concerto No. 1: Oistrakh; New York Philharmonic (Sony).

mode [1] The specific arrangement of whole and half steps in a DIATONIC SCALE. In the tonal music of the past four centuries, by far the most common modes have been the major and minor. But in earlier music—from chant to Renaissance polyphony—other scale arrangements were regularly used, and each was believed to have its own affective quality and character. During the late Middle Ages and Renaissance, a system of 12 modes and a highly complicated grammar was in place, which differentiated the modes according to their concluding scale DEGREE (called the "final," analogous to the TONIC of a major or minor scale) and their characteristic sound. Modes other than the major and minor remain common in some folk music, and classical composers of recent vintage have used these modes, or the old Renaissance and church modes, to invest their music with distinctive harmonic color. *See also* SCALE. [2] In medieval music, the relationship, expressed as a proportion, between the durations of the long and short notes. If the proportion was 3:1, the mode was "perfect"; if 2:1, "imperfect."

moderato (It., "moderate") A tempo generally viewed as falling between andante and allegro; also used as a modifier for either of those tempos, e.g., *Allegro moderato* (Rachmaninov, Symphony No. 2, first movement) and *Andante moderato* (Brahms, Symphony No. 4, second movement). Shostakovich chose *moderato* as the tempo marking for the first movement of his Symphony No. 5.

modulation (from Lat. *modulatio,* "measurement") Within a movement or a section of a piece, a clear change of key. Modulation occurs when a key other than the TONIC is established in the listener's perception as the "home" key. The notes and harmonies characteristic of the new key must be present long enough to be recognized; the shift is usually confirmed by means of a CADENCE in the new key. Essential to the aural and psychological impact of the key-area forms that have been employed in sonatas, concertos, symphonies, operas, and other large-scale compositions since the beginning of the 18th century, modulation has become one of the most important expressive devices in Western music. Its use led to a grand expansion of musical form in the 19th century, and without it the works of Mozart, Beethoven, Schubert, Wagner, and many others would be shorn of emotional complexity. Occasionally modulation serves as a purely coloristic device; the Folk Dance from Prokofiev's *Romeo and Juliet* is a good example.

Moiseiwitsch, Benno

(b. Odessa, February 22, 1890; d. London, April 9, 1963)

RUSSIAN PIANIST. He so impressed his teachers at the Imperial Music Academy in Odessa that at the age of nine he was awarded the Anton Rubinstein Prize. He later continued his studies in Vienna with Theodor Leschetitzky, the leading piano guru of the day, whose many students dominated piano playing from the last decades of the 19th century well into the first half of the 20th. Moiseiwitsch's mature playing exemplified the qualities of the Leschetitzky school: a fluid, brilliant technique coupled with a singing tone, and a broad, Romantic approach to interpretation.

Moiseiwitsch's large repertoire was based in the literature of the 19th century. His personal style was characterized by a remarkable fluency and musical suppleness, a beautiful, unforced sound, and highly refined musical taste. His playing was greatly admired by Sergey Rachmaninov, whose works Moiseiwitsch played to the avowed satisfaction of that daunting composer-pianist. Though equipped with a virtuoso technique, he was chiefly regarded as a lyric player. He continues to be held in high esteem by piano cognoscenti for his elegant and thoughtful playing, qualities reflected in the many recordings he made of works by Schumann and, especially, Chopin.

RECOMMENDED RECORDINGS

COLLECTIONS:

"GREAT PIANISTS OF THE 20TH CENTURY": WORKS OF CHOPIN, LISZT, PROKOFIEV, RACHMANINOV, MEDNER (PHILIPS).

PIANO RECORDINGS, VOLS. I–VII (NAXOS).

WORKS OF BEETHOVEN, CHOPIN, SCHUMANN, MUSSORGSKY (PEARL).

molto (It., "very") Descriptive term frequently used in tempo markings, e.g., *Allegro molto* (Beethoven, Symphony No. 3, finale), *Allegro molto moderato,* in which "molto" applies to "moderato" (Sibelius, Symphony No. 6, first movement), or to modify a dynamic or interpretive instruction (e.g., *molto espressivo, crescendo molto*).

monody Accompanied Italian song settings of the first half of the 17th century. The form grew naturally out of the last stages of the 16th-century polyphonic MADRIGAL, which had already begun to reflect a declamatory, highly expressive, and ornamental style; but the impetus for focusing on a single voice came from the Florentine Camerata, a group of poets, musicians, and scholars who were convinced that the emulation of ancient Greek solo song would lead to vocal settings of increased expressiveness and greater intelligibility.

In the vanguard of this new approach was the Florentine composer Giulio Caccini (ca. 1545–1618), whose first collection of monodies, *Le nuove musiche* (1601), not only exemplified the expressive, declamatory, highly ornamented "new style," but, in an important introduction, codified the manner in which this expressiveness should be achieved: by using a heightened, flexible approach to rhythm and tempo in the vocal line, as well as by harmonizing the accompanying bass (usually played on a string instrument such as the lute or chitarrone) in an improvisatory manner, so as to allow for unresolved dissonances. These two elements together were known as "sprezzatura," which can be loosely rendered in English as "elegant negligence" or "nonchalance." Oddly enough, Caccini's most famous monody, "Amarilli, mia bella," while manifesting the basic tenet of expressiveness, shows very little, if any, of the declamatory ornamental style which he stressed so clearly in his written introduction to *Le nuove musiche.*

Other important composers of monody (also involved in some of the earliest operas) were the Florentines Jacopo Peri (1561–1633) and Marco da Gagliano (1582–1643); significant contributions were made as well by Sigismondo d'India (d. 1629), Girolamo Frescobaldi, Giacomo Carissimi (1605–74), and Claudio Monteverdi, who brought the form to its apogee in his magisterial operas; a powerful and representative example is the aria "Possente spirto," from *L'Orfeo* (1607).

The concept of "monody" as a genre unto itself lost currency after about 1650, as by then its dramatic and expressive elements had been completely absorbed into the lexicon of opera.

RECOMMENDED RECORDINGS

"THE ITALIAN LUTE SONG" (CACCINI, MONTEVERDI, NEGRI, CARISSIMI, OTHERS): BAIRD, MCFARLANE (DORIAN).

"VIRTUOSO ITALIAN VOCAL MUSIC" (CACCINI, FRESCOBALDI, LUZZASCHI, CARISSIMI, OTHERS): BOTT; PICKETT AND NEW LONDON CONSORT (OISEAU-LYRE).

monophony (Gr., "single voice") Music written for a single voice, or voices singing in unison. The repertoire encompasses PLAINCHANT, medieval songs of the troubadours, trouvères, and Minnesingers, as well as any unaccompanied song for solo voice. Monophony also describes pieces of solo instrumental music where there is one melodic line and no harmony.

monothematic Term used to describe a piece of music or an individual movement whose content is derived from a single melodic idea. Examples include the finales of Haydn's Symphony No. 104 in D (*London*) and Mozart's Symphony No. 39 in E-flat, K. 543.

Monteux, Pierre

(b. Paris, April 4, 1875; d. Hancock, Me., July 1, 1964)

FRENCH/AMERICAN CONDUCTOR. One of the most capable conductors of the 20th century, he was present at the creation of some of its most important music. He began lessons on the violin at the age of six and entered the Paris Conservatoire when he was nine, studying violin, harmony, and counterpoint and taking a first prize in violin in 1896. By then he was already a professional, having been engaged as a violist by both the Opéra-Comique and the Concerts Colonne orchestra in 1890. He rose to principal in both groups, taking on the additional role of assistant conductor and choirmaster with the Colonne ensemble in 1894, and playing in the premiere of Debussy's *Pelléas et Mélisande* at the Opéra-Comique in 1902. From 1894 to 1911 he also played viola in the Quatuor Geloso.

Monteux found himself a participant in the birth of musical modernism when, in 1909, the Russian impresario Sergey Diaghilev engaged the Colonne orchestra to play in the pit for his newly formed Ballets Russes. The first work commissioned by the company was Igor Stravinsky's *The Firebird,* which received its premiere on June 25, 1910, under the baton of the Colonne orchestra's principal conductor, Gabriel Pierné. Monteux got his golden opportunity the following season when Diaghilev, having engaged a Russian conductor for the premiere of Stravinsky's *Petrushka,* had the nerve to ask Pierné to conduct the preliminary rehearsals; Pierné refused and Monteux, eager to acquire the additional experience, stepped in. As the date of the premiere approached, Stravinsky, who had attended the rehearsals, insisted that Monteux remain on the podium for the performances, arguing that he knew the music better than anyone. Monteux was subsequently entrusted with the premieres of Stravinsky's *The Rite of Spring* (1913) and *Le chant de rossignol* (1917), Ravel's *Daphnis et Chloé* (1912), and Debussy's *Jeux* (1913).

Monteux served in the French military during the early years of World War I. He visited the United States in 1916 and was active at the Metropolitan Opera during the seasons of 1917–19 (he would resurface at the Met in 1953–56 and again in 1958–59). As music director of the Boston Symphony Orchestra from 1919 to 1924, he introduced numerous contemporary works to the orchestra's repertoire, including scores by Debussy, Milhaud, Bridge, Falla, Gian Francesco Malipiero (1882–1973), and Szymanowski. Monteux spent ten years (1924–34) as second conductor of the Concertgebouw Orchestra of Amsterdam, sharing the podium with Willem Mengelberg, and served as music director of the San Francisco Symphony Orchestra from 1936 to 1952. He became an American citizen in 1942.

Pierre Monteux, elegance incarnate

During the 1950s, Monteux maintained a busy schedule as guest conductor, working with the Chicago Symphony Orchestra and appearing regularly with his old ensemble in Boston. In 1961, at the age of 86, he accepted his final appointment, as chief conductor of the London Symphony Orchestra—insisting, with characteristic flair, on a 25-year contract with an option to renew for another 25 years. He remained active as a performer until the final year of his life, and on one of his last trips to the podium conducted *The Rite of Spring* on the 50th anniversary of its premiere.

Monteux's vast repertoire included the major works of the Austro-Germanic tradition as well as the French; he was considered a definitive interpreter of the early-20th-century scores in which he specialized. He got his way with orchestras not by being a tyrant, but by using an approach that was patient and authoritative, tempered by a wonderful sense of humor. Like many conductors of his era, he favored the use of expressive rubato and encouraged orchestras to play in long, supple phrases. Through much of his career he pursued a pedagogical interest, opening a school for conductors in Paris in 1932, whose work he later carried on at his home in Hancock, Maine. His pupils included Neville Marriner, André Previn, and David Zinman.

RECOMMENDED RECORDINGS

FRANCK, SYMPHONY IN D MINOR: CHICAGO SYMPHONY ORCHESTRA (RCA).

RAVEL, *DAPHNIS ET CHLOÉ*: LONDON SYMPHONY ORCHESTRA (DECCA).

STRAVINSKY, *PETRUSHKA*: BOSTON SYMPHONY ORCHESTRA (RCA).

TCHAIKOVSKY, SYMPHONY NO. 6 (*PATHÉTIQUE*): BOSTON SYMPHONY ORCHESTRA (RCA).

Monteverdi, Claudio

(b. Cremona, May 15, 1567; d. Venice, November 29, 1643)

ITALIAN COMPOSER, the most important musician of the first half of the 17th century. He absorbed the musical style of the late Renaissance and, in his early works, helped bring it to its highest expression. He pioneered new compositional techniques in his madrigals and other vocal works, effectively laying the foundation for many of the stylistic conventions of the Baroque. To the nascent genre of opera he brought the power of a musical imagination unrivaled in his own lifetime, together with formal skills and psychological insights among the most impressive of any composer in history. He created works of extraordinary stature in nearly every significant form of the day.

The son of a doctor, he studied with Marc'Antonio Ingegneri (ca. 1547–92) at the cathedral in Cremona, obtaining a thorough grounding in traditional "Palestrina-style" polyphony—the lush-sounding, rigorously constructed contrapuntal art of Palestrina and his circle. A precocious student, Monteverdi published several books of motets and madrigals in this conservative style before going to Mantua, in 1590 or 1591, to serve as a string instrumentalist at the court of Duke Vincenzo Gonzaga. There he came into contact with Giaches de Wert (1535–96), the master of the ducal chapel and a composer known for the daring, expressive use of chromaticism and dissonance in his madrigals. Wert's music would exert an important influence on Monteverdi, whose Third Book of madrigals, appearing in 1592, reveals a new boldness in approach and a much wider range of style. In 1599 Monteverdi was passed over as Wert's successor in favor of the more experienced Benedetto Pallavicino, but in 1601, following Pallavicino's death, he was appointed *maestro di cappella* in Mantua.

Monteverdi's fame spread rapidly, supported by the publication of his Fourth Book of madrigals in 1603 and his Fifth Book in 1605. Even before the madrigals of the Fourth Book appeared in print, the conservative theorist Giovanni Maria Artusi—having heard some of them in private performance—published a fierce diatribe excoriating Monteverdi for his modernistic excesses. While Artusi's attack did nothing but enhance Monteverdi's stature as a madrigalist, it cried out for rebuttal. In 1607, when Monteverdi published his *Scherzi musicali* (*Musical Jokes*; a collection of part-songs for three voices, written in a much simpler style than the madrigals), he included a lengthy declaration (signed by his brother, Giulio Cesare Monteverdi, also a musician in the service of the Gonzaga family) arguing that his works utilized a new way of writing—a so-called *seconda prattica,* to which the rules of the old *prima prattica,* the method of Palestrina and the traditionalists, did not apply. The "second practice" was based on the premise that in vocal music, expression of the emotional content of the words was paramount and could justify the sorts of transgressions to which Artusi objected.

The greatest achievement of Monteverdi's first 40 years was the completion, also in 1607, of his first opera, *L'Orfeo* ◉, widely acknowledged as the first great work in the history of the genre. A second opera, *Arianna,* the music to which is now lost (except for one aria, "Lasciatemi morire"), followed in 1608. Around this time Monteverdi became disenchanted with conditions at the Mantuan court. Feeling overworked and underappreciated, he retreated to the home of his father, Baldassare, in Cremona. But a petition written by Baldassare to Duke Vincenzo, seeking Claudio's release from the post of *maestro di cappella,* was rejected, and Monteverdi had no choice but to remain in the Gonzaga family's service until 1612—when, following Vincenzo's death, both he and his brother were sacked.

The deteriorating conditions in Mantua had already prompted Monteverdi to begin looking elsewhere for employment, and undoubtedly played a part in his decision to publish, in 1610, a grand collection of church music, including a mass in the old style and a set of Vespers ◉ demonstrating his mastery of the new style (in its use of basso continuo, voices and instruments in combination, dance forms, virtuoso solo singing, and operatic declamation) alongside elements of the old (cantus firmus technique, divided choirs, and strict a cappella polyphony). Monteverdi's dedication of the collection to Pope Paul V suggests he was hoping for an appointment in Rome, but, as things turned out, his future was in Venice. The death of Giulio Cesare Martinengo in July of 1613 left vacant the post of *maestro di cappella* at the Basilica of San Marco, the city's magnificent principal

CLAVDIO MONTE VERDE

FIORI POETICI
Raccolti nel Funerale
DEL MOLTO ILLVSTRE;
E Molto Reuerendo
SIGNOR CLAVDIO
Monte verde
Maestro di Cappella della Ducale di S. Marco.
Consecrati
DA D. GIO: BATTISTA
Marinoni, detto Gioue:
Maestro di Cappella del Domo di Padoua
ALL' ILLVSTRISSIMI
& Eccellentissimi
SIG. PROCVRATORI
Di Chiesa di S. Marco.
In VENETIA, Presso Francesco Miloco.
Con Lic. de Sup. MDCXLIV.

Title page of a collection of the poetic orations read at Monteverdi's funeral

church, and on August 19, 1613, following his successful audition with a performance of one of his masses, Monteverdi got the job.

Monteverdi would spend the remaining 30 years of his life in Venice. Much of the music he wrote for San Marco has been lost. A single retrospective volume of 40 sacred pieces was published in 1640, under the title *Selva morale e spirituale* (*Moral and Spiritual Forest*), with another, containing a mass and psalm settings, appearing posthumously in 1650. Three new books of madrigals were published during the composer's years in Venice. The Sixth Book, dating from 1614, is a collection of five-part settings, some coming fairly close to 16th-century style, others in the new soloistic manner known as the *stile concertato,* in which continuo instruments rather than voices fill out the texture. In the latter, Monteverdi delights in showing how one or two voices can be more expressive than four or five. The Seventh Book of madrigals (1619), titled *Concerto,* consists mostly of duets and trios in this new style, while the Eighth Book (1638), titled *Madrigali guerrieri, et amorosi* (*Warlike and Amorous Madrigals*), runs the gamut from large-scale polyphonic works for voices and instruments to pieces in the theatrical style. A Ninth Book, consisting of miscellaneous madrigals and canzonettas, was published posthumously in 1651.

Monteverdi was a few months shy of his 70th birthday when, during the winter of 1637, the world's first public opera house opened its doors in the Venetian parish of San Cassiano. Over the next four years Venice acquired three more opera houses. Competition was keen, and Monteverdi found his talents as an opera composer in demand once again. In 1640, his *Arianna* was revived at the Teatro San Moisè. That same season, for the Teatro San Cassiano, Monteverdi wrote *Il ritorno di Ulisse in patria* (*The Return of Ulysses to His Homeland*). In 1641, for the Teatro Santi Giovanni e Paolo, he composed *Le nozze d'Enea in Lavinia* (*The Marriage of Aeneas to Lavinia*), the music to which has been lost, and in 1643, also for Santi Giovanni e Paolo, he wrote *L'INCORONAZIONE DI POPPEA,* his crowning masterpiece. Encompassing a range of styles from heroic to lyrical to comic, and uniting seemingly disparate musical and formal approaches by sheer force of imagination, these grand works set the stage for Baroque opera, which composers of the next two generations would turn into the predominant musical genre of 17th-century Italy.

In a period of revolutionary change in musical style, much of which he helped bring about, Monteverdi was the art's most adventurous, eloquent, and influential voice. A brilliant innovator whose own language underwent a complete metamorphosis over the years, he was also a brilliant synthesizer whose work in established genres infused them with new vitality. To paraphrase his contemporary Shakespeare, he bestrode the musical world like a colossus, bridging not merely two centuries but two eras, the Renaissance and the Baroque. He was the Orpheus of his age.

RECOMMENDED RECORDINGS

IL COMBATTIMENTO DI TANCREDI E CLORINDA, IL BALLO DELLE INGRATE: ALESSANDRINI AND CONCERTO ITALIANO (OPUS 111).

L'INCORONAZIONE DI POPPEA: BORST, LAURENS, KÖHLER, LARMORE; JACOBS AND CONCERTO VOCALE (HARMONIA MUNDI).

L'INCORONAZIONE DI POPPEA: MCNAIR, OTTER, HANCHARD, CHANCE; GARDINER AND ENGLISH BAROQUE SOLOISTS (DG).

MADRIGALS, BOOKS 4 AND 8: ALESSANDRINI AND CONCERTO ITALIANO (OPUS 111).

L'ORFEO: DALE, LARMORE, SCHOLL, PEETERS; JACOBS AND CONCERTO VOCALE (HARMONIA MUNDI).

SELVA MORALE E SPIRITUALE: CHRISTIE AND LES ARTS FLORISSANTS (HARMONIA MUNDI).

VESPERS OF 1610: BAIRD, DAWSON, OTTER, ARGENTA, ROLFE JOHNSON; GARDINER AND ENGLISH BAROQUE SOLOISTS (DG).

VESPERS OF 1610: KIEHR, BORDEN, SCHOLL, TORRES; JACOBS AND NETHERLANDS CHAMBER CHOIR, CONCERTO VOCALE (HARMONIA MUNDI).

VESPERS OF 1610: MONOYIOS, CHANCE, ROBSON, TERFEL, MILES; GARDINER AND MONTEVERDI CHOIR, ENGLISH BAROQUE SOLOISTS (DG).

***Moonlight* Sonata** NICKNAME OF LUDWIG VAN BEETHOVEN'S PIANO SONATA IN C-SHARP MINOR, OP. 27, NO. 2, published in 1802. The name originated not with Beethoven himself, but with the poet Ludwig Rellstab, who likened the eerie calm of the sonata's opening movement to the experience of being in "a boat in the moonlight" on Lake Lucerne. Beethoven had paved the way for such speculation by placing the description "quasi una fantasia" ("like a fantasy") at the head of this sonata and its companion piece, the Sonata in E-flat, Op. 27, No. 1.

The *Moonlight* Sonata begins, atypically, with its slow movement. The famously repeated three-note figure that haunts this Adagio—a figure most likely inspired by the Act I trio of Mozart's *Don Giovanni* (another "fantastic" nocturnal scene)—produces a funereal ostinato under the actual melody, a tolling subject of great desolation. Engrossing as it is, the movement is essentially a prelude: The sonata's concluding Allegretto and Presto movements carry the weight of the argument and represent a Scylla and Charybdis of musical challenges for the performer.

RECOMMENDED RECORDINGS

GILELS (DG).
RUBINSTEIN (RCA).
RUDOLF SERKIN (SONY).

Moore, Gerald

(b. Watford, July 30, 1899; d. Penn., March 13, 1987)

ENGLISH PIANIST. One of the foremost accompanists of the 20th century, he signed with the English label HMV in 1921, following study in England and Canada. During a career spanning five decades, he worked with a veritable who's who of soloists, from Pablo Casals and John McCormack to Elisabeth Schwarzkopf, Dietrich Fischer-Dieskau, and Janet Baker; with the latter artists he recorded hundreds of songs by Schubert, Wolf, and Richard Strauss. He wrote several books on the interpretation of the art song literature, as well as other books of an autobiographical nature, including *The Unashamed Accompanist* (1943), *Am I Too Loud? Memoirs of an Accompanist* (1962), and *Farewell Recital* (1978).

RECOMMENDED RECORDINGS

"A SCHUBERT EVENING": BAKER (EMI).
SCHUBERT, GOETHE SONGS: FISCHER-DIESKAU (DG).
SCHUBERT, *DIE SCHÖNE MÜLLERIN*, *SCHWANENGESANG*, *WINTERREISE*: FISCHER-DIESKAU (DG).
WOLF, *SPANISCHES LIEDERBUCH*: SCHWARZKOPF, FISCHER-DIESKAU (DG).

mordent ORNAMENT consisting of a rapid single or double alternation between a written note and its neighbor a step below, beginning and ending on the written note. A good example of the use of mordents in the ornamentation of a vocal line is provided by François Couperin in the second of his *Leçons de Ténèbre.*

morendo (It., "dying") Expressive marking in very quiet passages, indicating that the sound is to be allowed to fade away. *See also* AGRÉMENTS.

Morris, James

(b. Baltimore, January 10, 1947)

AMERICAN BASS-BARITONE. He studied at the University of Maryland and the Peabody Conservatory, as well as privately with Rosa Ponselle, continuing his education at the Academy of Vocal Arts in Philadelphia under the tutelage of Nicola Moscona. He made his professional debut with the Baltimore Opera (as Crespel in Offenbach's *Les contes d'Hoffmann*) in 1967; in 1970, when he was 23, he signed with the Metropolitan Opera as its youngest solo artist, making his company debut on January 7, 1971, as the King in Verdi's *Aida.* Subsequent roles at the Met included both the Commendatore and Don Giovanni, Raimondo in Donizetti's *Lucia di Lammermoor,* the four villains in *Les contes d'Hoffmann,* and Claggart in Britten's *Billy Budd,* a role Morris brought off with mesmerizing intensity.

With his commanding, darkly resonant voice and imposing physical stature, Morris was destined for the big Wagner roles. Prior to making his debut as Wotan in *Die Walküre* (Baltimore, 1984), he coached intensively with Hans Hotter. He performed the three *Ring* cycle Wotans together for the first time in Munich in 1987, and starred in the Met's acclaimed "old-school" production of the *Ring* launched in 1989 (returning in sensational form for its revival in 2004). In 2001 he capped his Wagnerian career with the role of Hans Sachs in new productions of *Die Meistersinger von Nürnberg* in San Francisco

James Morris, the leading Wotan of his generation

and at the Met. Ironically, perhaps because of his success elsewhere, this great Wagner singer, the greatest Wotan of his generation, still has never sung at Bayreuth.

RECOMMENDED RECORDINGS

WAGNER, *SIEGFRIED*: BEHRENS, GOLDBERG, ZEDNIK, MOLL; LEVINE AND METROPOLITAN OPERA (DG).

WAGNER, *DIE WALKÜRE*: NORMAN, BEHRENS, LAKES, LUDWIG, MOLL; LEVINE AND METROPOLITAN OPERA (DG).

Moses und Aron (Moses and Aaron) **OPERA IN TWO ACTS BY ARNOLD SCHOENBERG,** to his own libretto, first performed (in concert) on March 12, 1954, in Hamburg, and first staged June 6, 1957, at the Stadttheater in Zurich. Though Schoenberg envisaged a third act that he never composed, the work is complete as it stands and has achieved a place in the repertoire in recent years, thanks in part to performances at the Metropolitan Opera and the Salzburg Festival. The Biblical tale of tongue-tied Moses and his eloquent brother, Aaron, becomes here a parable of the artist's role as prophet, focusing on the impediments life poses to faith and the question of what can and cannot be expressed.

RECOMMENDED RECORDING

MERRITT, PITTMAN-JENNINGS, POLGÁR; BOULEZ AND NETHERLANDS OPERA CHORUS, ROYAL CONCERTGEBOUW ORCHESTRA (DG).

mosso (It., "agitated") Descriptive term occasionally used as part of a tempo marking, e.g., *Andante mosso, quasi allegretto* (Sibelius, Symphony No. 5, second movement), but more commonly found in conjunction with the words *più* ("more") and *meno* ("less"), to indicate a modification of the designated tempo during the course of a movement, e.g., *più mosso* ("faster"), *meno mosso* ("slower").

motet A polyphonic vocal composition, usually with a sacred text. The motet emerged as a distinct genre in France during the 13th and 14th centuries, initially retaining many of the structural and technical characteristics of the liturgical polyphony from which it developed. The most sophisticated motets from this era typically presented a Latin text in slow-moving notes in the tenor voice, with additional text or texts—in Latin or the vernacular (i.e., French)—set to faster-moving notes in one, two, or three upper voices. The overlapping texts, sacred and secular, tended to comment upon one another in surprising ways; similarly, the overlapping metrical and melodic patterns produced by the use of isorhythmic elements in these settings surprised and delighted the medieval ear.

The motet reconnected with its sacred origins in the 15th century, acquiring a new gravitas and melismatic grace in the works of Du Fay and his contemporaries. It reached a peak of structural and contrapuntal sophistication, and of sonorous beauty, in the mature works of Josquin, written at the end of the 15th and beginning of the 16th century. Significant contributions to the genre were also made by Palestrina and Lassus later in the 16th century, before interest in the genre waned during the Baroque. Motets with instrumental accompaniment became the norm rather than the exception during the 17th century, and increasingly the use of choral forces, rather than solo voices one to a part, was preferred. Large choral motets in the style of cantatas, with orchestral accompaniment and parts for soloists, flourished in France from the middle of the 17th century to the middle of the 18th in the hands of Lully, Rameau, and others. Among the finest late contributions to the motet repertoire are the handful of works J. S. Bach composed, all with German texts, the majority for eight voices a cappella, between about 1712 and 1735. ◉ *See also* ISORHYTHM.

RECOMMENDED RECORDINGS

BACH, MOTETS: HERREWEGHE AND LA CHAPELLE ROYALE (HARMONIA MUNDI).
BACH, MOTETS: SCHOLARS BAROQUE ENSEMBLE (NAXOS).
BRAHMS, MOTETS: CREED AND RIAS-KAMMERCHOR (HARMONIA MUNDI).
DU FAY, MOTETS: VAN NEVEL AND HUELGAS ENSEMBLE (HARMONIA MUNDI).
JOSQUIN, MOTETS: HERREWEGHE AND LA CHAPELLE ROYALE (HARMONIA MUNDI).
"LOVE'S ILLUSION" (MOTETS FROM THE MONTPELLIER MANUSCRIPT): ANONYMOUS 4 (HARMONIA MUNDI).
POULENC, *QUATRE MOTETS POUR LE TEMPS DE NOËL*: CHRISTOPHERS AND THE SIXTEEN (VIRGIN CLASSICS).

moto perpetuo (It., "perpetual motion") A piece or a style of writing in which a melodic figuration consisting entirely of rapid notes is sustained without interruption. The finale of Schubert's Symphony No. 3 is a particularly energetic example. ◉

Mottl, Felix

(b. Unter-St. Veit, August 24, 1856; d. Munich, July 2, 1911)

AUSTRIAN CONDUCTOR AND COMPOSER. With Hermann Levi and Hans Richter, he was one of the "holy trinity" of conductors anointed by Richard Wagner and entrusted with carrying on the master's tradition at Bayreuth. Wagner determined each one's forte, declaring Richter to be matchless in *Die Meistersinger von Nürnberg,* Levi in *Parsifal,* and Mottl in *Tristan und Isolde.*

Mottl received his early music training at the Löwenburg Seminary in Vienna. He continued at the Vienna Conservatory (where he studied theory with Anton Bruckner) and was invited at the age of 19 to participate as an assistant conductor in the 1876 premiere of Wagner's *Ring* cycle at Bayreuth. From 1881 until 1903 he held the post of music director of the Karlsruhe Opera, turning it into one of the finest houses in Germany. During his tenure, the complete operas of Berlioz and Wagner were produced there. Mottl was engaged to conduct *Tristan und Isolde* at Bayreuth in 1886, and in 1888 was prevailed upon by Cosima Wagner, the composer's widow, to conduct *Parsifal* in place of Levi (an act of transparent anti-Semitism). It was not a happy experience, since Cosima had the role of artistic arbiter and interpreter, dictating tempi and creating considerable confusion for the agreeable but conflicted Mottl, to say nothing of Wagner's carefully trained musicians in the orchestra. Soldiering on, Mottl continued to carry the torch. He conducted an all-Wagner concert at Queen's Hall in London in 1894, and returned to England to conduct the *Ring* cycle at Covent Garden in 1898 and 1900. He was engaged by the Metropolitan Opera as general music director for its 1903–04 season, and conducted two Mozart operas, five Wagner operas, and ten performances of Bizet's *Carmen.* Totally dissatisfied with the experience, he never returned to the United States.

In 1903 Mottl became director of the Munich Opera, a position he kept until his death—which occurred as he was conducting his 100th performance of *Tristan und Isolde.* According to Bruno Walter, Mottl's assistant at the time (and soon to be his successor), Mottl suffered a heart attack on the podium during the first act of *Tristan,* just after Isolde sings, "Todgeweihtes Haupt! Todgeweihtes Herz! Was hältst du von dem Knechte?" ("Death-doomed head! Death-doomed heart! What think'st thou of the knave?"). The Isolde in that fateful performance was Mottl's wife, Zdenka Fassbender.

Mottl's compositions, now rarely performed, include three finished operas, two symphonies, two string quartets, and approximately 50 songs.

movement A complete section or subdivision of a piece of instrumental music, generally unified by tempo, key, mood, or affect.

Mozart, Leopold

(b. Augsburg, November 14, 1719; d. Salzburg, May 28, 1787)

GERMAN VIOLINIST AND COMPOSER, father of Wolfgang Amadeus Mozart. He attended high school in Augsburg and entered the Benedictine University in Salzburg in 1737, where he studied philosophy and law. In 1743, after a brief period of service to a Salzburg nobleman, he was appointed fourth violinist in the court orchestra of the Archbishop of Salzburg. He married Anna Maria Pertl, from nearby St. Gilgen, in 1747; they had seven children, of whom only two—Maria Anna (b. 1751, nicknamed "Nannerl") and Wolfgang (b. 1756)—survived to adulthood. In 1758 he became the orchestra's second violinist, and in 1763 he was promoted to the post of deputy Kapellmeister. His efforts to cultivate Wolfgang's talent and expand the boy's musical horizons, which involved lengthy periods of travel away from home, undoubtedly accounted for his lack of further advancement in the Salzburg musical hierarchy. In later years, as relations between his son and the archbishop grew strained, Leopold had to take much of the heat.

Leopold Mozart, portrait in oils, ca. 1765

Leopold Mozart was one of the finest fiddlers in Europe. He had a broad range of intellectual interests and an equally broad range as a composer: His oeuvre includes numerous symphonies (many now lost), as well as liturgical settings, serenades, divertimentos, and partitas, and a small number of chamber and solo keyboard works. Of his compositions that have retained a place in the repertoire, the most familiar are the Cassation in G (ca. 1760; an arrangement long attributed to Joseph Haydn, better known as the *Toy* Symphony), and the Trumpet Concerto in D (1762). In addition to presiding over the education of the greatest genius in the history of music—no small achievement—Leopold Mozart wrote the most important violin method of the mid-18th century: *Versuch einer gründlichen Violinschule* (*A Treatise on the Fundamental Principles of Violin Playing*), published in 1756, the same year Wolfgang was born.

RECOMMENDED RECORDINGS

SELECTED SYMPHONIES: ARMSTRONG AND NEW ZEALAND CHAMBER ORCHESTRA (NAXOS).

TOY SYMPHONY: TUROVSKY AND I MUSICI DI MONTREAL (CHANDOS).

TRUMPET CONCERTO: EKLUND; SPARF AND DROTTNINGHOLM BAROQUE ENSEMBLE (NAXOS).

Mozart, Wolfgang Amadeus

(b. Salzburg, January 27, 1756; d. Vienna, December 5, 1791)

AUSTRIAN COMPOSER, PIANIST, VIOLINIST, AND VIOLIST, music's supremely gifted creator, whose achievements mark a zenith of Western culture. The two main phases of his life were the period of his childhood, youth, and early maturity, from 1756 to 1781, and the decade he spent as a freelance musician in Vienna, from 1781 to his death. The first phase saw his emergence as the most astonishing child prodigy in the history of music up to that time, and included a halcyon period as the sensation of Europe. He traveled abroad in search of opportunity and a position, and spent several years in Salzburg as a desperately unhappy lackey. The second phase, a decade of incomparable glory, brought emancipation and the production of the concertos, symphonies, chamber works, and operas that represent not only the pinnacle of Classicism but, as the conductor Charles Dutoit has observed, "the summit of creation."

Wolfgang Mozart at the piano during his years as a traveling prodigy

"The miracle that God let be born in Salzburg," as Leopold Mozart more than once referred to his son, was cosmopolitan practically from birth. He received a thorough education from his father, a violin teacher and court musician in Salzburg, embracing not only music but a considerable range of the liberal arts and sciences. Following in the footsteps of his elder sister, Nannerl, he became a keyboard prodigy, performing for the first time when he was five years old; he also became an outstanding violinist. From his seventh to his 23rd year he was away from home more than half the time, displaying his talents on tours of Europe. The longest of these trips, to Munich, Paris, and London, lasted three and a half years, from the time Mozart was seven until shortly before his 11th birthday. While in London he met J. C. Bach and absorbed much from him. The three journeys to Italy he made with his father between 1769 and 1773 gave him a thorough exposure to Italian church music and allowed him to sample far more opera than could be heard in Salzburg. They also enabled him to assimilate the Italian symphonic style, of which he became a towering master while still in his teens. An extended trip to Mannheim and Paris in 1777–78 brought an opportunity to compose for two of the best ensembles in Europe: the orchestra of Elector Carl Theodor in Mannheim and that of the Concert Spirituel in Paris.

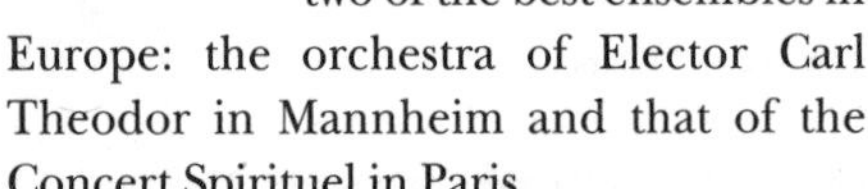

Between trips abroad, Mozart, like his father, worked as a court musician for the Prince-Archbishop of Salzburg. He was appointed concertmaster of the court orchestra, without pay, at the age of 13. Three years later, following the installation of Hieronymus Colloredo as archbishop, Mozart was confirmed in the post of court concertmaster at an annual salary of 150 gulden, and in 1779 the post of court organist was added to his dossier. Mozart's time in Salzburg was taken up with masses and other sacred settings, symphonies, serenades, divertimentos, and miscellaneous chamber pieces—the usual run of courtly duties. Though he felt confined in Salzburg and chafed at its provincialism and lack of opera, he nevertheless found outlets for his genius in such extraordinary works as his Symphony No. 25 in G minor, K. 183, an ambitious essay in the STURM UND DRANG style, and Symphony No. 29 in A, K. 201, whose courtly elegance, intimate yet intense expression, and supreme craftsmanship set it apart from all the other Salzburg symphonies. During the years 1773–76, he also composed a total of 37 movements for solo violin and orchestra—five violin concertos plus numerous concerted movements for violin embedded in serenades and other works—all for himself to play.

Child prodigies grow up eventually, and Mozart did so during the trip to Mannheim and Paris in 1777–78, on which he was accompanied by his mother. In Mannheim, he fell in love with the virtuosic, high-horsepower playing of the court orchestra, as well as with a gifted young singer named Aloysia Weber. Aloysia chose to marry the painter Joseph Lange, however, and Mozart eventually married Aloysia's younger sister Constanze. In Paris, Mozart's music, especially his Concerto for Flute and Harp, K. 299, and Symphony in D, K. 297 (*PARIS*), was enthusiastically received. But no job offer resulted, and soon after the symphony's premiere his mother fell ill and died. Alone for the first time in his life, the 22-year-old composer had not only to cope with a devastating loss but to carefully break the news to his father by mail. On his return to Salzburg, he composed several symphonies, the *Posthorn* Serenade, K. 320, a divertimento, a violin sonata, and the *Sinfonia concertante* in E flat for violin and viola, K. 364, one of the most beautiful string concertos in the literature. Its polished orchestral writing and cosmopolitan idiom (incorporating many of the effects favored in Paris and Mannheim) show Mozart at a new level of stylistic and technical accomplishment. One final proof of his stature remained: the opera seria *IDOMENEO, RE DI CRETA*, composed for Munich and premiered there in 1781. Its boldness, power, and dramatic authority are the hallmarks of a master.

Constanze Mozart

Mozart's life entered its second phase on June 8, 1781, the day on which, against his father's wishes and those of their mutual employer, he left the service of the Prince-Archbishop of Salzburg to make his way as a freelance musician in Vienna. With the uncertainty of life in the big city came the freedom to make decisions for himself; he married Constanze in 1782, joined the Freemasons in 1784, and spread his wings as a musician. His burning desire was to establish himself as an opera composer. Vienna was then the operatic center of the German-speaking world, and Mozart was soon engaged in his first project there, the

A view of Salzburg, from an 18th-century print

Singspiel *Die Entführung aus dem Serail* (*Abduction from the Seraglio*). The work's premiere in 1782 was a notable success. The following year Mozart met Vienna's new court poet and notorious free spirit, Lorenzo da Ponte. At first he was skeptical: "If he is in league with Salieri," Mozart wrote his father on May 7, 1783, "I will never get anything out of him. But I would dearly love to show what I can do in an Italian opera."

It would be two years before Mozart realized his dream, but during those years he showed Vienna what he could do as a pianist-composer. Between 1784 and 1786 he produced a dozen piano concertos that are among the glories of Western art. Written mostly for the Lenten season, when by decree the theaters were closed, these works contain music of a marvelously theatrical cast. Indeed, each of them is virtually an opera *manqué,* with witty, conversational exchanges between the piano and orchestra, beautiful slow movements patterned after arias of love, and—except in the minor-key works—bubbling *opera buffa* finales. By the time Mozart approached da Ponte with the idea of collaborating on an operatic setting of Beaumarchais's *Le mariage de Figaro,* most likely in the summer of 1785, he had taken the art of emotional characterization to new heights in his concertos. He was ready to write great operas. Da Ponte, keenly aware of his ability, agreed at once.

Commissioned by Emperor Joseph II, LE NOZZE DI FIGARO (*The Marriage of Figaro*) opened May 1, 1786, at the Burgtheater in Vienna and enjoyed substantial if not uproarious success. But it was a huge hit when it premiered later that year in Prague. On a visit to the Bohemian capital in January of 1787, Mozart was able to attend one performance of *Figaro* and conduct another, and to lead the premiere of his newly composed Symphony No. 38 in D, K. 504 (henceforth called the PRAGUE), a

Mozart as a young man, posthumous portrait by Barbara Krafft, 1819

work of high spirits and exquisite craftsmanship. By the time he left for Vienna, he had in his pocket the commission for his next opera, DON GIOVANNI. Its premiere in Prague, on October 29, 1787, would be the high-water mark of his career.

It is a myth that in his final years Mozart sank into poverty and died penniless and in despair. While it is true that he was never good at managing his finances and often lived beyond his means, the well-documented financial problems he faced during the years 1788–90 were mainly the result of hard times brought on by war between Austria and Turkey. As his earnings declined he gave top priority to creating works that he could sell on subscription or perform at concerts for his own benefit. The symphonies in E-flat, K. 543, G minor, K. 550, and C, K. 551, completed in six weeks in the summer of 1788, were probably composed for a benefit concert Mozart intended to give that fall. Finding it easier to borrow than tighten his belt, he directed a stream of letters to his Masonic lodge brother Michael Puchberg, asking for loans. Some relief came in December 1788, following the death of Christoph Willibald Gluck, when Mozart was appointed to the post of Imperial and Royal Chamber Composer. The 800 gulden he drew (to create dance music for the fancy court balls given during Carnival) was, he lamented, "too much for the services I give, and too little for what I am capable of."

Just what he was capable of Mozart showed in works like the Clarinet Quintet, K. 581 (1789), written for Anton Stadler, and the opera *COSÌ FAN TUTTE* (*All Women Are Like That*), a score utterly perfect in formal terms, rich, nuanced, and emotionally probing. The death of Joseph II in February of 1790 brought a halt to performances of *Così* just weeks after its premiere (they were resumed in the spring), but left Mozart with fresh hopes of achieving preferment at court after the accession of the new emperor, Leopold II. Soon enough these hopes were dashed, and the begging letters continued to go out to Puchberg. Mozart's fortunes improved dramatically in the spring and summer of 1791 with the arrival of commissions for *DIE ZAUBERFLÖTE* (*The Magic Flute*) and *La clemenza di Tito.* The latter, intended for festivities marking the coronation of Leopold II as King of Bohemia, required a rush job and another journey to Prague for its premiere on September 6. Mozart then had to hurry back to Vienna to put the finishing touches on *Die Zauberflöte* and ready it for its premiere on September 30. Once that was out of the way he took up the Clarinet Concerto, K. 622, for Stadler. Meanwhile, another commission, for a Requiem, had also arrived in the summer of 1791 from Count Franz Walsegg-Stuppach, a recently widowed, music-loving nobleman who wanted a suitable memorial for his wife. Mozart tried to shoehorn bits of the Requiem into his work on other pieces, but was unable to complete the task before becoming gravely ill around November 20, most likely with a recurrence of rheumatic fever, which he had first contracted as a child. He succumbed early in the morning of December 5 after having gathered friends at his bedside to sing through the unfinished Requiem.

No composer in history has achieved the absolute preeminence in the realms of theatrical and symphonic composition that Mozart did (the closest second is Richard Strauss), or contributed a comparable number of masterpieces to those two repertoires. Of the 19 stage works he completed, six are constantly performed today, and several others occasionally; of the nearly 50 symphonies, a dozen; and of the three dozen concertos, two dozen. For Mozart, opera was the most important and, to judge from his own words, most fulfilling of creative endeavors. He was a skilled dramatic composer before he encountered Lorenzo da Ponte, but da Ponte's plots, elegant verses, imagination, and professionalism clearly inspired Mozart to surpass himself and the rest of the world. The three comic masterpieces he composed in collaboration with da Ponte—*Le nozze di Figaro, Don Giovanni,* and *Così fan tutte*—are arguably his supreme musical achievements, remarkable in the richness and acuity of their characterization, the sophistication of their orchestration and musical imagery, and the elegance of their formal plans.

Mozart's brilliance is revealed most directly in the high profile he gives to individual characters and situations through constant and astonishingly clever allusion to the styles and topics of 18th-century music, and in his ability to comment on the action through the orchestra—as in the opening number of *Don Giovanni,* when the servant Leporello dreams of being a cavalier and the orchestra transforms his music from a foot march into a mounted gallop. Less obvious but no less telling is the way Mozart brings the long-range harmonic action of symphonic music to bear on individual numbers and entire scenes, thereby opening up and complicating the simple closed forms of Italian opera buffa and energizing the drama. One of the reasons the beginning of *Don Giovanni* (from the overture through Donna Anna's "Fuggi, crudele") has such power is that the entire span is constructed along the lines of a 20-minute symphony in D minor. In similar fashion, the finales of these works (e.g., the Act IV finale to *Le nozze di Figaro*) are built to unprecedented lengths, prolonging the suspense and excitement.

The concertos and symphonies are on the same exalted plane. In his piano concertos Mozart was less interested in display than in achieving integrity and formal perfection; one of the distinctive features of these works is the way the writing for the solo instrument remains substantive even in the most virtuosic passages. As with the operas, the concertos' scoring is exceptionally refined, the emotional range extraordinary, the play of topics and ideas inspired. The works run a remarkable gamut of expression: some are predominantly festive in tone (the concertos in C, K. 467 and 503, and in E-flat, K. 482), others playful and amorous, or gently poignant (the concertos in A, K. 488, and B-flat, K. 595), while the minor-key works convey much darker moods: seething, turbulent, and dramatic in one case (the concerto in D minor, K. 466), funereal and hauntingly desolate in the other (the concerto in C minor, K. 491). The concertos for horn and clarinet are the finest in the literature; the latter, a particularly wonderful late work, inhabits an expressive realm in which fantasy and gentle pathos prevail, and exhibits a unique richness and ambivalence of feeling. As a symphonist Mozart

Score of Mozart's Piano Concerto No. 24 in C minor, showing faces doodled by the composer

balanced bravura and serious argument with masterly ease. His youthful works are eclectic in the best sense, remarkable for the way they bring together elements of the Italian and German styles, incorporate tricks from Mannheim, and wear the latest fashions from Paris. When he was able to write for a large orchestra, as he was in Paris in 1778, and later in Vienna, he reveled in the sonority and power at his disposal and made especially colorful use of the winds. His final contributions to the genre—the *Prague* Symphony of 1786 and the three of 1788—are probing and quite personal in their expression. Each has its own sound—the clarinets dominate in Symphony No. 39 in E-flat, K. 543, imparting a luminous quality to the whole, while the absence of trumpets and drums in Symphony No. 40 in G minor, K. 550, shifts the mood from drama toward one of agitation and despair. Among orchestral works of the 18th century only Haydn's *London* symphonies merit comparison, though nothing Haydn or anyone since has written quite matches the intense emotional expression and contrapuntal brilliance Mozart achieved in these scores.

***Tom Hulce in Milos Forman's* Amadeus**

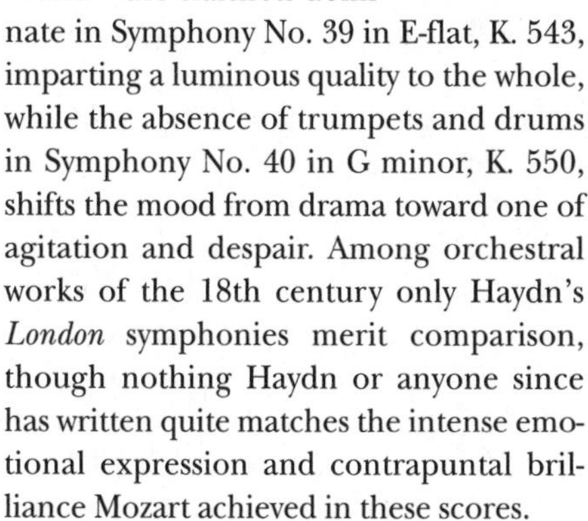

Mozart's chamber works—which include a number of outstanding string quartets and quintets, the best pieces written in the 18th century for wind ensemble, assorted divertimentos, cassations, and serenades, and many fine sonatas for one or more instruments—constitute an important tributary to the almost miraculous stream of his production. The six string quartets dedicated to Haydn (composed 1782–85) owe much to Haydn's example in their scintillating play of topic, and may do the master one better in the fluency of their part-writing. But it was in his quintets for two violins, two violas, and cello, particularly the two written during the spring of 1787—in C, K. 515, and G minor, K. 516—and the quintet for clarinet and strings written two years later that Mozart reached the pinnacle of his achievement as a chamber composer. One of the most remarkable features of the latter work is the utter transparency of its texture, which allows the clarinet to be absorbed in the harmony at certain points while subtly coloring the sound of the string ensemble.

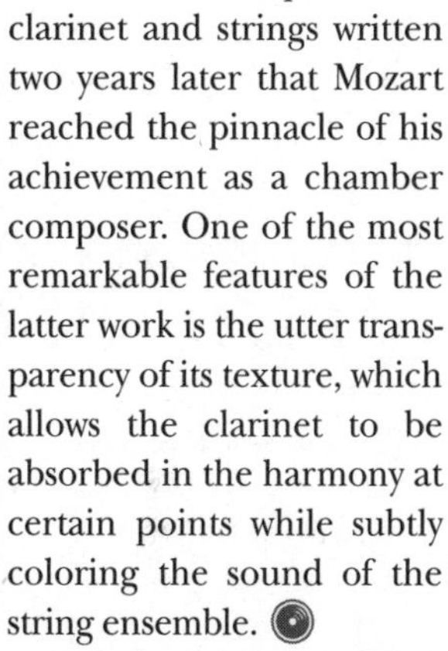

It is important to think of Mozart the man not as the childlike genius of Peter Shaffer's play *Amadeus* (to say nothing of the boob he becomes in Milos Forman's film version), but as someone with a worldly, mature insight into human nature. He could not have been otherwise and written works like *Le nozze di Figaro, Die Zauberflöte,* the late G minor Symphony, and the Clarinet Concerto. Mozart's contemporaries recognized that his music was different, and most if not all of them appreciated what set it apart: its harmonic and formal sophistication, the richness of its scoring and texture, its remarkable fantasy and emotional complexity. Yet during the 19th century, and for the first half of the 20th, Mozart was thought of either as the divinely innocent, porcelainized figure whose bust sat on the shelf, or as a modest precursor of the great Romantic composers. We now see him as a more penetrating artist whose music, in addition to having surface beauty, is lit from within by its intense engagement with the emotions. When we hear his music played today, it has an immediacy, clarity, and freshness that are wondrous and exhilarating, along with an ambiguity and tension, a fragility and poignancy, that bring us face-to-face with who we are, and at the same time take us outside ourselves to an ecstatic plane where gaiety, melancholy, and what Milan Kundera has called "the unbearable lightness of being" seem to coalesce.

RECOMMENDED RECORDINGS

CLARINET CONCERTO: PAY; HOGWOOD AND ACADEMY OF ANCIENT MUSIC (DECCA).

COSÌ FAN TUTTE: SOLTI (DECCA).

DON GIOVANNI: GIULINI (EMI).

LATE SYMPHONIES (NOS. 35–41): BÖHM AND BERLIN PHILHARMONIC (DG).

LATE SYMPHONIES (NOS. 35–41): WALTER AND COLUMBIA SYMPHONY ORCHESTRA (SONY).

LE NOZZE DI FIGARO: SOLTI (DECCA).

PIANO CONCERTOS NOS. 20, 23, 24, AND 25: MORAVEC; MARRINER AND ACADEMY OF ST. MARTIN-IN-THE-FIELDS (HÄNSSLER).

PIANO CONCERTOS NOS. 20, 23, 24, 26, 27: CURZON; KERTÉSZ AND LONDON SYMPHONY ORCHESTRA, BRITTEN AND ENGLISH CHAMBER ORCHESTRA (DECCA).

REQUIEM: BLASI, LIPOVSEK, HEILMANN, ROOTERING; DAVIS AND BAVARIAN RADIO SYMPHONY ORCHESTRA (RCA).

VIOLA QUINTETS: FEHÉRVÁRI AND ÉDER QUARTET (NAXOS).

WIND MUSIC: ENSEMBLE PHILIDOR (CALLIOPE).

DIE ZAUBERFLÖTE: LEAR, WUNDERLICH, PETERS, FISCHER-DIESKAU, OTTO; BÖHM AND BERLIN PHILHARMONIC (DG).

Mravinsky, Evgeny

(b. St. Petersburg, June 4, 1903; d. Leningrad, January 19, 1988)

RUSSIAN CONDUCTOR. He took part in the musical life of his native city as its name changed from St. Petersburg to Petrograd to Leningrad, and died as it was on the verge of once again being called St. Petersburg. For the final 50 years of his life he was the most important conductor in the Soviet Union. He studied composition and conducting at the Leningrad Conservatory, and took lessons in conducting from Nikolay Malko. From 1932 to 1938 he was conductor at the Leningrad Academic Opera and Ballet Theater (previously known as the Mariinsky, later the Kirov), and in 1938 he was appointed permanent conductor of the Leningrad Philharmonic Orchestra, whose leader he remained until his death. During the five decades he spent at its helm, he transformed the Leningrad Philharmonic into the Soviet Union's most prestigious and accomplished orchestra, leading blazing performances of the music of Beethoven, Wagner, Tchaikovsky, and many 20th-century masters, and adding to the group's prominence at home and abroad by arranging for it to give the premieres of several of Shostakovich's symphonies (Nos. 5, 6, 9, 10, and 12). Shostakovich showed his appreciation by dedicating his Symphony No. 8 to Mravinsky, who premiered it on November 4, 1943, in Moscow (Leningrad then being under siege) with the State Symphony Orchestra of the U.S.S.R.

Autocratic and imperious, but undeniably brilliant, Mravinsky cultivated hair-trigger responsiveness from his musicians, often pushing them to the limits of speed and volume. He rehearsed fanatically yet managed to summon playing of electrifying spontaneity in performance. When he was on the podium, the Leningraders produced a sound unlike that of any other orchestra, characterized by an astonishing dynamic range—from a barely audible pianissimo to a huge, floor-rattling fortissimo—and coloration running the gamut from blinding to sepulchral.

RECOMMENDED RECORDINGS

SHOSTAKOVICH, SYMPHONY NO. 10: LENINGRAD PHILHARMONIC (MELODIYA).

TCHAIKOVSKY, SYMPHONIES NOS. 4–6: LENINGRAD PHILHARMONIC (DG).

Muck, Karl

(b. Darmstadt, October 22, 1859; d. Stuttgart, March 3, 1940)

GERMAN CONDUCTOR. He was one of the greatest Wagnerians of the generation immediately following those who knew and worked directly with the composer, and was responsible for leading the performances of *Parsifal* at Bayreuth from 1901 until 1930. He received his earliest musical instruction from his father, and subsequently studied piano in Würzburg and at the Leipzig Conservatory. Prior to beginning his career in music, he also studied classical philology at the universities of Heidelberg and Leipzig, earning his doctorate in 1880. That same year he made his debut with the Leipzig Gewandhaus Orchestra. In 1886 he became chief conductor at the German National Theater in Prague, and in 1892 he was appointed chief conductor of the Berlin Court Opera, where he served 20 years (becoming the company's general music director in 1908) and molded the orchestra into a superb ensemble. From 1906 to 1908, and again from 1912 to 1918, he was music director of the Boston Symphony Orchestra. His tenure in Boston came to an astonishing end when, following America's entry into World War I and a smear campaign in the newspapers, he was arrested and interned as an enemy alien. Returning to Germany after the Armistice, he closed out his career conducting the Hamburg Philharmonic (1922–33).

Muck had a prodigious repertoire as an opera conductor; in Berlin alone, during his 20 years there, he conducted 1,071 performances of 103 different operas. He also had a willingness to conduct new music. He led the first Boston performances of Debussy's *La mer* (in 1907) and Sibelius's First and Fourth Symphonies, as well as the American premiere of Schoenberg's *Five Pieces for Orchestra.* A hardworking musician famed for his painstaking preparation of every detail, Muck was able to coax performances of enormous grandeur and radiance from the orchestras he faced. His recordings of sizable sections of *Parsifal,* made in 1927 and 1928, reflect the glow of a golden age in Wagner interpretation.

RECOMMENDED RECORDING

WAGNER, *PARSIFAL* (EXCERPTS): VARIOUS SOLOISTS (NAXOS).

Mühlfeld, Richard

(b. Salzungern, February 28, 1856; d. Meiningen, June 1, 1907)

GERMAN CLARINETIST. He became principal clarinet of the Meiningen Court Orchestra in 1879, retaining that post until his death. His extraordinary virtuosity and the exquisite beauty of his tone inspired Brahms—who heard him play during a visit to Meiningen in March of 1891—to come out of retirement and begin composing after a lapse of more than a year. Brahms completed both the Trio in A minor, Op. 114, for clarinet, cello, and piano, and the Quintet in B minor, Op. 115, for clarinet and strings during the summer of 1891, and in 1894 he composed the two Sonatas for Clarinet and Piano, Op. 120, premiering them with Mühlfeld in Vienna on January 7, 1895. These sonatas for "Fräulein Klarinette," as Brahms had affectionately come to call the instrument, were the last ones he would write and served as his farewell to instrumental composition.

Clarinet virtuoso Mühlfeld in 1900

Munch, Charles

*(b. Strasbourg, September 26, 1891;
d. Richmond, Va., November 6, 1968)*

FRENCH CONDUCTOR. The son of a respected organist and choirmaster, he was born in Alsace and studied violin at the Strasbourg Conservatory and then in Paris with Lucien Capet. He spent World War I in a German uniform, surviving a gas attack at Peronne and sustaining a wound at Verdun. After the war he became professor of violin at the Strasbourg Conservatory and a naturalized French citizen; he also undertook further study of the violin with Carl Flesch in Berlin. In 1926 he was appointed professor of violin at the Leipzig Conservatory and concertmaster of the Gewandhaus Orchestra, then under the direction of Wilhelm Furtwängler. He moved to Paris in 1933 and made his conducting debut there. Over the next 15 years he worked with several Parisian orchestras, serving as director of the Société Philharmonique (1935–38) and the Société des Concerts du Conservatoire (from 1937). He remained in Paris during World War II, conducting and working behind the scenes to support the Resistance. He was awarded the Légion d'Honneur in 1945.

Munch's American conducting career began in 1946 when he was invited to guest conduct the Boston Symphony Orchestra. In 1948 he led the French National Radio Orchestra on a successful U.S. tour, and in 1949 he succeeded an ailing Serge Koussevitzky as music director of the Boston Symphony. Munch maintained the orchestra's high standard and introduced many new works to its repertoire. He took the BSO on its first European tour in 1952 and on another in 1956 that included the U.S.S.R., sharing the podium honors on both occasions with Pierre Monteux, who had led the orchestra from 1920 through 1924. Munch retired from Boston in 1962 and returned to France, looking forward to a less demanding career of guest conducting. In 1967, however, he became deeply involved in launching the newly founded Orchestre de Paris. Leading the orchestra on a North American tour in 1968, he died in Richmond, Virginia, the morning of a concert.

A spontaneous and passionate interpreter, Munch was magnificent in the French repertoire, particularly the music of Berlioz, Debussy, and Ravel. His recordings of the *Symphonie fantastique* and the Berlioz Requiem, of *La mer, Daphnis et Chloé,* and Saint-Saëns's *Organ* Symphony are still considered benchmarks. He also enjoyed programming works by 20th-century French composers such as Roussel, Honegger, and Milhaud, and was an ardent champion of the Czech composer Martinů, who wrote his Symphony No. 6 (*Fantaisies symphoniques*) especially for him. Munch's performances, characterized by a rare mix of discipline and an almost improvisatory "in the moment" feeling, were notable for their clarity, brilliance, and energy. A kindly figure on and off the podium, Munch was admired by musicians and beloved by his public. In 1954 he recounted his life in music in the book *Je suis chef d'orchestre.*

RECOMMENDED RECORDINGS

BERLIOZ, REQUIEM: BOSTON SYMPHONY ORCHESTRA (RCA).

BERLIOZ, *SYMPHONIE FANTASTIQUE*: BOSTON SYMPHONY ORCHESTRA (RCA).

DEBUSSY, *LA MER* (WITH IBERT, *ESCALES . . .* AND SAINT-SAËNS, *ORGAN* SYMPHONY): BOSTON SYMPHONY ORCHESTRA (RCA).

musette [1] A small bagpipe popular in France in the 17th and early 18th centuries. [2] In 18th-century music, a dancelike piece or passage that mimics the sound of a bagpipe, usually by means of a drone bass. The final movement of Haydn's Symphony No. 104 is an example.

Musica Antiqua Köln *See box on pages 310–13.*

Musical Offering (Musikalische Opfer) SET OF SOLO AND ENSEMBLE PIECES BY **J. S. BACH (BWV 1079),** prepared in 1747 as contrapuntal studies on a theme by Frederick the Great. The king, an accomplished flutist and composer, had asked Bach to improvise on the theme at sight, when Bach visited the Prussian court in May of 1747. Bach had done so, but when asked for a six-part fugue on the subject, demurred, realizing that such a complex realization would require time and thought. Promising the king that he would produce the desired fugue, Bach returned to Leipzig. By July 7, 1747, he had completed the undertaking: a *Musical Offering* to Frederick that neatly summarized Bach's knowledge of the art and theory of music, consisting of two keyboard fugues—one in three voices, the other in the promised six—a sonata for flute, violin, and continuo, and a set of five canons for flute, violin, and keyboard, all based on the royal theme. The collection was headed by an acrostic: ***R**egis **I**ussu **C**antio **E**t **R**eliqua **C**anonica **A**rte **R**esoluta* ("At the king's request, the fugue and the remainder resolved with canonic art"), *ricercar* being another word for "fugue."

RECOMMENDED RECORDINGS

SAVALL AND LE CONCERT DES NATIONS (ALIA VOX).

VARIOUS SOLOISTS; CAPPELLA ISTROPOLITANA (NAXOS).

Music for Strings, Percussion, and Celesta COMPOSITION BY **BÉLA BARTÓK,** commissioned by Paul Sacher and the Chamber Orchestra of Basel, and first performed by them on January 21, 1937. It is arguably Bartók's finest and most concentrated orchestral work, and also one of the most difficult of his scores to perform. The string ensemble is divided into two main groups (each consisting of first and second violins, violas, cellos, and basses) that are occasionally divided even further within the parts, producing a very dense texture. The writing for the string groups is frequently antiphonal, often canonic, and metrically complicated at many points in the score. In performance, the strings are seated around a central cluster of celesta and percussion (including harp, piano, xylophone, timpani, bass drum, tam-tam, large and small cymbals, side drum, and snare drum).

The slow opening movement of *Music for Strings, Percussion, and Celesta* is a rigorous fugue built on a sinuous, eerily chromatic subject. The structure is that of a palindrome: Following a potent crescendo, at the midpoint of the fugue, the entries reverse themselves and begin to render the subject in contrary motion, after which the voices begin to drop out in a gradual decrescendo. The second movement is an energetic Allegro in sonata form full of dazzling interplay between the string groups; it contains a marvelous episode marked by pulsating pizzicato chords. The ensuing Adagio is a hauntingly atmospheric utterance spiced by eerie portamentos in the timpani and strings. In the dancelike finale, Bartók's love of folk music comes to the fore. Toward its end, there is a reprise of the opening movement's fugue subject, now shorn of its unsettling chromaticism, before a fast-moving coda sweeps the piece to its close.

RECOMMENDED RECORDING

REINER AND CHICAGO SYMPHONY ORCHESTRA (RCA).

Musiciens du Louvre, Les *See box on pages 310–13.*

Musikverein Building on the Karlsplatz in Vienna belonging to the Gesellschaft der Musikfreunde (Society of the Friends of Music; founded in 1812), site of the hall in which the Vienna Philharmonic regularly

Vienna's Musikverein, New Year's Day 1987—the Vienna Philharmonic with Kathleen Battle and Herbert von Karajan

performs. The Greek revival–style building, opened in 1870, was designed by Danish-born architect Theophil Hansen. It houses a multipurpose room (the Gottfried-von-Einem-Saal, opened in 1996) and two concert halls: the Brahms-Saal (inagurated with a recital by Clara Schumann), seating just over 600, and the Grosser Musikvereinssaal, with 1,744 seats and room for 300 standees. The Grosser Musikvereinssaal, home to the VIENNA PHILHARMONIC, is considered one of the finest concert halls in the world, with a shoe box shape that contributes to near-perfect acoustics. The interior, which Eduard Hanslick worried might be "too sparkling and magnificent for a concert hall," is adorned with golden caryatids and has an ornately decorated wooden ceiling with paintings depicting Apollo and the nine muses. A row of arched windows over the balcony allows daylight to flood the hall during afternoon concerts.

Among the holdings of the music library at the Musikverein are the manuscript scores of Beethoven's *Eroica* Symphony, Mozart's Symphony in G minor, K. 550, and all of Schubert's symphonies save the Fifth.

Mussorgsky, Modest

(b. Karevo, March 21, 1839; d. St. Petersburg, March 28, 1881)

RUSSIAN COMPOSER. Though sometimes crude in execution—and handicapped by his addiction to alcohol—Mussorgsky was an innovator of the first magnitude, with a profoundly original musical imagination and remarkably prescient notions of harmonic function and musical structure. His major accomplishments were in opera and song, where his interest in capturing the inflections of spoken Russian contributed to the emergence of a musical idiom unlike any other. Yet his sizable reputation rests on just a handful of works, only a few of them authentic.

Mussorgsky grew up on his well-to-do family's lakeside estate, about 250 miles south of St. Petersburg. He started piano lessons with his mother when he was six, performed at nine (a Field concerto, at home), and the next year was taken to St. Petersburg, where he spent two years in a private school for children of the gentry. In 1852 the teenager enrolled in the Cadet School of the Guards to train for a military career. He continued piano lessons for a couple more years, developing into a capable performer with no more than a dilettante's knowledge of theory. He graduated in 1856 with a commission as an officer in the Russian Imperial Guard, and joined the tsar's personal regiment. That fall he met Aleksandr Borodin, who came away with the impression of a dashing young officer who already had a way with the ladies. A few months later he met Aleksandr Dargomizhsky, through whom he soon became acquainted with César Cui, Mily Balakirev, and the critic Vladimir Stasov. In December 1857 he began composition lessons with Balakirev, concentrating on the analysis of scores by Beethoven, Schumann, Liszt, and others.

Mussorgsky resigned his commission in 1858, in the midst of what appears to have been a nervous breakdown, and decided to devote himself fully to music. His emotional problems continued on and off for several more years; in 1861 he broke with Balakirev and began teaching himself composition through exercises and transcriptions.

The emancipation of the serfs that same year brought Mussorgsky's family to the brink of financial ruin. The aspiring composer spent most of the next year on the estate trying to stabilize things. To support himself he moved to St. Petersburg and entered the civil service in 1863; he began to have problems with alcohol around 1865. In 1867 he finished his first significant orchestral composition, a tone poem he described as "hot and chaotic," called *St. John's Night on Bald Mountain* (in English usually shortened to *NIGHT ON BALD* [sometimes *Bare*] *MOUNTAIN*). ◉ He hoped Balakirev would conduct it, but his former mentor wanted changes to the score that Mussorgsky refused to make, and the work went unperformed. (The same year, following a concert given for a pan-Slavic congress in St. Petersburg, Stasov coined the term "Mighty Handful," a.k.a. THE FIVE, to refer to the Balakirev circle, which included Mussorgsky and another newfound friend, Rimsky-Korsakov.) Annoyed that Balakirev was blocking his way as an orchestral composer, Mussorgsky busied himself with some songs and a preliminary effort to set Nikolay Gogol's *The Marriage,* trying for the first time to develop a style of operatic declamation based on speech rhythms and inflection. He composed several scenes before abandoning the project and turning to what would be the most important undertaking of his career, a setting of Aleksandr Pushkin's *BORIS GODUNOV.*

He had just begun it when he got a job in the Forestry Department of the Ministry of State Property, early in 1869. For the next 11 years he would hold clerical jobs that paid increasingly well and left ample time for composition. This newfound stability helped Mussorgsky make rapid progress on *Boris.* The first version (seven scenes), completed by the end of 1869, was set in declamatory style. It was rejected just over a year later by the Mariinsky Theater on the grounds that it lacked a leading female role. Mussorgsky began a revision at once. Whereas his first version had been faithful to Pushkin, the second (in a prologue and four acts) was looser, more operatic, and included scenic elements not in Pushkin, as well as the added love interest. The composer finished this version in 1872 (at the time, he and Rimsky-Korsakov were living together as roommates). The Mariinsky eventually accepted the work and it received its premiere, heavily cut, in 1874.

The completion of the second version of *Boris* was followed by a long period of frequently interrupted work on another

Modest Mussorgsky, painting by Ilya Repin

historically themed opera, *KHOVANSHCHINA*. By the summer of 1873 Mussorgsky was again having drinking problems. In 1874 he composed his grandly imaginative suite for piano, *PICTURES AT AN EXHIBITION*, a tribute to a close friend, the recently deceased painter Victor Hartmann. The next year he began work on his most important song cycle, *Songs and Dances of Death* for bass and piano, and in 1876, having already reworked *Night on Bald Mountain* to include a "demonic chorus," he revised it yet again for use in an operatic setting of Gogol's short story *Sorochintsy Fair*—one of many instances in which he threw recycled material into a compositional breach.

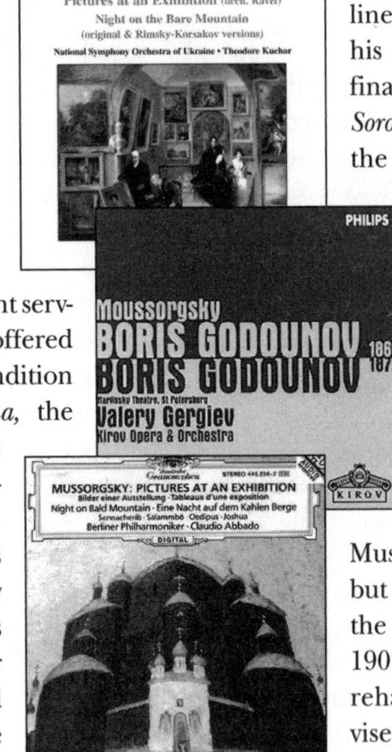

Heavy drinking disrupted Mussorgsky's life again in 1878, and within two years he was dismissed from government service. Two groups of friends offered him stipends, one on the condition that he finish *Khovanshchina*, the other on the condition that he finish *Sorochintsy Fair*. He completed neither. In early 1881 he suffered alcoholic seizures and was taken to a military hospital, where he spent his last month, dying a week after turning 42. A portrait painted by Ilya Repin just before the end shows the composer in his dressing gown, hair unkempt, nose reddened, a crazed look in his eyes.

At his death Mussorgsky left an oeuvre in disarray, having published little besides a handful of songs and the vocal score to *Boris Godunov*. It is rare today that a piece of his is heard as he wrote it. What looms largest in the repertoire are posthumous editions of his work, much of it tidied up and "corrected" by Rimsky-Korsakov. *Songs and Dances of Death* appeared in 1882, edited by Rimsky-Korsakov, and *Khovanshchina* was completed and orchestrated by Rimsky-Korsakov in 1883. (Ravel and Stravinsky would team up on a new version of *Khovanshchina* in 1913, and Shostakovich would try his hand in 1958–59, the version prefered today.) Rimsky's edition of *Night on Bald Mountain* was brought out in 1886. Mussorgsky's original version—the one Balakirev would not perform—was indeed flawed: a disheveled clump of gestures with no convincing line of action. Rimsky based his edition on Mussorgsky's final version, the one for *Sorochintsy Fair*, eschewing the choral parts and making flamboyant use of his skills as an orchestrator, he created what amounted to a new work.

Most striking was Rimsky's complete refashioning of *Boris Godunov*, undertaken in spite of the fact that Mussorgsky had left not one but two finished versions of the opera. Between 1892 and 1907, Rimsky reorchestrated, reharmonized, cut, and revised the score numerous times, arriving finally at the version that was used by Sergey Diaghilev in his Paris production of 1908. This was considered the "standard" version of the score until the 1980s, when Mussorgsky's 1872 version began a comeback. *Pictures at an Exhibition*, never intended as an orchestral piece, is now best known in that form thanks to Ravel's splendid 1922 orchestration, one of more than 20 such treatments of the piece.

Mussorgsky held a utilitarian view of art and believed that its essential purpose was to communicate truth, although his focus in opera shifted from naturalistic modes of declamation to a more conventional approach that allowed some artifice. Because he was largely self-taught and developed a quirky idiom, he was dismissed by many (but not all) of his contemporaries as an idiot savant. That perception yielded in the 20th century to the recognition that Mussorgsky possessed a powerful intellect and was keenly aware of his surroundings—attuned to the innovations of Liszt and Wagner, and able to adapt the scenic and dramatic strategies of Meyerbeer and Verdi to his chosen material. He made his own notable innovations, concentrating in typically Russian fashion on the bold dramatic possibilities inherent in tableau structure, while tapping into the continuous, dynamic development of character and plot across individual acts that is characteristic of Western opera. *Boris Godunov,* in particular, exerted a powerful influence on 20th-century Russian composers—including Shostakovich and Prokofiev—as well as on Debussy, Ravel, Janáček, and Britten.

With the 20th century also came new appreciation for the modernity of Mussorgsky's idiom—the side-slipping progressions that weaken the bonds of tonality, the distinctive use of modes and scales, and the prevalence of tritone relationships. As much as his novel harmonic language, what made Mussorgsky a protomodernist was his pessimistic view of human nature, his interest in isolated individuals with complex characters and motives, caught in the grip of political forces. To these characters and their situations he brought penetrating psychological insights, conveying "truth" with vivid imagination.

RECOMMENDED RECORDINGS

Boris Godunov (1869 and 1872 versions): Putilin, Vaneev, Borodina, Okhotnikov, others; Gergiev and Kirov Opera (Philips).

Boris Godunov (Rimsky-Korsakov version): Ghiaurov, Vishnevskaya, Maslennikov, Talvela, Spiess; Karajan and Vienna Philharmonic (Decca).

Khovanshchina: Minjelkiev, Glausin, Borodina, Okhotnikov; Gergiev and Kirov Opera (Philips).

Night on Bald Mountain (original and Rimsky-Korsakov versions): Kuchar and Ukraine Symphony Orchestra (Naxos).

Pictures at an Exhibition (Ravel orchestration): Karajan and Berlin Philharmonic (DG); Sinopoli and New York Philharmonic (DG).

Pictures at an Exhibition (piano): Richter (Philips).

Pictures at an Exhibition: *Songs and Dances of Death* (original version): Christoff, Moore (Pearl).

Songs and Dances of Death (Shostakovich orchestration): Aleksashkin; Solti and Chicago Symphony Orchestra (Decca).

mute Device used to soften, or alter, the sound of a string or brass instrument. Typical mutes for string instruments fit over the strings at the bridge, damping their vibration and thus absorbing some of the energy that would otherwise be transmitted to the resonating body of the instrument. While the volume of sound is reduced, the more important change that results from the use of a mute is that the tone color is radically altered; the sound acquires an ethereal glaze and seems vaguely disembodied.

Mutes for brass instruments vary greatly in appearance and construction, as well as in the effects they produce. The most common is the straight mute, basically a cone-shaped hollow plug of cardboard, wood, or aluminum that is inserted into the bell of the instrument. (When one of these mutes is placed in a tuba, it looks as if a giant cork has been stuck in the bell.) The use of a straight mute produces a pinched, metallic sound, and in forte a bright buzz rather than a clarion tone. Trombonists also make use of a plunger mute, which is nothing more than the piece of reddish rubber at the business end of a standard toilet plunger. It is held in front of the bell and produces a muffled, rather dry sound. As with the strings, the main purpose of using mutes on brass instruments is not to make the tone softer, but to produce a different tone color, from disembodied growls and buzzes in soft dynamics to hair-raising snarls in loud ones.

Muti, Riccardo

(b. Naples, July 28, 1941)

ITALIAN CONDUCTOR. He studied piano and composition in his native city and at the Giuseppe Verdi Conservatory in Milan before embarking on conducting studies with Franco Ferrara in Venice in 1965. In 1967 he won the Guido Cantelli conducting competition and the following year he made his debut with the RAI (Radio Televisione Italiana) Orchestra; he was appointed principal conductor of the Maggio Musicale festival in Florence in 1969 and became principal conductor at the Teatro Communale in Florence in 1970. In 1972 he made his American debut, with the Philadelphia Orchestra, and his British debut, with the New Philharmonia Orchestra. He served as principal conductor of the latter ensemble (renamed the Philharmonia in 1977) from 1973 to 1982.

Riccardo Muti in rehearsal, 2000

Muti succeeded Eugene Ormandy as music director of the Philadelphia Orchestra in 1980, remaining until 1992. During his tenure, he systematically hardened and coarsened the orchestra's sound in a misguided effort to make it a leaner and meaner ensemble better suited to the 20th century. He was at sea in American music and exhibited a startling lack of sympathy for large parts of the standard repertoire, but he achieved some notable successes with concert performances of opera, particularly Verdi and Wagner. In 1986 he was appointed music director of La Scala in Milan, where for nearly two decades he maintained a high standard of performance. His attempts to consolidate his power by tampering with the theater's management alienated La Scala's all-powerful unions, and he was forced to resign in 2005. The test of wills made international headlines, and resulted in Muti's being publicly excoriated for his vanity by no less a colleague than Franco Zeffirelli.

RECOMMENDED RECORDINGS

CASELLA, *PAGANINIANA* (WITH WORKS OF BUSONI AND MARTUCCI) LA SCALA ORCHESTRA (SONY).

VERDI, *AIDA*: CABALLÉ, DOMINGO, COSSOTTO, GHIAUROV; NEW PHILHARMONIA ORCHESTRA (EMI).

Mutter, Anne-Sophie

(b. Rheinfelden, June 29, 1963)

GERMAN VIOLINIST. She started piano studies at the age of five, but switched to the violin almost immediately, winning first prize in a competition for young musicians when she was six. She studied with Erna Honigberger and Aida Stucki, both pupils of Carl Flesch, and began her international career at the age of 13, playing a recital at the 1976 Lucerne Festival and appearing as soloist with Herbert von Karajan and the Berlin Philharmonic at the 1977 Salzburg Easter Festival. Her debut recording with Karajan and the BPO—of Mozart's Violin Concertos in G and A, K. 216 and 219—appeared in 1978.

Mutter made her American debut in January 1980 as an angelic 16-year-old, playing with consummate musicality and poise in concerts with the New York Philharmonic, under Zubin Mehta, and the National Symphony Orchestra, under Mstislav Rostropovich. Engagements with most of the major European and American orchestras soon followed, as did recital tours of Europe and North America, festival appearances, and a steady procession of highly acclaimed recordings. Mutter's partnership with Karajan continued until his death in 1989. She has also worked closely with Kurt Masur and André Previn; in recital, her accompanist is the American pianist Lambert Orkis, with whom she devoted the whole of 1998 to performing the Beethoven sonatas in North and South America, Europe, and the Far East.

Mutter has been a steadfast champion of new music for most of her career, and has premiered and recorded works written for her by Witold Lutosławski (*Chain 2*; 1986), Wolfgang Rihm (*Gesungene Zeit*; 1992), and Krzysztof Penderecki (Violin Concerto No. 2; 1995), among others. No other violinist of her generation has had such a noticeable impact on the repertoire. She has faced some formidable challenges in her personal life, notably the pressures of stardom at an early age and the loss of her first husband to cancer in 1995, which left her the single parent of two young children. In the years since then her playing, which was always beautiful, has taken on a new quality of urgency and immediacy, exhibiting greater emotional and intellectual depth, sharper insight, and fuller humanity. These factors have made Mutter, who in the summer of 2002 married André Previn, one of the outstanding musicians of our day. She plays the 1710 "Lord Dunn-Raven" Stradivarius.

Anne-Sophie Mutter at Carnegie Hall, 1998

RECOMMENDED RECORDINGS

Brahms, Violin Concerto: Masur and New York Philharmonic (DG).

Korngold, Violin Concerto; Tchaikovsky Violin Concerto: Previn and London Symphony Orchestra, Vienna Philharmonic (DG).

Mozart, Violin Concertos in G, K. 216, and A, K. 219: Karajan and Berlin Philharmonic (DG).

Sibelius, Violin Concerto: Previn and Staatskapelle Dresden (DG).

Muzio, Claudia

(b. Pavia, February 7, 1889; d. Rome, May 24, 1936)

ITALIAN SOPRANO. She was brought up in an operatic family: Her mother was a member of the chorus and her father worked as a stage director at both Covent

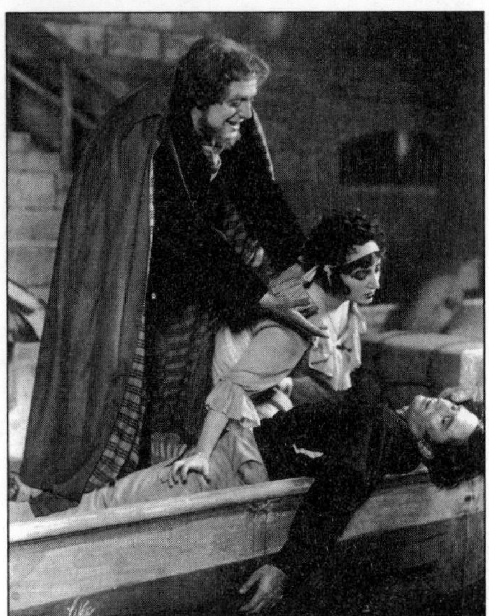

Claudia Muzio as Giorgetta in the world premiere of Puccini's **Il tabarro,** *1918*

Garden and the Metropolitan Opera. She made her debut in Arezzo in 1910, as Massenet's Manon, and sang at the Teatro Regio in Turin after that. She made her debut at La Scala in 1913 and appeared at Covent Garden in 1914 as Desdemona in Verdi's *Otello,* Margherita in Boito's *Mefistofele,* and the heroines of Puccini's *Tosca* and *La bohème,* opposite Caruso. Her strengths in Verdi, Puccini, and verismo brought her acclaim during her heyday at the Met, where she made her debut on December 4, 1916, as Tosca. In 1918 she created the role of Giorgetta in the world premiere of Puccini's *Il tabarro* at the Met, and during her seven seasons on the company's roster she was its leading Aida. Her other Met roles included Leonora in Verdi's *Il trovatore,* Nedda in Leoncavallo's *Pagliacci,* and Fiora in *L'amore dei tre re* by Italo Montemezzi (1875–1952). In the later years of her career she sang mainly in Rome.

As an interpreter Muzio displayed a compelling intensity and dramatic flair without stooping to histrionics. One of Toscanini's favorite collaborators, she was sensitive, subtle, and unfailingly musical.

Nabucco **OPERA IN FOUR PARTS BY GIUSEPPE VERDI,** to a libretto by Temistocle Solera, premiered March 9, 1842, at La Scala in Milan; the original title, *Nabucodonosor,* was shortened to the more manageable *Nabucco* in 1844. Verdi's third opera, *Nabucco* essentially launched its young composer's career and in many ways marks the emergence of his distinctive dramatic voice. Set in Jerusalem and Babylon in 587 B.C. (the year of the fall of Jerusalem and the beginning of Israel's "Babylonian Captivity"), its plot is driven by the conflicts among Nabucco (Nebuchadnezzar), the Babylonian king, Zaccaria, the high priest of the Hebrews, and Abigaille, Nabucco's vicious and power-hungry daughter (sung, in the original production, by Verdi's lover, Giuseppina Strepponi, whom he would marry in 1859). The chorus, representing the oppressed Hebrews, plays a crucial role in the proceedings, most notably with its lament "Va pensiero sull'ali dorate" ("Fly, thought, on wings of gold"), which gives voice to the captives' longing for their homeland. This number, the most famous piece of music Verdi would ever pen, became an anthem of the Risorgimento and was sung at Verdi's funeral in 1901, some 60 years after its composition.

RECOMMENDED RECORDINGS

CAPPUCCILLI, DIMITROVA, NESTERENKO, DOMINGO; SINOPOLI AND DEUTSCHE OPER BERLIN (DG).

GOBBI, SOULIOTIS, CAVA, PREVEDI; GARDELLI AND VIENNA PHILHARMONIC (DECCA).

Nachtmusik (Ger. "night music") A serenade. The most familiar use of the term occurs in the title Wolfgang Amadeus Mozart gave to his Serenade in G, K. 525, for string quartet with added double bass, *Eine kleine Nachtmusik.* Mozart also referred to his Wind Serenades in E-flat, K. 375, and C minor, K. 388, as "Nacht Musik." More than a century later, Mahler designated the second and fourth movements of his five-movement Symphony No. 7 (1908) as "Nachtmusik." The first of those movements presents an unsettling brand of "night music," but the second, with its solos for mandolin and guitar, offers a charming parody of an Italian serenade. *See also* SERENADE.

Nancarrow, Conlon *See box on pages 708–11.*

natural [1] In music notation, a sign indicating the cancellation of a sharp or flat [♮]. [2] In music for string instruments or harp, an instruction following a passage in harmonics indicating that what follows is to be played with a normal tone. [3] Term used to identify a horn or trumpet without valves.

neoclassicism Stylistic trend in 20th-century music involving an appropriation of the forms and, to a limited extent, the rhythmic, melodic, and harmonic gestures of CLASSICAL music. In many cases the mimicry, or parody, of the stylistic trappings of Classical music went hand in hand with a renewal of interest in contrapuntal procedures and a restoration of clarity to orchestral textures, which proved of great value—much greater than the short-term "fun" of dressing up as someone else, as Prokofiev claimed to be doing in his *Classical* Symphony of 1917. The most important figure in the movement was Stravinsky (whose approach, in many ways, was really neo-Baroque rather than neoclassical), but before his ballet *Pulcinella* appeared in 1920 ◉, Respighi had already penned *La boutique fantasque* (1918), based on music of Rossini, as well as the first set of *Antiche danze ed i arie per liuto* (*Ancient Airs and Dances for Lute*; 1917), actually a suite for small orchestra based on various 16th-century lute pieces; serving as the direct precedent for Stravinsky was the ballet *Le donne de buon humore* (*The Good Humored Ladies*) by Vincenzo Tommasini (1878–1950), composed in 1916 for Sergey Diaghilev's Ballets Russes, and based on keyboard sonatas of Domenico Scarlatti. Even before this, Debussy had leaned in a neoclassical direction with his chamber sonatas of 1915–17, as had Ravel with *Le tombeau de Couperin* (1914–17).

Stravinsky's many explorations of the idea eventually resulted in his assimilation of the classical spirit in works as distinctive and exalted as the *Symphony of Psalms* (1930), the *Dumbarton Oaks Concerto* (1937–38) ◉, *Symphony in C* (1938–40), *Danses concertantes* (1940–42), the ballets *Apollo* (1927–28) and *Jeu de cartes* (1936), and the opera *The Rake's Progress* (1947–51). These scores influenced many Americans, among them Walter Piston, Irving Fine, and David Diamond (1915–2005), whose own approaches, different from one another, proved equally intriguing.

neume (fr. Gr. *neuma,* "gesture") In medieval chant notation, a variety of graphic symbols representing a single note

or a grouping of several notes, thought to derive from hand gestures showing the shape of a melody. Surviving manuscripts show that the shapes of neumes varied widely from one part of Europe to another. The revolutionary invention of two staff lines, by Guido d'Arezzo in the 11th century, provided a reference point for pitches, and by the 13th century, neumes had simplified into the commonly seen square chant notation, eventually becoming separate notes.

Neveu, Ginette

(b. Paris, August 11, 1919; d. San Miguel, Azores, October 28, 1949)

FRENCH VIOLINIST. She studied with her mother, and performed as a soloist with the Concerts Colonne orchestra under the

Ginette Neveu in the late 1940s

direction of Gabriel Pierné when she was seven. She trained at the Paris Conservatoire, taking a first prize when she was 11, and studied with George Enescu and Carl Flesch. In 1935 she won the Wieniawski Competition in Warsaw, ahead of second-place winner David Oistrakh, and began an international career with tours of Poland and Germany, followed in 1936 by performances in the Soviet Union and in 1937 by appearances in the United States and Canada. She gave an acclaimed series of concerts in London following the war; there, on November 21, 1945, she also made the first of what sadly would turn out to be a mere handful of recordings for EMI—committing to disc a brilliant account of Sibelius's Violin Concerto with the Philharmonia Orchestra conducted by Walter Susskind. She subsequently recorded the Brahms Violin Concerto and the Chausson *Poème* with the Philharmonia and Issay Dobrowen, as well as pieces for violin and piano by Debussy and Ravel with her brother, pianist Jean Neveu. In 1947 she made successful debuts in Boston and New York, resulting in immediate return engagements for the 1949–50 season. She died in a plane crash on her way to the United States to fulfill those engagements.

Hailed in Europe and America as one of the greatest talents of her generation, Neveu continues to hold a place in the violinistic pantheon thanks to her recordings, which testify to a sure technique, a passionate interpretive stance, and a strong, bold style.

RECOMMENDED RECORDING

SIBELIUS, VIOLIN CONCERTO: SUSSKIND AND PHILHARMONIA ORCHESTRA (EMI, DUTTON LABS).

New England Triptych ORCHESTRAL WORK IN THREE MOVEMENTS BY WILLIAM SCHUMAN, composed on a commission from André Kostelanetz and premiered by the University of Miami Symphony Orchestra with Kostelanetz conducting, on October 28, 1956. The individual movements, based on anthems by the 18th-century American singing master William Billings, are: "Be Glad Then, America," "When Jesus Wept," and "Chester." The outer movements are virtuosically scored in Schuman's typical proclamatory manner; the solemn middle movement, for solo oboe, solo bassoon, muted strings, and tenor drum, is strikingly desolate.

RECOMMENDED RECORDINGS

LITTON AND DALLAS SYMPHONY ORCHESTRA (DORIAN).
SEREBRIER AND BOURNEMOUTH SYMPHONY ORCHESTRA (NAXOS).

New York Philharmonic ENSEMBLE FOUNDED IN 1842 by a group of New York musicians led by the American-born Ureli Corelli Hill. Originally called the Philharmonic Society of New York, it is America's oldest orchestra and one of the oldest in the world. The Philharmonic gave its first concert on December 7, 1842, under Hill's direction. In 1844 it gave the American premiere of Beethoven's Eighth Symphony, and in 1846 the American premiere of his Ninth. It presented the American premiere of Berlioz's *Symphonie fantastique* in 1866, when the composer was still alive, and gave the first U.S. performance of Act I of Wagner's *Die*

Castle Garden, site of the American premiere of Beethoven's Ninth Symphony

Walküre in 1876, the same year the *Ring* cycle was performed for the first time at Bayreuth.

German-born Theodore Thomas, one of the most important figures in American music during the 19th century, served as the Philharmonic's music director from 1877 to 1891; during his tenure, the orchestra gave the American premieres of Brahms's Symphony No. 4, Tchaikovsky's Violin Concerto, and Richard Strauss's *Tod und Verklärung,* as well as the world premiere of Tchaikovsky's Piano Concerto No. 2. Under the direction of Thomas's successor, Wagner disciple Anton Seidl (music director 1891–98), the Philharmonic took up residence in Carnegie Hall, where, on December 16, 1893, it gave the world premiere of Dvořák's Symphony *From the New World,* with the composer in attendance.

The 20th century brought a parade of extraordinary musicians to the Philharmonic's podium, either as music director, principal conductor, or music adviser, beginning with Gustav Mahler (1909–11) and continuing with Willem Mengelberg (1922–30), Arturo Toscanini (1928–36), John Barbirolli (1936–41), Artur Rodzinsky (1943–47), Bruno Walter (1947–49), Leopold Stokowski (1949–50), Dimitri Mitropoulos (1949–58), Leonard Bernstein (1958–69), George Szell (1969–70), Pierre Boulez (1971–77), Zubin Mehta (1978–91), and Kurt Masur (1991–2002). Lorin Maazel became music director at the beginning of the 2002–03 season and plans to serve until the end of the 2008–09 season.

Although his tenure was short and stormy, Mahler succeeded in elevating the level of the orchestra's playing by insisting on, among other things, proper intonation and rigorous rehearsal. His Philharmonic programs offered much Beethoven and Wagner, a generous amount of music by contemporaries such as Pfitzner, Debussy, and Richard Strauss, and even some American music. Naturally, he conducted a few of his own works (Symphony No. 1 and the *Kindertotenlieder* among them), and, in 1910, he led the orchestra in the world premiere of Rachmaninov's Piano Concerto No. 3, with the composer as soloist. In 1928, as Toscanini began his tenure, the Philharmonic Society merged with the Symphony Society of New York (founded in 1878 by Leopold Damrosch), becoming the Philharmonic Symphony Society of New York, still the name by which the ensemble is officially known. With Toscanini at the helm, the combined orchestra undertook a historic tour of Europe in 1930. That same year it became the first orchestra to be heard in a live coast-to-coast radio broadcast. Toscanini's impact on the orchestra was definitive. He imposed the highest standard of discipline on the players, molding them into a virtuosic body that responded to his ministrations with performances of breathtaking power and intensity.

The Philharmonic's modern era began in 1958, when Leonard Bernstein became director. Bernstein's debut with the orchestra in 1943—as a young assistant conductor substituting on short notice for an ailing maestro—had made him a media darling and marked him as a major talent when he was just 25. During the Bernstein years, the orchestra was in the public eye as never before. Its televised Young People's Concerts became the toast of the nation, and it recorded prolifically. Bernstein was a persuasive and dynamic leader, though no stickler for orchestral discipline. His devotion to American music and to the symphonies of Mahler was particularly intense, and resulted in many incandescent performances.

In 1962, after 70 seasons in Carnegie Hall, the ensemble took up residence in Philharmonic Hall (later renamed Avery Fisher Hall) at Lincoln Center. Following Bernstein's departure, it spent seven years in the care of Pierre Boulez, making a difficult adjustment to the precise demands of a musician some of the ensemble's members called "the French Correction." Flamboyance returned with the arrival of Zubin Mehta as music director, and the orchestra marked its 10,000th concert with a glorious performance of Mahler's *Resurrection* Symphony in 1982. But by the end of Mehta's tenure, the Philharmonic's playing had severely deteriorated and morale was low. Kurt Masur, in his 11 seasons as music director, turned the group's fortunes around. Restoring discipline and rebuilding the ensemble, he left the Philharmonic sounding newly burnished.

The New York Philharmonic has performed an enormous body of music by American-born composers, from Charles Ives to Aaron Jay Kernis (b. 1960). It plays approximately 150 concerts a year for an aggregate audience of nearly one million listeners, has made nearly 2,000 recordings since 1917, and gave its 14,000th concert on December 18, 2004—a milestone no other orchestra has approached.

RECOMMENDED RECORDINGS

Barber, *Adagio for Strings* (with other works): Schippers (Sony).

Brahms, *Ein Deutsches Requiem*: Seefried, London; Walter (Sony).

Brahms, Symphonies Nos. 1–4: Masur (Teldec).

Brahms, Violin Concerto: Mutter; Masur (DG).

Copland, *El Salón México*, *Billy the Kid*, *Rodeo*, *Appalachian Spring*: Bernstein (Sony).

Gershwin, *An American in Paris*: Bernstein (Sony).

Ives, Symphony No. 2: Bernstein (Sony).

Mahler, Symphonies Nos. 6, 7, and 9: Bernstein (Sony).

Mahler, Symphony No. 1: Mehta (Sony).

Ravel, *Daphnis et Chloé*: Boulez (Sony).

Nicolai, Otto

(b. Königsberg, June 9, 1810; d. Berlin, May 11, 1849)

German composer and conductor. A peripatetic childhood and adolescence, during which his father tried, unsuccessfully, to turn him into a prodigy, was followed by a peripatetic professional life as organist at the chapel of the German embassy in Rome, Kapellmeister at the Kärntnertortheater in Vienna, freelance opera composer in Italy, principal conductor at the Vienna Court Opera, and, finally, Kapellmeister at the Berlin Court Opera. His fame as a composer rests on a single extremely popular work, the opera *Die lustigen Weiber von Windsor* (*The Merry Wives of Windsor*), which received its first performance at the Court Opera House in Berlin on March 9, 1849.

Nicolai's legacy as a conductor is also defined by a single but very important endeavor. On March 28, 1842, he gathered 64 players from his orchestra at the Vienna Court Opera to perform Beethoven's Symphony No. 7. Thus was born the Vienna Philharmonic, which to this day honors its founder with an annual "Nicolai Concert." Nicolai's accounts of Beethoven's symphonies in Vienna during the next five years, especially his renditions of the Ninth in 1843, set the highest standard for the performance of "classical" music, which the orchestra he founded continues to uphold.

RECOMMENDED RECORDINGS

Die lustigen Weiber von Windsor: Ridderbusch, Brendel, Donath; Kubelík and Bavarian Radio Symphony Orchestra (Decca).

Mathis, Wunderlich, Frick; Heger and Bavarian State Opera Orchestra (EMI).

Nielsen, Carl

(b. Sortelung, June 9, 1865; d. Copenhagen, October 3, 1931)

Danish composer. He emerged as one of the leading musical figures in Scandinavia at the beginning of the 20th century, an innovative thinker whose aesthetic was radically distinct from the dominant trends of Romanticism. Rejecting voluptuousness and sentimentality, he clung to an intellectual pessimism that ran counter to the era's prevailing optimism. His compositional language, while acknowledging contemporary developments in harmony and scoring, remained rooted in the rhythmic and melodic conventions of Classicism, emphasizing the reiteration and protean transformation of outwardly simple material.

Nielsen's childhood, on the Danish island of Fyn, was modest but happy. Nielsen's father, a house painter, earned extra money as a village musician and endowed his naturally talented son with a love of music making and folk song. Nielsen learned to play the violin and cornet, and in 1879, soon after he turned 14, became a regimental bugler in the Danish army. In 1884 he won admission to the Conservatory in Copenhagen—then under the supervision of Niels Gade—where he remained until 1886, studying violin and music theory. He spent three years in the capital as a freelance musician, during which he produced his first mature efforts as a composer, including several string quartets and the Suite for Strings in A minor, Op. 1 (1888).

From 1889 to 1905 Nielsen played second violin in the orchestra of the Royal Theater in Copenhagen. Less than a year after joining the orchestra, he won a travel scholarship that allowed him to take a nine-month leave of absence from the opera pit, during which he met and married the Danish sculptress Anne Marie Brodersen, who had received a similar scholarship to study in Paris. Shortly after the couple returned to Denmark, Nielsen completed his Symphony No. 1 in G minor, a vibrant if still fairly traditional work. Bolder and more distinctive works soon followed, beginning with the opera *Saul og David* (*Saul and David*), finished in 1901, the Symphony No. 2, *De fire temperamenter* (*The Four Temperaments*), composed 1901–02, and the *Sinfonia Espansiva*.

During the first decade of the 20th century, Nielsen's overriding concern as a composer was dramatic characterization. This phase of his career culminated with one of his masterpieces, the comic opera *Maskarade* (1904–06). By the time of its premiere, Nielsen's years of drudgery as a workaday orchestral player were over: He had begun receiving a state pension in 1901, and his publisher, Wilhelm Hansen, had started to pay him an annuity in 1903. In 1908 he was named second conductor at the Royal Theater. When he was passed over for the post of first conductor, in 1914, Nielsen left the Royal Theater and once again became a free agent.

Carl Nielsen in 1908 and (facing page) *as regimental bugler, age 14*

There had been strains in the marriage, and as World War I broke over the rest of Europe, Nielsen and his wife separated. A period of introspection and personal reappraisal followed, out of which emerged Nielsen's strongest, most disturbing, and most valuable works, his Fourth and Fifth Symphonies. In the Fourth (1914–16), which he titled *Det Uudslukkelige* (*The Inextinguishable*) ◉, the spirit of the time is readily felt. Nielsen suggests in the symphony's trajectory from discordant strife to hymnlike affirmation that life's positive forces can triumph over destructive ones. The Fifth Symphony (1921–22) can also be understood as a response to violence and disorder, though on a more abstract and psychologically probing level. ◉ This score marked a turning point in Nielsen's development, and afterward his works took on more of the intimate character and quieter expressiveness of chamber music.

In addition to his two operas and six symphonies, Nielsen composed concertos for violin, flute, and clarinet, many songs and choral pieces, a small number of keyboard works, several short orchestral pieces, and some outstanding chamber music, capped by the Wind Quintet, Op. 43, of 1922. Outside Denmark, his reputation rests squarely on the symphonies. Whereas Sibelius, Nielsen's great contemporary, tried to make his symphonies as organic and tightly constructed as possible, Nielsen was interested in liberating the centrifugal elements of musical expression. He was not a great melodist—his melodies are rhythms, textures, arabesques—and in any case he was against making things too soft or easy on the listener. In fact, many of his scores have a sharp edge: In some, the music rings with irony and sarcasm, in others it produces a charged atmosphere in which one gradually becomes aware of troubling thoughts behind the pastoral surface of the notes. Yet in every work he wrote, Nielsen captured beauty, a muted, haunting beauty that is utterly Scandinavian.

RECOMMENDED RECORDINGS

Concertos for violin, clarinet, flute: Various soloists; Schønwandt and Danish National Radio Symphony Orchestra (Chandos).

Maskarade: Haugland, Resmark, Henning, Jensen, Skovhus; Schirmer and Danish National Radio Symphony Orchestra (Decca).

Symphonies (complete): Blomstedt and San Francisco Symphony Orchestra (Decca).

Symphony No. 4 (with overtures): Martinon and Chicago Symphony Orchestra (RCA).

Symphony No. 5: Bernstein and New York Philharmonic (Sony).

Violin Concerto: Salonen and Swedish Radio Symphony Orchestra (Sony).

Wind Quintet: Westwood Wind Quintet (Crystal).

Night on Bald Mountain, A SYMPHONIC POEM BY MODEST MUSSORGSKY, his first large-scale orchestral composition. The score, whose full title translates as *St. John's Night on Bald Mountain,* underwent a complicated process of formulation and revision spanning a quarter century. Some of the material that eventually made its way into the finished work may have originated in incidental music Mussorgsky drafted in 1860 for *The Witch,* a play by Baron Georgy Mengden, one of his army comrades. Returning to that material in April 1866 with the idea of transforming it into a free-standing orchestral work, Mussorgsky composed a first version of the tone poem, completing the orchestration in June 1867. In 1872 he prepared a second version of the piece for use in his planned opera *Mlada,* arranged for orchestra with a chorus of "demonic" voices. Although that opera was eventually abandoned, Mussorgsky was able to recycle this choral-orchestral version of the score, with further revisions, into another opera, *Sorochintsy Fair* (1880), which was left incomplete at his death. Using this last version of the piece as a guide (rather than Mussorgsky's original tone poem of 1867), Nikolay Rimsky-Korsakov produced a thoroughly revamped and reorchestrated version of the work in 1886, with the aim of correcting the "unsuccessful scoring" and "artistic transgressions" he felt had marred his friend's work. This is the form in which *A Night on Bald Mountain* is usually heard today.

St. John's Night, which occurs around the time of the summer solstice, is traditionally the night in northern climes when witches gather to hold their sabbath on the slopes of the local mountain. Mussorgsky's terrifyingly elemental vision of this ritual, in Leopold Stokowski's Technicolor adaptation of the Rimsky-Korsakov orchestration, was used by Walt Disney for the movie *Fantasia.*

RECOMMENDED RECORDINGS

ORIGINAL VERSION (1867) AND RIMSKY-KORSAKOV VERSION (1886): KUCHAR AND NATIONAL SYMPHONY ORCHESTRA OF UKRAINE (NAXOS).

RIMSKY-KORSAKOV VERSION (ARR. STOKOWSKI): KNUSSEN AND CLEVELAND ORCHESTRA (DG).

RIMSKY-KORSAKOV VERSION: SINOPOLI AND NEW YORK PHILHARMONIC (DG).

Nights in the Gardens of Spain *See* NOCHES EN LOS JARDINES DE ESPAÑA.

Nikisch, Arthur

(Lébényszentmiklós, October 12, 1855; d. Leipzig, January 23, 1922)

AUSTRO-HUNGARIAN CONDUCTOR, the most influential and widely admired podium figure of his era. A child prodigy, he studied violin with Joseph Hellmesberger at the Vienna Conservatory and became a member of the Vienna Court Opera Orchestra when he was 18. Appointed second conductor at the Leipzig Opera in 1878, he moved up to chief conductor the following year, staying 11 seasons. He served as music director of the Boston Symphony Orchestra (1889–93) and director of the Budapest Opera (1893–95), reaching the zenith of his career in 1895, when he accepted the principal conductorships of both the Gewandhaus Orchestra of Leipzig (succeeding Reinecke) and the Berlin Philharmonic (succeeding Bülow). He held both posts for the rest of his life, managing to work in frequent appearances as a guest conductor in London, as well as engagements with the orchestras of Amsterdam and Vienna, in effect becoming the prototype of the jet-set conductor before the advent of commercial aviation. During the final two decades of his life, he also served as director of the Leipzig Conservatory and appeared regularly as accompanist to the singer Elena Gerhardt, his former student.

As a conductor, Nikisch was famed for an economy of gesture and his ability seemingly to mesmerize an orchestra, drawing committed and impassioned playing from musicians with a minimum of physical exertion on his part. As an interpreter, he represented the Wagnerian ethos, espousing a broad, flexible approach to tempo, conducting in phrases rather than beats, encouraging the utmost beauty of sound and a singing legato from the strings, and striving to impart an emotionally charged rhetorical urgency to the music's line of action. He was peerless in Wagner's orchestral music, and was celebrated for his accounts of Beethoven, Schumann, and Brahms as well. He conducted the premiere of Bruckner's Seventh Symphony on December 30, 1884, in a towering performance that instantly established the work's stature, and a few years later he redeemed Tchaikovsky's Fifth Symphony in St. Petersburg after the composer's own account failed to impress the public. He was an important advocate of younger contemporaries such as Mahler and Richard Strauss.

Nikisch had a potent influence on many younger conductors, among them Wilhelm Furtwängler, his successor both in Berlin and Leipzig, Adrian Boult, who learned much from observing him during a year of study in Leipzig, Clemens Krauss, and Václav Talich. His orbit also included Bruno Walter, who in spite of being Mahler's protégé took after Nikisch both in the elegance of his technique and the collegial manner he favored when rehearsing.

Nikolayeva, Tatyana

(b. Bezhitza, May 4, 1924; d. San Francisco, November 22, 1993)

RUSSIAN PIANIST. She studied piano with Alexander Goldenweiser at the Moscow Conservatory, graduating in 1947 but remaining at the academy another three years to pursue studies in composition. She gained international recognition as the winner of the piano competition at the Leipzig Bach Festival in 1950. Shostakovich, one of the judges, was so taken with her playing—and so impressed by her offer to play from memory not only the single Bach prelude and fugue the rules required, but any one of the 48 preludes and fugues from *Das wohltemperirte Clavier*—that on his return to Moscow he began the composition of his own *24 Preludes and Fugues,* Op. 87. Nikolayeva premiered the complete set in Leningrad in 1952, and subsequently recorded it three times. She also recorded a large swath of Russian repertoire.

For more than 30 years, Nikolayeva's career was confined to the Soviet bloc, but in the 1980s she began to concertize in Western Europe, earning high praise for her performances of Bach's keyboard music. She was enthusiastically received at her New York recital debut in November 1993, but died two weeks later, after suffering a cerebral hemorrhage during a performance of the Shostakovich Preludes and Fugues in San Francisco.

RECOMMENDED RECORDING

SHOSTAKOVICH, *24 PRELUDES AND FUGUES* (HYPERION).

Nilsson, Birgit

(b. Västra Karups, May 17, 1918; d. Västra Karups, December 25, 2005)

SWEDISH SOPRANO. She was the dominant Wagnerian soprano of the 1960s and 1970s, and among the greatest ever in the roles of Isolde and Brünnhilde. She studied at the Royal Academy of Music in Stockholm and made her debut in Stockholm in 1946, as Agathe in Weber's *Der Freischütz.* In 1954, with the Royal Opera in Stockholm, she sang the role of Brünnhilde in *Götterdämmerung* for the first time; that same year she also began long associations with both the Vienna Staatsoper and the Bayreuth Festival. She was a regular at Bayreuth

Birgit Nilsson as Turandot

in the roles of Sieglinde, Brünnhilde, and Isolde from 1957 to 1970, and was captured at her peak in recordings of the *Ring* cycle and *Tristan und Isolde* made there in the mid-1960s under the baton of Karl Böhm. Her American debut took place with the San Francisco Opera in 1956. On December 18, 1959, she bowed at the Metropolitan Opera, as Isolde, returning every season through 1975 and making a stunning comeback in 1980 as Richard Strauss's Elektra. While at the Met, she owned the role of Turandot, and at the end of her career she thrilled New Yorkers a final time with four performances as the Dyer's Wife in Strauss's *Die Frau ohne Schatten.*

Nilsson's voice was one of the wonders of the operatic world, astonishing in its magnitude and intensity. It had the power to carry over an orchestra of any size and a steely brilliance at the top that could make one feel weak in the knees. Her intonation was perfect, her focus laser sharp, and she sang with compelling musicianship and artistry. She was also a convincing actress, capable of investing a character such as Elektra, Turandot, or Isolde with a mythic reality far preferable to mere verisimilitude.

RECOMMENDED RECORDINGS

STRAUSS, *ELEKTRA*: RESNIK, COLLIER, KRAUSE, STOLZE; SOLTI AND VIENNA PHILHARMONIC (DECCA).

WAGNER, *TRISTAN UND ISOLDE*: WINDGASSEN, LUDWIG, WAECHTER, TALVELA; BÖHM AND BAYREUTH FESTIVAL ORCHESTRA (DG).

WAGNER, *DIE WALKÜRE*, ACT III, SC. 3 (WITH EXCERPTS FROM *DER FLIEGENDE HOLLÄNDER*, *TANNHÄUSER*, AND *LOHENGRIN*): HOTTER; LUDWIG AND PHILHARMONIA ORCHESTRA (TESTAMENT).

Nixon in China **OPERA IN TWO ACTS BY JOHN ADAMS,** to a libretto by Alice Goodman, premiered October 22, 1987, at the Houston Grand Opera. The work, conceived by Peter Sellars, takes as its point of departure the 1972 visit of President Richard Nixon to China. Rather than making any attempt at historical accuracy, the work philosophizes about history itself, and the often petty personal drives that end up giving it direction. The opera's central characters—Richard and Pat Nixon, Henry Kissinger, Mao Tse-tung, Chou En-lai, and Mao's wife Chiang Ch'ing—are

Nixon in China: ***original cast members Sanford Sylvan (Chou En-lai), James Maddalena (Richard Nixon), Thomas Hammons (Henry Kissinger), and Carolann Page (Pat Nixon)***

caricatured with varying degrees of sympathy, caught in a fanciful scenario that explores the differences between Eastern and Western attitudes toward duty and power. Adams's minimalist score imbues the proceedings with energy and life, if not profound meaning. Highlights include the impressive opening scene, as *Air Force One* arrives at an airport outside Beijing, and a finale in which the principal characters meditate on their lives, and their moment in history, while lying in bed.

RECOMMENDED RECORDING

SYLVAN, CRANEY, MADDALENA; DEWAART AND ORCHESTRA OF ST. LUKE'S (NONESUCH).

noces, Les (The Wedding) **FOUR "RUSSIAN CHOREOGRAPHIC SCENES" BY IGOR STRAVINSKY** for soprano, mezzo-soprano, tenor, and bass soloists, chorus, four pianos, and 17 percussion instruments, to texts from a collection of Russian wedding songs by P. V. Kireyevsky, premiered June 13, 1923 in Paris, with Ernest Ansermet conducting. The French versions of the texts sung at the premiere were supplied by C. F. Ramuz, who also provided the text for *L'HISTOIRE DU SOLDAT*. The most "Russian" of Stravinsky's theatrical works—in terms of its subject, a Russian peasant wedding, and its folkish and chantlike musical content—*LES NOCES* (*SVADEBKA*, in Russian) proved to be one of his most important scores as well. An amalgam of ballet and cantata, it marked a new direction in his thinking, away from the savage grandeur of *THE RITE OF SPRING* and toward a new intimacy and economy. In addition, the diamondlike glint of its percussion-driven sonorities exerted a profound influence on the development of 20th-century musical language. *Les noces* is also a work of great expressiveness, not the first thing one normally associates with Stravinsky. In the concluding tableau, for example, at the very end of the piece, the happiness of the wedding day is touched with an ineffable sadness—one of many moments that reveals the composer's ability to elicit deep and complex emotion.

Felia Doubrovska in the premiere of Les Noces, *1923*

RECOMMENDED RECORDINGS

ARGERICH, FRANCESCH, KATSARIS, ZIMERMAN; BERNSTEIN AND ENGLISH BACH FESTIVAL ORCHESTRA AND CHORUS (DG).

INTERNATIONAL PIANO QUARTET; CRAFT AND LONDON PHILHARMONIA ORCHESTRA (KOCH).

Noches en los jardines de España (Nights in the Gardens of Spain) **CONCERTO-LIKE SET OF THREE SYMPHONIC "IMPRESSIONS" FOR PIANO AND ORCHESTRA BY MANUEL DE FALLA,** completed in 1915. The three movements of the score, a coloristic homage to Andalusia, are titled "En el Generalife" ("In the Generalife"), "Danza lejana" ("Distant Dance"), and "En los jardines de la Sierra de Córdoba" ("In the Gardens of the Sierra de Córdoba"). The piano plays a role midway between foreground (as in a conventional concerto) and background in all three movements, often presenting material that is more decorative than substantive. The result is a unique integration of the pianistic and orchestral personalities, almost as if the two were engaged in a love scene. While this may sound like a romanticized notion, Falla himself indicates that it is the correct one when, at the climax of the first movement, he quotes the four-note motif associated with the love potion from Wagner's *Tristan und Isolde.*

Although the score is dedicated to the pianist Ricardo Viñes, a close colleague of Ravel and Debussy as well as of Falla, *Noches en los jardines de España* was premiered by José Cubiles, in a performance at the Teatro Real in Madrid on April 9, 1916, Enrique Arbós conducting.

RECOMMENDED RECORDINGS

Larrocha; Frühbeck de Burgos and London Philharmonic Orchestra (Decca).

Soriano; Frühbeck de Burgos and Conservatory Concert Society Orchestra (EMI).

nocturne A quiet, meditative piece, usually for piano, built on a simple harmonic structure geared to the elaboration of a melodic line by ornament, generally over an arpeggiated bass. Most nocturnes are in three-part (ABA) form. The first pieces using the name appeared in the 18th century, but it was the appropriation of the term by the early-19th-century Irish composer John Field, and subsequently by Chopin, that established the nocturne as a genre. Among the composers who later made contributions to the literature were Liszt, Fauré, Tchaikovsky, Grieg, and Scriabin.

The 18 nocturnes Field composed between 1813 and 1835 foreshadow those of Chopin in their texture and nostalgic expression, though Chopin's grasp of form goes beyond Field's, and the mood of Chopin's essays is generally more somber and melancholy. While Chopin could mimic the Field manner with supreme skill, as in the Nocturne in B-flat minor, Op. 9, No. 1, he shows increasing resourcefulness in later works, which on the whole are more speculative and elaborate. He does this by enriching the harmonic content, extending the left hand across the whole range of the keyboard (as in the Nocturnes in C-sharp minor, Op. 27, No. 1 —a work of remarkable complexity and power—and E-flat, Op. 55, No. 2), even allowing the accompaniment to take on a melodic character itself. At other times, for example in the Nocturne in G, Op. 37, No. 2, he transforms the right-hand material into etude-like figures that seem to dart through the texture without sounding melodic at all, saving the more conventional melody for the contrasting middle section.

An influence on both Field and Chopin was the florid vocal style of Italian bel canto, best exemplified by the cavatinas in Bellini's operas. It is marvelously evoked in the melodic embellishments of several of Chopin's essays, particularly the Nocturnes in E-flat, Op. 9, No. 2, and F-sharp, Op. 15, No. 2, as well as the Nocturne in D-flat, Op. 27, No. 2 (where the technique is translated into more pianistic terms by the use of parallel thirds).

RECOMMENDED RECORDINGS

Chopin: Rubinstein (RCA).

Field: Frith (Naxos).

Nocturnes **Three pieces for orchestra by Claude Debussy,** composed in 1897–99 and first performed as a set on October 27, 1901, at the Concerts Lamoureux, under the baton of Camille Chevillard. The individual pieces are titled "Nuages" ("Clouds"), "Fêtes" ("Festivities"), and "Sirènes" ("Sirens"); the latter calls for wordless vocalizing by a small, eight-part women's choir placed behind the scene. The *Nocturnes* owe their inspiration about equally to several lines from the poetry of

Henri de Regnier, a friend of the composer, and to the paintings of the American artist James McNeill Whistler. Originally, Debussy planned to call the pieces *Trois scènes au crépuscule* (*Three Scenes at Twilight*), after a group of ten poems by Regnier. In ultimately deciding on the title, Debussy was thinking not of the nocturnes of Chopin or Fauré, but of a series of canvases by Whistler called *Nocturnes* that he found highly evocative. It was these works he had in mind when he described his own *Nocturnes* as being "an experiment in the different arrangements of a single color, like a study in gray in painting." For all that, there is little grayness but much flamboyance in the scoring of "Fêtes," one of Debussy's most brilliant creations.

RECOMMENDED RECORDINGS

DUTOIT AND MONTREAL SYMPHONY ORCHESTRA (DECCA).
HAITINK AND CONCERTGEBOUW ORCHESTRA (PHILIPS).
SALONEN AND LOS ANGELES PHILHARMONIC (SONY).

Norma **OPERA IN TWO ACTS BY VINCENZO BELLINI,** to a libretto by Felice Romani, premiered December 26, 1831, at La Scala in Milan. Equally notable for its graceful lyricism and its dramatic coherence, it is Bellini's supreme accomplishment. The story, set in ancient Gaul, derives its impetus from the clash of two cultures, Druid and Roman. The parallel to Italy, under Austrian domination at the time, is clear, but the point is made without the patriotic flamboyance that would erupt on Italy's stages later in the 19th century. In defiance of her vows, Norma, a Druid priestess, has become involved with the Roman proconsul Pollione, who has fathered two infant sons whom Norma must keep hidden. When Norma learns that Pollione has meanwhile fallen in love with Adalgisa, a novice priestess and her friend, she becomes enraged. As the opera's second act begins, Norma is on the point of killing her two children rather than let them be taken off to Rome. Bellini's treatment of this scene ("Dormono entrambi") is a virtuosic portrayal of agitation and shifting emotions. Norma's florid yet touching Act I address to the moon goddess, "Casta diva," is a sublime nocturne gently accompanied by the orchestra and the chorus, while her ardent duet with Adalgisa, "Sì, fino all'ore estreme," conveys the courage that is also a part of her character, and that will emerge full force in her eventual self-immolation.

In the original La Scala production of *Norma,* the title role was created by Giuditta Pasta and that of Adalgisa by Giulia Grisi, who went on to become a celebrated Norma in her own right. Since then, the role of Norma has attracted a host of great divas, including Rosa Ponselle, Maria Callas, and Joan Sutherland.

RECOMMENDED RECORDINGS

CALLAS, STIGNANI, FILIPPESCHI; SERAFIN AND LA SCALA ORCHESTRA (EMI).
SUTHERLAND, HORNE, ALEXANDER; BONYNGE AND LONDON SYMPHONY ORCHESTRA (DECCA).

Norman, Jessye

(b. Augusta, Ga., September 15, 1945)

AMERICAN SOPRANO. Endowed with one of the most imposing voices in history, she distinguished herself on stage, in recital, and on records as a singer of exceptional intelligence and perception. She studied music as an undergraduate at Howard University in Washington, D.C., and continued her training at the Peabody Conservatory and the University of Michigan. In 1968 she took first-place honors at the Munich International Music Competition; she made her operatic debut the following season at the Deutsche Oper Berlin, as Elisabeth in Wagner's *Tannhäuser.* In 1972 she appeared at La Scala, as Aida, and at Covent Garden, as Cassandre in Berlioz's *Les Troyens.* Cassandre was again

Jessye Norman as Strauss's Ariadne at the Metropolitan Opera

the vehicle when she made her Metropolitan Opera debut on September 26, 1983, the opening night of the company's centennial season. That same season, on February 18, 1984, she made Met history by singing both Cassandre and Didon in the same performance of *Les Troyens.* Unlike many vocalists, who seem untroubled by their size, she limited her stage appearances over the years to those roles in which she could look the part; in addition to Cassandre, she portrayed Emilia Marty in Janáček's *The Makropulos Case,* Judith in Bartók's *Bluebeard's Castle,* Kundry in Wagner's *Parsifal,* and the title character in Richard Strauss's *Ariadne auf Naxos,* roles that were all appropriate to her statuesque embodiment. A noted concert artist, she was admired for her renditions of Wagner's *Wesendonck* Lieder, Mahler's *Des Knaben Wunderhorn,* and above all for her sublime interpretation of Strauss's *Vier letzte lieder.* Though her regal manner was at times off-putting, she was a gracious and effective recitalist.

Norman's voice was phenomenal in its size, range, and coloration. Her diction was impeccable, her sound uniquely opulent and effortlessly supported, enabling her to sing long phrases with matchless ease. But what set her apart was the intelligence with which she used her gifts.

RECOMMENDED RECORDINGS

RAVEL, *CHANSONS MADECASSES*: BOULEZ AND ENSEMBLE INTERCONTEMPORAIN (SONY).

"SALZBURG RECITAL" (SONGS OF BEETHOVEN, DEBUSSY, WOLF): LEVINE (PHILIPS).

SCHUMANN, *FRAUENLIEBE UND LEBEN, LIEDERKREIS*: GAGE (PHILIPS).

STRAUSS, *ARIADNE AUF NAXOS*: GRUBEROVÁ, VARADY, FREY, FISCHER-DIESKAU; MASUR AND GEWANDHAUS ORCHESTRA (PHILIPS).

STRAUSS, *VIER LETZTE LIEDER*: MASUR AND GEWANDHAUS ORCHESTRA (PHILIPS).

Norrington, Sir Roger

(b. Oxford, March 16, 1934)

ENGLISH CONDUCTOR. He attended Cambridge as a choral scholar and studied conducting with Sir Adrian Boult at the Royal College of Music. His first post as conductor was that of director of the Schütz Choir, which he founded in 1962. From 1969 to 1982 he was music director of the Kent Opera, where his repertoire extended from Monteverdi (he prepared his own edition of *L'incoronazione di Poppea*) to Tippett. In 1978 he founded the London Classical Players, devoted to the performance of 18th- and 19th-century music on period instruments. His landmark recorded cycle of the Beethoven symphonies with that ensemble helped bring the period instrument movement into the mainstream, and had the salutary effect of focusing the attention of even the most traditionally minded performers on new scholarly insights into matters of tempo and articulation. Norrington was one of the first to apply performance-practice notions to the music of the 19th century, blazing what has since become a well-traveled trail in his recordings of Rossini and Wagner overtures, and of symphonies by Berlioz,

Mendelssohn, Schumann, and Brahms. In recent years he has devoted a large part of his time to working with full-size orchestras on music of the 19th and 20th centuries, particularly the scores of Beethoven, Vaughan Williams, and Walton. He was knighted in 1997.

Sir Roger Norrington: not too loud

RECOMMENDED RECORDINGS

BEETHOVEN, SYMPHONIES (COMPLETE): LONDON CLASSICAL PLAYERS (VIRGIN CLASSICS).

ROSSINI, OVERTURES: LONDON CLASSICAL PLAYERS (EMI).

Nose, The OPERA IN THREE ACTS BY DMITRY SHOSTAKOVICH, to a libretto written by the composer in collaboration with Evgeny Zamyatin, Gyorgy Ionin, and Aleksandr Preis (based on the short story by Nikolay Gogol), composed 1927–28 and premiered January 18, 1930, at the Maly Opera House in Leningrad, Samuil Samosud conducting. Closely following Gogol's satire, the opera, set in St. Petersburg in the 1830s, tells the story of a barber who unwittingly shaves the nose off one of his customers (the collegiate assessor Kovalyov, an important man), who reports his missing nose to the chief of police. The Nose (a tenor) finds a new home on the face of a State Councillor (an even more important man), complicating Kovalyov's efforts to get it back. The nose is eventually captured, but the Doctor advises against attempting to reattach it. In the end, miraculously, it reappears on Kovalyov's face. Gogol's story is an allegory of guilt, envy, suspicion, and self-pity, which Shostakovich's score takes to the limits of modernism and parody. With 78 sung roles, plus spoken roles and chorus, the work is almost impossible to perform, but that didn't stop the composer from having some very high-handed musical fun. There were no smiles from the Soviet critics, however, and the work was quickly shelved.

Nouvel Ensemble Moderne *See box on page 272.*

nozze di Figaro, Le (The Marriage of Figaro) OPERA IN FOUR ACTS BY WOLFGANG AMADEUS MOZART, to a libretto by Lorenzo da Ponte based on *La folle journée, ou le mariage de Figaro* (*The Madcap Day, or The Marriage of Figaro*) by Pierre-Augustin Beaumarchais, premiered May 1, 1786, at the Burgtheater in Vienna, with the composer conducting from the keyboard. The play on which the opera is based had appeared in 1778 as a sequel to the wildly successful *Le barbier de Seville* (1775). While it involved more or less the same characters as its predecessor, it presented a sharper and more critical assessment of the social order, and for that reason Louis XVI kept it off the French stage until 1784, when he reluctantly allowed a production at the Comédie-Française. His normally liberal-minded brother-in-law, Emperor Joseph II, followed suit, banning performances of the play in Austria but allowing the text to be published and to circulate freely. Mozart came across it in 1784 and immediately saw its potential. He was aware of the success Giovanni Paisiello (1740–1816) had had with his operatic adaptation of *Le barbier de Seville*—the Italian's *Il barbiere di Siviglia* had been the hit of the 1783 season in Vienna—and he knew the public wanted a sequel.

Mozart began work on *Figaro* in September 1785, finishing the score in April 1786. Listeners at the third performance of the opera called for so many encores that the emperor had to issue a decree allowing only arias to be encored. But the opera's finer qualities eluded the Viennese, who took greater pleasure in *Una cosa rara* by Vicente Martín y Soler (1754–1806), which premiered on the same stage six months later. *Figaro* dropped out of the repertoire after nine performances and was not revived in Vienna until 1789. The story was different in Prague, where *Figaro* premiered in December 1786 and enjoyed a huge success. The opera's triumph in the Bohemian capital, and the commission for *Don Giovanni* that resulted directly from it, proved to be the high-water mark of Mozart's career.

With *Le nozze di Figaro,* Mozart carried the architecture of opera and the art of characterization into new realms. The arias are brilliant crystallizations of feeling and humor, for example, the title character's "Non pìu andrai" at the end of Act I, but *Figaro*'s greatest significance lies in the ensemble numbers and the astonishing extended finales to Acts II and IV. Here, utilizing the principles of key organization and symphonic argument he had mastered in his instrumental compositions, Mozart generated a dramatic and comedic thrust unprecedented in the history of opera.

RECOMMENDED RECORDINGS

SCHWARZKOPF, MOFFO, COSSOTTO, TADDEI, VINCO, WAECHTER; GIULINI AND PHILHARMONIA ORCHESTRA (EMI).

TE KANAWA, POPP, VON STADE, RAMEY, ALLEN, MOLL; SOLTI AND LONDON PHILHARMONIC ORCHESTRA (DECCA).

nuits d'été, Les (Summer Nights) SET OF SIX SONGS BY HECTOR BERLIOZ, to poems by Théophile Gautier, composed in 1840–41. Originally set for mezzo-soprano and piano, the songs were orchestrated between 1843 and 1856 and published, with transpositions for several different voice types, as Berlioz's Op. 7. The best known of the six, "Le spectre de la rose," is a reverie in the style of a French Romance. In it, the ghost of a rose speaks with melancholy resignation to the young woman who picked it the day before and wore it to a ball. The scoring, which features muted strings, is a miracle of delicacy.

RECOMMENDED RECORDING

CRESPIN; ANSERMET AND L'ORCHESTRE DE LA SUISSE ROMANDE (DECCA).

Nutcracker, The BALLET IN TWO ACTS BY PYOTR IL'YICH TCHAIKOVSKY, OP. 71, composed in 1891–92 to a scenario by Marius Petipa (based on an adaptation by Dumas père of the story *Nussknacker und Mausekönig* by E. T. A. Hoffmann), and premiered on December 18, 1892, at the Mariinsky Theater in St. Petersburg. Originally intended as half of an opera-ballet double bill, it was presented that way at its premiere, sharing a program with Tchaikovsky's newly composed one-act opera *Iolanta.* The opera, for which the composer had high hopes, was damned by the critics, while the ballet met with a mixed reception, though Tchaikovsky himself did not think particularly highly of the subject, or, at least while he was working on it, of the music he had written for it.

The need to compose decorative music for a trite story in which there is no real human drama, together with the almost measure-by-measure instructions Petipa included at many points in the scenario, freed Tchaikovsky from having to worry about content and allowed him to indulge his gift for memorable melody and his remarkable imagination as an orchestrator. *The Nutcracker* is typical of Tchaikovsky's later music in its delicate use of the strings, which provide muted, shimmering backdrops to many of the scenes. Other striking orchestrational touches are the use of high flutes over gruff low bassoons in the "Chinese Dance" (the bassoons had been used this way in *Swan Lake,* but the flutes add an entirely new quality of tone); the dark wind colors (emphasizing double reeds) and subdued string background in the "Arabian Dance," which produces an effect of Orientalism in spite of the fact that the tune is actually from a Georgian lullabye; and the use of three low flutes in chordal voicing for the "Dance of the Mirlitons." The music of the ballet reaches an emotional peak in the second act's radiant Pas de Deux. Moments later, in the magically charming "Dance of the Sugar Plum Fairy," the solo celesta suggests the drops of water "spurting from fountains" called for in the scenario.

Prior to the ballet's premiere, Tchaikovsky extracted a suite from the score, the first performance of which he conducted in St. Petersburg on March 19, 1892. It is in this form that the most characterful numbers of *The Nutcracker* have attained universal popularity. The suite (designated Op. 71a) begins with the overture to the ballet, followed by the march from Act I and the "Dance of the Sugar Plum Fairy" from the Act II pas de deux. The next four numbers are drawn from the Act II divertissement, set in the Kingdom of Sweets. They are the "Russian Dance" (a *trepak*), the "Arabian Dance," the "Chinese Dance," and the "Dance of the Mirlitons." The suite concludes with the "Waltz of the Flowers" from Act II, one of the best known of all Tchaikovsky's waltzes.

RECOMMENDED RECORDINGS

COMPLETE BALLET: DORATI AND CONCERTGEBOUW ORCHESTRA (PHILIPS).

COMPLETE BALLET: GERGIEV AND KIROV ORCHESTRA (PHILIPS).

SUITE: ROSTROPOVICH AND BERLIN PHILHARMONIC (DG).

O

obbligato (It. "necessary") In instrumental music, a part that is essential as opposed to one that is optional or ad libitum. The term is commonly used to refer to prominent parts for solo instruments in the accompaniment of arias, especially in Baroque music. Examples include the solos from the trumpet, violin, cello, oboe d'amore, and two oboes da caccia in Bach's Cantata No. 147 (*Herz und Mund und Tat und Leben*), and the expressive solo for violin in the alto aria "Erbarme dich, mein Gott" from his *St. Matthew* Passion. Mozart put two obbligato arias in his opera *La clemenza di Tito,* one ("Non più di fiori") for basset-horn, the other ("Parto, parto") for the basset clarinet, and Beethoven honored the tradition in the opera *Fidelio* by setting Leonore's "Komm, Hoffnung" with an obbligato for the whole horn section. Verdi included a melancholy solo cello obbligato in the aria "Ella giammai m'amò!," sung by Philip II in *Don Carlo,* to help convey the poignancy of the king's heartsick realization that his wife never loved him.

Reconciliation of Oberon and Titiana

Oberlin, Russell *See box on pages 155–57.*

Oberon Opera in three acts by Carl Maria von Weber, to a libretto in English by James Robinson Planch (based on C. M. Wieland's poem "Oberon"), premiered April 12, 1826, in London at Covent Garden. Despite the severity of his tuberculosis, Weber agreed to travel to England to oversee production of the opera (he succumbed to his illness shortly after the premiere, on the eve of his return to Germany); in order to set the libretto confidently, he took more than 150 English lessons. The work was enthusiastically received, but has kept a precarious place in the repertoire, owing to the libretto's curiously masque-like structure and feeble plot.

The opera's title figure is the same fairy personage as Shakespeare's Oberon. The action revolves around the romance of Sir Huon of Bordeaux and Reiza, the daughter of the Caliph of Baghdad. They endure interminable trials and tribulations until Oberon and Titania save the day. If *Der Freischütz* reflected the dark side of Romanticism and its view of nature, life, and love, *Oberon* celebrates the happier aspects. The best part of the opera by far is its overture, the most evocative and subtly scored of any Weber wrote and one of the earliest 19th-century scores that can rightly be called a virtuoso showpiece. Its use of delicately animated figures in the woodwinds and muted strings provided a model for the fairy music of Mendelssohn and Berlioz.

RECOMMENDED RECORDINGS

COMPLETE OPERA: MARTINPELTO, KAUFMANN, DAVISLIM; GARDINER AND MONTEVERDI CHOIR, ORCHESTRE RÉVOLUTIONNAIRE ET ROMANTIQUE (PHILIPS).

COMPLETE OPERA: NIELSEN, SEIFFERT, VAN DER WALT, SKOVHUS; JANOWSKI AND DEUTSCHES SYMPHONIE-ORCHESTER BERLIN (RCA).

OVERTURE: JÄRVI AND PHILHARMONIA ORCHESTRA (CHANDOS).

OVERTURE: KARAJAN AND BERLIN PHILHARMONIC (DG).

oboe Customarily defined as a treble woodwind instrument with a double reed and conical bore, the oboe is better known to the musicians who play it as "the ill wind that nobody blows good." The oboe's name is a corruption of the French *hautbois,* originally one of the names of the *shawm,* a raucously loud outdoor instrument of medieval and Renaissance ceremony that can be traced back to ancient Middle Eastern ancestors. (*Hautbois* means "high wood," but "high" in the sense of "loud" rather than "high-pitched.") There are many instruments related to the oboe or considered by courtesy to belong in its family, among them the English horn and the heckelphone.

Made of grenadilla wood, the modern oboe has a slightly flared bell and measures approximately 25½ inches in length, not counting the reed, which protrudes 2½ inches from the top of the instrument. The oboe's range extends from B-flat below middle C to the A two octaves and a sixth above.

Today's oboe is a direct descendant of the Baroque oboe, which emerged in mid-17th-century France as a result of efforts by members of the Hotteterre and Philidor families to develop a softer, better-behaved alternative to the *shawm* for use indoors with stringed instruments. This type of oboe became, by the end of the 17th century, the principal wind instrument of the orchestra and, after the violin, the leading solo instrument of the time. Early examples had only two or three keys and a two-octave range. By the time of Mozart, the instrument's range had been extended to the F two octaves and a fourth above middle C. By 1840 the oboe had ten keys, facilitating a range of nearly three octaves.

Changes in musical style and the evolution of the orchestra into a larger and more brilliant ensemble spurred a simultaneous development of the oboe's tone quality and carrying power, which was achieved by refinements to its bore and the narrowing of its reed. By the middle of the 19th century the experiments of Guillaume Triébert and his son Frédéric produced an instrument almost identical to the expressive, bright-toned oboe in nearly universal use today. In 1872 the firm of Triébert devised a key system for its oboes that was soon adopted by the Paris Conservatoire as its standard, and by 1925 oboes using this system had made the instruments of German and Austrian makers nearly obsolete (except in Vienna, where to this day the Sellner-style oboe, a relic of the early 19th century, is the only oboe played in the Vienna Philharmonic and Vienna Staatsoper orchestras). In spite of its pinched and rather plangent tone, the Viennese oboe is indisputably authentic, the right oboe for the repertoire in which the Viennese excel.

The orchestral literature contains a handful of solos that are ideally rendered on the Viennese oboe, including the remarkable 11-note cadenza in the first movement of Beethoven's Fifth Symphony, the poignant melody in dotted rhythm in the second movement of Schubert's Ninth, and the sweet little tune in the *Allegretto grazioso* third movement of Brahms's Third. Among the many notable passages that favor the sound of the standard oboe, some of the best are the glorious extended solo in G major that comes in the middle of Richard Strauss's *Don Juan,* the seductive riffs that accompany "The Dance of the Seven Veils" in that composer's *Salome,* the meandering opening subject of the second movement of Tchaikovsky's Symphony No. 4, and the Moorish-flavored motif prominent in the second movement of Debussy's *Ibéria.* Among the highlights of the oboe's recital and chamber repertoire are Mozart's Quartet in F, K. 370, for oboe and strings, Schumann's *Drei Romanzen* for oboe and piano, and Britten's *Six Metamorphoses After Ovid* and Berio's *Sequenza VII,* both for unaccompanied oboe; the concerto literature, while modest, includes works by Mozart, Strauss, and Vaughan Williams, as well as Françaix's lovely *L'horloge de flore.*

While experts cite many reasons for the oboe's highly individualized sound, most agree that the role of the reed is paramount. Having the right cane is all-important, and that is a further reason the French oboe has set the standard for the world. Oboe reeds must be cut from a specific cane, *Arundo donax,* which resembles bamboo in appearance; though the cane grows in warm temperate or subtropical regions, only the crops in the southern French *départements* of Var and Vaucluse are satisfactory for reed making. Despairing American oboists almost gave up their profession during World War II, when occupied France, their source of cane, was cut off.

Detail on the bell of a Baroque oboe

Another reason for the supremacy of the French oboe, and for its reputation as an instrument of extraordinary color and flexibility, was the teaching of the French-born, Conservatoire-trained Marcel Tabuteau. A member of the Metropolitan Opera orchestra from 1908 to 1914, he joined the Philadelphia Orchestra as its principal oboist in 1915, at the invitation of Leopold Stokowski, and held that post until his retirement in 1954. He taught for more than 25 years at the Curtis Institute of Music in Philadelphia, where he trained an entire generation of oboists—including his successor in Philadelphia, John De Lancie, the longtime principal of the New York Philharmonic, Harold Gomberg, and the Cleveland Orchestra's estimable John Mack. Many of their students hold principal positions in major American orchestras.

Other leading solo oboists of recent years are the Swiss-born Heinz Holliger, who is also a composer of note, France's Maurice Bourgue, and the Americans Ray Still (for many years the principal of the Chicago Symphony Orchestra), Joseph Robinson (principal of the New York Philharmonic), and Alex Klein (Still's successor in Chicago, who had to step down in 2004 after developing dystonia). The period-instrument movement has led to renewed interest in the Baroque oboe and the emergence of several virtuoso players, among them England's Paul Goodwin.

oboe d'amore (It., "oboe of love") Mezzo-soprano oboe pitched in A (i.e., midway between the standard oboe and the English horn), with a slightly bulbous bell. (The term *d'amore,* when used in conjunction with the name of an instrument, denotes a softer or lower-sounding member of that instrument's family.) Developed in southern Germany during the second decade of the 18th century, it was prized for its warm, delicately veiled tone color. Bach was particularly fond of the instrument's sound: He included parts for two oboes d'amore in many of his Leipzig cantatas, and in the *Mass in B Minor* he fashioned a beautiful obbligato solo for oboe d'amore to accompany the alto aria "Qui sedes." The revival of interest in Bach's music in the late 19th century led to the manufacture of an updated variety of oboe d'amore with keywork similar to that of the modern oboe. The first orchestral work to make use of the new instrument was Richard Strauss's *Symphonia domestica* (1903), where, fittingly, it is entrusted with the theme representing "the Child." Solos for oboe d'amore also appear in Debussy's *Gigues* (1913) and Ravel's *Boléro* (1928).

Ockeghem, Johannes

(b. Saint Ghislain, ca. 1410; d. Tours [?], February 6, 1497)

FRANCO-FLEMISH COMPOSER. Acknowledged as one of the greatest composers of the 15th century, he came from the region of Hainaut, near the present-day border between Belgium and France, and spent most of his career in the service of the French court. Little is known about his early life. He probably received his education at one of the churches in Mons, the nearest sizable town to his place of birth. The earliest document in which he is mentioned by name records a yearlong appointment as *vicaire chanteur* at the church of Notre Dame in Antwerp in 1443. It seems likely that in the summer of 1444 he went to Moulins, where he served until 1448 as lead singer in the chapel of Charles I, Duke of Bourbon. In 1451, as the Hundred Years' War was winding down, he was offered a place, again as lead singer, in the newly reorganized chapel of the French king, Charles VII. By 1454, Ockeghem was listed in court documents as *premier chapelain,* indicating the high esteem in which he was held by the king. Within a few years Charles appointed Ockeghem to the lucrative office of treasurer of the collegiate church of St. Martin at Tours, a favor intended to make the composer a rich man at the church's expense.

Johannes Ockeghem, wearing eyeglasses and a hood, leads his singers.

Ockeghem continued in the service of the crown throughout the reign of Louis XI (1461–83), Charles's son, remaining in extraordinary favor at court and reaping the benefits of various prebends (ecclesiastical incomes). In 1464, on a visit to Cambrai, the seat of his home diocese, he appears to have been ordained; his decision to enter the priesthood at such a late stage in his life (he would have been in his 50s) may have been prompted by a desire for the position of *maître de chapelle* at the royal court. Whatever the motive, Ockeghem played an increasingly important role in the king's inner circle, eventually acquiring the title of counselor and taking on a number of diplomatic missions for Louis and his successor, Charles VIII (reigned 1483–98).

Endowed with an unusually deep and sonorous bass, Ockeghem was a superbly accomplished singer as well as a brilliant composer, whose character was by all accounts generous, warm, and gracious. He formed close friendships with Guillaume Du Fay and other musical figures of the day. His death occasioned an outpouring of laments, including the poem "Nymphes des bois" ("Wood nymphs") by Jehan Molinet (later set by Josquin) and an elegy from Erasmus. Ockeghem's music had a profound impact on composers of the younger generation, including Josquin and Jacob Obrecht (ca. 1450–1505), who were among the many to base mass settings on one or another of his chansons.

The stellar reputation Ockeghem enjoyed in his day is supported by a mere handful of surviving works: 13 masses, a Requiem (the earliest surviving polyphonic setting of the Requiem), five motets, and a few chansons, all of exceptional quality. Little is known of the circumstances surrounding their composition, and their chronology is uncertain because Ockeghem utilized a variety of compositional techniques throughout his career, which makes it impossible to date his works by stylistic analysis.

The Chigi Codex is the only manuscript that preserves all 13 of the masses, and is the unique source both for the Requiem and for Ockeghem's remarkable *Missa prolationum,* which ranks among the supreme achievements of contrapuntal art in Western music. (While scholars have questioned whether the Chigi Codex transmits the most accurate versions of these works, it is certainly one of the most beautifully finished manuscripts of the period. It was produced for the court of Philip the Fair, ca. 1498–1503, perhaps as a memorial to Ockeghem.) The *Missa prolationum* consists entirely of double canons in which pairs of voices sing the same music but in different meters; what is more, the canons occur at different intervals for each section of the mass. That such technical artifice could be woven into so beautiful a musical tapestry is astonishing, even today.

With the exception of this one work, Ockeghem's music relies hardly at all on the use of strict imitation, on which so much Renaissance sacred music is based. The melodic lines, unusually long by Renaissance standards, have a rhapsodic, seemingly improvisatory quality that makes their contrapuntal elaboration all the more extraordinary. Ockeghem's entire approach can vary markedly from one work to the next. More than half of his masses are based on an existing melody—from a song or PLAINCHANT—treated as a CANTUS FIRMUS. Yet in every case what he does with the borrowed material is different. In his *Missa "L'homme armé,"* whose cantus firmus is taken from a popular song, Ockeghem's treatment is fairly straightforward. His technique in the *Missa "De plus en plus"* (based on a chanson by Binchois) is more varied, and he becomes even subtler in his *Missa "Ma maistresse"* and *Missa "Fors seulement"* (both based on chansons of his own). Ockeghem was every bit as inventive in his motets, which show considerable imagination in their musical workings and their treatment of the texts.

As Ockeghem's music dropped out of the active repertoire during the 16th century, knowledge of it became the province of the theorists. The complexity of his work was admired, its beauty and vitality forgotten. With the revival of interest in early music, especially since the 1970s, Ockeghem has come in for a great deal of scholarly attention, and now, thanks to recordings, nearly all of his work can be heard and enjoyed by anyone, a privilege only the French court could claim when he was alive.

RECOMMENDED RECORDINGS

Missa "L'homme armé": Summerly and Oxford Camerata (Naxos).

Missa prolationum: Wickham and The Clerk's Groups (ASV).

Motets: Wickham and The Clerk's Group (ASV).

Requiem, Missa Mi-Mi: Hilliard Ensemble (EMI).

octave Interval between any two notes that are seven diatonic steps (12 semitones) apart. Tones an octave apart have a frequency ratio of 2:1 and, for reasons that are not completely understood, sound to our ears like the same pitch, differing only in register. This acoustic phenomenon, known as "octave equivalence," is common to all human cultures. To illustrate: Middle C on the piano vibrates at a frequency of 256 hertz (cycles per second), while the notes an octave above it and below it vibrate at 512 and 128 respectively, but we hear them all as C.

octet A piece for eight instruments. The instrumental disposition of most octets falls into one of three categories: all winds, all strings, or mixed winds and strings. During the final two decades of the 18th century, the wind octet (called a *Harmonie* in German, consisting of two oboes, two clarinets, two bassoons, and two horns) became a common formation in and around Vienna. Such groups usually performed outdoors, providing music for special occasions at the estates of the nobility or hiring themselves out to play serenades in the street. Pieces written for wind octet went by a variety of names; the most common were divertimento, cassation (from the German *gassatim gehen*, meaning "to go into the streets"), serenade, and partita (sometimes "parthia"). Among those who contributed to the genre were Mozart, Beethoven, Schubert, Josef Mysliveček (1737–81), Franz Krommer (1759–1831), and Joseph Triebensee (1772–1846); later additions to the repertoire came from Franz Paul Lachner (1830–90), Bruch, and Carl Reinecke (1824–1910). In the 20th century the wind-octet formula was expanded to include a variety of other instruments. Notable examples are Stravinsky's Octet (for flute, clarinet, two bassoons, two trumpets, trombone, and bass trombone) and Varèse's *Octandre* (for flute doubling piccolo, clarinet doubling E-flat clarinet, oboe, bassoon, horn, trumpet, trombone, and string bass). Both works date from 1923.

The string octet (four violins, two violas, two cellos) was born with Mendelssohn's brilliant Octet in E-flat, Op. 20, composed in 1825 when he was 16. Subsequent contributions to the genre were made by Gade, Johan Svendsen (1840–1911), Joachim Raff (1822–82), Enescu, and Glière. Between 1823 and 1847, Louis Spohr (1784–1859) produced four octets conceived of as double string quartets, in which the discourse was divided between two standard string foursomes. A century later this idea was taken to its logical but nonetheless mind-boggling conclusion by Milhaud, whose Quartets Nos. 14 and 15, Op. 291 (1949), were written so that they could be played separately, as string quartets, or simultaneously, as an octet.

Works for a mixed complement of winds and strings have tended to follow the instrumentation chosen by Schubert in his Octet in F, D. 803, for clarinet, horn, bassoon, two violins, viola, cello, and double bass (1824). Composers who have favored this disposition include Xenakis, Boris Blacher (1903–75), Siegfried Matthus (b. 1934), and Jean Françaix, whose delightful *À huit* (1972) is a particularly valuable contribution to the literature. *See also* CHAMBER MUSIC.

RECOMMENDED RECORDINGS

FRANÇAIX: GAUDIER ENSEMBLE (HYPERION).

MENDELSSOHN: GUARNERI AND ORION QUARTETS (ARABESQUE).

MENDELSSOHN: HAUSMUSIK (VIRGIN CLASSICS).

SCHUBERT: GAUDIER ENSEMBLE (HYPERION).

VARÈSE, *OCTANDRE*: BOULEZ AND ENSEMBLE INTERCONTEMPORAIN (SONY).

ode In ancient times, a poem intended to be sung on a special occasion, or as part of a dramatic performance. In modern times, a vocal work, usually in several sections, offered in praise of an august personage or as a gesture of thanksgiving. The ode became an important genre in England in the years following the Restoration (1660). English court odes typically called for solo voices, chorus, and orchestra, and were written for the celebration of royal birthdays and other special occasions, as well as for the court's New Year's Day festivities; odes in honor of St. Cecilia, the patron saint of music, whose feast day is November 22, constituted an especially charming subgenre. Leading 17th-century composers of odes included Henry Cooke (ca. 1615–72), John Blow (1649–1708), and Purcell ◉, whose two dozen surviving works in the form, including three odes to St. Cecilia, are particularly admirable. The tradition was carried on during the 18th century by William Boyce (1711–79) and Handel, among others, and survived into the 20th century in works such as Britten's *Hymn to St Cecilia* (1942), an a cappella setting of a text by W. H. Auden.

RECOMMENDED RECORDING

PURCELL, "ODES AND WELCOME SONGS" (8 VOLS.): AINSLEY, BONNER, BOWMAN, CHANCE, COVEY-CRUMP, OTHERS; KING AND KING'S CONSORT, CHOIR OF NEW COLLEGE, OXFORD (HYPERION).

O'Dette, Paul

(b. Pittsburgh, Penn., February 2, 1954)

AMERICAN LUTENIST. A prominent interpreter of solo lute music, he has also collaborated as an ensemble partner in several early-music groups, and is co-artistic director of the biennial Boston Early Music Festival. A self-taught rock guitar player, he moved on to classical guitar and then became interested in the repertoire and sonority of the lute. He studied guitar with Christopher Parkening and lute with Eugen Dombois, and took instruction in medieval and Renaissance performance practice from Thomas Binkley at the Studio der frühen Musik of the Schola Cantorum Basiliensis in Switzerland. In 1976, O'Dette joined the faculty of the Eastman School of Music, where he is director of early music. He has made award-winning recordings, including a traversal of the complete lute works of John Dowland. He has published numerous articles on historical performance practice, and is a member of the continuo ensemble Tragicomedia. O'Dette and Stephen Stubbs, his Boston Early Music Festival co-director, jointly lead performances of Baroque operas, a practice they began in 1997 with Luigi Rossi's *Orfeo*.

Paul O'Dette, from rock to Renaissance

RECOMMENDED RECORDINGS

"ALLA VENEZIANA" (16TH-CENTURY VENETIAN LUTE MUSIC) (HARMONIA MUNDI).

DOWLAND, COMPLETE WORKS FOR LUTE (5 VOLS.) (HARMONIA MUNDI).

Oedipus rex STAGED ORATORIO IN TWO ACTS FOR NARRATOR, vocal soloists, men's chorus, and orchestra by Igor Stravinsky, with scenario and text by Jean Cocteau (after Sophocles), premiered in concert form on May 30, 1927, in Paris, the composer conducting. One of several stage works that Stravinsky created in the years following *The Rite of Spring* as part of an effort to blur the lines between traditional genres, it is a hybrid of opera, oratorio, and ritualistic theater.

RECOMMENDED RECORDING

NORMAN, MOSER, NIMSGERN; DAVIS AND BAVARIAN RADIO SYMPHONY ORCHESTRA (ORFEO).

Offenbach, Jacques [Jacob]

(b. Cologne, June 20, 1819; d. Paris, October 5, 1880)

GERMAN/FRENCH COMPOSER. His father, a bookbinder, was a capable musician and served as cantor at a synagogue in Cologne. Jacob first studied violin, then took up the cello at the age of nine so he could play in a trio with his older brother and sister. In 1833 he enrolled as a cello student at the Paris Conservatoire; from then on he was known as Jacques. A year later he joined the orchestra of the Opéra-Comique, spending four years in the pit while continuing his cello studies privately and receiving some lessons in composition from Fromental Halévy. During the 1840s he made his way as a virtuoso cellist, playing in Parisian salons, touring to London, and triumphantly returning to his hometown to perform with Franz Liszt.

Jacques Offenbach, comic master, cancan composer

In 1855, having had little success getting his stage works accepted for performance at Parisian theaters, he went into business for himself, opening a theater called the Bouffes-Parisiens in rented space. Presenting his own works as well as those of others, he brought forth a series of hits, capped in 1858 by the triumphant premiere of his two-act comedy *Orphée aux enfers* (*Orpheus in the Underworld*). By the 1860s his fame as a composer of light opera had spread to Vienna and London. Keeping up a furious pace, penning three or four works a year, he achieved his greatest success in the genre with *La belle Hélène* (1864), *La vie parisienne* (1866), and *La Grande-Duchesse de Gerolstein* (1867).

Offenbach's production declined during the 1870s, even as his fame grew. In 1876 he embarked on a lengthy tour of the U.S., conducting performances of *La vie parisienne* and giving concerts in New York and Philadelphia. He spent the final years of his life working on the "opéra fantastique" *LES CONTES D'HOFFMANN*. With this score Offenbach surprisingly eclipsed his own reputation as a composer of operetta. Posthumously premiered in 1881, it has become one of the most successful of all French operas, performed more frequently than any other save *Carmen*.

Few composers in history have fit the times in which they lived as neatly as Offenbach. Wherever there was vanity, frivolity, or immorality in the Second Empire, he found it and set it to music, with every bit as much wit and imagination as Honoré Daumier and Gustave Doré showed in their art.

RECOMMENDED RECORDINGS

La belle Hélène: Norman, Aler, Alliot-Lugaz; Plasson and Orchestre du Capitole de Toulouse (EMI).

Les contes d'Hoffmann: Alagna, Dessay, Veduva, Dubosc, Jo, Van Dam; Nagano and Lyon National Orchestra (Erato).

Les contes d'Hoffmann: Sutherland, Domingo, Tourangeau, Bacquier; Bonynge and L'Orchestre de la Suisse Romande (Decca).

Selected overtures: Karajan and Berlin Philharmonic (DG).

Offertory Chant sung at Mass to accompany the "presentation of the offerings" (i.e., the procession in which bread and wine are brought to the altar to be offered by the celebrant in the name of Christ as the Eucharistic sacrifice). In musical settings of the Mass, the Offertory follows the Credo and precedes the Sanctus.

Oistrakh, David

(b. Odessa, September 30, 1908; d. Amsterdam, October 24, 1974)

RUSSIAN VIOLINIST AND CONDUCTOR. He was one of the preeminent Russian violinists of the 20th century. Like other Soviet musicians of his generation, he was already a well-established and seasoned artist by the time of his American debut, which came in 1955, at the height of the Cold War. He worked closely with the leading Soviet composers of his day, including Prokofiev, Shostakovich, Nikolay Miaskovsky (1881–1950), and Khachaturian; he premiered Khachaturian's popular Violin Concerto, both of Shostakovich's violin concertos, and Prokofiev's D major sonata.

Born into a Jewish family in prerevolutionary Russia, Oistrakh took lessons at the Odessa Conservatory with Pyotr Stolyarsky and made his debut at the age of five. In 1923, while still a student, he served as concertmaster of the Odessa Symphony Orchestra and performed as soloist with that group in the Bach A major concerto. Graduating in 1926, he made his Kiev debut the following year under Aleksandr Glazunov, and gave his Leningrad debut in 1928. Shortly after that he moved to Moscow, making his debut there in 1929.

Oistrakh became professor of violin at the Moscow Conservatory in 1934, a post he held until the mid-1960s. He entered several international competitions, coming in second to Ginette Neveu at the Wieniawski Competition in Warsaw in 1935 and taking first prize at the Concours Ysaÿe (later renamed the Queen Elisabeth Competition) in Brussels in 1937. Like many Soviet artists he performed at the front as well as in hospitals, factories, schools, and communities throughout the country during World War II. He was named a People's Artist of the Soviet Union in 1954 and received the Lenin Prize, his country's highest honor, in 1960.

The American public first heard Oistrakh play on November 20, 1955, at Carnegie Hall, when he gave the U.S. premiere of Shostakovich's Violin Concerto No. 1 with Dimitri Mitropoulos and the New York Philharmonic. He thus became the second in a triple-barreled Soviet "surprise" that floored the American musical establishment and began the thaw in the Cold War—Gilels and Oistrakh in 1955, Rostropovich in 1956. Easier for the authorities to control than many of his colleagues, Oistrakh was allowed to take frequent trips to the West and collaborate with the likes of Karajan and the Berlin Philharmonic, Szell and the Cleveland Orchestra, and Ormandy and the Philadelphia Orchestra. Some of his finest recordings resulted from these encounters. During the final decade of his life, Oistrakh also made occasional appearances as a conductor, often accompanying his son Igor (b. 1931), himself a first-class violinist.

Oistrakh's playing, infallibly musical, was marked by great warmth and sincerity of expression, and by a faithfulness to the written notes that only a few of his colleagues cared to display. He had fabulous fingers, and there was an extraordinary quality to his vibrato: richly expressive in a vocal way, intense and focused, but never unduly sweet. In an age of hyper-Romanticism and interpretive self-indulgence, his straightforward yet ardent interpretations stood out as beacons.

RECOMMENDED RECORDINGS

BEETHOVEN, TRIPLE CONCERTO; BRAHMS, DOUBLE CONCERTO: RICHTER, ROSTROPOVICH; KARAJAN AND BERLIN PHILHARMONIC; SZELL AND CLEVELAND ORCHESTRA (EMI).

KHATCHATURIAN, VIOLIN CONCERTO: GAUK AND USSR STATE ORCHESTRA (PEARL).

SHOSTAKOVICH, VIOLIN CONCERTO NO. 1: MITROPOULOS AND NEW YORK PHILHARMONIC (SONY).

TCHAIKOVSKY AND SIBELIUS, VIOLIN CONCERTOS: ORMANDY AND PHILADELPHIA ORCHESTRA (SONY).

ondes martenot *See box on pages 496–97.*

On Hearing the First Cuckoo in Spring TONE POEM BY FREDERICK DELIUS. The first of his *Two Pieces for Small Orchestra,* it was composed in 1912 and premiered at the Gewandhaus in Leipzig on October 23, 1913, under the baton of Arthur Nikisch. *On Hearing the First Cuckoo in Spring* naturally enough mimics the bird's distinctive two-note call and also quotes a tune from Grieg's *Norwegian Folk Songs* for piano ("In Ola Valley, in Ola Lake").

RECOMMENDED RECORDINGS

BEECHAM AND ROYAL PHILHARMONIC ORCHESTRA (EMI).

HANDLEY AND PHILHARMONIA ORCHESTRA (CHANDOS).

open string Any string that is allowed to vibrate freely from bridge to nut, without being stopped at some point on its length by being pressed against the fingerboard or a fret. The open strings on the violin are tuned to the following pitches: G, D, A, E; those on the viola C, G, D, A; the cello C, G, D, A; the string bass E, A, D, G. The guitar's open strings sound the pitches E, A, D, G, B, and E.

opera (It., "work") Drama with singing and the accompaniment of an orchestra or instrumental ensemble. The form was described in 1645 by the English diarist John Evelyn as "one of the most magnificent and expensive diversions the wit of man can invent." Like much of the Renaissance, opera was a Florentine invention, but it took the Venetians, republican, savvy, and commercial, to make it a success. The first public opera house in the world opened in Venice in 1637, in the parish of San Cassiano, and by 1650 the city had four companies operating at once. During the 17th century at least 16 opera theaters were built in Venice, and in them some 388 different operas were performed.

Opera had many forerunners in the musical and theatrical milieu of the Middle Ages and Renaissance: mysteries and liturgical dramas; the masque and other visual spectacles in which music played an adjunct role; the lavish 16th-century Italian *intermedii* (spoken plays on classical models, with musical numbers added); the Italian pastorale, which had begun to displace other forms of dramatic poetry by the middle of the 16th century; and the madrigal comedy that emerged from the commedia dell'arte in the latter part of the 16th century. A key element fell into place at the very end of the 16th century with the development of MONODY, a new form of dramatic solo song that emphasized intelligibility of text and natural declamation, and relied on the expression of a whole passage rather than successive emotions or images alluded to in the text, as the madrigal had done. The catalyst for this new style of singing—called *STILE RAPPRESENTATIVO,* or "theatrical style"—was an attempt on the part of a group of musicians, poets, and scholars, known as the Florentine Camerata, to re-create the experience of ancient Greek theater. The attempt failed for the most part, but opera was born.

In the final decade of the 16th century, the Florentine poet Ottavio Rinuccini created the first libretto, based on the myth of Apollo and Daphne, "solely to test the power of modern music." Its setting by Jacopo Corsi and Jacopo Peri in 1597–98, can be regarded as the first opera, though scarcely any of the music survives. Peri followed this with *Euridice* in 1600, the first opera for which all the music does survive, and other works by a number of composers—among them Marco da Gagliano and Giulio Caccini—soon appeared. As surprising and delightful as these first operas were, they were mainly spectacle and had several musical defects, among which were weak characterization, limited emotional range, lack of consistent organization, and monotonous vocal writing.

L'ORFEO
FAVOLA IN MVSICA
DA CLAVDIO MONTEVERDI
RAPPRESENTATA IN MANTOVA
l'Anno 1607. & nouamente data in luce.
AL SERENISSIMO SIGNOR
D. FRANCESCO GONZAGA
In Venetia Appresso Ricciardo Amadino.
M D C IX.

The title page from the first edition of Monteverdi's* L'Orfeo *(1607), published in Venice in 1609

All of this changed in 1607 with Claudio Monteverdi's *L'Orfeo*. In its effective mix of madrigalism and monody, its eloquence, strong characterization, and internal cohesion, and in the grand symmetry of its dramatic and musical design, *L'Orfeo* marked the beginning of opera as an art form. Monteverdi's transformation of the nascent genre continued during his years in Venice, where the metamorphosis of opera into a public spectacle brought about a significant changes in librettos and music. While opera's princely patrons had spared no expense, the hard realities of commerce required that resources be carefully husbanded. Smaller orchestras were used, the role of the chorus was reduced, and the virtuoso soloist gained in importance. Only two of Monteverdi's Venetian operas, *Il ritorno di Ulisse in patria* (1640) and *L'incoronazione di Poppea* (1643), have survived. Written at the height of his maturity, *Poppea,* with a libretto by Giovanni Francesco Busenello, was the first opera to have a historical rather than a mythological subject, and is perhaps the greatest of all Baroque operas. Gone are the abrupt contrasts of mood of the early days of opera—instead, each scene is linked to the next in a way that builds potent cumulative tension, with several comic scenes providing relief.

Because of the purity and inventiveness of his style, Monteverdi cast a long shadow over the rest of 17th-century Italian composers. But opera did not stand still. The second half of the century saw a formalization of the art along with the establishment of conventions and the emergence of a common style. The Renaissance interest in antiquity gradually faded, until often only the shell of the classical subject remained. Myths were supplanted by the epics of Ariosto and Tasso, abstraction and complication became the norm, and special effects calling for sophisticated stage machinery were utilized as often as possible, since impresarios insisted that every ducat they spent on a production be evident. In the works of Francesco Cavalli (1602–76)—whose career centered in Venice and whose *Giasone* (1649) was the most popular opera of the 17th century—the aria and the overture began to crystallize into musical and formal concepts, and by the end of the 17th century the division of scores into individual musical "numbers" was clearly established.

During the 17th century opera spread quickly from Italy to the rest of Europe. Its rise in France can be attributed to the work of a transplanted Italian, Jean-Baptiste Lully (born Giovanni Battista Lulli), who in 1672 convinced his patron, Louis XIV, to award him what amounted to a monopoly on opera in France. Lully proved himself worthy of that extraordinary favor. In such works as *Atys* (1676) and *Armide* (1686), composed, as were nearly all of his operas, to librettos by Philippe Quinault, he achieved an extremely elegant yet vibrant fusion of ballet, choral music, Italian recitative, and orchestral colorism. Elaborate choreography was de rigueur in Lully's operas, and it remained so in the works of his contemporaries and successors, André Campra (1660–1744) and Jean-Philippe Rameau.

In 1627, Heinrich Schütz composed what is generally regarded as the first opera in German, a setting of *Dafne* based on Rinuccini's libretto. From 1678 to 1738, German-language opera found a home in Hamburg and a champion in Reinhard Keiser (1674–1739), but vulgar poetry eventually spelled the end of the idyll. In most German cities during the 17th and 18th centuries, the proper language for opera was Italian. Italian composers such as Antonio Cesti (1623–69), Antonio Draghi (1634–1700), and Niccolò Jomelli (1714–74), along with two Italian-trained Germans, Karl Heinrich Graun and Johann Adolf Hasse, dominated the Austrian and German scene from the mid-17th to the mid-18th century.

Meanwhile, during nearly the whole of the 17th century, England remained an operatic backwater, even as English letters enjoyed a golden age. It was only by sheer luck that Henry Purcell, one of the greatest composers in England's history, emerged in the closing decades of the century, in full possession of one of the keenest theatrical sensibilities of the age. His SEMIOPERAS have enjoyed a full-blown revival in recent years, and his vibrant *Dido and Aeneas*, composed prior to 1689, remains one of the jewels of the repertoire.

The emergence of Italian comic opera—OPERA BUFFA—as a viable genre distinct from serious opera—opera seria—was perhaps the most important musical development of the first half of the 18th century. The century also saw the continued rise of the virtuoso singer and marked the heyday of the CASTRATI, male singers with voices of trumpet-like power in the mezzo-soprano range, several of whom became the world's first international musical superstars. A truly international style of opera emerged that could comfortably cross national boundaries; that style, in both the serious and the comic sectors, was Italian.

Alessandro Scarlatti (1660–1725) was the last "old master" of the serious Italian school and the most important operatic composer of the early 18th century in Italy. In Scarlatti's works, the use of the sinfonia (the three-part overture known as an

***You've come a long way, baby—a scene from Richard Strauss's* Salome**

"Italian" overture) was firmly established, along with such devices as accompanied recitative, a hallmark of opera seria, and the full DA CAPO aria, (in which the opening section of an aria is repeated, with inventive and demanding embellishments added by the singer.) Because of his large output (66 known works) and the high quality of his music, Scarlatti was seen as a model at the time, and even by such illustrious successors as Hasse and George Frideric Handel.

It was a double paradox that Handel, a German working in England, should have become one of the most accomplished composers of Italian opera seria in the 18th century. Yet Handel spent the greater part of his career toiling in the vineyard of Italian opera, contributing roughly 60 works to the form during the course of 36 years. He was a consummate master of dramatic composition who, without sacrificing an ounce of grandeur, was able to make his music convey an extraordinary range of emotion. Handel brought the best Italian singers to London to perform his works, enjoying many triumphs, but in the end not even he could halt the march of opera buffa.

Hapsburg Vienna remained a bastion of opera seria well into the 18th century; it was there, under the influence of the poets Apostolo Zeno (1668–1750) and Pietro Metastasio, that the literary conventions of the genre were firmly fixed. But around 1750, the formula started to come under fire; in his *Saggio sopra l'opera in musica* (*Essay on the Opera*; 1755), Francesco Algarotti (1712–64) criticized the dominance of the singer in much of Italian opera, damned Metastasio's ornate librettos with faint praise, and characterized the collaboration of Quinault and Lully as ideal between poet and composer. Behind Algarotti's broadside was a conviction that all aspects of opera, including the vocal, should be subordinate to a central poetic conception. The same idea stood behind the reforms championed by the librettist Rainieri Calzabigi (1714–95) and the composer Christoph Willibald Gluck. Calzabigi, whose progressive ideas had been influenced by J. C. Noverre's *Lettres sur la danse* (1760), found in Gluck a composer willing to put his music at the service of the words, yet able to write music of considerable emotional and descriptive power.

In France, too, change was in the air as the 18th century reached its midpoint, precipitating a pamphlet war in which two questions were incessantly debated: should opera proceed primarily from literary considerations or musical ones, and should subjects be drawn from myth or real life? The high-water mark of the debate came in 1752 with the *Querelle des Bouffons,* a controversy sparked by the first performances in Paris of Pergolesi's *La serva padrona,* in which the partisans of Italian opera buffa were pitted against the champions of French *tragédie lyrique.* The quarrel raged for three years, but in the end the box office spoke louder than the philosophers; by the 1760s the style of Lully, Rameau, and their followers had gone the way of the dinosaur.

As the 18th century came to an end, the static social order and grandiose moral posturing of opera seria struck most bourgeois listeners as a thing of the past. The genre was already archaic when Mozart penned *Idomeneo, re di Creta* (1780) and *La clemenza di Tito* (1791), and soon it simply faded away. Mozart himself, along with gifted colleagues such as Giovanni Paisiello (1740–1816), Domenico Cimarosa (1749–1801), and Vicente Martín y Soler (1754–1806) effectively nailed shut its coffin with their contributions to opera buffa—works which, as William Mann has pointed out, were "overtly comic yet fundamentally serious." The greatest of these by far were Mozart's three collaborations with the court poet Lorenzo da Ponte, *Le nozze* di *Figaro, Don Giovanni,* and *Così fan tutte.* In their symphonic construction, deft characterization, and richness of texture (both musical and dramatic), they set a new standard for what could be achieved in opera.

The dawn of the 19th century saw the emergence of the first international lion of the operatic stage, Gioachino Rossini. In works like *Il barbiere di Siviglia* and *La cenerentola* he revitalized the *buffa* style, creating situations in which uproarious hilarity and believable emotion coexisted with miraculous ease. One of the hallmarks of his vocal writing, and that of his near-contemporaries Gaetano Donizetti and Vincenzo Bellini, was its adherence to the precepts of BEL CANTO ("beautiful singing"), which emphasized a light, mellifluous tone and effortless delivery in florid passages. Bellini, a meticulously slow worker, was perhaps the greatest master of bel canto, and the three masterpieces he contributed to the literature, *La sonnambula, Norma,* and *I puritani* (1835), are the paragons of that style. Donizetti's music stands at the crossroads between bel canto and the more direct, sensational and melodramatic manner of the mid-19th century, soon to find its greatest exponent in Verdi. His range as a composer was remarkable, allowing his pen to fly from the high Romantic agitation of *Lucia di Lammermoor* to the effervescent comedy of *L'elisir d'amore* and *Don Pasquale.*

Otello ***at the Met, with Renée Fleming and Plácido Domingo***

The early decades of the 19th century also witnessed the rise of German Romantic opera. One finds hints of the new order in the colorism and high idealism of Mozart's two great singspiels, *Die Entführung aus dem Serail* and *Die Zauberflöte,* as well as in the philosophical stance of Beethoven's *Fidelio.* But the composer who achieved the real breakthrough in style was Carl Maria von Weber. Even if the only one of Weber's works that has held a place in the repertoire is *Der Freischütz,* the influence of that score and of Weber's *Euryanthe* and *Oberon* on Wagner and others—not just Germans, and not just composers of the 19th century—was decisive.

It was in Paris during the 1830s and 1840s—after the Revolution and the Restoration had both run their course, and the quiet counterrevolution of the bourgeoisie had set in—that the most important operatic developments of the first half of the 19th century took place. Audiences needed something spectacular, and French GRAND OPERA rose up to fill the need. Among the composers and works that made the spectacular a nightly occurrence at the Opéra were Daniel-François-Esprit Auber, whose *La muette de Portici,* premiered in 1828, effectively launched grand opera; Rossini, who bowed out of the operatic limelight with *Guillaume Tell* in 1829; and Giacomo Meyerbeer, the master of masters, whose string of hits included *Robert le diable* (1831), *Les Huguenots, Le prophète* (1849) and *L'Africaine* (posthumously premiered in 1865). Grand opera would provide a blueprint for many of the finest works of Wagner and Verdi.

Those two operatic titans of the 19th century, both born in 1813, grew up as Europe's destiny was being reshaped by strong revolutionary and reactionary currents. Wagner, the consummate man of the theater, was a pragmatic idealist who sought nothing less than to change the world through the power of his music. His talent was up to the task, and the scenic grandeur and emotional sweep of the works he placed in the repertoire—*Der fliegende Holländer, Tannhäuser, Lohengrin, Der Ring des Nibelungen* (consisting of *Das Rheingold, Die Walküre, Siegfried,* and *Götterdämmerung*), *Tristan und Isolde, Die Meistersinger von Nürnberg,* and *Parsifal*—has yet to be equaled, let alone surpassed. Verdi, the preeminent figure in Italian opera during the second half of the 19th century, was also perhaps the greatest dramatist the art of music has yet known. His contribution to the repertoire proved as impressive as Wagner's, and includes more than a dozen works that are regularly performed—among them *Nabucco, Ernani, Rigoletto, Il trovatore, La traviata, Luisa Miller, Un ballo in maschera, La forza del destino, Simon Boccanegra, Don Carlo, Aida, Otello,* and *Falstaff.*

Italian opera spread to Russia during the 18th century, with French opera close on its heels. The first Romantic operas by Russian composers adopted many of the conventions of these genres. Mikhail Glinka's *A Life for the Czar* and *Ruslan and Lyudmila* are regarded as the first important works of Russian national opera. Aleksandr Dargomïzhsky's *The Stone Guest* (posthumously premiered in 1872) marked a step toward the forging of an operatic language that followed the inflections of Russian speech, and Borodin's *Prince Igor* (also posthumously premiered, in 1890) carried on the epic tradition of *Ruslan and Lyudmila* while showing that Russian opera could also be melodious.

As the century wore on, the elements of spectacle, national history, and myth that had characterized the first Russian operas were retained in works that attempted a more profound psychological portraiture. Following in the footsteps of *Ruslan and Lyudmila,* many of these operas were derived from the works of Pushkin, including Tchaikovsky's two great contributions to the genre, *Eugene Onegin* and *The Queen of Spades.* Rimsky-Korsakov contributed a substantial number of works to the repertoire, showing remarkable aptitude for the fantastical. Mussorgsky's two most important operas, *Boris Godunov* and *Khovanshchina* (premiered posthumously in 1886), are, on one level, free interpretations of grand opera, and on another, probing psychological and social commentaries. Elements of the structure and musical language of *Boris* have echoed in the operas of Debussy, Janáček, Shostakovich, and Prokofiev, making it one of the most influential of all 19th-century operas.

France, in the years following the heyday of grand opera, saw composers attempting to escape the formulas of the genre while retaining some of its most appealing scenic elements. Among the leaders in this effort was Charles Gounod, whose *Faust,* once among the most popular operas in the repertoire, draws on *opéra comique* in its characterization of

Leontyne Price as Aida

Méphistophélès. In *Samson et Dalila,* Saint-Saëns sought to probe intimate emotions without sacrificing a grand opera backdrop, as did Delibes in his *Lakmé.* Miraculously, the best works of Jules Massenet, *Manon* and *Werther,* managed to distance themselves both from grand opera and the influence of Wagner (which by the end of the 19th century had become all but ubiquitous in French musical life), achieving an emotional warmth and idiomatic fluency that were decidedly French. By far the most original and important voice in French opera at this juncture was that of Georges Bizet, whose *Carmen,* based on a story by Prosper Mérimée, transformed *opéra comique* into a serious, passionate, and realistic genre.

***Poster art for Bizet's* Carmen**

At precisely the same time as Mussorgsky and Bizet were advancing opera into new psychological realms, in essence creating the first modern operas, two others, Jacques Offenbach and Johann Strauss Jr., were holding up the mirror of their art to the frivolities of their age while still striking a nerve. The latter's *Die Fledermaus,* with its heavily contrived plot and lilting Viennese waltzes, is one of the most popular pieces in the repertoire. Offenbach produced many exuberant farces, but his greatest achievement was the part fantasy, part romance, part comedy *Les contes d'Hoffmann,* which is more frequently performed today than any opera in French save *Carmen.*

The vacuum left in Italian opera by Verdi's exit in 1893 (the year his swansong, *Falstaff,* received its premiere) was quickly filled by Giacomo Puccini, whose first great success, *Manon Lescaut,* had its premiere the same year. Puccini possessed a stupendous melodic gift and outstanding theatrical instincts, and his best operas—a lineup that includes *La bohème, Tosca*, *Madama Butterfly, La fanciulla del West, Il Trittico* (*Il tabarro, Suor Angelica,* and *Gianni Schicchi*), and *Turandot*—have become staples of the repertoire not only in Italy but throughout the world. In many of these works Puccini tried to mimic real life on the stage (which is why he is often considered a representative of the VERISMO style), but the best of them succeed as much through their fine use of scenic and musical detail as by the (occasionally improbable) workings of their plots. Other important figures in Italy at the close of the 19th century were Amilcare Ponchielli (1834–86), the composer of *La gioconda,* and Umberto Giordano, whose most famous work is *Andrea Chénier* (1896). The purest expression of verismo came in Pietro Mascagni's *Cavalleria rusticana* and Ruggero Leoncavallo's *Pagliacci,* regularly presented as a double bill.

The early years of the 20th century witnessed a new kind of sensationalism in the opera house, thanks in large part to Richard Strauss. His *Salome,* a bombshell of an opera based on the play by Oscar Wilde, put perversity and depravity front and center and contained some of the most virtuosic, suggestive, and complex music ever penned. His next opera, *Elektra,* to a libretto by Hugo von Hofmannsthal, was even fiercer, an onslaught in which the orchestra is as much a star as any of the singers. Then came *Der Rosenkavalier,* a study of love from three angles, beautifully conceived by

Hofmannsthal and limned by Strauss, in waltz time, with the most opulent colors his palette contained. Strauss remained in the game following Hofmannsthal's death. With *Daphne* (1938), he brought German opera full circle back to the subject of the first opera in German, outdoing himself in the atmospheric final scene. His *Capriccio,* an opera-about-opera within an opera that premiered in Munich in the darkening autumn of 1942, proved an utterly appropriate valedictory gesture.

Most 20th-century opera has had to deal one way or another with the enormous impact of Wagner and Verdi. Like other French composers of his generation, Debussy fell under Wagner's spell in his youth. Unlike them, he was able to write a great opera that was not Wagnerian—even though *Pelléas et Mélisande* utilized leitmotifs, relied on short orchestral interludes to link scenes as *Parsifal* had done, and veered perilously close to the ecstasies of *Tristan und Isolde* in its climactic scene. In spite of those outward trappings, Debussy's *Pelléas* is all about what is going on inside its characters' minds, a drama not of action but of symbols transmuted into music. ◉ Maurice Ravel, the miniaturist par excellence, found his own way as well, showing remarkable originality, sensitivity, and flair in his two brief operas, *L'heure espagnole* (1911) and *L'enfant et les sortilèges.*

***Poster art for Puccini's* La bohème**

The mature operas of Leoš Janáček, including *Jenůfa* ◉, *Kát'a Kabanová, The Makropulos Case, The Cunning Little Vixen* (1924) and *From the House of the Dead,* are wonderful examples of art that was virtually sui generis. Janáček devised speech-based rhythms and melodies, and employed a strikingly colorful orchestral language far ahead of its time, much leaner than that of late Romanticism. The combination makes these works sound unlike anything written before or since.

In 20th-century Russia, the stylistic free-for-all of the early Soviet years was quickly followed by Stalinist repression and a long period of interference that put a damper on operatic expression. Yet two composers were talented enough to rise above the confusion. Shostakovich got into trouble for the frank subject matter and edgy music of *Lady Macbeth of Mtsensk District*; but of all the operas created throughout the history of the Soviet Union, it will probably be remembered as the best. Prokofiev's great achievement was to take a "safer" subject, Tolstoy's *War and Peace,* pay lip service to the doctrine of Socialist Realism, and still write an opera that was musically rich and profound in its assessment of character. Several of Prokofiev's other operas are now gaining a foothold in the international repertoire, including *The Love for Three Oranges* (1921), *The Flaming Angel* (1928), and *Betrothal in a Monastery* (1946), testimony to the liveliness of his musical imagination.

For Austrian and German composers of the late 19th and early 20th century, it was not easy to stand in the shadow of Wagner and be blinded by the brilliance of Strauss at the same time. Among those who managed to bring successful works to the stage, the most Wagnerian was Engelbert Humperdinck, whose *Hänsel und*

Gretel graciously tells the popular fairy tale in the language of the Bayreuth master. Hans Pfitzner achieved majesty in *Palestrina* without an excess of melodrama, while Arnold Schoenberg solved the problem by forging a new syntax, and doing his best to adapt it to the stage in works like *Erwartung* (1924) and *Moses und Aron.* Alexander von Zemlinsky clung to the superheated chromaticiscim that was part of Wagner's legacy, and wrote powerful, affecting works such as *Eine florentinische Tragödie* (1917) and *Der Zwerg* (1922). In *Wozzeck* and *Lulu,* Alban Berg proved much more adept at utilizing Schoenberg's new language on the stage than Schoenberg himself. Both works have established themselves in the repertoire. The eclectic Kurt Weill, with clever librettos from Bertolt Brecht, had no problem fascinating audiences with his *Aufstieg und Fall der Stadt Mahagonny* and *Die Dreigroschenoper;* the Nazis put an end to his career in Germany, but the works themselves have endured, and Weill's final American effort, *Street Scene* (1946), is once again attracting interest. Erich Wolfgang Korngold, who appreciated Strauss's achievement, simply went ahead and outdid the old man at his own game, penning early sensations *Violanta* and *Der Ring des*

***Lotte Lenya in Weill's* Die Dreigroschenoper (Threepenny Opera)**

Willard White and Cynthia Haymon in* Porgy and Bess, *1992

Polykrates in 1914, when he was barely out of his crib, and producing his masterpieces *Die tote Stadt* and *Das Wunder der Heliane* (1927) by the time he was 30.

The 20th century saw a belated but extraordinary flowering of opera in England and America. Indeed, one would be hard pressed to find greater stylistic variety in any place or period than in the operas written in English during the 20th century. George Gershwin's *Porgy and Bess* is the first great American opera, a marvelous fusion of an American subject with innately American music. The American repertoire has subsequently been enriched by Douglas Moore (1893–1969), Samuel Barber, Gian Carlo Menotti, Robert Ward (b. 1917), Carlysle Floyd (b. 1926), Dominick Argento (b. 1927), Conrad Susa (b. 1935), William Bolcom, John Corigliano, Philip Glass, and John Adams. In some of the best works by these composers—Argento's *Postcard from Morocco* (1971) and Susa's *Transformations* (1973)—opera has returned to its roots as a chamber form, with marked success.

England was particularly lucky in the 20th century to have not only Michael Tippett and Sir Peter Maxwell Davies, both notably successful in the operatic sphere, but the greatest theatrical composer in its history, Benjamin Britten. Britten's first masterpiece, *Peter Grimes,* was completed in 1945 and remains the most popular of his operas. Britten borrowed from the traditions of grand opera in it and in such works as *Billy Budd* (1951) as part of a strategy to deal with the underlying ambivalence of his dramatic material. He showed a gift for comedy in *Albert Herring* (1947) and a mastery of psychological suspense in *The Turn of the Screw* (1954). Stravinsky's *The Rake's Progress,* set to a libretto by W. H. Auden, is certainly one of the great works in the English language. It is also one of the few works written since 1950 to have attained a place in the international repertoire.

There has been spotty brilliance in Europe and Scandinavia during the past few decades: a few works of Hans Werner Henze (b. 1926) have achieved a kind of permanence, as has György Ligeti's *Le grand macabre* (1978). Some argue for the greatness of Messiaen's *St. François d'Assise* (1983). But the past 50 years have not seen the emergence of a single great opera composer in Italy, France, Germany, or Russia. It appears that theaters and directors in these countries would now rather reconstruct and deconstruct the works of the past than foster the creation of new ones. *See also entries for individual works and composers mentioned.*

opera buffa (It. "comic opera") Comic style of opera first developed in Naples in the early decades of the 18th century. Rather than being a completely new invention, it was a refinement of comic strategies first employed in 17th-century Roman and Venetian works. Even so, the impact of the first works to realize the potential of the medium (particularly Pergolesi's 1733 *La serva padrona*) was revolutionary. Whereas the dramatic action of opera seria was constantly being retarded by elaborate da capo arias, opera buffa bubbled along with a series of short, quick-hitting, often dancelike numbers. The typical plot was farcical, and full of incongruous elements, machinations, and near-anarchy . . . all accommodated in structures of immaculate symmetry, with repetitions of clockwork regularity. The adoption of a melodic approach emphasizing short motifs and a disjunct line called for singers who were flexible, sensitive to the declamation of words, and capable of conveying meaning in both tone and gesture. The style put a premium on a singer's acting ability and allowed situations to develop much more quickly and move in a much more fluid way than was possible in opera seria.

In the second half of the 18th century, the buffa genre conquered the north of Italy and the rest of Europe, and completely eclipsed the serious. Many composers, not all of them Italian, contributed masterpieces to the burgeoning repertoire. Among the finest were *Il barbiere di Siviglia* (1782) and *Il re Teodoro in Venezia* (1784) by Giovanni Paisiello (1740–1816), *Fra due litiganti* (1782) by Giuseppe Sarti (1729–1802), *Una cosa rara* (1786) by Vicente Martìn y Soler (1754–1806), *Il matrimonio segreto* (1792) by Domenico Cimarosa (1749–1801), and Mozart's three matchless creations to librettos by Lorenzo Da Ponte: *Le nozze di Figaro* (1786), *Don Giovanni* (1787), and *Così fan tutte* (1790).

Opera buffa petered out in the 19th century, but not before Rossini and Donizetti had gotten into the act. Rossini's *Il barbiere di Siviglia* (1816) and *La cenerentola* (1817) established him as one of opera's brightest stars, while Donizetti's *L'elisir d'amore* (1832) and *Don Pasquale* (1843) brought an enlargement of the orchestra and allowed the genre's century-old comic formulas to bask for a brief but glorious moment in the glow of Romanticism.

ophicleide (from Gr. *ophis,* "snake") Brass instrument patented by Jean Hilaire Ast, in 1821, the bass member of the family that includes the keyed bugle. Its resonant, somewhat impertinent and buzzy sonority served the needs of a number of early 19th-century composers, among them Mendelssohn, who included a part for the instrument in his Overture to *A Midsummer Night's Dream,* and Berlioz, who used two of them in his *Symphonie fantastique* and called for four in his *Grande messe des morts.* In modern performances these parts are usually played by tubas.

opus (Lat., "work"; abbreviated op.; plural *opera,* opp.) A work or group of works that has been published. The use of opus numbers by publishers to identify collections of instrumental music became common in the 18th century: Famous examples are Corelli's 12 Concerti Grossi, Op. 6, and Vivaldi's *Il Cimento dell'Armonia e dell'Inventione,* Op. 8, which includes *The Four Seasons.* In the 19th century, instrumental works almost always received opus numbers when they were published, but the choice of numbers was often arbitrary, and works were frequently published in a different order from that in which they were written. As a result, opus numbers cannot be trusted as a guide to the chronology of most composers' works. The use of opus numbers continued in the 20th century, but was far from universal. For example, most of the works of Schoenberg, Hindemith, Shostakovich, and Britten carried opus numbers, but those of Stravinsky (after 1910), Bartók (after 1920), and Walton did not. Today opus numbers are rarely used.

Silhouette of Handel conducting an oratorio from the keyboard

oratorio An extended musical setting of a text usually based on scripture (but occasionally drawn from classical literature, epic poetry, or some other source), intended for concert performance. The form gets its name from the Congregazione dell'Oratorio, a religious order founded in Rome in 1575 by Filippo Neri, devoted to prayer and spiritual exercises that included singing in an oratory, or prayer hall. One of the most important efforts of the order's early years was the staging, in 1600, of the sacred drama *Rappresentatione di Anima, et di Corpo* by Emilio de' Cavalieri (ca. 1550–1602), which, while technically not an oratorio (because it involved scenery, costumes, and acting), provided a musical template for the nascent genre.

The devotional oratorio developed quickly in the hands of composers such as Giacomo Carissimi (1605–74) and Domenico Mazzocchi (1592–1665), but by the end of the 17th century it had grown into something rather far removed from the Church—a hybrid that clothed religious figures and moral teachings in magnificent operatic trappings, intended not only for edification but also as entertainment. Giovanni Legrenzi (1626–90), Alessandro Stradella (1644–82), Alessandro Scarlatti, and Antonio Caldara (ca. 1670–1736) played the key roles in this transformation, and Handel followed their lead when as a young musician he composed his first oratorios during a brief residency in Rome. In the 1730s and 1740s, facing up to the demise of Italian opera in England, he would turn once again to the oratorio in the hope it might prove a cost-effective substitute for opera.

Handel's English oratorios not only succeeded where his operas had failed (on the bottom line), they established the oratorio genre as one of the central interests of English musical life. The salient qualities of his best works—the vivid pictorialism of *Israel in Egypt* (1739), the uplifting grandeur and spirituality of *Messiah* (1742), the majestic pageantry of *Solomon* (1749)—ensured that they would live for each new generation; as time went by, those qualities also inspired emulation by other composers, beginning with Haydn.

***Paul McCartney* (right) *and Carl Davis, creative team behind the* Liverpool Oratorio**

Haydn's oratorios *The Creation* (1796–98) and *The Seasons* (1799–1801) were the splendid late-ripening fruit of his visits to London between 1791 and 1795, when he came into contact with Handel's oratorios and developed a profound admiration for their power and breadth of expression. Both of the Haydn works are based on English librettos; the score to *The Creation* was published as a bilingual edition, with the oratorio's text engraved in German and English under the notes.

Romantic contributions to the literature included works by Liszt, Ferdinand Hiller (1811–85), Joachim Raff (1822–82), and Carl Loewe (1796–1869), as well as Mendelssohn's *Paulus* (*St. Paul*; 1836) and *Elijah* (1846), both influenced by the Handelian model. *Elijah,* composed to a text in English and premiered to vociferous acclaim at the Birmingham Festival, was thereafter performed almost annually in England until about 1930 and remains a staple of the repertoire. On the European continent, the oratorio flourished amid the revival of religious sentiment and the rise of nationalism that occurred in the second half of the 19th century. In England, meanwhile, the popularity of choral festivals such as those of Birmingham and Leeds, and—most important of all—the annual Three Choirs Festival (based alternately in Gloucester, Worcester, and Hereford) led, during the final years of the 19th century, to a new golden age for the oratorio. Dvořák's *St. Ludmilla* received its premiere at Leeds in 1886, but the crowning achievements of this era were the admirably polished settings of British composers John Stainer (1840–1901), Hubert Parry (1848–1918), Charles Villiers Stanford (1852–1924), and, above all, Elgar, whose *The Dream of Gerontius* (1900) ranks as one of the supreme masterpieces of the genre.

In the 20th century, Elgar further enriched the literature with *The Apostles* (1903) and *The Kingdom* (1906). Other important works from the first half of the century include Honegger's *Le roi David* (1923); Frank Martin's *Golgotha* (1945–48); *Das Buch mit sieben Siegeln* (*The Book of the Seven Seals*; 1935–37) by Franz Schmidt (1874–1939), a sweeping vision of the Apocalypse; and Tippett's *A Child of Our Time* (1939–41), based on the event that precipitated the Kristallnacht of 1938—the shooting of a German diplomat by a Jewish teenager, a story taken right from the front page of the newspaper. Tippett also composed one of the most important and successful works of the century's second half, *The Mask of Time* (1980–82), though a countryman of his, Paul McCartney (b. 1942), got far more attention for his pop-flavored *Liverpool Oratorio* (1991).

orchestra A large instrumental ensemble consisting of bowed strings with more than one player to a part, plus various wind, brass, and percussion instruments. The origin of the word is Greek: the *orchestra* was the flat semicircular area meant for dancing in front of the stage of a Greek theater. The concept of the orchestra as a large body of diverse instruments sounding together can be traced back further than that and is memorably preserved in the words of Psalm 150, which calls for the Lord to be praised "with the sound of the trumpet" as well as with the psaltery and harp, with stringed instruments and organs, and upon loud and high-sounding cymbals.

The modern symphony orchestra is of more recent vintage, having developed out of the string consorts and court ensembles of the Renaissance and early Baroque. The most important forerunner of this orchestra was the court "chapel" (in Italian, *cappella*; in German, *Kapell*) maintained by princes and prelates throughout the Middle Ages and Renaissance, which survived well into the 19th century. At first, chapels were nothing more than choirs, since instruments other than the organ were banned from use in church owing to their association with dancing, dining, and other secular pursuits. During the Renaissance, instruments began to appear in court chapels throughout Europe, and as the climate of the times grew more secular, the number of instrumentalists employed at court grew as well, along with the literature for instrumental ensembles. By the beginning of the 18th century the court chapel had in fact become an orchestra, especially in Germany, and the musician in charge of it—known there as KAPELLMEISTER and in Italy as *maestro di cappella*—was likely to be occupied not with church services but with concerts, operas, and chamber performances.

A parallel development occurred in the opera pit during the 17th century, as the accompanying ensemble grew from a miscellany of lutes, viols, violins, and keyboard instruments into a large, homogeneous group with well-defined parts for different members of the violin family (violin, viola, and cello) and for the string bass (a member of the viol family). The term *orchestra* came into standard use around 1700 to identify the sort of body both the court chapel and the opera orchestra had become.

The 18th century saw the establishment of the orchestra as the star of a thriving court and public concert scene. Whether played by the enormous, regally liveried array of the Concert Spirituel in Paris, the virtuoso court bands of Carl Theodor in Mannheim and Munich, or the Collegium Musicum Bach conducted at Zimmermann's coffeehouse in Leipzig, orchestral music

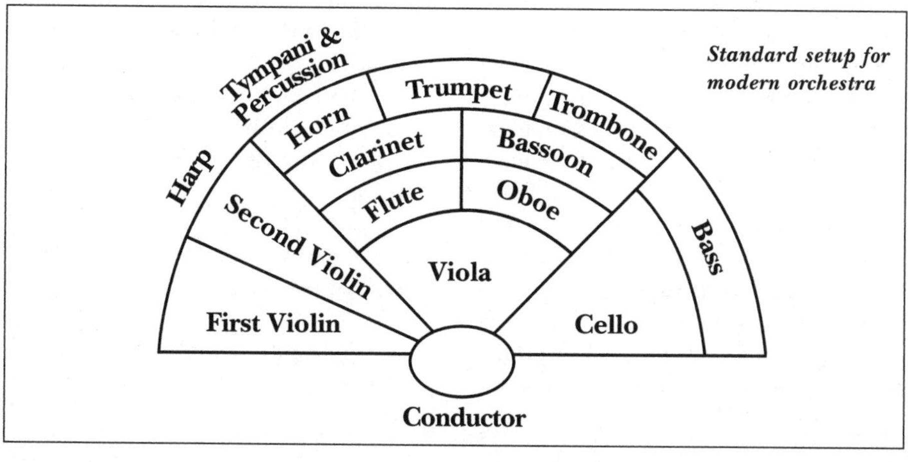

Standard setup for modern orchestra

offered a taste of the magnificent and sublime. For ears unaccustomed to anything louder than hoofbeats and church bells, hearing 50 or 60 instruments playing all at once was a breathtaking experience, beyond comparison with anything in nature or the imagination. Little wonder that composers eagerly sought to exploit the effect.

The orchestra of the 18th century was dominated by the strings, which were usually divided into four groups: first violins, second violins, violas, and basses (consisting of cellos and string basses playing together). The most commonly encountered woodwinds were flutes, oboes, and bassoons; since the same musicians often played both flute and oboe, scores would call for one or the other but rarely both, unless extra players were on hand. In all but the largest ensembles the clarinet was a rarity until the end of the century. Most orchestras had a pair of horns and could muster two trumpets and timpani for festive occasions. Trombones, a familiar presence in the opera house, had to wait until early in the 19th century to gain admission to the symphony orchestra.

The orchestra doubled in size during the Romantic era, achieving its present disposition of approximately 100 players at the end of the 19th century. As it grew, and as improvements in the construction and tone quality of the wind and brass instruments were made, the volume of its sound increased dramatically, and the balance shifted away from the strings toward the winds and brass. Instead of woodwinds in pairs, one could expect to find three or four of each variety, along with such auxiliary instruments as piccolo, English horn, bass clarinet, and contrabassoon. A full brass section consisted of as many as eight or ten horns, four trumpets, three trombones, and tuba. In addition to timpani, the percussion section routinely included cymbals, bass drum, and triangle, and on demand could produce such paraphernalia as tam-tam, snare drum, tubular bells, sleighbells, cowbells, glockenspiel, castanets, tambourine, rute, ratchet, and wind machine. Two harps were standard, and a large body of strings—on the order of 18 first and 16 second violins, 14 violas, 12 cellos, and 10 double basses—was essential if the string parts were to be heard at all in the loudest passages.

For a few 19th-century composers, among them Brahms and (surprisingly) Liszt, the orchestra Beethoven had known continued to be sufficient. But for the likes of Berlioz, Bruckner, Mahler, and Richard Strauss, dramatic effects and emotionally charged expression were de rigueur. Berlioz, for example, specified an apocalyptically huge orchestra in his *Grand messe des morts,* insisting on, among other things, eight sets of timpani played by ten timpanists. Strauss, in his opera *Elektra,* was more modest, knowing that only so many musicians would fit into even the largest opera pit; still, his note at the head of the score calls for 109 players.

As the 20th century unfolded, electronic instruments such as the theremin and ondes martenot began to appear in the orchestra (the latter plays a very important part in Messiaen's *Turangalîla-symphonie*), followed at century's end by synthesizers and a new influx of exotic percussion, from wind chimes and water gongs to brake drums and "tubaphones" (large resonators played by plastic clappers the size of tennis rackets). Even so, the regular disposition of the orchestra at the beginning of the 21st century remains essentially what it was at the end of the 19th. *See also box on pages 496–97.*

Orchestra of the Age of Enlightenment
See box on pages 310–13.

ordre (Fr.) A SUITE, almost always for a keyboard instrument such as the harpsichord.

The term was originally used by François Couperin and his contemporaries to refer to a group of pieces in the same key.

Orfeo, L' **OPERA IN A PROLOGUE AND FIVE ACTS BY CLAUDIO MONTEVERDI,** to a libretto by Alessandro Striggio (modeled on Ottavio Rinuccini's *Euridice* of 1600). Composed for carnival festivities at the court at Mantua, it was first presented on February 24, 1607, in a performance at the ducal palace sponsored by Francesco Gonzaga, eldest son of the Duke of Mantua. Described by Monteverdi as a "favola in musica" ("musical fable"), it tells the familiar story of Orpheus and Eurydice.

In the grand symmetry and cohesion of its design, the strength of its characterization, and above all the eloquence of its music, *L'Orfeo* marks a watershed in the development of opera, surpassing the achievement of the Florentine Camerata in a way that must have struck contemporary listeners as miraculous. Monteverdi's dramatic use of the florid solo style of singing—especially in Orfeo's Act III plea to Charon ("Possente spirto," an aria meant to illustrate the power of music, both in the story and to those in the seats)—set a new standard and opened an emotional door through which all later opera composers would have to pass.

RECOMMENDED RECORDINGS

DALE, BEN-NUN, LARMORE, SCHOLL; JACOBS AND CONCERTO VOCALE (HARMONIA MUNDI).

ROLFE JOHNSON, BAIRD, DAWSON, OTTER; GARDINER AND ENGLISH BAROQUE SOLOISTS (ARCHIV).

Orfeo ed Euridice **OPERA IN THREE ACTS BY CHRISTOPH WILLIBALD GLUCK,** to a libretto by Ranieri Calzabigi, premiered October 5, 1762, at the Burgtheater in Vienna. It was the first of the "reform" operas Gluck composed in collaboration with Calzabigi, in which plot and music were meant to proceed with a "noble simplicity," as a corrective to the ornate poetry and musical style of opera seria. In 1774, Gluck produced a French version of the opera (*Orphée et Eurydice*) for Paris, enlarging the score, revising the orchestration, and changing Orpheus from a castrato role to one for *haute-contre,* high tenor. Both versions of the opera were notably successful, Gluck's dignified music proving well suited to the mythic action. The most familiar passage is the "Dance of the Blessed Spirits" from Act II (of the French version), a gentle minuet in which strings and a pair of flutes evoke the pastoral bliss of the Elysian Fields.

RECOMMENDED RECORDING

RAGIN, MCNAIR, SIEDEN; GARDINER AND ENGLISH BAROQUE SOLOISTS (PHILIPS).

Orff, Carl

(b. Munich, July 10, 1895; d. Munich, March 29, 1982)

GERMAN COMPOSER. With the exception of yearlong appointments in Mannheim and Darmstadt following the end of World War I, he spent his entire life in and around Munich. He graduated from its Academy of Music in 1914, and made his living teaching in the city during the 1920s. Conscious from early in his career of the roots music has in dance, and deeply attuned to the sheer physicality of sound, by 1930 he had developed an idiom that exulted in the repetition of simple rhythmic patterns and short melodic cells. These traits are readily apparent in the three cantatas he wrote that year, on texts by Franz Werfel, for mixed chorus, pianos, and percussion, as well as in *Schulwerk,* a collection of teaching pieces begun in 1930 and further extended in the 1950s.

All that remained was to put a full orchestra to work in the idiom and expand the scale of the endeavor by turning a series of vignettes into an epic cycle. This

Carl Orff, composer of **Carmina Burana**

Orff accomplished in 1936 with CARMINA BURANA, the work that defined him as a composer. There are echoes of PLAINCHANT in the declamatory, incantatory way in which some of the texts are set, and the conception admittedly owes much to Stravinsky's *Les noces* and *Oedipus rex*, ceremonial works in which a ritualistic repetition of rhythmic patterns was pioneered. While Orff's treatment appears less sophisticated and more procedural than Stravinsky's—a quality that places him among the many grandfathers of modern minimalism—it nonetheless produced an explosive effect. *Carmina Burana* has become an iconic work, receiving countless performances, its distinctive sound an emblem of power mimicked in a thousand commercials.

Had it not been for *Carmina Burana,* Orff might have been better known for scores such as *Der Mond* (*The Moon*; 1939) and *Die Kluge* (*The Clever One*; 1943), two parable-operas based on fairy tales by the brothers Grimm, or for the trilogy of *Antigone* (1949), *Oedipus der Tyrann* (1959), and *Prometheus desmotes* (1968) inspired by tragedies of Sophocles and Aeschylus—in short, as one of the more interesting stage composers of the 20th century. On the other hand, were it not for *Carmina Burana,* these works might not be known at all outside the confines of German musicology. They might appear as mere footnotes in the biography of Carl Orff, the music educator who dabbled in opera. For in spite of the success of *Carmina Burana,* Orff probably had a greater impact on the music of the 20th century as an educator than as a composer. His method, based on the concept that music should be taught in connection with physical movement, won acceptance throughout the world; of his contemporaries, only Zoltán Kodály had a comparable pedagogical influence.

On the compositional front, Orff made no effort to escape the pull of *Carmina Burana.* He even wrote two sequels—*Catulli carmina* (*Songs of Catullus*; 1943) and *Trionfo di Afrodite* (*The Triumph of Aphrodite*; 1953), based on the poetry of Catullus and others—which he eventually appended to *Carmina Burana* to create a "theatrical triptych" called *Trionfi.* What is paradoxical is that this remarkably original composer had so little interest in originality. He put it best when he likened himself to "a relay runner who lights his torch from the fires of the past and brings it into the present."

RECOMMENDED RECORDINGS

CARMINA BURANA: FISCHER-DIESKAU, STOLZE, JANOWITZ; JOCHUM AND DEUTSCHE OPER BERLIN (DG).

CARMINA BURANA: KUEBLER, KEENLYSIDE, OELZE; THIELEMANN AND DEUTSCHE OPER BERLIN (DG).

CATULLI CARMINA, TRIONFO DI AFRODITE: SCHELLENBERGER, CHANCE, HENDRICKS; WELSER-MÖST AND MUNICH RADIO SYMPHONY ORCHESTRA (EMI).

organ INSTRUMENT OF ANCIENT ORIGIN, consisting of a keyboard, wind supply, and pipes tuned to different pitches, along with a mechanism linking the keyboard to shunts that direct air from the wind supply to specific pipes, allowing them to sound. Ctesibius of Alexandria, an engineer of the third century B.C., is credited with the invention of the earliest known pipe organ, the *hydraulos,* in which water pressure was used to regulate the flow of air to the pipes. Instruments of this type were difficult to construct and maintain, and later designs utilized bellows compressed by the weight of men or boys standing on or pumping them. During the early Middle Ages, Constantinople became a center of organ building; in 757, at the request of Pepin the Short (the father of Charlemagne), Constantine VI, the Byzantine emperor, sent a large organ to France, along with an assembly crew and an organist trained in Constantinople. This was the first documented organ in Western Europe. Charlemagne received a second instrument, fitted with bronze pipes and leather bellows, at Aachen in 812. Around 900, organs began to come into use in churches. The "keys" on early medieval organs were really levers and were most likely hand-operated, but by the end of the 13th century an arrangement resembling the modern keyboard, with broad finger-operated keys, had been introduced.

During the 14th and 15th centuries the art of organ building advanced gradually on many fronts, the general trend being toward larger instruments with greater numbers of pipes and an increasing variety of stops (ranks of pipes that have a specific sonic character or timbre). By 1500, a typical large northern European organ had two or three manuals (keyboards), as many as 15 different stops, a pedalboard capable of engaging several stops, and between 750 and 1,000 pipes. Innovation accelerated during the early years of the 16th century: new stops imitating the sounds of various flutes, brass, and reed instruments were added, and the organ's palette was further enriched by the increasingly common deployment of mixtures (stops combining two or more ranks of pipes that "harmonize" above a given note, usually by reinforcing the octave, fifth, or third, sometimes by highlighting one of the weaker overtones). The process of aggrandizement and refinement (both mechanical and tonal) continued through the 17th century, on a trajectory that reached its apogee in the works of the German Baroque builders Arp Schnitger (1648–1719) and Andreas (1678–1734) and Gottfried (1683–1753) Silbermann. The younger Silbermann's instruments in particular synthesized the best of the French and German traditions; magnificent achievements, they possessed the power, clarity, and brilliance to delineate the polyphonic textures of two distinctively complex forms of the era, the passacaglia and the fugue. Subsequent 18th-century builders were able to match the power of the best early-18th-century organs, but not always their "rationality," their balance, and the beauty of their sound.

The next major developments in organ design and construction came via the efforts of the French builder Aristide Cavaillé-Coll (1811–99). After winning the competition to build the new organ for the basilica of St. Denis in Paris in 1833, the young Cavaillé-Coll made the first practical use of

a pneumatic assist that overcame the hardness of touch common on large organs. This important change in the instrument's action led to the development of the so-called "symphonic style" organs of the later part of the century. Cavaillé-Coll went on to build many fine instruments in Paris, including those at Notre Dame, St. Sulpice, and St. Clothilde, as well as organs in Sheffield and at the Royal Albert Hall in London.

By the beginning of the 20th century, the electrification of mechanical parts of the organ led to the creation of instruments of monstrous power and size that found homes outside the church. The innovative builders who developed the modern theater organ included Henry Willis, Robert Hope-Jones, and the American Ernest M. Skinner. At the other end of the spectrum from these behemoths, as a response to the 20th-century revival of Baroque performance practice, interest focused on rediscovering the secrets of the pipework and mechanics of 17th- and 18th-century organs. Brilliant, clear, and versatile instruments have been produced along these lines by the firms of C. B. Fisk, Walter Holtkamp, and G. Donald Harrison of the United States, by Walcker, Steinmeyer, Klais, and Kemper in Germany, by the Dutch firm of Flentrop, and by Marcussen and Frobenius in Denmark.

The organ was originally regarded as a foundation instrument, its main purpose to support voices or accompany other instruments during church services. As the practice of preluding grew more popular, the solo capabilities of the organ captured the interest of many of the great keyboard composers of the 16th and 17th centuries—John Bull (ca. 1562–1628), Sweelinck, Louis Couperin (1626–61), Pachelbel, Frescobaldi, Louis-Claude Daquin (1694–1772), Handel, and J. S. Bach. The greatest master of organ music in the late 17th century was the Danish-born Dietrich Buxtehude, organist at the Marienkirche in Lübeck from 1668 to his death in 1707. He was also the single greatest influence on Bach, whose contributions to the literature (among them the Passacaglia and Fugue in C minor) are unsurpassed. With the emergence of the *galant* style, the organ lost favor with composers. Mozart wrote a small number of church sonatas calling for organ accompaniment, and a handful of pieces for "mechanical" organ; Beethoven wrote nothing for the instrument. The next composer of importance to the repertoire was Mendelssohn, a fine organist whose most significant contributions were his Six Sonatas, Op. 65, and Three Preludes and Fugues, Op. 37. Brahms penned the Fugue in A-flat minor (1856) and a set of 11 chorale preludes (1896), while Liszt made numerous arrangements for organ of pieces by other composers, and composed some impressive original works. Other notable contributions from German Romantic composers were made by Julius Reubke (1834–58), Joseph Reinberger (1839–1901), and Reger, who wrote many highly chromatic and densely textured works.

During the second half of the 19th century, some of France's best composers found positions (and a measure of financial security) as organists in Parisian churches. At the Church of la Madeleine, Camille Saint-Saëns presided over the organ from 1857 to 1877, followed by Théodore Dubois (1837–1924) and Gabriel Fauré; at St. Clothilde, César Franck was the incumbent from 1858 until his death in 1890; at St. Jean-St. François, Léo Delibes from 1861 until 1872; and at St. Sulpice, Charles-Marie Widor (1844–1937) played from 1870 until 1934, an astonishing tenure of 64 years. The chief successors to this generation included Maurice Duruflé, Jehan Alain (1911–40), and Olivier Messiaen, who was appointed organist at La Trinité in 1930 and continued to play there until shortly before his death in 1992. Of all the brilliant creations by the French organist-composers of the 19th and 20th centuries—whose number also includes Alexandre Guilmant (1837–1911), Louis Vierne (1870–1937), Marcel Dupré (1886–1971), and Jean Roger-Ducasse (1873–1954)—the works of Franck, Widor, Messiaen, and Alain are the most significant.

As the 21st century begins, innovations to the organ are still being made, the most significant and controversial of which is the incorporation of electronically produced tones. While synthesized sound is embraced by many, champions of authentic performance practice favor historically faithful sound and construction. Above all, organs continue to evolve in response to the specific needs and limitations of their venues.

***Organ* Symphony** NICKNAME OF SYMPHONY NO. 3 IN C MINOR BY CAMILLE SAINT-SAËNS, completed in 1886. Conceived on the grandest scale, and clearly influenced by the innovative compositional techniques of Liszt (to whose memory the score is dedicated), it is called the *Organ* Symphony because of the important role that instrument plays in the work—not as a solo instrument, but as a complement to the orchestra.

Within the symphony's unorthodox two-part layout can be found the conventional division of material into four movements: the first part consists of an Allegro prefaced by a brief slow introduction, followed by a Poco adagio (the equivalent of a typical slow movement), while the second part combines a scherzo and a Presto finale. A striking feature of the music is the degree to which Saint-Saëns makes use of the process of thematic transformation, a technique developed by Berlioz and Liszt in which a thematic cell from one movement is modified to produce a new theme in a subsequent one. There are two motto themes in the *Organ* Symphony. One is an ascending four-note motive first heard in the slow introduction, voiced by the oboe over a plaintive harmonization in the strings; it later appears in expanded form as the consoling theme of the Adagio and as the grand, chorale-like subject of the finale. The other appears initially in the guise of an accompaniment, a scurrying, sixteenth-note line in the violins that launches the Allegro portion of the first movement. It reappears in altered form at many points in the score—in two different transformations within the Adagio, as both the opening and a subsequent theme in the scherzo, and as a subsidiary theme in the finale.

The structural unity achieved in this fashion offsets the remarkable boldness and variety of Saint-Saëns's orchestral palette, and further serves to integrate the organ into the overall scheme of the work. The organ's majestic full voice is saved for the final portion of the symphony, where it sounds triumphant chords amid a bracing proclamation of the first motto theme by the orchestra. But its most beautiful moment comes at the beginning of the Adagio, where its pedal tones support a hushed, beautifully lyrical treatment of the same subject in the strings.

organum (Lat., from Gr. *organon,* "instrument," "tool," "organ") A "vertical" elaboration of PLAINCHANT in which additional vocal lines at one or two different pitch levels (usually above, sometimes below) move at the same pace as the line of chant and in a fashion more or less parallel to it; hence, it is a form of troping (or "following") of the chant. Early organum, from about A.D. 700 to 900, was expected to produce consonance according to strict rules handed down from Pythagorean theory. As time went by, organum became increasingly free in its allowance of passing dissonance, so that by 1050 or 1100 there was no longer much use for the strict form. Pérotin's four-voice setting of *Viderunt omnes* is an example of the freer style that flourished at Notre Dame in Paris during the 12th century.

By establishing an orderly scheme for the sounding of two or more consonant pitches simultaneously, organum provided the conceptual breakthrough necessary for the development of true POLYPHONY. With organum, music acquired a new dimension, in which the interaction of separate strands of sound allowed musicians to create harmony and a novel sense of space and musical structure.

Ormandy, Eugene [Blau, Jenő]

(b. Budapest, November 18, 1899; d. Philadelphia, March 12, 1985)

HUNGARIAN/AMERICAN CONDUCTOR. He studied violin at the National Hungarian Royal Academy of Music in Budapest with Jenő Hubay, graduating at the age of 14 and becoming a professor at 17. He came to the United States in 1921 on a concert tour that fizzled; he stayed to work in movie theaters, later radio. He quickly rose through the ranks to become concertmaster of the orchestra of the Capitol Theater in New York, where he made his conducting debut in 1924. In 1927 he became an American citizen, and in 1930 he was engaged by the Philadelphia Orchestra for its summer concerts at the Robin Hood Dell. He made his regular season debut with the Philadelphia Orchestra on October 30, 1931, substituting for an indisposed Arturo Toscanini. He was subsequently engaged as music director of the Minneapolis Symphony Orchestra (1931–36), where he became widely known for his pioneering recordings, including the first ever of Kodály's *Háry János* Suite and, in 1934, the first electrical recording of Mahler's Symphony No. 2 (*Resurrection*). Recalled to Philadelphia, he shared the podium with Leopold Stokowski for two years (1936–37), and served as sole music director for 42 years after that (1938–80), the longest such tenure in American history. By the time he stepped down, there was no one left in the orchestra who predated him: He had auditioned every one of his players. With the Philadelphians, Ormandy made nearly 400 long-playing records, a staggering discographic achievement.

Eugene Ormandy, molding the Philadelphia sound

Ormandy was among the 20th century's most capable and wide-ranging conductors. His strengths were Rachmaninov, Tchaikovsky, Sibelius, Brahms, and Shostakovich, but his repertoire was huge. He championed American composers such as Harris, Hanson, Paul Creston (1906–85), and Vincent Persichetti (1915–87), and boldly programmed new music, even thorny pieces like Penderecki's *Threnody to the Victims of Hiroshima* (1960). During his long career he conducted the premieres of Bartók's Third Piano Concerto, Barber's Violin Concerto, Webern's *Three Pieces for Orchestra,* and Rachmaninov's *Symphonic*

Dances, as well as the U.S. premieres of Britten's *A Young Person's Guide to the Orchestra* and Shostakovich's Cello Concerto No. 1 and Symphonies Nos. 4, 13, 14, and 15.

Standing only five feet, four inches, he walked with a limp, the result of a boyhood soccer injury, and was rarely given to podium acrobatics. He had a compact beat, somewhat stiff but clear. He was all business in rehearsal and performance, a thorough, meticulous craftsman with the sharpest of ears. As an interpreter, what he may have lacked in excitability and imagination he made up for in attention to detail and sonority, and his best performances were almost always characterized by fierce concentration and a passionate if chaste engagement with the music. He did nothing to deserve the neglect his recordings have suffered since his death, except to make music the old-fashioned way: faithfully, with one orchestra at a time.

RECOMMENDED RECORDINGS

RACHMANINOV, PIANO CONCERTOS NOS. 2 AND 3: RACHMANINOV; PHILADELPHIA ORCHESTRA (NAXOS).

SHOSTAKOVICH, CELLO CONCERTO NO. 1: ROSTROPOVICH; PHILADELPHIA ORCHESTRA (SONY).

SHOSTAKOVICH, SYMPHONY NO. 15: PHILADELPHIA ORCHESTRA (RCA).

SIBELIUS, *FOUR LEGENDS*: PHILADELPHIA ORCHESTRA (EMI).

SIBELIUS, SYMPHONY NO. 1: PHILADELPHIA ORCHESTRA (SONY).

STRAUSS, *DON QUIXOTE*: MUNROE, COOLEY; PHILADELPHIA ORCHESTRA (SONY).

TCHAIKOVSKY, *SWAN LAKE* (EXCERPTS): PHILADELPHIA ORCHESTRA (SONY).

TCHAIKOVSKY, SYMPHONY NO. 4: PHILADELPHIA ORCHESTRA (SONY).

ornaments In vocal and instrumental music, embellishments that are applied by the performer to a particular note—either by convention or at the direction of the composer—to draw attention to that note. If executed in a tasteful manner, they serve to heighten the expressive effect, display virtuosity, vary repetition, or otherwise enhance the listener's experience. Ornaments are often indicated in the score by means of signs and symbols, and they may also be improvised according to custom or whim. Among the more commonly encountered ornaments are the TRILL, APPOGGIATURA, GRACE NOTE, TURN, and MORDENT. At various times vibrato has also been considered an ornament. *See also* AGRÉMENTS.

ostinato (It. "obstinate") A short melodic or rhythmic figure repeated persistently throughout a passage or a whole composition; when such a figure serves as the bass, it is called a *basso ostinato. See also* CHACONNE.

Otello **OPERA IN FOUR ACTS BY GIUSEPPE VERDI,** to a libretto by Arrigo Boito based on William Shakespeare's *Othello,* premiered February 5, 1887, at La Scala in Milan. Shakespeare's story of the jealous Moor, brilliantly adapted by Boito, elicited Verdi's most powerful score. From its explosive opening storm scene to the frenzied finale in Desdemona's bedroom, the opera is a masterpiece of continuous development that encompasses traditional scenic and formal elements in an unbroken musical outpouring of overwhelming cumulative effect.

Verdi's portrayal of the central characters is gripping. From the moment he appears, Otello is a stunning presence (his opening "Esultate!" is one of the most commanding entrances in opera), a figure whose music freezes one in fear every time he turns to threaten Desdemona or Iago. Yet the Act I duet of Otello and Desdemona, "Già nella notte densa," contains some of the most gorgeous love music in Italian opera, suffused with a tender passion that mounts like a giant wave. Desdemona is deeply sympathetic, with a touching vulnerability, while the villainous Iago is given huge stature by Verdi's music, most notably in his "Credo in un Dio crudel" and the Act II oath swearing with Otello ("Sì, pel ciel"), a carryover from the friendship duets of bel canto opera that becomes ironically twisted when Iago, no longer the subordinate, takes the lead.

The first performance of *Otello* brought one of the greatest triumphs in Verdi's career. The evening's handpicked cast included Francesco Tamagno as Otello, Romilda Pantaleoni as Desdemona, and Victor Maurel as Iago, all of whom Verdi had carefully coached in their roles. When, at opera's end, the applause began, the 73-year-old composer and his librettist were obliged to take some 20 curtain calls.

RECOMMENDED RECORDINGS

Del Monaco, Tebaldi, Protti; Karajan and Vienna Philharmonic (Decca).

Domingo, Milnes, Scotto; Levine and National Philharmonic (RCA).

Otter, Anne Sofie von

(b. Stockholm, May 9, 1955)

SWEDISH MEZZO-SOPRANO. Born into the family of a high-ranking Swedish diplomat, she studied in Stockholm and at the Guildhall School of Music in London. Her first professional engagement was with the Basel Opera. She made her Covent Garden debut in 1985 and her Metropolitan Opera debut in 1988, both times appearing as Cherubino in Mozart's *Le nozze di Figaro.* She has distinguished herself on stage and in recordings in a wide range of operatic parts, from Purcell's Dido to Baba the Turk in Stravinsky's *The Rake's Progress,* but with special emphasis on works of the 18th century. Particularly noted for her recordings of Handel, Gluck, and Mozart, she is also a fine lieder artist with a repertoire that includes the songs of Schubert, Schumann, Brahms, Grieg, Sibelius, Korngold, and Zemlinsky.

Swedish mezzo Anne Sofie von Otter

RECOMMENDED RECORDINGS

Gluck, *Iphigénie en Aulide*: Van Dam, Dawson, Aler; Gardiner and Lyon Opera Orchestra (Erato).

Monteverdi, *Orfeo*: Rolfe Johnson, Baird, Dawson, Argenta; Gardiner and English Baroque Soloists (Archiv).

Mozart, *Così fan tutte*: Fleming, Lopardo, Bär; Solti and Chamber Orchestra of Europe (Decca).

Sibelius, songs: Forsberg (BIS).

Stravinsky, *The Rake's Progress*: Bostridge, York, Terfel; Gardiner and London Symphony Orchestra (DG).

overture [1] An orchestral movement that serves to introduce a staged musical work such as an opera or ballet or an oratorio. [2] A freestanding orchestral work in a single movement, often with a title suggesting some literary or pictorial association, or alluding to a specific occasion (e.g., Beethoven's *Consecration of the House* Overture). [3] In Baroque music, a suite for orchestra, so designated because such suites typically began with a movement in the style of a French overture.

Ozawa, Seiji

(b. Fenytien [now Shenyang], China, September 1, 1935)

JAPANESE CONDUCTOR. He graduated from Tokyo's Tōhō School of Music, where he was a student of Hideo Saito, with first prizes in composition and conducting. In 1959 he won first prize

Seiji Ozawa conducting at Tanglewood, 1997

at the International Competition of Orchestral Conductors in Besançon, and came under the wing of Charles Munch. Successive mentors included Herbert von Karajan and Leonard Bernstein, who appointed him assistant conductor of the New York Philharmonic for the 1961–62 season. After making his American debut in San Francisco in 1962, he quickly joined the guest-conducting circuit of the world's top orchestras. He served as music director of the Chicago Symphony Orchestra's Ravinia Festival for five years beginning in 1964, and held music directorships in Toronto (1965–69) and San Francisco (1970–76) prior to being named music director of the Boston Symphony in 1973. During his many years in Boston—his departure at the end of the 2001–02 season was long overdue—he continued to conduct in Europe, appearing with the Philharmonics of Berlin and Vienna and the Orchestre de Paris, among others, and making occasional but generally successsful forays into the opera pit. In 1994 the Boston Symphony named its new 1,180-seat concert hall at Tanglewood the Seiji Ozawa Hall in his honor. Ozawa became music director of the Vienna Staatsoper in 2002.

A master of technique, possessing a choreographic flamboyance and control of gesture that are second to none, Ozawa has always been impressive in the coloristic, virtuoso repertoire of the late 19th and early 20th centuries. His insights into the standard repertoire, at least that part of it he prefers to conduct—Beethoven, Brahms, and Mahler—while not particularly profound, have deepened with experience, and he has established himself as a major champion of mid- and late-20th-century composers such as Sessions, Lutosławski, Davies, and Messiaen, whose opera *Saint François d'Assise* (1983) he conducted in its world premiere.

At his best, Ozawa is a conductor who combines athletic grace with an extraordinary mental and musical aptitude. Too often, though, he seems to know scores from the outside in, rather than the inside out, communicating their every detail but not their emotional meaning. His respect for authority (Bernstein for Mahler and Karajan for Bruckner), while admirably Japanese, has had the unfortunate effect of sometimes turning him into a mere technician.

RECOMMENDED RECORDINGS

BERG, VIOLIN CONCERTO; STRAVINSKY, VIOLIN CONCERTO: PERLMAN; BOSTON SYMPHONY ORCHESTRA (DG).

FAURÉ, *DOLLY SUITE*, *PELLÉAS ET MÉLISANDE* (INCIDENTAL MUSIC): BOSTON SYMPHONY ORCHESTRA (DG).

LISZT, PIANO CONCERTOS NOS. 1 AND 2: ZIMERMAN, BOSTON SYMPHONY ORCHESTRA (DG).

MESSIAEN, *TURANGALÎLA-SYMPHONIE*: Y. LORIOD, J. LORIOD; TORONTO SYMPHONY ORCHESTRA (RCA).

P Q

Pachelbel, Johann

(b. Nuremberg, September 1, 1653; d. Nuremberg, March 9, 1706)

GERMAN COMPOSER AND ORGANIST. He was one of the most important figures in German music of the generation before Bach, but is known today almost exclusively for a single piece—actually, half a piece—his Canon in D, originally for three violins and continuo. Were it not for this one composition, his fame might never have spread beyond musicological circles, despite his important contributions to the Baroque organ repertoire and to Protestant liturgical music in particular. An outstanding student with broad intellectual horizons, he received the bulk of his musical education in Regensburg and Vienna, where he was exposed to the work of leading Catholic composers of southern Germany and Italy. He was a celebrated church organist and held several important positions during his career, beginning with a post as deputy at St. Stephen's in Vienna (1673–77), and culminating in his appointment in 1695 as organist at the cathedral of St. Sebaldus in his native Nuremberg, a title he held until the end of his life.

Pachelbel composed a sizable amount of music for the organ, for both liturgical and nonliturgical use, as well as keyboard suites, German and Latin motets, and more than a dozen settings of the Magnificat. While he was capable of composing in the most rigorous contrapuntal styles, he preferred a more direct, uncomplicated manner. His Canon in D ◉, one of the few chamber pieces ascribed to him, shows this style to good effect. Although called a canon, it is also a CHACONNE—a series of embellishments on a repeating melodic line in the bass.

RECOMMENDED RECORDINGS

"BAROQUE COLLECTION" (CANON AND GIGUE, WITH WORKS BY HANDEL, VIVALDI, BACH, AND OTHERS): VARIOUS SOLOISTS (EMI).

CHAMBER WORKS, INCLUDING CANON AND GIGUE: MANZE, SEIFERT, EGARR AND LONDON BAROQUE (HARMONIA MUNDI).

Pacific 231 ORCHESTRAL WORK BY ARTHUR HONEGGER, completed in 1923, the first of his three *Mouvements symphoniques.* It received its premiere May 8, 1924, in Paris, under the baton of Serge Koussevitzky. The title refers to the locomotive used in the 1920s and 1930s by the Compagnie du Nord to haul wagon-lit carriages from Le Havre, where Honegger was born, to Paris.

A Pacific 231 in the livery of the Compagnie du Nord

The music portrays the brawny 100-ton steam engine heaving itself from a standstill to high speed, then rapidly screeching to a halt; in the words of Harry Halbreich, the composer's biographer, *Pacific 231* is one of Honegger's "most original, radical, and carefully constructed works." The play of rhythms is intricate and exhilarating throughout the piece, which Honegger himself likened to a chorale prelude.

RECOMMENDED RECORDINGS

BERNSTEIN AND NEW YORK PHILHARMONIC (SONY).

ZINMAN AND TONHALLE-ORCHESTER ZURICH (DECCA).

Other works named for trains, planes, and wheeled vehicles: Alkan's *Le chemin de fer* (1844); Villa-Lobos's *The Little Train of the Caipira* (Bachianas Brasileiras No. 2); Martinů's *Thunderbolt P-47* (honoring the World War II American fighter-bomber built by Republic Aviation); Walton's *Spitfire Prelude and Fugue*; *Adventures in a Perambulator* by John Alden Carpenter (1876–1951); Adams's *Short Ride in a Fast Machine*; *Motown Metal* by Michael Daugherty.

Paderewski, Ignacy Jan

(b. Kuryłówka, November 18, 1860; d. New York, June 29, 1941)

POLISH PIANIST, COMPOSER, AND STATESMAN. Paderewski's serious studies began in 1872 at the Warsaw Conservatory. He complained that due to the new curriculum, he was compelled to spend too much time practicing secondary instruments and not allowed to concentrate sufficiently on the piano. Nevertheless, he received his diploma in 1878 and was appointed to the faculty shortly thereafter. He pursued further study in theory and composition in Berlin in 1881, and in 1884 went to Vienna to study with Theodor Leschetizky, the greatest piano teacher of the day. The lessons were a revelation to Paderewski, and he became obsessed with the idea of a career as a virtuoso. Because of Paderewski's late start (he was then 24), he lacked both repertoire and a virtuoso technique, and Leschetizky was less than sanguine about his chances. The young Pole's industry and determination paid off, however, and if Paderewski was not the best student Leschetizky ever taught, he certainly became his most famous. Paderewski's Paris debut in 1888 was a huge success, prompting concerto engagements with both Edouard Colonne and Charles Lamoureux, the two major conductors at the time. Since he had only one concerto in his repertoire, he quickly finished one he had begun composing in 1882, his Concerto in A minor, Op. 17; it remains the best of the "overlooked" Romantic concertos. From this point, Paderewski's career unfolded as a series of triumphs—London in 1890 and Carnegie Hall in New York in 1891, which launched an American tour of 117 concerts, the first of many grueling slogs through the provinces. He was an indefatigable touring artist, and he became one of the greatest box-office stars in the history of the piano, a cult figure par excellence. By 1910, after two decades of heavy touring, his playing had lost much of its finish and he was getting by on personality and willpower alone. His stage presence could carry the day—he was the perfect embodiment of the soulful poet-pianist, with a leonine mane of wavy hair and breathtakingly dignified bearing, and even his detractors had to concede that his playing had both imagination and an emotional depth that came through in spite of his less than perfect technique. His

Polish patriot and pianist Ignacy Jan Paderewski

recordings, made after 1911, do him little justice.

As a composer Paderewski was equally industrious. His opera *Manru* was produced in Dresden in 1901 and at the Metropolitan Opera in 1902, with subsequent productions in Philadelphia, Boston, Pittsburgh, Chicago, and Baltimore. In 1903 he wrote a piano sonata, a set of piano variations, and 12 songs, and in 1907–08 he completed his loose-jointed Symphony in B minor, Op. 24, a programmatic work of epic proportions describing the history and fate of Poland. It received its premiere with the Boston Symphony Orchestra, and was then played in Paris, London, and Warsaw.

Paderewski's energy and intellect found further expression in the humanitarian and diplomatic arenas. He was an ardent patriot and a brilliant orator, and spoke frequently in support of Polish independence and various charitable causes. In 1919 he became, for one year, the prime minister of Poland, and in that role was a signatory to the Treaty of Versailles. Though his pianistic powers had greatly diminished, his popularity endured, and in 1922 he returned to the concert stage. For the next two decades he continued to perform, giving away much of what he earned to philanthropic causes. He was in New York when Poland fell to the Nazis in 1939, and he died there while his country was still under occupation. Despite the fact that he can be considered in many ways a failure as performer, composer, *and* statesman, Paderewski remains an iconic figure in the history of music, and for Poles an enduring symbol of the artist as hero.

RECOMMENDED RECORDINGS

Polish Fantasia, Concerto for Piano and Orchestra: Hobson; Maksymiuk and Sinfonia Varsovia (Zephyr).

Polish Fantasia, Concerto for Piano and Orchestra, overture: Fialkowska; Wit and Polish National Symphony Orchestra (Naxos).

Paganini, Niccolò

(b. Genoa, October 27, 1782; d. Nice, May 27, 1840)

ITALIAN VIOLINIST AND COMPOSER. He was the first Romantic virtuoso, a man whose larger-than-life talents and personality sparked the imagination of his contemporaries, inspired adulation and imitation, and changed forever the public's notion of what musical performance was about.

He learned to play the violin, mandolin, and guitar as a youth, and by the age of 18 had already attracted attention for his sensational if unorthodox playing. He spent 1801–09 in Lucca, where he played for a time in the court orchestra and wrote his first important work for violin and orchestra, a theme-and-variations piece titled *Napoléon*. From 1810 to 1827 he toured the length and breadth of Italy, appearing in concerts and recitals and creating a repertoire for himself with the composition of his first three violin concertos and three sets of variations on tunes by his friend Rossini. He spent 1828–34 performing throughout Austria, Germany, France, and England. Around 1832 he shifted his attention for a time to concertizing on the viola, and in an effort to commission a blockbuster, approached Hector Berlioz for a concerto. Although he rejected the proffered

Niccolò Paganini, by Ingres

work, *Harold en Italie,* as unsuitable, and never played it, he later rewarded the French composer with a check for 20,000 francs.

Among the techniques Paganini either coined or advanced were the use of double harmonics, left-hand PIZZICATO, and ricochet bowing. His favorite instrument was a 1742 Guarneri del Gesù nicknamed "Il cannone" for its powerful sound.

Nearly all of Paganini's music was intended for the violin, either as a solo instrument or in chamber music partnerings with other strings and guitar. His 24 Caprices, Op. 1, for unaccompanied violin are still considered the touchstone of the repertoire in terms of sheer technical difficulty; the last of them, in A minor ◉, has had a significant impact on the piano repertoire as well, as the subject of an etude or a set of variations by Schumann, Liszt, Brahms, Rachmaninov, and Lutosławski, among others. With his six concertos for the violin, which are still occasionally encountered on concert programs, Paganini dispensed with the idea of integrating virtuosity and musical substance. In these works, virtuosity *is* the substance.

Much as the painters Jacques-Louis David and Jean-Auguste-Dominique Ingres had been drawn to Napoleon, and glorified him in oils, so Eugène Delacroix, the quintessential Romantic, captured Paganini's intense, brooding charisma in his famous portrait of the violinist in action. Liszt openly modeled his own manner of playing on Paganini's, continuing the revolution his exemplar had begun. Liszt and other composers of the day, confronted with the Italian's technique, were compelled to change the way they wrote for solo instruments, knowing that the public would demand virtuosity, whether it was in good taste or not.

PAGANINI
The 6 Violin Concertos
Die Violinkonzerte · Les Concertos pour violon
Salvatore Accardo
London Philharmonic Orchestra
Charles Dutoit

RECOMMENDED RECORDINGS

"THE BEST OF PAGANINI" (COLLECTION) (NAXOS).

CAPRICES: PERLMAN (EMI).

VIOLIN CONCERTOS (COMPLETE): ACCARDO; DUTOIT AND LONDON PHILHARMONIC (DG).

VIOLIN CONCERTOS NOS. 1 AND 2: KALER; GUNZENHAUSER AND NATIONAL SYMPHONY ORCHESTRA OF POLISH RADIO AND TELEVISION (NAXOS).

Pagliacci **OPERA IN A PROLOGUE AND TWO ACTS BY RUGGERO LEONCAVALLO,** to his own libretto (based on a tabloid crime report), premiered May 21, 1892, at the Teatro Dal Verme in Milan. With Mascagni's *Cavalleria rusticana* it shares the theme of murder committed by a jealous husband. Set in Calabria, *Pagliacci* (Italian for "players") centers around the volatile Canio, chief of the theatrical troupe from which the opera gets its name; it features a play within a play and is musically and dramatically the better of the "Cav and Pag" combo. For most of its length, Canio chafes over suspicions of his wife's infidelity, while Nedda, his wife, is in fact cheating on him with the unfortunate Silvio. The clown Tonio, spurned by Nedda, revenges himself by exposing her adultery. In the end, both Silvio and Nedda catch the point of Canio's dagger. The score to *Pagliacci* reaches impressive heights in the prologue ("Si può?") sung by Tonio, and in Canio's celebrated "Vesti la giubba," which opens the second act. ◉ *Pagliacci* is among the finest embodiments of the VERISMO style in opera.

RECOMMENDED RECORDINGS

CARLYLE, BERGONZI, TADDEI, PANERAI; KARAJAN AND LA SCALA ORCHESTRA (DG).

DOMINGO, MILNES, CABALLÉ, MCDANIEL; SANTI AND LONDON SYMPHONY ORCHESTRA (RCA).

Paine, John Knowles

(b. Portland, Me., January 9, 1839; d. Cambridge, Mass., April 25, 1906)

AMERICAN COMPOSER, ORGANIST, AND TEACHER. Having received his early training in Portland, Paine went to Berlin at 19 to continue his studies at the Hochschule, remaining for three years. The organ was his performance instrument, and during his European sojourn, he also gave piano recitals in England and Germany. He settled in Boston in 1861; in March of that year Harvard hired him to teach to the end of the academic year. His appointment was renewed, and in 1873 he was appointed assistant professor, responsible for courses in harmony and counterpoint. In 1875 he was appointed full professor of music, becoming the first person to hold a chair in music at any American university. From 1862 to 1882 Paine also performed as college organist. In 1869 he was awarded an honorary M.A. from Harvard; that was followed in 1890 by an honorary D. Mus. from Yale.

During his tenure at Harvard, he not only introduced the music of Bach, Beethoven, Schumann, and Brahms to his students, he helped establish music as an area of scholarly endeavor, a concept he brought back from his own studies in Germany, where musicology was becoming a serious academic pursuit. Among his composition students were John Alden Carpenter, Frederick S. Converse, Arthur Foote, Daniel Gregory Mason, and Carl Ruggles. He also taught Olin Downes, Hugo Leichtentritt, and Henry Lee Higginson, the founder of the Boston Symphony.

Paine was a careful and painstaking composer whose works were extremely conservative. Among his larger compositions were his Mass in D, which he performed with the Singakademie in Berlin in 1867; an oratorio, *Saint Peter,* premiered in 1873; two large symphonies written in 1875 and 1879, which were championed by Theodore Thomas; and a cantata, *Song of Promise,* written for the Cincinnati May Festival in 1888. It was as an educator, however, that Paine exerted the greatest influence, legitimizing music in the eyes of the American academic community.

RECOMMENDED RECORDING

SYMPHONIES NOS. 1 AND 2: MEHTA AND NEW YORK PHILHARMONIC (NEW WORLD).

Palestrina, Giovanni Pierluigi da

(b. Palestrina, February 3, 1525; d. Rome, February 2, 1594)

ITALIAN COMPOSER. He was one of the outstanding masters of the second half of the 16th century, a prolific composer of masses and motets whose music demonstrated both a remarkable technical refinement and an uplifting spirituality. He received his training at one of Rome's principal churches, Santa Maria Maggiore, and at 19 began a seven-year tenure as organist at the church of San Agapito in his hometown. He married during that time; there were three children. In 1551 he returned to Rome, where he spent the rest of his life, occupying a succession of positions at prestigious churches: St. Peter's, San Giovanni in Laterano, and Santa Maria Maggiore. Palestrina published his first book of masses in 1554, offering the dedication to Pope Julius III; the following January the pope took the

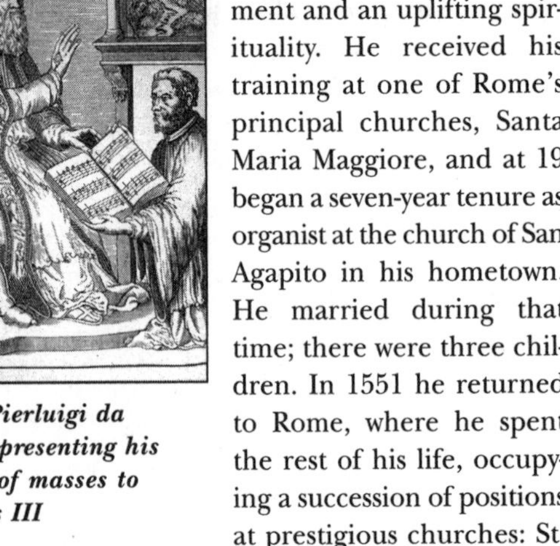

Giovanni Pierluigi da Palestrina presenting his first book of masses to Pope Julius III

unusual step of appointing him to the Sistine Chapel (his personal chapel) even though he was married. Palestrina remained there during the brief three-week reign of Julius's successor, Pope Marcellus II, in April 1555, but was booted out (along with two other married singers) by the newly enthroned Paul IV in September. From then to 1560, Palestrina served as *maestro di cappella* of San Giovanni in Laterano; he subsequently worked at Santa Maria Maggiore (1561–66), served as *maestro di cappella* at the Seminario Romano, and in 1571 returned to St. Peter's, where he remained to the end of his life.

During the 1570s, Palestrina lost his brother and two of his sons to a plague then rampant in Rome. In 1580, after the death of his wife, he considered joining the priesthood, but instead the next year married the well-to-do widow of a Roman fur merchant. For the last 13 years of his life he took a lively interest in the fur business and was well enough off financially to invest in real estate and become something of an entrepreneur.

Palestrina composed, according to the latest count, 104 masses (almost half of which were published during his lifetime), more than 300 motets and smaller church compositions, and more than 140 madrigals (including two books of spiritual madrigals). He also produced four or five settings of the *Lamentations of Jeremiah*, including a splendid set published in 1588, as well as about 70 hymns, 68 offertories, and 35 settings of the Magnificat.

Just as Josquin towered over his time some eight decades earlier, Palestrina stood out as the leading musician of the Counter-Reformation. To a degree, his liturgical settings reflect the directives of the Council of Trent (1545–63), which urged that the music be less intricate and mannered so that the words of the liturgy could be clearly understood. In his mass settings, including his most famous one, the *Missa Papae Marcelli*, written to commemorate the reign of Marcellus II, Palestrina accomplished this without sacrificing beauty of sound. Indeed, by paring back the counterpoint, limiting the amount of dissonance, and imposing his own strict rules on the succession of intervals to assure smoothness of melodic flow and sweetness of harmony—the essence of what would come to be known as "the Palestrina style"—he produced what many regard as the most beautiful sonority ever achieved in vocal music.

RECOMMENDED RECORDINGS

MISSA PAPAE MARCELLI: SUMMERLY AND OXFORD CAMERATA (NAXOS).

"MUSIC FOR MAUNDY THURSDAY" (*LAMENTATIONS OF JEREMIAH*): MUSICA CONTEXTA (CHANDOS).

VARIOUS MASSES (INCLUDING *MISSA PAPAE MARCELLI*): PHILLIPS AND TALLIS SCHOLARS (GIMELL).

Palestrina "MUSICAL LEGEND" IN THREE ACTS BY HANS PFITZNER, to his own libretto, composed 1912–15 and premiered June 12, 1917, at the Prinzregententheater in Munich, conducted by Bruno Walter. Set in Rome and Trent during the autumn of 1563, as the Council of Trent is drawing to a close, the action revolves around the council's debate over whether polyphonic music should be allowed in settings of the liturgy, and on Palestrina's reluctant composition of the *Missa Papae Marcelli* as the demonstration piece whose chaste beauty finally wins the day for the polyphonic camp. The opera's ample cast includes minor functionaries, numerous prelates, a Pope (Pius IV), and the apparitions of nine dead Masters of the Art of Music, one of whom is Josquin. But the principal figure, aside from Palestrina, is Cardinal Borromeo, the composer's ambitious friend and champion who turns on him when he shrinks

***An angelic choir intones the Kyrie, a scene from Pfitzner's* Palestrina**

from the task of composing the mass. In the opera the worthy composer is rescued from his despair when the music of the opening Kyrie comes to him via an angelic choir.

Palestrina represents a fascinating, if fanciful, blending of German Romantic philosophy and antiquarianism with the principles of Wagnerian music drama. Its turgid storyline and labored musical syntax have kept it from enjoying anything more than an occasional revival, but it contains some ineffably beautiful pages, especially in the prelude and the final scene of Act I. Pfitzner is said to have worked so hard on the score that tears of exhaustion fell onto the manuscript and blotted out some of the notes.

RECOMMENDED RECORDINGS

COMPLETE OPERA: GEDDA, FISCHER-DIESKAU, PREY, DONATH; KUBELÍK AND BAVARIAN RADIO SYMPHONY ORCHESTRA (DG).

ORCHESTRAL EXCERPTS: THIELEMANN AND DEUTSCHE OPER BERLIN (DG).

pants role In opera, a male character played by a female singer, usually a mezzo-soprano. Famous pants roles include those of Cherubino in Mozart's *Le nozze di Figaro,* Romeo in Bellini's *I Capuleti e i Montecchi,* Oscar in Verdi's *Un ballo in maschera,* Hänsel in Humperdinck's *Hänsel und Gretel,* Octavian in Richard Strauss's *Der Rosenkavalier,* and the Composer in Strauss's *Ariadne auf Naxos.* Others less frequently encountered are Annio in Mozart's *La clemenza di Tito,* the title role in Rossini's *Tancredi,* Urbain in Meyerbeer's *Les Huguenots,* and the roles of Silla and Ighino in Pfitzner's *Palestrina.*

Paray, Paul

(b. Le Tréport, May 24, 1886; d. Monte Carlo, October 10, 1979)

FRENCH CONDUCTOR AND COMPOSER. He received his early training from his father, an organist and choirmaster. Despite family objections to a musical career, he entered the Paris Conservatoire in 1904, and in 1911 won the Prix de Rome. While serving in the French army during World War I, he was captured at the Marne and spent the rest of the conflict in a prisoner of war camp. In 1920 he was appointed assistant conductor of the Lamoureux Orchestra, and in 1923 became its principal conductor. In 1928 he was named music director of the Monte Carlo Municipal Orchestra (an ensemble with which he made many recordings in later years), and in 1933 he became conductor of the Concerts Colonne. He fled Paris ahead of the German occupation in 1940, eventually finding his way back to Monte Carlo, where he worked for the French Resistance. Paray led the Colonne Orchestra again after the war, and in 1952 he became the music director of the newly revamped Detroit Symphony, a position he held until 1963. These were glory years for Paray and the Detroit Symphony—the recordings they made on the Mercury "Living Presence" label remain landmarks, high-fidelity registrations that document the conductor's breezy style and unique insight with remarkable sonic clarity. Paray conducted with a small, precise beat and great incisiveness, imparting to his accounts a rhythmic edge tempered by his native Gallic elegance. His programs did not venture much beyond the music of Roussel (his own well-crafted, if rather academic, compositions reflect the aesthetic of Chausson and d'Indy), but in French repertoire, his interpretations were engaging and memorable.

RECOMMENDED RECORDINGS

Chabrier, orchestral works: Detroit Symphony Orchestra (Mercury).

Suppé, overtures: Detroit Symphony Orchestra (Mercury).

***Paris* Symphonies** Set of six symphonies (**Nos. 82–87**) by **Joseph Haydn,** composed 1785–86 for the Concert de la Loge Olympique on a commission from the Count d'Ogny. The Loge Olympique was a masonic organization and its orchestra was large and well staffed, with 20 first and 20 second violins and ten double basses; the musicians, among the best in the world, wore fashionable light blue dress coats and played with swords at their sides. For each symphony Haydn received a fee of 25 louis d'or, plus five more for publication rights (by comparison, Mozart had been paid only five louis d'or for his *Paris* Symphony of 1778). It was an especially sweet deal for a composer whose music had long been illicitly performed and published in the French capital.

In their virtuosity and brilliant use of musical imagery, the *Paris* Symphonies mark an important advance in Haydn's style. Symphony No. 83, for example, shows a new sureness of argument and craftsmanship, a new directness in expression, and a melodic generosity that is remarkable even for Haydn. As a group they proved so successful that d'Ogny quickly commissioned an additional set of three works from Haydn, Symphonies Nos. 90–92.

RECOMMENDED RECORDING

Kuijken and Orchestra of the Age of Enlightenment (Virgin Classics).

***Paris* Symphony** Name associated with **Wolfgang Amadeus Mozart's Symphony No. 31 in D, K. 297,** composed for the Concert Spirituel (second only to the Concert des Amateurs among Parisian orchestras of the day) and premiered by it on June 18, 1778. It was the first of Mozart's symphonies to make use of a full wind section, including clarinets, and in concept and execution it was the grandest of his works up to that time, with some very demanding passages for the full ensemble.

One element of the Parisian style was the *premier coup d'archet*—the practice of launching a work with a unison bow stroke in the strings. Mozart obliged, using this feature as a unifying element throughout his symphony's opening movement. His original slow movement bothered the director of the orchestra, who claimed it was too subtle and sophisticated, so Mozart composed a simpler substitute, and, as it was not customary in Paris to have minuets in symphonies, Mozart dispensed with one in this case. But when it came to the finale, he intentionally tweaked the French taste. "As I had heard that all the last Allegros here begin with all the instruments together, usually in unison," he wrote his father, "I began mine with the violins alone, *piano* for the first eight bars—after which came a *forte*. This made the audience, as I expected, say 'Ssh!' at the *piano*. When they heard the *forte* they at once began to clap." The symphony was a huge success, which Mozart celebrated by going "to the Palais Royal, where I had a large ice cream and said a rosary, as I had promised."

RECOMMENDED RECORDINGS

MARRINER AND ACADEMY OF ST. MARTIN-IN-THE-FIELDS (EMI).

WORDSWORTH AND CAPPELLA ISTROPOLITANA (NAXOS).

parlando (It. "speaking") In vocal music, an instruction that a passage should be semi-vocalized, almost as if speaking rather than singing; it is mostly commonly found in operatic scores.

In instrumental music, an instruction indicating that a passage is to be articulated in a manner that is distinct and eloquent, but not lyrical. A good example comes at the end of "Mi chiamano Mimì" in Puccini's *La bohème.*

parody mass A setting of the mass in which the music of a preexisting polyphonic composition—such as a MOTET, a MADRIGAL, or a CHANSON—is recognizably incorporated. The weaving of portions of the entire polyphonic texture of another work into its musical fabric is what distinguishes a parody mass from a CANTUS FIRMUS mass, in which a single voice line (such as a chant melody or a popular tune) serves as the armature around which a free polyphonic treatment is built. During the 16th century, the parody mass, also referred to as "imitation" mass, became the dominant type of mass setting, reaching its zenith in the late works of Josquin and in the masses of Lassus and Palestrina.

Parsifal "STAGE CONSECRATION PLAY" IN THREE ACTS BY RICHARD WAGNER, to his own libretto, first performed July 26, 1882, in the Festspielhaus at Bayreuth. The composer sketched his first thoughts for its libretto in 1857, having read a modern edition of Wolfram von Eschenbach's medieval epic *Parzival* in 1845. He fashioned a working draft of the libretto in the spring of 1877, and composed the music between September 1877 and April 1879. The full orchestral score was completed December 25, 1881, after two and a half years of work. Wagner envisioned *Parsifal* as a ceremonial work to consecrate the theater he had built at Bayreuth in the 1870s. Following his death in 1883, a 30-year moratorium was placed on staged performances outside Bayreuth, which, with a few notable exceptions (e.g., the work's first Metropolitan Opera production in 1903), was honored by the world's opera houses.

Wagner had touched on the character of Parsifal once before, in his opera *Lohengrin* (1850). There, in the final scene, Lohengrin announces that he is Parsifal's son, and that his father presides over the knights of the Holy Grail. The idea of telling Parsifal's own story—how he was elevated to the leadership of the knights of the Grail—remained in the back of Wagner's mind during the years that separated the two works, while his musical language changed profoundly. In *Parsifal,* the chromaticism of *Tristan und Isolde* is applied with remarkable subtlety, and the treatment of LEITMOTIF is even more organic than it had been in the *Ring* cycle. The scoring is extraordinarily refined and transparent, resulting in a tissue of sound that appears to be "lit from behind" (Debussy's description). The music's long-breathed lines seem to arise out of nothingness and then return to it.

The story of Parsifal, the "pure fool," is full of religious overtones, but Wagner handled them without the bombast that marked his philosophical writings on religion. His music, brilliantly evocative in the Act II portrayal of the evil Klingsor and his magic domain, rises to great heights of expressiveness in the final act, as Parsifal and his old mentor Gurnemanz bear witness to the magic of Good Friday, and as Parsifal's acts of compassion win salvation for the suffering Amfortas, the humble Kundry, and the fellowship of the Holy Grail.

RECOMMENDED RECORDINGS

COMPLETE OPERA: JERUSALEM, MEIER, HÖLLE, VAN DAM, TOMLINSON; BARENBOIM AND BERLIN PHILHARMONIC (TELDEC).

PRELUDE AND "GOOD FRIDAY" MUSIC: WALTER AND COLUMBIA SYMPHONY ORCHESTRA (SONY).

Pärt, Arvo

(b. Paide, September 11, 1935)

ESTONIAN COMPOSER. He attended the Tallinn Conservatory, graduating in 1963. In the works of his student years, most of them for piano, he leaned stylistically toward neoclassicism, but soon turned to serialism, which, as the 1960s progressed, he began to leaven with Baroque-style contrapuntal procedures. Toward the end of the decade he realized that he could not express what he wanted to say using serial techniques; following several years of silence in the 1970s, he found his true voice in a greatly simplified, austere, and essentially tonal style. His breakthrough came with the hauntingly beautiful *TABULA RASA*, composed in 1977 for the Latvian violinist Gidon Kremer. In this work and others composed around the same time, Pärt coined a technique that he calls "tintinnabulation," in which one voice in a two-voice texture carries the melody (usually moving in stepwise fashion around a central pitch), while the other voice "rings out" the notes of the tonic triad around it.

Holy minimalist Arvo Pärt

Since 1980 most of Pärt's music has utilized vocal forces. Nearly all of it has been liturgical in nature or shaped in some fashion by religious texts and imagery, and a great deal of it has been put on disc, making Pärt one of the best documented of living composers. Pärt remains among the most important and successful practitioners of a style sometimes referred to as "holy minimalism," in which the procedures of MINIMALISM are fused with an intense spiritual pleading rooted in orthodox Christianity.

RECOMMENDED RECORDINGS

FRATRES: WERTHEN AND I FIAMMINGHI (TELARC).

PASSIO (*ST. JOHN* PASSION): HILLIARD ENSEMBLE, DAWSON; HILLIER AND WESTERN WIND CHAMBER CHOIR (ECM).

TABULA RASA: HATFIELD, HIRSCH; YUASA AND ULSTER ORCHESTRA (NAXOS).

TABULA RASA: KREMER, GRIDENKO, TEPP; KREMER AND KREMERATA BALTICA (NONESUCH).

TE DEUM, *MAGNIFICAT*, *BERLINER MESSE*: KALJUSTE AND ESTONIAN PHILHARMONIC CHAMBER CHOIR, TALLINN CHAMBER ORCHESTRA (ECM).

partita (from Lat. *pars*, "part" or "piece") A SUITE. The term came into common use during the second half of the 17th century, particularly among Austrian and German composers. Bach's partitas for solo violin epitomize the Baroque genre. By the mid-18th century a partita tended to be an orchestral suite with a modest number of movements (usually no more than four or five) or a suite for wind instruments. A celebrated example of the latter is Mozart's seven-movement Serenade in B-flat, K. 361 (370a), for 12 winds and double bass, which acquired the name *Gran Partita* shortly after it was written in the early 1780s. By the 19th century the term had become anachronistic, though several 20th-century composers used it in favor of weightier designations such as "symphony" for multimovement works. Among these was Sir William Walton, whose *Partita* (1957), composed to honor the 40th

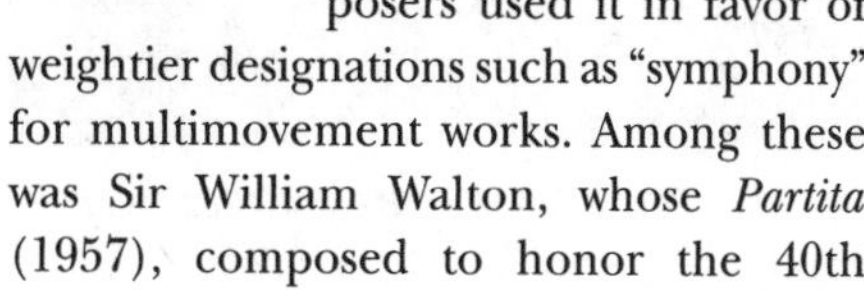

anniversary of the Cleveland Orchestra, is an exuberant, three-movement showpiece made to virtuoso measure. By contrast, the *Partita* (1937) of American composer Paul Creston (1906–85) is a true orchestral suite, whose five slender movements, with solo parts for violin and flute, clearly look back to 18th-century models.

RECOMMENDED RECORDINGS

BACH, COMPLETE PARTITAS: MILSTEIN (DG).

BACH, COMPLETE PARTITAS: PODGER (CHANNEL CLASSICS).

MOZART, SERENADE, K. 361: HOGWOOD AND AMADEUS WINDS (DECCA).

WALTON, *PARTITA FOR ORCHESTRA*: SZELL AND CLEVELAND ORCHESTRA (SONY).

passacaglia (from Sp. *pasar* and *calle,* "to walk the street") Originally a short interlude played on the guitar between strophes of a song; during the 17th century, the term became attached to an instrumental (mainly keyboard) and orchestral genre in which a series of variations unfold over a recurring harmonic progression, usually taking up eight bars in $\frac{3}{4}$ or $\frac{3}{2}$ time. Examples include Bach's Passacaglia in C minor, BWV 582, for organ, the fourth movement of Brahms's Symphony No. 4 in E minor, Op. 98, and the opening movement of William Schuman's Symphony No. 3. Britten uses a passacaglia as an orchestral interlude to ratchet up the tension at the climax of his opera *Peter Grimes.*

The New York Baroque Dance Company "walks the street."

passing tone In tonal music, a note not belonging to the harmony that is sounded in the course of stepwise melodic motion (usually descending) between two notes that do belong to the harmony, thus producing a momentary ("passing") dissonance.

Passion A musical work (usually calling for chorus, vocal soloists, and orchestra) based on one of the four Gospels, telling the story of Christ's crucifixion. Over the years, the Gospel according to St. Matthew has inspired numerous passion settings, probably more than Mark, Luke, or even John. The most celebrated of them is J. S. Bach's *St. Matthew* Passion (1727). In addition to this work and Bach's *St. John* Passion (1724), notable contributions to the genre have been made by Schütz, C. P. E. Bach, Penderecki, Pärt, and Osvaldo Golijov (b. 1960).

Pasta, Giuditta

(b. Saronno, October 26, 1797; d. Como, April 1, 1865)

ITALIAN SOPRANO. She studied in Milan and made her debut there in 1816, subsequently appearing in Paris and London in operas by Mozart, Ferdinando Paer (1771–1839), and Domenico Cimarosa (1749–1801). In 1821 she triumphed as Desdemona in Rossini's *Otello* at the Théâtre Italien in Paris; during the next few seasons, she continued her conquest of the Rossini repertoire, singing Desdemona in London, Tancredi and Elisabetta in Paris, and creating a sensation as Semiramide. Her singing so impressed Rossini that at the 1825 premiere of *Il viaggio a Reims* he assigned her the part of Corinna. By the end of the 1820s she was regarded throughout the world of Italian opera as the leading soprano of her day.

Pasta's career reached its zenith in the early 1830s, with her creation of some of the most important roles in the bel canto repertoire. On December 26, 1830, she sang the title role of Donizetti's *Anna Bolena* at the Teatro Carcano in Milan. On March 6, 1831, at the same theater, she sang Amina in the premiere of Bellini's *La sonnambula.* On December 26, 1831, for her debut at La Scala in Milan, she created the title role of Bellini's *Norma.* And on March 16, 1833, at La Fenice in Venice, she created the title role in Bellini's *Beatrice di Tenda.* She retired in 1835.

Few artists of any era have accomplished as much as Pasta and still managed to retire in their 30s. Her impact on the music of her time was considerable, and the blend of agility, range, timbre, and bravura she brought to her singing helped define the notion of bel canto. She was an extraordinary actress, and her embellishments were the epitome of good taste, according to no less an observer than Stendhal. But what electrified the audiences of her day was the sincerity of her singing and her intelligent command of vocal and dramatic nuance.

Giuditta Pasta

pastorale A movement or piece that evokes a rural scene, usually through music of a rustic and placid character. In instrumental and vocal pieces of the 17th and 18th centuries, music in the pastoral vein typically appears in the key of F, sometimes C or G, and utilizes meters such as $\frac{6}{8}$ and $\frac{12}{8}$. Drones and gently rocking DOTTED RHYTHMS are the most common features of the style, exemplified by the Sinfonia from Bach's *Christmas* Oratorio.

***Pastorale* Symphony** TITLE OF LUDWIG VAN BEETHOVEN'S SYMPHONY NO. 6 IN F, OP. 68, composed in 1808 and premiered December 22, 1808, on the same program as the Fifth Symphony. The score was published in 1809 with a dedication to Prince Franz Joseph Lobkowitz and Count Andreas Razumovsky. In terms of orchestral color and texture, the *Pastorale* is the most forward-looking of all Beethoven's symphonies. It opened an entire new expressive realm in music, and its pictorialism inspired imitation by a long line of 19th-century composers. Each of the symphony's five movements carries a brief descriptive heading: *I. Awakening of cheerful feelings on arrival in the country; II. Scene by the brook; III. Merry gathering of country folk; IV. Thunderstorm; V. Shepherds' Song: Happy, thankful feelings after the storm.* Despite this use of titles and occasional references to natural sounds, the *Pastorale* is not really a programmatic symphony. Rather, as Beethoven himself said in an explanatory note at the head of the score, it is "mehr Ausdruck der Empfindung als Malerei"—more the expression of feeling than painting.

In structural terms, the *Pastorale* Symphony follows the underlying premise of the Fifth, which is that a symphony should develop through a series of movements along a single dynamic arc. But while the structure is similar, the conceptual foundation of the two works is entirely different. In the *Pastorale,* texture and sonority are the organizing principles, not conflict of key. The restlessness of the earlier work is replaced by a flowing musical discourse in which Beethoven seems willing to inhabit a series of tonal regions as if time were standing still. The state of mind evoked by the music is that of Romantic contemplation, as opposed to the vigorous goal-directed action of Classicism.

As the 19th century unfolded, lesser composers would imitate the birdcalls or the storm, while the great ones saw the grand design of the *Pastorale* and realized that it represented a doorway into a different sort of musical experience, one in which sound itself was the fundamental element of the conception. Beethoven's recollection of happy thoughts on visiting the country would thus exert a profound influence on the subsequent development of the symphony, leaving its mark on the world of Schubert's Ninth, on Berlioz's *Symphonie fantastique* and *Harold en Italie*, on the gigantic symphonies of Bruckner and Mahler, and even on the operas of Wagner.

Beethoven by a Brook, ***lithograph from 1834***

RECOMMENDED RECORDINGS

BÖHM AND VIENNA PHILHARMONIC (DG).

WALTER AND COLUMBIA SYMPHONY ORCHESTRA (SONY).

***Pastoral* Symphony** TITLE INSCRIBED BY RALPH VAUGHAN WILLIAMS on his inward-looking Symphony No. 3, completed in 1921 and first performed on January 26, 1922, by the Royal Philharmonic Society Orchestra conducted by Adrian Boult. The symphony's finale, one of Vaughan Williams's finest achievements, includes a rhapsodic wordless solo for soprano.

RECOMMENDED RECORDINGS

HANDLEY AND ROYAL LIVERPOOL PHILHARMONIC ORCHESTRA (CFP).

PREVIN AND LONDON SYMPHONY ORCHESTRA (RCA).

***Pathétique* Sonata** TITLE GIVEN BY LUDWIG VAN BEETHOVEN (in full: *Grande Sonate pathétique*) TO HIS PIANO SONATA IN C MINOR, OP. 13. Completed in 1798 and published the following year with a dedication to Prince Karl von Lichnowsky, it decisively established Beethoven's reputation in Vienna. The first movement's slow introduction, with its mix of French overture, funeral march, and operatic recitative, is a masterpiece of the fantasy style in which poignant emotion and dramatic foreboding are conveyed with equal force. The main body of the movement is vehement and intense, with a restless agitation that foreshadows some of Beethoven's later treatments of the key of C minor (in particular, the first movements of the String Quartet, Op. 18, No. 4, and the Fifth Symphony). The ensuing Adagio, marked *cantabile,* offers a reprieve, but the troubled feeling of the opening movement returns in the concluding Allegro. As in the first movement, the structural seams are neatly fused by the intensity of Beethoven's expression.

RECOMMENDED RECORDINGS

GILELS (DG) AND SERKIN (SONY).

***Pathétique* Symphony** TITLE OF PYOTR IL'YICH TCHAIKOVSKY'S SYMPHONY NO. 6 IN B MINOR, OP. 74, composed in 1893 and premiered in St. Petersburg on October 28, 1893. The title, suggested to Tchaikovsky by his brother Modest after the score's completion, fits the piece well, since the primary meaning of "pathetic" in Russian corresponds to the word's secondary meaning in English, usually rendered as "affecting or moving the feelings." From the psychological standpoint, and in formal terms as well, the *Pathétique* is a revolutionary work. The mood of utter despair in which it ends marks a fundamental turning point in the history of the symphony—a rejection of the heroic aspiration and transcendent spirituality that had been key elements of symphonic thinking since Beethoven. In addition, Tchaikovsky's handling of the structure of the first and last movements reflects a new way of thinking, a departure from the rhetorical succession of ideas characteristic of Classicism and Romanticism.

The first movement, with its remarkable compression of development and recapitulation into a single span, is virtually a new species. The choice of an Adagio as the concluding movement is equally bold and devastatingly effective. This crushing valedictory opens with a descending scale motive representing Fate. The second subject, a hymnlike lament, appears to offer consolation; it builds to an impassioned climax, but is soon stifled. There is no development. Instead, out of the fragments of the lament, the Fate motive returns. Anguish mounts in a second climax of feverish intensity. There is a solemn cadence, and Fate's final blow is delivered by a single, chillingly soft stroke on the tam-tam. The lament returns, now in the minor key and but an echo, sinking lower and lower until it is extinguished and the symphony ends.

In these two extraordinary movements, and in the symphony's middle ones as well—a waltz subtly disfigured by its $\frac{5}{4}$ meter, and a scherzo which, in its fleeting images and manic energy, amounts to a march gone mad—Tchaikovsky's mastery of form and content is absolute. Also absolute is the sense of finality the music projects, as though Tchaikovsky, who died nine days after the symphony's premiere, knew that this would be his last work. Its impact, metaphysically and formally, on the subsequent course of the symphonic genre has been profound, and can be felt in the works of Sibelius, Mahler, and Shostakovich, among others.

RECOMMENDED RECORDINGS

Karajan and Berlin Philharmonic (DG).

Mravinsky and Leningrad Philharmonic (DG).

Patti, Adelina

(b. Madrid, February 19, 1843; d. Craig-y-Nos Castle, Wales, September 27, 1919)

Italian soprano. Both of her parents were professional singers (her mother is said to have sung a performance of Bellini's *Norma* the night before Adelina was born). She studied in New York with her half brother, the baritone Ettore Barilli, and made her debut there in 1859 in Donizetti's *Lucia di Lammermoor.* She made her debut at Covent Garden in 1861, as Amina in Bellini's *La sonnambula,* a role she reprised for her debuts in Paris (1862) and Vienna (1863). In 1876 she sang the title role in the London premiere of Verdi's *Aida,* and in 1877 she made her La Scala debut as Violetta in the composer's *La traviata.* Famous for commanding the highest fees of her day, she returned on several occasions to the United States, and in the spring of 1892 she was showcased along with members of her own ensemble in five different productions at the Metropolitan Opera, singing Rosina in Rossini's *Il barbiere di Siviglia,* the title role in *Lucia di Lammermoor,* Lady Harriet in Friedrich Freiherr von Flotow's *Martha,* the title role in Rossini's *Semiramide,* and Violetta. In 1895, 35 seasons after first appearing there, she gave her farewell performances at Covent Garden in operas of Rossini, Verdi, and Mozart.

Adelina Patti, 1882

Paul Bunyan OPERA IN A PROLOGUE AND TWO ACTS BY BENJAMIN BRITTEN, to a libretto by W. H. Auden based on American folklore, premiered May 5, 1941, at Columbia University in New York. Auden's libretto, gently satirizing the American myth of a country hewn by wisdom and might from virgin forest, portrays Bunyan more as an idea than a man. In the opera his role is a speaking part—he is not seen on stage and does not sing. The piece marked Britten's first foray into opera. Its music is an eclectic mix of Broadway and popular song with more serious elements.

RECOMMENDED RECORDING

COLEMAN-WRIGHT, CRANHAM, ROBINSON, WATSON; HICKOX AND ROYAL OPERA (CHANDOS).

pavane Courtly dance of the 16th and early 17th centuries, always in duple meter and typically at a moderate to slow tempo. The dance originated in Italy (most likely taking its name from the town of Padua), and enjoyed its greatest popularity as an instrumental form in England between about 1580 and 1625, particularly in the hands of Dowland.

Pavane pour une infante défunte (Pavane for a Dead Princess) PIECE FOR PIANO BY MAURICE RAVEL, composed in 1899. Ravel later said he chose the title simply for its alliterative value. Nonetheless, the music's modal harmonies and simple, balladelike melody lend it a psuedo-archaic quality, the aural equivalent of a pre-Raphaelite sensibility in painting. Ravel orchestrated the work in 1910, and in this form it has become a familiar presence on concert programs. Alfredo Casella conducted the premiere of the orchestral arrangement on December 25, 1911, in Paris.

RECOMMENDED RECORDINGS

PIANO: THIOLLIER (NAXOS).

ORCHESTRA: DUTOIT AND MONTREAL SYMPHONY ORCHESTRA (DECCA).

Pavarotti, Luciano

(b. Modena, October 12, 1935)

ITALIAN TENOR. In his prime one of the greatest lyric tenors in history, he devoted the later years of his career to being merely one of the most popular and ended up almost a pariah. He studied in Modena and Mantua and made his professional debut in 1961 as Rodolfo in Puccini's *La bohème.* He first appeared at Covent Garden in 1963, and in 1965 he made his La Scala debut, also as Rodolfo. After appearing in Miami and with the San Francisco Opera he made his Metropolitan Opera debut in 1968, once again as Rodolfo. During many seasons at the Met, he specialized in a handful of Donizetti operas and the lighter Verdi and Puccini roles, delighting audiences as Tonio in *La fille du régiment* (opposite Joan Sutherland) and Nemorino in *L'elisir d'amore,* and making a distinguished Riccardo in *Un ballo in maschera.*

Pavarotti's career as a recording artist took off in the late 1960s and remained strong through the 1970s, a decade which saw him partnered with Mirella Freni in recordings of Puccini's *Madama Butterfly* and *La bohème* under the baton of Herbert von Karajan, and with Joan Sutherland in recordings of Donizetti's *Lucia di Lammermoor* and Bellini's *I puritani* conducted by Richard Bonynge, as well as a spectacular *Turandot* conducted by Zubin Mehta. For a few years he enjoyed a thriving career as a recitalist; though his programs were unusually heavy with opera arias, audiences nonetheless loved what they heard, swooning at the emotion with which he clutched the ubiquitous white handkerchief in his left hand. By the 1980s, Pavarotti's recital programs had retreated to the songs of Paolo Tosti and various Neapolitan ditties, though always with the obligatory "Nessun dorma" as one of the encores. It was a small step from doing that, for $100,000 a pop, to stepping in front of thousands of spectators in sports arenas with the television cameras tracking every move, for millions: thus, joined by Plácido Domingo and José Carreras, Pavarotti reached a new plateau of fame and fortune as the most celebrated of the "Three Tenors."

During the 1990s, Pavarotti was pursued by the Italian government for underpayment of taxes (he agreed to pay back $12 million), and late in the decade he endured a humiliating brouhaha over whether he could actually read music, with challenges and rebuttals flying in the press. There were also reports of his lip-synching some performances, and in the spring of 2002 he backed out of what was to have been his farewell appearance at the Met, as Cavaradossi in Puccini's *Tosca,* less than an hour before curtain time. In the spring of 2004, with his vocal powers clearly diminished, he gained a measure of redemption by returning to the house, in the same role, for four final performances on its stage. The coup de grâce came in the autumn of 2004, when he was trashed in a biography written by his former manager.

In the early years of his career Pavarotti's warmth, charisma, and instinctive expressiveness were immensely attractive to audiences. The delicately tempered edge he brought to his top notes—placing them in a way that made his voice sound as though it were a hair's breadth from ruin—proved emotionally compelling on a purely visceral level. When he sang his nine full-voice high C's in *La fille du régiment* with Sutherland, it seemed as if the fate of the world was hanging on each one. His best roles were Rodolfo in *La bohème,* well suited to his sound, and Nemorino in *L'elisir d'amore,* where his corpulence was no disadvantage. By his own admission, the most challenging of his roles was that of Arturo in *I puritani,* with its climactic high D's; getting through it, he said, made him feel as if he had beaten Bjorn Borg in tennis. If Pavarotti is remembered kindly, it will be for achievements such as that, characteristic of his early career, and not for the avarice and professional sloth that marked his later years.

Luciano Pavarotti

RECOMMENDED RECORDINGS

DONIZETTI, *L'ELISIR D'AMORE*: SUTHERLAND, COSSA, MALAS; BONYNGE AND ENGLISH CHAMBER ORCHESTRA (DECCA).

DONIZETTI, *LA FILLE DU RÉGIMENT*: SUTHERLAND, SINCLAIR, MALAS; BONYNGE AND ROYAL OPERA (DECCA).

PUCCINI, *LA BOHÈME*: FRENI, HARWOOD, PANERAI, GHIAUROV; KARAJAN AND BERLIN PHILHARMONIC (DECCA).

PUCCINI, *MADAMA BUTTERFLY*: FRENI, LUDWIG, KERNS; KARAJAN AND VIENNA PHILHARMONIC (DECCA).

VERDI, *UN BALLO IN MASCHERA*: PRICE, BRUSON, LUDWIG, BATTLE; SOLTI AND NATIONAL PHILHARMONIC ORCHESTRA (DECCA).

Peacock Variations ORCHESTRAL WORK BY ZOLTÁN KODÁLY consisting of an introduction, a theme with 16 variations, and finale, composed in 1939 for the 50th anniversary of the Concertgebouw Orchestra, and premiered in Amsterdam on November 23, 1939, Willem Mengelberg conducting. Based on a Hungarian folk song, "The Peacock," and scored for a large but not extravagantly sized orchestra, the work is Kodály's masterpiece. The opening pages of the score subject the pentatonic folk tune to a series of brilliant transformations in writing that is by turns hymnlike, playful, and atmospheric. The tone becomes powerfully somber in a pair of slow variations in D minor (vars. 12 and 13), the second of which is a funeral march. The work ends with a joyous conclusion in which Kodály's gifts as an orchestrator are revealed in all their splendor.

RECOMMENDED RECORDINGS

KERTÉSZ AND LONDON SYMPHONY ORCHESTRA (TESTAMENT).

SOLTI AND VIENNA PHILHARMONIC (DECCA).

Pears, Peter

(b. Farnham, June 22, 1910; d. Aldeburgh, April 3, 1986)

ENGLISH TENOR. In his student years he excelled as a pianist, and though it is reported that he sang well enough (and played organ, bassoon, and viola), it is likely that the only real rival to his piano studies was a keen interest in cricket. A modest undergraduate career at Lancing College (1923–28) was followed by an unsuccessful year at Keble College, Oxford, after which he taught music, among other subjects, for four years at Grange, his old prep school. In 1933 he was accepted as an opera student at the Royal College of Music, but he left after two terms to sing professionally for the BBC. He first met the composer Benjamin Britten in 1934, at a rehearsal of Britten's *A Boy Was Born* by the BBC Singers; it was the April 1937 funeral of a mutual friend, the writer Peter Burra, that marked the start of the artistic and domestic relation-

Peter Pears as General Sir Philip Wingrave in Britten's* Owen Wingrave*, 1971

ship that would connect them for nearly 40 years. During that time, they were frequent collaborators in concert (with Britten as conductor) and recital (Britten as pianist). Most of all, they would become collaborators in opera, with Pears's voice the inspiration for numerous leading parts. The majority of Britten's operas explore a theme that fascinated the composer throughout his career: innocence undone by the power of evil. Pears made lasting impressions in a string of widely varied parts that dealt, one way or another, with this theme: the tortured title character in *Peter Grimes* (1945) and his shy alter ego, Albert, in *Albert Herring* (1947); duty-bound Captain Vere in *Billy Budd* (1951); Peter Quint, the ghostly seducer in *The Turn of the Screw* (1954); and the obsessed figure of Aschenbach in Britten's last opera, *Death in Venice* (1973). Pears also gave first performances of a number of nonoperatic works by Britten, including the song sets *Les Illuminations* (1939), *Seven Sonnets of Michelangelo* (1940), the *Serenade* for tenor, horn, and strings (1943), *The Holy Sonnets of John Donne* (1945), and *Winter Words* (1953); the "church parables" *Curlew River* (1964), *The Burning Fiery*

Furnace (1966), and *The Prodigal Son* (1968); and the *War Requiem* (1962).

Pears championed the work of Michael Tippett as well, singing in the premieres of *A Child of Our Time* (1944), *Boyhood's End* (1943), and *The Heart's Assurance* (1951). Also outside the Britten canon, his operatic repertoire included Ferrando in *Così fan tutte,* Alfredo in *La traviata,* Vašek in *The Bartered Bride,* Tamino in *Die Zauberflöte,* and Idomeneo. He was a frequent oratorio performer, specializing in the Evangelist parts in Bach's passions, and an insightful interpreter of the lieder of Schubert and Schumann.

By the time of *Peter Grimes,* Pears's voice had grown in strength and flexibility, and though its unconventional, non-Italianate timbre was not universally loved, there was no denying the musicality, intelligence, scholarship, and emotional commitment behind it. Numerous recordings have preserved many of his interpretations in opera, song, and concert repertoire. In 1948 he was a cofounder (with Britten, among others) of the Aldeburgh Festival; three decades later he took part in establishing Aldeburgh's School for Advanced Musical Study. Pears was made a Commander of the British Empire in 1957, and knighted for his services to music in 1977. In 1986, ten years after Britten's death, he suffered a heart attack and died at the Red House, his home with Britten for almost 30 years.

RECOMMENDED RECORDINGS

BRITTEN, *SERENADE*: BRAIN; BRITTEN AND BOYD NEEL STRING ORCHESTRA (PEARL).

BRITTEN, *SERENADE* (WITH *LES ILLUMINATIONS* AND *NOCTURNE*): TUCKWELL; BRITTEN AND ENGLISH CHAMBER ORCHESTRA (DECCA).

PETER GRIMES: C. WATSON, J. WATSON, EVANS; BRITTEN AND ROYAL OPERA (DECCA).

SCHUBERT, *WINTERREISE*: BRITTEN (DECCA).

WAR REQUIEM: VISHNEVSKAYA AND FISCHER-DIESKAU; BRITTEN AND LONDON SYMPHONY ORCHESTRA (DECCA).

pedal [1] A lever or a set of actuators operated by the foot on instruments such as the piano, organ, and harp. [2] A note or figure in the bass that is sustained under changing harmonies in the upper parts of a musical composition; a notable example is the pedal C sustained through eight measures in slow tempo at the beginning of Brahms's Symphony No. 1 in C minor, Op. 68.

Peer Gynt VERSE DRAMA BY HENRIK IBSEN, first staged February 24, 1876, in Oslo. The play's central figure is a Scandinavian Everyman whose exploits, cynically related, echo those of Homer's Odysseus and Voltaire's Candide. After years of searching for the meaning of life he returns home and finds Solvejg—the woman who was right for him all along—waiting for him on the doorstep. Ibsen asked Edvard Grieg to provide incidental music for the play early in 1874; the composer, thinking that only a small amount of music would be required, readily agreed. But the project turned out to be a mammoth undertaking, occupying most of Grieg's time during 1874–75. When it was finished, the score amounted to well over an hour of music.

Grieg understood both the idealism and the irony at the heart of the play, but wisely chose to let his music set the mood of various scenes rather than trying to probe more deeply into the characters and their motives. Nonetheless, his score shows commendable insight. There is plenty of profile in the dramatic scenes—such as "Peer Gynt and the Boyg" and "In the Hall of the Mountain King"—as well as affecting emotion in "Åse's Death" and an almost cinematic richness to "Morning Mood" and "Night Scene." The keys to the score's appeal can be found in the liveliness of its dance movements and the pastoral quality of Grieg's orchestration.

RECOMMENDED RECORDINGS

INCIDENTAL MUSIC: BONNEY, EKLÖF; JÄRVI AND GOTHENBURG SYMPHONY ORCHESTRA (DG).

INCIDENTAL MUSIC: HOLLWEG; BEECHAM WITH ROYAL PHILHARMONIC ORCHESTRA (EMI).

INCIDENTAL MUSIC: MALMBERG, HAEGGANDER; BLOMSTEDT AND SAN FRANCISCO SYMPHONY ORCHESTRA (DECCA).

Pelléas et Mélisande SYMBOLIST DRAMA BY THE BELGIAN PLAYWRIGHT MAURICE MAETERLINCK, published in 1892. It provoked a number of musical responses, the most important of which came from Debussy, Fauré, Schoenberg, and Sibelius.

Debussy saw the play at its first performance, in Paris, on May 17, 1893, and immediately started to work on an operatic setting, even before getting the author's permission, which he received after visiting Maeterlinck in Ghent at the end of 1893. Composition of the opera occupied Debussy for nearly a decade (though it was essentially sketched by 1895), making it the central work of his career. Sadly, it would also be the only operatic project Debussy brought to completion. The finished work, in five acts, an almost word-for-word setting of the drama, received its premiere on April 30, 1902, at the Opéra-Comique in Paris.

In *Pelléas et Mélisande,* Debussy avoids conventional singing most of the time in favor of a recitative-like vocalizing of the words. Lyrical treatment of the text is "reserved for certain points," such as the scene in which Pelléas and Mélisande declare their love for each other. Most of the time, the melodic fabric of the opera is provided by the orchestra, whose role is not to accompany the singers but to express what is going on inside the characters' heads, to convey the emotions only hinted at in the words. The score is a masterpiece of subtlety and refinement, and achieves what is perhaps the most intimate connection between word and music in the history of opera.

Fauré's incidental music for *Pelléas et Mélisande* was the first music inspired by the drama to reach the public. It was composed on a commission from London, where Maeterlinck's play was presented (in translation) in 1898, five years after its Paris premiere. The original incidental music was orchestrated by Fauré's student Charles Koechlin. Subsequently, Fauré extracted three movements—the Prélude, an Andantino ("La Fileuse"), and an Adagio ("La mort de Mélisande")—to form a suite, revising the orchestration himself. This was first performed in 1901. In 1909 he added a fourth movement, "Sicilienne." This final version of the suite received its first performance in 1912.

Following his composition of *Gurre-Lieder* in 1901, Schoenberg toyed with the idea of setting *Pelléas et Mélisande* as an opera, unaware that Debussy had already done so. He ultimately decided instead to create a symphonic poem based on the play. Work on the piece occupied him from July 1902 until February 1903. Densely scored, hyper-Wagnerian in its chromaticism and extension of motivic material, Schoenberg's *Pelleas und Melisande* compresses Maeterlinck's drama into a superheated paroxysm lasting three quarters of an hour, at the same time telescoping a four-movement symphonic design into a single sprawling utterance.

Sibelius's incidental music for *Pelléas och Mélisande,* Op. 46, was commissioned by the Swedish Theater in Helsinki for a production of Maeterlinck's play in a translation by Bertel Gripenberg. The score, consisting of ten numbers, was composed during the autumn and winter of 1904–05 amid work on the Third Symphony and the revised version of the Violin Concerto, and received its premiere on March 17, 1905, with the composer conducting. Using a small orchestra of flute (doubling piccolo), oboe (doubling English horn), two clarinets, two bassoons, two horns, timpani, triangle, and strings, Sibelius is able to convey the gentleness and dark foreboding that coexist in Maeterlinck's drama. The score includes a setting for mezzo-soprano of the song "De trenne blinda systrar" ("The Three Blind Sisters"), which Mélisande sings from the castle tower in Act III, sc. 2 of the play.

RECOMMENDED RECORDINGS

DEBUSSY: EWING, LE ROUX, VAN DAM, COURTIS; ABBADO AND VIENNA PHILHARMONIC (DG).

DEBUSSY: VON STADE, VAN DAM, RAIMONDI; KARAJAN AND BERLIN PHILHARMONIC (EMI).

FAURÉ: DUTOIT AND MONTREAL SYMPHONY ORCHESTRA (DECCA).

FAURÉ: OZAWA AND BOSTON SYMPHONY ORCHESTRA (DG).

SCHOENBERG: KARAJAN AND BERLIN PHILHARMONIC (DG).

SIBELIUS: KARAJAN AND BERLIN PHILHARMONIC (DG).

Penderecki, Krzysztof

(b. Debica, November 23, 1933)

POLISH COMPOSER AND CONDUCTOR. The paradoxical and brilliant author of some of the 20th century's most powerful music, he leapt to the forefront of the postwar avant-garde when he was in his 20s with his *Threnody to the Victims of Hiroshima,* an intense study in dissonance for orchestra-sized string ensemble. Fascinated by sonority, he has produced a remarkable body of innovative works for choral and orchestral forces that display writing of striking rhythmic complexity and searing expressiveness, much virtuosic brilliance and energy, and, often, profound religious feeling.

Having completed his studies at the Kraków Conservatory just the year before, Penderecki arrived on the scene literally overnight in 1959, when he swept all three prizes in a Polish composition contest. One of the entries, *Strophen,* is a classic essay in post–World War II malaise that revealed the 25-year-old composer's already sure feeling for sound and gesture. In 1960 Penderecki composed *Threnody to the Victims of Hiroshima,* which won the UNESCO prize, and his reputation was made. Further very successful compositions followed that remain in the repertoire: The *St. Luke* Passion, from 1966, was commissioned for the 700th anniversary of the Münster cathedral; Penderecki's first opera, *The Devils of Loudon* (based on a Huxley novel), dates from 1969. (His second opera, *Paradise Lost* [1978], really a semi-staged oratorio, never got a foothold in the repertoire, and the jury is still out on his third and fourth operas, *Die schwarze Maske* [1986] and *Ubu Rex* [1991].) The composer became director of the Kraków Conservatory in 1972, the same year he accepted a teaching appointment at Yale and embarked on a career as conductor.

Penderecki's *Partita,* a sort of modern *Brandenburg* Concerto written in 1971, shows how far he carried the quest for sonority, rhythmic complexity, and density of texture in a dozen years—a solo group consisting of harpsichord, harp, electric guitar, and electric and string basses is set against a conventional chamber orchestra to produce a fascinating interplay of surface and background activity. Although he began the 1970s as one of the most adventurous of young compositional insurgents, Penderecki turned during that decade toward an assertion of tonality in his scores; by the 1980s, in works such as the Viola Concerto, Symphony No. 2 (called the *Christmas* Symphony), and the oratorio-like *The Seven Gates of Jerusalem,* he had embraced the gloomy, minor-mode chromaticism and more conventional treatment of motive and texture of an artist who, once the enfant terrible, woke up one morning realizing he had become the heir to a tradition. Other symphonies and concertos have followed suit. But many of

Krzysztof Penderecki, composer and left-handed maestro, on the podium

these pieces, notably the Viola Concerto, still have the passages of skittering fast notes and ominous pedal tones that have long characterized Penderecki's music, and in all respects they remain remarkable studies in sound.

Penderecki once said, "We must go back to Mahler and start over." While this may have been meant chiefly to provoke, it clearly signaled rejection of 12-tone and serial procedures, i.e., what most of the European avant-garde has been interested in since the 1950s. The composer himself has firmly embraced a variety of neo-Romanticism that evokes the symphonic constructs of Mahler, and also of Zemlinsky, Richard Strauss, Schmidt, and Shostakovich. In spite of this remarkable (and, under the circumstances, courageous) turn, Penderecki remains one of the world's most adventurous musical thinkers, writing the music he feels compelled to write, and caring not at all about any establishment's idea of fashion.

RECOMMENDED RECORDINGS

ORCHESTRAL WORKS (INCLUDING SYMPHONIES NOS. 1–5, VIOLIN CONCERTOS NOS. 1 AND 2, *THRENODY,* OTHER WORKS): WIT AND POLISH NATIONAL RADIO SYMPHONY ORCHESTRA (NAXOS).

THRENODY, PARTITA (WITH OTHER WORKS): PENDERECKI AND POLISH NATIONAL RADIO SYMPHONY ORCHESTRA (EMI).

pentatonic scale A scale with five tones to the octave, common to many types of folk music. One of its characteristics is that it contains no sharply dissonant intervals. Among the many works in which pentatonic melodies appear are Copland's *Billy the Kid,* Mendelssohn's *Scottish* Symphony ◉, and Dvořák's *Symphony from the New World.*

Perahia, Murray

(b. New York, April 19, 1947)

AMERICAN PIANIST AND CONDUCTOR. He began playing the piano at the age of four, and later attended Mannes College, where he majored in conducting and composition. He spent summers at the Marlboro Festival in Vermont, where he had the opportunity to collaborate with Rudolf Serkin, Pablo Casals, and the members of the Budapest Quartet; he also studied with Mieczylsaw Horszowski. In 1972 he won the Leeds International Piano Competition, and in 1973 he gave his first concert at the Aldeburgh Festival, which brought him into contact with Benjamin Britten and Peter Pears; he subsequently served as co-artistic director of the festival from 1981 to 1989. In 2000 he was appointed principal guest conductor of the Academy of St. Martin-in-the-Fields.

Perahia has been a luminary of the concert stage, and one of classical music's most successful recording artists, for more than 30 years. Throughout his career he has been admired for his distinctively poetic playing, characterized by subtle shadings of tone and dynamics, extraordinary precision of touch, and an innate, unforced lyricism. Reluctant to take on the most virtuosic repertoire, he has always seemed more comfortable in music that is intimate and nuanced—Mozart, Schubert, Chopin, Mendelssohn, and Schumann—where his penetrating interpretations have won universal praise. While sidelined by a hand injury for several years during the 1990s, he devoted himself to a thorough reexamination of the solo keyboard works of Bach. His recent performances and recordings of this music have been revelatory.

RECOMMENDED RECORDINGS

BACH, *GOLDBERG VARIATIONS* (SONY).

CHOPIN, ETUDES, OPP. 10 AND 25 (SONY).

MOZART, PIANO CONCERTOS (COMPLETE): ENGLISH CHAMBER ORCHESTRA (SONY).

Keyboard poet Murray Perahia

percussion Instruments that are played by being shaken, scraped, or struck; in the latter category, the surface that is struck may be a membrane, or a plate or bar of metal, wood, or some other sound-emitting material. In addition to playing legitimate instruments, orchestral percussionists are usually the ones who get to fool around with toys, as in the *Metropolis* Symphony (1988–93; based on the Superman comic books) by Michael Daugherty, (b. 1954) where members of the percussion section are periodically called upon to blow police whistles.

Pergolesi, Giovanni Battista

(b. Iesi, January 4, 1710; d. Pozzuoli, March 16, 1736)

ITALIAN COMPOSER. He was an important figure in the development of 18th-century Italian opera buffa. His extraordinary influence and posthumous fame were a direct result of the popularity of his two-act comic intermezzo, *La serva padrona* (1733), which by the 1750s had become known throughout Europe. After his initial studies in Iesi, Pergolesi went to Naples sometime between 1720 and 1725 to study at the Conservatorio dei Poveri di Gesù Cristo. His first opera seria, *Salustia* (1732), was met with indifference, mostly because the celebrated castrato Nicolini, who had been engaged to sing the lead role, fell ill and died before the performance. Later that year Pergolesi's three-act comedy *Lo frate 'nnamorato,* written in Neapolitan dialect, was a runaway hit. Soon after its premiere, earthquakes rattled Naples; at services of public atonement on December 31, 1732, a Mass in F by Pergolesi and his settings of several vesper psalms were performed in the church of Santa Maria della Stella. Pergolesi's second effort at opera seria, *Il prigioniero superbo,* composed in the summer of 1733, was not a success, but it contained as its intermezzo *La serva padrona,* which created a sensation.

In 1734 Pergolesi fashioned his third opera seria, *Adriano in Siria,* using a libretto by Metastasio. Again, the interpolated intermezzo, *La contadina astuta,* was the more successful work. A new opera, *L'olimpiade,* also to a libretto by Metastasio, was produced the following January in Rome and was initially a failure. (According to one report, the composer, seated at the harpsichord, was hit by an orange during a performance.) Pergolesi returned to Naples. By the summer of 1735 his health was failing, but in his final months he managed to write a new opera buffa, *Il Flaminio,* the cantata *Orfeo,* and settings of the *Stabat mater* and *Salve regina.* In January 1736 he was taken to a Franciscan monastery in Pozzuoli, where he died two months later. In the years following his death, the rampant popularity of *La serva padrona* caused many pieces of music that were circulating in manuscript to be wrongly attributed to Pergolesi. Their number includes several of the tunes that Stravinsky used in *Pulcinella.*

Perlman, Itzhak

(b. Tel Aviv, August 31, 1945)

ISRAELI VIOLINIST. He taught himself to play on a toy violin, then received his initial training on a real one at the Academy of Music in Tel Aviv. In 1958, following two appearances on the *Ed Sullivan Show* in which he dazzled American television audiences, he moved to New York to continue his education at the Juilliard School. He studied with Ivan Galamian and Dorothy DeLay, made his Carnegie Hall debut in 1963, and in 1964 won the Leventritt competition. Over the next few years he made an impressive series of debuts in North America and Europe.

Since then, Perlman has filled engagements as a soloist with every major orchestra in the world and appeared in recitals in nearly all of its most important venues. He has recorded most of the leading works in the concerto repertoire, garnering 15 Grammys in the process, and committed to disc a good deal of the solo and chamber literature as well, in partnership with colleagues such as pianists Vladimir Ashkenazy and Daniel Barenboim, fellow violinist (and violist) Pinchas Zukerman, and cellist Lynn Harrell. Over the years he has also enjoyed a close association with the Israel Philharmonic. In 1993 he contributed the poignant violin solos to John Williams's score for the Steven Spielberg film *Schindler's List.*

Itzhak Perlman

Stricken with polio at the age of four, Perlman has long been an eloquent spokesman for the disabled. He remains the greatest living exponent of the Romantic approach to the violin, unmatched in the broad, grand gestures he can achieve in music that is close to his heart. His playing is characterized by intense emotion and heated expression—his warm vibrato and carefully placed portamentos are hallmarks—and by an unfailingly lyrical impulse that allows him to phrase even the most treacherous passages in a seamless line, and to produce soaring climaxes and tender, haunting pianissimos with little apparent effort. Yet despite possessing what can only be called a supreme technique, he often skates by on talent and showmanship.

RECOMMENDED RECORDINGS

BEETHOVEN, *ARCHDUKE* TRIO: HARRELL, ASHKENAZY (EMI).

BEETHOVEN, VIOLIN CONCERTO: GIULINI AND PHILHARMONIA ORCHESTRA (EMI).

BEETHOVEN, VIOLIN SONATAS, OPP. 24 (*SPRING*) AND 47 (*KREUTZER*): ASHKENAZY (DECCA).

BERG, VIOLIN CONCERTO: OZAWA AND BOSTON SYMPHONY ORCHESTRA (DG).

BRAHMS, VIOLIN CONCERTO: GIULINI AND CHICAGO SYMPHONY ORCHESTRA (EMI).

WILLIAMS, *SCHINDLER'S LIST* (FILM SCORE) (MCA).

Pérotin

(fl. Paris, ca. 1200)

FRENCH COMPOSER. Also known as Magister Perotinus or Perotinus Magnus, he was Léonin's younger contemporary and successor at the Cathedral of Notre Dame. From two important treatises of the late 13th century, by Johannes de Garlandia and the English theorist Anonymous 4, we know that Pérotin revised and added to the compilation begun by Léonin called the *magnus liber organi,* and that he was associated with the poet Philip the Chancellor (d. ca. 1237), some of whose texts he set.

Anonymous 4 identifies by name seven works by Pérotin, including four groundbreaking organa—*Alleluia: Nativitas* and *Alleluia: Posui* for three voices, and *Viderunt omnes* and *Sederunt omnes* for four voices. A number of other works have been attributed to him on stylistic grounds. With the exception of a single, fairly simple French three-voice piece found in the Codex Calixtinus in Spain, these are the first known works for more than two voices.

In keeping with the extraordinary musical developments at Notre Dame, Pérotin's organa are highly sophisticated. Going well beyond the earlier style of *organum purum,* in which an upper voice moves rhapsodically in free rhythm over a slow-moving tenor, Pérotin's upper voices are distinctly rhythmic, with repeated patterns intertwining to create a kaleidoscopic effect. Techniques such as note-against-note *conductus* style and the use of overlapping melodic and rhythmic patterns create an amazing vitality, turning what appears to be a relatively static form into something quite dynamic. Conceptually, the approach reveals an exquisite sensitivity to tonal architecture, one perfectly aligned with the aesthetic of the Gothic cathedral itself. The works of Pérotin and his contemporaries at Notre Dame had a decisive influence on the development of polyphonic music; even in our own time, composers such as Steve Reich have looked to Pérotin's music for inspiration.

RECOMMENDED RECORDINGS

"PÉROTIN": HILLIARD ENSEMBLE (ECM).

"THE SCHOOL OF NOTRE DAME": ORLANDO CONSORT (ARCHIV).

Peter and the Wolf **PIECE FOR NARRATOR AND ORCHESTRA BY SERGEY PROKOFIEV, OP. 67,** commissioned by the Moscow Central Children's Theater and premiered on May 2, 1936. The story, by Prokofiev himself, was conceived in collaboration with Natalia Satz, the theater's director. Uncompromising in its musical craftsmanship and without condescension as a piece of storytelling, *Peter and the Wolf* is one of Prokofiev's most effective scores. The characters are clearly delineated by the music: The bird is represented by excited, flighty runs on the flute; the duck, its music in a minor key, by the plaintive oboe; the cat, whose sultry, gliding steps are to be articulated *con eleganza,* by the clarinet; Peter's crusty grandfather by lurching figures in the bassoon; the wolf, its music also in the minor, by snarling brass; the not-so-smart hunters by their errant gunfire in the timpani and bass drum; and Peter himself by the string section, with its warmth and added expressive dimension. The suspense of Peter's confrontation with the wolf is resolved in a happy concluding march that brings all the characters together again, with a reprise of their music.

RECOMMENDED RECORDINGS

BERNSTEIN, NARRATOR; BERNSTEIN AND NEW YORK PHILHARMONIC (SONY).

PREVIN, NARRATOR; PREVIN AND ROYAL PHILHARMONIC ORCHESTRA (TELARC).

STING, NARRATOR; ABBADO AND CHAMBER ORCHESTRA OF EUROPE (DG).

Peter Grimes OPERA IN A PROLOGUE AND THREE ACTS BY BENJAMIN BRITTEN, to a libretto by Montagu Slater based on George Crabbe's "The Borough" (1810), a poem about life in an early-19th-century English fishing village. Composed in 1944–45 on a commission from Serge Koussevitzky, it received its premiere June 7, 1945, at Sadler's Wells, London; its American premiere took place at Tanglewood in 1946, with the young Leonard Bernstein conducting. *Peter Grimes* was Britten's second opera, and his first great success as a theatrical composer. It is a study of isolation, paranoia, and cruelty, insightfully probing the relationship between Grimes, a moody, sometimes violent, loner, and the Borough, a society determined to enforce its norms. Britten set the libretto along conventional lines (the opening tableau with chorus is typical of grand-opera scene structure), but his music is extraordinarily resourceful in its use of the orchestra and of modern harmonic language. At the end of the opera's prologue, for example, in a duet sung by Peter and Ellen Orford, the schoolmistress whom he hopes to marry, their conflicting viewpoints are vividly suggested by the fact that Peter sings in F minor, Ellen in E major, though eventually they come together on a note common to both tonalities, G-sharp.

Four brilliantly scored orchestral interludes contribute to the potent effect the work achieves in the theater, and Britten's deft use of folk elements imparts a typically English color to the proceedings. Among the composer's most impressive accomplishments is the way he devises a distinctive musical signature for each of the dozen principals. And in no other opera in the repertoire does the chorus have as large or difficult a part. Together, these touches add up to a work full of emotional resonance, a gripping piece of musical theater that is one of the finest operatic achievements of the mid-20th century.

RECOMMENDED RECORDINGS

PEARS, C. WATSON, J. WATSON, EVANS; BRITTEN AND ROYAL OPERA (DECCA).

VICKERS, HARPER, SUMMERS, BAINBRIDGE; DAVIS AND ROYAL OPERA (PHILIPS).

Peters, Roberta

(b. New York, May 4, 1930)

AMERICAN SOPRANO. A singer of notable gifts and intelligence, she was the darling of the Metropolitan Opera throughout the administrations of Rudolf Bing, Schuyler Chapin, and Anthony Bliss. Engaged by the company when she was 19, she made her debut on November 17, 1950, as a last-minute substitute in the role of Zerlina. Later the same season she appeared as both the Queen of the Night in Mozart's *Die Zauberflöte* (which was to have been her official debut role) and Rosina in Rossini's *Il barbiere di Siviglia.* She made her Covent Garden debut in 1951, sang at Salzburg and Vienna in 1963, and appeared at the Kirov and Bolshoi theaters in 1972, but her career remained focused in New York. By 1985, after 34 seasons with the Met, she had appeared in 512 performances and sung 24 different roles; in addition to Rosina, Zerlina, and the Queen of the Night, these included Gilda in Verdi's *Rigoletto,* the Donizetti roles of Norina in *Don Pasquale,* Adina in *L'elisir d'amore,* and the title part in *Lucia di Lammermoor,* Adele in Johann Strauss Jr.'s *Die Fledermaus,* and the Mozart roles of Despina in *Così fan tutte* and Susanna in *Le nozze di Figaro.* She possessed a soprano of remarkable beauty with a clear and light coloratura.

RECOMMENDED RECORDINGS

MOZART, *DIE ZAUBERFLÖTE*: WUNDERLICH, LEAR, OTTO, FISCHER-DIESKAU, CRASS; BÖHM AND BERLIN PHILHARMONIC (DG).

ROSSINI, *IL BARBIERE DI SIVIGLIA*: MERRILL, VALLETTI, TOZZI, CORENA; LEINSDORF AND METROPOLITAN OPERA (RCA).

Petrushka **Ballet in four scenes by Igor Stravinsky,** composed on a commission from Sergey Diaghilev and the Ballets Russes, and premiered at the Théâtre du Châtelet in Paris on June 13, 1911, Pierre Monteux conducting. The scene is set in St. Petersburg of the 1830s, during Mardi Gras, and the action revolves around a fatal ménage à trois, with an added wrinkle: The three principal characters—Petrushka, a Ballerina, and a Blackamoor—are all puppets. At the first performances, Tamara Karsavina was the Ballerina, Vaslav Nijinsky the Petrushka.

Petrushka had its origins in a concert piece for piano and orchestra that Stravinsky began to sketch soon after completing *The Firebird.* In his autobiography, the composer noted that he had been inspired by the image of a puppet "suddenly endowed with life, exasperating the patience of the orchestra with diabolic cascades of arpeggios. The orchestra in turn retaliates with menacing trumpet blasts. The outcome is a terrific noise which reaches its climax and ends in the sorrowful and querulous collapse of the poor puppet." Stravinsky played his sketches for Diaghilev in the summer of 1910. The impresario immediately saw their theatrical potential and persuaded Stravinsky to transform the material into a ballet; Alexandre Benois was assigned to assist Stravinsky in developing the scenario.

In comparison with that of *The Firebird,* the musical language of *Petrushka* is audaciously iconoclastic. The score does indeed make a terrific noise, partly because in Stravinsky's orchestration the strings are dominated by the wind, brass, and percussion instruments, producing a harder, edgier sonority. Even more important is the composer's revolutionary treatment of rhythm and harmony. The frequent shifting and mixing of meter, and the use of asymmetrical phrases and sharp, disruptive syncopations, goes far beyond anything that had been attempted previously in orchestral composition. ◉ The result is that for the first time in modern Western music, rhythm rather than harmony becomes the driving force in the long-range development of a piece, freeing harmony to be used in new ways. And the new uses Stravinsky found for harmony in *Petrushka* were startling ones, particularly his superimposition of chords of different keys, an effect known as POLYTONALITY. He later wrote that he had devised the juxtaposition of triads in C major and F-sharp major that permeates the score as a means of representing Petrushka's insults to the audience at the Shrovetide fair.

Mikhail Baryshnikov* (right) *as Petrushka in an ABT performance of Stravinsky's ballet

As he had in *The Firebird,* Stravinsky made use of existing material in *Petrushka.* At least five melodies are borrowed from various anthologies of Russian folk song, and the French tune "Elle avait un' jambe en bois" appears in the score as well. The material is more thoroughly assimilated than in *The Firebird,* better fulfilling Stravinsky's maxim that "a good composer steals," making whatever he takes from another his own. But in the third tableau, the transformation of tunes from *Die Schönbrunner* Waltz and *Steyrische Tänze* by Joseph Lanner (1801–43) into a waltz for the Ballerina and the awkward Blackamoor is not so much an appropriation as a conscious parody. With it, Stravinsky hit upon a process that would mark his idiom for the rest of his life.

RECOMMENDED RECORDINGS

COMPLETE BALLET:

DAVIS WITH CONCERTGEBOUW ORCHESTRA (PHILIPS).

BOULEZ WITH NEW YORK PHILHARMONIC (SONY).

SUITE:

STRAVINSKY AND COLUMBIA SYMPHONY ORCHESTRA (SONY).

Pfitzner, Hans

(b. Moscow, May 5, 1869; d. Salzburg, May 22, 1949)

GERMAN COMPOSER AND CONDUCTOR. Though he believed that he was the greatest German musician of his day, he was in fact overshadowed at every stage of his career by bolder, more talented figures who wielded pen and baton to greater effect, most notably Richard Strauss and Wilhelm Furtwängler. His towering ego, vituperative personality, and strident anti-Semitic views turned his life as both an artist and a man into a twisted tale of hand-wringing embitterment. Pfitzner's father, an orchestral violinist of Saxon stock, was concertmaster of the Frankfurt Stadttheater orchestra. Pfitzner attended Frankfurt's Hoch Conservatory from 1886 to 1890, studying piano with James Kwast and composition with Iwan Knorr. His earliest stylistic beacons were Schumann and Wagner, which aligned him with the more idealistic, progressive wing of 19th-century German Romanticism. As time went by his aesthetic and political views became increasingly hidebound and reactionary.

Over the years Pfitzner supported himself by teaching and conducting. In 1908 he was appointed director of the conservatory and the symphony orchestra in Strasburg, then part of Germany. In 1910 he was put in charge of that city's opera as well, where part of his job was to oversee the work of three younger conductors: Furtwängler, Otto Klemperer, and George Szell. Expelled from these posts at the end of World War I—when Alsace was ceded back to France—a humiliated and virtually penniless Pfitzner relocated to Munich, where he dwelt in a small house provided by admirers and wrote polemics attacking what he viewed as decadent modernist trends in contemporary composition and musicology.

Hans Pfitzner on the podium

The composer actively—and with a characteristic mix of indignation and obsequiousness—sought preferment from the Nazis once they came to power. While he was too much of an elitist ever to join the party, he was highly honored by the regime, though invariably shunned by its top dogs. After the end of World War II he had to ride out a denazification proceeding. He died still believing that "world Jewry" was responsible for most of Germany's and the world's ills.

Pfitzner composed assiduously in standard forms, which he approached in many cases with a turgid formality, but on occasion filled with music that was surprisingly soulful and at times quite modern, even dissonant, in its language. He bequeathed a single important work to the repertoire, the opera *PALESTRINA* (1912–15), premiered in Munich in 1917 under the baton of Bruno Walter. Its densely woven contrapuntal fabric and luminous scoring attest to Pfitzner's mastery of his metier. Other pieces of interest include his incidental music (1905) to Kleist's play *Das Kätchen von Heilbronn,* and the nationalistic cantata *Von deutscher Seelen* (*Of German Souls*; 1921), based on Eichendorff. He also composed concertos for the piano, violin, and cello; sonatas for violin and cello; three string quartets; and a smattering of songs. Pfitzner's music has few present-day champions outside Germany; even there, advocacy of his music tends to be seen as a coded acknowledgment of reactionary political views.

RECOMMENDED RECORDINGS

ORCHESTRAL EXCERPTS, *PALESTRINA, DAS HERZ,* AND *DAS KÄTCHEN VON HEILBRONN*: THIELEMANN AND DEUTSCHE OPER BERLIN (DG).

ORCHESTRAL WORKS (INCLUDING CONCERTOS): ALBERT AND BAMBERG SYMPHONY ORCHESTRA (CPO).

PALESTRINA: GEDDA, FISCHER-DIESKAU, WEIKL, RIDDERBUSCH; KUBELÍK AND BAVARIAN RADIO SYMPHONY ORCHESTRA (DG).

SONGS: PREY, BARITONE; SAWALLISCH (ORFEO).

Philadelphia Orchestra ENSEMBLE FOUNDED IN **1900.** Its first conductor, Fritz Scheel, was succeeded in 1907 by Carl Pohlig, a pupil of Franz Liszt who had served as an assistant to Gustav Mahler in Vienna. The orchestra's rise to national and international prominence began in 1912 with the appointment of Leopold Stokowski as music director. Stokowski built an ensemble of crack virtuosity and glowing confidence during his 24-year tenure. Within a few years of taking the reins, he led the orchestra in the U.S. premieres of Mahler's Eighth Symphony and *Das Lied von der Erde,* Schoenberg's Chamber Symphony No. 1, and Scriabin's Symphony No. 3 (*Divine Poem*). Other important first performances during the Stokowski era included the world premieres of Rachmaninov's Third Symphony and Fourth Piano Concerto and the American premieres of Sibelius's Sixth and Seventh Symphonies, Schoenberg's *Gurre-Lieder* and Violin Concerto, Stravinsky's *The Rite of Spring,* and Berg's *Wozzeck.*

Eugene Ormandy, who shared conducting duties with Stokowski in 1936–37 and served as music director from 1938 to 1980, built on the foundation Stokowski had prepared. He enhanced the orchestra's already luxurious tonal palette and cultivated what came to be known as "the Philadelphia sound." In the history of American orchestras, there has been nothing quite like the Philadelphia sound. Incomparably rich, deep-hued, and glowing, it got much of its character from the full, fat sound that the Philadelphia string players, using heavy bow pressure, had to develop in order to project in the dry-as-dust acoustic of the Academy of Music, the orchestra's home from 1900 to 2001. The Philadelphians also developed a unique pizzicato that was fleshier than usual and produced more tone, again to compensate for the dryness of their home hall. Complementing the Philadelphia strings was an exquisite wind section, strongly influenced by the French tradition, which played with character and elegance, as well as a gloriously burnished brass section, its sound weighty but never strident. Together, these forces could produce rainbow colors, but always with transparency (an effect quite different, oboist John De Lancie once remarked, from that of a rainbow "painted on a brick wall").

Among the luminaries of the Philadelphia Orchestra in its finest years—the

Eschenbach and the Philadelphia Orchestra start a new season.

1950s, 1960s, and 1970s—were concertmasters Anshel Brusilow and Norman Carol; principal violist Joseph de Pasquale; cellists Samuel Mays, Lorne Munroe, and Elsa Hilger; principal wind players De Lancie, William Kincaid, Murray Panitz, Marcel Tabuteau, Anthony Gigliotti, and Bernard Garfield; principal horn Mason Jones; harpist Marilyn Costello; and brass players Gilbert Johnson and Henry Charles Smith. Not since Mannheim in the 1760s had the world seen an orchestra of stars such as these, and no orchestra in the world could play the lavish, coloristic late-19th- and early-20th-century Russian, Czech, French, and Scandinavian repertoire any better.

In 1980 the music director's baton passed to Riccardo Muti, who served until the end of the 1991–92 season; in 1993 he was succeeded by the German-born Wolfgang Sawallisch. Both Muti and Sawallisch made the mistake of working against the orchestra's opulent grain, Muti by coarsening the sonority, Sawallisch by appointing key players whose tone was leaner and more Germanic (or, as one disgusted old-timer put it, more "effeminate") than the caloric Philadelphia brand. In December 2001 the orchestra moved to a new home, the 2,500-seat Verizon Hall at the Kimmel Center for the Performing Arts. Christoph Eschenbach became the ensemble's seventh music director at the beginning of the 2003–04 season.

RECOMMENDED RECORDINGS

RACHMANINOV, PIANO CONCERTOS NOS. 1 AND 4, *RHAPSODY ON A THEME OF PAGANINI*: RACHMANINOV; STOKOWSKI, ORMANDY (RCA, NAXOS).

RACHMANINOV, PIANO CONCERTOS NOS. 2 AND 3: STOKOWSKI, ORMANDY (RCA, NAXOS).

RACHMANINOV, SYMPHONY NO. 3, *VOCALISE*, *ISLE OF THE DEAD*: RACHMANINOV (RCA, PEARL).

RESPIGHI, *FONTANE DI ROMA*, *PINI DI ROMA*, *FESTE ROMANE*: MUTI (EMI).

SIBELIUS, *FOUR LEGENDS*: ORMANDY (EMI).

Philharmonia Baroque Orchestra *See box on pages 310–13.*

Philip Glass Ensemble *See box on page 272.*

phrase A sequence of notes articulated as a single, coherent, usually melodic gesture; a unit of musical syntax corresponding to a sentence in a prose work or to a line of verse. Phrasing—the art of shaping individual phrases so as to give them coherence and meaning within the larger musical context of a particular passage or movement—is an integral aspect of the performer's interpretation of a piece.

piano Keyboard instrument with strings of graduated size and length (usually running perpendicular to the keyboard) strung over a wooden soundboard and enclosed in a wooden case. Actually more a machine than an instrument, the piano was developed in Italy early in the 18th century using a mechanism invented by Bartolomeo Cristofori (1655–1732). The heart of this mechanism was its linkage of keys to hammers and its use of an escapement that allowed strings to continue vibrating after they were struck. The piano's major advantage over the harpsichord was that it could produce dynamic gradations from soft to loud, hence its original name, *pianoforte.* The size, sound, and construction of the piano all changed dramatically in the 19th century, turning what had been a rather soft-spoken drawing-room instrument into a thundering dreadnought of the concert stage. Today's concert grand, while marginally more brilliant, is little changed from the concert instruments of a century ago.

The rapid rise of the piano to the status it still enjoys as the world's most widely used musical instrument was a phenomenon of the later 18th and early 19th centuries, fueled both by social forces—the piano was the ideal instrument of the bourgeoisie because it stayed at home—and by the Industrial Revolution, which permitted significant improvements in the construction of pianos, among them the development of a steel frame. But the most important factor contributing to the piano's ascendancy was its adoption by a succession of virtuoso composer-performers as their instrument of choice. The efforts of Mozart, Beethoven, Clementi, and other late-18th- and early-19th-century pianists to provide themselves and their instrument with a repertoire of sonatas and concertos—which meant something quite different from answering the enormous demand for easier music that the piano-owning public could play—eventually led to the piano's establishment as a vehicle for professional soloists as well as amateurs.

The process of repertoire building was continued by the composer-pianists of the 19th century. Led by Schumann, Chopin, Mendelssohn, and, most imposing of all, Liszt, they intended nearly all of their keyboard music for public performance. For them the piano was the perfect extension of self. In the hands of Chopin and Schumann it was the soul of poetry, though Liszt could make it roar with Promethean authority. The sonata and concerto, while still important forms for these composers, shared the spotlight with a host of miniature genres and pieces patterned on dances.

With Liszt, the piano's conquest of the world reached its goal: The solo recital by the virtuoso pianist was confirmed as one of music's sacraments. After Liszt, thanks to the establishment of a "standard" repertoire, it was possible for virtuoso pianists who were not the primary creators of their own repertoire—i.e., specialists in performance—to come into their own. Indeed, it was almost necessary, since the executant standard Liszt had set was so high it proved difficult to compete unless one was devoted full-time to the effort. During the late 19th and early 20th century, figures such as Hans von Bülow (a student of Liszt), Vladimir de Pachmann (1848–1933), Móriz Rosenthal (another student of Liszt), and Josef Hofmann dazzled and delighted audiences without adding much of their own to the repertoire.

The 20th century was as much the era of the virtuoso as the composer, dominated by pianists such as Arthur Rubinstein, Benno Moiseiwitsch, Vladimir Horowitz, and their followers. Still, numerous composer-performers flourished, among them Albéniz, Granados, Leopold Godowski

(1870–1938), Busoni, and Rachmaninov. The 20th century saw the literature enriched in a variety of ways by these composers and many others. Debussy and Bartók, in particular, broke new ground in their exploration of the piano's sonority and its potential as a percussion instrument, while Rachmaninov, Scriabin, Ravel, and Prokofiev expanded in compelling ways upon the virtuoso technique of the 19th-century masters.

The piano has benefited throughout its history from the efforts of talented builders to improve its action, compass, tone, and carrying power. Even if no one has been able to overcome its single greatest limitation—the inability to sustain notes that has led to its being characterized as a "box of diminuendos"—the piano continues to be a musical wonder, with the capacity to convey complex textures across seven octaves and to fill a large hall with its sound. Among the most important builders engaged in the making of pianos have been Johann Andreas Stein and the firms of Streicher, Broadwood, Erard, Pleyel, Bösendorfer, and Steinway.

piano quartet A composition for piano and string trio (violin, viola, and cello). The best-known work in the form is probably Brahms's Piano Quartet in G minor, Op. 25 (1861). Other notable contributions to the literature have been made by Mozart, Schumann, Brahms, and Fauré, whose Piano Quartet in C minor shows him at his most ardent and lyrical. ◉ *See also* CHAMBER MUSIC.

RECOMMENDED RECORDING

BRAHMS, PIANO QUARTET IN G MINOR, OP. 25: GILELS AND AMADEUS QUARTET (DG).

piano quintet A composition for piano and string quartet (two violins, viola, and cello). Schumann's sparkling Piano Quintet in E-flat, Op. 44 (1842) ◉, was the first important essay in the genre, and it became the model for many subsequent efforts, not least Brahms's potent Piano Quintet in F minor, Op. 34 (1862)—a work of symphonic proportions that points to the mature composer's formal mastery and weight of argument. Important contributions to the literature were made by Dvořák, Franck, Fauré, and Elgar, and the repertoire also includes interesting works by Dohnányi, Korngold, and Shostakovich, among others. *See also* CHAMBER MUSIC.

RECOMMENDED RECORDING

SCHUMANN, BRAHMS, PIANO QUINTETS: JANDÓ AND KODÁLY QUINTET (NAXOS).

piano trio A composition for piano, violin, and cello. The foundation of the repertoire was laid by Joseph Haydn, Beethoven (his very first opus was a set of three piano trios and he crowned his work in the genre with the formidable *Archduke* Trio, Op. 97 ◉), and Schubert, who composed two outstanding works in the form, his Trios in B-flat, D. 898, and in E-flat, D. 929, in 1827. Mendelssohn added a pair of masterpieces to the canon with his Trios in D minor, Op. 49 (1839) and C minor, Op. 66 (1845). Brahms labored mightily to produce three trios he was willing to share with the world—his Opp. 8, 87, and 101—while Dvořák had an easier time writing his four, capped by the unconventional Trio in E minor, Op. 90 (*Dumky*), in six movements. Shostakovich's Trio No. 2 in E minor, Op. 67, written in 1944, is one of his greatest achievements in the chamber medium, on a par with the best of his string quartets. Among those who contributed a single important effort to the genre are Smetana (1855; rev. 1857), Chausson (1881), and Ravel, whose Trio in A minor (1914) is one of the masterpieces of the literature. *See also* CHAMBER MUSIC.

RECOMMENDED RECORDINGS

BEETHOVEN, *ARCHDUKE* TRIO: ASHKENAZY, PERLMAN, HARRELL (EMI).

BRAHMS, TRIOS: TRIO FONTENAY (TELDEC).

RAVEL, TRIO IN A MINOR: BEAUX ARTS TRIO (PHILIPS).

Piatigorsky, Gregor

(b. Yekaterinoslav Dnetropetrovosk, April 17, 1903; d. Los Angeles, August 6, 1976)

RUSSIAN-BORN CELLIST. He first began playing the cello at seven, was accepted at the Moscow Conservatory at nine, and became principal cellist of the Bolshoi Ballet at 15, an astonishingly rapid development. In 1921, he fled Russia for Germany, where he took lessons in Leipzig with Julius Klengel (also the teacher of Emmanuel Feuermann). Not especially impressed with Klengel, he moved to Berlin in 1922, where he earned a living playing trios in a Russian café. He was heard by Feuermann and also by Furtwängler, who engaged him as principal cellist of the Berlin Philharmonic in 1924; he remained in that post until 1928. He made his American debut in 1929, performing with the Philadelphia Orchestra under Leopold Stokowski and the New York Philharmonic under Willem Mengelberg.

Piatigorsky enjoyed a brilliant solo career and performed frequently in chamber music settings with the greatest players of the age, including Artur Schnabel, Carl Flesch, Vladimir Horowitz, Nathan Milstein, and especially Arthur Rubinstein, Jascha Heifetz, and William Primrose, with whom he made many recordings. Early in his career he gave the premieres of concertos by Castelnuovo-Tedesco and Hindemith, and in 1957, with Charles Munch and the Boston Symphony, he premiered William Walton's Cello Concerto, one of the finest string concertos of the 20th century. His recording of the work with Munch is legendary, as are the recordings he made of the Brahms sonatas with Rubinstein. Piatigorsky handled the cello with violinistic ease, and excelled as a recitalist, where his grace and humor were most evident, especially in the smaller pieces that he played inimitably. He owned two magnificent Stradivari cellos, the "Batta" of 1714, and the "Baudiot" of 1725. In later years he taught at the University of Southern California in Los Angeles.

RECOMMENDED RECORDINGS

BRAHMS, CELLO SONATAS: RUBINSTEIN (RCA).

BRAHMS, DOUBLE CONCERTO: HEIFETZ; WALLENSTEIN AND RCA VICTOR SYMPHONY ORCHESTRA (RCA).

WALTON, CELLO CONCERTO: MUNCH AND BOSTON SYMPHONY ORCHESTRA (RCA).

Piave, Francesco Maria

(b. Murano, May 18, 1810; d. Milan, March 5, 1876)

ITALIAN LIBRETTIST. The son of a Venetian glass artist, he studied for the priesthood but chose to make his living with the pen. Despite having little previous experience, he became Verdi's librettist in 1844, with *Ernani,* and continued in that capacity through *Macbeth, RIGOLETTO, LA TRAVIATA (The Woman Who Strayed), Simon Boccanegra,* and *LA FORZA DEL DESTINO (The Power of Fate),* to name only the best known of their collaborations. The secret of his success was his willingness to accept a steady barrage of minutely detailed instructions from Verdi, and provide the economical versifications the composer demanded. In 1859, on Verdi's recommendation, he became stage director at La Scala in Milan. In 1867 he suffered a stroke that left him paralyzed and unable to speak for the rest of his life.

piccolo (abbreviation of It. *flauto piccolo,* "little flute") Auxiliary member of the FLUTE family with a range an octave above that of the standard flute. It uses the same key system and fingering as the flute, but is slightly under half its length. The piccolo first came into use in France in the 18th century; initially, its role was to provide colorful special effects in the opera house. It entered the symphony orchestra via Beethoven's Symphonies Nos. 5, 6, and 9.

The piccolo adds brightness to the uppermost strands of an orchestral texture when employed as part of the tutti. In a solo capacity it can penetrate the texture and sound sparklingly clear or pastoral and sweet, depending on how it is used; it can have a magical effect when played softly. Orchestral players want an instrument that sounds brilliant and speaks clearly, but many prefer wooden piccolos to the metal variety familiar from use in bands—their less piercing, rounder tone is more appealing. Notable solo passages for the piccolo can be found in Donizetti's *Don Pasquale*; Weber's *Der Freischütz* (adorning Caspar's salacious drinking song "Hier im ird'schen Jammerthal"); Tchaikovsky's Fourth Symphony (third movement ◉); Dvořák's Sixth Symphony (the trio section of the scherzo); the prologue to Holst's opera *The Perfect Fool*; and, most famous of all, Sousa's *Stars and Stripes Forever*, in which the part is traditionally played by *all* the members of the flute section, standing.

Pictures at an Exhibition **SUITE FOR PIANO BY MODEST MUSSORGSKY,** composed in June 1874 as a memorial to a friend, the painter Victor Hartmann, who had died the previous year. The music takes as its point of departure ten images displayed at a posthumous exhibition of roughly 400 of the artist's works. Hartmann's originals were mostly modest sketches and watercolors. A whimsical costume sketch for a children's ballet called *Trilby*, showing a young dancer peering out of an oversize eggshell, became the "Ballet of Chicks in Their Shells." Similarly, a quaint design for a clock in the shape of a cabin built on chicken's feet inspired "The Hut on Fowl's Legs." According to Russian folklore, this peculiar structure is the abode of Baba Yaga, a witch who liked to fly around in a glowing iron mortar, the Slavic equivalent of a broomstick. Rather than portray the hut itself, Mussorgsky decided to depict the hag on one of her intimidating rides. In the grandest gesture of all, Mussorgsky turned Hartmann's lopsided, ornately decorated drawing of a city gate in the old Russian style (with a cupola in the shape of a helmet surmounting the gate house) into "The Great Gate of Kiev," the most breathtaking and at the same time most touching part of his tribute. To link the various elements of the suite, the composer used a theme he called "Promenade" to open the piece and to depict the viewer's passing from one work to the next. ◉

Though pianistically crude, Mussorgsky's *Pictures at an Exhibition* conveys the vitality, fantasy, and darkness of Hartmann's pictures with great imaginative force. From the moment the score was published (in 1886, edited by Rimsky-Korsakov), its symphonic potential was tantalizingly apparent, and over the years at least 20 orchestral realizations of the piece have been put forward by other musicians. Rimsky was the godfather of the first orchestration, undertaken by his pupil Mikhail Tushmalov in 1891. Subsequent scorings have been made by Sir Henry Wood, Leo Funtek, Maurice Ravel, Leonidas Leonardi, Lucien Cailliet, Leopold Stokowski, Sergey Gorchakov, Lawrence Leonard, and Vladimir Ashkenazy, among others. Although there are good things to be said for several of them, especially the Stokowski and Gorchakov, Ravel's remains far and away the most frequently performed, and is still, on many levels, the most satisfactory.

Ravel's orchestration was commissioned by the conductor Serge Koussevitzky for the Concerts Koussevitzky in Paris, and introduced by him there in October 1922. Ravel's scoring faithfully amplifies both the wit and feeling of the piano piece. His use of an alto saxophone for the melody of "The Old Castle"—strange as it might have sounded to Mussorgsky's ears—seems entirely apposite. Similarly, in the passage portraying Schmuyle, the poor Jew, in "Samuel Goldenberg and Schmuyle," his use of a muted trumpet triple-tonguing the sixteenth notes in a querulous fortissimo—and playing all the grace notes as well, which makes it more difficult for the instrument—imparts just the right tone of kvetch to the proceedings. The "Ballet of Chicks in Their Shells" becomes a lively piece of scene painting in Ravel's scoring, which, with its clucking oboes and scurrying scale passages in the bassoon and strings, transforms the children in their eggshell costumes into real chicks. In "The Hut on Fowl's Legs," Ravel marshals the heavy brass and a businesslike array of percussion to create a thunderous, heart-pounding chase that makes *A Night on Bald Mountain* seem polite by comparison. And in Ravel's magnificent rendering of "The Great Gate of Kiev," Mussorgsky's tribute to a gate that was never built becomes one of the architectural wonders of the world, brought to life by full brass, pulsing strings, pealing bells, and triumphant tam-tam and cymbal crashes.

RECOMMENDED RECORDINGS

PIANO VERSION:
HOROWITZ (RCA).
JANDÓ (NAXOS).
RICHTER (PHILIPS).
RAVEL ORCHESTRATION:
KARAJAN AND BERLIN PHILHARMONIC (DG).
SINOPOLI AND NEW YORK PHILHARMONIC (DG).
STOKOWSKI ORCHESTRATION:
KNUSSEN AND CLEVELAND ORCHESTRA (DG).

Pierrot lunaire CYCLE OF 21 SONGS ("thrice seven," to quote the work's title page) **FOR SPEAKER AND CHAMBER ENSEMBLE BY ARNOLD SCHOENBERG,** composed in 1912. The song texts—German translations by O. E. Hartleben of poems from Albert Giraud's *Pierrot lunaire*—are intoned according to a distinctive notation that indicates the precise rhythmic values as well as the relative pitches at which individual syllables are to be inflected. The accompanying ensemble consists of flute (doubling piccolo), clarinet (doubling bass clarinet), violin (doubling viola), cello, and piano.

Rudolf Nureyev as Pierrot

Pierrot lunaire, whose settings penetrate the disturbing fantasy of Giraud's poetry in a remarkably animated and suggestive manner, is the classic example of Schoenberg's atonal, expressionistic style. Its imaginative melding of voice and small instrumental ensemble—particularly the kaleidoscopic coloring Schoenberg achieves within the ensemble—has had an enormous influence on subsequent chamber-vocal settings, not least those of Boulez and Carter. Much of Schoenberg's later work seems stale in comparison to *Pierrot lunaire*'s madcap vitality.

RECOMMENDED RECORDING

SCHÄFER; BOULEZ AND ENSEMBLE INTERCONTEMPORAIN (DG).

Pinza, Ezio

(b. Rome, May 18, 1892; d. Stamford, Conn., May 9, 1957)

ITALIAN BASS. His innate vocal talent and love of music got the better of an early interest in cycling, and he studied music in

Ravenna and at the Bologna Conservatory. He made his debut in 1914 at Soncino, as Oroveso in Bellini's *Norma.* World War I, in which he served as a captain in the Italian army, postponed further career steps, but in 1920 he was heard in Rome as King Marke in Wagner's *Tristan und Isolde.* At Toscanini's invitation he sang Pogner in the 1922 La Scala revival of Wagner's *Die Meistersinger von Nürnberg.* He made his debut at the Metropolitan Opera on November 1, 1926, as Pontifex Maximus in Spontini's *La vestale.* For the next 22 years the Met would be his artistic home; he would sing 52 roles in 878 performances in New York and on the annual Met tour. A basso cantante with a sizable voice of silken suaveness, he specialized in French and Italian roles such as Mozart's Figaro, Don Basilio in Rossini's *Il barbiere di Siviglia,* Méphistophélès in Gounod's *Faust,* and the Verdi roles of Ramfis in *Aida,* Fiesco in *Simon Boccanegra,* and Padre Guardiano in *La forza del destino.* His Don Giovanni and Boris Godunov were both widely famed.

Pinza left the Met in 1948 for the less stressful and more lucrative artistic milieux of Broadway, film, and television. His continental charm, winning personality, and still-dashing good looks helped make him one of the few opera singers of any era to achieve success as a crossover artist. His portrayal of Émile de Becque in the original production of Rodgers and Hammerstein's *South Pacific* won him a Tony Award in 1950, and in 1954 he returned to Broadway to star with Walter Slezak in Harold Rome's *Fannie.* Between 1950 and 1951, he starred in two musicals for MGM: *Mr. Imperium,* with Lana Turner, and *Tonight We Sing,* a musical biopic in which he played the Russian bass Fyodor Chaliapin.

Ezio Pinza, whose singing provided operagoers with many an enchanted evening

Piston, Walter

(b. Rockland, Me., January 20, 1894; d. Belmont, Mass., November 12, 1976)

AMERICAN COMPOSER AND TEACHER. His paternal grandfather, Antonio Pistone, was a Genoese sailor who settled in Maine. Piston's family moved to Boston when he was 11; his early interest was in art. A self-taught and self-employed musician, he joined the Navy Band as a saxophonist following America's entry into World War I. He matriculated at Harvard when he was 26 and graduated when he was 30. From 1924 to 1926 he studied in Paris at the École Normale de Musique with Paul Dukas, George Enescu, and Nadia Boulanger; while there he played viola in the school orchestra. He returned to Boston in 1926 and taught at Harvard, where he spent the rest of his career (his students included Elliott Carter, Leroy Anderson, Irving Fine, Leonard Bernstein, and John Harbison). During the 1940s and 1950s, he wrote texts on harmony, counterpoint, and orchestration that are still in use.

Piston's ballet *The Incredible Flutist* (1938) put him on the map as a composer, and his Symphony No. 2 (1943) secured his reputation. The latter work, premiered by Hans Kindler and the National Symphony Orchestra in 1944 and played the same year by the Boston Symphony and the New York Philharmonic, brought Piston a New York Music Critics' Circle Award.

Both works are still in the repertoire. Perhaps the greatest of his achievements is his Symphony No. 4 (1950), one of the finest scores of the 20th century. As a composer, Piston spent his life searching for challenge and variety within established forms. His five string quartets and eight symphonies are the heart of his oeuvre, and all his works are remarkable for their discipline and craft. Piston embraced a neoclassicism very different from the fanciful, speculative, and essentially parodistic manner of Stravinsky; his was sober, rugged, densely contrapuntal in places, but essentially lyrical and always lucid—a neoclassicism with the emphasis on "classicism" rather than "neo."

RECOMMENDED RECORDINGS

The Incredible Flutist: Goff, Mann; Schwarz and Seattle Symphony Orchestra (Naxos).

Symphony No. 2: Thomas and Boston Symphony Orchestra (DG).

Symphony No. 4 (with other works): Schwarz and Seattle Symphony Orchestra (Naxos).

più (It., "more") Term used to modify a tempo or dynamic instruction, e.g., *più piano* is "softer"; *più mosso* is "faster."

pizzicato (It., "pinched") Instruction in music for bowed string instruments indicating that the player is to sound a note, chord, or passage by plucking the appropriate string(s) with his finger(s), rather than by using the bow. Various kinds of pizzicato are possible. In most cases a player will pluck the string using the fleshy part at the tip of the index or middle finger in order to produce a pleasantly full and rounded tone. For a "snap" pizzicato (sometimes called a "Bartók" pizzicato), the string is plucked more forcefully, so that it rebounds against the fingerboard. Paganini was among the first composers to call for left-hand pizzicato, a virtuoso technique that enables a performer to play a note or group of notes pizzicato (usually on an open string) either simultaneously or in alternation with bowed notes.

Pizzicato accompaniments are not uncommon in Baroque vocal music, but the use of pizzicato as a standard element of orchestral writing did not occur until the Classical period. Notable effects in the orchestral literature include the third movement of Tchaikovsky's Symphony No. 4 ◉, where all the strings play exclusively pizzicato, and the final movement of Debussy's *Ibéria,* where violins and violas are instructed to play widely spaced chords *quasi guitara,* strummed like a guitar, with the instrument held under the arm.

plainchant (from Lat., *cantus planus*) Generic term for the unaccompanied monophonic chant of the Western Christian liturgy. There were numerous local and regional varieties of plainchant in the early church, including Gregorian or Roman chant, Gallican chant in France, Mozarabic chant in Spain, Ambrosian chant in Milan, and the Sarum Use in England. But it was the Roman variety that eventually attained primacy. According to medieval legend, its melodies were miraculously transmitted by the Holy Spirit to Pope Gregory the Great (reigned 590–604), who in turn dictated them to a scribe; this is why it was customarily called Gregorian chant. But current scholarship has discounted the role Gregory played in the emergence of "Gregorian" chant, holding that the process of standardization occurred well after his papacy, some time between the end of the seventh century and the beginning of the ninth. An important factor in that process was the establishment in Rome, during the second half of the seventh century, of the Schola Cantorum (school of singing), dedicated to instructing singers in the proper performance of chant. It is now thought that the melodic formulas of the Roman repertoire were to a great extent defined there during the reign of Pope Gregory II (715–31). The impetus to make the Roman usage standard throughout Western Christendom came largely from the Carolingian monarchs, beginning with Pépin the Short (reigned 751–68), and continuing with Charlemagne (reigned 768–814) and his descendants. In 789 Charlemagne issued a "general admonition" instructing Frankish clergy to hew to the Roman form of chant; during his reign, he established schools of singing modeled on the Roman Schola Cantorum. It was not until about 1100, however, long after the Franks were gone, that Gregorian chant came into universal use in the Western church.

While the origins of plainchant may not have been miraculous, the effort to develop mnemonic aids for singing chant melodies produced something that was: written notation. Early notation, using shaped notes called NEUMES, began to be systematized during the ninth century and continued to develop over the next two centuries into the staff-and-clef notation still in use today.

Sanctified by its association with the liturgy and by its supposedly divine origin, plainchant became the principal source material for most of the liturgical music of the Middle Ages. As time went by, the desire to devise increasingly elaborate and impressive settings of the liturgy—and to achieve in music a representation of divine order, proportion, beauty, and harmony—had much the same effect on medieval musicians as the urge to erect increasingly spacious and beautiful cathedrals had on medieval builders. Plainchant melodies were put to use as building blocks in the development of ever more intricate musical constructs over a period of 700 years or more, culminating in the extraordinarily complex and beautiful polyphonic creations of the 16th century. *See also* CANTUS FIRMUS, MONOPHONY, ORGANUM.

RECOMMENDED RECORDINGS

CHANT: MONKS OF SANTO DOMINGO DE SILOS (EMI).

MONASTIC CHANT: HILLIER AND THEATRE OF VOICES (HARMONIA MUNDI).

OLD ROMAN CHANT (7TH–8TH CENTURIES): PÉRÈS AND ENSEMBLE ORGANUM (HARMONIA MUNDI).

Planets, The "SEVEN PIECES FOR LARGE ORCHESTRA" BY GUSTAV HOLST, composed 1914–16 and premiered September 29, 1918, at a private reading by the Queen's Hall Orchestra conducted by Adrian Boult. It was Holst's friend Clifford Bax who gave him the idea of attempting a large-scale piece depicting the planets not in terms of their physical characteristics but their astrological significance, focusing on the attributes long associated with their mythological namesakes. At the time Holst began working on the piece, astronomers had not yet discovered Pluto; the one known planet not written about was Earth, so the score consists of seven movements. The paradox is that the music of the "other" planets in every case reflects some aspect of earthly existence. The suite opens with a portrait of "Mars, the Bringer of War." The ensuing movements are "Venus, the Bringer of Peace," "Mercury, the Winged Messenger," "Jupiter, the Bringer of Jollity," "Saturn, the Bringer of Old Age," "Uranus, the Magician," and "Neptune, the Mystic."

At the first performance of *The Planets,* listeners assumed that "Mars"—with its uneasy, marchlike tread and ferociously loud climaxes—was an effigy of World War I, then still raging. But Holst had actually finished the movement before the August 1914 outbreak of hostilities. The jollity of "Jupiter" expresses itself in an accent remarkably like that of English folk music; at the heart of the movement is a hymnlike tune scored for unison strings, doubled by six horns, that Holst later set to the words "I Vow to Thee My Country." The final pages of "Neptune," with a wordless offstage female chorus, made the greatest impression on the first audiences, but Holst himself rightly judged "Saturn," whose sharp dissonances and glaring cacophony portray old age as a state of confusion, anxiety, and torment, to be the finest movement.

RECOMMENDED RECORDINGS

Boult and London Philharmonic Orchestra (EMI).

Gardiner and Philharmonia Orchestra (DG).

Previn and London Symphony Orchestra (EMI).

Pletnev, Mikhail

(b. Arkhangelsk, April 14, 1957)

Russian pianist and conductor. The son of musicians, he received his training at the Central Music School in Moscow and, from 1974, at the Moscow Conservatory, where his principal teacher was Jacob Flier. In 1978 he won the gold medal at the Tchaikovsky International Piano Competition in Moscow. In short order he came to be recognized as one of the premier pianists of his generation, a deliberate rather than spontaneous musician, gifted with a commanding technique (even Horowitz would have had difficulty duplicating his crystalline articulation in pianissimo), a big sonority, and a sometimes formidable interpretive instinct. Specializing in the virtuoso repertoire, particularly the works of Chopin, Liszt, Rachmaninov, and Prokofiev, he has uncorked gripping performances of works such as the Liszt B minor Sonata, but in recent years has shown a tendency toward exaggerated dynamics, a mannerist rubato, and the self-indulgent milking of emotion. In June of 1990 he performed at the personal invitation of Mikhail Gorbachev at the Soviet leader's summit with George Bush in Washington, D.C. He made a long-awaited Carnegie Hall recital debut in 2000.

Pletnev's conducting career began in 1980. In 1990, as the old Soviet system was giving way, he founded the Russian National Orchestra, the first entirely independent orchestra to exist in Russia since 1917; in 1993 he embarked with the ensemble on a series of recordings for Deutsche Grammophon, concentrating on the music of Russian composers, especially Tchaikovsky and Rachmaninov. To date, his conducting style has been more reserved and matter-of-fact than his pianism, though in scores such as Tchaikovsky's *Manfred* Symphony and *The Sleeping Beauty* and Rachmaninov's Symphony No. 2 he has achieved admirable results. In 2003, after temporarily ceding the role of chief conductor to Vladimir Spivakov, he was appointed artistic director of the Russian National Orchestra. He takes up the chief conductor's baton once again in 2006–07.

RECOMMENDED RECORDINGS

As pianist:

Prokofiev, Piano Sonatas Nos. 2, 7, and 8 (DG).

Tchaikovsky, Piano Concerto No. 1: Fedoseyev and Philharmonia Orchestra (Virgin Classics).

As conductor:

Tchaikovsky, *Manfred Symphony*: Russian National Orchestra (DG).

Tchaikovsky, *Sleeping Beauty*: Russian National Orchestra (DG).

Pleyel, Ignaz

(b. Ruppersthal, June 18, 1757; d. Paris, November 14, 1831)

Austrian composer, music publisher, and pianoforte maker. The child of a schoolmaster, he was taken to Vienna, where he received his early musical education from Johann Baptist Vanhal. Count Erdödy became Pleyel's patron and sent him to study composition with Joseph Haydn,

The Music Lesson ***by Matisse, 1917, with piano by Pleyel***

who later referred to him as his "dearest and most efficient pupil." Pleyel spent a couple of years in Italy at the beginning of the 1780s, and in 1784 he accepted a position in Strasbourg as assistant Kapellmeister at the cathedral, becoming Kapellmeister in 1789. Late in 1791, jobless as a result of the French Revolution, he arrived in London as conductor of the Professional Concert and found himself, much to his surprise, in competition with his old master Haydn, who was being presented at the same time by Johann Peter Salomon. Haydn maintained much affection for his former pupil, and wrote from London, "We are often together, and it does him honor to find that he knows the worth of his old father. We shall each take our share of success, and go home satisfied."

Pleyel's return to France the following year was rather ill timed; according to some sources he was declared an enemy of the Republic, though eventually he managed to clear himself of the charges by writing, while under arrest, a humdrum patriotic hymn. He settled in Paris in 1795, establishing himself as a music seller and later as a publisher; in 1802 his firm issued the first "miniature" scores ever published. Ever the entrepreneur, he secured in 1801 the first publication rights to all of Haydn's quartets written to date. By this time Pleyel's own work as a composer was largely finished. During the 1780s and 1790s, he produced a prodigious number of symphonies, concertos, and chamber pieces, especially string quartets and piano trios. His early works showed much taste and craft, but many of his compositions from about 1792 on exhibit an overly derivative style with little substance or imagination.

In 1807 Pleyel established his pianoforte factory, an enterprise that carried his name well beyond his death; his son, Camille, continued what became a highly successful business. Pleyel pianos were known for their silvery, singing quality and light touch. They were the preferred piano of Chopin, who made his Paris debut in the Pleyel rooms. The company continued to make instruments under its own name well into the 20th century.

RECOMMENDED RECORDINGS

SYMPHONIES: BAMERT AND LONDON MOZART PLAYERS (CHANDOS).

SYMPHONIES: GRODD AND CAPPELLA ISTROPOLITANA (NAXOS).

Pli selon pli (Fold upon Fold) WORK IN FIVE MOVEMENTS FOR SOPRANO AND LARGE ORCHESTRA (including multiple percussion) by Pierre Boulez, composed 1957–62. Subtitled "portrait de Mallarmé," the score represents both in its substance and technique an homage to the refractory, sensually suggestive language of the 19th-century French symbolist Stéphane Mallarmé.

RECOMMENDED RECORDING

SCHÄFER; BOULEZ AND ENSEMBLE INTERCONTEMPORAIN (DG).

poco (It., "[a] little") Term used to modify a dynamic, tempo, or expressive marking, e.g., *poco marc.* is "somewhat marcato"; *poco forte* is "somewhat loud"; *poco a poco diminuendo* is "diminuendo little by little"; *cresc. poco a poco* is "crescendo little by little."

Poem of Ecstasy, The SYMPHONIC MEDITATION IN ONE MOVEMENT BY ALEKSANDR SCRIABIN, OP. 54, composed 1905–08 and premiered December 10, 1908, by the Russian Symphony Society in New York under the baton of Modest Altschuler. The score, in effect the composer's Fourth Symphony, is a luxurious exercise in post-Wagnerian chromaticism aimed at evoking that transcendental state which, for Scriabin, represented the culmination of human potential in the ecstasy of artistic creation, a condition more or less indistinguishable from sexual ecstasy. It calls for an expansively large orchestra—including quadruple winds, eight horns, five trumpets, bells, and organ—which Scriabin uses in a manner that ranges from hyperrefined (one passage, at mm. 156–59, is marked "très parfumé") to orgiastic. Sensuous washes of sound, by turns languorous, feverish, and delirious, succeed one another until, at the end of the piece, a huge chord of C major—marked *fff* and sustained for upward of ten seconds—provides the long-awaited climax.

RECOMMENDED RECORDINGS

ASHKENAZY AND BERLIN RADIO SYMPHONY ORCHESTRA (DECCA).

MEHTA AND LOS ANGELES PHILHARMONIC ORCHESTRA (DECCA).

MUTI AND PHILADELPHIA ORCHESTRA (EMI).

Pohjola's Daughter (Pohjolan tytär) SYMPHONIC FANTASIA BY JEAN SIBELIUS, OP. 49, based on a story from the *Kalevala*. Composed during 1905–06, it was premiered December 29, 1906, in St. Petersburg by the Mariinski Theater Orchestra, the composer conducting. Sibelius conceived the music after hearing Richard Strauss conduct his own *Ein Heldenleben* and *Symphonia domestica* in Berlin; while working on the score he wrote to his wife, Aino, "This is my genre!! Here I can move without feeling the weight of tradition." The title might better be translated as "The Daughter of the North Farm," since according to Finnish mythology, Pohjola was a prosperous Viking farm community in the gloomy north.

RECOMMENDED RECORDING

BERNSTEIN AND NEW YORK PHILHARMONIC (SONY).

Pollini, Maurizio

(b. Milan, January 5, 1942)

ITALIAN PIANIST. The son of a music-loving architect, he began playing the piano at the age of five; his teachers included Carlo Lonati and Arturo Benedetti Michelangeli. He played his first concert in 1953, in Milan, and subsequently studied at the Milan Conservatory, graduating in 1959. The following year, at the age of 18 the youngest of 89 competitors, he won the Warsaw Chopin Competition. Recognizing that he needed to mature artistically, he withdrew from performing after a few months in order to extend his repertoire and work on his technique. He returned to the concert stage in the mid-1960s, and in 1968 gave his Carnegie Hall debut. Since 1971 he has recorded exclusively with Deutsche Grammophon. He has appeared in recital in most of the world's major venues and performed as soloist with many of the world's top orchestras. His repertoire includes the piano concertos of Beethoven and Brahms as well as Bach's *Das wohltemperirte Clavier,* nearly all of the solo piano music of Beethoven, large amounts of Schumann and Chopin, and works by such 20th-century composers as Debussy, Schoenberg, Stravinsky, Berg, Webern, Boulez, and Stockhausen.

Maurizio Pollini gets down to business in a recital.

Pollini has refused throughout his career to put his phenomenal technical abilities at the service of music that he believes lacks substance. He has also been unapologetic in his commitment to the postwar European avant-garde, particularly such figures as Luigi Nono (1924–90), Boulez, and Stockhausen; he sees idiomatic complexity as a gauge of musical value and views serialism in its various manifestations as the logical and necessary outcome of the past four centuries of stylistic development.

Among virtuoso pianists, Pollini is a master at turning restraint into a virtue. He is capable of astounding accuracy and velocity, yet one senses in his playing a fear of letting go, which has led to performances and recordings that are sometimes too cool and controlled. In spite of this he is able to suggest that even where there's little smoke there may still be fire. He has the ability to play Beethoven in a way that is truly annunciatory, and to take Schumann out of the hothouse and place him in the avant-garde of the 1830s. Insights such as these are rare in any era and particularly rare today.

RECOMMENDED RECORDINGS

BEETHOVEN, PIANO SONATAS, OPP. 101, 106, 109, 110, 111 (DG).

BOULEZ, PIANO SONATA NO. 2 (WITH WORKS BY PROKOFIEV, WEBERN, STRAVINSKY) (DG).

SCHUMANN, *SYMPHONIC ETUDES* (DG).

polonaise Polish dance in $\frac{3}{4}$ time typically exhibiting a "martial" or processional character, with a fanfare rhythm placing the accent on the second beat. Chopin's polonaises, written for the piano, are the best-known examples in the literature; among the most direct and emotionally assertive of his works, their character ranges substantially, from pensive pieces to utterly triumphant ones. Examples from the orchestral and operatic repertoire include the final movement of Beethoven's Triple Concerto, Op. 56, billed as a *Rondo alla Polacca*; the polonaises Tchaikovsky inserted in his opera *Eugene Onegin* and in the final movement of his Suite No. 3; and the Act III polonaise from Mussorgsky's *Boris Godunov.*

The most celebrated of Chopin's polonaises is the so-called *Heroic* Polonaise in A-flat ◉, Op. 53. Majestic, outgoing, and virtuosic, it is a quintessential example of the flamboyant approach to the genre. The piece's middle section, with its grand crescendo built on demonically fast left-hand octaves, is a litmus test of technique and endurance.

Polovtsian Dances, The *See* PRINCE IGOR.

polyphony (Gr., "many voices") The simultaneous sounding of two or more distinct musical lines (or "voices") that are rhythmically independent of one another. The style exemplified in Palestrina's masses, such as *Missa Papae Marcelli* ◉, has for centuries been considered the gold standard.

polytonality The simultaneous use of two or more tonal centers in a polyphonic texture. Ives was the first to explore polytonal effects in any methodical way, e.g., in his setting of Psalm 67 for eight-part chorus (ca. 1898–99). Other examples include the primarily chordal polytonality employed by Stravinsky in parts of *Petrushka* and *The Rite of Spring*; Britten's opposition of the keys of F minor and E major during the initial duet between Peter and Ellen Orford in *Peter Grimes*; and Ravel's brief, mainly coloristic setting of the tune in his *Boléro* in three keys at once: C major in the first horn and celesta, E major in first piccolo, and G major in second piccolo.

Pomp and Circumstance FIVE MILITARY MARCHES BY EDWARD ELGAR; the title they share comes from a line in Shakespeare's *Othello,* in which the word "circumstance" means pageantry. There is certainly plenty of that in these works. Elgar composed the first four between 1901 and 1907, but the fifth not until 1929–30. March No. 1, in D major, opens boisterously; its middle section has the tune familiar from so many graduation ceremonies. With its reliance on the strings, March No. 2, in A minor, is the most symphonic of the set—one would scarcely expect to actually *march* to this music, though it is martial enough in its swagger. The shadowy third march, in C minor, has been likened to a scherzo, while March No. 4, in G major, is another first-rate processional (composed in 1907, at the same time as Elgar's First Symphony, it shares some of the melancholy feeling of that work). The fifth march, in C major, completes the circle in a lighthearted, almost nostalgic fashion.

RECOMMENDED RECORDING

MENUHIN AND ROYAL PHILHARMONIC ORCHESTRA (VIRGIN CLASSICS).

Ponce, Manuel

(b. Fresnillo, December 8, 1882; d. Mexico City, April 24, 1948)

MEXICAN COMPOSER AND PIANIST. Born into a musical family, he began taking piano lessons from his sister when he was six; by the time he was 16 he was a church organist in Aguascalientes. He studied in Mexico City (1900–01), at the Liceo Musicale in Bologna (1904–05), and in Berlin (1905–07). At the end of 1907 he accepted a post as piano teacher at the Conservatorio Nacional in Mexico City, where he taught Carlos Chávez, among others. In 1912 he gave a concert of his own works (including the premiere of his Piano Concerto) that confirmed him as Mexico's leading serious composer, and he wrote the song "Estrellita," which instantly made him Mexico's most popular composer as well. His failure to secure the copyright cost him the financial independence he craved.

Ponce spent 1925–33 in Paris, where he studied with Paul Dukas and founded the review *Gaceta musical.* He formed a close friendship with Andrés Segovia, for whom he would write a group of sonatas and preludes for guitar that is perhaps the most important contribution to the instrument's 20th-century repertoire. Ponce returned to Mexico City in 1933 to serve as director of the Conservatorio Nacional. The 1930s and 1940s saw the premieres of several major works, including the symphonic poems *Chapultepec* (1934) and *Ferial* (1943), the *Suite en estilo antiguo* (1935), the *Concierto del sur* for guitar and orchestra (with Segovia as soloist, in 1941), and the Violin Concerto (with Szeryng as soloist, in 1943).

Like many Latin American composers of his generation, Ponce sought to create a national musical tradition for his country. He succeeded in doing so, and his success inspired younger colleagues, including Chávez and Revueltas, to contribute their best efforts to the cause as well.

RECOMMENDED RECORDINGS

CONCIERTO DEL SUR (WITH GUITAR CONCERTOS OF RODRIGO AND VILLA-LOBOS): ISBIN; SEREBRIER AND NEW YORK PHILHARMONIC (WARNER CLASSICS).

GUITAR SONATAS: VIEAUX (AZICA).

VIOLIN CONCERTO, *CONCIERTO DEL SUR*: SZERYNG; MORENO; BATIZ AND ROYAL PHILHARMONIC ORCHESTRA; PIANO CONCERTO: OSORIO; BATIZ AND STATE OF MEXICO SYMPHONY ORCHESTRA (ASV).

Pons, Lily

(b. Draguignan, April 12, 1898; d. Dallas, February 13, 1976)

FRENCH/AMERICAN SOPRANO. Born Alice Joséphine Pons, she entered the Paris Conservatoire as a pianist. Her education was interrupted by ill health and the onset of World War I, following which she was engaged by Paris's Théâtre des Variétés. As "Lily" Pons she played ingenue roles until 1923 when she left the house to marry August Mesritz. At his encouragement she began serious vocal training with Alberti di Gorostiaga in 1925, making her debut as Delibes's Lakmé at the Mulhouse Opera in 1928. Despite a lack of experience, she auditioned in 1930 for Giulio Gatti-Casazza, general manager of the Metropolitan Opera, who, with the recent retirement of Amelita Galli-Curci, found himself in need of a leading coloratura soprano. Begrudgingly engaged, and with no publicity fanfare from the reluctant Met, Pons made a spectacular debut in Donizetti's *Lucia di Lammermoor* on January 3, 1931. She remained at the Met in virtual ownership of a small list of roles (Lakmé and Marie in *La fille du régiment* among them) until the silver anniversary of her debut, in 1956. She was a petite, glamorous presence on the stage in an era when those qualities were in short supply. Her voice was small, but it had considerable focus and carrying power. From time to time critics would carp about the accuracy of her pitch and her musical taste, but her vocal agility and extended upper register, combined with her considerable onstage charm, left an overall impression that dazzled the public. Between 1935 and 1937 she starred in three films, including RKO's *I Dream Too Much,* with Henry Fonda and Lucille Ball. Divorced in 1933, she married conductor André Kostelanetz in 1938. They were frequent collaborators in concerts, broadcasts, and recordings; up to the time of their divorce in 1958, they made numerous tours in the United States and abroad, giving many performances for U.S. armed forces during World War II. Pons was awarded the Légion d'Honneur in 1938. Varieties both of rose and water lily bear her name, as does Lilypons, a town in Maryland. She officially retired from the operatic stage in November 1962 with a performance of *Lucia di Lammermoor* in Ft. Worth, but, collaborating with Kostelanetz, she made several concert appearances in her mid-70s, before her death from cancer at 77.

Lily Pons

RECOMMENDED RECORDING

ARIAS FROM *LAKMÉ, LUCIA DI LAMMERMOOR, IL BARBIERE DI SIVIGLIA, RIGOLETTO,* OTHERS (PEARL).

Ponselle, Rosa

(b. Meriden, Conn., January 22, 1897; d. Green Spring Valley, Md., May 25, 1981)

AMERICAN SOPRANO. One of the greatest singers of the 20th century, she was born Rosa Melba Ponselle to parents who had immigrated from near Naples. As a teenager she worked in a variety of musical jobs, including silent-movie accompanist and sheet music demonstrator. She eventually joined her older sister, Carmella, in New York City, where they enjoyed a successful career in vaudeville, billed as "Those Italian Girls with Operatic Voices." Carmella had operatic aspirations, and began formal vocal training with teacher-coach William Thornton in New York (she would eventually spend nine seasons on the roster at the Metropolitan Opera). When Rosa, who had had some informal music lessons with her mother, began studying with Thornton, her improvement was rapid and impressive. Fortuitously, owing to America's entry into World War I, the Met had been unable to import a European soprano to sing the role of Leonora opposite Enrico Caruso in its long-planned premiere of Verdi's *La forza del destino.* Though sources are divided on the role Thornton played, it is clear that Caruso, upon meeting and hearing Ponselle, was impressed enough to arrange an audition with the Met's general manager Giulio Gatti-Casazza, who, after a second audition, engaged the 21-year-old despite her vaudeville background and lack of experience. Ponselle's debut, on November 15, 1918, was the beginning of a sensational Met career that would last 19 seasons. During the 1920s, she established herself as a singer of distinction, excelling in lyric-dramatic roles such as Elisabetta in Verdi's *Don Carlo* and Elvira in *Ernani,* Santuzza in Mascagni's *Cavalleria rusticana,* Maddalena in Giordano's *Andrea Chénier,* and Rachel in Halévy's *La Juive.* Her portrayal of Giulia in Spontini's *La vestale* in 1925 revealed a singer coming into her prime, and her performance in the title role of Bellini's *Norma,* in 1927, established her absolutely. In recordings made at the time, one can hear the Ponselle trademarks: a voice of nobility and stature capable of perfect legato and flawless fioriture, rich and warm with an unusually full low range that ascended seamlessly to a radiant high B-flat. Onstage, her abilities as an actress made her the living embodiment of the emotions to which she gave voice.

A young Rosa Ponselle

Ponselle sang at Covent Garden (1929–31) and at Florence's first Maggio Musicale in 1933, but while considering an offer from La Scala, she heard tenor Giacomo Lauri-Volpi booed over a botched high note in a performance of Bellini's *I puritani,* and reportedly wired her agent: "Forget Milan. Only in America!" She continued to sing at the Met, adding such important roles as Violetta, Donna Anna, and Luisa Miller to her repertoire, but the trepidation with which she had always approached the top of her voice, plus an ongoing battle with stage fright, haunted her. In 1935 her beloved Gatti-Casazza retired, and Edward Johnson, for whom Ponselle felt no warmth, became the new general manager. In that same year, Ponselle introduced her last new role, Carmen, to the New York audience. Though successful at the box office, it generated a critical backlash that greatly upset her. She married Carle A. Jackson in 1936, and at the end of the 1936–37 season, at age 40 and still in her vocal prime, she retired from the stage. From that time until her death she occupied Villa Pace, her house in Green Spring Valley, north of Baltimore. Divorced from Jackson in 1951, she served as artistic director of the Baltimore Civic Opera, and in later years coached a handful of lucky up-and-coming singers, including James Morris.

RECOMMENDED RECORDING

"CASTA DIVA" (ARIAS FROM *NORMA, AIDA, ERNANI,* SONGS) (PEARL).

Popp, Lucia

(b. Uhorská Ves, November 12, 1939; d. Munich, November 16, 1993)

SLOVAK/AUSTRIAN SOPRANO. Her initial career interests in medicine and theater were superseded after a voice teacher recognized her potential when she sang in

Lucia Popp in the recording studio

a student theatrical production. She studied at the Bratislava Music Academy and made her professional debut at 23 as the Queen of the Night in Mozart's *Die Zauberflöte* with the Bratislava Opera. She was soon engaged at the Vienna Staatsoper, where her debut role was Barbarina in Mozart's *Le nozze di Figaro*. Her success with that small part led to her being cast in numerous larger roles during her lifetime tenure at the Staatsoper. She made her Metropolitan Opera debut in 1967 as the Queen of the Night, and returned to sing the roles of Pamina in *Die Zauberflöte* and Sophie in *Der Rosenkavalier*. Retaining her specialization in Mozart and Richard Strauss, she moved on as her voice matured to more substantial parts such as Susanna in *Le nozze di Figaro*, the title role in Strauss's *Arabella*, and the Marschallin in *Der Rosenkavalier*. She also was a memorable exponent of Marzellina (*Fidelio*), Janáček's Vixen, and Adina (in *L'elisir d'amore*). Equally at home in concert and recital, where her repertoire included songs of Schubert and Schumann, she possessed a pure, argent tone that caressed the ear whether in seamless legato or rapid passagework. The sound became more ample as she aged, while retaining a limpid clarity. Popp was a marvelously communicative actress. She received the title of Kammersängerin from the Austrian government in 1979, and kept an active performing schedule until shortly before her death, at 54, from a brain tumor.

RECOMMENDED RECORDINGS

BEETHOVEN: *FIDELIO*: JANOWITZ, KOLLO, FISCHER-DIESKAU; BERNSTEIN AND VIENNA PHILHARMONIC (DG).

"CHILDREN'S SONGS AND LULLABIES" (ORFEO).

JANÁČEK, *THE CUNNING LITTLE VIXEN*: RANDOVÁ, JEDLICKÁ; MACKERRAS AND VIENNA PHILHARMONIC (DECCA).

MOZART, *LE NOZZE DI FIGARO*: TE KANAWA, VON STADE, RAMEY, ALLEN; SOLTI AND LONDON PHILHARMONIC ORCHESTRA (DECCA).

SCHUBERT, SONGS: JOHNSON (HYPERION).

Porgy and Bess OPERA IN THREE ACTS BY GEORGE GERSHWIN, to a libretto by DuBose Heyward based on his novel *Porgy*, with additional lyrics by Ira Gershwin, premiered October 10, 1935, at the Alvin Theater in New York. The first act opens on a craps game in the fictitious locale of Catfish Row. Crown, a lowlife, and his woman, Bess, join the game. Sportin' Life, the local drug dealer, also joins the game. When one of the players wins, a drunken Crown fights with him and stabs him with a cotton hook. Crown bolts, leaving Bess stranded. Nobody in Catfish Row offers to help Bess except the crippled Porgy, who lets her stay with him. Bess falls in love with Porgy, who eventually stabs Crown during a fight and is sent to prison. At the end of the opera, Bess takes up with Sportin' Life, and the pair set off for New York. Upon his release from jail, Porgy decides that he, too, must go to New York to find her. The realistic plot elements and strongly etched characters of *Porgy and Bess* owe much to Heyward's close study of the African-

American communities of coastal South Carolina, where the action is set. But what places *Porgy and Bess* in the pantheon of great operas is Gershwin's music. In order to attune himself to the subject, the composer went to live on an island outside Charleston while he was working on the score. The melodies he produced are some of the most memorable in all of 20th-century opera—"Summertime," "My man's gone now," "I got plenty o' nuttin'," "Bess, you is my woman," "It ain't necessarily so"—and they endow the drama with a powerful sense of atmosphere. Although it took the Metropolitan Opera 50 years to acknowledge Gershwin's achievement (its first production of *Porgy and Bess* was in1985), *this* is the great American opera, a marvelous fusion of an American subject with innately American music.

RECOMMENDED RECORDINGS

EXCERPTS: PRICE, WARFIELD, SILLS; HENDERSON AND RCA VICTOR SYMPHONY ORCHESTRA (RCA).

WHITE, HAYMON, BLACKWELL, EVANS; RATTLE AND LONDON PHILHARMONIC (EMI).

portamento (from It. *portare*, "to carry") A seamless slide connecting one pitch to another. *See also* GLISSANDO.

posthorn Small brass instrument used as a signal horn for postal coaches. The classic posthorn of the late-18th and 19th centuries was coiled in three turns; for ease of playing, many instruments were equipped with keys or valves. The instrument receives a solo in the second trio of the second minuet of the Serenade in D of Mozart, K. 320 ◉, known as the *Posthorn* Serenade. It is also featured in a pastoral interlude in the third movement of Mahler's Symphony No. 3, where its use creates a fleeting sense of nostalgia. The characteristic triadic call of a posthorn is evoked in the piano accompaniment to the song "Die Post," in Schubert's *Winterreise.*

RECOMMENDED RECORDINGS

MAHLER, SYMPHONY NO. 3: MEHTA AND LOS ANGELES PHILHARMONIC ORCHESTRA (DECCA).

MOZART, SERENADE IN D, K. 320: MACKERRAS AND PRAGUE CHAMBER ORCHESTRA (TELARC).

Poulenc, Francis

(b. Paris, January 7, 1899; d. Paris, January 30, 1963)

FRENCH COMPOSER AND PIANIST. Many of his best pieces exude the smoky aroma of the nightclub and café, which often masks their concomitant sincerity and seriousness. Much like some composers of the Classical era, he worked with topics, only his were those of 20th-century Paris: jazz, silent movies, cabaret, folk song. He was influenced by the music of Satie and Stravinsky, though the Stravinskian elements in his oeuvre are similar to a virus that has been weakened for purposes of inoculation.

Poulenc was born into a well-to-do bourgeois family. His father, a devout Roman Catholic from the Aveyron district in the south of France, managed the family pharmaceutical firm (which later became Rhône-Poulenc, and is today's Aventis, maker of Allegra); his mother, Parisian through and through and a talented amateur pianist, came from a line of artists and craftsmen. Poulenc's artistic nature combined his mother's effervescence and his father's deep faith. When he was five he began piano lessons with his mother, and from 1914 to 1917 was a student of the brilliant Ricardo Viñes, preferred interpreter of Debussy and Ravel. World War I and the early loss of his parents (both of whom died when he was in his teens) forced Poulenc to abandon his plan to study at the Paris Conservatoire, but his untutored gift for composition had already begun to show when he was 18: His *Rapsodie nègre* for baritone and chamber ensemble caught the ear of both Stravinsky and Diaghilev. He was drafted in 1918 and spent the next three years in uniform, in no real danger and composing all the while. In 1920, with his works already being published and successfully making the rounds of cutting-edge Parisian salons, he was anointed one of LES SIX. Despite this dollop of celebrity, he began private studies the following year with Charles Koechlin, feeling that he relied too much on instinct, not enough on method.

He was still studying with Koechlin when Diaghilev commissioned him to write the ballet *Les biches* (*The Does*; 1923) for his Ballets Russe. The jaunty score that resulted is vintage Poulenc: spirited, irreverent, half Stravinsky, half circus. During the 1930s, Poulenc's music took a more serious turn, after he came to grips with his homosexuality and weathered the first of several depressions. He sat out World War II in occupied France, but enjoyed a blazing summer of productivity and fresh inspiration in the 1950s and early 1960s, cut short by a fatal heart attack just weeks after he turned 64.

Poulenc's songs (most composed between 1935 and 1959) were his major achievement. The stimulus for two-thirds of them was his association as a recital partner with the baritone Pierre Bernac. Poulenc's favorite poet was Paul Éluard, whose work he set in *Cinq poèmes de Paul Éluard,* the enchanting love-song cycles *Tel jour, telle nuit* (*Such a Day, Such a Night*) and *Miroirs brûlants* (*Burning Mirrors*), both from the 1930s, and *La fraîcheur et le feu* (*The Coolness and the Fire*), from 1950. A close second was Guillaume Apollinaire, whose surrealist play *Les mamelles de Tirésias* (*The Breasts of Tiresias*) inspired Poulenc to his first operatic effort, an *opéra bouffe* that received its premiere in 1947. Where *Tirésias* flirted with absurdity in music of both high and low style, Poulenc's next opera, *Dialogues des Carmélites* (1953–56), was utterly serious. A sensitive, compelling

***Francis Poulenc, master of* mélodie**

drama about a group of nuns put to death during the French Revolution, it is one of the operatic masterpieces of the 20th century. Poulenc showed yet another side of his genius in his final work for the stage, *La voix humaine* (1958; libretto by Jean Cocteau), a poignant one-person tragedy whose single prop is a telephone.

As bookends around *Dialogues des Carmélites,* Poulenc composed two of the most surprising, beautiful, and innovative sacred works of the 20th century: his settings of the *Stabat mater* (1950) and *Gloria* (1959). The *Stabat mater* is a potpourri of childlike sentiment, Mozartean grace, and salty cabaret harmonies, in which genuine devotion is expressed in the vernacular of a 20th-century *mélodiste* and bon vivant who did not confine his religious feelings to church. The *Gloria* is symphonic in conception and bold in execution—what stand out are the Stravinskian colors, textures, and rhythms. In both works, the dreadful Latin scansion is intentional, reflecting Poulenc's disdain for the dead language and his desire to put feeling first.

Poulenc created several instrumental works of high quality. One of his first major works was the *Concert champêtre* (*Rustic Concerto*; 1927–28) for harpsichord and orchestra, written for Wanda Landowska. During the 1930s, he composed two concertos on commission, one for two pianos and one for the unusual disposition of organ, strings, and timpani. The latter is more serious, at times religious in tone. The Concerto for Two Pianos, which Poulenc wrote for himself and his friend Jacques Février, is altogether light: its first movement, a humorous mutilation of D minor, ends with a weird apostrophe reminiscent of some gamelan music Poulenc had heard in 1931, while the second movement curdles Mozart's C major concerto, K. 467, with uniquely bittersweet harmonies and melodic twists.

Among Poulenc's gifts to the repertoire for woodwinds are a trio for oboe, bassoon, and piano and the *Aubade* for piano and 18 wind instruments, both from the 1920s, as well as a marvelous sextet for flute, oboe, clarinet, bassoon, horn, and piano, from the 1930s. Late in his career, secure in his idiom and seeking nothing more than to delight, he revisited the winds in a series of sonatas: The one for flute and piano (1957) was composed for Rampal and has entered the repertoire of every flutist ◉; the sonatas for clarinet and for oboe, from the early 1960s, are nearly as fine.

The fact that Poulenc's music is often a send-up of something else, or that it happily evokes, with feigned naïveté, a world of straw boaters and canes, makes it easy to overlook the genuine nostalgia, ambivalence, and heartbreak that so frequently lie within. With his great gift for melody and almost equally remarkable harmonic intuition—which enabled him to season an essentially diatonic idiom with tangy chromaticisms—Poulenc was born to write songs and music that sings. In a time and place where emotion in music was viewed with suspicion, he was not afraid to give pleasure or confess pain. The result was music that is often witty, insouciant, a bit naughty, occasionally unsettling, but never boring.

RECOMMENDED RECORDINGS

Les Biches (with other works): Prêtre and Philharmonia Orchestra (EMI).

Chamber music (complete): Nash Ensemble (Hyperion).

Chamber music (complete): Tharaud, others (Naxos).

Dialogues des Carmélites: Duval, Crespin, Gorr, Berton; Dervaux and Paris Opera (EMI).

Flute Sonata: Pahud, Le Sage (EMI).

Gloria, *Stabat Mater*: Choeur Régional Vittoria; Borst and Orchestre de la Cité (Naxos).

Gloria, *Stabat Mater*: Westminster Singers with Hickox and London Sinfonia (Virgin Classics).

Songs (complete): Ameling, Souzay, others; Baldwin (EMI).

Prague Symphony Name associated with Wolfgang Amadeus Mozart's Symphony No. 38 in D, K. 504, completed December 6, 1786, in Vienna and possibly premiered there before being performed in Prague for the first time, on January 19, 1787. Although long overshadowed by the last three symphonies Mozart wrote, the *Prague* is their equal in the vitality and development of its ideas, the brilliance of its counterpoint and orchestration, and the mastery of form Mozart displays in it. The slow introduction that prefaces its first movement is the most impressive such design in all of Classical music, a masterpiece of cumulative tension in which the rhythmic irregularity and harmonic vagueness of the first 15 measures and the extraordinary textural complexity of the following 21 (anchored solidly in the demonic D minor of *Don Giovanni*) combine to create a sense of high drama and expectation. The main body of the first movement incorporates a remarkable range of topics—the learned, brilliant,

Sturm und Drang, and singing styles are all embraced, with dazzling virtuosity and an amazing sureness of connection from one idea to the next. The writing displays a contrapuntal dexterity exceeding anything that had been tried in a symphony before, particularly in the movement's development section, whose severity places it on the order of the most advanced chamber music (which, with a string complement of no more than 14 in the Prague orchestra, may have been just what it sounded like). Yet there is a symphonic richness to Mozart's scoring that makes the overall effect grand indeed.

The G major Andante opens with what in other hands might have been a simple, aria-like subject in the strings. But in Mozart's hands, it quickly takes on a chromatic inflection and is spun out almost in the manner of a fantasy, through a series of highly profiled episodes in which sharp pathos and pastoral gentleness succeed one another with surprising swiftness. The music of the effervescent concluding Presto is cut from the same cloth as "Aprite presto," the lively duet between Susanna and Cherubino in Act II of *Le nozze di Figaro,* which at the time of the symphony's premiere was all the rage in Prague. The opera buffa brilliance of the writing must have delighted those who already knew *Figaro,* and sent those who didn't scurrying off to hear it.

Mozart looking over Prague

RECOMMENDED RECORDINGS

BÖHM AND BERLIN PHILHARMONIC (DG).

BRITTEN AND ENGLISH CHAMBER ORCHESTRA (DECCA).

WALTER AND COLUMBIA SYMPHONY ORCHESTRA (SONY).

prelude Literally, "to play before." Often the introductory movement to a suite or to a more involved essay such as a fugue. In the 19th century the term came increasingly to be applied to freestanding keyboard miniatures in a variety of simple forms (mainly two- or three-part), and to the suggestive, mood-setting introductions that took the place of full-blown opera overtures (e.g., in works such as Verdi's *La traviata* and *Un ballo in maschera* and in Wagner's operas from *Lohengrin* on).

Improvised preludes for organ and other keyboard instruments date back to the middle of the 15th century, and in the 16th and 17th centuries the prelude emerged as a common musical genre; notable examples can be found in the works of Frescobaldi, Sweelinck, and Buxtehude. But it was J. S. Bach who elevated the keyboard prelude to a place of distinction in the musical cosmos. The protean nature of his preludes for organ, and especially of the preludes that appear in the two books of *Das wohltemperirte Clavier,* provided an example for numerous followers, and showed that preludes could be works of interest in themselves, rather than mere setup pieces. Chopin took this idea a step further in his 24 *Préludes,* Op. 28 (1838–39), for piano. These brief essays are preludes to nothing but themselves. Striking in their variety of style, texture, and mood, they are among the most modern pieces Chopin wrote—though a few of them are not so much pieces but, as the poet Alfred de Vigny said (about poetry), "pearls of thought." Aphoristic, even cryptic, each is its own little universe.

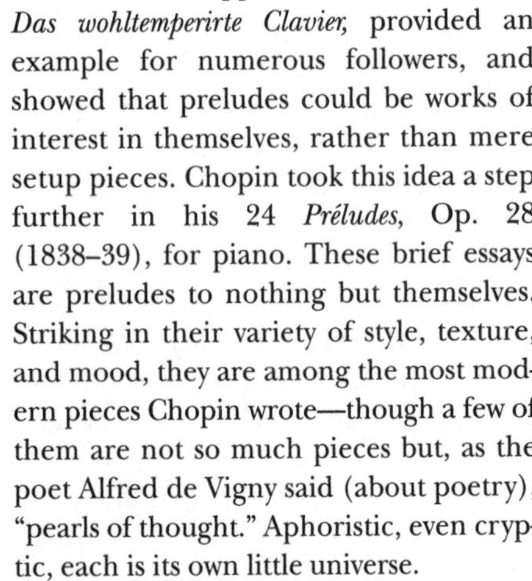

Alkan (1847), Busoni (1881), César Cui (1903), and Rachmaninov (between 1892 and 1910) also produced cycles of preludes for the piano in all of the major and minor keys (some of Rachmaninov's amount to small symphonic poems for the ivories). Numerous others have composed individual preludes or sets, including Scriabin, Szymanowski, Gershwin, and Ginastera. With Debussy's 24 preludes (in two books, published in 1910 and 1913), the genre may well have reached its apex. In these dreamy works key no longer matters: Debussy tantalizes the listener by appending titles to each one, but only at the end of the pieces, in parentheses, so that each becomes not merely an abstraction or an evocation, but the memory of one. Many of the titles contain literary referents (e.g., the fourth prelude from Book I is titled "Les sons et les parfums tournent dans l'air du soir," a line from Charles Baudelaire's "Harmonie du soir") and the music itself is full of fanciful allusions to popular and vernacular styles, assembled in a way that produces an inexhaustible fascination. The pieces in the second book, even more aphoristic, rarefied, and atmospheric than those of the first, verge on atonality.

Prélude à l'après-midi d'un faune (Prelude to the Afternoon of a Faun) Orchestral work by Claude Debussy, completed in 1894, inspired by a poem by Stéphane Mallarmé. The quintessential work of musical impressionism, it is also one of the seminal works of modernism, in which the elements of harmony, meter, rhythm, and timbre are treated in an astonishingly advanced and innovative manner. Most apparent to the ear, and certainly among the score's most wonderful attibutes, is the coloristic finesse of Debussy's orchestration—the way he paints a sonic canvas with fragments of motive and color. But the way the composer *frames* the canvas is equally remarkable. Calling for a slow tempo (initially, *Très modéré*), and utilizing a metric scheme that is "stretched out" (mainly $\frac{9}{8}$ and $\frac{12}{8}$ in the early pages), he introduces a host of rhythmic complications and irregularities whose purpose is to suppress a sense of regular pulse. The harmony is intentionally elusive, the direction of any given phrase or passage ambivalent, vague. The drowsy, suffocating warmth alluded to early in the poem is superbly rendered by Debussy in a languorous flute solo that unfolds against a dappled background of muted strings and feathery tremolos, made all the more effective by the absence of a clear pulse in the first pages of the score; the feeling of desire and passion barely suppressed at the climax of the poem is mirrored by the music's gradually intensifying lyricism; and the dreamy oblivion into which the Faun sinks at its end is evoked by the gradual fragmentation of overlapping melodies from earlier in the piece.

Debussy's evocative genius was recognized by Mallarmé himself, for whom the composer played the prelude shortly after he finished it. "I had not expected anything like that," the poet remarked: "The music prolongs the emotion of the poem and fixes the scene more vividly than colors could have done."

préludes, Les Symphonic poem by Franz Liszt, originally drafted in 1848 and recast in the early 1850s, and premiered in Weimar in 1854. It is the most popular of Liszt's twelve symphonic poems. The composer originally intended the work as an introduction to a choral composition, but eventually settled on the idea of making it a free-standing piece and linking it programmatically to one of Alphonse de Lamartine's *Méditations poétiques.* The score is in four broad sections, roughly corresponding to the divisions of Lamartine's poem. The music of the first section is intended to suggest "moods of spring and love," the second, "storms of life." There is a long "peaceful idyll" followed by a militant celebration of "strife and victory." Two recurrent melodies dominate the work, which Liszt varies substantially so that each time they appear in a different guise, they possess an entirely different expressive character. The composer himself called the process "thematic transformation."

The music of *Les préludes* is tremendously effective, so much so that during the 20th century several passages from the work became Hollywood stock-in-trade, turning up in everything from *Flash Gordon* serials to the Loony Toons. Liszt's treatment of the orchestra is nearly as inventive as his manipulation of the thematic material, and the work's blazingly scored concluding pages are among the most triumphant in the Romantic literature.

presto (It., "fast") Tempo marking that usually indicates a more rapid pace than *allegro* or *vivace. Prestissimo,* meaning "very fast," calls for the utmost speed, and is the quickest tempo in normal use.

Previn, André [Priwin, Andreas Ludwig]

(b. Berlin, April 6, 1929)

GERMAN/AMERICAN CONDUCTOR, COMPOSER, AND PIANIST. In 1938 his family left Germany for Paris, giving Previn the opportunity to study briefly at the Conservatoire, en route to settling in California in 1939. Previn became an American citizen in 1943; as a young man he studied composition in Los Angeles with Ernst Toch and Mario Castelnuovo-Tedesco, and took conducting lessons in San Francisco with Pierre Monteux. During the 1950s, he made a name for himself both as a jazz pianist and as an arranger and conductor of film music. By the time he was 35 he had received four Academy Awards for his work

***Rex Harrison and Audrey Hepburn in a scene from* My Fair Lady**

on the film scores to *Gigi* (1958), *Porgy and Bess* (1959), *Irma La Douce* (1963), and *My Fair Lady* (1964).

Previn made his concert conducting debut in 1962 with the Saint Louis Symphony Orchestra. In 1967 he succeeded Sir John Barbirolli as music director of the Houston Symphony Orchestra, and from 1968 to 1979 he served as principal conductor of the London Symphony Orchestra. His subsequent posts have included the music directorships of the Pittsburgh Symphony Orchestra (1976–84) and the Los Angeles Philharmonic (1985–89), and a brief stint as music director of the Royal Philharmonic Orchestra (1985–87). He has also enjoyed productive relationships with the Vienna Philharmonic and Staatskapelle Dresden.

As a composer, Previn has concentrated in recent years on matching his music to the talents of favorite performers: He has written song cycles for Kathleen Battle (*Honey and Rue*; 1992) and Barbara Bonney (*Sallie Chisum Remembers Billy the Kid*; 1994), an opera for Renée Fleming (*A Streetcar*

Named Desire, based on Tennessee Williams's play and premiered in San Francisco in 1998), a piano concerto for Vladimir Ashkenazy (1985), and sonatas for Yo-Yo Ma (1993) and Gil Shaham (1994). One of his latest works is a concerto for violinist Anne-Sophie Mutter, whom he married on August 1, 2002.

RECOMMENDED RECORDINGS

As conductor:

Britten, *Sinfonia da Requiem, Peter Grimes* (orchestral excerpts); Holst, *Egdon Heath*: London Symphony Orchestra (EMI).

Korngold, violin concerto; Tchaikovsky, Violin Concerto: Mutter with London Symphony Orchestra, Vienna Philharmonic (DG).

Vaughan Williams, symphonies (complete): London Symphony Orchestra (RCA).

Walton, Symphony No. 1: London Symphony Orchestra (RCA).

As composer:

Sallie Chisum Remembers Billy the Kid: Bonney, soprano; Previn and London Symphony Orchestra (DG).

A Streetcar Named Desire: Fleming, Futral, Gilfry; Previn and San Francisco Opera (DG).

Violin Concerto: Mutter; Previn and Boston Symphony Orchestra (DG).

Prey, Hermann

(b. Berlin, July 11, 1929; d. Krailling vor München, July 23, 1998)

German baritone. He was a student of Gunther Baum and Jaro Prohaska at Berlin's Hochschule für Musik. In 1952 his victories in competitions sponsored by the U.S. Armed Services Assistance Program for German youth and by Hessischer Rundfunk of Frankfurt resulted in both his German recital debut and—in concert with Eugene Ormandy and the Philadelphia Orchestra—his first appearance in the U.S. In 1952 he made his operatic debut in Wiesbaden, as Monuccio in *Tiefland* by Eugen d'Albert (1864–1932). He rapidly established himself on the international scene, taking his first bows at the Metropolitan Opera in 1960, as Wolfram in Wagner's *Tannhäuser,* and enjoying regular engagements in Munich, Berlin, Salzburg, Vienna, Paris, and London. He was especially admired for his portrayal of comic, lyric baritone roles, including Figaro (Mozart's and Rossini's), Eisenstein in *Die Fledermaus,* Papageno in *Die Zauberflöte,* Guglielmo in *Così fan tutte,* and Harlekin in *Ariadne auf Naxos*; his repertoire extended to Germont in Verdi's *La traviata,* the title role in Tchaikovsky's *Eugene Onegin,* and, later, the Speaker in Mozart's *Die Zauberflöte* and Beckmesser in Wagner's *Die Meistersinger von Nürnberg,* which he performed brilliantly at Bayreuth from 1981. With his characteristic warm, beautiful sound, excellent diction, and clear projection, he was also a natural on the recital and concert platform, settings in which the avuncular warmth of his personality readily came across to audiences. A notable soloist in works of Bach, Brahms, and Mahler, he was also one of the most widely respected lieder singers of the century; his insightful interpretations of the songs of Schubert

Hermann Prey enjoying a happy moment in rehearsal

were particularly admired. He recorded extensively throughout his career. From 1982 he taught at Hamburg's Musikhochschule. His 1981 autobiography, *Premierenfieber,* was issued in English in 1986 as *First Night Fever.*

RECOMMENDED RECORDINGS

MAHLER, *LIEDER EINES FAHRENDEN GESELLEN*: HAITINK AND CONCERTGEBOUW ORCHESTRA (PHILIPS).

MOZART, *LE NOZZE DI FIGARO*: JANOWITZ, MATHIS, TROYANOS, FISCHER-DIESKAU; BÖHM AND DEUTSCHE OPER BERLIN (DG).

ROSSINI, *IL BARBIERE DI SIVIGLIA*: BERGANZA, ALVA, DARA; ABBADO AND LONDON SYMPHONY ORCHESTRA (DG).

STRAUSS, SONGS: SAWALLISCH (ORFEO).

Price, Leontyne

(b. Laurel, Miss., February 10, 1927)

AMERICAN SOPRANO. She possessed one of the great voices of the 20th century—in its richness of timbre, the purity of its upper register, the resonance of its chest tones, and above all in its sheer size it was a phenomenal instrument—and during a career spanning more than three decades, she dazzled opera audiences in Europe and North America with both the splendor of her singing and the power of her characterization.

Both of Price's grandfathers were Methodist ministers; her father was a carpenter and her mother a nurse-midwife. She studied music at Central State College in Wilberforce, Ohio, and moved to New York in 1949 to pursue vocal studies at Juilliard. While there, she was singled out by composer-critic Virgil Thomson in a student performance of Verdi's *Falstaff*; Thomson offered her the role of Saint Cecilia in a 1952 revival of his opera *Four Saints in Three Acts,* which in turn led to her being cast as Bess in a touring production of Gershwin's *Porgy and Bess.* Price was chosen by conductor Peter Hermann Adler to sing the title role in an NBC television production of Puccini's *Tosca* in 1955, and reengaged the following year as Pamina in Mozart's *Die Zauberflöte.* In 1957 she made her debut with the San Francisco Opera, singing the role of the New Prioress (Madame Lidoine) in the American premiere of Poulenc's *Dialogues des Carmélites.* The following season, again with the San Francisco company, she appeared for the first time in two roles that would be central to her career: Aida, and Leonora in Verdi's *Il trovatore.*

Price made her Covent Garden debut in 1958, as Aida, and with Herbert von Karajan in the pit she sang the same role at her debut with the Vienna Staatsoper in 1959—an appearance that turned out to be the sensation of the season. She was subsequently engaged in Verona, Milan, and Salzburg, and made her Metropolitan Opera debut, in Verdi's *Il trovatore,* on January 27, 1961, shortly before her 34th birthday. During the 1960s and 1970s, she was a regular at the Met; she created the role of Cleopatra in Barber's *Antony and Cleopatra* for the opening of the company's 1966 season, and virtually owned the roles of Leonora, Aida, and Tosca during her prime.

While known especially for her memorable embodiments of the major Verdi and Puccini heroines, Price was also a superb recitalist. The range and size of her voice at times seemed superhuman, but her expression was deeply and intensely human, never histrionic. In that regard, she was the equal of Ponselle

Leontyne Price in 1973

and Farrar. In addition to a compelling voice and a highly cultivated artistry, Price had star quality. While she may not have been a great actress, hers was the kind of stage presence that comes along once or twice in a generation. So far, only one American-born soprano has achieved greater notoriety on the world's opera stages, and that was Maria Callas.

RECOMMENDED RECORDINGS

BARBER, *HERMIT SONGS*: BARBER; *KNOXVILLE, SUMMER OF 1915*, ARIAS FROM *ANTONY AND CLEOPATRA*, OTHERS: SCHIPPERS AND NEW PHILHARMONIA ORCHESTRA (RCA).

VERDI, *AIDA*: GORR, VICKERS, MERRILL, TOZZI; SOLTI AND ROME OPERA ORCHESTRA (DECCA).

VERDI, PUCCINI, ARIAS FROM *AIDA, IL TROVATORE, MADAMA BUTTERFLY, TOSCA, TURANDOT*: FABRITIIS AND ROME OPERA ORCHESTRA (RCA).

prima donna (It., "first lady") The principal soprano in the cast of an opera or in a company of singers.

Primrose, William

(b. Glasgow, August 23, 1904; d. Provo, Utah, May 1, 1982)

SCOTTISH VIOLIST AND TEACHER. His first lessons were on the violin with his father, then with Camillo Ritter, who had studied under Joseph Joachim. At 15, he moved to London to study violin at the Guildhall School with Max Mossel, receiving the Gold Medal upon his graduation in 1924. He then went to Eugène Ysaÿe, with whom he studied from 1925 through 1927; it was Ysaÿe who encouraged him to pursue his desire to be a violist. In 1930 Primrose became the violist in the London String Quartet, playing with the group until it was forced to disband in 1935. For the next two years he played wherever he could find work, ranging from the pit of Covent Garden to solo appearances on the concert stage, including a performance of the Walton Viola Concerto with Thomas Beecham (in which the conductor got lost in the scherzo). In 1937 Primrose joined Arturo Toscanini's NBC Symphony as principal violist. He remained in that chair for five years before committing himself full-time to a career as a soloist. Over the years, he appeared with many major orchestras in the United States and Great Britain. In a bid to enrich the repertoire he commissioned a viola concerto from Bartók in 1944; the work, unfinished at Bartók's death the following year, was completed by Tibor Serly, and Primrose premiered it in 1949. Primrose performed and recorded chamber music with some of the most illustrious musicians of the 20th century, among them Heifetz, Piatigorsky, and Kapell. Following a heart attack in 1963, his performing tapered off, but he remained active as a teacher, serving on the faculties of the University of Southern California, Indiana University, the Tōhō Gakuen School in Tokyo, and Brigham Young University, which houses his archives. He was an erudite, cultivated man and an articulate writer, as shown in his pedagogical publications.

William Primrose, doyen of the viola

One of the first to bring the viola into the spotlight as a solo instrument, Primrose captured in his performing the kind of drama and excitement more commonly associated with the violin. Short, sturdily built, and with enormous hands, he played effortlessly, with tremendous sweep and drive, and with a luminous tone. Of his many recordings, perhaps the finest was his blazing account of Berlioz's *Harold en Italie* with Serge Koussevitzky and the Boston Symphony; notable as well are his soulful renditions of Brahms's Sonata in E-flat,

Op. 120, No. 2, with Gerald Moore, and Zwei Gesänge, Op. 91, for alto, viola, and piano, with Marian Anderson.

RECOMMENDED RECORDING

BERLIOZ, *HAROLD EN ITALIE*: KOUSSEVITZKY AND BOSTON SYMPHONY ORCHESTRA (DUTTON).

Prince Igor OPERA IN A PROLOGUE AND FOUR ACTS BY ALEKSANDR PORFIR'YEVICH BORODIN, to his own libretto after a scenario by Vladimir Stasov (based on the 12th-century epic *The Lay of the Host of Igor*), posthumously premiered on November 4, 1890, at the Mariinsky Theater in St. Petersburg. Begun in 1869 and left unfinished at Borodin's death 18 years later, the work carries on the picturesque tradition of Glinka's *Ruslan and Lyudmila*, but with a strongly nationalist bent. Its score is a farrago of numbers written and scored by Borodin, passages retouched and orchestrated by Rimsky-Korsakov, and an entire act (the third) composed pretty much out of whole cloth by Glazunov; what there is by Borodin himself, most of it in the second act, is masterly. The plot of the opera deals with the defeat of the Russian prince Igor by the Polovtsians, his captivity, and his eventual escape. The score is best known for the dance sequence that ends Act II, the celebrated "Polovtsian Dances." In this finale, the warrior khan Konchak, leader of the Polovtsians, seeks to entertain the captive prince and his son by staging a series of dances in their honor. Some of the dances are gentle and exotic, while others are splendid and warlike. The Polovtsian women and children take part in the festivity alongside the men, and the whole affair builds to a rousing conclusion.

RECOMMENDED RECORDINGS

COMPLETE OPERA: KIT, GORCHAKOVA, OGNOVIENKO, MINJELKIEV; GERGIEV AND KIROV OPERA (PHILIPS).

POLOVTSIAN DANCES: BEECHAM AND ROYAL PHILHARMONIC ORCHESTRA (EMI).

program music Music that seeks to portray physical actions, objects, or scenes in a narrative manner, without the use of words. Good examples of program music include Vivaldi's *Four Seasons,* Berlioz's *Symphonie fantastique,* Rimsky-Korsakov's *Sheherazade,* Richard Strauss's *Till Eulenspiegel,* Vaughan Williams's *The Lark Ascending,* and Grofé's *Grand Canyon Suite. See also* SYMPHONIC POEM.

progression A series of chords related to one another within the context of a single key.

Prokofiev, Sergey

(b. Sontsovka, Ukraine, April 23, 1891; d. Moscow, March 5, 1953)

RUSSIAN COMPOSER AND PIANIST. He was the last great composer to grow up in tsarist Russia and one of the first artists of any stature to leave the Soviet Union after the Revolution. A musically precocious only child, he was raised in comfort by doting parents, his father a country estate manager, his mother artistically inclined and a capable pianist. At 13 he entered the St. Petersburg Conservatory, where he studied composition; by his late teens he had become a provocative and powerful "modernistic" pianist. In 1914, after a decade as a student, he left his turbulent homeland for London, where he got a commission from Sergey Diaghilev for the ballet *Ala and Lolli* (which the impresario later rejected) and heard Stravinsky's *Firebird, Petrushka,* and *The Rite of Spring.* By 1915 he had begun work on an opera based on Dostoyevsky's *The Gambler.* He returned home to find Russia in much worse turmoil than when he left, and he witnessed the Revolution of 1917 firsthand. His compositions from this time range widely, from prickly and dense piano scores to the inviting, accessible and exuberant *CLASSICAL SYMPHONY*. Motivated mainly by the desire to compose in peace, away from the chaos

The young Sergey Prokofiev, looking hardly like an enfant terrible

of war-ravaged Europe and Bolshevik-run Russia, he left his homeland for America (by way of Japan) in May 1918, with the blessing of the newly created Soviet ministry of culture. He expected to be gone for only a short time, but did not set foot on Russian soil again until 1927, and did not return for good until 1936. He did not care for Americans' musical conservatism, and the press found his work "barbaric" and "discordant." In 1921 his opera *THE LOVE FOR THREE ORANGES* received its premiere in Chicago, in French; he returned to Europe the following year, settling first in Germany, and in 1923, newly married, moved to Paris.

In Paris, Prokofiev continued to perform and compose. Conductor Serge Koussevitzky became his publisher and commissioned several works from him. It was at one of Koussevitzky's Paris concerts that the first Violin Concerto received its premiere, in 1923. Over time, Prokofiev began to change his style. The enfant terrible whose iconoclastic compositions left audiences electrified and confused through the 1920s gave way to a composer who, in his own words, had "gone down into the deeper realms of music" in search of a simpler, more direct style in which the emphasis was on emotional expression rather than novelty of syntax.

Much has been said about the forces that compelled Prokofiev to return to his native land at a time when Stalin and his minions were cracking down on artists, but financial concerns were not the main reason the prodigal son chose to come home. Starting in 1932, Prokofiev had been making increasingly frequent trips back and found the atmosphere in the U.S.S.R. more in tune with his development toward a simpler style. He also missed working with artists who shared his view of the world, and hungered for the feeling of belonging—to a people and a land—that a Russian can experience only in Russia. Commissions for the score to the film *LIEUTENANT KIJÉ*, the children's piece *PETER AND THE WOLF*, and the ballet *ROMEO AND JULIET* all came his way between 1933 and 1936. One of the most important projects of his first years back in Russia was his collaboration with the director Sergey

Prokofiev **(right)** ***with Sergei Eisenstein*** **(center)** ***and Edward Tisse, in 13th-century costumes, during the filming of*** **Alexander Nevsky**

Eisenstein on the film *Alexander Nevsky*, premiered in 1938. Prokofiev's score, one of the most vibrantly descriptive and dramatic in the history of cinema, combines symphonic grandeur and edgy modernism in a way that would typify Prokofiev's Soviet production; for concert use he extracted the meat of the score and turned it into a cantata.

In 1940 Prokofiev received a commission from the Kirov Theater in Leningrad to compose a ballet based on the Cinderella tale. The German invasion of the Soviet Union in June 1941 brought a temporary halt to the project, and Prokofiev turned to patriotic undertakings and an opera on Tolstoy's *War and Peace*. The siege of Leningrad forced the evacuation of the Kirov company to the city of Molotov in the Urals, where Prokofiev finished his *Cinderella* in 1944. During the war years Prokofiev experienced a number of life-changing experiences: He suffered his first heart attack, and had an affair with a younger woman that ended his marriage. By 1944, when he composed his Fifth Symphony, which he described as "the culmination of a long period of my creative life," the tide of World War II had turned, and Prokofiev had reached a new maturity as a composer.

His more direct approach had already manifested itself in *Romeo and Juliet*, *Alexander Nevsky*, and the Violin Concerto No. 2, but in this symphony it achieved its most powerful expression yet. A work of epic scope and noble character, the Fifth belongs to the grand Romantic tradition yet is clearly in touch with the spirit of its time. The war's grim presence can be felt in many parts of the score, most graphically in the concluding pages of the first movement, where the thunder of heavy guns is evoked in a towering, percussive climax. Here and elsewhere in the symphony one senses a disquieting ambivalence—feelings of triumph and tragedy are interlinked, neither clearly predominant.

Back in the U.S.S.R.—Prokofiev relaxing with score in hand; oil painting by Pyotr Konchalovsky (1934)

Having won a Stalin Prize for the Fifth Symphony, Prokofiev took a darker, edgier tone in his Symphony No. 6 (1947), a brooding work of remarkable power and originality. He got the shock of his life when, on February 10, 1948, he was censured in a brutal purge of the Union of Composers. The crackdown, masterminded by Stalin's henchman Andrey Zhdanov and ruthlessly carried out by Tikhon Khrennikov, the union's first secretary, left Prokofiev, Shostakovich, Khachaturian, and others in official disgrace. That the composer of *Peter and the Wolf* could be branded a "decadent formalist" remains one of the supreme ironies of 20th-century art, but as the reality of his predicament set in, Prokofiev's spirit began to crumble. From this point most of his output was "celebratory" music written on commission, its tone shaped by the dictates of "socialist realism." Only in the

Symphony Concerto for cello and orchestra, Op. 125 (1952), written for Rostropovich, did some of the old fire return.

Prokofiev, though dead for more than 50 years, remains (like Shostakovich) a victim of cultural politics. Assertions that he opportunistically sold out to the Soviets in the 1930s are not supported by the historical record. And despite the fact that he accommodated the apparatchiks in some of his later works, the best of them still speak forcefully to the emotions. His greatest scores from the Soviet period, including *Alexander Nevsky,* the Fifth Symphony, and *War and Peace,* clearly transcend any political context. As his music becomes more distanced from the times in which it was written, Prokofiev will only gain in stature.

RECOMMENDED RECORDINGS

Alexander Nevsky: Obraztsova, mezzo-soprano; Abbado and London Symphony Orchestra; *Lt. Kijé* and *Scythian Suite*: Chicago Symphony Orchestra (DG).

Piano Concertos Nos. 1, 3, 5: Bronfman; Mehta and Israel Philharmonic Orchestra (Sony).

Piano Sonatas Nos. 6–8: Richter (Russian Revelation).

Romeo and Juliet: Maazel and Cleveland Orchestra (Decca).

Romeo and Juliet: Previn and London Symphony Orchestra (EMI).

Symphonies Nos. 1 and 5: Karajan and Berlin Philharmonic (DG).

Symphonies Nos. 1 and 5: Thomas and London Symphony Orchestra (Sony).

Symphony Concerto for Cello and Orchestra: Rostropovich; Ozawa and London Symphony Orchestra (Warner Classics).

Violin concertos (2 vols.): Vengerov; Rostropovich and London Symphony Orchestra (Teldec).

Violin Concertos Nos. 1 and 2 (with Stravinsky, Violin Concerto): Lin; Salonen and Los Angeles Philharmonic Orchestra (Sony).

Violin Sonatas Nos. 1 and 2: G. Shaham; O. Shaham (Vanguard).

Proms Nickname for the Henry Wood Promenade Concerts, inaugurated in 1895 and held since 1941 in London's capacious Royal Albert Hall. The summertime series features the BBC Symphony Orchestra.

Patrons link arms and sing on the last night of the Proms.

Protecting Veil, The Piece for solo cello and string orchestra by John Tavener, composed in 1987 on a commission from the BBC for the 1989 Proms. It received its premiere September 4, 1989, in a performance by Steven Isserlis and the BBC Symphony Orchestra conducted by Oliver Knussen. A strikingly original and beautiful piece, lyrical in feeling and luminous in sound, *The Protecting Veil* is Tavener's most significant instrumental work to date. Inspired by the Orthodox feast celebrating the apparition of Mary in Constantinople in the early 10th century, it seeks to evoke the cosmic power and beauty of Mary, the Mother of God, through a sort of musical portrait of her life. The score is laid out in eight continuous sections, and the cello part is conceived as an unending song, an attempt on Tavener's part "to make a lyrical icon in sound, rather than in wood." Part VI, "Christ is risen!," brings an extraordinary, ecstatic climax.

RECOMMENDED RECORDINGS

ISSERLIS; ROZHDESTVENSKY AND LONDON SYMPHONY ORCHESTRA (VIRGIN CLASSICS).

KLIEGEL; YUASA AND ULSTER ORCHESTRA (NAXOS).

Puccini, Giacomo

(b. Lucca, December 22, 1858; d. Brussels, November 29, 1924)

ITALIAN COMPOSER. He was the most successful operatic composer of the 20th century and is arguably the greatest figure in the history of Italian opera after Verdi. Melancholy, haunted, and in his work an unyielding perfectionist, he possessed a stupendous melodic gift and outstanding theatrical instincts. Because of his keen interest in scenic detail, he has often been considered a representative of the VERISMO style; and because even the best of his works exhibit a certain melodramatic fervor, he has often been unfairly dismissed as a second-rate musical dramatist.

***Cover art for the score to* Madama Butterfly**

He was born into a family that had dominated music in Lucca for four generations. In 1880 he became a student at the Milan Conservatory, immersing himself in the musical and intellectual life of the city, befriending figures such as Alfredo Catalani and Arrigo Boito, and absorbing everything he could from the operatic repertoire on display at La Scala. His first opera, *Le villi* (*The Villas*), completed in 1883, attracted the attention of the publisher Giulio Ricordi, who thenceforth poured his resources and considerable personal clout into furthering the composer's career.

Puccini had his first great success with *MANON LESCAUT* (1893), derived from the novel by Abbé Prévost on which Massenet's *Manon* was also based. Here for the first time Luigi Illica was involved in shaping a libretto for the composer, and the results were so impressive that he was asked to collaborate, along with Giuseppe Giacosa, on the next three operas Puccini composed. The first of these, and the first of Puccini's works to fully reveal his genius, was *LA BOHÈME* (*Bohemian Life*; 1896). The imaginative treatment of character and situation, the sure instinct shown by Puccini for dramatic and comic effects, and above all the score's radiant, supremely expressive music, have made *La bohème* one of the most popular operas in the repertoire. Puccini followed this bittersweet comedy with *TOSCA* (1900), a thunderously dramatic work teeming with passion, jealousy, betrayal, and revenge—all the usual elements one finds in a good Italian opera. The same elements, but painted in extraordinary pastel colors, informed the final work on which Illica and Giacosa would team with Puccini, *MADAMA BUTTERFLY* (1904).

In the remaining 20 years of his life, Puccini's

Puccini in Oberammergau, 1922

Giulio Gatti-Casazza, David Belasco, Arturo Toscanini, and Puccini, at the time of the premiere of* La fanciulla del West, *1910

love of the exotic led him to compose operas set in times and places as remote from run-of-the-mill locales as Gold Rush–era California (*La fanciulla del West* [*The Girl of the Golden West*]), 13th-century Florence (*GIANNI SCHICCHI*), and legendary Peking (*TURANDOT*). Premiered by the Metropolitan Opera in 1910, *La fanciulla del West* remains Puccini's most underrated opera. The Met was again the venue for the 1918 premiere of Puccini's penultimate offering, *IL TRITTICO,* a grouping of three remarkably different one-act operas—*IL TABARRO* (*The Cloak*), *SUOR ANGELICA* (*Sister Angelica*), and *Gianni Schicchi*—each with its own personality brought home by compelling music.

Fierce, splendidly barbaric, unsettling, and exotic, *Turandot* was Puccini's last creation. ◉ He did not live to complete it, but he filled it with some extraordinary and notably advanced music, and in the figures of Turandot, Calaf, and Liù created three of his most memorable characters. It remains one of the few works of Puccini about which there is any real disagreement: For some, it is the greatest of all his operas, for others, a bold effort that misfired.

Puccini was an inveterate theatergoer who found many of his inspirations in stage plays. His genius was visual as well as musical—he created operas that need to be seen as much as heard, in which the atmosphere engendered by each scene is as important to the overall effect as the plot itself. The first act of *Tosca* would be inconceivable without the interior of Sant' Andrea della Valle, just as the second act of *La bohème* depends absolutely for its effect on the Parisian crowd scene that serves as its backdrop. Even so, the success of Puccini's works is ultimately attributable to the extraordinarily evocative quality of his music. Each opera he wrote had its own distinctive musical signature, its own characteristic combination of harmonic language and orchestral color (the Italian word *tinta* gets the idea across most effectively), chosen from an exceptionally rich palette. Few composers in the history of opera have shown anything like his resourcefulness and imagination.

RECOMMENDED RECORDINGS

La bohème: Freni, Pavarotti, Harwood, Panerai; Karajan and Berlin Philharmonic (Decca).

La fanciulla del West: Tebaldi, Del Monaco, MacNeil, Tozzi; Capuana and Accademia di Santa Cecilia (Decca).

Madama Butterfly: Freni, Pavarotti, Ludwig, Kerns; Karajan and Vienna Philharmonic (Decca).

Manon Lescaut: Freni, Pavarotti, Croft, Taddei; Levine and Metropolitan Opera (Decca).

Il Trittico: Gheorgiu, Alagna, Schicoff, Van Dam; Pappano and London Symphony Orchestra, Philharmonia Orchestra (EMI).

Tosca: Callas, Di Stefano, Gobbi; de Sabata and La Scala Orchestra (EMI).

Pulcinella **BALLET BY IGOR STRAVINSKY FOR CHAMBER ORCHESTRA AND SINGERS,** commissioned by Sergey Diaghilev in 1919 and premiered May 15, 1920 at the Paris Opéra, Ernest Ansermet conducting. The work was done in collaboration with Pablo

Picasso, who designed the decor and costumes, and Léonide Massine, who provided the choreography. It was Diaghilev who came up with the concept of using some pieces thought to be by Giovanni Battista Pergolesi (but later shown to include music written by Domenico Gallo, Fortunato Chelleri, and Carlo Ignazio Monza) as the basis for a ballet with a *commedia dell'arte* theme. At the premiere, Massine danced the title role, and Tamara Karsavina was the Pimpinella.

Stravinsky's imagination was fired by the material, which was typical of 18th-century chamber music in its regular phrases, light texture, and uncomplicated counterpoint. He went to work on it, turning what might in other hands have been a simple arrangement of another composer's ideas into a groundbreaking essay that essentially defined the NEOCLASSICAL style. The act of recomposing such straightforward music, within the limitations of a chamber-orchestral scoring, made Stravinsky keenly aware of how potent an effect could be achieved by the subtle dislocation and alteration of rhythmic and harmonic elements. The score he produced is charming, lively, full of cheeky "wrong-note" dissonances and quirky color (especially the grotesque gavotte variation set as a duet for trombone and double bass)—and it led Stravinsky in a direction that was utterly new, and whose myriad possibilities would occupy him for the next three decades.

Purcell, Henry

(b. prob. London, ca. September 10, 1659; d. Westminster, November 21, 1695)

ENGLISH COMPOSER. He was the outstanding English musician of the second half of the 17th century, and is regarded by many as the greatest composer England has ever produced. Born a year before the restoration of Charles II to the English throne, he served that music-loving monarch early in his career. When, following Charles's death in 1685, the musical scene at court went into decline, Purcell successfully redirected his energies toward the theater.

Henry Purcell

The son of a court musician, Purcell lived all his life in London. His father died in 1664; a few years later, probably in 1668 or 1669, young Henry became a choirboy in the Chapel Royal. After his voice broke, in 1673, he was taught by Christopher Gibbons (1615–76), the son of England's outstanding Renaissance composer Orlando Gibbons, and most likely by John Blow (1649–1708), whose music, along with that of Matthew Locke (ca. 1621–77), had a particularly strong influence on him. In 1679 he succeeded Blow as organist of Westminster Abbey, a post he retained for the rest of his life, and in 1682 he was appointed a member of the Chapel Royal. Between 1679 and 1685 he composed a large amount of ceremonial music for court. With the accession of James II in 1685 his production ebbed, and the arrival of William and Mary in 1688 brought this phase of his career to an end. By 1690 Purcell had made the transition from genteel court composer to celebrated man of the theater; he was so productive and successful that in 1695, the year of his death, his music was heard in 11 different London productions—not even Andrew Lloyd Webber has matched that.

In spite of the turmoil at court and the professional and financial uncertainties it created, Purcell remained a prolific composer throughout his career. He composed hundreds of songs and more than 50 pieces of instrumental and keyboard music, 24 odes and welcome songs for ceremonial occasions at court (including three brilliant tributes written for St. Cecilia's Day, *Welcome to all the pleasures*, *Laudate Ceciliam,* and *Hail, bright Cecilia*), and more than 100 anthems for the Chapel Royal and Westminster Abbey. He also composed or contributed to more than 50 works for the stage, of which the most important were the opera *DIDO AND AENEAS* (1689) and the semioperas *Dioclesian* (1690), *King Arthur* (1691), *The Fairy Queen* (1692), and *The Indian Queen* (1695).

Purcell had an unparalleled ability to set English in a felicitous manner. His sense of melody sprang in part from the English language itself and, as a singer, he knew how to make use of the skills of adult and boy vocalists. His youthful idiom was angular, highly chromatic, peppered with piquant dissonances. Much of his early vocal and instrumental music had its roots in the style of the mid-17th-century Italians—Giacomo Carissimi (1605–74), Michelangelo Rossi (ca. 1601–56), Antonio Cesti (1623–69), and Giovanni Legrenzi (1626–90)—rather than in the work of such contemporaries as Corelli and Alessandro Scarlatti. In the 1680s Purcell absorbed the influence of French courtly dance styles and began to incorporate some of the newer Italian formal procedures into his music, which stands apart from that of other English composers of the day due to its imagery, its more advanced long-range harmonic thinking, and its unique character. One can almost always recognize Purcell's music by its daring expressiveness—not grand and exuberant in the manner of Handel, but tinged with melancholy and a mixture of elegance, oddness, and wistfulness.

RECOMMENDED RECORDINGS

DIDO AND AENEAS: BAKER, HERINCX, CLARK; LEWIS AND ENGLISH CHAMBER ORCHESTRA (DECCA).

DIDO AND AENEAS: HUNT-LIEBERSON, SAFFER, DEAN, DEAM; MCGEGAN AND PHILHARMONIA BAROQUE ORCHESTRA (HARMONIA MUNDI).

THE FAIRY QUEEN: HARRHY, SMITH, NELSON; GARDINER AND ENGLISH BAROQUE SOLOISTS (DG).

FANTASIAS FOR VIOLS: FRETWORK (VIRGIN CLASSICS).

KING ARTHUR: GENS, MCFADDEN, PADMORE, BEST; CHRISTIE AND LES ARTS FLORISSANTS (ERATO).

ODES AND WELCOME SONGS (8 VOLS.): AINSLEY, BONNER, BOWMAN, CHANCE, COVEY-CRUMP, OTHERS; KING AND KING'S CONSORT, CHOIR OF NEW COLLEGE, OXFORD (HYPERION).

Quantz, Johann Joachim

(b. Oberscheden, January 30, 1697; d. Potsdam, July 12, 1773)

GERMAN FLUTIST AND COMPOSER active in Dresden and at the court of Frederick the Great. The son of a blacksmith, he began his musical education in 1708, studying principally with J. A. Fleischhack in Merseburg. As an apprentice and later journeyman he learned to play several string instruments, as well as the oboe and the trumpet; with these qualifications he became a member of the Dresden municipal band in 1716 at the age of 19. He traveled to Vienna in 1717 to study counterpoint with Jan Dismas Zelenka, and in 1718 he was appointed oboist in the Polish *Kapelle* of Augustus II, Elector of Saxony and the King of Poland. In 1719, after realizing that there were more oboists than positions to be filled, Quantz turned his attention to the transverse flute, a relatively new instrument, studying with Pierre-Gabriel Buffardin but modeling his playing style more on that of Johann Georg Pisendel, the leading violinist at the Dresden court. During a three-year period of travel and study in Italy, France, and England (1724–27), he came into contact with Alessandro Scarlatti, Johann Adolf

Hasse (1699–1783), and Handel, and sought to further develop his skills as a composer.

In March 1728 Quantz joined the Dresden court orchestra as flutist. He continued in the employ of Augustus II and his successor Augustus III until 1741, when Frederick the Great, the newly crowned king of Prussia and a professional-caliber flutist, succeed in luring him to Berlin with an offer of two and a half times his salary and comparatively light duties. Quantz spent the rest of his career at the Prussian court, presiding over the king's private evening concerts and coaching him in the fine points of flute playing, which by then he knew better than anyone alive.

Quantz composed more than 300 concertos and 200 sonatas for the flute, and a large number of other works that feature the instrument. He also wrote one of the most important musical treatises of the 18th century, *Versuch einer Anweisung die Flöte traversiere zu spielen* (*On Playing the Flute*), published in Berlin in 1752. Considerably broader in scope than its title implies, the *Versuch* offers practical advice on ornamentation and contains much of interest about music making in general and various national styles of the mid-18th century.

RECOMMENDED RECORDINGS

FLUTE CONCERTOS: BROWN; GOODMAN AND BRANDENBURG CONSORT (HYPERION).

FLUTE SONATAS: BROWN, JOHNSTONE, CAUDLE (CHANDOS).

FLUTE SONATAS: OLESKIEWICZ, VIAL, SCHULENNBERG (NAXOS).

quartet [1] A composition for an ensemble of four instruments. The most common formation is the STRING QUARTET, for which an enormous literature exists. [2] In vocal music, a passage or a number involving four singers.

Quartetto Italiano ITALIAN STRING QUARTET FOUNDED IN **1945** as the Nuovo Quartetto Italiano (the "Nuovo" was dropped in 1951). For many years the membership consisted of violinists Paolo Borciani and Elsa Pegreffi (who were married in 1952), violist Piero Farulli, and cellist Franco Rossi. The ensemble cultivated a lush, meaty sound that gave almost symphonic weight to its playing of Beethoven and Schubert. For the Philips label it recorded complete cycles of the Mozart and Beethoven quartets, a survey of the mature works of Schubert, and renditions of the Debussy and Ravel quartets that are still touchstones of the catalog. The group disbanded in 1980.

RECOMMENDED RECORDINGS

BEETHOVEN, STRING QUARTETS (COMPLETE) (PHILIPS).

DEBUSSY, RAVEL, STRING QUARTETS (PHILIPS).

Quasthoff, Thomas

(b. Hildesheim, November 9, 1959)

GERMAN BASS-BARITONE. He was born with severe deformities of the limbs as a result of his mother's use of thalidomide during her pregnancy. He was brought up in an environment that nurtured his talent, and he began musical studies in Hanover in 1972, taking voice lessons with Charlotte Lehmann and courses in music theory and history with Ernst Huber-Contwig. He was denied entrance to Hanover's Staatliche Hochschule für Musik und Theater on the lamentable grounds that, because he had only seven fingers, he could not possibly pass the qualifying exam in piano. He continued private singing lessons, worked as a radio disc jockey for several years, and in 1988 won first prize in the ARD International Music Competition in Munich. One of his earliest champions was the conductor Helmuth Rilling, who engaged him as a soloist with his Gächinger Kantorei and Bach Collegium Stuttgart; Rilling subse-

German bass-baritone Thomas Quasthoff

quently brought Quasthoff to the Oregon Bach Festival, where he made his American debut in 1995. In 1996 he became a professor in the vocal department at the Musikhochschule in Detmold, and in 2004 he was appointed professor at the Hanns Eisler Musikhochschule in Berlin. He signed an exclusive recording contract with Deutsche Grammophon in 1999. In recent seasons he has appeared as a soloist with many of the world's top orchestras, including the Berlin Philharmonic, Vienna Philharmonic, New York Philharmonic, Boston Symphony, Chicago Symphony, and Cleveland Orchestra, and has given recitals in major venues in Europe and the United States. He sang the role of Don Fernando in Beethoven's *Fidelio* at the Salzburg Easter Festival in 2003 and made his Vienna Staatsoper debut, as Amfortas in Wagner's *Parsifal,* in April 2004.

Quasthoff has a voice of remarkable size, range, and purity—as well as the technique and musical intelligence to use it to supreme effect. Listeners are often reminded of Dietrich Fischer-Dieskau when they encounter his honeyed tone and dramatic delivery for the first time; and like Fischer-Dieskau, Quasthoff confronts the repertoire and his audience with a formidable combination of seriousness and emotional penetration. But Quasthoff as an artist and in every other way is his own man, and every phrase he sings testifies to that individuality. His phenomenal diction, extraordinary control of dynamics, and, above all, the expressiveness of the voice itself, place him among the greats.

RECOMMENDED RECORDINGS

"EVENING STAR" (ARIAS BY LORTZING, WEBER, WAGNER, AND STRAUSS): THIELEMANN AND DEUTSCHE OPER BERLIN (DG).

SCHUBERT, GOETHE SONGS: SPENCER (RCA).

SCHUBERT, *WINTERREISE*: SPENCER (RCA).

Quattro pezzi sacri (Four Sacred Pieces) **COLLECTION OF CHORAL WORKS BY GIUSEPPE VERDI,** composed 1889–97 and published in 1898, when the composer was 85. The four parts of this musical offering embrace a broad range of emotion and gesture, from the hushed musings of the opening *Ave Maria,* for unaccompanied chorus, to the thunderous outbursts of the concluding Te Deum, for soprano, double chorus, and full orchestra. Verdi felt so close to the latter that he asked in his will to have the score buried with him.

The *Ave Maria* is written in the so-called "enigmatic" scale, which embraces the tones C, D-flat, E, F-sharp, G-sharp, A-sharp, and B, and is thus neither major nor minor, but an ethereal-sounding mix of whole tones, semitones, and an augmented second; the effect is made even more mysterious by Verdi's unaccompanied setting. The second of the four pieces is a *Stabat mater* for chorus and orchestra. In the third, an a cappella setting for female chorus titled "Laudi alla Vergine Maria," Verdi pays homage to the style of Palestrina while invoking the spirit of Dante (the text is drawn from the final canto of the poet's *Paradiso*). The first performance of three of the four pieces—the *Stabat mater,* "Laudi alla Vergine Maria," and Te Deum—took place in Paris on April 7, 1898.

RECOMMENDED RECORDINGS

BAKER; GIULINI AND PHILHARMONIA ORCHESTRA (EMI).

CARTER; SHAW AND ATLANTA SYMPHONY ORCHESTRA (TELARC).

Quatuor pour la fin du temps (Quartet for the End of Time) **COMPOSITION BY OLIVIER MESSIAEN FOR VIOLIN, CLARINET, CELLO, AND PIANO,** created in 1940 during his internment as a prisoner of war and first performed January 15, 1941, behind the barbed wire of Stalag VIII A at Görlitz in Silesia, for an audience of several hundred fellow POWs and the camp commander and staff. Messiaen himself played the piano; the other performers were Jean Le Boulaire (violin), Henri Akoka (clarinet), and Etienne Pasquier (cello). Inspired by a passage in the Book of Revelation, the quartet consists of eight movements whose titles refer to events of the Apocalypse, as imagined by the composer: 1) "Liturgie de cristal" ("Liturgy of Crystal"); 2) "Vocalise, pour l'ange qui annonce la fin du temps" ("Vocalise for the Angel Who Announces the End of Time"); 3) "Abîme des oiseaux" ("Abyss of the Birds"); 4) "Intermède" ("Interlude"); 5) "Louange à l'éternité de Jésus" ("Praise to the Eternity of Jesus"); 6) "Danse de la fureur, pour les sept trompettes" ("Dance of Frenzy, for the Seven Trumpets"); 7) "Fouillis d'arcs-en-ciel, pour l'ange qui annonce la fin du temps" ("Tumult of Rainbows, for the Angel Who Announces the End of Time"); 8) "Louange à l'immortalité de Jésus" ("Praise to the Immortality of Jesus").

With its complex play of rhythms and motives and strangely modal harmonies, the *Quatuor pour la fin du temps* truly seems not to belong to this world; and with his astonishing ear for color Messiaen does indeed make rainbows of sound shimmer through the piece. The work remains a classic expression of its composer's unique brand of musical mysticism, and, in "Abîme des oiseaux," contains one of the finest and most challenging pieces in the literature for solo clarinet.

RECOMMENDED RECORDINGS

AMICI ENSEMBLE (NAXOS).

SHAHAM, MEYER, WANG, CHUNG (DG).

TASHI (RCA).

quaver An eighth note. The term is common usage among English musicians. Further subdivisions of the quaver's value are referred to, in England, as semiquaver (sixteenth note), demisemiquaver (thirty-second note), and hemidemisemiquaver (sixty-fourth note), which takes much longer to say than to play.

Queen of Spades, The **OPERA IN THREE ACTS BY PYOTR IL'YICH TCHAIKOVSKY,** to a libretto by Modest Tchaikovsky (based on Aleksandr Pushkin's story), premiered December 19, 1890, at the Mariinsky Theater in St. Petersburg. The score, one of Tchaikovsky's supreme masterpieces, was created in an astonishingly short 44 days during a sojourn in Florence, proof, if any were needed, of the white heat of inspiration that kept the composer going as he clothed Pushkin's tale in the most resplendent operatic colors. By changing certain elements of the story—so as to create a believable love interest between Hermann, the young officer-protagonist determined to wrest from an old Countess her secret of winning at cards, and Lisa, the Countess's granddaughter—Tchaikovsky transformed

The Queen of Spades from an ironic tale of horror with a supernatural twist to a gripping portrait of tragic obsession that destroys all in its path. The music has a disturbing, dark beauty that suggests a cross between Mozart and Shostakovich.

RECOMMENDED RECORDING

GOUGALOFF, VISHNEVSKAYA, RESNIK, SCHWARZ, WEIKL, POPP; ROSTROPOVICH AND ORCHESTRE NATIONAL DE FRANCE (DG).

Quinault, Philippe

(b. Paris, ca. June 5, 1635; d. Paris, November 26, 1688)

FRENCH DRAMATIST AND LIBRETTIST. He wrote the librettos for nearly all of Lully's operas, drawing upon mythology and medieval legend for his subject matter. Among his best efforts were the books for *Cadmus et Hermione* (1673), *Alceste* (1674), *Atys* (1676), and *Armide* (1686; also set by Gluck, in 1777).

Philippe Quinault

quintet [1] A composition for an ensemble of five instruments. The literature has given rise to a variety of standard complements, of which the most common are quintets for instruments of the same family (i.e., string quintets) or of similar type, such as wind and brass quintets. There are two common formations for string quintet: two violins, two violas, and cello (which Mozart favored), or two violins, viola, and two cellos (the arrangement Boccherini preferred). Mozart, while a master of the string quartet, preferred the rich texture and more complex part-writing possible in the quintet medium, and it was there that he achieved his greatest successes in the field of chamber music. His Quintets in C, K. 515, and G minor, K. 516, both dating from 1787, are arguably his finest chamber works, though a pair from 1790–91—in D, K. 593, and in E-flat, K. 614—have their adherents, as does the sublime Quintet in A, K. 581, for clarinet and strings (1789). Schubert followed the Boccherini model in composing his late Quintet in C, D. 956, for an ensemble with two cellos, producing his greatest chamber work. Dvořák reverted to the two-viola formula in his sunny, outgoing Quintet in E-flat, Op. 97, a companion work to the celebrated String Quartet in F, Op. 96, and like it composed in America in 1893.

The wind quintet literature also presents several possible formations—the standard one is flute, oboe, clarinet, bassoon, and horn. In Paris, between 1817 and 1820, Reicha published four sets of six works each for this complement (Opp. 88, 91, 99, and 100), all of them gems. Other outstanding works for wind quintet include Nielsen's Quintet, Op. 43 (1922), Ibert's *Trois pièces brèves* (1930), Fine's *Partita* (1948), and Barber's lovely *Summer Music* (1956). Brass quintets also come in a variety of configurations; the most common involve two trumpets, horn, trombone, and tuba, or two trumpets, horn, and two trombones. The best works, all of fairly recent vintage, include those by Ingolf Dahl (1944), Malcolm Arnold (1961), and Gunther Schuller (1961, 1993).

Wind quintet

Among the most frequently performed quintets for mixed ensembles are the quintets for clarinet and strings by Mozart and Brahms (1891); Schubert's *Trout* Quintet, D. 667 (1819) ◉, for piano and a string foursome with double bass; and the quintets for piano and winds by Mozart (1784) and Beethoven (1796). Quintets for piano and strings are a particularly important subgenre with a large repertoire. *See also* PIANO QUINTET, CHAMBER MUSIC.

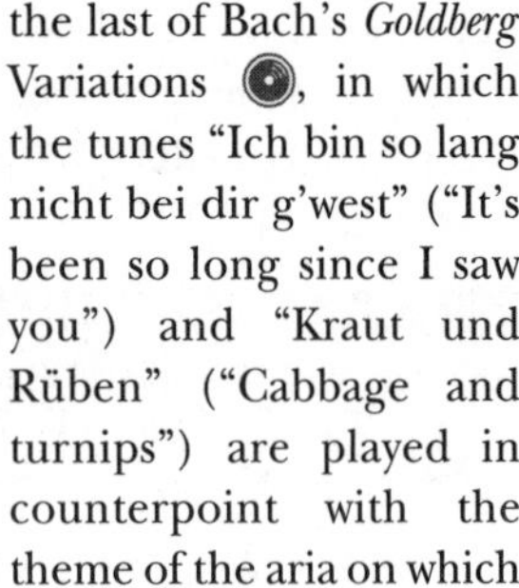

[2] In vocal music, a passage or a number involving five singers. Celebrated operatic quintets include "Di scrivermi ogni giorno" in Act I of Mozart's *Così fan tutte,* and "Selig, wie die Sonne" in the third act of Wagner's *Die Meistersinger von Nürnberg.*

quodlibet (Lat., "whatever pleases") A piece in which different popular melodies are sounded either polyphonically or in succession. An example of the former is the last of Bach's *Goldberg* Variations ◉, in which the tunes "Ich bin so lang nicht bei dir g'west" ("It's been so long since I saw you") and "Kraut und Rüben" ("Cabbage and turnips") are played in counterpoint with the theme of the aria on which the variations are based. Brahms's *Academic Festival* Overture, an example of the latter kind, trundles out one student song after another: "Wir hatten gebauet ein stättliche Haus" ("We had built a stately house"), the "Hochfeierlicher Landesvater" ("Most solemn song to the father of the country"), "Was kommt dort in der Höh?" ("What comes there from on high?"), and finally, "Gaudeamus igitur" ("Let us therefore rejoice").

Rachmaninov, Sergey

(b. Semyonovo, April 1, 1873; d. Beverly Hills, March 28, 1943)

RUSSIAN/AMERICAN COMPOSER AND PIANIST. Although he was one of the most capable pianists in history and certainly among the foremost virtuosos of his own era, he thought of himself primarily as a composer. He was a transitional figure between Romanticism and modernism, and can fairly be characterized as the last composer-virtuoso, the end of a line that stretched from Mozart and Beethoven through Chopin, Liszt, and Scriabin. His music runs the emotional gamut from somber introspection and romantic yearning to triumph and celebration, and his brilliant concertos and solo works for the piano are more firmly entrenched in the concert repertoire than those of any other 20th-century figure.

A studious Sergey Rachmaninov, with friend

Rachmaninov was born into an aristocratic, military, piano-playing family whose misfortunes required moves to St. Petersburg—where at nine he began study at its Conservatory—and a few years later to Moscow. By his late teens he had written his first works: the opera *Aleko* (completed in a mere three weeks as his final composition exam, it won the Moscow Conservatory's gold medal), a piano concerto, and sets of songs and piano fantasy pieces, including the hugely popular Prelude in C-sharp minor, Op. 3, No. 2.

Anguish followed this early acclaim. The premiere of his First Symphony, in 1897 in St. Petersburg, was a disaster. A drunk Aleksandr Glazunov conducted, critics raked the piece over the coals, and the sensitive, relentlessly serious Rachmaninov had a nervous breakdown, becoming so severely depressed that he was unable to compose for three years. (The symphony was not published or performed again during the composer's lifetime.) He remained functional enough to serve as conductor of the Moscow Private Russian Opera Company, and in 1899 he made his international debut as a pianist, at Queens Hall in London. But his artistic self-confidence was so shaken that eventually he sought psychotherapy, which included hypnosis.

The treatment had the desired effects, and by 1900 Rachmaninov began composition of his Piano Concerto No. 2 as well as the quasi-symphonic Suite No. 2, Op. 17, for two pianos. The concerto's second and third movements were premiered in Moscow, and in 1901 Rachmaninov completed both it and the suite, dedicating the concerto to his therapist. The next year he married his first cousin Natalia Satina, who proved a rock of stability even though the

Rachmaninov* (center) *with aviation pioneer Igor Sikorski* (right) *and Baron Nikolas Solovieff

marriage had been opposed by friends, family, and church because of their kinship.

The next decades were productive. The Ten Preludes, Op. 23, were finished in 1903, and the following year Rachmaninov signed a contract to conduct at the Bolshoi Theatre. While there he completed and premiered two operas (*Francesca da Rimini* and *The Miserly Knight*). In 1906 the family (a daughter had been born) moved to Dresden, where the composer worked on his Symphony No. 2, which he introduced in St. Petersburg in 1908; in 1907 a second daughter was born. The ensuing years in Dresden, with summers back in Russia, also saw completion of the symphonic poem *The Isle of the Dead* and the Piano Concerto No. 3, the premiere of which he gave (with Mahler on the podium) in 1909 in New York. Outstanding works of this period include the choral symphony *The Bells* (1913), inspired by Edgar Allan Poe, and the glowingly beautiful *All-Night Vigil* (1915), a vespers setting for a cappella chorus.

Sergey Rachmaninov as a young man and* (facing page) *in later years

Following the 1917 Revolution and the loss of his family's estate and revenue, Rachmaninov left Russia and began a career as a touring concert pianist. He signed a contract with the Victor label, eventually recording his Piano Concerto No. 2 (with the Philadelphia Orchestra) and other works through the 1920s. During the 1930s, he built a lakeside villa called Senar (an acronym for **Se**rgey and **Na**talia **R**achmaninov) outside Lucerne; composed perhaps his best-known work, the *Rhapsody on a Theme of Paganini*, as well as his Symphony No. 3; and recorded most of his major works. He continued composing and recording into the early 1940s, when his health began to fail. He gave his final concert in 1943, in Knoxville, Tennessee. Seriously ill (though unaware that the cause was cancer), he returned to Beverly Hills, where he died, days short of his 70th birthday, and just weeks after attaining American citizenship.

Rachmaninov's keyboard technique was formidable and his compositions for the piano capitalize on it, exploring the instrument's full range of dynamic and expressive effects. Invariably, there is a pronounced lyricism to his writing, sometimes tender in its expression, at other times grand and soaring. Underlying everything is a strength of sonority: No composer has ever drawn a more powerful sound from the piano. Rachmaninov's own playing, well captured on phonograph recordings and piano rolls, shows awesome power and dexterity, steely fingers moving with dazzling velocity, the phrasing extraordinarily flexible yet without excessive rubato.

Rachmaninov continues to be thought of as a throwback, a Romantic who was left at the station when the 20th Century Limited pulled out. In fact, as scores such as the *Rhapsody on a Theme of Paganini* and the *Symphonic Dances* (1940) show, he was a reluctant modernist, seeking to convey emotion, and perhaps a sense of nostalgia, in an idiom that took into account a good many 20th-century trends in rhythm, harmony, and scoring. For no other reason than that his music has always been popular and is melodically generous, Rachmaninov has regularly been dismissed by critics and musical scholars as second-rate. It is an assessment that can no longer be defended.

RECOMMENDED RECORDINGS

The Bells: Mescheriakova, Larin, Chernov; Pletnev and Russian National Orchestra (DG).

Piano concertos (complete): Hough; Litton and Dallas Symphony Orchestra (Hyperion).

Piano concertos, *Rhapsody on a Theme of Paganini*: Rachmaninov; Stokowski, Ormandy and Philadelphia Orchestra (RCA, Naxos).

Piano works (including Preludes, Op. 32, and Sonatas Nos. 1 and 2): Rodriguez (Elan).

Preludes: Weissenberg (RCA).

Symphonic Dances (with Symphony No. 3): Pletnev and Russian National Orchestra (DG).

Symphony No. 1: Pletnev and Russian National Orchestra (DG).

Symphony No. 2: Pletnev and Russian National Orchestra (DG).

Symphony No. 2: Sanderling and Leningrad Philharmonic (DG).

Symphony No. 3: Rachmaninov and Philadelphia Orchestra (RCA).

Symphony No. 3: Stokowski and National Philharmonic Orchestra (EMI).

Vespers (*"All-Night Vigil"*): Chernushenko and St. Petersburg Cappella (Le Chant du Monde).

Ragin, Derek Lee *See box on pages 155–57.*

Rake's Progress, The Opera in three acts and an epilogue by Igor Stravinsky, to a libretto by W. H. Auden and Chester Kallman based on *A Rake's Progress,* eight satirical engravings published by William Hogarth in 1735. *The Rake's Progress* tells the story of Tom Rakewell, who, convinced by a mysterious stranger named Nick Shadow that he could lose his inheritance, leaves Anne Trulove for London to tend to his fortune. After Tom confesses his ignorance when it comes to the management of money, Nick offers to become Tom's "financial adviser" for a year and a day, and then he will tell Tom how much he is owed for the service. Nick leads Tom through a variety of misadventures and squanders his fortune. When the year has passed, Nick reveals himself as the devil, and the price for his services is Tom's soul. Tom ends up in Bedlam, and dies, insane, in the arms of Anne, who has indeed been true.

Composed between 1947 and 1951, *The Rake's Progress* was premiered under the composer's baton on September 11, 1951, at La Fenice in Venice. The idea of utilizing Hogarth's scenes as the storyboard for a mock comic opera was Stravinsky's own, inspired by his encounter at an exhibit in Chicago in 1947. Acknowledging Mozart as his model (but borrowing from the whole of operatic tradition, as well as from himself), Stravinsky sought in *The Rake's Progress,* as in so many of his works, to create a parody of the past. The opera's structure and use of set pieces self-consciously recall the conventions of 18th-century opera. Against this background the central characters—Tom, Anne, Baba the Turk (a bearded lady), and Nick—stand out as humorously idealized figures in an allegory of death and rebirth. Synthetic though it is, the score is an exceptionally vital piece of modern musical theater.

RECOMMENDED RECORDINGS

Bostridge, York, Terfel, Otter; Gardiner and London Symphony Orchestra (DG).

Young, Raskin, Reardon, Sarfaty; Stravinsky and Royal Philharmonic Orchestra (Sony).

rallentando (It.) Slowing down.

Rameau, Jean-Philippe

(b. Dijon, September 25, 1683; d. Paris, September 12, 1764)

FRENCH COMPOSER AND THEORIST. He started out as an organist and clavecinist, settling in Paris in 1722 and establishing a solid reputation as a composer and teacher of keyboard music. With the premiere of his tragedy *Hippolyte et Aricie* at the Paris Opéra on October 1, 1733, he began—at the age of 50—a brilliant second career as a dramatic composer. During the next 30 years, he produced more than two dozen dramatic works, mostly *tragédies lyriques* and *opéra-ballets,* including *Les Indes galantes* (1735), *Castor et Pollux* (1737), *Dardanus* (1739), *Zaïs* (1748), and *Les boréades* (1763). The integration of music and drama would prove closer in some than in others, but all are grand and elegant works in a majestic, elevated style notable for its lyric beauty.

In addition to his works for the stage, Rameau composed a handful of motets and cantatas, three collections of solo keyboard suites, a volume of chamber pieces for harpsichord and accompanying instruments titled *Pièces de clavecin en concerts* (1741), and a set of harpsichord arrangements of music from *Les Indes galantes.* The keyboard music, which still holds a place in the repertoire of harpsichordists, is bright, light, and colorful—neither as weighty nor as densely contrapuntal as that of Rameau's German contemporaries. While the operas and keyboard pieces may be the only part of Rameau's production that modern audiences are likely to encounter, he set great store by his theoretical writings, of which the most important was his *Traité de l'harmonie* (*Treatise on Harmony*; 1722). His influence upon theorists from his own time through the present has been substantial.

Baroque dance, before the king

RECOMMENDED RECORDINGS

CASTOR ET POLLUX: CROOK, CORRÉAS, MELLON, GENS; CHRISTIE AND LES ARTS FLORISSANTS (HARMONIA MUNDI).

DARDANUS: AINSLEY, GENS, NAOURI, DELUNSCH; MINKOWSKI AND MUSICIENS DU LOUVRE (DG).

LES INDES GALANTES: MCFADDEN, PIAU, POULENARD, RIME; CHRISTIE AND LES ARTS FLORISSANTS (HARMONIA MUNDI).

SOLO KEYBOARD SUITES: ROUSSET (OISEAU-LYRE).

SUITES FROM *ANACRÉON, DAPHNIS ET EGLÉ*: TEREY-SMITH AND CAPELLA SAVARIA (NAXOS).

Ramey, Samuel

(b. Colby, Kan., March 28, 1942)

AMERICAN BASS-BARITONE. He studied music in high school and college and took part in apprentice programs at the Central City Opera and Santa Fe Opera during the 1960s. He made his debut with the New York City Opera in 1973 as Zuniga in Bizet's *Carmen,* and remained on the company's roster until 1986. In 1979 he bowed for the first time in Chicago and San Francisco, on both occasions as Colline in Puccini's *La bohème,* and in 1981 he made his debuts at La Scala and the Vienna Staatsoper, both times as Figaro in Mozart's

Le nozze di Figaro. He has been a regular at the Metropolitan Opera since 1984, when he made his debut as Argante in Handel's *Rinaldo.*

Ramey has made a career of portraying devils, libertines, and troubled souls. He has sung the role of Méphistophélès in Gounod's *Faust* in more than 200 performances worldwide and has enjoyed notable success as well in the title role of Boito's *Mefistofele.* One of the great triumphs of his years at the Met came in 1992 when, on the opening night of the season, he sang all four villains in the company's production of Offenbach's *Les contes d'Hoffmann.* Other roles for which he is known include Olin Blitch in *Susannah* by Carlisle Floyd (b. 1926), Nick Shadow in Stravinsky's *The Rake's Progress,* Verdi's Attila, the title role in Mozart's *Don Giovanni,* Philip II in Verdi's *Don Carlo,* and Bluebeard in Bartók's *Bluebeard's Castle.* Ramey commands a sonorous, dark-hued voice notable for its deep bass resonance, and brings an electrifying athleticism to his stage portrayals. In recent years he has also shown himself to be a compelling recitalist.

RECOMMENDED RECORDINGS

COLLECTION:

BARTÓK, *BLUEBEARD'S CASTLE*: MARTÓN; FISCHER AND HUNGARIAN STATE ORCHESTRA (SONY).

"A DATE WITH THE DEVIL" (SCENES AND ARIAS FROM WORKS BY BERLIOZ, BOITO, GOUNOD, MEYERBEER, OFFENBACH): RUDEL AND MUNICH RADIO ORCHESTRA (NAXOS).

OFFENBACH, *LES CONTES D'HOFFMANN*: ARAIZA, STUDER, NORMAN, LIND, OTTER; TATE AND STAATSKAPELLE DRESDEN (PHILIPS).

Rampal, Jean-Pierre

(b. Marseille, January 7, 1922; d. Paris, May 20, 2000)

FRENCH FLUTIST. In a career lasting more than 50 years he brought the flute international popularity and a place of honor as a solo instrument, something it had not enjoyed in nearly two centuries. As a teenager he studied with his father, Joseph Rampal, who was professor of flute at the conservatory in Marseille and principal flute in the city's orchestra. In 1939 he entered the University of Marseille, intending to prepare for a career in medicine. He received a diploma in sciences in 1941, but had to forgo medical school owing to the German occupation of France. In 1943, when the authorities attempted to conscript him for forced labor in Germany, he went underground, hiding out in Marseille and later in Paris. Though a fugitive, he managed to enroll in the Paris Conservatoire, where, in May 1944, he took a first prize in flute. Following the liberation of France that summer, he began a rapid rise to prominence as an orchestral player, concert soloist, and chamber musician. He served as principal flute of the Vichy Opera (1946–50) and the Paris Opéra (1956–62), thereafter devoting himself full-time to a solo career that combined engagements with the world's leading orchestras and recital tours accompanied primarily by the harpsichordist Robert Veyron-Lacroix (his duo partner for more than 30 years) and the pianist John Steele Ritter. In later years he collaborated in performances and recordings of trio repertoire with Isaac Stern and Mstislav Rostropovich.

Rampal, the premier flutist of his generation, possessed an impeccable technique until late in his career. He played with an amplitude and suavity of tone that few of his colleagues could match, had remarkably fast fingers, and was incomparable in the way he turned a phrase. His playing was graceful and limpid in the best French manner, his sound luminous. He cared little for rhythmic animation in Baroque music; instead, he favored a softening of profile, both rhythmic and melodic. Yet to everything he played he brought a wonderful sense of fluidity, of motion without haste, along with a masterful exploitation of dynamic contrasts.

Among the works written for Rampal are concertos by Martinon, André Jolivet (1905–74), David Diamond (1915–2005), Jean Rivier (1896–1937), and Jean Françaix, Copland's Duo for Flute and Piano (1971), Boulez's *Sonatina for Flute and Piano* (1946)—which Rampal detested and never played—Jolivet's Sonata for Flute and Piano (1958), and, most precious of all, the Sonata for Flute and Piano by Poulenc (1956–57). He made more than 350 commercial recordings, on which more than 1,000 compositions are represented—a sweeping traversal of the flute repertoire. As delightful offstage as on, Rampal was a gourmet and bon vivant of the first rank (with a special passion for sushi), as well as a model of Gallic charm. His autobiography *Music, My Love,* written with Deborah Wise, was published in 1989.

RECOMMENDED RECORDINGS

Collection: "Flute Masterpieces of the 20th Century" (includes concertos by Ibert, Khachaturian, Jolivet and sonatas by Martinů, Hindemith, Prokofiev, Poulenc) (Erato).

Mozart, flute concertos: Mehta and Israel Philharmonic (Sony).

Mozart, flute quartets: Accardo, Stern, Rostropovich (Sony).

Rapsodie espagnole (Spanish Rhapsody)

Orchestral work in four movements by Maurice Ravel, published in 1907. The virtuosic scoring—especially the idiomatic use of percussion (including such distinctively "Spanish" instruments as castanets and tambourine) and the deft touches of muted strings and brass—makes the *Rapsodie espagnole* one of Ravel's most appealing works. The opening "Prélude à la nuit" ("Prelude to the Night") is a slow, hypnotic evocation of the Iberian evening, fragrant with color: As a descending four-note motif (F–E–D–C-sharp) repeats itself in the background, passion blooms briefly, like a nocturnal flower, in an ardent phrase for the strings, before cadenzas for paired clarinets and bassoons bring the movement to a close. Flashes of tambourine punctuate the shadowy "Malagueña," which fills the role of a scherzo and vanishes into the night as quickly as it came. With the ensuing "Habanera," a sultry piece originally composed for two pianos, Ravel shows his craft as an orchestrator to striking effect, creating a mosaic of delicate color. The finale, entitled "Feria" ("Festival"), is a brilliantly scored showpiece with dizzily shifting rhythms in its outer sections and a languorous central section featuring serpentine solos by the English horn and clarinet. Amid echoes of the four-note "night" motif from the first movement, the festivities become increasingly lively until, with his sure sense of climax, Ravel brings the whole affair to a dazzling conclusion.

RECOMMENDED RECORDINGS

Dutoit and Montreal Symphony Orchestra (Decca).

Martinon and Chicago Symphony Orchestra (RCA).

Rattle, Sir Simon

(b. Liverpool, January 19, 1955)

English conductor. In September 2002 he stepped into what is traditionally regarded as the most important post in European musical life, that of music director of the Berlin Philharmonic. Raised by parents who were musical enthusiasts, he absorbed music by listening to the radio and recordings, reading books and scores, and going to concerts; a performance of Mahler's Symphony No. 2 he attended when he was 11 proved to be the spark that ignited a burning desire to conduct. He entered the Royal Academy of Music at the age of 16, studied piano, percussion, and conducting, and in 1974 won first prize in the John Player International Conducting Competition. He spent three years as assistant conductor of the Bournemouth Symphony Orchestra and the Bournemouth Sinfonietta, then became assistant conductor of the BBC Scottish Symphony and associate conductor of the Royal Liverpool Philharmonic. In 1980 he was appointed principal conductor of the City of Birmingham Symphony Orchestra, where he remained for 18 seasons—the last eight as music director—and presided over the orchestra's rise from the third tier of English ensembles to at least the second.

Rattle made his debut at Glyndebourne in 1977 with Janáček's *The Cunning Little Vixen* and appeared for the first time at Covent Garden in 1990, again with *Vixen.* His American debut came in 1979 with the Los Angeles Philharmonic, and he subsequently served as that orchestra's principal guest conductor (1981–94). His work in the United States included guest conducting engagements with the orchestras of Cleveland (whose players did not care for him), Chicago, San Francisco, Philadelphia (where for a while he was rumored to be in line to succeed Wolfgang Sawallisch), and Boston. He brought the City of Birmingham Symphony Orchestra on tour to New York in 1988, but made the mistake of programming Beethoven symphonies in America's musical capital with a provincial orchestra; the critics greeted those performances in tones ranging from polite dismissal to righteous indignation.

Things went more smoothly for Rattle in Europe, where, in addition to his widely acclaimed stewardship of the Birmingham Orchestra, he enjoyed, from 1992, a fruitful working relationship with the Orchestra of the Age of Enlightenment (including a cycle of Mozart operas at Glyndebourne) and auspicious debuts with the continent's top orchestras: the Berlin Philharmonic in 1986, leading Mahler's Symphony No. 6, and the Vienna Philharmonic in 1993, with Mahler's Symphony No. 9. In June 1999, following Claudio Abbado's decision to step down as music director of the Berlin ensemble, Rattle was chosen by the orchestra's players to succeed him (surprising many who thought Daniel Barenboim would get the nod) and was granted a remarkably generous ten-year contract.

In the early years, Rattle's career was boosted by a concerted effort on the part of his record label, EMI, and the British media to anoint him the Next Great English Conductor. By the time he was tapped for the Berlin job he had made more than 60 recordings, a sizable number for a conductor in his mid-40s. Nearly all received glowing coverage in the British press, though American reviewers were often more reserved in their assessments. With the passing of time, Rattle has shown himself to be a skilled and perceptive orchestra leader, a thoughtful programmer, and an astute communicator. His music

Sir Simon Rattle

making, always energetic and rhythmically alert, exhibits scrupulous attention to dynamics and phrasing; yet for all its punctilio and polish, up to now it has offered few compelling interpretive insights and often lacks emotional depth.

Rattle's repertoire is unusually adventurous and reflects his wide-ranging intellect and broad musical sympathies, which include a fondness for jazz and contemporary music (notably the works of English composers Nicholas Maw, Colin Matthews, Mark-Anthony Turnage, and Thomas Adès, and of the American John Adams), and for the idiosyncratically colorful idioms of Janáček and Szymanowski. He has an excellent knowledge of the recorded repertoire and a keen understanding of 18th- and 19th-century performance practice, along with a refreshing habit of taking musical scholarship into account in his work; for example, when he recorded the Beethoven symphonies with the Vienna Philharmonic in 2002, one of his most impressive achievements to date, he used the critical edition of Jonathan Del Mar published by Bärenreiter between 1999 and 2001, then hot off the press. Rattle was named a Commander of the British Empire in 1987 and knighted in 1994.

RECOMMENDED RECORDINGS

BEETHOVEN, SYMPHONIES (COMPLETE): VIENNA PHILHARMONIC (EMI).

SCHOENBERG, *GURRE-LIEDER*: MATTILA, OTTER, MOSER, LANGRIDGE, QUASTHOFF; BERLIN PHILHARMONIC (EMI).

SZYMANOWSKI, *KING ROGER*, SYMPHONY NO. 4: HAMPSON, SZMYTKA, LANGRIDGE, MINKIEWICZ; CITY OF BIRMINGHAM SYMPHONY ORCHESTRA (EMI).

Rautavaara, Einojuhani

(b. Helsinki, October 9, 1928)

FINNISH COMPOSER. In 1954, having attended schools in his home city and Turku and earned a master's degree at the University of Helsinki, he joined the composition class of Aarre Merikanto at Helsinki's Sibelius Academy. The following year he received a singular honor when Jean Sibelius, then 90, nominated him for a Koussevitzky Foundation grant to study in the United States. During 1955 and 1956 he studied composition at the Juilliard School with Vincent Persichetti and at Tanglewood with Roger Sessions (1955) and Aaron Copland (1956). Additional studies took place in Switzerland, with Wladimir Vogel, and in Cologne, with Rudolf Petzold. Upon his return to Finland he taught at the Sibelius Academy (1957–59), served as music archivist for the Helsinki Philharmonic (1959–61), and subsequently rejoined the faculty of the Sibelius Academy as a lecturer (1966–76) and as professor of composition (1976–90). Since 1990 he has devoted himself full-time to composition.

Rautavaara, communing with angels

One of the most imaginative and productive composers of his generation, Rautavaara has absorbed numerous influences and explored a wide range of styles during his career, always balancing a constructivist impulse with a mystical strain. His journey began with early forays into neoclassicism and serialism, and became more colorful as his interests extended to jazz, aleatoric procedures, and the use of taped sounds—the latter figuring prominently in what is still his best-known work, the "concerto for birds and orchestra" titled *Cantus Arcticus* (1972). Rautavaara's willingness to experiment with different styles and compositional methods has been tempered by a commonsense desire to make his music attractive to performers and appealing to listeners. Since the mid-1970s his works have reflected not only his developing postmodernist aesthetic—characterized by a reengagement with tonality verging on a new Romanticism—but also an upwelling of nondoctrinal spirituality, evident in his "Angel Series" of compositions that includes *Angels and Visitations* (1978) for orchestra, the double bass concerto *Angel of Dusk* (1980), *Playgrounds for Angels* (1981) for ten brass instruments, and the symphony *Angel of Light* (1994).

Serving as his own librettist, Rautavaara has written ten operas or chamber operas, of which the best known are *Thomas* (1985), *Vincent* (1987; based on the life of Vincent van Gogh), *Aleksis Kivi* (1997, based on the life of the eponymous Finnish writer), and *Rasputin* (2003). He has composed eight symphonies—the most recent, Symphony No. 8 (*The Journey*), was premiered by the Philadelphia Orchestra in April 2000—as well as 11 concertos, including his highly regarded Violin Concerto (1976–77) and the Piano Concerto No. 3 (*Gift of Dreams*), written in 1998 on a commission from Vladimir Ashkenazy. He has also created more than a dozen works for string ensemble, numerous chamber and solo instrumental pieces, and a large body of choral works. What stands out about almost all of his music is its human scale and unfettered communicativeness, in which spontaneity of gesture and sudden emotional frissons underscore Rautavaara's oft-stated conviction that he is essentially a conduit for his music, and that there is an aspect of the process that is, and should be, beyond the composer's control.

RECOMMENDED RECORDINGS

ANGELS AND VISITATIONS, *ISLE OF BLISS*, VIOLIN CONCERTO: OLIVEIRA; SEGERSTAM AND HELSINKI PHILHARMONIC ORCHESTRA (ONDINE).

CANTUS ARCTICUS, SYMPHONY NO. 3, PIANO CONCERTO NO. 1: MIKKOLA; LINTU AND ROYAL SCOTTISH NATIONAL ORCHESTRA (NAXOS).

SYMPHONY NO. 7 (*ANGEL OF LIGHT*), *CANTUS ARCTICUS*, FLUTE CONCERTO: ALANKO; VÄNSKÄ AND LAHTI SYMPHONY ORCHESTRA (BIS).

Ravel, Maurice

(b. Ciboure, March 7, 1875; d. Paris, December 28, 1937)

FRENCH COMPOSER. One of the most successful composers of the 20th century, to judge from the number of works that have entered the repertoire, he delighted in imagery and evocation, yet had a typically French passion for clarity, balance, and restraint. Wherever he looked—to Spain, classical antiquity, the French Baroque, or jazz—he found raw material for his craftsmanlike talent, a talent that expressed itself in the transformation and shaping of conventional ideas into the most viscerally exciting of musical gestures.

Maurice Ravel at the piano

Ravel's mother was of Basque descent, his father Swiss, a music-loving engineer. He was born in Basque country, in the southwestern corner of France a short distance from the Spanish border, but was only a few months old when the family moved to Paris. At 14 he entered the Paris Conservatoire, meeting Emmanuel Chabrier and Erik Satie, and eventually studying composition with Gabriel Fauré, who discerned in him "a musical nature very taken with novelty, with a disarming sincerity." The fascination with novelty caused Ravel to fail in his five attempts to win the coveted Prix de Rome. By the time of the last attempt, in 1905, he was already an established composer, having produced the exquisite *Jeux d'eau* (*Fountains*) for piano, a magnificent string quartet, and the song cycle SHÉHÉRAZADE. The fluency of idiom and consummate command of form exhibited in these works mark them as products of a mature and original musical thinker. Ravel's failure to win the Prix de Rome boosted his cachet among the cognoscenti and made him a central figure in the antiestablishment crowd; in 1909 he took a leading role in founding the Société Musicale Indépendente, created in opposition to the conservative Société Nationale, under the control of d'Indy.

Henri Matisse's* L'Asie, *1940

In the years 1905–14 Ravel produced some of his finest works, including the piano pieces *Miroirs*, *GASPARD DE LA NUIT*, *MA MÈRE L'OYE* (*Mother Goose*), and *VALSES NOBLES ET SENTIMENTALES*, the extraordinarily accomplished Piano Trio, the orchestral *RAPSODIE ESPAGNOLE*, the ballet *DAPHNIS ET CHLOÉ*, and the opera *L'heure espagnole* (*Spanish Time*). Following the outbreak of World War I, Ravel volunteered for the air corps but was turned down after failing his physical (he was underweight and had a hernia). Eventually he saw action as a driver in the motorized transport, but in 1916 he came down with dysentery and had to be hospitalized. During a long recuperation in Paris, he completed the piano suite *LE TOMBEAU DE COUPERIN*, dedicating each of its six movements to a friend or acquaintance who had fallen in the war. The experience of war, his illness, and his mother's death, early in 1917, cast a pall, and it is tempting to see the first major work Ravel produced after the war—the menacing and surprisingly violent symphonic poem *LA VALSE*—as an effort to exorcise some demons. For Serge Koussevitzky he created a brilliantly fantastic orchestration of Mussorgsky's piano cycle *PICTURES AT AN EXHIBITION* in 1922, but the main work of the early 1920s was the remarkable operatic evocation of childhood dreams and fears, *L'ENFANT ET LES SORTILÈGES* (*The Child and the Magic Spells*).

Ravel's postwar interest in jazz and in such coloristic devices as bitonality stimulated him further, markedly influencing certain pages in his famous orchestral showpiece, *BOLÉRO*, from 1928. Between 1929 and 1931 Ravel worked simultaneously on two piano concertos—one in D for the left hand, brooding and focused, and one in G major, airy and effervescent. The latter Ravel intended for his own use; its scoring is brilliant, and there is a jazzy flavor to much of the writing that lends a sultry feel to the concerto's quieter pages and imparts a wonderful vibrancy to its climaxes. The left-hand concerto is a striking contrast in its solemnity, power, and predominantly dark orchestral textures. In the fall of 1932 Ravel was in a traumatic taxi accident that may have triggered the onset of Pick's disease; he experienced increasing debilitation and died five years later, after brain surgery.

Ravel's musical language exhibits a penchant for harmonies saturated by sevenths and ninths that reflects his indebtedness to Fauré. To everything he did, he brought a meticulous, lapidary quality, achieving a kind of clockwork precision in the musical processes (which his sometime collaborator Stravinsky teased him about) without sacrificing panache. His gift for combining cool sensuality with unhindered display was remarkable.

Ravel's piano music synthesizes numerous elements, among them the flowing figurations of Fauré and the virtuosic etude technique of Chopin and Liszt. Ravel made much of Debussy's evocative harmony and also pioneered keyboard effects that the elder composer later extended, notably the illusory, shimmering textures of *Jeux d'eau* (1901). He participated on equal footing with Debussy in making the period 1902–19 the golden age of French piano music.

Much of Ravel's music looks toward Spain, which for him represented not only a fascinating, remote, dreamlike realm, but also an inexhaustible source of exotic musical ideas and colorful aural imagery. Childhood, whose innocence appealed deeply to Ravel, proved another realm of inspiration, tapped in works such as *Ma mère l'oye* and *L'enfant et les sortilèges.* Secretive in everything, especially his emotions, Ravel kept himself in some ways a perpetual child, masked and game-playing. The most important human relationship of his life was the one he had with his mother; in his relationships with others, and, through his music, with the world at large, he maintained a chaste tone of impassioned restraint.

RECOMMENDED RECORDINGS

Boléro: Karajan and Berlin Philharmonic (DG).

Collected Orchestral works: Dutoit and Montreal Symphony Orchestra (Decca).

Daphnis et Chloé (complete): Martinon and Orchestre de Paris (EMI).

Daphnis et Chloé (Suite No. 2), *Rapsodie espagnole,* and other works: Martinon and Chicago Symphony Orchestra (RCA).

L'enfant et les sortilèges: Stephen, Owens, Futral, Lascarro, Wilson-Johnson; Previn and London Symphony Orchestra (DG).

Gaspard de la nuit (with works of Chopin and Prokofiev): Pogorelich (DG).

Piano Concerto in G, Concerto for the Left Hand: Thibaudet; Dutoit and Montreal Symphony Orchestra (Decca).

Piano Trio: Beaux Arts Trio (Philips).

Piano Trio: Florestan Trio (Hyperion).

Shéhérazade: Graham; Tortelier and BBC Symphony Orchestra (Warner Classics).

String Quartet: Guarneri Quartet (RCA).

String Quartet: Quartetto Italiano (Philips).

Razumovsky Quartets Set of three string quartets by Ludwig van Beethoven, his Opus 59, written for Count Andreas Razumovsky (1752–1836), the Russian ambassador to the Hapsburg court. Razumovsky was an amateur violinist of considerable merit whose substantial wealth enabled him to maintain a resident quartet that included among its members the outstanding violinist Ignaz Schuppanzigh and the cellist Joseph Linke. The three *Razumovsky* Quartets were commissioned toward the end of 1805 and completed within a year. Razumovsky's commission called for Beethoven to make use of actual Russian themes, which he did in the first two works of the set. In the scherzo to the Quartet in E minor, Op. 59, No. 2, he quotes the patriotic hymn "Slava," which Mussorgsky would later insert in the "Coronation" Scene of *Boris Godunov.* And in the finale to the

Quartet in F, Op. 59, No. 1, he uses a Russian tune as the subject of what amounts to a monothematic sonata.

The *Razumovsky* Quartets exhibit the hallmarks of Beethoven's middle-period style: Expansive, energetic, symphonic in approach, they are among the supreme achievements in the genre. It is hard to understand how their initial reception could have been so discouraging, yet the pieces provoked consternation and ridicule, even among Beethoven's musically literate friends. One perceptive review in a Viennese journal reported of these works that "the conception is profound and the construction excellent, but they are not easily comprehended—with the possible exception of the third in C major, which cannot but appeal to intelligent lovers of music because of its originality, melody, and harmonic power."

RECOMMENDED RECORDINGS

GUARNERI QUARTET (RCA).

KODÁLY QUARTET (NAXOS).

TAKÁCS QUARTET (DECCA).

recapitulation Third section of a movement in SONATA FORM, in which material from the exposition reappears and the home key of the movement is confirmed.

recitative [1] A declamatory style of singing, often conversational in its pacing and inflection, found in opera and other musico-dramatic forms, or a passage that calls for this style of singing. A good example is the recitativo "leporello, ove sei?" from Mozart's Don Giovanni. [2] An instrumental passage that resembles vocal recitative.

Max Reger: defiant traditionalist

recorder Woodwind instrument with seven finger holes and a thumbhole, belonging to the family of duct, or "fipple" flutes (i.e., those with a notched mouthpiece like that of a police whistle). It was among the most popular instruments of the Renaissance and Baroque periods. There are four common sizes: sopranino, descant (or soprano), treble (or alto), and tenor. Bass and contrabass instruments are also found, their use generally restricted to consort music. The repertoire for solo recorder is slight, but it includes concerted works by Vivaldi, Sammartini, and Telemann, as well as solo sonatas by Handel and Telemann. Bach called for recorders in 19 of his cantatas and showcased the instrument in two of his *Brandenburg* Concertos: No. 2 in F, which features a concertino group of violin, oboe, trumpet, and treble recorder, and No. 4 in G, with a solo group of violin and two treble (in some instances, sopranino) recorders.

Reger, Max

(b. Brand, March 19, 1873; d. Leipzig, May 11, 1916)

GERMAN COMPOSER. After early studies in Weiden, he entered the Sondershausen Conservatory in 1890 and became a student of Hugo Riemann, who instructed him using the works of Brahms and Bach as models. He followed Riemann to the Wiesbaden Conservatory, where he completed his studies and held a faculty position teaching theory. A year of compulsory military service (1896–97) caused him great psychological and physical harm, and he returned to Weiden for three years to recuperate. In 1901 he moved to Munich, where he taught privately and, later, at the Akademie der Tonkunst. In a characteristic display of contentiousness, Reger openly rejected the teaching of Riemann and publicly declared a "war of progress" that alienated him from his colleagues and made critics bristle. His vast output of organ compositions dates mostly from this period, and though these works never achieved much critical acclaim, Reger found a champion in the great organist Karl Straube, who performed them in spite of their difficulties. In 1907 Reger became professor of composition at the Leipzig Conservatory and director of music at the University of Leipzig; he quit the university after a year but remained at the conservatory until 1911. Some of his finest orchestral works—including the *Variations and Fugue on a Theme of J. A. Hiller* (1907), Violin Concerto (1907–08), and *Symphonisches Prolog zu einer Tragödie* (1908)—date from these years. He became director of the court orchestra at Meiningen in 1911, succeeding Hans von Bülow and Richard Strauss; in declining health, he stepped down in 1915 and retired to Jena. Among his last works was the one most frequently heard on concert programs today, the *Variations and Fugue on a Theme of Mozart* (1914), based on the opening theme of Mozart's Piano Sonata in A, K. 331.

Reger was a rigid traditionalist, a driven and compulsive worker with a prickly personality and an undiplomatic tongue, who could be strident in defense of his aesthetic. His compositional style was an extension of the language of Brahms, steeped in the formal structures of the past. He was strongly attracted to variation form and was a master at the contrapuntal elaboration of material. His harmonic vocabulary was often densely chromatic, given to rapid, unprepared modulations that impart a tonal vagueness to his music. His output was sizable, amounting to nearly 150 opuses and touching on nearly every standard genre except opera.

RECOMMENDED RECORDINGS

ORGAN WORKS: HAAS, LOHMANN, KAISSER (NAXOS).

VARIATIONS AND FUGUE ON A THEME OF J. A. HILLER: JÄRVI AND CONCERTGEBOUW ORCHESTRA (CHANDOS).

VARIATIONS AND FUGUE ON A THEME OF MOZART: BÖHM AND BERLIN PHILHARMONIC (DG).

Reich, Steve

(b. New York, October 3, 1936)

AMERICAN COMPOSER. Raised in New York and California, he took piano lessons as a child and from the age of 14 studied percussion with Roland Kohloff, percussionist and subsequently principal timpanist of the New York Philharmonic. He graduated with honors in philosophy from Cornell University in 1957, then enrolled in the Juilliard School, where from 1958 to 1961 he studied composition with William Bergsma and Vincent Persichetti. He continued his compositional studies with Darius Milhaud and Luciano Berio at Mills College, receiving an M.A. in music in 1963.

Reich's first important works were tape pieces such as *It's Gonna Rain* (1965) that make use of a technique Reich called "phasing," in which two tape loops (in *It's Gonna Rain,* the voice of a black preacher named Brother Walter delivering a sermon on the Flood) are set in motion at slightly different speeds, beginning in unison and gradually drifting out of phase, creating rhythmic complexities. Reich subsequently incorporated the technique in compositions for standard instruments. After a period of immersion in Ghanaian drumming, Reich composed *Drumming* (1971), a lengthy (57 to 86 minutes long) elaboration of a single rhythmic cell for an ensemble of tuned bongos, marimbas, glockenspiels, vibes, piccolo, and two female voices.

Drumming was followed by *Music for 18 Musicians* (1974–76), a landmark work in the history of minimalism and a watershed in Reich's career. The piece, for an ensemble of two clarinets, four pianos, three marimbas, two xylophones, vibraphone, violin, cello, and four female voices, is a progression of 11 "chords" (voicing somewhat variable) in which each chord is explored individually, with textures developing and morphing according to minimalist techniques (i.e., constantly changing, but almost imperceptibly). With its lush textures (which have been described as "tropical") and its expansion of a static harmonic situation into something very dynamic, *Music for 18 Musicians* brought elements of "maximalism" to minimalism.

Throughout his career, Reich's style has evolved in a "circular" rather than linear manner: He has borrowed concepts from 12th-century ORGANUM, made use of techniques from African and Indonesian music, picked up threads of Stravinsky and Orff. In the three decades since he conceived *Music for 18 Musicians,* he has also gone back over his own tracks, returning to the idea of "phasing" in such works as *Vermont Counterpoint* (1982) for flute and tape, *New York Counterpoint* (1985) for clarinet and tape, and *Different Trains* (1988) for string quartet and tape, but treating it in a much more complex manner. His maximal tendencies have asserted themselves in works such as *Tehillim,* a 1981 setting of psalms for voices and ensemble that has a percussive rhythmic pulse but eschews repeated melodic patterns, and *City Life* (1995), a richly scored piece for an ensemble of sampling keyboards, percussion, winds, and strings that conveys an undercurrent of despair and uneasiness.

Reich remains in love with sound, a composer who still revels in surface beauty and hypnotic fluctuations of rhythm and texture. But for some time he has also been interested in sustained harmonic development, large-scale structure, and expressive richness. Long admired as an innovator, he has managed to reaffirm traditional values while cavorting—marching would be far too predictable—to the beats of many different drummers. *See also box on page 272.*

Steve Reich, modern American master

RECOMMENDED RECORDINGS

CITY LIFE: ENSEMBLE MODERN (RCA).

DIFFERENT TRAINS: KRONOS QUARTET (NONESUCH).

DRUMMING: SŌ PERCUSSION (CANTALOUPE).

MUSIC FOR 18 MUSICIANS: ENSEMBLE MODERN (NONESUCH).

MUSIC FOR 18 MUSICIANS: STEVE REICH ENSEMBLE (ECM).

"STEVE REICH 1965–1995" (10 CDS): VARIOUS ARTISTS (NONESUCH).

VERMONT COUNTERPOINT: WILSON (EMI).

Reicha, Antoine

(b. Prague, February 26, 1770; d. Paris, May 28, 1836)

CZECH/FRENCH COMPOSER, TEACHER, AND THEORIST. Raised by his uncle Josef Reicha, a composer and conductor, and his French-born aunt, he grew up speaking both German and French. The family moved to Bonn in 1785, where the young Reicha played flute in the orchestra, becoming fast friends with one of his contemporaries in the viola section, Ludwig van Beethoven. Reicha studied composition against his uncle's wishes, and entered Bonn University in 1789. Following the French invasion of the Rhineland in 1794, he moved to Hamburg, where he devoted himself to teaching, composition, and the study of mathematics and philosophy. Reicha earned recognition as an important figure in Vienna's musical life during the years he lived there (1801–08): He made contact with Haydn, renewed his friendship with Beethoven, and wrote an opera, *Argine, regina di Granata* (1802), commissioned by Empress Maria Theresa. With a second Napoleonic invasion of Austria looming, he moved to Paris in 1808 and was appointed professor of counterpoint and fugue at the Paris Conservatoire in 1818. Among his students were Berlioz, Liszt, and Franck. He was named to the Légion d'Honneur in 1831, and became a member of the Académie in 1835.

Antoine Reicha, engraving from the **Journal des Artistes**

Reicha contributed hundreds of works to the chamber music catalog, most notably works for wind instruments alone or in novel combinations with strings. What his music may lack in genius it more than makes up in melodic charm and harmonic daring. He also wrote several influential theoretical works, the most important the *Traité de melodie* (*Treatise on Melody*; 1814) and *Traité de haute composition musicale* (*Treatise on Serious Musical Composition*; 1824–26).

RECOMMENDED RECORDINGS

WIND QUINTETS (COMPLETE): ALBERT SCHWEITZER QUINTET (CPO).

WIND QUINTETS (SELECTION): MICHAEL THOMPSON WIND QUINTET (NAXOS).

Reiner, Fritz

(b. Budapest, December 19, 1888; d. New York, November 15, 1963)

HUNGARIAN/AMERICAN CONDUCTOR. He began his study of music with his mother, a fine amateur pianist. In 1903 he enrolled simultaneously at the Royal University in Budapest, where in deference to his father he took courses in law, and the Hungarian National Royal Academy of Music. Following his father's death a year later, he left the university to devote himself full-time to the study of music. He remained at the academy until 1909; his piano teacher during the last two years was the young Béla Bartók. He worked for a year after graduation as rehearsal pianist for a local light opera company, and spent a year as staff conductor at the municipal theater in Laibach (now Ljubljana, Slovenia), working under Václav Talich. In 1911 he accepted a post with the Népopera in Budapest, where he conducted a varied repertoire running from Rossini, Donizetti, and Meyerbeer through Verdi, Wagner, and Puccini. Following the death of Ernst von Schuch in 1914, Reiner was summoned to Dresden, where he worked as staff conductor through the end of 1921. While in Dresden he conducted Mozart, Wagner, Verdi, and a number of contemporary works; in 1919 he presided over the German premiere of Richard Strauss's *Die Frau ohne Schatten.* He observed Strauss conducting his own works on many occasions and learned much from attending concerts of Arthur Nikisch in Berlin.

In 1922, after being passed over as music director in Dresden (Fritz Busch got the job), Reiner became conductor of the Cincinnati Symphony Orchestra, succeeding Eugène Ysaÿe. Finding it necessary to shake up the orchestra's personnel in order to raise its standard of playing, he quickly gained a reputation as an abusive disciplinarian. By 1928, however, the year he became an American citizen, Reiner had lifted the Cincinnati ensemble to a new level. In 1930 he filed for divorce in order to marry the spirited American actress Carlotta Irwin (his third marriage); the orchestra's board, facing a storm of indignation, let him go. The following year he became head of the orchestra and opera departments at the Curtis Institute of Music in Philadelphia, where his students included Leonard Bernstein. His career remained in a holding pattern until 1938, when he was named music director of the Pittsburgh Symphony Orchestra. During the decade he spent in Pittsburgh (1938–48), Reiner conducted more than 500 works, including much contemporary music.

In 1948 Reiner joined the staff of the Metropolitan Opera in New York. He made his Met debut conducting Strauss's *Salome* on February 4, 1949, and during five seasons on the roster led 113 performances, including the Met premiere of Stravinsky's *The Rake's Progress* (in 1953) and acclaimed renditions of Wagner's *Tristan und Isolde* and Strauss's *Der Rosenkavalier.*

Reiner became music director of the Chicago Symphony Orchestra in 1953. Already an outstanding orchestra, though one in turmoil, it became a stupendous one under Reiner's command—in the opinion of Stravinsky, "the most precise and flexible orchestra in the world." During his ten seasons with the ensemble, he again conducted nearly 500 works, many of them new to his own repertoire. He championed the music of dozens of living American and European composers, and made a series of monumental recordings for RCA Victor, including magnificent readings of major works by Beethoven, Brahms, Strauss, and Bartók. In ill health and wearied by battles with the orchestra's management, he resigned in 1962 and died the following year.

Famous for his small beat, sparing gestures, hawklike gaze, and sullen temper, Reiner was a stern taskmaster but also a brilliantly gifted conductor who, while he intimidated a few, commanded the respect and devotion of the majority of his associates, and as a result was able to draw exceptional playing from them. Always prepared, he came to rehearsal knowing exactly what he wanted and communicated it with great clarity and minimum verbiage. In performances and in front of the microphone he could light a fire under his players without exerting himself (something he learned from Nikisch) or losing control of balances and pacing. His advocacy was particularly important in establishing the music of Bartók in the orchestral repertoire. Together with violinist Joseph Szigeti, he persuaded Serge Koussevitzky to offer Bartók a $1,000 commission for what became the *Concerto for Orchestra*; he subsequently made the first recording of the

Fritz Reiner in rehearsal, showing how the passage should go

score (with the Pittsburgh Symphony in 1946) and the greatest (with the Chicago Symphony in 1955).

RECOMMENDED RECORDINGS

BARTÓK, *MUSIC FOR STRINGS, PERCUSSION, AND CELESTA, CONCERTO FOR ORCHESTRA*: CHICAGO SYMPHONY ORCHESTRA (RCA).

BRAHMS, VIOLIN CONCERTO: HEIFETZ; CHICAGO SYMPHONY ORCHESTRA (RCA).

MUSSORGSKY, *PICTURES AT AN EXHIBITION*: CHICAGO SYMPHONY ORCHESTRA (RCA).

PROKOFIEV, *ALEXANDER NEVSKY* (CANTATA): ELIAS; CHICAGO SYMPHONY ORCHESTRA (RCA).

STRAUSS, *ALSO SPRACH ZARATHUSTRA, EIN HELDENLEBEN*: CHICAGO SYMPHONY ORCHESTRA (RCA).

reprise A part of a movement or composition that repeats an earlier theme or section.

Requiem Properly, a musical setting of the Latin Mass for the Dead; more generally, any musical work with a text intended to commemorate the dead. The earliest surviving polyphonic setting is by Ockeghem; it is incomplete (lacking a Sanctus, Agnus Dei, and Communion), and was composed some time after 1450, quite possibly after 1470. A setting by Du Fay, believed to date from around 1470 and now lost, may have been the model for Ockeghem's work. Several subsequent settings from the late 15th and early 16th centuries are clearly indebted to Ockeghem. Important settings from the late 16th and early 17th century include two by Lassus (published in 1578 and 1580) and two by Tomás Luis de Victoria (1583 and 1605). The most significant Requiem of the 18th century was Mozart's dark-hued and vividly expressive but, alas, unfinished setting of 1791. Other interesting settings include youthful works by François-Joseph Gossec (1734–1829; 1760) and Joseph Martin Kraus (1756–92; 1775).

The 19th century saw a number of ambitious and grandly scaled Requiems, including two by Cherubini—the boldly scored C minor of 1816 and the gloomy D minor of 1836, written for himself—and the astounding creations of Berlioz (1837) and Verdi (1874), among the most impressive choral-orchestral works in the literature. Fauré took a more intimate tack in his Requiem (final version 1900) and Duruflé returned to plainchant for the basis of his 1947 setting. Britten showed characteristic acuity in setting the text of his *War Requiem* (1961), which interweaves the Latin Mass with antiwar poetry by Wilfred Owen. Noteworthy among recent contributions to the genre is Penderecki's *Polish Requiem* (1984; rev. 1993), a work that bears witness equally to Poland's strong Catholic faith and troubled 20th-century history.

Standing outside the tradition of the Latin Requiem, Brahms's *Ein deutsches Requiem* (*A German Requiem*), completed in 1868, used as its text Old and New Testament passages from the Lutheran Bible. Similarly, Hindemith's post-Holocaust (1946) Requiem, subtitled "For Those We Love," was based on Walt Whitman's poignant lament for Civil War dead, "When Lilacs Last in the Dooryard Bloom'd." *See also* MASS.

Respighi, Ottorino

(b. Bologna, July 9, 1879; d. Rome, April 18, 1936)

ITALIAN COMPOSER. His orchestral works—including suites for chamber ensemble, as well as some of the largest and gaudiest symphonic blockbusters ever written—stand as the most successful contributions to the repertoire by any Italian of the 20th century. Born into a musical family, he received his musical education at the Liceo Musicale in Bologna. Between 1900 and 1903, while working as an orchestral violist in Russia, he had the opportunity to study composition and orchestration with Rimsky-Korsakov, whose colorful palette would have a profound impact on his own approach to scoring. (In 1902, he studied briefly, though without much benefit, with Max Bruch in Berlin.) From 1903 to 1908 he continued to make his living as a violist, playing in orchestras as well as in the Magellini Quartet, while composing on the side. In 1913, after failing to land a permanent teaching position in Bologna, he was appointed professor of composition at the Liceo Musicale di Santa Cecilia in Rome, where he would live the rest of his life; in 1919 he married one of his students, the singer and composer Elsa Olivieri Sangiacomo (1894–1996). In 1932 the government of Mussolini honored him with a membership in the Reale Accademia d'Italia. While the extraordinary popularity of his symphonic poems *Fontane di Roma* (*Fountains of Rome*; 1915–16) and *Pini di Roma* (*Pines of Rome*; 1923–24) made it unnecessary for him to hold a "day job" during the 1920s and 1930s, he nonetheless served as director of the Conservatorio di Santa Cecilia (successor to the Liceo) from 1923 to 1926, and taught an advanced composition class at Rome's prestigious Accademia di Santa Cecilia until the year before he died. From the mid-1920s he traveled extensively, appearing frequently as pianist and conductor in performances of his own music.

After Puccini, Respighi was the most famous Italian composer of his day. Though he dutifully and repeatedly sought success in the operatic sphere, none of the eight works he completed in the genre has attained a place in the repertoire; some have never even been performed. As an orchestral colorist, however, he was unsurpassed. He deservedly achieved worldwide fame with *Fontane di Roma*, whose brilliant pictorialism he trumped in the even more successful *Pini di Roma*, complete with a recorded twittering nightingale and offstage flugelhorns depicting the advance of a triumphal consular army. Both works partake of the harmonic subtleties of Debussy, Ravel, and Richard Strauss, but are decked out in splashy orchestrations that recall the Russians—Rimsky-Korsakov and Stravinsky in particular. Following the breakthrough with *Fontane di Roma*, Respighi showed his range in scores reflecting a variety of approaches: In 1917 he produced the first of three collections of *Antiche danze ed arie per liuto* (*Ancient Dances and Airs for Lute*), spirited transcriptions for small orchestra of Italian Renaissance lute pieces; in 1918, he wrote a breezily scored ballet for Diaghilev called *La boutique fantasque*, based on music by Rossini. The luminously scored *Vertrate di chiesa* (*Church Windows*) and *Trittico botticelliano* (*Botticelli Triptych*) appeared in 1925–27, followed in 1928 by the sumptuous *Impressioni brasiliane* (*Brazilian Impressions*) and in 1932 by the unabashedly opulent ballet *Belkis, regina de Saba* (*Belkis, Queen of Sheba*), a tour de force of symphonic belly dance that repays Respighi's debt to Rimsky-Korsakov with exuberant interest. Respighi

Ottorino Respighi

had an intimate side as well, which he showed in *Il tramonto* (1918), a lovely chamber cantata (text by Shelley) for mezzo-soprano and string quartet, and in his Violin Sonata (1917). His pronounced antiquarian streak is exhibited not only in the *Antiche danze ed arie* but in a number of works that make use of plainchant and church modes—including *Tre preludi sopra melodie gregoriani* (1919–21), the *Concerto gregoriano* (1921) for violin and orchestra, the *Concerto in modo misolidio* (1925) for piano and orchestra, and the *Quartetto dorico* (1924) for string quartet—as well as in the charming 1928 orchestral suite *Gli uccelli* (*The Birds*), based on Baroque keyboard pieces. Whether in works such as these, where his touch was light as a feather, or in more grandiose efforts—not least *Feste romane* (1928), the over-the-top three-quel to *Fontane di Roma* and *Pini di Roma*—Respighi showed his mettle as an orchestrator, developing an arsenal of effects that Hollywood soundtrackers have been looting ever since.

Detail from Botticelli's* Primavera, *1477

RECOMMENDED RECORDINGS

Antiche danze ed arie per liuto (*Ancient Dances and Airs for Lute*): Dorati and Philharmonia Hungaria (Mercury).

Gli uccelli: Dorati and London Symphony Orchestra (Mercury).

Impressione brasiliane (*Brazilian Impressions*), *Vetrate di chiesa* (*Church Windows*): Simon and Philharmonia Orchestra (Chandos).

Pini di Roma, Fontane di Roma, Feste romane: Maazel and Pittsburgh Symphony Orchestra (Sony).

Pini di Roma, Fontane di Roma, Gli uccelli: Kertész and London Symphony Orchestra (Decca).

responsory A chant used as a postlude to the reading of lessons at Matins and Vespers. The first part of a chant in responsory form is called the *respond,* the following part the *verse.*

rest Symbol in music notation indicating a measured silence. Like notes, rests have specific rhythmic values that can be lengthened by the use of a dot (e.g., a dotted eighth rest indicates a pause equal to three sixteenth notes). In addition to serving a purely utilitarian function—to provide performers with a "rest" for breath or to avert finger fatigue—rests are an essential part of proper musical punctuation, often used to assist performers in articulating a phrase clearly and with the correct rhythm. Rests also play an essential part in musical expression, because silence can be, and often is, as important to the communication of mood and emotion as sound. Two celebrated examples of this are the rests that occur throughout the first 15 measures of the prelude to Act I of Wagner's *Tristan und Isolde,* and the rest in measure 6 of Debussy's *Prélude à l'après-midi d'un faune.*

***Revolutionary* Etude** Nickname of Frédéric Chopin's Etude in C minor, Op. 10, No. 12. Legend has it that Chopin penned this demonic essay in a mood of despair upon hearing of the capture of Warsaw by the Russians. But the piece was probably composed in September 1830, a full year before that event. The turbulent figuration for the left hand is the work's most striking feature.

Revueltas, Silvestre

(b. Santiago Papasquiaro, December 31, 1899; d. Mexico City, October 5, 1940)

Mexican composer. He studied violin as a child in Colima, continuing his education in Mexico City and at St. Edward College in Austin, Texas, and the Chicago

Musical College. After a brief hiatus in Mexico he returned to Chicago as a graduate student in violin (1922–26). Between 1926 and 1928 he played in a theater orchestra in San Antonio and conducted a community orchestra in Mobile, Alabama. In 1929 his countryman Carlos Chávez summoned him to Mexico City to serve as assistant conductor of the Mexico Symphony Orchestra, where he remained until 1935. Drawn to Spain in 1937 following the outbreak of its Civil War, he worked on behalf of the Republican government. He returned to Mexico and died of the effects of alcoholism.

Only after he became Chávez's assistant at the Mexico Symphony Orchestra did Revueltas begin to compose. His output, while small, was colorful and *muy picante,* reflecting the influence of Stravinsky (particularly *The Rite of Spring* and *Petrushka*) and bearing a resemblance—in its slightly impudent tone and burlesque quality—to the music of Ibert and Poulenc. In much of his music Revueltas made use of folklike melodies, though he did not actually quote real Mexican folk tunes. *Sensemayá* (1938), his most popular work, was clearly influenced by *The Rite of Spring*: Inspired by a poem about the killing of a tropical snake, it builds like a Mexican *Boléro* to a roaring climax. Revueltas's masterpiece, *La noche de los Mayas* (1939), was written as movie music. In effect a four-movement symphony with a beautiful slow movement ("Noche de Yucatán"), it is expressive, imaginative, and strikingly poetic.

Revueltas is often contrasted with Chávez, his exact contemporary and the leading establishment figure in 20th-century Mexican music. Their personalities were notably different and so was their music. Revueltas was cynical, individualistic, a leftist, and a loner; not surprisingly, his music was more dissonant and modernistic, denser and darker than Chávez's. Undoubtedly, part of what makes the music of Revueltas resonate with today's audiences is that there is something menacing and malevolent beneath its surface. If, in listening to the music of Chávez, you come away with the impression that the Indians are happy, in Revueltas you get the feeling that they are about to tear the beating heart out of your chest.

RECOMMENDED RECORDING

ORCHESTRAL AND SMALL ENSEMBLE WORKS (INCLUDING *SENSEMAYÁ, LA NOCHE DE LOS MAYAS*): SALONEN AND LOS ANGELES PHILHARMONIC ORCHESTRA (SONY).

rhapsody (from Gr. *rhapsodos,* "a reciter of unaccompanied epic poetry") An extended musical piece that is freely organized or episodic in nature rather than rigorously argued. Since the middle of the 19th century, when Liszt's *Hungarian Rhapsodies* attained widespread popularity, the term has frequently been applied to pieces of a folkish or nationalistic cast and to works that make virtuosic demands on orchestras and instrumentalists (e.g., Dvořák's three *Slavonic Rhapsodies,* Op. 45, Enescu's two *Romanian Rhapsodies,* Op. 11, and Debussy's *Rapsodie* for saxophone and orchestra).

Rhapsody in Blue COMPOSITION FOR JAZZ ORCHESTRA AND SOLO PIANO BY GEORGE GERSHWIN, premiered February 12, 1924, in New York's Aeolian Hall by Paul Whiteman and his band, with the composer as soloist. Gershwin drafted the piece in great haste after reading in the newspaper that a work of his was going to be performed by Whiteman at a concert billed "An Experiment in Modern Music." Whiteman's arranger, the multitalented Ferde Grofé, scored the piece for a large dance band that included eight violins along with the customary reeds, brass, and percussion of a jazz ensemble. At the time of the premiere, Gershwin had not yet written out the solo piano part.

In the hands of another composer, the *Rhapsody in Blue* could easily have been an exercise in dressing up jazzy rhythms and melodic figures in symphonic garb. But Gershwin's sense of timing and his gift for memorable melody turned the work into something more—a piece that communicated an entirely new range of moods and emotions on the classical wavelength, and did so with instantaneous appeal. Gershwin would show greater formal aptitude in later works (the tunes in the *Rhapsody in Blue* are stitched together in places), but he would never surpass the freshness of inspiration that marks this effort. In 1926 Grofé rescored the piece for full symphony orchestra and piano, the version in which it is usually heard in concert and on record.

RECOMMENDED RECORDINGS

BERNSTEIN AND COLUMBIA SYMPHONY ORCHESTRA (SONY).

LITTON AND DALLAS SYMPHONY ORCHESTRA (DELOS).

Rhapsody on a Theme of Paganini THEME-AND-VARIATION WORK FOR PIANO AND ORCHESTRA BY SERGEY RACHMANINOV, composed in 1934. Based on Paganini's celebrated 24th Caprice for unaccompanied violin, it consists of an introduction, the theme, and 24 variations. The theme is not stated until *after* the introduction and first variation have been played; fittingly, it is given to the violins when it appears. The ensuing variations, exploring a scintillating range of pianistic and orchestral textures, flow marvelously from one to the next. In variations 7, 10, and 24, Rachmaninov indulges in one of his favorite compositional quirks, quoting the theme of the DIES IRAE from the Latin Mass for the Dead (he does the same thing in *The Isle of the Dead* and the *Symphonic Dances*). His sense of *diablerie* is palpable in the driving energy of variations 8 and 9, which come between two references to the *Dies irae,* and again in the final pages of the score. Elsewhere, particularly in the cavalry charge of variation 14, one recognizes the grand Romantic sweep of Rachmaninov's piano concertos. The 15th variation is a fleet scherzo, at the start of which the piano has the stage to itself. Then, with the 18th variation, comes one of the most celebrated of all Rachmaninov's melodies: Romantic, wistful, yearning, it is no more than the theme played upside down and with a slightly altered rhythm. The piano rightly introduces this inspired idea, which is then given to the first violins and cellos in octaves. The final variations build in momentum and excitement to a conclusion that would have left even Paganini a bit breathless, capped by an excuse-me ending as delightful as it is brief.

RECOMMENDED RECORDINGS

HOUGH; LITTON AND DALLAS SYMPHONY ORCHESTRA (HYPERION).

RACHMANINOV; STOKOWSKI AND PHILADELPHIA ORCHESTRA (RCA).

Rheingold, Das OPERA IN FOUR SCENES BY RICHARD WAGNER, composed 1853–54 as the "preliminary evening" of his tetralogy *DER RING DES NIBELUNGEN,* and first performed September 22, 1869, at the National Theater in Munich. Two and a half hours long, it is short by comparison with the other *Ring* operas. Its opening scene takes place at the *bottom* of the Rhine—during the orchestral introduction, the river's majestic ground tone (E-flat) is sustained by the basses as the rest of the orchestra paints a spectacular portrait of the rolling current and shafts of sunlight piercing the depths, illuminating a lump of gold. The drama commences with the dwarf Alberich's theft of the gold from the Rhine Maidens, followed by a scene in which Wotan, the chief of the gods, contracts for the building of Valhalla with a pair of giants. Possession of a ring formed from the Rhine gold confers unlimited power on Alberich (the Nibelung of the title), so Wotan must steal the ring, along with the hoard of gold the dwarf has amassed. Before surrendering the ring, Alberich lays a curse on it. Wotan wants to keep the ring, but Erda, the nicest of the *Ring*'s chthonic characters, rises up to tell him that's a bad idea. The curse is quickly fulfilled when Fasolt and Fafner, the two giants (who have decided to be paid for their labor with the gold stolen from Alberich), fall to arguing over who will get the ring. Fafner kills Fasolt. The opera ends with the gods' emptily victorious march across a rainbow bridge into Valhalla.

The continuous musical structure of *Das Rheingold* is itself a gigantic achievement. Into it Wagner sets the main motifs of the *Ring* cycle—identifying various objects (e.g., Valhalla, the ring, the Rhine), as well as key concepts (brooding, the curse, the contract) and personages—with all the skill of a master builder, preparing the listener for what is to come on the following three evenings. Equally impressive is the miraculous suggestiveness of Wagner's scoring, which conveys everything from the flow of a river to the flickering malevolence of fire, and even—with radiant brass, shimmering strings, and *six* offstage harps—the hues of the rainbow bridge.

RECOMMENDED RECORDING

LONDON, FLAGSTAD, SVANHOLM, NEIDLINGER; SOLTI AND VIENNA PHILHARMONIC (DECCA).

***Rhenish* Symphony** TITLE OF ROBERT SCHUMANN'S SYMPHONY NO. 3 IN E-FLAT, OP. 97; despite its designation, it was the fourth (and last) work he completed in the form. The symphony was composed at breakneck speed over five weeks in the autumn of 1850, shortly after Schumann and his wife, Clara, had moved from Dresden to the city of Düsseldorf on the Rhine. The optimism with which Schumann greeted this move (and his assumption of the post of municipal music director in Düsseldorf) can be felt in many pages of the score, especially in the energetic opening and closing movements. The symphony is laid out along conventional lines, except for the insertion of an additional slow movement prior to the finale. The festive opening movement, marked *Lebhaft* ("lively"), establishes a mood of sunny ebullience, juxtaposing passages of choralelike majesty and breathless animation. The second movement, though called a scherzo, is a freewheeling Ländler that Schumann considered calling "Morning on the Rhine" or "Rhine Wine Song." A tranquil intermezzo follows. The only outright allusion to the symphony's "Rhenish" origins comes with the penultimate movement, supposedly inspired by a scene Schumann witnessed at the cathedral in nearby Cologne—a ceremony marking the elevation of an archbishop to the rank of cardinal. The music here, in contrast with that of the rest of the symphony, is solemn and grave, suggesting a processional in the immense interior spaces of a Gothic nave. The finale, which contains a reminiscence of the cathedral music near its end, closes the symphony on a joyful note.

RECOMMENDED RECORDINGS

BERNSTEIN AND VIENNA PHILHARMONIC (DG).
KARAJAN AND BERLIN PHILHARMONIC (DG).

rhythm The regular pattern of strong and weak beats (or a recognizable ordering of longer and shorter durations) that characterizes a musical phrase, passage, or period.

RIAS Kammerchor *See box on pages 934–36.*

Richter, Hans

(b. Raab, April 4, 1843; d. Bayreuth, December 5, 1916)

AUSTRIAN CONDUCTOR. His parents were both musicians. In 1854, following the death of his father, he was sent to Vienna to be trained in the profession, first as a choirboy and subsequently at the conservatory of the Gesellschaft der Musikfreunde. He learned to play numerous instruments, and following his graduation in 1862 joined the orchestra of the Kärntnertortheater as a horn player. In 1866, at the age of 23, he apprenticed himself to Richard Wagner, staying with the composer in his Swiss exile (at Tribschen, outside of Lucerne) to copy the score of *Die Meistersinger von Nürnberg,* and serving as Wagner's assistant at the opera's premiere in Munich in 1868. Back in Tribschen in 1870, he helped copy the score to *Siegfried* and surreptitiously rehearsed the small ensemble that, on Christmas morning, gave the premiere of the *Siegfried Idyll* on the stairway leading to the second floor of the villa, where he played the viola and, for good measure, tossed off the short trumpet solo at the work's climax. Richter became music director of the National Theater in Pest the following year. In 1875 he was appointed conductor at the Vienna Court Opera, at the same time becoming the Vienna Philharmonic's first permanent conductor, a post he held until 1898.

In the summer of 1876 Richter conducted the first integral performances of Wagner's *Ring* cycle at Bayreuth. His association with the Bayreuth Festival continued through the summer of 1912, by which time he was a resident of Bayreuth. In addition to serving as Wagner's chief acolyte, Richter proved a distinguished interpreter of the symphonies of Brahms, who tapped him to conduct the premieres of Nos. 2 (1877) and 3 (1883), and of Dvořák, whose Sixth Symphony (1880) is dedicated to him. During his years at the helm of the Vienna Philharmonic, he also became a leading advocate of the music of Bruckner, conducting the premieres of the second version of the Fourth Symphony (1881), the Te Deum (1886), and the final version of the Eighth Symphony (1892). In later years, Richter championed the works of Elgar, conducting the premieres of both the *Enigma* Variations (1899) and *The Dream of Gerontius* (1900) and receiving the dedication of the composer's First Symphony (1908).

Richter was among the first of the great locomotive-set conductors whose impact extended beyond a single city to the European continent as a whole. Following his inauguration of the Richter Concerts in London, in 1879, he was a presence on the English musical scene for more than 30 years, an era climaxed by his tenure as music director of the Hallé Orchestra (1899–1911) and concomitant service as a principal conductor both of the London Symphony Orchestra (1904–11) and at Covent Garden (1903–10). In his heyday, in the closing years of the 19th century, only the names of Bülow and Nikisch could be mentioned in the same breath as his. Unlike both of them, however, Richter was evenly balanced between the symphonic and operatic spheres.

Hans Richter, in an 1893 lithograph

Richter, Sviatoslav

(b. Zhitomir, Ukraine, March 20, 1915; d. Moscow, August 1, 1997)

RUSSIAN PIANIST. Among pianists, he was widely regarded as the greatest of the 20th century. Known for his astonishing virtuosity and penetrating interpretive insight, the reclusive Russian became a mythic figure to music lovers on both sides of the Iron Curtain, his performances and recordings a litmus test for the sublime.

Richter's parents were German; his father, Teofil, was a professional musician and his mother was musically inclined. Shortly after he was born, the family moved to Odessa, where Richter effectively taught himself to play the piano. He worked as a *répétiteur* at the city's opera house, and for a time was interested in conducting. At the age of 22, however, he decided to embark on a serious study of the piano and moved to Moscow to enroll in the master class of Heinrich Neuhaus at the Moscow Conservatory. Under the tutelage of Neuhaus he developed a formidable technique that, in combination with his powerful musical intelligence, made him a master even as a student. He was ultimately expelled from the conservatory for failing a required course in dialectical materialism. Not long after, on the night of October 7, 1941, Richter's 69-year-old father was executed by an NKVD (Communist secret police) firing squad in Odessa on trumped-up charges of counterrevolutionary activity.

Richter gave the first public performances of two of Prokofiev's three wartime piano sonatas, No. 6 in A, Op. 82 (in 1940), and No. 7 in B-flat, Op. 83 (in 1942). He would later also become a champion of Sonata No. 8 (premiered by Gilels), and would receive the dedication of Prokofiev's last work in the form, Sonata No. 9 in C, Op. 103. On February 18, 1952, with Mstislav Rostropovich as soloist, he conducted the world premiere of Prokofiev's *Symphony-Concerto* for cello and orchestra, the one and only time he ever performed without a piano, and a courageous act: Prokofiev had been censured on Stalin's orders in a purge of the Composers' Union in 1948.

In the years that followed, Richter occasionally partnered with Rostropovich and violinist David Oistrakh in recital programs and on record. Because his homosexuality and the fact that he had family in the West (his mother had remarried after World War II and was living in Germany) drew extra scrutiny from the authorities, Richter was the last of the major Soviet artists of the Stalin era to be permitted to perform abroad. His growing reputation did enable him to travel with some frequency inside the Soviet Bloc, and those appearances quickly became the stuff of legend. At a 1958 recital in Sofia, Bulgaria, for example, he gave what many aficionados consider to be the finest account of Mussorgsky's *Pictures at an Exhibition* ever captured on tape, a performance as celebrated in pianistic

Sviatoslav Richter in rehearsal

circles as Callas's Lisbon *Traviata* is in vocal ones. Eventually, a delegation of high-level artists and friends—including Rostropovich, Oistrakh, and the conductor Kirill Kondrashin—was able to convince the authorities that the longer they waited to let Richter out, the greater the eventual international embarrassment would be. In 1960 Richter was allowed to perform in Finland as a test; following his return to Moscow, he was immediately sent on a tour of the U.S. Thereafter he was authorized to travel on a regular basis and to perform and record with Western orchestras such as the London Symphony and the Berlin Philharmonic.

As his career progressed, Richter, who was prone to depression, became increasingly idiosyncratic as a performer and withdrawn as a person. In later years he lived and worked as much outside Russia as in it. He loved Italy and France, where in 1965 he established a festival in a stone barn near Tours, and was also quite fond of Japan. Richter's domestic partnership with the lyric soprano Nina Dorliac (the two were never formally married), though in large part necessitated by stringent Soviet laws against homosexuality, remained cordial to the end of the pianist's life.

Richter possessed a phenomenal memory and was master of a colossal repertoire. He was deeply introspective, capable of penetrating the emotional depths of any piece. He was also mercurial and imaginative, which led some to characterize his playing as quirky, others as willful and imperious. The more difficult a piece was, the more dazzlingly Richter played it. His tone, never hard or clangorous, had a steely brilliance that turned to thunder as it got loud.

The music of Schubert and Schumann stood at the center of Richter's pianistic universe. He was also known for his fulminant Liszt and aristocratic Beethoven, and for his authoritative interpretations of Scriabin and Prokofiev. In performance Richter had the rare ability to completely inhabit the moment yet never lose sight of the musical architecture, a piece's line of argument and its long-term goal. Seeing a piece as a whole, as well as its details, and seizing on both of these aspects in performance, he could give a kind of "composer's-eye view" of the music, no matter who the composer was. At its best his playing was characterized by a sense of flow that was not so much inexorable (which would imply force) as inevitable, unescapable, irresistible.

RECOMMENDED RECORDINGS

COLLECTION: "GREAT PIANISTS OF THE 20TH CENTURY": INCLUDES MUSSORGSKY, *PICTURES AT AN EXHIBITION;* PROKOFIEV, SONATAS NOS. 6–8; WORKS BY SCHUBERT, CHOPIN, LISZT, RACHMANINOV (PHILIPS).

LISZT, PIANO CONCERTOS NOS. 1 AND 2, B MINOR SONATA: KONDRASHIN AND LONDON SYMPHONY ORCHESTRA (PHILIPS).

"Ride of the Valkyries, The" POPULAR TITLE GIVEN TO THE PRELUDE TO ACT III OF RICHARD WAGNER'S *DIE WALKÜRE.* Daughters of Wotan, the Valkyries ride winged steeds into battle, where their mission is to retrieve the bodies of fallen heroes and carry them off to Valhalla. Wagner's exultant depiction of the Valkyries' aerial horsemanship precedes a rendezvous of eight of the nine maidens (Brünnhilde being absent) on the summit of a rocky mountain.

Rienzi GRAND OPERA IN FIVE ACTS BY RICHARD WAGNER, to his own libretto (based on Edward Bulwer-Lytton's novel *Rienzi, the Last of the Tribunes*), composed 1838–40 and premiered October 20, 1842, in Dresden. Set in Rome around the middle of the 14th century, against a backdrop of feuding families and civil unrest, the plot deals with the efforts of Cola Rienzi, a papal notary, to bring order to the city, placate the unruly populace, and survive various attempts on his life. He ultimately fails on all counts. The mob sets fire to the Capitol, and as the building collapses (a grand-opera denouement if ever there was one), Rienzi dies clasping his beloved Irene in his arms.

The Overture to *Rienzi* is a popular concert piece, but the opera itself—owing to its long-windedness, extravagant scenic demands, and impenetrable plot—is rarely performed. Wagner's intention was to outdo all previous grand operas in sumptuousness and scale—that is, to beat Meyerbeer at his own game. That he failed was not for lack of either talent or ambition; his gift simply lay in another direction, which *Der fliegende Holländer* was about to make clear. Wagner's actual manuscript vanished at the end of World War II. The last person known to have had it in his possession was Adolf Hitler, who claimed that *Rienzi* had a profound impact on him in his teens.

RECOMMENDED RECORDINGS

COMPLETE OPERA:

KOLLO, MARTIN, ADAM; HOLLREISER AND STAATSKAPELLE DRESDEN (EMI).

OVERTURE:

BARENBOIM AND CHICAGO SYMPHONY ORCHESTRA (TELDEC).

KLEMPERER AND PHILHARMONIA ORCHESTRA (EMI).

Rigoletto **OPERA IN THREE ACTS BY GIUSEPPE VERDI,** to a libretto by Francesco Maria Piave (based on Victor Hugo's 1832 play *Le roi s'amuse*), premiered March 11, 1851, at La Fenice in Venice. Hugo's volatile plot, revolving around the amoral behavior of a ruler, gave Verdi a great deal of trouble with the censors. In the end, Hugo's king (François I) became the Duke of Mantua, who in Verdi's treatment emerges as a complex, reflective, introspective character, shifting the emotional ground of the original. But the real focus of the story remains the hunchback Rigoletto, whom Verdi treats as a tragic figure of compelling stature, willful yet noble in the vein of King Lear. Gilda, the daughter Rigoletto tries to protect and ends up destroying, is also a substantial figure, one who reaches a new level of awareness as a result of her unhappy experiences. Her role, verging on the coloratura range, presents some unusual technical challenges.

Verdi's score is marvelously alive. As befits the subject, its music is often tough, at times brutal. This was a revolutionary departure from the smoothness of bel canto, but Verdi was always more interested in emotional intensity and dramatic thrust than he was in pretty sound. Among the opera's highlights are its taut opening scene, with its grand dramatic crescendo, and the final act's brilliantly evocative storm scene. Gilda's "Caro nome" and the Duke's "La donna è mobile" are justly celebrated arias, but it is with the quartet "Bella figlia dell'amore" that Verdi scales the heights of characterization, limning four personalities—Rigoletto, the Duke, Gilda, and Maddalena—simultaneously.

RECOMMENDED RECORDING

DOMINGO, CAPPUCCILLI, COTRUBAS, GHIAUROV; GIULINI AND VIENNA PHILHARMONIC (DG).

Rihm, Wolfgang

(b. Karlsruhe, March 13, 1952)

GERMAN COMPOSER. From 1968 to 1972 he studied piano and composition at the Hochschule für Musik in Karlsruhe. He pursued further studies in composition with Karlheinz Stockhausen, Klaus Huber, Wolfgang Fortner, and Humphrey Searle, returning to teach in Karlsruhe from 1973 to 1978 and becoming professor of composition there in 1985. Since 1978 he has also served on the faculty of the summer course in Darmstadt.

Rihm is one of the most widely performed and frequently commissioned composers in Europe. Eclectic and remarkably

Wolfgang Rihm

wide-ranging, he has produced more than 150 works to date, including concertos and orchestral music, numerous works for instrumental ensembles of various sizes and dispositions, ten string quartets, and a variety of solo and vocal pieces. He has also written five major works for the stage, including the music dramas *Oedipus* (1987) and *Die Eroberung von Mexico* (*The Conquest of Mexico*; 1992). While opposed to the purely procedural aims of serialism, Rihm has assimilated many elements from the sound worlds of prewar modernism and the postwar avant-garde, combining them with methods and approaches rooted in the Austro-Germanic tradition. In this way, he has developed a syntactically complex and gesturally surprising idiom, which at times can be powerfully expressive, though in an abstract rather than subjective vein.

RECOMMENDED RECORDINGS

DIE EROBERUNG VON MEXICO (THE CONQUEST OF MEXICO): SALTER, BEHLE, FUGISS, OTTO; METZMACHER AND HAMBURG STATE OPERA (CPO).

TIME CHANT: MUTTER; LEVINE AND CHICAGO SYMPHONY ORCHESTRA (DG).

Rimsky-Korsakov, Nikolay

(b. Tikhvin, March 18, 1844; d. Lyubensk, June 21, 1908)

RUSSIAN COMPOSER AND TEACHER. He came from a well-to-do family with a tradition of military service, and received his primary schooling at home, including, as with any well-rounded youth of his station, piano lessons. The boy showed aptitude for music but no passion. His family determined that he would follow his elder brother Voin into a career as a naval officer and enrolled him in the St. Petersburg Naval College in 1856. There he continued his study of piano and also took in performances at the opera. Voin, having become the director of the Naval College, called a halt to his younger brother's piano lessons in 1861 (Nikolay and his teacher obediently shifted to the rudiments of theory and composition); but that same year, Balakirev offered to become Nikolay's musical mentor, introducing him to the influential critic Vladimir Stasov and the young composers Mussorgsky and Cui.

In his captivating fashion, Balakirev took a taskmaster's approach to guiding Rimsky-Korsakov's musical development. His young charge's first assignment was to write a symphony, with a lot of input from Balakirev. Work on this had just begun when, in 1862, the newly minted midshipman was sent on a long training cruise aboard a clipper that took him to England and the Americas. Rimsky-Korsakov played through scores on a piano he had brought aboard, read literature, and tinkered with his symphony. He returned to St. Petersburg in 1865 and quickly finished the piece, which was premiered on New Year's Eve by Balakirev and his orchestra at the Free School of Music.

Portrait of Nikolay Rimsky-Korsakov by Valentin Serov, 1898

By 1867, the year Stasov identified him as one of the "Mighty Handful," Rimsky had produced a couple more symphonic works, including the tone poem *Sadko,* and he was already showing remarkable abilities as an orchestrator. Symphony No. 2 (*Antar*), in which his great gifts as a storyteller and scene painter emerged for the first time, appeared in 1868. Three years later came a watershed: He completed *The Maid of Pskov,* the first of his 15 operas, and accepted what he termed an "undeserved" professorship at the St. Petersburg Conservatory. Painfully aware of the limitations of his own training (particularly, gaping holes in his knowledge of harmony and counterpoint), he assigned himself remedial exercises and spent three years in the mid-1870s relearning compositional technique. (Aside from himself, his students at the conservatory would include Anatoly Lyadov and Aleksandr Glazunov and a host of lesser but important lights; in 1902, he would take on the 20-year-old Igor Stravinsky as a private pupil.)

In 1873 the position of Inspector of Naval Bands was created for Rimsky-Korsakov, and he dutifully learned to play wind and brass instruments, advancing his already informed knowledge of orchestration even further. He assiduously studied and collected folk songs and made use of them in his work. The claim that he didn't assimilate the essence of Russian folk music to the extent Mussorgsky and Borodin did is a canard; Rimsky did a better job of that than any of his contemporaries, and his accomplishments in this area served as a model for Stravinsky.

One finger in a mighty handful: composer Nikolay Rimsky-Korsakov

More opera ensued at the end of the decade, with *May Night* (1878–79), followed by the brilliantly orchestrated *Snow Maiden,* which premiered at the Mariinsky Theater in 1882 and was a huge success. Completion of this work brought Rimsky to a compositional standstill, believing he had nothing more to say. Over the next several years he busied himself revising earlier work, writing a harmony textbook, and finishing and editing the music of others. The first task was to complete Mussorgsky's *KHOVANSHCHINA* (a project begun shortly after that composer's death in 1881, and completed in 1883), followed by *NIGHT ON BALD MOUNTAIN* (1886). After Borodin's death in 1887, he teamed with Glazunov to finish *PRINCE IGOR,* Glazunov completing the vocal score while Rimsky orchestrated the whole work. Waiting for a suitable operatic project to come his way, he also penned the orchestral works for which he is best known in the West: the *CAPRICCIO ESPAGNOL* ◉, *SHEHERAZADE* ◉, and the *Russian Easter* Overture, all of them polished, self-assured showpieces that show just how thoroughly the composer had overcome his earlier technical deficiencies.

The catalyst in Rimsky-Korsakov's return to opera was the Russian premiere of Wagner's *Ring* cycle, performed in St. Petersburg during the 1888–89 season by a visiting company conducted by Karl Muck. His imagination fired, Rimsky immediately composed *Mlada,* using burnished, brass-heavy colorings from the Wagnerian palette in its scoring. Once again, following its completion, he felt he had reached the end of his creative road, and he turned to

Mussorgsky's *Boris Godunov,* which between 1892 and 1896 he completely rewrote, in essence producing a new work. A decade later he revised "his" version of *Boris,* restoring cuts and adding new passages. It was this work, presented in Paris by Sergey Diaghilev in 1908, that introduced *Boris* to Europe and secured Mussorgsky's reputation in the West. But while Rimsky's remodeling of *Boris* can be admired as a brilliant work in its own right, there is no longer any question that it allows Mussorgsky's edgy, lean, and notably grim tone to be lost in the resplendent colorism and softer harmonic language.

From 1894 to the end of his life, Rimsky-Korsakov crowned his career with more than a half dozen major operas. Several were allegorical fairy tales, some with religious undercurrents. A new nationalist style emerged in *The Tale of Tsar Saltan* (1899–1900) and *The Legend of the Invisible City of Kitezh* (1903–04), which were folkloristic not just in melodic content but in overall manner, again pointing toward Stravinsky. In all of these late works, Rimsky showed himself a master of illustrative music, and capable of deep emotion as well.

Rimsky-Korsakov started out as a poster boy for Balakirev and his philosophy of musical dilettantism. But his personality, shaped by a deeply ingrained sense of duty and discipline, recoiled from all that was amateurish, and he became one of the most successful and accomplished composers of his day, certainly among the most professional, with a systematic approach to his craft and a penchant for polishing previous work.

Though outside Russia he is thought of as the composer of *Sheherazade* and *Capriccio espagnol* and little else, his real importance is to be found in the operatic sphere. He brought the historical-dramatic style (pioneered by Glinka) to its peak with *The Maid of Pskov,* brought the fairy-tale genre (also pioneered by Glinka) to *its* peak with such late works as *The Tale of Tsar Saltan* and *The Golden Cockerel* (1906–07), and produced what were for many years, and in some cases remain, the standard performing versions of major operas of Aleksandr Dargomïzhsky (1813–69), Mussorgsky, and Borodin. Without him, a Russian repertoire would hardly exist.

RECOMMENDED RECORDINGS

Capriccio espagnol: Kondrashin and RCA Victor Orchestra (RCA).

Capriccio espagnol: Maazel and Berlin Philharmonic (DG).

The Legend of the Invisible City of Kitezh: Gorchakova, Galusin, Putilin, Ohotnikov; Gergiev and Kirov Opera (Philips).

Overtures and suites: Järvi and Scottish National Orchestra (Chandos).

Sheherazade: Gergiev and Kirov Orchestra (Philips).

Sheherazade: Kondrashin and Concertgebouw Orchestra (Philips).

The Tsar's Bride: Bezzuhenkov, Shaguch, Hvorostovsky, Borodina; Gergiev and Kirov Opera (Philips).

Ring des Nibelungen, Der (The Ring of the Nibelung) **Operatic tetralogy by Richard Wagner,** described as a "stage festival play for three days and a preliminary evening," premiered as a cycle August 13–17, 1876, at the Festpielhaus in Bayreuth. Work on the *Ring* occupied Wagner for a quarter of a century. He wrote the librettos of the four operas in reverse order: starting in 1848 with *Götterdämmerung* (which he originally entitled *Siegfrieds Tod*), then drafting *Siegfried* (originally *Jung-Siegfried*), *Die Walküre,* and *Das Rheingold.* The four "poems," as Wagner called them, took four years to write; their texts were published in 1853 before a note of the music had been set down. Wagner composed the operas' music in the order in which it was to be heard: first *Das Rheingold* (1853–54)—which he called a *Vorabend,* literally "Fore-evening," a kind of prologue—then *Die Walküre* (1854–56), *Siegfried* (1856–71), and *Götterdämmerung* (1869–74). His work on the score to *Siegfried* was broken off in 1857 and resumed in 1869; during that 12-year hiatus he composed *Tristan und Isolde* and *Die Meistersinger von Nürnberg.*

The *Ring* is an allegory of the economic, political, and social conditions of Wagner's day. It also marks the zenith of 19th-century grand opera. Its characters, situations, and complications, all brilliantly treated, emerge from the rich soil of that tradition, even if Wagner's musical architecture and dramaturgy surpass anything that had previously been put on the stage. The theme of the *Ring* is one of redemption through love and death—a theme Wagner had touched on repeatedly, and explored most trenchantly in *Tristan und Isolde.* A subsidiary theme is that of the freedom of the individual to act outside the bounds of higher authority or law, and the consequences of such actions.

RECOMMENDED RECORDINGS

Flagstad, Nilsson, Hotter, London, others; Solti and Vienna Philharmonic (Decca).

Nilsson, Rysanek, Adam, Talvela, others; Böhm and Bayreuth Festival (Philips).

Rinuccini, Ottavio

(b. Florence, January 20, 1562; d. Florence, March 28, 1621)

TUSCAN POET AND LIBRETTIST. During the 1590s, he created the world's first opera libretto, based on the myth of Apollo and Daphne, "solely to test the power of modern music." Rinuccini's *Dafne* was a libretto in search of a score, and its setting by Jacopo Corsi (1561–1602) and Jacopo Peri (1561–1633) in 1598 was the first opera, though scarcely any of the music survives. Marco da Gagliano (1582–1643) created a new setting of *Dafne* in 1608, for which the music does survive. Rinuccini's second libretto, *Euridice* (1600), was set by Peri and served as the model for Alessandro Striggio's libretto for Claudio Monteverdi's *L'Orfeo* (1607). Monteverdi set Rinuccini's *Arianna* in 1608 (nearly all of the music is lost), and the same year created *Il ballo delle ingrate,* a song-and-dance entertainment for the Mantuan court, using verses by Rinuccini. Another libretto, *Narciso,* was never set. In 1627 Heinrich Schütz composed what is generally regarded as the first opera in German, *Dafne,* using a German adaptation of Rinuccini's original libretto. None of Schütz's *Dafne* survives.

ripieno (It., "filled") In Baroque orchestral music, particularly concertos, the group that plays the tutti passages, i.e., the main body of the ensemble, as distinct from the solo group, known as the *concertino.*

ritardando (It., "slowing down") Instruction indicating a momentary slowing or broadening of tempo.

Rite of Spring, The (Sacre du Printemps, Le) BALLET IN TWO PARTS BY IGOR STRAVINSKY, composed 1911–13 on a commission from Sergey Diaghilev and the Ballets Russes, and premiered May 29, 1913, at the Théâtre des Champs-Elysées in Paris, Pierre Monteux conducting. The oddly bestial nature of the choreography by Vaslav Nijinsky, in tandem with the revolutionary sound and syntax of Stravinsky's score, sparked a riot among first-night listeners that remains among the most talked-about events in musical history.

Subtitled "Pictures from Pagan Russia," *The Rite of Spring* was composed to a two-part scenario drawn up during the summer of 1910 by the Russian painter and archaeologist Nikolay Roerich, to whom the score is dedicated. Whereas Stravinsky's two prior ballets for the Diaghilev company, *The Firebird* and *Petrushka,* had emerged from fairly specific narrative frameworks, this one grew out of an essentially scenic conception centering around primitive springtime fertility rites (the focus of the ballet's first part, "Adoration of the Earth") and human sacrifice (a concession to sensationalism with no basis in anthropological fact, but nonetheless the culmination of the ballet's second part, "The Sacrifice"). Rather than marking a total break with the past, as has often been claimed (by the composer himself, among others), the score represents a continuation of Stravinsky's development from *The Firebird,* and such shorter and earlier works as *Fireworks* and the *Scherzo fantastique,* through *Petrushka,* whose preoccupation with rhythm as both a structural and expressive device is carried further—indeed, to an extreme of metric complexity and violent offbeat accentuation. At the same time, dissonance, also taken to an extreme, is so prevalent that the functional bonds of conventional harmony are effectively dissolved. For all that, *The Rite of Spring* is a strikingly lyrical work. Much of the melodic material of the ballet is derived from folk song; at least nine specific songs have been identified as sources.

The orchestra employed in *The Rite of Spring* is one of the largest in any standard repertoire work: three flutes with additional parts for two piccolos and alto flute, four oboes, two English horns, three clarinets, two bass clarinets, E-flat clarinet, four bassoons, two contrabassoons, eight horns, four trumpets, piccolo trumpet, bass trumpet, three trombones, two tenor tubas, two bass tubas, two sets of timpani, expanded percussion requiring five or six players, and strings, frequently divided. Stravinsky's writing calls for effects of unprecedented loudness and for many instruments to play at the limits of their range. The opening bassoon solo—which begins on a high C, includes several high D's, and is written entirely above middle C—is one of the most notable examples, the first of many surprises, some subtle, some shocking, contained in the score.

Paul Robeson

RECOMMENDED RECORDINGS

BOULEZ AND CLEVELAND ORCHESTRA (SONY).

STRAVINSKY AND COLUMBIA SYMPHONY ORCHESTRA (SONY).

ritornello (from It. *ritorno,* "return") [1] A repeat of a passage or section within a piece of music. [2] An instrumental episode within a vocal piece, especially an aria. An example is provided by the prologue to Monteverdi's *L'Orfeo.* [3] In 18th-century music, a tutti passage in a concerto.

Robeson, Paul

(b. Princeton, N.J., April 9, 1898; d. Philadelphia, Penn., January 23, 1976)

AMERICAN BASS-BARITONE AND ACTOR. The son of a former slave, he grew up in New Jersey and won a scholarship to Rutgers University, where he excelled in both athletics and academics, and was class valedictorian in 1919. After graduating from Columbia Law School in 1923, he worked briefly at a New York law firm, but then turned to acting. Imposingly tall, and possessing a booming, sonorous bass, Robeson played leading roles on Broadway in *All God's Chillun Got Wings* (1924) and Eugene O'Neill's *The Emperor Jones* (1925). He gave his first concert in 1925, made a cross-country tour in 1926, and became extremely popular as a concert singer in the U.S. and Europe, specializing in folk songs, spirituals, labor songs like "Joe Hill," and what was to become his trademark song, "Ol' Man River," from Jerome Kern's *Show Boat.* He starred in *Othello* on Broadway, and made several movies, including *The Emperor Jones* (1933), *Song of Freedom* (1936), and *Show Boat* (1936).

During World War II, Robeson entertained Allied troops and spoke out against fascism. He was admired and befriended by such prominent personalities as Eleanor Roosevelt, W. E. B. Du Bois, Joe Louis, Pablo Neruda, and Harry Truman. Despite his success and enormous popularity, Robeson was constantly aware of racism in America, and he embraced Communism following a tour of the "workers' paradise" of the Soviet Union. His denunciations of segregation and his praise for the Soviet system made him suspect amid the growing tensions of the Cold War. He was summoned to testify in the McCarthy hearings, and public opinion turned against him. Unable to work in his own country, he undertook a lengthy tour of Europe in the summer of 1958 and lived in England until 1963. The final years of his life, spent back in the U.S., were shadowed by illness.

Rococo (from Fr. *rocaille,* referring to the ornamental working of rock, stone, stucco, and other materials) Term occasionally used to identify a mid-18th-century musical style representing a transitional phase between the Baroque and Classical periods. Music referred to as "rococo" tended to be characterized by predictably short, symmetrical phrases in which the melodic figures were highly ornamental, imparting a quaint, superficial elegance to the expression. The style often emphasized pastoral elements and favored lighter textures.

Rodeo BALLET BY AARON COPLAND, composed in 1942 on a commission from the Ballets Russes de Monte Carlo and premiered October 16, 1942, at the Metropolitan Opera in New York. The dancer Agnes de Mille, who choreographed the work and performed the lead role at its premiere, provided the following scenario: "Throughout the American Southwest, the Saturday afternoon rodeo is a tradition. On the remote ranches, as well as in the trading centers and the towns, the 'hands' get together to show off their skill in roping, riding, branding and throwing. . . . The afternoon's exhibition is usually followed by a Saturday night dance at the Ranch House. The theme of the ballet is basic. It deals with the problem that has confronted all American women, from earliest pioneer times, and which has never ceased to occupy them throughout the history of the building of our country: how to get a suitable man." As in *Billy the Kid,* Copland made use of traditional cowboy songs in the score to *Rodeo,* among them the well-worn favorite "Old Paint." Yet *Billy the Kid* "has a certain 'grand opera' side," the composer once noted, while "*Rodeo* is closer to musical comedy."

Subsequent to the ballet's premiere, Copland extracted an orchestral suite from *Rodeo* for concert performance. The suite, *Four Dance Episodes from Rodeo,* was premiered by the New York Philharmonic on June 22, 1943, and is one of the most frequently programmed of all Copland's works. The four sections of the suite are titled "Buckaroo Holiday," "Corral Nocturne," "Saturday Night Waltz," and "Hoe-Down." "Buckaroo Holiday" is a razzle-dazzle Allegro that in some ways follows the sonata-form structure typical of the first movement of a symphony. The "Corral Nocturne" is an atmospheric slow movement in Copland's most pensive style. "Saturday Night Waltz" opens with a passage reminiscent of string instruments being tuned; its loping waltz includes a couple of references to "Old Paint." The concluding "Hoe-Down," based on the square dance tunes "Bonyparte" and

"McLeod's Reel," is a kick-up-your-heels tour de force of rhythmic verve and orchestral boldness.

RECOMMENDED RECORDINGS

COMPLETE:

SLATKIN AND SAINT LOUIS SYMPHONY ORCHESTRA (EMI).

FOUR DANCE EPISODES:

BERNSTEIN AND NEW YORK PHILHARMONIC (SONY).

SCHWARZ AND SEATTLE SYMPHONY ORCHESTRA (DELOS).

Rodrigo, Joaquín

(b. Sagunto, November 22, 1901; d. Madrid, July 6, 1999)

SPANISH COMPOSER. He was not only the last of the great Spanish nationalists, but the last representative of the creative axis that linked France and Spain during the 40 years between Albéniz's arrival in Paris and the death of Ravel. Blind from the age of three, Rodrigo found a world of color and beauty in music. In 1927 he became a pupil of Paul Dukas in Paris; during the 1930s, he studied at the Sorbonne and the Paris Conservatoire. Soon after returning to Spain in 1939 he composed his *Concierto de Aranjuez* for guitar and orchestra, the defining work of his career and a score whose Mozartean qualities have made it universally popular. Every page exhibits a classical poise and economy of means—the rhythms have a dancelike spring, the lyricism never wears out its welcome, and the orchestration is sublime. In his subsequent scores, including the nearly-as-popular *Fantasía para un gentilhombre* (1954), Rodrigo never attempted, as Falla had done, to tap the emotive core of Spanish folk and popular idioms; rather, he tried to endow his works with a picturesque quality, something that would give his music, essentially neoclassical, a Spanish flavor. Mixing elements of folk music with allusions to Renaissance and Baroque practice, his approach to orchestral colorism was decidedly French-influenced.

Joaquín Rodrigo at the piano

Rodrigo remained a productive composer into his 80s. His output, consisting mainly of concertos for various instruments, solo works for guitar, piano, violin, and cello, and about 60 song settings, includes an impressive number of pieces likely to find a permanent place in the repertoire.

RECOMMENDED RECORDINGS

CONCIERTO DE ARANJUEZ, FANTASÍA PARA UN GENTILHOMBRE: PARKENING; LITTON AND ROYAL PHILHARMONIC ORCHESTRA (EMI).

CONCIERTO DE ARANJUEZ, FANTASÍA PARA UN GENTILHOMBRE: PEPE ROMERO; MARRINER AND ACADEMY OF ST. MARTIN-IN-THE-FIELDS (PHILIPS).

Rolfe Johnson, Anthony

(b. Tackley, November 5, 1940)

ENGLISH TENOR. He studied at the Guildhall School with Ellis Keeler and subsequently with Vera Rozsa, Richard Lewis, and Peter Pears. He made his debut with the English Opera Group in 1973, as Vaudemont in Tchaikovsky's *Iolanta,* and sang Lensky in *Eugene Onegin* at Glyndebourne in 1974. He has been associated with the role of Aschenbach in Britten's *Death in Venice*—which he first sang in 1983 at both the Geneva Opera and the Scottish Opera, and later performed at the Metropolitan—as well as the title role in *Idomeneo,* which he sang in 1991 at the Salzburg Festival under Seiji Ozawa, at the Vienna Staatsoper with Nikolaus Harnoncourt, and at the Met with James Levine, his house debut. He sang his first *Peter Grimes* with the Scottish Opera in 1994. Other roles include Don Ottavio, Tamino, Titus, Ferrando, Belmonte, Essex (in Britten's *Gloriana*), the Male Chorus (in Britten's *The Rape of Lucretia*), Florestan, Jupiter (in Handel's *Semele*), Tom Rakewell, and the title roles in Monteverdi's *L'Orfeo* and *Il ritorno di Ulisse in patria.* Rolfe Johnson has had a distinguished career as an oratorio singer, performing and recording works of Handel and Haydn, and his repertoire includes the parts of the Evangelist in both the *St. Matthew* and *St. John* Passions of Bach. He is also a renowned singer of lieder and English song, as well as a founding member of the Songmaker's Almanac (1976), a touring vocal ensemble. He was appointed director of singing studies at the Britten-Pears School in 1990, and was made a Commander of the British Empire in 1992.

RECOMMENDED RECORDINGS

BACH, *ST. MATTHEW* PASSION: BONNEY, OTTER, CHANCE, CROOK, HAUPTMANN; GARDINER AND ENGLISH BAROQUE SOLOISTS (ARCHIV).

MONTEVERDI, *L'ORFEO*: BAIRD, DAWSON, OTTER, ARGENTA: GARDINER AND ENGLISH BAROQUE SOLOISTS (ARCHIV).

Romani, Felice

(b. Genoa, January 31, 1788; d. Moneglia, January 28, 1865)

ITALIAN LIBRETTIST. After studies in Pisa and Genoa he settled in Milan, where he was engaged as a librettist by the Teatro alla Scala. In a career reaching from 1813 to 1855, he created more than 80 librettos and worked with many of the most successful composers of the day, including Rossini, Donizetti, and Bellini. His librettos were admired for the elegance and economy of their language as well as their dramatic coherence; among his finest were those for Bellini's *NORMA* and *LA SONNAMBULA* (both 1831) and Donizetti's *L'ELISIR D'AMORE* (1832).

***Romantic* Symphony** [1] Title of Anton Bruckner's Symphony No. 4 in E-flat (1874, rev. 1880). [2] Title of Howard Hanson's Symphony No. 2, Op. 30, premiered by Serge Koussevitzky and the Boston Symphony Orchestra in 1930.

RECOMMENDED RECORDINGS

BRUCKNER: BÖHM AND VIENNA PHILHARMONIC (DECCA).

HANSON: SCHWARZ AND SEATTLE SYMPHONY ORCHESTRA (DELOS).

HANSON: SLATKIN AND SAINT LOUIS SYMPHONY ORCHESTRA (EMI).

Romanticism Style period in Western music extending from about 1820 to 1910, lagging behind, though to a degree shaped by, the literary Romanticism that emanated from Germany at the end of the 18th century in works such as Goethe's *Die Leiden des jungen Werthers* (1774) and *Wilhelm Meisters Lehrjahre* (1796). Other sources include the early poetry of Wordsworth, the novels of Scott, and the writings of Rousseau and Chateaubriand. One can find elements of "Romanticism" in the music of many 18th-century composers, including Mozart and Haydn, and a potent sense of the new direction in the works of Beethoven, whose career straddled the divide between the Classical and Romantic eras.

The Beethoven biographer Maynard Solomon has suggested that Romanticism can be defined as a yearning for a state of mind or feeling beyond one's ordinary capacities and experience, a useful notion that points up the connections between the literary and musical manifestations of the movement. The first generation of true Romantics was headed by Berlioz, Schumann, Mendelssohn, Chopin, Liszt, Wagner,

Donizetti, Bellini, and Verdi, born between 1797 and 1813, who reached their maturity as composers in the 1830s and 1840s. It was these composers whose music gave voice to the grand themes of Romanticism: the celebration of nature's vastness and its indifference to man's strivings, a fascination with elements of the bizarre and fantastic, and the rejection of rationalism. In the Romantic view, sense and experience took precedence over reason, and the notion of good and evil as moral poles represented by God and the devil gave way to a more nuanced and subjective view of human nature in which the impulses toward good and evil, and the conflict they produce, are seen to exist mainly within the individual.

Typical of the era's concerns were the musings on nature's grandeur and the sense of spiritual elevation that characterize Wordsworth's "Lines Composed a Few Miles Above Tintern Abbey" (1798) and "Ode: Intimations of Immortality" (1802–04), Vigny's "Le cor" (1825), and Liszt's *Bénédiction de Dieu dans la solitude* (1848–53) and *Années de pèlerinage—Suisse* (1848–55), and that periodically come to the fore in the course of Wagner's *Der Ring des Nibelungen* (1848–74). Géricault's outsize and dramatic painting *Le radeau de la Méduse* (*The Raft of the Medusa*; 1819) portrayed nature in a more threatening way, as did the desolate images of Caspar David Friedrich. This view found an echo in "Scène aux champs," the third movement of Berlioz's *Symphonie fantastique* (1830), and in Mendelssohn's *Hebrides* Overture (1830–32). The abandonment of self to the liberating—though usually destructive—power of the emotions, and the philosophical burden of isolation, disillusionment, and loss were other themes that reverberated through Romantic art. Byron, the poet of wildness, exoticism, and disdain, was the spokesman for this side of Romanticism; his portrayals of heroic suffering provided inspiration for works by Berlioz, Schumann, Verdi, Tchaikovsky, and others. His posture of ironic detachment was a typically Romantic one, and the impassioned language and gloomy tone of his *Childe Harold's Pilgrimage* (1812) had numerous counterparts in the styles of others, for example in Berlioz's moody *Harold en Italie* (inspired by Byron's epic), and in Delacroix's canvases, whose swirling colors and violent, distorted imagery were the painterly equivalent of Berlioz's orchestral palette and Byron's verbal one. For each of these creators the aim was to excite powerful, unsettling emotions in the observer.

The Cornfield ***(1826), painting by John Constable***

Wagner's *Tristan und Isolde* (1856) was the quintessential treatment of the theme of surrender to all-consuming passion. Its aesthetic impact and the influence it exerted on the language of music and the other arts was enormous; it can lay a strong claim to being the dominant art work of the entire Romantic era. Yet another recurrent theme of Romanticism was the penetration and disruption of the natural order by the supernatural, exemplified in the fantastic stories of E. T. A. Hoffmann, the nightmarish vision of the Wolf's Glen in Weber's *Der Freischütz* (1821), and the spectral terrors of the Dutchman's ship in Wagner's *Der fliegende Holländer* (1840–41).

The music of Romanticism often strove for largeness of scale and powerfully expressed emotion, but not always. At the opposite extreme from expansiveness was the search for intimacy and poetry that one finds in nearly all of Chopin and in a great deal of Schumann, Mendelssohn, and Liszt. For these figures and for many other Romantics the vignette was an elevated genre. Sound itself emerged in the Romantic era as a determinant of musical structure and a powerful influence on form. With new instrumental and coloristic resources available, imagining and exploring new worlds of sound became a primary mission, particularly in music for the piano and for the orchestra.

Wagner and Verdi dominated opera to the end of the 19th century, but in the sphere of instrumental music there was significant generational change during the Romantic period. At the outset, with Paganini and Liszt in the vanguard, an altogether new emphasis was placed on the soloist as interpreter and protagonist. In performance, as in composition, spontaneity and the abandonment of studied orderliness carried the day. The later Romantics saw things a bit differently. While many of them—including Brahms, Tchaikovsky, Dvořák, Bruckner, Mahler, Richard Strauss, Franck, Saint-Saëns, Elgar, Sibelius, and others born between 1820 and 1865—retained a fondness for large-scale structures and emphatic emotional expression, quite a few sought at the same time to convey a more "studied" and rational impression, or at least to change the balance between form and feeling and to allow for greater expressive ambivalence. Each in his own way, Brahms, Dvořák, Bruckner, and Mahler looked back to Beethoven and Schubert in an effort to temper passion with rigorous argument. Strauss took the flamboyance of Liszt and Berlioz to new heights before seeking a kind of Mozartean poise in his late works, while Sibelius compressed an opulent early idiom further and further, until nearly all its Romantic trappings yielded to a radically austere, yet emotionally intense, modernist abstraction.

Romeo and Juliet BALLET IN FOUR ACTS BY **SERGEY PROKOFIEV,** composed 1935–36 and premiered December 30, 1938, in Brno. The idea for a ballet based on William Shakespeare's play was suggested to Prokofiev late in 1934 by Sergey Radlov, director of the Leningrad State Academic Theater of Opera and Ballet (formerly the Mariinsky Theater and soon to be named the Kirov). In the spring of 1935, after Radlov was sacked, the project was taken on by Moscow's Bolshoi Theatre. The original scenario imposed a happy ending on the story, owing to choreographic necessity: As the composer acidly put it, "living people can dance, but the dead cannot dance lying down." Working with remarkable efficiency through the spring and summer of 1935, Prokofiev completed the ballet in less than five months. But the score was rejected by the Bolshoi company as unfit for dancing, and controversy swirled around the ending, which struck many as too great a liberty to take with Shakespeare. After being assured that the dying, if not the dead, could indeed dance, Prokofiev agreed to a restoration of Shakespeare's tragic ending and wrote music to suit it. But it was not until 1938, after the Bolshoi balked a second time, that *Romeo and Juliet* received its first production, in Czechoslovakia. The first Soviet performances took place at the Kirov, on January 11, 1940, with Galina Ulanova dancing the part of Juliet, as she had in Brno.

With its airborne excitement, vivid characterizations, and scenes built upon a perfectly gauged succession of quick-hitting, brilliantly orchestrated numbers, *Romeo and Juliet* ranks among the greatest scores ever composed for the stage. Passionately brutal and tender, it conveys the richness of feeling in Shakespeare's original as few settings have, sustaining the high drama of tragedy while telling a love story full of humor, ardor, and transcendent lyricism.

RECOMMENDED RECORDINGS

Ashkenazy and Royal Philharmonic Orchestra (Decca).

Maazel and Cleveland Orchestra (Decca).

Previn and London Symphony Orchestra (EMI).

***Romeo and Juliet* "Fantasy overture" by Piotr Il'yich Tchaikovsky,** composed to a scenario by Mily Balakirev based on Shakespeare's *Romeo and Juliet.* The idea of a work based on Shakespeare's tragedy probably came up during discussions Tchaikovsky and Balakirev had in the summer of 1869, and when Tchaikovsky did not immediately proceed with it, Balakirev put pressure on him by letter, sending an outline of how he would organize the score, even including the first four bars that he would use if he were writing the piece himself. Within six weeks of receiving Balakirev's letter, Tchaikovsky finished the entire score. When Balakirev saw it, he found much to praise in it, but had some criticisms. After the first performance in March 1870, Tchaikovsky decided to take Balakirev's advice and thoroughly rewrite the work. Ten years later, still dissatisfied with the score, he revised it again. It is this version from 1880 that is most commonly performed.

In its tightly wound argument and insightful handling of the emotional currents of Shakespeare's story, Tchaikovsky's score reveals for the first time the balance between symphonic logic and expressive power that mark the composer's finest efforts. The slow introduction is rich in thematic material, and the characterization is sharply drawn: the somber opening wind chorale, with its phrasing reminiscent of plainchant, does double duty by establishing the tragic atmosphere of the story while also evoking the religious presence behind the scene, that of the long-suffering Friar Lawrence. Other motives suggest the tides of enmity and passion that will draw the star-cross'd lovers to their doom. There is a powerful buildup to the main Allegro, culminating in a repeated B minor chord that grows more intense with each iteration. The violent, martial theme depicting the strife of the Montague and Capulet families erupts with full fury, to be followed, inevitably, by the music representing Romeo and Juliet in the intentionally remote key of D-flat major.

The idea of putting the young couple in a world of their own, harmonically distant from the warring families, had been Balakirev's, but Tchaikovsky does his would-be mentor one better by forging a thematic link between the strife theme and that of the two lovers, so that the fatal nature of the relationships can be felt on a subliminal level from the start. Tchaikovsky's development of the material is assured and emotionally gripping, and he builds the overture to a climax made devastatingly effective in the revision of 1880: after the music of the feuding Montagues and Capulets overwhelms that of Romeo and Juliet, a pained echo of the love theme, now wrenchingly recast in B minor, the "martial" key from earlier, issues from the strings. The tragic feeling of this passage foreshadows the end of the *"Pathétique"* Symphony, also in B minor, though Tchaikovsky does not allow his lovers a quiet end. Instead, he summons a series of tumultuous *fortissimo* chords, and closes the overture with a reminiscence of the pitiless violence that had driven Romeo and Juliet to their deaths.

Sean Lavery and Suzanne Farrell in Paul Mejia's **Romeo and Juliet**

RECOMMENDED RECORDINGS

BERNSTEIN AND NEW YORK PHILHARMONIC (WITH FESTIVAL OVERTURE *1812*, *CAPRICCIO ITALIEN*, AND OTHER WORKS) (SONY).

GERGIEV AND KIROV ORCHESTRA (WITH SYMPHONY NO. 6) (PHILIPS).

Roméo et Juliette [1] **"DRAMATIC SYMPHONY" IN SEVEN MOVEMENTS FOR CHORUS, SOLOISTS, AND ORCHESTRA BY HECTOR BERLIOZ** based on the play by Shakespeare, composed in 1839 and premiered in Paris at the Conservatoire on November 24, 1839, the composer conducting. The score is dedicated to Niccolò Paganini, whose magnanimous gift of 20,000 francs following an 1838 performance of *Harold en Italie* enabled Berlioz to undertake the composition. *Roméo et Juliette* represents a bold extension of the symphonic conquests Berlioz had begun with his *Symphonie fantastique* and *Harold en Italie.* It is the work that makes sense not just of his symphonies, but of his entire canon—that shows him most clearly as both a symphonist in search of the theater and a dramatist most comfortable with the language of music.

Among the most celebrated portions of the score are two purely instrumental sections: the "Scène d'amour" ("Love Scene") and the scherzo "La Reine Mab" ("Queen Mab"). The "Scène d'amour" parallels the balcony scene in Shakespeare's play and contains some of the most ethereally beautiful pages in all of Romantic music. Passion hangs in the air like perfume, while the raptures of young love swell in successive waves until the music reaches a radiant paroxysm of emotion. "La Reine Mab" takes its imagery from Mercutio's famous Act I soliloquy, in which he describes the night ride of the fairy queen "through lovers' brains" in a nutshell coach "drawn with a team of little atomi." Berlioz's scintillating interlude, conjuring a scene full of enchantment and gossamer lightness, is one of the finest display pieces of the 19th century.

[2] **OPERA IN FIVE ACTS BY CHARLES GOUNOD,** to a libretto by Jules Barbier and Michel Carré (after William Shakespeare's play), composed 1865–66 and premiered April 27, 1867, at the Théâtre Lyrique in Paris. The most successful operatic treatment of the play yet to have entered the repertoire, it is, after *Faust,* the most frequently performed of Gounod's 12 operas.

RECOMMENDED RECORDINGS

BERLIOZ: BORODINA, MOSER, MILES; DAVIS AND VIENNA PHILHARMONIC (PHILIPS).

GOUNOD: ALAGNA, GHEORGHIU, VAN DAM, KEENLYSIDE; PLASSON AND ORCHESTRE DU CAPITOLE DE TOULOUSE (EMI).

rondo [1] A multisection form in which the melodic material heard at the beginning returns one or more times within the body of the rondo, always in the tonic key, and makes a final appearance at the end to "round" off the form. These recurrent appearances of the initial material, called refrains, are interspersed with episodes of contrasting character. A schematic representation of a typical rondo might look like this: A B A C A D A. In order for the form to work, the main subject (A) must be an easily grasped "tune" or subject. [2] A movement in which rondo form or a close approximation of it is employed. The final movements of concertos are frequently cast in rondo form, with the designation *Rondo* often appearing at the head of the score. Movements in rondo form are also encountered in many sonatas (e.g., Beethoven's Piano Sonata in A, Op. 2, No. 2, fourth movement) and symphonies (e.g., Mahler's Symphony No. 7, finale).

Rorem, Ned

(b. Richmond, Ind., October 23, 1923)

AMERICAN COMPOSER. His father, C. Rufus Rorem, was a medical economist whose work led to the creation of Blue Cross; his mother, Gladys Miller, was a civil rights advocate. He grew up in Chicago, where he studied piano as a child (the music of Debussy and Ravel had a transformative impact on him) and later received instruction in harmony from Leo Sowerby. He entered the School of Music at Northwestern University in 1940, transferring two years later to the Curtis Institute of Music in Philadelphia, where he studied with Rosario Scalero (who had earlier taught Samuel Barber). In 1944 he moved to New York and became a composition student of Bernard Wagenaar at Juilliard, receiving his B.A. in 1946 and his M.A. in 1948.

Composer-diarist Ned Rorem

While in New York he worked as Virgil Thomson's copyist in return for $20 a week and orchestration lessons. He came of age when he moved to Paris in 1949; he subsequently spent a couple of years in Morocco and returned to live in Paris from 1952 to 1958. Since then he has lived and worked in the United States, mainly in New York City. He has received numerous commissions, awards, and fellowships (including a Fulbright and a Guggenheim); in 1976 he was awarded the Pulitzer Prize for his orchestral work *Air Music,* commissioned by the Cincinnati Symphony Orchestra and conductor Thomas Schippers.

Rorem has written a substantial amount of orchestral music (including three symphonies, four piano concertos, and concertos for violin, organ, and English horn), two dozen chamber pieces, six operas, numerous works for chorus, pieces for piano and organ, and roughly 400 songs that rank with the finest by any American composer. Among the highlights of his career have been the premiere of his Symphony No. 3 by the New York Philharmonic and Leonard Bernstein in 1959, the premiere of his opera *Miss Julie* (based on the Strindberg play) by the New York City Opera in 1965, the publication of his first book, *The Paris Diary,* in 1966, and the premiere of his evening-length song-cycle *Evidence of Things Not Seen* in 1998. The latter, a collection of 36 songs on poems by 24 different authors, marks the culmination of his work as a composer of song. At their best, Rorem's songs—from every period in his career—are approachable, melodically memorable, and richly nuanced. By comparison, his instrumental music tends to be prolix and discursive. So far, Rorem has written 15 books, including five volumes of diaries (the most recent, *Lies,* covering 1986–99) and several collections of lectures and criticism.

RECOMMENDED RECORDINGS

CONCERTO FOR ENGLISH HORN AND ORCHESTRA: STACY; PALMER AND ROCHESTER PHILHARMONIC ORCHESTRA (NEW WORLD).

EVIDENCE OF THINGS NOT SEEN: MCDONALD, ZIEGLER, MÜLLER, OLLMANN, BARRETT, BLIER (NEW WORLD).

SELECTED SONGS: FARLEY, ROREM (NAXOS).

SELECTED SONGS: GRAHAM, MARTINEAU (ERATO).

SYMPHONIES NOS. 1–3: SEREBRIER AND BOURNEMOUTH SYMPHONY ORCHESTRA (NAXOS).

Rosamunde, Fürstin von Zypern (Rosamunde, Princess of Cypress) PLAY IN FOUR ACTS BY HELMINA VON CHÉZY, with incidental music by Franz Schubert, premiered December 20, 1823, at the Theater an der Wien in Vienna. Schubert's music consisted of an overture originally composed in 1822 for the opera *Alfonso und Estrella* and ten additional numbers, several also recycled from earlier pieces. Oddly, following Schubert's death, performers eager to present the *Rosamunde* music in concert began substituting another of his overtures for the one he had pressed into service at the time of the play's premiere; this was the overture he had composed as a prelude to Georg von Hoffmann's play *Die Zauberharfe* (*The Magic Harp*), premiered at the Theater an der Wien on August 19, 1820. Posterity's second-guessing turned out to have merit, for it gave new life to one of Schubert's finest orchestral essays. With its solemn slow introduction, ebullient Allegro, and festive coda, the overture to *Die Zauberharfe,* now commonly referred to as the *Rosamunde* Overture, has become a fixture of the concert repertoire, similar in sound and spirit to the opening movement of Schubert's Ninth Symphony, with which it shares the brilliant key of C major.

RECOMMENDED RECORDINGS

INCIDENTAL MUSIC:

AMELING; MASUR AND GEWANDHAUS ORCHESTRA (PHILIPS).

OTTER; ABBADO AND CHAMBER ORCHESTRA OF EUROPE (DG).

OVERTURE:

KARAJAN AND BERLIN PHILHARMONIC (EMI).

Rosbaud, Hans

(b. Graz, July 22, 1895; d. Lugano, December 29, 1962)

AUSTRIAN CONDUCTOR, important as a champion of the composers of his time, especially Schoenberg, Webern, Berg, and, toward the end of his career, Boulez and Stockhausen. He studied piano and composition in Frankfurt and was named director of the Frankfurt Radio Orchestra in 1929. His taste for contemporary music proved unpopular with the Nazis and he sat out the World War II years at posts in Münster and Strasbourg, effectively silenced. In 1948 he took charge of the newly formed orchestra of the Southwest German Radio (SWF) in Baden-Baden, which became his bully pulpit for the remainder of his life; that same year he helped organize the opera festival at Aix-en-Provence, where he appeared every summer until 1959. During the 1950s, he was also a fixture at the Donaueschingen Festival.

Although he specialized in 20th-century repertoire, Rosbaud was a musician of remarkable cultivation equally admired for his accounts of Mozart's operas and for his interpretations of symphonies by Haydn, Bruckner, and Mahler. Among the works he premiered during his career were Bartók's Second Piano Concerto (1933), with the composer at the keyboard, Schoenberg's *Moses und Aron* (both the concert premiere in 1954 and the stage premiere in 1957), and Boulez's *Le marteau sans maître* (1955).

RECOMMENDED RECORDINGS

BRUCKNER, SYMPHONY NO. 7: SOUTHWEST GERMAN RADIO SYMPHONY ORCHESTRA (VOX).

HAYDN, SYMPHONIES NOS. 92 AND 104: BERLIN PHILHARMONIC (DG).

Rosenkavalier, Der **OPERA IN THREE ACTS BY RICHARD STRAUSS,** to a libretto by Hugo von Hoffmansthal, premiered January 26, 1911, at the Court Opera in Dresden under the baton of Ernst von Schuch. What makes the opera especially remarkable is the way it succeeds in looking at love from three different viewpoints at once: those of the thirty-something Marschallin, her impetuous young lover Octavian, and the bourgeois girl with whom Octavian ultimately falls in love, Sophie. A comic element is added by the boorish machinations of the Marschallin's kinsman, Baron Ochs. The backdrop to all this is Vienna of the 1740s, during the epoch of Maria Theresa—a period Strauss and Hofmannsthal sought to evoke in a fashion "half real and half imaginary," to which the libretto and the music impart a mix of mannered elegance, Romantic passion, and nostalgia. To provide the musical motif through which both the glamour and the bittersweet emotions of the story could be brought to life, Strauss turned to the dance that did not exist at the time in which the opera is set, though it came to be emblematic of Viennese life a century later: the waltz. Somehow, the incongruity of waltz music in Maria Theresa's Vienna is swept aside by the radiance of Strauss's score and the utter fluency of his characterization.

Much of the opera is set in a conversational style and the action seems to flow like that of a stage play. The curtain goes up to one of the boldest and most sensuous orchestral prologues in all of music, a no-holds-barred portrait of the Marschallin and Octavian in bed, climaxed by orgasmic whoops from the horns. In the remaining 516 pages of the score Strauss generates a series of musical frissons and moves effortlessly between the serious and the burlesque. His orchestration is luminous and wonderfully imaginative, particularly in its shimmering depiction of the Silver Rose, the token of betrothal that Octavian (the cavalier of the opera's title) is asked to present to Sophie on behalf of Ochs. Strauss's assignment of the romantic leads to three female voices (Octavian is a pants role for mezzo-soprano) allows him to indulge in some of his most beautiful love music, climaxed by the Act III trio in which the Marschallin lets go of Octavian so that he may find happiness, for a while, with Sophie.

RECOMMENDED RECORDINGS

LUDWIG, SCHWARZKOPF, STICH-RANDALL, EDELMANN; KARAJAN AND PHILHARMONIA ORCHESTRA (EMI).

TE KANAWA, OTTER, HENDRICKS, RYDL; HAITINK AND STAATSKAPELLE DRESDEN (EMI).

Rosenthal, Moriz

(b. Lemberg, December 18, 1862; d. New York, September 3, 1946)

POLISH/AUSTRIAN PIANIST. At the age of ten he became a student of Karol Mikuli, who had studied with Chopin. In 1875 he moved to Vienna to study with Rafael Joseffy, and in 1877 he began private lessons with Liszt, which lasted until the master's death in 1886. During this time, he also took a degree in philosophy at the University of Vienna. He toured the United States for the first time in 1888–89 (performing with the violinist Fritz Kreisler), returned regularly thereafter, and eventually settled in New York in 1938. Among the students of his later years was Charles Rosen.

Rosenthal was one of the most brilliant virtuosos of the late 19th century, with a prodigious technique on the same level as Liszt's. He was capable of producing a thunderous fortissimo, but also of extraordinary delicacy, kaleidoscopic color, and the sort of freedom and flexibility rarely heard in the 20th century; in Romantic music he was an impeccable stylist. His recordings, all made after he had turned 60, convey merely a hint of the power he possessed in his prime.

Rossini, Gioachino

(b. Pesaro, February 29, 1792; d. Passy, November 13, 1868)

ITALIAN COMPOSER, whose comic gift was matched by his great productivity. In a mere 19 years (1810–1829) he composed 39 operas, many of them of the first rank. He brought an end to the old order in Italian opera—the stale plots, the formulaic characters—and laid a foundation for the Romantics through his emphasis on advancing the drama through music, without abandoning the art of "beautiful singing."

Both of Rossini's parents were musicians. His father, Giuseppe, a skilled horn player, was employed as a municipal trumpeter in Pesaro from 1790. His mother, Anna, was a capable soprano. In 1800, in the midst of the Napoleonic wars, Giuseppe was briefly imprisoned by the papal authorities for his lively republican sympathies; from 1801 until 1808, Giuseppe and Anna made the rounds of regional theaters—she as the prima donna, he as an instrumentalist. The young Rossini took part in some of these tours and was playing viola in opera orchestras before he turned nine. He composed his first sacred settings at the age of ten and by the time he was 12 had penned a charming set of six four-part string sonatas that are still in the active repertoire. An excellent singer, he was admitted to membership in Bologna's prestigious Accademia Filarmonica in 1806 at the age of 14. The following year he heard for the first time the Spanish soprano Isabella Colbran, whom he would marry in 1822 and for whom he would write some of his most demanding and dramatically potent roles.

Gioachino Rossini, engraving from 1820

Rossini received his first important operatic commission in 1810 from the Teatro San Moisè in Venice, for a one-act *farsa comica,* or comedy, titled *La cambiale di matrimonio* (*The Bill of Marriage*). Between November 1810 and January 1813 he composed five additional *farse,* ending with *Il Signor Bruschino.* In the midst of this, his first two-act opera, *La pietra del paragone* (*The Moral Touchstone*), received its premiere in 1812 at the Teatro alla Scala in Milan. By 1814, the year he was offered a lucrative contract by the Teatro San Carlo in Naples, Rossini was a young star. San Carlo was the best-financed house in Europe; its roster included Colbran, the tenors Manuel García and Andrea Nozzari, and the bass Michele Benedetti. Rossini was given heavy responsibilites involving composition, administration, and the preparation of performances of his own and other composers' works. His efforts at San Carlo, centering on opera seria, led to a string of successes beginning with *Elisabetta, regina d'Inghilterra* (1815) and including *La donna del lago* (1819), an imaginative treatment of Walter Scott's *The Lady of the Lake.* Even with a full plate in Naples, he had the energy to shuttle back and forth to Rome; it was for that city that he composed his two greatest comedies, *IL BARBIERE DI SIVIGLIA* (*The Barber of Seville*; 1816) and *LA CENERENTOLA* (*Cinderella*; 1817).

Rossini's last work for the Italian stage was the powerful melodrama *Semiramide* (1823), based on a tragedy by Voltaire set in ancient Babylon. In 1824, Rossini was installed as general manager of the Théâtre Italien in Paris, where Italian operas were performed in their original language. The following year he composed a royal entertainment, *Il viaggio a Reims* (*The Journey to Rheims*), to celebrate the coronation of Charles X; in 1826 he produced *Le siège de Corinthe,* a vivid reworking of *Maometto II* (1820), one of his few San Carlo failures. Rossini then capped his operatic career with *Le Comte Ory* (1828) and *GUILLAUME TELL* (1829), both written for the Paris Opéra. Having sent French grand opera on its way with *Tell,* Rossini, only 37 years old, retired.

Many factors played a role in Rossini's decision to quit. Chief among them were sheer physical exhaustion and, it now seems likely, emotional difficulties associated with either chronic depression or bipolar disorder. In addition, Rossini was troubled by what he viewed as a decline in the standards of singing and by the political upheaval surrounding the Revolution of 1830—which deposed Charles X and brought the "citizen king" Louis-Philippe to the French throne. As a result of the new bourgeois order, Rossini's contract with the Opéra was canceled; it took him six years to get his lost annuity restored. He wrote little music during the 1830s save for a series of songs called *Les soirées musicales* (1830–35) and an extraordinary setting of the *Stabat mater*, begun in 1832 and completed in 1841.

In 1846, following Colbran's death, Rossini married Olympe Pélissier, who had helped him through the worst of his years of malaise. He returned to composition with the *Péchés de vieillesse* (*Sins of Old Age*; 1857–68), and offered as his swan song the touchingly intimate *Petite messe solennelle* (1863).

To deal with the variety of situations he faced as a theatrical composer, Rossini borrowed from every convention; on many occasions he also lifted the best material from one work he had written and put it in another. He revitalized the buffa style, casting aside much of what he had inherited from Giovanni Paisiello (1740–1816) and Domenico Cimarosa (1749–1801). He also innovated, masterfully using the orchestra to create a scintillating, rhythmically vital backdrop to the vocal lines he spun with such seeming ease, bringing a sharpness to the art of characterization that rivaled Mozart's. He blazed a trail for the Romantics in his choice of material, seizing on Scott for *La donna del lago* before Donizetti looked to him for *Lucia de Lammermoor,* and turning to Schiller for *Guillaume Tell* long before Verdi got in the game.

In the best of Rossini's music, which is to say in nearly all of it, one finds lightness without frivolity—a sympathetic view of human nature from one who was himself frequently burdened by the weight of despair. Again and again, he achieved the kind of surprise that, as his biographer Stendhal well knew, induces laughter. There's hardly anything in opera funnier than Don Basilio's aria "La calunnia" from *Il barbiere di Siviglia,* in which the spread of rumor from a tiny whisper to a deafening roar is mimicked by a classic, brilliantly orchestrated Rossini crescendo, climaxed at the line "come un colpo di canone" ("like the ka-boom of a canon") by an explosive thwack on the bass drum. Rarely has a composer succeeded so marvelously in capturing the comic essence of words in music.

RECOMMENDED RECORDINGS

IL BARBIERE DI SIVIGLIA: BARTOLI, NUCCI, MATTEUZZI, FISSORE, BURCHULADZE; PATANÈ AND TEATRO COMMUNALE DI BOLOGNA (DECCA).

LA CENERENTOLA: BARTOLI, MATTEUZZI, CORBELLI, DARA; CHAILLY AND TEATRO COMUNALE DI BOLOGNA (DECCA).

GUILLAUME TELL: BACQUIER, CABALLÉ, GEDDA, MESPLÉ; GARDELLI AND ROYAL PHILHARMONIC ORCHESTRA (EMI).

STABAT MATER: PAVAROTTI, LORENGAR, MINTON, SOTIN; KERTÉSZ AND LONDON SYMPHONY ORCHESTRA (DECCA).

IL VIAGGIO A REIMS: RICCIARELLI, CUBERLI, ARAIZA, NUCCI, RAMEY; ABBADO AND CHAMBER ORCHESTRA OF EUROPE (DG).

SELECTED OVERTURES:

CHAILLY AND NATIONAL PHILHARMONIC ORCHESTRA (DECCA).

GIULINI AND PHILHARMONIA ORCHESTRA (EMI).

NORRINGTON AND LONDON CLASSICAL PLAYERS (EMI).

Rostropovich, Mstislav

(b. Baku, Azerbaijan, March 27, 1927)

RUSSIAN CELLIST, CONDUCTOR, AND PIANIST. The greatest cellist of the second half of the 20th century, he is universally regarded as one of the supreme string virtuosos in the history of music. He was born into a musical family: His father, Leopold, a student of Casals, was a distinguished cellist and teacher, his mother an accomplished pianist, and his elder sister a violinist. In 1931, at the age of four, he started to play the piano "without my parents' permission." That same year the family moved to Moscow. When Rostropovich was eight his father began teaching him the cello and enrolled him in a school for the musically gifted. Following the German invasion in 1941, the family was evacuated to the Urals. The death of Rostropovich's father in 1942 deprived the family of its breadwinner, and the teenager went to work playing for wounded Red Army soldiers in small towns and hamlets across Russia. In 1943 he entered the Moscow Conservatory, where he studied cello with Semyon Kozolupov, piano (playing Rachmaninov's Concerto No. 2 as his final exam), and composition with Dmitry Shostakovich and Vissarion Shebalin. Two years later, at the age of 18, he won a national competition and, though still a student, was catapulted into the front rank of Soviet performers. In 1948, following Stalin's crackdown on the Union of Soviet Composers—in which Prokofiev, Shostakovich, Khachaturian, Dmitry Kabalevsky (1904–87), and Nikolay Myaskovsky (1881–1950) were all censured and Shostakovich lost his professorship—Rostropovich left the conservatory in protest. He went to live with Prokofiev, in effect becoming a member of the composer's family for several months. Later, he assisted Prokofiev with the composition of the solo part of his *Symphony-Concerto* for cello and orchestra, Op. 125.

Mstislav Rostropovich in the 1960s

Rostropovich had to abandon early hopes of becoming a composer himself, "bombed flat," as he put it, by the sheer genius of his mentors Prokofiev and Shostakovich. But the 1950s brought a burgeoning of his solo career, aided by a first-place finish at the 1950 International Competition for Cellists in Prague and by major prizes from the Soviet government. In 1955 he met Galina Vishnevskaya, the Soviet Union's most celebrated prima donna, and married her after a four-day courtship. The following year he became one of the first Soviet artists sent to the West in the Cold War thaw that began after Stalin's death; his debuts in London and New York created a sensation among listeners and critics who had never heard the cello played as he could play it. In 1959 he gave the premiere of Shostakovich's Concerto No. 1, Op. 107, one of the most important works in the modern repertoire. Performing the concerto in London in 1960, he met and formed a close friendship with Benjamin Britten, who over the next 15 years favored him with some of his finest works. In 1960 Rostropovich became the youngest full professor at the Moscow Conservatory, where his title was professor of cello *and* double bass.

During the 1960s, Rostropovich made frequent trips to the West. As top athletes and mountain climbers will do, he began setting himself increasingly difficult challenges as a performer, programming marathon concert series in London, Moscow, and New York in which he played most of the existing works in the repertoire. In 1968 he made his official conducting debut, in Tchaikovsky's *Eugene Onegin* at the Bolshoi Theatre, with Vishnevskaya as his Tatyana. In 1969, Rostropovich and Vishnevskaya invited Aleksandr Solzhenitsyn—still an "allowed" author in the Soviet Union, but virtually penniless—to live and work at their dacha outside Moscow; he spent five winters there. Following the novelist's receipt of the Nobel Prize in 1970, when a campaign was mounted against him by the Soviet authorities, Rostropovich wrote an open letter

to the Soviet press, challenging the whole system of official interference in artistic and intellectual life. The letter went unpublished, but was widely circulated in the West. This act of defiance cost Rostropovich and Vishnevskaya their careers. Their engagements were canceled and their travel outside the Soviet Union was curtailed. With their two daughters they went into exile in 1974. Just before leaving, Rostropovich gave a final concert, leading a student orchestra in the Great Hall of the Moscow Conservatory in Tchaikovsky's *Pathétique* Symphony.

With little more than his cello and his talent, Rostropovich started over again. He made his American conducting debut with the National Symphony Orchestra in 1975 and became its music director in 1977, serving 17 years in that post. Overcoming his somewhat rudimentary baton technique, he developed into a very capable conductor and elevated the NSO to world-class level. Free to travel, he also rebuilt his solo career, performing as cellist everywhere in the world except the Soviet bloc and making numerous recordings. He and Vishnevskaya were stripped of their Soviet citizenship in 1978. But in 1990, with the door opened by Mikhail Gorbachev's policy of *glasnost,* Rostropovich returned in triumph to his homeland at the head of the National Symphony to lead tumultuously received performances in Moscow and Leningrad. After stepping down in Washington, he busied himself conducting opera in Vienna, Stockholm, Moscow, and St. Petersburg and maintained an active guest-conducting schedule with orchestras in Europe (especially the London Symphony Orchestra) and the United States, where he enjoyed enormous success in several mini-festivals with the Chicago Symphony. He and Vishnevskaya have also devoted considerable resources to humanitarian work, mainly focused on improving the quality of children's health care in Russia.

Rostropovich defined for his era the art and technique of playing the cello. Major works written for him include Prokofiev's *Symphony-Concerto* and Cello Sonata in C; Britten's *Cello Symphony,* Sonata for Cello and Piano, and three Suites for unaccompanied cello; concertos by Myaskovsky, Khachaturian, Glier, Dutilleux, Lutosławski, Penderecki, and Schnittke; and both of Shostakovich's cello concertos. As a cellist he has been celebrated for his powerful sonority and his projection in soft dynamics ("I like *piano, pianissimo* . . . where sound is born"); for his superior intonation and incomparably rich tone, which can take on an extraordinary intensity in the high register; and for the astonishing accuracy of his fingering and passagework.

Rostropovich* (right) *and the author at Lincoln Center, April 2002; above, the many faces of "Slava"

His style is wonderfully lithe, full of color, and capable of mercurial shifts in mood, and he brings to his playing an almost superhuman energy, ardor, and conviction. Among the instruments he has owned is the "Duport" Stradivari, formerly played by Jean-Louis Duport and Auguste Franchomme, one of the finest instruments in existence.

In his conducting, Rostropovich is passionate, sweeping, and emotionally direct. While his technique has never been especially refined, he possesses a sensational ear and is able to mold the sound of an orchestra with complete assurance. In certain repertoire (for example, the symphonies of Mahler) his readings can be burdened by details, but in the music of Tchaikovsky, Borodin, Mussorgsky, Rimsky-Korsakov, and his beloved Prokofiev, Shostakovich, and Britten, his interpretations are unmatched in their drama and color, intense emotional grip, and utter freedom from routine.

RECOMMENDED RECORDINGS

As cellist:

Bach, suites (EMI).

Beethoven, cello sonatas: Richter (Philips).

Dutilleux, Lutosławski, cello concertos: Baudo, Lutosławski and Orchestre de Paris (EMI).

Dvořák, Cello Concerto: Karajan and Berlin Philharmonic (DG).

Schubert, *Arpeggione* Sonata; Debussy, Sonata: Britten (Decca).

Shostakovich, Cello Concerto No. 1: Ormandy and Philadelphia Orchestra (Sony).

As conductor:

Shostakovich, *Lady Macbeth of Mtsensk*: Vishnevskaya, Gedda, Petkov, Tear, Haugland; London Philharmonic Orchestra (EMI).

Shostakovich, symphonies (complete): London Symphony Orchestra, National Symphony Orchestra, Moscow Academic Symphony Orchestra (Teldec).

Tchaikovsky, suites from *Swan Lake, The Sleeping Beauty, The Nutcracker*: Berlin Philharmonic (DG).

Rostropovich's mother, Sofia, carried him for ten months instead of nine. He used to ask her why, if she had taken all that time, she hadn't done a better job on his face. "Because I was working on your hands," she told him.

Rouse, Christopher *See box on pages 708–11.*

Roussel, Albert

(b. Tourcoing, April 5, 1869; d. Royan, August 23, 1937)

FRENCH COMPOSER. He came from a well-to-do family in the home-furnishings business in northern France. His childhood was unsettled; his father died shortly after his birth, and his mother never really recovered from the loss, dying when Roussel was eight. He was raised from the age of 11 by his maternal aunt and her husband.

In 1884 the 15-year-old Roussel entered the Collège Stanislas in Paris, preparing for a career as a naval officer but also receiving instruction in organ. His schooling entailed training voyages to French Indochina (Vietnam); after receiving his commission, his first duty as an officer was in the Atlantic on the last sailing ship in the French navy, the three-masted frigate *Melpomène.* Roussel's interest in music continued to develop, and when he received his discharge, in 1893, he became a student of Vincent d'Indy at the newly founded Schola Cantorum. While he was a student there, Roussel taught counterpoint to others, including Erik Satie and the much younger Bohuslav Martinů.

Roussel's first large-scale work was the four-movement symphony *La poème de la forêt* (1904–06)—a sort of sylvan *Four Seasons,* complete with descriptive titles and musical depictions of winter storms and the like. The composer married Blanche Preisach in 1908 and the couple took an extended honeymoon that included visits to India and southeast Asia; the composer would later draw upon his memories of this voyage in one of his most imaginative and striking works, the opera *Padmâvatî.*

Albert Roussel at work, 1937

Completed in 1918 and premiered in 1923, it succinctly retells—in classical opera-ballet format but employing Indian scales and exotic orchestration—a 13th-century Hindu tragedy. Prior to receiving the commission for *Padmâvatî,* Roussel had revealed his exceptional abilities as a composer of scenic music with the ballet *Le festin de l'araignée* (*The Spider's Feast*). Begun in 1912 and completed the next year, this inspired creation depicts a day in the garden as an insect drama.

During World War I, Roussel first served as an ambulance driver with the Red Cross, and later drove artillery-transport vehicles at Verdun and the battle of the Somme. He received a medical discharge early in 1918 and, after completing *Padmâvatî,* composed his Symphony No. 2 in B-flat. In 1920 he bought a villa in Brittany and with his wife spent the rest of his days there.

Arguably Roussel's greatest work, his Symphony No. 3 in G minor, was commissioned by Serge Koussevitzky for the Boston Symphony Orchestra's 50th anniversary; Roussel traveled to attend its premiere in 1930. In the next four years he wrote his finest ballet, *Bacchus et Ariane,* and the Symphony No. 4 in A. Other works of note include the *Sérénade* (1925) for flute, violin, viola, cello, and harp; the Trio (1929) for flute, viola, and cello; and a String Trio (1937). There also is much piano music of considerable charm.

Over the course of his career Roussel moved from impressionistic and programmatic pictorialism toward a neoclassical style rooted in the traditional forms of absolute music. His mature idiom is a blend of Franckian order and Debussyan color, but with a unique mixture of "orientalisms" and other refreshing elements drawn from his love of non-Western culture; his works, lucid in their structure, are unapologetically lyrical and characterized by a clear exposition and development of ideas. Harmonies have a salty tang and rhythms a motoric vitality, and the orchestration draws from a remarkable palette, often colored by a distinctively burnished red-gold glow of the brass. Almost all of Roussel's music is underperformed today.

RECOMMENDED RECORDINGS

Bacchus et Ariane, Le festin de l'araignée **(complete): Tortelier and BBC Philharmonic Orchestra (Chandos).**

Bacchus et Ariane, **Suite No. 2: Martinon and Chicago Symphony Orchestra (RCA).**

Symphonies Nos. 1–4: Dutoit and Orchestre National de France (Erato).

Symphony No. 3: Bernstein and New York Philharmonic (Sony).

Royal Academy of Music **CONSERVATORY FOUNDED IN LONDON IN 1822.** Generations of English musicians have been trained at the facility, which since 1911 has occupied premises on Marylebone Road alongside Regent's Park in central London. Among the school's alumni are Arthur Sullivan (who entered in 1856), the conductors Henry Wood, John Barbirolli, and Simon Rattle (a student from 1971 to 1974), and the composer Harrison Birtwistle (currently RAM's director of contemporary music).

Royal Concertgebouw Orchestra *See* CONCERTGEBOUW.

Royal Opera House, Covent Garden *See* COVENT GARDEN.

Royal Philharmonic Orchestra LONDON ORCHESTRA FOUNDED IN 1946 BY SIR THOMAS BEECHAM, who remained its music director until his death in 1961. Rudolf Kempe, appointed associate conductor in 1960, guided the orchestra from 1961 until 1975. Since then, the leadership has included Antal Dorati (chief conductor 1975–78), Walter Weller (principal conductor 1980–85), André Previn (music director 1985–87, principal conductor 1988–92), and Vladimir Ashkenazy (music director 1987–94). In 1996 Daniele Gatti became the orchestra's music director, and in 2005 Leonard Slatkin was appointed principal guest conductor. The RPO regularly performs at several venues in and around London, including the Royal Albert Hall, and recently acquired a new home—Cadogan Hall, Sloane Square.

RECOMMENDED RECORDINGS

DELIUS, ORCHESTRAL WORKS: BEECHAM (EMI).

GLAZUNOV, *THE SEASONS*: ASHKENAZY (DECCA).

GRIEG, *PEER GYNT* (EXCERPTS): BEECHAM (EMI).

WALTON, *BELSHAZZAR'S FEAST*: LUXON; PREVIN (CARLTON CLASSICS).

rubato (from It. *rubare,* "to steal") An element of phrasing that involves a departure, for expressive purposes, from the precise notated rhythm without a disturbance of the basic pulse. On a particular note or phrase one "steals" some of the durational value of adjoining notes, usually delaying or lingering slightly, then picking up the pace. Few performers today apply rubato with the kind of freedom that typified interpreters of bygone years such as Franz Liszt, but good examples of its use can be found

The Chairman (of rubato), Frank Sinatra, 1954

in the recordings of Wilhelm Kempff and Arthur Rubinstein. One of the most accomplished practitioners of the art of rubato was Frank Sinatra, who routinely "teased" the beat, holding a note longer than written, then catching up with the band.

During the 18th century, a more formalized application of rubato—in which the phrasing of a melodic line was advanced or delayed by half a beat while the accompaniment remained in strict time—was known as *tempo rubato.* This staggered effect was incorporated in many keyboard pieces of the era, and can be heard in the first movement variations of Beethoven's Piano Sonata in A-flat, Op. 26.

Rubinstein, Arthur [Artur]

(b. Lodz, January 28, 1887; d. Geneva, December 20, 1982)

POLISH/AMERICAN PIANIST. Famed as much for his gregarious personality and charismatic stage presence as for his spellbinding playing, he was one of the most inspired and distinctive musicians of the 20th century, and a man who loved life and lived it to the hilt. In a career spanning more than 80 years he was particularly admired for his glowing interpretations of the music of Chopin, but his repertoire, which was enormous by today's standards, embraced nearly all the significant works of the 19th and early 20th centuries.

Born into a Jewish merchant family in a section of Poland then under Prussian domination, Rubinstein fell in love with the piano as a child and developed rapidly into a prodigy. He first performed in public at the age of seven. Four years later the young pianist was taken to Berlin and presented to Joseph Joachim, who agreed to assume responsibility for his education. In 1900, at the age of 13, Rubinstein made his formal debut in Berlin performing Mozart's Concerto in A, K. 488, at a concert of the Berlin Philharmonic. He made his American debut in 1906 at Carnegie Hall playing Saint-Saëns's Concerto No. 2 in G minor with the Philadelphia Orchestra. He then toured the U.S., giving more than 40 concerts.

Returning to Europe, Rubinstein devoted himself to several more years of study, travel, and, as he put it, "hurdling the greatest obstacle in the path of a prodigy, that of shedding my immaturity." From 1910 until the outbreak of World War I he concertized extensively, playing throughout Europe and appearing in Moscow and St. Petersburg under the baton of Serge Koussevitzky. In 1916 he made his first visit to Spain; scheduled to play four recitals, he remained to give 120, beginning a lifelong love affair with Spain and its culture from which he would emerge as one of the foremost interpreters of Spanish music. His first concerts in South America followed in 1917.

Between the wars, Rubinstein's life centered on London and Paris, where he found himself in the salons of high society and on intimate terms with the likes of Coco Chanel, the Rothschilds, Pablo Picasso, Igor Stravinsky, and the American-born Princesse de Polignac. He made a triumphant return to the United States in 1937, touring under the aegis of Sol Hurok. When the Germans entered Paris in 1940, Rubinstein was on tour; he and his family subsequently moved to the United States, taking up residence, along with many other displaced artists, in Hollywood. In 1947, a year after becoming an American citizen, the pianist returned to Europe to concertize there for the first time since 1939. An idol before he left the Continent, he resumed his career to even greater acclaim, though he refused for the rest of his life to perform in Germany out of respect for the victims of the Holocaust, to which he lost a number of family members.

Rubinstein continued to concertize into his 90th year, when partial blindness compelled him to retire. He bade farewell to Carnegie Hall in March of 1976, and gave the final performance of his career, a recital at Wigmore Hall in London, two months later. Rubinstein published two autobiographical books, *My Young Years* (covering the first 29 years of his life) in 1973, and *My Many Years* (covering the next 64) in 1980. He received the Presidential Medal of Freedom in 1976, and was a charter

Arthur Rubinstein, reflecting on his many years

recipient of the Kennedy Center Honors in 1978.

In musical terms, there were really two Arthur Rubinsteins: the extroverted virtuoso who reached his peak in the 1930s and the sophisticated, cosmopolitan stylist of the 1950s onward, whose warmly aristocratic manner tended to delight rather than dazzle. Even so, the hallmarks of Rubinstein's pianism—supple phrasing, subtle rubato, gorgeous tone—changed little over the years. He was a master of the singing line, and at his best he achieved an emotional directness and a balance of the fiery and poetic that was as revealing as it was thrilling.

RECOMMENDED RECORDINGS

BRAHMS, PIANO CONCERTO NO. 1: LEINSDORF AND BOSTON SYMPHONY ORCHESTRA (RCA).

"RUBINSTEIN COLLECTION": CHOPIN, BALLADES, SCHERZOS, NOCTURNES, WALTZES, POLONAISES, OTHER WORKS (RCA).

Ruders, Poul

(b. Ringsted, March 27, 1949)

DANISH COMPOSER. He sang in the Copenhagen Boys Choir, studied piano and organ in Odense, and completed his training as an organist at the Royal Danish Conservatory in Copenhagen. He was a visiting professor at Yale in 1991 and lived in London from 1991 to 1994. His output, already substantial, includes more than a dozen works for orchestra, several concertos, numerous chamber and instrumental works, vocal pieces, and two operas. Among his most interesting achievements to date are *Solar Trilogy* (1992–95), consisting of three works for orchestra—*Gong, Zenith,* and *Corona*—inspired by different aspects of the sun; the *Concerto in Pieces* (1994–95), an exhilarating set of variations on music by Purcell, intended as a modern-day sequel to Britten's *Young Person's Guide to the Orchestra*; the opera *The Handmaid's Tale* (1998), based on Margaret Atwood's dystopian novel about a bleak, postholocaust future in which the West is ravaged by religious fundamentalism; and *Proces Kafka* (*Kafka's Trial*), based on the life and writings of Franz Kafka, which received its premiere at Copenhagen's newly opened Operaen opera house in March 2005. Prolific and imaginative, with an eclectic bent that enables him to range widely in pursuit of ideas, Ruders has emerged not only as the leading Danish composer of his generation, but as one of the most interesting musical voices on the scene today, a figure whose best works exhibit a striking, and rare, combination of cohesion, vitality, and expressive point.

RECOMMENDED RECORDINGS

CONCERTO IN PIECES: DAVIS AND BBC SYMPHONY ORCHESTRA (BRIDGE).

GUITAR MUSIC: STAROBIN (BRIDGE).

THE HANDMAID'S TALE: RORHOLM, FISCHER, ELMING, DAHL; SCHØNWANDT AND ROYAL DANISH OPERA (DA CAPO).

SOLAR TRILOGY FOR ORCHESTRA: *GONG, ZENITH, CORONA*; SCHØNWANDT AND ODENSE SYMPHONY ORCHESTRA (MARCO POLO).

Ruffo, Titta

(b. Pisa, June 9, 1877; d. Florence, July 5, 1953)

ITALIAN BARITONE. His baptismal name was Ruffo Cafiero Titta, which he changed to Titta Ruffo when he took the stage. He grew up in poverty, first in Pisa, then Rome, where the family moved when he was seven. He was destined to follow his father's path as a metalworker until, at 13, a performance of the Mascagni sensation *Cavalleria rusticana* at Rome's Teatro Costanze changed his life. Afterward, when imitating its melodies and the manner in which they were sung, he discovered (along with his entire neighborhood, presumably), that he had a prodigious talent for singing, and at 19 he was admitted to the Accademia di Santa Cecilia in Rome. He studied voice with Venceslao Persichini, teacher of another soon-to-be-famous baritone, Giuseppe de Luca, but Ruffo felt that Persichini doted on de Luca at his expense, and after a few months he left school, ending his only formal musical education. A Rome debut in 1898 as the Herald in Wagner's *Lohengrin* led to provincial engagements, and he began to build a repertoire that would include Verdi's Rigoletto and Germont, Barnaba in *La gioconda* by Amilcare Ponchielli (1834–86), Mozart's Don Giovanni, Rossini's Figaro, Gérard in Giordano's *Andrea Chénier,* and his career favorite, the title role in *Hamlet* by Ambroise Thomas (1811–96). By the end of the first decade of the 20th century, he had become a star throughout Europe and in South America. Though his acting was unsubtle and his style of singing could not be called bel canto, his robust physicality and onstage persona, plus the remarkable size and feral beauty of his voice, earned him the name "the Singing Lion."

Ruffo first performed in the U.S. in 1912, but did not appear at the Metropolitan Opera until 1922. It has been suggested (without real evidence) that his debut there might have been stalled by Enrico Caruso, who, despite an untroubled personal relationship with Ruffo, could have feared that the stentorian baritone's vocal presence would overshadow his own. But Caruso was dead when Ruffo first bowed at the Met, as Figaro in Rossini's *Il barbiere di Siviglia,* on January 19, 1922. Ruffo remained on the Met's roster for eight seasons, but his lack of vocal training had by then caught up with him, and the decline that would soon end his career was apparent after his first season at the Met. Following his return to Italy in 1929, his performances were confined mostly to concerts. "The lion is silent," he said upon retirement in 1936. Before and during World War II, Ruffo was persecuted in Italy for his strong antifascist views. His much-praised autobiography, *La mia parabola* (*My Parabola*), is an account of his youth and rise to fame, ending during the Met years. The conductor Tullio Serafin remarked: "In my lifetime there have been three miracles: Caruso, Ponselle, and Ruffo." De Luca's summation was similar: "It wasn't a voice, it was a miracle."

Rugby **ORCHESTRAL WORK COMPLETED IN 1928 BY ARTHUR HONEGGER,** the second of his three *Mouvements symphoniques.* It received its premiere October 19, 1928, at the inaugural concert of the Orchestre Symphonique de Paris, conducted by Ernest Ansermet. "I'm very fond of soccer, but rugby is closer to my heart," the composer wrote. "It seems to me more spontaneous, more direct, closer to Nature than soccer, which is more scientific. Certainly I'm not insensitive to soccer's carefully prepared plays, but I'm more keenly attracted to rugby's rhythm, which is savage, abrupt, chaotic, and desperate." Written for a large orchestra that, surprisingly, includes no percussion, *Rugby* is one of Honegger's most dynamic and rhythmically complex works. The score uses jagged rhythms and angular melodic contours as well as frequent sharp dissonance to suggest the raw athletic vigor and near anarchy on display in a typical match; as in a typical match, the action takes place in two "halves," the first centered around G major, the second on D major.

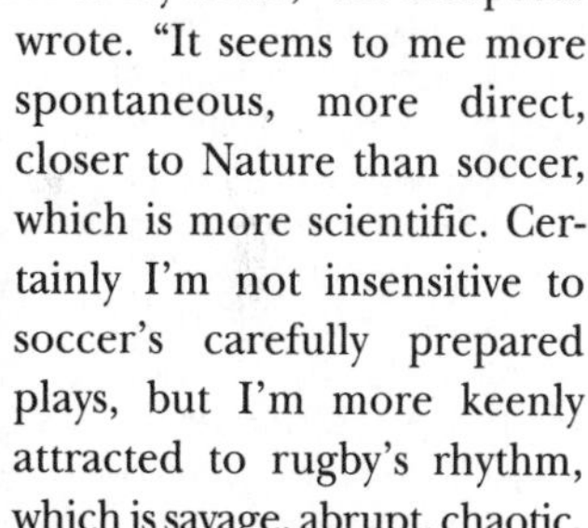

RECOMMENDED RECORDINGS

BERNSTEIN AND NEW YORK PHILHARMONIC (SONY).

ZINMAN AND TONHALLE-ORCHESTER ZURICH (DECCA).

Carl Ruggles

(b. East Marion, Mass., March 11, 1876; d. Bennington, Vt., October 24, 1971). A free-thinking New England individualist like his contemporary and good friend Charles Ives, he studied violin as a boy, attended some classes at Harvard, and composed music that sounded like nothing anybody had heard before: craggy, intense, upthrusting, and definitely not tonal. Also like Ives, he was drawn to the spiritual, nature-worshipping poetry of the English and American Romantics, some of which (e.g., Browning and Whitman) he set to music. He turned to a line from Blake for the title of his three-movement orchestral suite, *Men and Mountains* (1924; rev. 1936, 1941), and was indebted to Browning for the memorable tag he attached to his most ambitious orchestral score, the powerfully assertive, densely polyphonic, and unapologetically dissonant *Sun-Treader* (1926–31).

George Antheil

(b. Trenton, July 8, 1900; d. New York, February 12, 1959). He was precocious, studying composition with Ernest Bloch when he was in his teens; he was a pianist, traveling to Europe and making his London recital debut when he was 21; and he was a polymath, penning a treatise on criminology, a murder mystery, and an advice column for *Esquire.* Early on he came under the spell of Stravinsky, whose vigorous treatment of rhythm influenced his own driven, ostinato-dominated style—already evident, along with an obsessive interest in machines, in his Piano Sonata No. 2, subtitled the *Airplane Sonata,* of 1921. Stravinsky's *Les noces* provided the model for what would become Antheil's most celebrated work, the modernist *Ballet mécanique* for large percussion ensemble (including pianos, xylophones, several aircraft propellers, and a police siren) composed in Paris 1923–25 and premiered there in 1926. Antheil returned to the United States in 1933, and in 1936 he settled in Hollywood. Over the next two decades he composed numerous film and television scores and produced a substantial amount of concert music, shedding his "bad boy" image in the process. During World War II, Antheil teamed up with the brilliant Viennese-born actress Hedy Lamarr (1913–2000) to design a device for radio guidance of torpedos that would be immune to enemy jamming. Lamarr came up with the concept of "frequency-hopping," and Antheil figured out how to coordinate transmitters with a system using synchronized punched-paper rolls, similar to those of a player piano, that was based on a scheme he had worked out in his *Ballet mécanique.* The device received U.S. Patent number 2,292,387 under Lamarr's name. It became the basis for the spread spectrum technology first used by the U.S. military, and proved fundamental to practical modern-day applications such as garage door openers and cell phones.

Mark Blitzstein

(b. Philadelphia, March 2, 1905; d. Fort-de-France, Martinique, January 22, 1964). An excellent pianist, he studied composition with Rosario Scalero at the Curtis Institute, had a brief fling with 12-tone technique as a student of Schoenberg in Berlin, and in due course embraced neo-classicism, jazz, popular song, Communism, and a left-wing social agenda, all of which came to a boil in his musical-theater piece *The Cradle Will Rock* (1936–37), a satirical, irreverent and, for the time, dangerously controversial poke at the capitalist establishment. When America got into World War II, on the same side as Russia, Blitzstein threw himself into the war effort, penning his *Airborne Symphony* (1944–46) on a commission from the U.S. Air Force. He continued combining musical eclecticism and social commentary after the war in his opera *Regina* (1946–48) and in the musical plays *Reuben, Reuben* (1955) and *Juno* (1957–59). Another opera, *Sacco and Vanzetti* (1959–64), was left unfinished at his death, which resulted from injuries sustained in a barroom brawl.

AMERICAN CLASSICS

George
ANTHEIL
Ballet Mécanique
Philadelphia Virtuosi Chamber Orchestra
Daniel Spalding

Alan Hovhaness

Alan Hovhaness

(b. Somerville, Mass., March 8, 1911; d. Seattle, June 21, 2000). Of Scottish and Armenian ancestry (he was born Alan Vaness Chakmakjian), he began writing music in childhood and kept at it to the end of his life, composing more than 400 pieces, including more than 60 symphonies. His career received an early boost when his Symphony No. 2 (*Mysterious Mountain*)–commissioned by Leopold Stokowski for the opening of his first season as music director of the Houston Symphony Orchestra in 1955–was recorded by Fritz Reiner and the Chicago Symphony and became a runaway success. While his materials were his own, Hovhaness made use of procedures drawn from Indian and Asian music, Armenian chant, Renaissance polyphony, and medieval plainsong. Flavored by modal harmonies and ritualistic repetitions of figure, much of his music has a mystical, pseudo-archaic feel to it. This has caused many to characterize it as a kind of proto-minimalism, but it really has more in common with 20th-century primitivism in painting, especially its studied naïveté and predilection for patterns. At its best, it expresses rapture and achieves a majestic kind of flow; at its worst, it devolves into long-winded inanity. But it is never remote, and it always gives off a sonorous beauty.

Conlon Nancarrow

(b. Texarkana, Ark., October 27, 1912; d. Mexico City, August 10, 1997). He studied at the Cincinnati College Conservatory, and later took lessons with Roger Sessions, Walter Piston, and Nicolas Slonimsky. A committed Communist, he joined the International Brigades and fought in the Abraham Lincoln Battalion on the losing side in the Spanish civil war. In 1939, he escaped from Spain by stowing away on a freighter loaded with olive oil. He returned briefly to the United States; reading Henry Cowell's *New Musical Resources* changed his perspective radically, and he began to focus on producing music of extraordinary rhythmic intricacy. In 1940, he left the U.S., taking up residence in Mexico City (he became a Mexican citizen in 1956). Almost certainly a Communist agent, and by all accounts not a very nice man, he was later named in a Senate investigation of passport fraud. Nancarrow's visionary rhythmic conceptions, built on mathematical complexities even a computer would find challenging, were well beyond the capabilities of even the best pianists. Frustrated, he used a family bequest to purchase a player piano and began punching his own rolls, creating some of the most amazingly complicated music of the 20th century. His most important efforts were two large series of studies for player piano. In 1982, he received a "genius" grant from the MacArthur Foundation.

Frederick Rzewski

Frederick Rzewski

(b. Westfield, Mass., April 13, 1938). He studied at Harvard and Princeton, and spent time in Europe on a Fulbright grant, becoming one of the founders (in 1966) of Musica Elettronica Viva in Rome. In 1977, he was appointed professor at the Royal Conservatory of Music in Liège, Belgium. An exceptionally capable pianist, Rzewski has incorporated mathematical schemes and improvisational elements in his music (e.g. *Les Moutons de Panurge*, 1969), and

Conlon Nancarrow

made use of graphic notation and 12-tone techniques. His approach has been experimental, but also eclectic ... drawing on big-boned Romantic virtuoso techniques in his magnificent set of variations for piano, *The People United Will Never Be Defeated!* (1975). Recent works include his six-movement *Pocket Symphony* (2000), written for the contemporary chamber ensemble eighth blackbird.

Michael Daugherty

New Voices

Christopher Rouse

(b. Baltimore, February 15, 1949). He emerged from studies at Oberlin and Cornell as a master of percussive shock and awe, his music seething with manic energy and flaunting a virtuosity shaped by his acquaintance with hard rock and his own training as a percussionist. He had his first big successes with *The Infernal Machine* (1981) and *Gorgon* (1984), diabolically loud, fast, and clamorous. But since the mid-1980s he has embraced, with equal fervor, a darkly contemplative, at times pessimistic Romanticism that comes out of Bruckner, Mahler, Shostakovich, and Karl Amadeus Hartmann and Allan Pettersson. Rouse's works of the past two decades have proffered a mingling of visceral excitement with tragic visions, e.g. *Phaethon* (1987), his orchestral imagining of the calamitous ride in sun god's chariot, brought to an end by a thunderbolt from Zeus. Rouse had reached precisely that climactic point in the score on the morning of January 28, 1986, when the space shuttle *Challenger* blew up shortly after launch, and fell in pieces from the sky; he dedicated the piece to the memory of the fallen astronauts. Among his works are two symphonies (1986, 1994) and concertos for trombone (1991; winner of the 1993 Pulitzer Prize), violin (1991), cello (1992), flute (1993), guitar (1999), as well as a percussion concerto titled *Der gerettete Alberich* (*Alberich Redeemed*; 1997).

Kaija Saariaho

(b. Helsinki, October 14, 1952) and **Magnus Lindberg** *(b. Helsinki, June 27, 1958).* They are leading members of new wave in Finnish music. Saariaho studied at the Sibelius Academy and in Freiburg. In 1982 she settled in Paris, where she has shared in the exploratory work of IRCAM. One of the consistent characteristics of her music is its fascination with tone color. To this end she has made frequent use of experimental instrumental techniques and routinely opened the door to electronic and computer-generated sound; hers is a world of indirect but very palpable emotional expression. Among her most important works to date is the opera *L'amour de loin* (2000), based on the life of the 12th-century troubadour Jaufre Rudel. Lindberg also studied at the Sibelius Academy, and along with Saariaho and Esa-Pekka Salonen was one of the founding members of the Finnish new music society "Korvat auki" ("Ears Open"). He was captivated early on by the serialism of Stockhausen and Babbitt, but his mind quickly opened to other influences, particularly the music of Varèse and Berio and the spectral explorations of the modern French scene. His orchestral piece *Kraft* (1985) revels in a love of sonority at the same time it reveals an extraordinarily sensitive ear and keen intuition ... the intuition of one who can bring powerful masses of orchestral sound crashing in on the listener, yet understands the heartache in the crack of a snail's shell.

Michael Daugherty

(b. Cedar Rapids, April 28, 1954). He attended North Texas State University, studied with Earle Brown, Jacob Druckman, and György Ligeti, among others, and is currently on the faculty of the University of Michigan in Ann Arbor. The titles and inspiration for many of his works are drawn from American pop culture: the five-movement *Metropolis Symphony* and *Bizarro* are based on characters from the Superman comics, while such scores as *Sing Sing: J. Edgar Hoover* and *Elvis Everywhere* (both written for the Kronos Quartet), *Jackie O*, and *Le Tombeau de Liberace* all pay homage to deceased American icons. At least we think they're deceased. Daugherty's music is uninhibited, eventful, richly evocative, and fun.

Tan Dun

(b. Simao, August 18, 1957). He grew up in rural China, working as a rice planter on a government commune before joining a traveling Peking opera troupe. He later studied at Beijing's Central Conservatory. In 1985 he moved to New York as a doctoral student in composition at Columbia University; he worked with Chou Wen-chung (a disciple of Varèse) and discovered the downtown musical scene, finding much to stimulate his thinking in the music of John

Cage, Philip Glass, and Steve Reich. Since then, Tan Dun has taken an energetic and eclectic approach to composition, utilizing Asian and nontraditional instruments within works for conventional forces, and composing in a variety of genres. Best known for his film scores to *Fallen* (1998) and *Crouching Tiger, Hidden Dragon* (2000), he wrote *Ghost Opera* for the Kronos Quartet and made a splash with his *Water Concerto for Water Percussion and Orchestra*, premiered by the New York Philharmonic with Kurt Masur. In 2000 he was one of four composers commissioned by the Internationale Bachakademie Stuttgart to compose a passion in commemoration of the 250th anniversary of Bach's death (the others were Sofia Gubaydulina, Wolfgang Rihm, and Osvaldo Golijov). His response, *Water Passion After St. Matthew*, uses amplified bowls of water as percussion instruments. He has written several operas, including *Marco Polo* (1995–96), *Peony Pavilion* (1998), and *Tea: A Mirror of the Soul* (2002), in which ceramic, stone, and paper instruments are included in the orchestra. Among his most important commissions to date is one from the Metropolitan Opera for a work to be premiered in December 2006.

Aaron Jay Kernis

(b. Philadelphia, January 15, 1960). He studied at the San Francisco Conservatory, Manhattan School of Music, and Yale, and became composer in residence of the St. Paul Chamber Orchestra in 1993. A gentle, soulful musician of remarkable imagination, he won early celebrity with his *Dream of the Morning Sky* (1982–83). Since the late 1980s, Kernis has aimed for directness of utterance and produced a series of works in an approachable idiom that sounds like an outgrowth of Copland's "American" style; this vein includes scores like his *Lament and Prayer* (1996) for violin and orchestra. Kernis won the Pulitzer Prize in 1998 for his String Quartet No. 2.

Osvaldo Golijov

(b. La Plata, December 5, 1960). In 2006, *The New York Times* hailed this Argentine-born composer as "classical music's great globalist hope." Raised in a rich cultural environment that included the tangos of Astor Piazzolla and Jewish liturgical and klezmer music, as well as classical music, he moved to Israel in 1983 to study with Mark Kopytman, and on to the United States in 1986, earning a doctorate at the University of Pennsylvania and studying with George Crumb. His music is a wonderfully inventive mix of elements that includes folk and popular styles, Iberian and Latin American vernacular, and a zesty embrace of Jewish tradition. He has been on America's musical radar since his *Yiddishbbuk* for string quartet won first place in the 1993 Kennedy Center Friedheim Awards for chamber music. His *La Pasión según San Marcos* (2000), commissioned by the Internationale Bachakademie Stuttgart to honor the 250th anniversary of Bach's death, set the musical world on its ear with its vibrant introduction of street music into the passion framework. Recently completed scores include *Ayre*, written for the soprano Dawn Upshaw, and the opera *Ainadamar* (*Fountain of Tears*; 2003), about the legacy of Federico García Lorca.

Jennifer Higdon

(b. New York, December 31, 1962). Brooklyn-born but raised in Atlanta and Seymour, Tenn., she majored in flute at Bowling Green State University, did her graduate work at the University of Pennsylvania, and studied composition with George Crumb and Ned Rorem; she is currently a member of the composition faculty at the Curtis Institute. Martinů and Britten collide head-on with Bartók in Higdon's music, yet the resulting fireworks are as American as the Fourth of July. Her most widely heard work to date is the *orchestral blue cathedral* (2000), which has been recorded by the Atlanta Symphony Orchestra under Robert Spano, as has her *Concerto for Orchestra* (2002). Higdon drew inspiration for the latter work from the members of the Philadelphia Orchestra, many of whom are colleagues or former students at Curtis. The players liked the piece so much they called it "Ein Higdonleben," because it held its own on a program with Strauss's majestic *Ein Heldenleben*, no easy feat. Other works include *Cityscape* (2002), *An Exaltation of Larks* (2006, written for the Tokyo String Quartet), and a *Percussion Concerto* (2005, co-commissioned by the Philadelphia, Indianapolis, and Dallas Symphony Orchestras).

Osvaldo Golijov

Ruggles, Carl *See box on pages 708–11.*

Rusalka [1] OPERA IN THREE ACTS BY ANTONÍN DVOŘÁK, to a libretto by Jaroslav Kvapil (based on Friedrich de la Motte Fouqué's novel *Undine*), premiered March 31, 1901, at the National Theater in Prague. The composer's finest opera, *Rusalka* has been slow to make its way into theaters outside the Czech Republic, though its score contains some of the most beautiful music Dvořák ever wrote. The plot concerns the unrequited love of Rusalka, a water nymph, for the Prince, a human being whom she has seen swimming in her lake, which ultimately leads to their deaths. Rusalka's Act I "Song to the Moon", in which the lovesick nymph asks the moon to tell the Prince that she is waiting for him, is the opera's most celebrated number.

[2] OPERA IN FOUR ACTS BY ALEKSANDR DARGOMÏZHSKY (1813–69), to his own libretto (based on Aleksandr Pushkin's poem), premiered May 16, 1856, at the Circus Theater in St. Petersburg.

RECOMMENDED RECORDING

FLEMING, HEPPNER, HAWLATA, ZAJICK; MACKERRAS AND CZECH PHILHARMONIC (DECCA).

Ruslan and Lyudmila "MAGIC" OPERA IN FIVE ACTS BY MIKHAIL GLINKA, to a libretto by V. F. Shirkov (based on Aleksandr Pushkin's narrative poem *Ruslan i Lyudmila*), premiered November 27, 1842, at the Bolshoi Theatre in St. Petersburg. Glinka began work on the score in 1837, the year of Pushkin's death, shortly after the premiere of *A Life for the Tsar.* The plot—rich in fairy-tale elements and full of complications—concerns the fate of the beautiful Lyudmila, daughter of the grand duke of Kiev, after her abduction by the sinister dwarf Chernomor. Her father promises her hand in marriage to the man who will

Title page of **Ruslan and Lyudmila**

rescue her. As the opera's title foretells, it is Ruslan, a nobleman, who performs the heroic deed, awakening the princess from an enchanted sleep with the help of a magic ring. The work's overture has become a mainstay of the concert repertoire.

Glinka's setting is one of the seminal works of Russian opera, a prototype of the folk-epic approach that would dominate the genre up to the beginning of the 20th century. In both its music and its structure it exerted an influence on many subsequent works, especially those of Borodin and Rimsky-Korsakov. Rarely staged nowadays, it is known outside Russia only by its overture, a buoyant curtain-raiser with flying passages for the strings, rousing outbursts from the brass, and bold solo strokes on the timpani. In the coda to the overture Glinka makes pioneering use of the whole-tone scale, foreshadowing the music that accompanies Chernomor's sorcery later in the opera. This unusual scale would become a stock gesture of Russian composers from Rimsky-Korsakov to Stravinsky, who used it to evoke the oriental, the exotic, the magical, or the mysterious.

RECOMMENDED RECORDINGS

OPERA: OGNOVIENKO, NETREBKO, DIADKOVA, GORCHAKOVA; GERGIEV AND KIROV OPERA (PHILIPS).

OVERTURE: REINER AND CHICAGO SYMPHONY ORCHESTRA (RCA).

Rysanek, Leonie

(b. Vienna, November 14, 1926; d. Vienna, March 7, 1998)

AUSTRIAN SOPRANO. She studied in Vienna and made her debut in 1949, in Innsbruck, as Agathe in Weber's *Der Freischütz.* In 1951 she took part in the postwar reopening of the Bayreuth Festival, singing Sieglinde in *Die Walküre* under the baton of Wilhelm Furtwängler. After several seasons in Munich she joined the roster of the Vienna Staatsoper in 1954, rapidly becoming one of its most radiant and reliable stars. She made her Metropolitan Opera debut on February 5, 1959, replacing Maria Callas as Lady Macbeth in the Met premiere of Verdi's *Macbeth.* Vienna and New York remained Rysanek's principal bases for the duration of her career. At the Met, where she sang major roles well into the 1980s, she was revered no less by the critics than by her fans. By the time of her farewell appearance with the company, as the Countess in Tchaikovsky's *The Queen of Spades* on January 2, 1996, she had sung 299 performances in 24 different roles and had taken part in the Met premieres of Richard Strauss's *Ariadne auf Naxos* and *Die Frau ohne Schatten,* and of Janáček's *Kát'a Kabanová.* The roles in which she appeared most often included Chrysothemis in Strauss's *Elektra,* Leonore in Beethoven's *Fidelio,* and in Wagner the parts of Senta in *Der fliegende Holländer* and Elisabeth in *Tannhäuser.*

One of the reigning divas of the second half of the 20th century, Rysanek left an indelible impression with her powerful, well-controlled soprano. In addition to possessing superb technique and a highly developed sense of musical style, she was a magnificent actress with penetrating insight into character. Foremost among the qualities that made her unique was that she always brought out the best in others. Anyone who saw her sing Chrysothemis opposite the Elektra of Birgit Nilsson—in Vienna during the 1960s or in New York in 1980—will never forget the chemistry achieved in those performances.

RECOMMENDED RECORDINGS

BEETHOVEN, *FIDELIO*: HÄFLIGER, FISCHER-DIESKAU, FRICK, SEEFRIED; FRICSAY AND BAVARIAN STATE OPERA (DG).

WAGNER, *DIE WALKÜRE*: KING, NIENSTEDT, NILSSON, ADAM; BÖHM AND BAYREUTH FESTIVAL ORCHESTRA (PHILIPS).

Rzewski, Frederick *See box on pages 708–11.*

S

Sacher, Paul

(b. Basel, April 28, 1906; d. Basel, May 26, 1999)

SWISS CONDUCTOR AND PHILANTHROPIST who possessed generosity and good taste in equal and abundant measure. Among the performer-patrons of 20th-century music, he was the most important after Koussevitzky. He studied conducting with Felix Weingartner and founded the Basel Chamber Orchestra in 1926; he was instrumental in establishing and directing several other musical organizations in his hometown as well. He married the heiress to the major Swiss pharmaceutical fortune of Hoffmann-La Roche; with her support and encouragement, he was able to extend commissions to many of the finest composers of the 20th century. The result: more than 200 works and a list of masterpieces ranging from Bartók's *Music for Strings, Percussion, and Celesta* and Divertimento to Richard Strauss's *Metamorphosen,* Honegger's Second and Fourth Symphonies, and Stravinsky's Concerto in D.

Portrait of Paul Sacher

Of these and other works Sacher proved to be a more than capable interpreter, continuing to conduct into his 90s. His collection of manuscripts and correspondence was preserved and expanded after the Sacher Foundation was set up in 1973. It includes Berio's *Sequenza III,* Boulez's *Le marteau sans maître,* and Stravinsky's *The Rite of Spring.*

RECOMMENDED RECORDING

STRAVINSKY, VIOLIN CONCERTO: MUTTER; PHILHARMONIA ORCHESTRA (DG).

sackbut Renaissance brass instrument, forerunner of the modern TROMBONE.

Sacre du printemps, Le *See* THE RITE OF SPRING.

Saga, En (A Saga) SYMPHONIC POEM BY JEAN SIBELIUS, OP. 9 ◉, composed in 1892 and premiered February 16, 1893, by the Helsinki Orchestral Society, the composer conducting. Sibelius revised the score in 1902. The first performance of this version was given on November 3, 1902, by the Helsinki Philharmonic conducted by Robert Kajanus.

RECOMMENDED RECORDINGS

ASHKENAZY AND PHILHARMONIA ORCHESTRA (DECCA).
JÄRVI AND GOTHENBURG SYMPHONY ORCHESTRA (BIS).

Saint-Georges, Joseph Boulogne de

(b. Baillif, Guadeloupe, December 25, 1745; d. Paris, June 9, 1799)

FRENCH SWORDSMAN, SOLDIER OF FORTUNE, AND COMPOSER. The son of a planter and an African slave, he was raised from the age of seven in France. More is known about his training as a swordsman than about his musical studies. He was 19 when he became a Gendarme de la Garde du Roi and acquired the title "Chevalier"; by the time he was 20 he was recognized as the finest fencer in France and the equal of any in Europe. Also an excellent violinist, in 1769 he was invited to join the Concert des Amateurs, then Paris's finest orchestra, under the supervision of composer François-Joseph Gossec (1734–1829). Saint-Georges became its concertmaster and, in 1773, its director. After the Amateurs was disbanded in 1781, he founded the Concert de la Loge Olympique. In 1784 or early 1785, acting as agent for the lodge's grandmaster, the Count d'Ogny, he arranged the commissioning of Haydn's six *Paris* Symphonies. Revolutionary politics and various diplomatic and military adventures kept Saint-Georges occupied during the 1790s; early in the decade he spent 18 months in prison on orders of Robespierre and later he helped quell a slave revolt in Santo Domingo.

The Chevalier de Saint-Georges's output as a composer consists of half a dozen works for the stage (mainly comic operas), several sets of string quartets, a handful of symphonies, and more than a dozen violin concertos.

RECOMMENDED RECORDINGS

COLLECTION: "LE MOZART NOIR" (INCLUDING SYMPHONIES IN G AND D, OP. 11, NOS. 1 AND 2, VIOLIN CONCERTO IN D, OP. 3, NO. 1; WORKS OF LECLAIR AND GOSSEC): LAMON AND TAFELMUSIK (CBC).

VIOLIN CONCERTOS: NISHIZAKI; MÜLLER-BRÜHL AND COLOGNE CHAMBER ORCHESTRA (NAXOS).

St. Matthew Passion *(Passio secundum Matthaeum)*

SACRED WORK FOR SOLOISTS, CHORUS, AND ORCHESTRA BY J. S. BACH, composed in 1727 and probably first performed on Good Friday, April 15, 1729. Acknowledging its extraordinary size and splendor, members of Bach's own family called it "the great Passion." It consists of 68 separate numbers, many of them in several sections, and makes use of every manner of text setting common to the sacred music of Bach's day, including recitative, arioso, aria, chorus, and chorale, treating each with incomparable finesse. The structure operates on three levels simultaneously: The actual story of the Passion is related in the recitatives and in many of the settings for the chorus (where the choristers represent the bystanders of Biblical days); the emotional significance of what is happening, from the point of view of the devout Christian of any age, is examined in a series of poetic meditations set as arias; and the participatory response of the Lutheran congregation of Bach's own day is conveyed in the chorales.

The words of the Evangelist (St. Matthew) and Jesus are set as recitative and declaimed by tenor and bass soloists respectively. Following a custom honored by both Schütz and Telemann, Bach places a "halo" of string sound around the words of Jesus, which is pointedly extinguished at the words "Eli, Eli, lama asabthani?" ("My God, my God, why hast thou foresaken me?"). The score is full of such effects: When Jesus climbs the Mount of Olives, the bass line precedes Him, and when He says, "I will smite the shepherd, and the sheep of the flock shall be scattered," the strings are sent scurrying in all directions.

What is most striking about the *St. Matthew* Passion is the intense expressiveness of its arias, most of which are in da capo form, many featuring obbligato accompaniments—typical features of

Baroque operatic style. The elevated pathos of the alto's "Erbarme dich, mein Gott" ("Have mercy, Lord"), in which a dignified sarabande rhythm and chaconne bass are fused with an intensely expressive obbligato violin solo, is unmatched anywhere in music. It is a marvelous example of Bach's skill at slipping theatrical elements into a devotional setting.

RECOMMENDED RECORDING

ROLFE JOHNSON, SCHMIDT, BONNEY, OTTER, CHANCE, CROOK; GARDINER AND ENGLISH BAROQUE SOLOISTS (DG).

Saint-Saëns, Camille

(b. Paris, October 9, 1835; d. Algiers, December 16, 1921)

FRENCH COMPOSER AND PIANIST. From about 1870 to 1890 he towered over the musical life of France on the strength of his remarkable talent, intellectual brilliance, wide-ranging interests, enormous capacity for work, and cast-iron constitution. A world traveler before the advent of aviation, he visited the United States on several occasions, spent many winters in Northern Africa, and was still hardy enough to tour South America in his ninth decade. Though born before the invention of the telegraph, he lived long enough to become the first major composer in history to write film music.

His father died when Saint-Saëns was just three months old; he was raised by his mother and his great-aunt, who began teaching him to play the piano when he was three. At ten he made his debut at the Salle Pleyel on a program that included piano concertos of Mozart and Beethoven. He had an eidetic memory, which allowed him to master not only music but a huge variety of subjects: His interests included mathematics, archaeology, astronomy, and the natural sciences. He entered the Paris Conservatoire in 1848, winning first prize

Camille Saint-Saëns

in organ in 1851 and studying composition and orchestration with Fromental Halévy. He quickly gained admission to the elite musical circles of Paris, where his talents earned the admiration of Rossini, Berlioz, Liszt, Viardot, and Gounod. In 1857 he became organist at the church of the Madeleine, and as pianist and conductor he championed the music of the new school—Wagner, Liszt, and Schumann—as well as that of the old—Bach, Handel, and Mozart. In this he was noticeably ahead of his time.

From 1861 to 1865 he taught at the École Niedermeyer, where his students included Gabriel Fauré, and in 1871 he founded the Société Nationale de Musique, which would become one of the most important organizations in French musical life over the next three decades. The 1870s and 1880s were a period of remarkable productivity, during which Saint-Saëns wrote much of his best and enduringly popular music, including the opera *SAMSON ET DALILA* (finished in 1877), the *ORGAN SYMPHONY* (1886), several tone poems, a dozen concerted works, and a clutch of chamber works, including *Le Carnaval des animaux* (*The Carnival of the Animals*; 1886). During the 1890s, he supervised the publication of a complete edition of the works of Rameau; in 1908 he wrote music for the silent film *L'assassinat du duc de Guise.* He remained active as composer and performer to the end of his life—he gave his last concert two months before he turned 86—and in later years wrote essays on a variety of subjects, including botany, ancient instruments, early music, and the works of contemporary composers.

Saint-Saëns contributed to every major genre common in the 19th century. Of his 13 operas only one, *Samson et Dalila,* retains a place in the repertoire. Following the lead of Liszt, he was the first French composer to write symphonic poems—*Le rouet d'Omphale* (1871), *Phaëton* (1873), *Danse macabre* (1874), and *La jeunesse d'Hercule* (1877). He penned five symphonies, of which two, both early compositions, remained unpublished for many years. His most important work in the form was his Symphony No. 3 in C minor, known as the *Organ* Symphony because of the prominent role assigned to that instrument. Among Saint-Saëns's other important works are concertos for piano, violin, and cello, as well as numerous shorter concerted works, including the *Introduction and Rondo capriccioso* (1863) and the *Havanaise* (1887), both for violin and orchestra.

Saint-Saëns has been judged by posterity as a reactionary. In fact, he was one of his era's most astute and eclectic musicians, thoroughly acquainted with the works of his most forward-looking contemporaries. If he was more a consolidator than a pioneer, he nonetheless remained true to the spirit and traditions of French music by fusing the best of the new and old and by exhibiting consummate craftsmanship and a sensitive ear for sonority in all his works.

RECOMMENDED RECORDINGS

Le Carnaval des animaux: Bernstein and New York Philharmonic (Sony).

Piano concertos (complete): Hough; Oramo and City of Birmingham Symphony Orchestra (Hyperion).

Samson et Dalila: Domingo, Obraztsova, Bruson, Thau; Barenboim and Orchestre de Paris (DG).

Symphonies (complete): Martinon and French National Radio Orchestra (EMI).

Symphony No. 3 (*Organ* Symphony): Munch and Boston Symphony Orchestra (RCA).

Tone poems, *Introduction and Rondo Capriccioso, Havanaise*: Chung; Dutoit and Royal Philharmonic Orchestra (Decca).

Salerno-Sonnenberg, Nadja

(b. Rome, January 10, 1961)

American violinist. She emigrated to the United States with her family at the age of eight. She studied at the Curtis Institute and continued her work at the Juilliard School with Dorothy DeLay. Her career was launched when she won the Naumburg International Violin Competition in 1981; at the time, she was the youngest artist ever to receive the award. She has been the recipient of two other significant awards, an Avery Fisher career grant in 1983, and the Avery Fisher Prize in 1999. A favorite of the media, in part because of her cultivation of a renegade image, Salerno-Sonnenberg has made efforts to undo the mystique of the artistic persona by reaching out to a larger

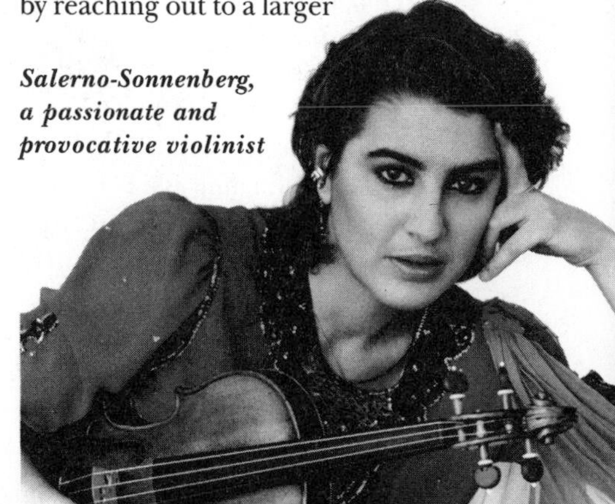

Salerno-Sonnenberg, a passionate and provocative violinist

audience through television appearances ranging from documentaries and children's programs to late-night talk shows. A violinist of undisputed gifts, her interpretations are intense and flamboyant, sometimes reckless, self-indulgent, and lacking in stylistic discernment. Her stage manner tends toward the histrionic, and she is given to miming the music as well as playing it, distracting some listeners even as she entertains many others. She has appeared with many of the world's major orchestras and has recorded widely. In 2005 she launched her own record label, NSS Music.

RECOMMENDED RECORDING

MENDELSSOHN, VIOLIN CONCERTO IN E MINOR (WITH WORKS OF SAINT-SAËNS AND MASSENET): SCHWARZ AND NEW YORK CHAMBER SYMPHONY (EMI).

Salieri, Antonio

(b. Legnago, August 18, 1750; d. Vienna, May 7, 1825)

ITALIAN COMPOSER. He studied violin and keyboard in his native town, continuing his musical education in Venice after the deaths of his parents around 1765. He became a protégé of the composer Florian Leopold Gassmann (1729–74), who brought him to Vienna, taught him composition, and introduced him to such important figures in the musical life of the Hapsburg capital as Metastasio, Gluck, and Emperor Joseph II; the music-loving monarch became one of his most enthusiastic supporters. Following several successful efforts in the comic vein, Salieri made his name as a composer of opera seria with *Armida,* which met with resounding acclaim at its Vienna premiere in 1771. In 1774 Salieri succeeded Gassmann as court composer and became head of the Italian opera in Vienna. In 1788 he became court Kapellmeister, a title he held until his retirement in 1824. Thanks to his talent and connections, Salieri also enjoyed considerable success in Paris during the 1780s. With the support of Gluck and the emperor (whose sister was Marie Antoinette), Salieri undertook the composition of *Les Danaïdes,* a five-act *tragédie lyrique,* and presided over its premiere at the Paris Opéra in 1784. That led to the commission for *Tarare,* with a libretto by Beaumarchais, which was an even greater hit at its premiere in 1787. Following Salieri's return to Vienna, Joseph commissioned an Italian version of *Tarare,* titled *Axur, re d'Ormus,* with a libretto by Lorenzo da Ponte; it received its premiere in 1788 and by 1805 had been performed more than 100 times in Vienna. None of Salieri's subsequent efforts enjoyed that degree of popularity, but he continued to produce works for the Viennese stage until 1804 and composed a good deal of sacred music after that.

Salieri in silhouette

At the time Salieri was active, the vast difference in quality between his best work and Mozart's best work was not as apparent as it is today. Salieri's music was rightly admired: It appealed to the tastes of the day, was easily assimilated, and made few demands. As one of the most highly placed musicians in Vienna during Mozart's ten years there (1781–91), Salieri almost certainly aroused more envy in Mozart than Mozart did in him; indeed, the Italian could afford to be, and often was, generous in the praise of his younger colleague's music. In 1789 he arranged for the first performance of Mozart's Clarinet Quintet and, in April 1791, he may well have conducted the Vienna premiere of one of Mozart's last symphonies—most likely No. 39 or 40—for it is known that a "grand symphony" by Mozart was played under Salieri's direction by an orchestra that included the brother clarinetists Anton and Johann Stadler. It is not known how the rumor originated that Salieri poisoned Mozart, though Mozart's own son dismissed it as false in 1829. That did not keep Pushkin from embracing the notion in his verse play *Mozart and Salieri* (1830) or Peter Shaffer from embellishing it still further in *Amadeus* (1984).

F. Murray Abraham as Salieri in **Amadeus**

In his later years Salieri devoted much of his time to teaching, passing along what he had learned about counterpoint, theory, and Italian vocal style to younger musicians, among them Beethoven, Schubert, and Liszt.

RECOMMENDED RECORDINGS

OVERTURES:

BÄMERT AND LONDON MOZART PLAYERS (CHANDOS).

DITTRICH AND SLOVAK RADIO SYMPHONY ORCHESTRA (NAXOS).

Salome **OPERA IN ONE ACT BY RICHARD STRAUSS,** to Hedwig Lachmann's German translation of the play by Oscar Wilde, premiered December 9, 1905, at the Dresden Court Opera. In spite of the difficulty of the music and the story's graphic portrayal of sexual perversity (which caused the work to be banned when Mahler tried to perform it in Vienna), the premiere was an overwhelming success. The score contains some of the most virtuosic, suggestive, and complex music ever penned, and Strauss's mastery of the orchestra is apparent on every page of it. His music is at its most febrile in portraying the distorted exoticism of Salome, the adolescent princess of Judea who covets the body of John the Baptist and becomes the instrument of his doom when he refuses her advances. Her insatiable desire is conveyed in music that scales the heights of passion, while the lurid necrophilia of her deranged final moments calls forth an orchestral paroxysm of operatically unprecedented magnitude. Jochanaan (as the Baptist is known in German) is himself a disturbing mix of madness and evangelical fervor, his solo pronouncements a blend of Lutheran chorale and the sepulchral tones of the Commendatore in *Don Giovanni.* The hasty, fast-talking Herod, haunted by phantasms of guilt and desire, is portrayed in music of fawning opulence; his wife, the spiteful Herodias, in much harsher tones.

The scene painting for which Strauss achieved celebrity in his symphonic poems is lifted to a new level in *Salome,* with passages such as those representing Herod slipping in a pool of blood or describing a wind that feels "like the beating of vast wings" strewn throughout the score. The luxurious pages of "THE DANCE OF THE SEVEN VEILS" set a new standard of symphonic eroticism ◉, and Strauss goes out of his way to get the severing of the Baptist's head just right: The score calls for repeated muffled high B-flats from a solo double bass, with the string pinched off by the thumb and forefinger so that the emerging sound, meant to represent the tendons of Jochanaan's neck being cut one by one, resembles "the suppressed, choked moaning of a woman." The composer's wish that Salome come across as "a 16-year-old princess with the voice of an Isolde" has rarely been fulfilled, but famous exponents of the role have included the devastatingly good-looking Finnish soprano Aïno Ackté, the sultry Ljuba Welitsch, and the steely Birgit Nilsson, as well as Maria Cebotari and Leonie Rysanek.

RECOMMENDED RECORDINGS

BEHRENS, BALTSA, BÖHM, VAN DAM; KARAJAN AND VIENNA PHILHARMONIC (EMI).

NILSSON, HOFFMAN, STOLZE, WAECHTER; SOLTI AND VIENNA PHILHARMONIC (DECCA).

Salomon, Johann Peter

(b. Bonn, February 20, 1745; d. London, November 28, 1815)

GERMAN VIOLINIST, COMPOSER, AND IMPRESARIO. The son of an oboist and court musician, he entered the ranks of musicians in service to the Bonn court in 1758, when he was 13. He subsequently held a position in Rheinsberg as music director to Prince Heinrich of Prussia. He moved to England in 1781 and became a concert promoter. In 1790, following the death of Joseph Haydn's patron, Prince Nikolaus Esterházy, the quick-thinking Salomon engaged Haydn for a series of six London concerts, with a new symphony to be performed at each. Salomon's offer required Haydn to travel to the English capital to supervise the performances; Salomon himself served as the orchestra's concertmaster. Haydn's first London sojourn, from early 1791 until the summer of 1792, was so successful that Salomon invited him back two years later on the same terms. As the catalyst in the composition of Haydn's 12 *London* symphonies, Salomon played a supporting role of immense importance in the history of music. He was rewarded not only with fame and fortune, but with a solo part in the finale to Haydn's Symphony No. 98 in B-flat, the solo violin part in Haydn's *Sinfonia concertante,* also in B-flat, and the six string quartets of Haydn's Opp. 71 and 74, dedicated to Count Apponyi but intended for Salomon and his quartet.

RECOMMENDED RECORDING

ENGLISH SONGS AND DUETS: KIRKBY, MÜLLER, ROBERTS, KELLY (WITH SONGS BY HAYDN, ARNOLD, OTHERS) (HYPERION).

Salonen, Esa-Pekka

(b. Helsinki, June 30, 1958)

FINNISH CONDUCTOR AND COMPOSER. He studied horn, conducting, and composition at the Sibelius Academy in Helsinki during the 1970s and made his conducting debut with the Finnish Radio Symphony Orchestra in 1979. He spent the next two years in Italy studying composition with Franco Donatoni and Niccolò Castiglioni. In 1983 he stepped in on short notice to conduct Mahler's Symphony No. 3 with the Philharmonia Orchestra of London and became an overnight sensation. His American debut, with the Los Angeles Philharmonic, followed in 1984 and he signed a recording contract with Sony in 1985. He became music director of the Los Angeles Philharmonic in the fall of 1992; he has also served as principal guest conductor of the Philharmonia (1985–94), and principal conductor of the Swedish Radio Symphony Orchestra (1985–95).

Esa-Pekka Salonen, Finnish conductor-composer

Known for his lively intellect and adventurous programming, Salonen has focused strongly on 20th-century classics in his work in Los Angeles. Early in his career he indulged a love of big pieces, but had a tendency to get carried away; over the last decade he has developed into a more authoritative presence on the podium, displaying a good ear for timbres and a precise, supple technique in his thoughtfully shaped interpretations. On disc he has given outstanding accounts of orchestral works by Sibelius, Nielsen, Mahler, Debussy, Bartók, and Revueltas; he has also made landmark recordings of Ligeti's opera *Le grand macabre*, Lutosławski's Symphony No. 3, and assorted works by Finnish composers Kaija Saariaho (b. 1952) and Magnus Lindberg (b. 1958). In order to devote more time to his own composing, Salonen took a sabbatical from his Los Angeles post during 2000. His output includes a song cycle for soprano and 14 instruments titled *Five Images After Sappho* (1999) and a small but growing number of orchestral and instrumental works. Among his recent compositions are his *L.A. Variations* (1997, commissioned by the Los Angeles Philharmonic), *Gambit* (1998, an orchestral piece composed as a 40th birthday present for Lindberg), and the cello concerto *Mania* (2000). In 2005, Salonen's contract with the Los Angeles Philharmonic was extended through the end of the 2007–08 season, with an evergreen clause to take effect following that season.

RECOMMENDED RECORDINGS

AS CONDUCTOR:

LINDBERG, *KRAFT*, PIANO CONCERTO: FINNISH RADIO SYMPHONY ORCHESTRA (ONDINE).

PROKOFIEV, VIOLIN CONCERTOS NOS. 1 AND 2: LIN; LOS ANGELES PHILHARMONIC (SONY).

REVUELTAS, ORCHESTRAL AND ENSEMBLE WORKS: LOS ANGELES PHILHARMONIC (SONY).

AS COMPOSER:

L.A. VARIATIONS, *FIVE IMAGES AFTER SAPPHO*, OTHER WORKS: UPSHAW; SALONEN AND LOS ANGELES PHILHARMONIC, LONDON SINFONIETTA (SONY).

Salón México, El ORCHESTRAL WORK BY AARON COPLAND composed in 1933–36 and premiered in Mexico City on August 27, 1937, by the Mexico Symphony Orchestra, Carlos Chávez conducting. Its raw material consists of Mexican songs and dance tunes that Copland drew from two different collections. In form, the piece resembles a scherzo. It has a bold, energetic opening section followed by a slower serenade-like episode full of the sultry atmosphere of a down-and-dirty dance hall. A gradual quickening of the pace leads to a return of the bright, brassy music of the opening, and a convulsive climax. The piece got its name from El Salón México, a Harlem-style dance hall in Mexico City that Copland visited in 1932.

RECOMMENDED RECORDINGS

BERNSTEIN AND NEW YORK PHILHARMONIC (SONY).

KOUSSEVITZKY AND BOSTON SYMPHONY ORCHESTRA (PEARL).

Salzburg Festival ANNUAL SUMMER FESTIVAL OF MUSIC AND DRAMA IN AUSTRIA, inaugurated in 1920. The idea of situating a festival in Salzburg took shape during the last two decades of the 19th century and the first decade of the 20th; between 1879 and 1910 a number of special-occasion festivals were organized in Salzburg under the leadership of conductors Hans Richter, Felix Mottl, Arthur Nikisch, Felix Weingartner, Gustav Mahler, and Richard Strauss. Plans to open a regular summer festival in 1914 had to be shelved as a result of the outbreak of World War I. Following the war the movement to establish a permanent festival was quickly advanced by a council of artistic visionaries, including Strauss, the stage director Max Reinhardt, scenic designer Alfred Roller, the playwright Hugo von Hofmannsthal, and Franz Schalk, the artistic director of the Vienna Staatsoper. For these five figures, led by Reinhardt, the nascent Salzburg Festival had a moral as well as a cultural mission. The first production, on August 20, 1920, was of *Jedermann* (*Everyman*), Hofmannsthal's dramatic adaptation of the English medieval morality play. It was performed on the steps and in the

A scene from Hoffmansthal's **Jedermann** *at the Salzburg Festival, 1996*

square of the Salzburg Cathedral, a tradition that has been maintained ever since.

From the start, Mozart, Salzburg's greatest native son, and Strauss, from nearby Bavaria, have been at the heart of the festival's offerings, and the Vienna Philharmonic has been its main musical engine. The first operatic productions were mounted in 1922. A major venue, the Festspielhaus, was opened in 1925, and enlarged the following year; there were further alterations in 1937 and 1939. The Salzburg Festival experienced a glorious era during the 1930s, with memorable performances conducted by Bruno Walter, Arturo Toscanini, Fritz Busch, Erich Kleiber, and Otto Klemperer. After the Anschluss in 1938, these conductors and many other artists were unable, or unwilling, to perform in Austria. Salzburg's offerings shrank during World War II, and because of wartime austerity measures the festival was canceled in 1944.

Activity resumed in 1945. In 1956, Herbert von Karajan was appointed the festival's artistic director, a position he held until a year before his death in 1989. Like Reinhardt, Karajan exerted an enormous influence on the character of the festival. He started an Easter Festival in 1967, for which the resident orchestra was his own Berlin Philharmonic, and presided over most of the summer festival's operatic offerings. During his tenure, the festival grew to become the darling not only of wealthy jet-setters but also of record companies, which contributed greatly to its commercial prospects.

After Karajan's death, the festival named Gérard Mortier (b. 1943) as artistic director, effective in 1991. Mortier radicalized programming at Salzburg in a way that was not to traditionalists' taste, bringing in productions of challenging 20th-century works such as Schoenberg's *Moses und Aron,* Berg's *Lulu,* Bartók's *Bluebeard's Castle,* and Janáček's *From the House of the Dead,* as well as unconventional stagings of standard repertoire—a clear departure from Karajan's typical slate of Mozart, Verdi, and Strauss. It can be argued that Mortier was simply trying to bring the festival back to its founding ideals and make it more relevant to its times, but his manner was every bit as imperious as Karajan's. In 2002 the German composer and arts administrator Peter Ruzicka (b. 1948) was summoned to succeed Mortier and put the festival back on a more traditional footing. He presented a five-year plan—through 2006, the 250th anniversary of Mozart's birth—focusing again on Mozart and Strauss and restoring the Vienna Philharmonic to a place of honor; in March of 2004, Ruzicka declared that he would step down at the end of the 2006 festival, and the festival announced that the director Jürgen Flimm (b. 1941) would succeed him.

Sammartini, Giovanni Battista

(b. Milan, 1700 or 1701; d. Milan, January 15, 1775)

ITALIAN COMPOSER AND ORGANIST. His father, Alexis Saint-Martin, was a French-born oboist who had emigrated to Italy. Sammartini studied with his father and was active as an oboist in the early years of his career. In 1728 he was appointed *maestro di cappella* for the Congregazione del Santissimo Entierro in Milan, in which post he continued to serve until shortly before his death; in 1768 he also became *maestro di cappella* to the ducal court. It is possible, though not certain, that between 1737 and 1741 he taught Christoph Willibald Gluck; in 1770, he befriended the young Wolfgang Mozart. Sammartini was one of the early masters of the symphony. In addition to composing at least 70 works in that nascent form—and thereby helping to imbue it with the Italianate liveliness that remained part of its character through the works of Mozart—he also wrote three operas, a number of concerti grossi, and reams of church music and chamber music. Altogether, his output totaled close to 2,000 compositions, many of which are now lost.

RECOMMENDED RECORDINGS

CONCERTOS FOR FLUTE, OBOE, HARPSICHORD: I MUSICI AMBROSIANI (DYNAMIC 2000).

SYMPHONY IN A (WITH CONCERTI GROSSI BY CORELLI, SCARLATTI, OTHERS): CAPPELLA ISTROPOLITANA (NAXOS).

Samson et Dalila **OPERA IN THREE ACTS BY CAMILLE SAINT-SAËNS,** to a libretto by Ferdinand Lemaire, premiered December 2, 1877, at the Ducal Theater in Weimar in a production mounted by Franz Liszt. The work received its belated premiere at the Paris Opéra in 1892. Saint-Saëns originally conceived of *Samson et Dalila* as an oratorio, which may partially account for its weaknesses as a piece of theater: The action is remarkably static and little in the way of character development occurs at any point. Nonetheless, much of the music is first-rate, and with only four important roles to worry about, Saint-Saëns was able to achieve a feeling of intimacy without sacrificing the grand-opera backdrop that makes the piece a favorite of audiences everywhere. Dalila's "Mon coeur s'ouvre à ta voix" is one of the finest arias in the mezzo-soprano playbook, ravishingly seductive. The opera's final scene is particularly outsized. It includes an extravagant bacchanale ◉ that is one of the greatest ballet sequences in opera, and it closes with nothing less than the collapse of the Temple of Dagon, as Samson calls on God for strength to vanquish his enemy—a scene that either astonishes and delights, or provokes titters, depending on the production.

RECOMMENDED RECORDINGS

DOMINGO, MEIER, RAMEY, FONDARY; CHUNG AND ORCHESTRE DE L'OPÉRA-BASTILLE (EMI).

DOMINGO, OBRAZTSOVA, BRUSON, THAU; BARENBOIM AND ORCHESTRE DE PARIS (DG).

San Francisco Opera **OPERA COMPANY INCORPORATED IN 1923.** It is the second oldest opera company in continuous operation in the United States. Gaetano Merola, recruited from Naples, who had previously worked at the Metropolitan Opera in New York, founded the company and served for 30 seasons as its general manager and principal conductor. Performances were initially given in the San Francisco Civic Auditorium; in 1932 the War Memorial Opera House (designed by Arthur Brown, architect of Coit Tower and San Francisco's City Hall) became the company's permanent home. In the years since Merola's death in 1953, the company has been led by Kurt Herbert Adler (1953–81), Terence A. McEwen (1982–87), Lotfi Mansouri (1988–2001), and Pamela Rosenberg, who in 2004 announced that she would step down in July 2006, at the expiration of her contract. David Gockley, for many years the director of the Houston Grand Opera, will take over at that time. On Rosenberg's watch the company moved to the forefront of the contemporary opera scene, giving the U.S. premieres of Messiaen's *Saint François d'Assise* in 2002, and Ligeti's *Le grand macabre* (sung in English) in 2004.

La traviata ***at the San Francisco Opera***

The American stage premiere of John Adams's *Doctor Atomic* took place in October 2005.

Currently the second largest opera company in the country, the San Francisco Opera has presented almost every major opera star in leading roles over the decades. Its high production values and musical standards make it one of the most respected establishments in the world. In 1983 (ten years before the Met), San Francisco became one of the first important companies to use English supertitles, now a routine fixture in American houses. In 1992 Mansouri introduced Pacific Visions, an ambitious program to commission new operas and present unusual and neglected repertoire. Since its inception, Pacific Visions has commissioned *Dangerous Liaisons* (1994) by Conrad Susa (b. 1935) and librettist Philip Littell; *Harvey Milk* (1996) by Stewart Wallace (b. 1960) and librettist Michael Korie (coproduced with the Houston Grand Opera and New York City Opera); *A Streetcar Named Desire* (1999) by André Previn and librettist Philip Littell, after the play by Tennessee Williams; and *Dead Man Walking* (2001) by Jake Heggie (b. 1961) and librettist Terrence McNally, after the book by Sister Helen Prejean.

Portrait of Sarasate by Felix Moscheles, 1879

sarabande Elegant, sinuous dance in slow triple time. Of Spanish origin, it was one of the standard dances of the suite during the 17th and 18th centuries. Bach's cello suites contain some of the most beautiful sarabandes ever written; the second movement of Mozart's *Jupiter* Symphony, with its courtly passion, offers a remarkably speculative treatment of the dance. *See also* SUITE.

Sarasate, Pablo de

(b. Pamplona, March 10, 1844; d. Biarritz, September 20, 1908)

SPANISH VIOLINIST AND COMPOSER. He began his study of the violin with his father, an artillery bandmaster, at the age of five and gave his first concert when he was eight. In 1856, after further study in Madrid, Sarasate and his mother set out for Paris in hopes of his gaining a spot in the class of Jean Alard at the Conservatoire; along the way, Sarasate's mother suffered a fatal heart attack and he became infected with cholera. The Spanish consul in Bayonne took the lad into his home until he recovered and financed the continuation of his journey to Paris. After hearing the youngster play, Alard became his teacher. The following year Sarasate won first prize in violin and solfège, and in 1859 he took a prize in harmony.

In the years that followed, Sarasate enjoyed a thriving career as a touring virtuoso and became one of the most famous musicians of his era. With his assured technique (which made his playing of even the most difficult pieces seemingly effortless) and a tone that was pure and sweet, if not particularly powerful, he represented a new breed of virtuoso. Many of the 19th century's most dashing works for the violin were composed for or dedicated to him, including Saint-Saëns's Violin Concertos Nos. 1 (1859) and 3 (1880), as well as his *Introduction and Rondo capriccioso* (1863), Lalo's *Symphonie espagnole* (1874), Bruch's Violin Concerto No. 2 (1878) and *Scottish* Fantasy (1880), and Wieniawski's Violin Concerto No. 2 (1862). Sarasate's own accomplishments as a composer included numerous works for violin and piano, though no concertos. His best-known work is *Zigeunerweisen* (*Gypsy Ways*), originally written for violin and piano, later orchestrated and published as his Op. 20 in Leipzig in 1878 (hence the German title). The brief rhapsody, one of the cornerstones of the virtuoso repertoire, is in three broad sections: a smoldering introduction in the best Hungarian café style; a slow, lyrical interlude; and a fulminant final dance that brings the piece to a brilliant conclusion. In 1884 the violinist's sultry elegance was immortalized by James McNeill Whistler in the portrait *Arrangement in Black: Pablo de Sarasate*.

RECOMMENDED RECORDINGS

Carmen Fantasy (with Paganini, Violin Concerto No. 1): Perlman; Foster and Royal Philharmonic Orchestra (EMI).

Zigeunerweisen: Heifetz; Steinberg and RCA Victor Symphony Orchestra (RCA).

Zigeunerweisen (with Wieniawski violin concertos): Shaham; Foster and London Symphony Orchestra (DG).

Satie, Erik

(b. Honfleur, May 17, 1866; d. Paris, July 1, 1925)

French composer. He had a difficult childhood: his mother died when he was six, and he was raised for a while by his paternal grandparents, then his grandmother died, then his father remarried. Satie's stepmother, a headstrong woman with musical interests, enrolled him in the Paris Conservatoire in 1879. He spent seven miserable years there, was a mediocre student, and eventually flunked out. In 1887 he left home and began living a bohemian life in Montmartre, hanging out in cabarets and styling himself an *artiste*. In 1898 he moved to Arcueil, on the southern outskirts of Paris, where he lived for the rest of his life in a sparsely furnished apartment. During the early 1900s he worked as a café pianist, walking the six miles into Paris every day and returning in the early-morning hours by train.

Erik Satie, postcard caricature by E. Renaudin

In 1905, hoping to improve his technique as a composer, Satie went back to "school"—this time the Schola Cantorum—to study counterpoint with Albert Roussel (his junior by three years) and composition and orchestration with Vincent d'Indy. He emerged from artistic obscurity in 1911 when Maurice Ravel played his three *Sarabandes* (1887) at a concert of the Société Musicale Indépendente; he came to be seen as a "precursor" of Ravel and Claude Debussy—who by then were ruling the roost in French musical life. With the public awakened, Satie produced between 1912 and 1917 a series of humorous piano works with strange names, e.g., *Vieux séquins et vieilles cuirasses* (*Old Coins and Old Armor*; 1914), continuing a conceit he had inaugurated with his three GYMNOPÉDIES (1888), six *Gnossiennes* (1889–97), and *Trois morceaux en forme de poire* (*Three Pieces in the Shape of a Pear,* consisting of seven pieces; 1903). After 1915 Satie received a major push from Jean Cocteau, who arranged for Diaghilev's Ballets Russes to commission *Parade* (1917), with story line by Cocteau, sets by Pablo Picasso, and choreography by Léonide Massine. The ballet, with its café-style music, was a succès de scandale. Out of this emerged, circa 1920 (with Cocteau serving as godfather), LES SIX, a Satie fan club of young composers. In the years that followed, Satie attempted unsuccessfully to come up with another ballet hit, joined the Communist Party, and had a fling with the Dada movement. He died of cirrhosis of the liver.

Until the 1960s, when his piano music made a comeback, Satie was viewed as the court jester of the early-20th-century Parisian musical scene—impoverished, barely professional, meriting little more than a dismissive smirk. Even Debussy treated him more like a lapdog than a friend. In some ways Satie was naive (in his basic ideas and their excessive repetition, and certainly in his grasp of musical structure), but he was insistent in a characteristically modern manner, and original in a way that, while not shocking, got under people's skin. It is clear that his *Sarabandes* had an influence on Debussy's much later *La cathédrale engloutie* (*The Sunken Cathedral*; 1910) as well as on pieces such as the sarabande from *Pour le piano* (1901); also clear is the debt Ravel's piano music owes to his. Satie's appropriation of music-hall elements anticipated Poulenc and others, and the sarcastic, cryptic, epigrammatic, and quasi-ecclesiastical trappings of his style found many echoes later in the 20th century.

Satie in later years

RECOMMENDED RECORDINGS

PARADE: DORATI AND LONDON SYMPHONY ORCHESTRA (MERCURY).

PIANO MUSIC (COMPLETE): CICCOLINI (EMI).

PIANO MUSIC (SELECTIONS): CICCOLINI (EMI).

PIANO MUSIC (SELECTIONS): ROGÉ (DECCA).

Satyagraha **OPERA IN THREE ACTS BY PHILIP GLASS,** to a libretto by the composer and Constance DeJong, premiered September 5, 1980, by the Netherlands Opera in Rotterdam. The opera examines Gandhi's development of a philosophy of nonviolent resistance—informed by the concept of *satyagraha* ("truth force")—during his years as a young lawyer in South Africa (1893–1914). The emergence of Gandhi's idea is seen through the lens of three guardian figures, one for each act, who observe the action silently, but, by their very presence, comment upon it: Leo Tolstoy, Rabindranath Tagore, and Martin Luther King Jr. The work incorporates six singing roles, a chorus of 40, and an orchestra consisting of strings, woodwinds, and organ.

Douglas Perry as Gandhi in **Satyagraha**

RECOMMENDED RECORDING

Perry, McFarland, Cummings, Reeve; Keene and New York City Opera (Sony).

Saul **Oratorio by George Frideric Handel,** to a text by Charles Jennens based on the Old Testament books of I Samuel and II Samuel, composed in 1738 and premiered January 16, 1739, at the King's Theatre Haymarket in London. The story focuses on King Saul's jealousy over David's popularity after his defeat of Goliath. When the King's attempt to kill the young upstart fails, Saul asks the Witch of Endor to summon the spirit of the prophet Samuel, who tells him that the following day both he and his son will be killed in a great battle and, inevitably, David will inherit the kingdom of Israel.

RECOMMENDED RECORDINGS

Davies, Scholl, Padmore, Argenta; McCreesh and Gabrieli Players (DG).

Dawson, Holton, Ainsley, Brown; Gardiner and English Baroqu e Soloists (Polygram).

Joshua, Zazzo, Ovenden, Bell, Saks; Jacobs and Concerto Köln (harmonia mundi).

Savall, Jordi

(b. Barcelona, August 1, 1941)

Catalan viol player and conductor. He has effectively reinstated the viola da gamba and its repertoire in the modern era. As a cellist in Barcelona, he came across the music of French Baroque composer Marin Marais (1656–1728), and in 1965 went in search of the instrument for which it was written. He studied treatises and microfilm of period manuscripts in order to learn the performance practices of the time. In 1968 he went to the Schola Cantorum Basiliensis in Switzerland and studied with August Wenziger, whom he succeeded as the institute's teacher of viola da gamba in 1974. Also that year, with his wife, soprano Montserrat Figueras, and two colleagues, he founded the ensemble Hespèrion XX to bring pre-Classical music, particularly that of the Iberian peninsula, back to life. (He updated the name to Hespèrion XXI at the turn of the century.) In 1987, he founded the vocal ensemble La Capella Reial de Catalunya, and in 1989 he launched yet another group, the period instrument orchestra Le Concert des Nations, dedicated to performing music of the Baroque and Classical periods. These three ensembles have enabled Savall to present an extraordinary amount of repertoire, ranging from medieval fiddle music, the swinging ensaladas of Matheo Flecha (ca. 1530–1604), and the viol concerts of William Lawes (1602–45) to the masses of Victoria and the symphonies of Beethoven, always in an energetic, informed, and committed fashion.

Savall directed and performed the music for Alain Corneau's 1991 film *Tous les matins du monde,* starring Gérard Depardieu—a dark tale about Marais and his teacher, the 17th century gambist-composer Jean de Sainte-Colombe (fl. 1658–87). Savall's soulful playing on that soundtrack brought the viol new exposure and popularity, encouraging a new generation of players to take it up. Savall and his ensemble colleagues (whose number now includes his daughter, Arianna, and son, Ferran) have made dozens of recordings. In 1998, Savall established his own label, Alia Vox.

RECOMMENDED RECORDINGS

"LES VOIX HUMAINES": WORKS FOR SOLO VIOLA DA GAMBA BY BACH, FORQUERAY, MARAIS, TELEMANN, OTHERS (ALIA VOX).

"TOUS LES MATINS DU MONDE" (FILM SOUNDTRACK): WORKS BY COUPERIN, LULLY, MARAIS, SAINTE-COLOMBE, SAVALL, OTHERS; SAVALL AND LE CONCERT DES NATIONS (VALOIS).

Sawallisch, Wolfgang

(b. Munich, August 26, 1923)

GERMAN CONDUCTOR AND PIANIST. His education at the Munich Hochschule für Musik was interrupted by World War II; he graduated in 1947 and took up his first appointment as a *répétiteur* in Augsburg. In 1953, at the age of 30, he was appointed director of the opera in Aachen, making him the youngest general music director in Germany. He next held top posts in Wiesbaden (1958–60) and Cologne (1960–63), and was engaged to conduct at the Bayreuth Festival from 1957 to 1961. He served as principal conductor of the Vienna Symphony (1960–70), and subsequently of L'Orchestre de la Suisse Romande (1970–80). His career in Germany reached its apogee with his two-decade tenure as general music director of the Bavarian State Opera in Munich (1971–92), during which he restored its reputation as one of the finest houses in the world.

Wolfgang Sawallisch at work with orchestra

Sawallisch became music director of the Philadelphia Orchestra in 1993, succeeding Riccardo Muti, and remained in that post for ten years. His efforts to make the orchestra sound leaner and cleaner—i.e., more like a German ensemble—were misguided and only partly successful.

Throughout his career as a conductor, Sawallisch continued to work, when his schedule allowed, as an accompanist and chamber music partner. Over the years he appeared in recital with Dietrich Fischer-Dieskau and Elisabeth Schwarzkopf, and made several fine recordings of the lieder repertoire. His catalog as an opera conductor is extensive; one of his earliest recordings, of Richard Strauss's *Capriccio* with an all-star cast headed by Schwarzkopf, remains legendary. Also notable are his recordings of Strauss's *Die Frau ohne Schatten* and Mozart's *Die Zauberflöte* with the Bavarian State Opera. A thoughtful and comprehensive musician, Sawallisch has been an outstanding exponent of the German and Austrian repertoire, particularly the operas of Mozart and Richard Strauss, and the symphonic works of Beethoven, Schumann, Brahms, and Strauss.

RECOMMENDED RECORDINGS

MOZART, *DIE ZAUBERFLÖTE*: ROTHENBERGER, MOSER, SCHREIER, BERRY, MOLL; BAVARIAN STATE OPERA (EMI).

SCHUMANN, SYMPHONIES (COMPLETE): STAATSKAPELLE DRESDEN (EMI).

STRAUSS, *CAPRICCIO*: SCHWARZKOPF, WAECHTER, GEDDA, FISCHER-DIESKAU, HOTTER; PHILHARMONIA ORCHESTRA (EMI).

saxophone Single-reed wind instrument invented by the Belgian-born instrument builder Adolphe Sax (1814–94) around 1840 and patented in 1846. Modern saxophones come in a variety of sizes, the most common of which are soprano, alto, tenor, and baritone (sopranino, bass, and contrabass models also exist, but are rarely used). The body of the instrument is made of metal, usually brass, and has a conical bore. The mouthpiece and key system resemble those of the clarinet.

Sax got his start building standard varieties of wind instruments. His skill was such that in 1830, when he was 15, flutes and clarinets he had made in his father's workshop were shown at the Brussels Industrial Exhibition. In 1838 he patented a bass clarinet superior to any then in existence. By the time he moved to Paris in 1842, he had developed two entirely new instrumental families: the saxophone and the saxhorn, a valved brass instrument intended primarily for military use. The impetus for both may have been the declining standards of French military music of the day. Recognizing the business potential, Sax went at the problem with singular energy. He prodded the French government into setting up a commission; in 1845 a competition was held between a small band, using Sax's instruments under his direction, and a much larger one of conventional disposition. Sax's band carried the day and he acquired what was, in effect, a monopoly in French military music.

While Sax intended the saxophone for a military career, he was aware that support from mainstream musicians would be valuable to its survival. One of the first composers he approached on his arrival in Paris was Hector Berlioz, who expressed interest, as did Giacomo Meyerbeer and Fromental Halévy (1799–1862), the grand duo at the Paris Opéra. It was ultimately through opera that the saxophone came into the hands of classical musicians. The Alsatian-born composer Jean-Georges Kastner (1810–67) included a solo for it in his 1844 opera *Le dernier roi di Juda*, the first "official" use of the instrument; he also wrote a sextet for saxophones that year. Before long, parts for saxophone had appeared in operas by Meyerbeer, Bizet, Massenet, and Ambroise Thomas (1811–96). It took a bit longer for the saxophone to gain a foothold in the concert repertoire. The first composer to include a part for saxophone in a symphony was the American William Henry Fry (1813–64), who did so in his *Santa Claus* Symphony of 1853; more frequently encountered orchestral works with parts for saxophone include Bizet's incidental music for *L'Arlésienne* ◉, Ravel's orchestration of Mussorgsky's *Pictures at an Exhibition*, Rachmaninov's *Symphonic Dances*, Walton's *Belshazzar's Feast*, Prokofiev's *Romeo and Juliet*, and Britten's *Sinfonia da Requiem*. Ferde Grofé's symphonic orchestration of Gershwin's *Rhapsody in Blue* calls for three saxophones, as does Ravel's *Boléro*. Several concerted works for saxophone have established themselves in the repertoire, of which the most notable are Debussy's *Rhapsody*, the concertos by Glazunov and Ingolf Dahl (1912–70), and Ibert's *Concertino*.

Only after it had been accepted in the classical sphere did jazz discover the saxophone and transform its sound, character, and reputation, in particular via the swing bands of the 1930s and 1940s.

Sayão, Bidú

(b. Rio de Janeiro, May 11, 1902; d. Lincoln, Me., March 12, 1999)

BRAZILIAN SOPRANO. Named Balduina de Oliveira Sayão after her grandmother, she adopted her mother's nickname, Bidú.

Plans to become an actress were discouraged by her family, so she turned to singing, studying with the Romanian soprano Elena Teodorini. After an early debut at 18 (as Donizetti's Lucia) at Rio's Teatro Municipal, she followed Teodorini to Europe, eventually going to Nice to train with the renowned Polish tenor Jean de Reszke, whom she later credited for her ability to blend words and sound into an integrated whole. She returned to Rio in 1925, making a well-received second debut in 1926 as Rosina in Rossini's *Il barbiere di Siviglia.* Between that time and 1937, the year of her Metropolitan Opera debut, she sang throughout Italy, in Paris, and in her native Rio. Arturo Toscanini, who had heard her in Milan as Violetta in Verdi's *La traviata,* engaged her for a 1936 New York Philharmonic performance of Debussy's *La damoiselle élue* at Carnegie Hall; her success in that engagement led directly to her 1937 Met debut as Massenet's Manon. In 16 seasons at the Met she performed a number of lyric and coloratura roles, including Susanna, Mimì, Violetta, Juliette, and Mélisande. Hers was a silvery, refined sound, small but focused, and her ability to breathe dramatic life into characters comic or tragic earned her a reputation as a fine singing actress.

Sayão was an avid recitalist and concert performer, and is credited with suggesting to Heitor Villa-Lobos that his *Bachianas Brasileiras* No. 5, originally conceived for solo violin and eight cellos, might work better with a wordless soprano on the solo line. The piece was recast for her, and the historic first recording was captured in a single take.

RECOMMENDED RECORDING

COLLECTION:

"LA DAMOISELLE ÉLUE": SONGS AND ARIAS BY DEBUSSY, MOZART, BELLINI, VERDI, AND PUCCINI (SONY).

Scala, La *See* TEATRO ALLA SCALA.

scala di seta, La (The Silken Ladder) COMIC OPERA IN ONE ACT BY GIOACHINO ROSSINI, to a libretto by Giuseppe Maria Foppa, premiered May 9, 1812, at the Teatro San Moisè in Venice. The silken ladder of the opera's title is one of several devices used in the course of this frothy little entertainment to bring about a happy end. The plot involves a secret marriage—that of Giulia and Dorvil—and the lengths these two go to in their effort to engineer a romance between his friend and her cousin, so as to keep their own liaison a secret.

RECOMMENDED RECORDING

CORBELLI, DE CAROLIS, RINGHOLZ, VARGAS; VIOTTI AND ENGLISH CHAMBER ORCHESTRA (CLAVES).

scale (from It. *scala,* "ladder") A stepwise succession of tones. The most common scales in use in Western music are the DIATONIC (with seven tones to the octave), CHROMATIC (12 tones to the octave, ascending and descending by half steps), PENTATONIC (five tones to the octave), and WHOLE-TONE (six tones to the octave, ascending and descending by whole steps).

Scarlatti, Alessandro

(b. Palermo, May 2, 1660; d. Naples, October 22, 1725)

ITALIAN COMPOSER. He was the last "old master" of the Italian Baroque and the most important operatic composer of the early 18th century in Italy. His parents were both musical and he received training in Palermo and, from 1672, Rome, where his talent quickly attracted important patrons and helped him become an established figure in the city's cultural life while he was still in his teens. Between 1679 and 1683 he served as *maestro di cappella* at two important Roman churches and basked in the favor of leading Roman

Alessandro Scarlatti

aristocrats, including Cardinal Pamphili and Sweden's Queen Christina. But his desire to compose operas, public performances of which were banned in Rome, led him to accept an offer of a position in Naples as *maestro di cappella* at the royal chapel there. Despite intrigues against him on the part of Neapolitan musicians who resented an outsider's being put in charge, and financial pressures associated with his growing family, Scarlatti flourished. He left Naples in 1703, for reasons having to do with what can best be described as political miscalculations, and spent several years in Rome and Venice before returning in 1708 to his old post as master of the royal chapel. He continued to crank out operas, his pace slower than before, his works less successful, and his debts still deep. He died famous, but in penury.

Scarlatti's output was voluminous. He composed masses, motets, and a large number of oratorios; sonatas, concerti grossi, and keyboard pieces; more than 600 secular cantatas, most of them for solo voice and instrumental accompaniment; and probably more than 100 operas, of which about 65 are known today. Because of his large output of cantatas and operas and the high quality of his music, Scarlatti was seen as a model by many younger composers who ended up more successful than he, including Handel, Johann Adolf Hasse (1699–1783), and Niccolò Jommelli (1714–74). His operas helped establish the use of the three-part overture known as a SINFONIA and such devices as accompanied recitative and the full DA CAPO aria.

RECOMMENDED RECORDINGS

CANTATA PER LA NOTTE DI NATALE: BERTINI, FEDI, CAVINA; ALESSANDRINI AND CONCERTO ITALIANO (OPUS 111).

CONCERTI GROSSI, OTHER WORKS: BIONDI AND EUROPA GALANTE (VIRGIN CLASSICS).

SECULAR CANTATAS: LESNE, PIAU; IL SEMINARIO MUSICALE (VIRGIN CLASSICS).

Scarlatti, Domenico

(b. Naples, October 26, 1685; d. Madrid, July 23, 1757)

ITALIAN COMPOSER AND HARPSICHORDIST, son of Alessandro Scarlatti. His father arranged for his musical education and, recognizing his special talent at the keyboard, saw to it that he was appointed organist of the royal chapel in Naples (where the elder Scarlatti was *maestro di cappella*) and that he received bonus pay for being court chamber harpsichordist as well. Alessandro continued to manage his son's early career, sending him to Venice and Rome (where the young man met George Frideric Handel, his exact contemporary—the two forming a warm friendship after a keyboard "duel" in which they played each other to a draw). But the father's dearest ambition—that his son follow in his footsteps as a composer of operas and vocal works—was not realized. While the younger Scarlatti did pen more than a dozen operas and a large number of

Domenico Scarlatti at the keyboard

oratorios and cantatas, he would find his natural expression not in vocal music, but at the keyboard, and not in his homeland, but on the Iberian peninsula. At the age of 34, he left Italy to take up duties in Lisbon as music master to the eldest daughter of King John V of Portugal, the Infanta María Bárbara de Braganza. When, in 1728, María Bárbara married the heir to the Spanish throne, Scarlatti went with her, first to Seville, and later to Madrid, where he spent the final 24 years of his life.

The Palace of Aranjuez, the primary residence of King Fernando VI and Queen María Bárbara, became the seat of a thriving musical establishment, at the center of which stood Scarlatti and the great Italian castrato Carlo Broschi, known as Farinelli. María Bárbara's interest in music, and her remarkable talent as both a harpsichordist and a pianist, was the stimulus that drew from Scarlatti the great work of his career, more than 500 single-movement keyboard sonatas. Under the queen's patronage, these were copied and bound, the collection eventually running to 15 volumes.

These sonatas, though nearly all in two-part form, show an extraordinary range of color, mood, and affect. In many, there is an identifiably Spanish cast, whether from the use of characteristic dance rhythms, inflections drawn from the flamenco style of singing, or figuration evocative of a guitar's strumming and repeated notes (such as are found in the Sonatas in A minor, K. 175, and E major, K. 206), or from the incorporation of actual Spanish melodies. Some of the sonatas focus on striking, often peculiar harmonic twists, which Scarlatti found far more interesting than spinning out conventional counterpoint, while others emphasize rhythmic figures or ornaments, a good example being the Sonata in C, K. 497. As a rule, the sonatas are earthy in character, inhabiting a suggestive rather than an abstract world. The majority are dashing and virtuosic, often calling for rapid hand-crossings, sudden jumps, and high-velocity fingerwork. These outward expressions of brio, along with the inner vitality of the musical ideas themselves, have ensured the works a place in the repertoires not only of harpsichordists, but of many pianists as well. In fact, the repeated-note figuration in the Sonata in D major, K. 96, works even better on piano.

RECOMMENDED RECORDINGS

KEYBOARD SONATAS:
HARPSICHORD:
PUYANA (HARMONIA MUNDI).
ROUSSET (DECCA).
PIANO:
HOROWITZ (SONY).
JANDÓ (NAXOS).
PLETNEV (VIRGIN CLASSICS).

Schelomo **"HEBREW RHAPSODY" FOR CELLO AND ORCHESTRA BY ERNEST BLOCH,** composed in Geneva 1915–16 and premiered May 3, 1917, in New York by Leopold Stokowski and the Philadelphia Orchestra, with Hans Kindler as soloist. The work's title is the Hebrew form of the name Solomon. It was not Bloch's intention to compose a work of Jewish music or even music based on Jewish themes. Rather, as he put it, his interest was in "the Jewish soul . . . the venerable emotion of the race that slumbers way down in our soul." There is nonetheless an exotic, almost Oriental quality to the work's melodic material. The piece calls for a large orchestra, opulently scored, against which the plaintive, despairing voice of the cello sounds a note of deep pessimism and spirituality. This is in keeping with what is supposed to have been Solomon's dual identity: As king he knew the fullest extent of power and splendor, while as the Preacher of Jerusalem heard in the first chapter of Ecclesiastes, he dismissed the worldly and the wise as vexation of the spirit, vanity of vanities. It was an interesting subject for a composer to take up, as the greatest vexation in history, World War I, raged around Switzerland.

RECOMMENDED RECORDING

FOURNIER; WALLENSTEIN AND BERLIN PHILHARMONIC (DG).

Scherchen, Hermann

(b. Berlin, June 21, 1891; d. Florence, June 12, 1966)

GERMAN CONDUCTOR AND AUTHOR. Largely self-taught, he began his musical career in 1907 as a violist in the Blüthner Orchestra and the Berlin Philharmonic. In 1911 he helped Arnold Schoenberg prepare the score of *Pierrot lunaire* for its Berlin premiere; the following year he made his conducting debut leading performances of the piece on tour. He became conductor of the Riga Philharmonic in 1914, and spent much of World War I interned in a Russian prisoner-of-war camp as an enemy alien. After the war, he served as music director of the Frankfurt Museum Concerts, general music director in Königsberg, and conductor of the East German Radio Orchestra; he was also instrumental in launching the journal *Melos,* which was concerned with contemporary music and ideas. He left Germany in 1933 and moved to Switzerland, where he worked with the Zurich Radio Orchestra and further developed a fruitful association with the Musikkollegium in Winterthur. Following World War II, he taught at the Venice Biennale and at Darmstadt, and in 1954 he opened an electronic music studio in Gravesano (funded by UNESCO). He made his American debut in 1964 as guest conductor of the Philadelphia Orchestra.

Hermann Scherchen at the podium

During his career Scherchen conducted an astonishing number of first performances, including Berg's *Three Fragments from Wozzeck* (in 1924), *Der Wein* (1930), and Violin Concerto (1936); Roussel's *Aeneas* (1935); Webern's *Variations,* Op. 30 (1943); Richard Strauss's wind symphony *Fröhliche Werkstatt* (*Happy Workshop*; 1946); Luigi Dallapiccola's (1904–75) *Il prigioniero* (1950) and *Canti di liberazione* (1955); Stockhausen's *Kontra-Punkte I* (1953); Varèse's *Déserts* (1954); and Xenakis's *Pithoprakta* (1957). In his spare time he wrote a *Handbook of Conducting* (1929), *The Nature of Music* (1946), and *Music for Everyman* (1950).

Scherchen was an anomaly among conductors of his day—a progressive intellectual with exceptional gifts and an unrelenting sense of curiosity. His passionate devotion to the experimental left him completely open to new ideas and unusually free of preconceptions—an attitude also reflected in his approach to the standard repertoire.

RECOMMENDED RECORDING

COLLECTION:
"GREAT CONDUCTORS OF THE 20TH CENTURY—HERMAN SCHERCHEN": WORKS OF HAYDN, BEETHOVEN, BRAHMS, SCHOENBERG, STRAVINSKY (EMI).

scherzo (It., "joke") [1] A movement in fast tempo, often dancelike in character, usually found as one of the inner movements of a symphony, a quartet, or any other instrumental form consisting of four or more movements. The term was used throughout the 17th century as a fanciful title for various kinds of vocal and instrumental pieces, but Haydn, in his Op. 33 string quartets, was the first to deploy a scherzo in place of a minuet. Beethoven adopted the scherzo as the standard dance movement in his sonatas and symphonies, reverting to the minuet only for anachronistic effect, as in his Eighth Symphony. Not all scherzos are lighthearted or funny—some, such as the scherzo to Beethoven's Fifth Symphony, are positively grim. Seeing this paradox as an opportunity for some mischief, Ives titled the scherzo of his Trio for Violin, Cello and Piano (1909–10) *"TSIAJ" or Medley on the Fence or on the Campus!*—leaving the performer to figure out that "TSIAJ" stands for "This Scherzo Is A Joke." [2] A freestanding single-movement composition in the style of a scherzo, usually for orchestra (e.g., Dvořák's *Scherzo capriccioso*, Stravinsky's *Scherzo fantastique*).

Schiff, Andras

(b. Budapest, December 21, 1953)

HUNGARIAN/BRITISH PIANIST. He began piano lessons at five, and continued his studies with Pál Kadosa, György Kurtág, and Ferenc Rados at the Ferenc Liszt Academy in Budapest, and later with George Malcolm in London. A prizewinner at the Tchaikovsky Competition in Moscow (1974) and at the Leeds International Competition (1975), he soon established a solo and recording career. He was quick to concentrate his efforts on projects built around the works of Bach, Mozart, and Beethoven in particular; his repertoire also includes a good deal of Haydn, Schubert, Schumann, Chopin, Bartók, and Janáček. In 2004, he began a series of performances of the 32 Beethoven piano sonatas presented in chronological order and recorded live for ECM New Series.

In 1999, Schiff created his own chamber orchestra, the Cappella Andrea Barca, for a seven-year series in which he performed the complete Mozart piano concertos at the Salzburg Mozarteum. His extensive discography, beginning with traversals of the Mozart sonatas and of Bach's *Das wohltemperirte Clavier* on Decca, continuing on Teldec, and most recently on ECM, includes two recordings of Bach's *Goldberg* Variations, and much else of value. He won Grammy Awards for his accounts of Bach's *English* Suites and of Schubert's *Schwanengesang* with tenor Peter Schreier. He became a British citizen in 2001 and lives in London and Florence.

RECOMMENDED RECORDINGS

BACH, *DAS WOHLTEMPERIERTE CLAVIER*, BOOKS I AND II (DECCA).

MOZART, PIANO SONATAS (DECCA).

SCHUBERT, *IMPROMPTUS*, *MOMENTS MUSICAUX*, OTHER WORKS (DECCA).

Schiøtz, Aksel

(b. Roskilde, September 1, 1906; d. Copenhagen, April 19, 1975)

DANISH TENOR/BARITONE AND TEACHER. In keeping with his father's wishes, he studied modern languages at the University of Copenhagen, and became a schoolmaster. His love of singing was well known to friends, and he was invited to join the Copenhagen Male Choir, with which he became a soloist. Encouraged to take formal vocal training, he worked with several teachers in Copenhagen, finally studying in Stockholm with John Forsell, Jussi Björling's teacher. His first song recital was in 1936, and he made his operatic debut in 1939 as Ferrando in Mozart's *Così fan tutte* at the Royal Opera in Copenhagen. A year earlier he had begun to record for HMV, but any boost that might have given to an international career was lost at the outbreak of World War II, when Denmark fell under German occupation. During the war years, Schiøtz performed widely and defiantly in Denmark, concentrating on Danish repertoire; toward the end of the war, after being warned that his life might be in danger, he briefly went into hiding. His international recording career resumed after the war, and sessions in England with Gerald Moore as accompanist resulted in extraordinary recordings of Schubert's *Die schöne Müllerin* and Schumann's *Dichterliebe.* His operatic debut outside Denmark came in 1946, singing the Male Chorus role in Britten's *The Rape of Lucretia* at the Glyndebourne Festival.

That same year a tumor was discovered near his vocal cords, necessitating an operation that left Schiøtz with partial paralysis of his face. Determined to overcome the infirmity, he recovered enough to return to the recital stage in 1948, but health issues reemerged in 1950, and treatment for a brain tumor caused a speech impairment. Once more he overcame his physical difficulties and, as a baritone, resumed performing. Schiøtz spent the latter part of his career teaching. Faculty appointments included professorships at the University of Minnesota, the Royal Conservatory of Music, the University of Toronto, the University of Colorado, and the Royal Danish School of Educational Studies in Copenhagen. *The Singer and His Art,* his book on song interpretation, was published in 1969. In his brief performing career Schiøtz was highly respected, especially in lieder circles, for his cultivation and musicality, his insightful and unmannered delivery of text, and his sweet, clear, unforced vocalism.

RECOMMENDED RECORDINGS

SCHUMANN, *DICHTERLIEBE*: MOORE (EMI, PEARL).

COLLECTIONS:

"THE COMPLETE AKSEL SCHIØTZ RECORDINGS," VOL. 2—SCHUBERT, *DIE SCHÖNE MÜLLERIN*: MOORE (DANACORD).

"THE COMPLETE AKSEL SCHIØTZ RECORDINGS," VOL. 3—SCHUMANN, *DICHTERLIEBE*: MOORE (DANACORD).

Schipa, Tito

(b. Lecce, January 2, 1888; d. New York, December 16, 1965)

ITALIAN TENOR. Born Raffaele Attilio Amadeo Schipa to a poor family from Apuglia, Schipa (whose nickname, Tito, derives from Italian slang for "little guy") exhibited sufficient vocal talent that his academic shortcomings were generally overlooked. He responded well to voice lessons from local maestros, and in 1909 a successful campaign was launched to send him to Milan, where he studied at the conservatory with Emilio Piccoli. In 1910, after only a year in Milan, he made his professional debut in nearby Vercelli as Alfredo in Verdi's *La traviata.* He worked in the provinces until his Rome debut in 1911, and by the time of his La Scala debut four years later, he had sung throughout Italy and in South America and Spain in a wide range of roles: Maurizio in *Adriana Lecouvreur* by Francesco Cilea (1866–1950), Turiddu in Mascagni's *Cavalleria rusticana,* the Duke in Verdi's *Rigoletto,* the title role in Gounod's *Faust,* Loris Ipanov in Giordano's *Fedora,* and Almaviva in

Rossini's *Il barbiere di Siviglia.* He created the role of Ruggero in the world premiere of Puccini's *La rondine* at Monte Carlo in 1917. He was first heard in the United States in 1919 at the Chicago Opera, where he scored an immediate string of successes in roles opposite soprano Amelita Galli-Curci. During his American years (1919–35), his stylish singing and winning stage personality helped turn him into a popular entertainment figure; in addition to his extensive activity as a recording artist, he made several movies for Paramount Studios.

Schipa spent the early part of his career building a wide repertoire, but he knew his limitations as a singer. Like Caruso, he lacked a high C, but he did not have, as compensation, Caruso's robust sound, nor could he boast great range or agility. In stylistic elegance, however, he was unmatched, and his ability to sing legato set a daunting standard for singers who came after him. Systematically dropping all but the most lyric roles from his repertoire, he spent his American years focusing on a narrow range of parts in which few tenors were his equal. Between 1932 and 1935, his golden years at the Metropolitan Opera, the Schipa roles (Nemorino, Ottavio, Ernesto, Almaviva, Des Grieux, and his personal favorite, Wilhelm Meister in Ambroise Thomas's *Mignon*) were much admired. He rejoined the Met in 1941, returning later that year to Mussolini's Italy. His popularity was so great, however, that his reappearance in the U.S. after World War II, when his pro-fascist sentiments were well known, elicited none of the controversy that made Kirsten Flagstad persona non grata on the American scene. Schipa retired from the stage in 1958 to teach voice, first in Budapest, then in New York City. At age 75, still in good vocal health, he undertook a final American concert tour. Also a composer, he left, in addition to some songs written during his Hollywood years, the operetta *La Principessa Liana* (1929) and some sacred music.

RECOMMENDED RECORDINGS

COLLECTIONS:

DONIZETTI, *DON PASQUALE*: BADINI, POLI, SARACENI; SABAJNO AND LA SCALA OPERA (OPERA D'ORO).

"PRIMA VOCE—SCHIPA": ARIAS BY BELLINI, DONIZETTI, MOZART, PUCCINI, OTHERS (NIMBUS).

"TITO SCHIPA FAVOURITES": ARIAS, NEAPOLITAN AND ITALIAN SONGS, SPANISH SONGS (ASV).

Schippers, Thomas

(b. Kalamazoo, Mich., March 9, 1930; d. New York, December 16, 1977)

AMERICAN CONDUCTOR. He studied piano and organ at the Curtis Institute of Music in Philadelphia, but was expelled when his intimate relationship with Gian Carlo Menotti came to light. His conducting career was launched when he got a gig as conductor of Menotti's *The Consul* in 1950, which was followed by his appointment as music director of Menotti's Festival of Two Worlds at Spoleto, Italy. He joined the staff of the New York City Opera in 1951, and in 1955 he made his conducting debuts at the New York Philharmonic and the Metropolitan Opera (leading a double bill that included Donizetti's *Don Pasquale*). He was later tapped to conduct the world premiere of Barber's *Antony and Cleopatra,* with which the new Metropolitan Opera House at Lincoln Center opened its doors in 1966. In 1970 he was appointed music director of the Cincinnati Symphony Orchestra, a position he retained until his death, from cancer, at the age of 47.

An articulate and gifted orchestra leader, Schippers was admired equally for his work in the opera house and on the concert stage. He made outstanding recordings of works by Barber and Menotti, of Ravel's orchestration of *Pictures at an Exhibition,* and of the music of Verdi and Puccini.

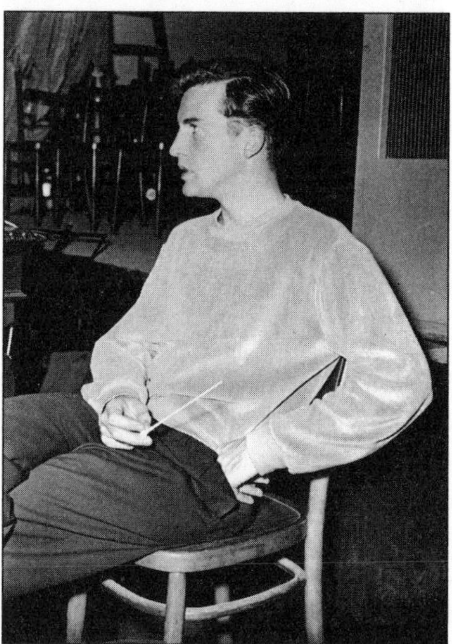

Thomas Schippers takes a break.

RECOMMENDED RECORDING

BARBER, *ADAGIO FOR STRINGS* (WITH OTHER WORKS BY BARBER AND MENOTTI): NEW YORK PHILHARMONIC (SONY).

Schnabel, Artur

(b. Lipnik, April 17, 1882; d. Axenstein, Switzerland, August 15, 1951)

AUSTRIAN/AMERICAN PIANIST AND COMPOSER. He was raised in Vienna, where he studied piano with Theodor Leschetizky and composition with Eusebius Mandyczewski. It was the former who told him: "You will never be a pianist; you are a musician." He made his debut in 1890 and moved to Berlin in 1900, where he lived and worked until Hitler became chancellor in 1933; during this period, he emerged as a leading interpreter of the works of Beethoven and Schubert, as well as those of Mozart, Schumann, and Brahms. From 1925 until 1930, he taught at the Hochschule für Musik in Berlin. In 1927, to mark the centennial of Beethoven's death, he played all 32 of Beethoven's piano sonatas in Berlin, a feat he later repeated there and in London. He emigrated to the U.S. in 1939 and taught at the University of Michigan from 1940 to 1945. He became an American citizen in 1944.

An advocate of repertoire that was not flashy and had largely been overlooked by a generation of daredevils, Schnabel offered a corrective to the self-indulgence and showiness of many a Romantic virtuoso. He was admired for his ability to produce a gentle tone and a wonderful singing line, and for his articulate playing, with its rigorous exposure of the music's inner-voice texture. Yet he was not a literalist, as even a cursory look at his edition of the Beethoven sonatas—full of markings not to be found in the original—will attest. He had a tendency to sectionalize large movements (by changes of tempo and intensity), giving them high expressive profiles but sometimes weakening them (e.g., the first movement of the Schubert B-flat sonata, D. 960). In 1932 he undertook the first-ever complete recording of the Beethoven sonatas, for HMV; he was also the first to regularly play Schubert's sonatas in recital and the first to record them. His pupils included Clifford Curzon, Leon Fleisher, and Claude Frank.

RECOMMENDED RECORDINGS

BEETHOVEN, THE "NAMED" PIANO SONATAS (PEARL).

SCHUBERT, *MOMENTS MUSICAUX* AND PIANO SONATAS NOS. 17, 20, AND 21 (GRAMMOFONO 2000).

Schnittke, Alfred

(b. Engels, November 24, 1934; d. Hamburg, August 3, 1998)

RUSSIAN COMPOSER of Jewish and Volga-German descent. He began his musical studies in 1946 in Vienna, where his father, a journalist and translator, had been posted after World War II. Following his family's return to Moscow in 1948, he received instruction in piano and choral conducting, and from 1953 to 1961 he studied at the Moscow Conservatory. In 1962 he joined the conservatory's faculty as an instructor of instrumentation, a position he held until 1972. After that he supported himself mainly by composing film scores, of which he completed more than 60. He suffered a stroke in 1985 and spent the rest of his life severely disabled, but nevertheless able to compose. He left Russia for Germany in 1990, maintaining dual citizenship while residing in Hamburg. During his last years, his productivity and the quality of his work declined as a result of chronic health problems.

Schnittke's major works include three operas, nine symphonies, six "concerti grossi," four violin concertos, and concertos for piano, viola, and cello, as well as a substantial amount of chamber music, including four string quartets, a piano quintet, and the poignant *Prelude in Memoriam Shostakovich* for two violins. He began as a follower of Shostakovich, then, like so many in his generation, became a serialist. But he soon chose, as he put it, to "alight from an already overcrowded train." He eventually settled on a decidedly idiosyncratic and eclectic idiom, a kind of referential postmodernism in which anything and everything could be used and parodied, even the most banal ideas, but often with such urgency that the listener might not know whether the effort was serious or ironic until, moments (or years) later, it became clear that it was both.

Schnittke's music often looked at itself in this way. His breakthrough work was the Violin Sonata No. 2 (1968), subtitled "Quasi una sonata" (a takeoff on the designation of Beethoven's *Moonlight* Sonata as a sonata *quasi una fantasia*). The composer described this piece as "a report of the impossibility of the sonata, made in the form of a sonata." Schnittke was championed by some of Russia's finest instrumentalists, including Gidon Kremer and Mstislav Rostropovich, whose performances often made an eloquent case for his work. What has become clear as a result of their advocacy, and with the passage of time, is that in most of his music Schnittke was trying to deal with the moral challenges facing modern man. He was concerned with the conflict between good and evil—about which, as someone who grew up in Stalin's U.S.S.R., he knew a great deal. Sometimes his take on things could be a little skewed. But one has to admire the inventiveness he showed in works such as his Faust cantata *Seid nüchtern und wachet* (*Be Sober and Attentive*; 1983), particularly his brilliant use of musical metaphor. Who else among late-20th-century composers would have thought of using a tango to depict Faust's final agonies?

RECOMMENDED RECORDINGS

Violin Sonata No. 2 (with *Concerti grossi* Nos. 1 and 5): Kremer; Dohnányi and Vienna Philharmonic (DG).

Piano Quintet: Berman with Vermeer Quartet (Naxos).

Schnorr von Carolsfeld, Ludwig

(b. Munich, July 2, 1836; d. Dresden, July 21, 1865)

GERMAN TENOR. He studied at the Leipzig Conservatory and was engaged by the Court Opera in Karlsruhe in 1854; he became the company's principal tenor in 1858. He moved to Dresden with his wife, the soprano Malvina Garrigues, in 1860, quickly establishing himself as a leading interpreter of the roles of Tannhäuser and Lohengrin. Schnorr and his wife subsequently learned the title roles of Wagner's *Tristan und Isolde*—which had been published but not yet performed—and sang them for the composer in 1862. Wagner, much taken with Schnorr's musicianship and understanding of the part, arranged for the tenor and his wife to sing at the work's premiere on June 10, 1865, in

Munich, presided over by Hans von Bülow. The heavyset Schnorr gave his all in rehearsals and performance, carrying the day. But the physical strain was too much for him: He soon became ill and died five weeks later, delirious, singing, and calling out Wagner's name on his deathbed.

With his baritonal resonance and color—a sound that Wagner described as "full, soft, and gleaming"—and his dramatic projection, Schnorr was the Heldentenor Wagner had been waiting for. Had he lived, he most likely would have become the first Siegfried.

Schoenberg, Arnold

(b. Vienna, September 13, 1874; d. Los Angeles, July 13, 1951)

AUSTRIAN COMPOSER. The son of a Jewish tradesman (his father ran a small shoe-manufacturing concern), he began violin lessons in 1882, and soon was composing little duos for the instrument in the popular style, later marches and polkas in imitation of the repertoire played by bands in the parks. In 1890, after his father's death, he left school to apprentice with a private bank, remaining unhappily in its employ until 1895. Musically he was largely self-taught; he studied Beethoven scores he bought secondhand and read about sonata form in an encyclopedia the family purchased in installments.

In 1894, playing in an amateur orchestra, Schoenberg met Alexander von Zemlinsky, who would become his artistic mentor. He soon left the bank job and in 1895 became conductor of several amateur choral societies in and around Vienna. His composing picked up and in 1897 he submitted the manuscript of a string quartet to Zemlinsky, who arranged for it to be performed at the Musikverein. In 1898 Schoenberg converted from Judaism to Lutheranism, for spiritual rather than opportunistic reasons. During the summer of 1899, he became involved with Zemlinsky's sister, Mathilde, marrying her two years later. In September he wrote the string sextet *VERKLÄRTE NACHT* (*Transfigured Night*), Op. 4. The composition, a work of turbulent, superheated late Romanticism, was the first of Schoenberg's to gain a place in the repertoire, and remains one of his finest achievements.

Emboldened by its completion (and by a prize offered by the Vienna Composers Society), Schoenberg set to work on a symphonic song cycle, *GURRE-LIEDER* (*Songs of Gurre*), which took a decade to complete. He and Mathilde moved to Berlin in 1901, where he worked as a cabaret conductor while teaching harmony at the Stern Conservatory. *Verklärte Nacht* had its world premiere in 1902; the symphonic poem *PELLEAS UND MELISANDE,* Op. 5, followed in 1903. Schoenberg's reputation was such that Alban Berg and Anton Webern became his students the next year. In 1907 the String Quartet No. 1, Op. 7, and the Chamber Symphony No. 1, Op. 9, received their first performances, the latter showing clear signs—in its abundance of harmonies built on fourths rather than thirds—that Schoenberg was beginning to rethink conventional tonality.

With his String Quartet No. 2, Op. 10, Schoenberg moved toward even more intense expressionism and farther away from tonality. This pathbreaking piece, whose 1908 premiere provoked an uproar, was composed during a period when Mathilde had run off with the Schoenbergs' upstairs neighbor, the painter Richard Gerstl. Mathilde soon returned to her husband and their two children, Gerstl committed suicide, and Schoenberg chose a path of complete emotional denial about the affair. This phase of Schoenberg's musical development climaxed in the *Five Pieces for Orchestra* (*Fünf Orchesterstücke*), Op. 16, the expressionistic one-person opera *Erwartung*

Schoenberg on a visit to Russia

(*Anticipation*), Op. 17, both completed in 1909, and *PIERROT LUNAIRE,* Op. 21 (1912), a song cycle wherein the performer must vocalize not by singing, but with precisely pitched speech called *Sprechstimme.*

From 1907 Schoenberg devoted himself almost as intensely to painting as to music. His activity as a painter culminated in the formation of a friendship with Wassily Kandinsky and an invitation to participate in the 1911 Blaue Reiter exhibit in Munich, where four paintings of his were shown. Also in 1911 he completed *Harmonielehre,* a major treatise on harmony, dedicating it to Gustav Mahler. The premiere of *Gurre-Lieder* in Vienna in 1913 brought Schoenberg the greatest triumph of his life; with a characteristic bitterness over past slights, he refused to acknowledge the applause. The ensuing years, with World War I raging, were comparatively fallow.

Mathilde died in 1923. Schoenberg continued to systematize his revolutionary approach to harmony, and with the Five Piano Pieces, Op. 23 ◉, completed in 1923, introduced the 12-TONE method. Ten months after Mathilde's death, he married Gertrud Kolisch (some 25 years younger than he), and in 1925 he succeeded Ferruccio Busoni as professor of composition at Berlin's Akademie der Künste. The Variations for Orchestra, Op. 31, marking the first use of 12-tone technique in a composition for large orchestra, were finished in 1928 and premiered by Furtwängler and the Berlin Philharmonic that same year.

In 1929 Schoenberg completed the first stage work composed with the 12-tone technique, his one-act opera *Von Heute auf Morgen* (*From Today Until Tomorrow*), Op. 32. The following year he began composing the score to *MOSES UND ARON,* envisaged as a three-act opera; he quickly became bogged down in its conceptual and dramaturgical complexities. Nazi-fanned anti-Semitism in Berlin in 1933 forced the family to leave for Paris (where Schoenberg converted back to Judaism), and thence immediately for the United States. After a year on the East Coast, Schoenberg moved to Los Angeles and soon became a professor at UCLA, settling in Brentwood and befriending George Gershwin, among others. He composed his String Quartet No. 4, Op. 37, in 1936, and in 1939 completed the Chamber Symphony No. 2, Op. 38, which he had begun in 1906. In 1947, on a commission from the Koussevitzky Music Foundation, he wrote *A Survivor from Warsaw,* Op. 46, for narrator, male voices, and orchestra. Failing health limited his activities in the final years of his life, and while he composed a few small pieces, he was unable to travel to

Europe for celebrations of his 75th birthday or to finish *Moses und Aron.*

Even before he broke from the constraints of tonality, Schoenberg had explored the use of tone color and harmony as structural devices. In the Six Songs (1904–05), for example, each song called for a different instrumental complement, giving each a distinctive atmosphere; in "Farben" ("Colors"), the third of his *Five Pieces for Orchestra,* he explored the idea of *Klangfarbenmelodie,* the creation of a musical line based more on instrumental sonority than on changes in pitch. The masterly pieces he created in the expressionist style between 1907 and 1910 (the period of his psychological turmoil) showed a command of technique and color that his paintings from the same period lacked, fine as they were—even the very good ones, such as his self-portrait *Der rote Blick* (*The Red Gaze*) from 1910.

Schoenberg's aesthetic horizons opened considerably following his forced emigration to the United States, partly from necessity (no one was commissioning 12-tone works in the 1930s and 1940s) and partly from what some have called the composer's "latent desire" to write more consonant, tonal music. Schoenberg nonetheless took pains to minimize the importance of these essays and to preempt any suggestion that they marked a renunciation of his thornier 12-tone style. Some of the pieces from his 17 years in Los Angeles scarcely sound like the work of the man who wrote *Pierrot lunaire,* or, for that matter, the crabbed, dense works of the later 1920s.

Schoenberg left a singularly prominent mark on the music of the 20th century, as the composer and theorist responsible for the establishment of the 12-tone system of composition. He always maintained that his system represented not a break with the past—specifically, musical Romanticism—but a logical, inevitable continuation of it. Indeed, his historical position may turn out to be similar to that of Bach; each lived at a time of transition between two musical eras, trying to reconcile their divergent characteristics. If the intellect is also a passion, as has been asserted, Schoenberg's music, with its singular fixation on density, orderliness, and complexity, represents one of the most wanton expressions of passion ever committed to notes. Even Webern, his chief disciple, felt his music was too "hot," and audiences still have a difficult time drawing close to it.

RECOMMENDED RECORDINGS

CHAMBER SYMPHONIES NOS. 1 AND 2: HOLLIGER AND CHAMBER ORCHESTRA OF EUROPE (WARNER).

FIVE PIANO PIECES, OP. 23: JACOBS (NONESUCH).

FIVE PIANO PIECES, OP. 23: POLLINI (DG).

FIVE PIECES FOR ORCHESTRA: BOULEZ AND BBC SYMPHONY ORCHESTRA (SONY).

FIVE PIECES FOR ORCHESTRA: CRAFT AND LONDON SYMPHONY ORCHESTRA (KOCH).

GURRE-LIEDER: MATTILA, OTTER, MOSER, LANGRIDGE, QUASTHOFF; RATTLE AND BERLIN PHILHARMONIC (EMI).

PIERROT LUNAIRE AND *THE BOOK OF THE HANGING GARDENS*: DEGAETANI; WEISBERG AND CONTEMPORARY CHAMBER ENSEMBLE (NONESUCH).

PIERROT LUNAIRE: SCHÄFER; BOULEZ AND ENSEMBLE INTERCONTEMPORAIN (DG).

VARIATIONS FOR ORCHESTRA, OP. 31: KARAJAN AND BERLIN PHILHARMONIC (DG).

VERKLÄRTE NACHT (SEXTET): DINKIN, REHER WITH HOLLYWOOD QUARTET (TESTAMENT).

VERKLÄRTE NACHT (STRING ORCHESTRA): KARAJAN AND BERLIN PHILHARMONIC (DG).

Scholl, Andreas *See box on pages 155–57.*

schöne Müllerin, Die (The Lovely Mill-Maid) **CYCLE OF 20 SONGS BY FRANZ SCHUBERT, D. 795,** to poems by Wilhelm Müller, composed during October and November of 1823. Müller's simple and rather naive poetry—created in 1816–17 for a household skit inspired by the opera *La molinara* by Giovanni Paisiello (1740–1816)—proved ideal grist for Schubert's compositional mill, allowing the composer, through his music, to subtly delve into the darker emotions of the story. The resulting cycle is a springlike idyll of unrequited love with a tragic ending, in which the brokenhearted young hero, spurned by the maid of the mill in favor of a hunter, drowns himself in the millstream. Schubert makes the sound of the stream a recurrent motif of the cycle by means of the rippling, arpeggiated piano figuration used to accompany many of the songs.

RECOMMENDED RECORDING

FISCHER-DIESKAU, MOORE (DG).

Schöpfung, Die *See* THE CREATION.

Schorr, Friedrich

(b. Nagyvarád, September 2, 1888; d. Farmington, Conn., August 14, 1953)

HUNGARIAN/AMERICAN BASS-BARITONE. The son of a respected Jewish cantor, himself a fine baritone, Schorr studied with Adolph Robinson, who had been Leo Slezak's teacher. On Robinson's recommendation, he was engaged in the winter of 1912 by the Chicago Opera to sing small roles, but his official debut came later that year in Graz when, at 23, he appeared as Wotan in Wagner's *Die Walküre.* He sang in Graz for the next four seasons before moving on to Cologne (1918–23). He then joined the Berlin Staatsoper, where he spent seven seasons on the roster. Though it is his portrayals of Hans Sachs, Wotan, the Dutchman, and other Wagner roles for which he is remembered today, Schorr was also acclaimed in the Richard Strauss roles of Orestes, Barak, and Jochanaan, and as Beethoven's Pizarro. He was a regular at London's Covent Garden (1925–33), and was the Bayreuth Wotan from 1925 through 1931. During his 20-year career at the Metropolitan Opera (1924–43), he sang with such other "golden age" Wagnerians as Kirsten Flagstad, Helen Traubel, and Lauritz Melchior.

Considered the greatest heroic baritone of his generation, Schorr sang Wagner with a warm, Italianate legato and a delivery that emphasized clarity of diction. His voice was powerful but renowned as much for its beauty as for its grandeur. Thanks to his many recordings, Schorr's artistry, particularly as the Dutchman and Sachs, continues to be a benchmark. He was a fine coach and stage director, and served in the years following his retirement from singing as director of the Manhattan School of Music in New York.

RECOMMENDED RECORDING

COLLECTION:
"FRIEDRICH SCHORR SINGS WAGNER": ARIAS AND EXCERPTS FROM *DER FLIEGENDE HOLLÄNDER, DIE MEISTERSINGER VON NÜRNBERG,* THE *RING* CYCLE (PREISER).

Schreier, Peter

(b. Meissen, July 29, 1935)

GERMAN TENOR AND CONDUCTOR. His first musical instruction came from his father, a cantor and organist, and by his tenth birthday he was a member of the Dresden Kreuzchor. He remained with the choir as a tenor after his voice changed, and began serious musical training in singing and conducting. After studies at the Hochschule für Musik in Dresden and an apprenticeship with the Dresden State Opera's studio program, he made his debut in 1959 with the Dresden company as the First Prisoner in Beethoven's *Fidelio.* In 1961 he was given a spot on the company's roster, and in 1963 he joined the Berlin Staatsoper. Word of his remarkable affinity for Mozart tenor roles quickly spread beyond what was then East Germany, and by the end of the 1960s he had made successful debuts at the Vienna Staatsoper, Salzburg Festival, Hamburg State Opera, Covent Garden, La Scala, and

Metropolitan Opera, where he bowed for the first time on Christmas Day, 1967, as Tamino in Mozart's *Die Zauberflöte.* In addition to the Mozart roles for which he was best known—Belmonte, Tamino, Ferrando, and Tito—he achieved distinction in Wagner as David in *Die Meistersinger von Nürnberg* and Loge in *Das Rheingold,* as Almaviva in Rossini's *Il barbiere di Siviglia,* and as Fenton in Verdi's *Falstaff.* He also emerged as an outstanding oratorio singer—in the Bach passions he was perhaps the finest Evangelist of his day—and a distinguished lieder artist. His work in these fields is documented by many outstanding recordings.

Peter Schreier in 1992

Since the 1980s, Schreier has been active as a conductor, specializing, unsurprisingly, in the works of J. S. Bach and Mozart, and has made a number of first-rate recordings in that capacity. He retired from singing in 2000.

RECOMMENDED RECORDINGS

AS TENOR:

MOZART, *DIE ZAUBERFLÖTE*: ROTHENBERGER, MOSER, BERRY, MOLL, ADAM; SAWALLISCH AND BAVARIAN STATE OPERA (EMI).

SCHUBERT, *DIE SCHÖNE MÜLLERIN*: SCHIFF (DECCA).

AS CONDUCTOR:

MOZART, *REQUIEM*: M. PRICE, SCHMIDT, ARAIZA, ADAM; STAATSKAPELLE DRESDEN (PHILIPS).

Schubert, Franz

(b. Vienna, January 31, 1797; d. Vienna, November 19, 1828)

AUSTRIAN COMPOSER, regarded as the greatest song composer in history. The last in the line of Viennese Classical composers, he was also the first of the Romantics, for, while his musical style was rooted in Classicism, his sense of color, harmonic action, and musical time were new and surprising. Though he died at the age of 31, his oeuvre is one of the richest in all of music.

The son of a schoolteacher, he was not a child prodigy in the sense that Mozart had been, nor, for reasons of temperament, did he ever become a great virtuoso, though he played the violin, viola, and piano with professional competence. Less than five feet tall and overweight—his nickname, Schwammerl, meant "tubby"—with poor eyesight and a face pocked with scars, he was hardly an imposing figure. As an adult he was certainly no angel: He smoked constantly, drank excessively, and was wildly promiscuous (though in what directions remains a matter of speculation). But he was a good student, and he grew up in a family where music was spoken as a second language, easily absorbing everything he was taught. He began violin lessons with his father when he was eight. At 11, having earlier passed an audition with Antonio Salieri, he was accepted as a choirboy at the Imperial court chapel; for several years he took lessons in composition from Salieri while studying tuition-free at the Imperial and Royal City College, where he played in the second violin section of the school's orchestra. During these years, he formed a close friendship with the orchestra's founder, Josef von Spaun, who brought him into contact with an ever-widening circle of kindred spirits and ensured the much-needed encouragement of his talents. Later, it would be in Spaun's home that the "Schubertiade"—an evening devoted to Schubert's songs and chamber works—became an important facet of Viennese musical life.

Schubert's compositional genius erupted in the autumn of 1814, about the time he went to work as a teacher in his father's elementary school. By the end of 1815 he had produced almost 150 songs—including a brilliant treatment of Goethe's *ERLKÖNIG*, D. 328, his first masterpiece—and numerous other works, among them two symphonies, two string quartets, and two masses.

The winter of 1822–23 brought the great crisis in Schubert's life: He contracted syphilis. This is almost certainly the reason he left unfinished the extraordinary Symphony No. 8 in B minor he had begun in October of 1822. The two movements Schubert did complete of what has come to be known as his *UNFINISHED SYMPHONY*, D. 759 ◉, plumb the most extraordinary emotional depths, marking a new level of accomplishment in his work as a symphonist. Another work from this period, the *WANDERERFANTASIE*, D. 760, for piano, shows how rapidly and in what original directions his treatment of large-scale form was developing. Anxiety over his illness clouded Schubert's thoughts for the rest of his life, but he kept writing and breaking new ground to the end, drafting his greatest symphonic work, the monumentally vast Symphony No. 9 in C, D. 944 ◉, in the summer of 1825; penning two piano trios and the great song cycles *WINTERREISE* (*Winter Journey*) ◉, D. 911, in 1827 and *SCHWANENGESANG* (*Swan Song*), D. 957, in 1828; and producing the last three piano sonatas, D. 958–60, the sublime Quintet in C for strings, D. 956, and some of his finest songs, including *"DER HIRT AUF DEM FELSEN"* (*"The Shepherd on the Rocks"*), D. 965 ◉, in the final months of his life. He survived Beethoven by less than two years and was laid to rest near him in Vienna's Währing cemetery.

Franz Schubert, music in hand

Schubert's known songs for solo voice with piano accompaniment number 634, of which nearly 400 were published after his death. His enormous, deeply expressive output revolutionized the lied: He was among the first to exploit the possibilities of song cycles, like *DIE SCHÖNE MÜLLERIN* (*The Lovely Mill-Maid*), D. 795—within which a continuous narrative thread unifies the texts—and he brought a new level of sophistication and insight to the setting of poetry. The perfection with which both melody and accompaniment suit the text in so many of his songs has rarely been equaled.

Schubert had the ability to achieve in music what a poem achieved in language. And he made the piano an equal partner with the voice in the expressive work of the song. For him, writing a song was not a matter of setting the words *to* music, but of translating the poetry *into* music. His willingness to set poems of great emotional intensity was matched by his ability to conjure up harmonic twists and melodic turns that conveyed emotion with remarkable simplicity and force, so that without overextending his rhetoric he could, in a few lines of music, scale the heights of elation and probe the depths of suffering, longing, loneliness, and loss.

It was not until long after his death that Schubert's achievements in the field of instrumental music were properly appreciated, in part because many of his best works went unpublished and unknown for decades. His eight symphonies (in the conventional numbering there is no No. 7) have become staples of the symphonic repertoire;

Schubert* (standing, right) *and friends on an excursion to the country

the most frequently encountered are the probingly Mozartean Symphony No. 5 in B-flat, D. 485, composed when Schubert was 19 (but not published until 1885) ◉, the *Unfinished* (published in 1867), and the Ninth (published in 1840). Schubert's contributions to the chamber literature are equally formidable. They include a handful of fine works for violin and piano, the *Arpeggione* Sonata, D. 821 (1824), two magisterial piano trios, and several string quartets, of which the best are the Quartet in D minor (*DER TOD UND DAS MÄDCHEN*; *Death and the Maiden*), D. 810 (1824) and the Quartet in G, D. 887 (1826), a work of extraordinary spaciousness and energy. There are also the TROUT QUINTET, D. 667 (1819) ◉, the superb Octet in F, D. 803 (1824), and the Quintet in C, one of the half-dozen supreme masterpieces of the chamber genre.

A Schubertiade

In the keyboard literature of the 19th century, only the late sonatas of Schubert and the B minor sonata of Liszt stand on the same exalted plane as the great piano sonatas of Beethoven. Schubert's interest in the genre, like Beethoven's, extended from the beginning of his career to its end, though in Schubert's case a mere 13 years separate his earliest essays (unfinished sonatas in C and E, both dating from 1815) from the three sonatas of 1828 that bring the canon to a close. Viewed from this perspective, the scope of the later sonatas—their emotional depth and the mastery of form, gesture, and content they reflect—is astonishing.

Schubert's musical language was unique and often strange. Much has been said about the grace and suppleness of his melodies, but it is their immediacy—the directness with which they convey an emotional nuance—that is remarkable. What Mark Twain said about using the exactly right word in a piece of writing—that whenever we come upon it "the resulting effect is physical as well as spiritual, and electrically prompt"—perfectly describes Schubert's way with a melody. Schubert's use of harmony could also be revelatory. The coloristic impact of particular chords was as important to him as the functional role harmony played in anchoring musical syntax. His music is full of unusual progressions and his tendency to blur the distinction between the major and minor modes enriched the expressive possibilities of both.

For Schubert, the musical experience was not a transit from point A to point B, but a series of sojourns in different regions of sound, thought, and feeling. Just as Schubert's local use of harmony was unorthodox, so too was his long-range tonal thinking. His key schemes, rather than being polarized in the typical Classical manner, treat key areas as part of a broad continuum. This is essentially a Romantic trait, and Schubert's "late" instrumental works—from the Ninth Symphony on—

show it at its most pronounced. Their expansive, rhapsodic lines of action and affective combination of turbulence and tranquillity seem to arise from an entirely new concept of the purpose of music: the gradual revelation of an inner world, unfolded at "heavenly length" (Robert Schumann's words). With this approach, Schubert, showing that genres like the symphony, sonata, and string quartet could be something other than what Beethoven had made of them, exerted a profound influence on subsequent generations. Schumann, Liszt, and Brahms were all changed by their contact with his music, and the vastness and integrity of his designs boldly pointed the way for the symphonies of Bruckner and Mahler, among others.

RECOMMENDED RECORDINGS

ARPEGGIONE SONATA: ROSTROPOVICH, BRITTEN (DECCA).

GOETHE LIEDER: FISCHER-DIESKAU, MOORE (DG).

PIANO SONATAS (COMPLETE): KEMPFF (DG).

QUINTET IN C, D. 956: ROSTROPOVICH WITH EMERSON QUARTET (DG).

QUARTET IN D MINOR, D. 810, QUARTET IN G, D. 887: QUARTETTO ITALIANO (PHILIPS).

QUARTET IN G, D. 887: EMERSON QUARTET (DG).

DIE SCHÖNE MÜLLERIN, WINTERREISE, SCHWANENGESANG: FISCHER-DIESKAU, MOORE (DG).

SELECTED SONGS: BAKER, JOHNSON (HYPERION).

SYMPHONY NO. 8: WALTER AND NEW YORK PHILHARMONIC (SONY).

SYMPHONY NO. 9: SOLTI AND VIENNA PHILHARMONIC (DECCA).

TROUT QUINTET: SERKIN, LAREDO, NAEGELE, PARNAS, LEVINE (SONY).

WANDERERFANTASIE (WITH SONATA IN B-FLAT, D. 960): CURZON (DECCA).

WANDERERFANTASIE (WITH SONATA IN B-FLAT, D. 960): RUBINSTEIN (RCA).

WINTERREISE: FISCHER-DIESKAU, DEMUS (DG).

WINTERREISE: QUASTHOFF, SPENCER (RCA).

WINTERREISE: GOERNE, JOHNSON (HYPERION).

COLLECTION:

"A SCHUBERT EVENING": BAKER, MOORE, PARSONS (EMI).

Schuman, William

(b. New York, August 4, 1910; d. New York, February 15, 1992)

AMERICAN COMPOSER AND ADMINISTRATOR. He came to classical music through an interest in popular music and jazz that developed rapidly when he was in his teens. At the age of 19 he began his formal study of music with private lessons in harmony and counterpoint; he took summer courses in composition at the Juilliard School in 1932 and 1933 and studied with Roy Harris from 1936 until 1938. On the strength of an endorsement from Aaron Copland, his Symphony No. 2 (1937) was premiered by Serge Koussevitzky and the Boston Symphony in 1939. Koussevitzky immediately commissioned what would become Schuman's breakthrough work, his Symphony No. 3, and conducted its premiere in Boston on October 17, 1941. In the years that followed, Schuman composed another seven symphonies, numerous orchestral works including the popular *NEW ENGLAND TRIPTYCH* (1956), several ballets, a baseball opera titled *The Mighty Casey* (1953), works for chorus and band, and a smattering of chamber pieces. He also became one of America's most honored composers; in 1943, having already garnered two Guggenheim Fellowships (1939–41), he picked up the first Pulitzer Prize ever awarded in music for his cantata *A Free Song* (1942), and in 1973 he became a member of the American Academy of Arts and Letters. In 1981 he topped even that, becoming the first recipient of the William Schuman Award, a prize named for him by

William Schuman

Columbia University. Schuman also achieved distinction in academic life, teaching at Sarah Lawrence College (1935–45) and serving as the president of Juilliard (1945–61). From 1962 to 1969 he presided over Lincoln Center.

In a career spent for the most part fulfilling commissions rather than writing from inner necessity, Schuman broke little new ground but found interesting ways to adapt conventional forms and procedures. He was a brilliant orchestrator, with a penchant for scoring by choir (the winds doing one thing, the brass doing another, the strings another) and adept at building effective climaxes through the reiteration of brief rhythmic and motivic figures. He proved in works such as the *New England Triptych* and his Third, Fifth (*Symphony for Strings*), and Sixth Symphonies that he was capable of writing music of vibrant strength and energy, even if the daring dissonances and bold polytonal excursions now produce a certain aesthetic pleasure at odds with the jarring effect they undoubtedly had when the pieces were new. In many of his later works Schuman was content to pour old wine into new bottles, and even some of his finest scores have an element of bombast. Hailed in their time, most of his works now seem more impressive for their construction and scoring than for any communication of beauty or emotion, while some, such as the *American Festival* Overture (1939), are just plain hot air.

RECOMMENDED RECORDINGS

New England Triptych: Litton and Dallas Symphony Orchestra (Dorian).

Symphonies Nos. 3, 5, and 8: Bernstein and New York Philharmonic (Sony).

Symphonies Nos. 4 and 9: Schwarz and Seattle Symphony (Naxos).

Symphony No. 6: Ormandy and Philadelphia Orchestra (Albany).

Schumann, Clara [née Wieck]

(b. Leipzig, September 13, 1819; d. Frankfurt, May 20, 1896)

German pianist and composer, wife of Robert Schumann. She was the daughter of Marianne and Friedrich Wieck, both pianists; following their divorce in 1824, Friedrich, one of the great teachers of the day, was granted custody of five-year-old Clara and her brothers. Clara was taught to play the piano and quickly became a phenomenon. She made her debut at the Gewandhaus when she was 11, appeared in Paris when she was 12, and took Vienna by storm when she was 18.

In the spring of 1835, when she was 15, Clara became romantically involved with one of her father's students, the 25-year-old Robert Schumann. For the next five years the two rode an emotional roller coaster, in and out of love with each other, but eventually united in their determination to marry against the fierce opposition of Clara's father. Schumann ended up filing a suit against him; Wieck responded by claiming, among other things, that Schumann was a drunk, and managed to drag things out for a year before the courts ruled in Schumann's favor. Robert and Clara were married on September 12, 1840, one day before Clara's 21st birthday.

Over the next 14 years the couple had eight children, one of whom died in infancy. Clara took on the roles of wife, mother, and musical helpmate to her husband with exceptional purposefulness, managing a lively, welcoming household and continuing to perform and compose, though she put her husband's composing

Clara Schumann in 1853

needs first. She gave the premieres of many of Robert's works, including the Piano Concerto in A minor, Op. 54 (1846), and championed them on her concert programs. Following her husband's death, in 1856, she ceased her own composing and resumed the life of a touring virtuoso, making the case for Schumann's music across Europe. Johannes Brahms, whom she and Robert had befriended when he was a lad of 20, became something more than a friend to Clara after Robert's death; the relationship remained a close one for the rest of her life.

Clara's own music—mainly songs and piano pieces ◉—is of high quality, though it has always been overshadowed by that of her husband. As one of the 19th century's outstanding pianists, as a champion of Robert Schumann's works, and as a supportive muse to Brahms, her place in the musical firmament is assured.

RECOMMENDED RECORDINGS

LIEDER (WITH R. SCHUMANN, *LIEDERKREIS*): SKOVHUS; DEUTSCH (SONY).

PIANO CONCERTO IN A MINOR, PIANO TRIO IN G MINOR, *ROMANCES* FOR VIOLIN AND PIANO: JOCHUM, SILVERSTEIN, CARR; SILVERSTEIN AND BAMBERG SYMPHONY ORCHESTRA (TUDOR).

PIANO WORKS (*SOIRÉES MUSICALES*, OTHERS): V. JOCHUM (TUDOR).

PIANO WORKS (*TROIS ROMANCES*, SONATA IN G, *SOIRÉES MUSICALES*): IWAI (NAXOS).

Schumann, Elisabeth

(b. Merseburg, June 13, 1888; d. New York, April 23, 1952)

GERMAN SOPRANO. After vocal training in Dresden, Berlin, and Hamburg, she made her debut in Hamburg in 1909 as the Shepherd in Wagner's *Tannhäuser*, remaining with the Hamburg Opera until 1919, when Richard Strauss, a great admirer of her Sophie in *Der Rosenkavalier*, invited her to join the Vienna Staatsoper. Though her debut season at the Metropolitan Opera (1914–15) featured her in 50 performances of ten roles, she never again sang with that company; nonetheless, her career blossomed in Europe, where she would eventually be heard in more than 90 roles. In addition to Strauss portrayals (especially Sophie, which she sang for almost her entire operatic career), she was much loved in the Mozart roles of Susanna, Blonde, Zerlina, and Despina, and as Adele in *Die Fledermaus*. She also ventured into heavier, lyric roles such as Mimì in Puccini's *La bohème* and Gounod's Juliette, and had particular success as Eva in Wagner's *Die Meistersinger von Nürnberg*. Highly regarded as a recitalist, she made numerous recordings and tours (including a 1921 U.S. tour with Richard Strauss at the keyboard). Her 28-year career in opera came to an end with the Nazi takeover of Austria in 1938; still in excellent voice, she continued to sing in concert and on the recital stage into her 60s.

Silver-voiced soprano Elisabeth Schumann

Schumann's lively, winning personality was matched by a light yet irresistible, silvery voice. A musician of great intelligence, she used every vocal and dramatic resource at her command to bring each role and song to life; despite her pert appearance and delicate voice, she was capable of expressing deep emotion. And when it came to expressing youthful zest and gaiety, hardly anyone could touch her.

Schumann, Robert

(b. Zwickau, June 8, 1810; d. Endenich, July 29, 1856)

GERMAN COMPOSER AND CRITIC. A quirky, problematic genius, he wrote some of the greatest music of the Romantic era, and also some of the weakest. Severely affected by what was most likely bipolar disorder, he achieved almost superhuman productivity during his manic periods. His life ended early and miserably with a descent into insanity brought on by syphilis. He did his best work when younger, in small forms: piano pieces and songs.

Schumann's bookseller father was also a novelist and translator of Walter Scott and Byron; highly nervous, he married a violently passionate woman, and Schumann was brought up in an environment both literary and unstable. He began piano studies at seven, and studied Latin and Greek at school in Zwickau, developing a keen interest in literature and in writing as he entered his teens. He continued to develop as a pianist and wrote novels. When he was 16 his father died and in the same month his sister committed suicide. His father had stipulated that for Robert to receive his inheritance he had to take a three-year course of study at the university level, and the next year Schumann enrolled as a law student at the University of Leipzig. He spent his time reading Jean Paul Richter and soon became a piano student of (and boarder with) Friedrich Wieck, whose daughter, Clara, then nine, he would eventually marry. He developed a consuming interest in the music of Schubert, which opened a window on his own creative yearnings.

Robert Schumann, ca. 1826

In 1830 Schumann opted out of law and resumed his studies with Wieck. Despite incessant practice, he never became the virtuoso pianist he hoped to be, owing to a "numbness" in the middle finger of his right hand. The problem may have resulted from his use, over Wieck's objection, of a splint contraption to strengthen the hand, or from mercury poisoning related to the treatment of syphilis, which he probably contracted in his teens. Fortunately, he would not need to be a virtuoso —because he would marry one.

The 1830s were turbulent for Schumann. He fought with Wieck over his training and his relationship with Clara, which Wieck opposed. Under stress, he drank and smoked heavily and suffered his first bouts of depression. Gradually Schumann let go of the dream of keyboard virtuosity and became active as a critic, for which he was, during his lifetime, as well known as he was for his music. Simultaneously he developed into a very capable composer. In 1834 he founded the *Neue Zeitschrift für Musik,* turning it into a platform for his philosophizing on the music of the past and present and for notices and analyses of new works. Among his own important works of the decade were the majority of the pieces that established his reputation as a composer for the piano: *Carnaval,* the *Davidsbündlertänze,* the *Symphonic Etudes,* the Fantasy in C, *Kinderszenen* (*Scenes from Childhood*), *Kreisleriana,* and others. During this time, he befriended Chopin and Mendelssohn.

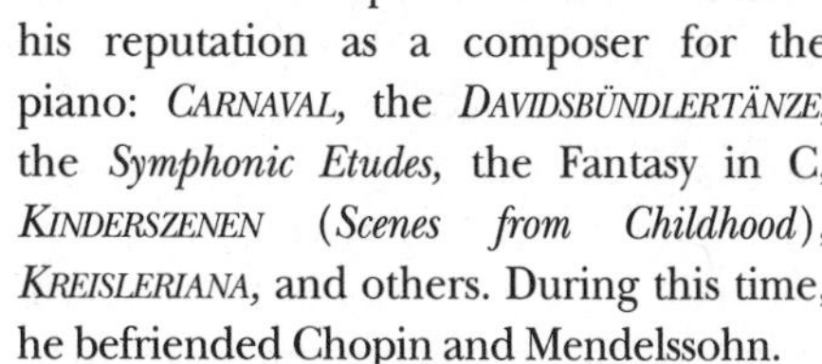

By 1840 Clara Wieck, 20, was a distinguished pianist and had been in the public eye for more than a decade. Schumann's marriage to her—which took place that year after he prevailed in a lawsuit against her father—resulted in an enormous creative outpouring. First came the "year of song." Anticipating marriage in a decidedly lyrical state of mind, Schumann focused his pent-up emotion on vocal music, composing nearly 140 songs in

1840, most of them in the anxious months before August, when the marriage-permission suit he and Clara had filed against her father was decided in their favor. The following year, in a mood of celebration, he turned to the orchestra. His works included two symphonies—No. 1 in B-flat (the SPRING SYMPHONY) and No. 4 in D minor—as well as the *Overture, Scherzo and Finale,* and a *Fantasie* in A minor for piano and orchestra. In 1842 Schumann focused on chamber music, composing three string quartets, the often heard Piano Quintet in E-flat, Op. 44, and the wonderful Piano Quartet in E-flat, Op. 47.

Such feverish concentration on a single genre at a time can be seen as typical manic behavior. The other side of the coin—phobias and terrifying slides into depression—turned up as the 1840s wore on, leaving the composer incapacitated. At the end of 1844 Schumann and Clara moved to Dresden, at one of the lowest of his low points. During the next few years, he completed the Piano Concerto in A minor, Op. 54 (an outgrowth of the earlier *Fantasie*), his Symphony No. 2 in C, Op. 61, his one opera, *Genoveva,* and an extraordinary "dramatic poem" for orchestra and speaker based on Byron's *MANFRED.*

In 1850 Schumann accepted a position as municipal music director in Düsseldorf. One of the first works he composed after his arrival was the Symphony No. 3 in E-flat, Op. 97, the *RHENISH,* inspired by the Rhineland and the majestic Cologne Cathedral. During the three seasons he held the job, Schumann experienced difficulties with city administrators and ultimately, owing to his increasingly erratic behavior on the podium, lost the respect of the orchestra and chorus. He was fired in the fall of 1853. A bright spot during that sad season was the time the Schumanns spent with the renowned violinist Joseph Joachim and the 20-year-old Johannes Brahms, whose budding genius Schumann immediately recognized.

Schumann in 1830

During the winter of 1854, Schumann's insanity manifested itself dramatically: He heard "angelic" voices that quickly morphed into a bestial noise of "tigers and hyenas." On a February morning he walked to a bridge over the Rhine and threw himself in; he was rescued by fishermen. Insisting that for Clara's protection he be institutionalized, he was placed in a sanatorium; his doctors prevented Clara from seeing him for more than two years, until days before his death.

Schumann's literary sensitivity and introspective nature led him to imbue nearly everything he wrote with personality—in the case of his best songs and piano pieces, often the multiple sides of his own personality. Nearly all of his piano music is referential, attempting to embody emotions aroused by literature or to characterize actors' interactions in some ongoing novel or lyric poem of the mind. One of Schumann's favorite conceits was the "Davidsbund" ("Tribe of David"), peopled by imaginary characters who, like the

Biblical David, were willing to stand up to the artistic Philistines of the day. The members of this society included Meister Raro, probably an idealization of his teacher and father-in-law, as well as Schumann's two major personae: the impetuous extrovert Florestan and the pale, studious, introverted Eusebius. The *DAVIDSBÜNDLERTÄNZE (Dances of the Tribe of David)* specifically chronicles an emotional and musical journey with these two alter egos at the wheel—but so do most of Schumann's works, especially those for piano.

Schumann's lyrical, intense musicality produced some of the most beautiful and moving lieder in the repertoire. His *DICHTERLIEBE* (*Poet's Love*) ◉, a setting of 16 poems by Heinrich Heine, is his best-known song cycle and a supreme achievement in German lied. Other cycles include *FRAUENLIEBE UND -LEBEN* (*Woman's Love and Life*) and two sets titled *Liederkreis* (one to poems of Heine, one to poems of Joseph von Eichendorff). There is a substantial amount of chamber music; the best pieces are the Piano Quintet (the first piece ever written for that complement), the Piano Quartet, and the *Three Romances* for oboe and piano. ◉

As a symphonic composer Schumann sports a long rap sheet: awkwardness in larger forms, muddy scoring, excessive doublings that always sound a little out of tune. But he was capable of achieving splendid orchestral effects, and his Third and Fourth Symphonies also reveal original and innovative approaches to form. In an effort to reinforce a feeling of unity in the Fourth Symphony, he specified that its four movements be played without a break, with the aim that the entire work would form a large cyclical structure. The underlying unity of the piece asserts itself in the treatment of key and in the thematic linking of the last movement to the first, and of parts of the third movement to the second. The material is so closely knit that musicologists have come to regard it as a landmark in the history of the genre. Of the concerted works, the Piano Concerto is Schumann at his best. The Cello Concerto is a solid piece, but the Violin Concerto, a late work of troubled delicacy, requires very sympathetic treatment to be effective. None of Schumann's efforts for the stage has found a place in the repertoire.

There is little doubt that Schumann will remain a canonic figure, though if quality of work is the only gauge, his importance has long been overrated. His abilities at times fell short of his ambitions, but he brought enthusiasm and a rare poetic genius to everything he attempted. As a critic he was remarkably astute in some judgments, wildly off the mark in others, and in all cases generous. He never became a great pianist, was a failure as a conductor, and at times was not even a very good composer. But his entire being was music, informed by dream and fantasy. He was music's quintessential Romantic, always ardent, always striving for the ideal.

RECOMMENDED RECORDINGS

CARNAVAL: RUBINSTEIN (RCA).

DAVIDSBÜNDLERTÄNZE: PERAHIA (SONY).

DICHTERLIEBE: FISCHER-DIESKAU, BRENDEL (PHILIPS).

DICHTERLIEBE: WUNDERLICH, GIESEN (DG).

KINDERSZENEN: JANDÓ (NAXOS).

KINDERSZENEN: LUPU (DECCA).

KREISLERIANA: EGOROV (EMI).

KREISLERIANA: LUPU (DECCA).

PIANO CONCERTO: PERAHIA; DAVIS AND BAVARIAN RADIO SYMPHONY ORCHESTRA (SONY).

PIANO QUINTET, PIANO QUARTET: BETTELHEIM, RHODES WITH BEAUX ARTS TRIO (PHILIPS).

SYMPHONIC ETUDES: POLLINI (DG).

SYMPHONIES: BERNSTEIN AND VIENNA PHILHARMONIC (DG).

SYMPHONIES: KARAJAN AND BERLIN PHILHARMONIC (DG).

SYMPHONIES: SAWALLISCH AND STAATSKAPELLE DRESDEN (EMI).

Schumann-Heink, Ernestine

(b. Lieben, June 15, 1861; d. Los Angeles, November 17, 1936)

AUSTRIAN/AMERICAN CONTRALTO. Born Ernestine Rössler to an Austrian army officer and his Italian wife, the famously headstrong contralto credited her father for her stubborn streak and her mother (her first voice teacher) for her love of the arts. She studied in Graz with Marietta Leclair and made her first public appearance there at the age of 15, as a soloist in Beethoven's Ninth Symphony. Her operatic debut came two years later in Dresden, as Azucena in Verdi's *Il trovatore.* Though the 17-year-old lacked the experience to make Verdi's mad old Gypsy credible, her performance identified her as a singer of promise. She sang with the Dresden Court Opera for four seasons (1878–82); following her marriage to Ernst Heink, she moved to Hamburg, and sang as Ernestine Heink until 1897. Performing frequently under the direction of Gustav Mahler, she began to build an operatic repertoire that would eventually include nearly 150 roles, and to develop the performance profile for which she would pass into history.

A singer of great power and expressivity, she was that rarest of voice types, a true contralto. But with her extensive range and remarkable physical stamina, she excelled in roles outside the relatively narrow contralto repertoire; in addition to deeply pitched staples such as Wagner's Erda, she sang with great success in roles with a higher tessitura such as Waltraute in Wagner's *Götterdämmerung,* Amneris in Verdi's *Aida,* and Fidès in Meyerbeer's *Le prophète.* After she and Heink were divorced, she married the actor Paul Schumann and created for herself the hyphenated stage name by which she would subsequently be known. Schumann, who died in 1904, is generally credited with bringing out his wife's acting talents by stressing the value of working with operatic texts as if they were scripts.

From 1896 to 1914 Schumann-Heink sang at the Bayreuth Festival, where she was a particular favorite of Wagner's widow, Cosima. Ortrud, the raging villainess in *Lohengrin,* was the vehicle for her Metropolitan Opera debut, which took place in Chicago on November 7, 1898, the opening night of the company's fall tour. A few days later she sang the role of Fricka, and on January 9, 1899, she made her New York debut, again as Ortrud. Henry E. Krehbiel, writing for the *New York Tribune,* remarked on that occasion, "When she wins admiration for the passages in which Wagner thought neither of contralto nor soprano, but only of his Frisian creation, half woman, half witch and all wickedness personified, she compelled it by virtue of

Ernestine Schumann-Heink at a War Bond rally, belting it out for the boys

her thrilling use of tonal color, her giving out of Wagner's ideal which she had absorbed completely." Enamored of the United States, Schumann-Heink canceled her standing contract with the Berlin Opera, and remained at the Met to sing (mostly) Wagnerian roles until 1903. Thereafter, she sang sporadically with the company until 1932.

Though her operatic career continued into her 72nd year and included among its highlights the creation in 1909 of the role of Klytemnestra in Richard Strauss's *Elektra,* Schumann-Heink spent most of the final three decades of her career as a concert singer, solidifying her reputation through numerous tours, extensive appearances on radio, and many justly prized records—as well as her enthusiastic support of American forces during World War I (she had become an American citizen in 1905). She retired as one of America's most beloved musical artists.

Schütz, Heinrich

(b. Köstritz, October 8, 1585; d. Dresden, November 6, 1672)

THE GREATEST GERMAN COMPOSER of the 17th century. His music, shaped by the Italian practice of the Renaissance and Baroque, served as the cornerstone of Baroque musical art in Germany.

Schütz came from a close-knit, respected bourgeois family of innkeepers and small businessmen. He grew up in Weissenfels and showed musical inclination early, learning to sing angelically as a child. When the local landgrave, Moritz of Hessen-Kassel, stayed at the inn and heard him, Schütz's destiny was changed. Moritz prevailed upon the boy's father to permit him to take charge of his education. At Kassel, Schütz served as choirboy and was schooled at an academy for noble children, where he excelled in languages. In 1608 he entered the University of Marburg to study law, acceding to his father's wish that he have a "secure profession." Again he was an outstanding student. But Moritz, quite convinced of his young protégé's unique musical gift, made an offer neither Schütz nor his father could refuse, proposing to pay Schütz's way with a two-year stipend (200 thalers a year) to study, in Venice, with Giovanni Gabrieli.

Schütz arrived in Venice in 1609. The bond between teacher and student became so close that Gabrieli persuaded Moritz to foot the bill for a third year, at the start of which Schütz published, as his Op. 1, his *Primo libro de madrigali,* a collection of five-voice madrigals dedicated to Moritz. Following Gabrieli's death in 1612, Schütz returned to Moritz's court as organist. But within a couple of years Johann Georg I, the Elector of Saxony, requested that Schütz come to Dresden as acting Kapellmeister. Moritz had little choice but to comply with the sovereign's wishes, and give up the musician whose talents he had done so much to develop. In Dresden, Schütz was responsible for music for court ceremonial functions. He published *Psalmen Davids* in 1619; also that year he married. (His wife died in 1625, leaving two daughters who were brought up by their maternal grandmother; Schütz never remarried.) In 1627 Schütz composed the earliest known opera in German, *Dafne,* based on the same libretto that had been used in Jacopo Peri's groundbreaking *Dafne* of 1598; the music does not survive. The following year Schütz made a second trip to Italy, his goal to familiarize himself with the nascent Baroque style in music. Monteverdi was his guide this time around. Schütz was particularly interested in dramatic monody, the new, highly expressive *concertato* style of solo vocal writing that made use of basso continuo. He immediately put it to use in his *Symphoniae sacrae,* which were published in Venice in 1629, shortly before he returned to Dresden. Two years later, music at the Dresden court came to a halt, as Saxony entered the Thirty Years' War (1618–48). Schütz soldiered on in service of the Saxon court for another 40 years, through good times and bad, but spent long periods in Denmark and at Wolfenbüttel, the court of the Duke of Brunswick-Lüneburg.

He continued writing music until shortly before his death, at 87, with no diminishment of ability. In 1670 he asked a former deputy to write a five-voice psalm setting "in the Palestrina style of counterpoint," by then a century old, for use at his funeral. The three other pieces performed on that occasion he wrote himself.

Schütz's endeavors over a long career were of huge importance to the development of music in Germany. By adapting the techniques of the new Italian theatrical style to German sacred music, he brought the Baroque revolution to his homeland, and infused its musical language with a new grace and expressiveness. The core of his achievement were the "sacred concertos"—sacred vocal works with continuo for a variable complement of solo voices, often with obbligato instruments (usually strings). Among these are the two sets of *Kleine geistliche Concerte* and the three sets of *Symphoniae sacrae,* the first with Latin texts, the latter two with German. Schütz wrote motets in both the old polyphonic style and the modern (i.e., with continuo). In addition to these there are the psalm settings of his *Psalmen Davids,* hybrid works for voices and basso continuo—part motet, part sacred concerto. He also composed three Passions, a Magnificat, a Requiem (the *Musicalische Exequien,* in German), and a *Christmas Story* (1660); the latter's joyous, colorfully Italianate music already points the way to Bach.

Schütz had a strong sense of duty, coping into his old age with difficulties not of his making, writing for what was available when war resulted in reduced performing forces. His works are informed by a spirit of resilience, endurance, and acceptance of both loss and opportunity. In his own life he drew comfort from Scripture, particularly the Psalms, and he wrote music that sought to convey that solace to others, as beautifully and economically as possible.

Heinrich Schütz

RECOMMENDED RECORDINGS

MUSICALISCHE EXEQUIEN: HOLTON, CHANCE, LANG, BIRCHALL; GARDINER AND MONTEVERDI CHOIR, ENGLISH BAROQUE SOLOISTS (DG).

SYMPHONIAE SACRAE (FIRST SET): BORDEN, COVEY-CRUMP, POTTER, VAN DER KAMP; DICKEY AND CONCERTO PALATINO (ACCENT).

SYMPHONIAE SACRAE (THIRD SET): ZEDELIUS, FRIMMER, CHANCE, PRÉGARDIEN, THOMAS; BERNIUS AND MUSICA FIATA, KAMMERCHOR STUTTGART (DEUTSCHE HARMONIA MUNDI).

WEIHNACHTSHISTORIE (*CHRISTMAS STORY*): AGNEW, CROOKES, MCCARTHY; SUMMERLY AND OXFORD CAMERATA (NAXOS).

WEIHNACHTSHISTORIE: KIRKBY, ROGERS, THOMAS; PARROTT AND TAVERNER PLAYERS (VIRGIN CLASSICS).

Schwanengesang (Swan Song) **Collection of 14 songs in two books by Franz Schubert, D. 957,** composed between August and October 1828 to poems by Ludwig Rellstab, Heinrich Heine, and Johann Gabriel Seidl.

RECOMMENDED RECORDING

Fischer-Dieskau, Moore (DG).

Schwantner, Joseph

(b. Chicago, March 22, 1943)

American composer. He learned to play the guitar and the tuba as a youth and was interested in both jazz and classical music in high school. He attended the American Conservatory in Chicago, receiving his bachelor's degree in 1964, and subesquently studied at Northwestern University, earning his master's (1966) and a doctorate in composition (1968). After brief teaching stints at universities in Washington and Indiana, in 1970 he joined the faculty at the Eastman School of Music in Rochester, New York. His first substantial orchestral work, *Aftertones of Infinity,* won the Pulitzer Prize in music in 1979; two years later, his *Music of Amber,* for flute, clarinet, violin, cello, piano, and percussion received first prize in the Kennedy Center/Friedheim Awards. From 1982 to 1985, Schwantner worked in partnership with conductor Leonard Slatkin as composer-in-residence with the Saint Louis Symphony Orchestra. Among the works to result from the association were *A Sudden Rainbow* (1986), the guitar concerto *From Afar . . .* (1987), written for Sharon Isbin, and a Piano Concerto (1988) composed for Emanuel Ax. Slatkin also conducted the premiere of Schwantner's Percussion Concerto (1995), written for the New York Philharmonic and its principal percussionist, Christopher Lamb. Among Schwantner's most recent works is *September Canticle,* a "poem" for organ, brass, percussion, and strings, commissioned by the Dallas Symphony Orchestra and premiered in 2002.

Schwantner's early works made use of serial techniques, but in a fairly loose way; he soon moved away from serialism toward an eclectic and loosely tonal style, one in which he was free to indulge his interest in unusual tone colors and instrumental groupings, along with his flair for executant virtuosity. As a composer of instrumental music he has earned the esteem of performers, audiences, and critics while continuing to write music that is challenging and surprising. His work is distinguished by fine craftsmanship, as one might expect from a composer who has likened his role to that of an artisan.

RECOMMENDED RECORDINGS

Aftertones of Infinity**: Slatkin and Julliard Orchestra (New World).**

From Afar . . . **: Isbin, Wolff and St. Paul Chamber Orchestra (Virgin Classics).**

Schwarz, Gerard

(b. Hoboken, N.J., August 19, 1947)

American conductor. He began his career as a virtuoso trumpet player. A student of William Vacchiano, he was a member of the American Brass Quintet (1965–73) and became co-principal trumpet of the New York Philharmonic in 1973. In 1977, he gave up the trumpet to focus entirely on conducting. That year he became music director of the Y Chamber Symphony in New York, later renamed the New York Chamber Symphony, which offered an alternative to the mainstream orchestral programming then dominant in New York. From 1978 to 1985 he also served as music director of the Los Angeles Chamber Orchestra. He made numerous recordings with both ensembles, establishing his credentials as a champion of American composers and an interpreter of the classics. In 1982 Schwarz became music director of

Lincoln Center's Mostly Mozart Festival, which he ably guided through two decades of growth and artistic achievement; in 2002 he was designated the festival's conductor laureate.

Schwarz became music adviser to the Seattle Symphony in 1983, and in 1985 he was named its music director. In Seattle he has developed an outstanding ensemble and continued his work on behalf of American composers, particularly 20th-century symphonists such as Howard Hanson, Alan Hovhaness (1911–2000), David Diamond (1915–2005), Walter Piston, and William Schuman, creating a distinctive profile for the orchestra. His recordings have set both interpretive and sonic benchmarks, and garnered considerable acclaim. Schwarz also pushed for the building of the orchestra's new home, Benaroya Hall, which opened in downtown Seattle on September 12, 1998. He became music director of the Royal Liverpool Philharmonic Orchestra in 2001.

RECOMMENDED RECORDINGS

AS INSTRUMENTALIST:

HAYDN, HUMMEL, TRUMPET CONCERTOS: SCHWARZ AND NEW YORK CHAMBER ENSEMBLE (DELOS).

"NEW MUSIC FOR TRUMPET": WORKS BY BRANT, CARTER, WOLPE, OTHERS; RANGER, ROSENZWEIG (PHOENIX USA).

AS CONDUCTOR:

COPLAND, *LINCOLN PORTRAIT, AN OUTDOOR OVERTURE, FANFARE FOR THE COMMON MAN* (WITH WORKS OF HARRIS): JONES; SEATTLE SYMPHONY ORCHESTRA (DELOS).

HANSON, SYMPHONIES NOS. 1 AND 2: SEATTLE SYMPHONY ORCHESTRA (DELOS).

HOVHANESS, SYMPHONY NO. 2 (*MYSTERIOUS MOUNTAIN*), *AND GOD CREATED WHALES*, OTHER WORKS: SEATTLE SYMPHONY ORCHESTRA (NAXOS).

"MADE IN THE USA": SYMPHONIC WORKS BY CRESTON, DIAMOND, HANSON, SCHUMAN, OTHERS; SEATTLE SYMPHONY ORCHESTRA (DELOS).

Schwarzkopf, Dame Elisabeth

(b. Jarotschin, Poland, December 9, 1915)

GERMAN SOPRANO. Among the most promising singers of her generation, she studied at the Berlin Hochschule für Musik beginning in 1934 and subsequently with Maria Ivogün and her husband, the pianist Michael Raucheisen. In 1935, at the age of 19, she joined the Nazi Student League. Her talent was recognized early on by the Reichstheaterkammer, which designated her an opera singer summa cum laude in 1938; that same year she was placed under contract with Berlin's Deutsches Opernhaus (known today as the Deutsche Oper Berlin). She made her stage debut with that company on April 15, 1938, as a Flower Maiden in Wagner's *Parsifal.* In 1940 she joined the Nazi Party, and thanks to a combination of talent, adroit maneuvering, and solid party credentials she enjoyed a flourishing career in the Third Reich as a darling of the brass hats, chief among them SS General Hugo Jury, Gauleiter of Lower Austria, her protector.

Following the war, she toured with the Vienna Staatsoper (whose home on the Ringstrasse had yet to be rebuilt), making her London debut at Covent Garden in 1947, as Donna Elvira in Mozart's *Don Giovanni,* and bowing at Milan's La Scala in 1948, as the Marschallin in Richard Strauss's *Der Rosenkavalier.* She subsequently sang with the resident companies of both houses on many occasions. In the summer of 1951 she sang under Wilhelm Furtwängler's baton in the performance of Beethoven's Ninth Symphony that reopened the Bayreuth Festival; later that year she created the role of Anne Trulove in the world premiere of Stravinsky's *The Rake's Progress,* in Venice. She sang at Carnegie Hall for the first time in 1953 and made her American

Elisabeth Schwarzkopf as Zerbinetta in **Ariadne auf Naxos**

stage debut in 1955, with the San Francisco Opera. In 1964 she made her belated debut at the Metropolitan Opera, as the Marschallin. By then the sun was setting on her career. She gave her last operatic performance in Brussels, on December 31, 1971, and retired from the recital stage in 1979.

In 1946, in Vienna, the 30-year-old Schwarzkopf had auditioned for the English record producer Walter Legge, who during the years that followed featured her in a number of important registrations for EMI—songs of Schumann, Brahms, and Wolf; Mozart's *Così fan tutte* and Strauss's *Ariadne auf Naxos* and *Der Rosenkavalier,* all with Karajan; Beethoven's Ninth and Brahms's *Ein deutsches Requiem,* also with Karajan; Strauss's *Capriccio* with Wolfgang Sawallisch; Strauss's *Vier letzte Lieder* with George Szell; a remake of the Brahms Requiem, with Klemperer conducting; and a remake of *Così,* with Karl Böhm. Schwarzkopf also provided the dubbed high C for Kirsten Flagstad in the legendary 1952 recording of Wagner's *Tristan und Isolde* conducted by Furtwängler. In 1953 Schwarzkopf and Legge married; he produced all of her recordings, the last one finished just months before his death in 1979. In 1992 Schwarzkopf was knighted by Queen Elizabeth II for her services to music.

Schwarzkopf possessed a formidable drive and ego. She brought the attributes of an accomplished lieder singer to everything she did: excellent intonation, intelligent phrasing, sharp delineation of character. In her prime she could produce a radiant, silver-toned sound of outstanding quality and expressiveness. At her best, in the Mozart and Strauss roles she favored and in a wide swath of German lieder, she was all but incomparable. But her technique began to erode by the late 1950s; in recordings made from that point on she often sounds hooty in the high reaches. Sadly, interpretive affectations crept into her singing as her voice deteriorated, resulting in the self-consciously "artsy" manner of her later years in the studio.

RECOMMENDED RECORDINGS

BRAHMS, *EIN DEUTSCHES REQUIEM*: FISCHER-DIESKAU; KLEMPERER AND PHILHARMONIA ORCHESTRA (EMI).

MAHLER, *DES KNABEN WUNDERHORN*: FISCHER-DIESKAU; SZELL AND LONDON SYMPHONY ORCHESTRA (EMI).

MOZART, *COSÌ FAN TUTTE*: LUDWIG, STEFFEK, KRAUS, TADDEI, BERRY; BÖHM AND PHILHARMONIA ORCHESTRA (EMI).

STRAUSS, *CAPRICCIO*: LUDWIG, WAECHTER, GEDDA, FISCHER-DIESKAU, HOTTER; SAWALLISCH AND PHILHARMONIA ORCHESTRA (EMI).

STRAUSS, *DER ROSENKAVALIER*: LUDWIG, STICH-RANDALL, EDELMANN, WAECHTER; KARAJAN AND PHILHARMONIA ORCHESTRA (EMI).

STRAUSS, *VIER LETZTE LIEDER*: SZELL AND BERLIN RADIO SYMPHONY ORCHESTRA (EMI).

WOLF, LIEDER: MOORE (EMI).

scordatura (from It. *scordare,* "to forget") On string instruments, a nonstandard tuning. The literature contains numerous examples of scordatura tuning, especially for the violin. No fewer than 14 of the so-called *Mystery* Sonatas (ca. 1675) by Baroque composer Heinrich BIBER call for scordatura tunings, each one different, whose purpose is to produce unusual tonal effects or to permit double stops, arpeggiated figures, and bariolage that would be impossible on a normally tuned violin. Mozart, in his *Sinfonia concertante* in E-flat, K. 364, for violin and viola, specifies that the strings of the solo viola be tuned a half tone higher, allowing the viola to sound the root and fifth of the E-flat major chord on open strings and thereby produce a more powerful and brilliant sound that more nearly balances that of the solo violin. To make the tuning work, Mozart writes the viola part a half step lower, as if the piece were in D. Examples of cello scordatura include Bach's Suite No. 5 in C minor (in which the A string is tuned down to G) and Kodály's Sonata, Op. 8 (in which the C and G strings are tuned down to B and F-sharp).

***Scottish* Fantasy** WORK FOR VIOLIN AND ORCHESTRA BY MAX BRUCH, OP. 46, composed 1879–80 and premiered February 22, 1881, in Liverpool. Bruch conducted and Joseph Joachim was the soloist. The full title of the work is *Fantasie unter freier Benutzung schottischer Volksmelodien* (*Fantasy with Free Use of Scottish Folk Melodies*). The score is dedicated to Joachim's archrival, the violinist Pablo de Sarasate.

RECOMMENDED RECORDINGS

CHUNG; KEMPE AND ROYAL PHILHARMONIC ORCHESTRA (DECCA).

HEIFETZ; STEINBERG AND RCA VICTOR SYMPHONY ORCHESTRA (NAXOS).

LIN; SLATKIN AND CHICAGO SYMPHONY ORCHESTRA (SONY).

***Scottish* Symphony** NICKNAME OF FELIX MENDELSSOHN'S SYMPHONY NO. 3 IN A MINOR, OP. 56, completed in Berlin in 1842 and first performed on March 3, 1842, in Leipzig, by the Gewandhaus Orchestra under the composer's direction. The work is a musical response to Scotland, whose rocky, Romantic land- and seascapes, viewed firsthand during the summer of 1829, had fascinated the young composer. A visit to Mary Stuart's chapel at Holyrood Castle in Edinburgh prompted the principal theme of the first movement, while the sound of Scottish folk music undoubtedly influenced the melody heard on the clarinet at the beginning of the scherzo.

RECOMMENDED RECORDINGS

KARAJAN AND BERLIN PHILHARMONIC (DG).

MAAG AND LONDON SYMPHONY ORCHESTRA (DECCA).

MASUR AND GEWANDHAUS ORCHESTRA (EURODISC).

Scriabin, Aleksandr

(b. Moscow, January 6, 1872; d. Moscow, April 27, 1915)

RUSSIAN COMPOSER AND PIANIST. Driven by an egomaniacal mysticism that eventually led to messianic delusions, he started out writing in a fairly conventional late-Romantic idiom and developed into a visionary modernist intent on pushing the envelope of tonality to its limits. His piano music was his most important achievement.

Scriabin's father, a lawyer and foreign service officer, came from a family with a long tradition of military service. His mother was an exceptionally talented pianist; she died of complications from his birth, less than a year afterward. The only child was raised by his two grandmothers and his doting aunt, living a pampered existence that surely helped form his delicate, nervous, egocentric personality. His aunt, also a pianist, became his first teacher. Taken to concerts and operas, Scriabin developed an interest in literature and the arts. He entered the army cadet corps as a boy, and began his formal musical education when he was 11, studying piano with Nikolay Zverev and following the customary regimen: He lived in his teacher's house (a fellow student was the young Rachmaninov), learned French and German and social etiquette, and practiced hard. He received help preparing for the Moscow Conservatory entrance examinations from Sergey Taneyev.

Though of diminutive stature and with hands that could barely span an octave, Scriabin attacked the most difficult repertoire during his years at the conservatory; in 1891 he severely strained his right hand with excessive practicing. Forbidden by a doctor to play, he focused on his left hand and developed a formidable technique. (His Prelude in C-sharp minor and Nocturne in D-flat, Op. 9, Nos. 1 and 2, written for the left hand only, date from 1894. ◉ Idiomatic and well wrought, they exhibit the young composer's gift for yearning lyricism as well as a marked predilection for dark moods.)

Scriabin's conservatory career came to a stormy end, with the 20-year-old in conflict with his fugue teacher Anton Arensky. Aiming to become a sort of latter-day Chopin, Scriabin promptly composed a clutch of preludes and his Piano Sonata No. 1—his first published works. He undertook travel outside of Russia and made his European debut in Paris in 1896; he also developed an unbridled lifestyle, including regular bouts of all-night drinking. In 1897 he married pianist Vera Isakovitch, who bore a child a year for four years. Scriabin's publisher kept him afloat until he landed a professorship at the Moscow Conservatory in 1898. Over the next three years, he wrote his first two symphonies, which were received with incomprehension and open hostility.

The watershed year was 1903. Scriabin began a love affair with the 20-year-old Tatiana de Schloezer, a pianist (and follower of philosophical cults), who would encourage his megalomania. In the glow of this relationship, his works for piano became infused with an extreme sensuality. The scintillating brilliance and feverish emotional intensity of the Piano Sonata No. 4 mark it as a breakthrough; on its heels, in 1904, Scriabin finished the hedonistically opulent Third Symphony, titled *Divine Poem*. Having also seduced a 15-year-old student, Scriabin had to leave Russia and seek temporary sanctuary in Switzerland. Tatiana soon moved in. The *Divine Poem* was premiered in Paris in 1905, the same year the couple moved to Italy, essentially destitute, with Tatiana pregnant (she would bear Scriabin three children in all). The composer was invited to New York for concerts during the winter of 1906–07 followed by a recital tour of the Midwest, in which he acquitted himself ably. But after Tatiana joined him the couple were disinvited from further musical appearances

Scriabin, sketch by Leonid Pasternak, 1907

and effectively kicked out of the country, as friends and colleagues of Scriabin now in the U.S. sided with Vera in the scandalous saga of infidelity and abandonment.

Scriabin and Tatiana next lived in Paris and Lausanne. From this time came two major orchestral works: The *Poem of Ecstasy*, scored for an enormous orchestra and based aesthetically on Scriabin's developing philosophy of art as a sexual act, and *Prometheus, the Poem of Fire,* for piano, large orchestra, wordless chorus, and color organ (an apparatus that bathed performers and audience in colored light, whose "tonalities" were closely coordinated with the music). In 1908 Scriabin met Serge Koussevitzky, who, fascinated by his theories associating colors with keys, became an enthusiastic champion as both conductor and publisher. They toured together in 1910 but afterward had a falling-out over money.

In 1909, when Scriabin returned to Russia, he was recognized as a prophet of modernism, his music finally embraced by the critics. His piano works of the next several years included five brilliant sonatas (Nos. 6 through 10) and *Vers la flamme* (1914), a *poème* for the piano. Scriabin was visited during the summer of 1913 in Switzerland by Igor Stravinsky, who pronounced the late piano pieces "incomparable." Scriabin now contemplated his "great work," which he referred to as the *Mysterium,* a vast, purifying musical happening that would lift participants to a higher spiritual plane; it would take place in India, land of swamis and sages (in 1914 he bought property in Darjeeling), and he would be at the center of it, playing the piano. His visionary music was to be a wonderful glimpse into the future. But that future never came, and in an instant Scriabin too was gone: In the spring of 1915 he developed an infection from a pimple on his mustachioed upper lip and died of sepsis.

The vast majority of Scriabin's compositional output involved the piano, which he played with exceptional finesse. The influence of Chopin and Liszt on his earlier piano works, scintillating pianistic miniatures, was to be expected. In later works the collagelike assembly of motifs into subjects, and the subsequent processes of recollection within a piece, also owed something to Liszt's notion of thematic transformation. The lugubriousness of earlier works was superseded by the languor of later ones, which became increasingly turbulent and almost telegraphically compressed.

Scriabin's other major musical endeavors were his manic, delirious, kaleidoscopic essays for orchestra. While his first two symphonies were nothing special—No. 1 is a sprawling six-movement hodgepodge, No. 2 a dark, slow-moving, minor-key meditation with the obligatory triumphant concluding movement in the major—with the *Divine Poem,* fulminant and compact, Scriabin hit his stride. Here, and even more so in the *Poem of Ecstasy* and *Prometheus,* the harmony is saturated to the point where there is complete freedom to maneuver yet nowhere to go, because every chord sounds pretty much like the one that preceded it, making a palette of shimmering tonal ambiguities. The result is music that at once conveys a longing for the unattainable and, paradoxically, attains it, luxuriating in the contemplation of its own sound.

RECOMMENDED RECORDINGS

Piano pieces: Horowitz (Sony).

Piano sonatas (complete): Hamelin (Hyperion).

***Poem of Ecstasy*: Mehta and Los Angeles Philharmonic Orchestra (Decca).**

***Prometheus*: Toradze; Gergiev and Kirov Orchestra (Philips).**

Symphony No. 3 (*Divine Poem*) and *Poem of Ecstasy*: Pletnev and Russian National Orchestra (DG).

Eugène Scribe, **spiritus rector** *of grand opera*

Scribe, Eugène

(b. Paris, December 24, 1791; d. Paris, February 20, 1861)

FRENCH LIBRETTIST. The son of a silk merchant, he studied for a career in law. Deflected by his love of the theater, he began writing vaudevilles at the age of 18. He produced his first comic opera libretto in 1813 and by the early 1820s had established himself as one of Paris's most successful dramatists. In 1828, in his second effort for the Paris Opéra, he hit pay dirt: he created the libretto for Auber's *La muette de Portici,* which launched the new style of Parisian grand opera and became an overnight sensation, quickly spreading its author's fame throughout Europe. That same year he wrote the libretto for Rossini's *Le comte Ory.*

Scribe's collaborations with Auber and Meyerbeer produced many of the most popular comic and grand operas of the 1830s, 1840s, and 1850s. For Auber, he wrote, among others, *Fra Diavolo* (1830), *Gustav III, ou Le bal masqué* (1833; later set by Verdi as *UN BALLO IN MASCHERA*), *Le cheval de bronze* (1835), and *Les diamants de la couronne* (1841). For Meyerbeer, he penned *Robert le diable* (1831), *LES HUGUENOTS* (1836), *Le prophète* (1849), and *L'Africaine* (1865). Among his other librettos were those for *La Juive* (1835) by Fromental Halévy (1799–1862), Donizetti's *La favorite* (1840), and Verdi's *Les vêpres siciliennes* (1855). As the *spiritus rector* of Parisian grand opera, Scribe set the standard to which all other writers aspired. He was a shrewd businessman and parlayed his box office successes into a fortune. His complete works were published, in 76 volumes, between 1874 and 1885.

Seasons, The [1] **ORATORIO (*DIE JAHRESZEITEN*) BY JOSEPH HAYDN,** to a text by Gottfried van Swieten, composed 1799–1801 and first performed April 24, 1801, in Vienna. [2] **SUITE FOR PIANO BY PYOTR IL'YICH TCHAIKOVSKY** (consisting of 12 pieces, one for each month of the year), composed 1875–76. [3] **BALLET IN ONE ACT BY ALEKSANDR GLAZUNOV,** to a scenario by Marius Petipa, composed in 1899 and premiered February 7, 1900, at the Hermitage Theater in St. Petersburg.

RECOMMENDED RECORDINGS

GLAZUNOV:
ASHKENAZY AND ROYAL PHILHARMONIC ORCHESTRA (DECCA).

HAYDN:
(IN GERMAN)
BONNEY, ROLFE JOHNSON, SCHMIDT; GARDINER AND ENGLISH BAROQUE SOLOISTS (DG ARCHIV).
(IN ENGLISH)
HARPER, DAVIES, SHIRLEY-QUIRK; DAVIS AND BBC SYMPHONY ORCHESTRA (PHILIPS DUO).

TCHAIKOVSKY:
PLETNEV (VIRGIN CLASSICS).

Sea Symphony, A [1] **TITLE OF RALPH VAUGHAN WILLIAMS'S SYMPHONY NO. 1 FOR SOPRANO AND BARITONE SOLOISTS, CHORUS, AND ORCHESTRA,** composed 1903–09 and premiered October 12, 1910 (Vaughan Williams's 38th birthday), at the Leeds Festival, conducted by the composer. The texts sung in the four movements are drawn from Walt Whitman's *Leaves of Grass.* [2] **SUBTITLE OF HOWARD HANSON'S SYMPHONY NO. 7 FOR CHORUS AND ORCHESTRA,** on texts by Whitman, composed in 1977.

RECOMMENDED RECORDINGS

VAUGHAN WILLIAMS:

HARPER, SHIRLEY-QUIRK; PREVIN AND LONDON SYMPHONY ORCHESTRA (RCA).

RODGERS, SCHIMELL; HANDLEY AND ROYAL LIVERPOOL PHILHARMONIC ORCHESTRA (CFP).

HANSON:

SCHWARZ AND SEATTLE SYMPHONY ORCHESTRA (DELOS).

Segovia, Andrés

(b. Linares, February 21, 1893; d. Madrid, June 2, 1987)

SPANISH GUITARIST. He established the guitar as a 20th-century concert instrument, rescuing it from years of neglect and creating a new technique, a new repertoire, and a new style of playing notable for its taste, musicality, poetic effects, and brilliance. He began his study of the guitar at the age of four and made his debut in Granada at 16. He performed in Madrid for the first time in 1913 and created a sensation with his first South American tour in 1919. Debuts in Paris (1924), Moscow (1926), and New York (1928) followed, and he toured Japan in 1929. His programs, consisting of works by Francisco Tárrega (1852–1909) and others along with his own transcriptions, primarily of Bach, astonished audiences that until then had had no reason to think of the guitar as a classical instrument; his success encouraged a number of contemporary composers to write for him, including Villa-Lobos, Rodrigo, Ponce, and Mario Castelnuovo-Tedesco (1895–1968). Among the major concert works composed for or premiered by him were Villa-Lobos's 12 *Etudes* (1929), Castelnuovo-Tedesco's Concerto in D (1939), Ponce's *Concierto del sur* (1941), Villa-Lobos's Guitar Concerto (1956), and Rodrigo's *Fantasía para un gentilhombre* (1958). He recorded prolifically (his first disc in 1927, his last in 1977) and was a regular presence on the recital circuit into his 80s. He played his last recital in April 1987, at the age of 94.

Segovia was a disciplined, serious artist. Few other performers have been as involved with the creation of new works for their instrument, and probably none have gone to such great lengths to adapt for their instrument the existing literature for other instruments. His virtuosity was on a par with that expected of violinists and pianists, which had never been the case with guitarists before Segovia. He inspired generations of younger musicians to become guitarists, and many of them came

Andrés Segovia, patron saint of the guitar

to him for validation in master classes and private coaching; he was never far from teaching. With his simple tweed suit, white shirt, and loosely bowed black ribbon tie he was the perfect image of a rustic, 19th-century Spanish gentleman. Gentle he was, and unfailingly kind to his audiences and admirers. He considered the peaks of his career to have been the first time he played his transcription of the D minor Chaconne by Bach (Paris, 1935), and the first performance of the Castelnuovo-Tedesco concerto (in Montevideo, Uruguay). He enjoyed many other great moments and a full measure of celebrity over the course of his long career, but he never forgot the primacy of music. "Each of us is an island," he said near the end of his life. "Music is the ocean."

RECOMMENDED RECORDINGS

BACH, SONATAS AND PARTITAS (MCA).

PONCE, SONATAS, PIECES FOR GUITAR (MCA).

SOR, STUDIES (MCA).

RECITAL:

"ANDRÉS SEGOVIA IN LONDON, 1949" (TESTAMENT).

Seidl, Anton

(b. Pest, May 7, 1850; d. New York, March 28, 1898).

AUSTRO-HUNGARIAN CONDUCTOR, NATURALIZED AMERICAN. An early fascination with the music (and the person) of Richard Wagner led him to become a missionary for the composer's works in the United States. After studying piano and composition at the Leipzig Conservatory, he became an apprentice of the conductor Hans Richter. He spent six years living with the Wagner family as the composer's amanuensis, preparing many of the singers for the premiere of the *Ring* at Bayreuth in 1876, and serving as understudy for Richter, who conducted the performances. In 1879, through Wagner's influence, he was named chief conductor of the Neues Theater in Leipzig; he subsequently toured Europe with Wagner's works, giving four complete performances of the *Ring* in Berlin in 1881. In 1885, Seidl moved to New York, where he became principal conductor of the Metropolitan Opera. In an era when all performances at the Met were sung in German, Seidl conducted the majority of the operas, many of them by Wagner, including the American premieres of *Die Meistersinger von Nürnberg, Tristan und Isolde,* and three of the *Ring* operas.

Seidl was also omnipresent as a concert conductor. He gave the world premiere of Dvořák's Symphony No. 9 (*From the New World*) in Carnegie Hall on December 16, 1893, with the New York Philharmonic. He also worked with many different ensembles of freelance musicians, conducted at the Brooklyn Academy of Music, led summer concerts of Wagner and Liszt at Brighton Beach on Coney Island, and toured the United States. One of his American protégés was the composer Victor Herbert (1859–1924), who was often his principal cellist and assistant conductor.

semibreve In medieval notation, a note with a duration half or third that of the BREVE (depending on the mensuration), represented by a diamond-shaped white note [◇]. In modern notation, a whole note [𝅝]. The term is in standard use in Britain and Italy.

semiopera A stage play with music, in which the central characters have speaking parts, the minor characters sing or dance, and the action includes numerous scenic effects. The composer Matthew Locke (ca. 1621–77) was an important figure in the early development of this uniquely English genre; he contributed music to the first successful semioperas, *The Tempest* (1674, based on William Shakespeare) and *Psyche* (1675, text by Thomas Shadwell). The best-known semioperas are four works with music by Henry Purcell: *Dioclesian* (1690), *King Arthur* (1691, text by John Dryden), *The Fairy Queen* (1692, based on Shakespeare's *A Midsummer Night's Dream*), and *The Indian Queen* (1695, text by Dryden). The most notable semiopera written after Purcell's death was *The Island Princess* (1699), to which Jeremiah Clarke (ca. 1674–1707) contributed some of the music. The genre died out following the introduction of Italian opera to the London stage in 1705.

semiquaver A sixteenth note [♬]. The term is commonly used by English musicians.

semitone The interval of a half step, also commonly referred to as a minor second. It is the smallest interval of the standard Western tuning system, in which 12 exactly equal semitones make up an octave. Semitones are found in all CHROMATIC and DIATONIC scales.

Semper Opera OPERA HOUSE IN DRESDEN designed by the architect Gottfried Semper (1803–73) and built in 1841, originally known as the Königliches Sächsisches Hoftheater (Royal Saxon Court Theater). The structure was destroyed by fire in 1869 and rebuilt in 1878. It was destroyed for the second time by the Allied firebombing of Dresden on the night of February 13, 1945, rebuilt yet again beginning in 1977, and reopened on the night of February 13, 1985, with a performance of Weber's *Der Freischütz*. It survived the flooding of the Elbe during the summer of 2002 with only minor damage. Long considered one of the finest and most beautiful opera houses in the world (the main reason it has been twice rebuilt to the original plan), it was the site of the world premieres of Wagner's *Rienzi* (1842), *Der fliegende Holländer* (1843), and *Tannhäuser* (1845), and of many of the operas of Richard Strauss.

The Semper Opera in Dresden

Senesino [Bernardi, Francesco]

(b. Siena [no date known]; d. Siena, ca. January 27, 1759)

ITALIAN CASTRATO. One of the most celebrated 18th-century castrati, he took his stage name from Siena, the town of his birth. He sang in Venice, Bologna, Genoa, Naples, and Dresden—where Handel, on a recruiting tour for his London company, heard him in 1719. Senesino came to London in 1720, and became the most admired male singer in town. Though he and Handel had a vigorous mutual disaffection for each other, he stayed with Handel through the collapse of his first company in 1728, and joined the second in 1730; in 1733 he left, with several other singers, to establish a competing company, the Opera of the Nobility. During his career, Senesino sang in 17 operas by Handel, as well as several by other composers; Handel wrote many of his greatest roles for him, including Julius Caesar, Orlando, Flavio, Andronicus in *Tamerlano*, and Bertarido in *Rodelinda*. Senesino returned to Italy in 1737, after the death knell had sounded for opera seria in London. He was wistfully remembered in a popular song, "The Lady's Lamentation for the Loss of Senesino."

septet A piece for seven instruments. There is no standard complement, but the vast majority of septets are for a mixed group of wind and string instruments. Beethoven established the prevailing mix in his Septet in E-flat, Op. 20, for clarinet, horn, bassoon, violin, viola, cello, and double bass (1799). Berwald used the same complement in his Septet in B-flat, composed around 1828. Hummel composed two septets, each for a different combination of instruments: his Septet in D minor, Op. 74 (ca. 1816), calls for flute, oboe, horn, viola, cello, double bass, and piano, and his *Septett militaire* in C, Op. 114 (1829), for flute, clarinet, trumpet, violin, cello, double bass, and piano. Ignaz Moscheles (1794–1870) included a particularly virtuosic piano part in his Septet in D, Op. 88 (1832–33), and countenanced a supporting ensemble consisting either of two violins, two violas, cello, and double bass, or clarinet, horn, violin, viola, cello, and double bass. Stravinsky, nothing if not a free thinker, opted for clarinet, bassoon, horn, violin, viola, cello, and piano in his 12-tone Septet (1953). *See also* CHAMBER MUSIC.

RECOMMENDED RECORDINGS

BEETHOVEN, SEPTET IN E-FLAT, OP. 20: GAUDIER ENSEMBLE (HYPERION).

BERWALD, SEPTET IN B-FLAT: GAUDIER ENSEMBLE (HYPERION).

STRAVINSKY, SEPTET: STRAVINSKY AND COLUMBIA CHAMBER ORCHESTRA (SONY).

sequence [1] In the Middle Ages, a piece of plainchant or polyphony in which each musical phrase was repeated to accommodate a text written in the form AA BB CC, etc. Sequences could be quite lengthy and did not always adhere strictly to the form; many had phrases of varying length as well as occasional phrases that did not repeat. Originally part of the Mass, the sequence eventually became a freestanding form. [2] A thematic device in which the same melodic figure is repeated several times in succession in an ascending or descending pattern, i.e., with each repetition beginning a step higher (the usual case, because it produces a feeling of tension) or a step lower.

serenade (from It. *serenata*) A piece of music intended to be performed outdoors in the evening, usually as a tribute to a particular individual. The term is derived from the Italian word *sereno,* poetic parlance for a "cloudless evening sky." During the 18th century, especially in Italy, Austria, and southern Germany, the serenade was a popular instrumental genre. Serenades written for orchestra typically consisted of five or more movements beginning with a substantial movement in sonata form, ending with a lively movement in fast tempo, and fitting a sequence of minuets and slow movements between them. Mozart's serenades of the 1770s and 1780s epitomized the genre; his contributions included not only works written for orchestra—most notably the *Haffner* Serenade, K. 250 (1776), and the *Posthorn* Serenade, K. 320 (1779)—but pieces for wind ensemble, such as the Serenades in E-flat, K. 375 (1781), C minor, K. 388 (1782), and B-flat, K. 361 (1784), the celebrated *Eine kleine Nachtmusik,* K. 525 (1787), for strings, and the beautiful Divertimento in D, K. 334, for strings and two horns (1779–80), a serenade in all but name.

During the 19th century, the serenade

gradually lost its nocturnal connotation and moved indoors, becoming a more generic form akin to the symphony, though less weighty. Serenades for strings proved increasingly popular; the finest were those written by Dvořák (1875), Tchaikovsky (1880), Suk (1892), and Elgar (1892), and Wolf's jaunty little *Italian Serenade* (1887). Wind serenades virtually disappeared, though Dvořák penned a lovely one for nine winds, cello, and string bass in 1878, and the young Richard Strauss paid the first of his many homages to Mozart with a serenade for 13 winds written in 1881. The most important orchestral serenades of the 19th century were the two that Brahms composed between 1857 and 1859, in D, Op. 11, and A, Op. 16. The A major work is noteworthy for its omission of violins.

Among the most appealing 20th-century examples of the genre are Wilhelm Stenhammar's (1871–1927) marvelously sunny Serenade in F, Op. 31 (1911–13), Sibelius's Serenade for Violin and Orchestra, Op. 69 (1912–13), and Roussel's intimate *Sérénade,* Op. 30 (1925), for flute, string trio, and harp. *See also* NACHTMUSIK, PARTITA.

RECOMMENDED RECORDINGS

BRAHMS, SERENADES NOS. 1 AND 2: KERTÉSZ AND LONDON SYMPHONY ORCHESTRA (DECCA).

DVOŘÁK, SERENADE FOR STRINGS AND SERENADE FOR WINDS: MARRINER AND ACADEMY OF ST. MARTIN-IN-THE-FIELDS (PHILIPS).

DVOŘÁK, SERENADE FOR WINDS: KERTÉSZ AND LONDON SYMPHONY ORCHESTRA (DECCA).

MOZART, *HAFFNER* AND *POSTHORN* SERENADES, *EINE KLEINE NACHTMUSIK*: MARRINER AND ACADEMY OF ST. MARTIN-IN-THE-FIELDS (PHILIPS).

MOZART, WIND SERENADES: ENSEMBLE PHILIDOR (CALLIOPE).

SUK, SERENADE FOR STRINGS: BĚLOHLÁVEK AND CZECH PHILHARMONIC (SUPRAPHON).

TCHAIKOVSKY, DVOŘÁK, SERENADES FOR STRINGS: KARAJAN AND BERLIN PHILHARMONIC (DG).

Serenade (after Plato's "Symposium") WORK FOR SOLO VIOLIN, STRING ORCHESTRA, HARP, AND PERCUSSION BY LEONARD BERNSTEIN. It was composed in 1954 and received its premiere on September 12 of that year in Venice, with the composer conducting the Israel Philharmonic Orchestra and Isaac Stern as soloist. The topic of Plato's *Symposium* is love, and the five movements of Bernstein's score—"Phaedrus/ Pausanius" "Aristophanes," "Eryximachus," "Agathon," and "Socrates/Alcibiades"—take their names from individuals who expound on that subject during the course of an imagined banquet and who themselves embody different aspects of the evening's topic. Musically, the *Serenade* is a combination of trenchant character sketches and an ongoing variation scheme, of concerto and symphony, of confession and entertainment. "Eryximachus" functions in many ways as a scherzo and incorporates some delicious fugato writing. The heartfelt lyrical expression of "Agathon," a slow hymn to love, stands in striking contrast to it. The impassioned climactic pages of "Agathon" are reprised in the introduction to the *Serenade*'s final movement, "Socrates/ Alcibiades," which builds to a jazzy uproar and ends the whole work on a note of joyful abandon.

RECOMMENDED RECORDINGS

HAHN; ZINMAN AND BALTIMORE SYMPHONY ORCHESTRA (SONY).

KREMER; BERNSTEIN AND ISRAEL PHILHARMONIC ORCHESTRA (DG).

Serenade to Music VOCAL ORCHESTRAL WORK BY RALPH VAUGHAN WILLIAMS, composed to mark the 50th anniversary of the conducting debut of Sir Henry Wood and premiered on October 5, 1938, with Wood conducting. It is a setting of lines from Act V, sc. 1 of William Shakespeare's *The Merchant of Venice* (beginning with "How sweet the moonlight sleeps upon this bank!"); this is the scene where Lorenzo and Jessica sit together by the side of a stream, look up at the stars, and listen to the sounds of music drifting over the night air. The piece was written for a specially gathered group of 16 well-known solo singers—four each of sopranos, mezzo-sopranos, and tenors, one baritone, and three basses—each of whose solos is identified in the score by their initials.

RECOMMENDED RECORDINGS

AINSLEY, CONNELL, DAVIES, DAWSON, HILL, OTHERS; BEST AND ENGLISH CHAMBER ORCHESTRA (HYPERION).

ALLIN, BALFOUR, DESMOND, HENDERSON, NASH, OTHERS; WOOD AND BBC SYMPHONY ORCHESTRA (PEARL).

serialism Compositional method in which various elements of a piece of music—most commonly the pitch, register, rhythmic duration, and timbre of its constituent notes—are stringently determined by means of a preestablished set of parameters chosen by the composer. The most common form of serialism is 12-TONE composition, a technique established by Arnold Schoenberg in the 1920s and subsequently adopted by his students Alban Berg and Anton Webern. It was Webern who pushed the technique the furthest and used it the most rigorously; his works laid the foundation for the pervasive or "total" serialism that became the dominant compositional technique of both the European avant-garde and of American academe beginning in the 1950s. This form of serialism, which involves the systematic treatment not only of pitch but of timbre, duration, and dynamics as well—thereby neutralizing rhythm, and to a degree melody, as elements of expression—was practiced most formidably by Pierre Boulez, Luigi Nono (1924–90), and (briefly) Karlheinz Stockhausen. Prevalent on both sides of the Atlantic until about 1980, it has rapidly lost its grip in America since then and is slowly giving up the ghost in Europe.

Composers of the younger generation, and many senior figures who once practiced it, have come to view serialism as a reductive, circumscribed, and needlessly arcane method of ordering a musical composition, one that almost inevitably results in works that, if not downright meaningless, are bereft of any recognizable emotion other than edginess. Among those who succeeded against the odds in showing some imagination with the techniques of serialism were Webern, Luigi Dallapiccola (1904–75), Boulez, and Stockhausen, and the Americans Milton Babbitt, George Perle (b. 1915), and George Rochberg (1918–2005). Rochberg, who abandoned serialism in the 1970s, became one of its sharpest critics; among the multitude of others who have turned their backs on the technique are Einojuhani Rautavaara and Arvo Pärt.

Serkin, Rudolf

(b. Eger, March 28, 1903; d. Guilford, Vt., May 8, 1991)

AUSTRIAN/AMERICAN PIANIST. One of the great pianists of the 20th century, he excelled in the roles of soloist, recitalist, and chamber musician, and was an eminent pedagogue. His parents, Mordko and Augusta Serkin, were Russian Jews who had fled the pogroms. He began to play the piano when he was four, and the family moved to Vienna so he could study there—piano with Richard Robert and composition with Joseph Marx and Arnold Schoenberg. He made his debut with the Vienna Symphony Orchestra in 1915 and began actively concertizing in 1920; among his earliest partners on the concert stage was the violinist Adolf Busch. During the 1920s, Serkin lived with Busch and his family in Berlin; he would later marry Busch's daughter Irene. After Hitler came to power the climate in Germany quickly became inhospitable; in 1934 the Nazis tried to discourage Busch (who was not Jewish) from performing with Serkin, causing the Busches and Serkin to emigrate to Switzerland. In 1935 Serkin made his first appearance in the United States, performing with Busch in Washington, D.C. The following year he made his debut with the New York Philharmonic under Arturo Toscanini, earning rave reviews, and in 1937 he played his first Carnegie Hall recital. In 1939 Serkin took a teaching post at the Curtis Institute of Music in Philadelphia and became an American citizen.

For many years Serkin headed the piano department at Curtis and from 1968 to 1976 he served as the school's director. He made an enormous contribution to American musical life when, in 1950, he joined Busch in founding the Marlboro Music Festival in Vermont; following Busch's death in 1952, he became the festival's director.

Rudolf Serkin, serious yet soulful, and the greatest Beethoven pianist of his day

A pianist of uncommon sensitivity and gifts, Serkin was noted for his authoritative interpretations of the Austro-Germanic repertoire—especially the music of Mozart, Beethoven, Schubert, and Brahms—and his strenuous approach to everything. His accounts of Beethoven and Schubert in particular were admired for their painstaking attention to detail, their "grand declamation," their grasp of form and content, their shapeliness (achieved through a magisterial use of rubato), and their spirituality. Though he was able to play difficult music, such as Brahms's *Variations on a Theme by Handel*, supremely well, Serkin was rarely hailed for his pianistic abilities; indeed, he was often criticized for his brittle tone, clumsy pedaling, and tendency to vocalize while he played. Where some found dryness, a pedantic quality, and, on occasion, an overemphasis of detail at the expense of flow, others found rapt concentration, profundity, and, on occasion, blazing imagination.

RECOMMENDED RECORDINGS

BEETHOVEN, PIANO CONCERTOS (COMPLETE): OZAWA AND BOSTON SYMPHONY ORCHESTRA (TELARC).

BEETHOVEN, PIANO SONATAS, OPP. 109, 110, 111 (SONY).

BEETHOVEN, SONATAS (*PATHÉTIQUE, WALDSTEIN,* AND *APPASSIONATA*) (SONY).

BRAHMS, CELLO SONATAS: ROSTROPOVICH (DG).

BRAHMS, PIANO CONCERTO NO. 2: SZELL AND CLEVELAND ORCHESTRA (SONY).

MOZART, PIANO CONCERTOS NOS. 19 AND 20: SZELL AND CLEVELAND ORCHESTRA (SONY).

MOZART, PIANO CONCERTO NO. 27: ORMANDY AND PHILADELPHIA ORCHESTRA (SONY).

Sessions, Roger

(b. Brooklyn, December 28, 1896; d. Princeton, N.J., March 16, 1985)

AMERICAN COMPOSER, one of the leading members (along with Gershwin, Copland, Piston, Harris, and Thomson) of the generation that established America's musical independence. He embraced rather than rejected the "accepted" forms of the sonata, symphony, and string quartet; in filling them, he was not satisfied with the conventional or the convenient, but sought the most rigorous content, language, and ideas.

An American eminence: Roger Sessions

Although Sessions was born in what was then the city of Brooklyn, his family came from Hadley, Massachusetts, and in outlook he remained more of a New Englander than a New Yorker. He entered Harvard when he was 14 and made quick work of the place. He had hoped to study with Ravel in Paris after graduating, but the outbreak of World War I sent Ravel into the ambulance corps, so Sessions took another bachelor's degree—at Yale, studying with Horatio Parker, Charles Ives's teacher—and subsequently had private lessons with Ernest Bloch. From 1925 to 1933 he lived the then-fashionable life of an expatriate in Paris, Berlin, and Florence, supporting himself on two Guggenheim awards, a Prix de Rome, and a Carnegie Fellowship. His Symphony No. 1—premiered in 1927 by the Boston Symphony Orchestra and Serge Koussevitzky—revealed his aptitude for the form, and during the course of a career lasting more than 60 years, he would write another eight symphonies, as well as a *Concerto for Orchestra* (which won the Pulitzer Prize in 1982), concertos for violin and piano, an assortment of orchestral song settings and chamber pieces, three piano sonatas, a cantata based on Walt Whitman's "When Lilacs Last in the Dooryard Bloom'd" (1964–70), and a small number of works for the stage, including incidental music for the play *The Black Maskers* (1923) and an opera, *Montezuma* (begun in 1935 but not finished until 1963).

Sessions taught at Smith College, Berkeley, Princeton, the Cleveland Institute of Music, and the Juilliard School. To judge from a list of his students, who included Vivian Fine, Milton Babbitt, David Diamond, David Del Tredici, Earl Kim, Leon Kirchner, Andrew Imbrie, Hugo Weisgall, and John Harbison, he was probably the most important composition teacher in America from the late 1930s to the late 1970s. The characteristics that mark his later work—rhythmic energy, spacious, open sonority, rich textures, and the occasional long-breathed melody—are already apparent in the music of his youth, as is a characteristic thorniness. An intellectual and a rugged individualist, Sessions did not care to make things easy for his listener; as Alfredo Casella said, his music was "born difficult."

RECOMMENDED RECORDINGS

The Black Maskers Suite: Ehrling and Juilliard Orchestra (New World).

Concerto for Orchestra: Ozawa and Boston Symphony Orchestra (Hyperion).

Piano Sonatas Nos. 2 and 3: Hodgkinson (New World).

When Lilacs Last in the Dooryard Bloom'd: Ozawa and Boston Symphony Orchestra (New World).

Seven Deadly Sins, The *See* Die sieben Todsünden.

sextet [1] A composition for an ensemble of six instruments. Notable examples include Brahms's two sextets for strings (two violins, two violas, two cellos)—in B-flat, Op. 18 (1859–60), and in G, Op. 36 (1864–65)—and Janáček's suite for winds titled *Mládí* (*Youth*), written in 1924 for an ensemble consisting of flute (doubling piccolo), oboe, clarinet, bassoon, horn, and bass clarinet. [2] In vocal music, a passage or a number involving six singers. Among the best-known operatic sextets are those from the third act of Mozart's *Le nozze di Figaro* ("Riconosci in questo amplesso"), the second act of his *Don Giovanni* ("Sola, sola in buio loco"), and the second act of Donizetti's *Lucia di Lammermoor* ("Chi mi frena in tal momento?"), which includes chorus. *See also* CHAMBER MUSIC.

RECOMMENDED RECORDINGS

BRAHMS, SEXTET IN B-FLAT, OP. 18: RAPHAEL ENSEMBLE (HYPERION).

JANÁČEK, MLÁDÍ: OSLO PHILHARMONIC WIND SOLOISTS (NAXOS).

sforzando A sudden, emphatic forte.

Shaham, Gil

(b. Champaign-Urbana, Ill., February 19, 1971)

AMERICAN VIOLINIST. Soon after his birth, Shaham's family moved to Israel, where he grew up. He received his first violin lessons from Samuel Bernstein at the Rubin Academy of Music in Jerusalem. In 1980 he played for Isaac Stern, who suggested that he study at Aspen with Dorothy DeLay. In 1981, at the age of ten, he made his debut with the Jerusalem Symphony Orchestra, Alexander Schneider conducting, which was quickly followed by a debut with the Israel Philharmonic, Zubin Mehta conducting. In 1982 he won first prize in the Claremont Competition, allowing him to study at the Juilliard School with DeLay and Hyo Kang. He made his European debut in 1986 at the Schleswig-Holstein Festival, and in 1989, substituting for an ailing Itzhak Perlman, performed the Bruch and Sibelius concertos with the London Symphony Orchestra conducted by Michael Tilson Thomas. In 1989 he began his undergraduate studies at Columbia University, and in 1990 he was awarded an Avery Fisher career grant. He made his Carnegie Hall debut in 1992, and has since performed with most of Europe's and America's major orchestras, under the batons of such conductors as Herbert Blomstedt, Sir Colin Davis, Charles Dutoit, Lorin Maazel, Zubin Mehta, Riccardo Muti, André Previn, and Giuseppe Sinopoli.

Shaham has made many fine recordings of repertoire ranging from the violin concertos of Barber, Korngold, and Bartók to Messiaen's *Quatuor pour la fin du temps,* and has appeared frequently in recital with his sister, the pianist Orli Shaham. He plays with an unruffled elegance that recalls the manner of Henryk Szeryng and Nathan Milstein, producing a warm, beautifully rounded sound that is richly expressive. His instrument is the "Countess Polignac," a Stradivari dated 1699.

RECOMMENDED RECORDINGS

BARTÓK, VIOLIN CONCERTO NO. 2 AND RHAPSODY FOR VIOLIN AND ORCHESTRA NO. 1: BOULEZ AND CHICAGO SYMPHONY ORCHESTRA (DG).

KORNGOLD, BARBER, VIOLIN CONCERTOS: PREVIN AND LONDON SYMPHONY ORCHESTRA (DG).

PROKOFIEV, VIOLIN SONATAS NOS. 1 AND 2: O. SHAHAM (VANGUARD).

sharp [1] sign indicating that a note is to be raised in pitch by one semitone [♯]. [2] Sounding higher than the correct pitch.

Shaw, Robert

(b. Red Bluff, Cal., April 30, 1916; d. New Haven, Conn., January 25, 1999)

AMERICAN CHORUSMASTER AND CONDUCTOR. The son and grandson of ministers, he attended Pomona College (1934–38), where he studied philosophy, literature, and religion, was an outstanding athlete, and sang in and conducted the school's glee club. It was there that the noted radio conductor Fred Waring discovered him: On campus to make a movie, Waring saw Shaw at work and tapped him to organize the Fred Waring Glee Club in

New York. Shaw conducted that group until 1945; meanwhile, in 1941, he formed his own 120-member chorus, the Collegiate Chorale, which he led until 1954. He received a Guggenheim Fellowship in 1944 and at about the same time was handpicked by Arturo Toscanini to prepare choruses for the NBC Symphony. In 1948 Shaw founded his most famous group, the Robert Shaw Chorale, an ensemble of 40 professional singers with which he worked until 1965, leaving as a legacy some of the most acclaimed choral recordings ever produced.

Robert Shaw, choral alchemist

Shaw's career as an orchestra conductor was slower to develop, but also reached the heights. He studied with Pierre Monteux and Artur Rodzinski in 1950 and worked with the San Diego Symphony Orchestra from 1953 to 1958. He spent 11 years (1956–67) as associate conductor of the Cleveland Orchestra, working closely with George Szell and establishing a top-notch chorus. He was appointed music director of the Atlanta Symphony Orchestra in 1967. During his 21 years at its helm, he turned the orchestra into a first-rate ensemble and created an outstanding chorus to perform and record with it. Upon stepping down in 1988, he was installed as the head of the newly founded Robert Shaw Institute at Emory University in Atlanta.

The composers from whom Shaw commissioned works included Bartók, Milhaud, Britten, Barber, and Copland. His most important commission was the Hindemith Requiem (*When Lilacs Last in the Dooryard Bloom'd*), which he premiered with the Collegiate Chorale in 1946.

Shaw was named "America's greatest choral conductor" by the National Association of Composers and Conductors in 1943, when he was 27. It turned out to be a designation that would fit for more than 50 years. Throughout his career he was hailed as a genius and magician, though it might have made more sense to call him a choral alchemist, since he repeatedly extracted—in rehearsal and performance—the secret ingredient that turns voices into gold.

RECOMMENDED RECORDINGS

BRITTEN, *WAR REQUIEM*: HAYWOOD, ROLFE JOHNSON, LUXON; ATLANTA SYMPHONY ORCHESTRA AND CHORUS (TELARC).

FAURÉ, DURUFLÉ, *REQUIEM*: BLEGEN, MORRIS; ATLANTA SYMPHONY ORCHESTRA AND CHORUS (TELARC).

VERDI, *REQUIEM*: DUNN, CURRY, HADLEY, PLISHKA; ATLANTA SYMPHONY ORCHESTRA AND CHORUS (TELARC).

COLLECTION:

"A FESTIVAL OF CAROLS": ROBERT SHAW CHORALE (RCA).

shawm Raucous outdoor instrument of medieval and Renaissance ceremony, descended from Middle Eastern ancestors. *See also* OBOE.

Shchedrin, Rodion

(b. Moscow, December 16, 1932)

RUSSIAN COMPOSER. Born to a family of musicians, he entered the Moscow Choir School, where his father taught, in 1945. At 15 he won a composition contest judged by Aram Khachaturian. He was accepted into the Moscow Conservatory in 1950, where he studied piano with Yakov Flier and composition with Yuri Shaporin, continuing with postgraduate studies until 1959. Shchedrin's first compositions were written in a conservative "Socialist realism" vein, as shown in his First Piano Concerto (1954) and *The Little Humpbacked Horse* (1956), a ballet. In the 1960s, Shchedrin began to experiment with taking short, humorous Russian folk songs called *chastushki,* and transforming them with neoclassical or serialist techniques. Two major compositions from this period, a three-act opera, *Not for Love Alone* (1961), and the Concerto for Orchestra No. 1 (*Naughty Limericks*; 1963), are examples of this original use of *chastushki.* Again experimenting with traditional forms, Shchedrin wrote his Second Symphony (1965) as a series of 25 preludes, each inspired by images of World War II.

By the 1970s Shchedrin had evolved a style that was a synthesis of neoclassical elements and some jazz and pop, which he defined as "post-avant-garde." Married in 1958 to the magnificent ballerina Maya Plisetskaya, he wrote frequently for the dance: the one-act *Carmen Suite* of 1967 (by far his most frequently performed work), *Anna Karenina* (1971), and two scores based on works of Anton Chekhov, *The Seagull* (1979) and *Lady with Lapdog* (1985), all for the Bolshoi Ballet. His second opera, *Dead Souls* (1976), with a libretto based on his own adaptation of the Nikolay Gogol novel, premiered at the Bolshoi Opera. Shchedrin's associations with many of Russia's stellar musicians have resulted in a number of fine works: for Vladimir Spivakov and the Moscow Virtuosi, *Russian Photographs* (1994), and for the brilliant violinist Maxim Vengerov, *Concerto Cantabile* for violin and string orchestra and *Balalaika* (both 1997) for violin solo without bow. The composer's long-standing friendship with cellist and conductor Mstislav Rostropovich has resulted in many collaborations and dedications, including *Stikhira for the Millennium of the Christianization of Russia* (1988), commissioned by the National Symphony Orchestra; the concerto *Sotto Voce* (1994); a sonata for cello and piano (1996); *Parabola Concertante* (2001) for cello, string orchestra, and timpani; and *Slava, Slava* (1997) for orchestra, written in honor of Rostropovich's 70th birthday. Rostropovich also conducted the premiere of Shchedrin's controversial opera *Lolita* (1994), based on the novel by Vladimir Nabokov. A pianist of considerable ability, Shchedrin has given the first performances of many of his piano compositions, including four of his five piano concertos. Notable recent commissions include *Dialogues with Shostakovich* (2001), a set of symphonic etudes for orchestra (for Mariss Jansons and the Pittsburgh Symphony), and *The Enchanted Wanderer* (2002), an opera for the concert stage for mezzo-soprano, tenor, bass, mixed chorus, and orchestra (for Lorin Maazel and the New York Philharmonic). Masterful in every medium, Shchedrin is one of the most significant and compelling Russian composers in the post-Soviet era. He currently lives and works in Germany.

RECOMMENDED RECORDINGS

CARMEN SUITE: DEPREIST AND MONTE CARLO PHILHARMONIC ORCHESTRA (DELOS).

CARMEN SUITE: SCHWARZ AND LOS ANGELES CHAMBER ORCHESTRA (CAPITOL).

CONCERTO CANTABILE FOR VIOLIN AND ORCHESTRA: VENGEROV; ROSTROPOVICH AND LONDON SYMPHONY ORCHESTRA (ANGEL).

CONCERTO FOR ORCHESTRA NO. 1 (WITH *CARMEN SUITE*): KUCHAR AND UKRAINIAN STATE ORCHESTRA (NAXOS).

CONCERTOS FOR ORCHESTRA NOS. 1 AND 2: PLETNEV AND RUSSIAN NATIONAL ORCHESTRA (DG).

SYMPHONY NO. 2 AND CONCERTO FOR ORCHESTRA NO. 3 (*OLD RUSSIAN CIRCUS MUSIC*): SINAISKY AND BBC PHILHARMONIC ORCHESTRA (CHANDOS).

Sheherazade SYMPHONIC SUITE BY NIKOLAY RIMSKY-KORSAKOV, **OP. 35,** composed in

1888 and inspired by *The Thousand and One Nights.* Named for the storytelling heroine of that remarkable compendium, *Sheherazade* resembles a symphony in structure. The four movements, each of which carries a descriptive title, share thematic material, including a sinuous melody portraying Sheherazade herself, played by the solo violin, and a stern motive that represents Sultan Shahriar, forcefully hurled out by strings and full brass at the start of the piece. Each of these is subjected to numerous transformations, a process greatly aided by Rimsky's brilliance as an orchestrator, so that the whole work is, as the composer claimed, "closely knit by the community of its themes and motives, yet presenting a kaleidoscope of images and designs."

The imagery of the opening movement, "The Sea and Sinbad's Ship," is easy to discern: The undulating accompaniment in the lower strings that underlies Shahriar's motive, here doing double duty for Sinbad, immediately shows the gallant sailor on the deck of his ship, riding out the swells portrayed by the timpani. "The Tale of the Kalendar Prince," with galloping rhythms, warlike fanfares, and flashing cymbals that glint like scimitars, tells of land-based adventure and takes the place of a conventional scherzo, while "The Young Prince and the Young Princess" is a tender romance with hints of arabesques and a processional. Wild revels and an undercurrent of urgency mark the finale, "The Festival at Baghdad—The Sea—Shipwreck on a Rock Surmounted by a Bronze Warrior." Toward the end, there is a cyclical return of the music depicting the sea and Sinbad's ship, only this time there is a storm upon the waters. Winds, strings, and percussion portray the billowing waves and spume in all their terrifying magnificence as the brass proclaim the theme of Shahriar/Sinbad. The ship crashes against the rocks and is destroyed—but it is only a story, and gentle Sheherazade has the last word, bringing comfort to her husband, the happy king who has spared her life.

RECOMMENDED RECORDINGS

GERGIEV AND KIROV ORCHESTRA (PHILIPS).

KONDRASHIN AND CONCERTGEBOUW ORCHESTRA (PHILIPS).

Shéhérazade **CYCLE OF THREE SONGS FOR VOICE (USUALLY MEZZO-SOPRANO) AND LARGE ORCHESTRA BY MAURICE RAVEL,** to texts by Tristan Klingsor, composed in 1903 and premiered in May 1904. "Tristan Klingsor" was the doubly Wagnerian pseudonym of Arthur Justin Léon Leclère (1874–1966), a friend of Ravel and fellow member of the Bohemian artistic circle known as Les Apaches; his poems, perfumed with forbidden sensuality, appealed to Ravel's love of the exotic and inspired the 28-year-old composer, fresh out of the Paris Conservatoire, to a masterly display of his talent. The luxuriously scored first song, "Asie" ("Asia"), builds through a series of colorful episodes touching on the Levant, Persia, India, and China to a grandly scaled climax on the words "Je voudrais voir mourir d'amour ou bien de haine" ("I would like to see [someone] die from love or, better yet, from hate"). The two remaining songs, "La flûte enchantée" ("The Magic Flute") and "L'indifférent" ("The Indifferent One"), are more modest in scope, if not more chaste in tone: Indeed, the longing expressed in "L'indifférent"—mysterious, wistful, and more than a little sad—is a rare instance of emotional confession in Ravel's music.

RECOMMENDED RECORDINGS

GRAHAM; TORTELIER AND BBC SYMPHONY ORCHESTRA (WARNER).

OTTER; BOULEZ AND CLEVELAND ORCHESTRA (INCLUDING *LE TOMBEAU DE COUPERIN, PAVANE POUR UNE INFANTE DÉFUNTE;* DEBUSSY, *DANSES*) (DG).

Shostakovich, Dmitry

(b. St. Petersburg, September 25, 1906; d. Moscow, August 9, 1975)

RUSSIAN COMPOSER. His 15 symphonies are the most important addition to the symphonic repertoire by any composer born in the 20th century. He contributed significantly to other genres as well, among them opera, ballet, the concerto, and the film score, and to chamber and instrumental forms including song. Among his greatest works are 15 string quartets, which like the symphonies reflect a career-long preoccupation with finding an appropriate balance between musical form and emotional content. As the scholar Richard Taruskin has pointed out, Shostakovich "embodied the idea of the artist in society," as distinct from the type of artist—aloof, hyper-intellectual, self-absorbed—represented by many of his contemporaries in the mid-20th-century European avant-garde.

Shostakovich came from a relatively well-off family. His father was a government scientist and decent amateur singer, his mother a conservatory-trained pianist. He began lessons with her in 1915, progressing with astonishing rapidity, to the point where he entered the Petrograd Conservatory at 13 and studied with Maximilian Steinberg, Rimsky-Korsakov's son-in-law. Shostakovich was a brilliant, talented, serious, yet irreverent student who quickly developed into a topflight pianist and composer of extraordinarily advanced, often sharp and satirical, music. His Symphony No. 1, composed in 1925, when he was 19, and premiered in May 1926, created an immediate international sensation. Grotesque elements in the scherzo presage later works, as do the overall tension, nervous energy, and youthful excitement. There is as well a hint of the iconoclastic attitude that would remain a part of the composer's makeup (e.g., the cheeky opening bars, which are almost a mockery of a "serious" symphonic introduction, and the obbligato part for piano in the second movement).

Shostakovich as a student

Shostakovich flourished in the permissive atmosphere of postrevolutionary iconoclasm that lingered through the 1920s. Modernism—with its credo of experimentation, its celebration of both the abstract and the synthetic, and its implicit negation of the past—was the dominant trend in all Soviet arts. Not everything he wrote was first-rate. The success of the First Symphony brought a commission from the propaganda section of the Soviet state music publishing house; the result was the much weaker Symphony No. 2 (*To October*). It was the first in a long line of "official" or commemorative works on politically appropriate subjects that would include his Symphony No. 3 (1930) and Symphony No. 12 (1961). But between 1927 and 1930, Shostakovich also composed a string of musically daring and aesthetically provocative scores, among them his first opera, *THE NOSE* (after Gogol), and his first ballet, *The Age of Gold.*

As the deadly 1930s unfolded, Shostakovich continued along his risky path of innovation. The decade saw the composition of two highly significant works: the full-length opera *LADY MACBETH OF MTSENSK DISTRICT* and the dissonant, sprawlingly Mahlerian Symphony No. 4. Nothing Shostakovich had attempted so far had been as large in scale or as powerful; now the young composer *did* want to be taken seriously. And when Stalin came to hear *Lady Macbeth,* in 1936, almost two years after its critically acclaimed Leningrad premiere, Shostakovich paid the price. The dictator ordered the publication of a review in *Pravda* excoriating the music and its creator. Never mind that *The Nose* had been far more radical—overnight, Shostakovich went from enfant terrible to pariah.

Dissatisfied with it and not wanting to risk running into another buzz saw, Shostakovich shelved the Fourth (it would not be premiered until 1961) and turned his energies to a new work. The Fifth Symphony would be different—an accessible, conventionally styled and structured work, beginning on a tragic note and leading to a triumphant, heroic conclusion. Shostakovich encouraged this view by allowing the piece to be declared "a Soviet artist's reply to just criticism." The Fifth created a sensation at its premiere in Leningrad in 1937, and Shostakovich was instantly rehabilitated. But those closest to the composer realized that there was a profound irony to the symphony's finale. The triumph it seemed to portray was that of the machine that had ground him up.

Shostakovich in a typically anguished moment

When, in the summer of 1941, Hitler invaded the Soviet Union, Leningrad came under attack and Shostakovich became a symbol of his country's spirited resistance (*Time* magazine ran a cover illustration of him in firefighter's gear). He was evacuated to Kuibyshev on the Volga, where he completed his Seventh Symphony (LENINGRAD). The score ("Dedicated to the city of Leningrad") received its premiere there on March 5, 1942. Shostakovich composed his powerful Symphony No. 8 at the height of the war, in 1943. The Eighth looks into the abyss, probing the psychological desolation and evoking the eerie detachment that war induces in its survivors. In its finale, the enormous energies of the Symphony's first four movements are not harnessed to a resolution—triumphant, tragic, or otherwise—but are left hanging, almost as if the symphony had ended with a question mark. The effect is utterly unexpected and as moving as anything Shostakovich wrote.

At the end of the war, in 1945, came Symphony No. 9. Many people expected a big work, exuding optimism and high purpose; instead the composer gave them something comical, quirky, a parody of Classical style. Dangerous it was not, yet . . . in 1948, Shostakovich, along with Prokofiev, Khachaturian, and others, was censured for "decadent formalism" by the authorities. For the next five years, until Stalin's death, Shostakovich kept his best music to himself. The Violin Concerto No. 1, composed for David Oistrakh, was withheld until 1955, and the Fourth and Fifth String Quartets and the song cycle *From Jewish Folk Poetry* were likewise locked in the drawer. In the months immediately following the tyrant's demise, Shostakovich composed his Tenth Symphony, one of the handful of indisputable masterpieces penned in the second half of the 20th century. It offers a glimpse into the darkest and most desolate corners of the composer's soul. In a gesture reserved for scores of special meaning to him, Shostakovich even signs his name, introducing his motto theme *DSCH* (D, E-flat, C, B) in the third movement and making it the

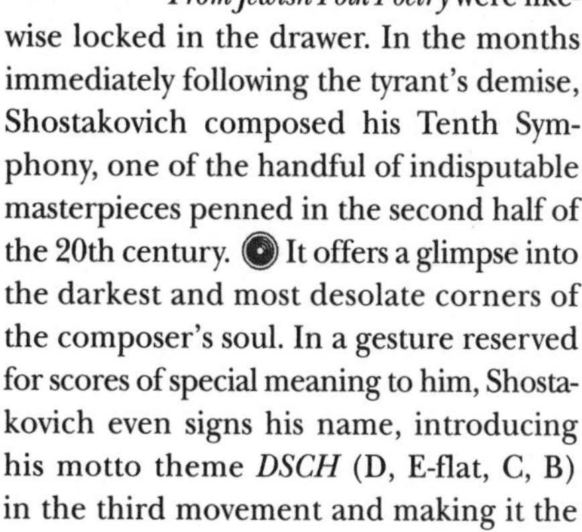

The young iconoclast at the keyboard

climactic ingredient of the finale, which ends with the timpani hammering out the initials in gloriously ebullient strokes. The chilling, haunting, desolately severe Symphony No. 11 was written in 1956–57 and subtitled *The Year 1905*. By 1962, Shostakovich felt safe enough to again be controversial. In his Symphony No. 13, with bass soloist and male chorus, he set five poems of Yevgeny Yevtushenko, choosing for the very powerful opening movement the poem "Babi Yar," an attack on anti-Semitism. Symphony No. 14 (1969), with bass and soprano soloists, is a song cycle on death, with texts by Federico García Lorca and Rainer Maria Rilke among others, and the final work in the canon, Symphony No. 15 (1971), is a waking dream, a haunted fantasy: whimsical, strange, touching, with much that is kept secret, like Shostakovich himself.

Shostakovich wrote two concertos for piano, but achieved more in his concertos for string instruments, starting with the Violin Concerto No. 1. His first Cello Concerto ◉, written for Rostropovich in 1959, is one of the supreme 20th-century contributions to that instrument's repertoire; his Cello Concerto No. 2 (1966), also written for Rostropovich, is more introspective and nearly as good. The Violin Concerto No. 2 (1967) was, like the first, composed for Oistrakh.

Nine of Shostakovich's 15 string quartets were composed during the 1960s and 1970s, when he again felt free to write absolute music and take compositional risks. By far the most frequently performed of the cycle, though hardly typical, is No. 8. Composed in three days during a visit to Dresden in 1960, it is pointedly tragic in tone and contains some of Shostakovich's most compelling music. The entire collection of 15 has been called biographical, the private as opposed to the public history that can be read in the symphonies. Shostakovich also wrote sonatas for cello, for violin, and for viola (his last work, from 1975); two piano trios, the second of which is a profoundly poignant essay, one of his finest efforts; and several collections of piano pieces, including the 24 Preludes and Fugues, again on the studied and cerebral side but capable of giving great intellectual pleasure.

Shostakovich died a shattered man, in terms of his health and nerves, but with his artistry intact. With every year that passes, it appears more likely that he—the heir of Mahler and an artist of mordant, ironic, nervous character who became increasingly dark in later works as he contemplated death—will come to be seen as one of the iconic composers of the 20th century, alongside Stravinsky and Schoenberg. While their works had a much greater influence on the development of style, it was his music, not theirs, which in its darkness and pain, its litany of hope crushed, its sense of the grotesque, the absurd, the paranoid, and the vicious—above all its grasp of suffering and sadness—revealed the essential truth of the time.

RECOMMENDED RECORDINGS

Cello Concerto No. 1: Rostropovich; Ormandy and Philadelphia Orchestra; Violin Concerto No. 1: Oistrakh; Mitropoulos and New York Philharmonic (Sony).

Lady Macbeth of Mtsensk District: Vishnevskya, Gedda, Petkov, Krenn; Rostropovich and London Philharmonic Orchestra (EMI).

Piano Trio No. 2: Ax, Stern, Ma (Sony).

Preludes and Fugues, Op. 87 for piano: Nikolayeva (Hyperion).

String quartets (complete): Eder Quartet (Naxos).

String quartets (complete): Emerson Quartet (DG).

Symphonies (complete): Rostropovich and London Symphony Orchestra, National Symphony Orchestra, Moscow Academic Symphony Orchestra (Teldec).

Symphonies Nos. 1 and 9: Rostropovich and National Symphony Orchestra (Teldec).

Symphony No. 5: Bernstein and New York Philharmonic (Sony).

Symphony No. 7: Bernstein and Chicago Symphony Orchestra (DG).

Symphony No. 10: Karajan and Berlin Philharmonic (DG).

Symphony No. 13: Rintzler, bass; Haitink and Concertgebouw Orchestra (Decca).

Symphony No. 15: Ormandy and Philadelphia Orchestra (RCA).

Violin Concertos Nos. 1 and 2 (with Prokofiev, Violin Concertos Nos. 1 and 2): Vengerov; Rostropovich and London Symphony Orchestra (Teldec).

Sibelius, Jean

(b. Hämeenlinna, December 8, 1865; d. Järvenpää, September 20, 1957)

FINNISH COMPOSER. The most widely admired artist Finland has produced, he is recognized in England, America, and Scandinavia as one of the great composers of the 20th century. Christened Johan Julius Christian Sibelius and called "Janne" by his family, he took the name "Jean" after a seafaring uncle who had preferred the French form. He began to play the violin as a boy and started lessons when he was 14. Later he would write, "The violin took me by storm and for the next ten years it was my dearest wish, my greatest ambition to become a great virtuoso."

Sibelius's dearest wish died hard. He spent four years as a violin student at the Helsinki Music Institute (now the Sibelius Academy), performing several concertos, including the Mendelssohn, and formed a close bond with new faculty member Ferruccio Busoni. In 1889 he took a year of study in Berlin and the following year did the same in Vienna. As late as 1891, the 25-year-old auditioned unsuccessfully for a spot in the Vienna Philharmonic.

But something more valuable did come Sibelius's way in Vienna, and that was a sense of his own Finnishness and of the importance of writing Finnish music. He would find inspiration for a number of his works in the myths, sagas, and folklore of his native country. A particularly rich source was the national epic, the *Kalevala*. In 1892 he completed a sprawling symphonic cantata based on the story of KULLERVO, one of the heroes of the *Kalevala*. During the years 1893–96, he composed four symphonic poems inspired by the tale of Lemminkäinen (another hero from the *Kalevala*); these were published under the title *Four Legends* and include *THE SWAN OF TUONELA*. Both early scores attest to his powers as an orchestrator and mark his developing command of symphonic form.

The Finland where Sibelius was born and grew to adulthood was a grand duchy of Russia, having been ceded by Sweden in 1809. (Sibelius grew up speaking Swedish.) By the end of the 19th century, the appetite of most Finns for independence had become a raging hunger, and national sentiment regularly bubbled up despite tsarist censorship. In 1899 Sibelius made a memorable contribution to the protest movement by composing the music for a set of six "historical tableaux," the performance of which was intended to benefit a national newspaper writers' pension fund. The music Sibelius wrote for the tableau "Finland Awakes!" proved so stirring that he decided to publish it separately, as FINLANDIA. It was not the composer's favorite piece, but it has remained so popular that it identifies him worldwide.

Sibelius, study for a painting by Akseli Gallen-Kallela, 1894

The Finn's first two symphonies were works of strong nationalist character as well. Like Brahms, Sibelius could hear the tread of giants behind him, and he hesitated until he was sure of his powers. He began fashioning his Symphony No. 1 in 1898, when he was 32. The work of Tchaikovsky was a particularly strong influence, especially the *Pathétique* Symphony. As Sibelius confided at the time to his wife, Aino, "There is much in that man that I recognize in myself." But what sets the First Symphony apart are the propulsive rhythms and almost savage expressiveness of its best pages, along with the elemental quality of its motives and scoring. The volatile Finnish spirit is clearly present in the mix. The First Symphony made a powerful impression at its premiere, in 1899. The Second followed closely, occupying Sibelius through the end of 1901.

By 1903, the year in which he undertook his Violin Concerto, Sibelius's hopes of becoming a concertizing artist had long since been abandoned. In their place stood the reality of being recognized as Finland's leading composer, with a developing international reputation. At the same time, the composer's heavy drinking took a toll on his creative capacities. Financial difficulties caused considerable domestic strain, even forcing Sibelius to set the date of the first performance of the concerto earlier than he would have liked. As a high-level violinist, he well knew how to get the most idiomatic and expressive effects out of the instrument. He also knew how to introduce virtuosic display into a serious work without cheapening it. But his first draft of the piece was prolix and loose-limbed, and it took Sibelius a year of brooding and a month of further hard, self-critical work to beat it into the powerful, tightly wound, splendidly dramatic concerto we have today. Richard Strauss led the premiere of the final version.

As Sibelius turned his back on both Romantic tradition and contemporary symphonic thinking, he began—in works like the Violin Concerto and the symphonic poem POHJOLA'S DAUGHTER (1905–06)—to pursue the formal concision and searching self-expression that had characterized the first two movements of the Second Symphony. The idyllic, aphoristic Third Symphony (1907) feels peculiarly neoclassical (Sibelius called it a "relapse"), but the grimly pessimistic Fourth Symphony (1910–11) is formidably compressed and emotionally intense. Inspired in part by a trip to Koli, a lakeside retreat, the Fourth expressionistically paints an inner landscape with great, sustained masses of sound welling up from the brass, timpani, and low strings, seemingly glacial in their flow. Throughout the astringent, restless work, Sibelius emphasizes the dissonant interval of the tritone, at times bringing his language to the edge of harmonic dysfunction. The third movement is one of the great slow movements of the 20th century, on a par with the best of Shostakovich, full of angst and despair drawn from the well of the composer's own experience.

An early version of the Symphony No. 5 received its premiere at the end of 1915 in a concert marking Sibelius's 50th birthday, which was proclaimed a national holiday. For some time the composer had been an international figure—the year before he had visited England and the U.S. to much celebration and been awarded a honorary doctorate at Yale. Still, he had to struggle artistically and financially while World War I raged in Europe. He heavily reworked the Fifth, completing it in its final form after the war and conducting that premiere in 1921. It had become a thing of stark beauty, strength, economy, and, with its famously powerful cadential chords at the close, affirmation.

Sibelius changed his approach yet again for the Sixth Symphony (1923). In its four slender, somewhat disembodied movements, Palestrina-style counterpoint informs strangely energetic, bass-shy musical ideas, apparently inspired by nature studies: "Pure spring water," the composer said of it. Sibelius's pursuit of concision in form culminated in the Seventh Symphony (1924) and the symphonic poem TAPIOLA (1926). Both are densely written single-movement essays in which the principal ideas develop out of one another in almost stream-of-consciousness fashion. All that remains in these scores of conventional four-movement symphonic layout or sonata design is a submerged outline. The Seventh ends with a crescendo and a pileup of snarling dissonances, only resolving to C major at the very end. *Tapiola,* a great tone painting of the realm of the Nordic Forest God, has angry moments as well, and conveys an extraordinary picture of nature—human as well as woodland—at its most elemental.

The perfectionist composer began working on an Eighth Symphony and continued into the 1930s, probably going through several drafts, but burned the manuscript a decade later. Sibelius's wife reported that he looked happy and peaceful after feeding the fire. In any event, there was nothing more from him.

Sibelius spent his creative life struggling with personal demons: first alcohol, then throat cancer, then alcohol again. These struggles permeate much of his music, with its overcoming of obstacles, volcanic emotion below a bleak surface, and inexorable drive. He composed a large number of songs and piano pieces, choral works, chamber pieces (including the string quartet *Voces intimae*), and a considerable amount of incidental music. His symphonic works are his greatest contribution to the repertoire. What makes them important is their integrity, the way they build upon and develop from powerful, generative ideas, in a manner that is the musical equivalent of a biological process. They illustrate, as Harry Halbreich has observed, "the possibilities of emancipating the technique of development from its inherited forms, with a concision unequalled since the classics." Part of this process Sibelius achieved through his scoring, by treating the winds, brass, and strings as separate choirs, each with its own material, so various ideas could be presented simultaneously in different parts of the orchestra without losing their identity. The overlapping of material in separate strata of the score, often moving at different rates, creates climactic passages of extraordinary visceral intensity.

RECOMMENDED RECORDINGS

Four Legends: Ormandy and Philadelphia Orchestra (EMI).

Four Legends: Vänskä and Lahti Symphony Orchestra (BIS).

Kullervo: Laukka, Paasikivi; Vänskä and Lahti Symphony Orchestra (BIS).

Symphonies (complete): Davis and Boston Symphony Orchestra (Philips).

Symphony No. 1: Ormandy and Philadelphia Orchestra (Sony).

Symphony No. 2: Barbirolli and Royal Philharmonic Orchestra (Chesky).

Symphony No. 2: Szell and Concertgebouw Orchestra (Philips).

Symphonies Nos. 4–7: Karajan and Berlin Philharmonic (DG).

Symphony No. 5: Bernstein and New York Philharmonic (Sony).

Tone poems (including *Tapiola*): Davis and London Symphony Orchestra (RCA).

Tone poems: Karajan and Berlin Philharmonic (DG).

Violin Concerto: Lin; Salonen and Philharmonia Orchestra (Sony).

Violin Concerto: Mutter; Previn and Staatskapelle Dresden (DG).

siciliana Dance type frequently encountered in instrumental pieces and arias from the late 17th century to the end of the 18th century, typically associated with an expression of revery or melancholy. Its characteristic dotted rhythm, set in a duple meter with triplet subdivisions (either $\frac{6}{8}$ or $\frac{12}{8}$), gives it a gently rocking quality that is immediately recognizable.

By the beginning of the 18th century the siciliana had become a stock gesture for depicting pastoral scenes in music; Bach and Handel both treated it in that fashion. One of the best examples can be found in the first movement of Mozart's Piano Sonata in A, K. 331.

***sieben Todsünden, Die* (The Seven Deadly Sins)** "Ballet chanté" by Kurt Weill, consisting of a prologue, seven parts, and an epilogue, for solo dancer, mezzo-soprano, men's chorus, and instrumental ensemble, to lyrics by Bertholt Brecht, premiered June 7, 1933, in Paris at the Théâtre des Champs-Elysées (with choreography by George Balanchine). One of Weill's most trenchant works, *Die sieben Todsünden* is a modern morality play with some typically Brechtian twists: The Everyman is a woman and, far from resisting the sins, she succumbs to all of them. Through a series of songs the heroine, named Anna (mezzo-soprano), tells how she and her sister, also named Anna (dancer), endure their downward spiral into ever-deepening depravity, portrayed as an odyssey across the same darkly mythologized American landscape that figured in *Aufstieg und Fall der Stadt Mahagonny* (*Rise and Fall of the City of Mahagonny*). Before leaving their home in Louisiana, they confront Sloth; on their journey they encounter Pride in Memphis, Wrath in Los Angeles, Gluttony in Philadelphia, Lust in Boston, Avarice in Baltimore, Envy in San Francisco. A "Greek" chorus of four men, singing most of the time in barbershop harmony, represents the family they left behind in Louisiana ("mother" is a bass). At the end, the two Annas return to Louisiana, where the family has built a house with the money the girls have sent back from their seven-year journey through the seven deadly sins.

RECOMMENDED RECORDINGS

Fassbaender; Garben and North German Radio Symphony Orchestra (harmonia mundi).

Lemper: Mauceri and RIAS Berlin Sinfonietta (Polygram).

Siegfried Opera in three acts by Richard Wagner, completed in 1871 and premiered as the third part of his tetralogy *Der Ring des Nibelungen* on August 16, 1876, at the Festspielhaus in Bayreuth. With *Siegfried*, which follows *Die Walküre* in the *Ring* cycle, Wagner picks up the thread of his story after about 20 years have elapsed. The young Siegfried, raised in the forest by Alberich's brother Mime (without knowledge of his heroic origin), reforges the fragments of his father Siegmund's sword and puts it to immediate use. He kills Fafner, who has been sitting on the gold hoard and the ring since the end of *DAS RHEINGOLD*; then he kills Mime, who had been planning to kill him and take the gold; then he defiantly shatters Wotan's spear. He wakes the sleeping Brünnhilde, woos her, and wins her. *Siegfried* is often thought of as the scherzo of the *Ring* cycle—not only because it comes third, but because it is a rather upbeat piece of theater in spite of the carnage. The music of the final act, which finds Wagner at the peak of his powers, is sublime, ecstatic. The sudden flowering of love is portrayed in a half-hour duet that only the composer of *Tristan und Isolde* could have written.

RECOMMENDED RECORDINGS

WINDGASSEN, NILSSON, ADAM, BÖHME, NEIDLINGER; BÖHM AND BAYREUTH FESTIVAL ORCHESTRA (PHILIPS).

WINDGASSEN, NILSSON, SUTHERLAND, HOTTER, STOLZE, NEIDLINGER; SOLTI AND VIENNA PHILHARMONIC (DECCA).

Siegfried Idyll INSTRUMENTAL PIECE BY RICHARD WAGNER, composed as a musical gift for his wife, Cosima, and premiered on December 25, 1870, her 33rd birthday, at the villa Tribschen, outside Lucerne, where the couple lived. Completed on December 4, 1870, the score made use of thematic material that Wagner had earlier envisaged as the basis of a trio or a string quartet and that subsequently found its way into Act III of the opera *SIEGFRIED*. In addition to these tunes, the lullaby "Schlaf, Kindchen, schlaf" is quoted, and there are musical reminiscences of the birdsong and the fiery sunrise that heralded the birth of Richard and Cosima's son Siegfried 18 months earlier. The composition of the score and preparations for its first performance were kept secret from Cosima. At night, Wagner's assistant, the young Hans Richter, slipped out of the house to rehearse the piece in town. By Christmas morning, all was ready. Fifteen musicians stood assembled on the narrow staircase leading to the second floor, and Cosima awoke to the strains of the *Siegfried Idyll*, her birthday present. *See also* AUBADE.

RECOMMENDED RECORDINGS

KARAJAN AND BERLIN PHILHARMONIC (DG).

WALTER AND COLUMBIA SYMPHONY ORCHESTRA (SONY).

Siepi, Cesare

(b. Milan, February 10, 1923)

ITALIAN BASSO. His innate vocal gift was recognized early, and cultivated by private teachers and a period of study at Milan's Verdi Conservatory. From the age of 14 he was a member of the Milan Madrigal Group, and he made his operatic debut only four years later at Schio, as Sparafucile in Verdi's *Rigoletto*. He was instantly heralded as a promising young artist, but the disruptions of World War II put his career on hold. Openly anti-fascist, he lived a virtual exile in Switzerland until the end of the war. Following the war he returned to vocal action in Italy's most prestigious opera houses, making his La Scala debut in 1946, as Zaccaria in Verdi's *Nabucco*. During more than a decade at La Scala, he honed his roles until their ownership seemed to have been handed him directly by his charismatic predecessor Ezio Pinza.

Siepi's debut at the Metropolitan Opera came about unexpectedly, after the bass Boris Christoff, barred from entering the country, was forced to withdraw from a new production of Verdi's *Don Carlo* slated for opening night of the Met's 1950–51 season. Siepi was thrown into the breach as Philip II by the company's new director, Rudolf Bing. That performance was the first of 488 that would follow over nearly a quarter of a century. Notable among Siepi's 20 Met roles were Verdi's Ramfis (*Aida*) and Padre Guardiano (*La forza del destino*), Gounod's Méphistophélès, Rossini's Don Basilio, Wagner's Gurnemanz, Mussorgsky's Boris Godunov, Oroveso in Bellini's *Norma,* Colline in Puccini's *La bohème,* and Mozart's Figaro and Don Giovanni—perhaps his most famous role. Siepi's was a sizable voice, a genuine bass, with crackling resonance in the lower notes and a healthy ping in his extended, nearly baritonal upper register. As an actor he excelled in roles requiring kingly bearing in one moment and emotional upheaval in the next; but he was also at home with the kind of goofy comedy required to make Don Basilio a success. In the 20 years following his Met farewell on April 19, 1973, he continued to sing professionally in opera, concert, musical theater, and recital.

RECOMMENDED RECORDINGS

MOZART, *DON GIOVANNI*: DELLA CASA, DANCO, CORENA, DERMOTA; KRIPS AND VIENNA PHILHARMONIC (DECCA).

MOZART, *LE NOZZE DI FIGARO*: DANCO, GUEDEN, DELLA CASA, POELL, CORENA; KLEIBER AND VIENNA PHILHARMONIC (DECCA).

PUCCINI, *LA BOHÈME*: TEBALDI, BERGONZI, BASTIANINI, D'ANGELO; SERAFIN AND ACCADEMIA DI SANTA CECILIA (DECCA).

Sills, Beverly

(b. New York, May 25, 1929)

AMERICAN SOPRANO. By the age of seven the future opera star had amassed considerable performing experience, and her birth name, Belle Miriam Silverman, had become the marquee-friendly Beverly Sills. A precocious child who would later describe herself as a compulsive talker, she appeared on radio in variety shows (including *Major Bowes' Amateur Hour*), serial drama, and commercials; in the 20th Century Fox short film *Uncle Sol Solves It* (1938), she sang "Il bacio," one of 22 arias she learned phonetically from her mother's cherished collection of Amelita Galli-Curci 78s. At seven she began formal vocal training with Estelle Liebling, a Marchesi pupil and a teacher of Galli-Curci; Liebling and Sills worked together for 34 years. By her middle teens, determined to become an opera star, Sills toured the country in operetta. Then, in 1951–52, on tours organized by impresario Charles Wagner, she sang her first signature operatic role, Violetta in Verdi's *La traviata,* a part she would repeat in nearly 300 career performances. After auditioning several times for the New York City Opera, Sills was engaged by the company for its 1955 season as Rosalinde in Johann Strauss Jr.'s *Die Fledermaus.* Sills quickly became a valuable member of the troupe, singing parts such as Philine in Ambroise Thomas's *Mignon,* Mme Goldentrill in Mozart's *Der Schauspieldirektor,* and the title role in Douglas Moore's *The Ballad of Baby Doe*—a role upon which she would leave an indelible artistic stamp. At about the same time, she married financial writer Peter Greenough. Due to the responsibilities that came with an inherited family (Greenough's three daughters from a previous marriage) plus those of her own new one (an autistic son, and a daughter with profound hearing loss), Sills slowed her performing schedule for a few years.

By 1963 she was back at the City Opera in force. New roles included all of the heroines in Offenbach's *Les contes d'Hoffmann,* Donna Anna, Konstanze, Marguerite, and Louise. Her exceptionally bright, medium-sized but well-focused voice was capable of spinning a seemingly endless legato line, or bursting with crystalline perfection into waves of dazzling fioratura and thrilling high notes. Her vocal skills, along with her increasingly affecting work as an actress, won her a strong following in the New York public and press, and set the stage for her arrival on the international scene, in 1966, when the City Opera celebrated its new quarters at Lincoln Center's New York State Theater by mounting Handel's rarely performed *Giulio Cesare*—simultaneously with the Metropolitan Opera's premiere of Samuel Barber's *Antony and Cleopatra*—with Norman Treigle in the title role and Sills as Cleopatra. Critics from around the world were there; they came, they saw, Sills conquered. In 1969 a spectacular debut as Pamira in La Scala's new production of Rossini's *Le siège de Corinthe* fulfilled what the City Opera *Giulio Cesare* had promised.

The Brooklyn-born, homegrown diva who had achieved international success without the Metropolitan Opera made the most of her late-breaking fame, performing about 100 nights a year in the world's great opera houses and concert halls, keeping the City Opera as her artistic base. Showcased in new productions there, she was Lucia, Manon, the Daughter of the Regiment, the Merry Widow; among her most successful vehicles were the roles of Anna Bolena, Maria Stuarda, and Elisabetta I in Donizetti's three Tudor tragedies. True to her childhood nickname, "Bubbles," the effervescent Sills was a popular guest on television network talk shows and variety specials, and the subject of cover stories in both *Time* and *Newsweek*. By the time she made her long-awaited debut at the Metropolitan Opera, in 1976 (repeating her La Scala triumph as Pamira), she was that rarest of all things for an opera star: a household name.

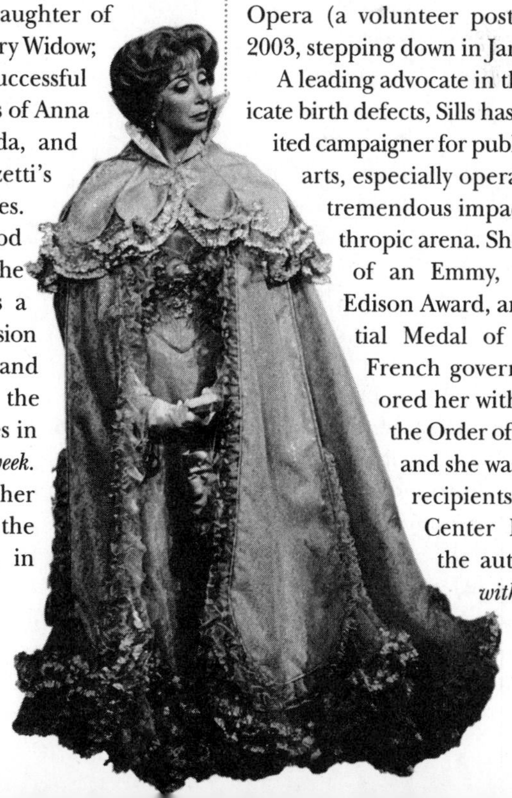

***Beverly Sills as Norina in* Don Pasquale**

She sang a handful of roles at the Met (Violetta, Thaïs, Norina, Lucia), but after nearly 50 years in the public eye, 25 of them as a professional opera singer, her best days were behind her. Wisely opting to leave the stage while she still commanded it, she retired from singing in October 1980 with a nationally televised gala at the City Opera. The next day she began in earnest her new job as the company's general director, a position she had held part-time in the final months of her singing career. She was instrumental in introducing supertitles to New York audiences (leading to their acceptance around the world) and in revamping the overall structure of the City Opera, putting it on firmer financial footing than it had previously enjoyed. She retired in 1991, but in 1994 she was back at Lincoln Center as its chairman, a post she held until 2002. She became chairman of the Metropolitan Opera (a volunteer post) in November 2003, stepping down in January 2005.

A leading advocate in the cause to eradicate birth defects, Sills has also been a spirited campaigner for public support of the arts, especially opera, and has had a tremendous impact in the philanthropic arena. She is the recipient of an Emmy, a Grammy, an Edison Award, and the Presidential Medal of Freedom. The French government has honored her with the insignia of the Order of Arts and Letters, and she was one of the first recipients of the Kennedy Center Honors. She is the author of *Children with Autism: A Parent's Guide* and three autobiographical works:

Bubbles; *Beverly: An Autobiography*; and *Bubbles: An Encore*.

RECOMMENDED RECORDINGS

HANDEL, *GIULIO CESARE*: TREIGLE, FORRESTER, WOLF, COSSA; RUDEL AND NEW YORK CITY OPERA (RCA).

COLLECTION:

"THE ART OF BEVERLY SILLS": ARIAS FROM *MIGNON*, *MANON*, *LOUISE*, *LUCIA DI LAMMERMOOR*, *LES CONTES D'HOFFMANN*, AND OTHERS (DG).

"THE VERY BEST OF BEVERLY SILLS": ARIAS FROM WORKS BY ROSSINI, DONIZETTI, LEHÁR, MASSENET, AND VERDI (EMI).

Simionato, Giulietta

(b. Forlì, May 12, 1910)

ITALIAN MEZZO-SOPRANO. After completing her studies in Rovigo, she won the 1933 Bel Canto Competition in Florence and readied herself for an operatic success that ended up taking a long time to materialize. Her formal debut came in 1935, in the world premiere of *Orsèolo* by Ildebrando Pizzetti (1880–1968) at the Florence Maggio Musicale, but when she was signed to a contract by La Scala in 1936, it was as a comprimario artist, relegated to small roles and supporting parts. In 1947, having "discovered" an important artist on its very own roster, La Scala assigned Simionato to the title role of *Mignon* by Ambroise Thomas (1811–96); she remained a leading mezzo at the house until her retirement from the stage in 1966.

Simionato had a rich, sizable voice with a strong upper extension and impressive low notes. She was an outstanding Amneris, and a memorable interpreter of the roles of Azucena, Carmen, Gioconda, Santuzza, Quickly, and the Principessa in Puccini's *Suor Angelica*. She had substantial range as an actress, and a style of singing well suited to the bel canto repertoire. She was much admired for both her Rosina and her Cenerentola and enjoyed notable success at La Scala as Adalgisa (which she performed to Callas's Norma) and Jane Seymour (to Callas's Anna Bolena). She sang in most of the great opera houses of the world, including Covent Garden, the Vienna Staatsoper, and the Metropolitan, where she appeared during the course of four seasons between 1959 and 1965.

RECOMMENDED RECORDINGS

VERDI, *AIDA*: TEBALDI, BERGONZI, MACNEIL; KARAJAN AND VIENNA PHILHARMONIC (DECCA).

COLLECTION:

"THE COLOR OF ONE VOICE": EXCERPTS FROM *AIDA*; ARIAS BY MASCAGNI, MASSENET, THOMAS, AND BIZET (FONO ENTERPRISE).

sinfonia Overture in three connected movements (fast-slow-fast) typically used in Italian operas of the early 18th century, characterized by thematic economy and a reliance on fugal or imitative procedures. It was one of the precursors of the modern symphony. *See also* SYMPHONY.

Sinfonia WORK FOR EIGHT AMPLIFIED VOICES AND ORCHESTRA BY LUCIANO BERIO, composed in 1968–69. The third movement is a collagelike deconstruction of the scherzo from Mahler's Symphony No. 2 as well as containing allusions to numerous other repertoire works.

RECOMMENDED RECORDINGS

LONDON VOICES; EÖTVÖS AND GOTHENBURG SYMPHONY ORCHESTRA (DG).

NEW SWINGLE SINGERS; BOULEZ AND FRENCH NATIONAL ORCHESTRA (ERATO).

Sinfonia antartica TITLE OF RALPH VAUGHAN WILLIAMS'S SEVENTH SYMPHONY, for soprano, small women's chorus, and orchestra, composed 1949–52 and premiered January 14, 1953, in Manchester by the Hallé Orchestra conducted by John Barbirolli. The score is based on material Vaughan Williams created for the film *Scott of the Antarctic* (1948).

RECOMMENDED RECORDINGS

ARMSTRONG; HAITINK AND LONDON PHILHARMONIC ORCHESTRA (EMI).

HARPER, RICHARDSON; PREVIN AND AMBROSIAN SINGERS, LONDON SYMPHONY ORCHESTRA (RCA).

RUSSELL; BAKELS AND BOURNEMOUTH SYMPHONY ORCHESTRA (NAXOS).

Sinfonia da Requiem **ORCHESTRAL WORK BY BENJAMIN BRITTEN, OP. 20,** composed in 1940 (while Britten was living in America) and premiered March 29, 1941, by the New York Philharmonic under the direction of John Barbirolli. The score consists of three connected movements, titled, after sections of the Latin Requiem, "Lacrymosa," "Dies irae," and "Requiem aeternam." The opening "Lacrymosa" is searing and intense, a powerful lament that begins with a hammer blow on the note D (for "Death") and builds to an agonized climax. Britten makes use of a piano in the orchestra to give added weight to the sound. The ensuing "Dies irae" movement, a dance of death, is fleet and angry, punctuated by fluttertongued snarls from the flutes and brass. The influence of Mahler can be felt in the finale, an elegy in which stabbing dissonances lend poignance to the plea for peace.

Britten's composition of the *Sinfonia da Requiem* was prompted by a commission from the Japanese government for a work to mark the 2,600th anniversary of Japan's ruling dynasty. Upon its completion the score was rejected by the Japanese on the grounds that the Christian liturgical references of its title and movement headings were insulting. Britten's music makes an even sharper point, registering his feelings about war and human slaughter, which the Japanese had perpetrated during their occupation of Manchuria in the years leading up to 1940.

RECOMMENDED RECORDINGS

PREVIN AND LONDON SYMPHONY ORCHESTRA (EMI).

SLATKIN AND LONDON PHILHARMONIC ORCHESTRA (RCA).

Sinfonia espansiva **TITLE OF CARL NIELSEN'S SYMPHONY NO. 3, OP. 27,** for soprano and tenor soloists and orchestra, composed 1910–11 and premiered February 28, 1912, in Copenhagen, the composer conducting. The work's success marked a turning point in Nielsen's fortunes with the Danish public and his critics. Nielsen gave the symphony its title shortly after the premiere, taking as his cue the tempo marking for the first movement: *Allegro espansivo.* The symphony's idyllic second movement, which incorporates a wordless aria for soprano and tenor soloists, was performed at Nielsen's funeral on October 9, 1931.

RECOMMENDED RECORDINGS

BERNSTEIN AND ROYAL DANISH ORCHESTRA (SONY).

BLOMSTEDT AND SAN FRANCISCO SYMPHONY ORCHESTRA (DECCA).

Sinfonietta **ORCHESTRAL WORK IN FIVE MOVEMENTS BY LEOŠ JANÁČEK,** first performed June 26, 1926, by the Czech Philharmonic conducted by Václav Talich. Janáček's editors at the newspaper *Lidové noviny,* for which he wrote occasional articles, had requested "some fanfares" for the Sokol Gymnastic Festival of 1926, a national celebration of the newly formed Czechoslovak Republic. Janáček, a fervent patriot, took advantage of the commission to write a work that conveyed his optimism and pride in the independence of his country, dedicating it "To the Czechoslovak Armed Forces" and insisting, at least in the beginning, on the title *Military Sinfonietta.* As the work took shape, it also became a tribute to Brno, the capital city of Moravia, which—as Brünn—had been under Austrian domination until the founding of the republic in 1918. Janáček intended for each movement after the first to portray a landmark or an aspect of the city's character.

The piece, Janáček's largest purely orchestral composition, is really more of a suite than a "little symphony." Each of the five movements is scored for a different combination of instruments, and the orchestration of the whole is bold, colorful, and, in spite of expanded wind and brass sections, characteristically lean.

RECOMMENDED RECORDINGS

Bělohlávek and Czech Philharmonic (Chandos).

Mackerras and Vienna Philharmonic (Decca).

singspiel (Ger., "sung play") A type of comic opera with text in the vernacular (normally German) in which musical numbers are interspersed with sections of spoken dialogue. Notable examples include *Die Jagd* by Johann Adam Hiller (1728–1804), Mozart's *Die Entführung aus dem Serail* (1782), *Der Schauspieldirektor* (1786), and *Die Zauberflöte* (1791), Dittersdorf's *Der Apotheker und der Doktor* (1786), and Weber's *Abu Hassan* (1811). Kodály's *Háry János,* with a text in Hungarian, is probably the best-known 20th-century successor to these scores. Because of their more serious tone, works such as Beethoven's *Fidelio* (1805, rev. 1806/1814) and Weber's *Der Freischütz* (1821), which also incorporate spoken dialogue, are not considered part of the genre.

Sinopoli, Giuseppe

(b. Venice, November 2, 1946; d. Berlin, April 20, 2001)

ITALIAN CONDUCTOR AND COMPOSER. He approached music with a rarefied and highly disciplined intellectualism that, on occasion, produced striking results. Sinopoli studied organ at the conservatory of Messina; as a university student, he simultaneously took courses in composition at the Venice Conservatory and in medicine and psychiatry at the University of Padua. He earned his medical degree (with a dissertation on criminal anthropology) and

Giuseppe Sinopoli in performance

became a professor of composition, both in 1972. After further composition studies with Franco Donatoni and Bruno Maderna, and conducting studies with Hans Swarowsky in Vienna, he began working as a conductor. In 1975 he founded the Bruno Maderna Ensemble, specializing in contemporary music. His operatic conducting debut came in Venice in 1978, with Verdi's *Aida.* From 1983 to 1987 he served as chief conductor of the orchestra of the Accademia di Santa Cecilia in Rome, and in 1984 he was named principal conductor of the Philharmonia Orchestra of London, subsequently serving as that orchestra's music director (1987–94). He was active at the Deutsche Oper Berlin throughout the 1980s and in 1985 made his debuts at the Metropolitan Opera, conducting Puccini's *Tosca,* and the Bayreuth Festival, conducting *Tannhäuser.* He became principal conductor of the Staatskapelle Dresden in 1992 and was preparing to assume the post of music director of the Dresden State Opera at the time of his death, from a heart attack that occurred while he was conducting a performance of *Aida* in Berlin. (He was also about to receive a second doctorate, in archaeology, in recognition of a thesis written on Babylonian royal cities.)

As a composer, Sinopoli was highly regarded in certain avant-garde circles. He composed a good deal of chamber music, several orchestral works, and an opera, *Lou Salomé,* about a pioneering female psychoanalyst who was a disciple of Freud. His podium career was largely a creation of Deutsche Grammophon in Hamburg. In spite of his great intelligence and thorough knowledge of music, he lacked, at least in the early years, many of the basic technical skills of an accomplished conductor, from being able to balance chords and give clear upbeats to the management of tempo and dynamics. He was nevertheless able to achieve reasonably, sometimes outstandingly, good results in the recording studio, working exclusively with world-class ensembles.

"THEY DIED WITH THEIR BOOTS ON"
Other conductors who perished on the podium: Felix Mottl (1911), Eduard van Beinum (1959), Dimitri Mitropoulos (1960), and Joseph Keilberth (1968).

RECOMMENDED RECORDINGS

MUSSORGSKY, *PICTURES AT AN EXHIBITION*: NEW YORK PHILHARMONIC (DG).

STRAUSS, *ARIADNE AUF NAXOS*: VOIGT, DESSAY, OTTER, HEPPNER; STAATSKAPELLE DRESDEN (DG).

Six, Les Group of 20th-century French composers consisting of Francis Poulenc, Darius Milhaud, Arthur Honegger, Georges Auric (1899–1983), Germaine Tailleferre (1892–1983), and Louis Durey (1888–1979), all of whom were, for a time, followers of Jean Cocteau. The name came from the title of an article written in 1920 by Henri Collet for the journal *Comoedia.*

Sixteen, The *See box on pages 934–36.*

Slatkin, Leonard

(b. Los Angeles, September 1, 1944)

AMERICAN CONDUCTOR. His parents, violinist Felix Slatkin and cellist Eleanor Aller, were founding members of the Hollywood String Quartet and top-notch studio musicians: Felix was concertmaster of the 20th Century Fox orchestra and Aller was principal cello of the orchestra at Warner Bros. After beginning his musical career on the piano, Slatkin first studied conducting with his father and continued with Walter Susskind at Aspen and Jean Morel at the Juilliard School. Susskind engaged him as assistant conductor of the Saint Louis Symphony Orchestra in 1968 and promoted him to associate in 1971. Slatkin made his European debut in 1974 with the Royal Philharmonic Orchestra in London; during the 1970s, he also began making regular appearances as a guest conductor with most of America's major orchestras and many European ensembles. In 1979, after serving two seasons as music director of the New Orleans Philharmonic, he was named music director of the Saint Louis Symphony Orchestra, a position he retained until 1996. He made his debut as an opera conductor with the Lyric Opera of Chicago in 1986, and in 1991 he was engaged by the Metropolitan Opera to conduct a new production of Puccini's *La fanciulla del West.* At the beginning of the 1996–97 season he succeeded Mstislav Rostropovich as music director of the National Symphony Orchestra in Washington, D.C. (he plans to step down from its podium at the end of the 2007–08 season). He served as music director of the BBC Symphony Orchestra

American conductor Leonard Slatkin

from 1999 to 2002, and in 2005 he was appointed principal guest conductor of the Royal Philharmonic Orchestra.

Slatkin's 28-year collaboration with the Saint Louis Symphony Orchestra changed the musical map of the United States. Under his baton a distinguished second-tier ensemble became a virtuosic, world-class orchestra admired for its warmth, polish, and stylistic versatility. Slatkin grew on the job, becoming a persuasive interpreter of the standard repertoire and an effective champion of much 20th-century music, particularly that of American, Russian, and British composers. Along the way he compiled an extensive discography, working not only with the Saint Louis ensemble but with several prominent London orchestras, including the London Philharmonic, the London Symphony Orchestra, and the Philharmonia. In Washington, he tightened the NSO's ensemble, brought greater focus to its programming, and cultivated a less colorful, but more burnished, sonority. His music making, like the remarks he enjoys making to his audiences, is characterized by pithiness and a burning intelligence.

RECOMMENDED RECORDINGS

BARBER, ORCHESTRAL WORKS (INCLUDING *ESSAYS*, *ADAGIO FOR STRINGS*, *OVERTURE TO THE SCHOOL FOR SCANDAL*): SAINT LOUIS SYMPHONY ORCHESTRA (EMI).

BARBER, VIOLIN CONCERTO; HANSON, SYMPHONY NO. 2: OLIVEIRA; SAINT LOUIS SYMPHONY ORCHESTRA (EMI).

BOLCOM, *SONGS OF INNOCENCE AND OF EXPERIENCE*: UNIVERSITY OF MICHIGAN SYMPHONY ORCHESTRA (NAXOS).

BRITTEN, *SINFONIA DA REQUIEM*, *YOUNG PERSON'S GUIDE TO THE ORCHESTRA*, *PASSACAGLIA*, "FOUR SEA INTERLUDES" FROM *PETER GRIMES*: LONDON PHILHARMONIC ORCHESTRA (RCA).

COPLAND, *BILLY THE KID*, *RODEO*: SAINT LOUIS SYMPHONY ORCHESTRA (EMI).

Sleeping Beauty, The BALLET IN A PROLOGUE AND THREE ACTS BY PYOTR IL'YICH TCHAIKOVSKY, with choreography by Marius Petipa to a scenario by Ivan Vsevolozhsky (based on the fairy tale by Charles Perrault), premiered January 15, 1890, at the Mariinsky Theater in St. Petersburg. The familiar plot centers on a young princess who, after a curse is placed upon her by a wicked fairy, falls asleep for 100 years and is awakened by a prince's kiss. The score, composed between December 1888 and September 1889, reveals Tchaikovsky at the peak of his powers: the structure is assured, the characterization brilliant and precise. Most remarkable is the way the composer manages, through his choice of musical ideas and extraordinary skill as an orchestrator, to evoke a specific atmosphere in each scene and thereby draw the listener into the enchanted world of the story.

Julie Kent as Aurora in Tchaikovsky's **The Sleeping Beauty**

RECOMMENDED RECORDINGS

(COMPLETE): DORATI AND CONCERTGEBOUW ORCHESTRA (PHILIPS).

(COMPLETE): PLETNEV AND RUSSIAN NATIONAL ORCHESTRA (DG).

(SUITE): ROSTROPOVICH AND BERLIN PHILHARMONIC (DG).

sleighbells *See box on pages 496–97.*

Slezak, Leo

(b. Mährisch-Schönberg, August 18, 1873; d. Egern am Tegernsee, June 1, 1946)

AUSTRIAN TENOR. He made his debut in Brünn (now Brno), as Lohengrin, in 1896. Gustav Mahler engaged him in Vienna in 1901, initiating a relationship between the singer and the Vienna Court Opera (later the Staatsoper) that would endure until 1933. In 1909, following a period of coaching with Jean de Reszke, Slezak made his Metropolitan Opera debut as Otello, with Arturo Toscanini in the pit. He remained on the Met's roster just four seasons, but dominated the Wagner and Verdi repertoire, appearing as Tannhäuser, Lohengrin, and Walther in *Die Meistersinger von Nürnberg,* and as Manrico in *Il trovatore* and Radames in *Aida*; in 1910 he sang Hermann in the U.S. premiere of Tchaikovsky's *The Queen of Spades,* under Mahler's baton.

With his imposing stature and girth, Slezak cut a formidable figure on stage. He had ample reserves of power and sang with a lustrous tone. Though usually cast in heroic roles, he was known for a clownish sense of humor and will be remembered for delivering one of the funniest lines ever uttered in front of the footlights. In the final moments of *Lohengrin,* noticing that the swanboat had begun to move off toward the wings before he could board it, he inquired in a stage whisper, much as someone who had missed a train might ask, "Wenn geht der nächste Schwann?" ("What time's the next swan?"), provoking gales of laughter from his audience. He was the father of actor Walter Slezak.

Leo Slezak and son Walter

Smetana, Bedřich

(b. Litomyšl, March 2, 1824; d. Prague, May 12, 1884)

CZECH COMPOSER. Displaying remarkable musical talent at an early age, he received instruction from his father, an enthusiastic amateur violinist, and from several local teachers; his formal musical education was scattered and rudimentary until, in 1844, he became a private student of Joseph Proksch in Prague. His lack of systematic training enabled him to think outside the conventions of the day, and his imagination was further stimulated by the music of Hector Berlioz and Franz Liszt, which he especially admired. Not surprisingly, programmatic elements in general, and the tone poems in particular, would figure prominently in Smetana's oeuvre. Smetana founded a music school of his own in Prague in 1848, married the following year, and began to assume an important role in Prague's musical life as teacher, performer, and concert organizer, though not to any great extent as composer. Feeling that his gifts in this area had gone unrecognized, he left Prague for a teaching job in Göteborg, Sweden, in 1856. Smetana's domestic life was filled with tragedy in these early years—three of his four daughters died between 1854 and 1856, and his wife, whose tuberculosis was aggravated by the wet Swedish winters, died in 1859 on the way home to Bohemia. In Sweden, Smetana found opportunities to conduct, and he advanced his craft as a composer with his first three symphonic poems: *Richard III, Wallensteins Lager,* and *Håkon Jarl* (1857–61). But musical life in Göteborg proved more provincial than Smetana could stomach, and news of the impending opening of the Provisional Theater in Prague, where Czech-language opera would be allowed to take root, hastened his return home at the end of 1861.

For Smetana, whose first language was German, the creation of a repertoire for the Provisional Theater (which opened its doors in 1862) proved both an opportunity and a challenge. He went at it with characteristic determination. He was appointed principal conductor at the Provisional Theater in 1866. The success earlier that same year of his first opera, *The Brandenburgers in Bohemia,* encouraged him to finish another, the comic opera THE BARTERED BRIDE (*Prodaná nevěsta*; 1866, rev. 1870), which became his most popular work for the stage. The charm, humor, and naturalness of this work soon found a devoted audience; Smetana never achieved comparable success with any of his later operas—*Dalibor* (1868), *Libuše* (1872), *The Two Widows* (1874), *The Kiss* (1876), *The Secret* (1878), and *The Devil's Wall* (1882). Smetana continued as principal conductor of the Provisional Theater through 1874, and introduced more than 40 new works to the repertoire. From 1874 to 1879 he composed *MÁ VLAST* (*My Country*), a series of six symphonic poems inspired by Czech legends and scenery; the second of the six, *Vltava* (*The Moldau*), is by far the best known of the set.

In 1874 Smetana lost his hearing, a secondary symptom of syphilis. In his String Quartet in E Minor (*From My Life*), written in 1876, the piercing high E harmonic sounded toward the end of the fourth movement represents the sudden onset of tinnitus that preceded his deafness. In 1875 Smetana received a pension, freeing him, to a degree, to compose unhindered by financial concerns. He remained productive nearly to the end.

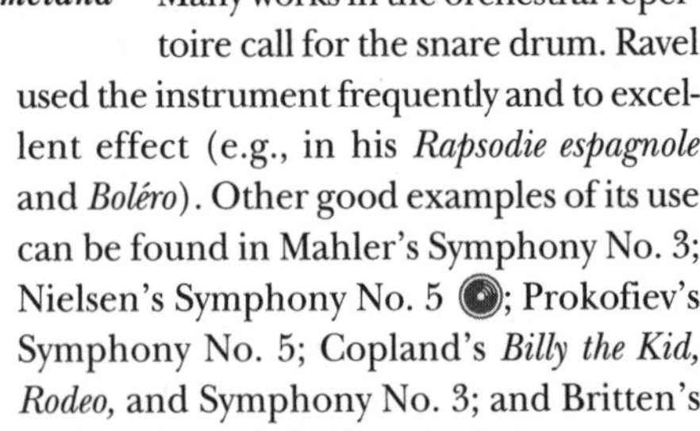

Bedřich Smetana

In 1882, while Smetana was still alive, *The Bartered Bride* received its 100th performance, a milestone in the history of Czech opera. By 1952 it had received 1,000 performances at Prague's National Theater alone. As the creator of an enduring operatic repertoire in Czech, Smetana holds pride of place among all composers of Czech birth. Though not as powerful a musical thinker as Dvořák, nor as versatile a creator, he imbued his music with a meaningful expression of the Czech nation's character and aspirations and gave musical voice to its language and history. For this achievement he is rightly considered, along with Dvořák and Janáček, one of the pillars of modern Czech culture.

RECOMMENDED RECORDINGS

THE BARTERED BRIDE (OVERTURE AND ORCHESTRAL EXCERPTS): KUBELÍK AND BAVARIAN RADIO SYMPHONY ORCHESTRA (DG).

MÁ VLAST: KUBELÍK AND CZECH PHILHARMONIC (SUPRAPHON).

STRING QUARTET IN E MINOR: MOYZES QUARTET (NAXOS).

snare drum A drum with heads of parchment about 14 or 15 inches in diameter, and a case, usually of metal, about six inches deep. The drumsticks are of hard wood, usually hickory, with oval-shaped tips. The "snares" are wires (formerly, gut strings) that can be brought into contact with the bottom head of the drum; they vibrate against it when the top head is struck, causing the characteristic rustling sound. The drum can also be played with the snares disengaged, in which case it sounds like a fairly high-pitched tom-tom. Many works in the orchestral repertoire call for the snare drum. Ravel used the instrument frequently and to excellent effect (e.g., in his *Rapsodie espagnole* and *Boléro*). Other good examples of its use can be found in Mahler's Symphony No. 3; Nielsen's Symphony No. 5; Prokofiev's Symphony No. 5; Copland's *Billy the Kid, Rodeo,* and Symphony No. 3; and Britten's *A Young Person's Guide to the Orchestra.*

Söderström, Elisabeth

(b. Stockholm, May 7, 1927)

SWEDISH SOPRANO. Following studies with Russian lyric coloratura Adelaíde Andreyeva de Skilondz, Söderström made her professional debut as Mozart's Bastienne in

1947 at the Drottningholm Court Theatre, outside Stockholm, where she would return to serve as artistic director from 1993 to 1996. In 1949 she joined the Swedish Royal Opera. She made her debut at Glyndebourne in 1957, as the Composer in Richard Strauss's *Ariadne auf Naxos,* and returned on a regular basis through 1979, singing the roles of Octavian in *Der Rosenkavalier* and the Countess in *Capriccio,* Leonore in Beethoven's *Fidelio,* and Susanna in Mozart's *Le nozze di Figaro,* the same role with which she made her Metropolitan Opera debut in 1959. In subsequent appearances at the Met she was Ellen Orford in Britten's *Peter Grimes* and Sophie and the Marschallin in *Der Rosenkavalier*; as recently as 1999 she bowed as the Countess in Tchaikovsky's *The Queen of Spades.* Long associated with the operas of Leoš Janáček, she has sung the title roles in *Kát'a Kabanová* and *Jenůfa,* and the role of Emilia Marty in *The Makropulos Case*; her outstanding interpretations of all three are preserved on recordings conducted by Sir Charles Mackerras.

Söderström's vast repertoire and experience, extraordinary musical intelligence, and compelling skills as an actress have all played a part in her success. Her stylistic range—from Monteverdi through Mozart and Strauss to Janáček, Ligeti, and Hans Werner Henze (b. 1926)—is little short of phenomenal, but what is most remarkable about her singing is the way she unfailingly creates fully realized characters on the stage. Her singing in concert and recital is equally remarkable for its emotional communication.

RECOMMENDED RECORDINGS

JANÁČEK, *JENŮFA*: OCHMAN, DVORSKY, RANDOVA, POPP; MACKERRAS AND VIENNA PHILHARMONIC (DECCA).

JANÁČEK, *THE MAKROPULOS CASE*: BLACHUT, DVORSKY, KREJCIK, CZAKOVA; MACKERRAS AND VIENNA PHILHARMONIC (DECCA).

RACHMANINOV, SONGS: ASHKENAZY (DECCA).

solfège Technique of singing passages at sight using the syllables associated with the notes of the scale (*do, re, mi, fa,* etc.) as a mnemonic device to correctly sound different intervals.

solo (It., "alone") [1] A piece or a passage played or sung by a single performer. [2] When used as a marking in an orchestral or vocal score, an indication that the passage is to be played by a single instrument, or sung by a solo voice, rather than taken by the whole section.

Solomon **ORATORIO BY GEORGE FRIDERIC HANDEL,** based on the Old Testament books of II Chronicles and I Kings, composed in 1748 and premiered March 17, 1749, at Covent Garden in London. Act I begins with the establishment of the Temple of Solomon and ends with the king and his bride romantically retiring to the bedchamber. Act II tells the famous story of two women who come to Solomon with a newborn son, arguing about which one is the mother. Act III depicts the visit of the Queen of Sheba and the splendor of Solomon's court and contains the oratorio's most famous music, the "Arrival of the Queen of Sheba."

RECOMMENDED RECORDING

WATKINSON, HENDRICKS, ARGENTA, ROLFE JOHNSON; GARDINER AND ENGLISH BAROQUE SOLOISTS (PHILIPS).

Solti, Georg

(b. Budapest, October 21, 1912; d. Antibes, September 5, 1997)

HUNGARIAN/BRITISH CONDUCTOR. A fascinating hybrid of old-school maestro and media celebrity, Solti was one of the most successful international star conductors of the second half of the 20th century and one of the last to come up through the opera house. He was noted for his interpretations of the Austro-Germanic symphonic repertoire, particularly Haydn, Beethoven, Mendelssohn, Brahms, and Mahler; for his exciting renditions of 19th- and 20th-century showpieces such as Mussorgsky's *Pictures at an Exhibition* and Bartók's *Concerto for Orchestra*; and, in opera, for his accounts of the most significant works of Mozart, Verdi, Wagner, and Richard Strauss.

Born into a middle-class Jewish family when Hungary was still a part of the Austro-Hungarian Empire, Solti took piano lessons as a child and at 13 enrolled in the Franz Liszt Academy in Budapest, where he studied with Béla Bartók, Zoltán Kodály, and Ernő Dohnányi. He graduated in 1930 and became a rehearsal pianist and coach at the Budapest Opera. By the age of 24 he was conducting rehearsals. Solti worked as an assistant to Arturo Toscanini at the Salzburg Festival in 1936 and 1937 (alongside Erich Leinsdorf), even playing the glockenspiel in performances of Mozart's *Die Zauberflöte.* He made his conducting debut on March 11, 1938 (the date Austria was absorbed by Germany in the Anschluss), leading Mozart's *Le nozze di Figaro* in Budapest.

In 1939 Solti left Hungary for Switzerland, where he spent the war years making his living as a pianist (only Swiss-born conductors were allowed to conduct there). He won the Geneva International Piano Competition in 1942. As part of the Allied effort to rebuild Germany's cultural life using artists free of any Nazi associations, Solti was engaged to conduct Beethoven's *Fidelio* at the Bavarian State Opera in Munich in 1945, a remarkable opportunity in view of his lack of experience. The following year he was placed in charge of the company. He remained in Munich for six years, leaving in 1952 to become general music director of the city of Frankfurt.

Solti's U.S. debut came in 1953, when he conducted Strauss's *Elektra* with the San Francisco Opera. He made his debut with the Chicago Symphony Orchestra the following year, and in 1956 conducted Wagner's *Die Walküre,* Strauss's *Salome,* and Verdi's *La forza del destino* at the Lyric Opera of Chicago. He took his first bows at the Metropolitan Opera on December 17, 1960, with Wagner's *Tannhäuser.* During his short-lived career at the Met, which ended in 1964 in a dispute over casting, he conducted 37 performances of seven works.

Georg Solti, the picture of podium intensity

Solti served as music director at Covent Garden from 1961 to 1971, raising the standard of orchestral playing at the house and leading a number of important premieres, including the first productions there of Wagner's *Ring* cycle, Strauss's *Die Frau ohne Schatten,* and Britten's *A Midsummer Night's Dream.* For his services to English music Solti was knighted in 1972.

The most important association of Solti's career was with the Chicago Symphony Orchestra. During his 22 years in charge (1969–91), he led the CSO to the foremost position among America's "top five" orchestras—traditionally those of New York, Boston, Philadelphia, Chicago, and Cleveland. Solti and the Chicagoans became famous for a uniquely dynamic, all-stops-out brand of music making, one that emphasized hard-hitting interpretations of big orchestral showpieces and amazing virtuosity from every section. Their annual visits to New York's Carnegie Hall in the 1970s and 1980s, when they would toss off the most demanding scores with the greatest of ease, were the toast of the town. In 1991, after he stepped down as its music director, Solti was named laureate conductor of the Chicago Symphony Orchestra. He died while on vacation in the south of France, weeks before he was scheduled to conduct his 1,000th concert with the CSO. His autobiography, intended to be part of the celebration of his 85th birthday, was published posthumously by Knopf.

Sir Georg was one of the most widely recorded conductors in history. His first recording of a complete symphonic work was made in 1949 with the London Philharmonic Orchestra (and marked the beginning of an association with the LPO that would culminate with Solti's engagement as principal conductor from 1979 to 1983), while his last, with the Budapest Festival Orchestra, went into the can in 1997. During the intervening 48 years, Solti committed a huge amount of the core symphonic repertoire to disc, along with the major operas of Mozart, Wagner, and Strauss, some Verdi, and numerous others. He won more Grammys (32) than any musician in history, classical or popular, including Elvis Presley, Michael Jackson, and Madonna. His stereo account of the complete *Ring* cycle for London Records (begun in 1958 and completed in 1965) is one of the greatest achievements in the history of recording.

On the podium Solti cut a figure that was impossible to miss. Tall, bald, and terrible, with deep-set eyes that made him look like a death's head in tails, he worked himself into a fury, his angular gestures and slashing baton conveying an incredible intensity, energy, and electricity. There were times when he missed the spirit of the music (brutalizing a gentle work like Schubert's Fifth Symphony, for example), but at other times he realized elements in the score that nobody else seemed to notice or to be able to achieve (like the final ritard in Bartók's *Music for Strings, Percussion, and Celesta,* and the huge structural crescendo at the climax of the first movement of Mahler's Symphony No. 8). Solti always gave of his best, and his best performances etched themselves vividly into the memory, testifying to an absolutely galvanic personality.

Solti dons fireman's helmet given by members of the Chicago Symphony after recording Mahler's Symphony No. 8.

RECOMMENDED RECORDINGS

BRAHMS, SYMPHONIES (COMPLETE): CHICAGO SYMPHONY ORCHESTRA (DECCA).

MAHLER, SYMPHONY NO. 8: AUGER, HARPER, POPP, KOLLO, TALVELA, SHIRLEY-QUIRK, ET AL.; CHICAGO SYMPHONY ORCHESTRA (DECCA).

MOZART, *LE NOZZE DI FIGARO*: POPP, VON STADE, TE KANAWA, RAMEY, ALLEN, MOLL; LONDON PHILHARMONIC ORCHESTRA (DECCA).

SCHUBERT, SYMPHONY NO. 9: VIENNA PHILHARMONIC (DECCA).

STRAUSS, *ELEKTRA*: NILSSON, RESNIK, STOLZE, KRAUSE; VIENNA PHILHARMONIC (DECCA).

WAGNER, *DER RING DES NIBELUNGEN*: FLAGSTAD, NILSSON, LUDWIG, STOLZE, HOTTER, WINDGASSEN, FISCHER-DIESKAU, LONDON, ET AL.; VIENNA PHILHARMONIC (DECCA).

sombrero de tres picos, El (The Three-Cornered Hat) BALLET BY MANUEL DE FALLA, composed 1916–19 and premiered July 22, 1919, at the Alhambra Theatre in London, with Ernest Ansermet conducting, choreography by Léonide Massine, and sets and costumes by Pablo Picasso. The music originated as a quasi-balletic pantomime for chamber orchestra and vocalist based on Pedro Antonio de Alarcón's novel *El corregidor y la molinera.* Following a commission from Sergey Diaghilev and the Ballets Russes, Falla revised the first part of the pantomime and expanded the instrumental palette to create a vivid, breezily ironic ballet score. Falla's writing is brilliantly virtuosic and warmly lyrical, spiced with extraordinary rhythmic and instrumental touches. Throughout the score, the sultry, changing moods and dynamic tempos of life and love under the Spanish sun are evoked with flair; the concluding *jota,* in particular, transmits the dizzying, coloristic whirl of an Iberian festival with visceral intensity.

RECOMMENDED RECORDING

DUTOIT AND MONTREAL SYMPHONY ORCHESTRA (DECCA).

sonata (from It. *suonare,* "to sound") A freestanding piece for solo instrument or instruments, with or without accompaniment. As early as the 13th-century words like *sonada* and *sonnade* appear in literary sources as designations for instrumental pieces; with the proliferation of instrumental music that occurred toward the end of the 16th century, the term "sonata" became one of many applied in a loose manner to individual pieces not patterned on specific dance types. The multimovement chamber genre familiar to modern-day listeners as the sonata emerged in Italy during the 17th century. Toward the end of that century it became customary to classify sonatas for one or more instruments with continuo as belonging to one of two genres: either *sonata da chiesa* ("church sonata") or *sonata da camera* ("chamber sonata"). The former were suitable for use in church (meaning they did not contain movements based on dances; Biber's *Mystery* Sonatas are an example), while the latter, which did contain such movements, and thus were similar to suites for solo instruments, were intended for concert use or domestic entertainment. Corelli published collections of both types, and his works came to be seen as models. A typical *sonata da chiesa* consisted of four movements in a slow-fast-slow-fast arrangement; the second movement was often fugal in character. A *sonata da camera* usually consisted of three to five movements, opening with a movement in slow tempo, and including in most cases at least one dance movement. Almost from the start, Corelli departed from his own templates, and by the beginning of the 18th century, in his works and those of others, the distinction between "church sonata" and "chamber sonata" had disappeared altogether.

The Baroque saw the heyday of the so-called trio sonata, a specific type within the broader sonata genre. These works were usually scored for two melody instruments (e.g., two violins) and a bass instrument (such as the cello), plus continuo; the "trio" designation referred to the number of melodic voices in the texture, not necessarily the number of musicians required to play such pieces. The three-voice texture could also be achieved using a single melody instrument (violin, oboe, flute, or cello) and a keyboard instrument (harpsichord or organ). Sonatas for unaccompanied string instrument (such as Bach's in G minor, A minor, and C, for the violin) were fashionable in the late 17th and early 18th century as well, particularly north of the

Bach Sonata No. 1 in G minor, for unaccompanied violin

Alps. But as the 18th century unfolded, it was the solo sonata—usually for accompanied violin, sometimes for keyboard (as in the case of Domenico Scarlatti's many brilliant essays)—that began to predominate.

During the Classical era the solo sonata completed its conquest of the chamber sphere, and the genre acquired the characteristics and formal layout that to a great extent it retains today. Most sonatas of the past 250 years have been large-scale works for the piano, or for one (or more) solo instruments with piano accompaniment, and have usually consisted of three or four movements, though sonatas in one or two movements are not uncommon. The opening movement, usually an Allegro, tends to be cast in "sonata" form (see following entry) and is usually followed by a movement in slow or moderate tempo and a finale in a lively tempo; an optional "dance" movement (minuet, scherzo) can appear after the first movement, before the finale, or as the finale. There are many variations on this plan.

The post-1750 sonata literature is vast, particularly when it comes to solo keyboard works. Any survey of important piano sonatas would include works by Haydn, Clementi, Mozart, Beethoven, Schubert, Chopin, Liszt, Brahms, Rachmaninov, Scriabin, and Prokofiev, and might touch as well on significant contributions by Berg, Stravinsky, and Boulez and by the Americans MacDowell, Ives, Griffes, Copland, and Carter. The repertoire for violin and piano includes sonatas by Mozart, Beethoven, Brahms, Franck, Fauré, Grieg, Elgar, Debussy, Ravel, Prokofiev, Ives, and Copland, while that for viola and piano is headed by works of Hindemith, Milhaud, and Shostakovich. The most important sonatas for cello and piano are those of Beethoven, Chopin, Mendelssohn, Brahms, Strauss, Debussy, Rachmaninov, Shostakovich, Prokofiev, and Britten. The repertoire for unaccompanied string instrument is smaller, but includes major works by Ysaÿe (the six sonatas, Op. 27, for violin), Kodály (his Op. 8 sonata for cello), and Bartók (the 1944 sonata for violin).

Among the most frequently encountered sonatas for wind instrument and piano are those of Brahms (his two Op. 120 sonatas for clarinet, also playable on the viola), Prokofiev (flute), and Poulenc (flute, oboe, and clarinet). Sonatas for unusual combinations of instruments abound, though, with the exception of Debussy's Sonata for Flute, Viola, and Harp (1915) and Ravel's Sonata for Violin and Cello (1920–22), few are staples of the repertoire.

sonata form In music from the Classical era to the present, an organizational plan discernible in many constituent movements—opening movements especially, but also slow movements and finales—of large-scale instrumental pieces such as symphonies, overtures, quartets, trios, and sonatas. The scheme should more properly be called "key area" form, because the principles on which it is based are harmonic, not melodic.

The hallmark of sonata form is its establishment of two (or more) well-defined key areas as the structural pillars of the first part of a movement, and its incorporation of a restatement, later in the movement, of material associated with the first part. Within the first part of a sonata-form movement (called the *exposition*), there is a departure from the TONIC to a closely related key: usually the DOMINANT, if the tonic is a major key, or the relative major, if the tonic is a minor key. Sometimes, as in Beethoven's *Pastoral* Symphony, the exposition involves three key areas (this approach can also be found in many works of Schubert, Bruckner, and Mahler, among others). Later (in what is called the *development*), there is an excursion through other keys, some of which may be remote from the movement's home key. In the final part of the movement (called the *recapitulation*), the tonic is reestablished, usually by means of a reprise of the opening material. The material associated with the second key area (and the third, if there is one), may be reprised as well, but in the home key, not the key in which it was originally heard. The departure from the home key that characterizes a sonata-form movement, particularly the harmonic peregrination in the development section, produces tension that acts a bit like centrifugal force: The further the harmony gets from the tonic, and the longer it stays away, the greater the tension and the greater the emotional impact when the home key is recaptured. The restatement of material from the second key area in the tonic (if it occurs) reinforces the feeling of a return and provides a sense of closure to the movement.

Sonata form has been one of the most important structural devices in the music of the past three centuries, serving as the template for individual movements in large-scale works and for whole works such as concert overtures and symphonic poems (Mendelssohn's *Hebrides* Overture and Richard Strauss's *Don Juan* and *Ein Heldenleben* are examples). It has proven extremely flexible, and adaptations of its basic design are legion. Because Haydn, Mozart, and Beethoven—whose works established the procedure as a paradigm—usually (though not always) employed first and second subjects of contrasting melodic character, sonata form has often been discussed and analyzed in thematic terms. This has tended to obscure the fact that what makes the form "work" is the harmonic tension caused by the departure from the tonic key and the sense of arrival that accompanies its reassertion and confirmation in the closing part of a movement.

sonatina (It., "little sonata") Generic term for a piece that resembles a sonata but is more modest in scale and content. Mozart's Piano Sonata in C, K. 545, is a particularly good example of the type (even though it is called a sonata), as are Beethoven's Piano Sonata in G, Op. 79, and Schubert's three Sonatinas for Violin and Piano. Among the most familiar pieces so named are Clementi's Six Sonatinas, Op. 36, which belong to the repertoire of nearly every beginning pianist, and Ravel's *Sonatine* (1903–05), a work of scintillating beauty and sophistication.

song cycle A group of songs that are thematically related, that tell a story, or that otherwise form a single musical and poetic entity, as opposed to a collection of individual songs. Examples include Beethoven's *An die ferne Geliebte* (1815–16), Schubert's

Die schöne Müllerin (1823) and *Winterreise* (1827), Schumann's *Frauenliebe und -leben,* Op. 42, and *Dichterliebe,* Op. 48 (both 1840), Berlioz's *Les nuits d'été* (1840–41), Mussorgsky's *Songs and Dances of Death* (1875–77), Mahler's *Lieder eines fahrenden Gesellen* (1883–85), and Schoenberg's *Pierrot lunaire* (1912).

sonnambula, La (The Sleepwalker) OPERA IN TWO ACTS BY VINCENZO BELLINI, to a libretto by Felice Romani (after Eugène Scribe's *La somnambule*), premiered March 6, 1831, at the Teatro Carcano in Milan. The original cast included Giuditta Pasta as Amina and Giovanni Battista Rubini as Elvino. The role of Amina quickly became a favorite of Maria Malibran and was later championed by Adelina Patti, Luisa Tetrazzini, Amelita Galli-Curci, and Maria Callas. Set in Switzerland in the early 19th century, the story deals with the complications that ensue when Amina, beloved of Elvino, sleepwalks into the bedroom of Count Rodolfo. Just as her somnambulism gets her into trouble in the first act, it gets her out of it in the second, and the opera ends happily, with Elvino awakening his bride-to-be by slipping a wedding ring onto her finger.

RECOMMENDED RECORDINGS

ORGONASOVA, GIMÉNEZ, D'ARTEGNA, PAPADJIAKOV; ZEDDA AND NETHERLANDS RADIO CHAMBER ORCHESTRA (NAXOS).

SUTHERLAND, ELKINS, PAVAROTTI, GHIAUROV; BONYNGE AND NATIONAL PHILHARMONIC ORCHESTRA (DECCA).

soprano (from It. *sopra,* "above") Situated in the highest musical range. The term is derived from the Latin *superius,* the designation for the highest voice in 15th-century polyphonic settings. It can refer to an instrument, such as the soprano saxophone or soprano recorder, but is most often used to describe a high female (occasionally juvenile or male) voice. There are various types of soprano voices and numerous fine shadings of character and quality within each type. The main categories are lyric and dramatic—the lyric being generally lighter and more maneuverable, the dramatic heavier and more powerful. The role of Susanna in Mozart's *Le nozze di Figaro* is a classic lyric part, as are Zerlina in Mozart's *Don Giovanni,* Amelia in Verdi's *Simon Boccanegra,* and Micaela in Bizet's *Carmen.* Among the outstanding lyric sopranos of recent years have been Lucia Popp, Elisabeth Söderström, Edith Mathis, and Dawn Upshaw; earlier generations thrilled to the lyric artistry of Jenny Lind and Elisabeth Schumann. The operatic literature is filled with great dramatic roles, including those of Leonora in Verdi's *La forza del destino,* the title roles in Verdi's *Aida,* Ponchielli's *La gioconda,* Puccini's *Tosca* and *Turandot,* Cio-Cio-San in Puccini's *Madama Butterfly,* and the Wagner heroines Brünnhilde and Isolde. The roster of noted dramatic sopranos includes Geraldine Farrar, Maria Jeritza, Kirsten Flagstad, Renata Tebaldi, Maria Callas, Leontyne Price, Hildegard Behrens, and Galina Vishnevskaya, to name just a few. Many roles do not fall neatly into one category or the other—for example, Donna Anna in *Don Giovanni* and Violetta in Verdi's *La traviata*—and many sopranos have voices that blend lyric and dramatic qualities, such as Rosa Ponselle, Lotte Lehmann, Mirella Freni, and Renée Fleming.

Other specialized role-and-voice types within the soprano domain are the coloratura, which excels in the highest part of the range, and the soubrette, a particularly light-voiced soprano suited for light-hearted characters. *See also* COLORATURA, SOUBRETTE, SPINTO.

Sorcerer's Apprentice, The (L'apprenti sorcier) ORCHESTRAL SHOWPIECE BY PAUL

DUKAS, who subtitled it "a symphonic scherzo after a ballade of Goethe." In this brilliantly conceived essay, which received its premiere on May 18, 1897, at a concert of the Société Nationale in Paris, Dukas pioneered harmonic usages that would later be taken up by Stravinsky (in his *Fireworks*) and Debussy (in the ballet *Jeux*). The Beethovenian tautness of Dukas's musical argument is complemented by orchestration of exhilarating brilliance, which picks up where Wagner left off in "The Ride of the Valkyries." Most delightful of all is the sheer exuberance with which *The Sorcerer's Apprentice* plays out Goethe's poem about a young magician casting spells before he has earned his wand. None other than Mickey Mouse was cast as the hapless conjurer in the Disney cartoon treatment of the music, one of the highlights of *Fantasia* (1940) and as virtuosic in its own way as the original.

RECOMMENDED RECORDINGS

LEVINE AND BERLIN PHILHARMONIC (DG).

SLATKIN AND ORCHESTRE NATIONALE DE FRANCE (RCA).

sostenuto (It., "sustained") [1] A direction to prolong a tone or slow the tempo. [2] A passage of music whose notes are significantly prolonged.

sotto voce (It., "under [the] voice") An instruction to a performer to sing or play a particular passage softly, as if in a whisper (e.g., Brahms, Intermezzo in E-flat minor, Op. 118, No. 6).

soubrette (Fr., "servant girl") In opera, a comic role sung by a light-voiced soprano, often an impertinent servant. Among the most familiar soubrette roles are Serpina in Pergolesi's *La serva padrona,* Despina in Mozart's *Così fan tutte,* Papagena in Mozart's *Die Zauberflöte,* and Adele in Johann Strauss Jr.'s *Die Fledermaus.*

Sousa, John Philip

(b. Washington, D.C., November 6, 1854; d. Reading, Penn. March 6, 1932)

AMERICAN BANDMASTER AND COMPOSER. His father, Antonio, born in Spain of Portuguese parents, was a trombonist in the U.S. Marine Band. He began his six-year-old son's musical education on various instruments, and in 1868, after the younger Sousa threatened to run away and play in a circus band, enrolled him as an apprentice in the Marine Band instead. At 18, Sousa wrote his first published composition, a waltz titled *Moonlight on the Potomac.* He left the Marine Band in 1875, and began conducting theater orchestras. In Philadelphia, during the Centennial Exposition of 1876, he played violin in an orchestra conducted by Jacques Offenbach; the following year he conducted Gilbert and Sullivan's *H.M.S Pinafore* on Broadway. He returned to Washington in 1880 to become the conductor of the Marine Band, which he led for 12 years, through five presidential administrations. In 1892, after two successful tours with the Marine Band, he formed his own civilian concert band, which gave its first performance in Plainfield, New Jersey. Sousa would tour nationally and internationally with the group for the remaining 39 years of his life. In 1910–11 he led his band on a world tour that included Great Britain, the Canary Islands, South Africa, Australia, New Zealand, Fiji, Hawaii, and Canada. Though he was 62 when the United States entered World War I, he took a job training musicians for the U.S. Navy, at a salary of one dollar a month. After the war, he continued to tour with his band and to work for the cause of music education. He was the recipient of several honorary degrees and became an honorary Ponca Indian chief; in 1927–28 he was among those who testified before Congress on behalf of protecting the rights of composers. Fittingly, he died on tour in Reading, Pennsylvania, after rehearsing a

A Sousa march, and staff surmounted by Marine emblem

local band for an anniversary concert; the last work he conducted was *The Stars and Stripes Forever.*

Over six decades, Sousa wrote 136 marches, including *The Stars and Stripes Forever, The Washington Post March,* and *Semper Fidelis.* He also wrote 15 operettas that enjoyed considerable success in their day, including *El Capitan* (1895), *The Bride Elect* (1897), and *The Charlatan* (produced in Montreal in 1898). He created 11 picturesque suites for orchestra, including *The Chariot Race* (based on Lew Wallace's *Ben-Hur*) and *The Last Days of Pompeii* (based on Edward George Bulwer-Lytton's book), and made hundreds of arrangements and transcriptions for band. With the Marine Band and his own touring band he gave approximately 15,000 performances, justly earning his designation as "The March King," and living up to his own job description as a "salesman of Americanism." *See also* MARCH.

RECOMMENDED RECORDINGS

MARCHES AND ORCHESTRAL WORKS: BRION AND VARIOUS ENSEMBLES (NAXOS).

MARCHES AND ORCHESTRAL WORKS: FENNELL AND EASTMAN WIND ENSEMBLE (MERCURY).

Spanish Caprice *See* CAPRICCIO ESPAGNOL.

Spano, Robert

(b. Conneaut, Ohio, May 7, 1961)

AMERICAN CONDUCTOR AND PIANIST. Considered one of the most gifted young conductors on the scene, he was born into a musical family, exhibiting at an early age gifts as a pianist, composer, violinist, and flutist. In 1984 he graduated from the Oberlin Conservatory, where he studied conducting with Robert Baustian. Postgraduate studies followed with Max Rudolf at the Curtis Institute of Music in Philadelphia, after which he joined the conducting faculty of Bowling Green State University and served as assistant conductor of the Boston Symphony Orchestra. As music director of the Brooklyn Philharmonic from 1996 to 2004, he proved adventurous in his choice of repertoire and had a dynamic presence on the podium; his work attracted widespread notice, and in 2001 he was appointed music director of the Atlanta Symphony Orchestra, whose podium he has turned into a bully pulpit for the advancement of American music. Spano's recording of Vaughan Williams's *A Sea Symphony* with the ASO and its chorus won Grammy Awards in 2003 for best classical and best choral album. His work is marked by an impressive blend of clarity, passion, and intelligence.

RECOMMENDED RECORDINGS

HIGDON, *CITY SCAPE, CONCERTO FOR ORCHESTRA*: ATLANTA SYMPHONY ORCHESTRA (TELARC).

"RAINBOW BODY": WORKS BY BARBER, COPLAND, THEOFANIDIS, HIGDON; ATLANTA SYMPHONY ORCHESTRA (TELARC).

Speculum Musicae *See box on page 272.*

spiccato (from It. *spiccare,* "to stand out") On string instruments, a short, off-the-string bow stroke.

spinto (from It. *spingere,* "to push") An essentially lyric voice (soprano or tenor) that exhibits greater power, particularly at the top of the range, than is generally expected. The term is also used to characterize roles that require a spinto quality, such as Leonora in Verdi's *La forza del destino* and Mimì in Puccini's *La bohème,* the title role in Giordano's *Andrea Chénier,* Ramerrez in Puccini's *La fanciulla del West,* and Alfredo in Verdi's *La traviata.*

Spontini, Gaspare

(b. Maiolati, November 14, 1774; d. Maiolati, January 24, 1851)

ITALIAN COMPOSER AND CONDUCTOR. Though he was the son of peasants, Spontini's early musical aptitude was noted and encouraged, and he was admitted to a Naples conservatory in 1793. Between 1796 and 1802 he led a peripatetic professional life, spending time in Rome, Florence, and Palermo and writing his first operas. He arrived in Paris at the end of 1802, and after struggling to find a foothold there enjoyed his first great success with the premiere of *La vestale* (*The Vestal Virgin*) in 1807. The work, an elaborate affair that required unprecedented amounts of rehearsal—largely caused by Spontini's endless changes and polishing—might not have reached the stage at all had it not been for the efforts of Empress Josephine, who received the dedication. Its triumph established Spontini as a major figure, and it was soon produced in Vienna and Berlin. In 1809, with talk of Napoleon planning a Spanish campaign, Spontini wrote *Fernand Cortez,* another huge spectacle, which again enjoyed sweeping acclaim in Paris. Wisely lowering his profile after Napoleon's downfall, he worked his way back into the graces of the restored Bourbon monarchy, but found his career path blocked. A new opera, *Olimpie,* based on Voltaire, was a failure at its premiere in 1819, and in 1820 Spontini moved to Berlin, accepting a longstanding offer from King Friedrich Wilhelm III to come to the Prussian capital and raise the standards of opera there. Spontini's Berlin years, however, were filled more with political intrigues and rivalries than musical creativity. Even the success he enjoyed in 1821 with a new mounting of *La vestale* lasted only a little over a month. Weber's *Der Freischütz* was premiered in Berlin on June 18, 1821, and the course of opera in 19th-century Germany changed with the stunning success of that masterpiece. Spontini completed only two more operas, *Alcidor* (1825) and *Agnes von Hohenstaufen* (1829). His egotism and despotic manner endeared him to few (even the gentle Mendelssohn found him insufferable), and he finally left Berlin in disgrace in 1842, a trail of personality clashes and lawsuits behind him. He returned to Paris, traveled aimlessly, and spent the final months of his life in his hometown.

With *La vestale,* Spontini rekindled the pure musical flame of Gluck's *tragédies lyriques,* the main reason Berlioz became such a devoted admirer of his work. (Interestingly, *La vestale* also served as Callas's vehicle in her first encounter with the director Luchino Visconti, at La Scala in 1954.) And with *Fernand Cortez,* Spontini anticipated many of the structural and scenic elements that would figure in French grand opera, which put Meyerbeer and even Wagner in his debt. Spontini had a sense of spectacle that appealed to the Romantic vanguard, and he was one of the first great autocrats of the podium, demanding an extraordinary standard of execution from the organizations with which he worked, both theatrically and orchestrally. This fact was not lost on Wagner, who interviewed Spontini in Dresden in 1844, and witnessed firsthand the lengths to which he went in preparing a performance. As vast as Spontini's ego was, he arranged for the poor to be the beneficiaries of his estate after his death.

RECOMMENDED RECORDING

La Vestale: Callas, Stignani, Corelli, Sordello; Votto and La Scala Orchestra (IDI).

***Spring* Sonata** Sobriquet attached to Ludwig van Beethoven's Sonata for Violin and Piano in F, Op. 24, composed in 1800. Although the nickname did not originate with the composer, it is apt: The four-movement work has a generously tuneful character and a sunny disposition, basking warmly in the major mode. It is the first of Beethoven's violin sonatas to incorporate a scherzo.

RECOMMENDED RECORDING

Perlman, Ashkenazy (Decca).

***Spring* Symphony** Nickname of Robert Schumann's Symphony No. 1 in B-flat, Op. 38, sketched January 23–26, 1841, and premiered March 31, 1841, by the Leipzig Gewandhaus Orchestra under the baton of Felix Mendelssohn.

Staatskapelle Dresden Ensemble founded on September 22, 1548, as the Hofkapelle (court ensemble) of the Elector of Saxony. It became known as the Sächsische Staatskapelle (Saxon State Orchestra) after World War I, and acquired its present name in 1947. It originally consisted of eight or nine trumpets and a set of drums, and was responsible for providing music for entertainment and ceremonial occasions. The composer Michael Praetorius (1571–1621) was named de facto conductor of the ensemble in 1613; he was succeeded in 1617 by Heinrich Schütz, who remained its chief until his death in 1672 and played a vital role in reviving the ensemble after it was disbanded during the Thirty Years' War. By 1680 the group could boast 19 trumpeters and one or two timpanists, but when the state was occupied with pressing matters such as wars, the number of players tended to shrink. Saxony's fortunes peaked in the 18th century under Friedrich August I (who ruled as King Augustus II, "the Strong," from 1694 to 1733) and his successor Friedrich August II (King Augustus III, from 1733 to 1763). Prominent musicians with ties to the Saxon court and its orchestra during their reigns included J. S. Bach (who filled the largely honorary position of "court composer" from 1736 to his death in 1750) and Johann Adolf Hasse, who held the title of Kapellmeister from 1734 to 1764.

As the orchestra of the Saxon Court Opera (from 1919, the Saxon State Opera), the Kapelle has participated in some of the most important developments in the history of opera. Carl Maria von Weber served as Kapellmeister from 1817 to his death in 1826, and was responsible for the German repertoire at the Court Opera (the Italian repertoire had a separate Kapellmeister); while in Dresden he composed *Der Freischütz* (1821), *Euryanthe* (1823), and most of *Oberon* (1826). Richard Wagner took up the post of second Kapellmeister following the successful premiere of his opera *Rienzi* (1842), serving from 1843 to 1849.

The conductor Ernst von Schuch became associated with the Dresden orchestra in 1872 and served as music director at the Court Opera from 1882 until his death in 1914. Schuch presided over a brilliant period in Dresden's musical history, taking charge of nine premieres of works by Richard Strauss, including *Feuersnot* (1901), *Salome* (1905), *Elektra* (1909), and *Der Rosenkavalier* (1911). His successors at the Opera were Fritz Reiner (1914–21) and Fritz Busch (1922–33), who continued Dresden's Strauss tradition by leading the premieres of *Intermezzo* (1924) and *Die ägyptische Helena* (1928) before losing his post as general music director when the Nazis came to power. Karl Böhm, an Austrian with a suitably compliant attitude toward the Nazi regime, was put in charge of the orchestra and opera in 1934, remaining there until 1943. He conducted the premiere of Strauss's *Daphne* in 1938. The principal conductors of the Staatskapelle Dresden during the postwar years were Joseph Keilberth (1945–50), Rudolph Kempe (1949–52), and Otmar Suitner (1960–64). Kurt Sanderling served as chief conductor from 1964 to 1967, and recent leaders have included Herbert Blomstedt (1975–85), Hans Vonk (1985–90), and Giuseppe Sinopoli (1992–2001).

RECOMMENDED RECORDINGS

BRAHMS, SYMPHONIES (COMPLETE): SANDERLING (EURODISC).

SCHUMANN, SYMPHONIES (COMPLETE): SAWALLISCH (EMI).

R. STRAUSS, COLLECTED ORCHESTRAL WORKS: KEMPE (EMI).

STRAUSS, *ARIADNE AUF NAXOS*: VOIGT, DESSAY, OTTER, HEPPNER; SINOPOLI (DG).

Stabat mater A 13TH-CENTURY FRANCISCAN TEXT, traditionally ascribed to Jacopone da Todi (d. 1306), used in the Roman liturgy as both a sequence and a hymn. A contemplation of the Crucifixion and a petition to the Virgin Mary for help, it is the musical equivalent of the Deposition in painting. The text, in Latin, consists of 20 three-line stanzas yoked in pairs in an AAB AAB rhyme scheme. Its first words are "Stabat mater dolorosa" ("sorrowfully [His] mother stood"). Written in not particularly good Latin with a meter ill suited to dramatic treatment, the text has nonetheless been set by many notable composers. Among the finest settings of the Renaissance are ones by Josquin, Palestrina, and Lassus. The best-known 18th-century settings are those of Alessandro Scarlatti (ca. 1715) and Pergolesi (1736). In the 19th century, Rossini took a flamboyantly operatic approach to the text (1841), Dvořák treated it as an oratorio (1877), and Verdi viewed it as an intimate meditation (1898; the second of his *Quattro pezzi sacri*). Important settings from the 20th century include those of Szymanowski (1925–26), Poulenc (1950), and Penderecki (1962; subsequently incorporated into his *St. Luke* Passion).

RECOMMENDED RECORDINGS

DVOŘÁK: BEŇAČKOVÁ, WENKEL, DVORSKY, ROOTERING; SAWALLISCH AND CZECH PHILHARMONIC (SUPRAPHON).

POULENC: DUBOSC; HICKOX AND CITY OF LONDON SINFONIA (VIRGIN CLASSICS).

ROSSINI: LORENGAR, MINTON, PAVAROTTI, SOTIN; KERTÉSZ AND LONDON SYMPHONY ORCHESTRA (DECCA).

SZYMANOWSKI: GADULANKA, SZOSTEK-RADKOWA, HIOLSKI; STYRJA AND POLISH NATIONAL PHILHARMONIC ORCHESTRA (NAXOS).

staccato (It., "detached") An articulation in which notes are separated from one another and often, though not always, lightly accented. The whole orchestra—first the bassoons, joined by the winds, then the strings and brass—plays staccato at the beginning of "Uranus" from Holst's *The Planets*.

Stadler, Anton

(b. Bruck an der Leitha, June 28, 1753; d. Vienna, June 15, 1812)

AUSTRIAN CLARINETIST. He was the elder brother of Johann Stadler (1755–1804), also a clarinetist. In 1779 the brothers became members of the Imperial Harmonie (the term denotes a six- or eight-part wind ensemble) in Vienna—Anton originally played second clarinet to Johann's first—and by 1781 they were full-time members of the Imperial Court Orchestra as well, with Anton playing first. Anton, keenly interested in the clarinet's lower register, played an important part in the development of the basset clarinet. It is likely that he got to know Wolfgang Mozart soon after Mozart took up residence in Vienna in 1781. Mozart subsequently composed several important works for Stadler, including the Quintet in E-flat, K. 452 (1784), for piano and winds, the Trio in E-flat, K. 498 (*Kegelstaat*; 1786) for clarinet, piano, and viola, the Quintet in A, K. 581 (1789), for clarinet and strings, and the Concerto in A, K. 622 (1791). He also intended the two obbligato arias in his opera *La clemenza di Tito,* K. 621, for Stadler, one ("Non più di fiori") written for the basset-horn, the other ("Parto, parto") for the basset clarinet, and it is likely that Mozart had the brothers Stadler in mind when he created his magnificent seven-movement Serenade in B-flat, K. 361, for 12 winds and string bass, in 1784.

Unlike the good-natured Joseph Leutgeb, for whom Mozart wrote his horn concertos, Anton Stadler was a scoundrel. He was in debt to Mozart for 500 gulden at the time of the composer's death—a sum greater than half Mozart's annual salary as court chamber musician—and he also lost the manuscripts of some works Mozart composed for him. Stadler alleged to Mozart's widow that they were stolen from him during a trip through Germany, but the clarinetist's Viennese acquaintances remained convinced that he pawned them shortly after the composer's death. Stadler must have played like an angel, for in spite of his roguish behavior Mozart loved him like a brother. The quintet and the concerto in particular show what the composer thought of his artistry.

Stamitz, Johann

(b. Nemecky Brod, June 19, 1717; d. Mannheim, March 27, 1757)

BOHEMIAN COMPOSER AND VIOLINIST. He attended a Jesuit high school and subsequently enrolled at the university in Prague. In 1741 he joined the Mannheim Court Orchestra, becoming concertmaster in 1745–46 and director of instrumental music in 1750. Under his leadership the Mannheim ensemble became the most highly respected in all of Europe, famous for its precision and command of brilliant effects. As a composer, Stamitz emphasized these effects in his symphonies, 58 of which survive. More important, he was among the first to write four-movement symphonies on a consistent basis, establishing the model that would be adopted by Haydn, Mozart, and everyone else who followed. By incorporating elements of the operatic sinfonia style into his concert symphonies (particularly in the treatment of thematic material and orchestration), Stamitz helped bring about the confluence of Italian and German practices that produced the Classical symphony.

RECOMMENDED RECORDINGS

FLUTE CONCERTO IN G (WITH WORKS BY HAYDN, C. STAMITZ, OTHERS): B. KUIJKEN; LAMON AND TAFELMUSIK (SONY).

SYMPHONIES (2 VOLS.): ARMSTRONG AND NEW ZEALAND CHAMBER ORCHESTRA; WARD AND NORTHERN CHAMBER ORCHESTRA (NAXOS).

Starker, Janos

(b. Budapest, July 5, 1924)

AMERICAN CELLIST OF HUNGARIAN DESCENT. A distinguished performer and teacher, he began cello lessons at six and taught his first student at eight. After graduating from the Ferenc Liszt Academy in Budapest, which he entered at the age of seven, he served as principal cellist of the Budapest Opera and Philharmonic; he later emigrated to France. In 1948, invited by Antal Dorati, he moved to the U.S. to become principal cellist of the Dallas Symphony (1948–49). He subsequently held the principal's chairs of the Metropolitan Opera Orchestra (1949–53) and the Chicago Symphony (1953–58), where he worked under Fritz Reiner. He left the CSO to pursue a career as a soloist, and in 1958 was appointed professor of cello at Indiana University, helping to make it a

Cellist Janos Starker

mecca for string players through his masterclasses. Starker became an American citizen in 1954. His core repertoire includes the Bach cello suites, which he has recorded several times (winning a Grammy for his 1998 traversal on RCA), Kodály's Sonata for solo cello, and numerous concertos and chamber works. He has given the premieres of several contemporary works, including concertos by Bernard Heiden (1910–2000) and Miklós Rózsa (1907–95), and of an adaptation for cello of Bartók's Viola Concerto. Starker has published teaching methods for string instruments and several performing editions, including one of the Bach suites. In 2004, Indiana University Press published his memoir, *The World of Music According to Starker.* His instruments have included cellos by Matteo Goffriller (1706) and Giuseppe Giovanni Battista Guarneri (1707).

RECOMMENDED RECORDINGS

BACH, SUITES FOR SOLO CELLO (RCA).

BRAHMS, CONCERTO IN A MINOR FOR VIOLIN, CELLO, AND ORCHESTRA: SZERYNG; HAITINK AND ROYAL CONCERTGEBOUW ORCHESTRA (POLYGRAM).

Steber, Eleanor

(b. Wheeling, W.V., July 17, 1916; d. Langhorne, Penn., October 3, 1990)

AMERICAN SOPRANO. She entered the New England Conservatory to study piano, eventually directing her attention toward voice. She studied with William Whitney, and after moving to New York in 1939, worked with the tenor Paul Althouse. Musical odd jobs as singer and pianist sustained her until she won the Metropolitan Opera Auditions of the Air in 1940, which led to her Met debut on December 7, 1940, as Sophie in Richard Strauss's *Der Rosenkavalier.* Over the next quarter century she would spend 22 seasons at the Met, appearing in 34 roles and 427 performances. In 1942 she made her debut as the Countess in Mozart's *Le nozze di Figaro,* the role she would sing most frequently during her Met career. Violetta, Marguerite, Rosalinde, and Eva followed, and by 1949 the Marschallin had replaced Sophie in the catalog of Steber roles, which included Desdemona, Tosca, Elisabeth in Verdi's *Don Carlo,* and Elsa in Wagner's *Lohengrin.* Steber became the Met's first Arabella (in 1955) and its first Marie in Berg's *Wozzeck* (1959). And, after the role had been turned down by both Maria Callas and Sena Jurinac, she scored a triumph as the vain title character in the world premiere of Barber's *Vanessa* (1955). Outside the Met, Steber kept a busy schedule of performances at the festivals of Edinburgh, Glyndebourne, Florence, and Bayreuth, as well as at the Vienna Staatsoper and the Chicago Lyric Opera, among other companies. The Met became less friendly to her after the arrival of general manager Rudolf Bing in 1950, and when her 1960–61 contract contained nothing but cover assignments, she wasn't interested. She made occasional appearances there until 1963, and on April 16, 1966, sang in the gala farewell at the old Metropolitan Opera House before the company's move to Lincoln Center. A few months earlier she had given her last performance of a lead role on the Met stage, as an 11th-hour replacement for an indisposed Dorothy Kirsten, appearing as Minnie in Puccini's *La fanciulla del West,* a part she hadn't sung in public in nearly a decade.

Steber was an indefatigable performer, and when her career at the Met slowed, she turned her attention to an area that had always appealed to her, the recital platform. There, singing well beyond the glory days of her voice, she presented large-scale recital programs featuring selections from virtually every genre of serious vocal music. Her programs included a work she had commissioned in 1947 and premiered the following year, Barber's elegiac *Knoxville: Summer of 1915.*

Eleanor Steber

Numerous recordings bear witness to Steber's radiant singing of Mozart. In the music of this most transparent of composers, hers was the defining voice of her generation, both technically and dramatically. Her portrayals of the Countess, Pamina, Donna Anna and Donna Elvira, Konstanze, and Fiordiligi continue to stand as benchmarks of interpretation. An avid teacher, Steber held positions at the Juilliard School, the New England Conservatory of Music, the American Institute of Vocal Studies in Graz, and the Cleveland Institute of Music, where she headed the voice department from 1963 to 1972.

RECOMMENDED RECORDING

RECITAL:
"ELEANOR STEBER IN CONCERT": BARBER, *KNOXVILLE, SUMMER OF 1915*; ARIAS BY BELLINI, MOZART, PUCCINI, STRAUSS, AND VERDI (VAI).

Steinway & Sons AMERICAN PIANO MANUFACTURERS. German-born Heinrich Steinweg (1797–1871), the founder of the company, developed an interest in piano making in 1820, and in 1825 he gave his bride his first piano, which he built in the kitchen of his home, as a wedding present. In 1839, Steinweg won first prize for his piano at a fair in Brunswick, but despite his skill, the business failed in Germany, and he and his family moved to New York, where he worked for various piano firms. He established his own company in 1853; the name of the highly successful firm was legally changed to Steinway in 1864. Steinway created a seven-octave piano of "American design," featuring a one-piece cast-iron frame and overstringing, which produced unusual clarity and power. Steinway Hall on 14th Street became a cultural center, presenting many European artists to New York concertgoers. Since 1871 the business of piano building has been carried on by Steinway's heirs, who have since added hundreds of patents for innovations in the design and function of the firm's pianos. Steinway & Sons continues to make superb instruments in both Astoria, New York, and Hamburg, Germany, instruments that are noted for their brilliance and responsiveness. They are judged by many demanding artists to be the gold standard for concert grand pianos. Among the many celebrated pianists who have been on the Steinway roster are Ignacy Jan Paderewski, Sergey Rachmaninov, Josef Hofmann, George Gershwin, Arthur Rubinstein, and Vladimir Horowitz. *See also* PIANO.

Stern, Isaac

(b. Kremenets, Ukraine, July 21, 1920; d. New York, September 22, 2001)

AMERICAN VIOLINIST. One of the most influential musicians in American history, he performed and recorded the violin literature from Vivaldi to Stravinsky and collaborated with virtually every major international orchestra and conductor of the postwar era. He spearheaded the campaign to save Carnegie Hall from the wrecker's ball in 1960 and presided over its growth and development as a nonprofit entity for the next 40 years, playing a key role in its renovation in 1986. Throughout his career he was passionately committed to the nurturing of younger talent.

Stern's family settled in San Francisco when he was one year old. He started taking piano lessons when he was six but switched to the violin because a friend who lived across the street had begun taking violin lessons. Between 1931 and 1937 he studied with Naoum Blinder, the concertmaster of the San Francisco Symphony Orchestra, and read chamber music with the first-desk players of the orchestra. On March 20, 1937, he played the Brahms concerto with the San Francisco Symphony and its music director, Pierre Monteux, in a concert broadcast nationwide. Later that year he made his New York debut at Town Hall. In 1940 he joined the stable of impresario Sol Hurok and began concertizing with the pianist Alexander Zakin, who would remain his recital partner for 33 years. Following America's entry into World War II, he formed a classical music unit for the USO; equipped with a truck and an upright Steinway painted olive drab and specially treated to withstand the humidity of the tropics, his unit went to Hawaii, Guadalcanal, and Espiritu Santo to play for the troops.

Stern made his Carnegie Hall debut on January 8, 1943, and signed his first contract with Columbia Records in 1945; for Columbia and its successor labels, CBS Masterworks and Sony Classical, he compiled a discography covering virtually the whole of the major solo and chamber repertoire for violin. He gave the first performance of William Schuman's Violin

Isaac Stern, bearing down in rehearsal

Concerto, with Charles Munch and the Boston Symphony, in 1950, and played the premiere of Leonard Bernstein's *Serenade (after Plato's "Symposium")*, with the composer conducting the Israel Philharmonic Orchestra, in Venice in 1954. He later gave the first performances of concertos by George Rochberg (1975), Penderecki (1977), Dutilleux (*L'arbre des songes*; 1985), and Davies (1986), all of which he recorded.

In 1956, a year after David Oistrakh and Emil Gilels had broken the ice by touring the United States, Stern became the first major American instrumentalist to tour the Soviet Union during the Cold War. In 1979 he made a historic visit to China, traveling with a film crew, lecturing, giving master classes, listening to young talent, and advising the political hierarchy on the integration of China's musical life with that of the West. More than 70 hours of film were subsequently edited into the 84-minute *From Mao to Mozart: Isaac Stern in China.* The film won the Academy Award for best feature-length documentary in 1981.

Stern made more than 100 trips to Israel; his many performances there included one, during the Persian Gulf War, when most in the audience were wearing gas masks. Following the Six-Day War of 1967 he performed the Mendelssohn E minor concerto with Bernstein and the Israel Philharmonic atop Mount Scopus, which became the focal moment of another film, *A Journey to Jerusalem.*

Stern was the ultimate career musician. But his celebrity and influence in musical circles sometimes obscured the fact that he was also one of the supreme masters of the violin. At his best, he combined the finest qualities of several exemplars: the dazzling virtuosity of Heifetz, the "golden sound" of Kreisler, the expressive warmth of Elman. Yet his style of playing, notable for its almost vocal approach to phrasing and inflection, was uniquely his own, an imitation of no one. His bow arm was fabled for its strength and steadiness, and he possessed a distinctive tone—sweet and warm, with an exceptionally expressive vibrato. Stern's concert instruments were two of the finest Guarneri del Gesù violins in existence.

RECOMMENDED RECORDINGS

BEETHOVEN, PIANO TRIOS OP. 70, NOS. 1 AND 2; PIANO TRIO, OP. 97: ISTOMIN, ROSE (SONY).

BEETHOVEN: SONATAS FOR VIOLIN AND PIANO (COMPLETE): ISTOMIN (SONY).

BRAHMS, VIOLIN CONCERTO: ORMANDY AND PHILADELPHIA ORCHESTRA (SONY).

BRUCH, VIOLIN CONCERTO; MENDELSSOHN, TCHAIKOVSKY, VIOLIN CONCERTOS: ORMANDY AND PHILADELPHIA ORCHESTRA (SONY).

MENDELSSOHN, PIANO TRIOS: ISTOMIN, ROSE (SONY).

WIENIAWSKI, VIOLIN CONCERTO NO. 2: ORMANDY AND PHILADELPHIA ORCHESTRA (SONY).

Stevens, Risë

(b. New York, June 11, 1913)

AMERICAN MEZZO-SOPRANO. She studied at the Juilliard School with Anna Eugénie Schön-René (herself a pupil of Pauline Viardot) from 1932 to 1935, then, turning down an offer from the Metropolitan Opera for the following year, went to Vienna for further study with Marie Gutheil-Schoder and Herbert Graf. Her professional career began with two roles that would become signature parts, Mignon and Octavian, the former in 1936 with the German Opera in Prague, the latter in 1938 at the Vienna Staatsoper and the Teatro Colón in Buenos Aires. On November 22, 1938, she bowed with the Metropolitan Opera on tour in Philadelphia, singing Octavian to Lotte Lehmann's Marschallin in *Der Rosenkavalier.* Her house debut, as Mignon, followed on December 17 of that year. Stevens remained a Metropolitan mainstay until 1961, her plummy vocalism and vibrant onstage personality much lauded; in her 23 seasons at the house, she virtually reigned over a small but important collection of lyric mezzo roles that included Cherubino, Orfeo, Hänsel, Dalila, Orlofsky, Laura in *La gioconda,* and the role with which she was most closely identified, Carmen, which she sang in 124 performances. During her career she also sang at the Paris Opéra, La Scala, Covent Garden, Glyndebourne, and with the opera companies of Chicago and San Francisco. In the 1940s Stevens achieved a degree of film success, starring in *The Chocolate Soldier* (1941) with Nelson Eddy; *Carnegie Hall* (1947) with Lily Pons and Arthur Rubinstein; and, most important, *Going My Way* (1944), in which she played opera singer Genevieve Linden to Bing Crosby's Oscar-winning Father Chuck O'Malley.

Following her retirement from the Met, Stevens continued to record and concertize, and as her own performing career drew to a close, she championed the cause of emerging young performers. She headed the short-lived Metropolitan Opera Touring Company until 1966 and was president of Mannes College of Music from 1975 to 1978. She returned to the Met in 1980 as director of its National Council Auditions, a position she held until 1988.

RECOMMENDED RECORDING

COLLECTION:
"LEGENDARY VOICES": ARIAS BY BIZET, DONIZETTI, MEYERBEER, MOZART, THOMAS, AND TCHAIKOVSKY (PREISER).

Steve Reich and Musicians *See box on page 272.*

stile antico (It., "old style") A generic term that came into use in the 1640s, signifying a compositional manner that was intentionally "old-fashioned," i.e., one that made prominent use of imitation, allowed limited dissonance, and avoided dance rhythms, hewing to the style of composition exemplified in the works of Palestrina. Monteverdi consciously reverted to the *stile antico* in his six-voice *Missa "In illo tempore"* of 1610, and many 18th- and 19th-century composers alluded to it in their works, including Bach in his *Mass in B Minor,* Handel in his *Messiah,* and Beethoven in his *Missa solemnis.* During the 19th century, the *stile antico* was put forward as a model by the Cecilian movement, a group seeking to reform Catholic church music.

stile concitato (It. "agitated style") A term used widely in the 17th century, derived from Monteverdi's theory of three styles—*concitato* (agitated), *temperato* (moderate), and *molle* (soft or relaxed)—which lent themselves to the expression of anger, moderation, and humility. He described these styles in the preface to his Eighth Book of madrigals, quoting Plato's *Republic* as his source. Musically, the *stile concitato* translated into the division of the semibreve (whole note) into 16th notes to represent a belligerent or agitated affect. Passages of rapid, repeated notes are characteristic of many of the works in Monteverdi's Eighth Book, particularly the dramatic semiopera *Il combattimento di Tancredi e Clorinda* (composed in 1623), and also occur in his later operas. The technique, which could be applied in vocal or instrumental writing, was used by contemporaries of Monteverdi including Heinrich Schütz.

stile rappresentativo (It., "theatrical style") The "new" style of dramatic recitative singing developed in Florence at the end of the 16th century by Vincenzo Galilei (ca. 1520–91), father of the astronomer Galileo Galilei, and other members of the group of Florentine musicians, poets, and scholars known as the Camerata. The style eschewed polyphony, sought to make the text intelligible, and relied on melody to express the feeling of a whole passage, rather than attempting to mimic successive emotions or the images alluded to in the text, as the 16th-century madrigal had typically done. This manner of singing became the chief ingredient in the musical form called opera. The catalyst for its development was an attempt on the part of the Camerata to re-create the experience of ancient Greek theater. Monteverdi's "Lamento d'Arianna" shows the style at its most exquisite.

Still, William Grant

(b. Woodville, Miss., May 11, 1895; d. Los Angeles, December 3, 1978).

AMERICAN COMPOSER AND ARRANGER. The son of college-educated teachers (his father had been the town bandmaster in Woodville), he was raised in Little Rock, Arkansas. He studied violin, and while he considered medicine as a career, his love for music won out. He attended Ohio's Wilberforce College (1911–15) and was enrolled at Oberlin in 1917 and again in 1919, with a stint in the navy in between. In 1915 and 1916 he played in dance bands in Ohio, and as a sideman in Memphis for

William Grant Still

W. C. Handy (1873–1958). Still followed Handy to New York City in 1919. There he played oboe in the pit band for Eubie Blake's "Shuffle Along," and became a successful arranger for theater orchestras and such artists as Sophie Tucker, Paul Whiteman, and Artie Shaw, while pursuing a career as a composer. He studied briefly with Chadwick, but his most important teacher was Varèse, who helped him develop his lyrical style and programmed his music on concerts of the International Composers' Guild.

Still was a gifted melodist whose music melded the influences of European impressionism, jazz and blues, popular music, Broadway, and, to a lesser extent, spirituals. His Symphony No. 1 (*Afro-American*) had its premiere in 1931, with Howard Hanson conducting the Rochester Philharmonic, the first symphony by a black composer to be performed by a major American orchestra. Still's career accelerated, and he received commissions from CBS, the New York World's Fair, and several major American orchestras. In 1934, with a Guggenheim Fellowship, he left New York for Los Angeles, where he devoted himself primarily to the composition of serious music. The first of eight operas, *Blue Steel* (1934), was followed by *Troubled Island* (1937–49), which was produced by the New York City Opera in 1949. In addition to his operas and five symphonies, Still's output included symphonic poems and some chamber music, as well as solo instrumental, choral, and vocal works.

RECOMMENDED RECORDINGS

CHAMBER WORKS FOR FLUTE, PIANO, VOICE (INCLUDING *SUMMERLAND, HERE'S ONE, SONG OF SEPARATION*): VIDEMUS CHAMBER ENSEMBLE (NEW WORLD RECORDS).

SYMPHONY NO. 1 (*AFRO-AMERICAN*); ELLINGTON, *THE RIVER* SUITE: JÄRVI AND DETROIT SYMPHONY ORCHESTRA (CHANDOS).

SYMPHONY NO. 2 (*SONG OF A NEW RACE*); DAWSON, *NEGRO FOLK SYMPHONY*: JÄRVI AND DETROIT SYMPHONY ORCHESTRA (CHANDOS).

Stockhausen, Karlheinz

(b. Burg Mödrath, August 22, 1928)

GERMAN COMPOSER. His effectiveness as a composer has been hampered by a megalomania rivaling that of Richard Wagner, without the corresponding genius. He is nonetheless one of the most celebrated figures of the old European postwar avant-garde. During a long career as a stylistic chameleon, he has composed serial and electronic works and explored indeterminacy and various conceptual approaches, including the use of "formula" technique, in which one or more musical formulas (which are something like super-leitmotifs, and can be quite lengthy) determine the melodic, rhythmic, harmonic, and dynamic parameters of a piece, as well as the articulations, structural subdivisions, and overall duration. In recent decades he has sought to create a "cosmic" music that transcends all stylistic definition.

Stockhausen's mother was committed to an insane asylum in 1933 and was subsequently liquidated by the Nazis; his father was killed during World War II in Hungary.

Stockhausen at a workshop in Rome, 1981

In the final months of the war Karlheinz served at a German military hospital, and in its destitute aftermath he worked as a farmhand for relatives. Between 1947 and 1951 he studied at the Hochschule für Musik in Cologne and at the University of Cologne; during this period, he took composition lessons from Frank Martin. He began composing in 1950, and in 1951 he moved to Paris, where he studied with Olivier Messiaen and, briefly, Darius Milhaud. He returned to Cologne in 1953, and began a long period of activity at the Studio for Electronic Music of Westdeutscher Rundfunk (WDR); from 1963 to 1977 he served as director of the studio.

For more than two decades, from 1953 to 1974, Stockhausen lectured at the summer course in new music at Darmstadt. He served as coeditor of *Die Reihe* (*The Row*), a publication devoted to serial music, from 1954 to 1959. He was a visiting professor at the University of Pennsylvania in 1965, and at the University of California, Davis, in 1966–67, and taught composition at his alma mater, the Hochschule für Musik in Cologne, from 1971 to 1977. From 1977 to 2001 he worked on the composition of a gigantic and flamboyantly disjunct music-drama cycle in seven parts called *Licht* (*Die sieben Tage der Woche*) (*Light* [*The Seven Days of the Week*]). The seven "days" of *Licht* were premiered piecemeal, beginning with parts of *Donnerstag aus Licht* (*Thursday from Light*; 1978–81), and ending with the final scene of *Sonntag aus Licht* in 2003. Among the more interesting—and impractical—portions of this gargantuan oeuvre is the *Helikopter-Streichquartett* (*Helicopter String Quartet*), premiered in 1994. The piece calls for the four members of a string quartet to play their individual parts while hovering over the performance area in four different helicopters, keeping together by using TV and audio relay equipment.

In the midst of much noise from Stockhausen there have been a few significant works: *Gesang der Jünglinge* (*Song of the Youths*; 1955–56), a 13-minute tape piece that is one of the seminal essays in electronic music; *Gruppen* (*Groups*; 1955–57), for three orchestras (with three conductors) arrayed on three sides of the audience, a landmark of spatial music; *Zyklus* (1959), a solo percussion piece that is spiral-bound and notated so that any one of its pages can serve as the beginning; several of the 11 *Klavierstücke* (*Piano Pieces*) composed between 1952 and 1956, especially *Klavierstück IX* (which, in its revised version of 1961, makes prominent use of the Fibonacci series as an organizing principle and begins with the same chord repeated more than 100 times in a long decrescendo). Stockhausen has described all of his music as "spiritual" music, though the theology behind it is nebulous and rather eccentric, if not downright loony. He has written music of incredible concentration (*Klavierstück III* lasts less than 30 seconds) and unbelievable sprawl (*Licht* takes about 25 hours to perform).

RECOMMENDED RECORDINGS

***Helicopter* Quartet: Arditti Quartet (Montaigne).**

***Klavierstücke*: Henck (Wergo).**

***Zyklus*: Faralli (Arts Music).**

Stokowski, Leopold

(b. London, April 18, 1882; d. Nether Wallop, September 13, 1977)

AMERICAN CONDUCTOR OF POLISH-IRISH DESCENT. The greatest magician the podium has ever known, and one of its most charismatic personalities, he tended to interpret the classics as though he were a god fond of creating the music in his own image. But during his years at the helm of the Philadelphia Orchestra (1912–38, the final two years as co-conductor with Eugene Ormandy) he fashioned it into the world's foremost symphonic ensemble, leading premieres of some of the century's most important works and cultivating a virtuosity and beauty of tone that were unsurpassed then and remain among the supreme examples of the conductor's art. He was capable of making any orchestra he faced into a vehicle for his extraordinary, coloristic interpretations, and he continued to be active both on the podium and in front of the microphone into his 90s.

He entered the Royal College of Music at the age of 13 and was active as a chorister, organist, and choir director in several London churches during his youth. In 1902 he was appointed choirmaster at St. James's Church, Piccadilly, and the following year he received his bachelor's degree in music from Queen's College, Oxford. In 1905 he became organist and choir director at St. Bartholomew's in New York. He left New York in 1908 and made his debuts as an orchestral conductor in Paris and London.

In 1909, despite his lack of experience, Stokowski was named music director of the Cincinnati Symphony Orchestra. He took over the Philadelphia Orchestra in 1912 and transformed it almost overnight into a paragon, achieving an incandescent standard of execution while cultivating the extraordinarily refined and opulent sonority that came to be known as "the Philadelphia sound." Part of the secret was the conductor's hiring of outstanding solo wind and string players, and part his application of new approaches such as free rather than uniform bowing to smooth out the string sound. During the 1930s, Stokowski's fondness for modern music began to grate on the conservative board in Philadelphia, and he and they eventually parted company.

Before leaving, Stokowski starred with the Philadelphians in Walt Disney's *Fantasia* (1940). He served as co-conductor of the NBC Symphony Orchestra with Arturo Toscanini (1942–44), clashing with the Italian maestro over rights to lead the American premiere of Shostakovich's *Leningrad* Symphony (he didn't win that one). He founded the New York City Symphony in 1944 and the Hollywood Bowl Orchestra in 1945, and was active as a guest conductor of the New York Philharmonic (1947–50). He subsequently served as music director of the Houston Symphony Orchestra (1955–61), and in 1962, at the age of 80, founded the American Symphony Orchestra in New York. In 1972 he returned to England, performing until 1975 and

Leopold Stokowski

recording almost until the day he died. In his final decade he would make his way to the podium with difficulty, shuffling along slowly, but when he lifted his hands to conduct, the years melted away.

During his remarkable career, Stokowski conducted hundreds of American and world premieres, including the American premieres of Mahler's *Symphony of a Thousand* (he had attended the world premiere in Munich conducted by the composer), Stravinsky's *The Rite of Spring,* Schoenberg's *Gurre-Lieder* and *Pierrot lunaire,* and Berg's *Wozzeck.* He gave the world premieres of Rachmaninov's Symphony No. 3, Piano Concerto No. 4, and *Rhapsody on a Theme of Paganini* (the latter two with the composer as soloist), of Schoenberg's Violin Concerto, and of works by Varèse, Ives (his Symphony No. 4, in 1965), and Alan Hovhaness (1911–2000). His repertoire was huge, but he was particularly comfortable in the music of Wagner, Tchaikovsky, Rachmaninov, and Shostakovich; he also gloried in his own orchestral transcriptions of organ works by Bach and various symphonic "syntheses" of celebrated operas. His account with the Philadelphia Orchestra of Debussy's *Clair de lune* (originally for piano) is one of the most beautiful three-minute sides ever recorded.

Throughout his career Stokowski cultivated an aura—that of conductor as idol—through various conceits, including a fake central-European accent and the use of theatrical lighting effects to draw attention to his face and hands while he was on the podium (he stopped using a baton in 1929). He socialized at the highest levels (the third of his three wives was Gloria Vanderbilt, and he had a well-publicized affair with Greta Garbo), becoming enough of a cult figure to be parodied by Bugs Bunny. But behind the facade was a phenomenal musician, an adventurous champion of contemporary composers, and a courageous innovator. During his years in Philadelphia, Stokowski developed a passionate interest in recording; in the 1920s he made the first electrical recordings of an orchestra, and in the 1930s he presided over the earliest stereo recordings, made in conjunction with Bell Labs. He was constantly tinkering with the seating of the orchestra, not always successfully, but his shifting of the second violins from the right of the conductor to the left—to sit alongside the first violins, for a richer, more homogeneous sound—has been accepted nearly everywhere.

More than Toscanini or Koussevitzky, his most prominent mid-20th-century contemporaries on the American scene, Stokowski defined for the public what a conductor was. When he appeared on the podium, audiences knew they were in the presence of a *conductor,* and musicians knew it, too.

RECOMMENDED RECORDINGS

BIZET, *L'ARLÉSIENNE* SUITE AND *CARMEN* SUITE (SONY).

RACHMANINOV, PIANO CONCERTO NO. 4 AND *RHAPSODY ON A THEME OF PAGANINI*: RACHMANINOV; PHILADELPHIA ORCHESTRA (RCA, NAXOS).

RACHMANINOV, SYMPHONY NO. 3: NATIONAL PHILHARMONIC ORCHESTRA (EMI).

TCHAIKOVSKY, *FRANCESCA DA RIMINI*: STADIUM SYMPHONY ORCHESTRA OF NEW YORK (EVEREST).

COLLECTION:

"DECCA RECORDINGS 1965–1972" (INCLUDING WORKS OF BERLIOZ, FRANCK, ELGAR, AND MESSIAEN, AS WELL AS TRANSCRIPTIONS) (DECCA).

Stolz, Teresa

(b. Elbekosteletz, June 2, 1834; d. Milan, August 22, 1902)

BOHEMIAN SOPRANO. She studied at the Prague Conservatory and made her operatic debut in Tiflis in 1857. Gifted with an enormous, luminous voice and compelling dramatic instincts, she became the first of the great Verdi dramatic sopranos.

She sang at the Italian premiere of *Don Carlo* in 1867 and, under Verdi's direct supervision, in the premiere of the revised version of *La forza del destino* in 1869. Verdi chose her to sing the title role in *Aida* in the work's Italian premiere at La Scala on February 8, 1872, and assigned her the soprano solos at the premiere of his Requiem in 1874, which she reprised on tour in Paris, London, and Vienna. Stolz's intimate personal relationship with Verdi was the source of much gossip during this period, and caused Verdi's wife, Giuseppina, great pain. By 1876 the two women had sorted things out, and Stolz remained a close friend of the family. She was at Verdi's side when he died in 1901. She died the following year.

Stradivari, Antonio

(b. Cremona, ca. 1644; d. Cremona, December 18, 1737)

ITALIAN LUTHIER. He was the foremost member of the great triumvirate of string instrument builders active in Cremona during the 17th and 18th centuries (Nicolò AMATI and Giuseppe GUARNERI "del Gesù" being the other two). He may have been apprenticed to Amati, and his earliest violins, dating from 1666, clearly reflect that maker's influence. In 1680 he moved to a house in the Piazza San Domenico, where he lived and worked the remainder of his life, specializing in the manufacture of violins and cellos. In the decade that followed he moved away from the Amati pattern, chiefly by designing firmer, heavier corners that promoted a more powerful tone. In the early 1690s he established a larger pattern for the violin (referred to as the "long Strad"), varying from 14 1/16 to 14 3/16 inches in length and with a back nearly always cut in one piece. At the same time, Stradivari's varnish took on a deeper color—a rich hue of amber, orange, and light red (as opposed to the yellowish cast of his earliest violins)—that became a hallmark of his style.

Stradivari used the long pattern almost exclusively until 1698. After that, his violins measure about 14 inches in length; their width is similar to that of the long Strads, with outlines that are more curved, a fuller body, and longer corners. Stradivari's greatest achievements date from the first two decades of the 18th century, when he also devised a hugely successful smaller pattern for his cellos (with a body length of about 30 inches) that became the standard for nearly all subsequent builders. About 20 of these magnificent instruments still exist, including the "Duport" (1711), named for the French cellist Jean-Louis Duport (1749–1819) and acquired by Mstislav Rostropovich in 1974. There are only about a dozen Stradivari violas in existence.

Bust of Stradivari by P. Foglia

Stradivari's label traditionally read: *Antonius Stradivarius Cremonensis Faciebat Anno* ______ (Made by Antonio Stradivari in Cremona in the year ______). Between 1666 and 1737 he made more than 1,100 instruments, of which about 550 survive today. While the proportions and appearance of his instruments have been much imitated, the craftsmanship and sound quality have only occasionally been equaled, and never surpassed. The tone of a Strad—whether violin, viola, or cello—is characteristically brilliant, rich, intense, and alive, and no builder has ever matched the exquisite refinement and beauty of these instruments. Among the finest examples of Stradivari's craftsmanship are the "Paganini" Strads (a set of two violins, viola, and cello once owned by

Niccolò Paganini) and the "Betts" (1704), all in the possession of the Library of Congress; the "Alard" (1715), possibly the finest of all Stradivari violins; and the "Messiah" (1716). For many of the world's finest string players, the Strad is still the touchstone of the luthier's art.

Stratas, Teresa

(b. Toronto, May 26, 1938)

CANADIAN SOPRANO, considered one of the greatest singing actresses of her time. Born to Greek immigrant parents who owned a restaurant in Toronto, she started studying voice at the age of 12 and sang her first professional role, Mimì in Puccini's *La bohème,* when she was 20. In 1959, after winning the Metropolitan Opera Auditions of the Air, she sang a small role in Massenet's *Manon* at the Met. She has since sung nearly 40 roles at the Met and more than 50 in the leading opera houses of the world, including Covent Garden, the Paris Opéra, Vienna Staatsoper, Deutsche Oper Berlin, Bavarian State Opera, Bolshoi Opera, and San Francisco Opera. In 1979 Pierre Boulez chose her to sing the title role in the first complete performance of Berg's *Lulu,* at the Opéra, which she soon reprised at the Met. Also at the Met, in 1991, she created the role of Marie Antoinette in the world premiere of *The Ghosts of Versailles* by John Corigliano. At the other end of her astonishing artistic spectrum, Stratas sang in the New York musical *Rags*—for which she received a Tony nomination—and inherited the mantle of Lotte Lenya (from Lenya personally) as the ideal interpreter of Kurt Weill, to whose songs she brings an almost unbearable intensity.

What makes a Stratas performance unique is the quality of raw, honest connection of artist to music, and a similar connection of the woman to the world makes her unique among artists: In 1981 she worked with Mother Teresa in India, nursing the terminally ill, and in the 1990s she went to Romania to work in a hospital caring for sick and dying orphans. She has said these experiences gave her a sobering intimacy with the realities of life and death, and help ground her as she deals with the sometimes superficial world of opera.

RECOMMENDED RECORDINGS

BERG, *LULU*: MINTON, SCHWARZ, MAZURA, RIEGEL, TEAR; BOULEZ AND PARIS OPERA (DG).

"STRATAS SINGS WEILL": SCHWARZ AND CHAMBER ORCHESTRA OF NEW YORK (NONESUCH).

"THE UNKNOWN WEILL": WOITACH (NONESUCH).

Strauss AUSTRIAN FAMILY OF COMPOSER-PERFORMERS famous for popularizing the Viennese WALTZ and creating many of its most splendid exemplars. For the better part of a century, from about 1830 to 1900, their music dominated the Viennese social scene. The family's origins were Jewish, a fact **Johann Strauss** *(b. Vienna, March 14, 1804; d. Vienna, September 25, 1849)* did his best to hide from the occasionally intolerant Viennese. Strauss, who became an accomplished violinist and violist, joined the dance band of Josef Lanner in 1819. Following his marriage in 1825, he struck out on his own. His rise to fame was quick; by 1829 he was already a celebrity in Vienna, and by 1833 he was touring with his orchestra to other countries. His career was unfortunately short; he died at the age of 45 after catching scarlet fever from one of his children. Among the many popular pieces he wrote, he is best known today for a single work—the *Radetzky* March, Op. 228, composed in 1848—the musical embodiment of the once-great military might of the Hapsburg monarchy.

Despite the elder Strauss's wish that he become a banker, **Johann Strauss Jr.** *(b. Vienna, October 25, 1825; d. Vienna, June 3, 1899)* followed in his father's footsteps

***Johann Strauss Jr. with Brahms at Bad Ischl, 1894; Josef Strauss* (right)**

and became known as the "Waltz King" during the dance's heyday in the mid-19th century. He entered the music business officially in 1844, requiring a special permit since he was still underage. His success quickly rivaled that of his father, and upon Johann Sr.'s death, the two Strauss orchestras were merged and Johann Jr. took over as leader. During the next five decades, the younger Strauss—who hid a melancholy nature behind his musical gaiety—conducted and toured with the family orchestra and on his own, turning out hundreds of waltzes, polkas, and quadrilles in a stream that reached its peak in the 1850s and 1860s. The best of his waltzes—including the *Emperor, Blue Danube, Roses from the South, Tales from the Vienna Woods*, *Vienna Blood, Artist's Life,* and *Wine, Women, and Song*—are among the triumphs of 19th-century Viennese music, perfect crystallizations of the cultural milieu in which they were written. Johann Jr. also contributed 16 works to the operetta repertoire, of which the most successful were *DIE FLEDERMAUS* (*The Bat*; 1874), *Eine Nacht in Venedig* (1883), and *Die Zigeunerbaron* (1885).

Josef Strauss *(b. Vienna, August 20, 1827; d. Vienna, July 22, 1870)* was perhaps an even more formidable composer than his elder brother. Pensive and introverted, he revealed in his works a profound musicality and sophisticated imagination. His best waltzes, which include *Music of the Spheres* and *Delirium,* combine remarkable poetic beauty with an almost neurotic expressiveness. Josef may well have ghostwritten some of the waltzes credited to his brother Johann Jr., and the two also teamed up on several occasions, most notably for the popular *Pizzicato* Polka.

Eduard Strauss *(b. Vienna, March 15, 1835; d. Vienna, December 28, 1916)* turned to music after receiving a classical education. By the time he came along, the family waltz business was going so well his participation was virtually required. He was only a fair violinist, but he became the best conductor of the three Strauss brothers. Less compelling as a composer than his two siblings, he nonetheless contributed more than 300 works to the canon, of which a few are occasionally performed today.

RECOMMENDED RECORDINGS

"THE COMPLETE NEW YEAR CONCERTS (1952–54)": KRAUSS AND VIENNA PHILHARMONIC (ARCHIPEL).

MUSIC OF JOHANN JR. AND JOSEF STRAUSS: KARAJAN AND BERLIN PHILHARMONIC (DG).

"NEW YEAR'S DAY 1987": BATTLE; KARAJAN AND VIENNA PHILHARMONIC (DG).

"A VIENNESE NEW YEAR—FAVORITE WALTZES, POLKAS, AND OVERTURES": WORKS OF JOSEF AND JOHANN STRAUSS JR. (NAXOS).

Strauss, Richard

(b. Munich, June 11, 1864; d. Garmisch-Partenkirchen, September 8, 1949)

GERMAN COMPOSER AND CONDUCTOR. In a long life as a productive composer, he took opera to new heights of expressiveness, and in his use of the orchestra boldly went where no one had gone before. His father, Franz Strauss, was principal horn in the Munich Court Orchestra. Richard began piano lessons at four, and two years later was composing, his father providing the notation. He began violin study with the leader of the Court Orchestra, and by the time he reached high school, works of his were being performed. Strauss entered the University of Munich in 1882 and for two terms studied philosophy, art history, and aesthetics. That same year saw the premiere of the Serenade in E-flat for 13 winds, Op. 7, the first of Strauss's works to earn a place in the repertoire. Soon after, Strauss conducted his Suite for Winds, Op. 4, with the Meiningen Court Orchestra, and his Symphony in F minor was played by the New York Philharmonic. In 1885 he became Hans von Bülow's assistant at Meiningen and within months filled in for him as principal conductor (beating out Mahler and Weingartner).

Strauss was on his way as both composer and conductor. By 1890 he had composed his First Horn Concerto, as well as the symphonic poems *Aus Italien, Macbeth,* *DON JUAN*, and *TOD UND VERKLÄRUNG* (*Death and Transfiguration*), and had received conducting appointments in Munich and in Weimar. In the final decade of the 19th century he continued to break ground with still more symphonic poems, full of color, virtuosity, and dazzling orchestral effects: *TILL EULENSPIEGEL*, *ALSO SPRACH ZARATHUSTRA* (*Thus Spake Zarathustra,* with its justly famous opening fanfare), *DON QUIXOTE*, and *EIN HELDENLEBEN* (*A Hero's Life*). The imagery ranges from roguery and midnight philosophy to bleating sheep and ranting music critics, and there is a similar range in forms, from variation and rondeau to expansive hybrids of symphony and sonata.

On January 17, 1892, "the most wonderful day of my life," Strauss conducted Wagner's *Tristan und Isolde* starring Pauline de Ahna, who had accepted his proposal of marriage that morning. He continued writing symphonic poems after the century turned—the sprawling *Symphonia domestica,* in which the hero of *Ein Heldenleben* has fully embraced a bourgeois existence (his father, Franz, did not care for the piece, and said it gave him a feeling like "bugs in your pants"), and *Eine Alpensinfonie,* which celebrates a day spent amid nature, its 22 sections chronicling the ascent and descent of an Alpine peak, with help from cow bells, wind machine, and organ. Strauss's conducting continued to flourish—he became Kapellmeister at the Berlin Court Opera in 1898, and made his New York debut in 1904—but as the century got under way, opera was the enterprise that engaged him most fully.

In *SALOME* (1905), Strauss's virtuosic use of the orchestra opened an entirely new era for opera, while the lavish descriptiveness of his setting and the decadence of the story itself made a wonderfully perverse comment on the heroic Wagnerian tradition. Equally gory and impassioned, *Elektra* (1909, to a libretto by Hugo von Hofmannsthal, who would become Strauss's trusted collaborator

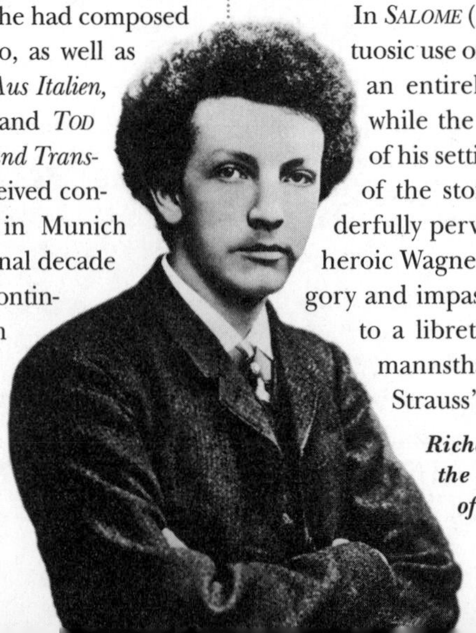

Richard Strauss at the good beginning of his career

in a series of great works) expanded on the theme of obsessive female jealousy and disordered sexuality, and veered even closer to the edge of musical cataclysm. With *Der Rosenkavalier* (1911) and subsequent operas, Strauss (and Hofmannsthal, through *Arabella*) turned away from depravity toward works that looked at human relationships and artistic and philosophical issues in a gentler light. *Der Rosenkavalier*, *Ariadne auf Naxos* (1912; rev. 1916), *Die Frau ohne Schatten* (*The Woman Without a Shadow*; 1919), *Intermezzo* (1924), *Die ägyptische Helena* (1928), *Arabella* (1933), and *Capriccio* (1942) are warmer in sentiment, more reticent in emotion, and somewhat more celebratory.

Strauss in later years

In the same decades, Strauss's conducting career took him on tours to North and South America and most of Europe. In 1933, following Hitler's installation as Chancellor of Germany, he was appointed president of the Reichsmusikkammer (state music bureau). With a Jewish daughter-in-law (whom he protected), he had to toe the line; though not a Nazi, his association with the regime left him politically compromised. In the spring of 1945, he wrote a beautiful lament for strings, *Metamorphosen*, in grief for the destruction of German culture. In other late works—such as the Second Horn Concerto (1942), the wind serenades *Aus der Werkstatt eines Invaliden* (*From the Invalid's Workshop*; 1943) and *Fröhlicher Werkstatt* (*Happy Workshop*; 1946), and the Oboe Concerto (1946)—he escaped into a blissful realm of Mozartean purity and grace. After the war he went to Switzerland to avoid having to testify in denazification proceedings. There he composed the autumnal *Vier letzte Lieder* (*Four Last Songs*). Cleared in 1948, he returned to Germany in 1949, where he died later that year.

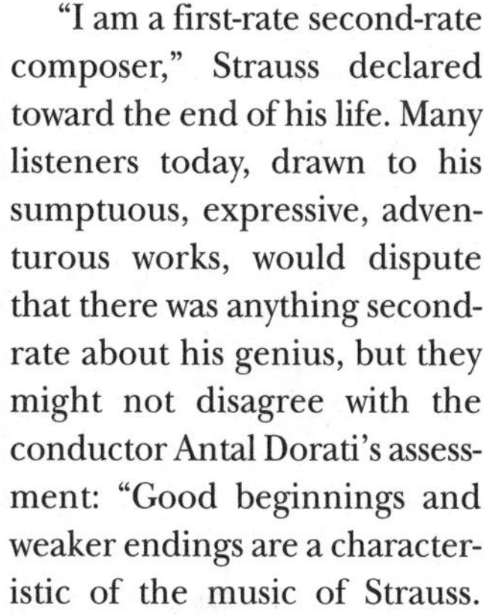

"I am a first-rate second-rate composer," Strauss declared toward the end of his life. Many listeners today, drawn to his sumptuous, expressive, adventurous works, would dispute that there was anything second-rate about his genius, but they might not disagree with the conductor Antal Dorati's assessment: "Good beginnings and weaker endings are a characteristic of the music of Strauss. And in all of Strauss's life it was this way—the beginning of his life . . . so exciting, so full of promise, and the end, under the Nazi shadow. But at least he was a marvelous beginner."

RECOMMENDED RECORDINGS

Also sprach Zarathustra, Ein Heldenleben: Reiner and Chicago Symphony Orchestra (RCA).

Collected orchestral music: Kempe and Staatskapelle Dreden (EMI).

Don Juan, Tod und Verklärung, Till Eulenspiegel: Karajan and Berlin Philharmonic (DG).

Don Juan, Tod und Verklärung, Till Eulenspiegel: Szell and Cleveland Orchestra (Sony).

Don Quixote: Rostropovich; Karajan and Berlin Philharmonic (EMI).

Eine Alpensinfonie: Kempe and Staatskapelle Dresden (EMI).

Elektra: Marc, Voigt, Schwarz, Jerusalem, Ramey; Sinopoli and Vienna Philharmonic (DG).

Elektra: Nilsson, Resnik, Collier, Stolze, Krause; Solti and Vienna Philharmonic (Decca).

Der Rosenkavalier: Schwarzkopf, Ludwig, Stich-Randall, Edelmann; Karajan and Philharmonia Orchestra (EMI).

Salome: Behrens, Van Dam, Böhm, Baltsa, Ochman; Karajan and Vienna Philharmonic (EMI).

Vier letzte Lieder (*Four Last Songs*): Norman; Masur and Gewandhaus Orchestra (Philips).

Vier letzte Lieder (*Four Last Songs*): Schwarzkopf; Szell and Berlin Radio Symphony Orchestra (EMI).

Stravinsky, Igor

(b. Oranienbaum, June 17, 1882; d. New York, April 6, 1971)

RUSSIAN COMPOSER. With his ballets *Petrushka* and *The Rite of Spring,* he forever changed the language of music by making rhythm the principal generative element of large-scale composition. In subsequent works he continued to innovate and rearrange the elements of music, helping to establish neoclassicism as a major stylistic direction of the 20th century and, late in his career, experimenting with 12-tone techniques. His influence on 20th-century music was comparable to Picasso's on painting, and like Picasso he was a master of the art of parody.

Stravinsky was born in a resort town on the Baltic near St. Petersburg, into a well-to-do family of the lesser nobility. His mother was a capable amateur pianist and singer; his father, Fyodor, had attended the St. Petersburg Conservatory and at the time of Stravinsky's birth was the leading bass-baritone of the Mariinsky Theater. Growing up in St. Petersburg, Stravinsky had considerable childhood exposure to opera and ballet and contact with leading figures of the city's musical life. He was educated at home until he was 11 and then attended private school and took piano lessons. He was a voracious reader, with wide-ranging interests.

In the fall of 1901 Stravinsky enrolled as a law student at University of St. Petersburg, continuing private instruction in piano as well as harmony and counterpoint. The next year he sought the guidance of Rimsky-Korsakov, who advised against his entering the conservatory and agreed to take him on as a private composition pupil. These weekly lessons continued along with Stravinsky's law studies. The young composer completed the first draft of his Symphony in E-flat in September 1905 (revised under Rimsky's supervision over the next couple of years); the models were Glazunov and Tchaikovsky.

In 1905 Stravinsky married his cousin Katya Nosenko. Rimsky continued to mentor Stravinsky and to see him regularly, and Stravinsky absorbed much from the colorful idiom of Rimsky's late works, especially *The Legend of the Invisible City of Kitezh* and *The Golden Cockerel.* His works testify to a rapid growth of mastery, particularly the *Scherzo fantastique* (inspired by Maeterlinck's *La vie des abeilles*) and *FIREWORKS,* which shows the influence of Scriabin's more radical concepts of harmony. These scores caught the attention of Sergey Diaghilev, who invited Stravinsky to orchestrate a couple of numbers for choreographer Mikhail Fokine's ballet *Les Sylphides,* created for the 1909 Paris season of the Ballets Russes. This led by a circuitous route to the commission that would change everything: *The Firebird.*

Premiered during the 1910 season, *THE FIREBIRD* is an extraordinarily skillful syn-

Igor Stravinsky, confrontationalist composer

thesis of elements from Rimsky-Korsakov and Glazunov, a masterpiece of orchestral colorism. While impressive, it was just a prologue to the astonishing revelation of genius that came with *Petrushka* (1911) and *The Rite of Spring* (1913), both brilliantly original: Nothing had ever sounded like these pieces.

Of the three ballets, *PETRUSHKA* exhibits the most perfect melding of music and scene, the most accomplished integration of the dance into a series of tableaux. But it was the magnificently calculated chaos of *THE RITE OF SPRING* that amazed and transformed the musical world—the Big Bang of modern music, whose noise is still being heard. For Stravinsky it embodied even more: a nexus of folkloristic elements (already adumbrated in *Petrushka*), extreme musical means (explosive, visceral, and disruptive), and a "ritualistic" manner of structuring and presenting material. The stylized-ritualistic direction was a new one and would become an important thread in Stravinsky's work, carried on in *LES NOCES* (*The Wedding*), whose first version was completed in 1917, and in several scores of the 1920s, including *SYMPHONIES OF WIND INSTRUMENTS*, *OEDIPUS REX*, and the *SYMPHONY OF PSALMS*.

Stravinsky's last prewar Paris premiere, in May 1914, was the "musical fairy tale" *Le rossignol*, based on Hans Christian Andersen's "The Nightingale." Stravinsky had begun the setting in 1908–09 and put it aside. Despite all that had happened in the interim, he was able to complete the piece by 1914 without departing far from the idiom in which he had begun it, essentially that of *The Firebird*.

World War I and the Russian Revolution brought an end to the good times. Summering with his wife and their children in Switzerland, Stravinsky was cut off from both Russia and France in August 1914; the family settled outside Lausanne and remained in exile until 1920. Straitened circumstances necessitated his cranking out pieces for cash, but the isolation, coupled with the loss of opportunity to produce anything for large forces, had a beneficial effect, allowing Stravinsky to try out new ideas and explore the possibilities inherent in smaller forms. Making a virtue of necessity, he went to work with a reduced palette, emphasizing the wind instruments, and avoiding massed strings, especially the violins. In addition to the original draft of *Les noces*, important works of this period include *Renard*, *L'HISTOIRE DU SOLDAT* (*The Soldier's Tale*), and *Symphonies of Wind Instruments*; just a couple years later came the Octet for winds.

During the 1920s, Stravinsky undertook a radical rethinking of musical form and structure. The most conspicuous development was his return to the forms and "constructive principles" of 18th-century music—a movement dubbed "neoclassicism." The stylistic breakthrough came with the "Pergolesi" ballet *PULCINELLA*, commissioned by Diaghilev and premiered in May 1920. Even as *Symphonies of Wind Instruments* was closing out the folkloric "Russian" chapter of Stravinsky's stylistic evolution, *Pulcinella* was opening the door to the cosmopolitan neoclassical idiom that would become his stylistic preoccupation for the next 30 years. The harvest was rich: the ballets *Apollo*, *LE BAISER DE LA FÉE* (*The Fairy's Kiss*; based on Tchaikovsky), and *JEU DE CARTES* (*Game of Cards*), along with purely instrumental compositions such as the Concerto in D for strings (commissioned by Paul Sacher), the Violin Concerto (also very much in D), and the *Dumbarton Oaks* Concerto. This last, for chamber orchestra, loosely modeled on the *Brandenburg* Concertos, is a kind of conversation with Bach in which Stravinsky, naturally, gets the last word.

Stravinsky* (second from right) *and the Hindemith Quartet, violist Paul Hindemith standing

The years 1938–39 brought upheaval and sorrow with the deaths of Stravinsky's eldest daughter, his mother, and his wife (though since 1922 the composer had been living openly with his mistress, Vera Sudeykina; they married in 1940). Within weeks of the outbreak of World War II, Stravinsky left Europe for America. He delivered lectures at Harvard, settled with Vera in West Hollywood, and hung out with other Russian émigrés, a small circle of friends from the world of the arts. Again he cranked out works on commission in order to survive, producing exquisite hackwork such as the *Circus Polka, Four Norwegian Moods, Ode* (commissioned by Serge Koussevitzky), and the *Ebony* Concerto (commissioned by Woody Herman). There also were works of higher aim and quality: the Symphony in C (1938–40), premiered by the Chicago Symphony Orchestra with Stravinsky conducting, a brilliant and assured refraction of the classical four-movement symphony; *DANSES CONCERTANTES* (1940–42), not a ballet but a suite for chamber orchestra; and the *SYMPHONY IN THREE MOVEMENTS* (1942–45), premiered by the New York Philharmonic with Stravinsky conducting, a vibrant, dramatic orchestral canvas. ◉ Major achievements after the war were the ballet *Orpheus* and the opera *THE RAKE'S PROGRESS.* Begun in 1947 and finished four years later, *The Rake's Progress* was the high-water mark of Stravinsky's immersion in neoclassicism and his first fling with opera since *Le rossignol* (two more dissimilar operas by the same composer would be hard to find). One of the great operas of the 20th century, it is also Stravinsky's greatest work of musical parody.

When Stravinsky conducted its premiere, in Venice in 1951, it marked the first time he had set foot on European soil since 1939. In the midst of work on *The Rake's Progress,* Robert Craft, a young American and Juilliard-trained conductor, became Stravinsky's assistant. Craft would serve as amanuensis, adviser, and apologist, preparing orchestras for Stravinsky to conduct, collaborating on numerous books and recordings, playing Boswell to Stravinsky's Johnson for the rest of the composer's life. In addition, Craft (a champion of Schoenberg and Webern) was the catalyst in Stravinsky's final stylistic transformation, which involved an embrace of Schoenbergian serialism and touched everything from the splendid Septet (1953) on. Stravinsky's serial works still sound Stravinskian, retaining his distinctive rhythmic animation. Some did turn out dry and dull, but there were successes such as the ballet *Agon* (1953–57), written for George Balanchine. Late works, from the 1960s, include the short cantata *A Sermon, a Narrative, and a Prayer* and *Requiem Canticles,* whose premiere Craft conducted.

Stravinsky had been conducting and recording his own work since the 1920s, but his most significant efforts as executant came during his frequent guest engagements in America, and while presiding over recordings of a large part of his oeuvre for Columbia Records. He moved to New York in 1969. Following his death, two years later, his body was flown to Venice and interred on the necropolitan island of San Michele.

Protean, stateless, uprooted, peripatetic—equal parts French and Russian, with a keen intelligence, malicious temperament, and acerbic wit—Stravinsky was one of the dominant figures in the formation of the aesthetic of modernism, an iconoclast who became an icon. He was also the model eclectic, stealing stuff everywhere without ever losing his identity. Indeed, throughout his long career Stravinsky actively sought external influence and ideas to work with, using anything he felt to be useful, and with each piece pointing in a different direction. He was a brilliant posturer, a skillful manipulator of materials and procedures, and a purveyor of feigned emotion (or none—"the play of the musical elements is the thing," he wrote), who, like the charlatan in *Petrushka,* was always present in and commenting on his creations.

Obsessed with his own importance, Stravinsky seemed, at least in his later years, perpetually irked by the way more glamorous conductors stole his thunder every time they performed one of his scores. And, in an odd way, Stravinsky's imagination ran backward, from an early fascination with the fantastic to a fixation on the parodistic to, in his final decade, a largely sterile preoccupation with technique. Even so, what we call "modern music" came into being with *Petrushka* and *The Rite of Spring.* In bringing about this sea change in the way music could function, Stravinsky became one of the most important composers in history, enlarging, as Debussy told him, "the boundaries of the permissible in the empire of sound."

RECOMMENDED RECORDINGS

EARLY ORCHESTRAL WORKS (INCLUDING SYMPHONY IN E-FLAT, *SCHERZO FANTASTIQUE, FIREWORKS, THE FIREBIRD* SUITE): ASHKENAZY AND ST. PETERSBURG PHILHARMONIC (DECCA).

THE FIREBIRD, PETRUSHKA, THE RITE OF SPRING: DAVIS AND ROYAL CONCERTGEBOUW ORCHESTRA (PHILIPS).

THE FIREBIRD, PETRUSHKA, THE RITE OF SPRING: STRAVINSKY AND COLUMBIA SYMPHONY ORCHESTRA (SONY).

L'HISTOIRE DU SOLDAT: BOHMER, ARMSTRONG, GOODWIN; WILSON AND SOLISTI NEW YORK (CHESKY).

L'HISTOIRE DU SOLDAT: COCTEAU, USTINOV, FERTEY; MARKEVITCH AND VARIOUS SOLOISTS (PHILIPS).

LES NOCES: BERNSTEIN AND VARIOUS SOLOISTS (DG).

PETRUSHKA, THE RITE OF SPRING: BOULEZ AND NEW YORK PHILHARMONIC, CLEVELAND ORCHESTRA (SONY).

PETRUSHKA, THE RITE OF SPRING: OZAWA AND BOSTON SYMPHONY ORCHESTRA, CHICAGO SYMPHONY ORCHESTRA (RCA).

THE RAKE'S PROGRESS: BOSTRIDGE, YORK, TERFEL, OTTER; GARDINER AND LONDON SYMPHONY ORCHESTRA (DG).

THE RAKE'S PROGRESS: YOUNG, RASKIN, REARDON, SARFATY; STRAVINSKY AND ROYAL PHILHARMONIC ORCHESTRA (SONY).

SYMPHONY OF PSALMS, SYMPHONY IN C, *SYMPHONY IN THREE MOVEMENTS*: STRAVINSKY AND VARIOUS SOLOISTS (SONY).

VIOLIN CONCERTO IN D: CHUNG; PREVIN AND LONDON SYMPHONY ORCHESTRA (DECCA).

stretto (It., "narrow," "tight") [1] An overlapping of entries in a FUGUE so as to heighten the musical tension. [2] The adoption of a faster tempo in the climactic or closing pages of a piece. Examples can be found at the end of the Act II finale in Mozart's *Le nozze di Figaro* and in the codas to the final movements of Brahms's Piano Quartet in G minor, Op. 25, and Mahler's Symphony No. 5.

Striggio, Alessandro

(b. Mantua, ca. 1573; d. Venice, June 15, 1630)

ITALIAN COURTIER AND POET. His father, also named Alessandro Striggio (ca. 1540–92), was a noted composer of madrigals; his mother was the singer Virginia Vagnoli. A capable musician, Striggio studied law at Mantua and spent most of his life in the service of the Gonzaga family, becoming the ducal secretary (to Vincenzo I) in 1611. He created the libretto for Monteverdi's *L'Orfeo* (1607), modeling it on Rinuccini's *Euridice* (1600), and also wrote librettos that were set by Marco da Gagliano (1582–1643).

string instruments Instruments belonging to several distinct families that produce sound when one or more strings are plucked or bowed. Instruments in which the strings are framed—such as harps, pianos, and harpsichords—are not considered part of this group. *See also* CELLO, DOUBLE BASS, GUITAR, VIOL, VIOLA, VIOLA DA GAMBA, VIOLA D'AMORE, VIOLIN.

string quartet [1] An ensemble consisting of two violins, a viola, and a cello. [2] A composition, usually in several movements, for string quartet. What has made the string quartet an ideal medium for serious instrumental composition for more than two centuries is the homogeneity of sound that four string instruments, all belonging to the same family, can achieve. In addition to balance and tonal refinement, the quartet has afforded composers great flexibility owing to the virtuosic capabilities both of the instruments themselves and of their best players.

Although Austrian and German composers, specifically Haydn, Mozart, and Beethoven, perfected the string quartet form, the Italians were the first to capitalize on the quartet as a medium, thanks to their idiomatic feeling for string writing and their supremacy in instrument making. The pioneering works of Tartini and Sammartini, dating from the mid-18th century (and displaying a clear development from the texture of the Baroque trio sonata with basso continuo), were elegant and well crafted. Even the quartets of Boccherini that appeared during the 1760s showed more finesse than those Haydn was writing at the same time, though Haydn would eventually go much further. Important work on the development of the string quartet also occurred in Mannheim during the 1750s and 1760s. By the early 1780s the quartet was well established as a form, with the most meaningful compositional activity centered in Paris, around Giovanni Battista Viotti (1755–1824), and at Esterháza, with Haydn.

Haydn effectively brought the Classical string quartet into its maturity with his Opus 33 set of six quartets, completed in 1781 and known as the *Russian* Quartets because they bore a dedication to Grand Duke Paul of Russia. With these works he outstripped his Italian and French colleagues in the animation and conversational repartee of his quartet textures, as well as in depth of expression. He consolidated his triumph during the next 20 years, capped by the six quartets of his Opus 76 (1799), works of freshness and subtlety, brilliant in their formal and melodic invention and full of striking departures from convention. The freedom they exhibit in the interplay of figures is notable, as is the independence of the parts. More remarkable still is the rhetorical power of the slow movements, which are of unprecedented profundity and scope.

Mozart built on Haydn's string quartet style in his six famous essays dedicated to the elder master (1785), his finest achievement in the genre. All six are characterized by an extraordinarily rich sense of melodic and harmonic invention, contrapuntal sophistication, warm expressiveness, and felicitous treatment of topic.

Beethoven's 16 contributions to the genre are the greatest body of works written for string quartet. During his career, Beethoven stretched the string quartet toward symphonic dimensions, while enriching the genre's expressive context through the use of parody and a breathtaking range of textures and topical devices. His six Op. 18 quartets (1800) assimilate the stylistic and formal accomplishments of his predecessors. But they also subvert the conventions of the Classical style. The astonishing quartets he wrote at the end of his career, between 1824 and 1826 (Opp. 127, 130, 131, 132, and 135, plus the *Grosse Fuge,* Op. 133) exhibit an exceptionally open, spontaneous, and visionary concept of structure. As a group, they are marked by a tendency toward concision; there is not a single grandly scaled opening movement among them. Yet there is a paradoxical expansion in all of them—of the expressive scope of individual works, of the domains of rhythm, harmony, and color, and of time itself, which even in short movements can seem to stand still. In no other music of any composer is the generative power of the imagination so strikingly evident.

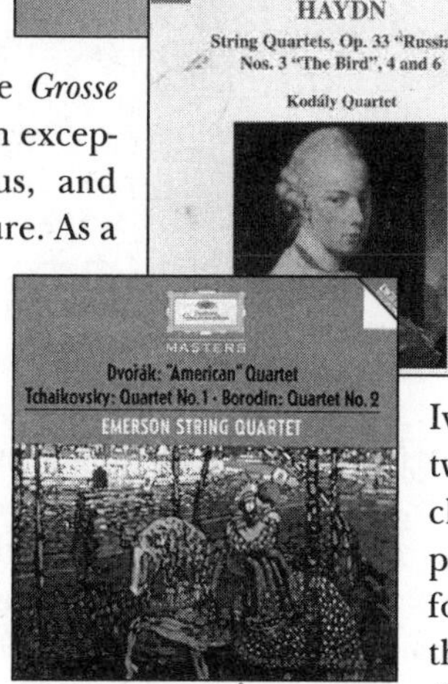

For other musicians, let alone audiences, Beethoven's late quartets were even more daunting than his symphonies. Schubert, however, was spared the agony later composers faced: He wrote his finest works in the form, the Quartet in D minor, D. 810 (*Der Tod und das Mädchen*; 1824), and the spacious Quartet in G, D. 887 (1826), before Beethoven's late works were known. Both Mendelssohn and Schumann, who fashioned several quartets each, found other chamber combinations more agreeable. Brahms was even more intimidated; in his three string quartets he tried to rise to the occasion, though he, too, found greater success with other groupings. Not so Dvořák, a string player and lifelong chamber musician, who contributed 14 works to the repertoire. His String Quartet No. 12 in F, Op. 96 (1893), subtitled the *American,* is his most celebrated work in the form, but several of his earlier works, and the magisterial pair he composed in 1895, are every bit as fine.

Important works were contributed to the quartet literature by Franck, Elgar, Debussy, and Ravel, each of whom composed one mature essay, almost as a proof of worthiness. Ives and Janáček each wrote two, producing works of great character. While some string players consider Schoenberg's four numbered quartets to be the best of the 20th century, there is broader support for viewing the six string quartets of Bartók and the 15 of Shostakovich as the century's most important.

Like Beethoven's, Bartók's quartets reflect their composer's growth and stylistic development over a period of three decades; also like Beethoven's, they served as the vehicle for their composer's self-discovery and his deepest, most intimate expression, revealing in microcosm the essence of his musical thinking. Composed between 1908 and 1939, they embrace a wealth of styles and folk idioms and make use of a range of advanced techniques, including fierce "snap" pizzicatos in which the plucked string rebounds off the fingerboard (also called a "Bartók" pizzicato), haunting glissandos, dramatic mutings, and extended passages in multiple stops. Each of the six has its own aims and character; taken together, they represent Bartók's most sophisticated exploration of complex rhythmic motifs and formal schemes.

Despite the modernity of his language, Shostakovich paid thoughtful homage to the Classical ideal in his quartets, which in their argument and structure are clearly descended from the works of Haydn and Beethoven. Touching on a remarkable variety of moods, the pieces speak to the listener in a manner that suggests they are entries in a private diary, as opposed to the more public memoirs of Shostakovich's symponies. Nine of the 15 were composed during the 1960s and 1970s, when Shostakovich, victimized twice during the Stalin years, again felt free to write "absolute" music and to take compositional risks. *See also* CHAMBER MUSIC *and entries for individual works and composers.*

Strozzi, Barbara

(b. Venice, 1619; d. Padua, November 11, 1677)

ITALIAN SINGER AND COMPOSER. She was the adopted (probably natural) daughter of the prominent librettist and poet, Giulio Strozzi (1583–1652), and her talents were nurtured within the highest circles of Venetian musical and literary society. A student of Francesco Cavalli, she became famous for her virtuosic performances at meetings of the Accademia degli Incogniti, the primary force behind the blending of music and drama that eventually became Baroque opera seria.

In 1644 she published a collection of madrigals, with texts by her father; after this, the majority of her published works were for solo voice and continuo, ranging in form from short, strophic ariettas to fully developed cantatas containing contrasting sections of recitative, arioso, and aria. Strozzi's command of vocal writing is evident in her ability to respond to her texts with a combination of lyricism, dramatic techniques such as unmeasured sections and *stile concitato,* and the sheer virtuosic vocalism of long melismas and intricate notated ornamentation—all of which attests to her own extraordinary talent as a singer. Strozzi was remarkable not only as a fully professional female composer, but also as a composer whose works were published and known within her lifetime, a rare accomplishment in the 17th century.

RECOMMENDED RECORDINGS

ARIAS AND DUETS: BRANDES, LANE, RICHARDS; MILNES AND NEW YORK BAROQUE (PGM).

CANTATAS: BOTT; CHATEAUNEUF, OTHERS (CARLTON CLASSICS).

IL PRIMO LIBRO DI MADRIGALI: LA VENEXIANA (GLOSSA).

Sturm und Drang (Storm and Stress)

Name of literary movement prominent in late-18th-century Germany, taken from the title of a tragedy about the American Revolution, *Der Wirrwarr, oder Sturm und Drang,* written in 1776 by Friedrich Maximilian Klinger. The style stressed passion, boldness, the expression of extreme feeling, and personal emotional experience. Johann Wolfgang von Goethe's play *Götz von Berlichingen* (1773) pointed the way to the Sturm und Drang sensibility, and Friedrich von Schiller became a key figure in the movement, authoring its greatest work, the 1781 play *Die Räuber* (*The Brigands*), later utilized by Verdi as the basis for his opera *I masnadieri* (1847). Musicologists have appropriated "Sturm und Drang" to identify a proto-Romantic musical style that actually preceded the literary phenomenon. It is exemplified by the symphonies Haydn composed between 1768 and 1772, with their fondness for "distant" keys, the minor mode, deep pathos, and dramatic extremes of expression and gesture—especially No. 44 in E minor (*Trauersinfonie*; 1772) and No. 49 in F minor (*La passione*; 1768)—as well as by Mozart's Symphony No. 25 in G minor, K. 183 (1773). The turbulent emotion of these works has much in common with the impassioned action of the Sturm und Drang tragedies.

RECOMMENDED RECORDINGS

HAYDN, *STURM UND DRANG* SYMPHONIES: HOGWOOD AND ACADEMY OF ANCIENT MUSIC (OISEAU-LYRE).

MOZART, SYMPHONY NO. 25 IN G MINOR: MACKERRAS AND PRAGUE CHAMBER ORCHESTRA (TELARC).

subdominant The fourth degree of a major or minor scale and, by extension, the chord whose root is that note. For example, in the C major scale the subdominant is F, and in the key of C major, the subdominant harmony is F major (a chord with the notes F–A–C). In the key of D minor, the subdominant harmony is G minor (G–B-flat–D), G being the fourth degree of the D minor scale.

suite [1] An instrumental composition consisting of several movements in dance form, usually in the same key, often preceded by a prelude or a full-blown overture. During the Baroque period, when the suite was a prominent genre in both orchestral and keyboard music, the dances customarily included an ALLEMANDE, COURANTE, SARABANDE, and GIGUE. Among the optional dances that could be encountered, the most common were the BOURRÉE, GAVOTTE, MINUET, and PASSEPIED. [2] A freestanding work consisting of excerpts from an opera, ballet, or other large work. [3] A multimovement orchestral piece (e.g., Grofé's *Grand Canyon* Suite and Holst's *The Planets*).

Suk, Josef

(b. Křečovice, January 4, 1874; d. Benešov, May 29, 1935)

CZECH COMPOSER AND VIOLINIST. After receiving basic musical training in violin, piano, and organ from his father, a schoolteacher and choirmaster, he pursued violin study at the Prague Conservatory in 1885, graduating in 1891. He remained another year to study composition with Dvořák and chamber music with Hanuš Wihan. In Wihan's class, he and three other colleagues formed the Czech Quartet, in which he played second violin. The quartet would tour extensively, giving more than 4,000 performances over 40 years, and enjoy considerable success. In the course of his work with Dvořák, Suk not only became Dvořák's favorite student but, in 1898, married the composer's daughter, Otilie. Not surprisingly, Suk's early style draws from Brahms and Dvořák; his compositions from this period already show remarkable command and assurance, as demonstrated in the popular Serenade for Strings, Op. 6 (1892), written when Suk was only 18. Over the course of the ensuing decade, a deepening emotional range becomes apparent in Suk's works, which can be tracked from his *Dramatic Overture,* Op. 4 (1892), through the Piano Quintet, Op. 8 (1893, rev. 1915), the String Quartet, Op. 11 (1896, rev. 1915), and Symphony No. 1 in E, Op. 14 (1899). Some especially fine orchestral works date from the first years of the 20th century, including *Pohádka* (*Fairy Tale*), Op. 16, completed in 1900, the Fantasy for Violin and Orchestra, Op. 24, and the *Fantastic Scherzo,* Op. 25, both dating from 1903. In 1904–05, Suk's life was shattered by the deaths, 14 months apart, of his father-in-law and his young wife. Deeply depressed, he eventually returned to composition with his Symphony No. 2 in C minor, Op. 27, completed in 1906 and titled *Asrael* after the angel of death (the score is dedicated to the memory of Otilie and her father). It was a long distance from the springlike beauty of the Serenade for Strings to the tragic splendor of the *Asrael* Symphony, and Suk traveled it in a terribly short time. Unfortunate as the symphony's genesis was, it is one of the great symphonic efforts of the post-Romantic era.

Suk soldiered on, and in 1922 he was appointed professor of composition at the Prague Conservatory, where he taught a generation of Czech composers, including Bohuslav Martinů. Over time, Suk's musical language became more and more complex; despite his Romantic temperament and outlook, he did not stand still. Deeply felt and finely crafted, his work deserves to be better known outside the Czech Republic.

RECOMMENDED RECORDINGS

Asrael Symphony: Bělohlávek and Czech Philharmonic (Chandos).

Asrael Symphony: Talich and Czech Philharmonic (Supraphon).

Pohádka, Serenade for Strings: Bělohlávek and Czech Philharmonic (Chandos).

Serenade for Strings: Kreček and Cappella Istropolitana (Naxos).

Serenade for Strings: Warren-Green and London Chamber Orchestra (Virgin Classics).

Sullivan, Arthur

(b. London, May 13, 1842; d. London, November 22, 1900)

British composer. Though he distinguished himself as the musical half of what many consider the greatest musical-comedy collaboration in the history of the theater, he wanted to be remembered for his serious compositions. The precocious son of a band musician, he won England's first Mendelssohn Prize, allowing him to study at the Royal Academy of Music from 1856 to 1858. He continued his studies at the Leipzig Conservatory, graduating in 1861, and returned to London. In April 1862 at the Crystal Palace, a performance of his orchestral suite *The Tempest* (composed as his graduation piece) met with huge success. Sullivan was launched as a serious composer, and over the next several years he turned out orchestral pieces, including the Symphony in E (*Irish*; 1866), a cello concerto, the oratorio *The Prodigal Son* (1869), numerous songs, and a number of hymns, among them "Onward Christian Soldiers" (1871).

To make ends meet Sullivan worked as a church organist and conducted an amateur choir, and in 1876 he became head of the newly established National Training School for Music. Along the way, still looking for a breakthrough, he met William S. Gilbert, a dramatist and satirist six years his senior, and began to collaborate with him on operettas.

Thespis, the first of Sullivan's 14 collaborations with Gilbert, was commissioned by London's Gaiety Theatre in 1871. It was a dismal failure, but the experience gave the pair a glimpse of how they might go about creating a piece, if a second opportunity presented itself. When, in 1875, it did (by way of Richard D'Oyly Carte, the theatrical producer who would produce all their subsequent collaborations), the resulting one-act satire on Britain's legal system, *Trial by Jury,* was an enormous success.

By the time their run was over, Gilbert and Sullivan would be 20 years older, barely speaking to each other, and considerably wealthier than when they had begun. In the wake of their often rocky relationship they would leave a priceless legacy, the Savoy Operas, so named for the London theater

Caricature of Sir Arthur Sullivan

that D'Oyly Carte built in 1881 expressly for them (it was the first London theater to be lit by electricity). Nearly all were formulaic, highly topical spoofs of a particular style (Japanese vogue in *The Mikado*; 1885), a trend (*Patience*, 1881, lampoons the Aesthetic Movement as embodied by Oscar Wilde), or an institution (the Royal Navy, nearly sunk by *H.M.S. Pinafore* in 1878). They retain much of their innate charm, spiky wit, political edge, and outright absurdity today, nearly a century and a half later. The other fruits of the collaboration were *The Sorcerer* (1877), *The Pirates of Penzance* (1879), *Iolanthe* (1882), *Princess Ida* (1884), *Ruddigore* (1887), *The Yeomen of the Guard* (1888), *The Gondoliers* (1889), *Utopia Limited* (1893), and *The Grand Duke* (1896).

Highly protective of his clever, quirky, but often thorny and arcane texts, Gilbert made sure that the music never overshadowed the lyrics; Sullivan was required to provide an enormously varied musical fabric that seemed nevertheless of a piece with the theatrical world it described. His work within the parameters his collaborator set for it is nothing short of a miracle.

Knighted in 1883 by Queen Victoria, who saw in him a great hope for British music, Sullivan continued conducting at the Leeds Festival and Philharmonic Society, and poured much energy into the composition of a grand-opera setting of Walter Scott's *Ivanhoe*, which failed to hold the stage after its premiere in 1891. Following the rift with Gilbert, he tried to maintain an active artistic and social life, composing two new, non-Gilbert operettas. Gout and a chronic kidney condition that had plagued him for years grew worse, and he was often debilitated by pain. He grew accustomed to relief from morphine, but after a while even that became ineffective. A final operetta, *The Emerald Isle*, left unfinished at Sullivan's death, was subsequently completed by Sir Edward German.

***Allan Corduner* (left) *and Jim Broadbent as Sullivan and Gilbert in Mike Leigh's film* Topsy-Turvy**

RECOMMENDED RECORDINGS

OPERETTA OVERTURES:

H.M.S. PINAFORE: SUART, ALLEN, EVANS, SCHADE, PALMER; MACKERRAS AND WELSH NATIONAL OPERA (TELARC).

MARRINER AND ACADEMY OF ST. MARTIN-IN-THE-FIELDS (DECCA).

PENNY AND ROYAL BALLET SINFONIA (NAXOS).

THE PIRATES OF PENZANCE: AINSLEY, EVANS, SUART, VAN ALLAN; MACKERRAS AND WELSH NATIONAL OPERA (TELARC).

sul ponticello (It., "on the [little] bridge") For bowed string instruments, an instruction to play close to the bridge, which produces a thin, raspy tone. This color can be very effective when produced by an entire string section, as occurs in the middle of Sibelius's *En Saga*.

sul tasto (It., "on the fingerboard") In string music, a direction indicating that a passage is to be played with the bow contacting the strings over the end of the fingerboard (i.e., farther from the bridge than in normal bowing), which produces a softening and gentle coloration of the sound. The effect was a particular favorite of Debussy, who used the equivalent

French marking *sur la touche* in works such as his *Prélude à l'après-midi d'un faune* and *Rondes de printemps*.

Suor Angelica (Sister Angelica) **OPERA IN ONE ACT BY GIACOMO PUCCINI,** composed in 1917 to a libretto by Giovacchino Forzano and premiered December 14, 1918, at the Metropolitan Opera in New York as the second part of *IL TRITTICO,* with Geraldine Farrar in the title role. The action, which takes place in a convent toward the end of the 17th century, centers on a young nun from a noble family who poisons herself after learning that the child she had borne out of wedlock has died. Her final moments are transfigured by an apparition of the Virgin Mary, surrounded by a host of angels, leading Angelica's child toward her. Puccini's musical treatment is sweet—nearly saccharine—and suffused with pastel orchestral colors.

RECOMMENDED RECORDINGS

GALLARDO-DOMAS, MANCA DI NISSA, PALMER, ROSCHMANN; PAPPANO AND PHILHARMONIA ORCHESTRA (EMI).

SUTHERLAND, LUDWIG, COLLINS, JONES; BONYNGE AND NATIONAL PHILHARMONIC ORCHESTRA (DECCA).

Suppé, Franz

(b. Spalato, Dalmatia, April 18, 1819; d. Vienna, May 21, 1895)

AUSTRIAN COMPOSER OF BELGIAN DESCENT. As a youth he spent time in Italy, where he heard the operas of Rossini and Donizetti (who was a distant relative). In 1835, following the death of his father, he settled in Vienna. He began his career in 1840 as a conductor at the Theater in der Josefstadt, becoming music director at the prestigious Theater an der Wien in 1845. In 1862 he moved to the Kaitheater, and from 1865 to 1882 he served as music director of the Carltheater.

Suppé was the first Viennese composer to absorb the musical influence of Offenbach, and during the 1860s, he became the founder of a new school of operetta in the Hapsburg capital. One of his greatest successes was the "military operetta" *Die leichte Kavallerie* (*The Light Cavalry*), premiered in 1866 at the Carltheater. The work is best known for its overture, a dashing and imaginative tone poem with a Hungarian accent and a jaunty cavalry march as its second subject. Other of Suppé's works whose overtures (at least) remain in the orchestral repertoire are *Ein Morgen, Mittag und Abend in Wien* (*Morning, Noon and Night in Vienna*; 1844), *Dichter und Bauer* (*Poet and Peasant*; 1846), *Die schöne Galathée* (*The Beautiful Galatea*; 1865), and *Boccaccio* (1879).

RECOMMENDED RECORDINGS

OVERTURES:

MARRINER AND ACADEMY OF ST. MARTIN-IN-THE-FIELDS (EMI).

PARAY AND DETROIT SYMPHONY ORCHESTRA (MERCURY).

***Surprise* Symphony** **NICKNAME OF JOSEPH HAYDN'S SYMPHONY NO. 94 IN G,** the second of 12 composed on commission from Johann Peter Salomon for performance in London. One can imagine at least a few among the audience at the premiere, on March 23, 1792, in the Hannover Square Rooms, being startled out of their seats by the "surprise"—an explosive *fortissimo* accompanied by a timpani stroke that is dropped like a bomb 16 bars into the mildest of Andantes. The rest of the symphony is hardly less delightful. After a slow introduction, the Vivace first movement offers up a laughing first subject and a second group that titters for a few measures, then brays outright. The waltzlike minuet is full of high spirits, and the finale, one of Haydn's most exuberant, shows that music that is light at heart can also be well crafted and virtuosic.

RECOMMENDED RECORDING

DAVIS AND CONCERTGEBOUW ORCHESTRA (PHILIPS).

suspension A dissonance created when a melodic note that belongs to one harmony is sustained while the harmony below it shifts; the note is thus "suspended" above a harmony to which it does not belong. Typically, a suspension resolves downward, by stepwise motion. Monteverdi made use of suspensions in the "Duo Seraphim" of his 1610 *Vespro della Beata Vergine.*

Sutherland, Dame Joan

(b. Sydney, November 7, 1926)

AUSTRALIAN SOPRANO. Melbourne gave the world a great soprano in Nellie Melba, but Sydney brought forth a greater one still in Joan Sutherland, a singer of monumental stature and one of the 20th century's most accomplished musical artists. In a career spanning four decades, Sutherland added a new dimension to the art of bel canto—"beautiful singing"—with her dazzling performances as Lucia, Norma, Violetta (in Verdi's *La traviata*), and in dozens of other roles. Her incomparable vocal dexterity and beauty of tone, ideally suited to the demands of coloratura singing, made her appearance a sensation.

Sutherland began singing as a child, working with her mother, an accomplished mezzo-soprano, until she was 19, then studying with Aida Summers on scholarship while she held down various secretarial jobs. In the summer of 1947 she appeared in her first opera productions (Handel's *Acis and Galatea* and Purcell's *Dido and Aeneas*) with the Singers of Australia. She moved to London in 1951 to continue her studies. She made her Covent Garden debut in 1952 as the First Lady in Mozart's *Die Zauberflöte,* and later that year sang Clotilde opposite Callas's Norma. In 1954 she married the Australian pianist and conductor Richard Bonynge, a friend from her student years, who was to become not only her lifelong companion but her most frequent collaborator in performance and on disc.

As a member of the Royal Opera Company during the 1950s, Sutherland sang a variety of secondary roles, ranging from Handel to Verdi. She later said that at that time, "I fancied myself a second Flagstad." But her gift lay in another direction. With Bonynge's help she continued to work on her technique and to develop the notes in the upper register that were essential to the coloratura repertoire. Her sensational London debut in the title role of Donizetti's *Lucia di Lammermoor,* on February 17, 1959, marked the turning point in her career. The opera had not been staged at Covent Garden since 1925, and Sutherland's performance (in Franco Zeffirelli's graphic production) bowled over public and critics alike. After a similarly thrilling stand as Handel's Alcina in Venice in 1960, she was dubbed by the Italian press "La Stupenda," a title that aptly conveyed both the size of her talent

Joan Sutherland as Amina in **La sonnambula**

and the magnitude of her stage presence. She was named a Commander of the Order of the British Empire in 1961, the same year that also saw her make her debuts at La Scala in Milan and the Metropolitan Opera, both times in the role of Lucia.

For 30 years, until her retirement in 1990, Dame Joan performed leading roles in opera houses all over the world, recording more than 30 complete operas, including such rarities as Massenet's *Esclarmonde* and *Le roi de Lahore.* An exceptionally versatile soprano, able to sing coloratura, lyric, and dramatic roles with equal authority, she was particularly well regarded as an exponent of Italian bel canto (where her specialties included the roles of Amina in Bellini's *La sonnambula,* Semiramide, Norma, and, of course, Lucia) and the French repertoire (she was without equal as Marie in Donizetti's *La fille du régiment* and as Marguerite de Valois in Meyerbeer's *Les Huguenots*). Sutherland also achieved distinction as Turandot—a role she never performed onstage, but recorded to magnificent effect—and was a resplendent Suor Angelica. With her enormous range, remarkable purity of tone, breathtaking agility, and trills that were considered the best in the business, she was a paragon of technical accomplishment. She was also a fine actress, whose statuesque height (five feet, nine inches) and regal bearing made an unforgettable impression upon audiences.

Sutherland penned her autobiography in 1997, documenting her formidable career with disarming candor and confirming what legions of fans the world over had long suspected: that in addition to being one of the century's greatest singers, she was also a delightful, outgoing personality of extraordinary grace and warmth.

RECOMMENDED RECORDINGS

BELLINI, *LA SONNAMBULA*: PAVAROTTI, JONES, GHIAUROV; BONYNGE AND NATIONAL PHILHARMONIC ORCHESTRA (DECCA).

BELLINI, *NORMA*: HORNE, ALEXANDER, CROSS, MINTON; BONYNGE AND LONDON SYMPHONY ORCHESTRA (DECCA).

DONIZETTI, *LUCIA DI LAMMERMOOR*: PAVAROTTI, MILNES, GHIAUROV, DAVIES; BONYNGE AND ROYAL OPERA (DECCA).

MASSENET, *ESCLARMONDE*: ARAGALL, TOURANGEAU, DAVIES; BONYNGE AND NATIONAL PHILHARMONIC ORCHESTRA (DECCA).

PUCCINI, *SUOR ANGELICA*: LUDWIG, COLLINS, JONES; BONYNGE AND NATIONAL PHILHARMONIC ORCHESTRA (DECCA).

PUCCINI, *TURANDOT*: PAVAROTTI, CABALLÉ, GHIAUROV, PEARS; MEHTA AND LONDON PHILHARMONIC ORCHESTRA (DECCA).

"THE ART OF THE PRIMA DONNA": ARIAS BY ARNE, HANDEL, BELLINI, GOUNOD, MOZART, VERDI, OTHERS; MOLINARI-PRADELLI AND ROYAL OPERA (LONDON).

Swan Lake BALLET IN FOUR ACTS BY PYOTR IL'YICH TCHAIKOVSKY, composed 1875–76 and premiered March 4, 1877, at the Bolshoi Theatre in Moscow. The literary source for the ballet is unknown. It may have been a story from an 18th-century collection of German folk tales by J. K. A. Musäus. Tchaikovsky had fashioned a domestic ballet after this story in 1871 for his sister Alexandra's children. When, in the spring of 1875, the management of the Imperial Theaters in Moscow approached him with a commission for a full-length ballet, he proposed the same subject. Once the idea had been

Riolanna Lorenzo and Zachary Henck in a scene from Swan Lake approved, Tchaikovsky eagerly set to work, and the music that poured out was characterful and inspired. But the ballet's initial reception was less than enthusiastic. The sets, the choreography, even the dancers were substandard, and Tchaikovsky was criticized for music that was deemed too complex and "undanceable." The score *was* complex, if not unduly so, and much more symphonic than what Russian ballet audiences were used to. It was also better organized in terms of its key scheme, brilliantly orchestrated, and saturated with memorable melodies.

Precisely because it embodied these traits, *Swan Lake* revolutionized the art of composing for the dance, transforming the music of the ballet from a grand decorative gesture into an essential component of the drama onstage. Yet for quite a while the intensely self-critical Tchaikovsky failed to see the value of his own score. Later in 1877, after hearing Delibes's *Sylvia* in Vienna, he wrote to Sergey Taneyev: "What charm and elegance, what riches in the melody, the rhythm, the harmony! I was ashamed. If I had known this music before, I would, of course, not have written *Swan Lake.*"

RECOMMENDED RECORDINGS

(COMPLETE): DUTOIT AND MONTREAL SYMPHONY ORCHESTRA (DECCA).

(SUITE): ORMANDY AND PHILADELPHIA ORCHESTRA (SONY).

(SUITE): ROSTROPOVICH AND BERLIN PHILHARMONIC (DG).

Swan of Tuonela, The TONE POEM BY JEAN SIBELIUS, composed in 1895. It is the second of his *Four Legends* based on the exploits of the hero Lemminkäinen, as told in the Finnish national epic, the *Kalevala.* The music depicts a scene that Sibelius, in a note printed in an early edition of the score, described in these words: "Tuonela, the land of death, the Hades of Finnish mythology, is surrounded by a large river with black waters and rapid current, on which the singing Swan of Tuonela floats majestically." Sibelius's scoring is somber and dark—no flutes or trumpets are used, and of the clarinets, only the bass. The Swan, as it glides upon the black waters with the serenity of death, is represented by the English horn, which intones a haunting solo against the poignantly sustained harmonies of the muted strings. The score is a masterpiece of orchestral colorism, not of the brilliant, kaleidoscopic variety, but nocturnal—much like the canvases James McNeill Whistler painted in black and gray. In its austerity and darkness of tone it foreshadows Sibelius's last major symphonic scores, the Seventh Symphony and *Tapiola.*

RECOMMENDED RECORDINGS

KARAJAN AND BERLIN PHILHARMONIC (DG).

ORMANDY AND PHILADELPHIA ORCHESTRA (EMI).

Sweelinck, Jan Pieterszoon

(b. Deventer, May 1562; d. Amsterdam, October 16, 1621)

DUTCH COMPOSER, ORGANIST, AND TEACHER. He received his early musical training from his father, Pieter, who was organist for the Oude Kerk (Old Church) in Amsterdam. Sweelinck succeeded his father around 1577; upon his death the position passed to his son, Dirck Janszoon (1591–1652), also an excellent organist. Sweelinck was the preeminent composer and most influential keyboard artist of his day in the Netherlands. He was renowned as a teacher and referred to as a "maker of organists." Samuel Scheidt (1587–1654), one of the most important organist-composers of the following generation,was his student, and the influence of Sweelinck reaches even into the 18th century through Handel and J. S. Bach. From Sweelinck the composer, 254 vocal works survive, ranging from lighthearted secular settings to deeply felt sacred ones. He observed the traditional imitative practice of the Renaissance in most of his vocal writing. In his keyboard works he made the break toward a more modern idiom, with contrapuntal techniques that would become well established in Baroque instrumental music. His 72 known instrumental compositions, all for the organ or harpsichord, testify to a remarkably innovative genius. Among these influential works are fantasias, echo fantasias, toccatas, and variations. In the toccatas Sweelinck brought the elements of display to an unprecedented level of brilliance; the fantasias, worked out in countrapuntal style, foreshadow the keyboard fugues of the later 17th and early 18th centuries. Though he spent his entire life in or near Amsterdam, Sweelinck was greatly admired by the English virginalists (John Bull wrote a lament upon his death), and manuscripts of his works have been found in England, France, Germany, Italy, even Hungary. His contributions to the development of the fugue and the chorale variation were part of the foundation on which subsequent musical architects, including J. S. Bach, would build in the century following his death.

Sweelinck, engraving by Jan Muller, 1624

RECOMMENDED RECORDINGS

Cantiones Sacrae (2 vols.): Marlow and Cambridge Trinity College Choir (Hyperion).

Choral works (3 vols.): Christie, Koopman, Phillips; Van Nevel and Netherlands Chamber Choir (NM Classics).

Keyboard music (complete): Koopman (Philips).

Selected organ works: J. D. Christie (Naxos).

Symphonic Metamorphoses After Themes of Carl Maria von Weber *See Symphonische Metamorphosen nach Themen von Carl Maria von Weber.*

symphonic poem A freestanding orchestral work, usually in a single movement, based on a literary or descriptive program; the genre enjoyed great popularity between about 1850 and 1920. The antecedents to the symphonic poem can be found in the concert overtures of the early 19th century, particularly such works as Beethoven's *Coriolan* (1807) and Mendelssohn's *Hebrides* (1830–32)—the former a character study of the legendary Roman general doomed by his pride, the latter an attempt to portray a scene from nature. The term "symphonic poem" (*symphonische Dichtung*) was coined by Liszt, who wrote a dozen works in the form between 1848 and 1858, and added a thirteenth—*Von der Wiege bis zum Grabe* (*From the Cradle to the Grave*)—in 1883. The best known of his contributions are *Les préludes* (1848), *Prometheus* (1850), *Mazeppa* (1851), and *Hamlet* (1858). Liszt was mainly interested in portraying moods and states of mind in his symphonic poems, but many of those who followed found the challenge of conveying a detailed narrative or painting a dramatic scene more interesting. Smetana, who admired Liszt enormously, was quick to appropriate the genre for his own use; his *Má vlast* (1872–79) is a cycle of six symphonic poems touching on Bohemian legend. Though better known for his concert overtures, Dvořák also embraced the storytelling possibilities of the symphonic poem in four late works inspired by folk tales of K. J. Erben—*The Water Goblin, The Noonday Witch, The Golden Spinning Wheel,* and *The Wood Dove.* Sibelius found the symphonic poem perfectly suited to his visionary, myth-based musical style and remained interested in it throughout his career, from *En saga* (1892) and the four symphonic poems that make up the *Lemminkäinen* Suite (1895), through *Pohjola's Daughter* (1905–06), *Night Ride and Sunrise* (1908), *Luonnotar* (1913), and *The Oceanides* (1914), to *Tapiola* (1926), the latter a work of especially remarkable concentration that testifies to its composer's dazzling sonic imagination. Saint-Saëns was the first French composer to write symphonic poems, proving a highly competent musical illustrator in *Le rouet d'Omphale* (1871), *Phaëton* (1873), and *Danse macabre* (1874). Franck delved more deeply into the psychology of his subjects in *Les Éolides* (1875–76), *Le chasseur maudit* (1882), and *Psyché* (1887–88). The genre established itself fairly late in England, but in Bax found a particularly compelling advocate: His best works in the form, all wonderfully evocative, are *The Garden of Fand* (1913–16), *November Woods* (1917), and *Tintagel* (1917–19), arguably his masterpiece. Liszt's influence was particularly strong in Russia, where many composers were encouraged to try their hand at symphonic poetry. Most successful were Tchaikovsky, with *Francesca da Rimini* (1876), and Rachmaninov, whose *Isle of the Dead* (1909), inspired by Arnold Böcklin's painting, in some ways returns to the Lisztian ideal of portraying states of mind rather than a sequence of events.

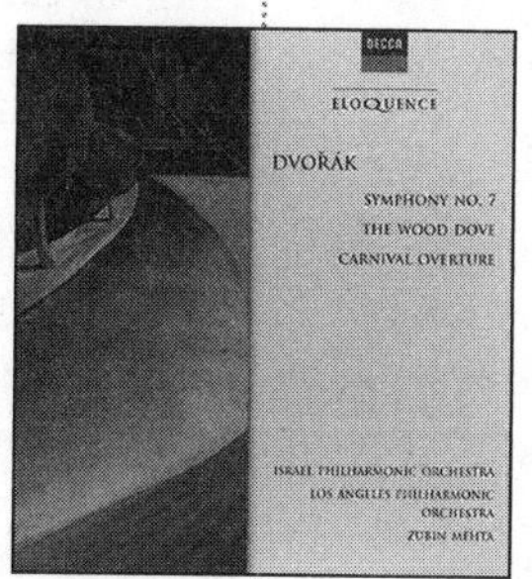

No composer, not even Liszt, made more important or impressive contributions to the development of the symphonic poem than Richard Strauss, the master tone painter of the orchestral literature. His love affair with the genre began with *Aus Italien* (1886) and culminated with the *Symphonia domestica* (1902–04) and *Eine Alpensinfonie* (1911–15)—vast descriptive canvases in which every bell and whistle (and thunder machine) of the orchestrator's art is put to use. The central works of his canon—*Don Juan* (1888–89), *Tod und Verklärung* (1888–89), *Till Eulenspiegel* (1894–95), *Also sprach Zarathustra* (1896), *Don Quixote* (1897), and *Ein Heldenleben* (1897–98)—are definitive of the genre.

Symphonie espagnole CONCERTO FOR VIOLIN AND ORCHESTRA IN FIVE MOVEMENTS BY **ÉDOUARD LALO, OP. 21,** composed in 1874 for the Spanish violinist Pablo de Sarasate and premiered by him in Paris at the Concerts Colonne on February 7, 1875. Lalo's colorful scoring, together with the melodic and rhythmic audacity of his material, lends the work a convincingly Spanish cast.

RECOMMENDED RECORDINGS

CHANG; DUTOIT AND ROYAL CONCERTGEBOUW ORCHESTRA (EMI).

ZUKERMAN; MEHTA AND LOS ANGELES PHILHARMONIC (SONY).

Symphonie fantastique (Fantastic Symphony) SYMPHONY IN FIVE MOVEMENTS BY **HECTOR BERLIOZ,** composed 1829–30 and premiered December 5, 1830, at the Paris

Conservatoire, François-Antoine Habeneck conducting. The work began to take shape in the composer's mind after he attended a performance of *Hamlet* at the Odéon in which the Irish-born actress Harriet Smithson performed the role of Ophelia. Berlioz was overwhelmed by her beauty and fell desperately in love. Seeking a release for his pent-up emotions, and hoping to attract her attention, he hit upon the idea of writing a "fantastic symphony" that took as its subject the experiences of a young musician in love. The detailed program, written by Berlioz himself and published prior to the work's premiere, shows that he conceived of his *Symphonie fantastique* as a romantically heightened self-portrait.

The *Symphonie fantastique* is one of the earliest and greatest programmatic works in the repertoire. It is also, in nearly every respect, a work of revolutionary originality. Berlioz's use of an IDÉE FIXE to unify the score was a significant innovation that would influence the works of Franz Liszt and, later on, the music of numerous Russian composers. Equally remarkable was his coruscatingly brilliant orchestration, which made groundbreaking use of multiple timpani, orchestral bells, an augmented brass section, and unusual effects such as COL LEGNO *battuto* bowing, in which the string players bounce the wood of their bows off the strings. Strange, wonderful, and extravagant, the *Symphonie fantastique* heralded a new era in orchestral music and established Berlioz as one of the seminal figures of Romanticism.

RECOMMENDED RECORDINGS

DAVIS AND CONCERTGEBOUW ORCHESTRA (PHILIPS).

MUNCH AND BOSTON SYMPHONY ORCHESTRA (RCA).

Symphonies of Wind Instruments COMPOSITION BY IGOR STRAVINSKY for 24 wind and brass instruments, composed 1918–20 and premiered at the Queen's Hall in London on June 10, 1921, under the direction of Serge Koussevitzky. Stravinsky was so disenchanted with early performances of the piece (including Koussevitzky's) that in 1924 he imposed a ban on its being conducted by anyone other than Ernest Ansermet and himself. The score—the last of a long line of compositions by Stravinsky in an identifiably Russian or nationalist idiom—incorporates an unusual symphonic structure in which nine distinct motivic units of varying length and character are "shuffled" with one another (some are heard twice, some as many as five times) to form a chain of episodes within a single movement.

RECOMMENDED RECORDING

CRAFT AND PHILHARMONIA ORCHESTRA (KOCH).

Symphonische Metamorphosen nach Themen von Carl Maria von Weber (Symphonic Metamorphosis After Themes of Carl Maria von Weber) ORCHESTRAL SHOWPIECE IN FOUR MOVEMENTS BY PAUL HINDEMITH, composed in 1943 and premiered January 24, 1944, by the New York Philharmonic under the direction of Artur Rodzinski. Hindemith found several of the themes he treats here in a volume containing Weber's original compositions and arrangements for piano duet, among them *Six petites pièces faciles,* Op. 3, composed in 1801, and *Huit pièces,* Op. 60, dating from 1818–19. The jaunty opening movement is based on the fourth piece in the latter group, while the powerful march-finale is derived from the seventh. In between comes a scherzo, the longest of the score's four movements, and a slightly melancholy Andantino spun out from the second of the *pièces faciles.* The scherzo is based on an overture Weber wrote for an adaptation by Friedrich von Schiller of Carlo Gozzi's *Turandot*—the same play on which Puccini's opera is based. Weber got its "Chinese" theme from Jean-Jacques Rousseau's *Dictionnaire de musique.* Rousseau, in turn, appropriated it from the writings of the 18th-century sinologist Father Jean-Baptiste du Halde. Hindemith's treatment of this thrice-derived material, climaxed by a brilliant fugato passage announced by the trombones, is virtuosic in the extreme.

RECOMMENDED RECORDINGS

BLOMSTEDT AND SAN FRANCISCO SYMPHONY ORCHESTRA (DECCA).

SZELL AND CLEVELAND ORCHESTRA (SONY).

symphony (from Lat. *symphonia,* "sounding together") A large-scale composition for orchestra, usually consisting of more than one movement, sometimes incorporating passages to be spoken or sung by soloists and/or chorus. As a genre the symphony was an outgrowth of several Italian orchestral genres of the Baroque—particularly the SINFONIA and the CONCERTO GROSSO—and of the chamber sonata as it existed in Italy and Germany at the end of the 17th century. Shaped by many hands during the course of the 18th century, most ably by Mozart and Haydn, it became the dominant orchestral format of the 19th century thanks to the impact of Beethoven's visionary essays.

The most popular early variety of symphony was the three-movement Italian symphony, basically a glorified opera overture with a fast-slow-fast arrangement of movements using short, binary forms. These works generated a fair degree of rhythmic excitement and featured striking orchestral effects. This format was gradually superseded, primarily in Austria and Germany, by a four-movement plan: an opening movement in lively tempo (usually Allegro) often preceded by a slow introduction; a lyrical slow movement; a minuet; and a brisk finale. Nearly always, the first movement was in SONATA FORM.

The orchestra of the Royal Academy of Music, rehearsing in Duke Hall, 1999

Often, the slow movement and finale were cast in sonata form as well. This was the type of symphony that took root in Mannheim, Vienna, and other centers and was perfected in the works of Mozart and Haydn. Departures from the four-movement model began with Beethoven's *Pastorale* and continued through the 19th century and into the 20th, yet the model remained operative in the works of Mahler, Nielsen, Sibelius, Shostakovich, Prokofiev, and Vaughan Williams, the most important symphonists of the past 100 years. The predominant aim of most 19th-century symphonies, strongly influenced by the example of Beethoven, was to create a dramatic trajectory; this effort was carried on during the 20th century by Mahler and Shostakovich, among others. Certain late-19th-century works, and many of the 20th century, pursued a different though not incompatible goal: to reflect upon material in a manner that achieved a sense of closure and organic coherence. Sibelius and Vaughan Williams tended to take this approach.

Beethoven had an enormous impact on the evolution of the symphony. His models were the late works of Mozart and Haydn, which, brilliant as they were, he surpassed in his *Eroica*. But far more important was the way Beethoven redefined the symphony as a genre, by fashioning works that made philosophical and even metaphysical statements—thus not only expanding the form of the symphony but transforming its character.

Every symphonist since Beethoven has had to contend with his achievement or consciously step back from it. Schubert at first had difficulty with the expansiveness of Beethoven's designs, possibly one of the reasons he abandoned his *Unfinished* Symphony; but in his Symphony No. 9 in C, D. 944 (1825–28), he found a solution, a way to approach Beethoven's scale and grandeur without imitating Beethoven's manner. Berlioz, one of the few Frenchmen of his day who understood *why* Beethoven was so great, also devised his own way of responding in the *Symphonie fantastique* (1830), which makes use of a detailed program and displays, for the time, an extraordinarily bold approach to orchestration. It was harder for Mendelssohn and Schumann, but the former's *Scottish* Symphony (No. 3 in A minor; 1842) is one of the most successful works in the genre, combining the absolute and the programmatic—conventional argument and deft pictorial imagery—in a remarkably effective way. Brahms felt the weight of Beethoven's greatness so acutely that it restrained him from coming forward with his First Symphony until he was 43, a middle-aged man by 19th-century standards, and older than Beethoven was when he finished the Eighth Symphony. Brahms cast his First Symphony in a Beethovenian mold, and then broke it. He was shrewd enough, and a sufficiently powerful thinker, to find new things to say in his remaining three essays. Bruckner, as Deryck Cooke has pointed out, took up the "metaphysical challenge" of Beethoven's Ninth in his own works, particularly his Fifth, Eighth, and Ninth Symphonies, setting the stage for Mahler and Shostakovich to do likewise in a way suited to the 20th century.

By the time Shostakovich finished his last symphony in 1971, the symphony as a genre had long since come to be questioned. Many composers felt that its possibilities had been exhausted, or, siding with Stravinsky, that they had to be radically reinterpreted. After an early effort while he was still a student, Stravinsky shied away from writing symphonies that smacked of the conventional and used the term for works that weren't symphonies; still, his *Symphony in C* (1938–40), a parody of the Classical style, and *Symphony in Three Movements* (1942–45) are outstanding. Most 20th-century composers who wrote numbered symphonies—the list includes Roussel, Martinů, Hanson, Piston, Sessions, Walton, Edmund Rubbra (1901–86), Honegger, Franz Schmidt (1874–1939), Karl Amadeus Hartmann (1905–63), Alan Hovhaness (1911–2000), Andrzej Panufnik (1914–91), George Rochberg (1918–2005), and Penderecki, as well as Vaughan Williams, Prokofiev, and Shostakovich—tended to be considered throwbacks. Yet in the symphonies of the two greatest Scandinavian composers of the 20th century, Sibelius and Nielsen, one hardly gets the feeling that one is treading water. Indeed, with Sibelius, for example in his Symphony No. 4 ◉, we see what is essentially a new approach to the entire notion of musical development, an approach that stresses the organic evolution of material during the course of a work.

Since the end of World War II several composers have contributed importantly to the quest for new symphonic directions, among them Dutilleux, Lutosławski, and Davies. That a whole galaxy of avant-garde figures wedded to serial and spectral techniques has done nothing should hardly be surprising. For the time being it is not fashionable to write symphonies. The production of orchestral music continues, but concertos—in which a soloist can carry part of the burden of convincing the audience—and pieces with suggestive names and fuzzy musical logic seem to be the current vehicles of choice. Few of today's composers possess the granitelike confidence Sibelius had to let their music speak for itself. *See also entries for individual works and composers.*

Symphony in Three Movements ORCHESTRAL WORK BY IGOR STRAVINSKY, composed 1942–45 and premiered January 24, 1946, by the New York Philharmonic with the composer conducting. While Stravinsky declared in his program note for the work's first performance that the symphony "has no program," he later confided that the music at various points in the score had been suggested to him by newsreel footage of Japan's invasion of Manchuria and of the German blitzkrieg in Europe, and that the whole feeling of the work was bound up with his emotional reactions to World War II. The first movement has the most direct link to these extramusical associations: It was, according to remarks later made by Stravinsky, "inspired by a war film" documenting the Japanese scorched-earth tactics in China. The middle part of the movement is especially closely related to a sequence that had made a strong impression on the composer, showing Chinese peasants scratching and digging in the fields. ◉ The symphony's gentle Andante was derived in large part from music Stravinsky had originally written for a film adaptation of Franz Werfel's *The Song of Bernadette,* a project he eventually abandoned (the scene in question depicts the apparition of the Virgin). Again in the symphony's finale, war is the backdrop: Stravinsky later claimed that the beginning of the movement was associated in his mind with images of goose-stepping soldiers, while the fugue that appears later on had a comic "immobility" he likened to the "overturned arrogance" of the Germans as their war machine ran out of gas. The exuberant, "rather too commercial" conclusion of the work on a bracing D-flat sixth chord, the composer said, was his way of cheering the success of the Allies. These things aside, the *Symphony in Three Movements* is one of the most gripping and effectively executed scores of the 20th century, a dynamic, tightly constructed work that deserves more frequent hearing.

RECOMMENDED RECORDINGS

CRAFT AND PHILHARMONIA ORCHESTRA (KOCH).

STRAVINSKY AND COLUMBIA SYMPHONY ORCHESTRA (SONY).

Symphony of Psalms WORK FOR MIXED CHORUS AND ORCHESTRA BY IGOR STRAVINSKY, composed in 1930 on a commission from Serge Koussevitzky and the Boston Symphony Orchestra to mark the 50th anniversary of the orchestra's founding. Due to a postponement of the Boston premiere, the first performance was given at the Palais des Beaux-Arts in Brussels, on December 13, 1930, by the Brussels Philharmonic Society conducted by Ernest Ansermet. The American premiere, conducted by Koussevitzky, followed on December 19, 1930, in Boston. For his texts, Stravinsky selected verses from Psalms 39 and 40 and the whole of Psalm 150, using the wording of the Vulgate. In his preface to the score, he specified that the words should always be sung in Latin, though he subsequently revealed that he had begun with a Russian text and later switched to Latin. According to Stravinsky, the whole work was penned "in a state of religious and musical ebullience."

Stylistically, the *Symphony of Psalms* represents a bridge between the ritualistic manner of *Oedipus rex* and the kineticism of the *Symphony in Three Movements.* Stravinsky's aim was to fashion an extended work that would permit elaborate contrapuntal development without necessarily conforming to any academic or historical convention. But to facilitate the process of writing contrapuntally, he did, in a sense, look back to the choral works of the Baroque: He established the chorus and orchestra as opposing groups and placed them on an equal footing. To better balance the two groups, and, perhaps, to lend a sense of gravity and austerity to the setting, he chose (some time after he had begun work on the score) to use a string section without violins and violas. And, most likely because of their warm timbre, he banished the clarinets from an otherwise large wind section. In the program accompanying the work's premiere, the three movements of the *Symphony of Psalms,* which are played without a break, were given the titles "Prélude," "Double Fugue," and "Allegro symphonique." Although these titles were later dropped, and do not appear in the score, they provide some insight into the way the work is constructed. The score, composed "to the glory of God," was dedicated to the Boston Symphony Orchestra.

RECOMMENDED RECORDING

STRAVINSKY AND CBC SYMPHONY ORCHESTRA AND CHORUS (SONY).

Symphony of a Thousand NICKNAME ATTACHED TO GUSTAV MAHLER'S SYMPHONY NO. 8 IN E-FLAT, composed during the summers of 1906 and 1907, and premiered September 12, 1910, in Munich, the composer conducting. The name was dreamed up prior to the symphony's premiere as a promotional slogan by Emil Gutmann, the impresario who produced the event. The actual number of performers involved was 1,029. The Eighth Symphony, Mahler's largest tonal edifice, is still the hardest of his symphonies to perform, as it requires an enormous orchestra, two-part mixed chorus, boys' choir, and eight vocal soloists. In essence, the score is a disquisition on love ascending from the immediate to the eternal. Its first movement is a huge setting of the hymn "Veni, Creator spiritus" by Hrbanus Maurus (776–856). Brilliant as this opening paean is, it is the finale—a setting of the last pages of Goethe's *Faust,* lasting the better part of an hour—that makes the symphony one of the pinnacles of the literature. While its line of action often appears to be episodic, if not sprawling—the critic Theodor W. Adorno famously skewered the composition as a "symbolische Riesenschwarte" ("symbolic monsterpiece")—the Eighth is sonically the richest and motivically the most thoroughly integrated of all Mahler's symphonies.

RECOMMENDED RECORDING

AUGER, HARPER, POPP, KOLLO, TALVELA, SHIRLEY-QUIRK, OTHERS; SOLTI AND CHICAGO SYMPHONY ORCHESTRA (DECCA).

Symphony of Sorrowful Songs (Symfonia piesni żałosnych) TITLE GIVEN BY HENRYK GÓRECKI TO HIS SYMPHONY NO. 3 for soprano and orchestra, composed during the final three months of 1976 and premiered in April 1977 by the Orchestra of the Southwest German Radio (Baden-Baden), with soloist Stefanie Woytowicz, under the direction of Ernest Bour. It became one of the most popular classical compositions of the 1990s, thanks to the runaway success of the Nonesuch recording featuring soprano Dawn Upshaw with the London Sinfonietta conducted by David Zinman. Released in 1992, the CD went to the top of the charts in England and in the U.S., selling hundreds of thousands of copies.

The work is in three nominally slow movements, all marked *Lento,* all archlike structures, all touching in some way on the figure of the Virgin Mary. The first movement, lasting the better part of half an hour, consists of a canon for strings (which builds up from two parts to eight parts and back down to two) flanking a setting of a 15th-century prayer known as the "Holy Cross Lament"—in essence, a *Stabat mater.* The second movement sets a prayer to Mary written on the wall of a Gestapo prison cell by an incarcerated 18-year-old Polish girl—her words echo those of the *Ave Maria.* The third movement is based on a folk song of the Opole region in southwest Poland in which a mother mourns the loss of her son—making it the musical equivalent of a pietà.

In his writing for the orchestra Górecki effectively creates a music of stasis with tremulous dissonances that hover like incense in the air; at the same time, he maintains a sense of urgency through the use of luminous and dark sonorities.

RECOMMENDED RECORDINGS

KILANOWICZ; WIT AND POLISH NATIONAL RADIO SYMPHONY ORCHESTRA (NAXOS).

UPSHAW; ZINMAN AND LONDON SINFONIETTA (NONESUCH).

syncopation (from Gr. *synkope,* "a cutting short") The regular shifting or displacement of a rhythm's normal accent from a strong beat to a weak one, or to a position between beats.

Szell, George

(b. Budapest, June 7, 1897; d. Cleveland, July 30, 1970)

HUNGARIAN/AMERICAN CONDUCTOR AND PIANIST. He grew up in Vienna, where his family moved when he was three. Precociously gifted, he studied piano with Richard Robert (whose students would include Clara Haskill and Rudolf Serkin) and took lessons in theory and composition from Eusebius Mandyczewski (a friend and colleague of Brahms) and, for a brief time, Max Reger. He made his debut as a pianist and composer with the Vienna Tonkünstler Orchestra in 1908. During 1909 and 1910, he made a ten-concert tour of Europe as a pianist. He made his conducting debut at the age of 17, with the Blüthner Orchestra in Berlin, appearing on the program as pianist and composer as well.

In time-honored fashion Szell then worked his way up the conducting ladder through a succession of opera-house positions: unpaid pianist-coach at the Berlin Court Opera under Richard Strauss (1915–17); first conductor in Strasbourg under Hans Pfitzner (1917–18); assistant conductor at the German Opera in Prague (1919–21), at Darmstadt (1921–22), and at Düsseldorf (1922–24); first conductor at the Berlin Staatsoper under Erich Kleiber (1924–29); and finally, chief conductor at the German Opera in Prague (1929–37), where he also got the opportunity to conduct concerts with the Czech Philharmonic. Szell made his American debut in 1930, with the Saint Louis Symphony Orchestra, and appeared for the first time with the Concertgebouw Orchestra of Amsterdam in 1936. Keeping several steps ahead of the Fascists, he held simultaneous appointments as conductor of the Scottish Orchestra in Glasgow and the Residentie-Orkest in The Hague (1937–39); during 1938 and 1939 he also was active as a conductor with the Australian Broadcasting Corporation.

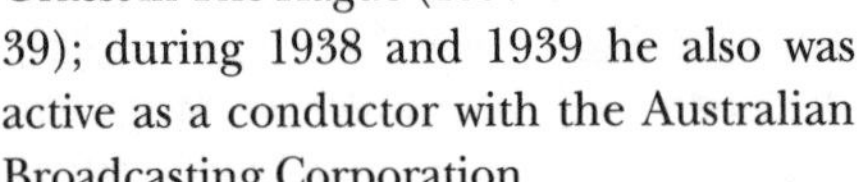

Szell settled in the United States in 1939. He spent a year teaching at the Mannes School in New York, and in 1941, at the invitation of Arturo Toscanini, made his New York debut with the NBC Symphony Orchestra; the following year he made his Metropolitan Opera debut conducting Richard Strauss's *Salome.* Between 1942 and 1946 he was a regular conductor at the Met and a guest conductor with the New York Philharmonic, Boston Symphony, Philadelphia Orchestra, and Cleveland Orchestra. In 1946 he was named music director of the Cleveland Orchestra and became a U.S. citizen.

For the rest of his life, apart from routine guest-conducting, Szell painstakingly cultivated the Cleveland Orchestra, turning it into one of the most magnificent ensembles in musical history. Placing rigorous emphasis on intonation, rhythmic precision, and balance—qualities one expects in chamber music—he established the virtuoso standard to which all major orchestras have subsequently had to aspire. The approach came naturally, for Szell was a superb chamber musician himself, noted for his collaborations with the Budapest String Quartet and violinist Joseph Szigeti. Ever the perfectionist, he had a prickly personality that frequently made others chafe.

Szell cut an impeccable figure on the podium, elegantly fitted out in his tails, shoes immaculately shined. He possessed a masterly baton technique, his gestures always under control, never showy. He knew how to phrase, if not always how to breathe, had the keenest of ears, and could draw on an astonishingly intimate knowledge of the techniques and limitations of orchestral instruments. He was a great Mozartean—his favorite turf was the piano concertos—and nearly as great in Haydn. His Beethoven was a masculine figure, portrayed in brilliantly chiseled, dry-eyed accounts of the symphonies and concertos, as virtuosic in their way (and as muscular) as Michelangelo's *David.* An outstanding interpreter of Schumann and Brahms, he was brilliant in the symphonic poems of Richard Strauss. In the works of Sibelius and Mahler that he conducted he was authoritative, though he had less affinity for Debussy and Ravel. Szell also conducted the music of many contemporaries, and was particularly noted for his accounts of orchestral works by Hindemith and Walton—he commissioned the latter's *Partita* for the 40th anniversary season of the Cleveland Orchestra, conducting its debut performance in 1958. Toward the end of his career he presided over the world premiere of Dutilleux's *Métaboles* (1965).

Szell's compositions, mostly youthful works, have long since fallen by the wayside, but his vibrant 1940 symphonic transcription of Smetana's String Quartet in E

George Szell

minor (*From My Life*), recorded by him with the Cleveland Orchestra, testifies to his skill as an orchestrator.

RECOMMENDED RECORDINGS

BEETHOVEN SYMPHONIES (COMPLETE): CLEVELAND ORCHESTRA (SONY).

BRAHMS, PIANO CONCERTO NO. 2: FLEISHER; CLEVELAND ORCHESTRA (SONY).

HINDEMITH, *SYMPHONISCHE METAMORPHOSEN NACH THEMEN VON CARL MARIA VON WEBER*: CLEVELAND ORCHESTRA (SONY).

MAHLER, SYMPHONY NO. 4: RASKIN; CLEVELAND ORCHESTRA (SONY).

MOZART, PIANO CONCERTOS NOS. 21 AND 24: CASADESUS; CLEVELAND ORCHESTRA (SONY).

SCHUMANN, SYMPHONIES NOS. 1–4: CLEVELAND ORCHESTRA (SONY).

SIBELIUS, SYMPHONY NO. 2: CONCERTGEBOUW ORCHESTRA (PHILIPS).

STRAUSS, *DON JUAN, TOD UND VERKLÄRUNG, TILL EULENSPIEGEL*: CLEVELAND ORCHESTRA (SONY).

WALTON, *PARTITA*: CLEVELAND ORCHESTRA (SONY).

Szeryng, Henryk

(b. Warsaw, September 22, 1918; d. Kassel, Germany, March 3, 1988)

POLISH/MEXICAN VIOLINIST. His performance of the Mendelssohn concerto at the age of nine convinced Bronisław Huberman to recommend that the family send the young prodigy to Berlin to study with Carl Flesch. He made his debut in Warsaw in 1933, playing the Beethoven Violin Concerto, with Bruno Walter conducting; debuts in Bucharest, Vienna, and Paris followed. In 1933, Szeryng moved to Paris to study composition with Nadia Boulanger. Fluent in several languages, he volunteered for the Polish army-in-exile in 1939 as a translator for General Sikorski, and during the war helped arrange for the emigration of 4,000 Polish refugees to Mexico. Szeryng ultimately settled in Mexico and in 1946 accepted a professorship at the University of Mexico, with the idea of investing himself in the cultural life of his adoptive country. This self-imposed artistic isolation came to an end in 1953 when Arthur Rubinstein played sonatas with him after a concert in Mexico City, and realized that a world-class violinist was languishing out of sight. Rubinstein called his agent, Sol Hurok, to make arrangements to present Szeryng to the musical world. The violinist returned with a vengeance, playing in New York in 1956 and quickly building an international career. During the 1960s and 1970s, he performed with most of the world's major orchestras and conductors, and was the dedicatee of new works by Chávez, Maderna, and Penderecki, among others.

Szeryng's many recordings testify to his extensive repertoire and authority in many styles. His recording of the Bach sonatas and partitas for unaccompanied violin won France's Grand Prix du Disque in 1954; he was also responsible for the modern revival of Paganini's Concerto No. 3 in E minor, thought to be lost, which he subsequently recorded. In addition to all the major violin concertos, he recorded the Mozart sonatas for piano and violin with Ingrid Haebler, and the Schubert piano trios with Rubinstein and cellist Pierre Fournier.

Szeryng's playing combined intelligence with considerable warmth and temperament. His tone was burnished, his technique irreproachable. If raw excitement was occasionally lacking in his performances, it was by conscious choice, to avoid anything that might detract from the elegant precision and steely strength that were the violinist's stock-in-trade.

RECOMMENDED RECORDINGS

BEETHOVEN, ROMANCES: HAITINK AND CONCERTGEBOUW ORCHESTRA (PHILIPS).

BRAHMS, VIOLIN CONCERTO: HAITINK AND ROYAL CONCERTGEBOUW ORCHESTRA (PHILIPS).

MOZART, SONATAS FOR VIOLIN AND PIANO: HAEBLER (PHILIPS).

PAGANINI, VIOLIN CONCERTO NO. 3: GIBSON AND LONDON SYMPHONY ORCHESTRA (PHILIPS).

Szymanowski, Karol

(b. Tymoszówka, Ukraine, October 6, 1882; d. Lausanne, March 29, 1937)

POLISH COMPOSER. The leading figure in Polish music during the first half of the 20th century, he suffered from depression and a dependence on nicotine and alcohol that undermined his health early on and led to numerous personal crises and professional setbacks. He nonetheless produced an impressive body of work that included masterpieces in a broad range of genres.

Szymanowski began his study of music in the Ukraine, moving to Warsaw in 1901 for private lessons in harmony and counterpoint. He underwent an early immersion in musical Teutonicism—his Concert Overture in E, composed 1904–05, sounds like a close cousin of Richard Strauss's *Don Juan,* complete with 32 cymbal crashes. Looking for a way to free himself from the

Karol Szymanowski

sound and aesthetics of German Romanticism, Szymanowski embraced the Impressionism of Debussy and Ravel and the intense expressionism and harmonic ambiguity of Scriabin. Simultaneously, as the result of a series of Mediterranean holidays, he developed a consuming interest in the cultures of antiquity, early Christendom, and Islam. The most fascinating byproduct of this mix of influences was his Symphony No. 3 (1914–16), subtitled *The Song of the Night.* A luxuriously prurient setting for tenor, chorus, and orchestra of an amorous stanza by the 13th-century Sufi mystic Jalal ad-Din ar-Rumi, *The Song of the Night*—its almost militant eroticism leaving Wagner and Scriabin far behind—was the last overripe fruit to fall from Szymanowski's tree. After a period of quiescence, he turned to folk music and adopted the leaner harmonic language of such 20th-century modernists as Stravinsky and Bartók. This later style, marking Szymanowski's emergence as a nationalist, is exemplified by his two ballet scores—*Mandragora* (1920; after Molière's *Le bourgeois gentilhomme*), and

Harnasie (1923–31), derived from a folk legend of the Tatra Mountains—and by his opera *Król Roger* (*King Roger*; 1920–24).

With his growing reputation it was perhaps inevitable that Szymanowski would be given an opportunity to reshape the musical institutions of the newly independent, post–World War I Poland. He served as director of the Warsaw Conservatory (1927–29) and as rector of its successor institute, the Warsaw Academy of Music (1930–32), but due to resistance from the establishment and his own shaky health, he was largely ineffective in both positions. Financially strapped and in need of a vehicle for his own concertizing, he composed the *Symphonie concertante,* Op. 60, for piano and orchestra (sometimes referred to as his Symphony No. 4), in 1932. His writing here and in his final orchestral work, the Violin Concerto No. 2 (1933), is bold, fresh, and unfettered, marking his closest approach to the later Bartók and Prokofiev.

In addition to his contributions to the symphonic and stage repertoire, Szymanowski composed more than a dozen sets of songs for voice and piano as well as a handful of chamber works, among which the best known are the three *Mity* (*Myths*), Op. 30 (1915), for violin and piano. He also created some superb music for solo piano—in particular, the Mazurkas, Opp. 50 and 62, the Etudes, Op. 33, and the cycles *Metopy* (*Metopes*; 1915) and *Maski* (*Masks*; 1915–16).

RECOMMENDED RECORDINGS

HARNASIE, MANDRAGORA, AND ETUDE FOR ORCHESTRA IN B-FLAT: STRYJA AND POLISH STATE PHILHARMONIC ORCHESTRA (NAXOS).

KING ROGER: HIOLSKI, OCHMAN, ZAGORZANKA, GRYCHNIK; STRYJA AND POLISH CHAMBER PHILHARMONIC (NAXOS).

ORCHESTRAL WORKS: SEMKOW, WIT, KASPRZYK AND POLISH NATIONAL RADIO SYMPHONY ORCHESTRA (EMI).

PIANO WORKS: ANDERSZEWSKI (VIRGIN CLASSICS).

SYMPHONIES NOS. 1–4: STRYJA AND POLISH STATE PHILHARMONIC ORCHESTRA (NAXOS).

T

tabarro, Il (The Cloak) **OPERA IN ONE ACT BY GIACOMO PUCCINI,** to a libretto by Giuseppe Adami (based on the play *La houppelande* by Didier Gold), composed 1915–16 and premiered December 14, 1918, at the Metropolitan Opera in New York as the first part of *IL TRITTICO,* with Claudia Muzio as Giorgetta. The action takes place on a barge in the Seine, and is driven by tensions in the relationship between the brooding, middle-aged barge owner, Michele, and his unhappy young wife, Giorgetta, who is carrying on an affair with a young stevedore, Luigi. The opera ends with a fatal altercation between Michele and Luigi, followed by a Grand Guignol moment in which Giorgetta, longing for a reconciliation with her husband, asks him to wrap her in his cloak: In response, he opens it wide to reveal Luigi's corpse. A masterfully drawn vignette in the verismo style, *Il tabarro* is one of Puccini's finest works. Its score achieves an extraordinary evocation of mood, using as one of its leitmotifs a melancholy chordal melody set over recurrent descending triplet figures representing the cheerless passage of the Seine.

RECOMMENDED RECORDING

GHEORGHIU, ALAGNA, SHICOFF, GUELFI; PAPPANO AND LONDON SYMPHONY ORCHESTRA (EMI).

table (Fr.) The wooden soundboard of the HARP, which ascends from the pedestal to the neck of the instrument at approximately a 45-degree angle, narrowing as it goes. The instruction *près de la table* means that the strings are to be plucked close to the soundboard, which produces a somewhat metallic, guitarlike tone.

table

Tabula Rasa **CONCERTINO FOR TWO VIOLINS, STRINGS, AND PREPARED PIANO BY ARVO PÄRT,** composed in 1977 for the violinist Gidon Kremer. The work, in two exquisitely slow sections, casts an unforgettable spell with the purity and fragility of its gestures. At the end of the piece's first section, Pärt employs one of his trademark techniques, "tintinnabulation"—the ringing of a single chord.

RECOMMENDED RECORDING

KREMER, GRIDENKO, TEPP; KREMER AND KREMERATA BALTICA (NONESUCH).

tacet (Lat., "[it] is silent") Direction to the performer of a vocal or instrumental part to be silent, usually for an entire number or movement.

Tafelmusik (Ger., "table music") [1] Generic term for music intended to accompany dining. An abundance of *Tafelmusik* was produced between the mid-16th century, when the term came into use, and the mid-18th, when it began to go out of fashion (the term, not the custom of dining with background music). During the latter part of the 18th century, elaborate collections of *Tafelmusik*—such as the three sets issued by Telemann in 1733—came to be supplanted by plain old suites and divertimentos, often featuring tunes from the latest operas played by a small ensemble of woodwind instruments. Mozart parodied this manifestation in the "supper scene" of *Don Giovanni,* where an onstage wind band plays excerpts from Martín y Soler's *Una cosa rara* (1786), Sarti's *Fra i due litiganti* (1782), and Mozart's own *Le nozze di Figaro* while Leporello serves and the Don dines. By the beginning of the 19th, the idea of writing music for people to listen to while eating was frowned upon by serious composers.

[2] **Canadian period instrument orchestra founded in 1979.** *See box on pages 310–13.*

RECOMMENDED RECORDINGS

Telemann, *Tafelmusik* (complete): Goebel and Musica Antiqua Köln (DG).

Telemann, *Tafelmusik* (complete): Orchestra of the Golden Age (Naxos).

Takemitsu, Toru

(b. Tokyo, October 8, 1930; d. Tokyo, February 20, 1996)

Japanese composer. Born at a time when Japan was starting to immerse itself in Western culture, he became fascinated by Western music at an early age. He remained largely self-taught, but throughout his career drew lovingly on the sonic explorations of Debussy and Messiaen as inspiration for his own. Beginning in 1948, Takemitsu studied composition informally under Yasuji Kiyose and Fumio Hayasaka, in whose memory he wrote his *Requiem* (1957) for string orchestra. In 1951 he helped found the Jikken Kobo (Experimental Workshop) to support the creation of mixed-media works. He wrote prolifically for film, creating more than 90 scores—his best-known efforts are *Woman in the Dunes* (1964), directed by Hiroshi Teshigahara, and *Ran* (1985), directed by Akira Kurosawa. Though he was sparing in his reliance on the traditional instruments of his country, he made striking use of the biwa and the shakuhachi in *Eclipse* (1966), and in *November Steps* (1967), which was commissioned for the 125th anniversary of the New York Philharmonic by Leonard Bernstein (Seiji Ozawa conducted the premiere).

In 1975 Takemitsu was invited to teach at Yale as a visiting professor, and in 1984 he was elected an honorary member of the American Academy and Institute of Arts and Letters. He died of cancer in 1996, leaving unfinished an opera, *La Madrugada* (*The Dawn*), commissioned by the Lyon National Opera for the fall of 1998.

Takemitsu thought of himself as a vessel through which inspiration flowed, and he referred to music as "a stream of sounds." The role of the composer was "to curve and shape them into the form of what we call music," he argued. His large and eclectic output reflects many influences and moods: not only the coloristic soundscapes of Debussy and Messiaen, but also the kind of sparseness found in Webern and the freewheeling techniques of John Cage. His instrumental combinations were original, his sensitivity as an orchestrator masterful.

RECOMMENDED RECORDINGS

Chamber and solo works for flute: Aitken and Toronto New Music Ensemble (Naxos).

***A Flock Descends into the Pentagonal Garden*: Tashi; Ozawa and Boston Symphony Orchestra (DG).**

***From Me Flows What You Call Time*: St. Clair and Pacific Symphony Orchestra (Sony).**

Tale of Tsar Saltan, The **Opera in a prologue and four acts by Nikolai Rimsky-Korsakov,** to a libretto by Vladimir Belsky (based on Aleksandr Pushkin's poem "The Tale of Tsar Saltan"), premiered in Moscow on November 3, 1900. Considered the most beautiful of Rimsky's operas, *The Tale of Tsar Saltan* was composed in honor of the Pushkin centenary; its score captures the wonder and magic of Pushkin's verse to perfection, while the fantastic imagery of the narrative is clothed in the spectacular colors only this greatest of Russian orchestrators could bring to it. The most famous excerpt from the opera is the entr'acte between the two scenes of Act III, known as "THE FLIGHT OF THE BUMBLEBEE." It depicts the aerial journey of Prince Guidon—the opera's hero and the son of Tsar Saltan—who has been transformed into a bumblebee so that he can fly across the ocean to visit his father's court unobserved. Because its rapid notes make it an ideal virtuoso showpiece, "The Flight of the Bumblebee" is frequently performed in solo arrangements.

***Costume design for* The Tale of Tsar Saltan**

RECOMMENDED RECORDINGS

SUITE:

ASHKENAZY AND PHILHARMONIA ORCHESTRA (DG).

BÁTIZ AND PHILHARMONIA ORCHESTRA (NAXOS).

Talich, Václav

(b. Kromeřěříž, Moravia, May 28, 1883; d. Beroun, March 16, 1961)

CZECH CONDUCTOR AND VIOLINIST. He began his study of the violin with his father, a music teacher and composer, and attended the Prague Conservatory—where he studied violin with Jan Marak and, later, Otakar Ševčik—until 1903. He served under Arthur Nikisch as concertmaster of the Berlin Philharmonic in 1903–04, and subsequently became concertmaster at the Odessa Opera and, in 1905, professor of violin in Tiflis. From 1908 to 1912 he was principal conductor of the Slovenian Philharmonic in Ljubljana, and in 1912 he was appointed chief conductor of the opera in Plzeň, where he worked for the next three years. During this period, Talich studied conducting with Nikisch and theory with Max Reger, both a short distance away in Leipzig. His growing reputation resulted in several invitations to guest-conduct the Czech Philharmonic; in 1918, on one of his visits, he led the premiere of Suk's tone poem *Zrani* (*Ripening*), to great acclaim. In 1919 Talich was named the orchestra's principal conductor, and over the next few years he turned it into an enviable ensemble, worthy of comparison with the best in Europe. While he was at it, he became the first Czech conductor to enjoy an international career, directing the Scottish Orchestra in Glasgow (1926–27) and the Stockholm Concert Society Orchestra (1926–36). In 1935 he took charge of the National Theater in Prague, serving until it was shut down by the Germans in 1944. Under considerable pressure throughout the German occupation during World War II, he gave up his responsibilities at the Philharmonic in 1941 and did his best to distance himself from the Nazis in his work at the National Theater. But the fact that he had remained active in Czech musical life made him a target of the Communists when they took over after the war. Effectively banished from Prague, Talich in 1949 founded the Slovak Philharmonic Orchestra in Bratislava. He returned to Prague in 1952, his reputation somewhat restored, and continued to be active until 1956, when failing health forced him off the podium; in these final years he made some of his greatest recordings.

More than anyone else, Talich was responsible for establishing the Czech Philharmonic as a world-class orchestra, and for cultivating its luminous string sound and the uniquely characterful playing style of its winds. Even during the years of his banishment, he was able to make recordings with the Philharmonic that show his remarkable sensitivity to color, his natural musicality, and his outstanding interpretive gift. He advanced the cause of Czech composers, too, acquitting himself magnificently in the music of Dvořák and Smetana, and championing Janáček (whose *Sinfonietta* he premiered in 1921), Vítězslav Novák (1870–1949), and Suk.

RECOMMENDED RECORDINGS

DVOŘÁK, CELLO CONCERTO: ROSTROPOVICH AND CZECH PHILHARMONIC (SUPRAPHON).

DVOŘÁK, *SLAVONIC DANCES*: CZECH PHILHARMONIC (SUPRAPHON).

JANÁČEK, *TARAS BULBA*; SUITE FROM *THE CUNNING LITTLE VIXEN* (WITH NOVÁK, *MORAVIAN-SLOVAK SUITE*): CZECH PHILHARMONIC (SUPRAPHON).

SUK, SYMPHONY IN C MINOR (*ASRAEL*; DVOŘÁK, *STABAT MATER*): CZECH PHILHARMONIC (SUPRAPHON).

Tallis, Thomas

(b. Kent, ca. 1505; d. Greenwich, November 20 or 23, 1585)

ENGLISH COMPOSER. Little is known about his youth and training; the earliest mention of his name is as an organist serving at the Benedictine priory of Dover in 1530–31. By 1537 he was in London, presumably working as the organist at the church of St. Mary-at-Hill. He subsequently served at Waltham Abbey in Essex and at Canterbury Cathedral, where he was employed as a singer in, and perhaps leader of, the cathedral's 22-voice choir. From his late 30s until his death he was a Gentleman of the Chapel Royal, a position he may have owed to a recommendation from Thomas Cranmer, then Archbishop of Canterbury and one of Henry VIII's most trusted advisers. His duties included playing the organ and rehearsing the men of the chapel choir. By the end of his career Tallis had served four monarchs; he died halfway through the reign of Elizabeth I.

Tallis remained a Catholic through the Elizabethan suppression of the church, serving his queen loyally in spite of it and being rewarded, in 1575, with a royal grant of letters patent—an exclusive license to print and publish music, which he shared with his younger colleague William Byrd. While the monopoly on music publishing did nothing to improve Tallis's finances, he was by then reasonably well off.

Even though it was rooted in the "old" style of Josquin, Tallis's music spoke with an unmistakably English accent in its harmonies and voicings; its spirituality and otherworldliness seem a carryover from the time of modes and plainchant. In works like the anthems and the astonishing 40-voice motet *Spem in alium*, Tallis showed remarkable ingenuity and craftsmanship. Ever innovative as a composer, he remained open to contemporary Italian influences and developed an increasingly fluent and accomplished technique. In his work, which covered a wide range of genres—from settings in Latin of the Mass and the *Lamentations of Jeremiah* to English anthems and settings for the English church service—he tended to convey a feeling of gentleness and poignancy, what some have described as a "penitential mood." This quality is echoed in his epitaph: "As he did live, so also did he die, / In mild and quiet sort (O happy man)." *See also box on pages 934–36.*

Thomas Tallis in an 18th-century engraving

RECOMMENDED RECORDINGS

COMPLETE ENGLISH ANTHEMS: PHILLIPS AND TALLIS SCHOLARS (GIMELL).

LAMENTATIONS OF JEREMIAH: PHILLIPS AND TALLIS SCHOLARS (GIMELL).

SPEM IN ALIUM: SUMMERLY AND OXFORD CAMERATA (NAXOS).

SPEM IN ALIUM (WITH OTHER MOTETS): PHILLIPS AND TALLIS SCHOLARS (GIMELL).

Tallis Scholars, The *See box on pages 934–36.*

Tamagno, Francesco

(b. Turin, December 28, 1850; d. Varese, August 31, 1905)

ITALIAN TENOR. The son of an innkeeper, he studied with Carlo Pedrotti at the Turin Conservatory and first sang in the chorus of the Teatro Regio in Turin. His high register was noted in an 1872 performance of *Poliuto* by Donizetti, when he delivered an effortless and commanding high B. His first major role was Riccardo in Verdi's *Un ballo in maschera,* undertaken in Palermo in 1874; his *Ernani* at Milan's La Scala in 1880 drew the attention of the composer. Though Verdi had misgivings about Tamagno's narrow musical background and lack of cultivation, he also recognized an intuitive stage animal with fearless acting instincts and a stentorian upper register.

In 1887 at La Scala, Verdi played his hunch: He chose Tamagno to create the demanding role of Otello, to which the tenor brought the requisite vocal steel. It was the high point of Tamagno's career. He repeated his success in London at the Lyceum Theater in 1889, the Metropolitan Opera in 1894, and Covent Garden in 1895, as well as in Buenos Aires, Madrid, Monte Carlo, and Moscow. Tamagno made a few recordings between 1903 and 1905, in the paleolithically primitive years of the medium. As a sideline, he was a passionate butterfly collector. He donated his vast collection to the city of Varese upon his death.

tambourine Percussion instrument of Middle Eastern origin. The standard tambourine has a single calfskin head about 10 inches in diameter that is stretched over a circular wooden shell. The shell has narrow openings in which pairs of thin brass discs called "jingles" are affixed to the frame by wires. The tambourine can be shaken or struck (with the knuckles, fingers, or base of the hand, or against the knee), and rolls can be produced by sliding a moistened thumb across the head. Precise rhythmic figures can easily be articulated using the fingers or a combination of strokes between hand and knee. The French name of the instrument, *tambour de Basque,* gives an indication of the context in which it is often used in orchestral music—to provide an element of Spanish, Moorish, or Mediterranean color: It is a fixture in works such as Rimsky-Korsakov's *Capriccio espagnol,* Ravel's *Rapsodie espagnole* ◉ and *Alborada del gracioso,* Falla's *El sombrero de tres picos,* and Tchaikovsky's *Swan Lake* and *The Nutcracker* (which has outstanding parts for the tambourine in its Act II divertissement). The tambourine imparts bacchanalian frenzy to Wagner's *Tannhäuser* Overture and more generalized flashiness to Dvořák's *Carnival* Overture and Prokofiev's Symphony No. 5. The

The **tambour de Basque** *goes native*

instrument plays a crucial role in Stravinsky's *Petrushka*: In a novel effect, the composer calls for it to be held close to the floor and dropped, to represent Petrushka falling and breaking his skull after the Moor has struck him with his saber.

tam-tam Percussion instrument derived from gongs of indefinite pitch that originated in China. It consists of a thickish disc of bronze with a rolled rim, which prevents the outer edge from vibrating. The disc is suspended in a frame and is struck with a stick covered with chamois or felt. Orchestral tam-tams come in two sizes: a large one measuring 28 inches in diameter and a small one about 20 inches in diameter. When struck forcibly, the tam-tam is the loudest instrument in the orchestra, a veritable sun capable of obliterating the sound of a hundred instruments in the glare of its distinctive noise. It can also be tremendously effective when played softly, producing a sound that is ominous and dreadful, e.g., the chilling single stroke that marks the climax of the final movement of Tchaikovsky's Symphony No. 6 in B minor. ◉ Tam-tam strokes lend a feeling of menace to the heaving sea in the third movement of Debussy's *La mer* and add an oriental flavor to "Laideronnette, Impératrice des Pagodes" in Ravel's *Ma mère l'oye*. In *The Rite of Spring*, Stravinsky calls for the tam-tam to be scraped with a triangle beater during "The Glorification of the Chosen One," which produces a sound like the dry scream of a low-flying jet. Other notable uses of the instrument can be found in Copland's *Fanfare for the Common Man*, Lutosławski's *Concerto for Orchestra*, and Rachmaninov's *Symphonic Dances*, where, following a *fortissimo* stroke in the final bar of the piece, the tam-tam is allowed to ring after the rest of the orchestra has fallen silent.

Tanglewood FESTIVAL BASED IN LENOX, MASSACHUSETTS, in the Berkshires, the summer home of the Boston Symphony Orchestra. It began with a series of concerts given by the New York Philharmonic in the summer of 1934. In 1936, the Boston Symphony was invited to give its first concerts in the Berkshires at Holmwood (an estate once belonging to the Vanderbilts), and in the winter of 1936 the Tappan family offered Tanglewood, its 210-acre estate, as a gift to the orchestra and its music director, Serge Koussevitzky. The first official Tanglewood concerts were given under a tent during the summer of 1937. The variable summer weather made the need for a more substantial structure rapidly apparent, and money was raised for the construction of a "music shed," which was inaugurated on August 4, 1938. The shed was improved in 1959 with the addition of a canopy over the orchestra, and in 1988 was renamed The Serge Koussevitzky Music Shed. In 1984, the BSO acquired the adjacent Highwood estate, enlarging the grounds by 40 percent and allowing for the construction of a new performance facility, Seiji Ozawa Hall, inaugurated in 1994.

In 1940, the educational arm of the festival, then called the Berkshire Music Center (now the Tanglewood Music Center), began its operations. Thanks to it, Tanglewood became a festival where American musicians—especially composers—could learn their craft. Leonard Bernstein was among the first to study there; among the luminaries who taught at Tanglewood in the early years were Aaron Copland and Paul Hindemith. For several generations now, the most promising young composers and top young orchestral players have flocked to Tanglewood to study with its faculty, one of the most distinguished in the country. Students have gone on to teach, establishing a tradition of enormous value that is joyously renewed each summer.

The Tanglewood Festival runs for eight weeks in July and August. Since it opened, it has been a place where people can hear world-class musicians play in gorgeous surroundings. Unlike many summer festivals that cater to a more casual audience, Tanglewood has always offered "serious" programs. Given its magnificent sylvan setting and the caliber, it is no wonder that it attracts more than 350,000 visitors each season.

Tannhäuser **"Grand Romantic opera" in three acts by Richard Wagner,** to his own libretto, composed 1843–45 and premiered October 19, 1845, at the Dresden Court Theater; for the Paris premiere, in 1861, Wagner made substantial revisions to the score, extending the overture to include a ballet interlude (with women's chorus), de rigueur for any work that hoped to please a Parisian audience. The opera's story is based on two legends that originally had no connection: In one, which had been treated satirically in a poem by Heinrich Heine, the medieval knight Tannhäuser tires of the affections of the goddess Venus and makes his way to Rome to seek the Pope's forgiveness for a life of ease and lust. In the other, updated by E. T. A. Hoffmann, the knight Heinrich von Ofterdingen receives demonic inspiration in a singing contest that takes place at the Wartburg. Wagner merged the characters of Heinrich and Tannhäuser and created the figure of Elisabeth to serve as a foil to Venus, representing the pole of spiritual love as Venus does that of physical love.

Tannhäuser, like the Flying Dutchman, is a doomed man who can be redeemed only by the self-sacrificing love of a woman. The trial of that love lies at the heart of *Tannhäuser,* where it is surrounded by the kind of spectacle one would expect in a work that still adheres to the conventions of grand opera. The opera's second act, which centers on the singing contest, opens with one of the finest set pieces in all of Wagner, Elisabeth's pulsating "Dich, teure Halle," and includes a classic grand-opera processional. The title part is extremely demanding, a challenge for any tenor. But the most beautiful (albeit conventional) number in the score is given to the gentle-hearted Wolfram von Eschenbach, whose hymn to the evening star, "O du, mein holder Abendstern," is one of the gems of the baritone repertoire.

RECOMMENDED RECORDINGS

Opera:

Domingo, Studer, Baltsa, Schmidt, Salminen; Sinopoli and Philharmonia (DG).

Overture and "Venusburg" music:

Walter and Columbia Symphony Orchestra (Sony).

Tapiola **Symphonic poem by Jean Sibelius, Op. 112,** commissioned by the New York Symphony Society and premiered December 26, 1926, in New York, Walter Damrosch conducting. Like many of his earlier works, *Tapiola,* the last of Sibelius's major scores, was inspired by material from the *Kalevala.* According to Finnish legend, Tapiola is the realm of the forest god, Tapio, whose mythical domain is described in lines that preface the score:

> Wide-spread they stand, the
> Northland's dusky forests,
> Ancient, mysterious, brooding savage
> dreams;
> Within them dwells the Forest's
> mighty God,
> And wood-sprites in the gloom
> weave magic secrets.

The stark, tightly confined melodic utterance in the strings with which *Tapiola* opens immediately establishes a "brooding" atmosphere and serves as the germinal motif of the entire work. Out of this cell, Sibelius develops a seamless symphonic argument of remarkable coherence and cumulative intensity. Midway through the piece, a searing climax pits wind, brass, and strings against each other in a chaotic confrontation. But the emotional zenith of the work is not reached until very near the end, as tremolando strings unleash a storm of near-hysterical violence. After an intense, unison lament by the massed strings, playing in their highest register, the work closes with a somber epilogue.

RECOMMENDED RECORDINGS

DAVIS AND LONDON SYMPHONY ORCHESTRA (RCA).

KARAJAN AND BERLIN PHILHARMONIC (DG).

tarantella Frenzied southern Italian dance in $\frac{3}{8}$ or $\frac{6}{8}$ time, named after the city of Taranto in Apulia. While an alternate theory of how the dance got its name—that its wild gyrations were thought to cure the bite of a tarantula—is more attractive, there is no solid evidence to support it. Nonetheless, the breathless pace of the dance and its tendency to jump between the major and the minor mode suggest the kind of feverish behavior one might expect from an encounter with *Lycosa tarantula* (which was also named after the city). The final movement of Mendelssohn's *Italian* Symphony (No. 4 in A major) incorporates a tarantella rhythm in one of its themes.

Tartini, Giuseppe

(b. Pirano, April 8, 1692; d. Padua, February 26, 1770)

ITALIAN VIOLINIST, COMPOSER, AND TEACHER. Though Tartini's family wished him to take holy orders, they allowed him to attend the University of Padua to study law. His real passions, however, were fencing and the violin, and he was extremely good at both. At the age of 18, he fell in love with Elisabetta Premazore and secretly married her. Forced to leave Padua, he sought refuge in Assisi, and was sheltered in a convent supervised by a priest he knew from Pirano. During the three years he spent hiding out, he practiced furiously, experimenting with the violin, bow, and string thicknesses; he was also able to work with the composer Bohuslav Cernohorský (1684–1742)—known as Il Padre Boemo, "the Bohemian priest"—who was organist at the basilica of Assisi.

By 1714 Tartini was once again at large, playing in various opera orchestras and continuing to refine his technique. In 1721 he was appointed *primo violino* in charge of all instrumental music at the Basilica of San Antonio in Padua, and in 1723 he was allowed to travel to Prague to participate in the musical activities accompanying the coronation of Emperor Charles VI as king of Bohemia. He remained in Prague for three years in the service of Count Kinsky. Suffering from the chilly climate, he returned to Padua in 1726, where he spent the rest of his life. In 1727 he opened an academy for violinists, which became famous throughout Europe. A tireless teacher, often instructing ten students a day, he exerted an enormous influence on the development of the Franco-Italian style that would dominate violin playing in the late 18th and early 19th century. His playing was characterized by a sweet and expressive tone, impeccable intonation,

Giuseppe Tartini

perfect bowing, and the discreet use of vibrato.

As a composer, Tartini lived through the mid-18th-century shift from the late Baroque to the *GALANT,* and was accomplished in both styles. His output consisted almost entirely of concertos and sonatas for the violin, and his reputation today rests primarily on his fiendishly difficult Sonata in G minor, known as the *Trillo del diavolo* (*Devil's Trill*). Inspiration for the piece came to him in a dream in which he sold his soul to the devil, whereupon his servant played the violin in the most extraordinary way, which he tried to recapture upon waking. Though fanciful, this account is in keeping with what we know of Tartini, who had a taste for mysticism, poetry, and romance, and whose thoughts on music often veered in a speculative direction.

RECOMMENDED RECORDINGS

VIOLIN CONCERTOS: WALLFISCH; KRAEMER AND RAGLAN BAROQUE PLAYERS (HYPERION).

VIOLIN SONATAS (INCLUDING *DEVIL'S TRILL*): MANZE (HARMONIA MUNDI).

Tauber, Richard

(b. Linz, May 16, 1891; d. London, January 8, 1948)

AUSTRIAN/BRITISH TENOR. A celebrated tenor of the 1920s and 1930s, especially remembered as a distinguished Mozart singer, he was one of the first artists to combine careers in both opera and operetta, maintaining artistic credibility in the former and elevating the artistic standards of the latter. He was a child of the theater figuratively and literally: His (unwed) parents were both professional actors. Tauber's father eventually sent him to the Hoch Conservatory in Frankfurt and later to Freiburg, where he studied with Carl Beines, who convinced Tauber that his voice was best suited to Mozart, not Wagner (Tauber's first love). Tauber made his debut in 1913 at Chemnitz, singing Tamino in *Die Zauberflöte* and Max in *Der Freischütz.* The director of the Dresden Opera heard him and immediately offered him a five-year contract. Because he readily acquired useful theatrical skills and was a remarkably quick study, Tauber was frequently called upon to substitute on short notice in unfamiliar, often difficult, roles. He became known as the "SOS tenor" and sang more than 60 roles. In 1922 he accepted a contract at the Vienna Staatsoper, which allowed him to conduct at the Volksoper and sing at the Berlin Staatsoper as well. In his prime, Tauber was considered the greatest Mozart tenor around—tasteful, stylish, flexible, and wonderfully musical—a distinct achievement in roles that pose vocal challenges without offering much in the way of dramatic opportunity.

Around 1925 Tauber began a long and happy collaboration with Franz Lehár. He became such a star that in every new Lehár operetta, there was a "Tauber song" specially tailored to the tenor's unique vocal gifts. Tauber himself tried his hand at composition and wrote three operettas, as well as songs and some film music. A fine actor, he appeared in several movies, and he became a prolific recording artist with some 730 sides to his credit; of his contemporaries, only John McCormack recorded more. But Tauber never received a penny in royalties for his many immensely popular operetta recordings, having negotiated only a straight fee.

Tauber started performing in England in 1931, singing in Lehár's *Das Land des Lächelns* at Drury Lane; in 1938 he made his Covent Garden debut in

Richard Tauber

Die Zauberflöte, with Thomas Beecham conducting. He married the English starlet Diana Napier in 1936. Because Tauber's father was half Jewish, the couple was forced to flee Austria in 1938 at the time of the Anschluss. They settled in London, and he became a British subject in 1940. Having left everything behind, Tauber spent the war years conducting and singing, mostly the lighter music for which he was so famous, in an effort to stabilize his finances. His last appearance was as Don Ottavio in *Don Giovanni* with the Vienna Staatsoper, on tour at Covent Garden in 1947. He sang the role to perfection; a week later, his left lung, ravaged by cancer, was removed. He died the following year, having established himself—along with McCormack and Caruso—among his era's most beloved tenors.

RECOMMENDED RECORDINGS

EXCERPTS:

LEHÁR, *DAS LAND DES LÄCHELNS, DER GRAF VON LUXEMBURG, DAS FÜSTENKIND*: LEHÁR AND ZURICH RADIO SYMPHONY ORCHESTRA (KOCH/SCHWANN).

LEHÁR, *DIE LUSTIGE WITWE*: REINING, NOVOTNÁ; LEHÁR AND VIENNA PHILHARMONIC (PREISER).

COLLECTIONS:

ARIAS AND DUETS (INCLUDING SELECTIONS FROM *MARTHA, CARMEN, TOSCA, IL TROVATORE, MIGNON*): LEHMANN, RETHBERG, VARIOUS SOLOISTS (PREISER).

ARIAS BY MOZART, WAGNER, TCHAIKOVSKY, VERDI, AND PUCCINI (PEARL).

Tavener, Sir John

(b. London, January 28, 1944)

ENGLISH COMPOSER. One of the most popular of contemporary composers, he has created a large body of vocal and instrumental works inspired by English poetry, English Renaissance choral music, and the contemplative spirituality of the Eastern Orthodox Church. By the time he entered Highgate School, Tavener was already a proficient pianist and organist. He subsequently studied at the Royal Academy of Music (where his teachers

Sir John Tavener in 1993

included Sir Lennox Berkeley), developing an accomplished technique as a composer. His early works include the cantata *The Whale* (1965–66)—its successful premiere in 1968 at the inaugural concert of the London Sinfonietta led to Tavener's getting a contract with Apple, the Beatles' record label—the *Celtic* Requiem (1969), and the opera *Thérèse* (1973–76), which deals with the crisis of conscience of the young nun St. Thérèse of Lisieux. At this point, Tavener started looking toward the Eastern church—the a cappella *Canticle of the Mother of God* (1976) and the chamber opera *A Gentle Spirit* (1977) show his developing orientation—and in 1977, at the age of 33, he converted to the Russian wing of the Orthodox Church. His music began to assume a more austere, transcendental, and mystical quality, hewing to simpler structures and textures with no loss of emotional intensity. Since finding his voice as a composer—a voice at once meditative, rapturous, and incantatory—Tavener has become one of the most celebrated and productive figures on the English musical scene. His best-known work, *The Protecting Veil* (1987), for cello and string orchestra, has been recorded half a dozen times to date. Several other works have achieved notable popularity, including his *Akathist of Thanksgiving* (1988), *Song for Athene* (1993)—performed at the funeral of Princess Diana—and *Eternity's Sunrise* (1997), composed for soprano and 18th-century instrumental ensemble, with a text drawn from two poems of William Blake.

Tavener's music eschews the conventional concept of "development" in favor of a rhapsodic unfurling of ideas and their cyclical return—a treatment emblematic of the kind of spiritual development the composer seems interested in. Tavener's music has an extraordinary lyricism, a true vocal quality, and great beauty of texture and color. Above all, it is music that seems to be suffused with light—not bad for a composer whose enterprise has been described as the creation of icons in sound. Tavener was knighted in 2000.

RECOMMENDED RECORDINGS

Akathist of Thanksgiving: Bowman, Wilson; Neary and BBC Symphony Orchestra (Sony).

Eternity's Sunrise: Rozario; Goodwin and Academy of Ancient Music (harmonia mundi).

The Protecting Veil: Isserlis; Rozhdestvensky and London Symphony Orchestra (Virgin Classics).

The Protecting Veil: Kliegel; Yuasa and Ulster Orchestra (Naxos).

Taverner, John

(b. South Lincolnshire, ca. 1490; d. Boston, October 18, 1545)

English composer. He is first mentioned in 1524 in the archives of the collegiate church at Tattershall, Lincolnshire, as a member of the choir. In 1526 he moved to Oxford to serve as first instructor of the choristers at Cardinal College, founded by Henry VIII's chief adviser, Cardinal Wolsey. In 1530, following Wolsey's fall from power, Taverner returned to Lincolnshire to work as a singer at the church of St. Botolph in Boston, which supported a choir of substantial size and probably paid him handsomely. Indeed, Taverner was well enough off that when spending on the church's choir was curtailed in the mid-1530s, he was able to retire and live comfortably. Toward the end of his life he served as one of Boston's 12 town aldermen.

It is likely that most of Taverner's church music—mainly settings of the Mass and the Magnificat, large-scale votive antiphons, and shorter liturgical pieces—was composed during 1520–30, when elaborate polyphonic settings of the liturgy still had a prominent place in the English church. Taverner wrote masses in six, five, and four voices; of these the most splendid are the six-voice *Missa Corona spinea* and *Missa Gloria tibi Trinitas*, and the four-voice *The Western Wind*, based on a secular tune.

RECOMMENDED RECORDINGS

Missa Corona Spinea, Gloria tibi Trinitas, The Western Wind: Christophers and The Sixteen (Hyperion).

Missa Gloria tibi Trinitas, The Western Wind: Phillips and Tallis Scholars (Gimell).

Taverner Consort, Choir, and Players *See box on pages 310–13.*

Tchaikovsky, Pyotr Il'yich

(b. Votkinsk, May 7, 1840; d. St. Petersburg, November 6, 1893)

Russian composer. He was the most accomplished and professional Russian composer of the 19th century: conservatory trained, literate, astutely critical of his own work and others', and highly disciplined. His music, always popular with audiences and rightly valued by musicians such as Rachmaninov, Stravinsky, and Shostakovich, is no longer subject to the critical disparagement it suffered at times during the 20th century, when it was dismissed by some as maudlin or hysterical, by others as irrelevant or merely pretty.

The son of a mining engineer, Tchaikovsky had a sheltered childhood, and his preternaturally sensitive nature and talent for self-expression were apparent early on; music would remain in the background, however, until he was in his 20s. In 1852 he was sent to board at the School of Jurisprudence in St. Petersburg, from which he graduated in 1859. He spent a couple of years in the tsarist ministry of justice, and in 1861, still working at the ministry, he signed up for a theory class at the Russian Musical Society. In 1862 he entered the newly opened St. Petersburg Conservatory, where he studied with Anton Rubinstein. In September of 1865, shortly after his graduation, he was offered a teaching post at the Moscow Conservatory by Nikolay Rubinstein, Anton's brother. He moved to Moscow in January 1866 and took up his duties as an instructor of music theory when the conservatory opened the following September.

Pyotr Il'yich Tchaikovsky as a young man

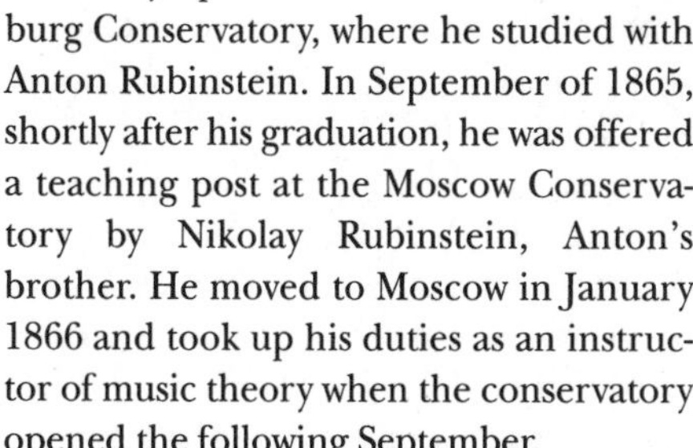

Despite his teaching obligations and a less than optimal domestic situation (for the first five years he boarded with Rubinstein), Tchaikovsky composed prolifically over the next decade, penning, among other works, his first three symphonies, several tone poems, the *Romeo and Juliet* Fantasy Overture, the Piano Concerto in B-flat minor, three operas, and two string quartets. In the summer of 1876 he traveled to Bayreuth to attend the first performances of Wagner's *Ring* cycle. The following year brought tumultuous changes in Tchaikovsky's life. In December 1876 came the unforeseen appearance of a benefactress—the elusive Nadezhda von Meck, widow of a railroad baron—who was to provide much-needed encouragement, financial and emotional support, and above all an outlet for Tchaikovsky's communicative urge. In July 1877, swayed from his better judgment by thoughts of Aleksandr Pushkin's fatally cold-hearted hero Eugene Onegin (soon to be the subject of an opera), the homosexual Tchaikovsky married Antonina Milyukova. The marriage proved to be disastrous and short-lived. By the end of September, the composer had made a halfhearted attempt at suicide and suffered a complete nervous breakdown. His younger brother Anatoly arranged a quick separation, then hustled Tchaikovsky out of the country, in the hope that he could work in peace and recover his sanity.

During the months that followed, Tchaikovsky visited Paris and Vienna and traveled widely in Italy. He completed his Fourth Symphony and the opera *Eugene Onegin*, and he learned that Mme von Meck was willing to provide him with an annual stipend of 6,000 rubles. Out of respect for her wishes Tchaikovsky never met his mysterious patroness, but during the 14 years of their curious, arm's-length relationship, carried on entirely by correspondence, they were often in close proximity. In 1878, during a joint but separate sojourn in Florence, he noted that she stopped in front of his villa every morning to try to catch a glimpse of him. "How should I behave?" he wrote his brother. "Should I go to the window and bow?"

The stipend from Mme von Meck brought Tchaikovsky a measure of financial independence and allowed him to leave his job at the conservatory. The epistolatory relationship that went with it provided him with a sounding board. He nonetheless would always struggle to recapture his emotional equilibrium. Free to travel, he wandered in Russia and through much of Europe for six years. Realizing that he needed to put down roots, he settled in Klin, about 60 miles northwest of Moscow, in 1885. There he would live for the rest of his life, composing according to a rigorous daily routine, with frequent breaks for travel: Italy in 1890; the United States in 1891 for a tour of the East Coast and the opening of Carnegie Hall, at which he conducted; England in 1893, to receive an honorary doctorate from Cambridge. Stability, of a sort, returned in his final years, enabling him to compose several works of towering greatness—including the ballet *The Sleeping Beauty* (1889), the opera *The Queen of Spades* (1890), and the *Pathétique* Symphony (1893)—in blazingly concentrated bursts of creativity.

Tchaikovsky around the age of 50

Tchaikovsky's death so soon after the premiere of the latter work was long believed to have been caused by cholera, but suicide cannot be ruled out. Theories abound as to why the composer might have chosen to end his own life, including one that Tchaikovsky took poison after being confronted by his old schoolmates from the School of Jurisprudence with a letter that would have exposed him as a homosexual. The true circumstances of his death may never be known.

At the very outset of his career, Tchaikovsky learned to sketch and score his works quickly, to polish and revise those that did not initially satisfy him (in the case of Symphonies Nos. 1 and 2 and *Romeo and Juliet*, several times), and to resist the temptation to rush a score to completion. He composed numerous solo piano pieces, a small number of chamber works, and more than 100 songs, many of them quite lovely. But it was in the larger forms that he excelled. Here his output was evenly balanced between works for the stage—operas and ballets—and symphonic ones, the orchestra being the common denominator. Unlike many of his colleagues, who practiced orchestration as if it were a sartorial exercise, Tchaikovsky thought directly in terms of orchestral color. His resourcefulness in the use of instruments was unsurpassed, but for him it was the orchestra itself, not individual instruments, that had a sound—which is why all of his orchestral scores have a lustrous sonority that can be immediately identified as "Tchaikovskian."

Like Mozart, whose music he admired, Tchaikovsky responded eagerly to the challenge of characterization in his stage music. Of his ten operas, the ones now most likely to be encountered are *Eugene Onegin* (1879), *The Maid of Orleans* (1881, derived from Schiller), *Mazeppa* (1884), and *The Queen of Spades*. *Eugene Onegin* and *The Queen of Spades*, both based on Pushkin, summoned music of extraordinary richness and vitality from the composer and have become standard repertoire works outside Russia. Their central characters—the one (Onegin) fatalistic and disdainful, the other (Hermann) feverishly obsessed with winning at cards—resonated powerfully with Tchaikovsky, in part, no doubt, because both spurn love when it is offered. The composer can hardly be blamed for turning Pushkin's cynical detachment from those characters into something much more emotionally involving.

Among the most beautiful of all Tchaikovsky's works are his three ballets, *Swan Lake* (1877), *The Sleeping Beauty*, and *The Nutcracker* (1892), which inhabit a fairy-tale world, albeit one with a dark side. Thanks to his extraordinary skill as an orchestrator, Tchaikovsky was able to evoke a specific atmosphere in each and draw listeners into the enchanted stories. But while the plots are fanciful, the emotions touched on in the music are profoundly human. By transforming the role of music in the ballet from a grand decorative gesture into an essential component of the drama on the stage—first in *Swan Lake* and to an even greater extent in *The Sleeping Beauty*—Tchaikovsky revolutionized the art of composing for the dance.

As a symphonist Tchaikovsky enriched the repertoire and exerted a vital influence on later composers as diverse as Sibelius, Prokofiev, and Shostakovich. Of his first three symphonies, all accomplished exercises, the second (known as the *Little Russian*) has had the greatest success, mainly because of its rip-roaring finale and memorable melodic material. But it was only when he set to work on his Symphony No. 4 in F minor (1877) that Tchaikovsky discovered—in the expression of heated emotion—the key to both melodic inspiration and mastery of form, and as a consequence found his voice as a symphonic composer. His technique had become noticeably more assured by the time he penned the programmatic *Manfred* Symphony (1886), even if his ideas weren't quite so striking. His final two works in the form, with interior programs known only to the composer, are notably dark. The funereal opening, wide swings of mood, and feverish—though, in the end, implausibly festive—climax of the Fifth Symphony (1888) convey a psychological drama that could hardly be put into words in any case. With the *Pathétique* (Symphony No. 6 in B minor), Tchaikovsky went much deeper, fashioning a symphony of the most profound personal confession, as original in method and formal concept as it was in tone and emotional content. The English musicologist David Brown has rightly characterized it as "the most truly original symphony to have been composed in the seventy years since Beethoven's Ninth."

Tchaikovsky was like Racine's Phèdre, desperately trying throughout his adult life to hide from the light of day the dark flame of passion—in his case, a passion for young men. That he was troubled by and ashamed of his sexuality to the depths of his soul, in a way we can scarcely imagine today, has been well documented. Deeply religious, he viewed it as a sickness: To say otherwise would be to graft a late-20th-century attitude onto his preternaturally sensitive 19th-century character. What he dreaded more than anything was public exposure.

Mikhail Baryshnikov in* The Nutcracker; *American Ballet Theater

Music was Tchaikovsky's salvation. He saw the expression of emotion as the central concern of his art and found in the act of composition the freedom to emote, and the means to control emotion, that he sorely missed in his personal life. It is true that not all of his music is top-drawer; some of his scores appear to be formally awkward or short on content, and sometimes the process of argument seems feeble. But the best of his music is supremely accomplished, undeniably moving, and more than occasionally transcendent.

RECOMMENDED RECORDINGS

Eugene Onegin: Kubiak, Weikl, Burrows, Ghiaurov; Solti and Royal Opera Orchestra (Decca).

Festival Overture 1812: Dorati and Minneapolis Symphony Orchestra (Mercury).

Festival Overture 1812: Solti and Chicago Symphony Orchestra (Decca).

Manfred Symphony: Pletnev and Russian National Orchestra (DG).

Piano Concerto No. 1: Cliburn; Kondrashin and RCA Symphony Orchestra (RCA).

Piano Concerto No. 1: Gilels; Reiner and Chicago Symphony Orchestra (RCA).

The Queen of Spades: Gougaloff, Vishnevskaya, Resnik, Schwarz, Weikl, Petkov, Popp; Rostropovich and L'Orchestre National de France (DG).

Romeo and Juliet (Fantasy Overture): Karajan and Vienna Philharmonic (Decca).

Serenade for Strings: Karajan and Berlin Philharmonic (DG).

The Sleeping Beauty (complete): Pletnev and Russian National Orchestra (DG).

Swan Lake, The Sleeping Beauty, The Nutcracker (suites): Rostropovich and Berlin Philharmonic (DG).

Symphonies (complete): Karajan and Berlin Philharmonic (DG).

Symphonies Nos. 4–6: Mravinsky and Leningrad Philharmonic (DG).

Violin Concerto: Milstein; Abbado and Vienna Philharmonic (DG).

Teatro alla Scala Opera house designed by Giuseppe Piermarini and built in 1778 on the site of the demolished church of Santa Maria della Scala, in the heart of Milan. In the past two centuries the venerable theater—which Stendhal used to say made a trip to Italy worth the trouble—has come to occupy a place at the heart of Italian opera as well. La Scala opened August 3, 1778, with a performance of *L'Europa riconosciuta* by Antonio Salieri, an opera written for the occasion. (Gluck had been invited to provide the opening opera, but refused.) The land for the theater was given by Maria Theresa, the Austrian empress, and construction was underwritten by Milan's first families, who reserved ownership of the boxes for themselves. Set in the Piazza della Scala, facing a statue not of Verdi or Bellini but of Leonardo da Vinci, La Scala is particularly famous for its horseshoe-shaped auditorium, in which six golden tiers rise above the parterre. In 1807 the stage was enlarged; two side wings were added in 1830. Gas lights were installed in 1860, electric lighting in 1883. An orchestra pit was installed in 1907 and the stage was modernized in 1921. The theater was transformed from a municipal department to a foundation in 1997; it runs on a $100 million annual budget, 45 percent of which is supplied by the city of Milan.

Thanks mainly to La Scala, Milan became the center of Italian musical life in the 19th century, as Venice had been in the 17th century and Rome and Naples in the 18th. Among the works that have been premiered there are Bellini's *Il pirata* (1827) and *Norma* (1831), and Verdi's *Oberto* (1839), *Nabucco* (1842), and *I Lombardi* (1843), the final version of *La forza del destino* (1869), the revised *Simon Boccanegra* (1881), and, most important, *Otello* (1887) and *Falstaff* (1893). La Scala has also been the point of introduction to Italy of numerous operas by foreign composers; among its most important nights have been the Italian premieres of works by Wagner, Richard Strauss, Tchaikovsky, Mussorgsky, and Debussy.

Arturo Toscanini was active as a conductor at La Scala from 1898, serving as artistic director from 1921 to 1929. The house, damaged by Allied bombing on the night of August 16, 1943, was rebuilt immediately after the end of World War II. Toscanini, absent for 16 years, was invited to conduct the gala reopening concert on May 11, 1946, which featured works by Rossini, Verdi, Boito, and Puccini. The list of conductors who have served as music director at La Scala includes, in addition to Toscanini, Herbert von Karajan, Victor de Sabata, Claudio Abbado, and Riccardo Muti, who held the post from 1986 to 2005. Every great singer of Italian opera from Maria Malibran to the present has sung there.

The opera season at La Scala traditionally opens on December 7, the feast day of St. Ambrose, Milan's patron saint. On December 31, 2001, the house was closed for a $75 million renovation. It reopened on schedule, on December 7, 2004, with a gala performance conducted by Muti of the same work with which La Scala originally opened, Salieri's *L'Europa riconosciuta.*

Teatro alla Scala

RECOMMENDED RECORDINGS

MASCAGNI, *CAVALLERIA RUSTICANA*; LEONCAVALLO, *PAGLIACCI*: BERGONZI, TADDEI, COSSOTTO, ALLEGRI; KARAJAN (DG).

PUCCINI, *TOSCA*: CALLAS, DI STEFANO, GOBBI; DE SABATA (EMI).

VERDI, *SIMON BOCCANEGRA*: CAPPUCCILLI, FRENI, CARRERAS, GHIAUROV, VAN DAM; ABBADO (DG).

Tebaldi, Renata

(b. Pesaro, February 1, 1922; d. Republic of San Marino, December 19, 2004)

ITALIAN SOPRANO. At the height of her career her only rival was Maria Callas, and even then she had a large part of the repertoire to herself. Stricken with polio when she was three, and unable to participate in the usual outdoor activities, she became interested in music. From 1939 she studied at the Conservatory of Parma, and in 1944 in Rovigo she made her debut, as Helen of Troy in Boito's *Mefistofele.* She auditioned for Arturo Toscanini in 1946 and sang under his baton in the gala concert that reopened La Scala on May 11 of that year; she returned during the 1946–47 season to sing the role of Mimì in Puccini's *La bohème,* and performed frequently at La Scala from 1949 to 1954. In 1950 she made her London debut, singing with the La Scala company at Covent Garden, and her American debut, as Aida in San Francisco. In her Metropolitan Opera debut, on January 31, 1955, she sang the role of Desdemona in Verdi's *Otello* opposite Mario del Monaco. Between 1955 and 1973 she appeared in 267 performances at the Met, most frequently as Mimì, Desdemona, Tosca, Violetta in Verdi's *La traviata,* Maddalena in Giordano's *Andrea Chénier,* and as the heroines in Cilea's *Adriana Lecouvreur,* Ponchielli's *La gioconda,* and Puccini's *Tosca.* Her last new role at the Met was Minnie in Puccini's *La fanciulla del West,* which she sang in 1970, and she went out as she had come in—as Desdemona, in a farewell performance of *Otello* on January 8, 1973. Over the next few years she made a few concert appearances, before taking her leave with a 1976 concert at La Scala.

Tebaldi's repertoire included some Mozart and Rossini, even rarities by Spontini, but it centered on Verdi, Puccini, and such specialty roles as Maddalena, Adriana Lecouvreur, and the title role in *La Wally* by Alfredo Catalani (1854–93). Her voice, a classic *lirico spinto,* was one of the loveliest of the 20th century, an instrument of ravishing beauty and vibrant color—rich, pure, and golden-toned—that she used with magnificent artistry.

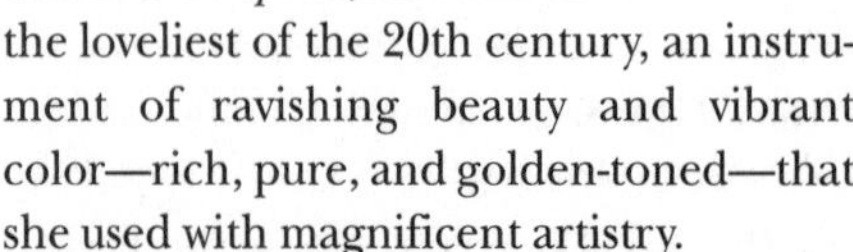

Renata Tebaldi as Tosca

RECOMMENDED RECORDINGS

PUCCINI, *LA FANCIULLA DEL WEST*; DEL MONACO, MACNEIL; CAPUANA AND ORCHESTRA DELL' ACCADEMIA DI SANTA CECILIA (DECCA).

PUCCINI, *TURANDOT*: NILSSON, BJÖRLING, TOZZI; LEINSDORF AND ROME OPERA ORCHESTRA (RCA).

VERDI, *AIDA*: BERGONZI, SIMIONATO, MACNEIL; KARAJAN AND VIENNA PHILHARMONIC (DECCA).

Te Deum A song of praise to God sung at the conclusion of Matins on Sundays and feast days, and as a hymn of thanksgiving at the consecration of a bishop or after a military victory. The Latin text, which dates from the early Middle Ages, borrows phraseology from the Mass and the Psalms; its plainchant melody was fixed at an early date and remained substantially unchanged thereafter. Polyphonic settings of the text began to appear in the 14th century but were relatively rare until the 16th century. The Baroque brought an upsurge of interest in the Te Deum as a text for festive occasions, and numerous settings date from the 18th century, among them two by Haydn (1765 and 1800) and several by Handel—of which the best known are his *Utrecht* Te Deum (1713), written in honor of the Peace of Utrecht, and the *Dettingen* Te Deum (1743), celebrating the English victory at Dettingen. Important settings of the 19th and 20th centuries include those by Berlioz (1849), Bruckner (1885), Dvořák (1896), Verdi (1897), and Walton (1953, written for the coronation of Elizabeth II). Also noteworthy is Puccini's inclusion of a Te Deum in his opera *Tosca* (1900), where it forms the grand conclusion to Act I.

RECOMMENDED RECORDINGS

BERLIOZ: DAVIS AND LONDON SYMPHONY ORCHESTRA (PHILIPS).

BRUCKNER: JOCHUM AND BERLIN PHILHARMONIC (DG).

HANDEL, *DETTINGEN* TE DEUM: PINNOCK AND ENGLISH CONCERT (ARCHIV).

Te Kanawa, Dame Kiri

(b. Gisborne, New Zealand, March 6, 1944)

BRITISH SOPRANO. The adopted daughter of a Maori father and an Irish mother, she left New Zealand in 1965, already a rising star, to study at the London Opera Centre, where she was accepted without an audition. She made a sensational debut in 1971 at Covent Garden as the Countess in Mozart's *Le nozze di Figaro* and debuted in 1974 at the Metropolitan Opera as Desdemona in Verdi's *Otello,* replacing an indisposed Teresa Stratas. Other roles closely associated with Te Kanawa are Mozart's Pamina, Fiordiligi, and Donna Elvira, Elizabeth of Valois in Verdi's *Don Carlo,* and Amelia in Verdi's *Simon Boccanegra.* Of Richard Strauss's magnificent soprano roles, she has sung the Countess in *Capriccio,* the title role in *Arabella,* and the Marschallin in *Der Rosenkavalier.* Te Kanawa sang to her largest audience (estimated at 600 million people) when she performed Handel's "Let the Bright Seraphim" at the wedding of Lady Diana Spencer to Charles, Prince of Wales, in Westminster Cathedral in 1981. In 1982 she was created a Dame of the British Empire by Queen Elizabeth II. Te Kanawa is one of the few classical singers who have made successful crossover recordings of show music, a genre she has sung with real style and affection from the very beginning of her career in London's West End.

Dame Kiri Te Kanawa

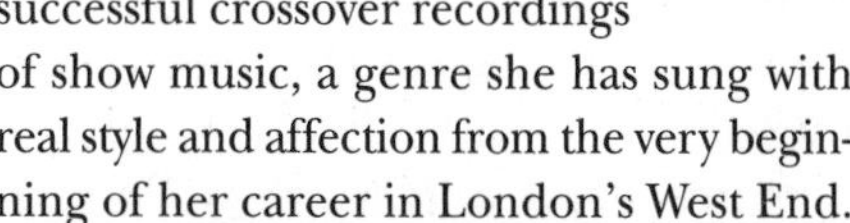

RECOMMENDED RECORDINGS

MOZART, *LE NOZZE DI FIGARO*: POPP, VON STADE, ALLEN, RAMEY; SOLTI AND LONDON PHILHARMONIC ORCHESTRA (DECCA).

J. STRAUSS, *DIE FLEDERMAUS*: GRUBEROVA, FASSBAENDER, LEECH, BRENDEL, BÄR; PREVIN AND VIENNA PHILHARMONIC (PHILIPS).

R. STRAUSS, *CAPRICCIO*: FASSBAENDER, HEILMANN, HAGEGÅRD, HOLLWEG, BÄR; SCHIRMER AND VIENNA PHILHARMONIC (DECCA).

R. STRAUSS, *DER ROSENKAVALIER*: HENDRICKS, OTTER, RYDL; HAITINK AND STAATSKAPELLE DRESDEN (EMI).

COLLECTION:

ARIAS BY PUCCINI AND VERDI: PRITCHARD AND LONDON PHILHARMONIC ORCHESTRA (SONY).

Telemann, Georg Philipp

(b. Magdeburg, March 14, 1681; d. Hamburg, June 25, 1767)

GERMAN COMPOSER. Regarded in his day as Germany's most important composer, he was one of the most productive musicians in history, writing works in virtually every form of significance to the 18th century, including opera. He successfully united the elements of different national styles in a fluent, cosmopolitan idiom that influenced many of his colleagues and represented an important link between the late Baroque and the emerging aesthetic of Classicism.

Unlike J. S. Bach, his slightly younger contemporary, he did not come from a distinguished musical family. His father was a schoolmaster and member of the clergy, his mother the daughter of a Protestant minister. He was interested in music from childhood, received a thorough general education, and in 1701 enrolled in the University of Leipzig to study law. His talent—he was an accomplished performer on many instruments, particularly the violin, and a fine singer—quickly drew him into Leipzig's musical life. In 1702 he founded an association of student musicians (a *collegium musicum*) and became director of the city's opera. His successful ventures quickly brought him into conflict with the Kantor of the Thomaskirche, Johann Kuhnau, who clearly did not enjoy having someone of Telemann's talent encroaching on his territory. In 1705, following several complaints from Kuhnau to the Leipzig town council, Telemann found it expedient to leave for Poland, where he served as Kapellmeister to the Count of Promnitz at Sorau. Between 1708 and 1712 he worked in Eisenach at the court of Johann Wilhelm, Duke of Saxe-Eisenach, serving first as director of instrumental music and subsequently as Kapellmeister. While in Eisenach he got to know Bach, who in 1714 asked him to stand as godfather to his son Carl Philipp Emanuel. From 1712 to 1721 Telemann served as music director for the city of Frankfurt, taking a cut in pay in order to have a job that offered greater artistic freedom than a court appointment. Hamburg, with its great opera tradition, beckoned in

Georg Philipp Telemann

1721. Here Telemann remained for the rest of his life, enjoying many productive years, building a thriving music publishing business, and keeping up with the latest musical developments via personal contacts and an active correspondence with many other musicians.

Telemann composed into his 80s, and the sheer volume of his output is staggering. He may have created as many as 50 operas, most of which are lost; their disappearance is a double shame since these works represent, along with the operas of Reinhard Keiser (1674–1739), the most important contribution to the German-language repertoire in the first half of the 18th century. His output of church cantatas, estimated at around 1,700, dwarfs that of Bach or anyone else—he composed at least 20 annual cycles, of which 12 survive more or less intact. He also penned numerous passions, ten oratorios, and more than a dozen masses, making him easily the most prolific composer of church music in history.

Telemann's instrumental works include about 125 orchestral suites, 125 concertos ◉, 40 quartets, 130 trios, around 90 solo sonatas, and 145 keyboard pieces. Among them are several pieces that remain popular, including his "water music," titled *Hamburger Ebb und Fluth* (1723), three collections of *Musique de table* (published in 1733), a set of six quartets for flute, violin, viol, and continuo known as the *Paris* Quartets (1730), and a set of 12 Fantasies for Solo Flute (1732–33). These works exemplify Telemann's remarkable fluency and his command of various national styles, in particular his affinity for the French style and the emerging *GALANT*.

In spite of his range and fecundity, Telemann's reputation has suffered from the tendency of latter-day listeners to compare his works with those of Bach or Handel in the same genres. Whenever such comparisons are made, it is Telemann's music that sounds "generic," Bach's and Handel's that seems alive and inspired. By the standards of his day, Telemann was a great composer. In comparison with Bach and Handel, he was merely good.

RECOMMENDED RECORDINGS

CHAMBER CANTATAS: BRANDES, LANE; MUSICA PACIFICA (DORIAN).

FANTASIAS (12) FOR SOLO FLUTE: GUIMOND (FLEUR DE LYS).

PARIS QUARTETS: HAZELZET; HUGGETT AND TRIO SONNERIE (VIRGIN CLASSICS).

TAFELMUSIK: GOEBEL AND MUSICA ANTIQUA KÖLN (ARCHIV).

WASSERMUSIK: GOEBEL AND MUSICA ANTIQUA KÖLN (ARCHIV).

WASSERMUSIK (OVERTURE IN C MAJOR—*HAMBURGER EBB UND FLUTH*); HANDEL, *WATER MUSIC*: KING AND KING'S CONSORT (HYPERION).

temperament The tuning of the notes of various scales so as to produce musically or theoretically appropriate concords. The standard temperament in modern Western music is called "equal temperament," in which every half step is exactly the same distance from its neighbor up and down the scale. It took centuries for equal temperament to emerge from the fog of ancient philosophy and medieval music theory, which held that certain intervals, especially fourths and fifths, had to be "perfect," their pitches fixed according to simple numerical ratios. The problem was that stacking perfectly tuned fourths and fifths on top of each other did not in the end produce a satisfactory octave. For instruments with a fixed tuning, especially keyboard instruments, this eventually became an insurmountable problem. Among the early solutions to this problem were "just" intonation (in which fifths and thirds are kept pure) and "mean-tone" temperament (in which the fifths are shortened but the seconds are of uniform size). Even with these adjustments, certain keys or tonalities sounded much more pleasing to the ear than others, which as time went by proved an increasingly onerous limitation. The proponents of equal temperament included the composers Adrian Willaert and Vincenzo Galilei (father of the astronomer), the scientist Daniel Bernoulli, and the composer-theorist Jean-Philippe Rameau. In part to prove the viability of this temperament, J. S. Bach composed his magnum opus for the keyboard, *DAS WOHLTEMPERIRTE CLAVIER,* which contains preludes and fugues in all 24 of the major and minor keys. The value of equal temperament, as Bach showed, was not so much that it allowed music in all keys to sound equally "good," but that it gave composers the freedom to modulate from one key to another (even a distant key) within a given piece. This led to a grand expansion of musical form and proved fundamental to the psychological and emotional impact of much of the music of the past three centuries. Still, there is much to be said for so-called nonequal (or "ill-tempered") tunings, which are capable of producing extraordinarily beautiful concords, in some cases, with an entirely unique visceral and emotional impact. Many experimental composers still work with these tuning systems, always trying to find new sounds from the realm of pitches that lie in the cracks between the piano keys.

tempo (It., "time") The pace of a particular section or piece of music.

tenor (from Lat. *tenere,* "to hold") Originally, the vocal part that carried or "held" the CANTUS FIRMUS in medieval and Renaissance polyphony. By the 15th century, the term had come to signify the type of voice—a male voice midway between bass and alto—that sang this part. During the later 17th and early 18th centuries, the tenor remained in the shadow of the castrato on the opera stage, but by the end of the 18th century it had emerged as the heroic male voice type. Tenor parts, especially in operas of the last two centuries, are generally classified as either lyric or dramatic, depending upon how forcefully passages lying in the upper register must be sung. Notable parts for lyric tenor include the roles of Tamino in Mozart's *Die Zauberflöte,* Alfredo in Verdi's *La traviata,* Don José in Bizet's *Carmen,* and Rodolfo in Puccini's *La bohème.* Of the many tenors who have specialized in lyric roles, some of the finest have been Jussi Björling, Nicolai Gedda, Carlo Bergonzi, Alfredo Kraus, and Fritz Wunderlich. Among the best-known dramatic parts are the Verdi roles of Manrico, in *Il trovatore,* and Otello, Wagner's Lohengrin, and Calaf in Puccini's *Turandot.* Singers who have specialized in these and similar dramatic roles include Francesco Tamagno (the first Otello), Giacomo Lauri-Volpi, Leo Slezak, and Mario del Monaco. Enrico Caruso was that rare singer capable of doing equal justice to lyric and dramatic parts; his closest counterpart today is Plácido Domingo. The HELDENTENOR (Ger., "heroic tenor") is a more robust type of dramatic tenor, with the stamina to sing for extended periods, and with power, in the mid-to-upper part of the range (around the break between head and chest voice). Parts that demand this type of voice include the Wagner roles of Tristan and, in the final two operas of the *Ring* cycle, Siegfried, the title role in Richard Strauss's *Guntram*, and the Emperor in his *Die Frau ohne Schatten*. The classic Heldentenor voice was that of Lauritz Melchior, whose powerful, ringing high notes had a baritonal resonance. Others who have distinguished themselves in the Heldentenor repertoire include Wolfgang Windgassen, Jon Vickers, and, in recent years, Ben Heppner.

tenuto (from It. *tenere,* "to hold") Instruction indicating that a note is to be held (i.e., sustained) for its full rhythmic value. In scores up through the early 19th century, the word *tenuto* or its abbreviation, *ten.*, was used as the marking for this articulation (e.g., Beethoven's Symphony No. 7, second movement). In modern usage, the symbol showing that a note is to be played tenuto is a horizontal stroke placed above or below the note head.

Terfel, Bryn

(b. Pwllheli, November 9, 1965)

WELSH BASS-BARITONE. Born into the Welsh tradition in which singing is as natural as breathing, Terfel eventually entered the Guildhall School of Music and Drama in 1984 and studied with Arthur Reckless and then Rudolf Piernay. He graduated in 1989, winning the school's gold medal and several other awards. In the years that followed he made a series of career-building debuts: at the Welsh National Opera in 1990, as Guglielmo in Mozart's *Così fan tutte*; the English National Opera in 1991, in the title role of *Le nozze di Figaro*; at Covent Garden in 1992, as Masetto in *Don Giovanni*; and at the Salzburg Festival in 1992, as Jochanaan in Richard Strauss's *Salome,* a significant professional breakthrough. This led to engagements in London, Amsterdam, Vienna, and Paris, as well as a recording contract with Deutsche Grammophon. In 1994, he returned to Covent Garden to sing Mozart's Figaro, which he reprised in his Metropolitan Opera debut later that season. Terfel has appeared frequently in recital—at London's Wigmore Hall, the Salzburg Festival, and Carnegie Hall—and has performed as a soloist with many leading orchestras. His growing discography has garnered several Grammy nominations and awards, and includes recordings of oratorio (Mendelssohn's *Elijah* and Walton's *Belshazzar's Feast*), opera and opera arias, English songs, and various lieder of Schubert and Schumann. In recent years he has moved cautiously from his early Mozart successes into the weightier roles to which his large, darkly resonant voice seems well suited, including Falstaff, Wolfram in *Tannhäuser,* and Scarpia in *Tosca.* With his imposing physical stature, fine dramatic instincts, innate musicality, and larger-than-life vocal presence, he seems destined, with time, to command most of the major Wagner and Verdi roles.

Bryn Terfel, big man with a big voice, in recital at Carnegie Hall, 1996

RECOMMENDED RECORDINGS

Mozart, *Le nozze di Figaro*: Gilfry, Hagley, Stephen, Martinpelto; Gardiner and English Baroque Soloists (Archiv).

Collections:

Arias by Donizetti, Mozart, Offenbach, Verdi, Wagner, others: Levine and Metropolitan Opera Orchestra (DG).

"The Vagabond": Songs of Vaughan Williams, Butterworth, Finzi, Ireland; Martineau (DG).

tessitura (It., "weaving") In vocal music, the place in the singer's range where a particular passage or an entire part lies (i.e., not the overall compass that is required to sing the part, but the area where most of the notes are found—high, low, or in the middle of the range).

Tetrazzini, Luisa

(b. Florence, June 29, 1871; d. Milan, April 28, 1940)

ITALIAN SOPRANO. Along with Amelita Galli-Curci, she was one of the first to be designated specifically as a coloratura. She studied with her elder sister, Eva, and made her professional debut in 1895 at Florence's Teatro Pagliano, in Meyerbeer's *L'Africaine.* Thereafter she toured Italy and Europe to great acclaim. She made her Covent Garden debut in 1907 as Violetta in *La traviata,* and later added Gilda in *Rigoletto* and Donizetti's Lucia to crown her triumph. Tetrazzini made her U.S. debut in 1908 and sang eight performances at the Metropolitan Opera in the winter of 1911–12. Though she never returned to the Met, she enjoyed enormous popularity in America: She once sang on Christmas Eve for a crowd of more than 100,000 fans in the square in front of the *San Francisco Chronicle* building—subsequently renamed Tetrazzini Square. Her voice was warm and vibrant, becoming absolutely dazzling as it went higher. Her fioritura was extremely accurate and agile, though in the few recordings extant, some of her embellishments are in questionable taste. Tetrazzini maintained freshness and flexibility well into her middle years, and because she was able to command huge fees amassed a considerable fortune—which, due to poor management and unfortunate choices in husbands, was soon dissipated. Despite her formidable artistic gifts, Tetrazzini's interests were simple: Her favorite pastimes were playing dominoes, eating, and going to the movies. She was also extremely superstitious, and regardless of the fee offered, would sing only on Mondays and Thursdays, her "lucky" days. The pasta dish chicken (or veal) tetrazzini was named in her honor, and she returned the compliment by becoming its biggest fan.

RECOMMENDED RECORDING

Collection:

Arias by Bellini, Donizetti, Rossini, Verdi (Nimbus).

Teyte, Maggie

(b. Wolverhampton, April 17, 1888; d. London, May 26, 1976)

ENGLISH SOPRANO. She left London in 1903 to study in Paris with the tenor Jean de Reszke. In 1906 she made her debut singing in an all-Mozart concert conducted by Reynaldo Hahn, in the company of Lilli Lehmann, Mario Ancona, and Édouard de Reszke; in 1907 she joined the Opéra-Comique. In 1908 she was cast as Debussy's Mélisande, replacing the magnificent Mary Garden, who had created the part. In order to prepare for the role, Teyte was coached daily by the composer for six months, covering not only the opera but all of his songs. Teyte scored a triumph in *Pelléas et Mélisande* and reprised the role at Covent Garden in 1910, with Thomas Beecham conducting. She also sang Cherubino and Blonde in *Le nozze di Figaro* and *Die Entführung aus dem Serail,* as well as the title roles in Massenet's *Cendrillon* and *Manon.* During the war years, Teyte sang with the Chicago Opera Company in Chicago, Philadelphia, and

New York, and with the Boston Opera—but never with the Metropolitan Opera. Following her marriage in 1921, she went into semiretirement; when the marriage fell apart in 1931, she found herself forgotten by the public and frustrated in her efforts to reestablish her career. In 1936 she made a landmark recording of Debussy songs for EMI with Alfred Cortot. This not only confirmed her as one of the leading exponents of French art song but jump-started her career. Although opportunities were again circumscribed by World War II, in 1948 she sang a recital in New York's Town Hall and finally got to present her signature role, Mélisande, in New York at the City Opera; she was a mere 60 years old. She retired from the stage in 1951, and from concert activity in 1955. She was created a Chevalier de la Légion d'Honneur in 1957 and a Dame Commander of the Order of the British Empire in 1958. Listening to the recordings she made, one is immediately struck not only by the purity of her sound and the perfect placement of the voice, but by the exquisite legato and the beauty of her French diction. With the voice not of an operatic extrovert but more of an ingenue, Teyte seemed destined never to reach a huge audience, nor to enjoy as successful a career as she deserved; she was nonetheless a singer of exquisite taste and rare sensibility.

RECOMMENDED RECORDINGS

"Maggie Teyte in Concert": Britten, *Les Illuminations* (complete); Debussy, *Pelléas et Mélisande* (excerpts); works by Fauré, Hahn, R. Strauss, others (VAI).

"Maggie Teyte: A Vocal Portrait": Debussy, *Chansons de Bilitis*, *Les fêtes galantes*; Ravel, *Shéhérazade*; songs by Berlioz, Duparc, Tchaikovsky, others; Moore (Naxos).

Thaïs Opera in three acts by Jules Massenet, to a libretto by Louis Gallet (based on a novel by Anatole France published in 1890), composed 1892–93 and premiered March 16, 1894, at the Paris Opéra. The story, set in and around Alexandria in the 4th century A.D., deals with the attempt of a monk, Athanaël, to convert the courtesan Thaïs and save her from her wicked ways. Thaïs does convert, dying a saint in the opera's final scene. This is too much for Athanaël, who, unable to overcome his long-suppressed lust, casts off his spiritual moorings and abandons himself to a pitiable apostasy. The opera's best-known music is the orchestral interlude between the first two scenes of Act II, titled "Méditation," which depicts Thaïs's conversion and features a surpassingly lovely solo for the violin.

RECOMMENDED RECORDINGS

Fleming, Hampson, Sabbatini; Abel and L'Orchestre National de Bordeaux (Decca).

Méditation: Bell; Litton and Royal Philharmonic Orchestra (Decca).

theme (from Gr. *thema*, "subject") A musical idea or statement that is capable of standing as a complete musical "thought" and that serves as the subject, or one of the subjects, of a piece. Themes can run the gamut from short and pithy, e.g., the famous theme of Paganini's Caprice in A minor, subject of numerous variation works, to long and discursive, as in Tchaikovsky's Piano Concerto in B-flat minor, whose opening pages unfold a theme of remarkably expansive character over 107 measures . . . one that is never heard again after that.

theme and variations *See* VARIATION(S).

theorbo A large lute with a long neck and two sets of strings—one a regular set of stopped strings positioned over the fingerboard, the other a set of long, unstopped bass strings. The theorbo was used primarily during the 17th century as both a solo instrument and a continuo instrument; in the latter capacity it frequently appeared in the instrumental groups that accompanied operas, its long neck towering over the ensemble like a misplaced telephone pole.

theremin *See box on pages 496–97.*

Thomas, Michael Tilson

(b. Los Angeles, December 21, 1944)

AMERICAN CONDUCTOR AND PIANIST. He belongs to an artistic family: his grandfather, Boris Tomashefsky, was a superstar of the Yiddish theater whose name is still invoked satirically to describe those who overemote. Thomas studied piano with John Crown and composition and conducting with Ingolf Dahl at the University of Southern California, becoming music director of the Young Musicians Foundation Debut Orchestra at 19 and working with Stravinsky, Boulez, Stockhausen, and Copland on premieres of their compositions. In 1969, at the age of 24, he won the Koussevitzky Prize at Tanglewood and was appointed assistant conductor of the Boston Symphony Orchestra; ten days into the job he made his New York debut, replacing an ailing William Steinberg in mid-concert. He was later promoted to associate conductor, then principal guest conductor, of the BSO. He served as music director of the Buffalo Philharmonic (1971–79), principal guest conductor of the Los Angeles Philharmonic (1981–85), and principal conductor of the London Symphony Orchestra (1988–95). In 1988 he founded and became artistic director of the New World Symphony, a professional training orchestra based in Miami. He was named the 11th music director of the San Francisco Symphony Orchestra in 1995.

Michael Tilson Thomas

One of today's princes of the podium, Thomas (known as MTT in the music business) has presided over a musical golden age in San Francisco. With his incredible ear for orchestral detail, thoroughness in rehearsal, and accomplished technique, he has honed the San Francisco ensemble to a fine edge; it produces a clean, transparent sound in the most difficult repertoire and plays a wide variety of 19th- and 20th-century fare with a convincing sense of style. Thomas's strengths as an interpreter are broad, ranging from Tchaikovsky and Mahler to Stravinsky, Schoenberg, and Ives. He is strongly committed to American music and has featured even fairly obscure works to great advantage on international tours with the orchestra and in the American Mavericks series he conducts in San Francisco. He also has a formidable gift for talking about music and communicating his insights and excitement without pedantry, much as Leonard Bernstein did. To his credit, he has done all this, and done it tastefully, without losing his sense of fun and flair for showmanship.

RECOMMENDED RECORDINGS

COPLAND, ORCHESTRAL WORKS: SAN FRANCISCO SYMPHONY ORCHESTRA (RCA).

GERSHWIN, ORCHESTRAL WORKS: SAN FRANCISCO SYMPHONY ORCHESTRA (RCA).

IVES, ORCHESTRAL WORKS: SAN FRANCISCO SYMPHONY ORCHESTRA (RCA).

IVES, *THREE PLACES IN NEW ENGLAND* (WITH PISTON, SYMPHONY NO. 2; RUGGLES, *SUN-TREADER*): BOSTON SYMPHONY ORCHESTRA (DG).

MAHLER, SYMPHONIES: SAN FRANCISCO SYMPHONY ORCHESTRA (SAN FRANCISCO SYMPHONY).

Thomas, Theodore

(b. Esens, October 11, 1835; d. Chicago, January 4, 1905)

GERMAN/AMERICAN CONDUCTOR. He played a pivotal role in the development of orchestral tradition in the United States, essentially fathering the Chicago Symphony Orchestra. The son of a *Stadtpfeifer* (town bandleader), he learned to play the violin as a child and was already an experienced performer when, at the age of ten, he emigrated with his family to the United States. He played in several New York theater orchestras and by the time he was 15 had toured the country as a violin recitalist. In 1854 he joined the New York Philharmonic Society as a violinist, and the following year he established a chamber series in New York with pianist William Mason, giving the world premiere of Brahms's Piano Trio in B, Op. 8, at the first concert. Thomas became co-conductor of the Brooklyn Philharmonic Society in 1862 and in 1866 became the organization's sole conductor, forming the Theodore Thomas Orchestra to serve as its resident ensemble. Thomas remained at the helm of his orchestra, touring with it far and wide, until 1891. In 1873 he founded the Cincinnati May Festival, and in 1877 he was named conductor of the New York Philharmonic, retaining that post until 1891 as well.

Theodore Thomas

But the New York Philharmonic was not a full-time, permanently established orchestra. When a group of businessmen in Chicago offered to set up just such an ensemble for Thomas to conduct, he leapt at the chance. The result was the Chicago Orchestra (today's Chicago Symphony Orchestra), which gave its first concerts on October 16 and 17, 1891, with Thomas on the podium. During his tenure in Chicago, Thomas gave the American premieres of works by Bruckner, Dvořák, Elgar, Glazunov, Smetana, Tchaikovsky, and Richard Strauss, who in 1904, at Thomas's invitation, became the first musician to guest-conduct the orchestra. That same year, at Thomas's urging, a new concert hall designed by Chicago architect Daniel H. Burnham was built for the orchestra. Thomas and the CSO christened Orchestra Hall—still the ensemble's home—on December 14, 1904. The conductor, who had contracted influenza while preparing the dedicatory concert, died of pneumonia less than a month later, after conducting just two weeks of subscription concerts in the new hall. For six years after his death, the Chicago Orchestra called itself the Theodore Thomas Orchestra in tribute.

Hardworking, knowledgeable, well organized, and highly principled, Thomas was the most influential American conductor of the 19th century. He presented the classics with a high-minded insistence that they be played well and taken seriously—disciplining audiences as well as orchestras in the process—and programmed new music with evangelical fervor. The rise of America's top orchestras to the artistic pinnacles they reached in the 20th century was in large part his legacy.

Thomaskirche (St. Thomas's Church)

MAIN LUTHERAN CHURCH IN LEIPZIG, built in the 13th century, remodeled between 1482 and 1496 (when it acquired a high, very steeply pitched roof) and again in 1639. It came through World War II substantially unscathed and is still standing. The Thomaskirche was the base of operations for J. S. Bach, who served as Kantor from

1723 to his death in 1750. Six years prior to taking its top musical job, Bach had served as consultant to the church, testing the new organ that Johann Scheibe had built for it between 1710 and 1716.

Interior and exterior views of the Thomaskirche

Thompson, Randall

(b. New York, April 21, 1899; d. Cambridge, Mass., July 9, 1984)

AMERICAN COMPOSER. He attended Harvard University, where he received a B.A. in 1920 and an M.A. in 1922, and studied privately with Ernest Bloch. In 1922 he was the recipient of a Prix de Rome, which enabled him to study with Gian Francesco Malipiero; during a long career in academe, he received two Guggenheim Fellowships and did teaching stints at Wellesley, Berkeley, the Curtis Institute, the University of Virginia, and Princeton. In 1948 he returned to Harvard, where he remained until his retirement in 1965. His most important music was choral rather than instrumental, including the work for which he became best known, the four-voice a cappella *Alleluia* he composed in 1940 for the opening exercises of the Berkshire Music Center in Tanglewood. Of the three symphonies he wrote, only the second has remained in the repertoire. It was premiered in 1932 by Howard Hanson and the Rochester Philharmonic, and quickly entered the repertoire of other American orchestras, including the New York Philharmonic, which first played it in 1933 under the baton of Bruno Walter.

RECOMMENDED RECORDINGS

ALLELUIA, THE PEACEABLE KINGDOM, TWELVE CANTICLES, OTHER WORKS: SHEWAN AND ROBERTS WESLEYAN COLLEGE CHOIR (ALBANY).

SYMPHONY NO. 2: BERNSTEIN AND NEW YORK PHILHARMONIC (SONY).

Thomson, Virgil

(b. Kansas City, November 25, 1896; d. New York, September 30, 1989)

AMERICAN COMPOSER AND CRITIC. He learned to play the piano and organ as a boy. Following America's entry into World War I, he enlisted in the army. He was being trained as a pilot and was headed for France when the war ended. He eventually got to France, by way of Harvard, where he studied composition and served as assistant conductor of the Harvard Glee Club; following a European tour by the glee club in the summer of 1921, he remained in Paris to study with Nadia Boulanger. In Paris he became acquainted with Jean Cocteau, Erik Satie, and the members of Les Six. He graduated from Harvard in 1923, and after further study with Rosario Scalero returned to Paris, where he lived from 1925 to 1940. His emergence as one of the most important American composers of the 20th century was hastened by his fellow expatriate Gertrude Stein, whom he met in 1926, and who furnished him with librettos for his operas *FOUR SAINTS IN THREE ACTS* (1934) and *The Mother of Us All* (1947). During the 1930s, Thomson also achieved considerable renown for his scores to two documentary films written and directed by Pare

Lorentz for the U.S. Resettlement Administration, part of the Roosevelt administration's New Deal: *The Plow That Broke the Plains* (1936), about the abuses that led to the Dust Bowl, and *The River* (1938), which laid out the case for flood control that had led to the creation of the Tennessee Valley Authority. Following his return to America, Thomson served from 1940 to 1954 as music critic of the *New York Herald-Tribune,* where he wrote brilliantly, with insight and wit, skewering countless celebrated composers and performers and becoming the champion of a new generation of American musicians and writers that included John Cage, Lou Harrison, and Ned Rorem; later on he mentored critics Alan Rich, John Rockwell, and many others. While working as a critic, he continued to compose, and in 1948 his score for the Robert Flaherty documentary *Louisiana Story* won the Pulitzer Prize for music. He spent the last 35 years of his life as an eminence, holding court in his apartment at the Chelsea Hotel in New York, receiving numerous honors, and urging his fellow journalists to be muckrakers and "expose them all."

Virgil Thomson with his **Musical Portrait of Gertrude Stein**

Thomson was a master at using whatever materials came to hand and proved remarkably adept at weaving vernacular elements—the Americana of cowboy songs, Baptist hymn tunes, the blues, popular dance forms—into his music. The resulting patchwork, so distinctively American in its blithe eclecticism and homespun informality, reflected both the earthiness of Thomson's midwestern roots and the sophistication of the New York scene. That his music often came across with an exasperating silliness simply shows how hard Thomson tried not to take himself too seriously, part of the airy legacy of the Parisian salons he frequented as a young man. He was one of the sharpest, most elegant music critics ever to write in the English language, and that, too, owes something to the taste for simplicity and elegance of expression he acquired during his years in France.

RECOMMENDED RECORDINGS

The Plow that Broke the Plains (with *Acadian Songs and Dances from Louisiana Story*): Corp and New London Orchestra (Hyperion).

Symphony on a Hymn Tune (with Symphonies Nos. 2 and 3): Sedares and New Zealand Symphony Orchestra (Naxos).

Threepenny Opera, The *See* DIE DREIGROSCHENOPER.

Three Places in New England SUBTITLE OF *ORCHESTRAL SET NO. 1* BY CHARLES IVES, a symphonic triptych composed between 1912 and 1921 and premiered January 10, 1931, in New York in a version for small orchestra conducted by Nicolas Slonimsky. The first movement bears the title "The 'St Gaudens' in Boston Common (Col. Shaw and His Colored Regiment)," the reference being to the Shaw Memorial created in 1897 by the American sculptor Augustus Saint-Gaudens. Out of a nebulous opening, strains of Stephen Foster's "Old Black Joe" begin to crystallize, dreamily over-

***Detail from the Shaw Memorial, subject of the first of Ives's* Three Places in New England**

lapped by fragments of Civil War marching tunes. The meditative mood is broken by a single forceful outburst, and the restless meditation concludes. The second movement, "Putnam's Camp, Redding, Connecticut," is a portrait of the Revolutionary War encampment of Israel Putnam, a general in the Continental Army. In this wild mix of ragtime and martial fantasy, snatches of several familiar patriotic tunes are heard. The final movement, "The Housatonic at Stockbridge," gets its title from a poem by Robert Underwood Johnson. Ives revealed that the piece is a reminiscence of "a Sunday morning walk that Mrs. Ives and I took near Stockbridge the summer after we were married. We walked in the meadows . . . and heard the distant singing from the church across the river. The mists had not entirely left the river and the colors, the running water, the banks and trees were something that one would always remember." The score is one of Ives's most remarkable creations, an almost impressionistic collage of hymn tunes that builds to a chaotic climax and quickly vanishes into the mists of memory.

RECOMMENDED RECORDING

THOMAS AND SAN FRANCISCO ORCHESTRA (RCA).

Tibbett, Lawrence

(b. Bakersfield, Calif., November 16, 1896; d. New York, July 15, 1960)

AMERICAN BARITONE. Tibbett was just a boy when his father, the sheriff of Bakersfield County, was shot dead in a gun battle; he went on to become the first American-born, American-trained baritone to achieve a major international career. Pursuing an early interest in theater, he worked with the Shakespeare group organized by Tyrone Power Sr. He first sang in public in Los Angeles at 21; a stipend enabled him to go to New York to study with Frank La Forge. In 1923, after his second audition, he was hired by the Metropolitan Opera to sing minor roles such as Lavitsky in *Boris Godunov,* Morales in *Carmen,* the Marquis d'Obigny in *La traviata,* and the Herald in *Lohengrin.* The major baritone roles were being sung at the time by such heavyweights as Chaliapin, De Luca, Ruffo, Schorr, and Antonio Scotti. In a performance on January 2, 1925, opposite Scotti's Falstaff, Tibbett as Ford sang his monologue with such unprecedented fervor that it brought down the house; the show stopped for ten minutes until Tibbett was finally brought out from behind the curtain to accept a solo bow. He became an overnight celebrity and was embraced by the American operagoing public. Tibbett eventually came to sing the major baritone roles that had been the exclusive property of European singers—Wolfram, Germont, Amonasro, Scarpia, and Rigoletto, making perhaps his greatest impression as Verdi's Simon Boccanegra. Though he also eventually sang with opera companies in Chicago and San Francisco, the Met was his home base for 27 seasons. He made his first international tour with the company in 1937, singing the title role in Verdi's *Rigoletto* and the role of Iago in *Otello,* and he sang in the world premieres of several

American operas, including *The Emperor Jones* by Louis Gruenberg (1884–1964), *The King's Henchmen* by Deems Taylor (1885–1966), and Howard Hanson's *Merry Mount.* Tibbett's reputation profited from the growing popularity of radio and movies; he appeared in singing roles in half a dozen films, including *A Rogue Song, New Moon, The Southerners, Cuban Love Song,* and *Metropolitan,* which made him a household name. He started to experience a vocal decline in the 1940s and sang his last Met performance, in Mussorgsky's *Khovanshchina,* in 1950. With his all-American good looks and engaging demeanor, and with a distinctively mellow yet resonant voice that could float all the way up to a high B and comfortably down to a low F, Tibbett was as much at home in a Broadway musical as he was a few blocks down the street on the Met's stage. His popularity did much to open the doors for the next generations of American-born and -trained singers, especially those great American baritones who followed in his footsteps, including Leonard Warren, Robert Merrill, Sherrill Milnes, and Samuel Ramey.

RECOMMENDED RECORDINGS

VERDI, SCENES FROM *SIMON BOCCANEGRA* AND *OTELLO*: BAMPTON, MARTINELLI, JEPSON, WARREN; PELLETIER AND METROPOLITAN OPERA (PEARL).

COLLECTION:

"LAWRENCE TIBBETT—FROM BROADWAY TO HOLLYWOOD": GERSHWIN, *PORGY AND BESS* (EXCERPTS); WORKS BY DVOŘÁK, LEHÁR, HANSON, STRAUS, YOUMANS (NIMBUS).

Till Eulenspiegels lustige Streiche (Till Eulenspiegel's Merry Pranks) SYMPHONIC POEM BY **RICHARD STRAUSS, OP. 28,** composed 1894–95 and premiered November 5, 1895, in Cologne, Franz Wüllner conducting. The title page of the score states: "Composed for large orchestra after the old roguish manner—in rondeau form." The orchestra Strauss uses is very large indeed, calling for triple winds, eight horns, and an unusually large battery that includes a ratchet. The musical imagery that fills the work is roguish to say the least. Till Eulenspiegel is a character out of German folklore, supposedly a real-life practical joker and miscreant who died in Lübeck around 1350—in bed, not on the gallows as Strauss has it. Tales of his exploits began to enter the folk literature around 1500, and he came to symbolize a much-needed and rarely encountered farcical lightness in the German temperament. His high-spirited pranks included riding through the marketplace and upsetting the stalls, dressing up as a priest, chasing after girls, and mocking the good townspeople, all of which Strauss characterizes in the most vivid manner.

In the end, at least according to the composer, Till is caught and tried. The full orchestra, with the snare drum rolling ominously, indicts him. At first he answers cavalierly; then, realizing the seriousness of his predicament, he whimpers for mercy. His judges, the trombones, condemn him to death with the fierce proclamation of a descending seventh—taken from the scene in Mozart's *Don Giovanni* where Donna Anna and the other characters, having just captured Leporello, sing "Morrà!" ("He dies!"). Unlike Leporello, who gets off, Till is hanged. But, in a sweet epilogue to the tone poem, Strauss confirms that the rogue's spirit lives on.

RECOMMENDED RECORDINGS

KARAJAN AND BERLIN PHILHARMONIC (DG).

SZELL AND CLEVELAND ORCHESTRA (SONY).

Time Cycle WORK FOR SOPRANO AND ORCHESTRA BY **LUKAS FOSS,** composed 1959–60 to texts (on the topic of time) by W. H. Auden, A. E. Housman, Franz Kafka, and Friedrich Nietzsche, and premiered October 1960, by the New York Philharmonic and Leonard Bernstein, with Adele Addison as soloist. Foss also produced a version of the score for chamber ensemble and voice. The four songs of *Time Cycle* are notated, but the instrumental interludes that connect them are improvised. The work, which put Foss on the map as a composer, gained instant notoriety at its premiere when Bernstein announced from the podium that he intended to conduct the entire piece twice, "even if there are only 12 people in this house who want to hear it again."

RECOMMENDED RECORDING

ADDISON; BERNSTEIN AND COLUMBIA SYMPHONY ORCHESTRA (SONY).

time signature A figurative or numerical sign placed at the beginning of a piece of music (immediately after the clef and key signature), indicating the music's meter. In most cases the time signature is expressed as a pair of numbers, one above the other. The lower number represents the note value that is being counted as a metric (in the sense of time) unit, and is always a power of two. The upper number indicates how many units of that value are present in each measure (not, it must be emphasized, how many *beats* there are). Thus a time signature of $\frac{3}{2}$ indicates that there are three half notes per measure, while a time signature of $\frac{6}{8}$ indicates that there are six eighth notes per measure. Most music in $\frac{6}{8}$, however, is felt in two beats to the measure. Occasionally, symbols derived from medieval mensuration markings are used to denote meters of $\frac{4}{4}$ (known as "common time" [C]) and $\frac{2}{2}$ (sometimes called "cut time" or ALLA BREVE [¢]). *See also* METER.

timpani Pitched drums with large-diameter heads of calfskin or plastic stretched across deep, bowl-shaped copper shells (hence the name "kettledrums") that impart considerable resonance. The drums come in four standard sizes with overlapping ranges. The largest has a head 30 inches in diameter and a range from low D to the A a fifth above; the rest of the family consists of drums with head diameters of 28 inches (yielding F to C), 25 inches (B-flat to F), and 23 inches (D to the A below middle C). Increasing the tension on the drumhead raises the pitch. For the past century the best drums have been built with pedal-operated mechanical tensioning systems that allow the timpanist to make tuning changes quickly and accurately. The sound produced by a drum is affected by many things: the forcefulness of the stroke, where the drumhead is struck (close to the rim or more toward the center), and most of all by the hardness of the sticks used. Timpanists keep a variety of sticks on hand with heads of different materials, from wood, the hardest, to sponge, the softest. The heads of most sticks are covered by varying thicknesses of felt, flannel, or cotton yarn; in the absence of specific instructions in the score or from the conductor, the timpanist chooses the type of stick most appropriate to the musical requirements of a particular passage, often changing sticks several times in the course of a piece. The resonance of timpani is such that even after soft strokes the drumhead must be damped by the player's fingers, to keep it from resounding past the written duration of the note. This resonance is also what makes rolls on

Cross-handed strokes, with sword

the timpani (written as trills in the score) so effective.

Kettledrums of various kinds have been used in music making and ceremony since ancient times. The European practice (borrowed from the Ottoman Turks) of mounting them on horseback for use in processionals dates back to the mid-15th century and can still be witnessed when French cavalry bands march down the Champs-Elysées on national holidays. It was customary for a phalanx of trumpets to be used alongside the kettledrums, establishing an association between these instruments that has endured for centuries in countless pieces of classical music. The timpani's main use in concert music is the reinforcement of the bass line, especially at cadences, where their presence adds weight and emphasis along with clear delineation of the rhythm. In keeping with their ceremonial heritage they are frequently used in support of the brass for music aiming to suggest pomp, festivity, and splendor. The use of two drums, tuned to the tonic and dominant notes of the harmony, was standard until Beethoven, who was among the first to use the timpani soloistically (e.g., the octave F's hammered out at the beginning of the second movement of the Ninth Symphony ◉) and to apply more imaginative tunings (such as the tritone A–E-flat in the dungeon scene of *Fidelio,* producing a "wrong" sound that chillingly conveys the horror of the place). In his *Symphonie fantastique,* Berlioz, who played the timpani, revolutionized their role in the orchestra, calling for the use of sponge and wood heads at various points in the score and deploying multiple drums and players with great specificity: four drums, each tuned to a different note, and four players in the third movement; five drums, three players, in the fourth. He would outdo himself in his Requiem, whose "Tuba mirum" requires 16 drums and ten players.

Striking uses of the timpani can be found in the works of many 19th- and 20th-century composers. Brahms has the timpanist pound out the pedal C's at the beginning of his Symphony No. 1, eight measures of relentless *forte* strokes. Mahler uses two timpanists on four drums to similarly reinforce the cadential quarter notes at the end of his Symphony No. 3, and he instructs the timpanist to use two sticks at a time to sound the powerful eighth-note figures on three drums that mark the climax of the slow movement of his Symphony No. 4. To open the finale of his Seventh Symphony, he gives the timpanist a six-measure solo on four drums to be played "with bravura," one of the great moments in the literature. ◉ Strauss makes virtuosic demands on the timpanist in many of his tone poems (starting with the first page of *Don Juan*) and in several of his operas, particularly *Salome* and *Elektra*; these include not only the execution of rhythmically tricky passages but lightning changes of sticks and tunings. In the special-effects department, Stravinsky calls for a small *timpano piccolo* to get a jolting high B-natural in *The Rite of Spring,* while Nielsen, telling the players to make a "menacing" sound even in *piano,* creates a battle between two sets of timpani throughout the final movement of his Symphony No. 4 (*The Inextinguishable*), achieving visual as well as musical impact. Among the most intriguing timpanic effects are the glissandi Bartók calls for in his *Music for Strings, Percussion, and Celesta* and Sonata for Two Pianos and Percussion (1937), where the timpanist changes the pitch while the drum head is sounding.

There are a handful of concertos for the timpani, none dating from earlier than the mid-20th century; of note is the *Timpani Concerto* (1983) by William Kraft (b. 1923), who for two decades was principal timpanist of the Los Angeles Philharmonic. Timpani are treated soloistically in several multiple concertos, including Poulenc's *Concerto for Organ, Strings, and Timpani* (1938) and Frank Martin's *Concerto for Seven Wind Instruments* (1949). The timpani's chamber repertoire includes, in addition to the Bartók sonata, Carter's *Eight Pieces for Four Timpani* (two of the eight, "Canaries" and "Saeta," are particularly popular recital pieces) and numerous 20th-century pieces for mixed percussion.

Tippett, Michael

(b. London, January 2, 1905; d. London, January 8, 1998)

ENGLISH COMPOSER. His father was a liberal lawyer and his mother a suffragette; he was educated in English "public" (i.e., private) schools and came to music relatively late, taking piano lessons as a teenager and singing in the local church choir. The experience of hearing an orchestra concert conducted by Malcolm Sargent led him to decide to become a composer, and he enrolled at the Royal College of Music in 1923. He left the RCM in 1928 to live and work in Surrey, where he taught French at a preparatory school and conducted the local concert and opera society. In 1930 he returned to the RCM for further study with R. O. Morris, concentrating on counterpoint; this training would lay the groundwork for his first mature compostions—the String Quartet No. 1 (1935; rev. 1944) and Piano Sonata No. 1 (1936–37; rev. 1942, 1954)—and would continue to bear fruit throughout his career. During the 1930s, he became involved in radical politics, joining the Communist Party (as a Trotskyist) in 1935 and organizing the South London Orchestra of Unemployed Musicians. He became a committed Jungian, underwent analysis, and saw his aesthetic ideas begin to come into focus following several informal encounters with T. S. Eliot. All of this searching led to the oratorio *A Child of Our Time* (1939–41), a passionate protest against Fascism and the work that put Tippett's name on the map.

In nearly all his early music Tippett showed a willingness to build on tradition by using structural, harmonic, and textural elements of earlier styles to achieve his expressive ends. The Concerto for Double String Orchestra (1938–39), a particularly fine example of this process, follows the formal model of the Baroque concerto grosso and is also clearly indebted to the kind of fugal procedures explored by Beethoven in his late works.

Tippett became musical director of Morley College, London, in 1940, remaining until 1951. While at Morley he encouraged the performance of much early music and composed several choral pieces as well as his Symphony No. 1 (1944–45). In 1943 he was sentenced to three months' imprisonment for refusing, as a pacifist, to comply with the British government conditions of exemption from active war service. (His relationship with the government would improve over time, leading to a knighthood in 1966.) After leaving Morley, Tippett devoted himself entirely to composition and to work on radio, enjoying a slow-growing fame. He reached a major milestone with the completion, in 1952, of his radiant first opera, *The Midsummer Marriage*; the work's 1955 premiere at the Royal Opera House, with the young Joan Sutherland as Jenifer, cemented his position as one of England's leading composers. Over the next 20 years he composed three more operas: *King Priam* (1958–61), *The Knot Garden* (1966–69), and *The Ice Break* (1973–76). Tippett remained active through his 80s, painstakingly fulfilling a steady stream of large commissions, including several from the United States. For the Chicago Symphony Orchestra he composed his Symphony No. 4 (1976–77) and *Byzantium,* a setting of the Yeats poem, for soprano and orchestra (1989–90); for the Boston Symphony Orchestra his oratorio *The Mask of Time* (1980–82); and for the Houston Grand Opera his final opera, *New Year* (1986–88). The premiere of *Byzantium* in 1991 ignited a small scandal when, to Sir Georg Solti's immense displeasure, Jessye Norman refused to learn the soprano part and had to be replaced by Faye Robinson. Among the composer's last works were a Fifth String Quartet (1990–91) and *The Rose Lake,* described as "a song without words for orchestra," the premiere of which was given by the London Symphony Orchestra under Sir Colin Davis in Tippett's 90th birthday year.

Michael Tippett in a reflective moment

In much of his music, and for much of his life, Tippett felt the need for words. But he was not always successful in setting them musically. His text for *A Child of Our Time* is cumbersome, and the one for *The Mask of Time,* largely of his making, verges on the inscrutable; even his musical deconstruction of Yeats's "Byzantium" is not to the poem's advantage. The need for words was part of a larger problem for Tippett, having to do with the Manichean worldview he absorbed from Jung, in which light and dark, good and evil have equal claims. In attempting to make his art express this duality, he often loaded it with heavier moralistic freight than it could bear and forced upon it a complexity that was aimless and off-putting. In the best of his works, from early and late in his career, he was saved from this modernist obsession with density, complication, and dismay—and from his own intellectual pretentiousness—by his honest feeling for beauty and his respect for the past.

RECOMMENDED RECORDINGS

A Child of Our Time: Robinson, Walker, Garrison, Cheek; Tippett and City of Birmingham Symphony Orchestra (Naxos).

The Midsummer Marriage: Bainbridge, Burrows, Carlyle, Harwood; Davis and Royal Opera (Lyrita).

toccata (from It. *toccare,* "to touch") A work, nearly always for a keyboard instrument, intended as a display of manual dexterity. Most toccatas feature rapid passages requiring clean fingerwork and long sections of continuous movement in short note values. The toccata was a fixture of Baroque organ music from Frescobaldi on; Buxtehude wrote many, but the most famous example is Bach's Toccata in D minor, BWV 565, composed ca. 1702. The French composer Charles-Marie Widor (1844–1937), whose ten organ symphonies are his crowning achievement, served up a splendid toccata as the finale to the best of them, Symphony No. 5 in F minor, Op. 42, No. 1 (1887). Among the most notable toccatas written for the piano are Schumann's Toccata in C, Op. 7 (1829–33), and the final movements of Debussy's *Pour le piano* (1901) and Ravel's *Le tombeau de Couperin* (1917).

Toch, Ernst

(b. Vienna, December 7, 1887; d. Los Angeles, October 1, 1964)

AUSTRIAN/AMERICAN COMPOSER. He was largely self-taught as a composer—a process that began when he copied out several Mozart string quartets and, without looking ahead, started testing his thoughts against Mozart's on how the material should be developed. He won a composition prize named for Mozart in 1909; the purse allowed him to move to Germany and study at the Hoch Conservatory in Frankfurt. In 1913 he began to teach music in Mannheim, but at the outbreak of World War I he was called into the Austrian army. Following the war he returned to Mannheim a changed man, no longer a late Romantic but a confirmed modernist. He composed a variety of cutting-edge works in the 15 years that followed, including three string quartets, two collections of songs, and the *Geographic Fugue* (1930), a fascinating exercise in rhythmic declamation for chorus, which speaks the words of the fugue, all place names. He left Germany in 1933, wiring his wife a coded message from Paris—"I have my pencil"—to let her know it was safe for her to follow. After a brief period in London, where he wrote his *Big Ben* Variations, Op. 62 (1935), for orchestra, Toch made his way to Los Angeles, joining many other dispossessed Europeans. He composed 16 film scores (three of which were nominated for Academy Awards) and taught at the University of Southern California. Following a massive heart attack (which forced him to think about his legacy), he channeled all his energy into composition, producing seven symphonies, an opera, and a number of solo and chamber works. His Third Symphony won the Pulitzer Prize in 1955. Though few people took notice of Toch while he was alive and working in L.A.—he once called himself "the world's most forgotten composer"—his music is now making a comeback, both in Europe and America, because it is fresh, imaginative, and well written.

RECOMMENDED RECORDINGS

PIANO CONCERTO NO. 1 (WITH *BIG BEN VARIATIONS* AND OTHER WORKS): CROW; BOTSTEIN AND NDR SYMPHONY ORCHESTRA (NEW WORLD).

SYMPHONIES NOS. 2, 3, 5–7 (2 VOLS.): FRANCIS AND BERLIN RADIO SYMPHONY ORCHESTRA (CPO).

Tod und das Mädchen, Der (Death and the Maiden) [1] SONG BY FRANZ SCHUBERT, **D. 531,** to a text by Matthias Claudius, composed in February 1817.

[2] NICKNAME OF SCHUBERT'S STRING QUARTET IN D MINOR, **D. 810,** composed in March 1824, which includes a variation movement based on the melody of the song. A dramatic work that exhibits an almost Beethovenian drive in its opening movement, it is one of Schubert's finest contributions to the genre.

RECOMMENDED RECORDINGS

SONG: BAKER, PARSONS (EMI).

STRING QUARTET:

EMERSON QUARTET (DG).

GUARNERI QUARTET (ARABESQUE).

Tod und Verklärung (Death and Transfiguration) SYMPHONIC POEM BY RICHARD STRAUSS, **OP. 24,** composed 1888–89 and premiered June 21, 1890, in Eisenach, the composer conducting. In a letter written to Friedrich von Hausegger in 1894, Strauss provided the following program:

> The idea came to me to write a tone poem describing the last hours of a man who had striven for the highest ideals, presumably an artist. . . . He recalls his past life; his childhood passes before his eyes; his youth with its striving and passions and then, while the pains return, there appears to him the goal of his life's journey, the Ideal which he attempted to embody in his art, but which he was unable to perfect because such perfection could be achieved by no man. The fatal hour arrives. The soul leaves his body, to discover in the eternal cosmos the magnificent realization of the Ideal that could not be fulfilled here below.

In his vivid portrayal of the final agony, Strauss's use of the orchestra is particularly virtuosic. With brutal force the trombones and timpani hammer out the convulsive rhythms of the struggle until the end comes and the music almost literally evaporates. Out of the ether of a single note—C—the music of Transfiguration arises, building to a huge C-major climax and subsiding with a gentle last glimpse of the Ideal.

RECOMMENDED RECORDINGS

HORENSTEIN AND LONDON SYMPHONY ORCHESTRA (CHANDOS).

KARAJAN AND BERLIN PHILHARMONIC (DG).

SZELL AND CLEVELAND ORCHESTRA (SONY).

tombeau de Couperin, Le SUITE IN SIX MOVEMENTS FOR PIANO (four of which were subsequently orchestrated) by Maurice Ravel, composed 1914–17 and first performed April 11, 1919, by Marguerite Long. Well before Ravel gave it a new lease on life, the *tombeau* (literally "tomb," here signifying a work intended as a memorial) had served as a vehicle for many of France's finest poets and composers to pay tribute to their deceased predecessors. As a poetic genre it was particularly important during the 16th and 17th centuries; musicians, especially lutenists and harpsichordists, took it up in the 17th and 18th centuries. In 1914, with France reeling from the German onslaught, Ravel, like many of his countrymen, felt the need to assert the value of French culture. Not surprisingly, his thoughts turned to the epoch of Louis XIV, a golden age in the history of France, and to the music of the master clavecinist of the French Baroque, François Couperin. *Le tombeau de Couperin*—consisting of a Prélude, Fugue, Forlane, Rigaudon, Menuet, and Toccata loosely patterned on Baroque models—was to be his tribute to the French spirit and to the enduring values of clarity and elegance that have characterized French art. By the time Ravel finished the score, toward the end of World War I, he had something else to commemorate—the lives of fallen friends. Each of the movements of the suite is dedicated to an individual who perished in the conflict.

In 1919, in response to a request from Rolf de Maré's Swedish ballet, Ravel orchestrated four movements of *Le tombeau de Couperin* (the Prélude, Forlane, Menuet, and Rigaudon) for a small complement similar in size to an 18th-century orchestra: two flutes, two oboes (second doubling English horn), two clarinets, two bassoons, two horns, trumpet, harp, and strings. The scoring is typically brilliant—particularly the fleet, exquisitely challenging writing for winds in the Prélude, and the flamboyant treatment of strings and trumpet in the Rigaudon. The orchestral suite (which does not include the Fugue and the Toccata, the two most pianistic movements of the original) received its premiere on February 28, 1920, at a concert of the Pasdeloup Orchestra conducted by René Baton. The version of the score best known to listeners today, it has become one of the most popular of Ravel's works. The ballet (consisting of the orchestral suite minus the Prélude) received its premiere November 8, 1920, at the Théâtre des Champs-Elysées in Paris, with Désiré-Emile Inghelbrecht conducting. Ravel himself conducted the 100th performance of the ballet in 1923, also at the Théâtre des Champs-Elysées.

RECOMMENDED RECORDINGS

PIANO:

THIBAUDET (DECCA).

THIOLLIER (NAXOS).

ORCHESTRA:

DUTOIT AND MONTREAL SYMPHONY ORCHESTRA (DECCA).

MARTINON AND ORCHESTRE DE PARIS (EMI).

tonality The system of major and minor keys in use in Western music since the 17th century. *See also* KEY.

tone poem *See* SYMPHONIC POEM.

tone row A succession of notes, usually with no pitch repeated, used as a generative motif for a piece of music. Most of the works that employ tone rows are 12-TONE compositions.

tonic [1] The first degree of a major or minor scale and, by extension, the chord whose root is that note. [2] The central or "home" key of a given piece, or of a section of a piece.

Tosca **OPERA IN THREE ACTS BY GIACOMO PUCCINI,** to a libretto by Giuseppe Giacosa and Luigi Illica (based on the play by Victorien Sardou written for Sarah Bernhardt), premiered January 14, 1900, at the Teatro Costanzi in Rome. The drama is set in Rome in June 1800; the unseen presence behind the action is Napoleon, whose Italian campaign has polarized Roman society. On one side is Cavaradossi, a painter with Republican sympathies who, almost before his colors are mixed, plunges into the quickest-hitting tune in all of opera, "Recondita armonia," remarking on the mysterious beauty of his lover, Tosca, while he paints a portrait of the Madonna. On the other side, contra Napoleon, is Scarpia, the chief of police, a menacing, powerful figure used to manipulating others, but consumed by lust for Tosca. In the middle is Tosca, the celebrated diva, vulnerable and violent, whose "Vissi d'arte" stops the show in the second act. Her confrontation with Scarpia, which ends badly for that elegantly treacherous thug, is music drama at its finest.

Tosca manages to work several of Rome's landmarks into its action, which has its advantages: In no other locale could a prima donna leap to her death from as imposing an edifice as the Castel Sant' Angelo, where the third act is set. But the conflicts that make *Tosca* gripping, and much more than the "shabby little shocker" Joseph Kerman once called it, could occur anywhere jealousy and betrayal coexist. In the three principal roles—as impressive a love triangle as there is in opera—one finds everything necessary for an audience pleaser.

RECOMMENDED RECORDINGS

CALLAS, DI STEFANO, GOBBI; DE SABATA AND LA SCALA ORCHESTRA (EMI).

GHEORGHIU, ALAGNA, RAIMONDI; PAPPANO AND ROYAL OPERA (EMI).

PRICE, DI STEFANO, TADDEI; KARAJAN AND VIENNA PHILHARMONIC (DECCA).

Toscanini, Arturo

(b. Parma, March 25, 1867; d. New York, January 16, 1957)

ITALIAN CONDUCTOR. During a podium career that lasted nearly 70 years, he established himself as the most important conductor of his generation and one of the most influential musicians of the 20th

Eagle-eyed Arturo Toscanini

century, enjoying in the process fame and fortune that were unprecedented for a classical performer. In the early 1930s, when Babe Ruth was making $80,000 a year with the New York Yankees, Toscanini earned a cool $100,000 for a four-month season with the New York Philharmonic. Blessed with a phenomenal memory—and forced to rely on it in performance due to his extreme nearsightedness—he knew almost 600 works down to the last detail and could explode at the slightest deviation from the score he carried in his head. But while his fiery temper cowed quite a few musicians, his relentless pursuit of perfection and incandescent performing style inspired many others and had a transformative impact on the art of interpretation.

Toscanini began his musical studies at the age of nine at Parma's Royal School of Music, graduating in 1885 with highest honors in cello and composition. The following year he was engaged by the Rossi Opera Company, a touring organization, as principal cellist and assistant chorusmaster. At a performance of Verdi's *Aida* in Rio de Janeiro on June 30, 1886, he was thrust into the limelight for the first time, after the evening's scheduled conductor withdrew due to "indisposition" and the Brazilian audience erupted with catcalls and commotion at the announcement that he was to be replaced by the company's assistant conductor. Knowing that Toscanini had memorized the score, several of the singers shouted out his name; the 19-year-old novice walked to the podium, sat down, and conducted. Toscanini's spontaneous debut was met with thunderous ovations, and he was hired to lead the orchestra for the remainder of the season. He made his Italian debut later in 1886 and quickly came to be recognized as a conductor of uncommon gifts.

Between 1886 and 1894, Toscanini solidified his reputation, conducting opera in the major Italian houses. One of the high-water marks of this period came on May 21, 1892, when he presided over the premiere of Leoncavallo's *Pagliacci.* Toscanini became director of Turin's Teatro Regio in 1895; he immediately caused a sensation by leading the first performance by an Italian opera company of Wagner's *Götterdämmerung.* Less than six weeks later, on February 1, 1896, he conducted the world premiere of Puccini's *La bohème,* again at the Regio.

In 1898 Toscanini was appointed music director of Italy's leading opera company, La Scala in Milan. He remained there until 1903, and returned, after a short stint in Buenos Aires, for the company's 1906–08 seasons. He came to the United States in 1908 to take the principal conductor's post at the Metropolitan Opera; while in New York, he led the world premiere of Puccini's *La fanciulla del West,* in 1910, and the American premiere of Mussorgsky's *Boris Godunov,* in 1913. Also in 1913, he made his American debut as a symphonic conductor with a New York performance of Beethoven's Ninth. He returned to Italy in 1915 and spent the remainder of World War I there. He resumed his duties at La Scala in 1920, taking its orchestra and chorus on a North American tour and making his first recordings for the Victor Talking Machine Co. He conducted the world premiere of Puccini's *Turandot* at La Scala in 1926.

On January 5, 1926, Toscanini made his debut with the New York Philharmonic, conducting the American premiere of Respighi's *Pini di Roma.* In 1929 he resigned from La Scala to become the Philharmonic's music director, a post he held until 1936. In 1937 the Radio Corporation of America (RCA) formed the NBC Symphony Orchestra specifically for Toscanini to conduct. During the next 17 years, he and the orchestra made numerous recordings and gave hundreds of broadcasts, and by the 1950s an estimated 8 million listeners were regularly tuning them in on the radio.

In the summer months Toscanini kept up a grueling schedule, conducting at the Bayreuth Festival (1930–31), the Salzburg Festival (1934–37), in London (1935–36), and at the newly established Lucerne Festival (1938–39). He toured South America with the NBC Symphony in 1940 and, following the end of World War II, returned to Italy to conduct the first concert in the rebuilt La Scala opera house. His last major campaign with the NBC Symphony, in the spring of 1950, was a coast-to-coast tour by train that found the 83-year-old maestro leading a total of 21 concerts (with five different programs) in 44 days. In 1954, at the age of 87, he resigned the directorship of the NBC Symphony following a memory lapse during a live broadcast of the *Tannhäuser* Overture, and the orchestra was quickly disbanded. Toscanini died in New York three years later, two months shy of his 90th birthday.

Toscanini at work in later years

Toscanini was a complicated and in many ways paradoxical figure. He was the ultimate old-school conductor, dominating orchestras with a combination of belligerence (swearing at and even scuffling with musicians who didn't meet his expectations), personal charisma, and sheer musical willpower. Yet he was also the first modern conductor—a musician whose career was tied to the media and whose name was known to millions of Americans who never actually saw him perform, but who listened worshipfully to his phonograph records and radio broadcasts. He was obsessed with energy and force, yet he constantly exhorted his players to "sing." And, though stiff and undemonstrative in his physical gestures, he could elicit phenomenal responses from his players with a glance or the slightest change of facial expression. He rehearsed intensively and demanded absolute perfection. Sometimes he got it, often he didn't, but there was an electricity in his performances and recordings that few conductors since his time have been able to generate.

RECOMMENDED RECORDINGS

BEETHOVEN, SYMPHONIES (COMPLETE): NBC SYMPHONY ORCHESTRA (RCA).

RESPIGHI, PINI DI ROMA, FONTANE DI ROMA, FESTE ROMANE: NBC SYMPHONY ORCHESTRA (RCA).

VERDI, *REQUIEM*: NELLI, BARBIERI, DI STEFANO, SIEPI; NBC SYMPHONY ORCHESTRA (RCA).

tote Stadt, Die (The Dead City) OPERA IN THREE ACTS BY **ERICH WOLFGANG KORNGOLD,** to a libretto by the composer and his father (based on the novel *Bruges* *la morte,* by Georges Rodenbach), composed in 1920 and premiered simultaneously in Hamburg and Cologne on December 4, 1920. The "dead" city is Bruges, where the action takes place at the end of the 19th century. The opera follows the half-imagined, half-real interaction between Paul, recently widowed, and Marietta, a dancer whom he has just met, and who bears an uncanny resemblance to Paul's deceased wife, Marie. At one point, Marie's apparition tells Paul to stop living in the past and move on with his life; later, Paul dreams of being seduced by Marietta, then murdering her after an argument. Having fantasized a horrible end to his imagined relationship with Marietta, Paul is able, at the end of the opera, to renounce the possibility of a real relationship with Marietta, and to make up his mind to leave Bruges. Korngold's rapturous vocal writing and luxuriant use of the orchestra are perfectly suited to a plot in which fantasy and reality seductively intertwine.

RECOMMENDED RECORDING

NEBLETT, WAGERMANN, LUXON, KOLLO, PREY; LEINSDORF AND MUNICH RADIO SYMPHONY ORCHESTRA (RCA).

Tower, Joan

(b. New Rochelle, N.Y., September 6, 1938)

AMERICAN COMPOSER. Part of her childhood was spent in South America, beginning at the age of nine when her father, a geologist, took a job as a mining engineer in La Paz, Bolivia. She was there for the next nine years and, after overcoming the initial trauma of dislocation, quickly fell in love with the Latin culture. In addition to studying the piano she learned to play all sorts of exotic percussion instruments. She studied at Bennington College, receiving her B.A. in 1961, and at Columbia University, where she earned an M.A. in 1965 (and was awarded a D.M.A. in 1978). An expert pianist and chamber musician, she founded the Da Capo Chamber Players in 1969 and subsequently composed a number of works for that group.

Joan Tower

Tower started out in composition as a serialist, but beginning with *Black Topaz* (1976) she turned away from that toward a new idiom, emotionally more direct, influenced by Messiaen, among others. She served as composer in residence with the Saint Louis Symphony Orchestra from 1984 to 1987, working closely with conductor Leonard Slatkin; while there, she composed her *Fanfare for the Uncommon Woman* (1986), using the same instrumentation as Copland's familiar work. She has since created several sequels playing off that catchy title, emerging not only as a role model for women composers but as an eminent figure in American musical life. Her strong brief of commissions includes concertos for the piano (1985), clarinet (1988), flute (1989), and violin (1992), and a sizable number of works for varied chamber formations. Among her recent works are *Tambor* (1998) and *Strike Zones* (2001), both concerto-like pieces for percussion and orchestra, and *In Memory* (2002), written for the Tokyo String Quartet.

Tower has formidable skills as an orchestral composer, but is more inclined to write chamber music, where greater intimacy of expression is possible. She cites Beethoven as the composer who has had the greatest influence on her musical thinking, and acknowledges Stravinsky, Copland, Shostakovich, and Messiaen as her 20th-century musical idols.

RECOMMENDED RECORDINGS

CONCERTOS FOR FLUTE, CLARINET, VIOLIN, PIANO: WINCENC, SHIFRIN, OLIVEIRA, OPPENS; SILVERSTEIN, BRAGADO-DARMAN AND LOUISVILLE ORCHESTRA (D'NOTE CLASSICS).

FANFARES FOR THE UNCOMMON WOMAN NOS. 1–5: ALSOP AND COLORADO SYMPHONY ORCHESTRA (KOCH).

***Toy* Symphony** [1] NICKNAME OF THE CASSATION IN G PRESUMED TO BE BY LEOPOLD MOZART (though formerly attributed to Joseph Haydn), so called because it features little obbligato solos by toy instruments such as birdcalls, a rattle, and so on. [2] WORK FOR CHILDREN BY THE AMERICAN COMPOSER TOD MACHOVER (B. 1953), using hyperviolin, beat bugs, and other esoteric instruments, premiered in 2003.

RECOMMENDED RECORDING

MOZART:

HAGER AND LUXEMBOURG RADIO SYMPHONY ORCHESTRA (FORLANE).

***Tragic* Overture** CONCERT OVERTURE BY JOHANNES BRAHMS, OP. 81, composed in 1880 and premiered December 26, 1880, in Vienna. As weighty and serious as its counterpart, the *Academic Festival* Overture, Op. 80, is lively and effervescent, it stands in the line of Beethoven's *Coriolan* and *Egmont* as a portrait of stoic resistance to the dark tide of destiny. That the title is intentionally vague—not referring to any specific literary or historical figure—is typical of Brahms. The overture is cast as a tightly wound sonata-form movement, dominated by a brooding, grimly urgent exordium in D minor. Even so, its consoling second subject is one of the most beautiful in all of Brahms's orchestral music.

RECOMMENDED RECORDINGS

ABBADO AND BERLIN PHILHARMONIC (DG).

SZELL AND CLEVELAND ORCHESTRA (SONY).

transcription [1] The copying of a piece of music from one form of notation to another. [2] The arrangement of a piece of music for a medium or forces different from those for which its composer intended it (e.g., Franz Liszt's transcriptions of the Beethoven symphonies for piano, or Leopold Stokowski's transcriptions of Bach organ pieces for orchestra).

transposition The notation or performance of music at a pitch different from that at which it was originally intended to sound.

Traubel, Helen

(b. St. Louis, June 20, 1899; d. Santa Monica, Calif., July 28, 1972)

AMERICAN SOPRANO. The daughter of a pharmacist and an enthusiastic amateur singer, Traubel studied in St. Louis with Vetta Karst and made her debut with the Saint Louis Symphony in 1925. When she subsequently sang at Lewisohn Stadium in New York, she came to the attention of Giulio Gatti-Casazza, general manager of the Metropolitan Opera, who offered her a contract. She refused it and returned to St. Louis to continue her studies and gain experience. She finally sang at the Met in 1937 in a new opera by Walter Damrosch (1862–1950), *The Man Without a Country.* The opera is long forgotten, but Traubel went on to become one of the greatest Wagnerian sopranos of the day. In 1939 she sang her first Sieglinde at the Met opposite Kirsten Flagstad's Brünnhilde, and when Flagstad left the Met in 1941 to return to Norway, Traubel assumed all of Flagstad's roles. Traubel had a big, handsome voice of exceptional warmth that soared over the orchestra without strain or stridency. Even during the golden age of Wagnerian singers at the Met, between 1930 and 1950, amid an array of legendary heroic singers such as Flagstad, Lotte

Lehmann, Frieda Leider, Kerstin Thorborg, Friederich Schorr, and Lauritz Melchior, Traubel stood out, and was especially admired for the impetuous passion she brought to the role of Isolde, which she sang 44 times on the Met stage. Traubel had no pretenses about, and made no apologies for, singing lighter, popular fare, and enjoyed occasional Broadway and nightclub appearances, much to the dismay of Rudolf Bing, the Met's general manager from 1950. In a contract letter sent to Traubel in 1953, he included a not-so-veiled warning that she might consider missing a season or two until she turned her attention completely to serious art. Traubel, incensed by Bing's snobbery, had his letter published in the press, refused to sign the contract, and never again sang at the Met. She continued to sing both in concert and on Broadway, and appeared in several movies. An openhearted, generous personality, with a voice that knew no limits, she was one of America's greatest home-grown talents.

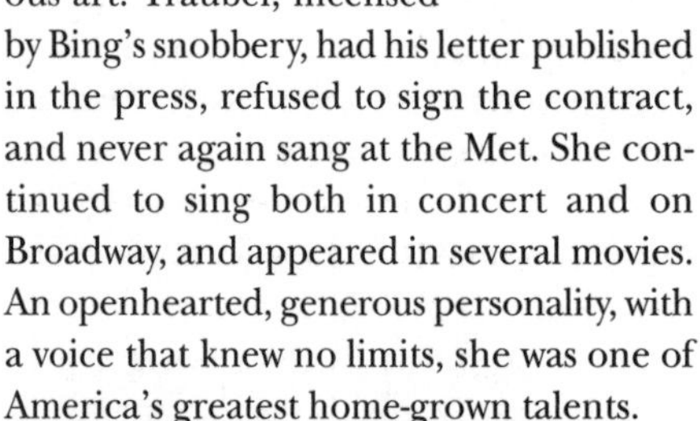

RECOMMENDED RECORDINGS

WAGNER, SCENES FROM *LOHENGRIN* AND *TRISTAN UND ISOLDE*: MELCHIOR, VARNAY, BAUM, OTHERS; KNOCH, BUSCH AND METROPOLITAN OPERA ORCHESTRA; LEINSDORF AND COLUMBIA SYMPHONY ORCHESTRA (SONY).

COLLECTION:

"LEGENDARY VOICES" (2 VOLS.): ARIAS AND SONGS BY GLUCK, MOZART, WAGNER, STRAUSS, VERDI (PREISER).

"Träumerei" ("Reverie") TITLE OF THE SEVENTH MOVEMENT OF ROBERT SCHUMANN'S *KINDERSZENEN* (*Scenes from Childhood*). Among the most popular encore pieces in the piano repertoire, it was a particular favorite of Vladimir Horowitz.

traviata, La (The Woman Who Strayed) OPERA IN FOUR PARTS BY GIUSEPPE VERDI to a libretto by Francesco Maria Piave. Based on the play *La dame aux camellias* by Alexandre Dumas *fils*, it was composed in 1853 and premiered at La Fenice in Venice the same year. The play on which the opera was based was hot off the press when Verdi got hold of it: Marie Duplessis, the real-life courtesan on whom the character Violetta Valéry is based, had just died, in 1847, at age 23. At the time Verdi finished his setting in 1853, he and the soprano Giuseppina Strepponi had been living together out of wedlock for six years. The similarities between their situation and that of Violetta and Alfredo Germont, the lovers at the heart of *La traviata*, were unmistakable—and no doubt part of the reason Verdi responded so fervently to the story. He was intrigued as well by the complicated triangle, in which the father, Giorgio Germont, is the "other man."

Cover of first edition of **La traviata**

The opera is full of glorious intimate moments and conveys a telling insight into the uncertainty, fragility, and painful vulnerability of love. Thanks to Verdi's sympathetic treatment, the thrust of the drama becomes not whether the lead character will die—that is known from the beginning—but whether she will have the experience of real, joyous redeeming love before she does. Verdi's understanding of the character's complex feelings can be crushing in its impact: The whole work is a gripping emotional crescendo, and the character of Violetta, the consumptive young woman who sacrifices everything for her lover's sake, is among Verdi's supreme achievements.

RECOMMENDED RECORDINGS

Cotrubas, Domingo, Milnes; Kleiber and Bavarian State Orchestra (DG).

Highlights:

Sutherland, Bergonzi, Merrill; Pritchard and Florence Maggio Musicale (Decca).

Treigle, Norman

(b. New Orleans, March 6, 1927; d. New Orleans, February 16, 1975)

AMERICAN BASS-BARITONE. He studied voice with Elizabeth Wood in his native New Orleans, and made his professional debut with the New Orleans Opera in 1947. His debut with the New York City Opera, as Colline in *La bohème* in 1953, went largely unnoticed. Then, in September 1956, he sang the role of Olin Blitch opposite Phyllis Curtin in the City Opera production of Carlisle Floyd's (b. 1926) *Susannah,* and became an instant star. A singer of enormous dramatic force and electrifying stage presence, he became an anchor of the company through 1972. Subsequent City Opera triumphs included *Boris Godunov* in 1964 and the title role in Handel's *Giulio Cesare* in 1966, the production that launched Beverly Sills into starry orbit and laid the foundation of an important stage partnership for Sills and Treigle. In 1969, the City Opera mounted Boito's *Mefistofele* for Treigle; it became one of the company's greatest critical and financial successes. Treigle's final City Opera production was Offenbach's *Les contes d'Hoffmann,* in which he played the four villains (1972); he recorded the opera with Sills that same year under the baton of Julius Rudel. After his departure from the City Opera, Treigle sang in Europe, making his Covent Garden debut with *Faust* in 1973, and appearing in Hamburg and Milan.

RECOMMENDED RECORDINGS

Boito, *Mefistofele*: Caballé, Domingo; Rudel and London Symphony Orchestra (EMI).

Handel, *Giulio Cesare*: Sills, Forrester, Wolff, Malas; Rudel and New York City Opera Orchestra (RCA).

tremolo (from It. *tremolare,* "to tremble") A rapid reiteration of a single note, or an alternation between two notes at least a minor third apart. When a tremolo is played in such a way as to produce rhythmically precise subdivisions of a given time value, it is described as a measured tremolo; when the effect is that of a sustained "shimmering" on a note, it is said to be unmeasured. The most common form of tremolo is unmeasured bowed string tremolo on a single note or chord (as in the beginning of the *Blue Danube* Waltz). A timpani roll is a species of tremolo.

triad A chord consisting of three notes: the "root," the third above, and the fifth above, in any arrangement or inversion.

triangle Percussion instrument named for its shape. The standard triangle is a steel rod bent in the shape of an equilateral triangle, six to seven inches on a side and open at one corner. It is played with a metal beater. If properly struck, the instrument's tone is high, clear, and luminous. Individual notes can be played with a stroke that contacts the instrument on the base or along one of the sides near the apex, depending on the tone one wishes to produce. Rolls, which can be notated either as trills or tremolos, are played by executing rapid strokes within one of the angles, producing a sparkling, penetrating sonority that blends beautifully with the upper partials of the orchestral harmony. The triangle entered the arsenal of Western classical music in the Middle Ages, but became a fixture in the orchestra only toward the middle of the 18th century, after being popularized by the Janissary bands of the Ottoman Empire. Mozart used the triangle, along with cymbals, in his overture to *Die Entführung aus dem Serail* (1782), and Haydn included these instruments in his Symphony No. 100 in G (1794), nicknamed the *Military*—both composers intending to suggest a Turkish element. When Beethoven deployed the triangle (along with cymbals and bass drum) in the finale of his Ninth Symphony, he broadened its context from the topical to the coloristic, opening the door to widespread use of the instrument in the orchestral music of the 19th and 20th centuries. Notable passages involving the triangle can be found in Schumann's *Spring* Symphony (1841), Liszt's Piano Concerto No. 1 (1853), Tchaikovsky's Symphony No. 4 (1877), Brahms's Symphony No. 4 (1884–85), Rimsky-Korsakov's *Capriccio espagnol* (1887), and Dvořák's Symphony *From the New World* (1893). The triangle contributes to the splash of color that begins Respighi's *Pini di Roma* (1923–24) and to the final moments of any number of works, including Ravel's orchestration of *Pictures at an Exhibition* (1922) and Shostakovich's Symphony No. 5 (1937).

trill An ornament applied to a specific note, consisting of a moderate to very rapid alternation between that note and another note either a half step or a whole step above it. *See also* AGRÉMENTS; ORNAMENTS.

trio [1] In instrumental music, a composition for three performers; in opera, a scene or number in which three singers participate. [2] The middle section of a minuet or scherzo.

trio sonata In Baroque music, a sonata written for two melody instruments and continuo. The standard complement, from the late 17th century on, was two treble instruments and harpsichord, with or without a bass instrument such as cello, violone, or string bass. On keyboard instruments, a trio sonata texture could be achieved without additional instruments, with two principal "voices" or lines, plus a bass line. *See also* SONATA.

Tristan und Isolde OPERA IN THREE ACTS BY RICHARD WAGNER, to his own libretto (based on the medieval romance by Gottfried von Strassburg), composed 1857–59 and premiered June 10, 1865, at the National Theater in Munich. In *Tristan und Isolde,* arguably the most important opera of the 19th century, Wagner explored the relationship of passion and free will in terms that prepared him for the completion of *Siegfried* and *Götterdämmerung,* the final two operas of his *Ring* cycle, in the process bringing about a sea change in aesthetics and revolutionizing musical thought.

Tristan und Isolde is the story of two neurotic lovers undone yet ultimately transfigured by their love. The opera has only six principal roles, two of which are fairly small, a brief chorus (of men only) at the end of the first act, and a minimum of scenery. Its orchestra is not unduly large, although the score does call at one point for 12 offstage horns. Yet the challenge of putting on *Tristan* was, and has remained, one of the greatest in the theater. Wagner coined a new musical language when he wrote the work, entrusted the orchestra with a more important and more taxing part in the proceedings than it had had in any previous opera, and demanded of his two leading singers herculean endurance, compass, and vocal power. The harmonic syntax of *Tristan* has a degree of CHROMATICISM unprecedented in tonal music, fundamentally changing the way harmonic implications and tensions are dealt with. Chords calling for resolution are allowed to stand unresolved, producing in the listener a psychological yearning that mirrors the unsatisfied longings of the opera's protagonists. The dysfunctional treatment of harmony, sustained across four hours, allows Wagner to open up a whole new world of expression.

Since its first performance, *Tristan und Isolde* has held a place apart in the world of opera. In imagining the seething confrontations of its title characters in the first act, their voluptuous love music in the second, and, most of all, Tristan's feverish longings and Isolde's ecstatic love-death in the finale, Wagner came as close as he ever would to the elusive goal of creating an ideal music drama.

RECOMMENDED RECORDINGS

FLAGSTAD, SUTHAUS, THEBOM, FISCHER-DIESKAU; FURTWÄNGLER AND PHILHARMONIA ORCHESTRA (EMI).

NILSSON, WINDGASSEN, LUDWIG, WAECHTER, TALVELA; BÖHM AND BAYREUTH FESTIVAL ORCHESTRA (DG).

tritone The interval of an augmented fourth (or diminished fifth), so called because it spans three whole tones. Because it falls between two "perfect" intervals—the fourth and the fifth—and generates a glaring dissonance when sounded, it was called the "Devil's interval" in medieval music. In his *War Requiem* (1961), Britten made prominent use of the tritone, allowing its dissonance to hang like smoke in the air of the opening pages.

trittico, Il (The Triptych) OPERATIC TRILOGY BY GIACOMO PUCCINI, consisting of the one-act operas *IL TABARRO, SUOR ANGELICA,* and *GIANNI SCHICCHI,* premiered December 14, 1918, at the Metropolitan Opera in New York.

RECOMMENDED RECORDING

GHEORGHIU, PALMER, ROSCHMANN, ALAGNA, SCHICOFF, VAN DAM; PAPPANO AND LONDON SYMPHONY ORCHESTRA, PHILHARMONIA ORCHESTRA (EMI).

trombone Brass instrument with a mostly cylindrical bore that becomes conical toward the bell, a shallow, cup-shaped mouthpiece, and a distinctive U-shaped slide operated by the right hand. Its design has remained essentially unchanged since the 1500s. Prior to the 18th century the trombone was known as the SACKBUT, a name derived from an unlikely mix of Spanish and Teutonic roots meaning "push-pull." Early trombones came in a variety of sizes and were typically deployed as a kind of "choir" consisting of tenor, bass, and alto voices—a division that has survived in the notation of some orchestral trombone parts, where the first and second trombones share a staff in tenor clef, and the part for third trombone is notated on a separate staff, in bass clef. The standard modern trombone is the tenor, pitched in B-flat, with a 9-foot tube length when the slide is fully retracted. Many tenor trombones come with an additional length of tubing called an "F attachment," allowing the instrument's range to be extended down a fourth, to low C. For players specializing in lower parts, "tenor-bass" trombones are often built with a wider bore, a larger bell, and an F attachment that permits a low B-natural. Orchestral players may keep several different instruments in their arsenal, including a small-bore trombone known as a "pea-shooter" for high solo work.

The trombone has an astonishing dynamic range, from soft to shatteringly loud (it can generate more sonic energy than any other nonpercussion instrument), and is capable of an equally remarkable range of coloration. In the hands of a good player it can proclaim in full, ringing tones with a brassy glint, threaten with menacing, edgy snarls, or deliver a rich, cantabile baritone.

Until the middle of the 18th century the trombone was used mainly in church (routinely doubling the lower parts in vocal music) and in civic and courtly ceremony, its sound adding heft to fanfares. It entered the orchestra by way of the opera house, where its solemn tone had long served to symbolize solemnity, foreboding, and the supernatural. Beethoven was the first composer to use the trombone in a symphony, and he did it with typical panache, hurling three of them into the finale of his Fifth Symphony. He used them again in the Sixth and the Ninth to add weight to the orchestral sonority, and after that there was no turning back. Schubert made very effective use of trombones in his final two symphonies, employing them as much for color as weight; Berlioz the conductor let them run wild in his orchestra, and as a composer he had the delicacy of imagination to use eight of them, in unison, to provide solemn pedal tones under an ethereal trio of flutes in the "Hostias" section of his Requiem. Trombones do a lot of heavy lifting in Wagner's operas, but he also uses them for their subtle color, as in the hushed chords, marked *ppp,* at the very beginning of the "Liebestod" in *Tristan und Isolde.*

The Russian orchestral literature is rich in flamboyant writing for the trombone section, particularly the works of Tchaikovsky, Rimsky-Korsakov, Stravinsky, and Shostakovich. Debussy and Ravel were more circumspect, but they too could cut the bones loose, as Debussy does at the end of his *Ibéria,* calling on the three trombones to blast out a G-major chord, slide up an octave, and drop back down. Other great licks in the trombone book include the beginning of the "chase" scene in Bartók's *The Miraculous Mandarin,* where two muted trombones trade off against each other; the lengthy *fortissimo* solo for trombone in the first movement of Mahler's Third Symphony (mm. 166–208), depicting nature at its most primordial, which is finished off *fff* by all four players in the section; and the marvelous unison proclamation for three trombones that begins Walton's *Belshazzar's Feast.* The trombone's recital repertoire includes Hindemith's Sonata for Trombone and Piano (1941) and Berio's unaccompanied *Sequenza V* (1966). Despite the trombone's many merits, there is a dearth of concerted works for the instrument. Among the best in the repertoire are Frank Martin's *Ballade* (1941) for trombone and small orchestra, the Trombone Concerto (1955) by the English composer Gordon Jacob (1895–1984), and the concerto *Birds and Bells* (1995) by Danish composer Bent Sorensen (b. 1958), written for today's ranking classical player, the Swedish virtuoso Christian Lindberg.

trope (from Gr. *tropos,* "turn") A musical phrase or an element of a musical setting of a text that is based on a preexisting source. In much early music, the preexisting source was PLAINCHANT. Troping, as used in a vast amount of medieval music, was a reference to authority, a means of giving legitimacy to a new idea.

troubadours and trouvères Two related groups of poet-musicians of 12th- and 13th-century France. The troubadours, from the south, were Western culture's earliest authors of vernacular poetry set to music. Their approximately 2,600 surviving poems, exemplars of technical and rhetorical virtuosity, were written in *langue d'oc* (also known as Occitan or Provençal) and set to MONOPHONIC melodies, of which only about 300 have survived. Usually from high ranks of society, the troubadours were the first to realize the concept of *fin' amors,* now commonly called "courtly love," in which the poet, through adoration of an unattainable object of love, is refined by the experiences associated with being a worthy, courteous lover. Some of the most famous and influential troubadours were Bernart de Ventadorn (fl. ca. 1147–70), Jaufre Rudel (fl. ca. 1125–48), and Raimbaut de Vaqeiras (fl. ca. 1180–1205). Unusual in medieval society, a group of women troubadours, or "trobairitz," also contributed a body of poems, although only about 45 survive, all without music except for one *canso* by the Comtessa de Dia (fl. late 12th and early 13th centuries).

Throughout the 13th century, the northern trouvères followed the model begun by their southern compatriots, writing music and poems in *langue d'oil,* an early form of French. A little more than 2,000 trouvère poems are known, about two-thirds of them with music. One of the earliest trouvères, the lyric poet Chrétien de Troyes (fl. 1160–90), was also the author of the first Arthurian romances. The monk Gautier de Coincy (ca. 1177–1236) composed both *fine amour* and religious chansons as well as a major verse narrative with

A troubador before a royal couple

songs, *Les miracles de nostre-dame*; trouvère songs with religious texts were quite common. Probably most famous of the trouvères was Adam de La Halle (ca. 1240–88), who wrote both trouvère songs and polyphonic works, as well as one of the best-known medieval plays with music, *Le jeu de Robin et de Marion.*

The melodies of troubadour and trouvère songs range from elegant and declamatory to simpler, folk song–like tunes. Most were notated without rhythm (in a fashion similar to PLAINCHANT), sparking in modern times a century-long debate over whether to perform them freely or in a defined meter; recent opinion is that the varying types of verse should be the determining factor, so many choices are open to the performer. An argument between scholars Pierre Aubry (1874–1910) and Jean Beck (1881–1943), who both hypothesized that the songs should be rhythmic, resulted in history's strangest outcome of musicological research: Aubry's death while fencing with foils, preparing to fight a duel with Beck over who came up with the theory first.

RECOMMENDED RECORDINGS

BINKLEY AND STUDIO DER FRÜHEN MUSIK (ELEKTRA).

"CANSOS DE TROBAIRITZ" (SONGS OF WOMEN TROUBADOURS): FIGUERAS; HESPERION XX (EMI).

"LE JEU D'AMOUR": AZÉMA, KAMMEN, FLEAGLE (ELEKTRA).

POSCH AND ENSEMBLE UNICORN (NAXOS).

"SWEET IS THE SONG": BOTT (OISEAU-LYRE).

***Trout* Quintet** NICKNAME OF FRANZ SCHUBERT'S QUINTET IN **A, D. 667,** for piano, violin, viola, cello, and double bass. The work was composed during the summer of 1819, on a commission from Sylvester Paumgartner, an amateur cellist and chamber music enthusiast, for a musical evening at his home. The commission specified only that the instrumentation be the same as that of Hummel's Quintet in

E-flat, Op. 87, and that the new work contain a set of variations on Schubert's own song "Die Forelle" ("The Trout"), written in 1817 and apparently a great favorite of Paumgartner's. While conceived of as *Hausmusik,* intended entirely for pleasure, the resulting essay shows remarkable resourcefulness in the way it handles the unusual complement of string trio with added piano and double bass. The variety and clarity of texture Schubert achieves throughout the piece make it one of the marvels of the chamber literature, and even though the classic Biedermeier qualities of simplicity and easygoing lyricism inform the musical expression, there are moments when Schubert's treatment of harmony and line allow a glimpse of something deeper. The quintet's serenade-like character is clearly reflected in its five-movement design, and its essential leisureliness is underscored by its two Andantes framing the lone dance movement, a reversal of the usual pattern. The work's fourth movement is a set of six decorative variations on the theme of "Die Forelle."

RECOMMENDED RECORDINGS

SAWALLISCH, POSPICHAL, KLOS, REHM, WEISSENSTEINER (PROFIL).

SERKIN, LAREDO, NAEGELE, PARNAS, LEVINE (SONY).

trovatore, Il (The Troubadour) OPERA IN FOUR "PARTS" BY GIUSEPPE VERDI, to a libretto by Salvatore Cammarano (based on Antonio García Gutiérrez's play *El trovador*), premiered January 19, 1853, at the Teatro Apollo in Rome. Though dramatically less fine than either *Rigoletto* or *La traviata,* it nonetheless became one of the most popular operas of the 19th century—so popular that its "babies switched at birth" plot twist could be parodied by Gilbert and Sullivan in *The Gondoliers* and the music itself by the Marx Brothers in *A Night at the Opera. Il trovatore* is a blood-and-thunder opera of the old style, with a libretto that relies more on passion and complication than it does on real character. But there is still much great music in the opera, in addition to the famous "Anvil Chorus." The Gypsy Azucena's "Stride la vampa," which follows that chorus, will always make people's hair stand on end, and Manrico's "Di quella pira" remains the finest exit aria Verdi ever wrote. But the heart of the opera lies in its heroine Leonora's two great arias, "Tacea la notte" and "D'amor sull'ali rosee." In fact, there are enough great arias in the work to keep everyone happy, which is what inspired Enrico Caruso's memorable dictum to the effect that all *Il trovatore* needs to be a success is the four greatest singers in the world.

RECOMMENDED RECORDING

PRICE, COSSOTTO, DOMINGO, MILNES; MEHTA AND NEW PHILHARMONIA ORCHESTRA (RCA).

Troyanos, Tatiana

(b. New York, September 12, 1938; d. New York, August 21, 1993)

AMERICAN MEZZO-SOPRANO. As a child she was surrounded by vocal music: Her parents were both amateur singers and she participated in many church and school choirs, but her family could not afford serious musical training for her. When study finally became possible, she first gravitated to the piano, but her discovery of the recordings of another Greek-American, Maria Callas, and of standing room at the Metropolitan Opera, led her to apply to the Juilliard School in hopes of studying with Hans Heinz. Juilliard accepted her, but not to study with Heinz, so she circumnavigated school

Tatiana Troyanos

policy and took lessons from him privately; he remained her teacher for many years, through the beginning of her professional career. Her debut came in 1963 as Hippolyta in Britten's *A Midsummer Night's Dream* in its New York premiere at the New York City Opera. The same season she also sang Jocasta in Stravinsky's *Oedipus Rex*. She felt artistically frustrated at the City Opera, and with its music director Julius Rudel's support and that of Heinz, she sought work in Germany. A contract with the Hamburg State Opera materialized in 1965, and in the ensuing decade there, and at prominent European festivals and opera houses such as Aix-en-Provence and Covent Garden, she developed the vocal and dramatic skills that would earn her a place at the top of her profession. She had a rich, burnished sound with no perceptible break from the bottom to the considerably high top of her vocal range. Her voice was also wide-ranging in the spectra of color, volume, and flexibility it would allow. Coupled with Troyanos's emotional palette and statuesque glamour, it made her a singing actress of extraordinary versatility. Her activity at the Metropolitan Opera began in 1976 as Octavian in Richard Strauss's *Der Rosenkavalier*, a pants role with which she was strongly associated for most of her career; but she also gave the Met audience memorable portrayals of Charlotte, Eboli, Santuzza, Kundry, the Countess Geschwitz, Hänsel, Venus, and Adalgisa. Add the roles she performed in contemporary and early opera, and one finds a legacy of operatic diversity matched by few artists in history.

Troyanos appeared often and with success in recital and on the concert platform, and she recorded extensively throughout her too short career. Her final operatic performance, less than two months before her death from cancer, was with the San Francisco Opera as Clairon in Strauss's *Capriccio*.

Troyens, Les **GRAND OPERA IN FIVE ACTS BY HECTOR BERLIOZ,** to his own libretto (based on Virgil's *Aeneid*), composed 1856–58 and premiered December 6, 1890, in Karlsruhe, Felix Mottl conducting. The hero of *Les Troyens* is Aeneas, and the opera's story encompasses the denouement of the Trojan War, the flight of Aeneas and his followers to Carthage, and the establishment of ancient Rome. In the gigantic score Berlioz paints an orchestral canvas worthy of Delacroix, revealing an extraordinary theatrical vision in the process. His portrayal of the conflicted character of Aeneas and the tragic love of Dido are among the greatest achievements in French music.

From the beginning, *Les Troyens* was intended for the stage of the Paris Opéra. But the conception proved a little *too* grand for that house: The score was rejected by the management and remained unpublished until 1969, the centennial of Berlioz's death. In order to see at least a part of his magnum opus performed in his lifetime, Berlioz reluctantly agreed to a division of the work into two parts: *La prise de Troie*, consisting of the first two acts, and *Les Troyens à Carthage*, comprising the final three. Even then, when *Les Troyens à Carthage* was finally staged, at the Théâtre Lyrique on November 4, 1863, it survived only one night before being heavily cut. Berlioz never saw the first part of the opera staged.

RECOMMENDED RECORDINGS

COMPLETE:

HEPPNER, DE YOUNG, LANG, MINGARDO, MATTEI; DAVIS AND LONDON SYMPHONY ORCHESTRA (LSO LIVE).

VICKERS, VEASEY, BAINBRIDGE, LINDHOLM, GLOSSOP, THAU; DAVIS AND ROYAL OPERA (PHILIPS).

SELECTED SCENES:

LAKES, POLLET, VOIGT; DUTOIT AND MONTREAL SYMPHONY ORCHESTRA (DECCA).

trumpet Brass instrument with a mainly cylindrical bore, a conical bell flared at the opening, and a shallow, cup-shaped mouthpiece. Its origins are ancient, and its metamorphosis from the natural instrument of medieval and Renaissance pageant to the valved wonder of the orchestral brass section has been a complex one, involving not only changes in the instrument's construction but profound shifts in the style of music written for it and the technique and artistry expected of its players.

The sound of trumpets was a symbol of military and civil authority, and Renaissance princes often kept large contingents of trumpeters in courtly employ. The trumpet made the jump from ceremonial to art music during the Baroque era while retaining its identity as a festive instrument. Thanks to the strength of the guilds that regulated its teaching and use, professional players achieved a high technical standard and remarkable proficiency in the stratospheric reaches of the instrument's range, known as the *clarino* register. During the Classical era—as the guilds faltered and musical style moved away from the ornate virtuosity of the Baroque—this skill was gradually lost. The trumpets of the Baroque and Classical eras were large instruments, with tube lengths of seven or eight feet, depending on their key. The Baroque instrument was usually pitched in D—hence the overwhelming number of pieces in D major from that era—while instruments of the latter half of the 18th century came in a variety of keys, most commonly C, D, E-flat, and F. The instruments were limited to the notes of the natural harmonic series; but while Baroque players could sound notes up to the 20th harmonic and even beyond, Classical players rarely went above the 12th, restricting what could be written for them to fanfare figures and notes safely within the harmony.

The landscape changed dramatically when the valve trumpet appeared in the 1820s. Pitched in F (giving it a tube length of about six feet), with two, later three valves, it allowed a larger chromatic range and produced a heavy, warm sound with great nobility of tone. Its qualities were immediately seized upon by French composers, and used to magnificent effect by Berlioz in the overture to *Les francs-juges* (1826) and the *Waverley* Overture (1827–28) and by Rossini in his opera *Guillaume Tell* (1829). By the middle of the 19th century the valve trumpet in F was established as the standard instrument, likely to be used even when composers specified trumpets in D, E, or some other key, a practice that continued through the end of the 19th century (e.g., in the works of Brahms and Dvořák).

The modern valve trumpet (in B-flat or C) used today, with a tube length of about four feet, superseded the F trumpet in the early years of the 20th century. Smaller and more agile, it has a usable range from F sharp below middle C to the C (and occasionally D) two octaves above. Its most notable attributes are the edge, carrying power, and heroic brilliance of its tone. Piston valves are standard, though trumpets with rotary valves continue to be used in some European orchestras.

From the proclamatory flourishes that open Monteverdi's *L'Orfeo*, to the obbligato in "The Trumpet Shall Sound" from Handel's *Messiah* and the trumpet writing in the celebratory choruses of Bach's *Mass in B Minor* (the epitome of Baroque style in orhestral music), to the offstage clarion calls in Beethoven's *Leonore* Overtures

Nos. 2 and 3, fanfares have continued to be the trumpet's stock-in-trade. But composers have found many other uses for it. Its sustained glow is captured by Wagner in the leitmotif depicting "The Sword" in *Die Walküre,* while its jazzy flair in scale runs and repeated-note figures is exploited by Tchaikovsky in the "Spanish Dance" from *The Nutcracker.* An outstanding range of effects is possible with the mute—from atmospheric soft tones (e.g., the plaintive solo with English horn in Debussy's *La mer* or the procession-like approach of three muted trumpets in the "Fêtes" movement of his *Nocturnes*) to electrifyingly loud ones (e.g., Stravinsky's two muted trumpets and two muted cornets, *fff,* in the second tableau of *Petrushka*).

The trumpet's concerted literature includes a part in Bach's *Brandenburg* Concerto No. 2 as well as solo concertos by Leopold Mozart, Joseph Haydn, Hummel, and the Armenian composer Alexander Arutiunian (b. 1920). Many of the most notable soloists of the modern era have been orchestral players, including Roger Voisin (Boston Symphony Orchestra), Adolph "Bud" Herseth (Chicago Symphony Orchestra), Timofey Dokshitser (Bolshoi Ballet), and Gerard Schwarz, who was principal with the New York Philharmonic before embarking on his conducting career. Among those who have specialized as solo artists are the French virtuoso Maurice André, Sweden's Håkan Hardenberger, Germany's Ludwig Güttler, and the American Philip Smith. Jazz has its own pantheon of great players, including Louis Armstrong, Miles Davis, Clark Terry, Dizzy Gillespie, Chet Baker, and Wynton Marsalis.

tuba Brass instrument with a pronounced conical bore favoring the production of its lowest notes, a widely flared bell, and a deep, cup-shaped mouthpiece. Of the many sizes of tuba that have been produced, two are in standard orchestral use: the nine-foot tenor tuba in F (called a *euphonium* when used in a band), with a practical range from low F sharp to the C above middle C, and the 14-foot bass tuba in C, with a range from low D to F above middle C. For certain orchestral applications, such as the music of Wagner, a contrabass tuba in B-flat is often preferred for its added weight of tone. Tubas come with a variety of valve schemes; there are usually four valves, sometimes five or six, occasionally seven. Piston and rotary valves are found about equally, American players tending to prefer the former. The bass tuba weighs 20 to 25 pounds.

The tuba is a comparatively recent arrival as an orchestral instrument. Berlioz was the first important composer to call for tubas in his works, finding their sound preferable to that of the ophicleide, a forerunner of the bass tuba that he had used to sensational effect in the *Symphonie fantastique.* Wagner embraced the tuba early on, including one in the orchestra for *Der fliegende Holländer* and requiring a large contrabass tuba in *Der Ring des Nibelungen.* Though stereotyped as sluggish and crude, the tuba is capable of great agility and beauty of tone. It can sing mellifluously in legato passages in its middle register and thunder with earth-shaking authority. Whatever it does, it requires a lot of air from the player. In a typical orchestral texture it provides a solid foundation for the brass, often reinforcing the bass line. It is frequently teamed with the trombones as the bass voice in a brass quartet.

The orchestral literature includes a number of virtuoso tuba parts, such as the solo in the "Bydlo" section of Ravel's orchestration of *Pictures at an Exhibition.* In the "Turandot" scherzo in his *Symphonische Metamorphosen nach Themen von Carl Maria von Weber,* Hindemith writes several passages that show off the tuba's agility, while in *Don Quixote,* Richard Strauss makes its droll depiction of Sancho Panza (a solo doubled by bass clarinet) a tour de force of legato phrasing with wide skips thrown in. Though the tuba gets few opportunities to take center stage for an entire piece, its repertoire contains excellent concertos by Ralph Vaughan Williams (1954) and John Williams (1985). The list of notable tuba virtuosos includes William Bell (for many years principal with the New York Philharmonic), Chester Schmitz (longtime principal of the Boston Symphony), Harvey Phillips, and Sam Pilafian.

Tucker, Richard

(b. New York, August 28, 1913; d. Kalamazoo, Mich., January 8, 1975)

AMERICAN TENOR. With his brilliant, stentorian voice and remarkable endurance he made a lasting contribution to America's musical life and helped to show that Americans could do opera as well as anybody. Educated in Brooklyn public schools, he began singing in synagogues at the age of six. Turning his back on various business ventures, he studied voice with Paul Althouse and started performing in concerts and on the radio, making an early appearance on Chicago's *Theater of the Air* broadcast. In 1941, after placing second in the Metropolitan Opera Auditions of the Air, he was offered a contract by Met director Edward Johnson—after Johnson was persuaded to hear him sing a service at the Brooklyn Jewish Center that held the congregation of 2,000 enraptured. Tucker made his Met debut in the role of Enzo in Ponchielli's *La gioconda* in 1945. He added more roles from the French and Italian repertoire, and by the end of his career at the Met had sung 31 roles in 31 seasons, amassing a total of 734 performances. In 1949 he was singularly honored by being tapped to sing the part of Radames in a broadcast performance of Verdi's *Aida* by the NBC Symphony under Arturo Toscanini.

Richard Tucker, showing a "can belto" attitude

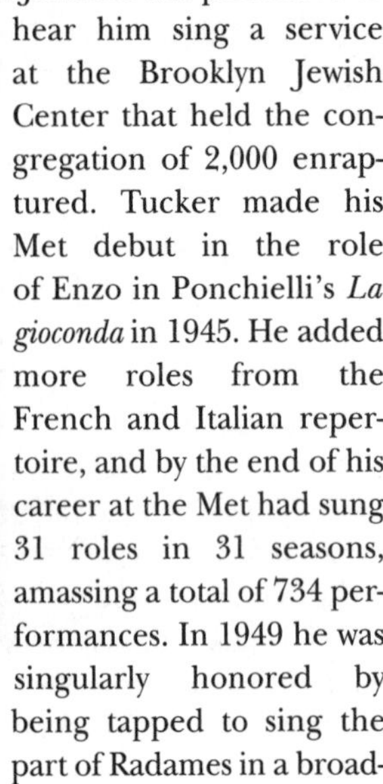

Tucker's voice was a reliable instrument of undisputed quality with a clarion upper register. He was especially noted for the Verdi roles of the Duke in *Rigoletto,* Rodolfo in *Luisa Miller,* and Manrico in *Il trovatore*; the Puccini roles of Rodolfo in *La bohème* and Cavaradossi in *Tosca*; and Don José in Bizet's *Carmen.* Though not noted for his acting, which was somewhat wooden and old-fashioned, he had a lively sense of humor, and was always a gracious colleague. A deeply religious man, he went to Vietnam during the war to lead a Passover seder for the Jewish troops. He was married to Sara Perelmuth, the sister of another brilliant tenor of the day, Jan Peerce. Tucker died of a heart attack in 1975 in Kalamazoo, preparing a concert with his friend and colleague, the baritone Robert Merrill. He is the only singer to have been honored with a funeral on the stage of the Metropolitan Opera.

Tuckwell, Barry

(b. Melbourne, March 5, 1931)

AUSTRALIAN HORN PLAYER AND CONDUCTOR, considered the foremost horn virtuoso of his generation. He began playing in the Sydney Symphony Orchestra when he was 15 and still a student at the conservatory. In 1950 he left for Great Britain, where he played in the Hallé Orchestra, Scottish National Orchestra, and the Bournemouth Symphony Orchestra before becoming principal horn of the London Symphony Orchestra in 1955, at the age of 24. He held that chair until 1968, when he embarked on an enormously successful solo career. He became the most recorded solo horn player ever, with more than 45 recordings to his credit, including multiple accounts of the Mozart concertos. Among the works composed for him were concertos by Oliver Knussen (b. 1952) and Richard Rodney Bennett (b. 1936); his repertoire encompassed all the standard works for his instrument, including Britten's *Serenade* for tenor, horn, and strings, the concertos of Mozart and Richard Strauss, and the Brahms trio. In everything he played he acquitted himself brilliantly, his signature tone remarkable for its heroic size and solidity.

Tuckwell served on the faculty of the Royal Academy of Music in London from 1962 to 1972. In the 1980s he turned his attention to conducting, serving as music director of the Tasmanian Symphony Orchestra (1981–83) and as founder and music director of the Maryland Symphony Orchestra, based in Hagerstown (1982–98). He received the Order of the British Empire in 1965.

Barry Tuckwell, the hornist and his horn in their prime

RECOMMENDED RECORDINGS

MOZART, HORN CONCERTOS: TUCKWELL AND ENGLISH CHAMBER ORCHESTRA (DECCA).

STRAUSS, HORN CONCERTOS: KERTÉSZ AND LONDON SYMPHONY ORCHESTRA (DECCA).

Turandot **OPERA IN THREE ACTS BY GIACOMO PUCCINI,** to a libretto by Giuseppe Adami and Renato Simoni (based on the play by Carlo Gozzi), composed 1921–24 and premiered posthumously April 25, 1926, at La Scala in Milan, Arturo Toscanini conducting. Puccini died before he could complete the final act of the opera. At the premiere—which ended with Toscanini turning to the audience and saying, "At this point, the master laid down his pen"—the opera was performed as Puccini left it. The score was published with an ending composed by Franco Alfano (based on Puccini's pencil sketches), which was subsequently shortened when a second edition of the score was prepared. It is this version of the opera that is usually heard today.

Set in legendary Peking, *Turandot* is a love story in which cruelty plays a large part. The title character, a princess, icily requires anyone who would be her suitor to answer three riddles or lose his head. She meets her match in Calaf, the son of the Tatar king Timur, who, like Mozart's Tamino, falls hopelessly in love with her picture and resolves to win her hand at any cost. Calaf succeeds in answering Turandot's riddles, and his misplaced affection is made all the more poignant when Liù, the slave girl who truly loves him, dies in order to protect him from Turandot's wrath. The opera ends with Turandot inexplicably submitting to Calaf's love, amid joyous celebration. The music of *Turandot* is by turns powerful and disquieting, colorful and exotic, and remarkably advanced in its harmonic and rhythmic orientation. Throughout the score, elements of musical modernism borrowed from the explorations of Debussy and Stravinsky are masterfully handled. Yet for all its marvelous theatricalism, and in spite of the brilliance of Puccini's scoring, *Turandot* marks a falling off in taste and dramatic effectiveness. It remains popular with audiences in houses worldwide because the leading roles are star vehicles of the first magnitude, anchored by two of the highest-voltage arias ever written, Turandot's "In questa reggia" and Calaf's "Nessun dorma."

Cover of the libretto to **Turandot**

RECOMMENDED RECORDINGS

NILSSON, BJÖRLING, TEBALDI, TOZZI; LEINSDORF AND ROME OPERA ORCHESTRA (RCA).

SUTHERLAND, PAVAROTTI, CABALLÉ, PEARS, GHIAUROV; MEHTA AND LONDON PHILHARMONIC ORCHESTRA (DECCA).

Turangalîla-symphonie SYMPHONY IN TEN MOVEMENTS BY OLIVIER MESSIAEN, composed 1946–48 on a commission from Serge Koussevitzky, and premiered December 2, 1949, by the Boston Symphony Orchestra under the baton of Leonard Bernstein. The symphony's name comes from two Sanskrit words: *turanga,* meaning "time," and *lîla,* "play." Messiaen described the piece as a love song, titling two of its movements "Chant d'amour"; it is an apt characterization for a work that makes such ecstatic and hedonistic use of the orchestra, here augmented by multiple percussion and solo parts for piano and ONDES MARTENOT. The work, which has become one of Messiaen's most popular, was conceived as the middle member of a trilogy based on the Tristan legend, between the song cycle *Harawi* (1945) and the *Cinq rechants* (1948) for 12 mixed voices.

RECOMMENDED RECORDINGS

Y. LORIOD, J. LORIOD; OZAWA AND TORONTO SYMPHONY ORCHESTRA (RCA).

THIBAUDET, HARADA; CHAILLY AND ROYAL CONCERTGEBOUW ORCHESTRA (DECCA).

turn An ornament applied to a specific note, consisting of a fairly quick alternation between it and the notes a step above it and below it. In the most common type of turn, the main note is sounded, followed by the note a step above, followed by the main note again, followed by the note a step below, and ending on the main note. *See also* AGRÉMENTS, ORNAMENTS.

Turn of the Screw, The OPERA IN A PROLOGUE AND TWO ACTS BY BENJAMIN BRITTEN, to a libretto by Myfanwy Piper (based on Henry James's tale), premiered September 14, 1954, at La Fenice in Venice. A chamber opera requiring an orchestra of 13 and a cast of only six (including a boy soprano as Miles), it is one of the most effective and easily presented of Britten's many stage works. James's story of demonic possession elicits music of appropriate edginess from Britten, full of menace (suggested by unsettling chromatic inflections of the melody) and agitation. The underlying theme, of innocence threatened and corrupted, is a common one in Britten's work.

RECOMMENDED RECORDINGS

Bostridge, Rodgers, Henschel, Tierney; Harding and Mahler Chamber Orchestra (Virgin Classics).

Donath, Tear, Harper, Watson; Davis and Royal Opera (Philips).

Lott, Langridge, Pay, Hulse; Bedford and Aldeburgh Festival Orchestra (Naxos).

tutti (It., "all") [1] In orchestral music, a passage played by all the instruments in a section, as opposed to a solo. [2] In Baroque concertos, any section in which the solo instrument or instruments and the accompanying group (known as the RIPIENO) come together and play in unison, rather than separately.

12-tone A method of composition in which ordered arrangements of the 12 notes of the chromatic scale serve as the principal melodic and harmonic building blocks of a piece. Schoenberg is credited with devising the system and launching it with his Five Piano Pieces, Op. 23 (1923). *See also* SERIALISM, TONE ROW.

U V

una corda (It., "one string") Pedal on the piano (farthest to the left on a typical concert grand) that, when depressed, shifts the keyboard and action slightly to one side, so that the hammers in the middle range of the instrument come into contact with only a single string, rather than two. At the upper end of the keyboard, where there are three strings per note, the hammers strike only two when the pedal is employed. The bass range, with one string per note, is not affected. Use of the una corda pedal does more than limit the volume of sound a piano will produce; it eviscerates the instrument's tone quality, making it softer and grayer, which can be a telling effect in certain passages, e.g., the second movement of Beethoven's Piano Concerto No. 4, which the piano plays entirely *una corda.*

Unanswered Question, The WORK FOR STRINGS, TRUMPET, AND FOUR FLUTES BY CHARLES IVES, composed in 1908 (and revised sometime in the 1930s) and first performed May 11, 1946, in New York, on the same program as his *Central Park in the Dark.* John Kirkpatrick, an authority on Ives, suggested that the two movements are "perhaps an anti-symphony." Both works involve two orchestral groups that proceed as if unaware of each other. In *The Unanswered Question,* the background (strings) is tonal, the foreground (trumpet and flutes) atonal; in *Central Park in the Dark,* the background is atonal, while familiar tunes occupy the foreground.

In the score to *The Unanswered Question,* Ives gave this account of the piece:

The strings play *ppp* throughout with no change in tempo. They are to represent "The Silences of the Druids—Who Know, See and Hear Nothing." The trumpet intones "The Perennial Question of Existence," and states it in the same tone of voice each time. But the hunt for "The Invisible Answer" undertaken by the flutes and other human beings, becomes gradually more active, faster and louder through an *animando* to a *con fuoco* [actually, for the successive "answers," Ives gives tempo markings of *Adagio, Andante, Allegretto, Allegro,* and *Allegro molto* with an accelerando to *Presto con fuoco,* while strings and trumpet remain at *Largo molto sempre*]. "The Fighting Answerers," as time goes on, and after a "secret conference," seem to realize a futility, and begin to mock "The Question"—the strife is over for the moment. After they disappear, "The Question" is asked for the last time, and "The Silences" are heard beyond in "Undisturbed Solitude."

RECOMMENDED RECORDINGS

BERNSTEIN AND NEW YORK PHILHARMONIC (SONY).
SINCLAIR AND NORTHERN SINFONIA (NAXOS).
THOMAS AND SAN FRANCISCO SYMPHONY ORCHESTRA (RCA).

***Unfinished* Symphony** NICKNAME OF FRANZ SCHUBERT'S SYMPHONY NO. 8 IN B MINOR, D. 759, consisting of two movements—an Allegro in B minor and an Andante in E major—composed in the autumn of 1822.

It is clear from Schubert's sketches for a third movement that his intention was to compose a four-movement symphony on a grand scale, one that would depart dramatically from the models of Mozart, Haydn, and early Beethoven, which he had followed up to that point, and visit a strikingly subjective new realm of expression. The tone is grim, yet surprisingly subdued, the orchestration dark and weighty. The subtle overlay of woodwinds and brass—which for the first time in any symphony are allowed a sonic presence equal to that of the strings—lends a poignant coloration to the texture, which Schubert heightens by means of unusual doublings and combinations. For example, the clarinet and oboe play the haunting main subject of the first movement in unison, rather than one or the other playing it as a solo. The trombones, which Beethoven had saved for climactic moments, are part of the orchestra from the start, and are used with great skill to darken its sonority and to add force to the violently impassioned outbursts that occur in both movements.

It is not certain why Schubert abandoned the symphony in midcourse. During the winter of 1822–23, he fell desperately ill, and it is possible he left the score incomplete because of the association it bore with that traumatic experience. An equally plausible explanation is that the symphony had become problematic in a purely formal sense. Because its ideas are melodic rather than motivic, they resist the kind of expansion and reconfiguration that typified Beethoven's procedures in sonata form; Schubert may have felt that by attempting to develop them in the manner of Beethoven, forcefully and dramatically, he was going against his own grain. His solution, hit upon two years later in the Ninth Symphony, would be to use pithier and more malleable material.

RECOMMENDED RECORDINGS

Böhm and Berlin Philharmonic (DG).
Jochum and Boston Symphony Orchestra (DG).
Walter and New York Philharmonic (Sony).

Upshaw, Dawn

(b. Nashville, July 17, 1960)

AMERICAN SOPRANO. She studied at the Manhattan School of Music and made her debut at the Metropolitan Opera on October 11, 1984, as Countess Ceprano in Verdi's *Rigoletto.* She quickly graduated from small roles to more significant ones, including Gretel in Humperdinck's *Hänsel und Gretel* and Blanche in Poulenc's *Dialogues des Carmélites.* Her portfolio as a Mozartean is particularly distinguished, with engagements at the Met as Ilia in *Idomeneo,* Zerlina in *Don Giovanni,* Pamina in *Die Zauberflöte,* Despina in *Così fan tutte,* and Susanna in *Le nozze di Figaro.* She has also sung the roles of Anne Trulove in Stravinsky's *The Rake's Progress* and the Angel in Messiaen's *Saint François d'Assise.* An accomplished recitalist whose knack for exploring the more interesting corners of the repertoire has led to some imaginative programs (and recordings) over the years, she is known as a champion of living composers, including Robert Beaser (b. 1954), John Harbison, and Kaija Saariaho. Her singing combines purity of tone, superb diction, and exceptional musical intelligence.

Dawn Upshaw

RECOMMENDED RECORDINGS

BARBER, *KNOXVILLE, SUMMER OF 1915*: ZINMAN AND ORCHESTRA OF ST. LUKE'S (NONESUCH).

HARBISON, *MIRABAI SONGS*: ZINMAN AND ORCHESTRA OF ST. LUKE'S (NONESUCH).

MESSIAEN, *SAINT FRANÇOIS D'ASSISE*: ALER, MERRITT, KRAUSE, VAN DAM; NAGANO AND HALLÉ ORCHESTRA (DG).

SONGS OF SONDHEIM, WEILL, BLITZSTEIN (NONESUCH).

"VOICES OF LIGHT" (SONGS OF DEBUSSY, FAURÉ, MESSIAEN): KALISH (NONESUCH).

"WHITE MOON: SONGS TO MORPHEUS" (WORKS BY CRUMB, DOWLAND, HANDEL, SCHWANTNER, SEEGER, WARLOCK, OTHERS): ORCHESTRA OF ST. LUKE'S (NONESUCH).

"THE WORLD SO WIDE" (WORKS BY ADAMS, BARBER, BERNSTEIN, COPLAND, OTHERS): ORCHESTRA OF ST. LUKE'S (NONESUCH).

Uudslukkelige, Det *See* THE INEXTINGUISHABLE.

valse, La (The Waltz) "CHOREOGRAPHIC POEM" FOR ORCHESTRA BY MAURICE RAVEL, composed 1919–20 and first performed December 12, 1920, in Paris, by the Lamoureux Orchestra under the baton of Camille Chevillard. The score is dedicated to Misia Sert. The idea of writing a large-scale symphonic work based on the waltz had intrigued Ravel since 1906; at the time, he thought of calling such a work *Wien,* the German name for the city of Vienna. World War I intervened before Ravel could take up the planned composition, but in 1918, when the Russian impresario Sergey Diaghilev offered him a commission to compose a ballet to his own choice of subject, Ravel saw his opportunity and went to work. The orchestration of the score, fittingly begun on New Year's Eve, was finished by the end of March 1920. Since French sensibilities were still tender, he decided to use a different title, calling the finished ballet simply *La valse.* After hearing Ravel play the score through in a two-piano arrangement, Diaghilev pronounced it a masterpiece, but quickly added: "It's not a ballet!" Ravel picked up the music and walked out, ending forever his association with the mercurial manager.

Diaghilev had a point. Rather than balletic, Ravel's treatment of the waltz is breathtakingly cinematic. Throughout the work his scoring suggests the swirling color and irresistible momentum of a ballroom dance. There is, as well, an element of menace as the piece builds to its intoxicating, ultimately frenzied conclusion. The embodiment of that menace comes in the final pages, the most violent in Ravel's entire oeuvre, as the orchestra exults in a waltz-death of apocalyptic and frightening splendor. By contrast, the first two minutes of the work are all mystery and suggestion, a masterly evocation of a scene described by a note in the printed score: "Through a swirling mist one discerns, in brief moments of clearness, waltzing couples. Little by little the vapors dissipate: one is able to make out an immense hall filled by a whirling throng. The scene becomes progressively clearer. The light of chandeliers bursts forth. An Imperial Court, around 1855."

RECOMMENDED RECORDINGS

BOULEZ AND NEW YORK PHILHARMONIC (SONY).

DUTOIT AND MONTREAL SYMPHONY ORCHESTRA (DECCA).

Valses nobles et sentimentales PIANO PIECE BY MAURICE RAVEL consisting of eight sections connected to one another in the manner of a waltz chain, composed in 1911. The first performance was given that May by Louis Aubert (1877–1968), whom Ravel had known since they were students in Gabriel Fauré's composition class at the Paris Conservatoire (as a lad of 11, Aubert had sung the treble solo in the first performance of Fauré's Requiem). Ravel orchestrated the piece in March

1912 for a ballet, *Adélaïde, ou Le langage des fleurs,* which received its premiere on April 22, 1912, at the Théâtre du Châtelet in Paris. The yearning, dreamlike music of *Valses nobles et sentimentales* is arguably more "sentimental" than "noble" (Ravel borrowed the two words from the music of Schubert), but "sentimental" in the French sense: ambivalent, unsettling, tinged with regret.

RECOMMENDED RECORDINGS

PIANO:
ROGÉ (DECCA).
RUBINSTEIN (RCA).
THIOLLIER (NAXOS).
ORCHESTRA:
BOULEZ AND NEW YORK PHILHARMONIC (SONY).
DUTOIT AND MONTREAL SYMPHONY ORCHESTRA (DECCA).

Van Dam, José

(b. Brussels, August 25, 1940)

BELGIAN BASS-BARITONE. He studied at the Brussels Conservatory and made his debut in 1960 in Liège, as Don Basilio in Rossini's *Il barbiere di Siviglia.* He was subsequently engaged by both the Opéra and the Opéra-Comique in Paris, and in 1967 he became a principal singer at the Deutsche Oper Berlin. He made his American debut, as Escamillo in Bizet's *Carmen,* with the San Francisco Opera in 1970, singing the same role in his first appearance at Covent Garden and at his Metropolitan Opera debut on November 21, 1975. An engaging actor endowed with a voice that was suave, richly resonant, yet free at the top, he achieved notable success as Golaud in Debussy's *Pelléas et Mélisande,* as the four villains in Offenbach's *Les contes d'Hoffmann,* and, on the concert stage, as Mephistopheles in Berlioz's *La damnation de Faust.* He created the title role in Messiaen's *Saint François d'Assise* at the Paris Opéra in 1983.

José Van Dam as Mozart's Don Giovanni

RECOMMENDED RECORDINGS

DEBUSSY, *PELLÉAS ET MÉLISANDE*: VON STADE, STILWELL, RAIMONDI; KARAJAN AND BERLIN PHILHARMONIC (EMI).
MESSIAEN, *SAINT FRANÇOIS D'ASSISE*: UPSHAW, ALER, MERRITT, KRAUSE; NAGANO AND HALLÉ ORCHESTRA (DG).
COLLECTION:
"MÉLODIES FRANÇAISES"; COLLARD (EMI).

Varèse, Edgard

(b. Paris, December 22, 1883; d. New York, November 6, 1965)

FRENCH/AMERICAN COMPOSER. His freely atonal idiom, with its uninhibited approach to sonority and rhythm, had a profound impact on the aesthetics of 20th-century music. His bold experimentation with orchestral and instrumental sound during the 1920s paved the way for composers as disparate as Boulez, Cage, Messiaen, and Frank Zappa (1940–93); he took another influential step in the 1950s when he assembled some of the first pieces to be created in the medium of magnetic tape.

Varèse spent his early childhood in Paris and Burgundy. His family settled in Turin when he was nine and he began studying music there when he was 16. At the age of 20 he returned to Paris and enrolled in the Schola Cantorum, where he studied composition with Albert

Edgard Varèse, seminal modernist

Roussel and conducting with Vincent d'Indy. The latter's patronizing attitude rubbed him the wrong way, and in 1905 he transferred to the Paris Conservatoire to study composition with Charles-Marie Widor. He moved to Berlin in 1907, where, with the help of Richard Strauss, his symphonic poem *Bourgogne* (*Burgundy*) received its premiere in 1910 (Varèse destroyed the score in the 1960s). While in Berlin, Varèse came into the orbit of Ferruccio Busoni, whose aesthetic views had a profound impact on his subsequent development. He also encountered the music of Arnold Schoenberg, which he quickly brought to the attention of Claude Debussy, in a remarkable case of musical cross-pollination. Varèse settled in Paris in 1913, but after failing to secure a permanent position, he left for the United States.

Varèse arrived in the U.S. at the end of December 1915 and immediately got to work on what he saw as his mission: to create an American audience for new music. He founded the New Symphony Orchestra in New York in 1919 and conducted its concerts until it abandoned the policy of playing new works. In 1921, together with the eminent French-born harpist-composer Carlos Salzedo (1885–1961), he founded the International Composers' Guild, the first organization in America to give concerts exclusively of contemporary music. During the six seasons it existed it presented works by 56 composers, including the first American performances of Schoenberg's *Pierrot lunaire* and Stravinsky's *Les noces,* as well as the premieres of Varèse's *Offrandes* (1921) for soprano and chamber orchestra; *Hyperprism* (1922–23) for nine wind instruments and percussion; *Octandre* (1923) for flute (doubling piccolo), clarinet (doubling E-flat clarinet), oboe, bassoon, horn, trumpet, trombone, and double bass; and *Intégrales* (1924–25) for 11 wind instruments and percussion. During these years Varèse's music was enthusiastically championed by Leopold Stokowski, who had conducted the premiere of *Intégrales*; in four successive seasons (1923–27) with the Philadelphia Orchestra, Stokowski led performances of *Hyperprism, Intégrales,* and the world premieres of Varèse's most substantial orchestral works, *Amériques* (1918–21) and *Arcana* (1925–27).

Varèse returned to Paris in 1928. He spent five years there, during which he occupied himself with a number of projected works that failed to materialize. Back in the United States, he created one of his shortest but greatest works, *Density 21.5* for solo flute, written in 1936 (rev. 1946) for the French-born flutist Georges Barrère, to celebrate the "inauguration" of his platinum flute (the specific gravity of platinum, thought at the time to be 21.5 grams per cubic centimeter, was later calculated to be 21.45). Frustrated in his efforts to create a center for electronic music—he had returned to the United States in the teeth of the Depression, not a good time to seek funding for such an esoteric project—Varèse became depressed; after *Density 21.5,* he wrote almost nothing for ten years. He conducted early music (a passion since his days at the Schola Cantorum), gave lectures at Columbia University, and taught at Darmstadt during the summer of 1950. In 1953 the gift of an Ampex tape recorder from an anonymous donor enabled him at last to realize some of the notions of organized sound he had been developing for four decades. The result was *Déserts,* for 14 wind instruments, piano, five percussion instruments, and tape, which Varèse completed in Paris in 1954. He returned to Europe in 1957 to work at the Philips laboratories in Eindhoven, where he created the *Poème électronique* on three-track tape for the Philips Pavilion at the 1958 Brussels World's Fair. In his final years Varèse revised the *Déserts* tape at the Columbia-Princeton Electronic Music Center.

By the end of his life, Varèse had produced only 12 finished compositions. Small as it was, his output was essential to the 20th century—even more so, it can be argued, than that of Webern. Varèse's imaginative deployment of overlapping sound planes—i.e., multiple streams of sound proceeding simultaneously in a single piece—revolutionized musical thinking. In works such as *Amériques* (calling for 27 winds, 29 brass, and a phenomenally large battery) and *Arcana* (for 20 winds, 19 brass, 68 strings, and six percussionists), he expanded the universe of orchestral sound geometrically. The extraordinarily loud climaxes, timbral juxtapositions, and spatial effects of these works are still striking more than 75 years after they were created. In the pieces not for full orchestra—*Hyperprism, Octandre, Intégrales, Ionisation* (1929–31) for a percussion ensemble of 13 players, and *Ecuatorial* (1932–34) for voice, four trumpets, four trombones, piano, organ, ONDES MARTENOT, and percussion—Varèse had an even greater impact. These are among the seminal works of modern music, both in their treatment of sonority and texture and in the way they harness the energy of basic rhythmic cells. *See also box on pages 496–97.*

RECOMMENDED RECORDINGS

ARCANA: MARTINON; CHICAGO SYMPHONY ORCHESTRA (RCA).

ARCANA, OCTANDRE, INTÉGRALES, DÉSERTS: LYNDON-GEE AND POLISH NATIONAL RADIO SYMPHONY ORCHESTRA (NAXOS).

COMPLETE WORKS FOR ORCHESTRA AND ENSEMBLE: CHAILLY; ROYAL CONCERTGEBOUW ORCHESTRA AND AKSO ENSEMBLE (DECCA).

variation(s) A formal procedure in which the "possibilities" of a given theme, which is usually stated at the beginning of the process, are explored through a series of discrete modifications. The variation process typically investigates the structure of the theme—its intervallic, rhythmic, and harmonic makeup—and seeks to tease out some of its rhetorical and expressive implications. As the French theorist Jérôme-Joseph de Momigny made clear in his *Cours complet d'harmonie et de composition* of 1806: "Variation is scientific, embroidery [i.e., embellishment] is tasteful." Variation can involve dressing a still-recognizable tune in different guises, altering its mood or character, and can also involve far more speculative and probing transformations of its rhythmic and harmonic identity, radically changing its nature.

The art of variation, especially through improvisation, has been a part of Western music from the beginning. As a formal procedure it has its roots in the Renaissance, and actual sets of variations appeared for the first time in the 16th century. The parade of major works founded on the variation principle begins with Bach's *Goldberg* Variations (1741), the towering achievement of Baroque keyboard music. Beethoven incorporated numerous variation movements in his works; significant examples include the second movement of the Fifth Symphony, the final movements of the *Eroica* and Ninth Symphonies, and movements in several of the piano sonatas (Opp. 26, 57, 109, and 111) and string quartets (Op. 18, No. 5, and Opp. 127 and 131). Beethoven also composed several sets of stand-alone variations for piano, the greatest of which are the *Diabelli* Variations, Op. 120, of 1823.

Brahms composed a dozen variation works for piano, as well as the magisterial *Variations on a Theme by Haydn,* Op. 56 (1873), which exists in two versions: for orchestra and for two pianos. Other important variation works for orchestra include Dvořák's *Symphonic Variations,* Op. 78 (1877); Richard Strauss's *Don Quixote,* Op. 35 (1897), for cello and orchestra; Elgar's *Enigma* Variations, Op. 36 (1898–99); Reger's *Variations and Fugue on a Theme by J. A. Hiller* (1907) and *Variations and Fugue on a Theme by Mozart* (1914); Schoenberg's Variations, Op. 31 (1928); Kodály's *Peacock* Variations (1938–39); Ginastera's *Variaciones concertantes,* Op. 23 (1953); Carter's *Variations for Orchestra* (1955); and Walton's *Variations on a Theme by Hindemith* (1962–63).

Rachmaninov contributed several variation works to the literature, most important the *Variations on a Theme by Corelli,* Op. 42 (1931), for solo piano, and the *Rhapsody on a Theme of Paganini,* Op. 43 (1934), for piano and orchestra. Other well-known variation works for piano and orchestra are Franck's *Variations symphoniques* (1885) and Dohnányi's *Variations on a Nursery Tune,* Op. 25 (1914). Bartók's Violin Concerto No. 2 (1937–38) presents a special case: Asked by his soloist, Zoltán Székely, to write a traditional concerto rather than the set of variations for violin and orchestra that he wanted to write, Bartók produced a three-movement work in which the second movement is a straightforward set of variations and the finale is actually a macrovariation of the first movement.

Copland's gritty *Piano Variations* (1930), for solo piano, not only stands among the finest variation works of the 20th century but is one of the landmarks of the keyboard literature. Notable variation works for piano of more recent vintage include the 50-minute set of variations on *The People United Shall Never Be Defeated!* (1975) by Frederic Rzewski (b. 1938) and the *Partita-Variations* (1976) by George Rochberg (1918–2005).

Variations on a Theme by Haydn Work in variation form by Johannes Brahms, composed in 1873. Two versions of the score were produced more or less simultaneously: Op. 56a, for orchestra (published 1874), and Op. 56b, for two pianos (published 1873). The two-piano version marks the culmination of Brahms's efforts as a composer of large-scale piano pieces, while the orchestral version sets the stage for his work as a symphonist and holds the distinction of being the first freestanding set of variations for orchestra ever written.

The "theme by Haydn" on which the variations are based came from a wind octet thought at the time to have been by Haydn, but more likely to have been composed by his pupil Ignaz Pleyel. The theme is identified in the octet's manuscript as

"Chorale St. Antonii," suggesting that its source is yet another, now unknown, work. Brahms sketched the two-piano version of the score first. Even though it does not pose technical challenges comparable to those in two of Brahms's earlier variation works for solo piano, on themes of Paganini and Handel, it is a remarkably successful venture, among the most fluent and perfect of Brahms's creations. There is a subtle internal coherence, achieved partly through repetition of basic rhythmic motifs, partly through the progressive relationship of tempos from one variation to the next. Brahms's treatment of texture and harmony is quite sophisticated, as is his exploitation of the two-piano sonority. Most impressive of all is the characterization of the individual variations, which shows remarkable inventiveness and speculative depth. There are eight variations and a final supervariation, a passacaglia, which brings the work to a festive conclusion.

The orchestral transcription of the score, much better known than the original version for two pianos, represents an important watershed in its composer's development. Turning the piano piece into an orchestral essay was Brahms's way of facing up to his uncertainties as an orchestrator and preparing the ground for the symphonies he felt obliged to produce. Like a painter doing studies before attempting a large canvas, he had already orchestrated three of his *Hungarian Dances*; with the *Variations on a Theme by Haydn* he took the final step toward the realization of his First Symphony, which had been a work-in-progress since 1862. The scoring is extraordinarily clear, allowing the contrapuntal constructions that are characteristic features of Brahms's variation technique to be heard to their best advantage.

The orchestral version of the *Variations on a Theme by Haydn* was premiered November 2, 1873, at a concert of the Vienna Philharmonic, with the composer conducting. The two-piano version of the score received its premiere on February 10, 1874, also in Vienna. This performance was followed two days later by one in Manchester, England, with Charles Hallé and Hans von Bülow.

RECOMMENDED RECORDINGS

TWO PIANOS:
PERAHIA, SOLTI (SONY).
ORCHESTRA:
ABBADO AND BERLIN PHILHARMONIC (DG).
KERTÉSZ AND VIENNA PHILHARMONIC (DECCA).

Astrid Varnay as Strauss's Elektra

Varnay, Astrid

(b. Stockholm, April 25, 1918)

AMERICAN SOPRANO OF HUNGARIAN DESCENT. Her parents, both professional singers, emigrated to America in 1920. She studied first with her mother, subsequently with Paul Althouse and the conductor Hermann Weigert (whom she married in 1944). She made her professional debut on December 6, 1941, hours before the attack on Pearl Harbor, standing in for Lotte Lehmann as Sieglinde in a Saturday matinee performance of Wagner's *Die Walküre* at the Metropolitan Opera in New York; a week later she stepped into the role of Brünnhilde as a replacement for Helen Traubel. With Kirsten Flagstad back in Norway, she became a mainstay of the Met's Wagner productions during the war years, particularly in the roles of Elsa, Sieglinde, Elisabeth, and Isolde. Her career was centered in Europe during the 1950s and 1960s—she was a regular at Bayreuth from 1951 to 1967—but she came back to the Met in the 1970s to sing such character roles as Herodias in Richard Strauss's *Salome,* Klytamnestra in Strauss's *Elektra,* Kostelnička in Janáček's *Jenůfa,* and Leocadia Begbick in Weill's *Aufstieg und Fall der Stadt Mahagonny.*

RECOMMENDED RECORDINGS

WAGNER, *DIE WALKÜRE* (SELECTIONS): LONDON; WEIGERT AND BAVARIAN RADIO SYMPHONY ORCHESTRA (ORFEO).

WAGNER, *GÖTTERDÄMMERUNG*: SCHWARZKOPF, HÖNGEN, ALDENHOFF, UHDE, WEBER; KNAPPERTSBUSCH AND BAYREUTH FESTIVAL ORCHESTRA (TESTAMENT).

Vaughan Williams, Ralph

(b. Down Ampney, October 12, 1872; d. London, August 26, 1958)

ENGLISH COMPOSER. Throughout a long career he demonstrated the ability to invest conventional orchestral forms with deeply personal, even visionary expression. Many of his works speak in a rhapsodic tone and communicate a feeling of timeless spiritual transcendence.

Ralph (pronounced "rafe") Vaughan Williams was the son of the Reverend Arthur Vaughan Williams and Margaret Wedgwood, great-granddaughter of the ceramicist Josiah Wedgwood and niece of Charles Darwin. Following the death of Vaughan Williams's father in 1875, his mother moved with the children back to her family home, outside Dorking, Surrey. In 1878, Ralph began taking music lessons with his aunt Sophy Wedgwood, learned violin the following year, and then piano. Just before turning 15 he entered the Charterhouse School, where he played violin and viola in the orchestra. In 1890 he enrolled at the Royal College of Music, where he studied composition with Sir Hubert Parry and Charles Villiers Stanford, and met and became friends with fellow student Gustav Holst. After two years he entered Trinity College, Cambridge, and took degrees in music (1894) and history (1895). He then resumed studies at the RCM and took a church-organist post. He married Adeline Fisher in 1897; on their extended honeymoon, in Germany, Vaughan Williams studied briefly with Max Bruch.

In 1904 he was asked to edit the English Hymnal. The job took two years instead of the expected two months, and the research led Vaughan Williams to a profound appreciation of the Tudor composers, especially Thomas Tallis. In 1908, still feeling the need to polish his technique, Vaughan Williams went to Paris to study with the slightly younger Maurice Ravel, who would later say that he was the only student of his "who didn't try to write

Ralph Vaughan Williams in 1922

my music." Works of these years included a wonderfully vivacious suite of incidental music created for a Cambridge University production of Aristophanes' *The Wasps,* and *A Sea Symphony,* the first of Vaughan Williams's nine symphonies and a gloriously unbridled response to some of Whitman's most grandiose poetry. Capping this period, in 1910, was the first of his masterpieces, the *Fantasia on a Theme by Thomas Tallis* for double string orchestra. In the rapt quietude of this study we get our first look into the expressive universe that Vaughan Williams would explore for the rest of his career.

Three years later *A London Symphony* cemented Vaughan Williams's standing as an orchestral composer. With the outbreak of World War I he enlisted as a private in the field ambulance service, seeing action in France and Greece. He received a commission in the Royal Garrison artillery and in 1918 became director of music for the First Army BEF in France. He was deeply affected by the carnage, and grief-stricken over the death of a friend, the composer (and fellow folk-song collector) George Butterworth.

Following the war, Vaughan Williams was appointed professor at the RCM and awarded an honorary doctorate from Oxford. The year 1921 saw the first performance of his popular *The Lark Ascending,* written before the war, and the *Pastoral* Symphony, which reflected upon the war as a kind of requiem, also expressing, via wordless soprano, a mutedly emotional longing for home. In the later 1920s the composer and his wife moved to the countryside of his childhood for the sake of her health, and his production slowed somewhat; his major work of the period was *Job,* a "masque for dancing" after William Blake.

In 1934 Vaughan Williams was devastated by the death of Holst, and when Elgar and Delius died that same year, the 62-year-old composer was faced with the unwelcome burden of being the leading figure in English musical life. He was far too protean to rest on his laurels; proof came in 1935 with the premiere of the Fourth Symphony, a violent, agitated, uneasy, dark work dedicated to Arnold Bax. Vaughan Williams's goal in the piece was fully met: to come up with a rigorously argued symphonic statement that unfolds according to the established principles of 19th-century composition—employing clearly defined and differentiated "subjects," standard formal architecture, and motivic development—but uses modern, angular syntax and language, much as Walton had done in his First Symphony, and as Stravinsky would do in his *Symphony in Three Movements.*

Utterly different are the *Fantasia on "Greensleeves"* (1934), for flute, harp, and strings, and the *Serenade to Music* (1938), a gorgeous setting of lines from *The Merchant of Venice.* Vaughan Williams's central work of the prewar and early-war period was the Symphony No. 5, his greatest. Dedicating the piece "without permission to Jean Sibelius," the composer conducted the premiere in 1943. Personal, unshowy, saturated with the spirit of folk song and hymn, the Fifth Symphony is a work of calm and bucolic beauty, with a quietly contained (though sometimes not so quiet or contained) ecstasy. The piece develops organically, with the thematic material tightly woven and related to two motifs set out right at the beginning. The harmony has a modal feel through the first three movements, which gives the symphony's ending, in a serene and brightly diatonic D major, the comforting finality of a blessing.

Film scores also occupied Vaughan Williams during the war, including *49th Parallel, Coastal Command,* and *Story of a*

Flemish Farm. His music for the 1948 documentary *Scott of the Antarctic* would later be transformed into the Seventh Symphony, SINFONIA ANTARTICA, completed in 1950, the same year as his Sixth. Despite origins in other film music, the Sixth is a bleak, agonized effort, from its starting cry to the ten icy minutes that end it.

In 1951, Adeline, Vaughan Williams's wife of more than 50 years, died. In 1953 he married the writer Ursula Wood. Gerald Finzi's death in 1956 left the composer once again demoralized by the loss of a talented and sympathetic colleague, but the flame continued to burn. Symphonies Nos. 8 and 9 received their premieres in 1956 and 1958. The 85-year-old composer died the day before he was to attend a recording session for the latter. Although he had turned down a knighthood more than 20 years earlier, at his death there was no doubt of Vaughan Williams's stature, and his ashes were interred in Westminster Abbey near the tomb of Henry Purcell.

Vaughan Williams's shorter orchestral works are among the gems of the repertoire, and beautifully consistent with the symphonies and other extended works. There are wonderful later concertos, too, for oboe and tuba, that reflect the joy of writing with nothing left to prove; five operas, of which the best is *Sir John in Love* (1928); choral works; and songs. Though agnostic, Vaughan Williams wrote some of the most moving and beautiful sacred settings of the 20th century, including the *Five Mystical Songs* (to poems of George Herbert) for baritone solo, chorus, and orchestra; the *Mass in G Minor*; several anthems and psalm settings; and two lovely Christmas works—the *Fantasia on Christmas Carols* and *Hodie.*

Although self-critical and lacking confidence during his early years, Vaughan Williams never lacked faith in his talent or ability. He was able to chart a career of constant organic growth, yet one full of surprises, opening unexpected vistas as he glimpsed new expressive possibilities. He was important not only for the high quality of his work, but for showing how a composer of the 20th century could relate to tradition yet be altogether of his time. Following his lead, Grainger, Finzi, Holst, and others began tapping into the wellsprings of English folk music, capturing not only its accents but its directness, simplicity, and energy. His influence extended to the Beatles and other popular musicians of the British Invasion. As important, if not more, Vaughan Williams also spearheaded, with Britten and Tippett, a reengagement with the tradition of Tallis, Byrd, and Purcell, forging a link between one golden age of English music and another.

RECOMMENDED RECORDINGS

FANTASIA ON A THEME BY THOMAS TALLIS, FANTASIA ON GREENSLEEVES, THE LARK ASCENDING: BROWN; MARRINER AND ACADEMY OF ST. MARTIN-IN-THE-FIELDS (ARGO).

FANTASIA ON A THEME BY THOMAS TALLIS, NORFOLK RHAPSODY NO. 1, *IN THE FEN COUNTRY*: MARRINER AND ACADEMY OF ST. MARTIN-IN-THE-FIELDS (PHILIPS).

FILM MUSIC: GAMBA AND BBC PHILHARMONIC ORCHESTRA (CHANDOS).

FIVE MYSTICAL SONGS, SERENADE TO MUSIC: ALLEN; BEST AND ENGLISH CHAMBER ORCHESTRA (HYPERION).

THE LARK ASCENDING: BEAN; BOULT AND NEW PHILHARMONIA ORCHESTRA (EMI).

MASS IN G MINOR (WITH WORKS OF BAX AND FINZI): WILLCOCKS AND KING'S COLLEGE CHOIR (EMI).

SIR JOHN IN LOVE: MAXWELL, GRITTON, CLAYCOMB, OWENS, PADMORE WITH HICKOX AND NORTHERN SINFONIA (CHANDOS).

SYMPHONIES (COMPLETE): BOULT AND LONDON PHILHARMONIC ORCHESTRA (EMI).

SYMPHONIES (COMPLETE): HANDLEY AND ROYAL LIVERPOOL PHILHARMONIC ORCHESTRA (CFP).

SYMPHONIES (COMPLETE): PREVIN AND LONDON SYMPHONY ORCHESTRA (RCA).

SYMPHONY NO. 2 (ORIGINAL VERSION): HICKOX AND LONDON SYMPHONY ORCHESTRA (CHANDOS).

Vengerov, Maxim

(b. Novosibirsk, August 15, 1974)

RUSSIAN VIOLINIST. He started playing the violin when he was four and gave his first recital at the age of five. In 1984 he won first prize in the Junior Wieniawski Competition in Poland, and in 1990—after making his debuts in Moscow and London—he won top honors at the International Carl Flesch Violin Competition in London. He made his U.S. debut with the New York Philharmonic in 1991 and quickly became a favorite guest artist with many of Europe's and America's top orchestras, including the Chicago Symphony Orchestra and the Royal Concertgebouw Orchestra of Amsterdam. He was appointed an envoy for music by UNICEF in 1997; in that role he has played for abducted child-soldiers in Uganda, children suffering from drug addiction in Thailand, and disadvantaged youths in Kosovo and Harlem. In 2000 he became a professor of violin at the Musikhochschule des Saarlands in Saarbrücken.

Vengerov's playing combines deep musicality with a phenomenal command of his instrument. He has had an astonishingly successful career to date and, with top-notch partners, has already made compelling recordings of many of the literature's most important concertos: Brahms with Barenboim and the Chicago Symphony, Mendelssohn and Bruch with Masur and the Gewandhaus Orchestra, Shostakovich and Prokofiev with Rostropovich and the London Symphony. Good as they are, most of them fall short of capturing the electricity he routinely generates on stage. With his prodigious technique, his outsize yet unfailingly beautiful tone, and his exquisite way of shaping a phrase, Vengerov is one of the most promising young violinists on the scene today. He currently plays the "Ex-Kreutzer" Stradivarius (1731).

Maxim Vengerov

RECOMMENDED RECORDINGS

BRAHMS, VIOLIN CONCERTO: BARENBOIM AND CHICAGO SYMPHONY ORCHESTRA (TELDEC).

SHOSTAKOVICH, PROKOFIEV, VIOLIN CONCERTOS (COMPLETE) (2 VOLS.): ROSTROPOVICH AND LONDON SYMPHONY ORCHESTRA (TELDEC).

WALTON, VIOLA CONCERTO; BRITTEN, VIOLIN CONCERTO): ROSTROPOVICH AND LONDON SYMPHONY ORCHESTRA (EMI).

RECITAL:

"VENGEROV": WORKS BY KREISLER, PAGANINI, SARASATE, AND WIENIAWSKI: BROWN (EMI).

verbunkos (from Ger. *Werbung*, "[military] draft") Marchlike Hungarian recruiting dance. It was used by Hussars to attract recruits in Hungarian villages from the 18th until the mid-19th century; Gypsy musicians typically provided the accompaniment. The style was so popular it became a fixture in later 19th- and 20th-century Hungarian music. Examples include the opening subject of the first movement of Bartók's Violin Concerto No. 2 (1938) and the Intermezzo from Kodály's *Háry János*.

Verdi, Giuseppe

(b. Roncole, October 9, 1813; d. Milan, January 27, 1901)

ITALIAN COMPOSER. He was the preeminent figure in Italian opera during the second half of the 19th century and arguably the greatest dramatist the art of music has yet known. After years of hard work, frequently mingled with frustration, he achieved in middle and later life a stunning series of successes, crafting his finest work when he was well into his 70s.

After he became famous, Verdi liked to say he was just a peasant, but his origins

Verdi in 1886; pastel by Giovanni Boldoni

weren't quite so humble. His father, a small landowner, kept an inn of respectable size in the crossroads settlement of Roncole; his mother, too, came from a family of innkeepers. Verdi grew up amid some of the finest farmland in Italy, under foreign domination, first French and later Austrian. When he was four Verdi's father found him a tutor from whom he learned, in addition to his ABCs, to play the organ.

From the age of ten, Verdi attended school in Busseto, boarding in town and walking the short distance back to Roncole on Sundays to be with his family and play the organ in the parish church. By the time he was 13, he was committed to music and came into contact with Antonio Barezzi, a well-to-do patron of Busseto's Philharmonic Society. Verdi lived in the Barezzi home from the time he was 17, and became attached to Barezzi's daughter Margherita. Encouraged by Barezzi to pursue his music studies in Milan, Verdi left Busseto in 1832, but failed the entrance examination for the Milan Conservatory. He ended up studying privately with Vincenzo Lavigna, Barezzi footing the considerable bill. Lavigna's tutelage included study of 18th-century counterpoint and fugue, modeled on Paisiello, as well as free composition in the modern style. During his three years in Milan, Verdi attended many performances at the Teatro alla Scala and smaller theaters.

In 1836 Verdi was named director of Busseto's Philharmonic Society, and two months later he married Margherita Barezzi. Over the next couple of years they had two children, both of whom died shortly after their first birthdays. In 1839 the composer, now based in Milan, premiered his first opera, *Oberto,* at La Scala. Margherita died suddenly the next year, probably of encephalitis. The grief-stricken composer threw himself into his work, but the modest success of *Oberto* was followed by the fiasco of *Un giorno di regno* (*King for a Day*), his first attempt at a comedy—such a severe blow that he nearly gave up composing.

NABUCCO (1842), Verdi's first outright triumph, marked the beginning of what he would later refer to as his years as a "galley slave." Over the next decade—collaborating with several librettists, chiefly Temistocle Solera, Francesco Piave, and Salvatore Cammarano—he cranked out 16 operas. With *Ernani,* based on a play by Victor Hugo, he began a lifelong quest for literary material of the highest merit to serve as the basis for his work. He would turn again to Hugo for the story behind *Rigoletto,* and to Friedrich von Schiller for *I masnadieri, Giovanna d'Arco, LUISA MILLER,* and *DON CARLO.* The raw material for *I due Foscari* and *Il corsaro* would come from Byron; Voltaire gave him *Alzira.* The source for *Macbeth,* of course, was Shakespeare, whose work would again figure importantly at the end of Verdi's career.

At rehearsals for the premiere of *Nabucco,* Verdi met the soprano Giuseppina Strepponi, who had stepped in at the last minute to take over the role of Abigaille. The two became an item in the mid-1840s, living together in Paris for two years and, more scandalously, shacking up back in Busseto in 1849. Fed up with gossiping tongues, Verdi bought land in Sant'Agata—a couple of miles outside of town, in the lush Parmesan countryside where his ancestors had been tenant farmers—and began building a villa. From 1851 he and Strepponi lived there; they were secretly married in 1859.

Giuseppina Strepponi

Verdi reached his artistic maturity with RIGOLETTO, IL TROVATORE (*The Troubadour*), and LA TRAVIATA (*The Woman Who Strayed*), his three back-to-back masterpieces of the early 1850s. *Rigoletto* marked a breakthrough in his ability to build drama through structure—to limn character and create tension with striking manipulations of standard forms and equally striking juxtapositions of contrasting musical styles. By comparison, *Il trovatore* seems regressive in formal terms, but it unleashed an entirely new kind of power, a kinetic, coiled intensity. Part of its impact comes from the way it puts the pressure of extremely heated emotion on the standard, closed forms. *La traviata,* the most intimate of the three, is the only one of Verdi's operas with a more or less contemporary setting, with situations that dramatically reflect the composer's growing interest in social questions and their relation to characterization. Musically, it shows him building on the techniques of characterization mastered in *Rigoletto* and successfully injecting into the mold of Italian opera the new ideas that were transforming French music at mid-century—subtler and more sophisticated forms for individual numbers than the standard, squarish Italian ones.

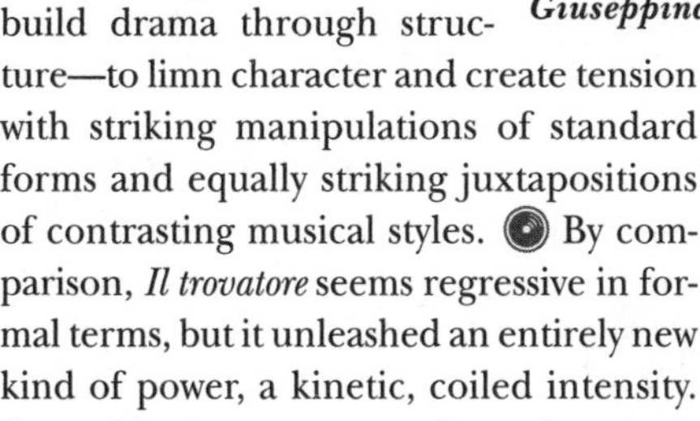

Verdi's name as acronym, standing for the Risorgimento's rallying cry: Vittorio Emanuele, Re d'Italia

Though Verdi had broken the shackles of convention with these works, he remained chained to the galley oars for the rest of the decade. In *Les vêpres siciliennes* (libretto by Eugène Scribe, for the Paris Opéra), the influence of French structural models is even more apparent; it also exhibits an expansion of scale that clearly owes something to grand opera. From this point on, Verdi's works would tend to be louder, more powerfully scored, longer, grander in scope. The next were *Simon Boccanegra* (1857; libretto by Piave, after García Gutiérrez) and UN BALLO IN MASCHERA (*A Masked Ball*; 1859; based on the libretto Scribe had written for Auber's *Gustave III, ou le bal masqué*). *Ballo* capped Verdi's first 20 years as an opera composer with a triumphant demonstration of mastery.

In his last four decades Verdi would compose just five new operas. During the 1860s, he devoted much time to work on the estate at Sant'Agata, where he instituted modern farming methods, and to politics. At the urging of Count Camillo Cavour—publisher of the newspaper *Il risorgimento* (the Risorgimento was the movement for the unification of Italy)—Verdi served as a deputy in the first Italian parliament from 1861 to 1865. Composing was not neglected: *LA FORZA DEL DESTINO* (*The Power of Fate*; 1862), written for St. Petersburg, proved a work of great power with the most symphonic overture Verdi would ever write; *Don Carlo* (1867), his second work for the Paris Opéra, was not only the greatest of Verdi's Schiller-inspired works but one of his mightiest creations for the stage, a synthesis of French and Italian opera styles possessing a political and dramatic vision virtually unique in the repertoire.

By the 1870s, Verdi was securely established as Italy's greatest composer. Famous throughout the world, he had no need to prove himself or, indeed, to make a living writing operas. But a generous commission from the Khedive of Egypt, the equivalent of at least $250,000 today, turned him to the composition of what has remained his most popular work, *AIDA*. It marked Verdi's most successful transformation of Meyerbeerian grand opera and its scenic formulas into a masterpiece of, among many other touches, color.

There would not be another new opera for almost 16 years, but Verdi kept busy. Shortly after Rossini's death, in 1868, he had written his publisher, Tito Ricordi, to suggest that a Requiem in Rossini's memory be compiled as a collaborative effort by Italy's leading composers. Ricordi had jumped on the idea, and 13 composers were asked to contribute sections of the mass; Verdi's assignment was the final *Libera me.* The composite *Messa per Rossini* stood complete in September 1869, but a performance planned for the first anniversary of Rossini's death never occurred. (Indeed, the work was not premiered until 1988.) In 1873 Ricordi returned the score of the *Libera me* to Verdi. The death that same year of Alessandro Manzoni—author of the novel *I promessi sposi* (*The Betrothed*) and one of the towering figures of the Risorgimento—affected Verdi even more deeply than Rossini's. In response, he decided to reverse engineer a complete Requiem in memory of Manzoni from the *Libera me* he had fashioned for the earlier mass, using some of its most salient material to build the *Dies irae* and *Requiem aeternam* sections of the new work. He devoted the summer of 1873 to completing it, bore the cost of printing the music, and presided over the first performance, at the Church of San Marco in Milan, on May 22, 1874. It is a monumental composition, imaginative and powerfully theatrical—not so much a statement of belief or consolation as a translation of the Latin text's rich dramatic possibilities into the language of opera.

In 1879 Giulio Ricordi, Tito's son, arranged a meeting between the aging Verdi and the poet-musician Arrigo Boito, with the aim of tempting the composer back into opera. Thus began one of the most fruitful partnerships the lyric stage has ever known. Initially Boito assisted Verdi in a major revision of *Simon Boccanegra,* contributing the text for a new Act I finale, a climactic council chamber scene that elicited music of almost unprecedented ferocity. But it was Boito's libretto for a new opera, based on Shakespeare's *Othello,* that

Verdi in the late 1890s

really set Verdi on fire. Premiered at La Scala in 1887, *OTELLO* represented a stylistic sea change, with newly sustained energy and dramatic tension, and far greater compression (achieved in part because the set pieces are fully integrated into the structure of each act). The action is continuous, as though events are happening in real time. The operatic world was stunned that an artist in his 70s evinced such powers.

And Verdi was not finished. In 1889 he took up a new Shakespeare project, again with Boito, this time a comedy. Completed four years later, *FALSTAFF,* based on *The Merry Wives of Windsor,* was Verdi's last work for the stage, his most ensemble-dominated opera, and the only comic opera from his mature years. Centering on the figure who is arguably Shakespeare's richest "character," Sir John Falstaff, Verdi's opera is similarly rich in its musical trappings, and shows conclusively that character, not action, is what the greatest opera is about.

Projects of Verdi's final years included the Casa di Riposo, a musicians' rest home in Milan. Verdi bought the land, had plans drawn up by Boito's brother Camillo, and set aside huge sums to build and endow it. He closed out his lifework with *QUATTRO PEZZI SACRI* (*Four Sacred Pieces*), written during the 1890s. His wife died at the end of 1897, and Verdi followed just over three years later. At his funeral, on February 26, 1901, Arturo Toscanini conducted a choir of 900 in the chorus "Va, pensiero" from *Nabucco*; mourners in the thousands lined the streets as the procession made its way through Milan.

No composer has contributed more great and near-great operas to the repertoire than Verdi. Any one of his works from *Nabucco* on—a total of 24 operas, not counting revisions—can today be found holding the stage in the world's opera houses. A dozen rank as absolute masterpieces. In considering Verdi's work, what stands out is the way it reflects the steady development of his powers as a dramatist and his amazing capacity for self-renewal. In his early efforts he worked straight from librettos he was provided. Once he established himself he took an active role in shaping them, always with a view toward advancing the drama on the stage. Increasingly, he focused on speed, on cutting away text, getting to the point, often resorting to the equivalent of jump cuts in cinema: his mature works have a pace, *velocità,* that is striking. The musical language and theatrical style of his early works are an outgrowth of Donizetti's, augmented by scenic elements of grand opera: climactic tableaux with massed forces, allowing the individuals' emotions and conflicts to be projected against a backdrop of group sentiment. Later works move with force, with a breathtaking sense of sweep and continuity, the structural seams absorbed within the orchestral fabric. Significantly, this permits a more intense focus on private moments (e.g., in *Don Carlo, Aida, Otello*).

While Verdi cared passionately about singing and obsessed over the capabilities of the vocalists who would realize his roles, the drama was paramount. Like Mozart, Verdi understood and was able to musically reveal the complexity of emotion. He was a master of gesture, both topical and stylistic, of the delineation of character through formal means. The sentimental bel canto delivery of Germont in *La traviata* symbolizes the manner of expression one would expect of the "older generation." In that same opera the changes in Violetta's attitude and feelings from one act to the next are reflected in the different styles of her delivery—from flighty coloratura of "Sempre libera" in the first act to the weightier spinto of the second and the ethereal tenderness of the third. Other examples include the varying vocal styles of principal characters in

Otello, what has been called the "energetic, hard, and icy glitter" of Lady Macbeth's music, and the quartet in *Rigoletto*—not just four parts harmonizing, but four distinct characters emoting simultaneously.

Verdi had an uncanny ability to shoot for the gallery and hit the heart. In true Aristotelian fashion he created terror and pity on the stage. Masterfully depicting raw feeling, every nerve exposed, he was unique among opera composers in his range of both characterization and emotion. For such theatrical potency his only rival was Shakespeare.

RECOMMENDED RECORDINGS

AIDA: CABALLÉ, COSSOTTO, DOMINGO, CAPPUCCILLI, GHIAUROV; MUTI AND NEW PHILHARMONIA ORCHESTRA (EMI).

UN BALLO IN MASCHERA: M. PRICE, PAVAROTTI, LUDWIG, BATTLE, BRUSON, LLOYD; SOLTI AND NATIONAL PHILHARMONIC ORCHESTRA (DECCA).

FALSTAFF: SCHWARZKOPF, BARBIERI, GOBBI, ALVA, MOFFO; KARAJAN AND PHILHARMONIA ORCHESTRA (EMI).

NABUCCO: CAPPUCCILLI, DOMINGO, DIMOTROVA; SINOPOLI AND DEUTSCHE OPER BERLIN (DG).

OTELLO: DOMINGO, MILNES, SCOTTO; LEVINE AND NATIONAL PHILHARMONIC ORCHESTRA (RCA).

REQUIEM, QUATTRO PEZZI SACRI: CURRY, DUNN, HADLEY, PLISHKA; SHAW AND ATLANTA SYMPHONY ORCHESTRA (TELARC).

REQUIEM, QUATTRO PEZZI SACRI: SCHWARZKOPF, GEDDA, LUDWIG, GHIAUROV; GIULINI AND PHILHARMONIA ORCHESTRA (EMI).

RIGOLETTO: CAPPUCCILLI, COTRUBAS, DOMINGO, GHIAUROV; GIULINI AND VIENNA PHILHARMONIC (DG).

SIMON BOCCANEGRA: CAPPUCCILLI, CARRERAS, FRENI, VAN DAM; ABBADO AND LA SCALA ORCHESTRA (DG).

LA TRAVIATA: COTRUBAS, DOMINGO, MILNES; KLEIBER AND BAVARIAN STATE OPERA ORCHESTRA (DG).

IL TROVATORE: PRICE, DOMINGO, MILNES, COSSOTTO; MEHTA AND PHILHARMONIA ORCHESTRA (RCA).

verismo (from It. *verità,* "truth") Originally, a movement in Italian literature of the late 19th century that emphasized objectivity and realism, by means of characters and situations drawn from the lower social strata. It became an operatic style during the 1890s, propelled by the success of two works that are still "twinned" on many bills, *Cavalleria rusticana* (1890), by Pietro Mascagni, and *Pagliacci* (1892) ◉, by Ruggero Leoncavallo. In these operas and the many works they influenced—such as Massenet's *La Navarraise* (1894), Giordano's *Fedora* (1898), and *Tiefland* (1903) by Eugen d'Albert (1864–1932)—the stage is supposed to portray real life, real people, and violent passions. Puccini absorbed many elements of the verismo manner into his style, an influence particularly clear in works such as *Tosca* (1900) and *Il tabarro* (1918).

Verklärte Nacht (Transfigured Night) TONE POEM FOR STRING SEXTET—TWO VIOLINS, TWO VIOLAS, AND TWO CELLOS—BY ARNOLD SCHOENBERG, OP. 4, completed in December 1899 and premiered March 18, 1902, in Vienna, by the Rosé Quartet and two colleagues. The piece's title comes from a poem by Richard Dehmel that appeared in the collection *Weib und Welt* (*Woman and World*). Dehmel's transcendent, intensely spiritual verse appealed to a number of German post-Romantic composers, among them Reger, Pfitzner, Richard Strauss, and Webern, all of whom made vocal settings of it. It deeply affected Schoenberg, who in addition to setting eight of Dehmel's other poems as songs, used "Verklärte Nacht" as the basis for this work, his most enduring chamber composition.

Verklärte Nacht combines the expressive, chromatic harmony of Wagner's *Tristan und Isolde* with the lush textures and painstaking motivic development of Brahms's late chamber works. It closely follows the expressive curve of the poem, in which, on a moonlit night among the trees, a woman confesses to her lover that she is pregnant by another man; he reassures her that through their love for each other the child will be as his.

One of the few full-blown pieces of program music in the chamber repertoire, *Verklärte Nacht* has an unconventional layout that calls to mind Strauss's highly effective plan for *Tod und Verklärung.* Its five sections (corresponding to the stanzas of Dehmel's poem) form two large spans; the first, rooted in D minor, expresses the woman's despair and the turbulent emotion of her confession, while the second, in D major and full of the paroxysmal expression of *Tristan und Isolde,* evokes the transfiguration the couple's love has brought to the night.

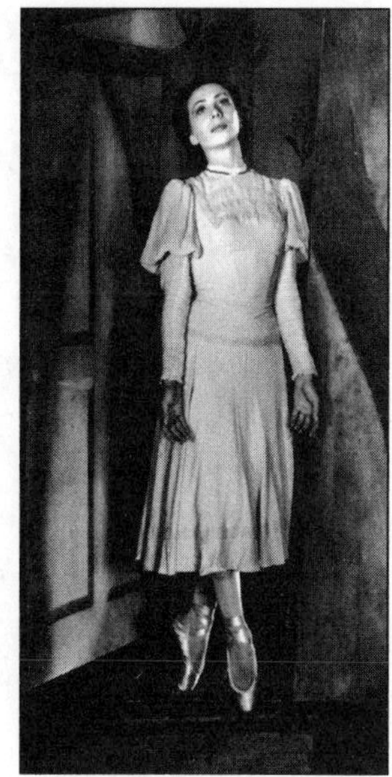

***Scene from Anthony Tudor's* Pillar of Fire**

Schoenberg was an accomplished cellist with an insider's knowledge of the chamber metier, and his writing for the strings throughout the sextet is idiomatic and colorfully effective. In 1917 he made an arrangement of the score for string orchestra, which he revised in 1943. In 1942, for New York's Ballet Theater, the choreographer Anthony Tudor created the ballet *Pillar of Fire* to the music of *Verklärte Nacht.*

RECOMMENDED RECORDINGS

SEXTET:

RAPHAEL ENSEMBLE (HYPERION).

STRING ORCHESTRA:

KARAJAN AND BERLIN PHILHARMONIC (DG).

MEHTA AND LOS ANGELES PHILHARMONIC ORCHESTRA (DECCA).

Viardot, Pauline

(b. Paris, July 18, 1821; d. Paris, May 18, 1910)

FRENCH MEZZO-SOPRANO OF SPANISH DESCENT. The daughter of the renowned singer and voice teacher Manuel García and sister of the celebrated singer Maria Malibran, she studied with her father up to his death in 1832, and after that with her mother; she also studied piano with Franz Liszt and composition with Antoine Reicha. She made her debut in a recital at the age of 16, and in 1839 sang the role of Desdemona in Rossini's *Otello* in Paris and London. She was much acclaimed; Hector Berlioz noted that her voice encompassed contralto, mezzo-soprano, and soprano ranges equally well. In 1840, she married the writer Louis Viardot, who became her manager. Her career took her across Europe as far as St. Petersburg. Among its highlights was her creation of the role of Fidès in Meyerbeer's *Le prophète* at the Paris Opéra (1849) and her memorable embodiment of the role of Orphée in Berlioz's adaptation of Gluck's *Orphée et Eurydice* at the Théâtre Lyrique (1859), which she sang 150 times in three years. In 1863, she moved to Baden-Baden to teach, returning to Paris in 1871 after the fall of Napoleon III. Viardot composed several operettas, some on librettos by Turgenev, whom she met in Russia (and with whom she carried on an affair that lasted until the writer's death in 1883). In the course of her lifetime, she also composed more than 100 songs in Italian, German, Spanish, and French.

RECOMMENDED RECORDINGS

AS COMPOSER:

***CENDRILLON*: PIAU, RIGBY, WATERS, VIDAL, VIALA; KOK AND GEOFFREY MITCHELL CHOIR (OPERA RARA).**

SONGS: BAYRAKDARIAN, KRADJIAN (ANALEKTA).

vibrato In the performance of vocal and instrumental (especially string) music, a manner of sounding individual notes so that their pitch fluctuates slightly "around" the written pitch. Vibrato was originally a kind of ornament, an expressive device applied selectively to certain notes to draw attention to them. Around the beginning of the 20th century it became the norm rather than the exception, to be utilized at all times unless an instruction like *senza vibrato* ("without vibrato") appears in the score. This kind of vibrato, known as "continuous" vibrato, has been standard practice for singers and for players of bowed string instruments for about a century; properly done, it lends warmth and body to a sustained line, and brings string playing closer to the effect of vocal singing. Vibrato can be narrow ("tight") or wide, relatively fast or slow, and can be varied according to the style of the music being played and the taste of the performer. Pronounced vibrato is generally considered a flaw. Lack of vibrato (a "straight" tone), which used to be the norm (and is still appropriate to a good deal of early music), is now considered an expressive device, and can impart a haunting, desolate, or ethereal quality to a line that might otherwise sound plain or merely pretty.

Vickers, Jon

(b. Prince Albert, Sask., October 29, 1926)

CANADIAN TENOR. One of seven children of a lay preacher in a small northern Saskatchewan town, he became a leading Heldentenor on the stages of the world's major opera houses during the 1960s and 1970s. He received his training at the Royal Conservatory of Music in Toronto with Herman Geiger-Torel, the founder of the Canadian Opera Company, and in 1956, within a self-imposed time limit of one month of auditioning (at the end of which, if unsuccessful, he would have pursued a business career), he landed a contract at the Royal Opera, Covent Garden. Over the next several seasons at his new artistic home, he sang many of the dramatic tenor roles for which he became famous: Radames, Don José, Siegmund, Canio, Parsifal, and Samson, as well as less well-known roles, such as Jason in Cherubini's *Médée,* and the taxing role of Énée in Berlioz's *Les Troyens,* which he considered his finest achievement. He debuted at Bayreuth in 1958 (as Siegmund), at the Metropolitan Opera in 1960 (as Florestan in *Fidelio* and Canio in *Pagliacci*), at the Vienna Staatsoper in 1959 (*Andréa Chenier*), and at Buenos Aires in 1963 (*Otello*). Among Vickers's most memorable achievements was his characterization of Britten's Peter Grimes, which he sang at the Met in 1967 and subsequently at Covent Garden.

Jon Vickers as Vašek in Smetana's **The Bartered Bride**

Vickers had an utterly unique timbre—rough, steely, with a distinctive burr, and so hot it practically glowed. In his prime his voice was huge, giving the impression of an unstoppable force of nature. He paid close attention in roles such as Otello and Grimes to both music and language, which accounted for the dramatic intensity he brought to his acting. His intellectual and emotional qualities had many critics comparing his stage presence to that of Callas and Chaliapin, and he belongs with them among the great vocal actors and compelling interpreters of the 20th century.

RECOMMENDED RECORDINGS

Beethoven, *Fidelio*: Ludwig, Crass, Frick, Berry; Klemperer and Philharmonia Orchestra (EMI).

Britten, *Peter Grimes*: Harper, Bainbridge, Summers, Allen, Van Allan; Davis and Royal Opera (Philips).

Verdi, *Otello*: Glossop, Freni; Karajan and Berlin Philharmonic (EMI).

Victoria, Tomás Luis de

(b. Avila, 1548; d. Madrid, August 20, 1611)

Composer of the Spanish Renaissance. He was brought up in a fairly prosperous and well-connected family in Ávila, also the birthplace of St. Teresa, whose mystical experiences began in 1554, when Tomás was a little boy. He was educated at a newly opened Jesuit school and sang as a choirboy at the Ávila Cathedral. In 1565, after his voice had broken, he was sent for further study to the Jesuit-run Collegio Germanico in Rome, where he was enrolled as a singer. He undoubtedly came to know Palestrina and may even have been taught by him; his rapid mastering of the older composer's style is apparent from his earliest published compositions, such as his first collection of motets (1572). Victoria served as a singer and organist of the church of Santa Maria di Monserrato in Rome from 1569 to 1574, and as *maestro di cappella* of the Collegio Germanico from 1573 until the end of 1576. He was ordained on August 28, 1575. From 1578 to 1585 he served as chaplain of the church of San Girolamo della Carità in Rome. During these years, he published collections of motets, masses, and Magnificat settings, as well as a splendid set of Lamentations and other works for Holy Week. He was recalled to Spain in 1586 by Philip II, to serve as chaplain to the king's sister, the Empress María, at the convent to which she had retired in Madrid. Following the empress's death in 1603, he composed in her memory what would be his last work, the *Officium defunctorum* of 1605. He was comfortably provided for during the rest of his life.

Victoria's output consists of 20 masses, 16 Magnificat settings, 56 motets, plus various settings of psalms, hymns, antiphons, sequences, two passion settings, and the *Officium Hebdomadae Sanctae,* music for Palm Sunday and the last three days of Holy Week, which includes his Lamentations. Though he was not as prolific as Palestrina (with 700 works) or Lassus (with an astonishing 2,000 works), Victoria was productive, and his output of a bit less than 180 works maintains a consistently high standard. In beauty and expressiveness, his music rivals Palestrina's, and its sound is in some ways similar—not surprising, as both were in the service of a conservative Rome during the Counter-Reformation. But where Palestrina tends toward an otherworldly elevation, Victoria conveys a more fervent kind of emotion, sometimes poignant and mystical, at other times intensely joyful.

RECOMMENDED RECORDINGS

Officium defunctorum: Phillips and Tallis Scholars (Gimell).

Selected masses and motets: Carwood and Cardinall's Musick (ASV).

Selected masses and motets: Summerly and Oxford Camerata (Naxos).

vida breve, La (The Short Life) **Opera in two acts by Manuel de Falla,** to a libretto by Carlos Fernández Shaw, premiered April 1, 1913, at the Casino in Nice. Set in Granada, where the composer would later make his home, the story centers around a young Gypsy girl, Salud, who dies of a broken heart when her lover marries another girl.

RECOMMENDED RECORDING

LOS ANGELES, HIGUERAS, COSSUTTA, MORENA; FRÜHBECK DE BURGOS AND NATIONAL ORCHESTRA OF SPAIN (EMI).

Vienna Philharmonic Ensemble founded in 1842 under the leadership of Otto Nicolai. Gathering 64 players from his orchestra at the Vienna Court Opera, Nicolai conducted a symphonic concert for subscribers on March 28 of that year, offering Beethoven's Symphony No. 7 as part of the program. Nicolai stayed only a few more years in Vienna, returning in 1847 to Berlin in his native Germany to take over its opera. But to this day, the Vienna Philharmonic honors its founder with the annual Nicolai Concert, the proceeds of which support its pension fund.

From 1842 until 1854, concerts took place only occasionally; between 1854 and 1860 the orchestra appeared annually. The regular Philharmonic Subscription Concerts, as they are still called, were introduced in 1860 under the direction of Otto Dessoff, who remained the orchestra's conductor until 1875. In 1870, the year of the Beethoven centenary, the Philharmonic moved into its permanent home in the main hall of the new building of the Gesellschaft der Musikfreunde (Society of the Friends of Music), the Grosser Musikvereinssaal.

In 1875 Hans Richter, a disciple of Wagner, became the Philharmonic's first permanent conductor. Richter, who had been a horn player with the orchestra before he took up conducting, led the Philharmonic in 214 performances during his 23-year tenure and championed the music of contemporary composers including Wagner, Bruckner, Brahms, and Dvořák. He was succeeded in 1898 by Gustav Mahler. While Mahler served only three seasons as the orchestra's conductor, he stayed on in Vienna as director of the Court Opera until 1907, and so (by an arrangement reserving two subscription concerts each year for the Opera's conductor) continued to lead the orchestra.

In 1908 the Philharmonic chose as its permanent conductor Felix Weingartner, who had replaced Mahler at the Court Opera and who remained with the Philharmonic until 1927. Weingartner was succeeded by Wilhelm Furtwängler and Clemens Krauss. In the years prior to the 1938 annexation of Austria by Germany, the membership of the Philharmonic was predominantly pro-Nazi, though this did not prevent the orchestra from collaborating with one of the finest conductors of the day, Bruno Walter, who happened to be Jewish.

During World War II, the Philharmonic became a plaything of the Nazis and their minions; nevertheless it was led by some outstanding conductors, notably Herbert von Karajan, Karl Böhm, Furtwängler, and Krauss. After the war, Walter returned to direct a number of performances with the orchestra he so deeply loved, and so did most of the wartime old guard, including Furtwängler, Böhm, and Karajan. The latter two continued to work with the orchestra into the 1980s. As time went by the orchestra reached out to many of the leading podium talents of the postwar years, among them Leonard Bernstein, Georg Solti, István Kertész, Claudio Abbado, Carlos Kleiber, Zubin Mehta, and Lorin Maazel. The postwar years saw the Philharmonic become remarkably active as a recording orchestra, producing distinguished work with all these figures.

The Vienna Philharmonic is today, as it has been from the very beginning, also the orchestra of the Vienna Staatsoper. For

The Vienna Philharmonic at home in the Grosser Musikvereinssaal

300 evenings a year, during the opera's enormous 10-month season, it plays in the pit of the city's opera house (designed by Gottfried Semper and opened in 1869), which is one of Austria's state theaters. Because of that, the members of the Philharmonic are government employees, under contractual obligation to the Staatsoper. Apart from this obligation, the Vienna Philharmonic as a concert orchestra is a private society, run by its members. It arranges its own concerts and tours and takes responsibility for planning its extensive recording activities. The orchestra is totally self-governing (all decisions are made by four-fifths vote of the membership), and the managerial functions are handled by a committee composed of players who, while continuing to perform their other duties, serve three-year terms; the full-time administrative staff consists only of three secretaries and an accountant. The ensemble has historically been all-male, departing from this tradition only a few years ago with the hiring of a female harpist. Women now may apply to audition, though the odds of their becoming members are as long as a Bruckner symphony.

In more ways than one the Philharmonic remains a bastion of conservatism. Over the years it has premiered a relatively small number of important new works, the most significant being Bruckner's Symphonies Nos. 4, 6, and 8, Brahms's Symphonies Nos. 2 and 3, and Mahler's Symphony No. 9; in 1880 the players' committee turned down the chance to premiere Dvořák's Symphony No. 6, which had been written at the behest of the orchestra's principal conductor, Hans Richter. The Philharmonic also painstakingly cultivates an "old-fashioned" sound through the use of wind and brass instruments that retain the characteristics of 19th-century models. The Viennese oboe, a throwback played nowhere else in the world, has a different bore from the modern oboe, uses a differently shaped reed, and requires different fingerings. Its sound is plangent and rather piercing. The trombones used by the Philharmonic have a narrower bore than standard modern instruments, as do the horns and trumpets, giving them all a somewhat brighter, more penetrating sound. The strings of the Philharmonic have long been famed for their burnished beauty and for the range of tone and color the players can achieve—the result not of any superiority in the instruments themselves, but of the ensemble's adherence to a style of string playing entirely its own, which is passed on from generation to generation and is characterized by an uncanny unanimity of bowing and attack. Taken together, these factors give the Philharmonic a unique sound, one that can be all wrong for Ravel and Debussy, but is utterly right for certain repertoire, such as Brahms, Bruckner, Richard Strauss, and the waltzes of Johann Strauss Jr.

RECOMMENDED RECORDINGS

BEETHOVEN, *FIDELIO*: JANOWITZ, POPP, KOLLO, SOTIN; BERNSTEIN (DG).

BEETHOVEN, SYMPHONIES (COMPLETE): BÖHM (DG).

BEETHOVEN, SYMPHONY NO. 5: FURTWÄNGLER (EMI).

BRAHMS, SYMPHONIES (COMPLETE): KERTÉSZ (DECCA).

BRUCKNER, SYMPHONIES NOS. 7 AND 8: KARAJAN (DG).

"STRAUSS HEROINES" (SCENES FROM *DER ROSENKAVALIER, ARABELLA, CAPRICCIO*): FLEMING, BONNEY, GRAHAM; ESCHENBACH (DECCA).

MUSIC OF JOHANN STRAUSS JR.: KARAJAN (DG).

MUSIC OF JOHANN STRAUSS JR.: C. KLEIBER (SONY).

MUSIC OF JOHANN STRAUSS JR.: KRAUSS (DECCA).

WAGNER, *DER RING DES NIBELUNGEN*: FLAGSTAD, NILSSON, HOTTER, LONDON, OTHERS; SOLTI WITH VARIOUS SOLOISTS (DECCA).

WAGNER, *DIE WALKÜRE*, ACT I: LEHMANN, MELCHIOR, LIST; WALTER (EMI).

Vier letzte Lieder (Four Last Songs) SONG CYCLE FOR SOPRANO AND ORCHESTRA BY RICHARD STRAUSS, completed in 1948 and premiered in London by Kirsten Flagstad and the Philharmonia Orchestra, Wilhelm Furtwängler conducting, on May 22, 1950, eight months after the composer's death. The final song in the set, "Im Abendrot" ("At Twilight"), to a poem by Joseph von Eichendorff, was the first to be sketched and scored. Strauss followed it with settings of three poems by Hermann Hesse: "Frühling" ("Spring"), "Beim Schlafengehen" ("Going to Sleep"), and "September." Never one to miss a felicitous connection between life and art, he finished the score to "September," his last work, on September 20, 1948.

The *Vier letzte Lieder* were Strauss's valedictory to composition, the beautiful culmination of his lifelong love affair with the soprano voice and the symphony orchestra. The texts of the songs are introspective and subdued, yet in all four settings the music is ardent, full of heartfelt sentiment. As always, Strauss achieves an effortless melodic outpouring: The vocal line stretches out serenely, without need for ornamentation, gently supported by an orchestra of ample but not exaggerated size. The scoring is magisterial, the coloration subtle, the contrapuntal fabric lighter than in Strauss's tone poems but as intricately woven as ever. "Beim Schlafengehen," the third song in the cycle, contains what are surely some of the most exquisite pages of the 20th century. The poem's final line—"Tief und tausendfach zu leben" ("To live deeply and a thousandfold")—elicits a lyrical extension on the word "tausend" that goes beyond the bounds of human breath, so that the word and the idea it represents become a single expressive entity, the very highest achievement of the songwriter's art.

RECOMMENDED RECORDINGS

NORMAN; MASUR AND GEWANDHAUS ORCHESTRA (PHILIPS).

SCHWARZKOPF; SZELL AND BERLIN RADIO SYMPHONY ORCHESTRA (EMI).

Vieuxtemps, Henry

(b. Vérviers, February 17, 1820; d. Mustapha-lez-Alger, Algeria, June 6, 1881)

BELGIAN VIOLINIST AND COMPOSER, one of the great touring virtuoso violinists of the post-Paganini generation. His first teacher was his father. He later studied with Charles de Bériot in Brussels and Paris; the lessons came to an end in 1831, when Bériot left Paris to concertize in Italy and continue his long-standing affair with the celebrated singer Maria Malibran. With his father, the 13-year-old Vieuxtemps started his peripatetic life with an 1833 tour of Germany. He settled in Vienna for the winter of 1833–34, came into contact with musicians who had been part of Beethoven's circle, and performed the master's violin concerto in March 1834, after only two weeks of study. Later in the season the young violinist played in London for Paganini, the reigning wizard of the violin, who predicted a great future for him. In 1835 the family moved to Paris, where Vieuxtemps studied composition with Antoine Reicha. At this time he composed his Concerto No. 2 in F-sharp minor, in which he tried to fuse the classical form of the French violin concerto with the brilliant technical innovations of Paganini. In 1837 Vieuxtemps toured Vienna, Warsaw, and Russia with the pianist Adolph von Henselt; he went on the road the following year with the French cellist Adrian François Servais. In 1840 he wrote what would be designated his Concerto No. 1, in E, which he presented in St. Petersburg and Brussels to great acclaim. In 1843–44 he undertook his first American tour; his potboiler fantasy for violin and piano on "Yankee Doodle" scored a hit with the relatively unsophisticated audiences he encountered. Upon his return he composed his Concerto No. 3 in A, and married Josephine Elder, a Viennese pianist.

Henry Vieuxtemps

In 1846, having accepted the position of soloist to the tsar and professor of violin, Vieuxtemps moved to St. Petersburg, where he and his wife remained for five years, the most settled period of his life. During this Russian sojourn he composed his Concerto No. 4 in D minor, one of his finest works. In 1855, after a short stay in Belgium the couple settled near Frankfurt, moving to Paris in 1866. Vieuxtemps toured the U.S. in 1857–58 with the pianist Sigismond Thalberg, and in 1861 composed his Concerto No. 5 in A minor. Following his wife's death, he undertook a third U.S. tour during the 1870–71 season. He returned to Brussels, accepted a professorship at the conservatory, and devoted himself to teaching. Among his students was the young Eugène Ysaÿe, who became his heir as the great master of the Franco-Belgian school. In 1874 Vieuxtemps suffered a stroke that paralyzed his left side; his recovery was only partial, and in 1879 he resigned his teaching position to resume his travels. He wrote two final concertos near the end of his life, and died in a sanatorium in Algeria in 1881.

Vieuxtemps represented a new kind of violin virtuoso, who, like Heinrich Wilhelm Ernst, and later Wieniawski and Joachim, played works by other composers with intelligence and taste, not just his own showpieces. As a composer, Vieuxtemps rejuvenated the violin concerto by raising the contribution of the orchestra to a more symphonic level. In his hands virtuosic display attained eloquence, especially in the Fourth and Fifth Concertos, which remain staples in the repertoire of every violinist.

RECOMMENDED RECORDING

VIOLIN CONCERTOS NOS. 5, 6, AND 7: KEYLIN; MOGRELIA AND SLOVAK RADIO SYMPHONY ORCHESTRA; YUASA AND ARNHEM PHILHARMONIC ORCHESTRA (NAXOS).

Village Romeo and Juliet, A "LYRIC DRAMA IN SIX PICTURES" BY FREDERICK DELIUS, to his own libretto (loosely based on a novel by Gottfried Keller), composed 1900–01 and premiered February 21, 1907, at the Komische Oper in Berlin. The opera's London premiere, on February 22, 1910, was conducted by Thomas Beecham, who also presided over the first recording of the work in 1948. The story, set in Switzerland around 1850, concerns the ill-fated attempt of two young lovers to find happiness together despite a feud between their families over an unused piece of land. In the final scene, realizing that the world is no place for passions as idealistic as theirs, they hijack a hay barge and head it out into the river, where they scuttle it and are pulled under by the current. *A Village Romeo and Juliet* was the work with which Delius reached maturity as a composer; in characteristic fashion, its tale of innocence undone is refracted in music of radiant tenderness.

The most frequently encountered excerpt from the opera is "The Walk to the Paradise Garden," which Delius composed in 1906 to serve as an intermezzo between the fifth and sixth scenes at the opera's Berlin premiere. More like a tone poem than an interlude, its Wagnerian orchestral colors and rapturous lyricism place it among the most compelling of Delius's scores.

RECOMMENDED RECORDINGS

COMPLETE:

HARWOOD, TEAR, LUXON, SHIRLEY-QUIRK; DAVIES AND ROYAL PHILHARMONIC ORCHESTRA (EMI).

"THE WALK TO THE PARADISE GARDEN" (DELIUS, ORCHESTRAL WORKS, VOL. 2): BEECHAM AND ROYAL PHILHARMONIC ORCHESTRA (EMI).

Villa-Lobos, Heitor

(b. Rio de Janeiro, March 5, 1887; d. Rio de Janeiro, November 17, 1959)

BRAZILIAN COMPOSER. The most important figure in Brazilian musical life of the 20th century, he is one of the few Latin American composers to have captivated European and North American audiences. His interest in music was encouraged by his father, an amateur musician, who taught him to play the cello. He subsequently taught himself to play guitar, and from the age of 12 was active as guitarist in the *chorões*—roving street bands—of Rio. He had little formal education; he left home, and school, at the age of 16 and supported himself by playing cello at the Odeon (Rio's leading theater) and in various hotels. Between

Brazil's Heitor Villa-Lobos loved a good cigar.

1905 and 1913, when he married, he made several trips into the Brazilian interior and along the Amazon. By 1917 he had amassed an impressive portfolio of works in various genres, including string quartets, symphonies, and pieces for piano.

In spite of rough treatment from Brazil's conservative critics, who pounced on some of the early performances of his music, Villa-Lobos gradually began to acquire a following. One of his most important early champions was the pianist Arthur Rubinstein, whom he met in 1918 and to whom he dedicated his *Rudepoema* (1927), a substantial work for piano conceived as a portrait of its honoree. He developed another valuable friendship with the young French composer Darius Milhaud, who lived in Rio during 1917–18. Villa-Lobos spent the years 1923 through 1930 mainly in Paris, where he was acknowledged by leading figures of the avant-garde (including Stravinsky, Varèse, and Prokofiev) and his music embraced by performers such as Rubinstein and Segovia. In the process he became a celebrity, and in 1930 returned to Brazil as a prophet no longer without honor in his own country. He immediately got to work on the creation of a national music curriculum, receiving support from Brazil's newly installed dictatorship. In 1942 he founded a national conservatory of choral singing, and in 1945 he established the Brazilian Academy of Music, over which he presided until his death. In later years he devoted much of his time to conducting and made several visits to the United States and France.

Villa-Lobos was essentially self-taught as a composer, his aesthetics and approach shaped more by intuition and observation than by training. Like Haydn, he started out as a street musician (he might have been a rock musician in today's world), and his works retained an idiomatic naturalness and emotional directness. Included in his prodigious output—some of it wonderful, some of it not very good—were operas, ballets, film scores, 12 numbered symphonies, 17 string quartets, numerous concertos, suites, fantasias, and symphonic poems, dozens of chamber works, and more than 100 songs. Almost all of it was inspired to some degree by Brazilian popular music, and by Villa-Lobos's love of the great masters, especially Bach. This joint provenance was expressly acknowledged in the titling of the composer's best-known compositions, the *Bachianas brasileiras*—nine pieces composed between 1930 and 1945 for varied vocal and instrumental complements, in which formal schemes and textures characteristic of Baroque compositions, specifically Bach's, are fused with melodic and rhythmic elements drawn from urban and indigenous Brazilian music. The most famous of these pieces, No. 2, is subtitled *O trenzinho do Caipira* (*The Little Train of the Caipira* ◉) and depicts in its toccata-like final movement the chugging of a locomotive used in the state of São Paulo. Nearly as well known is No. 5, a vocalise for eight cellos and soprano. Villa-Lobos also penned an extensive series of *Chôros*, pieces in the character of (and paying tribute to) the freewheeling music of the street bands the composer knew and loved from his salad days. Not surprisingly, some of his best music was written for the instrument of his youth, the guitar, in particular the *Suite popular brasileira* (1908–12), the 12 *Etudes* (1929), and a set of five *Preludes* (1940). ◉ A good deal of the music he composed after 1945—including a number of concertos done on commission—is concerned with instrumental virtuosity.

There are times when one can't help thinking that much of what Villa-Lobos wrote sounds like bad movie music (e.g., the Prelude from *Bachianas brasileiras* No. 2). But then those Brazilian rhythms kick in, the melody soars, the little train comes whistling along, and one realizes that at its best, the music of Villa-Lobos is melodically inspired, intriguingly melancholy, and, in its decidedly unique way, hip, stylish, elegant, even sexy.

RECOMMENDED RECORDINGS

BACHIANAS BRASILEIRAS NOS. 1, 2, 5, AND 9: LOS ANGELES; VILLA-LOBOS AND FRENCH NATIONAL RADIO ORCHESTRA (EMI).

GUITAR CONCERTO, PRELUDES, ETUDES: BREAM; PREVIN AND LONDON SYMPHONY ORCHESTRA (RCA).

GUITAR MUSIC (INCLUDING PRELUDES, ETUDES): KRAFT (NAXOS).

PIANO MUSIC (*A PROLE DO BEBÊ, AS TRÊS MARIAS,* AND *RUDEPOÊMA*): HAMELIN (HYPERION).

PIANO MUSIC (SELECTIONS FROM *A PROLE DO BEBÊ*): RUBINSTEIN (RCA).

Viñes, Ricardo

(b. Lérida, February 5, 1875; d. Barcelona, April, 29, 1943)

CATALONIAN PIANIST. He received lessons in Barcelona prior to enrolling at the Paris Conservatoire, where, from 1887, he studied piano, chamber music, and harmony, receiving a first prize in piano in 1894. He made his professional debut in 1895 at the Salle Pleyel in Paris and toured Russia in 1900. A brilliant virtuoso with exceptional technique, he became best known for his

Ricardo Viñes at the piano; Ravel leaning on the piano; Roussel, bearded, standing; Debussy, bearded, sitting

advocacy of the music of Maurice Ravel—whom he met and befriended when they were both 13 years old—and Claude Debussy. His were the hands, and feet (he was a master in the use of the pedals), that shaped a golden age of French piano music at the beginning of the 20th century; among the works he premiered, between 1902 and 1913, were Debussy's *Pour le Piano, Estampes, Images* Books I and II, and *L'isle joyeuse* (in addition to six of the composer's *Préludes*), and Ravel's *Pavane pour une infante defunte, Jeux d'eau, Miroirs,* and *Gaspard de la nuit.* In many ways, Viñes acted as these composers' muse—and not only through his playing: For example, he introduced Ravel to the writings of Aloysius Bertrand on which *Gaspard* is based. Viñes also championed the music of Enrique Granados and Manuel de Falla, as well as that of Francis Poulenc, who was his piano student. Works dedicated to him include Falla's *Noches en los jardines de España,* Debussy's *Poissons d'or,* and Ravel's *Oiseaux tristes.*

viol *See* VIOLA DA GAMBA.

viola Contralto member of the violin family. The materials used in its construction are essentially identical to those used for the violin. Where the viola differs considerably from its sister instrument is in the ratio of its size to its tuning; its proportions are not quite optimal. The open strings of the viola, C–G–D–A, are pitched a fifth lower than those of the violin, and an octave above the open strings of the cello. In order to most closely match the tone of a violin in that range, a viola should be 25 inches long, which would make it impossible for musicians with arms of normal length to hold at the shoulder (indeed, Richard Wagner had twenty 19-inch instruments made for Bayreuth, and they could barely be played). By necessity, violas are built smaller than they ought to be, but because slight variations in size can produce big variations in tone, and because matters of tone are subjective, a "standard" length has never been defined. Though violins seldom depart much from their 14-inch body length, conventional violas range from 15 inches to more than 17 inches, and sometimes—in the case of some notably large and mellow-sounding instruments built by members of the AMATI family—approach 18 inches. Some of the earliest and best violas were made by Gasparo da Salò (1540–1609) and his pupil Giovanni Paolo Maggini (1580–1631), both active in Brescia. The instruments of the Cremonese makers Girolamo and Antonio Amati, and of Girolamo's son Nicolò, dating from the late 16th and early 17th centuries, are also particularly prized. Only about a dozen violas by Antonio STRADIVARI survive.

The viola is played like a violin, but it has its own distinctive voice: dusky in the middle range, and plaintive, sometimes nasal, in the upper. Many relate to this timbre less readily and less eagerly than to that of the violin or the cello, but it can be highly expressive in the right hands. Good players, even when playing in the upper part of the instrument's range, are capable of producing a richness of tone that is truly vocal.

Bach gave the lead parts in his *Brandenburg* Concerto No. 6 to two violas, but the solo repertoire for viola really begins with Mozart. His *Sinfonia concertante,* K. 364, for violin and viola, contains ravishing solos for the viola and marvelous duets. His two Duos for violin and viola, K. 423 and 424, and his six quintets with added viola place virtuosic demands on the instrument, as do the Divertimento, K. 563, for string trio, and the *Kegelstaat* Trio, K. 498, for clarinet, viola, and piano. Beethoven's string quartets have viola parts that are nearly as demanding as those for the first violin. After Mozart and Beethoven, nobody underestimated the viola.

Among the important concert works of the 19th century are Berlioz's *Harold en Italie,* a symphony with an obbligato viola part (written for Paganini), Schumann's *Märchenbilder* ("tales" for viola and piano), and Brahms's late sonatas, Op. 120 for viola (or clarinet) and piano. Outstanding works of the 20th century include Ralph Vaughan Williams's *Flos Campi* (1925; written for Lionel Tertis), William Walton's Viola Concerto (1929; written for Tertis but premiered by Paul Hindemith, history's finest violist-composer), and a pair of works Hindemith wrote for himself: a viola concerto titled *Der Schwanendreher* (1935), and *Trauermusik* (1936). Within the orchestral repertoire solos on the viola are abundant, and are often used to evoke melancholy, e.g., the solo at the beginning of the third movement of Zoltán Kodály's *Háry János* Suite ("Song"), the solo in Albert Roussel's *Bacchus et Ariane,* and the languorous solo in the middle movement of Walton's *Partita.* Richard Strauss used a solo viola to more humorous effect to portray Sancho Panza in his *Don Quixote.* The viola section frequently gets a workout in orchestral scores. Two notable examples: the *divisi* accompanimental passage that opens Mozart's Symphony in G minor, K. 550, and the taxing sectional passages in Wagner's *Tannhäuser* Overture, which repeatedly take the violas into nosebleed territory. The symphonies of Brahms and Mahler and the symphonic poems of Strauss are full of meaty parts for the viola section; the latter's operas also make wonderful use of the violas.

In the pantheon of great violists, pride of place goes to William Primrose, because without him there would not be a modern standard of playing: That he was on the level of Jascha Heifetz is demonstrated in their recordings of the Handel-Halvorsen duo and the Mozart duos, and of trios with Emanuel Feuermann and Gregor Piatigorsky. Hindemith was a star, but played less and composed more as time went by. Lillian Fuchs was important as a teacher, soloist, and chamber musician. Masters of the second half of the 20th century included Milton Katims, Joseph de Pasquale (a Primrose student), and Walter Trampler, who played not only the traditional chamber repertoire but also a good deal of contemporary music. Among the best players of recent years have been Michael Tree, Samuel Rhodes, Kim Kashkashian, Robert Vernon, Scott Nickrenz, Cynthia Phelps, and Geraldine Walther. Paul Neubauer, early in his career the principal violist of the New York Philharmonic, has emerged as a wonderful solo player, with a real connection to salon music and to the turn-of-the-century style popularized by Fritz Kreisler. Although there has not been anybody like Primrose since Primrose, Yuri Bashmet earned considerable acclaim as a soloist in the closing years of the 20th century. But by common consent, among violists at least, the finest violist alive today is Pinchas Zuckerman, who possesses, in the words of one distinguished colleague, "an incredible gift."

viola da gamba Family of fretted string instruments encompassing bass, tenor, and treble ranges that appeared in Europe toward the end of the 15th century and enjoyed immense popularity in solo and ensemble performance during the 17th century. Called the viol by the English, and known in Italy as the viola da gamba because it was usually held between the knees (*gamba* is the Italian word for "leg"), the instrument had a flat back and sloping shoulders, was bowed with an underhand grip, and was usually strung with six strings, though examples with five or seven strings were not uncommon. The gamba literature is large. One of the most important contributions to it was made by the French composer Marin Marais (1656–1728), who between 1686 and 1725 published five books of music for the viola da gamba, containing 596 pieces. Music for "a chest of viols" was particularly popular in England during the 17th century; of the many pieces fashioned for these consorts, far and away the greatest are the nine four-part fantasias created by Henry Purcell in the summer of 1680. ◉ As the viol consort was by then becoming an archaic formation, Purcell may well have written these magnificent works not for actual performance, but as exercises in counterpoint.

viola d'amore String instrument similar in size to a viola but more closely related to a VIOLA DA GAMBA, with a flat back and sloping shoulders. It is fitted with a main set of seven strings that are bowed and fingered in the conventional manner and a second set of seven sympathetic strings that run through the bridge and under the fingerboard to a separate set of pegs on the pegbox. When the instrument is played, these strings vibrate in sympathy with the strings above them. The scroll of a viola d'amore is often adorned with a carved figure of the blindfolded Cupid, a reminder that "love [*amore*] is blind." The instrument produces a gentle, plangent sound with an ethereal halo.

The viola d'amore was used widely as a solo and obbligato instrument in the 17th and 18th centuries. Telemann, Bach, and Vivaldi, among others, featured it as a solo instrument in multiple works. Because of its softness it has seen limited use in the

A scene from the film* Tous les matins du monde, *showing violas da gamba

modern era. Still, it was employed to great effect by Meyerbeer in *Les Huguenots* (1836) and later by Puccini in *Madama Butterfly* (1904) and Pfitzner in *Palestrina* (1917). Janáček used one in several late works as an allusion to Kamila Stösslová, his platonic love interest from 1917 on, including *Kát'a Kabanová* (1921), *The Makropulos Case* (1926), and the original version of his String Quartet No. 2 (*Intimate Letters*; 1928). Hindemith and Frank Martin both fashioned sonatas for the viola d'amore.

violin String instrument developed in Italy during the 16th century, the soprano member of the family that includes the viola as its alto (or, more properly, its contralto) and the cello as its bass. The elegantly rounded body of the violin consists of a front panel (the belly) made of pine or spruce, a back panel usually made of maple, and a casing (the ribs) to which the slightly convex belly and back are fitted. A neck of solid maple, terminating in a pegbox and carved scroll, is joined to the top of the body; a fingerboard, usually made of ebony and unfretted, is attached to the neck and extends out over the belly toward the bridge, which is made of maple and affixed to the belly near its midpoint. Below the bridge is the tailpiece, which holds the strings in place and is attached by means of windings to the bottom of the instrument. The shoulders are rounded and join the neck at what is essentially a perpendicular angle. Inside the body of the instrument, the belly is reinforced by a strip of spruce called the bass-bar; a wooden soundpost, also made of spruce, helps to support the bridge and to enhance its ability to transmit vibrations from the strings to the belly of the instrument. Characteristic sound holes, called F-HOLES, are cut into the belly to improve the violin's resonance and allow sound to radiate from the interior of the instrument. The violin has four strings that are anchored at the tailpiece, run across the bridge and over the fingerboard to the nut, and terminate at the pegs, which are used to tension them. The strings, tuned in fifths to the pitches G–D–A–E, are made of metal or gut: the G string usually has a gut core wound with silver or copper wire; the D may be of gut or have a gut core wound with aluminum wire; the A can be of metal or gut; and the E is usually made of steel. The violin is held between the chin and left shoulder (a chin rest and shoulder support are often attached), and played with a bow. It has a four-octave range, from the open G to a high G or G-sharp playable, if one has the nerve, on the E string.

Instruments recognizable as violins first appeared in northern Italy around 1505–10, and quickly became fashionable. Consorts of four "violins" of graduated sizes (usually consisting of a violin, two violas of different sizes, and a bass violin) were common by the middle of the 16th century, and were used to provide dance music at courts on both sides of the Alps. With the arrival of the 17th century the violin assumed new importance, both as a solo instrument and as the workhorse of an emerging ensemble that combined a large number of strings with other types of instruments: the orchestra. The manufacture of the finest 17th- and 18th-century violins was centered in the Italian towns of Brescia, with the workshops of Gasparo da Salò (1540–1609) and Giovanni Paolo Maggini (1580–1631), and Cremona, which gave rise to the three figures regarded as the most talented builders in the instrument's history—Nicolò AMATI,

Antonio STRADIVARI, and Giuseppe GUARNERI ("del Gesù"). Other makers of importance during this era were the Tyrolean master Jacob Stainer (1617–83), and Matteo Goffriller (1659–1742) and Domenico Montagnana (1686–1750, best known for his cellos), both of whom worked in Venice. Among 19th-century makers, perhaps the most famous, and certainly one of the finest craftsmen, was Jean-Baptiste Vuillaume (1798–1875), who was based in Paris from 1818; many of his best instruments were copies of older Italian models. The art of violin bowmaking was brought to its height during the 19th century by a pair of Frenchmen, Francois Xavier Tourte (1747–1835) and Dominique Peccatte (1810–74).

As the most prominent string instrument in Western culture, the violin has carried the essential message of classical music for 400 years. Its sound is vibrant and extraordinarily rich in overtones, and on a good instrument a good player can produce a tone that is radiant, full of life, and wondrously expressive, in every respect as nuanced and communicative as the human voice. Indeed, what the violin does best is sing. When it is played forcefully its tone can be gruff, ardent, or steely; when it is played softly its voice can become delicate and ethereal. The E string has exceptional carrying power and imparts a ringing brilliance to high-flying melodies and passagework. While the A and D strings are less powerful, the G string is remarkably sonorous. A passage played on it can sound meaty and warm (e.g., the celebrated melody beginning at measure 61 in the final movement of Brahms's Symphony No. 1). HARMONICS are easily produced and of good quality, and the pizzicato can be highly effective, if somewhat dry. Regardless of the dynamic, register, or method of production, the sound of the violin is always characterized by great immediacy, thanks to the instrument's nearly perfect acoustical properties.

The sound of massed violins—a sound unique in its presence and tone color—is the foundation on which virtually the whole of the concert and operatic repertoire is based, from the works of Lully and Corelli up to the present day. In the 18th century, half the instruments in the orchestra were violins; while the proportions changed somewhat during the 19th and 20th centuries with the addition of wind, brass and percussion instruments, violins still make up nearly a third of the complement of a modern orchestra. The symphonic literature contains so many glorious, idiomatic passages for the violin section that it would be foolish even to begin to list them; to appreciate the violins' irreplaceable role in the expressive scheme of things, all one needs to do is imagine the Andante theme from the opening movement of Tchaikovsky's *Pathétique* Symphony (first announced at measure 89) in any of its three appearances *without* the violins taking the lead. Imagine the principal subject of the second movement of Mozart's *Jupiter* Symphony, an Andante *cantabile,* played by any section other than muted violins, or the F-major "Alma" theme in the first movement of Mahler's Symphony No. 6 (beginning at measure 76), sounded other than by first and second violins, *fortissimo,* in rhapsodic unison. The stereotypes are correct: When composers wear their hearts on their sleeves, a violin is playing.

The violin has the deepest, most engaging solo repertoire of any orchestral instrument, testimony to its versatility and innate expressiveness. The highlights of that repertoire are major solo concertos by Vivaldi, Bach, Mozart, Beethoven, Mendelssohn, Bruch, Tchaikovsky, Brahms, Sibelius, Bartók, Berg, Prokofiev, Korngold, Shostakovich, and Barber, all of them technically challenging and emotionally probing.

Other works of importance, if somewhat less frequently encountered, are the concertos of Paganini, Wieniawski, Vieuxtemps, Dvořák, Glazunov, Schoenberg, Stravinsky, Walton, and Dutilleux; the repertoire also boasts a sunny array of concerto-like works that includes Lalo's *Symphonie espagnole* ◉, Saint-Saëns's *Introduction and Rondo capriccioso* and *Havanaise,* and the Chausson *Poème*; beautiful mood pieces such as Vaughan Williams's *The Lark Ascending*; and symphonic works with major parts for solo violin such as Rimsky-Korsakov's *Capriccio espagnol* and *Sheherazade,* and Richard Strauss's *Ein Heldenleben.* The violin's recital repertoire is dominated by the solo sonatas and partitas of Bach, the sonatas for violin and piano of Mozart, Beethoven, Brahms, Franck, Debussy, and Prokofiev, and such ravishing showpieces as Ravel's *Tzigane,* Paganini's Caprices, Ysaÿe's solo sonatas, and Szymanowski's *Mity* (*Myths*). The chamber music literature—trios, quartets, quintets, sextets etc.—is one vast playground for the violin.

Among the violin's great masters have been a number of composer-performers, including Arcangelo Corelli, Francesco Geminiani, Giuseppe Tartini, Giovanni Battista Viotti (1755–1824), Nicolò Paganini, Joseph Joachim, Henry Vieuxtemps, Henryk Wieniawski, Pablo de Sarasate, Eugene Ysaÿe, and Fritz Kreisler; great teachers such as Leopold Auer and Carl Flesch (1873–1944); and straight-out virtuosos like Mischa Elman, Joseph Szigeti (1892–1973), Efrem Zimbalist, Jascha Heifetz, Nathan Milstein, David Oistrakh, Henryk Szeryng, and Isaac Stern. Among the many luminaries on the scene today are Itzhak Perlman, Anne-Sophie Mutter, Joshua Bell, Gidon Kremer, Midori, Maxim Vengerov, Pinchas Zukerman, Gil Shaham, and Hilary Hahn.

violoncello *See* CELLO.

violone (It., "big viol") As used during the 16th century, a generic term for a VIOLA DA GAMBA of any size; by the beginning of the 17th century, at least in Italy, it had come to signify a large bass viola da gamba with six strings, the forerunner of the modern DOUBLE BASS.

A Young Lady Seated at a Virginal, ***painting by Jan Vermeer, ca. 1670***

virginal A single-manual HARPSICHORD enclosed in a boxlike case of rectangular or polygonal shape, with a single set of strings running perpendicular to the keys. Popular from the early 16th to the mid-17th century, especially among Flemish makers, the instruments came to be known as virginals because they were customarily used by women for domestic music making (and are so pictured by many a Netherlandish painter). The cases were often ornately decorated, with landscapes occasionally painted on the inside of the lid.

virtuoso (It., "virtuous") A musician with an extraordinarily well developed technique; an adjective used to describe passages or pieces that are particularly challenging from a technical standpoint, or playing that successfully meets such challenges.

Vishnevskaya, Galina

(b. Leningrad, October 25, 1926)

RUSSIAN SOPRANO. Her extraordinary interpretive abilities, no less than her natural musicality and the remarkable quality of her voice, made her the leading Russian soprano of her generation. Twice married as a teenager during World War II, she joined the Bolshoi Theatre in 1952 and quickly rose to stardom there. In 1955 she wedded for the third time, marrying the cellist Mstislav Rostropovich after a whirlwind four-day courtship in Prague—she without having heard him play, he without having heard her sing. Her schedule, when the government allowed, included dates in the major musical capitals of the West. She made her Metropolitan Opera debut as Aida, in 1961, her Covent Garden debut, also as Aida, in 1962, and her La Scala debut, as Liù in Puccini's *Turandot* (opposite Birgit Nilsson), in 1964. Her portrayals of Tatyana in Tchaikovsky's *Eugene Onegin* and Katarina in Shostakovich's *Lady Macbeth of Mtsensk District* were and are likely to remain unsurpassed, and she performed several Verdi and Puccini roles with great distinction as well, including Violetta in *La traviata,* Cio-Cio-San in *Madama Butterfly,* and Tosca. The solo soprano part in Britten's *War Requiem* was written for her (the Soviet authorities refused to let her sing at the work's premiere, but did allow her to take part in the recording under the composer's direction a few months later), as were some of Britten's songs. Shostakovich also had her uniquely expressive voice in mind when he fashioned the soprano solos of his Symphony No. 14, Op. 135. She sang at the symphony's premiere, on September 29, 1969, in Leningrad, and recorded the work under her husband's baton in 1973.

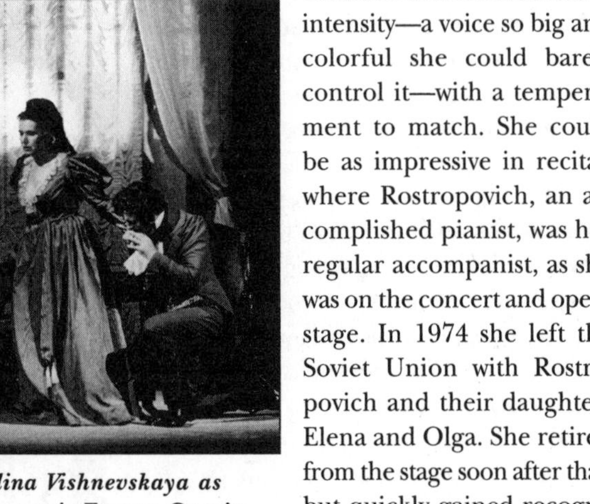

Galina Vishnevskaya as Tatyana in **Eugene Onegin**

Vishnevskaya possessed a voice of remarkable size, with a distinctive richness of timbre and communicative intensity—a voice so big and colorful she could barely control it—with a temperament to match. She could be as impressive in recital, where Rostropovich, an accomplished pianist, was her regular accompanist, as she was on the concert and opera stage. In 1974 she left the Soviet Union with Rostropovich and their daughters Elena and Olga. She retired from the stage soon after that, but quickly gained recognition as an author. Her autobiography, *Galina* (1984), is among the most compelling books written by any musician of modern times.

RECOMMENDED RECORDINGS

MUSSORGSKY, *BORIS GODUNOV*: GHIAUROV, SPIESS, MASLENNIKOV, TALVELA; KARAJAN AND VIENNA PHILHARMONIC (DECCA).

SHOSTAKOVICH, *LADY MACBETH OF MTSENSK DISTRICT*: GEDDA, TEAR, PETKOV; ROSTROPOVICH AND LONDON PHILHARMONIC ORCHESTRA (EMI).

TCHAIKOVSKY, *THE QUEEN OF SPADES*: DOBROWKSA, GOUGALOFF, RESNICK, WEIKL; ROSTROPOVICH AND L'ORCHESTRE NATIONAL DE FRANCE (DG).

COLLECTION:

MUSIC OF SHOSTAKOVICH AND MUSSORGSKY: PETKOV; ROSTROPOVICH AND LONDON PHILHARMONIC ORCHESTRA (EMI).

SONGS AND ARIAS BY MUSSORGSKY, RIMSKY-KORSAKOV, TCHAIKOVSKY: ROSTROPOVICH AND LONDON PHILHARMONIC (EMI).

Vitry, Philippe de

(b. Vitry, October 31, 1291; d. Meaux, June 9, 1361)

FRENCH COMPOSER AND THEORIST; after Machaut the most important figure of the ARS NOVA. He was a canon in several churches and cathedrals (toward the end of his life he was elevated to the post of Bishop of Meaux), a protégé of the Bourbons and counselor to the French royal court, and one of the most respected intellectuals of the 14th century. Already by about 1320 he was recognized as the leading representative of the new, rhythmically more complicated musical style examined in the treatise *Ars nova* (long thought to have been written by him, but probably a compilation of material from several sources). Only about a dozen works securely attributable to Vitry survive; all are motets. Several, including *Heu Fortuna, Quoniam secta,* and *In nova fert* found their way into the *Roman de Fauvel,* the most important single source of early-14th-century polyphony, which Vitry may have had a hand in compiling. Part moral fable and biting political satire—taking aim at the corruption of French governance—part chronicle, part musical entertainment, the *Roman de Fauvel* (ca. 1317) resembles an editorial cartoon come to life, with words, pictures, and music all on the same page, amplifying and enriching each other's meanings. Its central figure, Fauvel, is a horse who walks around like a man. Symbol of all that is vain and venal in the ruling elite, he rises from the stable to become one of the high and mighty, in the process despoiling the "fair garden of France." The phrase "to curry favor" is a corruption of "to curry Fauvel."

Vitry's most significant contribution to the art of music was his pioneering use of isorhythm, which remained an important device for large-scale polyphonic composition throughout the 14th and into the 15th century.

vivace Literally (in Italian) "lively," it generally indicates a faster tempo than ALLEGRO; also used as a modifier, as in *Allegro vivace.*

Vivaldi, Antonio

(b. Venice, March 4, 1678; d. Vienna, July 28, 1741)

ITALIAN COMPOSER, the most original and influential of his generation. He traveled widely, was eminently successful at getting his works published, and produced new offerings with astonishing fecundity; as a result, his music became known and emulated throughout Europe. His best-known work, four concertos for violin and strings known collectively as *THE FOUR SEASONS (LE Quattro Stagione)*, is among the earliest pieces of program music to have held on to a place in the repertoire.

Both of Vivaldi's grandfathers were tailors. His father, a professional violinist, joined the musical staff at the basilica of San Marco in Venice in 1685, remaining there for nearly 50 years. Antonio, the eldest of nine children, learned music from

Antonio Vivaldi, never far from his inkwell

The interior of the Basilica of San Marco in Venice

his father and trained for the priesthood; he was ordained in 1703, but ceased performing pastoral duties late in 1706. Also in 1703 he got his first full-time job as a musician, as *maestro di violino* at the Pio Ospedale della Pietà, one of four church-sponsored orphanages in Venice specializing in the musical training of girls. He gave instruction on violin as well as on the *viola all'inglese,* an instrument related to the VIOLA D'AMORE; in 1716 he was named *maestro dei concerti,* but soon after that he gave up regular teaching in order to spend more time abroad, though he continued to supply the Pietà with concertos on a regular basis until 1729.

During the early 1720s, he spent substantial amounts of time in Mantua and Rome, overseeing performances of operas he had written. By the end of the decade he was again on the road; he appears to have taken leave of Venice for lengthy stays in Vienna and Prague in the early 1730s, again related mainly to the production of newly written operas. The Venetian public began to lose interest in him by the late 1730s, and in 1740 he set off for Vienna once again, where he died in straitened circumstances.

Contemporary caricature of Vivaldi

Vivaldi composed voluminously in many genres: He wrote more than 50 operas, several dozen sacred works, four oratorios (of which the best known is *Juditha triumphans,* written for the girls of the Pietà in 1716), and more than 40 secular cantatas. He turned out solo sonatas and trio sonatas by the bushel and, most important, composed more than 500 concertos for solo and multiple instruments in all kinds of configurations. Of his operas a handful have been revived in modern times, and his buoyant setting of the *Gloria,* RV 589 (1708), is still immensely popular. But it is the concertos that had the greatest impact on Vivaldi's contemporaries and have kept his name alive for more than 250 years. Roughly 320 of them were written for a single solo instrument, the rest for various groupings of solo instruments. This emphasis on displaying the virtuosity of a single soloist was one of the most influential aspects of Vivaldi's work. Also important was the three-movement structure he favored, which became the norm. The techniques he used to keep these works interesting and lively—deftly varying texture and figuration, writing more "purposefully" for the RIPIENO, and favoring angular, energetic rhythms that packed considerable punch—were adopted by composers all over the continent. Even so, something in the sound of Vivaldi's music remained unique and impossible to imitate.

Vivaldi was among the most widely published composers of the first half of the 18th century. The collections of his Opp. 3 through 12—comprising 80 concertos for various groupings (Op. 8 includes *The Four Seasons* ◉)—were brought out between 1711 and 1729. Around 1730, when he was in his early 50s, Vivaldi decided not to publish any more concertos. It was more profitable for him to sell the actual manuscripts, which brought him a guinea per concerto. Instead of producing sets of concertos for the mass market, he began writing individual pieces for wealthy patrons, who purchased the works outright for their private delectation. The composer, amply rewarded for his labor, was content for these one-of-a-kind creations to disappear into the private collections of the rich and famous.

Unfortunately, these works were quickly lost to the world, since in many cases they were represented by only a single manuscript stashed in a library somewhere. The loss is particularly unfortunate because the pieces embodied the composer's most advanced thinking: They were individualistic and unconventional (if judged by the conventions Vivaldi himself helped to establish), emotionally probing, sophisticated, and surprising. In the final decade of his life, Vivaldi's style became a good deal more dramatic and provocative. Because he was mostly concerned with opera, his concertos tended to present material in a more theatrical manner than his earlier works had, and to exhibit an almost vocal fluency in the solo part. There is an increased interest in embellishment, beauty of line, and expressive freedom, which supersedes the concern for formal balance, symmetry, and correctness of manner that characterized the earlier concertos.

What set Vivaldi's concertos (whether early or late) apart from those of his contemporaries was the way they combined earthy vitality with virtuosic abandon and a seemingly inexhaustible supply of fantasy. These qualities, readily apparent to the more sophisticated among Vivaldi's patrons and peers, were undoubtedly what prompted J. S. Bach, the composer's junior by seven years, to study the works and make arrangements of several of them for his own use at the keyboard.

RECOMMENDED RECORDINGS

CONCERTOS FOR LUTE AND MANDOLIN:
PIANCA, GALFETTI; ANTONINI AND IL GIARDINO ARMONICO (TELDEC).

CONCERTOS FOR MANDOLIN AND OTHER INSTRUMENTS:
CONCERTOS FOR VIOLA D'AMORE: NENE CALABRESE; SCIMONE AND I SOLISTI VENETI (ERATO).

THE FOUR SEASONS: CARMIGNOLA; MARCON AND VENICE BAROQUE ORCHESTRA (SONY).

GLORIA, MAGNIFICAT, VIOLIN CONCERTOS: ALESSANDRINI AND CONCERTO ITALIANO (OPUS 111).

JUDITHA TRIUMPHANS: KOZENÁ, HERRMANN, TRULLO, CAMPARATO; DE MARCHI AND ACCADEMIA MONTRIS REGALIS (OPUS 111).

"Vocalise" **TITLE GIVEN BY SERGEY RACHMANINOV TO THE LAST OF HIS 14 SONGS FOR VOICE AND PIANO, OP. 34,** composed in 1912. Most of the songs in the collection are tailored to the abilities of, and bear dedications to, specific singers, among them the bass Fyodor Chaliapin and the tenor Leonid Sobinov. The wordless "Vocalise," in E minor, was written for Antonina Nezhdanova, a soprano celebrated for the beauty and instrumental purity of her voice; Rachmaninov subsequently made arrangements of it for soprano and orchestra, and for orchestra alone. Because of the music's lyric appeal, the piece has been arranged numerous times by other hands, for nearly every instrument that can play a melody.

With singing very likely being the oldest form of music making, it's not surprising that there are wonderful choirs and vocal ensembles of all kinds throughout the world. Nearly every European radio station and orchestra has an associated professional choir. In Britain, the tradition of university choirs of men and boys stretches far into the past, and the number of fine professional vocal groups is astounding. The United States, too, has an abundance of excellent college and professional choirs and chamber choruses.

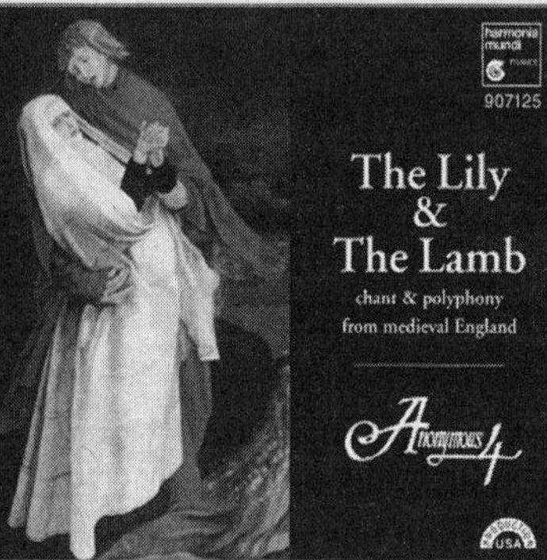

In recent decades the rapid growth of interest in early music has given rise to a number of vocal groups that specialize in that repertoire. Groups devoted to a cappella singing have become a strong force in the classical world as a wealth of vocal works from the Middle Ages and Renaissance have been dusted off and put back into currency. These works have in turn inspired a number of contemporary composers to turn their hand to the choral texture, adding even more riches to the repertoire.

Anonymous 4

New York–based female quartet founded in 1986 to specialize in medieval chant and polyphony. Named after a 13th-century treatise from the school of Notre Dame in Paris, the group is renowned for its haunting vocal blend, virtuoso ensemble singing, and elegantly crafted programs. With the immediate success of its 1992 debut release, *An English Ladymass,* the ensemble began a series of award-winning recordings, including its highly regarded 1997 release, *11,000 Virgins,* music of Hildegard von Bingen. The original members—sopranos Ruth Cunningham, Johanna Maria Rose, Marsha Genensky, and alto Susan Hellauer—performed together until 1998, when Irish-born Jacqueline Horner succeeded Cunningham. In recent years the group has commissioned works by Sir Peter Maxwell Davies, Steve Reich, and Sir John Tavener, and has collaborated with the Chilingirian String Quartet and early harp specialist Andrew Lawrence-King. A foray into gospel songs and the American shape-note tradition resulted in the chart-topping 2004 release *American Angels,* and in 2005 the group released a second Hildegard recording, *The Origins of Fire.*

RECOMMENDED RECORDING
***The Lily & The Lamb*: Chant and polyphony from medieval England (harmonia mundi).**

Chanticleer

12-voice male chamber chorus based in San Francisco, founded in 1978 by Louis Botto, who served as artistic director until his death in 1997. The ensemble's first focus was medieval and Renaissance repertoire; largely due to the inventive arrangements of music director Joseph Jennings, its repertoire expanded to include gospel, jazz, and popular music. With its suave homogeneous sound, the group has gained worldwide popularity, collaborating with Dawn Upshaw, Frederica von Stade, jazz pianist George Shearing, the San Francisco Symphony, New York Philharmonic, and St. Paul Chamber Orchestra; it has made more than 25 recordings. The ensemble has commissioned works by Jake Heggie, Sir John Tavener, John Musto, Tania Léon, Augusta Read Thomas, and Chen Yi, who was its composer-in-residence from 1993 to 1996. In 1994 Chanticleer presented a highly successful staged production of Britten's *Curlew River,* and in 2002 it premiered Tavener's full-length dramatic work *Lamentations and Praises.* The subsequent recording received a Grammy award, as did the group's 1999 release, *Colors of Love.*

RECOMMENDED RECORDING
***Colors of Love*: Works by Stephen Stucky, Chen Yi, John Tavener, Bernard Rands, Augusta Read Thomas, Steve Sametz (Teldec)**

Choir of King's College, Cambridge

One of the most venerable choral institutions in the world, it owes its existence to King Henry VI, who in 1441 laid the cornerstone for the magnificent King's College Chapel in Cambridge. Although the chapel was not completed until 1515, in the reign of Henry VIII, the original plan—to constitute a special choir to sing the chapel services—was carried out and remains in force to this day. The present-day choir, made up of 16 boy choristers, 14 choral scholars, and two organ scholars, working under such eminent directors as Sir David Willcocks, Philip Ledger, and, since 1982, Stephen Cleobury, has performed worldwide and made more than 75 recordings of repertoire ranging from Renaissance masses and English anthems to major works of

Handel, Bach, Mozart, Brahms, Vaughan Williams, and Messiaen, and has collaborated with the Academy of St. Martin-in-the-Fields, the English Chamber Orchestra, and the Academy of Ancient Music. The chapel's Christmas Eve service of Nine Lessons and Carols, devised by Dean Eric Milner-White in 1918, has become an international tradition since annual broadcasts were instituted in the 1930s.

RECOMMENDED RECORDINGS

Best Loved Hymns: Works by Vaughan Williams, Howells, Luther, Handel, Parry, and others; Cleobury (EMI).

Bax and Finzi, Anthems; Cleobury (EMI).

Collegium Vocale Ghent

Chamber chorus founded in 1970 by the Belgian conductor Philippe Herreweghe with the aim of applying the principles of historical performance practice to vocal music. Its performances of J. S. Bach's cantatas and major sacred works have earned widespread acclaim for their warm color, clarity, and sensitivity to text. The chorus, which has focused mainly on German Baroque repertoire, has collaborated with the Vienna Philharmonic, Royal Concertgebouw Orchestra, and La Petite Bande, as well as with its own instrumental ensemble, formed in the late 1980s. In 1977, Herreweghe formed the Paris-based ensemble La Chapelle Royale in order to perform French Baroque repertoire as well as the music of Flemish Renaissance masters such as Josquin and Lassus. The two groups now frequently join forces and have also ventured into the Classical and Romantic arena with recordings of the Mozart and Fauré Requiems and of Beethoven's Symphony No. 9.

RECOMMENDED RECORDING

J. S. Bach, cantatas and masses (Classics).

The Hilliard Ensemble

English male ensemble formed in 1974 and named for the famous 16th-century miniaturist Nicholas Hilliard. For the past 30 years it has been regarded as a peerless exponent of both early and contemporary music. The group's original music director, baritone Paul Hillier, left in 1990 for a teaching career in the U.S.; present members are countertenor David James, tenors Rogers Covey-Crump and David Harrold, and baritone Gordon Jones. In addition to making numerous recordings of impeccably sung medieval and Renaissance repertoire, the ensemble has enjoyed a long association the contemporary Estonian composer Arvo Pärt, beginning with its 1988 recording of his *Passio* for ECM. The group has commissioned works by Gavin Bryars, James MacMillan, Heinz Holliger, and Baltic composers Veljo Tormis and Erkki-Sven Tuur, and has performed with the London Philharmonic, the BBC Symphony Orchestra, and the Philadelphia Orchestra. An unusual collaboration with the Norwegian jazz saxophonist Jan Garbarek resulted in the 1994 release *Officium,* which became a very successful crossover album, followed in 1997 by *Mnemosyne.* The 2001 release *Morimur,* fascinating if somewhat controversial, was an amalgamation of Bach's violin Partita in D minor with chorale verses, based on research by Professor Helga Thoene.

RECOMMENDED RECORDING

Lassus: Missa Pro Defunctis; Prophetiae Sybillarum (ECM).

The King's Singers

Started in 1968 by six choral scholars at King's College Cambridge, the group devoted itself to a wide repertoire from the outset, and quickly became known for its ability to present anything from medieval and Renaissance masterpieces to witty arrangements of popular and traditional music, all in a winningly relaxed and humorous performance style. The group, which has had 19 members over the years, has built its immense popularity with worldwide tours, more than 70 recordings, and collaborations with a slate of fellow artists that includes Dame Kiri Te Kanawa, Emanuel Ax, Barbara Hendricks, Evelyn Glennie, and Bruce Johnston of the Beach Boys. The ensemble has performed with the London Symphony Orchestra, Chicago Symphony Orchestra, and the Cincinnati Pops in a recording of Beatles songs, and has commissioned works by Ned Rorem, Peter Maxwell Davies, Krzysztof Penderecki, and others. Fervently committed to education, the group has been the Prince Consort Ensemble-in-Residence at the Royal College of Music since 1996.

RECOMMENDED RECORDING

King's Singers Christmas: Traditional carols, works by Praetorius, Rutter, Bach, Pärt, Warlock, others (Signum).

RIAS Kammerchor

Founded in 1948, the chamber chorus played an important role in reviving the musical life of postwar Berlin, partnering with the Berlin Radio Symphony Orchestra and Berlin Philharmonic. The ensemble has worked under many illustrious conductors, including Karl Böhm, Herbert von Karajan, Lorin Maazel, Claudio Abbado, Daniel Barenboim, and James Levine. During the tenure of music director Günther Arndt in the 1980s, the group secured a reputation as one of the finest chamber choruses in Europe; since 1987, under Marcus Creed's direction, it has become a major force both in a cappella repertoire and in collaborations with Europe's most prestigious period-instrument orchestras. The ensemble frequently works with the Akademie für Alte Musik Berlin under the direction of René Jacobs, with which it has made a series of critically acclaimed recordings. Other frequent guest conductors are Philippe Herreweghe, Nikolaus Harnoncourt, and Sir John Eliot Gardiner. In 2003, the Dutch-born Daniel Reuss became artistic director;he has broadened the ensemble's repertoire to include 20th- and 21st-century works.

RECOMMENDED RECORDINGS
BRAHMS, SACRED CHORAL MUSIC: MOTETS, OP. 29, 74, 110; MISSA CANONICA, OTHER WORKS; CREED (HARMONIA MUNDI).
POULENC, *FIGURE HUMAINE, SEPT CHANSONS, UN SOIR DE NEIGE,* OTHER WORKS; REUSS (HARMONIA MUNDI).

The Sixteen

Formed in 1977 by conductor Harry Christophers to specialize in both Renaissance and contemporary choral repertoire, the 16-voice ensemble has become renowned not only for its precision but for the intense brilliance and drama it brings to performances. In 1992 the group began a series of recordings of the mostly neglected and devilishly difficult repertoire from the 15th-century Eton Choirbook; the first of the series, *The Rose and the Ostrich Feather,* won a Grammy award; four award-winning volumes followed. The group's multivolume sets of choral music of Britten and Poulenc have been hailed as models of interpretation. With its period instrument orchestra, the Symphony of Harmony and Invention, the group performs large-scale works such as Handel's *Israel in Egypt* and *Messiah,* Bach's *St. Matthew* Passion, and Purcell's *King Arthur* and *The Fairy Queen.* The chorus also collaborates regularly with the BBC Symphony Orchestra in performances of 20th-century works.

RECOMMENDED RECORDING
BLEST CECILIA: BRITTEN CHORAL WORKS (*REJOICE IN THE LAMB, TE DEUM IN C, FESTIVAL TE DEUM,* AND OTHERS). (CORO).

The Tallis Scholars

Founded in 1973 by director Peter Phillips, its members were choral scholars culled from the chapel choirs of Oxford and Cambridge. The ensemble is widely regarded as the world's finest exponent of Renaissance sacred choral repertoire, its fame resting on a distinctive purity of tone that unfailingly illuminates the complex interweaving lines of early polyphony. Since 1981 the group has made over 40 critically acclaimed recordings on its own record label, Gimell; its 1987 recording of Josquin's *Missa pange lingua* and *Missa La sol fa re mi* won Gramophone's coveted Record of the Year. While doing honor to the music of well-known composers such as Tallis, Byrd, and Palestrina, the group has also recorded works of less celebrated figures such as Tye. In 1994 the Tallis Scholars were invited to sing at the Sistine Chapel in festivities marking the completion of the restoration of Michelangelo's *Last Judgment,* and to perform at the church of Santa

Maria Maggiore in Rome, where Palestrina was both a choirboy and *maestro di cappella,* in honor of the 400th anniversary of the composer's death.

RECOMMENDED RECORDING
THE ESSENTIAL TALLIS SCHOLARS: WORKS OF ALLEGRI, VICTORIA, JOSQUIN, LASSUS, TALLIS, SHEPPARD, AND OTHERS. (GIMELL).

Theatre of Voices

Ensemble founded in 1990 by Paul Hillier at the University of California, Davis. Now based in Bloomington, Indiana, where Hillier directs Indiana University's Early Music Institute, it is flexible in number and focuses on several areas, among them medieval and Renaissance repertoire, American shape note songs and psalmody, and contemporary music. The group tours throughout the United States and Europe and has collaborated in concerts with Steve Reich & Musicians. Its recordings include *The Age of Cathedrals* (music of Pérotin and the school of Notre Dame), Lassus's *St. Matthew Passion,* Josquin's *Missa de Beata Virgine,* and two volumes of "Carols from the Old & New Worlds." Among its recordings of contemporary repertoire, "De Profundis", which contains a number of world-premiere recordings of works by Arvo Pärt, and "Litany for the Whale," a collection of works by John Cage, have drawn high praise.

RECOMMENDED RECORDING
PÄRT, "DE PROFUNDIS": *MISSA SILLABICA, SOLFEGGIO, CANTATE DOMINO, SEVEN MAGNIFICAT ANTHEMS,* OTHER WORKS (HARMONIA MUNDI).

Voigt, Deborah

(b. Chicago, August 4, 1960)

AMERICAN SOPRANO. She grew up outside Chicago and in Los Angeles. After a short-lived stint as a choral conducting major in college, she studied at California State University at Fullerton and then joined the San Francisco Opera's Merola Program, making her opera debut with the San Francisco company as the Celestial Voice in Verdi's *Don Carlo* in 1986. In 1988, she won the Luciano Pavarotti Vocal Competition, and in 1990, the gold medal at Moscow's Tchaikovsky International Competition. Voigt's career took off after a spectacular performance as Ariadne with the Boston Lyric Opera in 1989; in 1992, she made her Metropolitan Opera debut as Chrysothemis in *Elektra,* conducted by James Levine, who became a regular collaborator. Voigt's large, gleaming, and lustrous soprano has made her a natural for the Strauss and Wagner roles that make up the bulk of her repertoire, and has opened to her the doors of many if not all of the world's leading opera houses. Her regular roles include the Empress in *Die Frau ohne Schatten,* Sieglinde in *Die Walküre,* and Elsa in *Lohengrin*; she sang her first staged Isolde at the Vienna Staatsoper in 2003, receiving a 23-minute ovation on opening night. Voigt has also sung the roles of Aida, of Amelia in Verdi's *Un ballo in maschera,* and of Cassandre in the Met's staging of Berlioz's *Les Troyens* in 2003. She has made several aria recordings, including one of Wagner love duets with Plácido Domingo (her frequent partner in the Met's *Walküre*); among the complete operas she has recorded are Strauss's *Ariadne auf Naxos* with Giuseppe Sinopoli and *Die ägyptische Helena* with Leon Botstein, and Wagner's *Tristan und Isolde* with Christian Thielemann and the orchestra of the Vienna Staatsoper. After years of struggle with her weight, Voigt underwent bariatric surgery in June 2004.

Deborah Voigt

RECOMMENDED RECORDINGS

STRAUSS, *ARIADNE AUF NAXOS*: DESSAY, OTTER, HEPPNER; SINOPOLI AND DRESDEN STAATSKAPELLE (DG).

WAGNER, *TRISTAN UND ISOLDE*: MOSER, HOLL, WEBER; THIELEMANN AND VIENNA STAATSOPER (DG).

COLLECTION:

DUETS FROM WAGNER OPERAS: DOMINGO; PAPPANO AND ROYAL OPERA (EMI).

Von Stade, Frederica

(b. Somerville, N.J., June 1, 1945)

AMERICAN MEZZO-SOPRANO. She attended schools in the suburbs of New York City and Washington, D.C., and made her professional debut at New Haven's Long Wharf Theatre. She subsequently studied with Sebastian Engelberg at the Mannes College of Music in New York. With encouragement from Harold Schonberg, then the music critic of *The New York Times,* she entered the 1969 Metropolitan Opera auditions; during the course of the auditions, before the results were known, Met manager Rudolf Bing signed her to a three-year contract with the house. She made her Metropolitan Opera debut, as the Third Boy in Mozart's *Die Zauberflöte,* on January 10, 1970. Over the next three years she sang 19 other roles at the Met, in works by Mozart, Rossini, Verdi, Wagner, Gounod, Bizet, Offenbach, Puccini, and Richard Strauss, among others—an astonishing accomplishment for a singer still in her 20s. In 1973 she made her debut at the Paris Opéra, as Cherubino in Mozart's *Le nozze di Figaro,* and in 1975 she bowed for the first time at Covent Garden, as Rosina in Rossini's *Il barbiere di Siviglia.* She sang in the American premiere of Monteverdi's *Il ritorno di Ulisse in patria* during the 1974–75 season with the Washington Opera, and in 1974, with the Houston Opera, she created the role of Nina in *The Seagull* by Thomas Pasatieri (b. 1945).

Frederica Von Stade as Rossini's Cenerentola

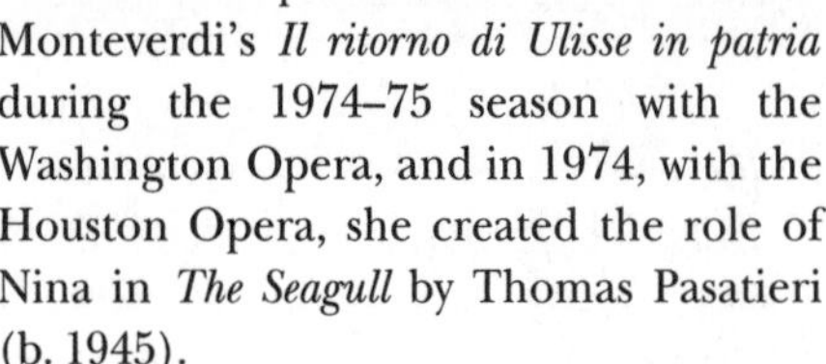

Von Stade's performance in the title role of Massenet's *Cendrillon* with the Washington Opera during its 1979–80 season elicited this comment from a local critic: "Her movement and expression are as subtle, as gracious and inviting, as a dream; her French is pure, perfect; her excursions into the upper register melting; and her lyrical reserves limitless. She is the kind of heroine Massenet must have wanted, able to bring to life what exists so abundantly in the music of *Cendrillon*—a tender beauty that merges with magic to become enchantment." Von Stade was a matchless Cherubino, the finest Mélisande of her generation, and a charming exponent of Rossini's Cenerentola. A superb recitalist, in recent years she has also enjoyed considerable success in a variety of crossover activities and has made memorable contributions to recordings of *Show Boat* by Jerome Kern (1885–1945) and Bernstein's *On the Town.*

RECOMMENDED RECORDINGS

Debussy, *Pelléas et Mélisande*: Stilwell, Van Dam, Raimondi; Karajan and Berlin Philharmonic (EMI).

Kern, *Show Boat*: Stratas, Hadley, Hubbard; McGlinn and London Sinfonietta (EMI).

Mozart, *Le nozze di Figaro*: Popp, Te Kanawa, Allen, Ramey, Moll; Solti and London Philharmonic Orchestra (Decca).

W

Wagner, Richard

(b. Leipzig, May 22, 1813; d. Venice, February 13, 1883)

GERMAN COMPOSER AND CONDUCTOR, author of the greatest German operas of the 19th century and of revolutionary advances in harmony, orchestration, musical dramaturgy, and aesthetics. Alone among the great figures in the history of opera, he never worked with a librettist, crafting the texts for all of his works himself. In addition to being one of the supreme geniuses in the history of opera he was, apart from Beethoven, the most influential composer of the 19th century. As an artist he was an unyielding perfectionist, governed by a visionary insight into character and emotions and by an unerring instinct for what could be achieved on stage and in sound. His early works carried forward the precepts of German Romanticism (owing much to Weber and Heinrich August Marschner [1810–53]), Italian bel canto (owing much to Bellini), and French grand opera (owing much to Auber and Meyerbeer), while boldly breaking new ground. His mature music dramas achieved an entirely novel synthesis of elements; in their scale, emotional intensity, and stunning disclosure of a glorious, hauntingly sensuous tonal language, they changed the course of history not only in music but in the other arts as well.

Richard Wagner with Cosima and Siegfried, ca. 1873

Precocious, intellectually gifted, and largely self-taught in composition, Wagner received his early schooling in Dresden and finished his education in Leipzig as a student at the Thomasschule (where he received training in harmony and counterpoint from Theodor Weinlig), and at the University of Leipzig. His father, Carl Friedrich Wagner, worked for the Leipzig police department and died when Richard was six months old; less than a year later Richard's mother married family friend Ludwig Geyer, an actor and painter based in Dresden, who died when Richard was eight. Though many have speculated that Geyer was the boy's actual father (citing the adult Wagner's physical resemblance to his stepfather and obvious artistic gift), there has never been any proof. What is certain is that Wagner had a love of literature, theater, and music, along with a powerful creative drive, from childhood. He spent his youth writing plays (corpse-ridden melodramas) and music (piano sonatas, songs, overtures, and a symphony). He was not yet 20 when he stepped into his first professional post, as chorusmaster and rehearsal conductor at a theater in Würzburg, and not quite 21 when he finished his first opera, *Die Feen* (*The Fairies*). He made his official debut as an opera conductor, with Mozart's *Don Giovanni,* in 1834; the following year, at the age of 22, he composed his second opera, *Das Liebesverbot* (*The Ban on Love*), a comedy based on Shakespeare's *Measure for Measure,* and began making notes for his autobiography.

In 1836, Wagner married the singer Minna Planer. During a brief stint as music director in Riga (1837–39), he began work on his third opera, RIENZI (a grand opera to end all grand operas based on Bulwer-Lytton's sprawling novel of medieval Rome), and conducted six of Beethoven's symphonies. His contract was not renewed, and in the summer of 1839 he and Minna slipped out of Riga to avoid creditors, enduring a difficult voyage across the Baltic and the North Sea to London before reaching Paris in September. There he finished the score to *Rienzi* and composed DER FLIEGENDE HOLLÄNDER (*The Flying Dutchman*), its overture a vivid depiction of a storm at sea much like the one he had braved on his crossing to London. Wagner returned to Germany in the spring of 1842 to prepare *Rienzi* for its premiere at the Dresden Court Opera. Its blazing success established his reputation in Germany and propelled his career to new heights. On January 2, 1843, he conducted the premiere of *Der fliegende Holländer* at the Dresden Opera; a month later he was appointed Kapellmeister of the royal Saxon court. In full stride as he turned 30, he moved quickly from one project to the next. In the spring of 1843 he began work on TANNHÄUSER, completing the score in 1845. He considered historical figures Frederick Barbarossa and Jesus of Nazareth as possible operatic subjects. These were both eventually dropped, but during the years 1845–48 work went forward on a new Romantic opera, LOHENGRIN.

Richard Wagner ca. 1870

The revolutionary unrest of 1848–49 deflected Wagner from his normally obsessive focus on composing; in the spring of 1849 he was actively associating with anarchists and revolutionaries, and there is evidence that he built improvised explosive devices. During the May 1849 uprising he climbed the tower of Dresden's Kreuzkirche to report on troop movements. After the insurrection failed, he had to flee Dresden to escape arrest, and for years a warrant for his arrest remained in force throughout Saxony. Wagner sought refuge in Switzerland (where he would live in exile, on and off, for more than two decades). He based himself in Zurich from the summer of 1849 until the summer of 1858. The year 1850 saw the premiere of *Lohengrin* in Weimar, under the baton of Franz Liszt, and the creation of Wagner's two best-known prose works: the anti-Semitic pamphlet *Das Judentum in der Musik* (*Jewishness in Music*) and the book-length *Oper und Drama* (*Opera and Drama*), laying out his artistic credo.

During his final months in Dresden, Wagner had begun drafting the prose outline for what would become the central work of his career, the four-opera cycle DER RING DES NIBELUNGEN (*The Ring of the Nibelung*). In Swiss exile he continued to work on the *Ring* text, bringing it to completion early in 1853. Without a position and with debts mounting, he found it expedient to cultivate patrons, the most important of whom was the retired businessman Otto Wesendonck, whom Wagner met in 1852. The composer quickly became infatuated with his benefactor's wife, Mathilde, a poet, and they began an affair that lasted six years. In 1857, Wagner set five of Mathilde's poems to music as his *WESENDONCK* LIEDER.

Meanwhile, Wagner forged ahead on the music for his *Ring* operas, completing *DAS RHEINGOLD* in 1854, *DIE WALKÜRE* in 1856, and finishing the first two acts of *SIEGFRIED* in 1857. But the affair with Mathilde Wesendonck had opened the composer's artistic eyes to the deepest realm of human passion, and in August of 1857 he reluctantly broke off work on *Siegfried*, leaving its hero asleep under a linden tree, and began to sketch the opera *TRISTAN UND ISOLDE*, based on the medieval romance by Gottfried von Strassburg. To tell the story of two lovers undone yet ultimately transfigured by their love, Wagner had to coin a new musical language, in which intense passion and unfulfilled longing could be conveyed, and sustained, across three acts and four hours. The score was finished in 1859, and marked a breakthrough in musical technique that would allow Wagner, ten years later, to create the incandescent love music of Act III of *Siegfried* and limn the monumentally intense drama of the final *Ring* opera, *GÖTTERDÄMMERUNG* (*Twilight of the Gods*).

In 1863 he fell in love with the 25-year-old Cosima von Bülow, daughter of Marie d'Agoult and Franz Liszt, and wife of Hans von Bülow. By 1864 he was living with her. Cosima and Wagner had three children—Isolde, Eva, and Siegfried—all born out of wedlock (as Cosima herself had been). In 1870, Bülow divorced her, and she and Wagner were married.

In a way that can only be described as operatic, fate intervened in Wagner's life in March of 1864, when an 18-year-old who was idolatrously devoted to the composer became King Ludwig II of Bavaria. Ludwig promptly summoned his hero to Munich, and paid off his debts. A starstruck friendship developed, one of the most important in the history of music. As generous with the crown's money as he was nutty, Ludwig wanted to erect a monumental stone opera house in Munich dedicated to Wagner's works, and commissioned the architect Gottfried Semper to draw up the plans. (Though that house was never built, within a decade Ludwig would provide Wagner with something even better.) In due course Ludwig paid for the premieres, in Munich, of *Tristan und Isolde* (1865) and *DIE MEISTERSINGER VON NÜRNBERG* (*The Mastersingers of Nuremberg*; 1868); over the 19 years between their first meeting and Wagner's death, the king lavished a total of 562,914 marks on the composer. From 1866 to 1872 Wagner lived in a lakeside house called Tribschen, just outside Lucerne, where in 1868 Cosima joined him. Those years would be the closest to an idyllic existence the composer would

Wagner at the Villa Wahnfried, with an allegory of his operas in the background

The Palazzo Vendramin in Venice, where Wagner died

ever enjoy. Wagner evoked the peace he felt at Tribschen in the calm, pensive music of his *SIEGFRIED IDYLL,* written as a birthday present for Cosima and first performed on the staircase outside her bedroom on Christmas Day, 1870.

At Tribschen, Wagner pressed toward the main goal of his life: completion of his *Ring* tetralogy and creation of the summer festival where it would be presented. Wagner and Cosima scouted Ludwig's Bavarian realm for a suitable site; following a visit in 1871, they chose the small Franconian town of BAYREUTH. The local authorities gave Wagner, free of charge, the land for a theater on a hill overlooking the town. Though Bayreuth already had one of the finest Baroque theaters in the world, Wagner had to have a venue built to his own specifications. The result, paid for by Ludwig, was the massive brick Festspielhaus, which still stands. Made almost entirely of wood on the inside, it has some of the finest acoustics in the world.

In 1872 the Wagners moved to Bayreuth, and in 1874 they settled into a new home there, the villa Wahnfried. Two summers of rehearsals were needed as run-up to the festival, made possible when Ludwig extended a loan of 100,000 thalers to the composer. The *Ring* cycle was premiered in August of 1876, with Hans Richter conducting (Liszt, Bruckner, Grieg, and Tchaikovsky attended). In 1877, Wagner began work on his final opera, *PARSIFAL.* The score was completed in 1882, and a second Bayreuth Festival was held for it. The premiere and most of that summer's 16 performances were conducted by Hermann Levi; at the final performance, Wagner secretly slipped into the pit, took the baton from Levi, and conducted the opera's conclusion. By then he was seriously ill, and the next February, on family vacation in Venice (moments after Cosima had gone ballistic over yet another one of his serial infidelities), he suffered a heart attack and died in Cosima's arms.

Wagner was not a pleasant human being. He had a voracious appetite for women, power, adulation, money, and fame, and was reptilian in his dealings with others. Like many Europeans of his day and class, he was also virulently anti-Semitic. But while in personal terms he was a horror, as an artist Wagner was honest and hardworking, and he never compromised. With a talent as large as his huge ego, he became the most prominent and influential musician of his era, and repaid his many artistic debts with interest, literally transforming music as it stood at the time of his youth into a new art form of sweeping emotive power. He revolutionized musical composition in a number of areas: architecturally, in the long-range harmonic thinking of the *Ring* operas and *Tristan und Isolde* and in the way those works are integrated through the systematic use of LEITMOTIFS; expressively, in the rhetorical and emotive power of his musical ideas and the richness of his harmonic language, particularly his telling use of CHROMATICISM; and coloristically, through his supremely accomplished orchestration. Wagner literally stood the orchestra on its head—where before the strings had dominated and the winds and brass augmented the orchestra's sound, in Wagner's music the winds and an expanded brass section are kept in constant use and do the heavy lifting, while the strings are given a more atmospheric role. The potency of this new division of labor is already apparent in *Der fliegende Holländer, Tannhäuser,* and *Lohengrin,* but the real change occurs with the *Ring* (a classic example of the new sound is the Act III prelude from *Die Walküre,* known as "THE RIDE OF THE VALKYRIES"). The many brilliant and colorful effects Wagner achieved turned the orchestra into the most formidable army in Europe, a force of overwhelming power capable of sweeping legions of listeners off their feet. While Wagner's approach tended to make his operas sound like orchestral music with voices riding on top, that too became a new trend, continued in the works of Richard Strauss and many others. It lives on in the movies, where underscoring of dialogue is a technique beloved of Hollywood composers.

Seen by musicians, and by artists in other disciplines, as the avatar of a new grandeur, heroism, and sensuality in the arts, Wagner was copied by many, and reviled by many others (Debussy was not alone in being in both camps). His influence extended to literature, philosophy, and the visual arts: the path taken by the French symbolists, by painters like Kandinsky, van Gogh, and Gaugin, and by writers and thinkers like D. H. Lawrence, Thomas Mann, and Claude Lévi-Strauss, would have been unimaginable without his music. Hitler, too, was influenced. Wagner's art can rightly be credited with having played an important, perhaps determinative, role in the birth of modernism, and Wagner himself with having pioneered the modernist approach to art. For he was not just interested in entertaining people, but in getting inside their thoughts and changing them. *See also* OPERA, ROMANTICISM.

RECOMMENDED RECORDINGS

DER FLIEGENDE HOLLÄNDER: HALE, BEHRENS, RYDL, PROTSCHKA; DOHNÁNYI AND VIENNA PHILHARMONIC (DECCA).

LOHENGRIN: DOMINGO, NORMAN, NIMSGERN, RANDOVÁ; SOLTI AND VIENNA PHILHARMONIC (DECCA).

DIE MEISTERSINGER VON NÜRNBERG: FISCHER-DIESKAU, DOMINGO, LIGENDZA, HERMANN; JOCHUM AND DEUTSCHE OPER BERLIN (DG).

DIE MEISTERSINGER VON NÜRNBERG: VAN DAM, HEPPNER, MATTILA, PAPE; SOLTI AND CHICAGO SYMPHONY ORCHESTRA (DECCA).

PARSIFAL: HOFFMAN, MOLL, NIMSGERN, VEJZOVIC, VAN DAM; KARAJAN AND BERLIN PHILHARMONIC (DG).

PARSIFAL: JERUSALEM, VAN DAM, HÖLLE, MEIER, TOMLINSON; BARENBOIM AND BERLIN PHILHARMONIC (TELDEC).

RIENZI: KOLLO, MARTIN, ADAM; HOLLREISER AND STAATSKAPELLE DRESDEN (EMI).

DER RING DES NIBELUNGEN: NILSSON, ADAM, RYSANEK, TALVELA, OTHERS; BÖHM AND BAYREUTH FESTIVAL (PHILIPS).

DER RING DES NIBELUNGEN: NILSSON, HOTTER, FLAGSTAD, LONDON, OTHERS; SOLTI AND VIENNA PHILHARMONIC (DECCA).

SELECTED OVERTURES AND PRELUDES: BARENBOIM AND CHICAGO SYMPHONY ORCHESTRA (TELDEC).

SELECTED OVERTURES AND PRELUDES: KARAJAN AND BERLIN PHILHARMONIC (EMI).

SELECTED OVERTURES AND PRELUDES: KLEMPERER AND PHILHARMONIA ORCHESTRA (EMI).

SELECTED OVERTURES AND PRELUDES: WALTER AND COLUMBIA SYMPHONY ORCHESTRA (SONY).

SIEGFRIED IDYLL: KARAJAN AND VIENNA PHILHARMONIC (DG).

SIEGFRIED IDYLL: WALTER AND COLUMBIA SYMPHONY ORCHESTRA (SONY).

TANNHÄUSER: DOMINGO, STUDER, BALTSA, SCHMIDT, SALMINEN; SINOPOLI AND PHILHARMONIA ORCHESTRA (DG).

TRISTAN UND ISOLDE: SUTHAUS, FLAGSTAD, THEBOM, FISCHER-DIESKAU, GREINDL; FURTWÄNGLER AND PHILHARMONIA ORCHESTRA (EMI).

TRISTAN UND ISOLDE: WINDGASSEN, NILSSON, LUDWIG, WAECHTER, TALVELA; BÖHM AND BAYREUTH FESTIVAL (DG).

WESENDONCK LIEDER: FLAGSTAD; FURTWÄNGLER AND PHILHARMONIA ORCHESTRA (EMI).

WESENDONCK LIEDER: NORMAN; DAVIS AND LONDON SYMPHONY ORCHESTRA (PHILIPS).

Wagner tuba Brass instrument designed by Richard Wagner for use in the operas of *Der Ring des Nibelungen.* Wagner's aim was to bridge the gap in the orchestral brass sonority between the horns and the trombones; though called a tuba, it in fact functions more like a horn. Wagner tubas have a distinctive elliptical shape and a gently flared bell that opens upward at a slight angle. They come in two sizes: a tenor in B-flat (with the same 9-foot tube length as a B-flat alto horn), and a bass in F (with the same 12-foot tube length as an F horn), in effect replicating on different instruments the B-flat and F divisions of the standard double horn. Their tone, less bright than that of the horns, is warm and glowing, in softer dynamics slightly sepulchral. Typically, two of each type are used in conjunction with a contrabass tuba to create a separate five-instrument choir within the brass section. Apart from their use in Wagner's *Ring,* Wagner tubas are required by Bruckner in his Symphonies Nos. 7, 8, and 9. They are also used in Richard Strauss's *Elektra, Die Frau ohne Schatten,* and *Eine Alpensinfonie.*

***Waldstein* Sonata** NICKNAME ATTACHED TO LUDWIG VAN BEETHOVEN'S PIANO SONATA IN C, OP. 53, composed 1803–04 and dedicated to Ferdinand Ernst Gabriel, Count Waldstein. The first of Beethoven's champions and a capable musician himself, Waldstein had arrived in Bonn in 1788 as a companion of the Elector, Max Franz. In 1792 he had written the famous lines in Beethoven's album urging him to go to Vienna and "receive Mozart's spirit from the hands of Haydn." His continued encouragement earned him the dedication of this sonata, one of the major keyboard works of Beethoven's middle years.

In brilliance, harmonic daring, and sheer virtuosity the *Waldstein* marks a new plateau in Beethoven's writing for the piano. Its first movement opens with a pulsating progression that approaches the home key by indirection, at the same time taking advantage of the resonant sound in the lower range of the early-19th-century fortepiano. Contrast and momentum are the hallmarks of the movement—an enormous amount of energy is released as it unfolds, the impetus of C major gaining from each harmonic digression. Instead of a slow movement of "normal" length and character, there is an Adagio introduction to the finale. Just as this Adagio appears to be spinning a melody in the warm middle range of the instrument, its progress is interrupted by a return of its opening phrase; then, out of the mists, a beautifully consoling, hymnlike tune materializes and builds by repetition into a paean of triumph. The effect of the finale's arriving in this way—quietly stealing upon the scene—is novel and transformative, an epiphany. The intervening episodes of the rondo set off the subject in a contrast of dark and light, major and minor, until the movement ends, *prestissimo,* in an exultant delirium of sound.

RECOMMENDED RECORDINGS

GILELS (DG).

R. SERKIN (SONY).

Waldteufel, Émile

(b. Strasbourg, December 9, 1837; d. Paris, February 12, 1915)

FRENCH COMPOSER AND PIANIST. Frequently referred to as the French Johann Strauss, he wrote more than 180 waltzes. He was trained at the Paris Conservatoire, but his professional beginnings were modest—his first job involved testing pianos in a piano factory. In 1865 he became pianist to the Empress Eugénie. As a composer of waltzes, Waldteufel hit his stride in the 1870s. Though his waltzes have never enjoyed the universal acclaim of Strauss's, their tunefulness and graceful charm reflect the taste of the Third Empire and its love of luxury. Waldteufel's best-known works are the waltzes *Les patineurs* (*The Skaters*; 1882), *Estudiantina* (1883), and *España* (1886), based on Chabrier's orchestral rhapsody.

RECOMMENDED RECORDINGS

WALTZES, POLKAS, GALOPS: SWIERCZEWSKI AND GULBENKIAN FOUNDATION SYMPHONY ORCHESTRA (NIMBUS).

WALTZES: A. WALTER AND SLOVAK STATE PHILHARMONIC ORCHESTRA (NAXOS).

Walküre, Die (The Valkyrie) **OPERA IN THREE ACTS BY RICHARD WAGNER,** composed 1854–56 as the second part of his tetralogy *DER RING DES NIBELUNGEN,* and first performed June 26, 1870, at the National Theater in Munich. In *Die Walküre,* the focus of Wagner's *Ring* drama shifts from the gods, giants, and dwarves of *DAS RHEINGOLD* to humans, specifically the warrior Siegmund and his twin sister, Sieglinde, who will become the parents of the central figure of the cycle, the hero Siegfried. The opera also focuses on the relationship between Wotan and his disobedient (but not disloyal) daughter Brünnhilde, the Valkyrie of the work's title. Ordered to see to the hero Siegmund's death, Brünnhilde goes against her father's command, but very much with his deeper feelings—since both Siegmund and Sieglinde, now pregnant, are Wotan's children as well—and spares the doomed man. For her rebellious act, Brünnhilde is sentenced to mortality: She will be left asleep on a rock surrounded by fire, until a hero dares the flames to awaken her. That hero, as yet unborn, will be Siegfried.

The most frequently performed of the *Ring* operas, *Die Walküre* is famous for its Act III prelude, known as "THE RIDE OF THE VALKYRIES." Its first act, one of the most cohesive and gripping in all of Wagner's work, ends with the impassioned love duet of Siegmund and Sieglinde. The tide of inspiration carries through the ensuing acts: The literature has few pages that compare with Wotan's emotional farewell to Brünnhilde at the end of Act III ◉ or with the imaginative "Magic Fire Music" of the work's final pages.

RECOMMENDED RECORDINGS

NILSSON, KING, CRESPIN, LUDWIG, HOTTER; SOLTI AND VIENNA PHILHARMONIC (DECCA).

NILSSON, KING, RYSANEK, BURMEISTER, ADAM; BÖHM AND BAYREUTH FESTIVAL ORCHESTRA (PHILIPS).

Walter [Schlesinger], Bruno

(b. Berlin, September 15, 1876; d. Beverly Hills, February 17, 1962)

GERMAN/AUSTRIAN/AMERICAN CONDUCTOR, among the most important and beloved of the 20th century. Walter was Gustav Mahler's acolyte in Hamburg and Vienna and a lifelong champion of his works. After establishing himself as a brilliant opera conductor in the early years of the 20th century, he developed into an eloquent interpreter of the symphonic

Bruno Walter in rehearsal smock

repertoire, crowning his career with a series of studio recordings of Mozart, Beethoven, Brahms, Wagner, Bruckner, and Mahler that remain among the glories of the stereo era.

Born into a middle-class Jewish family (the Schlesingers; he dropped the surname in 1911), Walter attended the Stern Conservatory in Berlin, where his mother had also studied, earning distinction as a pianist. At 12 he made his debut with the Berlin Philharmonic (Walter retained his keyboard skills and continued to put in appearances as an accompanist until late in his career). He decided to become a conductor after attending a concert led by Hans von Bülow. In 1893 he landed a job as an opera coach in Cologne, and in 1894, just 18, he joined the staff of the Hamburg Stadttheater, where Mahler was in charge. Walter spent two years in Hamburg, observing Mahler's rehearsals and performances; he was amazed by the titanic intensity of Mahler's conducting style and its communicative power, and by his ability to impose exacting standards upon an orchestra.

Following the usual route, Walter honed his skills in a progression of posts, spending a year or two in each: Breslau, Pressburg, Riga, and Berlin. In 1901 Mahler summoned him to the Vienna Court Opera to serve as his second-in-command, and in the ensuing years Walter became much more than that, taking on the role of trusted associate and confidant. Even after Mahler's 1908 departure from Vienna, Walter remained on close terms with his mentor; in essence, he was present at the creation of every one of Mahler's works from the Third Symphony to the end. Mahler valued Walter's insight and talent. Knowing that he would not live to conduct them himself, he entrusted to Walter the premieres of *Das Lied von der Erde* (in 1911) and the Ninth Symphony (1912). Walter made the first recordings of those works, during the 1930s, and later the premiere recording of Mahler's Fifth.

Walter took Austrian citizenship in 1911. In 1913 he was appointed general music director in Munich, a prestigious post that included responsibility for the Court Opera. During his years in the Bavarian capital, he led many premieres and forged a warm friendship with Thomas Mann, rekindled years later when the two lived in southern California. Walter left Munich in 1922. He made his American debut in 1923, as guest conductor of the New York Symphony Society (later the Philharmonic). Walter was regularly engaged as a guest conductor of the Berlin Philharmonic from 1919 on, and in 1929 he was entrusted with one of the top jobs in German musical life, succeeding Furtwängler at the helm of the Leipzig Gewandhaus Orchestra.

Walter's time at the summit would be short. In March 1933, only weeks after the Nazis came to power, he was forced from his position in Leipzig. Later that month, at Goebbels's instigation, he was dissuaded—by threat of physical harm—from making a scheduled appearance with the Berlin Philharmonic. He moved to France shortly before the Anschluss, saying farewell to Vienna and its Philharmonic with a harrowing performance of Mahler's Ninth. In 1939 he emigrated to the United States (he became a citizen in 1946), and from 1947 to 1949 he served as musical adviser to the New York Philharmonic.

Walter returned several times to Europe after World War II and gave his final performance with the Vienna Philharmonic in 1960. He had been slowed by a heart attack in 1957, but was able to spend the sunset years of his career near his home, in Beverly Hills, recording his core repertoire with a handpicked orchestra of top L.A. studio musicians.

Walter is best remembered for his devotion to Mahler and as an interpreter of the major Austro-Germanic symphonists—Haydn, Mozart, Beethoven, Schubert, Brahms, and Bruckner. Before settling in America, though, he was admired mainly for his work in the pit, where his specialties included not just Mozart but Verdi, Wagner, and Richard Strauss. He spurned atonal and serial music, and as time went by he conducted less 20th-century music and more of the standards. But it should be remembered that, when it was new, he championed the music not only of Mahler but of Debussy, Puccini, Pfitzner, Korngold, Shostakovich, Barber, and Miklós Rósza (1907–95). In addition to the Mahler scores he ushered into the world, his signature works included Bach's *St. Matthew* Passion, Wagner's *Tristan und Isolde,* Mozart's *Die Zauberflöte,* and Brahms's *Ein deutsches Requiem.* A magnificent 1935 recording of Act I of Wagner's *Die Walküre*—with Lauritz Melchior and Lotte Lehmann as Siegmund and Sieglinde, and a blazing Vienna Philhamonic in front of the microphone—shows what a superb opera conductor he was.

At their best, Walter's interpretations were revelatory. The passion and urgency that marked his conducting until he was well into his 70s (e.g., the amazing 1952 recording of *Das Lied von der Erde,* with the Vienna Philharmonic) gave way to a more measured approach: The accounts recorded by Columbia Masterworks during the conductor's Indian summer in Hollywood are still cohesive, if not quite as propulsive as the earlier efforts. But what these valedictory readings may sometimes lack in drive is compensated for by a new generosity of spirit, a philosophical softness and kindliness. And many are still fiery, athletic, luminous, robustly alive.

Like other performers of his generation, Walter was also a composer, producing among other works two symphonies and several song sets.

RECOMMENDED RECORDINGS

BEETHOVEN, SYMPHONIES (COMPLETE): COLUMBIA SYMPHONY ORCHESTRA (SONY).

BRAHMS, SYMPHONIES (COMPLETE): COLUMBIA SYMPHONY ORCHESTRA (SONY).

BRUCKNER, SYMPHONIES NOS. 4, 7, 9: COLUMBIA SYMPHONY ORCHESTRA (SONY).

MAHLER, *DAS LIED VON DER ERDE*: FERRIER, PATZAK; VIENNA PHILHARMONIC (DECCA).

MAHLER, *DAS LIED VON DER ERDE*: MILLER, HAEFLIGER; NEW YORK PHILHARMONIC (SONY).

MAHLER, SYMPHONIES NOS. 1, 2, 9: COLUMBIA SYMPHONY ORCHESTRA; NEW YORK PHILHARMONIC (SONY).

MOZART, SYMPHONIES NOS. 35–41: COLUMBIA SYMPHONY ORCHESTRA (SONY).

WAGNER, OVERTURES AND PRELUDES: COLUMBIA SYMPHONY ORCHESTRA (SONY).

WAGNER, *DIE WALKÜRE,* ACT I: LEHMANN, MELCHIOR, LIST; VIENNA PHILHARMONIC (EMI).

Walton, William

(b. Oldham, March 29, 1902; d. Ischia, March 8, 1983)

ENGLISH COMPOSER, who possessed one of the most vibrant and distinctive styles of the 20th century. Walton's father trained as a bass-baritone at the Royal Manchester College of Music, taught music at a local grammar school, and was a church organist and choirmaster; his mother taught voice and was a capable amateur contralto. As a child Walton sang and played the piano; at ten he won a scholarship as a chorister to Christ Church Cathedral School in Oxford, where he remained a student until 1918. That year, the 16-year-old enrolled as an undergraduate at Christ Church College, but left in two years without a degree, thrice failing a required exam.

At Oxford, Walton was befriended by Siegfried Sassoon, the World War I soldier turned pacifist poet, and through him came to know Sacheverall Sitwell, then a student at Balliol College. Sitwell, who had recently published his first volume of poems, introduced Walton to his elder

Heinkel He-111 and poster for 1969 film **The Battle of Britain,** *with music by Walton*

brother, Osbert, and sister, Edith; all three were soon creating a stir on London's literary scene. After Walton dropped out of Oxford, the Sitwells invited him to stay with them. A visit expected to last a few weeks turned into a residency of more than a decade. They introduced Walton to a circle that included T. S. Eliot, exposed him to jazz concerts and Diaghilev's Ballets Russes, and brought him to Italy.

One result of Walton's immersion in the Sitwells' world was *Façade* (1922–29), a large cluster of Edith's poems declaimed through a Sengerphone (a papier-mâché megaphone that covered mouth and nose) to sassy musical accompaniment. This drawing-room entertainment, showing the influence of jazz as well as modernist/expressionist/absurdist elements picked up from Stravinsky, Schoenberg, Ibert, Poulenc, and others, was Walton's breakthrough, and produced a delicious bit of scandal. It led to jazz-band arranging, but soon Walton was essaying conventional forms, notably the Viola Concerto (1929), written for Lionel Tertis, who, to his lasting sorrow, rejected it. It was premiered instead by Hindemith and brought Walton his first large-scale public success.

William Walton at home in Ischia

Walton didn't start to make money until he got into film work in the 1930s, but he got by with help from friends, chiefly Sassoon's generous patron, Lord Berners. The year 1931 saw the oratorio *Belshazzar's Feast* for baritone solo, mixed chorus, and a huge orchestra with augmented brass, its text cobbled together by Osbert Sitwell from various Old Testament scraps. The idea had been pushed by English conductor Malcolm Sargent. It was in this work that Walton developed his "grand manner," drawing on tradition—oratorio style, Elgar-like marches—while writing in a modern, clearly jazz-influenced vein. The result was an unabashedly flamboyant Biblical potboiler enlivened by cinematically vivid orchestral effects.

The Symphony No. 1 (1935) was another breakthrough. Composed during the dissolution of a stormy five-year love affair, it is a tough work of febrile intensity, where anxiety, melancholy, and malaise are swept away by the grand noise of a fugal finale. ◉ Walton presently began a happier liaison, with Alice Wimbourne, a viscountess 22 years his senior.

The march *Crown Imperial* (1937), for the coronation of King George VI, proved as good as Elgar's *Pomp and Circumstance* marches, on which it was modeled. The Violin Concerto (1939), written for Jascha Heifetz, was another success, brilliant and beautifully lyrical. Walton missed its premiere, in Cleveland, because England was by then at war. He busied himself during those days with work in support of the war effort, including such films as *Major Barbara, The First of the Few* (about Reginald Mitchell, designer of the Supermarine Spitfire), and *Henry V* (an hour of first-rate music behind Olivier). Walton continued the association with Olivier after the war, in *Hamlet* (1947) and *Richard III* (1955). Also after the war came chamber music—the String Quartet in A minor (1946) and Violin Sonata (1949) are both pieces of the first order.

Viscountess Wimbourne died in 1948, and later that year, on a trip to Argentina, the 46-year-old Walton met and fell in love with the 22-year-old Susana Gil Passo, social secretary to the British consul in Buenos Aires. Married in December, the couple soon moved to the island of Ischia, in the Bay of Naples.

There Walton worked on the opera *Troilus and Cressida,* which had been commissioned by the BBC in 1947. Set against the Trojan War, with a story full of treachery (derived from Chaucer, not Shakespeare) in which a woman is kept from the man she loves, the piece had a lengthy gestation, premiering at Covent Garden in 1954. It was a work in which Walton set great store and he wanted desperately for it to succeed; he spent years revising the score and, for a restaging of the opera in 1976, rewrote the part of Cressida so that it could be sung by mezzo-soprano Janet Baker. Although it contains some of Walton's most passionate and imaginative music, the opera has failed to gain a secure place in the repertoire.

Walton spent the remainder of the 1950s, indeed the rest of his life, soaking up the Mediterranean sun and composing on commission. The Cello Concerto (1956), for Gregor Piatigorsky, is sultry, bittersweet, and one of the finest string concertos of the 20th century. *Partita* (1957), commissioned for the 40th anniversary of the Cleveland Orchestra and premiered under the baton of George Szell, is a virtuoso romp suffused with "Mediterranean" light. Walton's Symphony No. 2 (1960), commissioned by the Royal Liverpool Philharmonic, shares the virtuosity of the *Partita* and, like it, was wonderfully realized by Szell and Cleveland, whose recording struck the composer as being "stupendous . . . absolutely right." In 1963 Walton repaid an old musical debt with his masterly *Variations on a Theme of Paul Hindemith.* His production fell off in his remaining two decades.

Walton was essentially self-taught and worked when the mood was upon him. Some of his finest pieces caused him a great deal of artistic trouble: He pondered for over half a year on how to set the word "gold" in *Belshazzar's Feast.* Yet the best of his music is characterized by a distinctive swagger, orchestral virtuosity, and, behind everything, genuine feeling.

RECOMMENDED RECORDINGS

Belshazzar's Feast: Shirley-Quirk; Previn and London Symphony Orchestra (EMI).

Cello Concerto: Piatigorsky; Munch and Boston Symphony Orchestra (RCA).

Crown Imperial, Orb and Sceptre (with Symphony No. 1): Previn and Royal Philharmonic Orchestra (Telarc).

Façade (complete): Lloyd-Jones and Nash Ensemble (Hyperion).

Façade (suites): Lloyd-Jones and English Northern Philharmonic (Hyperion).

Film music (including suites from *As You Like It* and *Henry V*). Carl Davis and London Symphony Orchestra (EMI).

Partita: Szell and Cleveland Orchestra (Sony).

Symphony No. 1: Previn and London Symphony Orchestra (RCA).

Symphony No. 2: Previn and London Symphony Orchestra (EMI).

Troilus and Cressida: Davies, Howarth, Howard, Robson, Bayley; Hickox and English National Philharmonia (Chandos).

waltz Dance in triple time (usually $\frac{3}{4}$) notable for its combination of grace and energy. As the most popular ballroom dance of the 19th century, both in Europe and America, it was embraced by classical composers from the 1820s until well into the 20th century. The waltz was an urban offshoot of 18th-century country dances such as the LÄNDLER and Deutscher of southern Germany, Austria, and Bohemia, and quickly became a craze after emerging in Vienna early in the 19th century. Part of its popularity stemmed from the fact that couples could hold each other closely and whirl around the dance floor together; as a socially acceptable form of physical intimacy for the unmarried, it was hard to beat until the tango came along. When it was new the waltz was considered a fast dance, and properly done it still is, moving smoothly and seductively, with two gliding steps for each downbeat. But behind the dance's liveliness there is often a hint of nervousness, something composers were quick to capitalize on as the waltz became an emblem for the dark truths that often lie behind carefree, worldly facades.

The waltz as a vehicle for ballroom dancing became the stock-in-trade of an enterprising group of Viennese composers, headed by Josef Lanner (1801–43) and Johann Strauss, whose sons Johann Jr. and Josef would come to dominate the waltz business in the latter half of the 19th century. The *Blue Danube* ◉ and *Tales from the Vienna Woods* ◉ are good examples. Other important figures in the production of ballroom waltzes were Émile Waldteufel and C. M. Ziehrer (1843–1922), known for his *Wiener Bürger* (1890).

Waltzes became a fixture of 19th- and early-20th-century operetta and ballet scores thanks to the work of such composers as Offenbach, Delibes, and Lehár. Tchaikovsky ladled some of the most exquisite waltzes ever written into his ballets *Swan Lake* ◉, *The Sleeping Beauty*, and *The Nutcracker*, and dropped another into the opera *Eugene Onegin*. Richard Strauss, every bit as partial to the waltz, made it the basis for Salome's "Dance of the Seven Veils" and gave it a starring role in *Der Rosenkavalier*.

The 19th-century piano repertoire is particularly rich in waltzes, beginning with Weber's *Invitation to the Dance* (1819), a virtuoso concert piece later magnificently orchestrated by Berlioz. Other interesting treatments include Beethoven's *Diabelli* Variations, Op. 120, based on a waltz by Anton Diabelli ◉; various sets of waltzes by Schubert; Chopin's 17 waltzes, including the so-called *Minute* Waltz in D-flat, Op. 64, No. 1 ◉; Brahms's two sets of *Liebeslieder* Waltzes for piano four-hands and vocal quartet; Liszt's *Mephisto* Waltz; and Ravel's *Valses nobles et sentimentales* (subsequently orchestrated). The concert repertoire includes Glazunov's two Concert Waltzes, Sibelius's *Valse triste* for strings, and Ravel's *La valse,* as well as innumerable works with waltz music embedded in them. Among the finest examples are Tchaikovsky's Symphonies No. 4 (first movement) and No. 6 (second movement, a remarkably speculative and melancholy meditation in $\frac{5}{4}$ time); the "Fête polonaise" from Chabrier's *Le roi malgré lui*; the "Conversation of Beauty and the Beast" in Ravel's *Ma mère l'oye*; Rachmaninov's *Symphonic Dances* (second movement); the Berg Violin Concerto (throughout); and the first movement of Shostakovich's Symphony No. 10, a haunting waltz-dream that turns terrifyingly violent.

***Wandererfantasie* (*Wanderer* Fantasy)** **TITLE OF FRANZ SCHUBERT'S FOUR-MOVEMENT FANTASY IN C FOR PIANO, D. 760,** composed in November 1822 and published as the composer's Op. 15 in 1823. The slow movement is based on thematic material from Schubert's song "Der Wanderer," D. 489, of 1816. The fantasy's "movements" are linked without traditional breaks through a recurrent rhythmic figure, and the finale incorporates a cyclical return of thematic elements from the first movement, effectively superimposing a sonata-form structure on the piece. This novel approach to unifying a multimovement work had an enormous influence on music written later in the 19th century, most notably that of Franz Liszt (who in addition made a virtuoso transcription of the *Wandererfantasie* for piano and orchestra in 1851), and Richard Strauss.

War and Peace **Opera in two parts by Sergey Prokofiev,** to a libretto by the composer and Mira Mendelson (based on Lev Tolstoy's novel written in 1869). It was composed primarily during 1941–42 and first performed complete on December 15, 1959, at the Bolshoi Theatre in Moscow; prior to that, the work had been presented in various abridgements or partial performances, the most important of which was the production of Part I of the final version (13 scenes and a choral epigraph) at the Maly Theater in Leningrad, premiered on June 12, 1946. Set in Russia during the years of Napoleon's bid for European hegemony, the opera compresses Tolstoy's epic story of betrayal, struggle, and redemption into a four-hour-long spectacle calling for an enormous cast (there are more than 70 roles, some silent) and hundreds of extras. Prokofiev poured some of his greatest music into the score, struggling mightily in the heat of World War II to forge a work that would stand up to the grandeur of its subject matter. Eventually, after rearranging the scene structure along lines suggested to him by the conductor Samuil Samosud, he succeeded in fashioning a masterpiece, one of the supreme achievements of Russian opera. Even so, its monumental scenic demands and requirement of a gigantic cast have made performances of it rare.

RECOMMENDED RECORDINGS

Gergalov, Prokina, Borodina, Gregorian; Gergiev and Kirov Opera (Philips).

Vishnevskaya, Miller, Ciesinski, Ochman, Gedda, Ghiuselev, Petkov; Rostropovich and French National Radio Orchestra (Erato).

Warren, Leonard

(b. New York, April 21, 1911; d. New York, March 4, 1960)

American baritone. Born in the Bronx to Russian immigrant parents (the family name was originally Warenoff), he intended to continue in the family fur business after his graduation from Columbia University, but instead became, in 1935, a member of the Radio City Music Hall choir. He studied singing with Sidney Dietch, and in 1937 entered the Metropolitan Opera Auditions of the Air; though he had only five arias in his repertoire, his singing so impressed the judges that he won. He spent the next six months in Milan studying with Giuseppe Païs and Riccardo Picozzi, and returned to accept a contract at the Met. Prior to making his debut as Paolo in Verdi's *Simon Boccanegra* in 1939, he was coached by the great baritone Giuseppe de Luca, learning seven roles in seven months. Though he also sang on occasion at La Scala, the Teatro Colón in Buenos Aires, and in Mexico City, Chicago, and San Francisco, he appeared primarily at the Met for the rest of his career, becoming the leading Verdi baritone of his day, and inheriting many of the roles of Lawrence Tibbett—among them Iago, Tonio, Amonasro, and Rigoletto (which became his signature role, undertaken in 89 performances). He collapsed and died on the Met stage during a performance of Verdi's *La forza del destino,* having just sung the aria "Urna fatale dal mio destino." Warren's voice was a velvet baritone of extraordinary size, ideally suited to Verdi. He was known for his forceful interpretations and his intractable personality, despite which he enjoyed the respect of his colleagues and the enthusiasm of a devoted public.

RECOMMENDED RECORDING

COLLECTION:
SCENES AND ARIAS FROM WORKS OF LEONCAVALLO, PONCHIELLI, ROSSINI, VERDI, OTHERS (PREISER).

War Requiem **WORK FOR ORCHESTRA, CHORUS, AND SOLOISTS BY BENJAMIN BRITTEN,** completed in 1961 and first performed on May 30, 1962, in Coventry, England, at the dedication of the new Coventry Cathedral, built next to the ruins of the cathedral bombed out by the Luftwaffe in 1940. The text is a conflation of the Latin Requiem and the poignant, disturbing, deeply personal antiwar verse of the English poet Wilfred Owen, who died at the front during the final week of World War I. The performing forces are immense: full symphony orchestra, chamber orchestra, mixed chorus, boys' choir, soprano, tenor, and baritone soloists, and two conductors—one for the main forces, the other for the chamber orchestra and the two male soloists, who are entrusted with the settings of Owen's poetry and represent soldiers (one German, one English) from opposite sides of the conflict in which Owen perished. The poems, filled with religious imagery, are used to amplify the message of the mass and move its focus from the abstract to the particular.

Musically, the *War Requiem* is a vast study of the TRITONE, the dissonant interval of the augmented fourth historically considered a symbol of the devil, to which Britten gives a haunting consonance and sonority as if to demonstrate evil's attraction. The score achieves a sweeping synthesis of style, one that encompasses everything from medieval mystery (the two soldiers representing a twin-voiced Everyman) to opera, symphony, and chamber idioms.

The Latin text is treated with a mysterious, spiritualized detachment in the settings for the children's voices, which are to be heard as if at a distance (in many performances the boys are placed in a choir loft or in the back of the hall, and they can indeed sound like angels). When the chorus or the solo soprano intones the Latin, it tends to become impersonally rigid and dogmatic, as in the soprano's "Liber scriptus proferetur," or airy and ironic, as in the chorus's fugal "Quam olim Abrahae." The *DIES IRAE*, mechanically sung and accompanied by frightful alarms in the brass and the thundering reports of cannon in the percussion, is a vision of apocalyptic power, one of the most harrowing pieces of music ever written. The beautiful *Recordare* has a trance-like quality.

The settings of Owen's poetry interspersed throughout the work show Britten at his most piquant. "It seemed that out of battle I escaped," the final interpolation of the work, contains a poignant confession that goes to the heart of the *War Requiem*'s meaning. In the shadowy netherworld of death the English soldier meets the German he killed the day before, who says to him:

> . . . Whatever hope is yours,
> Was my life also; I went hunting wild
> After the wildest beauty in the
> world.
>
> For by my glee might many men
> have laughed,
> And of my weeping something had
> been left,
> Which must die now. I mean the
> truth untold,
> The pity of war, the pity war distilled.

In passages such as these Britten's score makes a profound statement about the value of human life, while summing up both a vast musical tradition and the great historical experience of the 20th century; the *War Requiem* stands among the handful of indisputably great musical works from the second half of that century.

RECOMMENDED RECORDING

Vishnevskaya, Pears, Fischer-Dieskau; Britten and London Symphony Orchestra (Decca).

Water Music **Orchestral suite by George Frideric Handel,** composed in 1717 for the entertainment of George I and his guests during a royal procession by barge up the Thames on the evening of July 17, 1717. The king and his favorites listened as an ensemble of 50 musicians played Handel's music from another barge, while boats "beyond counting" crowded alongside. The idea of this spectacle originated with Johann Adolf, Baron Kielmansegg, the king's adviser; it was he who commissioned Handel, "His Majesty's principal Court Composer," to write the music.

Because the manuscript has been lost, and no authoritative first edition of the score exists, the order in which the various movements of the *Water Music* were played is uncertain. But it has been customary since Handel's time, based on the instrumentation and key relationships of the individual pieces, to group them in three suites: a large one in F consisting of ten movements and featuring two horns (this marked the first time that "French" horns had ever been used in English music), oboes, bassoon, and strings; one in D, consisting of five movements (including the celebrated "Hornpipe" ◉), with parts for trumpets, horns, oboes, bassoon, and strings; and one in G, in seven movements, for a softer complement of flute, recorder, oboes, bassoon, and strings. The festive suites in F and D were probably played on the barge. The G major grouping, without brass instruments and thus unsuited for outdoor performance, would have been played later, while the king dined.

Regardless of the order in which its movements are played, the *Water Music* ranks among the great offerings of occasional music. Its gestures are bracing, vital, grand—in every way fit for a king.

RECOMMENDED RECORDINGS

Gardiner and English Baroque Soloists (Philips).

Lamon and Tafelmusik (Sony).

Weber, Carl Maria von

(b. Eutin, November 19, 1786; d. London, June 5, 1826)

German composer, conductor, and pianist. He was among the first composers to discern and give voice to the grand themes of musical Romanticism. He was the son of an entrepreneurially minded town musician who in 1787 decided to form his own traveling music theater company; as a result, Weber spent his childhood and youth all over Germany. He received his initial musical training from his father and two older half-brothers, with subsequent instruction from Michael Haydn in Salzburg and Georg Vogler in Vienna.

Though he was sickly and nearsighted and limped, Weber was accomplished enough by the age of 17 to be awarded the post of opera conductor at Breslau (now Wrocław, Poland); a couple of years later he served a few months as court musician in Karlsruhe. In the summer of 1807 he landed a job as ducal secretary in Stuttgart and was joined there by his father, who had failed at his business ventures. In a scheme to repay some of his father's debts along with some of his own, Weber stuck his hand into the royal till, got caught, and was charged with embezzlement. He was jailed for several days and banished for life from Württemburg.

Chastened, Weber resolved to begin a new life. He adopted his father's peripatetic ways, traveling and living off his earnings as a concert pianist and the sale of works to various theaters and publishers. Passing through Prague in the winter of 1813, he was unexpectedly offered the music directorship of the Estates Theater, where, tasked with bringing the desultory opera company back to life, he made a valiant effort, but found himself frustrated both by his inability to cast important works and by the public's indifference. Weber's work did not go unnoticed, however, and on Christmas Day 1816 he was summoned to Dresden to create, under royal patronage, an official German-language opera company. Around the same time, he became engaged to Caroline Brandt, a soprano who had been a member of the Prague company; they married the following year.

Carl Maria von Weber, pencil sketch from 1822

Weber arrived in Dresden in 1817 and immediately went to work building an ensemble. His efforts met with only partial success and brought him into conflict with the long-established Italian-opera tradition in the Saxon capital. But it was in Dresden that he befriended the playwright Friedrich Kind, who would provide the libretto for Weber's most influential work, *DER FREISCHÜTZ* (*The Free* [i.e., "magical"] *Shooter*), which premiered in Berlin in 1821 and, four years later, in New York City—in English. In many ways *Der Freischütz* marked the coming-of-age of German Romantic opera. ◉ The social and moral issues woven into the fabric of its folktale plot, along with the elements of the bizarre and fantastic that enliven the drama, mark it as the product of a new artistic age. Weber's use of the orchestra throughout the work is brilliant and innovative; the overture is one of the most strikingly scored and evocative pieces of symphonic music from the first quarter of the 19th century.

The success of *Der Freischütz* greatly elevated Weber's standing in the musical world, but the stress of work and the progressive deterioration of his health—he was tubercular and after 1821 suffered increasingly frequent bouts of serious illness—limited his productivity during the last five years of his life. He completed the opera *EURYANTHE* in 1823, but the lukewarm reception accorded its premiere, in Vienna, left him embittered and discouraged. The next year, a commission from London for a new opera, *OBERON,* to be based on Christoph Martin Wieland's romance, brought a last burst of creative energy. Weber studied English in order to set the English libretto effectively, and traveled to London in the winter of 1826 to put the finishing touches on the score in preparation for the Covent Garden premiere. Exhausted by these efforts, he succumbed to tuberculosis less than eight weeks after the opera's first performance.

Weber's output included a good deal of incidental music, two symphonies, several concertos, a small amount of chamber music, numerous songs, and some sonatas and characteristic works for piano, including the celebrated "rondeau brillant" *Aufforderung zum Tanze* (*Invitation to the Dance*), later orchestrated by Berlioz. Several of his concerted works have secured a place in the repertoire: There are two particularly fine clarinet concertos (both composed in 1811), and the *Konzertstück* in F minor (1821) for piano and orchestra is a display piece of the first magnitude, completed on the morning of the premiere of *Der Freischütz.*

It was in the realm of opera and in his use of the orchestra that Weber made his most important contributions to the advancement of musical style. Even if the only one of his stage works that has held an unassailable place in the repertoire is *Der Freischütz,* its influence on the work of contemporaries such as Meyerbeer and on Weber's principal successor in the next generation, Wagner, was decisive. Weber's richly hued writing for the orchestra, notable for its almost unprecedently adventurous use of woodwind and brass—particularly the sparkle shown in such works as the *Konzertstück* and the elfin touches found in the overture to *Oberon* ◉—would have a profound effect on Berlioz, Mendelssohn, Wagner, Richard Strauss, indeed, on the whole lineage of 19th- and 20th-century composers concerned with color. *See also* ROMANTICISM.

RECOMMENDED RECORDINGS

CLARINET CONCERTOS: OTTENSAMER; WILDNER AND SLOVAK STATE PHILHARMONIC (NAXOS).

DER FREISCHÜTZ: JANOWITZ, MATHIS, SCHREIR, ADAM, WEIKL; C. KLEIBER AND STAATSKAPELLE DRESDEN (DG).

OVERTURES (INCLUDING *DER FREISCHÜTZ, EURYANTHE, OBERON, ABU HASSAN*): KUBELÍK AND BAVARIAN RADIO SYMPHONY ORCHESTRA (UNIVERSAL).

OVERTURES (INCLUDING *DER FREISCHÜTZ, EURYANTHE, OBERON*): KARAJAN AND BERLIN PHILHARMONIC (DG).

Webern, Anton

(b. Vienna, December 3, 1883; d. Mittersill, September 15, 1945)

AUSTRIAN COMPOSER. Exceptionally rarefied and severe, his music was the dominant influence on compositional trends of the 1950s and 1960s. On his paternal side Webern's family belonged to the minor nobility; his father served in high positions in the Hapsburg government. Webern's mother was an amateur pianist who gave him his first musical instruction. In 1890 the family moved from Vienna to Graz, and on to Klagenfurt four years later, where Webern studied theory, piano, and cello and played in the orchestra.

In the summer of 1902 the high-school graduate attended the Bayreuth Festival and was bowled over by *Parsifal.* That fall he entered the University of Vienna, earning his Ph.D. a mere four years later; his dissertation was an edition of the *Choralis constantinus* (vol. 2) of Heinrich Isaac, one of the *summae* of Renaissance contrapuntal, specifically canonic, art.

During his university studies, Webern began private composition lessons with Arnold Schoenberg, joined a few weeks later by the slightly younger Alban Berg. These three would be designated the Second Viennese School (the first, never referred to as such, comprising Haydn, Mozart, and Beethoven). Webern came to idolize Schoenberg. During the four years he spent under his tutelage, he composed numerous studies for string quartet, a couple of finished quartets, a string quintet, a group of five songs to poems of Richard Dehmel (the poet whose "Verklärte Nacht" had inspired Schoenberg's string sextet of that name), and, in 1908, the first work of his maturity, the *Passacaglia,* Op. 1, for orchestra. ◉

In 1908 Webern took a theater-conducting post at Bad Ischl. Finding himself unable to stay in a job anywhere for long (in no small part because he felt he *had* to be near Schoenberg), he held subsequent posts over the next five years in various German towns and cities; along the way he married his first cousin

Anton Webern, 1912

Wilhelmine Mörtl, in 1911; they had four children. Following World War I service, Webern settled with his family outside Vienna, where he taught composition and headed the Society for Private Musical Performances, which had been founded by Schoenberg to promote contemporary music. Following its dissolution, in 1922, Webern served for the next decade-plus as conductor of the Vienna Workers' Symphony Concerts and the Vienna Workers' Choral Society, became a regular conductor on state radio, and fulfilled guest engagements across Europe.

By 1926 Webern had mastered Schoenberg's 12-TONE technique and was producing works in the new manner. They culminated in 1928 in one of the most rigorous and disciplined of all Webern's compositions, the Symphony, Op. 21, whose rigid application of tone-row patterns (particularly in its palindromic second movement, which is a set of variations) marked a milestone in the development of SERIALISM. The work received its world premiere on December 18, 1929, at New York's Town Hall. Even more intense and reductive treatments of the 12-tone method lay ahead, particularly the Concerto (1934) for nine instruments.

Webern's 50th birthday found him at the zenith of his career, active as a conductor and productive as a composer, even if recognition of the value of his work remained limited. But things went downhill quickly. In 1934 the Social Democratic Party was declared illegal and its institutions—including the workers' orchestra and chorus—were shut down. Webern's isolation was compounded by Schoenberg's departure for America, in 1933, and the death of Berg, in 1935. For a while Webern, too, thought about emigrating, but he hung in, believing (like so many) that the rising tide of Fascism in Germany and Austria would eventually subside.

Soon his situation became dire. Webern's music (along with that of Schoenberg, Berg, and many others) was despised by the Nazis and was banned as "degenerate." Straitened finances and personal hardship lasted through the war years, with their steady succession of dashed hopes for performances and for recognition from anywhere in the Reich. Webern turned to cranking out piano reductions of minor operas. In April 1944, at 60, he was drafted into the air-raid police; the next February his son was killed in a strafing attack on a troop train. At the end of March, abandoning Vienna ahead of the advancing Red Army, Webern and his wife fled to Mittersill, in the heart of the Austrian Alps, where they spent the spring and summer with their daughters and grandchildren. One evening in September 1945, Webern stepped out onto the porch of his daughter's house to have a cigar and was shot and killed by a jumpy American soldier. The Americans had come to arrest Webern's son-in-law, who was involved in black-market activities.

Webern's early music is distilled, sounding like Mahler's textures pared to points and outlines. From 1909 his works were atonal, from 1924 rigorously serial, and eventually they moved beyond that to a kind of crystalline abstraction: reductive, extremely intimate, aphoristic. His explorations were perhaps most valuable in the realm of sonority, giving a view onto new timbral possibilities through pieces that last barely a few minutes.

Webern's systematic and concentrated approach to composition had important ramifications for 20th-century music. Following his death, he became a cult figure to at least two postwar generations of composers; his music exerted an enormous influence on Stockhausen, Boulez, Babbitt, Luigi Nono (1924–90), and Morton Feldman (1926–87). Now that these composers are either gone or fading, it remains to be seen whether Webern's music will become part of the repertoire—the *Passacaglia* is already there—or will grow ever more remote, arcane, and aesthetically isolated.

RECOMMENDED RECORDINGS

COLLECTED WORKS: BOULEZ AND VARIOUS SOLOISTS (DG).

CONCERTO: BOULEZ AND ENSEMBLE INTERCOMTEMPORAIN (DG).

ORCHESTRAL WORKS (INCLUDING *PASSACAGLIA*, SYMPHONY, OP. 21): DOHNÁNYI AND CLEVELAND ORCHESTRA (DECCA).

Wedding, The *See* LES NOCES.

Weill, Kurt

(b. Dessau, March 2, 1900; d. New York, April 3, 1950)

GERMAN/AMERICAN COMPOSER. Absorbing the influences of Hans Pfitzner and Max Reger, of cabaret, jazz, proletarian anthems, and a variety of other exotic elements, Weill composed in traditional classical genres but achieved his greatest fame as a master of musical theater, first in Germany, later on Broadway.

Kurt Weill, master of musical satire

His father was chief cantor at the synagogue in Dessau, and from early childhood Weill received musical training and regular exposure to opera and symphony concerts. Weill studied composition with Albert Bing from 1915; in the spring of 1918 he enrolled in Berlin's Hochschule für Musik, where he studied composition with Humperdinck and took lessons in counterpoint and conducting. He worked briefly at the Hoftheater in Dessau as an assistant conductor under Bing and Hans Knappertsbusch, and in 1920 took a post as conductor at a small theater in Lüdenscheid. In 1921 he embarked on a three-year master course in composition with Ferruccio Busoni at the Akademie der Künste in Berlin. Recognizing his talent, Busoni assigned him remedial work in counterpoint and watched over his rapid development as a symphonic and instrumental composer. His Divertimento, Op. 5, and *Sinfonia sacra,* Op. 6, were premiered by the Berlin Philharmonic during its 1922–23 season, and his first important stage work, the opera *Der Protagonist,* received its premiere in Dresden in 1926, under the baton of Fritz Busch.

In 1927 Weill began a collaboration with the Marxist playwright Bertolt Brecht that would lead to the production of his best-known works for the stage. A collection of five songs to texts drawn from Brecht's *Die Hauspostille* paved the way for the team's first opera, *Aufstieg und Fall der Stadt Mahagonny* (*Rise and Fall of the City Mahagonny*; 1927–29). Even before *Mahagonny* was finished, the duo turned out the work for which they are best known, *DIE DREIGROSCHENOPER (The Threepenny Opera),* a wonderfully clever updating of John Gay's 1728 *The Beggar's Opera* that proved a sensation at its Berlin premiere in 1928 and was quickly staged all over Europe. Meanwhile, in 1926, Weill had married the singer-actress Lotte Lenya, who created the role of Jenny in *Die Dreigroschenoper* and became the leading interpreter of his songs and the inspiration for many of his works. Weill and his music were perfect embodiments of the culture of Weimar Germany, but as national sentiment changed in the 1930s, Weill's road got rocky in a hurry. The 1930 Leipzig premiere of *Mahagonny* with its caustic social satire sparked a riot, and the rising influence of the Nazis put a damper on performances throughout Germany. The last of Weill's works to receive its premiere in Germany was the musical *Der Silbersee* (*The Silver Sea*), which opened simultaneously in three cities in February 1933. By then the Nazis were in charge and already promulgating laws against Jews. Weill left Berlin on March 21, 1933, less than a month after the Reichstag fire, and never returned to Germany.

His first stop was Paris, where in 1933 he created the "ballet chanté" *Die sieben Todsünden* (*The Seven Deadly Sins*), featuring Lenya in the lead role, with text by Brecht and choreography by the young George Balanchine. He came to America in 1935, and continued writing for the musical stage; he became a U.S. citizen in 1943. The musicals and the one opera—*Street Scene* (1946)—that Weill wrote in America were every bit as politically charged as his earlier collaborations with Brecht. In America as in Germany, Weill worked with outstanding wordsmiths: *Lost in the Stars* (1949), which deals with apartheid, utilized a book by Maxwell Anderson based on Alan Paton's *Cry the Beloved Country* (1948); *Lady in the Dark* (1940) had a book by Moss Hart and lyrics by Ira Gershwin; and *Street Scene,* about the dilemma of being a housewife, featured words by Langston Hughes.

In addition to roughly two dozen extant works for the stage, which contain his best songs, Weill composed a small number of free-standing songs and a handful of chamber works and orchestral pieces, including two symphonies, a Concerto for Violin and Wind Instruments, and the divertimento-like *Kleine Dreigroschenmusik* (1928–29) for winds, based on tunes from *Die Dreigroschenoper.*

Part of the interest of Weill's music lies in the way it melds high and low styles and reflects the composer's edgy, complex artistic nature. In it one encounters a successor to Mendelssohn and Mahler who readily embraced popular European and American dances and song styles, pointedly reconfiguring traditional harmonic language in the process. Weill's idiom abounds in classical gestures and textures, revels in a kind of pseudocounterpoint (based on the real thing, which he well knew), and flirts with high-style melodic ideas—some quite beautiful, but almost always a bit twisted. His work, often sardonic and bleak, was the product of one of the finest, most consistently inspired musical minds of the 20th century.

RECOMMENDED RECORDINGS

Die Dreigroschenoper: Lemper, Kollo, Dernesch; Mauceri and Berlin Radio Symphony Orchestra (Decca).

Kleine Dreigroschenmusik: Weisberg and Contemporary Chamber Ensemble (Nonesuch).

Die sieben Todsünden: Fassbaender; Garben and Northern German Radio Orchestra (harmonia mundi).

Die sieben Todsünden: Lemper; Mauceri and RIAS Berlin Sinfonietta (Polygram).

Songs: Lemper; Mauceri and Berlin Radio Symphony Orchestra (Decca).

Songs: Stratas; Schwarz and Chamber Orchestra of New York (Nonesuch).

Weingartner, Felix

(b. Zara, June 2, 1863; d. Winterthur, Switzerland, May 7, 1942)

Austrian conductor, composer, and author. He studied composition at Graz, then entered the University of Leipzig in philosophy. With the encouragement of the music critic Eduard Hanslick, he transferred to the Leipzig Conservatory, and proceeded to Weimar in 1883, where he became a part of Liszt's circle. His first opera, *Sakuntala,* was produced in Weimar in 1884. He quickly rose through the ranks as Kapellmeister—taking positions in Königsberg (1884), Danzig (1885), Hamburg (1887), and Mannheim (1889)—before settling in as director of the Berlin Opera and chief conductor of its orchestral concerts in 1891. He succeeded Mahler as director of the Vienna Court Opera in 1908. His appointment in Vienna lasted only three years, during which he alienated both critics and opera lovers, fired singers, and generally antagonized the administration. He did, however, retain his post as chief conductor of the Vienna Philharmonic until 1927. From 1927 to 1933 he was director of the Basel Conservatory, and during 1935–36, he served, again briefly, as director of the Vienna Staatsoper. Though he conducted many orchestra concerts in London over the years, Weingartner did not make his debut at Covent Garden until 1939, in Wagner's *Parsifal* and *Tannhäuser.* He appeared during three seasons as a guest conductor with the New York Philharmonic (1905–07), and in two with the Boston Opera (1912–13). A complete musician, he composed seven symphonies, three symphonic poems, and nine operas, as well as chamber works and songs, wrote several books on the art of conducting and interpretation, and helped in the editing of Berlioz's works for publication.

Felix Weingartner

Weingartner was one of the greatest and most influential conductors of his time, and the first in history to record prolifically, amassing a discography that touches on the symphonies of Mozart, Beethoven, and Brahms, as well as works by Mendelssohn, Liszt, and Wagner. Despite the importance of those latter two titans in his early years as a musician, Weingartner was a classicist in his outlook and practice, and eschewed all forms of self-indulgence and willfulness on the podium. His style and conducting technique were sober, dignified, tasteful, graceful, and aristocratic; judging by his recordings, his interpretations in many ways anticipated today's passion for musical rectitude. Weingartner's contempt for the heavy-handedness of many of his contemporaries, his differences of interpretive opinion with Bülow and Mahler, and his jealousy of Richard Strauss's success at the Vienna Staatsoper are recalled in his unvarnished memoirs, *Buffets and Rewards: A Musician's Reminiscences* (1937).

RECOMMENDED RECORDINGS

Beethoven, Symphonies (complete): London Philharmonic Orchestra and others (Naxos).

Collection:

"Great Conductors of the 20th Century—Felix Weingartner": Works of Beethoven, Berlioz, Liszt, Mozart, Wagner (EMI).

Welitsch, Ljuba

(b. Borissovo, July 10, 1913; d. Vienna, August 31, 1996)

Bulgarian soprano. Although her natural musical talent was evident at an early age—she was given a violin by her sister, and it was discovered that she had absolute pitch—she did not receive any formal vocal training until after she had entered the University of Sofia (as a philosophy and theology student) and became the soprano soloist at the nearby cathedral. She subsequently went to Vienna to study with Theodor Lierhammer, and in 1936 she made her professional debut with the Sofia Opera in the small role of Sophie in Charpentier's *Louise,* followed in 1937 by Nedda in Leoncavallo's *Pagliacci,* in Graz.

During World War II, Welitsch performed in the opera houses of Hamburg and Munich, adding the roles of Mimì, Musetta, Manon, Cio-Cio-San, and Elisabeth (in *Tannhäuser*) to her expanding repertoire, as well as the Mozart roles of Susanna, Donna Anna, and Fiordiligi. Her Musetta was a notorious show-stealer, much to the dismay of the often more famous Mimìs. Having performed the demanding role of the Composer in Richard Strauss's *Ariadne auf Naxos,* Welitsch received special coaching from Strauss for the role of Salome, which she sang at the Vienna Staatsoper in a 1944 performance in honor of the composer's 80th birthday. She joined the roster of the Staatsoper after the war.

When the Vienna company performed *Salome* on tour in London in 1947, Welitsch created a sensation. She duplicated her triumph in that role at her Metropolitan Opera debut in 1949. Welitsch's embodiment of Strauss's nubile, chillingly amoral temptress set the standard wherever she went. But she was also acclaimed in many other roles, including Jenůfa, Tosca, Aida, and Minnie in Puccini's *La fanciulla del West.* Welitsch's voice began to lose its remarkable luster in the early 1950s; not one to compromise the intensity and no-holds-barred approach of her singing and acting, she soon stepped out of starring roles on the operatic stage. She continued to sing character parts in Vienna for many years and returned to the Met in 1973 to make a cameo appearance in the role of the Duchess of Crakentorp in Donizetti's *La fille du régiment.* Welitsch was distinguished for her beautiful, silvery tone, impeccable diction (in half a dozen languages), and intensely musical, full-blooded approach to interpretation. Though her career was meteoric, she will be remembered as a singer who combined remarkable dramatic instincts with unflinching artistry, and who possessed a voice that was preternatural in its visceral impact.

Ljuba Welitsch as Strauss's Salome

RECOMMENDED RECORDINGS

"The Art of Ljuba Welitsch": Scenes and arias from works of Lehár, Mozart, Puccini, Tchaikovsky, Verdi, Weber (Preiser).

Strauss, *Salome* (final scene): Karajan and Vienna Philharmonic (EMI).

Well-Tempered Clavier *See* DAS WOHLTEMPERIRTE CLAVIER.

Welser-Möst, Franz

(b. Linz, April 22, 1960)

Austrian conductor. He studied violin, piano, and conducting in Linz, and from 1980 to 1984 was a conducting student at the Musikhochschule in Munich. In 1986 he made his debut with the London Philharmonic Orchestra and became music director of the Norköping Symphony Orchestra in Sweden. He made his debut at the Vienna Staatsoper in 1987 and his American debut in 1989 with the Saint Louis Symphony. In 1990 he was engaged as music director of the London Philharmonic, and in 1995 he became director of the Zurich Opera. His six-year tenure with the London Philharmonic was problematic (the musicians took to calling him Franz "Worse-than-Most") and, in the judgment of London's critics, artistically unsuccessful. Welser-Möst enjoyed smoother sailing during his seven years at the helm in Zurich, where he conducted 27 new productions and several revivals, including a complete *Ring* cycle during the 2001–02 season. In 1999, despite his spotty record in the symphonic sphere, he was tapped by the

Cleveland Orchestra to succeed Christoph von Dohnányi as music director, effective at the beginning of the 2002–03 season. In his first season in Cleveland, he conducted newly commissioned works by Oliver Knussen (b. 1952) and Rolf Wallin (b. 1957), and led the orchestra in concerts at Vienna's Musikverein. His work with the Clevelanders has yet to generate an outpouring of critical enthusiasm, but his openness to new repertoire and connection to the Austro-Germanic tradition are significant assets, ones he may well parlay into success.

Franz Welser-Möst

RECOMMENDED RECORDINGS

KORNGOLD, SYMPHONY IN F-SHARP MINOR: PHILADELPHIA ORCHESTRA (EMI).

ORFF, *CATULLI CARMINA, TRIONFO DI AFRODITE*: SCHELLENBERG, ODINIUS, REITER, LARSSON; MUNICH RADIO SYMPHONY ORCHESTRA (EMI).

Werther OPERA IN FOUR ACTS BY JULES MASSENET, to a libretto by Édouard Blau and Paul Milliet based on Goethe's 1774 novel *Die Leiden des jungen Werthers* (*The Sorrows of Young Werther*), composed 1885–87 and premiered February 16, 1892, at the Vienna Court Opera. It took the opera ten years to catch on; not until a 1903 revival at the Opéra-Comique in Paris did it find its legs. In the century since then it has had a secure place in the repertoire, standing alongside *Manon* as the most popular of Massenet's works. The action, set in Wetzlar (not far from Frankfurt) in the 1780s, involves the tender feelings that arise between the poet Werther and the lovely Charlotte, despite the fact that she is betrothed to another, and the painful course this infatuation takes after she marries, ending in Werther's suicide. Massenet's sensitive, finely crafted score is admirable for both its psychological insight and its melodic richness, apparent in numbers such as the Werther-Charlotte duet "Pourquoi me reveiller?" in the third act.

RECOMMENDED RECORDING

GHEORGHIU, PETIBON, ALAGNA, HAMPSON; PAPPANO AND LONDON SYMPHONY ORCHESTRA (EMI).

***Wesendonck* Lieder** SET OF FIVE SONGS FOR SOPRANO AND PIANO BY RICHARD WAGNER, composed 1857–58 to poems by Mathilde Wesendonck (with whom the composer was having an extramarital affair) and first performed July 30, 1862, in Laubenheim, near Mainz. Two of the songs, "Träume" and "Im Treibhaus," were conceived as "studies for *TRISTAN UND ISOLDE*." In them, Wagner touches on the feelings of languor and melancholy—and the dark, desolate longings—that would figure so prominently in the music of the opera. The songs are more frequently encountered today in orchestral arrangements made by Felix Mottl.

RECOMMENDED RECORDINGS

FLAGSTAD; FURTWÄNGLER AND PHILHARMONIA ORCHESTRA (EMI).

NORMAN; DAVIS AND LONDON SYMPHONY ORCHESTRA (PHILIPS).

whole-tone scale Scale with six tones to the octave, each a whole step apart. Because there are no half steps, the scale has no leading tone, no tonic, no point of departure or arrival; music that employs it has a mysterious quality and seems to float free of tonality. Russian composers of the 19th century pioneered the use of whole-tone melodies, starting with Glinka in his overture to *Ruslan and Lyudmila* (1842). Debussy carried the process considerably further, utilizing whole-tone textures with remarkable effectiveness in works such as *Pelléas et Mélisande* (1893–1902), *La mer* (1903–05), and in many of his piano pieces—e.g., *Voiles*, from the first book of *Préludes* (1910), and "Cloches à travers les feuilles," from the second book of *Images* (1907).

Wieniawski, Henryk [Henri]

(b. Lublin, July 10, 1835; d. Moscow, March 31, 1880)

POLISH VIOLINIST AND COMPOSER. He was born into an educated family—his mother and an uncle were professional pianists, and his father was an army surgeon. In 1843, at the age of eight, he was sent to study at the Paris Conservatoire. The following year he entered the advanced class of Lambert Massart, and at the age of 11 walked away with a *premier prix* and was awarded a Guarneri violin. He continued studying with Massart for two more years before going on tour to Russia and the Baltic in 1848; he returned to the Conservatoire in 1849 to study harmony. In 1851 he began the life of a touring virtuoso, playing roughly 100 concerts a year (many accompanied by his younger brother Józef, an accomplished pianist) and composing steadily. By 1853 he had completed 14 works, including several mazurkas, a set of etudes, and his brilliant Violin Concerto No. 1 in F-sharp minor, Op. 14—whose premiere at the Leipzig Gewandhaus cemented his reputation in Germany. In 1858 he played with Anton Rubinstein in Paris, and in 1859 he performed (as violinist and violist) with the Beethoven Quartet Society in London, an ad hoc group consisting of violinists Heinrich Wilhelm Ernst and Joseph Joachim, cellist Alfredo Piatti, and Wieniawski, a star-studded quartet if ever there was one. The following year he married Isabella Hampton, niece of the composer George Osborne. In 1860, Rubinstein persuaded Wieniawski to move to St. Petersburg and accept the posts of soloist to the tsar and professor of violin. His artistic development during the 12 years he spent there was substantial; he wrote his best works in Russia, including the *Etudes caprices*, Op. 18, for two violins, and the Concerto No. 2 in D minor, dedicated to Sarasate and one of the finest of all Romantic violin concertos. In a letter to Pauline Viardot, Turgenev recalled how beautifully Wieniawski played the Bach *Chaconne* and, on another occasion, the Op. 127 string quartet of Beethoven, signaling an artist of considerable depth.

Henryk Wieniawski, ca. 1870

In 1872 Wieniawski succumbed again to wanderlust, joining Rubinstein on a grueling American tour that entailed 215 concerts over the course of eight months. In 1875 he moved to Brussels to teach at its conservatory in place of Henry Vieuxtemps, who had suffered a stroke. One of his students there was the young Eugène Ysaÿe, who would strive to match his virtuosity without trying to emulate his style. While teaching, Wieniawski continued the demanding life of a touring violinist, tackling Germany in 1876 and playing concerts in London, Paris, Berlin, and Moscow in 1878. By that point his health had deterioriated drastically due to emphysema and a serious heart condition. At a Berlin performance of his D minor concerto on November 11, 1878, he had to be carried off the stage after collapsing midway through the piece. Joachim, who was in the audience, went onstage with his colleague's violin in hand and offered a performance of the Bach

Chaconne so that Wieniawski wouldn't lose the receipts for the concert. Gravely ill but in desperate financial need, Wieniawski continued on to Russia, where he gave his last performances in Moscow and Odessa. He spent his final days in the care of Nadezda von Meck, Tchaikovsky's famous patroness, at her home in Moscow.

Wieniawski was, in the estimation of knowledgeable contemporaries, the most brilliant violinist of the mid-19th century. Joachim recalled what a bold and committed performer he was, a daredevil with a left hand of dazzling accuracy. Leopold Auer saw him as absolutely unique. Wieniawski was the first to use what became known as the "Russian grip," with the index finger applying pressure to the top of the bow—a technique that added intensity to his tone and was adopted by many 20th-century violinists. Nearly everyone who heard him paid homage not only to his technique but to his extraordinarily powerful projection and fiery, outsized temperament, which left no doubt that a performer of the first magnitude was on the stage. Though he died young, he contributed significantly to the repertoire, to the development of technique, and to the notion that a virtuoso should also be a serious creative artist.

RECOMMENDED RECORDINGS

VIOLIN CONCERTOS NOS. 1 AND 2: BISENGALIEV; WIT AND POLISH NATIONAL RADIO SYMPHONY ORCHESTRA ORCHESTRA (NAXOS).

VIOLIN CONCERTOS NOS. 1 AND 2: SHAHAM; FOSTER AND LONDON SYMPHONY ORCHESTRA (DG).

Willaert, Adrian

(b. Bruges, ca. 1490; d. Venice, D ecember 17, 1562)

NETHERLANDISH COMPOSER, active mainly in Italy. He probably studied with Jean Mouton in Paris, and he may have been present in Rome ca. 1514–15. His first known post was in Ferrara, as a singer in the retinue of Cardinal Ippolito I d'Este. When Ippolito was assigned to a new see in Hungary, Willaert went with him; he spent a couple of years in Esztergom before returning to Ferrara. Following the cardinal's death in 1520, Willaert joined the staff of Duke Alfonso d'Este, the cardinal's brother. In 1527 he was appointed *maestro di cappella* at St. Mark's in Venice, a post he retained to the end of his life.

Willaert was an important composer of motets and madrigals, and his works in these genres exerted an influence on numerous composers, including Cipriano de Rore (ca. 1515–65; his student), Lassus, and Monteverdi. At present, about 175 motets and 56 madrigals can be securely attributed to him. Most of the motets were published in Venice during Willaert's lifetime, appearing in two books of four-voice settings (1539), one book of five-voice settings (1539), one of six-voice settings (1542), and in a final collection, *Musica nova* (1559), which contains some of Willaert's lengthier motet settings as well his finest madrigals. Nearly all of the 25 madrigals included in *Musica nova* (written around 1540, thus not really "new") are settings of complete sonnets of Petrarch. The works adhere closely to the sonnets' verse structure and show great virtuosity both in their treatment of word groupings and their projection of the poetic imagery—though their most striking feature is their continuous, densely woven contrapuntal texture. In addition to these works, about a dozen masses survive, along with several dozen psalm settings, numerous chansons, and a few instrumental pieces.

Willaert enjoyed a posthumous reputation second to none in his generation. Even 40 years after his death, Monteverdi, pushing musical style in an entirely new direction, acknowledged him as a paragon of what he called the *prima prattica*.

RECOMMENDED RECORDINGS

MADRIGALS, CHANSONS, VILLANELLE: MALFEYT AND ROMANESQUE (RICERCAR).

SELECTED SACRED WORKS (INCLUDING *MISSA CHRISTUS RESURGENS*): SUMMERLY AND OXFORD CAMERATA (NAXOS).

Williams, John (Towner)

(b. Floral Park, N.Y., February 8, 1932)

AMERICAN COMPOSER. He moved to Los Angeles with his family when he was 16, attending UCLA and taking private composition lessons from Mario Castelnuovo-Tedesco. After service in the Air Force, he returned to New York to attend the Juilliard School, where he was a piano student of Rosina Lhévinne. In 1956, Williams went to work as a pianist in Hollywood—he was responsible for the piano riff in Henry Mancini's theme music for the television series *Peter Gunn.* He became a staff arranger for Columbia Pictures and then 20th Century Fox, working on orchestrations for such film-scoring luminaries as Dmitri Tiomkin (1894–1979), Alfred Newman (1900–70), and Franz Waxman (1906–67). In the 1960s he started composing for television, writing themes for *Gilligan's Island, Lost in Space,* and *Land of the Giants.* He won Emmys for his scores for *Heidi* and *Jane Eyre,* and received his first Oscar for his adaptation of the music for the Broadway musical *Fiddler on the Roof* (1971). In the 1970s he supplied music for a number of disaster movies, including *The Poseidon Adventure, Earthquake,* and *The Towering Inferno,* but it was his score for the Steven Spielberg thriller *Jaws* (1975), with its iconic musical evocation of the shark, that secured his reputation and brought him an Oscar for best original score. Since then, Williams has provided the music for most of Spielberg's feature films. On Spielberg's recommendation, he was engaged by director George Lucas to score the *Star Wars* films. He has scored an impressive list of features, including *Superman, Raiders of the Lost Ark* (and two Indiana Jones sequels so far), *E.T. the Extra-Terrestrial* (Williams's third Oscar), *JFK, Jurassic Park, Schindler's List* (another Oscar winner), *Saving Private Ryan, Munich, Memoirs of a Geisha,* and the ongoing *Harry Potter* series. He also wrote the music for the *NBC Nightly News* (dubbed "The Mission") and penned fanfares for the Olympic summer games of 1984, 1988, and 1996.

John Williams responds to applause at Boston's Symphony Hall, 2002

Williams's concert music includes two symphonies, a cello concerto premiered by Yo-Yo Ma and the Boston Symphony Orchestra in 1994, *Tree Song* for violinist Gil Shaham, and concertos for violin, flute, clarinet, bassoon, horn, trumpet, and tuba. As conductor of the Boston Pops from 1980 to 1993 , he led the orchestra on three tours of the U.S. and three of Japan, and in 2003 he composed and conducted a new work, *Soundings,* to open the Walt Disney Concert Hall in Los Angeles. To date he has received five Oscars, 43 Academy Award nominations, 18 Grammys, three Golden Globes, two Emmys, and five BAFTA Awards (British Academy of Film and Television Arts).

A musician perfectly attuned to his métier, Williams is the most successful, versatile, and prolific film composer in the history of the medium, and probably the most highly compensated composer ever. He almost single-handedly revived the big-orchestra Hollywood film score, which had languished following the dissolution of the studio orchestras in the 1950s and 1960s. His style is eclectic in the best sense—the sweep of his ideas and grandeur of his orchestration clearly pay homage to the work of such soundtrackers as Erich Korngold, Alfred Newman, and Franz Waxman, but he has also made inspired use of elements drawn from the idioms of Holst, Walton, Prokofiev, Penderecki, and many others. The result, almost invariably, sounds apposite rather than derivative. Few living composers in any line of work can match him when it comes to creating atmosphere, drama, and a sense of adventure.

wind machine *See box on pages 496–97.*

Winterreise (Winter Journey) NARRATIVE CYCLE OF 24 SONGS (DIVIDED INTO TWO BOOKS OF 12 SONGS EACH) BY FRANZ SCHUBERT, to texts by Wilhelm Müller, set between February and December of 1827. It is among the supreme masterpieces of the art of song. The story concerns a lovelorn young man wandering through a desolate winter landscape, and the musical treatment is heavy with misery, noticeable in the way melodic lines tend to drop at the ends of phrases. The more outwardly expressive nature of the songs in Book II of the cycle (beginning with "Die Post" ◉) shows Schubert on a new plane of inspriration, capable of revealing to his listener, even in the gloom, marvelous emotional vistas.

RECOMMENDED RECORDINGS

FISCHER-DIESKAU, DEMUS (DG).

GOERNE, BRENDEL (DECCA).

QUASTHOFF, SPENCER (RCA).

wohltemperirte Clavier, Das (The Well-Tempered Clavier) TITLE GIVEN BY J. S. BACH TO A TWO-VOLUME COLLECTION OF KEYBOARD PIECES containing preludes and fugues in each of the 24 major and minor keys. Bach's aim was to prove the superiority for keyboard music of the tuning system known as equal temperament, in which the octave is divided into 12 exactly even half steps. Under the irregular and mean-tone temperaments still in wide use in Bach's day, keys such as B major or E-flat minor with more than four sharps or flats often sounded out of tune and usually had to be avoided on instruments with fixed tuning such as the organ or harpsichord. In contrast, the equal temperament system made all keys sound good (though thirds are all slightly out of tune), allowing modulatory freedom of unimagined scope. While several composers before Bach had sought to investigate its possibilities in systematic fashion, Bach's exploration in *Das wohltemperirte Clavier* proved to be of surpassing brilliance and thoroughness, and the collection is a touchstone of the keyboard literature.

Bach composed the 24 preludes and fugues of *Das wohltemperirte Clavier,* Book I, in 1722, as instructional pieces for his 12-year-old son, Wilhelm Friedemann. The writing encompasses a huge variety of styles and contrapuntal techniques, and the expressive range of the material is vast. The Prelude in C major, the celebrated opening piece of the set, uses an arpeggiated figuration throughout that is reminiscent of the lute style ◉, while the Prelude in C minor has the character of a fantasy. Frequently the character of a prelude contrasts markedly with that of the fugue in the same key—such is the case, for example, when the ebullient D major prelude gives way to a stately fugue with dotted rhythms typical of a French overture. The fugues in Book I range in complexity from two to five voices, though most are three- and four-voice settings. Several have chromatic subjects, more difficult to work with than diatonic ones, and a number manage to weave in melodic countersubjects.

Book II of *Das wohltemperirte Clavier,* dating from 1738–42, was assembled from a combination of newly composed pieces and various existing preludes and fugues going back a number of years, some of which Bach transposed so they would fit into the necessary scheme covering all 24 of the major and minor keys. There is less unity, and even greater variety, in this collection—Bach expands some of the preludes to almost monumental proportions; others are in binary form and aria style, neither of which had been utilized in the first book. In a few pieces, including the final fugue, Bach embraces the new *GALANT* style. *See also* TEMPERAMENT.

RECOMMENDED RECORDINGS

PIANO:

HEWITT (HYPERION).

SCHIFF (DECCA).

HARPSICHORD:

MORONEY (HARMONIA MUNDI).

Wolf, Hugo

(b. Windischgraz, Styria [now Slovenj Gradec, Slovenia], March 13, 1860; d. Vienna, February 22, 1903)

AUSTRIAN COMPOSER. One of the great masters of the lied, he brought remarkable inventiveness and expressive power to his works in the form. His mother was Slovenian, his father of German descent and sufficiently musical to give his son lessons on piano and violin. Wolf entered the Vienna Conservatory at 15, studying harmony and composition, and befriended Gustav Mahler, the same age as he. He attended performances at the Court Opera and became enthralled with the works of Wagner. The large-scale scores he attempted to write at this time were fraught with technical shortcomings. In 1877, after being kicked out of the conservatory for disciplinary reasons, he began to earn a living as a music teacher of children from well-to-do families. Most likely in 1878, one of his patrons arranged for his sexual initiation at a Viennese brothel, and he contracted syphilis. He became reclusive, fearing he might infect others. Increasingly he was drawn to song composition, modeling his efforts on Schumann, especially, and Schubert. But he was slow to develop and mature, musically and in other ways. An encounter with Brahms in 1879 at which he felt slighted led to a lifelong hostility for that towering figure.

Wagner was the other towering figure of the day, and Wolf attended performances of *Parsifal* at Bayreuth in 1882, the summer of its premiere, and again in 1883. Soon he became a music critic for the *Wiener Salonblatt* and during the next three years regularly attacked the music of Brahms ("the art of composing without ideas has decidedly found in Brahms its worthiest representative; [he] understands the trick of making something out of nothing"—and this is about the Fourth Symphony). But Wolf had penetrating views on much else, including Bruckner, and high praise for Wagner. The mid-1880s produced only a handful of songs, though of notable quality. Following the composition of the *ITALIAN SERENADE*, in the spring of 1887, a newly confident Wolf found his voice; the next winter the dam of inspiration broke open and he began feverishly setting texts by his favorite poet, Eduard Mörike.

Over the ensuing nine years—a period marked by cycles of manic creative activity and abysmal physical and mental exhaustion—Wolf composed what is essentially his life's work. The *Gedichte von Eduard Mörike*, 53 songs, emerged in 1888, as did a set of 20 songs to poems of Joseph von Eichendorff, and by early 1889 the *Gedichte von J. W. v. Goethe*, 51 songs, stood complete as well. It was a mind-boggling production for 12 months. The *Spanisches Liederbuch* took shape between fall 1889 and spring 1890, and Part I of the *ITALIENISCHES LIEDERBUCH* (*Italian Songbook*) followed between fall 1890 and the end of 1891. In 1896, Wolf added Part II of the *Italienisches Liederbuch*. In the autumn of 1897 he slipped into the insanity that he had known awaited him as a syphilitic; raving mad (he believed that he, not Mahler, was the director of the Vienna Court Opera), he was briefly placed in an asylum. In October 1898, after trying to drown himself in the Traunsee, he was permanently institutionalized, to waste away in the prison of his madness for the remaining four years of his life.

A sensitive nature, mood swings, and considerable other emotional turmoil—all of which caused Wolf so much grief in life—were also what made him a great songwriter. When it came to poetry Wolf's intuition was preternaturally acute, and it evoked musical responses of remarkable and often surprising intensity—striking melodic gestures, and bold harmonizations and musical imagery underscoring heightened states of feeling. Everything in a Wolf song seems incredibly vivid and telling; in effect, his songs are miniature symphonic poems for voice and piano. Wolf could depict complex emotion yet also saw the humor of life, and captured it like no other composer in history. A prime example is the "Elfenlied" from the *Mörike* lieder—truly something elfin, fitting for an artist who stood barely over five feet. The same quality is found in "Mein Liebster ist so klein" from the *Italienisches Liederbuch.* In their harmonic language his songs owe a debt to Wagner. But in their intimate penetration of the poetry, they mark him as a true successor to Schubert and Schumann.

RECOMMENDED RECORDINGS

ITALIAN SERENADE: AURYN QUARTET (CPO).

ITALIENISCHES LIEDERBUCH: BONNEY, HAGEGÅRD, PARSONS (TELDEC).

ITALIENISCHES LIEDERBUCH: LOTT, SCHREIER, JOHNSON (HYPERION).

MÖRIKE LIEDER: GENZ, RODGERS, VIGNOLES (HYPERION).

SPANISCHES LIEDERBUCH: SCHWARZKOPF, FISCHER-DIESKAU, MOORE (DG).

Wood, Henry J.

(b. London, March 3, 1869; d. Hitchin, August 19, 1944)

ENGLISH CONDUCTOR. After receiving his early musical training as an organist, he studied composition for six terms at the Royal Academy of Music before finding his way to the podium. In 1890 he was tapped by Arthur Sullivan to conduct rehearsals for the premiere of *Ivanhoe* at the Royal English Opera House. In 1895, two years after the opening of Queen's Hall in London, he was hired to conduct a series of summertime promenade concerts at the hall; with this engagement the 26-year-old stepped into a new role—that of the first British-born career conductor—and began a musical association that would last for the rest of his life. The Proms quickly became a venerated institution in London's musical life, and Wood one of the city's musical stars. Wood also conducted with great success in the provinces and abroad, making his New York Philharmonic debut in 1904. That same year, in an effort to enforce discipline and raise standards, he banned the use of "deputies" at rehearsals of the Queen's Hall Orchestra; a number of disgruntled players left to form the London Symphony Orchestra, but Wood shrugged off the setback and marched on. He was knighted in 1911, and in the years before World War I he presented many new works to London concertgoers, conducting the first performance of Elgar's Symphony No. 2 in 1911, the world premiere of Schoenberg's *Five Orchestral Pieces* in 1912, and the British premiere of Scriabin's *Prometheus* in 1913. After 1923 Wood spent time training young orchestral musicians at the Royal Academy of Music, and in 1925, 1926, and 1934 he guest conducted at the Hollywood Bowl. He was active with the BBC Symphony Orchestra from its inception in 1930, and continued in charge of the Proms after the BBC took them over. He donated his huge library of scores, parts, and books to the Royal Academy in 1938, the year of his jubilee. To celebrate the conductor's 50 years on the podium, Vaughan Williams wrote his *Serenade to Music* for 16 solo voices and orchestra, premiered by Wood at the Royal Albert Hall on October 5, 1938. In 1941, after the destruction of Queen's Hall, the Proms were moved to Albert Hall, where they remain to this day. In 1944, Wood conducted his final Proms performance, of Beethoven's Symphony No. 7, from the BBC's wartime base at Bedford. He died three weeks later, 49 years after first conducting the Proms.

Wood's strengths as an interpreter were Tchaikovsky, Wagner, and the music of his contemporaries Debussy, Richard Strauss, and Sibelius, all born in the same decade as he. He was a forceful champion of English music, particularly the works of Elgar, Delius, and Vaughan Williams, though he was not as closely identified with their music as Thomas Beecham and Adrian Boult became. Over the years, his passionate dedication to English musical life and his skills and vitality as an orchestra builder helped establish 20th-century London as a mecca for symphonic concerts; his importance can be gauged by the fact that he gave the premieres or first British performances of at least 717 works by 357 composers. Little wonder that, in tribute, the Proms concerts were named for him after his death.

RECOMMENDED RECORDING

VAUGHAN WILLIAMS, *SERENADE TO MUSIC*: TURNER, BALFOUR, JONES, WIDDOP, OTHERS; BBC SYMPHONY ORCHESTRA (PEARL).

woodwind instruments Handheld instruments that produce sound when the player blows air through a single or double reed (e.g., the OBOE), through a notched mouthpiece (e.g., the RECORDER), or across an open hole in the body of the instrument (e.g., the FLUTE). Woodwinds are not necessarily made of wood; flutes, for example, have at various times been made of glass, bone, wood, and metal. *See also* BASS CLARINET, BASSET CLARINET, BASSET-HORN, BASSOON, CLARINET, CONTRABASSOON, ENGLISH HORN, HECKELPHONE, PICCOLO, SAXOPHONE.

Wozzeck **OPERA IN THREE ACTS BY ALBAN BERG,** to his own libretto based on Georg Büchner's play *Woyzeck* (1836), premiered December 14, 1925, at the Berlin Staatsoper. A gripping, powerfully disturbing portrait of a soldier caught in the vortex of madness and despair (derived from events that actually took place in 1821), *Wozzeck* is one of the few post–World War I operas that have become established in the international repertoire. Its elaborate symmetry—three acts, each in five scenes, with a confrontation between Wozzeck and his common-law wife, Marie, at the center (Act II, sc. 3)—is buttressed by Berg's use of an array of standard musical forms as structural devices. The opera's first scene is constructed along the lines of a Baroque suite, with sections corresponding to a prelude, pavane, gigue, and gavotte. Subsequent scenes in the first two acts utilize rhapsody, passacaglia, rondo, sonata, fantasia and fugue, and scherzo as structural templates. Each of the five scenes of Act III is an invention, on a theme, note, rhythm, chord, and regular eighth-note pulse. But these are not merely structural exercises; Berg chooses his forms for their dramatic point. The clearest example is Act III, sc. 2, the climactic scene of the opera, in which Wozzeck stabs Marie to death. The repeated note B, heard in different parts of the orchestral texture, represents Wozzeck's insanity; as the scene builds to its murderous climax there is a huge crescendo on the note.

The harmonic language of *Wozzeck* is eclectic. It embraces the late-Romantic tonality of Mahler, the atonality of Schoenberg's *Pierrot lunaire,* and Schoenberg's 12-tone method (in the passacaglia)—all of which makes the opera's ending, in an unequivocally somber D minor, that much more troubling. The range of vocal delivery that Berg calls for includes *Sprechstimme* ("pitched speech," in which words are spoken, at a notated pitch and in specific rhythm, rather than sung) as well as conventional recitative and singing. The psychological insight Berg manages to convey through these myriad techniques is timeless and makes *Wozzeck* one of the most compelling dramas of the musical stage.

RECOMMENDED RECORDINGS

FISCHER-DIESKAU, LEAR, STOLZE; BÖHM AND DEUTSCHE OPER BERLIN (DG).

GRUNDHEBER, BEHRENS, HAUGLAND, LANGRIDGE; ABBADO AND VIENNA PHILHARMONIC (DG).

Wunderlich, Fritz

(b. Kusel, September 26, 1930; d. Heidelberg, September 17, 1966)

GERMAN TENOR. His parents were both musical, and his beautiful voice was noted by people who heard him singing in the bakery where he worked as a youth. He received from the town fathers of Kusel a scholarship to study at the Musikhochschule of Freiburg in Breisgau; in 1955 he sang Tamino in a student production of Mozart's *Die Zauberflöte,* and after graduating he received a contract from the Württemberg State Opera in Stuttgart, where he made his professional debut as Ulrich Eislinger in Wagner's *Die Meistersinger von Nürnberg.* When he replaced an ailing Josef Traxel as Tamino at a performance of *Die Zauberflöte* in Stuttgart, his remarkable rise to prominence began. Wunderlich's lyric tenor was an instrument of uncommon beauty and flexibility, with an endless legato and an easy top register ideal for the bel canto repertoire and for Mozart's demanding and unforgiving tenor roles. He also earned great respect as a Bach singer, and made matchless recordings of Schubert's *Die schöne Müllerin* and Schumann's *Dichterliebe.* By the mid-1960s, he had appeared with the Bavarian State Opera, the Vienna Staatsoper, and at Covent Garden, and was a regular participant at the Salzburg Festival. He enjoyed a successful concert tour of the United States in 1964, and was scheduled to make his Metropolitan Opera debut as Don Ottavio in Mozart's *Don Giovanni* on October 8, 1966. Tragically, he fell down a stone staircase at a friend's castle in Heidelberg and died of the injuries he sustained.

Though his career lasted only a decade, Wunderlich remains one of the most widely admired tenors in history, a reputation based not only on the beauty of his singing but on the promise of future greatness, which, sadly, went unfulfilled.

RECOMMENDED RECORDINGS

MOZART, *DIE ZAUBERFLÖTE*: FISCHER-DIESKAU, PETERS, OTTO, LEAR, CRASS, HOTTER; BÖHM AND BERLIN PHILHARMONIC (DG).

SCHUBERT, *DIE SCHÖNE MÜLLERIN*: GIESEN (DG).

SCHUMANN, *DICHTERLIEBE*: GIESEN (DG).

COLLECTION:

"THE VERY BEST OF FRITZ WUNDERLICH": ARIAS FROM OPERAS AND OPERETTAS, BY DONIZETTI, LEHÁR, MOZART, J. STRAUSS JR., TCHAIKOVSKY, OTHERS (EMI).

X Y Z

Xenakis, Iannis

(b. Brăila, Romania, May 29, 1922; d. Paris, February 4, 2001)

FRENCH COMPOSER OF GREEK DESCENT. His father, a well-to-do businessman, sent him to boarding school in Greece when he was ten. He spent his summer holidays exploring the plains of Attica on his bicycle, fascinated by the noise the cicadas made, rising and falling like the breath of a single creature, yet produced by countless insects hidden among the trees. He saw that nature was full of similar wonders: the pointillistic procession of raindrops during a shower, the ever-changing movement of clouds, the spontaneous geometric tracings of flocks of birds. Phenomena produced by myriad microscopic events would become his obsession.

Xenakis entered the Polytechnic Institute of Athens as an engineering student in 1940. During World War II, he was active in the Communist-led resistance to the German occupation, and in 1944, when the British came in, he took part in the street fighting against them, too, losing his left eye when a shell exploded in his face. He received his degree in engineering in 1946 and was promptly drafted. After discovering that resistance fighters were being rounded up and sent to concentration camps, he deserted and went into hiding. A court condemned him to death, but he escaped to Italy in 1947 and from there made his way to France, hoping to reach North America. Lacking proper papers, he was forced to remain in Paris, where good fortune finally found him.

To earn a living he worked in Le Corbusier's studio as an engineer and architect, remaining until 1959 and taking part in such projects as the convent at La Tourette and the Philips pavilion at the 1958 World's Fair. In Paris he also had an opportunity to pursue his interest in music. Though he lacked formal training, Xenakis gained admission to Olivier Messiaen's class in analysis at the Paris Conservatoire (1950–52), and during the 1950s and 1960s his compositional efforts received strong encouragement from the conductor Hermann Scherchen, a champion of new music.

Xenakis's unorthodox approach to composition owed much to his training as an architect. While diagramming a series of chord changes—drawing lines on a sheet of music paper to mark the path each voice takes as one chord follows another—he realized that he was looking at a structure, something resembling the skeleton of a ship. Wondering what would happen if the sounds actually followed the path marked on the paper, gradually rising and falling through the acoustic space rather than shifting abruptly, he came up with the idea for *Metastaseis* (1954), his first opus, which created a sensation at the 1955 Donaueschingen Festival. While the rest of the avant-garde was tinkering with complex pointillistic procedures, Xenakis stunned them with music that resembled a vibrating band of sound filaments. Other equally striking conceptions followed, including a series of works—*ST/4, ST/10,* and *ST/48*—organized with the help of an IBM computer. Structural linguistics, astrophysics, and set theory in turn provided generative principles for various works of the 1960s. During the 1970s, once again looking to nature for inspiration, Xenakis entered a new phase characterized by the elaborate polyphonic activity of "arborescent" forms, in which single musical lines open into multiple lines like branches of a tree. Important works in this vein included *Eridanos* (1973), *Cendrées* (1974), *Erikhthon* (1974), and *Jonchaies* (1977). During the 1980s and 1990s, Xenakis experimented with "sieve" structures, producing music of extraordinary sonic density and complexity, at once massive and chaotic.

RECOMMENDED RECORDINGS

JONCHAIES (WITH *SHAAR, LICHENS, ANTIKHTHON*): TAMAYO AND LUXEMBOURG PHILHARMONIC ORCHESTRA (TIMPANI).

METASTASEIS (WITH *PITHOPRAKTA, EONTA*): TAKAHASHI,; LE ROUX AND PARIS CONTEMPORARY ENSEMBLE (CHANT DU MONDE).

xylophone (from Gr. *xylon,* "wood") Percussion instrument consisting of a set of flat or slightly rounded rosewood bars of graduated size mounted on a trapezoidal frame; the bars are arrayed in two ranks like the white and black keys of a piano. Positioned below each bar is a tube resonator tuned to its pitch. The instrument is played using mallets with spherical heads of differing hardness; some heads are made of wood, some wrapped in yarn or felt. When struck with a hard mallet, the bars produce a bright, penetrating but fairly dry sound; softer mallets produce a duller, somewhat thuddy sound. Modern orchestral xylophones have a compass of three and a half (sometimes four) octaves, from the F (or the C) below middle C to the C three octaves above. Works with prominent parts for xylophone include Mahler's Symphony No. 6 (first and second movements), Debussy's *Ibéria* and *Gigues,* Stravinsky's *The Firebird,* Holst's *The Planets* ("Uranus"), Shostakovich's Symphony No. 5 and *Age of Gold* ◉, and Copland's *Appalachian Spring.* Boulez's *Le marteau sans maître* has an extremely challenging part for xylorimba, an instrument closely related to the xylophone but with the mellower sound of a marimba.

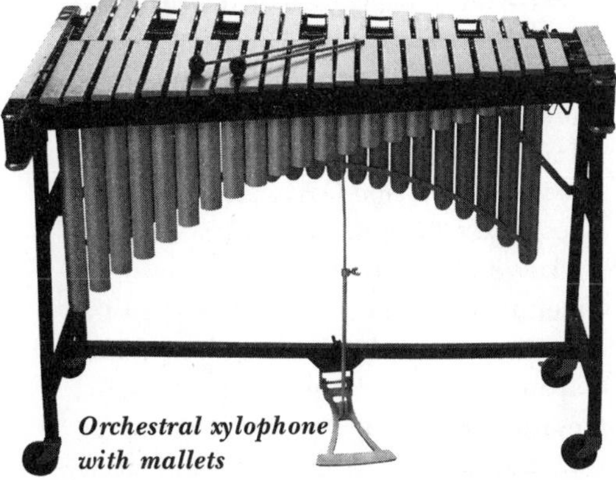

Orchestral xylophone with mallets

Ysaÿe, Eugène

(b. Liège, July 16, 1858; d. Brussels, May 12, 1931)

BELGIAN VIOLINIST AND COMPOSER. After receiving instruction from his father he attended the Liège Conservatory, taking a silver medal in 1874 and winning a scholarship that supported further study, first with Henryk Wieniawski in Brussels and subsequently with Henry Vieuxtemps in Paris. After serving in Berlin as concertmaster of the Bilsesche Kapelle (later re-formed as the Berlin Philharmonic) from 1879 to 1882, he returned to Paris in 1883 and quickly established himself as one of the most prominent musicians in the French capital. In 1886 he was appointed instructor of violin at the Brussels Conservatory, where, with

Eugène Ysaÿe, famed for the beauty of his tone

fellow faculty members, he formed the Quatuor Ysaÿe. Passionately committed to contemporary music, Ysaÿe and the quartet gave the first performances of works by Franck, d'Indy, Debussy, and Fauré. As a soloist, Ysaÿe premiered Franck's Sonata in A (1886), sent to him as a wedding gift, and Chausson's *Poème* (1896).

In the years following the outbreak of World War I, complications resulting from diabetes began to take their toll on Ysaÿe's playing, forcing him to turn his attention increasingly to conducting, teaching, and composition. From 1918 to 1922 he served as music director of the Cincinnati Symphony Orchestra, and in 1924, following his return from America, he produced what is regarded as his greatest work, the Six Sonatas, Op. 27, for unaccompanied violin. Each of the six is dedicated to a violinist of the younger generation—in order, the dedicatees are Joseph Szigeti, Jacques Thibaud, George Enescu, Fritz Kreisler, Mathieu Crickboom (second violin in the Quatuor Ysaÿe), and Manuel Quiroga. All are filled with rich and incredibly challenging writing, especially the flamboyant one-movement Sonata No. 3, subtitled *Ballade.* ◉ In 1929 Ysaÿe's right foot was amputated. He gave his last concert in 1930, and in the final year of his life completed an opera, *Piére li houïeu* (*Peter the Miner*), which received its premiere in Liège a few weeks before his death.

In every respect, Ysaÿe was an artist of the first rank. Generous, good-natured, and intensely dedicated, he was a supreme master of his instrument, yet he always insisted that virtuosity should serve the composer and the music, not the performer. A brilliant, penetrating interpreter, he preferred programs made up of substantive works rather than showpieces. One of the most notable aspects of his playing was his extraordinarily varied and expressive use of vibrato, which contributed much to his famed beauty of tone.

RECOMMENDED RECORDINGS

SONATAS FOR SOLO VIOLIN, NOS. 1–6: KAVAKOS (BIS).

SONATAS FOR SOLO VIOLIN, NOS. 1–6: SCHMID (ARTE NOVA).

Zauberflöte, Die (The Magic Flute) **SINGSPIEL IN TWO ACTS BY WOLFGANG AMADEUS MOZART,** to a libretto by Emanuel Schikaneder, premiered September 30, 1791, at the Theater auf der Wieden in Vienna. Schikaneder's sources included the story "Lulu, oder Die Zauberflöte" by A. J. Liebeskind, and a book titled *Sethos,* which claimed to be a translation of a Greek treatise on the ancient Egyptian mysteries of Isis and Osiris but was actually a forgery by the Abbé Jean Terrasson. This melange was infused with a substantial amount of Masonic allegory, much of it centering on the number three. Outwardly, the opera's plot is pantomime; inwardly, something far more meaningful, a parable of good (Sarastro and the brotherhood of the temples of Wisdom, Reason, and Nature) unmasking evil (the Queen of the Night and her entourage) through a felicitous alliance of Enlightened (Tamino and Pamina) and Natural Man (Papageno). Indeed, Goethe is reported to have said, "More knowledge is required to understand the value of this libretto than to mock it." He did not feel the need to defend Mozart's music: Its greatness was evident to all from the start.

The score opens with a mock-solemn overture that is one of the most brilliant instrumental movements Mozart ever fashioned; the numbers, ensembles, and set pieces that follow it are extraordinary in their variety and richness of character, in every case exhibiting the uncanny finesse that marked Mozart's late style. From settings as direct and folkish as Papageno's opening song, to the ornately old-fashioned first-act rage aria of the Queen of the Night, to the almost anachronistic cantus firmus duet for the Armed Men, to the strangely forward-looking Romanticism of Tamino's "Dies Bildnis ist bezaubernd schön" (for all that, a conventional *amoroso* aria) ◉, the writing is on the highest level. Mozart loved *Die Zauberflöte* perhaps more than any of his other operatic creations, and for good reason: It is a masterpiece, the happiest of syntheses. He died two months and a few days after the work's first performance.

Contemporary illustration portraying Papageno in **Die Zauberflöte**

RECOMMENDED RECORDINGS

LEAR, PETERS, OTTO, WUNDERLICH, FISCHER-DIESKAU, CRASS, HOTTER; BÖHM AND BERLIN PHILHARMONIC (DG).

MANNION, DESSAY, KITCHEN, BLOCHWITZ, SCHARINGER, HAGEN; CHRISTIE AND LES ARTS FLORISSANTS (ERATO).

Zelenka, Jan Dismas

(b. Lounovice pod Blaníkem, October 16, 1679; d. Dresden, December 22, 1745)

CZECH COMPOSER. The son of an organist, he studied at the Clementinum, one of Prague's Jesuit colleges. In 1710, after a period in the service of Count Joseph Ludwig Hartig, he joined the Dresden court orchestra as a string bass player. Between 1717 and 1718 he and other members of the orchestra accompanied their prince, Augustus II, on a yearlong courtship visit to Vienna; while in Vienna, Zelenka gave lessons in counterpoint to Johann Joachim Quantz while taking lessons in composition from the imperial Kapellmeister, Johann Joseph Fux.

Zelenka spent the remainder of his career in Dresden with the exception of an extended sojourn (1722–23) in Prague. During the later 1720s, he frequently deputized for the ailing Dresden Kapellmeister Johann David Heinichen, and following Heinichen's death in 1729 he served as acting Kapellmeister until the appointment of Johann Adolf Hasse in 1734. Zelenka's production as a composer consisted primarily of sacred music for the Catholic services of the Dresden court, though it is his instrumental music—almost all of it written between 1717 and 1723—that is usually encountered today. His output includes more than 20 masses, dozens of psalm settings, a large body of music for Holy Week, and numerous hymns and antiphons, as well as sonatas for many combinations of instruments and a handful of orchestral works. Whereas the sacred works look back to the style of the early Baroque, the instrumental pieces are more modern in feeling, proof of Zelenka's openness to elements of the *GALANT* style and to contemporary Italian fashion—particularly in the five *Capriccios,* akin to works by Vivaldi in their energy.

RECOMMENDED RECORDINGS

CAPRICCIOS (WITH OTHER ORCHESTRAL WORKS): SONNENTHEIL AND DAS NEU-ERÖFFNETE ORCHESTRE (CPO).

SELECTED SACRED WORKS: SAMPSON, BLAZE, GILCHRIST, GEORGE; KING AND KING'S CONSORT (HYPERION).

TRIO SONATAS FOR 2 OBOES, BASSOON, AND CONTINUO: BERNARDINI, GRAZZI, LISLEVAND, SENSI; ALESSANDRINI AND ZEFIRO (ASTRÉE).

Zemlinsky, Alexander von

(b. Vienna, October 14, 1871; d. Larchmont, N.Y., March 15, 1942)

AUSTRIAN COMPOSER AND CONDUCTOR. He studied at the Vienna Conservatory (1886–92) and quickly made a splash in the Austrian capital's musical life. Johannes Brahms was impressed by his earliest pieces and recommended him to his publisher, Simrock. Arnold Schoenberg sought him out as a teacher (he would later state that he owed almost all he knew "about composing technique and its problems" to Zemlinsky) and became a close friend, eventually marrying Zemlinsky's sister Mathilde. Gustav Mahler also took up the cause, premiering Zemlinsky's second opera, *Es war einmal . . .* (*Once Upon a Time . . .*), at the Vienna Court Opera in 1900. In addition to Schoenberg, Zemlinsky's circle of students included Berg, Webern, and Korngold, as well as the beautiful and talented Alma Schindler, with whom, in 1901, he fell hopelessly in love. Fascinated by his passionate advances yet repelled by his dwarfish, gnomelike appearance, Alma toyed with him for a while, then dumped him the minute she met Mahler.

The death of his father in 1900 brought an end to Zemlinsky's independence and forced him to take a series of posts as conductor. Though he lacked the charisma of a born performer, he was a first-rate interpreter. In 1904 he became chief conductor at the Vienna Volksoper (where, in 1906, he would give the Viennese premiere of Richard Strauss's *Salome*), and in 1907, at Mahler's invitation, he spent one season at the Court Opera. In 1911 he became music director of the German opera in Prague, remaining 16 years; among his assistants during that time were Erich Kleiber and George Szell. Otto Klemperer brought him to the Kroll Opera in Berlin in 1927. In 1933 he left Germany and returned to Austria, and in 1938, following the Anschluss, he fled Austria for the United States, where he died during World War II, essentially destitute and almost entirely forgotten in Europe.

As a composer, Zemlinsky cultivated an expressionistic, intensely emotional, but essentially tonal musical language, carrying on the tradition of Brahms and

Alexander von Zemlinsky, portrait by Arnold Schoenberg

Wagner in a more modern idiom. While he never embraced atonality or serialism, his music is harmonically advanced and often quite challenging. Of his operas, several appear from time to time in the repertoire of German houses, particularly the two one-act tragedies inspired by stories of Oscar Wilde: *Eine florentinische Tragödie* (*A Florentine Tragedy*; 1915–17) and *Der Zwerg* (*The Dwarf*; 1919–21), based on "The Birthday of the Infanta." Like the song "Das bucklichte Männlein" ("The Little Hunchback"), the latter work is emblematic of the autobiographical impulse that colors much of Zemlinsky's music and allowed him to convey with deep poignancy the feelings of wretchedness that well up in one whom others find repugnant, one whose hopes of love have been crushed. The best of Zemlinsky's orchestral works are his tone poem *Die Seejungfrau* (*The Mermaid*; 1902–03), based on the story by Hans Christian Andersen, a seething symphonic sublimation of his unhappiness over losing Alma; and the *Lyrische Symphonie* (*Lyric Symphony*; 1922–23) for soprano and baritone soloists with orchestra, on texts by Rabindranath Tagore.

RECOMMENDED RECORDINGS

EINE FLORENTINISCHE TRAGÖDIE (WITH SONGS BY ALMA MAHLER): VERMILLION, DOHMEN, KRUSE; CHAILLY AND ROYAL CONCERTGEBOUW ORCHESTRA (DECCA).

LYRISCHE SYMPHONIE: ISOKOSKI, SKOVHUS; CONLON AND COLOGNE PHILHARMONIC ORCHESTRA (EMI).

LYRISCHE SYMPHONIE: MARC, HAGEGÅRD; CHAILLY AND ROYAL CONCERTGEBOUW ORCHESTRA (DECCA).

DIE SEEJUNGFRAU: DAUSGAARD AND DANISH NATIONAL RADIO SYMPHONY ORCHESTRA (CHANDOS).

DIE SEEJUNGFRAU (WITH PSALM 23 "DER GUTE HIRT"): CHAILLY AND BERLIN RADIO SYMPHONY ORCHESTRA (DECCA).

DER ZWERG: ISOKOSKI, MARTINEZ, KUEBLER; CONLON AND COLOGNE PHILHARMONIC ORCHESTRA (EMI).

Zimbalist, Efrem

(b. Rostov-on-Don, April 21, 1889; d. Reno, Nev., February 22, 1985)

RUSSIAN/AMERICAN VIOLINIST AND TEACHER. A student of Leopold Auer at the St. Petersburg Conservatory (1901–07), he launched his international career with debuts in Berlin and London in 1907. Emigrating to the United States in 1911, he made his American debut with the Boston Symphony on October 27, 1911, playing the first American performance of Glazunov's Violin Concerto in A minor. In 1928 he joined the faculty of the recently opened Curtis Institute of Music in Philadelphia, where he later served as director (1941–68); his students there included Oscar Shumsky and Norman Carol. A thoughtful, probing interpreter, Zimbalist played with great nobility and a beautiful tone. He composed works for the stage and concert hall, and published a valuable method for the violin. In 1914 he married the singer Alma Gluck (1884–1938), with whom he had two children, both of whom became actors. In 1943 he married Mary Louise Curtis Bok, the founder of the Curtis Institute.

Efrem Zimbalist

Zimerman, Krystian

(b. Zabrze, December 5, 1956)

POLISH PIANIST. He studied at the conservatory in Katowice and in 1975 received first prize at the International Chopin Competition in Warsaw. Resisting the temptation to fill his calendar with engagements, he spent much of the following year coaching intensively with Arthur

Rubinstein. He made his American debut in 1979, with the New York Philharmonic, but in 1980, just as his career was getting under way, he took a lengthy sabbatical to reexamine his priorities. Self-critical and highly cultured, with an intellectual bent that is refreshing in a world of pianistic athletes, he combines in his playing an extraordinary command of technique and sonority with an equally extraordinary grasp of musical architecture. He has made a small number of recordings, most of which are outstanding, particularly his accounts of the Chopin *Ballades*—in which he conveys the music as if it had just come from the composer's pen, with a combination of poetic insight and sovereign technique that suits it perfectly—Liszt's two concertos and B minor sonata, and Lutosławski's Piano Concerto, which was written for him. In 1999, to mark the sesquicentennial of Chopin's death, Zimerman assumed the role of conductor as well as soloist for a recording (and subsequent performances on tour) of the two piano concertos; his readings, which stressed the improvisatory nature of the two works, were viewed as a revelation in some quarters, a noble failure in others owing to the sprawling treatment of the music.

Krystian Zimerman: combining technical prowess with intellectual penetration

RECOMMENDED RECORDINGS

CHOPIN, BALLADES (DG).

CHOPIN, PIANO CONCERTOS NOS. 1 AND 2: GIULINI AND LOS ANGELES PHILHARMONIC ORCHESTRA (DG).

LISZT, PIANO CONCERTOS NOS. 1 AND 2: OZAWA AND BOSTON SYMPHONY ORCHESTRA (DG).

LISZT, SONATA IN B MINOR (WITH OTHER WORKS) (DG).

Pinchas Zukerman, master of the violin and the viola

Zukerman, Pinchas

(b. Tel Aviv, July 16, 1948)

ISRAELI/AMERICAN VIOLINIST AND VIOLIST. The son of a violinist, he entered the Academy of Music in Tel Aviv at the age of eight. With Isaac Stern vouching for him (and serving as legal guardian), he came to New York as a teenager to study with Ivan Galamian at the Juilliard School. A victory at the Leventritt Competition in 1967 catapulted him into a high-flying career that has kept him on the go for almost four decades, playing engagements with virtually every major orchestra in the world and doing a substantial amount of conducting as well. As brilliant a violist as he is a violinist (in fact, many professional viola players say he is the best violist alive), Zukerman is admired for his intelligent and tasteful interpretations of the concerto literature. He is an excellent chamber musician, and has collaborated with pianists Daniel Barenboim, Vladimir Ashkenazy, and Mark Neikrug, cellists Jacqueline du Pré and Lynn Harrell, and as violist opposite his longtime friend Itzhak Perlman. From 1980 to 1987 he was music director of the St. Paul Chamber Orchestra, and in the summer of 1999 he became music director of the National Arts Centre Orchestra in Ottawa.

RECOMMENDED RECORDINGS

BEETHOVEN, VIOLIN SONATAS, NOS. 7–10: BARENBOIM (EMI).

BRAHMS, VIOLIN SONATAS, VIOLA SONATAS: BARENBOIM (DG).

BRUCH, VIOLIN CONCERTO NO. 1; LALO *SYMPHONIE ESPAGNOLE*: MEHTA AND LOS ANGELES PHILHARMONIC ORCHESTRA (SONY).

MOZART, DUOS FOR VIOLIN AND VIOLA; LECLAIR, SONATAS FOR 2 VIOLINS: PERLMAN (RCA).

Zwilich, Ellen Taaffe

(b. Miami, April 30, 1939)

AMERICAN COMPOSER, the first woman to receive the Pulitzer Prize in music. She studied at Florida State University and was a violin pupil of Ivan Galamian, then enrolled at the Juilliard School as a composition student of Elliott Carter and Roger Sessions. She was awarded a D.M.A. in composition in 1975. In 1983 she won the Pulitzer Prize for her Symphony No. 1, originally titled *Three Movements for Orchestra,* which received its premiere May 5, 1982, at a concert of the American Composers Orchestra conducted by Gunther Schuller. Scored for standard-sized orchestra with

Ellen Taaffe Zwilich in Carnegie Hall, 1995

expanded percussion complement, the engagingly contrapuntal work has an organic quality frequently aimed for in modern orchestral composition, but rarely achieved; much of its content is generated by the material of the first 15 measures of the first movement. Zwilich has written three further symphonies so far, numerous concertos for brass and wind instruments (including a smashing one for trombone ◉), and a handful of chamber pieces. Almost all of her music is accessible and reflects an innovative treatment of traditional genres and forms. From 1995 to 1999 Zwilich served as first occupant of the composer's chair at Carnegie Hall.

RECOMMENDED RECORDINGS

CONCERTO FOR HORN AND STRINGS, CONCERTO FOR BASS TROMBONE, STRINGS, TIMPANI AND CYMBALS, SYMPHONY NO. 4 (*THE GARDENS*): JOLLEY, VERNON; GREGORIAN AND MICHIGAN STATE UNIVERSITY CHORUS AND ORCHESTRA (KOCH).

SYMPHONY NO. 1 (WITH OTHER WORKS): NELSON AND INDIANAPOLIS SYMPHONY ORCHESTRA (NEW WORLD).

TRIPLE CONCERTO, DOUBLE CONCERTO, CONCERTO FOR PIANO: KALICHSTEIN, LAREDO, ROBINSON; STERN AND FLORIDA STATE UNIVERSITY ORCHESTRA (KOCH).

21C Media Group: 284 Mitch Jenkins(btm), 937 Joanne Savio; **The Academy of Ancient Music:** 310 Richard Haugton; **AKG Images:** 4(top), 18, 27(top), 33(btm), 34, 52, 57, 69, 71, 74(btm), 83(top), 95(top), 98, 110, 124, 127, 168, 174, 177, 178, 192(btm), 207(top), 219, 221, 223, 227, 229, 246, 277, 309, 328, 363, 392, 397, 405, 418, 440, 484, 489(top), 531, 538, 683(top & btm), 714, 718, 724(btm), 744, 778, 841, 911(top & btm), 955, 974; **AP/Wide World Photos:** 10, 46, 59, 68, 77, 109, 118, 184, 395, 424, 434, 501, 722, 810, 849, 871, 964; **Archiv fur Kunst und Geschichte, Berlin:** 646; **The Art Archive:** 478; **Artemis Picture Research Group:** 40; **Art Resource:** 7(top), 26, 53, 54, 61(btm), 107, 151, 170, 175, 207(btm), 358, 448, 499, 524, 675, 826, 862, 889, 896, 910; **Atlantic Records:** 909; **Austrian Cultural Institute:** 745(top); **Bibliothèque Nationale, Paris:** 61(top); **Bridgeman Art Library:** 283, 303(top & btm), 347, 355, 400, 671, 648(top), 655(top), 703, 847, 906, 929; **Brown Brothers:** 912; **Christie's Images:** 82, 421, 458; **Colbert Artists Management:** 521 Christian Steiner; **Columbia Artists Management:** 490 Malcolm Crowthers; Culver: 63(top), 73, 95(btm), 121(top & btm), 136, 201, 215(top), 252, 254, 259, 263, 265, 280, 285, 289, 291, 314, 336, 382, 386, 398, 412, 429, 468, 479, 487(top), 502, 507, 565, 591, 632, 633, 643, 668, 674, 716, 731, 761, 817, 818, 851, 856, 868, 921, 922, 940, 957, 959, 963, 972, 975; **Curtis Institute of Music:** 159; **Deutsche Grammophon:** 65, 919, 976(btm); **EMI Classics:** 700 Fayer Wein; **Everett Collection:** 319, 704; **The Granger Collection:** 112, 560; **Frédérick Chopin Museum:** 127(btm); **FrontRowPhotos/Jack Vartoogian:** 42, 180, 198, 212, 366, 401, 431, 477, 554, 571, 615, 623, 693, 727, 783, 857, 916; **Igor I. Sikorsky Historical Archives:** 658; **The Image Works:** 575, 578, 589; **Jan Yoors:** 162; **Julliard School:** 371; **Kasskara Fotografie Berlin:** 653; **Keith Saunders:** 449; **Kimbell Art Museum:** 666; **Königliche Porzellan-Manufaktur Berlin GmbH:** 139; **Lebrecht Music & Arts:** 3, 5, 12, 19, 20, 22, 30, 31, 37, 38, 56(top & btm), 75, 83(btm), 92, 96(right), 97, 123(btm), 133, 146(left & right), 153, 156(top & btm), 158, 165, 172, 173, 190, 196, 199(top & btm), 202, 204, 209, 217, 231, 236, 243, 256, 273, 284, 287, 294, 298, 300, 305, 311(top), 312(top right), 313(btm) 315, 316, 326, 330, 331, 333, 343, 345, 353(top), 368, 369, 390, 393, 399, 406, 409, 410(top & btm), 419, 422, 428 (top), 442, 451, 453, 464, 467, 471, 475, 486, 487(btm), 496(btm), 496 (top), 497, 503, 534, 540, 541, 551, 558, 561, 568, 594, 610, 616, 636, 638, 647, 664, 670, 687, 709(btm), 709 (top left), 709(top right), 710, 711, 712, 749, 813, 835, 840, 842, 853, 859, 884; **Library of Congress Prints and Photographs Division:** 2, 255, 262, 433, 592, 665, 816, 973; **Linkimage:** 588 Denise Grunstein; **Marco Caselli Nirmal-Ferrara:** 17; **Martyn Bane:** 590; **Mary Evans Picture Library:** 241, 725; **The National Gallery of Art:** 23; **National Portrait Gallery:** 90; **New York Baroque Dance Company:** 600 Beatriz Schiller; **New York Philharmonic:** 446 Chris Lee; **New York Public Library Picture Collection:** 9, 86(btm) BMW, 169(btm), 544, 577, 602, 915, 945; **Nonesuch:** 4(btm) Christine Alicino; **Opera News:** 45 James Heffernan, 930 Daniel Conde; **Paul Moor:** 513; **Photo Researchers:** 114 Fritz Henle; **Photos12.com:** 925; **Punchstock:** 210; **Richard Wagner Museum:** 939; **Rosalie O'Connor Photography:** 701(top & btm), 788, 830; **Royal College of Music:** 528; **Royal Danish Ministry:** 546; **Royal Danish Ministry:** 724(top); **Select Music and Video Distribution Limited:** 536; **Shirley Kirshbaum & Associates:** 976 Martha Swope; **Sound and Vision Archive:** 1,7(btm), 14, 21, 24, 25, 28(top & btm), 29, 33(top), 36, 41, 44, 48, 49, 51, 55, 64, 70, 72, 80, 81, 84, 85, 86(top), 88, 93, 94, 99, 101(top & btm), 102, 104, 106, 111, 115, 119, 123(top), 128, 130, 138, 140, 141, 149 (top), 164, 169 (top), 172(btm), 183, 185, 192 (top), 193, 195, 197, 211, 215(btm), 216, 220, 222, 227, 227, 237, 243, 253, 257, 261, 266, 267, 269, 281, 286, 290, 293, 306, 307, 317, 320, 321, 324, 334, 340, 341, 353(btm), 361, 362(top & btm), 365, 367, 375, 378, 387, 389, 403, 407, 408, 413, 416, 426, 428(btm), 435, 438(top & btm), 447, 454, 457, 463, 466, 481, 485, 489(btm), 492, 493, 494, 508, 516, 518, 525(btm), 526, 547, 550(btm), 550(top), 555, 569, 582, 586, 596, 599, 601, 603, 606, 612, 624, 634, 636, 641, 645(top), 650, 672, 679, 689, 695, 698, 705, 717, 720, 728, 732, 733, 737, 740, 743, 745(btm), 746, 747, 748, 750, 752, 754, 756, 759, 762, 768, 769, 774, 779(left), 786, 787, 789, 790, 792, 793, 795, 799(right), 805, 806, 811, 815(top), 829, 832, 852, 860, 865(btm), 867, 869(top), 870(btm), 870(top), 876, 880, 881, 890, 894, 895, 899, 901, 902, 905, 924, 931, 932(top), 938, 942, 948(btm), 950, 954, 961; **Sovfoto:** 74(top), 657, 776, 855; **Steve J. Sherman Photography:** 167, 270, 308, 444, 539, 630, 864, 882, 977; **Superstock:** 941 akg; **Transit:** 764; **Wilhelm Heckel GmbH, Wiesbaden:** 323; **Winne Klotz:** 182, 572(btm), 605; **Zubin Mehta:** 482.

Ted Libbey, who writes "lyrically and lucidly about music and music makers" *(Chicago Tribune),* is one of America's most highly regarded music critics and commentators. Known to millions of NPR listeners as the "curator" of *Performance Today's* Basic Record Library—where from 1989 to 2003 he was featured in a weekly segment on classical music and recordings—he has participated in America's musical life as a performer, composer, writer, editor, and teacher. At Yale University, where he received his B.A., he studied music history with

Leon Plantinga and conducting with John Mauceri and Gustav Meier, and sang in the European premiere of Leonard Bernstein's *Mass,* in Vienna, in 1973. After doing graduate work at Stanford University with Leonard Ratner, George Houle, and Leland Smith, he became the senior music critic of *The Washington Star.* From 1981 to 1984 he was a music critic for *The New York Times.* He later served as editor of *High Fidelity* and *Musical America* magazines, and in 2000 he became classical editor of the monthly *Schwann Inside.*

He brings to this book, which was eleven years in the making, not only an encyclopedic knowledge of music, but a firsthand acquaintance with many of the most important performers and composers of the 20th and 21st centuries. In addition to his best-selling *The NPR Guide to Building a Classical CD Collection,* he is the author of five books, including the official history of the National Symphony Orchestra. He reviews books for *The Washington Post* and *The Los Angeles Times,* and is a regular contributor to *The Absolute Sound.* Since September 2002, he has held the position of Director of Media Arts at the National Endowment for the Arts in Washington, D.C. He and his wife, Janet, live in Rockville, Maryland.